THE ROUGH GUIDE TO

# England

This tenth edition updated by

Jules Brown, Samantha Cook, Keith Drew, Matthew
Hancock, Emma Harrison, Rob Humphreys, Phil Lee,
Claire Saunders, Ann-Marie Shaw, Jos Simon, Helena
Smith, Matthew Teller, Amanda Tomlin and Steve Vickers

ROUGH
GUIDES

roughguides.com

# Contents

# Introduction to
# England

No one enjoys knocking England more than the English, but – modesty and self-deprecation aside – this little nation packs a powerful punch, and retains a boundless capacity to surprise, charm and thrill. England has a long history and heritage to be proud of, and a glorious regional diversity – from rugged coasts to ancient woodlands, offbeat festivals to artisan foods – that has few parallels. And for all the glories of the past, it's a nation that keeps moving forward, boasting vibrant cities, innovative modern architecture and a rich cultural scene that ensures it's as exciting a destination as any in Europe.

Whether you're in the market for city breaks and shopping sprees, or hanker after a hedonistic, muddy weekend at a music festival; whether you want to live like a lord in an aristocratic pile, or kip under canvas in one of the country's many cool campsites, there's an abundance of options for a fabulous break. England is also emerging as an increasingly foodie nation, with an ever-expanding choice of excellent food and drink – locally sourced and seasonally produced, championed in cafés, restaurants and pubs, at food festivals and farmers' markets in every corner of the nation – challenging every outmoded stereotype about dreary British cuisine.

The English do **heritage** amazingly well. There are first-class museums all over the country (many of them free), and what's left of the nation's green and pleasant land is protected with passion and skill. Indeed, ask an English person to define their nation in terms of what's worth seeing and you're most likely to have your attention drawn to the golden rural past – the village green, the duckpond, the hedgerow-fringed winding lane. And it really is impossible to overstate the bucolic attractions of the various regions, from Cornwall to the Lake District, or the delights they provide – from hiking trails and prehistoric stone circles to cosy pubs and arcane festivals. Don't be entirely misled by the chocolate boxes and the postcards, however – farming today forms just a tiny proportion of the national income and there's a

**ABOVE** ROBIN HOOD'S BAY, NORTH YORKSHIRE **RIGHT** LONDON EYE FROM JUBILEE GARDENS, LONDON

marked dislocation between the urban population and the small rural communities, many of which are struggling.

So perhaps the heart of England is found in its **towns and cities** instead? These, too, have more than their fair share of heritage and historic attractions, which, when matched with the buzzy energy of regeneration and innovation, can make a very heady mix – for every person who wants to stand outside the gates of Buckingham Palace or visit the Houses of Parliament, there's another who makes a beeline for the latest show at Tate Modern, the cityscape of downtown Manchester or the vibrant Liverpool waterfront. Urban civic pride is not a new phenomenon for the English, however. In fact, it's been steady since the Industrial Revolution, and **industry** – and the Empire it inspired – has provided a framework for much of what you'll see as you travel around. Virtually every town bears a mark of former wealth and power, be it a magnificent Gothic cathedral financed from a monarch's treasury, a parish church funded by the tycoons of the medieval wool trade, or a triumphalist civic building raised on the back of the slave and sugar trades. In the south of England you'll find old dockyards from which the Royal Navy patrolled the oceans, while in the north there are vast, hulking mills that employed entire towns. England's **museums and galleries** – several of them ranking among the world's finest – are full of treasures trawled from its imperial conquests. And in their grandiose stuccoed terraces and wide esplanades, the old seaside **resorts** bear testimony to the heyday of English holiday towns, at one time as fashionable as any European spa.

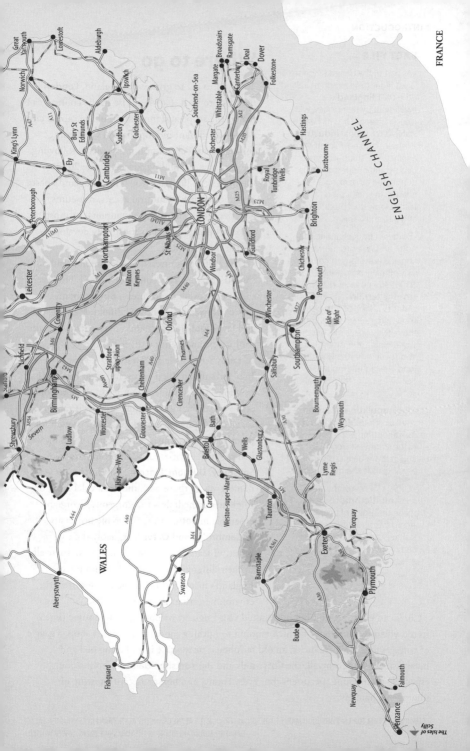

## FACT FILE

• As part of the United Kingdom of Great Britain and Northern Ireland ("the UK"), **England** is a parliamentary democracy, with Queen Elizabeth II as its head of state. Its traditional **industries** – fishing, farming, mining, engineering, shipbuilding – are in decline and business today is dominated by banking and finance, the media and technology, steel production, oil and gas, and tourism.

• Bordered by Scotland to the north and Wales to the west, England is the largest country in Great Britain, occupying an area of 50,085 square miles (129,720 sq km). The **terrain** is diverse, from plains to peaks, cliffs to beaches, though the superlatives, much like the natives, are all modest on a world scale – the largest lake, Windermere, is 10 miles (16km) long, the highest mountain, Scafell, just 3205ft (978m) above sea level.

• The **population** of around 54 million is dense for a country of its size. Settlement is concentrated in the southeast around London, and in the large industrial cities of the Midlands and the North.

• England is one of the world's most **multiethnic** countries, made up largely of people of Anglo-Saxon, Scots, Welsh and Irish descent, but with sizeable communities from the Caribbean, Africa, the Indian subcontinent, China, Southeast Asia and Eastern Europe.

# Where to go

To begin to get to grips with England, **London** is the place to start. Nowhere else in the country can match the scope and innovation of the capital city, a colossal, vibrant metropolis that's still going through a convulsion of improvements following the confidence-building success of the 2012 Olympics. It's here that you'll find England's best spread of nightlife, cultural events, museums, galleries, pubs, shops and restaurants, its most mixed population and its most fully developed tourist infrastructure.

The capital is an irresistible destination and should not, on any account, be missed. However, each of the other large cities – **Birmingham**, **Bristol**, **Newcastle**, **Leeds**, **Sheffield**, **Manchester** and **Liverpool** among them – makes its own claim for historic and cultural diversity, and you certainly won't have a representative view of England's urban life if you venture no further than London. And to some extent it's in these regional centres that the most exciting architectural and social developments are taking place, though for many visitors, as tourist attractions, they rank well behind ancient cities like **Canterbury**, **York**, **Salisbury**, **Durham**, **Lincoln** and **Winchester** – to name a few of those with the most celebrated of England's cathedrals – the gorgeous Georgian ensemble in **Bath**, or the venerable university cities of **Cambridge** and **Oxford**, arguably the two most beautiful seats of learning in the world. These all, in their different ways, provide a glimpse of England's history and heritage in a less frenetic environment than the capital.

Cities can be tiring, and nobody should visit England without spending some time in its old **villages**, hundreds of which amount to nothing more than a pub, a shop, a gaggle of cottages and, if you're lucky, an old farmhouse or wayside inn offering bed and breakfast. **Devon**, **Cornwall**, the **Cotswolds** and the **Yorkshire Dales** harbour some especially picturesque specimens, but every county can boast a decent showing of photogenic hamlets.

**CLOCKWISE FROM TOP LEFT** BOROUGH MARKET, LONDON; AFTERNOON TEA AT THE ORANGERY RESTAURANT IN KENSINGTON PALACE GARDENS; MOUNTAIN BIKING IN THE YORKSHIRE DALES, LOWER WINSKILL

## ENGLAND'S BEACHES

Although rarely mentioned in the same breath as the sun-baked sands of the Mediterranean or Caribbean, England's **beaches** can compare with the best of them, both in terms of natural beauty and for cleanliness. For a combination of decent climate and good sand, coastal **Cornwall** and **Devon**, in the southwest, are hard to beat. England's largely pebbly southeastern coast is perhaps less suitable for lounging, though it does boast the surreal shingle stretch of **Dungeness** and some glorious sandy strands around **Thanet** in Kent, while the low cliffs and gravel of East Anglia's shore give way to a string of wide sandy beaches between **Cromer** and **Hunstanton**. There are spectacular stretches of sand in the northeast, notably around Scarborough in Yorkshire and in **Northumberland**, though the stiff North Sea breezes may require a degree of stoicism. Offshore islands, too, have some stunning coves and beaches, notably the Isles of Scilly and the Isle of Man.

Almost every stretch of English coast is **walkable**, and mostly waymarked – check out in particular the Norfolk Coast Path, the Cleveland Way along the Yorkshire coast, or the 630-mile South West Coast Path, Britain's longest National Trail, which takes in some of the country's wildest and most picturesque scenery. And then there are the quintessentially English **resorts**: a good beach, a pier or two, the piercing screech of gulls, fish and chips, saucy postcards, donkey rides, and lobster-red flesh at every turn. Blackpool in the northwest is the apotheosis – full-on, glamorous and tawdry, and with seven miles of clean beach to boot. Other resorts blend the same basic family-friendly ingredients with, in varying degrees, old-fashioned gentility (including Scarborough, in Yorkshire – said to be the country's oldest resort – and Broadstairs in Kent); elegance (classy Southwold, in Suffolk); and vintage hipster appeal (Kent's Margate and Morecambe in Lancashire). On the south coast, meanwhile, Brighton has a fiercely independent identity that combines the Georgian charm of its architecture with a gay-friendly boho appeal.

---

Evidence of England's pedigree is scattered between its settlements, as well. Wherever you're based, you're never more than a few miles from a majestic **country house** or **ruined castle** or **monastery**, and in many parts of the country you'll come across the sites of civilizations that thrived here long before England existed as a nation. In the southwest there are remnants of a **Celtic** culture that elsewhere was all but eradicated by the **Romans**, and from the south coast to the northern border you can find traces of **prehistoric** settlers, the most famous being the megalithic circles of Stonehenge and Avebury.

Then of course there's the English **countryside**, a diverse terrain from which Constable, Turner, Wordsworth, the Brontë sisters and a host of other native luminaries took inspiration. Most dramatic and best known are the moors and uplands – **Exmoor**, **Dartmoor**, **Bodmin Moor**, the **North York Moors** and the **Lake District** – each of which has its over-visited spots, though a brisk walk will usually take you out of the throng. Quieter areas are tucked away in every corner, from the flat wetlands of the eastern Fens to the chalk downland of Sussex. It's a similar story on the coast, where a number of resorts take advantage of the choicest spots, but which also offers blissful pockets of peace and quiet – along the exposed strands of **Northumberland**, for example, the flat horizons of **East Anglia** or the crumbling headlands of **Dorset**.

### TOP TEN COASTAL BEAUTY SPOTS

# Author picks

**Fish and chips** You can get a lip-smacking seaside supper at *Yorkshire Fisheries*, Blackpool (see p.543), *Maggie's* (see p.157), on the beach in Hastings' Fishing Quarter – which has the biggest beach-launched fleet in Europe – or at Whitby's *Magpie Café* (see p.633), one of Rick Stein's favourites.

**Marvellous markets** Manchester's German Christmas Market is a magical wonderland, with Glühwein too (see p.527). Norwich's huge open-air market is always bustling (see p.394), but for the best foodie shopping in England it has to be Borough Market in London (see p.86).

**Boutique bolt holes** In a pretty Somerset village, *Lord Poulett Arms* combines history with contemporary chic (see p.304), while London's *Hazlitts* offers ravishing Georgian elegance in the heart of Soho (see p.108). You can luxuriate in Lincoln at the *Old Palace* (see p.501) or enjoy a posh retreat at *Randy Pike*, a cosy Lake District hideaway (see p.564).

**Glorious gardens** Vita Sackville-West's Sissinghurst, in Kent, is the artistic cottage garden to end them all (see p.150), while Stourhead in Wiltshire (see p.227) offers a slice of traditional England at its best. Find French and Italian influences at Mount Edgcumbe garden near Plymouth (see p.330) and offbeat charm at Alnwick Garden in Northumberland, with its topiary snakes and a poison garden (see p.670).

**Sandy beaches** You're spoilt for choice for glorious strands in the southwest, but stars include Studland Bay (see p.211) and Par Beach in the Isles of Scilly (see p.360). For vast expanses, head to Holkham Bay, where three miles of pancake-flat sands (see p.404) lie beyond the pines and dunes, or Northumberland's Bamburgh, which offers acres of sky, sea and dunes with a dramatic castle backdrop (see p.673).

> Our author recommendations don't end here. We've flagged up our favourite places – a perfectly sited hotel, an atmospheric café, a special restaurant – throughout the guide, highlighted with the ★ symbol.

**FROM TOP** *RANDY PIKE*; SISSINGHURST; FISH AND CHIPS

# When to go

Considering how temperate the English **climate** is it's amazing how much mileage the locals get out of the subject – a two-day cold snap is discussed as if it were the onset of a new Ice Age, and a week above 25°C (upper 70s °F) starts rumours of drought. In recent years, however, the Brits' weather obsession has had some grounding in serious reality: summer temperatures have been known to soar into the 30s (over 90°F) before dropping drastically the next day, while catastrophic winter and spring flooding, and violent coastal storms, has laid waste to many parts of the country.

However, as a rule, English summers rarely get very hot and the winters don't get very cold. There's not a great deal of regional variation (see box p.32), though there are small microclimates; in general it's wetter in the west than the east, and the south gets more hours of sunshine than the north. Regional differences are more marked in winter, when the south tends to be milder and wetter than the north.

The bottom line is that it's impossible to say with any certainty that the weather will be pleasant in any given month. Obviously, if you're planning to camp or go to the beach, you'll want to visit between June and September. That said, even August has been known to present weeks of rain on the trot. Elsewhere, if you're balancing the likely fairness of the weather against the density of the crowds, the best time would be between **April and early June** or in **September** or **October**. England in the springtime, and in the autumn, can be a very beautiful place.

## BEER AND BREWERIES

When you order a pint, you're doing more than having a drink – you're celebrating English heritage. Beer (see p.36) has been a staple of the local diet for centuries, dating back to times when water was too dangerous to drink, and in recent years there's been a huge resurgence in regional brewing that reflects the wider interest in locally sourced food and drink. England has a fantastic selection of beers (the best in the world – no argument), and there's no more quintessentially English experience than to sample a pint or two in the nation's one great surviving social institution, the **pub**.

While the major international breweries and pub companies are facing the economic squeeze, England's medium-sized and small **microbreweries** are flourishing. Each region has its own independent outfits, brewing beers that are sometimes confined to one particular area or even just one pub. Cumbria alone has more than thirty small breweries, with several pioneering one-pub outlets like the *Bitter End* in Cockermouth (see p.577), Hesket Newmarket's *Old Crown* (ⓦtheoldcrownpub.co.uk), said to be Britain's first cooperatively owned pub, and *Dipton Mill Inn* in Hexham (see p.666). The Hook Norton Brewery in Oxfordshire (ⓦhooky.co.uk) still uses a working steam engine in its beer production, while there can't be many more remote ale-making locations than that of the Dent Brewery (ⓦdentbrewery.co.uk), hidden in a secluded corner of the Yorkshire Dales National Park.

Elsewhere, many of the big beer names on the bar (like Boddington's of Manchester, or Tetley's from Leeds) started out as family businesses, though are owned by multinational conglomerates these days. Others with widely available beers – Adnams of Suffolk (ⓦadnams.co.uk), Shepherd Neame of Kent (ⓦshepherdneame.co.uk), Harveys of Sussex (ⓦharveys.org.uk), Yorkshire's Black Sheep (see box, p.606) and Timothy Taylor (ⓦtimothytaylor.co.uk) – are still independently owned and regionally based, though beer aficionados gravitate naturally towards the smaller, more idiosyncratic breweries. Many of these, along with smaller outfits including Jennings in Cockermouth (see p.576), offer guided tours – with the inevitable free tipple at the end.

**OPPOSITE** RIVERSIDE PUB, OXFORD; PORT ERIN, ISLE OF MAN

# 30

## things not to miss

It's not possible to see everything England has to offer in one trip – and we don't suggest you try. What follows is a selective taste of the country's highlights: stunning architecture, dramatic landscapes, fun activities and world-class museums. Each highlight has a page reference to take you straight into the Guide, where you can find out more. Coloured numbers refer to chapters in the Guide.

1

### 1 STONEHENGE
Page 225

Redolent of mystery and myth, this is the most important stone circle in England, attracting crowds of thousands, including white-robed druids, for the summer solstice.

### 2 EDEN PROJECT
Page 346

With its ecological agenda, the West Country's most popular attraction presents a refreshing alternative to the hard sell of many of the region's crowd-pullers.

### 3 SURFING IN NORTH DEVON
Page 341

The beaches strung along the northern coast of Devon offer some great breaks, with Woolacombe, Croyde and Saunton the places to see and be seen.

### 4 MALHAM
Page 603

A jewel of the Yorkshire Dales National Park, this pretty village is the perfect base for walks into the spectacular scenery of Malham Cove, Malham Tarn and Gordale Scar.

**5 DURHAM CATHEDRAL**
Page 641
Arguably the greatest Norman building in England, Durham's imposing cathedral perches on a peninsula overlooking the quaint, cobbled old town.

**6 HIKING IN THE PEAK DISTRICT**
Page 460
A stirring landscape of moors and peaks, deep-green dales, tumbling rivers and jagged cliffs, the Peak District attracts hikers and outdoors enthusiasts by the thousand.

**7 HAY FESTIVAL**
Page 440
A rural outpost on the English-Welsh border, tiny Hay cuts a bibliographic dash with its many bookshops and prestigious literary festival.

**8 THERMAE BATH SPA**
Page 291
Take a restorative soak in what is hands-down one of England's most beautiful cities.

**9 GLASTONBURY FESTIVAL**
Page 301
Mud, mud, glorious mud … More than forty years on, Glastonbury is still England's best, best-known and biggest music and arts fest.

**10 MARGATE**
Page 136
With its vintage shopping and its fabulous art gallery, its excellent restaurants and its broad sandy beach, Margate is a regenerating seaside resort to watch.

### 11 NORTHERN QUARTER, MANCHESTER
Manchester's old garment district is a buzzing area packed with indie shops, vintage emporiums and cool bars.

### 12 OXFORD COLLEGES
Admire the dreaming spires of this glorious historic university town.

### 13 BLACKPOOL PLEASURE BEACH
Donkey rides, illuminations and thrills galore at the mother of all English seaside resorts.

### 14 HAWORTH
This atmospheric Yorkshire village was home to the Brontë sisters; their Georgian home is now a museum.

### 15 BRADFORD CURRY HOUSES
Bradford's excellent curry restaurants run the gamut from cheap and cheerful balti houses to upmarket contemporary dining rooms.

### 16 SHOPPING IN BRIGHTON
Brighton's Lanes and quirky North Laine, packed with shops, cafés and bars, are at the heart of this warm-hearted, boho seaside resort.

### 17 DARTMOOR
Southern England's great expanse of wilderness is perfect for hikers and riders.

14

15

16

17

22

23

24

29

 **SOUTHWOLD**
25
Page 390

George Orwell didn't like the place, but everyone else does: Southwold is a charming seaside town with a wide sandy beach and brightly painted beach huts.

26 **NEW FOREST**
Page 201

Famed for its wild ponies, this ancient hunting ground is a fabulous destination for cyclists and walkers.

 **PEOPLE'S HISTORY**
27 **MUSEUM, MANCHESTER**
Page 518

A lively exploration of England's rich radical history, covering everything from antifascists to football fans.

28 **HADRIAN'S WALL**
Page 662

Walk or cycle the length of this atmospheric Roman monument, which snakes its way for 84 miles over rough, sheep-strewn countryside.

 **LONDON'S MARKETS**
29 Page 126

From the vintage stores and food stalls of Brick Lane (pictured) to the floral abundance of Columbia Road and the grand old Victorian hall at Spitalfields, London's East End markets could fill a weekend of browsing and bargain-hunting.

30 **ST IVES, CORNWALL**
Page 358

Sunny seaside resort with great beaches and the best arts collection in southwest England.

30

# Itineraries

England may be a small country, but between the bracing Cornish coast and the misty Northern peaks, it has an astonishing amount to offer. The following itineraries give you a taster of its top destinations, its offbeat corners, and its literary highlights.

## THE GRAND TOUR

You'll need at least two weeks to really enjoy the big-hit destinations, but if time is at a premium you could pick and mix from this round-up of England's must-sees.

❶ **London** Give yourself at least three nights in London, quite simply one of the world's greatest cities. **See p.48**

❷ **Brighton** You can keep up the pace in this vibrant coastal town: cool, quirky and with lashings of seaside fun. **See p.162**

❸ **St Ives** Cornwall's dramatic coastline is breathtaking; base yourself in this artistic little town to enjoy the best of it. **See p.358**

❹ **Bath** Few people can resist this elegant Georgian city, with its Roman baths, luxury spa and excellent foodie scene. **See p.288**

❺ **Ironbridge** Learn about England's Industrial Revolution at this World Heritage Site, and base yourself in Ludlow, one of the foodiest towns in the country. **See p.442 & p.448**

❻ **Liverpool** You don't have to be a Beatles fan to love "the Pool", which not only has some fantastic Fab Four sights, but also an excellent food and nightlife scene. **See p.531**

❼ **The Peak District** The Peaks offer wonderfully rugged outdoors country just a short hop away from the nearby cities. **See p.460**

❽ **York** This picturesque medieval city, with its glorious Minster, is one of the most beautiful in the country. **See p.611**

❾ **Lake District** The pretty village of Grasmere makes a perfect base for forays into the dramatic hills and lakes of the Lake District National Park. **See p.552**

## QUIRKY ENGLAND

This offbeat itinerary, which focuses on some loopy sights in some lovely places, will help uncover another side to England beyond Big Ben and Beefeaters.

❶ **Dennis Severs' House, London** The BM and the National Gallery are all very well, but this dilapidated East End treasure, where silent candle-lit tours propel you back to Huguenot East End, gives you a unique flavour of old London. **See p.81**

❷ **Dungeness, Kent** This wild shingle stretch, splashed with wildflowers, is home to a peculiarly English mix of artists, traditionalists and free spirits, all living in the shadow of a colossal nuclear power station. It's unlike anywhere else in England. **See p.148**

❸ **Postcard Museum, Isle of Wight** The Isle of Wight has an atmosphere all of its own – for a taster, check out the cheeky, and often surreal, British seaside humour at Ryde's retro postcard museum. **See p.190**

**ABOVE** ROYAL CRESCENT, BATH

**❹ Cerne Abbas Giant, Dorset** No visit to England, with its love of Carry On films and double-entendres, would be complete without a gawp at this large naked man carved into a green hillside. See p.214

**❺ Pitt Rivers Museum, Oxford** Eyes glazing over at the fancy china and Old Masters at stately home no. 32? Come here to peruse exhibits arranged like an exotic junk shop. Past "objects of the month" have included a disease demon mask from Sri Lanka and reindeer knickers from Siberia. See p.244

**❻ Southwold, Suffolk** Suffolk's poshest seaside town may seem frightfully refined, but head to the Under the Pier Show for offbeat arcade games and handmade slot machines – an inventive take on the traditional seaside pier. See p.390

**❼ Blackpool, Lancashire** England's loudest, brashest resort, where the sun never sets on the rollercoasters, karaoke bars and candy-floss kiosks. Waltz around the Blackpool Tower ballroom to the tones of a Wurlitzer organ and check out the chuckles on the Comedy Carpet. See p.540

## LITERARY ENGLAND

This itinerary, which touches upon the most famous of England's extraordinary literary highlights, could take at least two weeks – or longer, if you use the sites as jumping-off points into some of England's loveliest countryside.

**❶ Shakespeare's Globe, London** Shakespeare as it was meant to be experienced, outdoors, with a raucous crowd, full of verve. See p.85

**❷ Dickens Museum, Broadstairs** Dickens spent a lot of time in this Kentish seaside resort; this little house high on the cliff, inspiration for Miss Trotwood's house in *David Copperfield*, is full of memorabilia. See p.137

**❸ Chawton, Hampshire** The pretty village where Jane Austen lived in her later years is packed with sights relating to the perennially popular author. See p.201

**❹ Dorchester, Dorset** Thomas Hardy's town is a good base for the surrounding "Hardy country" that features so evocatively in his novels. See p.213

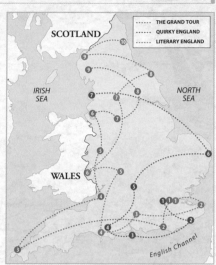

**❺ Stratford-upon-Avon, West Midlands** Not only can you see the Bard's works performed in the RSC theatres of his hometown, but you can also visit his birthplace and Anne Hathaway's picturesque cottage. See p.425

**❻ Hay-on-Wye, Herefordshire** Well worth a trip even if you can't make it to the world-famous literary festival, this riverside border town boasts a huge array of secondhand book stores. See p.440

**❼ Haworth, Yorkshire** A pilgrimage site for every Brontë fan: wander around the Parsonage where the sisters grew up – and stroll across the wild Yorkshire moorland that features so powerfully in their works. See p.599

**❽ Whitby, Yorkshire** Bram Stoker found spooky inspiration in this dramatically set fishing town – lure out your inner Goth and follow the Dracula trail around all the key sites. See p.630

**❾ Cockermouth, Cumbria** The Lake District, where Wordsworth wandered lonely as a cloud, is full of places related to the poet; a visit to his childhood home is a great starting point. See p.576

**❿ Seven Stories, Newcastle-upon-Tyne** Seven storeys crammed full of stories, focusing on the fine art of children's literature. See p.654

RURAL POSTBOX, LAKE DISTRICT NATIONAL PARK

# Basics

# Getting there

**London is one of the world's busiest transport hubs, and there are good deals from around the world on flights into the British capital. However, if you're planning to tour the southwest or north of England consider flying directly instead to more convenient international airports like Bristol, Birmingham or Manchester.**

London's biggest and best-known airports – **Heathrow** and **Gatwick** – take the bulk of transatlantic and long-haul flights into the UK, though there are also three smaller London airports (**Stansted**, **Luton** and **City**) and a host of useful regional British airports, many of which are served by low-cost flights from mainland Europe and Ireland. Principally, in England these are **Manchester** and **Liverpool** in the northwest; **Birmingham** in the West Midlands; **Bristol**, Newquay and Exeter in the West Country; **Leeds-Bradford** and Doncaster-Sheffield in Yorkshire; **Newcastle** and Durham Tees Valley in the northeast; **East Midlands**; and Bournemouth and Southampton in the south. There are also airports at Blackpool, Humberside, Nottingham and Norwich. The cheapest deals on all routes need to be booked well in advance and tend to have little or no flexibility, and taxes and fees can add significantly to any quoted price.

**Overland** routes from Europe include high-speed trains into London (with onward connections) through the Channel Tunnel – either passenger-only Eurostar services or the drive-on drive-off **Eurotunnel** shuttle train. There's also a range of useful ferry routes offering direct access to various regions.

## Flights from the US and Canada

Many airlines fly nonstop to London, Manchester and other British airports – flight time from the east coast is around seven hours, ten hours from the west. Flights on European airlines might be cheaper but tend to route through their respective European hubs, adding to the journey time.

Low-season round-trip **fares** from New York, Boston and Washington to London range from US$650–800, and in summer you can expect to pay more than US$1000 (add US$100–200 from other eastern cities). Low-season fares from the west coast can start at a little under US$1000, rising to more like US$1400 in summer and around Christmas. In **Canada**, the best deals involve flying to London from Toronto or Montreal (around Can$1000–1200 return). British Airways flies direct to Heathrow from Vancouver and Calgary while Air Canada has nonstop links from Vancouver, Calgary, Edmonton and Ottawa. From the west, fares range from Can$1200 to Can$1650.

## Flights from Australia, New Zealand and South Africa

Flight time from **Australia** and **New Zealand** to England is at least 22 hours. Flights via Southeast Asia or the Middle East to London are generally the cheapest. Average **return fares** from eastern Australian cities to London are Aus$1500–2500 depending on the season; from Perth or Darwin you'll pay around Aus$200 less. Return fares from Auckland to London range from NZ$2000–3000.

There are direct flights from **South Africa** to London Heathrow with South African Airways (Jo'burg and Cape Town), British Airways (Jo'burg and Cape Town) and Virgin Atlantic (Jo'burg). You might get a cheaper deal on indirect routes with Emirates (from Cape Town, Durban and Jo'burg), Ethiopian Airlines (from Jo'burg), KLM (from Jo'burg) and Lufthansa (from Jo'burg). Return fares are generally around ZAR7000–8000.

## Flights from Ireland

You can get a one-way flight between **Ireland** and England for around €50–80. There are routes out of Dublin, Cork, Knock, Kerry and Shannon to many English airports; airlines include Stobart Air (previously Aer Arann), Ryanair, Aer Lingus and British Airways. The cheapest options **from Belfast** and Derry are usually easyJet, flybe and Ryanair.

---

**A BETTER KIND OF TRAVEL**

At Rough Guides we are passionately committed to travel. We believe it helps us understand the world we live in and the people we share it with – and of course tourism is vital to many developing economies. But the scale of modern tourism has also damaged some places irreparably, and climate change is accelerated by most forms of transport, especially flying. All Rough Guides' flights are carbon-offset, and every year we donate money to a variety of environmental charities.

## Ferries

There are many ferry routes from mainland Europe and Ireland to England. The quickest, cheapest services are on the traditional cross-Channel routes **from the French ports** of Calais, Boulogne, Dieppe and Dunkerque to **Dover** and Folkestone in Kent. There are many other routes from elsewhere in France, plus Spain (Gijon, Santander and Bilbao), Belgium (Ostend and Zeebrugge) and the Netherlands (Hook of Holland, Amsterdam and Rotterdam) and Denmark (Esbjerg) into ports around the southern and eastern coasts of England, from Plymouth to Newcastle.

Ferry services from **Ireland** mainly run to England's northwest (Liverpool and the Isle of Man) and **Wales** (Holyhead, Fishguard and Pembroke).

**Fares** on all routes vary considerably, according to time of year, and time and type of crossing – some high-speed ferry services can cut journey times on the same route by up to half – while accommodation is often obligatory (and welcome) on night crossings from the continent.

For up-to-date **information** on routes and operators, check ⓦ discoverferries.com; to book direct, try ⓦ aferry.com.

## Trains

Direct **Eurostar trains** (ⓦ eurostar.com) run roughly hourly to London St Pancras International from Calais (1hr 10min), Lille (1hr 20min), Brussels (2hr) and Paris (2hr 20min), with connections into those cities from across Europe and direct seasonal services from southern France (Avignon in summer; Bourg St Maurice and Moutiers in winter). Fares start from around €75 one-way, though these special rates come with restrictions and you'll have to book well in advance. There are discounts on standard fares for travellers under 26 and over 60.

For drivers, the fastest and most convenient cross-Channel option is the **Eurotunnel** (ⓦ eurotunnel.com) drive-on-drive-off shuttle train from Calais to Folkestone (around 75 miles southeast of London), which runs 24 hours and takes 35–45 minutes. Booking is advised, especially at weekends or if you want the best prices. The standard fare for a car and all its passengers is €60–95 one way; more if booked at short notice. **Irish Ferries** (ⓦ irishferries.com) offers a very good "Rail Sail" deal, where you can book integrated train and ferry services from almost any station in Ireland to almost any station in England. Dublin to London, for example, takes under seven hours, with one-way

fares starting at €55. For the best train information online, check the **Man in Seat 61** at ⓦ seat61.com.

## Buses

**Eurolines** (ⓦ eurolines.co.uk) coordinates international bus services to London (with connections onwards) from dozens of **European cities**. This is the cheapest way of travelling, but you really do have to ask yourself how long you want to spend cooped up in a bus. Only routes from northern European cities are anything like bearable: the journey from Paris, for example, which takes around six hours to London Victoria Coach Station and costs from €25 one-way.

## Tours and organized holidays

**Package tours** of England, where all flights, accommodation and ground transport are arranged for you, can sometimes be cheaper than organizing things yourself. Many companies, for example, offer **coach tours** of the country's historic highlights, or help you explore some aspect of its heritage, such as art and architecture, or gardens and stately homes. Other operators specialize in **activity holidays** (see box, p.40) either escorted (ie, guide-led) or self-guided, the latter usually being slightly cheaper. Some companies offer budget versions of their holidays, staying in hostels or B&Bs, as well as hotel packages.

### AIRLINES

**Aer Lingus** ⓦ aerlingus.com
**Air Canada** ⓦ aircanada.com
**British Airways** ⓦ ba.com
**easyJet** ⓦ easyjet.com
**Emirates** ⓦ emirates.com
**Ethiopian Airlines** ⓦ ethiopianairlines.com
**flybe** ⓦ flybe.com
**KLM** ⓦ klm.com
**Lufthansa** ⓦ lufthansa.com
**Ryanair** ⓦ ryanair.com
**South African Airways** ⓦ flysaa.com
**Stobart Air** ⓦ aerarann.com
**Virgin Atlantic** ⓦ virgin-atlantic.com

### AGENTS AND OPERATORS

**North South Travel** UK ☎ 01245 608291, ⓦ northsouthtravel .co.uk. Friendly, competitive travel agency, offering discounted fares worldwide. Profits are used to support projects in the developing world, especially the promotion of sustainable tourism.
**STA Travel** UK ☎ 0333 321 0099, US ☎ 1800 781 4040, Australia ☎ 134 782, New Zealand ☎ 0800 474 400, South Africa ☎ 0861 781 781, ⓦ statravel.co.uk. Worldwide specialists in independent

travel; also student IDs, travel insurance, car rental, rail passes, and more. Good discounts for students and under-26s.

**Trailfinders** UK ☎ 020 7368 1200, Ireland ☎ 021 464 8800, Ⓦ trailfinders.com. One of the best-informed and most efficient agents for independent travellers.

**Travel CUTS** Canada ☎ 1800 667 2887, US ☎ 1800 592 2887, Ⓦ travelcuts.com. Canadian youth and student travel firm.

## PACKAGE TOURS

We have listed operators offering walking, cycling and activity holidays in our "Sports and outdoor activities" section (see p.39).

**Abercrombie & Kent** US ☎ 1800 554 7016, Ⓦ abercrombiekent .com. Classy travel specialist, with no-expense-spared escorted and independent trips, from a seven-night River Thames cruise to nine-day tours of English gardens.

**Contiki Holidays** UK ☎ 0845 075 0990, Ⓦ contiki.com. Lively, reasonably priced, budget-accommodation adventure tours for 18–35s, including 3- and 5-day London trips.

**Martin Randall Travel** UK ☎ 020 8742 3355, Ⓦ martinrandall .com. Wide-ranging all-inclusive historical and cultural tours led by experts – for example, 7 days walking Hadrian's Wall, 9 days exploring England's cathedrals or 4 days soaking up the Arts and Crafts heritage of the Cotswolds.

**Maupintour** US ☎ 1800 255 4266, Ⓦ maupintour.com. Quality, all-inclusive, themed escorted tours including a trip to London and southwest England.

# Getting around

**Almost every town and many villages in England can be reached by train or – if you have time and flexibility – bus, but public transport costs are among the highest in Europe and travel can eat up a large part of your budget. It pays to investigate all the special deals and passes, some of which are only available outside the UK and must be bought before you arrive. It may be cheaper to drive, though fuel and car rental rates are expensive and traffic can be bad in the cities and on the motorways.**

## By plane

For longer journeys across England such as London–Newcastle or Manchester–Newquay, you might consider **flying**, using airlines such as British Airways (Ⓦ ba.com), easyJet (Ⓦ easyjet.com), Ryanair (Ⓦ ryanair.com), flybe (Ⓦ flybe.com) and Cityjet (Ⓦ cityjet.com). Fares on popular routes such as London or Birmingham to Edinburgh and Glasgow London to Edinburgh, Birmingham to Glasgow, etc

with journey times of around just 1hr, can cost as little as £60 return – which can be less than the equivalent train fares, especially if you book early enough. That said, if you factor in travel to the airport and check-in procedures you won't always save much on total door-to-door journey time

## By train

Despite grumbles about the rail network, and the high cost of travel compared to other European rail systems, getting around England by train is still the best, most scenic and – usually – most painless way to travel. Most major towns in England have rail links, and mainline routes out of London in particular are **fast and frequent** – the 200-mile trips to York and Exeter, for instance, are covered in two hours. The fastest journeys head north from London on east- and west-coast mainline routes (to Birmingham, Manchester, Leeds and Newcastle, among others), and there are high-speed services to Kent from King's Cross St Pancras; other journeys, however, can be more complicated, particularly if you're travelling east–west across the country, which might involve a train change or two.

England's trains are run by a myriad of **operators**, but all are required to work as a single network with integrated ticketing. The **National Rail Enquiries** website (Ⓦ nationalrail.co.uk) is a useful first call for timetable, route and fare information; it lists all the regional operators and offers ticket-buying links from its journey planner. For an exhaustive rundown of train travel in the UK, check the excellent website **Man in Seat 61** (Ⓦ seat61.com).

### Buying tickets

As a rule, the earlier you book, the less you will pay. Always look out for **online offers** with **booking sites** like Ⓦ thetrainline.com or Ⓦ megatrain.com – the latter, in particular, offers a limited number of ridiculously low fares on certain popular routes. That said, it's also worth checking the websites of the individual operators, as occasionally their fares will trump those offered by the booking sites.

---

### TOP 5 TRAIN JOURNEYS

**Dartmouth Steam Railway** See p.324
**Isle of Wight Steam Railway** See p.191
**North Yorkshire Moors Railway** See box, p.627
**Ravenglass and Eskdale Railway** See p.575
**Settle to Carlisle Railway** See box, p.605

A **seat reservation** is usually included with the ticket. Just turning up and buying a ticket at the station is always the most expensive way to go (sometimes phenomenally so); it's always worth asking at the ticket desk about the cheapest option for your journey, as you may get discounts on groups or couples travelling together. If the ticket office is closed, or the automatic machines aren't working, you may buy your ticket on board from the inspector. In some cases, though, buying a ticket on the train when you had the opportunity to buy one beforehand could lead to a penalty of £20 – the stations from which penalty fares apply will have large posters advertising that fact.

Cheapest, wherever you buy them, are advance tickets, which are only available several weeks in advance and sell out quickly. They are restricted to use only on the specified train – miss it, and you pay a surcharge or have to buy another ticket. Off-peak fares can be bought in advance or on the day of travel, but are only valid for travel at quieter times (generally outside 5–10am and 3–8pm Mon–Fri). Most expensive are the fully flexible Anytime tickets.

### Rail passes

For overseas visitors planning to travel widely by train, a **BritRail England pass** could be a wise investment (🌐britrail.net). It gives unlimited travel throughout England and is valid for varied periods of from three to fifteen days in two months (not necessarily consecutive). There are first- and second-class versions, discounted Youth Passes and Senior Passes, and for every adult buying a full-priced ticket one child (aged 5 to 15) receives the same pass for free. Note that BritRail passes have to be bought before you enter the UK.

If you've been resident in a European country other than the UK for at least six months, an **InterRail pass** (🌐interrail.eu), allowing unlimited train travel in England, Wales and Scotland (for 3, 4, 6 or 8 days within one month), might be worth it – but note that you can't use the pass for travel in your own country of residence. **Eurail** passes are not valid in the UK, though they do provide discounts on Eurostar trains to England and on some ferry routes.

🌐nationalrail.co.uk details the many regional rail passes that can be bought by both locals and visitors in England itself. **Rover and Ranger passes** offer unlimited travel in single, multi-day or flexi-day formats – the Ride Cornwall Ranger, for example, which costs £10 for a day's worth of train travel in that county. There are numerous options when it comes to **annual railcards**, including the 16–25 Railcard, for full-time students and people between 16 and 25; the Senior Railcard for travellers over 60; the Two Together card for a couple travelling together (they don't have to be related); and the Family & Friends Railcard for groups of up to four adults and four children travelling together. Each costs £30 for the year and gives up to a third off most adult fares in England (more for children's fares).

## By bus

Travel by bus – long-distance services are known as "coaches" – is usually much cheaper than by train, though less comfortable, and traffic congestion can make the same journey much longer. The biggest **inter-city** bus operators in England are **National Express** (🌐nationalexpress.com) and Megabus (🌐megabus.com). On busy routes, and on any route at weekends and holidays, it's advisable to book ahead to get the best deal. Fares are very reasonable, with discounts for under-26s, over-60s and families, plus various advance-purchase fares, passes and special deals available. **Regional and urban** bus services are run by a huge array of companies. Check the official service **Traveline** (🌐traveline.info) for information and routes. In many cases, timetables and routes are well integrated, but operators tend to duplicate the busiest services, leaving the more remote spots neglected. As a rule, the further away from urban areas you get, the less frequent services become.

## By car

Your English driving experience will depend very much on where you drive. Slogging through the traffic from major city to major city is rarely an illuminating way to see the nation – motorways ("M" roads) and main "A" roads may have up to four lanes in each direction, but even these can get very congested, with long tailbacks a regular occurrence, especially at peak travel times and on public holidays. Driving in the countryside, on the other hand, is far more agreeable, though on "B" roads and minor roads there might only be one lane (single track) in both directions. Keep your speed down, and be prepared for abrupt encounters with tractors, sheep and other hazards in remote spots. Don't underestimate the English **weather**, either. Snow, ice, fog and wind can cause havoc – and there has been major flooding in the past few years – and driving conditions, on motorways as much as in rural areas, can deteriorate quickly. Local radio stations feature regularly updated traffic bulletins, as does the **Highways Agency** (ⓦhighways.gov.uk).

England currently just has one **Toll Road**, the M6 in the Midlands, but **congestion charging** applies in London (see box, p.106). **Fuel** is pricey – unleaded petrol (gasoline) and diesel in particular. Out-of-town supermarkets usually have the lowest prices, while the highest prices are charged by motorway service stations.

**Parking** in towns, cities and popular tourist spots can be a nightmare and often costs a small fortune. A yellow line along the edge of the road indicates **parking restrictions**; check the nearest sign to see exactly what they are. A double-yellow line means no parking at any time, though you can stop briefly to unload or pick up people or goods, while red lines signify no stopping at all. Fines for parking illegally are high – as much as £60 – and if you're wheel-clamped it will cost you £200 or so to have your vehicle released.

## Rules and regulations

Drive on the left. **Seatbelts** must be worn by everyone in a vehicle, front and back, while motorcyclists and their passengers must wear a helmet. You are not permitted to make a kerbside turn against a red light and must always give way to traffic (circulating clockwise) on a **roundabout** – this applies even for mini-roundabouts, which may be no more than a white circle painted on the road. **Speed limits** are 20 miles/hr in many residential streets, 30 miles/hr in built-up areas, 70 miles/hr on dual carriageways and motorways (freeways) and 60 miles/hr on most other roads – as a rule, assume that in any area with street lighting the speed limit is 30 miles/hr unless otherwise stated. Be alert to the signs, as **speed cameras** are everywhere.

Most foreign nationals can get by with their **driving licence** from home, but if you're in any doubt, obtain an **international driving permit** from a national motoring organization. Anyone bringing their own vehicle into the country should also carry vehicle registration, ownership and insurance documents.

The AA (ⓦtheaa.com), RAC (ⓦrac.co.uk) and Green Flag (ⓦgreenflag.com) all operate **24-hour emergency breakdown** services, and offer useful online route planners. You may be entitled to free assistance through a reciprocal arrangement with a motoring organization in your home country – check before setting out. You can make use of these emergency services if you are not a member, but you will need to join at the roadside and will incur a hefty surcharge.

## Vehicle rental

**Car rental** is best booked online through one of the large multinational chains (Avis, Budget, easycar, Hertz or National, for example) or through a site such as ⓦauto-europe.co.uk. **North Americans** might want to contact the independently owned Europe by Car (☎1 800 223 1516, ⓦeuropebycar blog.com), which has good deals on short and longer-term rentals.

If you rent a car from a company in the UK, expect to pay around £30 per day, £50 for a weekend, or £120–200 per week. Few companies will rent to drivers with less than one year's experience and most will only rent to people between 21 or 23 and 70 years of age. Rental cars will be manual (stick shift) unless you specify otherwise – if you want an **automatic transmission**, book well ahead and expect to pay at least £170 a week. **Motorbike rental** is even more expensive – around £350 a week. Try London-based Raceways (ⓦraceways.net) or Manchester-based New Horizons (ⓦnew horizonsbikehire.co.uk).

# By bike

Cycling around England can be a pleasant option, as long as you stick to the quieter "B" roads and country lanes – or, best of all, follow one of the **traffic-free trails** of the extensive National Cycle Network (see p.40).

**Cycle helmets** are not compulsory – but if you're hell-bent on tackling the congestion, pollution and aggression of city traffic, you're well advised to wear one. You do have to have a **rear reflector** and front and back **lights** when riding at night, and you are not allowed to carry children without a special **child seat**. It is also illegal to cycle on pavements and in most public parks, while **off-road** cyclists must stick to bridleways and by-ways designated for their use.

**Bike rental** is available at cycle shops in most large towns, and at villages within National Parks and other scenic areas. Expect to pay around £20–25 per day, or more for specialist mountain bikes and less for multi-day rents; you may need to provide credit card details or leave a passport as a deposit.

Accompanied bikes are allowed free on mainline trains, but you usually need to book the space in advance; check ⓦnationalrail.co.uk for individual company regulations. Bus and coach companies rarely accept cycles and even then only if they are dismantled and boxed.

# Accommodation

**Accommodation in England ranges from corporate chain hotels to crumbling castles, from budget backpacker hostels to chic boutique hotels. Characterful old buildings – former coaching inns, converted mansions and manor houses – also offer heaps of historic atmosphere. It also tends to be quite expensive, though there are bargains to be had.**

Although booking online is your best bet, many tourist offices will **reserve rooms** for you if you turn up without having done so. Using this service might incur a deposit that's deducted from your first night's bill (usually ten percent); in others the office will take a percentage or flat-rate commission of a few quid. If you turn up at a hotel or guesthouse on spec, don't be afraid to ask to see your room before committing – any place worth its salt, be it designer hotel or humble B&B, should have no objection.

A nationwide **grading system, annually upgraded,** awards **stars** to hotels, guesthouses and B&Bs. There's no hard and fast correlation between rank and price, but the system does lay down minimum levels of standards and service. However, not every establishment participates, and you shouldn't assume that a particular place is no good simply because it doesn't. In the rural backwaters in particular some of the best accommodation is to be found in **farmhouses** and other simple properties whose facilities may technically fall short of official standards.

## Hotels

English hotels vary wildly in size, style, comfort and price. The starting price for a basic hotel is around £80 per night for a double or twin room, breakfast

## TOP 5 QUIRKY HOTELS

**Belle Tout** Beachy Head. See p.159
**Cley Mill B&B** Norfolk. See p.402
**Old Dungeon Ghyll** Langdale. See p.565
**Pelirocco** Brighton. See p.167
**Rough Luxe** London. See p.109

usually included; anything more upmarket, or with a bit of boutique styling, will be around £100 a night, while at the top-end properties the sky's the limit, especially in London or in resort or country-house hotels. Many city hotels in particular charge a room rate only.

**Budget hotel chains** – including Premier Inn (Ⓦ premierinn.com), Holiday Inn Express (Ⓦ hiex press.com), Jurys Inn (Ⓦ jurysinns.com), Travelodge (Ⓦ travelodge.co.uk), Ibis (Ⓦ ibishotel.com) and Comfort/Quality/Sleep Inns (Ⓦ choicehotelsuk .co.uk) – have properties across the country. With no frills (and with breakfast charged extra), they are not always automatically the cheapest option, but they can be a good deal for families and small groups, and rates can get down to a bargain £40–50 per night if booked well in advance. Tune Hotels (London; Ⓦ tunehotels.com) and easyHotel (London; Ⓦ easyhotel.com) can be even cheaper, offering a simple "add-on" system whereby you book a minimal room online with the option of adding niceties including cleaning, windows, TVs, towels…

## B&Bs, guesthouses and pubs

At its most basic, the typical English **bed-and-breakfast** (**B&B**) is an ordinary private house with a couple of bedrooms set aside for paying guests. Larger establishments with more rooms, particularly in resorts, style themselves as **guesthouses**, but they are pretty much the same thing.

---

## ACCOMMODATION PRICES

Throughout this Guide we give a headline price for every accommodation reviewed, which indicates the lowest price you could expect to pay per night for a **double or twin room in high season** (basically, from Easter to the end of September, though local variations apply). We also give the high-season price for a dorm bed (and a double room, where available) in a **hostel** – note that for YHA hostels, prices quoted are for nonmembers (members get a £3 discount per night) – and per pitch or per person prices for **campsites**. For **self-catering**, we quote the minimum you might pay, for a night or a week, depending on the establishment, in high season. **Single occupancy** rates vary widely. Though they're typically around three-quarters of the price of a double, some places charge almost the full double rate and others charge only a little over half that. Rates in hotels and B&Bs may well drop between Sunday and Thursday, or if you stay more than one night, and some places will require a two-night minimum at the weekend and/or in high season.

At the extreme budget end of the scale – basic B&Bs under £60 a night – you'll normally experience small rooms, fairly spartan facilities and shared bathrooms (though there are some fantastic exceptions). You'll pay a few pounds more for en-suite shower and toilet, while at the top end of the range you can expect real style, fresh flowers, gourmet breakfasts, king-sized beds and luxurious bathrooms. Many top-notch B&Bs – say around £100 and up – offer more luxury and far better value pound for pound than more impersonal hotels. In this category you can also count **pubs** (or inns), and the increasingly popular "**restaurants with rooms**". Both will often have only a handful of rooms, but their atmosphere – and the lazy option of laying your head in the same place that you eat and drink – make them a good option.

## Hostels

The **Youth Hostels Association** (Ⓦ yha.org.uk) has hundreds of hostels across England, ranging from lakeside mansions to thatched country cottages. There are still shared bathrooms and traditional single-sex bunk-bed dormitories in most, though the majority also now offer smaller rooms (sometimes en-suite) of two to six beds for couples, families and groups. Some hostels have been purpose-built, or have had expensive refurbishments, and in cities, resorts and National Park areas the facilities are often every bit as good as budget hotels. Most offer self-catering kitchens, laundry facilities and lounges, while wi-fi access, cafés, bars, tour bookings and bike rental are common. The hostel will usually provide bed linen, pillows and duvet; towels and other necessities can often be rented.

You don't have to be a member to stay at a YHA hostel but nonmembers are charged an extra £3 a night. One year's membership, which is open only to residents of the EU, costs £15 per year for England and Wales and can be bought online or at any YHA hostel. Members gain automatic membership of the hostelling associations of the ninety countries affiliated to Hostelling International (HI; Ⓦ hihostels.com).

**Prices** are calculated according to season, location and demand, with adult dorm beds costing from £15–30 per night – prices can get higher than that in London and at peak holiday periods. A private twin room in a hostel goes for around £40–70, and family rooms sleeping four from around £70. **Meals** are good value – breakfast or a packed lunch for around £5, or £10–13 for dinner. Advance

> **TOP 5 HOSTELS**
> **Grasmere Independent Hostel**. See p.566
> **Kipps** Canterbury. See p.142
> **Meininger** London. See p.111
> **YHA Boscastle**. See p.367
> **YHA Whitby** See p.632

booking is recommended, and essential at Easter, Christmas and from May to August.

A large number of **independent hostels** offer similar prices. With no membership fees, more relaxed rules, mixed dorms and no curfew, many of them, in the cities at least, tend to attract a predominantly young, keen-to-party crowd, but there are family-friendly options, too. For news and reviews, check Ⓦ independenthostelguide.co.uk, which also lists primitive bunkhouses, bunk barns and camping barns in the most rural locations.

## Camping

There are hundreds of **campsites**, ranging from small, family-run places to large sites with laundries, shops and sports facilities. Costs start at around £5 per adult in the simplest sites, though at larger, more popular locations you can pay far more, and sometimes there are separate charges per car and tent. Many campsites also have accommodation in permanently fixed, fully equipped caravans, or in wooden cabins or similar. Perhaps in part due to the unreliable weather, Brits have taken **glamping** to their hearts, with more tipis, yurts, bell tents and camping "pods" than you could shake a billycan at. Some are downright lavish (with beds, plump duvets, private loos and wood-burners) and are priced accordingly.

In England's wilder places you will find **camping barns** and **bunkhouses**, many administered by the YHA, though with plenty of others operated by individual farmers and families. They are pretty basic – often in converted agricultural buildings, old crofters' cottages and the like – but they are weatherproof and cheap (from around £8–10 a night). **Farmers** may offer field-and-tap pitches for around £3 per night, but setting up a tent without asking first is counted as trespassing and seriously frowned upon. Camping wild is illegal in most National Parks and nature reserves – Dartmoor is one exception – check Ⓦ nationalparks.gov.uk/visiting/camping for more information.

*The Rough Guide to Camping in Britain* has detailed **reviews** of the best campsites, while

Ⓦcoolcamping.co.uk, Ⓦcampingandcaravanning club.co.uk and Ⓦukcampsite.co.uk are useful online resources.

## Self-catering

Holiday self-catering properties range from city penthouses to secluded cottages. **Studios and apartments**, available by the night in an increasing number of cities, offer an attractive alternative to hotels, with prices from around £90 a night (more in London). Rural **cottages and houses** work out cheaper, though the minimum rental period may be a week. Depending on the season and location, expect to pay from around £350 for a week in a small cottage, perhaps three or four times that for a larger property in a popular tourist spot.

### ACCOMMODATION CONTACTS

### B&BS, HOTELS, FARMS AND STUDENT ROOMS

**Bed&Fed** Ⓦ bedandfed.co.uk. Informal "homes from home", with your hosts providing a simple supper, bed and a light breakfast.

**CouchSurfing** Ⓦ couchsurfing.org. Huge worldwide directory listing people willing to let other members stay with them for free.

**Distinctly Different** Ⓦ distinctlydifferent.co.uk. B&B or self-catering in converted buildings across England, from cow sheds to lighthouses.

**Farm Stay** Ⓦ farmstay.co.uk. The UK's largest network of farm-based accommodation – B&B, self-catering and camping.

**LateRooms.com** Ⓦ laterooms.com. Thousands of rooms across England available at up to fifty percent discount.

**University rooms** Ⓦ universityrooms.co.uk. Student halls of residence in university towns from Cornwall to Northumberland, offering good-value rooms (mostly single) or self-catering apartments over the summer (July–Sept), Easter and Christmas holidays.

**Wolsey Lodges** Ⓦ wolseylodges.com. Superior B&B in grand properties throughout England, from Elizabethan manor houses to Victorian rectories.

### SELF-CATERING

**Airbnb** Ⓦ airbnb.com. Cool self-catering, with a huge variety of properties – seaside cottages to farmhouses, canal barges to warehouse apartments.

**Cottages4You** Ⓦ cottages4you.co.uk. A wide range of properties all over the UK.

**Landmark Trust** Ⓦ landmarktrust.org.uk. A preservation charity that lists pricey, rather special accommodation in England's most distinctive historic properties – castles, ruins, follies, towers and cottages.

**National Trust Holiday Cottages** Ⓦ nationaltrustcottages.co.uk and Ⓦ nts.org.uk. Self-catering holiday cottages, houses and farmhouses, most of which are set in the gardens or grounds of National Trust properties.

**Rural Retreats** Ⓦ ruralretreats.co.uk. Upmarket accommodation in restored historic buildings.

**Under the Thatch** ☎ 0844 500 5101, Ⓦ underthethatch.co.uk. A select choice of self-catering cottages and cabins, many beautifully restored, from traditional thatched cottages to Romany caravans and yurts.

# Food and drink

**England no longer has to feel ashamed of its culinary offerings. Over the last twenty years, changing tastes have transformed supermarket shelves, restaurant menus and pub blackboards, with an increasing importance placed on "ethical" and sustainable eating – not only sourcing products locally, but also using free-range, organic, humanely produced ingredients. London continues to be the main centre for all things foodie and fashionable, though great restaurants, gastropubs, farmers' markets and interesting local food suppliers can be found across England, often in surprisingly out-of-the-way places.**

## English cuisine

For some visitors the quintessential English meal is **fish and chips**, a dish that can vary from the succulently fresh to the indigestibly greasy: local knowledge is the key, as most towns, cities and resorts have at least one first-rate fish-and-chip shop ("chippie") or restaurant. Other **traditional English dishes** (steak and kidney pie, liver and onions, bacon sandwiches, roast beef, sausage and mash, pork pies) have largely discarded their stodgy image and been poshed up to become restaurant, and particularly gastropub, staples – comfort food still, but often cooked with the best ingredients and genuinely tasty. Many hitherto neglected or previously unfashionable English foods – from brawn to brains – are finding their way into top-end restaurants, too, as inventive restaurateurs, keen on using good, seasonal produce, reinvent the classics. The principles of this "nose to tail" eating crosses over with the increasingly modish **Modern British** cuisine, which marries local produce with ingredients and techniques from around the world. **Vegetarians** need not worry, either, despite all this emphasis on meat – veggie restaurants are fairly easy to find in towns and cities, and practically every restaurant and pub will have at least one vegetarian option, be it just a cheese sandwich or a plate of tomato pasta. As a failsafe, Italian, Indian and Chinese restaurants usually provide a decent choice of meat-free dishes.

The wealth of **fresh produce** varies regionally, from hedgerow herbs to fish landed from local boats, and, of course, seasonally. Restaurants are increasingly making use of seasonal ingredients – and in rural areas many farms offer "Pick Your Own"

## A FOODIE LEXICON

Whether you're curious about Cornish pasties or Lancashire hotpots, puzzled by Yorkshire puds or interested in Eccles cakes, you may have to learn a whole **lexicon** to figure out what you're eating. Foodie bafflers range from faggots (offal meatballs) to bubble-and-squeak (fried leftover potato and cabbage), toad in the hole (sausages in a batter pudding) and spotted dick (suet-pudding dessert with currants). Even the basics aren't straightforward – a simple bread roll, for example, may be referred to as a roll, cob, bap, barmcake, teacake or bread-bun, depending on which part of England you're in.

## TOP 5 CAFÉS

**Bar Italia** London. See p.111
**Betty's** York. See p.618
**Cookie's Crab Shack** Norfolk. See p.401
**Station Buffet Barter Books** Northumbria. See p.671
**Turl Street Kitchen** Oxford. See p.247

also have a few cheap **cafés** offering nonalcoholic drinks, all-day breakfasts, snacks and meals. Most are only open during the daytime, and have few airs and graces; the quality is not guaranteed, however. A few more genteel **teashops** or **tearooms** serve sandwiches, cakes and light meals throughout the day, as well, of course, as tea – the best of them will offer a full afternoon tea, including sandwiches, cakes and scones with cream and jam.

sessions, when you can come away with armfuls of delicious berries, orchard fruits, beetroot and the like. Year round you'll find superlative seafood – from crabs to cockles, oysters to lobster – fine cheeses and delicious free-range meat. Check out the growing profusion of farmers' markets (see Ⓦ localfoods.org.uk) and farm shops, usually signposted by the side of the road in rural areas, to enjoy the best local goodies and artisan products.

## Cafés, tearooms and coffee shops

Though still a nation of tea-heads, Brits have become bona fide **coffee** addicts, and international chain outlets, such as *Starbucks*, *Costa* and *Caffè Nero* line every high street. However, there will usually be at least one independent coffee shop, even in the smallest places, and artisan coffee, brewed with obsessive care by super-cool baristas, can be found in London, especially, along with some of the bigger cities. Despite the encroaching grip of the coffee chains, every town, city and resort in England should

## Pubs and gastropubs

The old-fashioned English **pub** remains an enduring social institution, and is often the best introduction to town or village life. In some places, it might be your only choice for food. While occasionally the offerings can be terrible, heavily reliant on frozen meals, microwaves and deep-fat fryers, England's foodie renaissance, and a commercial need to diversify, means that many have had to up their game. A new breed of **gastropubs** serve restaurant-quality food in country inns and city pubs alike. Some are really excellent – and just as expensive as a regular restaurant, though usually with a more informal feel – while others simply provide a relaxed place in which to enjoy a gourmet pork pie or cheese platter with your pint.

## Restaurants

Partly by dint of its size, London has the broadest selection of **top-class restaurants**, and the widest choice of cuisines, but there are some seriously fine

## ENGLISH BREAKFAST

The traditional **Full English** will keep you going all day. It kicks off with a choice of cereals, followed by any combination of eggs, bacon, sausage, tomatoes, mushrooms, baked beans and toast – all fried, though you can have your eggs scrambled or poached. Especially in northern England, it may also include "black pudding" (ie, blood sausage). Veggie alternatives are commonly available. Breakfasting anywhere in England, you may also be served kippers (smoked herring), haddock with a poached egg on top, omelettes and, increasingly, home-made muesli and yoghurt, fresh fruit salad and pancakes. A "continental" breakfast usually means cereal, toast and preserves, though often croissants, fruit and yoghurt too. The staple early morning drink is still tea, drunk strong, hot and with milk, though **coffee** is readily available everywhere.

**TOP 5 DESTINATION RESTAURANTS**

**Le Champignon Sauvage** Cheltenham. See p.268
**Medlar** London. See p.116
**L'Enclume** Cartmel. See p.558
**Lido** Bristol. See p.287
**Waterside Inn** Bray. See p.273

dining options in most major cities. Indeed, wherever you are in England you're rarely more than half an hour's drive from a really good meal – and some of the very best dining experiences are just as likely to be found in a suburban backstreet or sleepy village than a metropolitan hotspot. Heston Blumenthal's Michelin-star-studded *Fat Duck*, for example, touted as one of the world's best restaurants, is in the small Berkshire village of Bray, where you will also find the equally lauded *Waterside Inn* – while the best Indian food outside the Asian subcontinent is found in unsung cities like Bradford and Leicester.

While a great curry in Birmingham's Balti Triangle or a Cantonese feast in Manchester's Chinatown might **cost** you just £17 a head, the going rate for a meal with drinks in most modest restaurants is more like £27 per person. If a restaurant has any sort of reputation, you can expect to be spending £40–60 each, and much, much more for the services of a top chef – tasting menus (excluding drinks) at the best-known Michelin-starred restaurants cost upwards of £80 per person. However, **set meals** can be a steal, even at the poshest of restaurants, where a limited-choice two- or three-course lunch or a "pre-theatre" menu might cost less than half the usual price.

## Drinking

Originating as wayfarers' hostelries and coaching inns, **pubs** – "public houses" – have outlived the church and marketplace as the focal points of many a British town and village. They are as varied as the townscapes: in larger market towns you'll find huge oak-beamed inns with open fires and polished brass fittings; in remoter upland villages there are stone-built pubs no larger than a two-bedroomed cottage. In towns and cities corner pubs still cater to local neighbourhoods, while chain bars with cheap drinks, and cooler, more offbeat cocktail bars, offer sociable nights out. Most pubs and bars now serve food, in some shape or form (see p.35).

Most pubs are officially open from 11am to 11pm, though cities and resorts have a growing number of places with extended licences, especially at weekends. The legal **drinking age** is 18 and though many places will have a special family room or a beer garden, young children may not always be welcome.

### Beer and cider

**Beer**, sold by the pint (generally £2.50–4) and half pint (half the price), is England's staple drink, but ask simply for a "beer" and you'll cause no end of confusion. While lager is sold everywhere, England's unique glory is its **real ale**, a refreshing, uncarbonated beer brewed with traditional ingredients, pumped by hand from a cask and served at cellar temperature (not "warm", as foreign jibes have it). If it comes out of an electric pump (and especially if it's labelled "smoothflow" or similar), it isn't the real thing. The most common ale is known as **bitter**, with a colour ranging from straw-yellow to dark brown, depending on the brew. Other real ales include golden or **pale ales**, plus darker and maltier milds, stouts and porters. Controversy exists over the head of foam on top: in southern England, people prefer their pint without a head, and brimming to the top of the glass; in the north, flat beer is frowned on and drinkers prefer a short head of foam. You will also find "real" **cider**, made from fermented apple juice, and – particularly in England's West Country and Shropshire – **scrumpy**, a potent and cloudy beverage, usually flat, dry and very apple-y.

Many pubs are owned by large breweries who favour their own beers, though there should also be one or two "guest ales" available. For the best choice, however, you generally need to find a **free house** – an independently-run pub that can sell whichever beer it pleases. There are some fantastic choices, since England's small- and medium-sized microbreweries are flourishing – every region has its own independent outfits, brewing beers that are confined to one particular area or even just one pub. For more on English beer and pubs, check the website of the influential **Campaign for Real Ale** (ⓦ camra.org.uk).

### Wine

English **wine** is fast shucking off its image as inferior to its longer-established European counterparts, with a number of small-scale, award-winning vineyards producing delicious tipples. Around four hundred vineyards across England produce more than four million bottles a year between them. The speciality is sparkling wines, the best of which have beaten French Champagnes in tasting competitions. For more, see ⓦ englishwineproducers.com.

# The media

**The English remain fond of their newspapers, from national dailies to local weeklies, while there are hundreds of TV and radio stations, both terrestrial and digital.**

## Newspapers and magazines

From Monday to Saturday, four **daily newspapers** occupy the "quality" end of the English market: the Rupert Murdoch-owned *Times*, the staunchly Conservative *Daily Telegraph*, the left-of-centre *Guardian* and the centrist *Independent*. Among the high-selling **tabloid titles**, the most popular is the *Sun*, a muck-raking right-wing Murdoch paper whose chief rival is the traditionally left-leaning *Daily Mirror*. The middlebrow daily tabloids – the *Daily Mail* and the *Daily Express* – are equally muck-raking and noticeably xenophobic. England's oldest **Sunday newspaper** is *The Observer*, in the same stable as the *Guardian* and with a similar stance, while most other major papers publish their own Sunday editions.

Of the range of **specialist magazines and periodicals** covering just about every subject, *The Economist* is a sober business magazine; the left-wing-leaning *New Statesman* concentrates on social issues, and the satirical bi-weekly *Private Eye* prides itself on printing the stories the rest of the press won't touch – and on riding the consequent stream of libel suits.

## Television

UK **terrestrial television channels** are divided between the state-funded BBC (Ⓦbbc.co.uk), and the commercial channels ITV (Ⓦitv.com), Channel 4 (Ⓦchannel4.com) and Channel 5 (Ⓦchannel5.com). Despite periodic mutterings about the licence fee (paid by all British viewers), there's still more than enough quality to keep the **BBC** in good repute both at home and abroad. The commercial channels are united by a more tabloid approach to programme-making – if they don't get the advertising they don't survive.

The UK's **satellite** and **cable** TV companies are mounting a strong challenge to the erstwhile dominance of the terrestrial channels. Live sport, in particular, is increasingly in the hands of Rupert Murdoch's Sky, the major satellite provider, whose 24-hour rolling Sky News programme rivals that of CNN.

Most English homes and hotels get around forty "freeview" channels spread across the networks, including dedicated news, film, sports, arts and entertainment channels from the BBC, ITV, Channel 4 and 5.

## Radio

The BBC's **radio network** (Ⓦbbc.co.uk/radio) has five nationwide stations: **Radio 1** (almost exclusively devoted to chart and dance music); **Radio 2** (light pop and rock for an older audience); **Radio 3** (classical and jazz); **Radio 4** (current affairs, arts and drama); and **5 Live** (sports, news, live discussions and phone-ins). **Digital-only** BBC stations include the alternative-music 6 Music, and the BBC Asian Network. In addition, there are other national stations – like TalkSport and Classic FM – as well as a whole host of local stations in every region, both BBC and commercial.

# Festivals and events

**Many English festivals date back centuries, but the majority of the showpiece events marketed to tourists – from the military pageant of the Trooping of the Colour to the jolly bombast of the Last Night of the Proms say little about the country's folk history and even less about contemporary England. For a more instructive idea of what makes the English tick, you'd do better to catch some grassroots festivities, like London's exuberant Notting Hill Carnival or a wacky village celebration.**

## A festival calendar

### JAN–MARCH

**London Parade** (Jan 1) Ⓦlondonparade.co.uk. Floats, marching bands, clowns, cheerleaders and classic cars wend their way through the centre of London.

**Chinese New Year** (Feb 8, 2016; Jan 28, 2017). Processions, fireworks and festivities in the region's three main Chinatowns – London, Liverpool and Manchester.

**Shrove Tuesday** (47 days before Easter Sunday). The last day before Lent is also known as "Pancake Day" – it's traditional to eat thin pancakes, usually with sugar and lemon.

**Shrovetide Football** (Shrove Tuesday & Ash Wednesday) Ⓦashbourne-town.com. The world's oldest, largest, longest, craziest football game takes place in and around Ashbourne, Derbyshire.

**Rye Bay Scallop Week** (10 days end Feb/early March) Ⓦ scallop
.org.uk. Ten days of foodie events in the pretty Sussex town of Rye:
scallop tastings, cookery demos, barrow races and special menus.

**Six Nations Rugby tournament** (Feb & March) Ⓦ rbs6nations.com.
Tournament between England, Scotland, Wales, Ireland, France and Italy.

## APRIL–MAY

**St George's Day** (April 23) Ⓦ stgeorgesholiday.com. England's
national day is also, by chance, the birthday of William Shakespeare, so in
addition to Morris dancing and other traditional festivities in towns and
villages, there are also Bard-related events at Stratford-upon-Avon
(Ⓦ shakespeare.org.uk).

**Padstow 'Obby 'Oss** (May 1) Ⓦ padstowlive.com. Processions, music
and May Day dancing in Padstow, Cornwall, centring on the 'oss itself, a
curious costumed and masked figure with obscure origins. See p.364

**Helston Furry Dance** (May 8). Ancient custom involving a courtly
procession and "Floral Dance" through the Cornish town. See p.351

**Glyndebourne Opera Festival** (mid-May to late Aug)
Ⓦ glyndebourne.com. One of the classiest arts festivals in the country,
in East Sussex. See box, p.162

**Bath International Music Festival** (mid-May to June)
Ⓦ bathmusicfest.org.uk. Top-class, ten-day arts and music jamboree,
ranging from orchestral music to jazz and world music. See box, p.295

**Hay Festival** (last week in May) Ⓦ www.hayfestival.com. Bibliophiles
descend on this Welsh border town for a big literary shindig and its offshoot
HowTheLightGetsIn, a festival of philosophy and music. See p.440

## JUNE–JULY

**Trooping the Colour** (a Sat in June) Ⓦ royal.gov.uk. Massed bands,
equestrian pageantry, gun salutes and fly-pasts for the Queen's Official
Birthday on Horse Guards Parade, London.

**Aldeburgh Festival** (mid- to end June) Ⓦ aldeburgh.co.uk. Suffolk
jamboree of classical music, established by Benjamin Britten. See box, p.388

**Glastonbury** (late June) Ⓦ glastonburyfestivals.co.uk. This five-day
music and performing arts festival, taking place over the last weekend in
June on a beautiful site in Somerset, has grown from its hippie roots to
become the greatest music festival on the planet. See box, p.301

**Pride London** (end June/early July) Ⓦ prideinlondon.org.
England's biggest LGBT event, with parades, music and general gaiety.

Brighton (Ⓦ brighton-pride.org) and Manchester (Ⓦ manchesterpride
.com) have big Gay Pride events of their own in August.

**Latitude** (mid-July) Ⓦ latitudefestival.com. Set near the lovely
Suffolk seaside town of Southwold, Latitude music festival is a laidback,
family-friendly version of Glastonbury, and pulls nearly as many big
names. See p.390

**The Proms** (mid-July to mid-Sept) Ⓦ bbc.co.uk/proms. Top-flight
international classical music festival at the Royal Albert Hall, London,
ending in the famously patriotic Last Night of the Proms. See box, p.125

**WOMAD** (late July) Ⓦ womad.org. Renowned four-day world music
festival outside Malmesbury, Wiltshire.

**Whitstable Oyster Festival** (last week July) Ⓦ whitstable
oysterfestival.com. Street parades and music, and a beachside "blessing of
the oysters" — and heaps of fresh bivalves to snack on, of course. See p.135

**Cambridge Folk Festival** (end July/early Aug) Ⓦ cambridgefolk
festival.co.uk. Superb festival encompassing folk music in its broadest
sense, with a good mix of big names and interesting newcomers. See p.419

## AUG–SEPT

**Cowes Week** (1st week Aug) Ⓦ cowesweek.co.uk. Sailing extravaganza
in the Isle of Wight, with partying and star-studded entertainment. See p.195

**Broadstairs Folk Week** (mid-Aug) Ⓦ broadstairsfolkweek.org.uk.
Excellent folk and world music festival, with workshops, kids' events and a
torchlight parade.

**Great British Beer Festival** (mid-Aug) Ⓦ gbbf.org.uk. Colossal
booze-fest in London, featuring more than nine hundred real ales and
ciders from around the world.

**Notting Hill Carnival** (last Sun & bank holiday Mon Aug)
Ⓦ thenottinghillcarnival.com. Vivacious celebration led by London's
Caribbean community but including everything from Punjabi drummers
to Brazilian salsa, plus music, food and floats. See box, p.120

**Whitby Folk Week** (last week Aug) Ⓦ whitbyfolk.co.uk. A week's
worth of morris and sword dancing, finger-in-your-ear singing,
storytelling and more. See box, p.633

**Abbots Bromley Horn Dance** (early Sept) Ⓦ abbotsbromley
.com. Vaguely pagan mass dance in mock-medieval costume – one of
the most famous of England's ancient customs, in Staffordshire.

**Heritage Open Days** (2nd week Sept) Ⓦ heritageopendays.org
.uk. Annual opportunity to peek inside hundreds of buildings in England

---

## WEIRD AND WONDERFUL FESTIVALS

National nuttiness is displayed at dozens of local festivals around England every year. **Easter** is
particularly big on eccentricity, from the blacked-up Lancashire clog dancers doing the **Bacup
Nutters Dance** (Easter Saturday; Ⓦ coconutters.co.uk) to the **Hare Pie Scramble** and
**Bottle-Kicking** (Easter Monday), a chaotic village bottle-kicking contest at Hallaton,
Leicestershire. Meanwhile, Gawthorpe in Yorkshire sees the **World Coal-Carrying
Championship** (Easter Monday; Ⓦ gawthorpemaypole.org.uk), an annual race to carry 50kg of
coal a mile through the village. There's more odd racing at the **Brockworth Cheese Rolling**
(late May, bank holiday Monday; Ⓦ cheese-rolling.co.uk) when crowds of daredevils chase a
large cheese wheel down a murderous Gloucestershire incline. Later in the year, thousands
flock to Ashton, Northamptonshire, to watch modern-day gladiators fight for glory armed only
with a nut and twelve inches of string, in the **World Conker Championship** (mid-October;
Ⓦ worldconkerchampionships.com).

that don't normally open their doors to the public, from factories to Buddhist temples.

**Ludlow Food Festival** (mid-Sept) Ⓦ foodfestival.co.uk. High-profile fest in this foodie Shropshire town, with local producers, Michelin chefs and scores of events and masterclasses.

**St Ives September Festival** (last 2 weeks Sept) Ⓦ stivesseptemberfestival.co.uk. Eclectic Cornish festival of art, poetry, literature, jazz, folk, rock and world music.

### OCT–DEC

**Battle of Hastings reenactment** (weekend in mid-Oct) Ⓦ english-heritage.org.uk. Annual re-enactment of the famous 1066 battle in Battle, featuring over 1000 soldiers and living history encampments.

**Halloween** (Oct 31). Last day of the Celtic calendar and All Hallows Eve: pumpkins, plus a lot of ghoulish dressing-up, trick-or-treating and parties.

**Guy Fawkes Night/Bonfire Night** (Nov 5). Nationwide fireworks and bonfires commemorating the foiling of the Gunpowder Plot in 1605 – atop every bonfire is hoisted an effigy known as the "guy" after Guy Fawkes, one of the conspirators. Most notable events are at York (Fawkes' birthplace), Ottery St Mary in Devon and Lewes, East Sussex.

**Lord Mayor's Show** (2nd Sat in Nov) Ⓦ lordmayorsshow.org. Held annually in the City of London since 1215, and featuring a daytime cavalcade and night-time fireworks to mark the inauguration of the new Lord Mayor.

**New Year's Eve** (Dec 31). Big parties all over England; in London, there's a massive fireworks display over the Thames, and thousands of inebriates crowding Trafalgar Square.

# Sports and outdoor activities

**As the birthplace of football, cricket, rugby and tennis, England boasts a series of sporting events that attract a world audience. If you prefer participating to spectating, the UK caters for just about every outdoor activity, too: we've concentrated below on walking, cycling and watersports, but there are also opportunities for anything from rock climbing to pony trekking.**

## Spectator sports

**Football** (soccer) is the national game in England, with a wide programme of professional league matches taking place every Saturday afternoon from early August to mid-May, with plenty of Sunday and midweek fixtures too. It's very difficult to get tickets to Premier League matches involving the most famous teams (Chelsea, Arsenal, Manchester United, Liverpool), but tours of their grounds are feasible. You could also try one of the lower-league games.

Rugby comes in two codes – 15-a-side **Rugby Union** and 13-a-side **Rugby League**, both fearsomely brutal contact sports that can make entertaining viewing even if you don't understand the rules. In England, rugby is much less popular than football, but Rugby League has a loyal and dedicated fan base in the north – especially Yorkshire and Lancashire – while Union has traditionally been popular with the English middle class. Key Rugby Union and League games are sold out months in advance, but ordinary fixtures present few ticketing problems. The Rugby Union season runs from September to just after Easter, Rugby League February to September.

**Cricket** is English idiosyncrasy at its finest. Foreigners – and most Brits for that matter – marvel at a game that can last several days and still end in a draw, while many people are unfamiliar with its rules. International, five-day "Test" matches, pitting the English national side against visiting countries, are played most summers at grounds around the country, and tickets are usually fairly easy to come by. The domestic game traditionally centres on four-day County Championship matches between English county teams, though there's far bigger interest – certainly for casual watchers – in the "Twenty20" (T20) format, designed to encourage flamboyant, decisive play in short, three-hour matches.

Finally, if you're in England at the end of June and early July, you won't be able to miss the country's annual fixation with **tennis** in the shape of the Wimbledon championships. No one gives a hoot about the sport for the other fifty weeks of the year, but as long as one plucky Brit endures, the entire country gets caught up with tennis fever.

## Walking

**Walking routes** track across many of England's wilder areas, amid landscapes varied enough to suit any taste. Turn up in any National Park area and local information offices will be able to advise on anything from a family stroll to a full day out on the mountains. For shorter walks, you could check out the **National Trust** website (Ⓦ nationaltrust.org.uk), which details picturesque routes, of varying lengths, that weave through or near their properties, or if you are travelling on public transport, consult the user-generated site **Car Free Walks** (Ⓦ carfreewalks.org), which details hundreds of routes that set off and finish at train stations and

## ACTIVITY TOUR OPERATORS

There are numerous activity tours available taking in the best of England outdoors. We've listed some of the best below.

### BOATING AND SAILING

**Blakes Holiday Boating** UK ☎ 0844 856 7060, W blakes
.co.uk. Cruisers, yachts and narrowboats on the Norfolk Broads, the River Thames and various English canals.

**Classic Sailing** UK ☎ 01872 580022, W classic-sailing.co.uk.
Hands-on sailing holidays on traditional wooden boats and tall ships, including Cornwall and the Isles of Scilly.

### CYCLING

**The Carter Company** UK ☎ 01296 631671, W the-carter
-company.com. Gentle self-guided cycling and walking tours, including in London, Kent, Oxford and the Cotswolds, Devon, Cornwall and Dorset, in simple or luxury accommodation.

**Saddle Skedaddle** UK ☎ 0191 265 1110, W www.skedaddle
.co.uk. Biking adventures and classic road rides – including guided, self-guided and tailor-made tours in Cornwall, the Cotswolds, Northumberland and the New Forest, lasting from a weekend to a week.

### SURFING

**Big Friday** UK ☎ 01637 872512, W bigfriday.com. Surfing packages – some women-only – in England, with accommodation, travel and tuition laid on.

**Surfers World** UK ☎ 07540 221089, W surfersworld.co.uk.
Short breaks with surfing courses in Woolacombe, Croyde, and on the north Cornwall coast.

### WALKING

**Classic Journeys** US ☎ 1800 200 3887, W classicjourneys
.com. Upmarket guided "cultural walking adventures" in classic English and Scottish destinations, including the Cotswolds and the Cornish coast.

**Contours Walking Holidays** UK ☎ 01629 821900,
W contours.co.uk. Excellent short breaks or longer walking holidays and self-guided hikes in every region of England, from famous trails to lesser-known local routes.

**English Lakeland Ramblers** US ☎ 1800 724 8801,
W ramblers.com. Escorted walking tours in the Lake District and the Cotswolds, either inn-to-inn or based in a country hotel.

**Ramblers Worldwide Holidays** UK ☎ 01707 331133,
W ramblersholidays.co.uk. Sociable guided walking tours all over the UK, on a variety of themes, from dog-friendly to archeology, and for various fitness levels.

---

bus stops, providing OS map links and elevation profiles for each. Various **membership associations**, including the Ramblers Association (W ramblers.org.uk) and Walkers are Welcome (W walkersarewelcome.org.uk) also provide information and route ideas online.

Even for short hikes you need to be **properly equipped**, follow local advice and listen out for local weather reports – British weather is notoriously changeable and increasingly extreme. You will also need a good **map** – in most cases one of the excellent and reliable Ordnance Survey (OS) series (see p.45), usually available from local tourist offices, the best of which, along with outdoor shops, can also supply local maps, safety advice and guidebooks/leaflets.

### Hiking trails

England's finest **walking areas** are the granite moorlands and spectacular coastlines of Devon and Cornwall in the southwest, and the highlands of the north – notably the Yorkshire Dales, the North York Moors and the Lake District. Keen hikers might want to tackle one of England's twelve **National Trails** (W nationaltrail.co.uk). The most famous – certainly the toughest – is the **Pennine Way**

(268 miles; usual walking time 16–19 days), stretching from the Derbyshire Peak District to the Scottish Borders (see box, p.467), while the challenging **South West Coast Path** (630 miles; from 30 days) through Cornwall, Devon, Somerset and Dorset tends to be tackled in shorter sections (see box, p.309). Other English trails are less gung-ho in character, like the **South Downs Way** (100 miles; 8 days) following the chalk escarpment and ridges of the South Downs (see box, p.160) or the fascinating **Hadrian's Wall footpath** (84 miles; 7 days).

## Cycling

The **National Cycle Network** is made up of 14,500 miles of signed cycle route, mainly on traffic-free paths (including disused railways and canal towpaths) and country roads. You're never far from one of the numbered routes, all of which are detailed on the **Sustrans** website (W sustrans.org .uk), a charitable trust devoted to the development of environmentally sustainable transport. Sustrans also publishes an excellent series of waterproof cycle maps (1:100,000) and regional guides.

Major routes include the **C2C** (Sea-to-Sea), 140 miles between Whitehaven/Workington on the

## ENGLAND'S NATIONAL PARKS

England has ten National Parks (ⓦ www.nationalparks.gov.uk), ranging from Dartmoor in the southwest to Northumberland in the north. Check out the round-up below for the best things to do and see in each.

- **The Norfolk Broads** See box, p.398. The best place for a boating holiday – the rivers, marshes, fens and canals of Norfolk make up one of the important wetlands in Europe, and are also ideal for birdwatching. It's the one park where a car isn't much use – cyclists and walkers have the best of it. Don't miss: the long-distance footpath, Weavers' Way (see box, p.376).

- **Dartmoor** See pp.332–338. England's largest wilderness attracts back-to-nature hikers and tripped-out stone-chasers to Devon in equal measure – the open moorland walking can be pretty hardcore, and Dartmoor is famous for its standing stones, Stone Age hut circles and hill forts. Don't miss: Grimspound Bronze Age village (see p.334).

- **Exmoor** See pp.308–311. Exmoor straddles the Somerset/Devon border and on its northern edge overlooks the sea from high, hogback hills. Crisscrossed by trails and also accessible from the South West Coast Path, it's ideal for walking and pony trekking. Don't miss: the four-mile hike to Dunkery Beacon, Exmoor's highest point (see p.308).

- **Lake District** See pp.552–581. Many people's favourite National Park, the Lake District (in Cumbria, in northwest England) is an almost alpine landscape of glacial lakes and rugged mountains. It's great for hiking, rock climbing and watersports, but also has strong literary connections and thriving cultural traditions. Don't miss: Honister's hard-hat mine tour and Via Ferrata mountain traverse (see p.573).

- **New Forest** See pp.201–205. In the predominantly domesticated landscape of Hampshire, the country's best surviving example of a medieval hunting forest can be surprisingly wild. The majestic woodland is interspersed by tracts of heath, and a good network of paths and bridleways offers plenty of scope for biking and pony rides. Don't miss: camping in one of the stunning New Forest sites (see p.202).

- **Northumberland** See pp.662–675. Where England meets Scotland, remote Northumberland in England's northeast is adventure country. The long-distance Pennine Way runs the length of the park, and the Romans left their mark in the shape of Hadrian's Wall, along which you can hike or bike. Don't miss: the Chillingham cattle wildlife safari (see p.668).

- **North York Moors** See pp.623–627. A stunning mix of heather moorland, gentle valleys, ruined abbeys and wild coastline. Walking and mountain biking are the big outdoor activities here, but you can also tour the picturesque stone villages or hangout with Goths in Whitby. Don't miss: a day out at Ryedale Folk Museum (see p.626).

- **Peak District** See pp.460–471. England's first National Park (1951) is also the most visited, because it sits between the major population centres of the Midlands and the northwest. It's rugged outdoors country, with some dramatic underground caverns, tempered by stately homes and spa and market towns. Don't miss: a trip down Treak Cliff Cavern (see p.466).

- **South Downs** See box, p.160. England's newest National Park (established 2010) might not be as wild as the others – about 85 percent is farmland – but it offers a rural escape into West and East Sussex from one of the most densely populated parts of the country. Don't miss: a walk along the South Downs Way, which covers over 100 miles of the chalk uplands between Winchester and Beachy Head (see box, p.160).

- **Yorkshire Dales** See pp.599–609. The best choice for walking, cycling and pony trekking, Yorkshire's second National Park spreads across twenty dales, or valleys, at the heart of the Pennines. England's most scenic railway – the Settle to Carlisle line – is another great draw, while caves, waterfalls and castles provide the backdrop. Don't miss: the walk to dramatic Malham Cove (see p.603).

English northwest coast and Tynemouth/Sunderland on the northeast; the **Cornish Way** (123 miles), from Bude to Land's End, and the classic cross-Britain route from Land's End, in the far southwest of England, to John O'Groats, on the northeast tip of Scotland – roughly 1000 miles, which can be covered in two to three weeks, depending on which route you choose.

England's biggest cycling organization, the **Cycle Touring Club** (Ⓦctc.org.uk), provides lists of tour operators and rental outlets, and supplies members with touring and technical advice, as well as insurance.

## Watersports

**Sailing** and **windsurfing** in England are especially popular along the south coast (particularly the Isle of Wight and Solent) and in the southwest (around Falmouth in Cornwall, and around Salcombe and Dartmouth in Devon). Here, and in the Lake District, you'll be able to rent dinghies, boats and kayaks, either by the hour or for longer periods of instruction – from around £30 for a couple of hours of kayaking to around £150 for a two-day nonresidential sailing course.

Newquay in Cornwall is England's undisputed **surfing** centre, whose main break, Fistral, regularly hosts international contests. But there are quieter spots all along the north coast of Cornwall and Devon, as well as a growing scene on the more isolated northeast coast from Yorkshire up to Northumberland, with lots of action at the pretty seaside Teesside town of Saltburn. For more **information** on surfing in England, including a directory of surf schools and an events calendar, check Ⓦsurfinggb.com.

Another option is **coasteering**, a thrilling extreme sport that involves climbing, swimming, scrambling and cliff-jumping – with a guide – along the more spectacular stretches of rocky coast; Cornwall is a particularly good coasteering hot spot. Finally, if you can brave the often chilly temperatures, **wild swimming** has taken off in a big way, a wonderful way to experience England's many beautiful rivers, lakes, waterfall pools and sea caves – check Ⓦwild swimming.co.uk for a run-down of good places.

# Travel essentials

## Climate

Though it has seen some extreme storms, flooding and snowfall in recent years, overall England has a generally temperate, maritime climate, which means largely moderate temperatures and a decent chance of at least some rain whenever you visit. If you're attempting to balance the clemency of the weather against the density of the crowds, even given regional variations and microclimates the best months to come to England are April, May, September and October.

## Costs

Faced with another £4 pint, a £30 theatre ticket and a £20 taxi ride back to your £100-a-night hotel, England might seem like the most expensive place in Europe – in the cities, at least. Even if you're camping or hostelling, using public transport, buying picnic lunches and eating in pubs and cafés your

## AVERAGE DAILY MAXIMUM TEMPERATURES

### BIRMINGHAM

|      | Jan | Feb | Mar | Apr | May | Jun | Jul | Aug | Sep | Oct | Nov | Dec |
|------|-----|-----|-----|-----|-----|-----|-----|-----|-----|-----|-----|-----|
| °F   | 42  | 43  | 48  | 54  | 61  | 66  | 68  | 68  | 63  | 55  | 48  | 44  |
| °C   | 5   | 6   | 9   | 12  | 16  | 19  | 20  | 20  | 17  | 13  | 9   | 7   |

### LONDON

|      | Jan | Feb | Mar | Apr | May | Jun | Jul | Aug | Sep | Oct | Nov | Dec |
|------|-----|-----|-----|-----|-----|-----|-----|-----|-----|-----|-----|-----|
| °F   | 43  | 44  | 50  | 56  | 62  | 69  | 71  | 71  | 65  | 58  | 50  | 45  |
| °C   | 6   | 7   | 10  | 13  | 17  | 21  | 22  | 22  | 19  | 14  | 10  | 7   |

### PLYMOUTH

|      | Jan | Feb | Mar | Apr | May | Jun | Jul | Aug | Sep | Oct | Nov | Dec |
|------|-----|-----|-----|-----|-----|-----|-----|-----|-----|-----|-----|-----|
| °F   | 47  | 47  | 50  | 54  | 59  | 64  | 66  | 67  | 64  | 58  | 52  | 49  |
| °C   | 8   | 8   | 10  | 12  | 15  | 18  | 19  | 19  | 18  | 14  | 11  | 9   |

### YORK

|      | Jan | Feb | Mar | Apr | May | Jun | Jul | Aug | Sep | Oct | Nov | Dec |
|------|-----|-----|-----|-----|-----|-----|-----|-----|-----|-----|-----|-----|
| °F   | 43  | 44  | 49  | 55  | 61  | 67  | 70  | 69  | 64  | 57  | 49  | 45  |
| °C   | 6   | 7   | 10  | 13  | 16  | 19  | 21  | 21  | 18  | 14  | 9   | 7   |

minimum expenditure will be around £40 per person per day. Couples staying in B&Bs, eating at unpretentious restaurants and sightseeing should expect to splash out £70 per person, while if you're renting a car, staying in hotels and eating at fancier places, budget for at least £120 each. Double that last figure if you choose to stay in stylish city or grand country-house hotels, while on any visit to London work on the basis that you'll need an extra £30 per day.

### Discounts and admission charges

Many of England's **historic attractions** – from castles to stately homes – are owned and/or operated by either the **National Trust** (Ⓦ nationaltrust.org.uk; denoted as NT in the Guide) or **English Heritage** (Ⓦ english-heritage.org.uk; EH). Both these organizations usually charge entry fees, though some sites are free. If you plan to visit more than half a dozen places owned by any of them, it's worth considering an annual membership (£40–60) – you can join on your first visit to any attraction. US members of the Royal Oak Foundation (Ⓦ royal-oak.org) get free admission to all National Trust properties.

**Municipal art galleries and museums** across the UK often have free admission, as do the world-class **state museums** in London, Birmingham, Manchester and elsewhere, from the British Museum (London) to York's National Railway Museum. Private and municipal museums and other collections rarely charge more than £6 admission. Some **cathedrals** and churches either charge admission or ask for voluntary donations.

The admission charges given in the Guide are the full adult rate, unless otherwise stated. Concessionary rates – **generally half-price** – for **senior citizens** (over 60), under-26s and **children** (from 5 to 17) apply almost everywhere, from tourist attractions to public transport. Family tickets are often available, and children under 5 are usually free.

**Full-time students** can benefit from an International Student ID Card (ISIC; Ⓦ isic.org), and those under 26 from an International Youth Travel Card (IYTC), while **teachers** qualify for the International Teacher Identity Card (ITIC). Available from STA Travel (see p.28), all cost £12 and are valid for special air, rail and bus fares, and discounts at museums and other attractions.

## Crime and personal safety

Terrorist attacks and street riots in England may have changed the general perception of how safe it feels, but it's still extremely unlikely that you'll be at any risk as you travel around. There's heightened **security** in

## TIPPING

Although there are no fixed rules for **tipping**, a ten to fifteen percent tip is anticipated by restaurant waiters. Tipping taxi drivers ten percent or so is optional, but most people at the very least round the fare up to the nearest pound. Some restaurants levy a "discretionary" or "optional" **service charge** of 10 or 12.5 percent, which must be clearly stated on the menu and on the bill. However, you are not obliged to pay it, and certainly not if the food or service wasn't what you expected. It is not normal to leave tips in pubs, though more swanky cocktail bars will present their bills on a saucer, where some people choose to leave a few coins. The only other occasions when you'll be expected to tip are at the hairdressers, and in upmarket hotels where porters and bell boys expect and usually get a pound or two per bag or for calling a taxi.

place at airports and major train stations, and as a holiday-maker you can avoid the toughest urban areas where crime flourishes. You can walk more or less anywhere without fear of harassment, though all the big cities have their edgy districts and it's always better to err on the side of caution, especially late at night. Leave your passport and valuables in a hotel or hostel safe (carrying **ID** is not compulsory; though if you look particularly youthful and intend to drink in a pub or club it can be a good idea to carry it), and exercise the usual caution on public transport. If you're taking a taxi, always make sure it's officially licensed and never pick one up in the street – unless it's an official black taxi in London (see p.105). Bar or restaurant staff can usually provide a reliable recommendation or direct you to the nearest taxi rank.

Other than asking for directions, most visitors rarely come into contact with the **police**, who as a rule are approachable and helpful. Most wear chest guards and carry batons, though street officers do not normally carry guns. If you are robbed, report it straight away to the police; your insurance company will require a **crime report number**. For **police, fire** and **ambulance** services phone Ⓣ 999.

## Electricity

The **current** is 240V AC. North American appliances will need a transformer and adaptor; those from Europe, South Africa, Australia and New Zealand only need an adaptor.

## Entry requirements

Citizens of all European countries – except Albania, Bosnia and Herzegovina, Macedonia, Montenegro, Serbia and all the former Soviet republics (other than the Baltic states) – can enter England with just a **passport**, for up to three months (and indefinitely if you're from the EU). Americans, Canadians, Australians and New Zealanders can stay for up to six months, providing they have a return ticket and funds to cover their stay. Citizens of most other countries require a **visa**, obtainable from their British consulate or mission office. Check with the **UK Border Agency** (Ⓦukvisas.gov.uk) for up-to-date information about visa applications, extensions and all aspects of residency.

## Gay and lesbian travellers

England offers one of the most diverse and accessible **lesbian** and **gay** scenes anywhere in Europe. Nearly every sizeable town has some kind of organized gay life – from bars and clubs to community groups – with the major scenes found in London, Manchester and Brighton. Listings, news and reviews can be found at *Gay Times* (Ⓦgaytimes .co.uk), while for more information and useful links see Ⓦgaybritain.co.uk. The age of consent is 16.

## Health

No vaccinations are required for entry into England. Citizens of all EU and EEA countries are entitled to free medical treatment within the National Health Service (NHS), which includes the vast majority of hospitals and doctors, on production of their **European Health Insurance Card** (EHIC) or, in extremis, their passport or national identity card. The same applies to those Commonwealth countries that have reciprocal healthcare arrangements with the UK – for example Australia and New Zealand. If you don't fall into either of these catego-

ries, you will be charged for all medical services – except those administered by accident and emergency units at National Health Service hospitals – so health insurance is strongly advised.

Pharmacists (known as **chemists** in England) can advise you on minor conditions but can dispense only a limited range of drugs without a doctor's prescription. Most are open standard shop hours, though there are also late-night branches in large cities and at 24-hour supermarkets. For generic pain-relief, cold remedies and the like, the local supermarket is usually the cheapest option.

Minor complaints and injuries can be dealt with at a **doctor's (GP's) surgery** – your hotel should be able to point you in the right direction, though you may not be seen immediately. For serious injuries, go to the 24-hour **Accident and Emergency (A&E)** department of the nearest **hospital**, and in an **emergency**, call an ambulance on ☎999. If you need medical help fast but it's not a 999 emergency you can also get free advice from NHS 111, the health service's 24-hour helpline (☎111).

## Insurance

Even though EU health-care privileges apply in the UK, it's a good idea to take out an **insurance policy** before travelling to cover against theft, loss and illness or injury. Most exclude so-called dangerous sports unless an extra premium is paid: in England this can mean most watersports, rock climbing and mountaineering, though hiking, kayaking and jeep safaris would probably be covered. For non-EU citizens, it's worth checking whether you are already covered.

## Mail

**Stamps** are sold at post offices, as well as some supermarkets, newsagents and other stores. "First class" theoretically guarantees next-day UK delivery; "second class" delivery within three working days.

---

### ROUGH GUIDES TRAVEL INSURANCE

Rough Guides has teamed up with WorldNomads.com to offer great **travel insurance** deals. Policies are available to residents of over 150 countries, with cover for a wide range of adventure sports, 24-hour emergency assistance, high levels of medical and evacuation cover and a stream of travel safety information. Roughguides.com users can take advantage of their policies online 24/7, from anywhere in the world – even if you're already travelling. And since plans often change when you're on the road, you can extend your policy and even claim online. Roughguides.com users who buy travel insurance with WorldNomads.com can also leave a positive footprint and donate to a community development project. For more information go to Ⓦroughguides.com/travel-insurance.

## DISTANCES, WEIGHTS AND MEASURES

Distances (and speeds) on English signposts are in miles, and beer is still served in pints. For everything else – money, weights and measures – a confusing mixture of metric and imperial systems is used: fuel is dispensed by the litre, while meat, milk and vegetables may be sold in either or both systems.

Airmail to European destinations should arrive within three working days, and to countries outside Europe within five. A stamp for a first-class letter to anywhere in the British Isles currently costs 62p; second-class letters cost 53p. Note, though, that there are size restrictions: letters over 240 x 165 x 5mm are designated as "Large letters" and are correspondingly more expensive to send. A postcard to Europe Costs 97 pence, to rest of the world £1.28 To get an idea of how much you'll need to spend mailing letters to Europe and the rest of the world, check the Royal Mail website (W royal mail.com/price-finder).

## Maps

Petrol stations in England stock large-format **road atlases** produced by the AA, RAC, Collins, Ordnance Survey and others, which cover all of Britain, at a scale of around 1:250,000 and include larger-scale plans of major towns. The best of these is the Ordnance Survey road atlas, which handily uses the same grid reference system as their folding maps. Overall the Ordnance Survey (OS; W ordnance survey.co.uk) produces the most comprehensive maps, renowned for their accuracy and clarity. Their 1:50,000 (pink) Landranger series shows enough detail to be useful for most walkers and cyclists, and there's more detail still in the full-colour 1:25,000 (orange) Explorer series – both cover the whole of Britain. The full OS range is only available at a few big-city stores or online, but you can download high-res maps via the OS MapFinder app. A free useful website is W streetmon.rn.uk.

## Money

England's currency is the **pound sterling** (£), divided into 100 pence (p). Coins come in denominations of 1p, 2p, 5p, 10p, 20p, 50p and £1 and £2. Bank of England notes are in denominations of £5, £10, £20 and £50. For current **exchange rates**, consult W xe.com.

The easiest way to get hold of cash is to use your **debit card** in an **ATM**; there's usually a daily withdrawal limit, which varies depending on the money issuer, but starts at around £250. You'll find ATMs outside banks, at all major points of arrival and motorway service areas, at large supermarkets, petrol stations and even inside some pubs, rural post offices and village shops (though a charge of a few pounds may be levied on cash withdrawals at small, stand-alone ATMs – the screen will tell you and give you an option to cancel the operation). Depending on your bank and your debit card, you may also be able to ask for "cash back" when you shop at supermarkets.

**Credit cards** are widely accepted in hotels, shops and restaurants – MasterCard and Visa are almost universal, charge cards like American Express and Diners Club less so. Smaller establishments, such as B&Bs and some shops, may accept cash only. Remember that cash advances from ATMs using your credit card are treated as loans, with interest accruing daily from the date of withdrawal.

**Paying by plastic** involves inserting your credit or debit card into a "chip-and-pin" terminal, beside the till in shops, or brought to your table in restaurants, and then keying in your PIN to authorize the transaction; the only person handling your card is you. **Contactless** – or "wave and go" – payments, where you simply hold your credit or debit card on or near a card reader without having to key in a PIN, are increasingly available for transactions of up to £20. Contactless cards are marked with a little radio waves icon, similar to the wi-fi symbol, which you'll also see at establishments that accept this kind of payment. Note that the same overseas transaction fees will apply to contactless payments as to those made with a PIN. See W contactless.info for more details and a list of businesses that accept wave and go.

You cannot use **travellers' cheques** as cash – you'll always have to cash them first, making them an unreliable source of funds in an emergency or in remote areas. Outside banking hours, you can change currency or cheques at **post offices** and **bureaux de change** – the former charge no commission, while the latter tend to be open longer hours and are found in most city centres and at major airports and train stations. Avoid changing cash or cheques in hotels, where the rates are poor.

---

## PUBLIC HOLIDAYS

**Jan 1 (New Year's Day)**
**Good Friday**
**Easter Monday**
**First Mon in May ("May Day")**
**Last Mon in May**
**Last Mon in Aug**
**Dec 25 (Christmas Day)**
**Dec 26 (Boxing Day)**
Note that if January 1, December 25 or December 26 falls on a Saturday or Sunday, the next weekday becomes a public holiday.

---

# Opening hours and public holidays

Though traditional office hours are Monday to Saturday from around 9am to 5.30 or 6pm, many businesses, shops and restaurants throughout England will open earlier – or later – and close later. The majority of shops are open daily, and, in the towns at least might stay open late on a Thursday evening, but some places – even the so-called "24hr supermarkets" – are closed on Sunday, and businesses in remote areas and villages might even have an "early closing day" – often Wednesday – when they close at 1pm. Banks are not open at the weekend. We have given full **opening hours** for everything we review – museums, galleries and tourist attractions, cafés, restaurants, pubs and shops – throughout the Guide.

While many local shops and businesses close on **public holidays**, few tourist-related businesses observe them, particularly in summer. However, nearly all museums, galleries and other attractions are closed on Christmas Day and New Year's Day, with many also closed on Boxing Day (Dec 26). Several of England's public holidays are usually referred to as **bank holidays** (though it's not just the banks who have a day off).

# Phones

Every English landline number has a prefix, which, if beginning ☎01 or 02 represents an **area code**. The prefix ☎07 is for mobile phones/cellphones. A variety of ☎08 prefixes relate to the cost of calls – some, like ☎0800, are free to call from a landline, others (like ☎0845 and ☎0870) are more expensive than landlines, the actual price depending on your phone or phone operator. Beware, particularly, **premium-rate ☎09 numbers**, common for

pre-recorded information services (including some tourist authorities), which can be charged at anything up to £1.50 a minute.

The cheapest way to make calls on any landline is to buy a **phonecard**, available from many newsagents or online in denominations of £5, £10 and upwards. You dial the company's local access number, key in the pin number on the card and then make your call. Most hotel rooms have telephones, but there is almost always an exorbitant surcharge for their use. Public **payphones** – telephone boxes – are still found, though with the ubiquity of mobile phones, they're seldom used.

**Mobile phone** access is universal in towns and cities, and rural areas are well served too, though coverage can be patchy. To use your own phone, check with your provider that international roaming is activated – and that your phone will work in the UK (unless you have a tri-band phone, it's unlikely that a mobile bought for use in the US, for example, will work outside the States and vice versa). If you do bring your own phone, note that you are likely to be charged extra for incoming calls or texts when abroad. The cost of calls within the EU has decreased within recent years, but calls to destinations further afield are still unregulated and can be prohibitively expensive. If you're staying in England for any length of time, it's often easiest to **buy a mobile** and local SIM card in the UK – basic pre-pay ("pay as you go") models start at around £30, usually including some calling credit.

Dial ☎100 for the **operator**, ☎155 for the international operator.

# Smoking

**Smoking** is banned in all public buildings and offices, restaurants and pubs, and on all public transport. In addition, the vast majority of hotels and B&Bs no longer allow it.

---

## CALLING ABROAD FROM ENGLAND

**Australia** ☎0061 + area code minus the initial zero + number.
**New Zealand** ☎0064 + area code minus the initial zero + number.
**US and Canada** ☎001 + area code + number.
**Republic of Ireland** ☎00353 + area code minus the initial zero + number.
**South Africa** ☎0027 + area code + number.

---

# Time

**Greenwich Mean Time** (GMT) – equivalent to Co-ordinated Universal Time (UTC) – is used from the end of October to the end of March; for the rest of the year Britain switches to **British Summer Time** (BST), one hour ahead of GMT.

# Tourist information

England's tourism authority, VisitEngland (ⓦvisitengland.com) is a reasonable first stop for general information, while regional tourism boards concentrate on particular areas.

**Tourist offices** (also called Tourist Information Centres, or "TICs") exist in many English towns, though local cuts have led to some closures over recent years. They tend to follow standard shop hours (roughly Mon–Sat 9am–5.30pm), though are sometimes also open on Sundays, with hours curtailed during the winter season (Nov–Easter). We've listed opening hours in the Guide. Depending on the size of the office, staff will nearly always be able to book accommodation, reserve space on guided tours, and sell guidebooks, maps and walk leaflets.

The **National Parks** usually have their own dedicated information centres, which offer similar services to tourist offices but can also provide expert guidance on local walks and outdoor pursuits.

# Travellers with disabilities

On the whole, England has good facilities for travellers with disabilities. All new public buildings – including museums, galleries and cinemas – are obliged to provide **wheelchair access**; train stations and airports are accessible; many buses have easy-access boarding ramps; and dropped kerbs and signalled crossings are the rule in every city and town. The number of accessible hotels and restaurants is also growing, and reserved parking bays are available almost everywhere, from shopping malls to museums. If you have specific requirements, it's always best to talk first to your travel agent, chosen hotel or tour operator.

Wheelchair-users and blind or partially sighted people are automatically given thirty to forty percent reductions on train fares, and people with other disabilities are eligible for the Disabled Persons Railcard (£20/year; ⓦdisabledpersons -railcard.co.uk), which gives a third off the price of most tickets. There are no bus discounts for disabled tourists. In addition to the resources listed below, for detailed reviews of some of England's leading attractions – museums, markets, theatres – written by and for disabled people, download the *Rough Guide to Accessible Britain* (ⓦaccessible guide.co.uk).

## USEFUL CONTACTS

**Access-Able** ⓦ access-able.com. Online resource for travellers with disabilities, with links to UK operators and organizations.

**Open Britain** ⓦ openbritain.net. Accessible travel-related information, from accommodation to attractions.

**Tourism For All** ⓦ www.tourismforall.org.uk. Listings, guides and advice for access throughout England.

# Travelling with children

Facilities in England for travellers with children are similar to those in the rest of Europe. Breast-feeding is legal in all public places, including restaurants and cafés, and **baby-changing** rooms are widely available, including in shopping centres and train stations. Children aren't allowed in certain **licensed (ie, alcohol-serving) premises**, though this doesn't apply to restaurants, and many pubs and inns have family rooms or beer gardens where children are welcome. Some **B&Bs and hotels** won't accept children under a certain age (usually 12). Under-5s generally travel free on public transport and get in free to attractions; 5–16-year-olds usually entitled to concessionary rates of up to half the adult rate/fare.

# London

TATE MODERN AND MILLENNIUM BRIDGE

1

# London

For the visitor, London is a thrilling place. Monuments from the capital's glorious past are everywhere, from medieval banqueting halls and the great churches of Christopher Wren to eclectic Victorian architecture. You can relax in the city's quiet Georgian squares, explore the narrow alleyways of the City of London, wander along the riverside walkways, and uncover the quirks of what is still identifiably a collection of villages. The largest capital in the European Union, stretching for more than thirty miles from east to west, and with a population of over eight million, London is also incredibly diverse, ethnically and linguistically, offering cultural and culinary delights from right across the globe.

The capital's great historical **landmarks** – Big Ben, Westminster Abbey, Buckingham Palace, St Paul's Cathedral, the Tower of London and so on – draw in millions of tourists every year. Things change fast, though, and the regular emergence of new attractions ensures there's plenty to do even for those who've visited before. With Tate Modern and the Shard, the city boasts the world's most popular modern art museum and Western Europe's tallest building. And thanks to the 2012 Olympics, even the East End – not an area previously on most tourists' radar – has had a major overhaul.

You could spend days just **shopping** in London, mixing with the upper classes in the "tiara triangle" around Harrods, or sampling the offbeat weekend markets of Portobello Road, Brick Lane and Camden. The city's **pubs** have always had heaps of atmosphere, and **food** is now a major attraction too, with more than fifty Michelin-starred restaurants and the widest choice of cuisines on the planet. The **music, clubbing** and **gay and lesbian** scenes are second to none, and mainstream **arts** are no less exciting, with regular opportunities to catch outstanding theatre companies, dance troupes, exhibitions and opera.

London's special atmosphere comes mostly, however, from the life on its streets. A cosmopolitan city since at least the seventeenth century, when it was a haven for Huguenot immigrants escaping persecution in Louis XIV's France, today it is truly **multicultural**, with over half its permanent population originating from overseas. The last hundred years has seen the arrival of thousands from the Caribbean, the Indian subcontinent, the Mediterranean, the Far East and Eastern Europe, all of whom play an integral part in defining a metropolis that is unmatched in its sheer diversity.

ETHIOPIAN FOOD AT BRICK LANE MARKET

# Highlights

**❶ British Museum** Quite simply one of the world's greatest museums. **See p.70**

**❷ London Eye** The universally loved observation wheel is a key London landmark. **See p.83**

**❸ Tate Modern** London's huge modern art gallery is housed in a spectacularly converted power station. **See p.84**

**❹ Shakespeare's Globe Theatre** Catch a show in this amazing reconstructed outdoor Elizabethan theatre. **See p.85**

**❺ Highgate Cemetery** The steeply sloping terraces of the West Cemetery's overgrown graves are the last word in Victorian Gothic gloom. **See p.97**

**❻ Greenwich** Picturesque riverside spot, with a weekend market, the National Maritime Museum and old Royal Observatory. **See p.98**

**❼ Kew Gardens** Stroll amid the exotic trees and shrubs, or head for the steamy glasshouses. **See p.101**

**❽ Hampton Court Palace** Tudor interiors, architecture by Wren and vast gardens make this a great day out. **See p.102**

**❾ East End markets** Best visited on a Sunday – start at Spitalfields, head towards Brick Lane and end up at Columbia Road. **See p.126**

HIGHLIGHTS ARE MARKED ON THE MAP ON PP.52–53

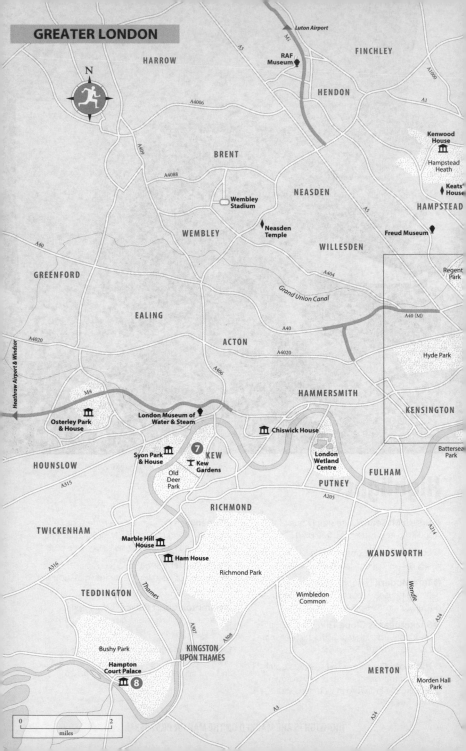

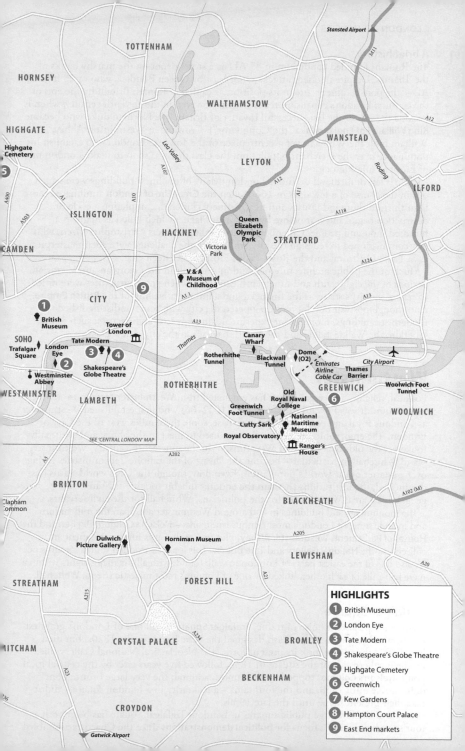

Stansted Airport

TOTTENHAM

HORNSEY

WALTHAMSTOW

HIGHGATE

WANSTEAD

Highgate
Cemetery

⑤

LEYTON

ILFORD

Lea Valley

Roding

ISLINGTON

Queen
Elizabeth
Olympic
Park

STRATFORD

CAMDEN

HACKNEY

Victoria
Park

V & A
Museum of
Childhood

CITY

⑨

① British
Museum

Tower of
London

Canary
Wharf

Dome
(O2)

City Airport

SOHO
Trafalgar
Square

London
Eye

② ③ ④

Tate Modern

Thames

Rotherhithe
Tunnel

Blackwall
Tunnel

Emirates
Airline
Cable Car

Thames
Barrier

Westminster
Abbey

Shakespeare's
Globe Theatre

ROTHERHITHE

GREENWICH

Woolwich Foot
Tunnel

WESTMINSTER

LAMBETH

Old
Royal Naval
College

⑥

WOOLWICH

Greenwich
Foot Tunnel

National
Maritime
Museum

SEE 'CENTRAL LONDON' MAP

Cutty Sark

Royal Observatory

Ranger's
House

BRIXTON

BLACKHEATH

Clapham
Common

Dulwich
Picture Gallery

Horniman Museum

LEWISHAM

STREATHAM

FOREST HILL

MITCHAM

CRYSTAL PALACE

BROMLEY

BECKENHAM

CROYDON

Gatwick Airport

**HIGHLIGHTS**

① British Museum
② London Eye
③ Tate Modern
④ Shakespeare's Globe Theatre
⑤ Highgate Cemetery
⑥ Greenwich
⑦ Kew Gardens
⑧ Hampton Court Palace
⑨ East End markets

**1**

## A brief history

The Romans founded **Londinium** in 47 AD as a stores depot on the marshy banks of the Thames. Despite frequent attacks – not least by Queen Boudica, who razed it in 61 AD – the port became secure in its position as capital of Roman Britain by the end of the century. London's expansion really began, however, in the eleventh century, when it became the seat of the last successful invader of Britain, the Norman duke who became **King William I of England** (aka "the Conqueror"). Crowned in Westminster Abbey, William built the White Tower – centrepiece of the Tower of London – to establish his dominance over the merchant population, the class that was soon to make London one of Europe's mightiest cities.

Little is left of medieval or Tudor London. Many of the finest buildings were wiped out in the course of a few days in 1666 when the **Great Fire of London** annihilated more than thirteen thousand houses and nearly ninety churches, completing a cycle of destruction begun the year before by the Great Plague, which killed as many as a hundred thousand people. Chief beneficiary of the blaze was Christopher Wren, who was commissioned to redesign the city and rose to the challenge with such masterpieces as St Paul's Cathedral and the Royal Naval Hospital in Greenwich.

Much of the public architecture of London was built in the Georgian and Victorian periods of the eighteenth and nineteenth centuries, when grand structures were raised to reflect the city's status as the financial and administrative hub of the **British Empire**. And though postwar development peppered the city with some undistinguished modernist buildings, more recent experiments in high-tech architecture, such as the Gherkin, the Walkie Talkie and the Shard, have given the city a new gloss.

# Westminster

Political, religious and regal power has emanated from **Westminster** for almost a millennium. It was Edward the Confessor (1042–66) who first established Westminster as London's royal and ecclesiastical power base, some three miles west of the City of London. The embryonic English parliament used to meet in the abbey and eventually took over the old royal palace of Westminster. In the nineteenth century, Westminster – and Whitehall in particular – became the "heart of the Empire", its ministries ruling over a quarter of the world's population. Even now, though the UK's world status has diminished, the institutions that run the country inhabit roughly the same geographical area: Westminster for the politicians, Whitehall for the civil servants.

The monuments and buildings in and around Westminster also span the millennium, and include some of London's most famous landmarks – **Nelson's Column**, **Big Ben** and the **Houses of Parliament**, **Westminster Abbey**, plus two of the city's finest permanent art collections, the **National Gallery** and **Tate Britain**. This is a well-trodden tourist circuit since it's also one of the easiest parts of London to walk round, with all the major sights within a mere half-mile of each other, linked by one of London's most majestic streets, **Whitehall**.

## Trafalgar Square

Despite the persistent noise of traffic, **Trafalgar Square** is still one of London's grandest architectural set pieces. John Nash designed the basic layout in the 1820s, but died long before the square took its present form. The Neoclassical National Gallery filled up the northern side of the square in 1838, followed five years later by the central focal point, **Nelson's Column**, topped by the famous admiral; the very large bronze lions didn't arrive until 1868, and the fountains – a real rarity in a London square – didn't take their present shape until the late 1930s.

As one of the few large public squares in London, Trafalgar Square has been both a tourist attraction and a focus for **political demonstrations** since the Chartists assembled

## LONDON ORIENTATION: WHERE TO GO

Although the majority of the city's sights are situated north of the **River Thames**, which loops through the centre of the city from west to east, there is no single focus of interest. That's because London hasn't grown through centralized planning but by a process of agglomeration. Villages and urban developments that once surrounded the core are now lost within the amorphous mass of Greater London.

**Westminster**, the country's royal, political and ecclesiastical power base for centuries, was once a separate city. The grand streets and squares to the north of Westminster, from **St James's** to **Covent Garden**, were built as residential suburbs after the Restoration in 1660, and are now the city's shopping and entertainment zones known collectively as the **West End**. To the east is the original City of London – known simply as **The City** – founded by the Romans, with more history than any other patch of the city, and now one of the world's great financial centres.

The **East End**, east of the City, is not conventional tourist territory, but has recently emerged as a bolt hole for artists and a destination for clubbers – and of course, in its far eastern reaches, the East End is now home to the **Olympic Park**. It's worth exploring the south bank of the Thames, too, from the **London Eye**, in the west, to **Tate Modern** and beyond. The **museums** of South Kensington are a must, as is Portobello Road market in trendy Notting Hill, literary Hampstead and Highgate, in north London, either side of half-wild **Hampstead Heath**, and **Greenwich**, downstream of central London, with its nautical associations, royal park and observatory. Finally, there are plenty of rewarding day-trips in west London along the Thames from **Chiswick** to **Windsor**, most notably to Hampton Court Palace and Windsor Castle.

here in 1848 before marching to Kennington Common. Since then, countless demos and rallies have taken place, and nowadays various free events, commemorations and celebrations are staged here.

Stranded on a traffic island to the south of the column, and pre-dating the entire square, is an **equestrian statue of Charles I**, erected shortly after the Restoration on the very spot where eight of those who had signed the king's death warrant were disembowelled. Charles's statue also marks the original site of the thirteenth-century **Charing Cross**, from where all distances from the capital are measured – a Victorian imitation now stands outside Charing Cross train station.

### St Martin-in-the-Fields

Trafalgar Square • Mon, Tues, Thurs & Fri 8.30am–1pm & 2–6pm, Wed 8.30am–1.15pm & 2–5pm, Sat 9.30am–6pm, Sun 3.30–5pm; concerts Mon, Tues & Fri lunchtime • Free • ☎ 020 7766 1100, ⓦ stmartin-in-the-fields.org • ⊖ Charing Cross

The northeastern corner of Trafalgar Square is occupied by James Gibbs's church of **St Martin-in-the-Fields**, fronted by a magnificent Corinthian portico. Designed in 1721, the interior is purposefully simple, though the Italian plasterwork on the barrel vaulting is exceptionally rich; it's best appreciated while listening to one of the church's free lunchtime **concerts**. There's a licensed café (see p.111) in the roomy **crypt**, along with a shop, gallery and brass-rubbing centre.

### National Gallery

Trafalgar Square • Daily 10am–6pm, Fri 10am–9pm • Guided tours daily 11.30am & 2.30pm, plus Fri 7pm, Sat & Sun 4pm • Free • ☎ 020 7747 2885, ⓦ nationalgallery.org.uk • ⊖ Charing Cross

The **National Gallery** was begun in 1824 by the British government. The gallery's canny acquisition policy has resulted in more than 2300 paintings, but the collection's virtue is not so much its size, but its range, depth and sheer quality. To view the collection chronologically, begin with the **Sainsbury Wing**, to the west. With more than one thousand paintings on permanent display in the main galleries, you'll need real stamina to see everything in one day, so if time is tight your best bet is to home in on your areas of special interest, having picked up a gallery plan at one of the information desks. **Audioguides**, with a brief audio commentary on each of the paintings on display are

1

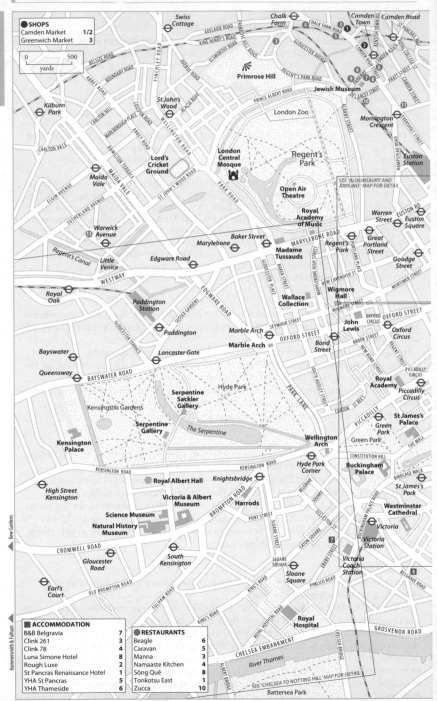

**SHOPS**

| | |
|---|---|
| Camden Market | 1/2 |
| Greenwich Market | 3 |

0 — 500 yards

**ACCOMMODATION**

| | |
|---|---|
| B&B Belgravia | 7 |
| Clink 261 | 3 |
| Clink 78 | 4 |
| Luna Simone Hotel | 8 |
| Rough Luxe | 2 |
| St Pancras Renaissance Hotel | 1 |
| YHA St Pancras | 5 |
| YHA Thameside | 6 |

**RESTAURANTS**

| | |
|---|---|
| Beagle | 6 |
| Caravan | 5 |
| Manna | 3 |
| Namaaste Kitchen | 4 |
| Sông Quê | 8 |
| Tonkotsu East | 1 |
| Zucca | 10 |

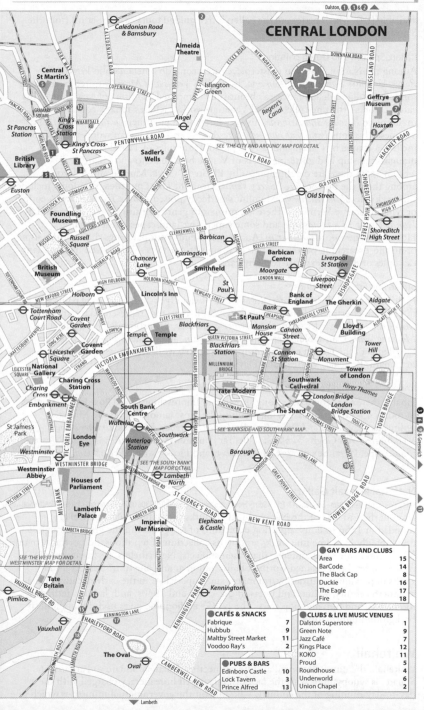

1

Dalston, ① ❶ & ❷ ▲

# CENTRAL LONDON

N

SEE 'THE CITY AND AROUND' MAP FOR DETAIL

SEE 'BANKSIDE AND SOUTHWARK' MAP

SEE 'THE SOUTH BANK' MAP FOR DETAIL

SEE 'THE WEST END AND WESTMINSTER' MAP FOR DETAIL

③ ⑥ ❾ & Greenwich ▶

▶

❶

▼ Lambeth

| ● GAY BARS AND CLUBS | |
| --- | --- |
| Area | 15 |
| BarCode | 14 |
| The Black Cap | 8 |
| Duckie | 16 |
| The Eagle | 17 |
| Fire | 18 |

| ● CAFÉS & SNACKS | |
| --- | --- |
| Fabrique | 7 |
| Hubbub | 9 |
| Maltby Street Market | 11 |
| Voodoo Ray's | 2 |

| ● PUBS & BARS | |
| --- | --- |
| Edinboro Castle | 10 |
| Lock Tavern | 3 |
| Prince Alfred | 13 |

| ● CLUBS & LIVE MUSIC VENUES | |
| --- | --- |
| Dalston Superstore | 1 |
| Green Note | 9 |
| Jazz Café | 7 |
| Kings Place | 12 |
| KOKO | 11 |
| Proud | 5 |
| Roundhouse | 4 |
| Underworld | 6 |
| Union Chapel | 2 |

**1**

available (£4). Much better are the gallery's free **guided tours**, which set off from the Sainsbury Wing foyer.

### Italian, Spanish and Dutch paintings

Among the National's **Italian** masterpieces are Leonardo's melancholic *Virgin of the Rocks*, Uccello's *Battle of San Romano*, Botticelli's *Venus and Mars* (inspired by a Dante sonnet) and Piero della Francesca's beautifully composed *Baptism of Christ*, one of his earliest works. The fine collection of Venetian works includes Titian's colourful early masterpiece *Bacchus and Ariadne*, his very late, much gloomier *Death of Acteon*, and Veronese's lustrous *Family of Darius before Alexander*. Later Italian works to look out for include a couple by Caravaggio, a few splendid examples of Tiepolo's airy draughtsmanship and glittering vistas of Venice by Canaletto and Guardi.

From **Spain** there are dazzling pieces by El Greco, Goya, Murillo and Velázquez, among them the provocative *Rokeby Venus*. From the **Low Countries**, standouts include van Eyck's *Arnolfini Marriage*, Memlinc's perfectly poised *Donne Triptych*, and a couple of typically serene Vermeers. There are numerous genre paintings, such as Frans Hals' *Family Group in a Landscape*, and some superlative landscapes, most notably Hobbema's *Avenue, Middleharnis*. An array of Rembrandt paintings that features some of his most searching portraits – two of them self-portraits – is followed by abundant examples of Rubens' expansive, fleshy canvases.

### British and French paintings

Holbein's masterful *Ambassadors* and several of van Dyck's portraits were painted for the English court; and there's home-grown **British** art, too, represented by important works such as Hogarth's satirical *Marriage à la Mode*, Gainsborough's translucent *Morning Walk*, Constable's ever-popular *Hay Wain*, and Turner's *Fighting Temeraire*. Highlights of the **French** contingent include superb works by Poussin, Claude, Fragonard, Boucher, Watteau and David.

### Impressionism and Post-Impressionism

Finally, there's a particularly strong showing of **Impressionists** and **Post-Impressionists** in rooms 43–46 of the East Wing. Among the most famous works are Manet's unfinished *Execution of Maximilian*, Renoir's *Umbrellas*, Monet's *Thames below Westminster*, Van Gogh's *Sunflowers*, Seurat's pointillist *Bathers at Asnières*, a Rousseau junglescape, Cézanne's proto-Cubist *Bathers* and Picasso's Blue Period *Child with a Dove*.

## National Portrait Gallery

St Martin's Place • Daily 10am–6pm, Thurs & Fri till 9pm • Free; audioguide £3.50 • ☎ 020 7306 0055, ⓦ npg.org.uk • ⊖ Leicester Square

Around the east side of the National Gallery lurks the **National Portrait Gallery**, founded in 1856 to house uplifting depictions of the good and the great. Though it undoubtedly has some fine works among its collection of ten thousand portraits, many of the studies are of less interest than their subjects. Nevertheless, it's fascinating to trace who has been deemed worthy of admiration at any one time: aristocrats and artists in previous centuries, warmongers and imperialists in the early decades of the twentieth century, writers and poets in the 1930s and 1940s, and, latterly, retired footballers, and film and pop stars. The NPG's **audioguide** gives useful biographical background information.

## Whitehall

**Whitehall**, the unusually broad avenue connecting Trafalgar Square to Parliament Square, is synonymous with the faceless, pinstriped bureaucracy charged with the day-to-day running of the country, who inhabit the governmental ministries which line the street. During the sixteenth and seventeenth centuries, however, Whitehall was the permanent residence of the kings and queens of England, and was actually synonymous with royalty.

The statues dotted about recall the days when Whitehall stood at the centre of an empire on which the sun never set. Halfway down, in the middle of the road, stands Edwin Lutyens' **Cenotaph**, a memorial to the war dead, erected after World War I and the centrepiece of the Remembrance Sunday ceremony in November. Close by are the gates of Downing Street, home to London's most famous address, **Number 10 Downing Street**, the seventeenth-century terraced house that has been the residence of the prime minister since it was presented to Sir Robert Walpole, Britain's first PM, by George II in 1732.

## Banqueting House

Whitehall • Mon–Sat 10am–5pm • £5 • ☎ 020 3166 6000, ⓦ hrp.org.uk • ⊖ Charing Cross

**Whitehall Palace** was originally the London seat of the Archbishop of York, confiscated and greatly extended by Henry VIII after a fire at Westminster forced him to find alternative accommodation. The chief section of the old palace to survive the 1698 fire was the **Banqueting House** begun by Inigo Jones in 1619 and the first Palladian building to be built in England. The one room open to the public has no original furnishings, but is well worth seeing for the superlative Rubens ceiling paintings glorifying the Stuart dynasty, commissioned by Charles I in the 1630s. Charles himself walked through the room for the last time in 1649 when he stepped onto the executioner's scaffold from one of its windows.

## Horse Guards: Household Cavalry Museum

Whitehall • Daily: March–Sept 10am–6pm; Oct–Feb 10am–5pm • £6 • ☎ 020 7930 3070, ⓦ householdcavalrymuseum.co.uk • ⊖ Charing Cross or Westminster

Two mounted sentries of the Queen's Household Cavalry and two horseless colleagues are posted to protect **Horse Guards**, originally the main gateway to St James's Park and Buckingham Palace. Round the back of the building, you'll find the **Household Cavalry Museum** where you can try on a trooper's elaborate uniform, complete a horse quiz and learn about the regiments' history. With the stables immediately adjacent, it's a sweet-smelling place, and – horse-lovers will be pleased to know – you can see the beasts in their stalls through a glass screen. Don't miss the pocket riot act on display, which ends with the wise warning: "must read correctly: variance fatal".

## Churchill War Rooms

King Charles St • Daily 9.30am–6pm • £17.50 • ☎ 020 7930 6961, ⓦ iwm.org.uk • ⊖ Westminster

In 1938, in anticipation of Nazi air raids, the basements of the civil service buildings on the south side of King Charles Street, south of Downing Street, were converted into the **Cabinet War Rooms**. It was here that Winston Churchill directed operations and held Cabinet meetings for the duration of World War II and the

---

### THE CHANGING OF THE GUARD

The Queen is Colonel-in-Chief of the seven **Household Regiments**: the Life Guards and the Blues and Royals are the two Household Cavalry regiments; while the Grenadier, Coldstream, Scots, Irish and Welsh Guards make up the Foot Guards.

The **Changing of the Guard** takes place at two London locations: the Foot Guards march with a band to Buckingham Palace (May–Aug daily 11.30am; Sept–April alternate days) – they're best sighted coming down the Mall around 11.15am, but remember there's no ceremony if it rains. The Household Cavalry have a ceremony at Horse Guards on Whitehall (Mon–Sat 11am, Sun 10am, with an elaborate inspection at 4pm), and they don't care if it rains or shines. A ceremony also takes place regularly at Windsor Castle (see p.272).

1

# THE WEST END AND WESTMINSTER

New Square · Lincoln's Inn · Royal Courts of Justice · Arundel Street · Temple · National Theatre · BFI IMAX Cinema · Hayward Gallery

Sir John Soane's Museum · Lincoln's Inn Fields · Hunterian Museum · LSE · St Mary-le-Strand · King's College · Somerset House · Waterloo Bridge · BFI Southbank · Queen Elizabeth Hall & Purcell Room · Royal Festival Hall · Hungerford Bridge

Holborn · KINGSWAY · ALDWYCH · Lancaster Place · Savoy Chapel · The Savoy · Embankment · Victoria Embankment Gardens

HIGH HOLBORN · Oasis · Donmar Warehouse · Royal Opera House · Covent Garden Market · London Transport Museum · STRAND · Charing Cross Station · Charing Cross

NEW OXFORD STREET · Centrepoint · St Giles-in-the-Fields · Covent Garden · St Paul's Church · Coliseum · St Martin-in-the-Fields · Nelson's Column · Admiralty Arch · WHITEHALL

Tottenham Court Road · CHARING CROSS ROAD · Foyles · Stanfords · Leicester Square · Hippodrome · National Gallery · TRAFALGAR SQUARE · Household Cavalry Museum

SOHO · Soho Theatre · St Anne's Church · CHINATOWN · Prince Charles Cinema · Odeon · National Portrait Gallery · Empire · Trocadero · Comedy Store · Guards' Crimean Memorial · ICA · Duke of York's Column

OXFORD STREET · All Saints · Liberty · REGENT STREET · Oxford Circus · Piccadilly Circus · Eros · Waterstone's · St James's Church · Royal Academy of Arts · ST JAMES'S · Fortnum & Mason · PALL MALL

Wigmore Hall · John Lewis · Handel House Museum · St George's Church · Sotheby's · NEW BOND STREET · MAYFAIR · Royal Institution · OLD BOND STREET · The Ritz · Green Park · PICCADILLY · BERKELEY SQUARE

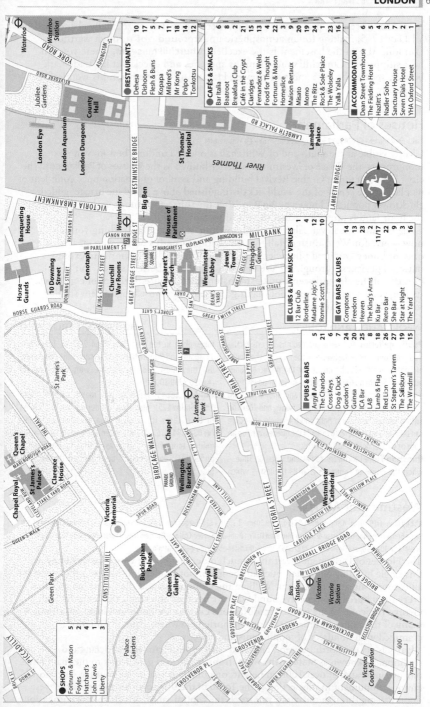

● RESTAURANTS
| | |
|---|---|
| Dehesa | 10 |
| Dishoom | 17 |
| Flesh & Buns | 5 |
| Kopapa | 7 |
| Mildred's | 11 |
| Mr Kong | 18 |
| Polpo | 14 |
| Tonkotsu | 12 |

● CAFÉS & SNACKS
| | |
|---|---|
| Bar Italia | 6 |
| Beatroot | 8 |
| Breakfast Club | 2 |
| Café in the Crypt | 21 |
| Claridges | 15 |
| Fernandez & Wells | 13 |
| Food for Thought | 4 |
| Fortnum & Mason | 22 |
| Homeslice | 3 |
| Maison Bertaux | 9 |
| Misato | 20 |
| Momo | 19 |
| The Ritz | 24 |
| Rock & Sole Plaice | 1 |
| The Wolseley | 23 |
| Yalla Yalla | 16 |

■ ACCOMMODATION
| | |
|---|---|
| Dean Street Townhouse | 6 |
| The Fielding Hotel | 5 |
| Hazlitt's | 4 |
| Nadler Soho | 3 |
| Sanctuary House | 7 |
| Seven Dials Hotel | 2 |
| YHA Oxford Street | 1 |

■ CLUBS & LIVE MUSIC VENUES
| | |
|---|---|
| 12 Bar Club | 1 |
| Borderline | 4 |
| Madame Jojc's | 12 |
| Ronnie Scott's | 10 |

■ GAY BARS & CLUBS
| | |
|---|---|
| Comptons | 14 |
| Freedom | 13 |
| Heaven | 23 |
| The King's Arms | 11/17 |
| Ku Bar | 8 |
| Retro Bar | 26 |
| She Bar | 9 |
| Star at Night | 3 |
| The Yard | 16 |

■ PUBS & BARS
| | |
|---|---|
| Argyll Arms | 5 |
| The Chandos | 21 |
| Cross Keys | 6 |
| Dog & Duck | 7 |
| Gordon's | 24 |
| Guinea | 20 |
| ICA Bar | 25 |
| LAB | 8 |
| Lamb & Flag | 18 |
| Red Lion | 26 |
| St Stephen's Tavern | 27 |
| The Salisbury | 19 |
| The Windmill | 15 |

● SHOPS
| | |
|---|---|
| Fortnum & Mason | 5 |
| Foyles | 2 |
| Hatchard's | 4 |
| John Lewis | 1 |
| Liberty | 3 |

**1**

rooms have been left pretty much as they were when they were finally abandoned on VJ Day 1945, making for an atmospheric underground trot through wartime London. Also in the basement is the excellent **Churchill Museum**, where you can hear snippets of Churchill's most famous speeches and check out his trademark bowler, spotted bow tie and half-chewed Havana, not to mention his wonderful burgundy zip-up "romper suit".

## Houses of Parliament

Parliament Square • ☎ 020 7219 3000, ⓦ parliament.uk • ⊖ Westminster

Clearly visible at the south end of Whitehall is one of London's best-known monuments, the Palace of Westminster, better known as the **Houses of Parliament**. The city's finest Victorian Gothic Revival building and symbol of a nation once confident of its place at the centre of the world, it's distinguished above all by the ornate, gilded clocktower popularly known as **Big Ben**, after the thirteen-tonne main bell that strikes the hour (and is broadcast across the world by BBC radio).

The original medieval palace burned down in 1834, and everything you see now – save for Westminster Hall – is the work of **Charles Barry**, who created an orgy of honey-coloured pinnacles, turrets and tracery that attempts to express national greatness through the use of Gothic and Elizabethan styles. You get a glimpse of the eleventh-century **Westminster Hall** en route to the public galleries, its huge oak hammer-beam roof making it one of the most magnificent secular medieval halls in Europe.

### INFORMATION AND TOURS                              HOUSES OF PARLIAMENT

**Public galleries** To watch proceedings in either the House of Commons – the livelier of the two – or the House of Lords, simply join the queue for the public galleries outside St Stephen's Gate. The public are let in slowly from about 4pm onwards on Mondays and Tuesdays, from around 1pm Wednesdays, noon on Thursdays, and 10am on Sitting Fridays. Security is tight and the whole procedure can take an hour or more, so to avoid the queues, turn up an hour or so later or on a Sitting Friday.

**Question Time** UK citizens can attend Question Time – when the House of Commons is at its liveliest – which takes place in the first hour (Mon 2.30pm, Tues–Thurs 11.30am) and Prime Minister's Question Time (Wed only), but they must book in advance with their local MP (☎ 020 7219 3000).

**Guided tours** Saturday year-round (9am–4.15pm; 1hr 15min; £25), plus Mon–Fri during school holidays. In both cases it's a good idea to book in advance (☎ 0844 847 1672). UK residents are entitled to a free guided tour of the palace, as well as up Big Ben (no under-11s); both need to be organized through your local MP.

## Westminster Abbey

Abbey Mon–Fri 9.30am–4.30pm, Wed till 6pm, Sat 9.30am–2.30pm • £18 **Verger tours** Mon–Fri times vary • £3 **Great Cloisters** Daily 9am–6pm • Free **Chapter House & Abbey Museum** Daily 10am–4pm • Free **College Garden** Tues–Thurs: April–Sept 10am–6pm; Oct–March 10am–4pm • Free • ☎ 020 7222 5152, ⓦ westminster-abbey.org • ⊖ Westminster

The Houses of Parliament dwarf their much older neighbour, **Westminster Abbey**, yet this single building embodies much of the history of England: it has been the venue for all coronations since the time of William the Conqueror, and the site of more or less every royal burial for some five hundred years between the reigns of Henry III and George II. Scores of the nation's most famous citizens are honoured here, too (though many of the stones commemorate people buried elsewhere), and the interior is crammed with hundreds of monuments and statues.

Entry is via the north transept, cluttered with monuments to politicians and traditionally known as **Statesmen's Aisle**, from which you gain access to the main **nave**: narrow, light and, at over 100ft in height, one of the tallest in the country. The most famous monument in this section is the **Tomb of the Unknown Soldier,** near the west door. Passing through the choir, you reach the central sanctuary, site of the coronations,

**1**

and the wonderful **Cosmati floor mosaic**, constructed in the thirteenth century by Italian craftsmen.

### Lady Chapel

The abbey's most dazzling architectural set piece, the **Lady Chapel**, was added by Henry VII in 1503 as his future resting place. With its intricately carved vaulting and fan-shaped gilded pendants, the chapel represents the final spectacular gasp of English Perpendicular Gothic.

### Poets' Corner

Nowadays, the abbey's royal tombs are upstaged by **Poets' Corner**, in the south transept, though the first occupant, Geoffrey Chaucer, was in fact buried here not because he was a poet, but because he lived nearby. By the eighteenth century this zone had become an artistic pantheon, and since then, the transept has been filled with tributes to all shades of talent.

### Great Cloisters and Coronation Chair

Doors in the south choir aisle (plus a separate entrance from Dean's Yard) lead to the **Great Cloisters**. On the east side lies the octagonal Chapter House, where the House of Commons met from 1257, boasting thirteenth-century apocalyptic wall paintings. Also worth a look is the Abbey Museum, filled with generations of lifelike (but bald) royal funereal effigies. After exploring the cloisters you can either exit via Dean's Yard, or via the West Door of the main nave, where you'll see Edward I's **Coronation Chair**, a decrepit oak throne dating from around 1300 and used for every coronation since.

## Tate Britain

Millbank • Daily 10am–6pm; first Fri bi-monthly until 10pm • Free • ☎ 020 7887 8888, ⓦ tate.org.uk • ⊖ Pimlico

A purpose-built gallery half a mile south of Parliament, founded in 1897 with money from Henry Tate, inventor of the sugar cube, **Tate Britain** is devoted to British art. As well as the collection covering 1500 to the present, the gallery also puts on large-scale temporary exhibitions (for which there is a charge) that showcase British artists.

The pictures have recently been rehung chronologically, so you begin with the richly bejewelled portraits of the Elizabethan nobility, before moving on to Britain's most famous artists – Hogarth, Constable, Gainsborough, Reynolds and Blake – plus foreign-born artists like Van Dyck who spent much of their career in Britain. The ever-popular **Pre-Raphaelites** are always well represented, as are established twentieth-century greats such as Stanley Spencer and Francis Bacon alongside living artists such as David Hockney and Bridget Riley. Lastly, don't miss the Tate's outstanding **Turner collection**, displayed in the Clore Gallery.

## Westminster Cathedral

Victoria St • **Cathedral** Mon–Fri 7am–7pm, Sat 8am–7pm, Sun 8am–8pm • Free **Campanile** Mon–Fri 9.30am–5pm, Sat & Sun 9.30am–6pm • £5 • ☎ 020 7798 9055, ⓦ westminstercathedral.org.uk • ⊖ Victoria

Begun in 1895, the stripey neo-Byzantine concoction of the Roman Catholic **Westminster Cathedral** was one of the last and wildest monuments to the Victorian era. It's constructed from more than twelve million terracotta-coloured bricks, decorated with hoops of Portland stone – "blood and bandages" style, as it's known – and culminates in a magnificent tapered campanile which rises to 274ft, served by a lift. The **interior** is only half finished, so to get an idea of what the place will look like when it's finally completed, explore the series of **side chapels** whose rich, multicoloured decor makes use of more than one hundred different marbles from around the world.

**1**

# St James's

**St James's**, the exclusive little enclave sandwiched between St James's Park and Piccadilly, was laid out in the 1670s close to St James's Palace. Regal and aristocratic residences overlook Green Park, gentlemen's clubs cluster along Pall Mall and St James's Street, while jacket-and-tie restaurants and expense-account gentlemen's outfitters line Jermyn Street. Hardly surprising then that most Londoners rarely stray into this area. Plenty of folk, however, frequent **St James's Park**, with large numbers heading for the Queen's chief residence, **Buckingham Palace**, and the adjacent Queen's Gallery and Royal Mews.

## The Mall

Laid out as a memorial to Queen Victoria, the tree-lined sweep of **The Mall** is at its best on Sundays, when it's closed to traffic. The bombastic **Admiralty Arch** was erected to mark the entrance at the Trafalgar Square end of The Mall, while at the Buckingham Palace end stands the ludicrous **Victoria Memorial**, Edward VII's overblown 2300-ton marble tribute to his mother, which is topped by a gilded statue of Victory. Four outlying allegorical groups in bronze confidently proclaim the great achievements of her reign.

## St James's Park

Daily 5am–midnight • Free • ☎ 0300 061 2350, ⓦ royalparks.org.uk

Flanking nearly the whole length of the Mall, **St James's Park** is the oldest of the royal parks, having been drained and enclosed for hunting purposes by Henry VIII. It was landscaped by Nash in the 1820s, and today its lake is a favourite picnic spot. Pelicans – originally a gift from the Russians to Charles II – can still be seen at the eastern end of the lake, and there are exotic ducks, swans and geese aplenty.

## Buckingham Palace

Daily: Aug 9.30am–7pm; Sept 9.30am–6pm • £20 • ☎ 020 7766 7300, ⓦ royalcollection.org.uk • ⊖ Green Park or Victoria

The graceless colossus of **Buckingham Palace** has served as the monarch's permanent London residence only since the accession of Victoria. Bought by George III in 1762, the building was overhauled in the late 1820s by Nash and again in 1913, producing a palace that's as bland as it's possible to be.

For two months of the year, the hallowed portals are grudgingly nudged open. The interior, however, is a bit of an anticlimax: of the palace's 750 rooms you're permitted to see twenty or so, and there's little sign of life, as the Queen decamps to Scotland every summer. For the rest of the year there's little to do here – not that this deters the crowds who mill around the railings, and gather in some force to watch the **Changing of the Guard** (see box, p.59), in which a detachment of the Queen's Foot Guards marches to appropriate martial music from St James's Palace and Wellington Barracks to the palace forecourt (unless it rains, that is).

## Queen's Gallery

Buckingham Palace Rd • Daily 10am–5.30pm • £9.50 • ☎ 020 7766 7300, ⓦ royalcollection.org.uk • ⊖ Victoria

A Doric portico on the south side of Buckingham Palace forms the entrance to the **Queen's Gallery**, which puts on temporary exhibitions drawn from the **Royal Collection**, a superlative array of art that includes works by Michelangelo, Raphael, Holbein, Reynolds, Gainsborough, Vermeer, Van Dyck, Rubens, Rembrandt and Canaletto, as well as the world's largest collection of Leonardo drawings, the odd Fabergé egg and heaps of Sèvres china.

**TOP 5 QUIRKY MUSEUMS**

**Dennis Severs' House** East End. See p.81

**Horniman Museum** Forest Hill. See p.99

**Hunterian Museum** Holborn. See p.73

**Old Operating Theatre and Herb Garret** Southwark. See p.86

**Sir John Soane's Museum** Holborn. See p.73

## Royal Mews

Buckingham Palace Rd • Feb, March & Nov Mon–Sat 10am–4pm; April–Oct daily 10am–5pm; • £8.75 • ☎ 020 7766 7302, ⓦ royalcollection.org.uk • ⊖ Victoria

Royal carriages are the main attraction at the Nash-built **Royal Mews**, in particular the Gold State Coach, made for George III in 1762 and used in every coronation since, smothered in 22-carat gilding and weighing four tonnes, its axles supporting four life-size figures.

## St James's Palace

Chapel Royal Oct to Good Friday services 8.30am & 11.15am **Queen's Chapel** Easter Sun–July Sun 8.30am & 11.15am • ⊖ Green Park

**St James's Palace**'s main red-brick gate-tower is pretty much all that remains of the Tudor palace erected here by Henry VIII. When Whitehall Palace burned down in 1698, St James's became the principal royal residence and, in keeping with tradition, every ambassador to the UK is still accredited to the "Court of St James's", even though the court has since moved down the road to Buckingham Palace. The modest, rambling, crenellated complex is off-limits to the public, with the exception of the **Chapel Royal**, situated within the palace, and the **Queen's Chapel**, on the other side of Marlborough Road; both are open for services only.

## Clarence House

Stable Yard Rd • Aug Mon–Fri 10am–4pm, Sat & Sun 10am–5.30pm; visits (by guided tour) must be booked in advance • £9.50 • ☎ 020 7766 7303, ⓦ royalcollection.org.uk • ⊖ Green Park

**Clarence House**, connected to the palace's southwest wing, was home to the Queen Mother, and now serves as the official London home of Charles and his second wife Camilla, but a handful of rooms can be visited over the summer when the royals are in Scotland. The interior is pretty unremarkable, so apart from a peek behind the scenes in a working royal palace, or a few mementos of the Queen Mum, the main draw is the twentieth-century British paintings on display by the likes of Walter Sickert and Augustus John.

# Mayfair

**Piccadilly**, which forms the southern border of swanky **Mayfair**, may not be the fashionable promenade it started out as in the eighteenth century, but a whiff of exclusivity still pervades **Bond Street** and its tributaries, where designer clothes emporia jostle for space with jewellers, bespoke tailors and fine art dealers. **Regent Street** and **Oxford Street**, meanwhile, are home to the flagship branches of the country's most popular chain stores.

## Piccadilly Circus

Anonymous and congested it may be, but **Piccadilly Circus** is, for many Londoners, the nearest their city comes to having a centre. A much-altered product of Nash's grand 1812 Regent Street plan and now a major traffic interchange, it may not be a

1

picturesque place, but thanks to its celebrated aluminium statue, popularly known as **Eros**, it's prime tourist territory.

The fountain's archer is one of the city's top attractions, a status that baffles all who live here. Despite the bow and arrow, it's not the god of love at all but his lesser-known brother, Anteros, god of requited love, commemorating the selfless philanthropic love of the Earl of Shaftesbury, a Bible-thumping social reformer who campaigned against child labour.

## Regent Street

**Regent Street**, drawn up by John Nash in 1812 as both a luxury shopping street and a triumphal way between George IV's Carlton House and Regent's Park, was the city's earliest attempt at dealing with traffic congestion, slum clearance and planned social segregation, something that would later be perfected by the Victorians. The increase in the purchasing power of the city's middle classes in the last century brought the tone of the street "down" and heavyweight stores now predominate. Among the best known are **Hamley's**, reputedly the world's largest toyshop, and **Liberty**, the upmarket department store that popularized Arts and Crafts designs.

## Piccadilly

**Piccadilly** apparently got its name from the ruffs or "pickadills" worn by the dandies who used to promenade here in the late seventeenth century. It's not much of a place for promenading today, however, with traffic nose to tail most of the day and night. Infinitely more pleasant places to window-shop are the various **nineteenth-century arcades** that shoot off to the north and south, originally built to protect shoppers from the mud and horse dung on the streets, but now equally useful for escaping exhaust fumes.

### Royal Academy of Arts

Piccadilly • Daily 10am–6pm, Fri till 10pm • £10–15 • ☎ 020 7300 8000, ⓦ royalacademy.org.uk • ⊖ Green Park

The **Royal Academy of Arts** occupies one of the few surviving aristocratic mansions that once lined the north side of Piccadilly. Rebuilding in the nineteenth century destroyed the original curved colonnades beyond the main gateway, but the complex has kept the feel of a Palladian *palazzo*. The country's first-ever formal art school, founded in 1768, the RA hosts a wide range of art exhibitions, and an annual **Summer Exhibition** that remains an essential stop on the social calendar of upper-middle-class England. Anyone can enter paintings in any style, and the lucky winners get hung, in rather close proximity, and sold. RA "Academicians" are allowed to display six of their own works – no matter how awful. The result is a bewildering display, which gets panned annually by highbrow critics, but enjoyed happily by everyone else.

---

### OXFORD STREET: THE BUSIEST STREET IN EUROPE

As wealthy Londoners began to move out of the City in the eighteenth century in favour of the newly developed West End, so **Oxford Street** – the old Roman road to Oxford – gradually became London's main shopping thoroughfare. Today, despite successive recessions and sky-high rents, Oxford Street remains Europe's busiest street, simply because this two-mile hotchpotch of shops is home to (often several) flagship branches of Britain's major retailers. The street's only real architectural landmark is **Selfridges** (see p.126) opened in 1909 with a facade featuring the Queen of Time riding the ship of commerce and supporting an Art Deco clock.

## Bond Street

While Oxford Street, Regent Street and Piccadilly have all gone downmarket, **Bond Street**, which runs parallel with Regent Street, has carefully maintained its exclusivity. It is, in fact, two streets rolled into one: the southern half, laid out in the 1680s, is known as Old Bond Street; its northern extension, which followed less than fifty years later, is known as New Bond Street. They are both pretty unassuming streets architecturally, yet the shops that line them are among the flashiest in London, dominated by perfumeries, jewellers and designer clothing stores. In addition to fashion, Bond Street is also renowned for its fine art galleries and its **auction houses**, the oldest of which is Sotheby's, 34–35 New Bond St, whose viewing galleries are open free of charge.

# Marylebone

**Marylebone**, which lies to the north of Oxford Street, is, like Mayfair, another grid-plan Georgian development – a couple of social and real-estate leagues below its neighbour, but a wealthy area nevertheless. It boasts a very fine art gallery, the **Wallace Collection**, and, in its northern fringes, one of London's biggest tourist attractions, **Madame Tussauds**, the oldest and largest wax museum in the world, plus the ever-popular **Sherlock Holmes Museum**.

## Wallace Collection

Manchester Square • Daily 10am–5pm • Free • ☎ 020 7563 9500, ⓦ wallacecollection.org • ⊖ Bond Street

Housed in a miniature eighteenth-century chateau, the splendid **Wallace Collection** is best known for its eighteenth-century French paintings, Franz Hals' *Laughing Cavalier*, Titian's *Perseus and Andromeda*, Velázquez's *Lady with a Fan* and Rembrandt's affectionate portrait of his teenage son, Titus. The museum has preserved the feel of a grand stately home, its exhibits piled high in glass cabinets, and paintings covering almost every inch of wall space. The fact that these exhibits are set amid priceless Boulle furniture – and a bloody great armoury – makes the place even more remarkable.

## Madame Tussauds

Marylebone Rd • Mon–Fri 9.30am–5.30pm, Sat & Sun 9am–6pm • Online tickets from £22.50 • ☎ 0871 894 3000, ⓦ madametussauds .com • ⊖ Baker Street

**Madame Tussauds** has been pulling in the crowds ever since the good lady arrived in London from Paris in 1802 bearing the sculpted heads of guillotined aristocrats. The entrance fee might be extortionate, the waxwork likenesses of the famous occasionally dubious and the attempts to relieve you of yet more cash relentless, but you can still rely on finding London's biggest queues here (book online to avoid waiting). You can choose to opt out of the Chamber of Horrors Live show, a piece of hokum designed to frighten the living daylights out of tourists.

## Sherlock Holmes Museum

239 Baker St • Daily 9.30am–6pm • £8 • ☎ 020 7224 3688, ⓦ sherlock-holmes.co.uk • ⊖ Baker Street

Baker Street is synonymous with Sherlock Holmes, the fictional detective who lived at no. 221b (the actual number on the door of the museum). Unashamedly touristy, the **Sherlock Holmes Museum** is stuffed full of Victoriana and life-size models of characters from the books. It's an atmospheric and very competent exercise in period reconstruction – you can even don a deerstalker to have your picture taken by the fireside, looking like the great detective himself.

**1**

# Soho

Bounded by Regent Street to the west, Oxford Street to the north and Charing Cross Road to the east, **Soho** is very much the heart of the West End. It's been the city's premier red-light district for centuries and retains an unorthodox and slightly raffish air that's unique for central London. It has an immigrant history as rich as that of the East End and a louche nightlife that has attracted writers and revellers of every sexual persuasion since the eighteenth century. Today it's London's most high-profile gay quarter, especially around **Old Compton Street**. Conventional sights are few, yet there's probably more street life here than anywhere in the city centre, whatever the hour. Most folk head to Soho to go the cinema or theatre, and to have a drink or a bite to eat in the innumerable bars, cafés and restaurants that pepper the area.

## Leicester Square

When the big cinemas and nightclubs are doing good business, and the buskers are entertaining the crowds, **Leicester Square** is one of the most crowded places in London, particularly on a Friday or Saturday when huge numbers of tourists and half the youth of the suburbs seem to congregate here. It wasn't until the mid-nineteenth century that the square actually began to emerge as an entertainment zone; cinema moved in during the 1930s, a golden age evoked by the sleek black lines of the Odeon on the east side.

## Chinatown

**Chinatown**, hemmed in between Leicester Square and Shaftesbury Avenue, is a self-contained jumble of shops, cafés and restaurants. Only a minority of London's Chinese live in these three small blocks, but it remains a focus for the community, a place to do business or the weekly shop, celebrate a wedding, or just meet up for meals, particularly on Sundays, when the restaurants overflow with Chinese families tucking into *dim sum*. **Gerrard Street** is the main drag, with telephone kiosks rigged out as pagodas and fake oriental gates or *paifang*.

## Old Compton Street

If Soho has a main road, it would be **Old Compton Street**, which runs parallel with Shaftesbury Avenue. The shops, boutiques and cafés here are typical of the area and a good barometer of the latest fads. Soho has been a permanent fixture on the **gay scene** for the better part of a century, and you'll find a profusion of gay bars, clubs and cafés jostling for position here and round the corner in Wardour Street.

# Covent Garden

More sanitized and commercial than neighbouring Soho, the shops and restaurants of **Covent Garden** today are a far cry from the district's heyday when the piazza was the great playground (and red-light district) of eighteenth-century London. The buskers in front of St Paul's Church, the theatres round about, and the **Royal Opera House** on Bow Street are survivors of this tradition, and on a balmy summer evening, **Covent Garden Piazza** is still an undeniably lively place to be.

## Covent Garden Piazza

London's oldest planned square, laid out in the 1630s by Inigo Jones, **Covent Garden Piazza** was initially a great success, its novelty value alone attracting a rich and

**1**

aristocratic clientele, but over the next century the tone of the place fell as the fruit and vegetable market expanded, and theatres, coffee houses and brothels began to take over the peripheral buildings. When the market closed in 1974, the piazza narrowly survived being turned into an office development. Instead, the elegant Victorian market hall and its environs were restored to house shops, restaurants and arts-and-crafts stalls. Of Jones's original piazza, the only remaining parts are the two rebuilt sections of north-side arcading, and **St Paul's Church**, to the west.

## London Transport Museum

Covent Garden Piazza • Mon–Thurs, Sat & Sun 10am–6pm, Fri 11am–6pm • Adults £15, under-16s free • ☎ 020 7379 6344, ⓦ ltmuseum .co.uk • ⊖ Covent Garden

A former flower-market shed on Covent Garden Piazza's east side is home to the **London Transport Museum**, a sure-fire hit for families with kids under 10. To follow the displays chronologically, head for Level 2, where you'll find a reconstructed 1829 Shillibeer's Horse Omnibus, which provided the city's first regular horse-bus service. Level 1 tells the story of the world's first underground system and contains a lovely 1920s Metropolitan Line carriage in burgundy and green with pretty, drooping lamps. On the ground floor, one double-decker **tram** is all that's left to pay tribute to the world's largest tram system, dismantled in 1952. Look out, too, for the first **tube** train, from the 1890s, whose lack of windows earned it the nickname "the padded cell".

## Royal Opera House

Bow St • **Floral Hall** Daily 10am–3.30pm • Free **Backstage tours** Mon–Fri 10.30am, 12.30pm & 2.30pm, Sat hourly 10.30am–2.30pm • £12 • ☎ 020 7304 4000, ⓦ roh.org.uk • ⊖ Covent Garden

The arcading on the northeast side of the piazza was rebuilt as part of the redevelopment of the **Royal Opera House**, whose main Neoclassical facade dates from 1811 and opens onto Bow Street. Now, however, you can reach the opera house from a passageway in the corner of the arcading. The spectacular wrought-iron **Floral Hall** serves as the opera house's main foyer, and is open to the public, as is the *Amphitheatre* bar/restaurant (from 90min before performance to the end of the last interval), which has a glorious terrace overlooking the piazza.

# Strand

Once famous for its riverside mansions, and later its music halls, the **Strand** – the main road connecting Westminster to the City – is a shadow of its former self. One of the few vestiges of glamour is **The Savoy**, London's first modern luxury hotel, built in 1889 on the site of the medieval Savoy Palace on the south side of the street. As its name suggests, the Strand once lay along the riverbank until the Victorians shored up the banks of the Thames to create the Embankment.

## Somerset House

Strand • **Courtyard** Daily 7.30am–11pm • Free **Riverside terrace** Daily 8am–6pm • Free **Embankment galleries** Daily 10am–6pm • £6 • ☎ 020 7845 4600, ⓦ somersethouse.org.uk • ⊖ Temple or Covent Garden

**Somerset House** is the sole survivor of the grandiose river palaces that once lined the Strand. Although it looks like an old aristocratic mansion, the present building was purpose-built in 1776 to house government offices. Nowadays, Somerset House's granite-paved courtyard, which has a 55-jet **fountain** that spouts little syncopated dances straight from the cobbles, is used for open-air performances, concerts, installations and, in winter, an ice rink.

The south wing has a lovely riverside terrace with a café/restaurant and the **Embankment Galleries**, which host innovative special exhibitions on contemporary

**1**

art and design. You can also admire the Royal Naval Commissioners' superb gilded eighteenth-century barge in the **King's Barge House**, below ground level in the south wing.

## Courtauld Gallery

Daily 10am–6pm • £6, £3 on Mon • ☎ 020 7848 2526, ⓦ courtauld.ac.uk • ⊖ Temple or Covent Garden

In the north wing of Somerset House is the **Courtauld Gallery**, chiefly known for its dazzling collection of Impressionist and Post-Impressionist paintings. Among the most celebrated is a small-scale version of Manet's *Déjeuner sur l'herbe*, Renoir's *La Loge*, and Degas' *Two Dancers*, plus a whole heap of Cézanne's canvases, including one of his series of *Card Players*. The Courtauld also boasts a fine selection of works by the likes of Rubens, Van Dyck, Tiepolo and Cranach the Elder, and has recently been augmented by the long-term loan of a hundred top-notch twentieth-century paintings and sculptures by, among others, Kandinksy, Matisse, Dufy, Derain, Rodin and Henry Moore.

# Bloomsbury

**Bloomsbury** was built over in grid-plan style from the 1660s onwards, and the formal bourgeois Georgian squares laid out then remain the area's main distinguishing feature. In the twentieth century, Bloomsbury acquired a reputation as the city's most learned quarter, dominated by the dual institutions of the **British Museum** and **London University**, but perhaps best known for its literary inhabitants, among them T.S. Eliot and Virginia Woolf. Today, the British Museum is clearly the star attraction, but there are other minor sights, such as the **Charles Dickens Museum**. Only in its northern fringes does the character of the area change dramatically, as you near the hustle and bustle of **Euston**, **St Pancras** and **King's Cross** train stations.

## British Museum

Great Russell St • Daily 10am–5.30pm, Fri till 8.30pm • Free • ☎ 020 7323 8299, ⓦ britishmuseum.org • ⊖ Tottenham Court Road, Russell Square or Holborn

The **British Museum** is one of the great museums of the world. With more than seventy thousand exhibits ranged over several miles of galleries, it boasts a huge collection of antiquities, prints and drawings – more than thirteen million objects (and growing). Its assortment of Roman and Greek art is unparalleled, its Egyptian collection is the most significant outside Egypt and, in addition, there are fabulous treasures from Anglo-Saxon and Roman Britain, from China, Japan, India and Mesopotamia.

The building itself, begun in 1823, is the grandest of London's Greek Revival edifices, dominated by the giant Ionian colonnade and portico that forms the main entrance. At the heart of the museum is the **Great Court**, with its remarkable, curving glass-and-steel roof, designed by Norman Foster. At the centre stands the copper-domed former **Round Reading Room**, built in the 1850s to house the British Library, where Karl Marx penned *Das Kapital*. More recently, it has been used for special exhibitions, which now take place in the new World Conservation and Exhibitions Centre.

### The highlights

The most famous of the **Roman and Greek antiquities** are the Parthenon sculptures, better known as the **Elgin Marbles**, after the British aristocrat who acquired the reliefs in 1801. The **Egyptian collection** of monumental sculptures is impressive, but it's the ever-popular **mummies** that draw the biggest crowds. Also on display is the **Rosetta Stone**, which finally unlocked the secret of Egyptian hieroglyphs. There's a splendid

1

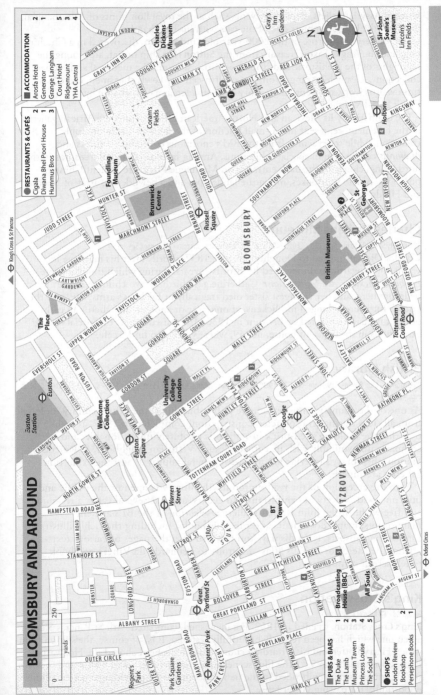

# BLOOMSBURY AND AROUND

■ ACCOMMODATION
| | |
|---|---|
| Arosfa Hotel | 2 |
| Generator | 1 |
| Grange Langham | 5 |
| Court Hotel | 3 |
| Ridgemount | 4 |
| YHA Central | |

● RESTAURANTS & CAFÉS
| | |
|---|---|
| Cigala | 2 |
| Diwana Bhel Poori House | 1 |
| Hummus Bros | 3 |

■ PUBS & BARS
| | |
|---|---|
| The Duke | 1 |
| The Lamb | 2 |
| Museum Tavern | 3 |
| Princess Louise | 4 |
| The Social | 5 |

● SHOPS
| | |
|---|---|
| London Review | 2 |
| Bookshop | |
| Persephone Books | 1 |

**1**

series of **Assyrian reliefs**, depicting events such as the royal lion hunts of Ashurbanipal, in which the king slaughters one of the cats with his bare hands.

The leathery half-corpse of the 2000-year-old **Lindow Man**, discovered in a Cheshire bog, and the Anglo-Saxon treasure from the **Sutton Hoo** ship burial, are among the highlights of the prehistoric and Romano-British section. The medieval and modern collections, meanwhile, range from the twelfth-century **Lewis chessmen**, carved from walrus ivory, to twentieth-century exhibits such as a copper vase by Frank Lloyd Wright.

The dramatically lit Mexican and North American galleries, plus the African galleries in the basement, represent just a small fraction of the museum's **ethnographic collection**, while select works from the BM's enormous collection of **prints and drawings** can be seen in special exhibitions. Among fabulous **Oriental treasures** in the north wing, closest to the back entrance on Montague Place, are ancient Chinese porcelain, ornate snuffboxes, miniature landscapes and a bewildering array of Buddhist and Hindu gods.

## Charles Dickens Museum

48 Doughty St • Daily 10am–5pm • £8 • ☎ 020 7405 2127, ⓦ dickensmuseum.com • ⊖ Russell Square

Charles Dickens moved to Doughty Street in 1837, shortly after his marriage to Catherine Hogarth, and they lived here for two years, during which time he wrote *Nicholas Nickleby* and *Oliver Twist*. Catherine gave birth to two children in the bedroom here, and her youngest sister died tragically in Dickens's arms. Much of the house's furniture belonged to Dickens, at one time or another, and there's an early portrait miniature painted by his aunt in 1830. The museum puts on special exhibitions in the adjacent house, no. 49, where you'll also find a café.

## British Library

96 Euston Rd • Mon & Wed–Fri 9.30am–6pm, Tues 9.30am–8pm, Sat 9.30am–5pm, Sun 11am–5pm • Free • ☎ 0843 208 1144, ⓦ bl.uk • ⊖ King's Cross

As one of the country's most expensive public buildings, the **British Library** took flak from all sides during its protracted construction, completed in 1997. Yet while it's true that the building's red-brick brutalism is resolutely unfashionable, and compares unfavourably with its cathedralesque Victorian neighbour, St Pancras Station, the library's interior has met with general approval, and the exhibition galleries are superb.

With the exception of the reading rooms, the library is open to the public and puts on a wide variety of exhibitions and events, and has several cafés, a restaurant and free wi-fi. In the John Ritblat Gallery a selection of the BL's ancient manuscripts, maps, documents and precious books, including the richly illustrated Lindisfarne Gospels, is on display. You can also turn the pages of various texts – from the Mercator's 1570s atlas of Europe to Leonardo da Vinci's notebook – on touch-screen computers.

## King's Cross Station

Euston Rd • ⊖ King's Cross

**King's Cross Station**, opened in 1852, is a mere shed, compared with St Pancras Station, albeit one which has been recently beautifully restored. It is, of course, the station from which Harry Potter and his wizarding chums leave for school aboard the Hogwarts Express from platform 9¾. The film scenes were shot between platforms 4 and 5, and a station trolley is now embedded in the new concourse wall, providing a perfect photo opportunity for passing Potter fans.

# Holborn

**Holborn**, on the periphery of the financial district of the City, has long been associated with the law, and its **Inns of Court** make for an interesting stroll, their archaic, cobbled precincts exuding the rarefied atmosphere of an Oxbridge college, and sheltering one of the city's oldest churches, the twelfth-century **Temple Church**. Holborn's gem, though, is the **Sir John Soane's Museum**, one of the most memorable and enjoyable of London's small museums, packed with architectural illusions and an eclectic array of curios.

## Temple

**Temple** is the largest and most complex of the Inns of Court, where every barrister in England must study (and eat) before being called to the Bar. A few very old buildings survive here and the maze of courtyards and passageways is fun to explore.

### Middle Temple Hall

Mon–Fri 10–11.30am & 3–4pm, phone to check access • Free • ☏ 020 7427 4800 • ⊖ Temple or Blackfriars

Medieval students ate, attended lectures and slept in the **Middle Temple Hall**, across the courtyard, still the Inn's main dining room. The present building, constructed in the 1560s, provided the setting for many great Elizabethan masques and plays – probably including Shakespeare's *Twelfth Night*, which is believed to have been premiered here in 1602. The hall is worth a visit for its fine hammer-beam roof, wooden panelling and decorative Elizabethan screen.

### Temple Church

Mon, Tues, Thurs & Fri 11am–4pm, Wed 2–4pm • £4 • ☏ 020 7353 3470, ⓦ templechurch.com • ⊖ Temple or Blackfriars

The complex's oldest building is **Temple Church**, built in 1185 by the Knights Templar, and modelled on the Church of the Holy Sepulchre in Jerusalem. The interior features striking Purbeck marble piers, recumbent marble effigies of medieval knights and tortured grotesques grimacing in the spandrels of the blind arcading. The church makes an appearance in both the book and the film of Dan Brown's *The Da Vinci Code*.

## Hunterian Museum

35–43 Lincoln's Inn Fields • Tues–Sat 10am–5pm • Free • ☏ 020 7869 6560, ⓦ www.rcseng.ac.uk • ⊖ Holborn

The **Hunterian Museum**, on the first floor of the Royal College of Surgeons, contains the unique specimen collection of the surgeon-scientist John Hunter (1728–93). The centrepiece is the Crystal Gallery, a wall of jars of pickled skeletons and body pieces – from the gall bladder of a puffer fish to the thyroid of a dromedary – prepared by Hunter himself. Among the most prized exhibits are the skeleton of the "Irish giant", Charles Byrne (1761–83), who was 7ft 10 inches tall, and the Sicilian dwarf Caroline Crachami (1815–24), who stood at just over 1ft 10 1/2 inches when she died at the age of nine.

## Sir John Soane's Museum

13 Lincoln's Inn Fields • Tues–Sat 10am–5pm, first Tues of the month candle-lit 6–9pm • Free • Guided tour Sat 11am, £10 • ☏ 020 7405 2107, ⓦ soane.org • ⊖ Holborn

A group of buildings on the north side of Lincoln's Inn Fields houses the fascinating **Sir John Soane's Museum**. Soane (1753–1837), a bricklayer's son who rose to be architect of the Bank of England, was an avid collector who designed this house not only as a home and office, but also as a place to stash his large collection of art and antiquities. Arranged much as it was in his lifetime, the ingeniously planned house has an informal, treasure-hunt atmosphere, with surprises in every alcove. Note that the

**1**

museum is very popular and you may have to queue to get in – and get here early if you want to go on a guided tour or on a candle-lit evening.

# The City

Stretching from Temple Bar in the west to the Tower of London in the east **The City** is where London began. It was here, nearly two thousand years ago, that the Romans first established a settlement on the Thames; later the medieval City emerged as the country's most important trading centre and it remains one of the world's leading financial hubs. However, in this Square Mile (as the City is sometimes referred to), you'll find few leftovers of London's early days, since four-fifths burnt down in the Great Fire of 1666. Rebuilt in brick and stone, the City gradually lost its centrality as London swelled westwards. What you see now is mostly the product of three fairly recent building phases: the Victorian construction boom; the postwar reconstruction following World War II; and the building frenzy that began in the 1980s and has continued ever since.

When you consider what has happened here, it's amazing that anything has survived to pay witness to the City's 2000-year history. Wren's spires still punctuate the skyline and his masterpiece, **St Paul's Cathedral**, remains one of London's geographical pivots. At the City's eastern edge, the **Tower of London** still boasts some of the best-preserved medieval fortifications in Europe. Other relics, such as Wren's **Monument** to the Great Fire and London's oldest synagogue and church, are less conspicuous, and even locals have problems finding modern attractions like the **Museum of London** and the **Barbican** arts complex.

## Fleet Street

**Fleet Street**'s associations with the printed press began in 1500, when Wynkyn de Worde, William Caxton's apprentice, moved the Caxton presses here from Westminster to be close to the lawyers of the Inns of Court (his best customers) and to the clergy of St Paul's. In 1702, the world's first daily newspaper, the now defunct **Daily Courant**, began publishing here, and by the nineteenth century, all the major national and provincial dailies had moved their presses to the area. Then in 1985, Britain's first colour tabloid, *Today*, appeared, using computer technology that rendered the Fleet Street presses obsolete. It was left to media tycoon Rupert Murdoch to take on the printers' unions in a bitter year-long dispute that changed the newspaper industry for ever. The press headquarters that once dominated the area have all now relocated, leaving just a handful of small publications and a few architectural landmarks to testify to 500 years of printing history.

### St Bride's Church

Fleet St • Mon–Fri 9am–6pm, Sat 11am–3pm, Sun 10am–6.30pm • Free • ☎ 020 7427 0133, ⓦ stbrides.com • ⊖ St Paul's

To find out more about Fleet Street's history, check out the exhibition in the crypt of **St Bride's Church**, the "journalists' and printers' cathedral", situated behind the former Reuters building. The church also features Wren's tallest, and most exquisite, spire (said to be the inspiration for the traditional tiered wedding cake).

### St Paul's Cathedral

Mon–Sat 8.30am–4.30pm • from £15 online • ☎ 020 7246 8348, ⓦ stpauls.co.uk • ⊖ St Paul's

Designed by Christopher Wren and completed in 1710, **St Paul's Cathedral** remains a dominating presence in the City, despite the encroaching tower blocks. Topped by an enormous lead-covered dome, its showpiece west facade is particularly magnificent.

1

---

**TOP 5 CITY CHURCHES**

The City of London is crowded with **churches** (ⓦ london-city-churches.org.uk), the majority of them built or rebuilt by Wren after the Great Fire. Weekday lunchtimes are a good time to visit, when many put on free concerts of classical and chamber music.

**St Bartholomew-the-Great** Cloth Fair; ⊖ Barbican. The oldest surviving pre-Fire church in the City and by far the most atmospheric.

**St Mary Abchurch** Abchurch Lane; ⊖ Cannon Street or Bank. Unique among Wren's City churches for its huge, painted, domed ceiling, plus the only authenticated reredos by Grinling Gibbons.

**St Mary Aldermary** Queen Victoria St; ⊖ Mansion House. Wren's most successful stab at Gothic, with fan vaulting in the aisles and a panelled ceiling in the nave.

**St Mary Woolnoth** Lombard St; ⊖ Bank. Hawksmoor's only City church, sporting an unusually broad, bulky tower and a Baroque clerestory that floods the church with light from its semicircular windows.

**St Stephen Walbrook** Walbrook; ⊖ Bank. Wren's dress rehearsal for St Paul's, with a wonderful central dome and plenty of original woodcarving.

---

The best place from which to appreciate St Paul's is beneath the **dome**, decorated (against Wren's wishes) with Thornhill's trompe-l'oeil frescoes. The most richly decorated section of the cathedral, however, is the **chancel**, where the gilded mosaics of birds, fish, animals and greenery, dating from the 1890s, are spectacular. The intricately carved oak and limewood **choir stalls**, and the imposing organ case, are the work of Wren's master carver, Grinling Gibbons.

### The galleries

A series of stairs, beginning in the south aisle, lead to the dome's three **galleries**, the first of which is the internal **Whispering Gallery**, so called because of its acoustic properties – words whispered to the wall on one side are distinctly audible over 100ft away on the other, though the place is often so busy you can't hear much above the hubbub. The other two galleries are exterior: the wide **Stone Gallery**, around the balustrade at the base of the dome, and ultimately the tiny **Golden Gallery**, below the golden ball and cross which top the cathedral.

### The crypt

Although the nave is crammed full of overblown monuments to military types, burials in St Paul's are confined to the whitewashed **crypt**, reputedly the largest in Europe. Immediately to your right is Artists' Corner, which boasts as many painters and architects as Westminster Abbey has poets, including Christopher Wren himself, who was commissioned to build the cathedral after its Gothic predecessor, Old St Paul's, was destroyed in the Great Fire. The crypt's two other star tombs are those of **Nelson** and **Wellington**, both occupying centre stage and both with even more fanciful monuments upstairs.

## Museum of London

150 London Wall · Daily 10am–6pm · Free · ☎ 020 7001 9844, ⓦ museumoflondon.org.uk · ⊖ Barbican or St Paul's

Over the centuries, numerous Roman, Saxon and medieval remains have been salvaged or dug up and are now displayed in the **Museum of London**, whose permanent galleries provide an educational and imaginative trot through London's past, from prehistory to the present day. Specific exhibits to look out for include the Bucklersbury Roman mosaic and the model of Old St Paul's, but the prize possession is the **Lord Mayor's Coach**, built in 1757 and rivalling the Queen's in sheer weight of gold decoration. Look out, too, for the museum's excellent temporary exhibitions, gallery tours, lectures, walks and videos it organizes throughout the year.

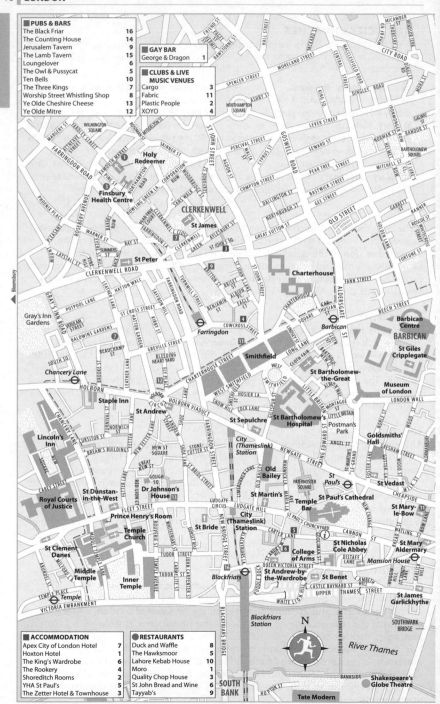

**PUBS & BARS**

| | |
|---|---|
| The Black Friar | 16 |
| The Counting House | 14 |
| Jerusalem Tavern | 9 |
| The Lamb Tavern | 15 |
| Loungelover | 6 |
| The Owl & Pussycat | 5 |
| Ten Bells | 10 |
| The Three Kings | 7 |
| Worship Street Whistling Shop | 8 |
| Ye Olde Cheshire Cheese | 13 |
| Ye Olde Mitre | 12 |

**GAY BAR**

| | |
|---|---|
| George & Dragon | 1 |

**CLUBS & LIVE MUSIC VENUES**

| | |
|---|---|
| Cargo | 3 |
| Fabric | 11 |
| Plastic People | 2 |
| XOYO | 4 |

**ACCOMMODATION**

| | |
|---|---|
| Apex City of London Hotel | 7 |
| Hoxton Hotel | 1 |
| The King's Wardrobe | 6 |
| The Rookery | 4 |
| Shoreditch Rooms | 2 |
| YHA St Paul's | 5 |
| The Zetter Hotel & Townhouse | 3 |

**RESTAURANTS**

| | |
|---|---|
| Duck and Waffle | 8 |
| The Hawksmoor | 5 |
| Lahore Kebab House | 10 |
| Moro | 1 |
| Quality Chop House | 3 |
| St John Bread and Wine | 6 |
| Tayyab's | 9 |

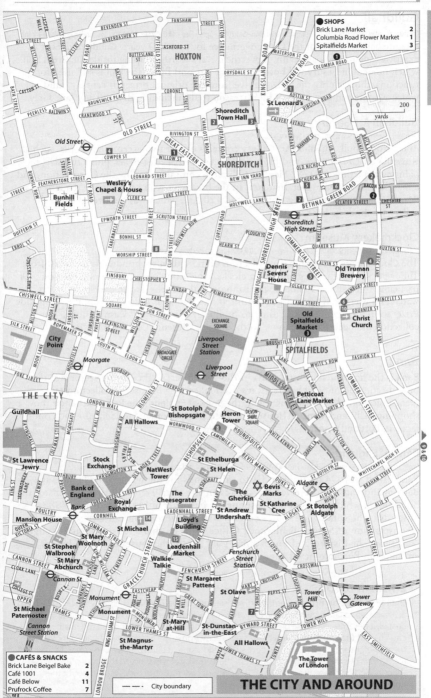

● SHOPS
| | |
|---|---|
| Brick Lane Market | 2 |
| Columbia Road Flower Market | 1 |
| Spitalfields Market | 3 |

0 — 200
yards

● CAFÉS & SNACKS
| | |
|---|---|
| Brick Lane Beigel Bake | 2 |
| Café 1001 | 4 |
| Café Below | 11 |
| Prufrock Coffee | 7 |

----- City boundary

**THE CITY AND AROUND**

**1**

# Guildhall

Gresham St • May–Sept daily 10am–5pm; Oct–April Mon–Sat 10am–5pm • Free • ☎ 020 7606 3030, ⓦ cityoflondon.gov.uk • ⊖ Bank

Despite being the seat of the City governance for over 800 years, **Guildhall** doesn't exactly exude municipal wealth. Nevertheless, it's worth popping inside the **Great Hall**, which miraculously survived both the Great Fire and Blitz. The hall is still used for functions, though only the walls survive from the original fifteenth-century building, which was the venue for several high-treason trials, including that of Lady Jane Grey.

## Guildhall Art Gallery

Mon–Sat 10am–5pm, Sun noon–4pm • Free • ⊖ Bank

The purpose-built **Guildhall Art Gallery** contains one or two exceptional works, such as Rossetti's *La Ghirlandata*, and Holman Hunt's *The Eve of St Agnes*, plus a massive painting depicting the 1782 Siege of Gibraltar, commissioned by the Corporation, and a marble statue of Margaret Thatcher. In the basement, you can view the remains of a **Roman amphitheatre**, dating from around 120 AD, which was discovered when the gallery was built in 1988.

## Clockmakers' Museum

Aldermanbury • Mon–Sat 9.30am–4.45pm • Free • ☎ 020 7332 1868, ⓦ clockmakers.org • ⊖ Bank

The **Clockmakers' Museum** has a collection of more than six hundred timepieces, from Tudor pocket watches to grandfather clocks, which ring out in unison on the hour. Of particular interest is H5, a marine chronometer that looks like an oversized pocket watch and was tested by George III himself. H4 had won John Harrison the Longitude Prize (see p.99) and he was required to produce H5 to prove it wasn't a fluke. The collection has been slated to move to the science Museum (see p.92) in 2015

# Bank

**Bank** is the finest architectural arena in the City. Heart of the finance sector and the busy meeting point of eight streets, it's overlooked by a handsome collection of Neoclassical buildings – among them, the **Bank of England**, the **Royal Exchange** (now a shopping mall) and **Mansion House** (the Lord Mayor's official residence) – each one faced in Portland stone.

## Bank of England

Threadneedle St • Mon–Fri 10am–5pm • Free • ☎ 020 7601 5545, ⓦ bankofengland.co.uk • ⊖ Bank

Established in 1694 by William III to raise funds for the war against France, the **Bank of England** wasn't erected on its present site until 1734. All that remains of the building on which Sir John Soane spent the best part of his career from 1788 onwards is the windowless, outer curtain wall. However, you can view a reconstruction of Soane's Bank Stock Office, with its characteristic domed skylight, read about the history, and touch a real gold bar, in the **museum**, which has its entrance on Bartholomew Lane.

---

### LONDON BRIDGE

Until 1750, **London Bridge** was the only bridge across the Thames. The medieval bridge achieved world fame: built of stone and crowded with timber-framed houses, a palace and a chapel, it became one of the great attractions of London – there's a model in the nearby church of **St Magnus the Martyr** (Tues–Fri 10am–4pm). The houses were finally removed in the mid-eighteenth century, and a new stone bridge erected in 1831; that one now stands in the Arizona desert, having been bought in the 1960s by a man who, so the story goes, thought he'd purchased Tower Bridge. The present concrete structure, without doubt the ugliest yet, dates from 1972.

**1**

---

### AIMING HIGH: CITY SKYSCRAPERS

Throughout the 1990s, most people's favourite modern building in the City was Richard Rogers' **Lloyd's Building**, on Leadenhall Street – a vertical version of his Pompidou Centre in Paris – an inside-out array of glass and steel piping. Lloyd's was upstaged in 2003 by Norman Foster's 590ft-high glass diamond-clad **Gherkin**, which endeared itself to Londoners with its cheeky shape. Despite the economic recession, the City skyline continues to sprout yet more skyscrapers, with **The Cheesegrater**, Richard Rogers' 737ft wedge-shaped office block, opposite the Lloyd's Building, leading the charge. Still to rise, close by, is the Scalpel, a 620ft twisted angular shard of glass due for completion in 2017. More controversial has been the rise of Rafael Viñoly's 525ft **Walkie Talkie**, on Fenchurch Street, which features a public "sky garden" on the top floor. Meanwhile, on the other side of the river, of course, is the tallest of the lot, Renzo Piano's 1016ft **Shard**, by London Bridge (see p.86).

---

## Bevis Marks Synagogue

Bevis Marks • Mon, Wed & Thurs 10.30am–2pm, Tues & Fri 10.30am–1pm, Sun 10.30am–12.30pm • Guided tours Wed & Fri noon, Sun 11am • £5 • ☎ 020 7626 1274, ⓦ bevismarks.org.uk • ⊖ Aldgate

Hidden away behind a red-brick office block in a little courtyard off Bevis Marks is the **Bevis Marks Synagogue**. Built in 1701 by Sephardic Jews who had fled the Inquisition in Spain and Portugal, this is the country's oldest surviving synagogue, and its roomy, rich interior gives an idea of just how wealthy the community was at the time. Nowadays, the Sephardic community has dispersed across London and the congregation has dwindled, though the magnificent array of chandeliers makes it popular for candlelit Jewish weddings.

## Monument

Monument St • Daily 9.30am–5.30pm • £2 • ☎ 020 7626 2717, ⓦ themonument.info • ⊖ Monument

The **Monument** was designed by Wren to commemorate the Great Fire of 1666. Crowned with spiky gilded flames, this plain Doric column stands 202ft high; if it were laid out flat it would touch the bakery where the Fire started, east of Monument. The bas-relief on the base, now in very bad shape, depicts Charles II and the Duke of York in Roman garb conducting the emergency relief operation. Views from the gallery, accessed by 311 steps, are somewhat dwarfed nowadays by the buildings springing up around it.

## Tower of London

March–Oct Sun & Mon 10am–5.30pm, Tues–Sat 9am–5.30pm; Nov–Feb closes 4.30pm • £20 • ☎ 0844 482 7799, ⓦ hrp.org.uk • ⊖ Tower Hill

One of Britain's main tourist attractions, the **Tower of London** overlooks the river at the eastern boundary of the old city walls. Despite all the hype, it remains one of London's most remarkable buildings, site of some of the goriest events in the nation's history, and somewhere all visitors and Londoners should explore at least once. Chiefly famous as a place of imprisonment and death, it has variously been used as a royal residence, armoury, mint, menagerie, observatory and – a function it still serves – a safe-deposit box for the Crown Jewels.

The lively free **guided tours** given by the Tower's **Beefeaters** (officially known as Yeoman Warders) are useful for getting your bearings. Visitors today enter the Tower along Water Lane, but in times gone by most prisoners were delivered through **Traitors' Gate**, on the waterfront. Immediately, they would have come to the **Bloody Tower**, which forms the main entrance to the Inner Ward, and which is where the 12-year-old Edward V and his 10-year-old brother were accommodated "for their own safety" in 1483 by their uncle, the future Richard III, and later murdered. It's also where **Walter Raleigh** was imprisoned on three separate occasions, including a thirteen-year stretch.

**1**

## Tower Green

At the centre of the Inner Ward is village-like **Tower Green**, where, over the years, seven highly placed but unlucky individuals have been beheaded, among them Anne Boleyn and her cousin Catherine Howard (Henry VIII's second and fifth wives). The **White Tower**, which overlooks the Green, is the original "Tower", begun in 1078, and now home to displays from the **Royal Armouries**. Even if you've no interest in military paraphernalia, you should at least pay a visit to the **Chapel of St John**, a beautiful Norman structure on the second floor that was completed in 1080 – making it the oldest intact church building in London.

## Crown Jewels

The **Waterloo Barracks**, to the north of the White Tower, hold the **Crown Jewels**; queues can be painfully long, however, and you only get to view the rocks from moving walkways. The vast majority of exhibits post-date the Commonwealth (1649–60), when many of the royal riches were melted down for coinage or sold off. Among the jewels are some of the largest cut diamonds in the world, plus the legendary **Koh-i-Noor**, which was set into the Queen Mother's Crown in 1937.

## Tower Bridge

Daily: April–Sept 10am–6pm; Oct–March 9.30am–5.30pm • £8 • ☎ 020 7403 3761, ⓦ towerbridge.org.uk • ⊖ Tower Hill

**Tower Bridge** ranks with Big Ben as the most famous of all London landmarks. Completed in 1894, its neo-Gothic towers are clad in Cornish granite and Portland stone, but conceal a steel frame, which, at the time, represented a considerable engineering achievement, allowing a road crossing that could be raised to give tall ships access to the upper reaches of the Thames. The raising of the bascules (from the French for "see-saw") remains an impressive sight – phone ahead or check the website to find out when the bridge is being raised. If you buy a ticket, you get to walk across the elevated walkways linking the summits of the towers and visit the Tower's Victorian Engine Rooms, on the south side of the bridge, where you can see the now defunct giant coal-fired boilers which drove the hydraulic system until 1976, and play some interactive engineering games.

# The East End

Few places in London have engendered so many myths as the **East End** (a catch-all title which covers just about everywhere east of the City). Its name is synonymous with slums, sweatshops and crime, as epitomized by figures such as Jack the Ripper and the Kray Twins, but also with the rags-to-riches success stories of a whole generations of Jews who were born in these cholera-ridden quarters and then moved to wealthier pastures.

Despite the transformation of much of the East End, and the fanfare around the 2012 **Olympic Park**, it's still not an obvious place for sightseeing, and – for the most part – still no beauty spot. Most visitors come here for its famous **Sunday markets**:

---

### HOXTON, SHOREDITCH AND DALSTON

Since the 1990s, the northern fringe of the City has been colonized by artists, designers and architects and transformed itself into the city's most vibrant artistic enclave, peppered with contemporary art galleries and a whole host of very cool bars, restaurants and clubs. **Hoxton** (to the north of Old Street) and **Shoreditch** (to the south) kicked off the East End transformation, but they have since been upstaged by **Dalston** (up Kingsland Road). There are few conventional sights as such in all three areas, though each one is stuffed full of art galleries, and their hip nightlife and shopping scenes keep them lively.

clothes and crafts in trendy Spitalfields, hip vintage gear around Brick Lane and flowers on Columbia Road. As for the East End **Docklands**, including the vast and awesome **Canary Wharf** redevelopment, most of it can be gawped at from the driverless, overhead **Docklands Light Railway** or DLR (see p.105), or from one of the boats that course up and down the Thames.

## Spitalfields

**Spitalfields**, within sight of the sleek tower blocks of the financial sector, lies at the old heart of the East End, where the French Huguenots settled in the seventeenth century, where the Jewish community was at its strongest in the late nineteenth century, and where today's Bengali community eats, sleeps, works and prays. If you visit just one area in the East End, it should be this, which preserves mementos from each wave of immigration. The focal point of the area is **Spitalfields Market**, the red-brick and green-gabled market hall built in 1893, which is busiest on Sundays.

### Dennis Severs' House

18 Folgate St • Mon noon–2pm • £7 • Sun noon–4pm • £10 • Silent Nights Mon & Wed 6–9pm • £14 • ☎ 020 7247 4013, Ⓦ dennissevershouse.co.uk • ⊖ Liverpool Street

You can visit one of Spitalfields' characteristic eighteenth-century terraced houses at 18 Folgate St, where the American artist **Dennis Severs** lived until 1999. Eschewing all modern conveniences, Severs lived under candlelight, decorating his house as it would have been two hundred years ago. The public were invited to share in the experience that he described as like "passing through a frame into a painting". Today visitors are free to explore the cluttered, candlelit rooms, which resonate with the distinct impression that the resident Huguenot family has just popped out: not least due to the smell of cooked food and the sound of horses' hooves on the cobbles outside.

## V&A Museum of Childhood

Cambridge Heath Rd • Daily 10am–5.45pm • Free • ☎ 020 8983 5200, Ⓦ www.museumofchildhood.org.uk • ⊖ Bethnal Green

The East End's most popular museum is the **V&A Museum of Childhood**. The open-plan, wrought-iron hall, originally part of (and still a branch of) the V&A (see p.89), was transported here in the 1860s to bring art to the East End. On the ground floor you'll see clockwork **toys** – everything from classic robots to a fully functioning model railway – marionettes and puppets, teddies and Smurfs and even Inuit dolls. The most famous exhibits are the remarkable antique **dolls' houses** dating back to 1673, now displayed upstairs, where you'll also find a play area for very small kids and the museum's special exhibitions.

---

### QUEEN ELIZABETH OLYMPIC PARK

The focus of the 2012 Olympics was the **Olympic Park** laid out over a series of islands formed by the River Lee and various tributaries and canals. Since the Olympics, the whole area has been replanted with patches of grass, trees and flowers and peppered with cafés, making it a great new park in which to hangout on a sunny day. The centrepiece of the park is the **Olympic Stadium**, set to become home to West Ham United football club in 2015. Standing close to the stadium is the **Orbit** tower (daily: April–Sept 11am–6pm; Oct–March 11am–5pm; £15), a 377ft-high continuous loop of red recycled steel designed by Anish Kapoor. But the most eye-catching venue is Zaha Hadid's wave-like **Aquatics Centre**, four times over budget, but looking very cool and costing under £5 for a swim. Other venues to lok out for are the curvy **Velodrome**, with its banked, Siberian pine track and adjacent BMX circuit, and the Copper Box, used for handball during the games, now a multi-sports centre. The nearest **tube** is Stratford, near the Olympic Village (now renamed East Village) and the Westfield shopping centre.

**1**

## Docklands

Built in the nineteenth century to cope with the huge volume of goods shipped along the Thames from all over the Empire, **Docklands** was once the largest enclosed cargo-dock system in the world. When the docks closed in the 1960s the area was generally regarded as having died forever, but regeneration in the 1980s brought luxury flats and, on the Isle of Dogs, a huge high-rise office development. Here, at **Canary Wharf**, Cesar Pelli's landmark stainless steel tower **One Canada Square** remains an icon on the city's eastern skyline. The excellent **Museum of London Docklands** (daily 10am–6pm; free), in an old warehouse in Canary Wharf, charts the history of the area from Roman times to the present day.

# The South Bank

The **South Bank** has a lot going for it. As well as the massive waterside **Southbank Centre**, it's home to a host of tourist attractions including the enormously popular **London Eye**. With most of London sitting on the north bank of the Thames, the views from here are the best on the river, and thanks to the wide, traffic-free riverside boulevard, the whole area can be happily explored on foot. Just a short walk away lies the absorbing **Imperial War Museum**, which will be commemorating the First World War over the next few years and contains the country's only permanent exhibition devoted to the Holocaust.

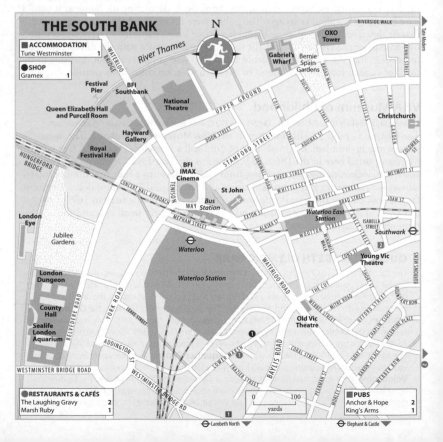

**1**

# Southbank Centre

Ⓦ southbankcentre.co.uk • ⊖ Waterloo or Embankment

In 1951, the South Bank Exhibition, on derelict land south of the Thames, formed the centrepiece of the national **Festival of Britain**, an attempt to revive morale postwar by celebrating the centenary of the Great Exhibition (when Britain really did rule over half the world). The most striking features of the site were the Ferris wheel (now reincarnated as the London Eye), the saucer-shaped Dome of Discovery (inspiration for the Millennium Dome), the Royal Festival Hall (which still stands) and the cigar-shaped steel-and-aluminium Skylon tower (yet to be revived).

The Festival of Britain's success provided the impetus for the creation of the **Southbank Centre**, home to artistic institutions such as the Royal Festival Hall, the Hayward Gallery, the BFI Southbank arts cinema, and the National Theatre (see p.123). Its unprepossessing concrete appearance is softened by its riverside location, its avenue of trees, its buskers and skateboarders, the weekend foodstalls behind the RFH and the busy secondhand bookstalls outside the BFI Southbank.

# London Eye

Daily: 10am–8.30pm or later • From £17 online • ☎ 0871 781 3000, Ⓦ londoneye.com • ⊖ Waterloo or Westminster

Despite being little more than ten years old, the **London Eye** is one of the city's most famous landmarks. Standing an impressive 443ft high, it's the largest Ferris wheel in Europe, weighing over two thousand tonnes, yet as simple and delicate as a bicycle wheel. It's constantly in slow motion, which means a full-circle "circuit" in one of its 32 pods (one for each of the city's boroughs) should take around thirty minutes: that may seem a long time but in fact it passes incredibly quickly. Book online (to save money), but note that unless you've paid extra you'll still have to queue to get on. Tickets are also sold from the box office at the eastern end of County Hall.

# London Aquarium

County Hall • Mon–Thurs 10am–6pm, Fri–Sun 10am–7pm • From £16 online • ☎ 0871 663 1679, Ⓦ visitsealife.co.uk • ⊖ Waterloo or Westminster

The most popular attraction in County Hall – the giant building beside the London Eye – is the **Sea Life London Aquarium,** spread across three subterranean levels. With some super-large tanks, and everything from dog-face puffers and piranhas to robot fish (seriously) and crocodiles, this is an attraction that is almost guaranteed to please kids, albeit at a price (book online to save a few quid and to avoid queuing or save £5 by buying an after 3pm ticket). Impressive in scale, the aquarium boasts a thrilling Shark Walk, in which sharks swim beneath you, as well as a replica blue whale skeleton encasing an underwater walkway.

# London Dungeon

County Hall • Mon & Wed–Fri 10am–5pm, Thurs 11am–5pm, Sat & Sun 10am–6pm; school holidays closes 7pm • from £22 online • ☎ 0871 423 2240, Ⓦ thedungeons.com • ⊖ Waterloo or Westminster

The latest venture to join in the shenanigans at County Hall is the **London Dungeon,** an orgy of Gothic horror and one of the city's major crowd-pleasers – to avoid queuing (and save money), buy your ticket online. Young teenagers and the credulous probably get the most out of the various ludicrous live-action scenarios through which visitors are herded, each one hyped up by the team of costumed ham-actors. These are followed by a series of fairly lame horror rides such as "Henry's Wrath Boat Ride" and a "Drop Dead Drop Ride", not to mention the latest "Jack the Ripper Experience".

## Imperial War Museum

Lambeth Rd • Daily 10am–6pm • Free • ☎ 020 7416 5000, ⓦ london.iwm.org.uk • ⊖ Lambeth North or Elephant & Castle

Housed in a domed building that was once the infamous lunatic asylum "Bedlam", the superb **Imperial War Museum** holds by far the best military museum in the capital. The treatment of the subject is impressively wide-ranging and fairly sober, with the main hall's militaristic display offset by the lower-ground-floor array of documents and images attesting to the human damage of war. The museum also has a harrowing **Holocaust Exhibition** (not recommended for children under 14), which you enter from the third floor. Pulling few punches, this has made a valiant attempt to avoid depicting the victims of the Holocaust as nameless masses by focusing on individual cases, and interspersing the archive footage with eyewitness accounts from contemporary survivors.

# Southwark

In Tudor and Stuart London, the chief reason for crossing the Thames to what is now **Southwark** was to visit the disreputable Bankside entertainment district around the south end of London Bridge. Four hundred years on, Londoners are heading to the area once more, thanks to a wealth of top attractions – led by the mighty **Tate Modern** – that pepper the traffic-free riverside path between Blackfriars Bridge and Tower Bridge. The area is conveniently linked to St Paul's and the City by the fabulous Norman Foster-designed **Millennium Bridge**, London's first pedestrian-only bridge.

## Tate Modern

Bankside • Daily 10am–6pm, Fri & Sat till 10pm • Free; multimedia guides £4 • ☎ 020 7887 8888, ⓦ tate.org.uk • ⊖ Southwark or Blackfriars

Bankside is dominated by the awesome **Tate Modern**. Originally designed as an oil-fired power station by Giles Gilbert Scott, this austere, brick-built "cathedral of power" was converted into a splendid modern art gallery in 2000. The best way to enter is down the ramp from the west so that you get the full effect of the stupendously large turbine hall. It's easy enough to find your way around the galleries, with levels 2, 3 and 4 displaying the permanent collection, and levels 2 and 3 also putting on fee-paying special exhibitions – level 7 is home to a bar/restaurant with a great view over the

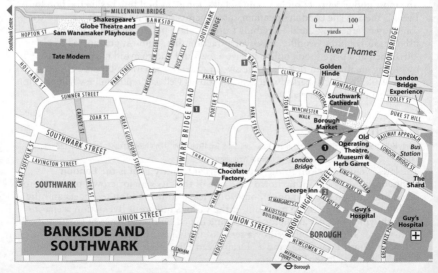

Thames. Along with the free guided tours and multimedia guides, various apps are available and the Tate has free wi-fi.

Works are grouped thematically and although the displays change every year or so, you're still pretty much guaranteed to see works by **Monet** and Bonnard, Cubist pioneers **Picasso** and Braque, Surrealists such as **Dalí**, abstract artists like **Mondrian**, Bridget Riley and Pollock, and Pop supremos **Warhol** and Lichtenstein. And such is the space here that several artists get whole rooms to themselves, among them Joseph Beuys, with his shamanistic wax and furs, and **Mark Rothko**, whose abstract "Seagram Murals", originally destined for a posh restaurant in New York, have their own shrine-like room in the heart of the collection.

## Shakespeare's Globe

21 New Globe Walk • Exhibition daily 9am–5.30pm • £13.50 • ☎ 020 7902 1400, ⓦ shakespearesglobe.com • ⊖ Southwark or London Bridge

Dwarfed by Tate Modern, but equally remarkable in its own way, **Shakespeare's Globe Theatre** is a reconstruction of the open-air polygonal playhouse where most of the Bard's later works were first performed. The theatre, which boasts the first new thatched roof in central London since the Great Fire of 1666 – and the first candle-lit indoor theatre since the advent of electricity – puts on plays by Shakespeare and his contemporaries, both outside and in the indoor Sam Wanamaker Playhouse. To find out more about Shakespeare and the history of Bankside, the Globe's stylish **exhibition** is well worth a visit. You can have a virtual play on medieval instruments such as the crumhorn or sackbut, prepare your own edition of Shakespeare, and feel the thatch, hazelnut-shell and daub used to build the theatre. There's also an informative **guided tour** round the two theatres – during the summer season, in afternoons, you get to visit the exhibition and the remains of the nearby Rose Theatre instead.

## Golden Hinde

St Mary Overie Dock • Mon–Sat 10am–5.30pm, Sun 10am–5pm, but phone ahead • £6 • ☎ 020 7403 0123, ⓦ goldenhinde.com • ⊖ London Bridge

An exact replica of the **Golden Hinde**, the galleon in which Francis Drake sailed

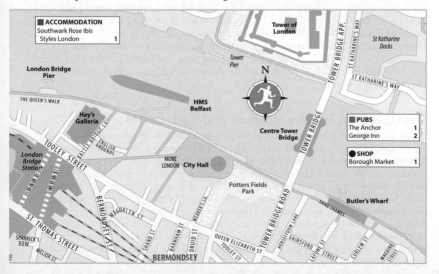

1

around the world from 1577 to 1580, nestles in St Mary Overie Dock, at the eastern end of Clink Street. The ship is surprisingly small, and its original crew of eighty-plus must have been cramped to say the least. There's a lack of interpretive panels, so it's worth paying the little bit extra and getting a guided tour from one of the folk in period costume – ring ahead to check that a group hasn't booked the place up.

## Southwark Cathedral

Mon–Fri 8am–6pm, Sat & Sun 11am–5pm • Free • ☎ 020 7367 6734, ⓦ southwarkcathedral.org.uk • ⊖ London Bridge

Close by the *Golden Hinde* stands **Southwark Cathedral**, built as the medieval Augustinian priory church of St Mary Overie, and given cathedral status only in 1905. Of the original thirteenth-century church, only the choir and retrochoir now remain, separated by a tall and beautiful stone Tudor screen, making them probably the oldest Gothic structures left in London. The nave was entirely rebuilt in the nineteenth century, but the cathedral contains numerous interesting monuments, from a thirteenth-century oak effigy of a knight to an early twentieth-century memorial to Shakespeare.

## Borough Market

8 Southwark St • Mon–Wed 10am–3pm, Thurs 11am–5pm, Fri noon–6pm, Sat 8am–5pm • ☎ 020 7407 1002, ⓦ boroughmarket.org.uk • ⊖ London Bridge

**Borough Market** is tucked beneath the railway arches between Borough High Street and Southwark Cathedral. The early-morning wholesale fruit and vegetable market winds up around 8am and is one of the few still trading under its original Victorian wrought-iron shed. But the market is best known nowadays for its busy specialist food market, with stalls selling top-quality and pricey produce from around the world – it's very popular so get there early on Friday and Saturday.

## The Shard

32 London Bridge • Daily 9am–10pm• From £25 online • ☎ 0844 499 7111, ⓦ theviewfromtheshard.com • ⊖ London Bridge

It's hard to justify the hubristic (Qatari-funded) Shard, London's – and the country's – tallest building. Even less justifiable are the ticket prices to reach the top floors of Renzo Piano's 1016ft-high, tapered, glass-clad skyscraper. Still, once you're there, if you can ignore the New Age muzak, the views are sublime, making everything else in London look small, from the unicycle of the London Eye to the tiny box that is St Paul's Cathedral, while the model railway of London Bridge is played out below you.

## Old Operating Theatre Museum and Herb Garret

St Thomas St • Daily 10.30am–5pm; closed mid-Dec to early Jan • £6.50 • ☎ 020 7188 2679, ⓦ thegarret.org.uk • ⊖ London Bridge

By far the most educative and the strangest of Southwark's museums is the **Old Operating Theatre Museum and Herb Garret**. Built in 1821 up a spiral staircase at the top of a church tower, where the hospital apothecary's herbs were stored, this women's operating theatre was once adjacent to the women's ward of St Thomas' Hospital (now in Lambeth). Despite being gore-free, the museum is as stomach-churning as the nearby London Dungeon (see p.83). The surgeons who used this room would have concentrated on speed and accuracy (most amputations took less than a minute), but there was still a thirty percent mortality rate, with many patients simply dying of shock, and many more from bacterial infection.

## London Bridge Experience

2–4 Tooley St • Mon–Fri & Sun 10am–5pm, Sat 10am–6pm • from £18 online • ☎ 0800 043 4666, ⓦ thelondonbridgeexperience.com • ⊖ London Bridge

With the London Dungeon now in County Hall (see p.83), Gothic horror fans should head instead to this slightly more historically pertinent scarefest. First off, it's a theatrical trot through the history of London Bridge, with guides in period garb hamming up the gory bits. Then, in case you're not scared enough yet, in the **London Tombs** section (no under 11s), more actors, dressed as zombies and murderers, leap out of the fog to frighten the wits out of you.

## HMS Belfast

The Queen's Walk • Daily: March–Oct 10am–6pm; Nov–Feb 10am–5pm • £14 • ☎ 020 7940 6300, ⓦ iwm.org.uk • ⊖ London Bridge

**HMS Belfast**, a World War II cruiser, is permanently moored between London Bridge and Tower Bridge. Armed with six torpedoes, and six-inch guns with a range of more than fourteen miles, the *Belfast* spent over two years of the war in the Royal Naval shipyards after being hit by a mine in the Firth of Forth at the beginning of hostilities. It later saw action in the Barents Sea during World War II and during the Korean War, before being decommissioned. The maze of cabins is fun to explore but if you want to find out more about the *Belfast*, head for the exhibition rooms in zone 5.

## City Hall

The Queen's Walk • Mon–Thurs 8.30am–6pm, Fri 8.30am–5.30pm • Free • ☎ 020 7983 4000, ⓦ london.gov.uk • ⊖ London Bridge

East of the *Belfast*, overlooking the river, Norman Foster's startling glass-encased **City Hall** looks like a giant car headlight or fencing mask, and serves as the headquarters for the Greater London Authority and the Mayor of London. Visitors are welcome to stroll up the helical walkway, visit the café and watch proceedings from the second floor.

# Kensington and Chelsea

**Hyde Park** and **Kensington Gardens** cover a distance of a mile and a half from Oxford Street in the northeast to Kensington Palace, set in the Royal Borough of **Kensington and Chelsea**. Other districts go in and out of fashion, but this area has been in vogue ever since royalty moved into **Kensington Palace** in the late seventeenth century.

The most popular tourist attractions lie in **South Kensington**, where three of London's top **museums** – the Victoria and Albert, Natural History and Science museums – stand on land bought with the proceeds of the 1851 Great Exhibition. Chelsea, to the south, has a slightly more bohemian pedigree. In the 1960s, the **King's Road** carved out its reputation as London's catwalk, while in the late 1970s it was the epicentre of the punk explosion. Nothing so rebellious goes on in Chelsea now, though its residents like to think of themselves as rather more artistic and intellectual than the purely moneyed types of Kensington.

## Hyde Park and Kensington Gardens

**Hyde Park** Daily 5am–midnight **Kensington Gardens** Daily 6am–dusk • ☎ 0300 061 2000, ⓦ royalparks.gov.uk • ⊖ Hyde Park Corner, Marble Arch, Knightsbridge or Lancaster Gate

Hangings, muggings, duels and the 1851 Great Exhibition are just some of the public events that have taken place in **Hyde Park**, which remains a popular spot for political demonstrations and pop concerts. For most of the time, however, the park is simply a lazy leisure ground – a wonderful open space that allows you to lose all sight of the city beyond a few persistent tower blocks.

**1**

The park is divided in two by the **Serpentine**, which has a pretty upper section known as the **Long Water**, which narrows until it reaches a group of four fountains. In the southern section, you'll find the popular **Lido** (mid-June to mid-Sept daily 10am–6pm; £4.50) on its south bank and the **Diana Memorial Fountain** (daily: March & Oct 10am–6pm; April–Aug 10am–8pm; Sept 10am–7pm; Nov–Feb 10am–4pm), less of a fountain and more of a giant oval-shaped mini-moat. The western half of the park is, in fact, officially known as **Kensington Gardens**; its two most popular attractions are the **Serpentine Gallery**, which puts on contemporary art exhibitions, and the overblown **Albert Memorial**.

## Marble Arch

At Hyde Park's treeless northeastern corner is **Marble Arch**, erected in 1828 as a triumphal entry to Buckingham Palace, but now stranded on a busy traffic island at the west end of Oxford Street. This is a historically charged piece of land, as it marks the site of **Tyburn gallows**, the city's main public execution spot until 1783. It's also the location of **Speakers' Corner**, a peculiarly English Sunday morning tradition, featuring an assembly of ranters and hecklers.

## Wellington Arch

Hyde Park Corner • Daily: April–Sept 10am–6pm; Oct 10am–5pm; Nov–March 10am–4pm • £4.20; EH • ⊖ Hyde Park Corner

At the southeast corner of Hyde Park, the **Wellington Arch** stands in the midst of **Hyde Park Corner**, one of London's busiest traffic interchanges. Erected in 1828, the arch was originally topped by an equestrian statue of the Duke himself, later replaced by Peace driving a four-horse chariot. Inside, you can view an exhibition on the history of the arch, and of London's outdoor sculpture, and take a lift to the top of the monument where the exterior balconies offer a bird's-eye view of the swirling traffic.

## Apsley House

149 Piccadilly • Wed–Sun: April–Oct 11am–5pm; Nov–March 11am–4pm • EH • £6.90 • ⊖ Hyde Park Corner

Overlooking the traffic whizzing round Hyde Park Corner is **Apsley House**, Wellington's London residence and now a museum to the "Iron Duke". The highlight is the **art collection**, much of which used to belong to the King of Spain. Among the best pieces, displayed in the Waterloo Gallery on the first floor, are works by de Hooch, Van Dyck, Velázquez, Goya, Rubens and Correggio. The famous, more than twice life-size, nude statue of Napoleon by Antonio Canova stands at the foot of the main staircase.

## Serpentine Gallery

Daily 10am–6pm; Teahouse mid-June to mid-Oct • Free • ⊖ Knightsbridge or South Kensington

In the southeast corner of Kensington Gardens stands the **Serpentine Gallery** built as a tearoom in 1908, but used as an a contemporary art gallery since the 1960s – and, more recently, the gallery has commissioned a leading architect to design a summer tea pavilion extension each year. A second exhibition space, the **Serpentine Sackler Gallery**, is housed in a former munitions depot nearby, with a permanent tearoom on the side, designed by Zaha Hadid.

## Albert Memorial

**Guided tours** March–Dec first Sun of month 2pm & 3pm; 45min; £7 • ☎ 020 7495 0916 • ⊖ Knightsbridge or South Kensington

Erected in 1876, the richly decorated, High Gothic **Albert Memorial** is as much a hymn to the glorious achievements of Britain as to its subject, Queen Victoria's husband, who died of typhoid in 1861. Albert occupies the central canopy, gilded from head to toe and clutching a catalogue for the 1851 Great Exhibition that he helped to organize.

### Royal Albert Hall

Kensington Gore • Guided tours from door 12 daily except Wed 10.30am–3.30pm; £8.50 • ☎ 020 7838 3105, ⓦ royalalberthall.com • ⊖ South Kensington or High Street Kensington

The 1851 Exhibition's most famous feature – the gargantuan glasshouse of the Crystal Palace – no longer exists, but the profits were used to buy a large tract of land south of the park, now home to South Kensington's remarkable cluster of museums and colleges, plus the vast **Royal Albert Hall**, a splendid iron-and-glass-domed concert hall with an exterior of red brick, terracotta and marble that became the hallmark of South Ken architecture. The hall is the venue for Europe's most democratic music festival, the Henry Wood Promenade Concerts, better known as the **Proms** (see box, p.125).

## Kensington Palace

Kensington Gardens • Daily: Easter–Oct 10am–6pm; Nov–Easter 10am–5pm • £15.40 • ☎ 020 3166 6000, ⓦ hrp.org.uk • ⊖ Queensway or High Street Kensington

Bought by William and Mary in 1689, the modestly proportioned Jacobean brick mansion of **Kensington Palace** was the chief royal residence for the next fifty years. KP, as it's fondly known in royal circles, is best known today as the place where Princess Diana lived from her marriage until her death in 1997. Today, it's the official residence of a number of royals including Prince William and Kate Middleton.

The palace is home to the **Royal Ceremonial Dress Collection**, which means you usually get to see a few of the frocks worn by Diana, as well as several of the Queen's dresses. The highlights of the King's state apartments are the trompe-l'oeil ceiling paintings by William Kent, particularly those in the Cupola Room, and the paintings in the King's Gallery by, among others, Tintoretto. Also of interest in the King's Gallery is the wind dial above the fireplace, connected to the palace weather vane, which was built for William III and is still fully functioning.

In the more modest Queen's state apartments, the curators have stepped up the multimedia theatrics to tell the sad story of Queen Anne, whose eighteen children all predeceased her. On the ground floor, you can learn about **Queen Victoria**, who spent an unhappy childhood in the palace, under the steely gaze of her strict German mother. According to her diary, her best friends were the palace's numerous "black beetles".

## Leighton House

12 Holland Park Rd • Daily except Tues 10am–5.30pm • £7 • ⓦ rbkc.gov.uk/museums • ⊖ High Street Kensington

Several wealthy Victorian artists rather self-consciously founded an artists' colony in the streets that lay to the west of Kensington Gardens. "It will be opulence, it will be sincerity", Lord Leighton opined before starting work on the remarkable **Leighton House** in the 1860s – he later became President of the Royal Academy and was ennobled on his deathbed. The big attraction is the domed **Arab Hall**, decorated with Saracen tiles, gilded mosaics and latticework drawn from all over the Islamic world. The other rooms are hung with paintings by Lord Leighton and his Pre-Raphaelite chums – there's even a Tintoretto.

## Victoria and Albert Museum (V&A)

Cromwell Rd • Daily 10am–5.45pm, Fri till 10pm • Free • ☎ 020 7942 2000, ⓦ vam.ac.uk • ⊖ South Kensington

For sheer variety and scale, the **Victoria and Albert Museum** is the greatest museum of applied arts in the world. Beautifully but haphazardly displayed across a seven-mile, four-storey maze of rooms, the V&A's treasures are impossible to survey in a single visit; get hold of a floor plan to help you decide which areas to concentrate on, and look out for the various free tours that set off from the main information desk in the

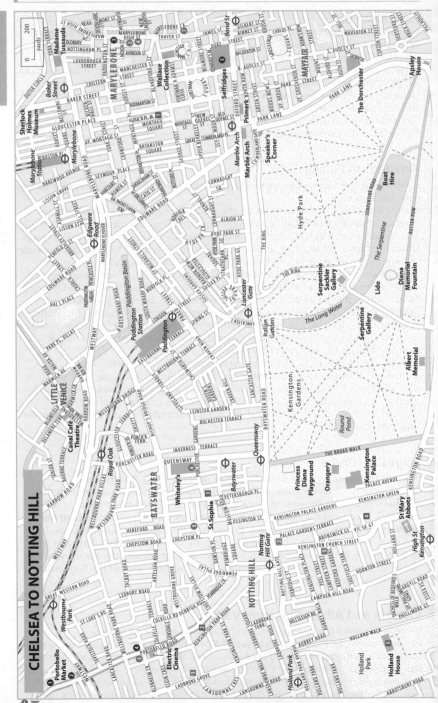

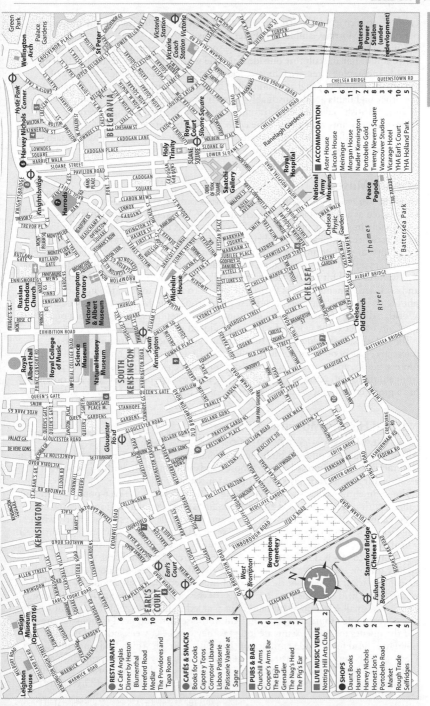

**■ ACCOMMODATION**
| | |
|---|---|
| Aster House | 9 |
| Lincoln House | 6 |
| Meininger | 11 |
| Morgan House | 7 |
| Nadler Kensington | 2 |
| Portobello Gold | 3 |
| Twenty Nevern Square | 8 |
| Vancouver Studios | 4 |
| Vicarage Hotel | 10 |
| YHA Earl's Court | 1 |
| YHA Holland Park | 5 |

**● RESTAURANTS**
| | |
|---|---|
| Le Café Anglais | 6 |
| Dinner by Heston Blumenthal | 8 |
| Hereford Road | 5 |
| Medlar | 10 |
| The Providores and Tapa Room | 2 |

**● CAFÉS & SNACKS**
| | |
|---|---|
| Books for Cooks | 3 |
| Capote y Toros | 9 |
| Comptoir Libanais | 7 |
| Lisboa Patisserie | 1 |
| Patisserie Valerie at Sagne | 4 |

**■ PUBS & BARS**
| | |
|---|---|
| Churchill Arms | 3 |
| Cooper's Arms Bar | 6 |
| The Elgin | 1 |
| Grenadier | 4 |
| The Nag's Head | 5 |
| The Pig's Ear | 7 |

**■ LIVE MUSIC VENUE**
| | |
|---|---|
| Notting Hill Arts Club | 2 |

**● SHOPS**
| | |
|---|---|
| Daunt Books | 3 |
| Harrods | 4 |
| Harvey Nichols | 6 |
| Honest Jon's | 2 |
| Portobello Road Market | 1 |
| Rough Trade | 5 |
| Selfridges | 5 |

**1**

Grand Entrance. And if you're flagging, head for the edifying café in the museum's period-piece Morris, Gamble & Poynter Rooms.

Whatever your taste, there's bound to be something to grab your attention: the finest collection of Italian sculpture outside Italy, the world's largest collection of Indian art outside India, plus extensive Chinese, Islamic and Japanese galleries; a gallery of twentieth-century objets d'art; and more Constable paintings than Tate Britain. Among the other highlights are the justifiably popular Jewellery section, the beautifully designed British Galleries, the Costume rooms and the fascinating Theatre & Performance rooms which house the collection of the former Covent Garden Theatre Museum. In addition, the V&A's temporary shows on art, photography and fashion – some of which you have to pay for – are among the best in Britain.

## Science Museum

Exhibition Rd • Daily 10am–6pm • Free • ☎ 0870 870 4868, ⓦ sciencemuseum.org.uk • ⊖ South Kensington

Established as a technological counterpart to the V&A, the **Science Museum** is undeniably impressive, filling seven floors with items drawn from every conceivable area of science, with hands-on galleries that appeal to adults and kids.

Stop first at the **information desk**, pick up a museum plan and check the daily events schedule; you can also sign up for a free **guided tour** on a specific subject. Most people will want to head for the **Wellcome Wing**, full of state-of-the-art interactive computers and an IMAX cinema (tickets £10), and geared to appeal to even the most museum-phobic teenager. To get there, you must pass through the Making of the Modern World, a display of iconic inventions from Robert Stephenson's *Rocket* train of 1829 to the Ford Model T, the world's first mass-produced car.

Those with kids should head for the popular Launchpad, the museum's busiest interactive gallery on Floor 3. The Challenge of Materials gallery, on Floor 1, is aimed more at adults, and is an extremely stylish exhibition covering the use of materials ranging from aluminium to zerodur (used for making laser gyroscopes), while Energy, on Floor 2, has a great "do not touch" electric-shock machine that absolutely fascinates kids.

## Natural History Museum

Cromwell Rd • Daily 10am–5.50pm • Free • ☎ 020 7942 5000, ⓦ nhm.ac.uk • ⊖ South Kensington

Alfred Waterhouse's purpose-built mock-Romanesque colossus ensures the status of the **Natural History Museum** as London's most handsome museum, both an important resource for serious zoologists and a major tourist attraction.

The main entrance leads to the **Blue Zone**, which includes the ever-popular Dinosaur gallery, with its grisly life-sized **animatronic dinosaurs**. Popular sections over in the **Green Zone** include the Creepy-Crawlies, and the excellent **Investigate** gallery, where children aged 7 to 14 get to play at being scientists (you need to obtain a timed ticket).

Little visited, compared to the rest of the museum, the **Darwin Centre** – also known as the **Orange Zone** – is dominated by the giant concrete **Cocoon**, home to more than twenty million specimens. Visitors can take the lift to the seventh floor and enter the Cocoon to learn more about the history of the collection, about taxonomy and the research and field trips the museum funds. In the nearby **Zoology spirit building**, you can view a small selection of bits and bobs pickled in glass jars, but if you want to join one of the **guided tours** that take you behind the scenes, you need to book on the day.

If the queues for the museum are long (as they can be at weekends and during school holidays), head for the side entrance on Exhibition Road, which leads into the former Geology Museum, now known as the **Red Zone**, a visually exciting romp through the earth's evolution. The most popular sections are the slightly tasteless Kobe earthquake simulator, and the spectacular display of gems and crystals in the Earth's Treasury.

**1**

## Chelsea

From the Swinging Sixties up until the era of Punk, **Chelsea** had a slightly bohemian pedigree; these days, it's just another wealthy west London suburb. Among the most nattily attired of all those parading down the King's Road nowadays are the scarlet- or navy-blue-clad Chelsea Pensioners, army veterans from the nearby **Royal Hospital**.

### Saatchi Gallery

King's Rd • Daily 10am–6pm • Free • ☎ 020 7811 3070, ⓦ saatchi-gallery.co.uk • ⊖ Sloane Square

On the south side of the King's Road, a short stroll from Sloane Square, the former **Duke of York's HQ**, built in 1801, is now the unlikely home of the **Saatchi Gallery**, which puts on changing exhibitions of contemporary art in its whitewashed rooms. Charles Saatchi, the collector behind the gallery, was the man who introduced Young British Artists (YBAs) like Damien Hirst, Sarah Lucas, Tracey Emin and Rachel Whiteread to the world in the 1990s.

### Royal Hospital

Royal Hospital Rd • Mon–Sat 11am–noon & 2–4pm, Sun 2–4pm • Free • ☎ 020 7881 5200, ⓦ chelsea-pensioners.co.uk • ⊖ Sloane Square

Founded as a retirement home for army veterans by Charles II in 1682, and designed by Christopher Wren, the **Royal Hospital**'s majestic red-brick wings and grassy courtyards became a blueprint for institutional and collegiate architecture all over the English-speaking world. The public are welcome to view the austere hospital chapel, and the equally grand, wood-panelled dining hall, opposite, where three hundred or so Pensioners still eat under the royal portraits and the vast allegorical mural of Charles II. On the east side of the hospital, a small **museum** displays Pensioners' uniforms, medals and two German bombs.

### National Army Museum

Royal Hospital Rd • Daily 10am–5.30pm • Free • ☎ 020 7881 6606, ⓦ nam.ac.uk • ⊖ Sloane Square

The concrete bunker next door to the Royal Hospital, on Royal Hospital Road, houses the **National Army Museum**. There are plenty of interesting historical artefacts, a top-class art gallery, plus an impressive array of uniforms and medals, a model of Waterloo and the skeleton of Napoleon's horse, Marengo, but for a more nuanced exploration of war, you're better off visiting the Imperial War Museum (see p.84).

# North London

Almost all of **North London**'s suburbs are easily accessible by tube from the centre, though just a handful of these satellite villages, now subsumed into the general mass of the city, are worth bothering with. First off, you should explore one of London's finest parks, **Regent's Park**, home to London Zoo; **Camden Town**, famous for its huge weekend market, is nearby. The highlights, however, are the village-like suburbs of **Hampstead** and **Highgate**, on the edge of London's wildest patch of greenery, **Hampstead Heath**.

## Regent's Park

Daily from 5am • Free • ☎ 0300 061 2300, ⓦ royalparks.org.uk • ⊖ Regent's Park, Baker Street, Great Portland Street, St John's Wood or Camden Town

**Regent's Park** is one of London's smartest parks, with a boating lake, ornamental ponds, waterfalls and some lovely gardens. Under the reign of the Prince Regent (later George IV), the park was to be girded by a continuous belt of terraces, and sprinkled with a total of 56 villas, including a magnificent royal palace. Inevitably, the plan was never fully realized, but enough was built to create something of the idealized garden city that Nash and the Prince Regent had envisaged. Within the Inner Circle, the **Queen Mary's Gardens** are by far the prettiest section of the park. Prominent on the skyline is the shiny copper dome of **London Central Mosque** at 146 Park Road, an entirely appropriate addition given the Prince Regent's taste for the Orient.

## London Zoo

Daily: March–Oct 10am–6pm; Nov–Feb 10am–4pm • £22 • ☎ 0844 225 1826, ⓦ zsl.org • ❷ Camden Town

The northeastern corner of the park is occupied by **London Zoo**. Founded in 1826 with the remnants of the royal menagerie, the enclosures here are as humane as any inner-city zoo could make them, and kids usually enjoy themselves. The invertebrate house, now known as BUGS, the Gorilla Kingdom, the African Bird Safari, and the walk-through rainforest and monkey enclosure are guaranteed winners.

# Camden Town

For all its tourist popularity, **Camden Market** remains a genuinely offbeat place. The sheer variety of what's on offer – from cheap CDs to furniture, along with a mass of street fashion and clubwear, and plenty of food stalls – is what makes **Camden Town** so special. More than 100,000 shoppers turn up here each weekend, and most parts of the market now stay open week-long, alongside a crop of shops, cafés and bistros.

## Jewish Museum

129 Albert St • Sat–Thurs 10am–5pm, Fri 10am–2pm • £7.50 • ☎ 020 7284 7384, ⓦ jewishmuseum.org.uk • ❷ Camden Town

Despite having no significant Jewish associations, Camden is home to London's purpose-built **Jewish Museum**. On the first floor, there's an engaging exhibition explaining Jewish practices, illustrated by cabinets of Judaica. On the second floor, there's a special Holocaust gallery which tells the story of Leon Greenman (1920–2008), one of only two British Jews who suffered and survived Auschwitz. The museum also puts on a lively programme of special exhibitions, discussions and concerts, and has a café on the ground floor.

# Hampstead

Perched on a hill to the west of Hampstead Heath, **Hampstead** village developed into a fashionable spa in the eighteenth century, and was not much altered thereafter. Later, it became one of the city's most celebrated literary *quartiers* and even now it retains its reputation as a bolt hole of the high-profile intelligentsia and discerning pop stars. Proximity to **Hampstead Heath** is, of course, the real joy of Hampstead; this mixture of woodland, smooth pasture and landscaped garden is quite simply the most exhilarating patch of greenery in London.

---

### REGENT'S CANAL BY BOAT

Three companies run daily **boat services** between Camden and Little Venice, passing through the Maida Hill tunnel. The narrowboat *Jenny Wren* (March Sat & Sun; April–Oct daily; ☎ 020 7485 4433, ⓦ walkersquay.com) starts off at Camden, goes through a canal lock (the only company to do so) and heads for Little Venice (with live commentary), while *Jason's* narrowboats (April–Oct daily; ☎ 020 7286 3428, ⓦ jasons.co.uk) start off at Little Venice (live commentary); the London Waterbus Company (April–Sept daily; Oct Thurs–Sun only; Nov–March Sat & Sun only, weather permitting; ☎ 020 7482 2550, ⓦ londonwaterbus.com) sets off from both places and calls at London Zoo. Whichever you choose, you can board at either end; **tickets** cost around £12 return, and journey time is 45 minutes one-way.

**1**

## Keats' House

Keats Grove • March–Oct Tues–Sun 1–5pm; Nov–Feb Fri–Sun 1–5pm • £5.50 • ☎ 020 7332 3868, ⓦ cityoflondon.gov.uk •
⊖ Hampstead or Hampstead Heath Overground

Hampstead's most illustrious figure is celebrated at **Keats' House**, an elegant, whitewashed Regency double villa off Downshire Hill at the bottom of the High Street. Inspired by the tranquillity of Hampstead and by his passion for girl-next-door Fanny Brawne (whose house is also part of the museum), Keats wrote some of his most famous works here before leaving for Rome, where he died of consumption in 1821, aged just 25. The neat, rather staid interior contains books and letters, Fanny's engagement ring and the four-poster bed in which the poet first coughed up blood, confiding to his companion, Charles Brown, "that drop of blood is my death warrant".

## 2 Willow Road

March–Oct Wed–Sun 11am–5pm • £6 • ☎ 020 7435 6166, ⓦ nationaltrust.org.uk • ⊖ Hampstead or Hampstead Heath Overground

An unassuming red-brick terraced house built in the 1930s by the Hungarian-born architect **Ernö Goldfinger** (1902–87), 2 Willow Road gives a fascinating insight into the modernist mindset. This was a state-of-the-art pad when Goldfinger moved in, and as he changed little during the following fifty years, what you see today is a 1930s avant-garde dwelling preserved in aspic, a house at once both modern and old-fashioned. An added bonus is that the rooms are packed with works of art by the likes of Bridget Riley, Duchamp, Henry Moore and Man Ray. Before 3pm, visits are by guided tour only (noon, 1 & 2pm); after 3pm, the public has unguided access.

## Freud Museum

20 Maresfield Gardens • Wed–Sun noon–5pm • £7 • ⓦ freud.org.uk • ⊖ Finchley Road

The **Freud Museum** is one of the most poignant of London's house museums. Having lived in Vienna for his entire adult life, the psychotherapist, by now semi-disabled and with only a year to live, was forced to flee the Nazis, arriving in London in the summer of 1938. The ground-floor study and library look exactly as they did when Freud lived here; the collection of erotic antiquities and the famous couch, sumptuously draped in Persian rugs, were all brought here from Vienna. Upstairs, home movies of family life are shown continually, and a small room is dedicated to his daughter, Anna, herself an influential child analyst, who lived in the house until her death in 1982.

## Hampstead Heath

Daily 24hr • Free • ☎ 020 7332 3322, ⓦ cityoflondon.gov.uk • Hampstead tube and Hampstead Heath or Gospel Oak Overground. Bus #210 from ⊖ Hampstead or Golders Green or Bus #24 from central London

**Hampstead Heath** may not have much of its original heathland left, but it packs a wonderful variety of bucolic scenery into its eight hundred acres. At its southern end are the rolling green pastures of **Parliament Hill**, north London's premier spot for kite flying. On either side are numerous ponds, three of which – one for men, one for women and one mixed – you can swim in. The thickest woodland is to be found in the **West Heath**, beyond Whitestone Pond, also the site of the most formal section, **Hill Garden**, a secretive and romantic little gem with eccentric balustraded terraces and a ruined pergola. Beyond lies **Golders Hill Park**, where you can gaze at pygmy goats and fallow deer, and inspect the impeccably maintained aviaries, home to flamingos, cranes and other exotic birds.

## Kenwood House

Daily 10am–5pm • Free • ☎ 020 8348 1286, ⓦ english-heritage.org.uk • Bus #210 from ⊖ Archway or Golders Green

Don't miss the landscaped grounds of Kenwood, in the north of the Heath, which are focused on the whitewashed Neoclassical mansion of **Kenwood House**. The house is now home to a collection of seventeenth- and eighteenth-century art, including a handful of real masterpieces by Vermeer, Rembrandt, Boucher, Gainsborough and

**1**

Reynolds. Of the period interiors, the most spectacular is Robert Adam's sky-blue and pink library.

## Highgate Cemetery

Swain's Lane · **East Cemetery** April–Oct Mon–Fri 10am–5pm, Sat & Sun 11am–5pm; Nov–March closes 4pm · £4 **West Cemetery** March–Nov Mon–Fri 1.45pm, Sat & Sun every 30min 11am–4pm · £12 · No under-8s · ☎ 020 8340 1834, ⓦ highgate cemetery.org · ⊖ Highgate

**Highgate Cemetery**, ranged on both sides of Swain's Lane, is London's best-known graveyard. The most illustrious incumbent of the **East Cemetery** is **Karl Marx**. Marx himself asked for a simple grave topped by a headstone, but by 1954 the Communist movement decided to move his grave to a more prominent position and erect the hulking bronze bust that now surmounts a granite plinth. To visit the more atmospheric and overgrown **West Cemetery**, with its spooky Egyptian Avenue and sunken catacombs, you must take a guided tour. Among the prominent graves usually visited are those of artist Dante Gabriel Rossetti, and lesbian novelist Radclyffe Hall.

## RAF Museum

Grahame Park Way · Daily 10am–6pm · Free · ☎ 020 8205 2266, ⓦ rafmuseum.org.uk · ⊖ Colindale

A world-class assembly of historic military aircraft can be seen at the **RAF Museum**, in the former Hendon Aerodrome beside the M1 motorway. Enthusiasts won't be disappointed, but anyone looking for a balanced account of modern aerial warfare should probably go to the Imperial War Museum (see p.84). Those with children should head for the hands-on Aeronauts gallery; those without might prefer to explore the often overlooked display galleries, ranged around the edge of the Main Aircraft Hall, which contain an art gallery and an exhibition on the history of flight, accompanied by replicas of some of the deathtraps of early aviation.

## Neasden Temple

105–119 Brentfield Rd · Daily 9am–6pm · Temple (with audioguide) · Free; exhibition £2 · ☎ 020 8965 2651, ⓦ londonmandir.baps.org · ⊖ Neasden

Perhaps the most remarkable building in the whole of London lies just off the North Circular, in the glum suburb of Neasden. Here, rising majestically above the surrounding semi-detached houses, is the **Shri Swaminarayan Mandir**, a traditional Hindu temple topped with domes and *shikharas*, erected in 1995 in a style and scale unseen outside of India for over a millennium. You enter through the Haveli (cultural complex) and, after taking off your shoes, proceed to the Mandir (temple) itself, carved entirely out of Carrara marble, with every possible surface transformed into a honeycomb of arabesques, flowers and seated gods. Beneath the Mandir, an **exhibition** explains the basic tenets of Hinduism and details the life of Lord Swaminarayan, and includes a video about the history of the building.

# South London

Now largely built up into a patchwork of Victorian terraces, **South London** nevertheless includes one outstanding area for sightseeing, and that is **Greenwich**, with its fantastic ensemble of the Royal Naval College and the Queen's House, the National Maritime Museum, the Royal Observatory, and the beautifully landscaped royal park. The only other suburban sights that stand out are the **Dulwich Picture Gallery**, a public art gallery even older than the National Gallery, and the eclectic **Horniman Museum**, in neighbouring Forest Hill.

**1**

# Greenwich

**Greenwich** draws tourists out from the centre in considerable numbers. At its heart is the outstanding architectural set piece of the **Old Royal Naval College** and the **Queen's House**, courtesy of Christopher Wren and Inigo Jones respectively. Most visitors, however, come to see the **Cutty Sark**, the **National Maritime Museum** and Greenwich Park's **Royal Observatory**. With the added attractions of its riverside pubs and walks – plus startling views across to Canary Wharf and Docklands – it makes for one of the best weekend trips in the capital. To reach Greenwich, you can take a **train** from London Bridge (every 30min), a **boat** from one of the piers in central London (every 20–30min), or the **DLR** to Cutty Sark station (every 4–10min).

## Cutty Sark

King William Walk • Daily 10am–5pm • £12 • ☎ 020 8858 6608, ⓦ rmg.co.uk • Cutty Sark DLR

Wedged in a dry dock by the river is the majestic **Cutty Sark**, the world's last surviving tea clipper. Launched in 1869, the *Cutty Sark* was actually more famous in its day as a wool clipper, returning from Australia in just 72 days. The vessel's name comes from Robert Burns' *Tam O'Shanter*, in which Tam, a drunken farmer, is chased by Nannie, an angry witch in a short Paisley linen dress, or "cutty sark"; the clipper's figurehead shows her clutching the hair from the tail of Tam's horse. After a devastating fire in 2007, the ship has been beautifully restored and now includes a museum beneath the ship's copper-lined keel displaying a collection of more than eighty ships' figureheads.

## Old Royal Naval College

Daily 10am–5pm • Free • ☎ 020 8269 4747, ⓦ ornc.org • Cutty Sark DLR

It's appropriate that the one London building that makes the most of its riverbank location should be the **Old Royal Naval College**, a majestic Baroque ensemble designed, for the most part, by Wren. Initially built as a royal palace, but eventually converted into the Royal Hospital for Seamen, the complex was later home to the Royal Naval College, but now houses the University of Greenwich and the Trinity College of Music. The two grandest rooms, situated underneath Wren's twin domes, are open to the public and well worth visiting. The **Chapel**, in the east wing, has exquisite pastel-shaded plasterwork and spectacular, decorative detailing on the ceiling, all designed by James "Athenian" Stuart after a fire in 1799 destroyed the original interior. Opposite the chapel is the magnificent **Painted Hall** in the west wing, which is dominated by James Thornhill's gargantuan allegorical ceiling painting, and his trompe-l'oeil fluted pilasters. Over in the Pepys Building, you can get a good overview of Greenwich's history in **Discover Greenwich**. The building also contains a tourist information office and the Royal Hospital's old brewhouse, which used to supply a ration of three pints to each seaman, and has now been revived and turned into a café/microbrewery.

## National Maritime Museum

Romney Rd • Daily 10am–5pm • Free • ☎ 020 8858 4422, ⓦ rmg.co.uk • Cutty Sark DLR

The main building of the excellent **National Maritime Museum** is centred on a spectacular glass-roofed courtyard, which houses the museum's largest artefacts, among them the splendid 63ft-long gilded **Royal Barge**, designed in Rococo style by William Kent for Prince Frederick, the much unloved eldest son of George II. The various themed galleries are superbly designed to appeal to visitors of all ages, but if you have kids, head for Floor Two, where the **Children's Gallery** gives kids a taste of life on the sea, loading miniature cargo, firing a cannon, learning to use Morse Code and so forth. Older children and adults alike will enjoy honing their ship-handling skills on the **Ship Simulator** next door.

1

Inigo Jones's **Queen's House**, originally built amid a rambling Tudor royal palace, is now the focal point of the Greenwich ensemble, and is an integral part of the Maritime Museum. As royal residences go, it's an unassuming country house, but as the first Neoclassical building in the country, it has enormous architectural significance. The interior currently houses the museum's **art collection** including works by painters as diverse as Reynolds and Lowry. Off the Great Hall, a perfect cube, lies the beautiful **Tulip Staircase**, Britain's earliest cantilevered spiral staircase – its name derives from the floral patterning in the wrought-iron balustrade.

## Royal Observatory

Blackheath Ave • **Astronomy Centre** Daily 10am–5pm • Free **Flamsteed House** Daily 10am–5pm • £7 **Planetarium** Mon–Fri 12.45–3.45pm; Sat & Sun & school holidays noon–4pm • £6.50 • ☏ 020 8312 6565, ⓦ rmg.co.uk • Greenwich DLR/train station

Perched on the crest of Greenwich Park's highest hill, the **Royal Observatory** was established by Charles II in 1675. It's housed in a rather dinky Wren-built red-brick building, whose northeastern turret sports a bright-red time-ball that climbs the mast at 12.58pm and drops at 1pm GMT precisely; it was added in 1833 to allow ships on the Thameslink to set their clocks.

Greenwich's greatest claim to fame, of course, is as the home of **Greenwich Mean Time** (GMT) and the **Prime Meridian**. Since 1884, Greenwich has occupied zero longitude – hence the world sets its clocks by GMT. The observatory housed the first Astronomer Royal, John Flamsteed, whose chief task was to study the night sky in order to discover an astronomical method of finding the longitude of a ship at sea. Beyond the Octagon Room, where the king used to show off to his guests, are the Time galleries, which display four of the clocks designed by **John Harrison**, including "H4", which helped win the Longitude Prize in 1763.

The **Astronomy Centre** houses high-tech galleries giving a brief rundown of the Big Bang theory of the universe and invites you to consider the big questions of astronomy today. You can also watch one of the thirty-minute presentations in the state-of-the-art **Planetarium**, introduced by a Royal Observatory astronomer.

## Dulwich Picture Gallery

Gallery Rd • Tues–Fri 10am–5pm, Sat & Sun 11am–5pm • £6 • ☏ 020 8693 5254, ⓦ dulwichpicturegallery.org.uk • West Dulwich (from Victoria) or North Dulwich (from London Bridge) train stations

**Dulwich Picture Gallery**, the nation's oldest public art gallery, was designed by John Soane in 1814. Soane created a beautifully spacious building, awash with natural light and crammed with superb paintings – elegiac landscapes by Cuyp, one of the world's finest Poussin series, and splendid works by Hogarth, Gainsborough, Van Dyck, Canaletto and Rubens, plus **Rembrandt**'s tiny *Portrait of a Young Man*, a top-class portrait of poet, playwright and Royalist, the future Earl of Bristol. At the centre of the museum is a tiny mausoleum designed by Soane for the sarcophagi of the gallery's founders.

## Horniman Museum

100 London Rd • Daily 10.30am–5.30pm • Free, aquarium £3.30 • ☏ 020 8699 1872, ⓦ horniman.ac.uk • Forest Hill train station from Victoria or London Bridge

The wonderful **Horniman Museum** was purpose-built in 1901 by Frederick Horniman, a tea trader with a passion for collecting. In addition to the museum's natural history collection of stuffed birds and animals, there's an eclectic ethnographic collection, and a music gallery with more than 1500 instruments from Chinese gongs to electric guitars. The state-of-the-art aquarium in the basement is definitely worth the entrance fee, as are the special ethnographic exhibitions the museum puts on.

# 1

# West London

Most visitors experience **West London** en route to or from Heathrow Airport, either from the confines of the train or tube (which runs overground at this point), or the motorway. The city and its satellites seem to continue unabated, with only fleeting glimpses of the countryside. However, in the five-mile stretch from Chiswick to Osterley there are several former country retreats, now surrounded by suburbia.

The Palladian villa of **Chiswick House** is perhaps the best known. However, it draws nothing like as many visitors as **Syon House**, most of whom come for the gardening centre and the indoor adventure playground rather than for the house itself, a showcase for the talents of Robert Adam, who also worked at **Osterley House**, another Elizabethan conversion.

Running through much of the area is the **River Thames**, once the "Great Highway of London" and still the most pleasant way to travel in these parts during summer. Boats plough up the Thames all the way from central London via the **Royal Botanic Gardens** at **Kew** and the picturesque riverside at **Richmond**, as far as **Hampton Court**.

## Chiswick House

Great Chertsey Rd • **House** April–Oct Mon–Wed & Sun 10am–6pm; Oct closes 5pm • £6.10; EH • **Gardens** Daily 7am–dusk • Free • ☎ 020 8995 0508, ⓦ chgt.org.uk • Chiswick train station from Waterloo or ⊖ Turnham Green

**Chiswick House** is a perfect little Neoclassical villa, designed in the 1720s by the Earl of Burlington, and set in one of the most beautifully landscaped gardens in London. Like its prototype, Palladio's Villa Rotonda near Vicenza, the house was created as a "temple to the arts" where, amid his fine art collection, Burlington could entertain artistic friends such as Swift, Handel and Pope. Entertaining took place on the **upper floor**, a series of cleverly interconnecting rooms, each enjoying a wonderful view out onto the gardens – all, that is, except the Tribunal, the domed octagonal hall at the centre of the villa, where the earl's finest paintings and sculptures would have been displayed.

## London Museum of Water & Steam

Corner of Kew Bridge Road and Green Dragon Lane • Daily 11am–4pm • £11.50 • ☎ 020 8568 4757, ⓦ waterandsteam.org.uk • Bus #237 or #267 from ⊖ Gunnersbury or Kew Bridge train station from Waterloo

Difficult to miss, thanks to its stylish Italianate standpipe tower, the **Museum of Water & Steam** occupies a former Victorian pumping station, 100yd west of Kew Bridge. At the heart of the museum is the Steam Hall, which contains a triple expansion steam engine and four gigantic nineteenth-century Cornish beam engines. The museum also has a hands-on **Waterworks** gallery in the basement, devoted to the history of the capital's water supply, and **Splash Zone** ideal for younger kids. The best time to visit is at weekends, when each of the museum's industrial dinosaurs is put through its paces, and the small narrow-gauge steam **Waterworks Railway** runs back and forth round the yard.

## Syon House

London Rd • **House** Mid-March to Oct Wed, Thurs & Sun 11am–5pm • £11.50 • **Gardens only** Mid-March to Oct daily 10.30am–5pm • £6.50 • ☎ 020 8560 0882, ⓦ syonpark.co.uk • Bus #237 or #267 from ⊖ Gunnersbury or Kew Bridge train station

From its rather plain castellated exterior, you'd never guess that **Syon House** contains the most opulent eighteenth-century interiors in London. The splendour of Robert Adam's refurbishment is immediately revealed, however, in the pristine **Great Hall**, an apsed double cube with a screen of Doric columns at one end and classical statuary

**RIVER TRANSPORT: HEADING WEST**

From April to October **Westminster Passenger Services** runs a scheduled service from Westminster Pier to Kew, Richmond and Hampton Court (3hr one-way; £15 single, £22.50 return; ☎020 7930 2062, ⓦwpsa.co.uk). In addition, **Turks** runs a regular service from Richmond to Hampton Court (April to mid-Sept Tues–Sun; £8 single, £9.50 return; ☎020 8546 2434, ⓦturks.co.uk). For the latest on boat services on the Thames, see ⓦtfl.gov.uk.

dotted around the edges. There are several more Adam-designed rooms to admire in the house, in particular the **Long Gallery** – 136ft by just 14ft – plus a smattering of works by Lely, Van Dyck and others.

While Adam beautified Syon House, Capability Brown laid out its **gardens** around an artificial lake, surrounding it with oaks, beeches, limes and cedars. The gardens' chief focus now, however, is the crescent-shaped **Great Conservatory**, an early nineteenth-century addition which is said to have inspired Joseph Paxton, architect of the Crystal Palace.

## Osterley House

Jersey Rd • **House** March & Oct Wed  Sun noon  4pm; April–Sept Wed–Sun 11am–5pm; Dec Sat & Sun noon–4pm • **Gardens** Daily: March & Oct–Dec noon–4pm; April–Sept 11am–5pm • £8.25; NT • ☎ 020 8232 5050, ⓦ nationaltrust.org.uk • ⊖ Osterley

Home to a colossal Elizabethan mansion redesigned by Robert Adam, **Osterley** is one of London's largest surviving estate parks, which still gives the impression of being in the countryside, despite the M4 motorway to the north. Osterley House boasts a characteristically cool **Entrance Hall**, followed by the so-called State Rooms of the south wing. Highlights include the **Drawing Room**, with Reynolds portraits on the damask walls and a coffered ceiling centred on a giant marigold, and the **Etruscan Dressing Room**, in which every surface is covered in delicate painted trelliswork, sphinxes and urns; Adam (and Wedgwood) dubbed the style "Etruscan", though it is in fact derived from Greek vases found at Pompeii.

## Kew Gardens

Kew Rd • Daily 9.30am–6.30pm or dusk • £15 • ☎ 020 8332 5655, ⓦ kew.org • ⊖ Kew Gardens

Established in 1759, Kew's **Royal Botanic Gardens** manage the extremely difficult task of being both a world leader in botanic research and an extraordinarily beautiful and popular public park. There's always something to see, whatever the season, but to get the most out of the place come sometime between spring and autumn, bring a picnic and stay for the day.

Of all the glasshouses, by far the most celebrated is the **Palm House**, a curvaceous mound of glass and wrought iron, designed by Decimus Burton in the 1840s. Its drippingly humid atmosphere nurtures most of the known palm species, while in the basement there's a small, excellent tropical aquarium. Elsewhere in the gardens, you'll find the **Treetop Walkway**, which lifts you 60ft off the ground, and gives you a novel view of the tree canopy.

The three-storey red-brick mansion of **Kew Palace** (April–Oct only), to the northwest of the Palm House, was bought by George II as a nursery and schoolhouse for his umpteen children. Later, George III was confined to the palace and subjected to the dubious attentions of doctors who attempted to find a cure for his "madness". There are one or two bits and bobs belonging to the royals, like the much-loved dolls' house, on the ground floor, which belonged to George III's daughters. Upstairs, you can view the chair in which Queen Charlotte passed away in 1818, while the top floor has been left pretty much untouched since those days.

**1**

# Richmond

**Richmond**, upriver from Kew, basked for centuries in the glow of royal patronage, with Plantagenet kings and Tudor monarchs frequenting the riverside palace. Although most of the courtiers and aristocrats have gone, it is still a wealthy district, with two theatres and highbrow pretensions.

## Richmond Park

Daily: March–Sept 7am–dusk; Oct–Feb 7.30am–dusk • Free • ☎ 0300 061 2200, ⓦ royalparks.gov.uk • Bus #371 or #65 from
⊖ Richmond to Petersham Gate

Richmond's greatest attraction is the enormous **Richmond Park**, at the top of Richmond Hill – 2500 acres of undulating grassland and bracken, dotted with coppiced woodland and as wild as anything in London. Eight miles across at its widest point, this is Europe's largest city park, famed for its red and fallow deer, which roam freely, and for its ancient oaks. For the most part untamed, the park does have a couple of deliberately landscaped plantations that feature splendid springtime azaleas and rhododendrons.

## Ham House

Ham St • **House** March–Oct daily except Fri noon–4pm • £10 • **Gardens** Daily: March–Oct 10am–5pm; Nov–Feb 10am–4pm • £4; NT •
☎ 020 8940 1950, ⓦ nationaltrust.org.uk • Bus #371 or #65 from ⊖ Richmond

Leave the rest of London far behind at **Ham House**, home to the earls of Dysart for nearly three hundred years. Expensively furnished in the seventeenth century, but little altered since then, the house is blessed with one of the finest Stuart interiors in the country, from the stupendously ornate Great Staircase to the Long Gallery, featuring six "Court Beauties" by Peter Lely. Elsewhere, there are several fine Verrio ceiling paintings, some exquisite parquet flooring and works by Van Dyck and Reynolds. Also glorious are the formal seventeenth-century **gardens**, especially the Cherry Garden, laid out with a pungent lavender parterre. The Orangery, overlooking the original kitchen garden, serves as a tearoom.

## Strawberry Hill

268 Waldegrave Rd • Mon–Wed 2–6pm, Sat & Sun noon–6pm (last admission 4.20pm) • £10.80 • ☎ 020 8744 1241,
ⓦ strawberryhillhouse.org.uk • Strawberry Hill train station from Waterloo

In 1747 writer, wit and fashion queen Horace Walpole, youngest son of former prime minister Robert Walpole, bought this "little play-thing house…the prettiest bauble you ever saw…set in enamelled meadows, with filigree hedges", renamed it **Strawberry Hill** and set about inventing the most influential building in the Gothic Revival. Walpole appointed a "Committee of Taste" to embellish his project with details from other Gothic buildings: screens from Old St Paul's and Rouen cathedrals, and fan vaulting from Henry VII's Chapel in Westminster Abbey. Walpole wanted visits of Strawberry Hill to be a theatrical experience, and, with its eccentric Gothic decor, it remains so to this day.

# Hampton Court

Daily: April–Oct 10am–6pm; Nov–March 10am–4.30pm • Palace, gardens & maze £16.50, free guided tours available (45min); gardens only £5.20; maze only £4 • ☎ 020 3166 6000, ⓦ hrp.org.uk • Hampton Court train station from Waterloo

**Hampton Court Palace**, a sprawling red-brick ensemble on the banks of the Thames thirteen miles southwest of London, is the finest of England's royal abodes. Built in 1516 by the upwardly mobile **Cardinal Wolsey**, Henry VIII's Lord Chancellor, it was purloined by Henry himself after Wolsey fell from favour. In the second half of the seventeenth century, Charles II laid out the gardens, inspired by what he had seen at

Versailles, while William and Mary had large sections of the palace remodelled by Wren a few years later.

There's not a lot of information in any of the rooms, but audioguides are available and free guided tours are led by period-costumed historians who bring the place to life. If your energy is lacking – and Hampton Court is huge – the most rewarding sections are: **Henry VIII's Apartments**, which feature the glorious double-hammer-beamed Great Hall; **William III's Apartments**; and **Henry VIII's Kitchens**.

Tickets to the Royal Apartments cover entry to the rest of the sites in the grounds. Those who don't wish to visit the apartments are free to wander around the gardens and visit the curious **Royal Tennis Courts** (April–Oct), but have to pay to try out the palace's famously tricky yew-hedge **Maze**, and visit the **Privy Garden**, where you can view Andrea Mantegna's colourful, heroic canvases, *The Triumphs of Caesar*, housed in the Lower Orangery, and the celebrated **Great Vine**, whose grapes are sold at the palace each year in September.

## ARRIVAL AND DEPARTURE                                                                 LONDON

### BY PLANE

The capital's five international airports – Heathrow, Gatwick, Stansted, Luton and City Airport – are all less than an hour from the city centre.

### HEATHROW

Fifteen miles west of central London, Heathrow (ⓦheathrowairport.com) has five terminals and three train/tube stations: one for terminals 1, 2 and 3, and separate ones for terminals 4 and 5. All stations are in Travelcard Zone 6.

**Heathrow Express** High-speed (ⓦheathrowexpress.com) trains travel nonstop to Paddington Station (daily 5am–midnight; every 15min; 15min; online tickets £21 single/£34 return).

**Heathrow Connect** Less pricey trains (ⓦheathrowconnect.com) travel to Paddington with several stops on the way (Mon–Sat 5am–midnight, Sun 6am–11pm; every 30min; 30–40min; £10 single).

**Underground** An even cheaper alternative is to take the tube (Piccadilly line) into central London (Mon–Sat 5am–11.45pm, Sun 6am–11.30pm; every 5min; 50min; £5.70 single/£8.90 for a One Day Off-Peak Travelcard).

**National Express** National Express bus services (ⓦnationalexpress.com) run direct to Victoria Coach Station (daily every 15–30min; 40–55min; £6 single, £11 return).

**Night buses** From midnight, you can take night bus #N9 (every 20min; 1hr 10min; £1.45). Heathrow to Trafalgar Square, with several other stops in West London en route.

### GATWICK

Around 30 miles south of London, Gatwick Airport (ⓦgatwickairport.com) has good transport connections with the city.

**Gatwick Express** The nonstop Gatwick Express (ⓦgatwickexpress.com) runs between the airport's South Terminal and Victoria Station (daily 4.30am–1.30am; every 15min; 30min; £20 single, £35 return).

**Overground trains** Other train options include Southern services to Victoria (every 15min–hourly; 35min) or Govia Thameslink services to various stations (every 15–hourly; journey 30–45min), including London Bridge and St Pancras; tickets for either cost around £10 single.

**Buses** easyBus (ⓦeasybus.co.uk) runs buses to West Brompton tube (daily 4.30am–midnight; every 20min; 1hr 10min), with online tickets from £2 single (£10 if you buy on board). National Express buses run from Gatwick direct to central London (daily 5am–9.30pm; hourly; 1hr 30min); tickets cost around £7 single, £13.50 return.

### STANSTED

Roughly 35 miles northeast of the capital, Stansted (ⓦstanstedairport.com) is commonly used by the budget airlines.

**Stansted Express** The most convenient way to get into town is by train on the Stansted Express (ⓦstanstedexpress.com) to Liverpool Street (daily 5.30am–12.30am; every 15–30min; 45min; £24 single, £33 return).

**Buses** All year round, 24 hours a day, Green Line and easyBus runs buses to Baker Street tube (daily 7am–1am; every 20min; 1hr 15min; online tickets from £2 single, £10 if you buy on board). National Express runs buses to Golders Green and Victoria Coach Station (24hr; every 30min; 1hr 30min–1hr 45min; £9 single).

### LUTON

Around 30 miles north of London, Luton (ⓦlondon-luton.co.uk) handles mostly charter flights.

**Luton Airport Parkway** A free shuttle bus (every 10min; 5min) transports passengers to Luton Airport Parkway train station, connected to St Pancras (every 15min–hourly; 25–35min; £15 single) and other central London stations.

**Buses** All year round, 24 hours a day, Green Line and easyBus run the #757 coach from Luton Airport to Baker Street and Victoria Coach Station (every 20–30min; 1hr 20min; from £2 online, or as much as £10).

**1**

## CITY AIRPORT

London's smallest airport, used primarily by business people, City Airport (⊛londoncityairport.com) is in Docklands, 10 miles east of central London. Docklands Light Railway (DLR) will take you straight to Bank in the City (Mon–Sat 5.30am–12.15am, Sun 7am–11.15pm every 8–15min; 20min; around £5), where you can change to the Tube.

## BY TRAIN

**From Europe** Eurostar (⊛eurostar.com) trains arrive at St Pancras International, next door to King's Cross.

**From Britain** Arriving by train from elsewhere in Britain, you'll come into one of London's numerous mainline stations, all of which have adjacent Underground stations linking into the city centre's tube network. As a rough guide, Charing Cross handles services to Kent; Euston to the Midlands, northwest England and Glasgow; Fenchurch Street to south Essex; King's Cross to northeast England and Scotland; Liverpool Street to eastern England; Marylebone to the Midlands; Paddington to southwest England; St Pancras for Eurostar and the southeast, plus trains to East Midlands and South Yorkshire; and Victoria and Waterloo to southeast England.

**Information** National Rail Enquiries (☎0845 748 4950, ⊛nationalrail.co.uk).

## DESTINATIONS

**London Charing Cross** to: Canterbury West (hourly; 1hr 40min); Dover Priory (Mon–Sat every 30min; 1hr 40min–1hr 50min); Hastings (every 30min; 1hr 30min); Rochester (every 30min; 1hr 10min).

**London Euston** to: Birmingham New Street (every 20min; 1hr 25min); Carlisle (every 2hr; 3hr 15min); Lancaster (hourly; 2hr 30min); Liverpool Lime Street (hourly; 2hr 10min); Manchester Piccadilly (every 20min; 2hr 10min).

**London King's Cross** to: Brighton (Mon–Sat 4 hourly, Sun 2 hourly; 1hr); Cambridge (every 30min; 45min); Durham (hourly; 2hr 40min–3hr); Leeds (hourly; 2hr 25min); Newcastle (every 30min; 3hr); Peterborough (every 30min; 45min); York (every 30min; 2hr).

**London Liverpool Street** to: Cambridge (every 30min; 1hr 15min); Norwich (every 30min; 1hr 55min).

**London Paddington** to: Bath (every 30min–hourly; 1hr 30min); Bristol (every 30–45min; 1hr 40min); Cheltenham (every 2hr; 2hr 15min); Exeter (hourly; 2hr 15min); Gloucester (every 2hr; 2hr); Oxford (every 30min; 55min); Penzance (every 1–2hr; 5hr 30min); Plymouth (hourly; 3hr 15min–3hr 40min); Windsor (change at Slough; Mon–Fri every 20min; Sat & Sun every 30min; 30–40min); Worcester (hourly; 2hr 20min).

**London St Pancras** to: Brighton (every 20min; 1hr 20min); Canterbury (every 30min; 1hr); Dover Priory (hourly; 1hr 5min); Leicester (every 30min; 1hr 10min); Nottingham (every 30min; 1hr 40min–2hr); Rochester (every 30min; 40min); Sheffield (every 30min; 2hr 10min–2hr 30min).

**London Victoria** to: Arundel (Mon–Sat every 30min, Sun hourly; 1hr 30min); Brighton (every 30min; 50min); Canterbury East (every 30min–hourly; 1hr 25min); Chichester (Mon–Sat 2 hourly; 1hr 35min); Dover Priory (Mon–Sat every 30min; 1hr 40min–1hr 55min); Lewes (Mon–Sat every 30min, Sun hourly; 1hr 10min); Rochester (every 30min; 45min).

**London Waterloo** to: Portsmouth Harbour (every 30min; 1hr 35min); Southampton Central (every 30min; 1hr 15min); Winchester (every 30min; 1hr); Windsor (Mon–Sat every 30min, Sun hourly; 50min).

## BY BUS

**Victoria Coach Station** Coming into London by coach (☎0870 580 8080, ⊛nationalexpress.com), you're most likely to arrive at Victoria Coach Station, a couple of hundred yards south down Buckingham Palace Road from the train and Underground stations of the same name.

**Information** Traveline (☎0871 200 2233, ⊛traveline.info).

Destinations Bath (hourly to every 1hr 30min; 3hr 30min); Birmingham (every 30min–hourly; 2hr 35min); Brighton (hourly; 2hr 10min); Bristol (hourly; 2hr 30min); Cambridge (hourly; 2hr); Canterbury (hourly; 2hr); Dover (hourly; 2hr 30min–3hr); Exeter (every 2hr; 4hr 15min); Gloucester (hourly; 3hr 20min); Liverpool (6 daily; 4hr 50min–5hr 30min); Manchester (9 daily; 4hr 50min–5hr 30min); Newcastle (5 daily; 6hr 25min–7hr 55min); Oxford (every 15min; 1hr 50min); Plymouth (6 daily; 5hr 20min); Stratford (4 daily; 3hr).

## GETTING AROUND

London's **transport network** is among the most complex and expensive in the world, but on the bright side you should be able to get to wherever you want, most hours of the day or night. Avoid travelling during the **rush hour** (Mon–Fri 8–9.30am & 5–7pm), when tubes become unbearably crowded, and some buses get so full that they won't let you on. Transport for London (TfL) provides excellent free maps and details of bus and tube services from its six **Travel Information Centres**: the most central is at Piccadilly Circus tube station (Mon–Fri 7.45am–7pm, Sat 9.15am–7pm, Sun 9.15am–6pm); there are other desks at the arrivals at Heathrow (terminals 1, 2 & 3) and various tube/train stations. There's also a 24-hour helpline and an excellent website for information on all bus and tube services (☎0843 222 1234, ⊛tfl.gov.uk/plan-a-journey).

## BY TUBE

Except for very short journeys, the Underground – or tube – is by far the quickest way to get about.

**Tube lines** Eleven different lines cross much of the metropolis, although London south of the river is not very well covered. Each line has its own colour and name – all you need to know is which direction you're travelling in: northbound, eastbound, southbound or westbound, and the final destination.

**Zones** London is divided into six concentric zones, with the vast majority of the city's accommodation, pubs, restaurants and sights in zones 1 and 2.

**Services** Services are frequent (Mon–Sat 5.30am–12.30am, Sun 7.30am–11.30pm), and you rarely have to wait more than five minutes for a train between central stations.

**Fares** Single fares are expensive – a journey in the central zone costs nearly £5 – so if you're intending to make more than one journey, an Oyster card or a Travelcard is by far your best option (see box below).

## BY BUS

London's red buses – most, but not all, of them, double-deckers – tend to get stuck in traffic jams, which prevents their running to a regular timetable. You must signal to get the bus to stop, and press the bell in order to get off.

**Services** Some buses run a 24-hour service, but most run between about 5am and midnight, with a network of Night Buses (prefixed with the letter "N") operating outside this period (every 20–30min).

**Fares** The standard walk-on fare is £1.45, but you cannot pay by cash, only with a card or pass (see box below).

## BY TRAIN

Large areas of London's outskirts are best reached by the suburban (overground) train network. Wherever a sight can only be reached by overground train, we've indicated in the guide the nearest train station and the central terminus from which you can depart.

## BY DLR

The Docklands Light Railway sets off from Bank, or from Tower Gateway, close to Tower Hill tube. The train, which cuts right through the middle of the office Canary Wharf buildings under a parabolic steel-and-glass canopy, is also a great way to get to Greenwich (see p.98).

## BY BOAT

Unfortunately, boat services on the Thames are not fully integrated into the public transport system. If you have a valid Travelcard (either in paper or Oyster form), you're entitled to a third off, but if you have a pay-as-you-go Oyster card, you get just ten percent off.

**Services** Timetables and services are complex, and there are numerous companies and small charter operators – for a full list pick up a booklet from a TfL information centre (see opposite) or visit ⓦ tfl.gov.uk. One of the largest companies is Thames Clippers (ⓦ thamesclippers.com), who run a regular commuter service (every 20–30min; around £6.50 single) between Waterloo and Greenwich; an off-peak hop-on, hop-off River Roamer on their services costs £15.

## BY TAXI

**Black cabs** Compared to most capital cities, London's metered black cabs are an expensive option unless there are three or more of you. The minimum fare is £2.40, and a ride from Euston to Victoria, for example, costs around £12–15 (Mon–Fri 6am–8pm). After 8pm on weekdays and all day during the weekend, a higher tariff applies, and after 10pm it's higher still. A yellow light over the windscreen tells you if the cab is available – just stick your arm out to hail it. To order a black cab in advance, phone

---

## GETTING ABOUT: OYSTER CARDS AND PASSES

The cheapest, easiest way to get about London is to use an **Oyster card**, London's transport smartcard, available from all tube stations and TfL Travel Information Centres, and valid on almost all networks .Use it either to store a weekly/monthly/yearly **Travelcard**, or as a pay-as-you-go deal; you can top it up at all tube stations and many newsagents. As you enter the tube or bus, simply touch in your card at the card reader – if you're using pay-as-you-go, the fare will be taken off. If you're using the tube or train, you need to touch out again, or a maximum cash fare of up to £8.60 will be deducted. A pay-as-you-go Oyster operates daily price-capping; you will stop being charged when you've paid the equivalent of a Day Travelcard, but you still need to touch in (and out). Oyster cards are free for those buying monthly or yearly tickets; everyone else needs to hand over a £5 refundable deposit.

**Children** under 11 travel for free; children aged 11–15 travel free on all buses and at child-rate on the tube; children aged 16 or 17 can travel at half the adult rate on all forms of transport. However, all children over 10 must have an Oyster photocard to be eligible for free travel – these should be applied for in advance online.

Various other travelcards and bus passes are available, too; check ⓦ tfl.gov.uk for details.

**1**

## THE CONGESTION CHARGE

All vehicles entering central London on weekdays between 7am and 6pm are liable to a **congestion charge** of £11.50 per vehicle. Drivers can pay the charge online, over the phone and at garages and shops, and must do so before midnight the same day or incur a £2.50 surcharge – 24 hours later, you'll be liable for a £130 Penalty Charge Notice (reduced to £65 if you pay within 14 days). Disabled travellers, motorcycles, minibuses and some alternative-fuel vehicles are exempt from the charge, and local residents get a ninety percent discount, but you must register in order to qualify. For more details, visit ⓦtfl.gov.uk.

☏0871 871 8710, and be prepared to pay an extra £2.

**Minicabs** Private minicabs are considerably cheaper than black cabs, but they cannot be hailed from the street. All minicabs must be licensed and able to produce a TfL ID on demand, but the best way to pick a company is to take the advice of the place you're at, unless you want to be certain of a woman driver, in which case call Lady Mini Cabs (☏020 7272 3300), or a gay/lesbian-friendly driver, in which case call London Cabs (☏020 7205 2677). If saving money (and time) is your main priority, then you might consider using the Uber app where the price varies according to supply and you can see which cabs are close by.

### BY BIKE

**Boris bikes** The easiest way to cycle round London is to use the city's cycle hire scheme – or Boris bikes, as they're universally known, after Boris Johnson, the Mayor of London at the time they were introduced. There are over 700 docking stations across central London. With a credit or debit card, you can buy 24 hours' access to the bikes for just £2, after which you get the first 30min free, so if you hop from station to station, you don't pay another penny. Otherwise, it's £1 for the first hour, increasing rapidly after that to £15 for three hours. If you're going to use the scheme a lot, you may be best off becoming a member and getting a key – for more details see ⓦtfl.gov.uk.

**Bike rental** Bikes can also be rented from the London Bicycle Tour Company,1a Gabriel Wharf on the South Bank (☏020 7923 6838, ⓦlondonbicycle. com), costing around £20 a day or £50 a week.

### INFORMATION

**City of London Information Centre** The City has the most central information office, situated on the south side of St Paul's Cathedral (Mon–Sat 9.30am–5.30pm, Sun 10am–4pm; ☏020 7332 1456, ⓦvisitthecity.co.uk; ⊖St Paul's).

**Maps** If you want to find your way around every nook and cranny of the city you'll need to invest in either an *A–Z Atlas* or a *Nicholson Streetfinder*, both of which have a street index covering every street in the capital. You can get them at most bookshops and newsagents for around £5. Stanfords, in Covent Garden at 12–14 Long Acre, WC2 (☏020 7836 1321, ⓦstanfords.co.uk) is a good map shop.

**Listings magazines** The most useful listings magazine for visitors is *Time Out*, a free weekly which comes out on Tuesday. It carries news and consumer features, along with critical appraisals of all the week's theatre, film, music, exhibitions, children's events and more; listings themselves are much more comprehensive on its website (ⓦtimeout.com).

### ACCOMMODATION

London **accommodation** is undeniably expensive, and will be by far your major outlay when visiting the city. The hostels are among the most costly in the world, while venerable institutions such as the *Ritz*, the *Dorchester* and the *Savoy* charge the very top international prices – from £300 per luxurious night. For a decent **hotel** room, you shouldn't expect much change out of £100 a night, and even the most basic **B&Bs** struggle to bring their tariffs down to £80 for a double with shared facilities. If you're not bothered about atmosphere or local flavour then the **chain hotels** are a safe bet – but they'll offer far less character than the places that we've reviewed below. *Premier Inn* (ⓦpremierinn.com), *Travelodge* (ⓦtravelodge.co.uk), *easyHotel* (ⓦeasyhotel.com) and *Tune* (ⓦtunehotels.com) all have hotels in central locations. Whatever the time of year, you should book as far in advance as you can if you want to stay within a couple of tube stops of the West End.

### BOOKING

**British Hotel Reservation Centre (BHRC)** If you arrive without having made plans (which is *not* a good idea), head for the BHRC (24hr helpline ☏020 7592 3055, ⓦbhrc.co.uk) desks at Heathrow airport, Victoria bus station and St Pancras and Victoria train stations. BHRC offices are open daily from early till late, and there's no booking fee.

**Useful websites** You can book accommodation for free at ⓦlondontown.com; payment is made directly to the hotel

**1**

and they offer good discounts. ⓦ couchsurfing.org puts young travellers in touch with people to stay with for free, while ⓦ airbnb.co.uk offers rooms and flats in interesting locations and properties, and ⓦ onefinestay.com offers a very luxurious version of the same.

## HOTELS

When choosing your area, bear in mind that as a rule the West End – Soho, Covent Garden, St James's, Mayfair and Marylebone – and the western districts of Knightsbridge and Kensington are dominated by expensive, upmarket hotels, whereas Bloomsbury is both less expensive and very central. For rock-bottom rooms, the widest choice is close to the main train termini of Victoria and Paddington, and among the budget B&Bs of Earl's Court.

### VICTORIA

**B&B Belgravia** 64–66 Ebury St, SW1 ☎ 020 7259 8570, ⓦ bb-belgravia.com; ⊖ Victoria; map pp.56–57. A B&B with flair, close to the train and bus stations. The rooms are comfy and all en suite, with sash windows and modern touches; those on the ground floor can be noisy. They also have nearby studios for similar rates. Free wi-fi and bike loan. **£120**

**Luna Simone Hotel** 47–49 Belgrave Rd, SW1 ☎ 020 7834 5897, ⓦ lunasimonehotel.com; ⊖ Victoria; map pp.56–57. Good-value B&B with friendly staff and plain, well-maintained en-suite rooms, including triples and quads. Big English breakfasts are included, and there's free wi-fi on the ground floor and in the lobby. **£140**

★ **Morgan House** 120 Ebury St, SW1 ☎ 020 7730 2384, ⓦ morganhouse.co.uk; ⊖ Victoria; map pp.90–91. A well above-average B&B in a comfortable Georgian building in a pretty street on the Chelsea/Victoria borders. Rooms are mostly en suite; the family room (£158) crams in a double and a bunk bed. Full breakfasts, and free wi-fi in the lobby. **£84**

### WESTMINSTER

**Sanctuary House** 33 Tothill St, SW1 ☎ 020 7799 4044, ⓦ sanctuaryhousehotel.com; ⊖ St James's Park; map pp.60–61. Run by Fuller's Brewery, above a Fuller's pub, with uncontroversial modernish decor. Breakfast is extra, and served in the pub, but the location, right by St James's Park, is terrific. Ask about special deals. Free wi-fi. **£160**

### MARYLEBONE

**Lincoln House** 33 Gloucester Place, W1 ☎ 020 7486 7630, ⓦ lincoln-house-hotel.com; ⊖ Marble Arch or Baker St; map pp.90–91. Dark wood panelling and nautical paraphernalia give this large Georgian guesthouse a quirky feel, and the rooms are en suite and comfortable, with tea and coffee facilities. Rates vary according to the size of the bed and length of stay; there are good online discounts. Breakfast costs extra. Free wi-fi. **£105**

### SOHO

**Dean Street Townhouse** 69–71 Dean St, W1 ☎ 020 7341775, ⓦ deanstreettownhouse.com; ⊖ Tottenham Court Road or Leicester Square; map pp.60–61. One of a chic set of hotels owned by the trendy Soho House members' club, this 1730s house offers "tiny" (at 160 square feet it's no exaggeration) "small", "medium" and "bigger" rooms – all of them doubles. Luxury details come with real style – handpainted wallpaper, funky toiletries and clawfoot tubs, some of which are in the bedrooms themselves. Free wi-fi. **£260**

★ **Hazlitt's** 6 Frith St, W1 ☎ 020 7434 1771, ⓦ hazlittshotel.com; ⊖ Tottenham Court Road; map pp.60–61. An early eighteenth-century building hiding a hotel of real character and charm, with en-suite, wonky-floored rooms decorated and furnished as close to period style as convenience and comfort allow. Breakfast (served in the rooms) is not included. Free wi-fi. **£210**

**Nadler Soho** 10 Carlisle St, W1 ☎ 020 3697 3697, ⓦ thenadler.com; ⊖ Tottenham Court Road; map pp.60–61. Glossy hotel offering good value for its excellent location. The rooms are modern and high-tech, if unexciting (the cheapest are pretty small), and each has a mini-kitchen – with espresso machine – which means you could effectively self-cater. **£170**

### COVENT GARDEN

**The Fielding Hotel** 4 Broad Court, Bow St, WC2 ☎ 020 7836 8305, ⓦ www.thefieldinghotel.co.uk; ⊖ Covent Garden; map pp.60–61. Quietly situated on a pedestrianized court, this simple hotel is a hidden gem. Its en-suite rooms are a firm favourite with visiting performers, since it's just a few yards from the Royal Opera House. No breakfast. Free wi-fi. **£140**

**Seven Dials Hotel** 7 Monmouth St, WC2 ☎ 020 7681 0791, ⓦ sevendialshotellondon.com; ⊖ Covent

## LONDON POSTCODES

A brief word on **London postcodes**: the name of each street is followed by a letter giving the geographical location (E for "east", WC for "west central" and so on) and a number that specifies the postal area. However, this is not a reliable indication of the remoteness of the locale – W5, for example, lies beyond the more remote sounding NW10 – so it's always best to check a map before taking a room in what may sound like a fairly central area.

Garden; map pp.60–61. Pleasant, family-run B&B in an attractive Covent Garden street. Rooms (singles to quads) are small, but all are clean and simple and most are en suite. Free wi-fi. **£105**

## BLOOMSBURY AND KING'S CROSS

**Arosfa Hotel** 83 Gower St, WC1 ☎020 7636 2115, ⓦarosfalondon.com; ⊖Goodge Street or Euston Square; map p.71. Fifteen en-suite B&B rooms. Some are tiny, but this is a clean, comfy and reliable option. Full breakfast, and free wi-fi in the lounge. **£120**

**Grange Langham Court Hotel** 31–35 Langham St, W1 ☎020 7436 6622, ⓦgrangehotels.com; ⊖Oxford Circus; map p.71. The rooms are small, but they're clean and comfortable, and the price, for this location – in a quiet spot near Regent Street – is reasonable. **£130**

★**Ridgemount** 65–67 Gower St, WC1 ☎020 7636 1141, ⓦridgemounthotel.co.uk; ⊖Goodge Street; map p.71. Old-fashioned, cosy, family-run guesthouse, with small, clean rooms (15 of the 32 have shared facilities – which are spotless). A reliable, basic Bloomsbury bargain. Full breakfast and free wi-fi. **£82**

**Rough Luxe** 1 Birkenhead St, WC1 ☎020 7837 5338, ⓦroughluxe.co.uk; ⊖King's Cross; map pp.56–57. This funky six-room guesthouse offers comfort and shabby chic style. Each room is different, and the aesthetic – peeling plaster, original artworks – is stronger in some than others. Free wi-fi. **£190**

**St Pancras Renaissance Hotel** Euston Rd, NW1 ☎020 7841 3540, ⓦmarriott.co.uk; ⊖King's Cross; map pp.56–57. The old St Pancras station, George Gilbert Scott's Gothic Revival masterpiece, is now a glamorous *Marriott*. The lofty public spaces and colossal lobby evoke the golden era of railway travel, but not all the rooms are in the main building and the others, in an annexe, aren't worth the price. Check online for dramatic deals. **£275**

## CLERKENWELL AND THE CITY

**Apex City of London Hotel** 1 Seething Lane, EC3 ☎0845 365 0000, ⓦapexhotels.co.uk; ⊖Tower Hill; map pp.76–77. Swish business hotel on a secluded street near the Tower of London. Room rates vary according to availability, so book early. Free gym, sauna and steam room, and free wi-fi. The nearby *Apex London Wall* (7–9 Copthall Ave, EC2; Moorgate tube) has more of a boutique feel but similar rates. **£160**

**The King's Wardrobe** 6 Wardrobe Place, Carter Lane, EC4 ☎020 7792 2222, ⓦbridgestreet.com; ⊖St Paul's; map pp.76–77. In a quiet courtyard just behind St Paul's Cathedral, this place is part of an international chain that caters largely for a business clientele – the apartments offer fully equipped kitchens and workstations, concierge service and housekeeping. Though housed in a

fourteenth-century building that once contained Edward III's royal regalia, the interior is modern. **£185**

**The Rookery** 12 Peter's Lane, Cowcross St, EC1 ☎020 7336 0931, ⓦrookeryhotel.com; ⊖Farringdon; map pp.76–77. Rambling Georgian townhouse on the edge of the City, in trendy Clerkenwell, that makes a delightful little hideaway. Rooms offer faded Baroque glam, with antique fittings, characterful bathrooms and creaky floorboards. **£185**

★**The Zetter Hotel & Townhouse** 86–88 Clerkenwell Rd, EC1 ☎020 7324 4567, ⓦthezetter.com; ⊖Farringdon; map pp.76–77. Glamorous warehouse conversion with a laidback edge, with gorgeous, colourful rooms with lots of eco touches; the on-site *Bruno Loubet* brasserie is a popular spot. The Georgian *Townhouse*, across the square, is more whimsical, with thirteen boudoirish rooms and a cosy cocktail bar. Free wi-fi. **£150**

## THE EAST END

**Hoxton Hotel** 81 Great Eastern St, EC2 ☎020 7550 1000, ⓦhoxtonhotels.com; ⊖Old Street; map pp.76–77. "The Hox" remains a youthful stalwart in this once edgy (but hurtling rapidly towards the mainstream) neighbourhood, with exposed brick and contemporary art in the public spaces, and simple, modern rooms. Rates include a light breakfast, free wi-fi and an hour's local calls a day, and there's a hip and popular brasserie. Rates depend on availability and vary wildly. **£90**

**Shoreditch Rooms** Shoreditch House, Ebor St, E1 ☎020 7739 5040, ⓦshoreditchrooms.com; Shoreditch High St Overground; map pp.76–77. From the same stable as the *Dean Street Townhouse* (see opposite) this hip little place has the same no-nonsense room-naming policy, with 26 options from "Tiny" up to "Small-plus". Rooms may be small but they're lovely, with lots of fresh, sun-bleached colours and vintage style. Staying here also allows you to hangout with the beautiful people in the members' club next door. Free wi-fi. **£165**

## SOUTH BANK AND SOUTHWARK

**Southwark Rose Ibis Styles London** 43–47 Southwark Bridge Rd, SE1 ☎020 7015 1480, ⓦibis .com; ⊖London Bridge; map pp.84–85. The *Southwark Rose* is a good central, budget option with design touches that raise the rooms a little above the bland chain hotels in this area. Rooms are generally comfortable and clean, and a buffet breakfast is included in rates, which vary widely depending on availability. Free wi-fi. **£120**

★**Tune Westminster** 118–120 Westminster Bridge Rd, London SE1 ⓦtunehotels.com; ⊖Lambeth North or Waterloo; map p.82. Doing away with fuss like tables, chairs and closets keeps rates low at this London outpost of the Asian cheapie chain. The pricing policy is smart

**1**

– simply opt to pay for extras, including towels, TV, hairdryers or wi-fi, on the booking site. Rooms are small and modern. **£70**

### KENSINGTON AND EARL'S COURT

★**Aster House** 3 Sumner Place, SW7 ☎ 020 7581 5888, Ⓦ asterhouse.com; ⊖ South Kensington; map pp.90–91. Pleasant, award-winning B&B, in a luxurious South Ken white-stuccoed street; one of the rooms opens out onto the lovely garden, and there's a large conservatory where a buffet breakfast is served. **£200**

**Nadler Kensington** 25 Courtfield Gardens, SW5 ☎ 020 7244 2255, Ⓦ thenadler.com; ⊖ Earl's Court; map pp.90–91. Good-value accommodation, with no fussy extras. Rooms range from "bijou singles" to "deluxe"; all are comfortable, clean and quiet, modern and attractive, with mini-kitchens and free wi-fi. A good choice for groups and families. **£130**

**Twenty Nevern Square** 20 Nevern Square, SW5 ☎ 020 7565 9555, Ⓦ 20nevernsquare.com; ⊖ Earl's Court; map pp.90–91. In an area of bog-standard B&Bs, this is an inexpensive boutique hotel with some style. Rooms are en suite; some, however, are teensy. Buffet breakfast included. Free wi-fi. **£90**

**Vicarage Hotel** 10 Vicarage Gate, W8 ☎ 020 7229 4030, Ⓦ londonvicaragehotel.com; ⊖ Notting Hill Gate or High Street Kensington; map pp.90–91. Nicely located B&B on a residential street a step away from Kensington Gardens. Clean rooms; some have shared facilities and quads are available. A full English breakfast is included. Free wi-fi. **£112**

### PADDINGTON, BAYSWATER AND NOTTING HILL

**Portobello Gold** 95–97 Portobello Rd, W1 ☎ 020 7460 4910, Ⓦ portobellogold.com; ⊖ Notting Hill Gate or Holland Park; map pp.90–91. A friendly option with five basic rooms and a small apartment above a lively pub-restaurant. Rooms are plain, and some are tiny, with miniature en suites; the apartment sleeps six – at a pinch – and has a little roof terrace. Breakfast not included. Free wi-fi. **£75**

**Vancouver Studios** 30 Prince's Square, W2 ☎ 020 7243 1270, Ⓦ vancouverstudios.co.uk; ⊖ Bayswater; map pp.90–91. Self-contained, smallish self-catering studios in a grand old Victorian townhouse with maid service and a pretty walled garden. They also have a couple of apartments, sleeping up to six. Free wi-fi. **£140**

### NORTH LONDON

**Hampstead Village Guesthouse** 2 Kemplay Rd, NW3 ☎ 020 7435 8679, Ⓦ hampsteadguesthouse.com; ⊖ Hampstead. Prettily located on a quiet residential street between Hampstead Village and the Heath, this is an unconventional guesthouse in a family home. Rooms (most en suite) are full of character, crammed with books, pictures and personal mementos. Breakfast costs extra. Free wi-fi. **£105**

### HOSTELS

London's official Youth Hostel Association (YHA) hostels (Ⓦ yha.org.uk) are generally the cleanest, most efficiently run in the capital. However, they often charge more than private hostels, and tend to get booked up months in advance. Independent hostels are cheaper and more relaxed, but can be less reliable in terms of facilities – some are noisy, not that clean, and essentially little more than places to flop after partying all night. A good website for booking independent places online is Ⓦ hostellondon.com.

### YHA HOSTELS

★**Central** 104 Bolsover St, W1 ☎ 0845 371 9154, Ⓦ yha.org.uk; ⊖ Great Portland Street; map p.71. Excellent 300-bed hostel in a quiet West End spot, with a kitchen and café-bar. Free wi-fi for members. Dorms only (mostly en suite). No groups. Dorms **£33**

**Earl's Court** 38 Bolton Gardens, SW5 ☎ 0845 371 9114, Ⓦ yha.org.uk; ⊖ Earl's Court; map pp.90–91. Better than a lot of accommodation in Earl's Court, this 186-bed hostel has a kitchen and café and patio garden. Single-sex dorms and private rooms. Dorms **£24**, doubles **£80**

**Holland Park** Holland Walk, W8 ☎ 0845 371 9122, Ⓦ yha.org.uk; ⊖ Holland Park or High Street Kensington; map pp.90–91. Idyllically situated in Holland Park and fairly convenient for the centre. Kitchen and café. Popular with groups. Dorms **£22**

**Oxford Street** 14 Noel St, W1 ☎ 0845 371 9133, Ⓦ yha.org.uk; ⊖ Oxford Circus or Tottenham Court Road; map pp.60–61. The Soho location and relatively modest size mean this hostel tends to fill quickly. The atmosphere is party central rather than family-friendly. Private rooms available. Free wi-fi for members. Dorms **£36**, doubles **£80**

**St Pancras** 79–81 Euston Rd, NW1 ☎ 0845 371 9344, Ⓦ yha.org.uk; ⊖ King's Cross St Pancras; map pp.56–57. Modern hostel on a busy road, popular with families. Rooms are clean, bright, double-glazed and en suite. No kitchen, but there is a café. No groups. Dorms **£28**, doubles **£80**

**St Paul's** 36 Carter Lane, EC4 ☎ 0845 371 9012, Ⓦ yha.org.uk; ⊖ St Paul's; map pp.76–77. A 215-bed hostel in a superb location opposite St Paul's Cathedral. No kitchen, but it has a café for breakfast (included in rates) and dinner. Small groups only. Dorms **£32**, doubles **£65**

**Thameside** 20 Salter Rd, SE16 ☎ 0845 371 9756, Ⓦ yha.org.uk; ⊖ Rotherhithe; map pp.56–57. London's largest YHA hostel, with 320 beds, is in a quiet spot near the river. It can feel a bit of a trek from the centre, but it's near the 02, has a good pub next door and often has space. Self-catering available, and a restaurant serving breakfast and dinner. Dorms £25, doubles £50

### INDEPENDENT HOSTELS
**Clink 78** 78 King's Cross Rd, WC1 ☎020 7183 9400, ⓦclinkhostels.com; ⊖ King's Cross; map pp.56–57. This huge party hostel is run by the same folk as *Clink 261*, with funky decor, a lively bar, and plenty of features from the days when it was a Victorian courthouse – you can even stay in an old cell. Dorms (4–16 beds) can be cramped, though partitions on the "pod" bunks increase privacy; special girls-only dorms include mirrors and clothes hangers. Plus private rooms, some en suite. Kitchen. Breakfast included. Dorms £17, doubles £65
**Clink 261** 261–265 Gray's Inn Rd, WC1 ☎020 7833 9400, ⓦclinkhostels.com; ⊖King's Cross; map pp.56–57. Clean, smallish hostel in a converted office block near King's Cross Station, with laundry and kitchen

facilities. Mostly 4–10 beds, with some private rooms that sleep up to three. Breakfast included. Dorms £17, doubles £60
**Generator** 37 Tavistock Place, WC1 ☎020 7388 7666, ⓦgeneratorhostels.com; ⊖ Russell Square or Euston; map p.71. A huge, funky party hostel, with more than 850 beds and bright, clubby decor. Dorms (some women-only) have 4–12 beds, and there are singles, twins, triples and quads – some of which are en suite. There's a late-night bar, a café and a laundry, but no kitchen. Free wi-fi. Groups welcome. Dorms £20, doubles £75
★**Meininger** 65–67 Queen's Gate, SW7 ☎020 3318 1407, ⓦmeininger-hostels.com; ⊖Gloucester Road; map pp.90–91. Cheery, secure 48-room modern hostel near the South Ken museums, run by a German chain. Dorms (4–12 beds), some women-only, plus singles and doubles. No kitchen; breakfast costs £6. There's a laundry. You can save a lot of money by booking early online. Dorms £35, doubles £125

## EATING

London is a great city for eating out. You can sample any kind of **cuisine** here, from Georgian to Peruvian, Modern British to fusion. And it needn't be expensive – even in the fanciest restaurants, set menus (most often served at lunch) can be a great deal, and modish "sharing plates" can be a godsend if you want to cut costs. The city's dynamic **street food** scene, meanwhile, with food trucks, carts and pop-up stalls dishing up artisan food at low prices, offers an amazing diversity. Keep track of the ever-shifting scene on ⓦkerbfood.com

### CAFÉS AND SNACKS
While the old-fashioned London caffs are a dying breed, the city has plenty of great little places where you can get quick, filling and inexpensive meals – especially good at lunchtime, most of them are open in the evenings too. Bear in mind also that many pubs (see pp.116–120) serve food, from simple pub grub to haute cuisine.

### WESTMINSTER
**Café in the Crypt** St Martin-in-the-Fields, Duncannon St, WC2 ☎020 7766 1158, ⓦstmartin-in-the-fields .org; ⊖ Charing Cross; map pp.60–61. Comfort food, with lots of veggie dishes, in a handy (and atmospheric) location – below the church in the eighteenth-century crypt. On sunny summer days you might want to have a drink or light lunch in the separate *Café in the Courtyard*, in the terrace behind the church. Mon & Tues 8am–8pm, Wed 8am–10.30pm (live jazz after 8pm), Thurs–Sat 8am–9pm, Sun 11am–6pm.

### MAYFAIR AND MARYLEBONE
★**Comptoir Libanais** 65 Wigmore St, W1 ☎020 7935 1110, ⓦlecomptoir.co.uk; ⊖ Bond Street; map pp.90–91. This cheap and cheerful, kitsch and stylish Middle Eastern deli/diner serves crunchy falafels, herby Lavosh breads, tagines and patisserie. The home-made lemonades are delicious. Mains from around £6.

Mon–Sat 8am–11.30pm, Sun 9am–10.30pm.
**Momo** 25 Heddon St, W1 ☎020 7434 4040, ⓦmomoresto.com; ⊖Piccadilly Circus; map pp.60–61. Reasonably priced, tasty snacks, honey-soaked pastries and aromatic mint tea in a wonderful Arabic tearoom/terrace stuffed with Moroccan memorabilia. The attached restaurant is good fun, too. Mon–Fri 8am–1am, Sat 10am–1am, Sun noon–1am.
**Patisserie Valerie at Sagne** 105 Marylebone High St, W1 ☎020 7935 6240, ⓦpatisserie-valerie.co .uk;⊖ Bond Street; map pp.90–91. Opened in 1926, this café – one of the best in the chain – is among Marylebone's finest. You can get light lunches and snacks, but it's the cakes that are to die for. There's another good branch on Old Compton Street in Soho. Mon–Fri 7am–8pm, Sat 8am–8pm, Sun 8.30am–7pm.
★**The Wolseley** 160 Piccadilly, W1 ☎020 7499 6996, ⓦthewolseley.com; ⊖ Green Park; map pp.60–61. The European brasserie-style food is delicious, though pricey – come for breakfast or afternoon tea – in this grand old café/restaurant with a stunning 1920s interior. Mon–Fri 7am–midnight, Sat 8am–midnight, Sun 8am–11pm.

### SOHO AND CHINATOWN
★**Bar Italia** 22 Frith St, W1 ☎020 7437 4520, ⓦbaritaliasoho.co.uk; ⊖Leicester Square; map pp.60–61. Tiny espresso bar that's been a Soho institution

**1**

## MORE THAN JUST A CUPPA: AFTERNOON TEA

The classic English **afternoon tea** – assorted sandwiches, scones and cream, cakes and tarts, and, of course, lashings of leaf tea – is available all over London. The most popular venues are the top hotels and swanky department stores; you should count on spending around £40 a head and book well in advance. Most hotels will expect "smart casual attire"; only *The Ritz* insists on jacket and tie. Prices quoted here are for the standard teas; most places offer champagne teas, or more substantial high teas, for a higher price.

**Claridges** Brook St, W1 ☎020 7629 8860, ⊛claridges.co.uk; ⊖Bond Street; map pp.60–61. Daily 3pm, 3.30pm, 5pm & 5.30pm. £50.

**Fortnum & Mason** 181 Piccadilly, W1 ☎0845 602 5694, ⊛fortnumandmason.com; ⊖Green Park or Piccadilly Circus; map pp.60–61. Mon–Sat noon–9pm, Sun noon–8pm. £40.

**The Ritz** Piccadilly, W1 ☎020 7300 2345, ⊛theritzlondon.com; ⊖Green Park; map pp.60–61. Daily 11.30am, 1.30pm, 3.30pm, 5.30pm & 7.30pm. £47.

**The Wolseley** 160 Piccadilly, W1 ☎020 7499 6996, ⊛thewolseley.com; ⊖Green Park; map pp.60–61. Mon–Fri 3–6.30pm, Sat 3.30–5.30pm, Sun 3.30–6.30pm. £23.75.

since the 50s, keeping many of its original features (including the Gaggia coffee machine) and its iconic neon sign. Daily 7am–5am.

**Beatroot** 92 Berwick St, W1 ☎020 7437 8591, ⊛beatroot.org.uk; ⊖Piccadilly Circus, Oxford Circus or Tottenham Court Road; ; map pp.60–61. Great little veggie/vegan café by the market, doling out savoury bakes, stews and salads (plus good cakes) in boxes of varying sizes, from around a fiver. Mon–Fri 9am–9pm, Sat 11am–9pm.

**Breakfast Club** 33 D'Arblay St, W1 ☎020 7434 2571, ⊛thebreakfastclubcafes.com; ⊖Oxford Circus; map pp.60–61. Comfy, battered, cheery and tattily retro, this laidback place is a fun (and popular) spot to linger over big all-day breakfasts, brunches, wraps, burgers, burritos and the like. Other branches around town. Mon–Sat 8am–10pm, Sun 8am–7pm.

**Fernandez & Wells** 73 Beak St, W1 ☎020 287 8124, ⊛fernandezandwells.com; ⊖Piccadilly Circus or Oxford Circus; map pp.60–61. Fabulous, freshly prepared sandwiches, artisan coffee and tempting cakes – most people take away, but there are one or two tables. Other branches around town. Mon–Fri 7.30am–6pm, Sat & Sun 9am–6pm.

★**Maison Bertaux** 28 Greek St, W1 ☎020 7437 6007, ⊛maisonbertaux.com; ⊖Leicester Square; map pp.60–61. Long-standing, old-fashioned and *très* French patisserie, with two floors and some outdoor seating. The decor is pretty, the cakes are out of this world, and a loyal, lingering clientele keeps the place bustlling. Mon–Sat 9.30am–10pm, Sun 9.30am–8pm.

**Misato** 11 Wardour St, W1 ☎020 7734 0808; ⊖Leicester Square; map pp.60–61. Simple, canteen-style Japanese place serving filling rice and noodle dishes, plus hearty bento boxes and sushi, for low prices. Daily noon–10.30pm.

**Yalla Yalla** 1 Greens Court, W1 ☎020 7287 7663, ⊛yalla-yalla.co.uk; ⊖Piccadilly Circus; map pp.60–61. The name is Arabic for "hurry, hurry!", and the ambience in this hole-in-the-wall is buzzy and fast. The Beirut street food includes good-value veggie meze and plenty of nicely spiced skewered meats. Meze from £3. Branches in Shoreditch and Fitzrovia. Mon–Fri 10am–11.30pm, Sat 11am–11pm.

### COVENT GARDEN

★**Food for Thought** 31 Neal St, WC2 ☎020 7836 0239, ⊛foodforthought-london.co.uk; ⊖Covent Garden; map pp.60–61. This minuscule veggie restaurant and takeaway has been dishing up hearty veggie/vegan soups, salads, hot dishes and desserts for some forty years, from a menu that changes twice daily. It's a crush at peak times. Mon–Sat noon–8.30pm, Sun noon–5.30pm.

**Homeslice** 13 Neal's Yard, WC2 ☎020 7836 4604, ⊛homeslicepizza.co.uk; ⊖Covent Garden; map pp.60–61. Funky little spot, which started its days as a streetfood truck, offering wood-fired thin-crust gourmet pizzas plus Prosecco on tap. £4 per slice, £20 for a 20" pizza. Mon–Sat noon–11pm, Sun noon–6pm.

**Rock & Sole Plaice** 47 Endell St, WC2 ☎020 7836 3785; ⊖Covent Garden; map pp.60–61. A rare survivor; a traditional fish-and-chip shop in central London. The fish is tasty, though not cheap. Eat in or at a pavement table, or take away. Daily noon–10.30pm.

### BLOOMSBURY

★**Diwana Bhel Poori House** 121–123 Drummond St, NW1 ☎020 7387 5556; ⊖Euston; map p.71. On a street lined with good Indian restaurants, this South Indian vegetarian diner wins for its scrumptious all-you-can-eat lunchtime buffets (daily; £6.95) and huge, fresh thalis (from £7). BYOB. Mon–Sat noon–10.30pm, Sun noon–9.30pm.

**Hummus Bros** 37–63 Southampton Row, WC1 ☎020 7404 7079, ⓦhbros.co.uk; ⊖Holborn; map p.71. Tiny "hummus bar"/takeaway, with a couple of benches and formica tables, offering hummus with warm pitta and toppings from guacamole to chunky beef, plus salads and falafels. From £4. Mon–Fri 11am–9pm.

### THE EAST END AND DALSTON

**Brick Lane Beigel Bake** 159 Brick Lane, E1 ☎020 7729 0616; ⊖Shoreditch High Street Overground; map pp.76–77. Classic bagel takeaway in the heart of the East End – very cheap, even for your top-end filling, smoked salmon and cream cheese. Daily 24hr.

**Café 1001** 91 Brick Lane, E1 ☎020 7247 6166, ⓦcafe1001.co.uk; ⊖Whitechapel or Shoreditch High Street Overground; map pp.76–77. This café-bar/club has kept going right through the East End's gentrification, and still keeps its laidback atmosphere, with sofas to crash on, used books to read and simple snacks and fattening cakes to sample. Frequent DJ sets and comedy nights. Daily 6am–midnight.

**Fabrique** Arch 385, Geffrye St, E2 ☎020 7033 0268, ⓦfabrique.co.uk; Hoxton Overground; map pp.56–57. Come to this simple, pretty Scandinavian bakery for spicy cinnamon buns, stone-oven-baked sourdough breads, cream cakes and Johan & Nyström coffee. Mon–Fri 8am–6pm, Sat & Sun 9am–6pm.

**Prufrock Coffee** 23–25 Leather Lane, EC1 ☎020 7242 0467, ⓦprufrockcoffee.com; ⊖Chancery Lane or Farringdon; map pp.76–77. This pared-down shrine to the coffee bean, brainchild of world barista champion Gwilym Davies, pioneered London's artisan coffee craze and still outdoes its rivals. Mon–Fri 8am–6pm, Sat & Sun 10am–5pm.

**Voodoo Ray's** 95 Kingsland High St, E8 ☎020 7249 7865, ⓦvoodoorays.co.uk; Dalston Junction Overground; map pp.56–57. Grungy late-night joints come and go in Dalston, but *Voodoo Ray's* seems set to stay – a post-party pizza/Margarita joint where the pizzas (from £3.50/slice) are huge and the Margaritas – usually being necked by a crowd who've had quite enough already – are strong. Mon–Wed & Sun 5pm–midnight, Thurs 5pm–1am, Fri 5pm–3am, Sat noon–3pm.

### THE CITY, DOCKLANDS AND THE EAST END

★**Café Below** Church of St Mary-le-Bow, Cheapside, EC2 ☎020 7329 0789, ⓦcafebelow.co.uk; ⊖St Paul's or Bank; map pp.76–77. A City gem: a cosy, good-value café in a Norman church crypt, serving modern Mediterranean food, with lots of veggie choices, and sticky breakfast pastries. Mains from £6. Mon–Fri 7.30am–2.30pm.

**Hubbub** 269 Westferry Rd, E14 ☎020 7515 5577, ⓦhubbubcafebar.com; Mudchute DLR; map pp.56–57. A real find in the otherwise drab Docklands eating scene,

this café-bar is housed in a former Victorian church, now an arts centre, and does decent burgers, sandwiches and tapas. Mon–Wed noon–11pm, Thurs & Fri noon–midnight, Sat 10am–midnight, Sun 10am–10.30pm.

### THE SOUTH BANK AND SOUTHWARK

**Maltby Street Market** Maltby St ⓦmaltby.st; ⊖London Bridge; map pp.56–57. Edgier and less expensive than nearby Borough Market, this street-food hot spot huddles under the railway arches south of Tower Bridge, with stalls, food carts and pop-ups serving everything from Mozambique sauces to artisan gin. Most action is on the lively Ropewalk. Sat 9am–4pm, Sun 11am–4pm.

**Marsh Ruby** 30 Lower Marsh, SE1 ☎020 7620 0593, ⓦmarshruby.com; ⊖Waterloo; map p.82. Terrific filling lunchtime curries for around a fiver: the food, on seasonally changing menus, is mostly organic/free range and the communal dining is basic but cheery. Mon–Fri 11.30am–3pm.

### KENSINGTON, CHELSEA AND NOTTING HILL

**Books for Cooks** 4 Blenheim Crescent, W11 ☎020 7221 1992, ⓦwww.booksforcooks.com; ⊖Ladbroke Grove or Notting Hill Gate; map pp.90–91. Tiny café within London's top cookery bookshop. Get there in time to grab a table for the set-menu lunch (noon–1.30pm). Tues–Sat 10am–6pm.

**Capote y Toros** 157 Old Brompton Rd, SW5 ☎020 7373 0567, ⓦcamblodetercio.co.uk; ⊖Gloucester Rd or South Kensington; map pp.90–91. The emphasis at this sunny bar is on Spain's wonderful sherries, with more than forty available by the glass, along with interesting tapas (£5–12). Tues–Sat 6–11.30pm.

★**Lisboa Patisserie** 57 Golborne Rd, W10 ☎020 8968 5242; ⊖Westbourne Park; map pp.90–91. Friendly, bustling Portuguese *pastelaria* selling the best custard tarts this side of Lisbon – along with coffee and a variety of cakes. *Café Oporto* at 62a Golborne Road is a good fallback if this place is full. Daily 7.30am–7.30pm.

### NORTH LONDON

**Brew House** Kenwood House, Hampstead Lane, NW3; ⊖Highgate. Handy café serving everything from full English breakfasts to gourmet sandwiches, cakes and teas, either in the house's old servants' wing or in the huge, sunny garden courtyard. Daily: spring & summer 9am–6pm; rest of year 9am–4pm.

★**Louis Patisserie** 32 Heath St, NW3 ☎020 7435 9908; ⊖Hampstead. For more than fifty years now this tiny, understated, and gloriously old-fashioned Hungarian tearoom/patisserie has been serving sticky cakes, tea and coffee to Heath-bound hordes and elderly locals. Daily 9am–6pm.

**1**

## WEST LONDON

**Pembroke Lodge** Richmond Park, Richmond TW10 ☎020 8940 8207, ⓦpembroke-lodge.co.uk; ⊖Richmond. In a gorgeous Georgian mansion in Richmond Park, this café has one of the best views in London and nice outdoor seating – there are some hot dishes, plus sandwiches and cakes. Daily 9am–5.30pm or 30min before dusk.

## RESTAURANTS

### MAYFAIR AND MARYLEBONE

★**Dehesa** 25 Ganton St, W1 ☎020 7494 4170, ⓦdehesa.co.uk; ⊖Oxford Circus or Piccadilly Circus; map pp.60–61. Very classy Spanish-Italian charcuterie and tapas bar serving rustic, robust food – try deep-fried courgette flowers with goat's cheese and honey, or salt cod croquettes, or just enjoy a plate of *jamón Ibérico* and a glass of Albariño. Tapas £5–10. Mon–Fri noon–3pm & 5–11pm, Sat noon–11pm, Sun noon–10pm.

**The Providores and Tapa Room** 109 Marylebone High St, W1 ☎020 7935 6175, ⓦtheprovidores.co.uk; ⊖Baker Street or Bond Street; map pp.90–91. Outstanding fusion restaurant, co-helmed by New Zealand celeb chef Peter Gordon, with the more casual, cheaper *Tapa Room* café downstairs. Mon–Fri 9am–10.30pm, Sat 9am–3pm & 4–10.30pm, Sun 9am–3pm & 4–10pm.

### SOHO AND CHINATOWN

**Mildred's** 45 Lexington St, W1 ☎020 7494 1634, ⓦmildreds.co.uk; ⊖Oxford Circus or Piccadilly Circus; map pp.60–61. *Mildred's* has a fresher and more contemporary feel than many veggie restaurants, and serves creative global cuisine. It's petite, and can get very busy, but takes no bookings. Mains £8–12. Mon–Sat noon–11pm.

★**Mr Kong** 21 Lisle St, WC2 ☎020 7437 7341, ⓦmrkongrestaurant.com; ⊖Leicester Square; map pp.60–61. Chinatown stalwart, with a very long menu of Cantonese food – don't miss the mussels in black bean sauce – and a good range of veggie dishes. Mains £7–25. Mon–Sat noon–2.45am, Sun noon–1.45am.

**Polpo** 41 Beak St, W1 ☎020 7734 4479, ⓦpolpo.co.uk; ⊖Piccadilly Circus; map pp.60–61. Warm, well-established restaurant modelled on a Venetian *bacaro*. Small plates from £3 – try grilled fennel with white anchovy, *pizzette* or any of the *polpette* (meatballs). Reservations for lunch only. Mon–Sat noon–11pm, Sun noon–4pm.

**Tonkotsu** 63 Dean St, W1 ☎020 7437 0071, ⓦtonkotsu.co.uk; ⊖Tottenham Court Road; pp.60–61. Slurpable, silky home-made ramen noodles in rich, savoury stocks, with pork belly, smoked haddock or veggie options. From £9. Mon–Fri noon–3pm & 5–10.30pm, Sat noon–10.30pm, Sun noon–10pm.

## COVENT GARDEN

**Dishoom** 12 Upper St Martin's Lane, WC2 ☎020 7420 9320, ⓦdishoom.com; ⊖Leicester Square or Covent Garden; map pp.60–61. Recreating the atmosphere of the Persian cafés of Old Bombay, *Dishoom* is witty and stylish, but most importantly, serves delicious food – don't miss the black dhal. Mains from £6.50, small dishes for less. Mon–Thurs 8am–11pm, Fri 8am–midnight, Sat 9am–midnight, Sun 9am–11pm.

**Flesh & Buns** 41 Earlham St, WC2 ☎020 7632 9500, ⓦfleshandbuns.com; ⊖Covent Garden; map pp.60–61. The boozy, hipster rock'n'roll vibe at this noisy Japanese izakaya-style basement restaurant belies the superlative quality of the food: the rice buns of the name are the stars here, served with succulent meat or delicious fish – perfect to soak up huge quantities of sake. Mon & Tues noon–3pm & 5–10.30pm, Wed–Fri noon–3pm & 5–11.30pm, Sat noon–11.30pm, Sun noon–9.30pm.

**Kopapa** 32–34 Monmouth St, WC2 ☎020 7240 6076, ⓦkopapa.co.uk; ⊖Covent Garden; map pp.60–61. Fusion food from the Kiwi team behind *Providores* (see opposite). Dishes like tempura spicy dahl-stuffed inari pocket on caramelised coconut with pickled green papaya offer fresh, complex flavours; many are designed to share. Small plates from £6. Good breakfasts and brunches, too. Mon–Fri 8.30–11.30am & noon–11pm, Sat 9.30am–4pm & 4.30–11pm, Sun 9.30am–4pm & 4.30–9.45pm.

## BLOOMSBURY

★**Caravan** 1 Granary Square, N1C ☎020 7101 7661, ⓦcaravankingscross.co.uk; ⊖King's Cross St Pancras; map pp.56–57. A trailblazer on the burgeoning King's Cross scene, this buzzy spot, occupying a huge old grain store, serves tempting Modern European/fusion breakfasts, brunches, small plates and coffee to a lively crowd, many of them from the next-door St Martin's School of Art. Small plates from £5. Mon & Tues 8am–10.30pm, Wed & Thurs 8am–11pm, Fri 8am–midnight, Sat 10am–midnight, Sun 10am–4pm.

**Cigala** 54 Lamb's Conduit St, WC1 ☎020 7405 1717, ⓦcigala.co.uk; ⊖Russell Square; map p.71. Simple dishes, robust flavours and Spanish flair at this sophisticated Iberian restaurant with daily changing menus. Mains from £12; two-/three-course set lunch menus £17.50/£19.50; tapas from £4. Mon–Fri noon–10.45pm, Sat 12.30–10.45pm, Sun 12.30–9.45pm.

## THE CITY AND CLERKENWELL

**Duck and Waffle** Heron Tower, 110 Bishopsgate, EC2 ☎020 3640 7310, ⓦduckandwaffle.com; ⊖Aldgate; map pp.76–77. Forty floors up, this smart place offers amazing City views and hipster comfort food (the signature dish features waffles, duck confit, fried duck egg and mustard maple syrup; £17). Small plates from £9. Daily 24hr.

★**Moro** 34–36 Exmouth Market, EC1 ☎020 7833 8336, ⓦmoro.co.uk; ⊖Farringdon or Angel; map pp.76–77. Gorgeous, welcoming restaurant that's a place of pilgrimage for disciples of Sam and Sam Clark's Moorish/Iberian cookbooks. The lamb dishes and the yoghurt cake are perennial hits, but all of it is tremendous, prepared with unusual ingredients. Booking essential. Mains £16–21, with tapas (around £5) served all day; they also have a tiny tapas bar, *Morito*, next door (where reservations are taken for lunch only). Mon–Sat noon–10.30pm, Sun 12.30–2.45pm.

**Quality Chop House** 88–94 Farringdon Rd, EC1 ☎020 7278 1452, ⓦthequalitychophouse.com; ⊖Farringdon; map pp.76–77. Beautiful old dining room, butcher's and slightly more casual wine bar with a daily changing menu focusing on the best cuts of British meat and freshest British produce. It's not cheap (weekday lunch mains from £13), but you can get set menus at dinner (£35) and Sun lunch (£28). Mon–Sat noon–3pm & 6–10.30pm, Sun noon–4pm; wine bar Mon–Sat noon–midnight.

**St John Bread and Wine** 94–96 Commercial St, E1 ☎020 7251 0848, ⓦstjohnbreadandwine.com; ⊖Liverpool Street; map pp.76–77. A simpler offshoot of the famed *St John*, with the same superlative British food on a regularly changing menu – featuring offal, pig's cheek and the like, but also wonderful veg and fish dishes, and simple breakfasts. Dishes £5–18. Mon–Fri 9–11am, noon–3pm & 6–11pm, Sat 9–11am, noon–4pm & 6–11pm, Sun 9 11am, noon–4pm & 6–9pm.

### THE EAST END AND DALSTON

**Beagle** 397–400 Geffrye St, E2 ☎020 7613 2967, ⓦbeaglelondon.co.uk; ⊖Hoxton; map pp.56–57. Occupying three railway arches, this Hoxton restaurant buzzes with a young crowd enjoying robust Modern British food and fashionable cocktails. Mains from £10. Mon & Tues 6–10.30pm, Wed–Fri noon–3pm & 6–10.30pm, Sat 11am–3pm & 6–10.30pm, Sun 11am–5pm.

**The Hawksmoor** 157 Commercial St, E1 ☎020 7426 4850, ⓦthehawksmoor.com; ⊖Liverpool Street or Shoreditch High Street Overground; map pp.76–77. Carnivores drool at the mention of this steakhouse, where the charcoal-grilled cuts of meat, impeccably sourced, are huge and succulent. A full meal could set you back well over £50, but the two-/three-course menu (Mon–Sat noon–3pm & 5–6pm) cuts costs at £23/£26. Mon–Sat noon–2.30pm & 5–10.30pm, Sun noon–4.30pm.

**Lahore Kebab House** 2–10 Umberston St, E1 ☎020 7481 9737, ⓦlahore-kebabhouse.com; ⊖Aldgate East; map pp.76–77. Famed Punjabi kebab house, just off Commercial Road. Go for the lamb cutlets and roti, and arrive hungry. BYOB. Mains £7–11. Daily noon–1am.

**Sông Quê** 134 Kingsland Rd, E2 ☎020 7613 3222, ⓦsongque.co.uk; Hoxton station; map pp.56–57. In a street crammed with budget Vietnamese restaurants, this simple place offers good *phô* (£8.50) and spicy seafood dishes. Mon–Fri noon–3pm & 5.30–11pm, Sat noon–11pm, Sun noon–10.30pm.

★**Tayyab's** 83–89 Fieldgate St, E1 ☎020 7247 9543, ⓦtayyabs.co.uk; ⊖Whitechapel; map pp.76–77. For more than forty years *Tayyab's* has been offering straightforward Punjabi food: good, freshly cooked and served without pretension. Prices have remained low (mains from £7) and booking is essential. BYOB. Daily noon–11.30pm.

**Tonkotsu East** Arch 334, 1a Dunston St, E8 ☎020 7254 2478, ⓦtonkotsu.co.uk; ⊖Haggerston; map pp.56–57. The Dalston branch of Soho's favourite Japanese noodle joint serves the same rich, silky home-made noodles in oily, savoury stocks, plus dumplings and *gyoza*, to a local hipster crowd sipping cocktails to while away what can be a long wait for a table. Mon 5–10pm, Tues–Fri noon–3pm & 5–10pm, Sat noon–10pm, Sun noon–9.30pm.

### SOUTHBANK AND SOUTHWARK

**The Laughing Gravy** 154 Blackfriars Rd, SE1 ☎020 7998 1701, ⓦthelaughinggravy.co.uk; ⊖Southwark; map p.82. Welcoming, cosy brasserie serving robust Modern English and Mediterranean food in a brick-lined dining room; a great find in this neck of the woods. Mon–Thurs noon–3pm & 5–10pm, Fri noon–3pm & 5–10.30pm, Sat noon–4pm & 5–10.30pm, Sun noon–4.30pm.

**Zucca** 184 Bermondsey St, SE1 ☎020 7378 6809, ⓦzuccalondon.com; ⊖London Bridge; map pp.56–57. Prices for the elegant modern Italian food in this lovely restaurant – fresh pasta, creamy risottos, grilled shellfish, all made with the freshest, simplest ingredients – are surprisingly low. Mains from £11. Tues–Fri noon–3pm & 6–10pm, Sat noon–3.30pm & 6–10pm, Sun noon–4pm.

### KENSINGTON AND CHELSEA

★**Dinner by Heston Blumenthal** Mandarin Oriental Hotel, 66 Knightsbridge, SW1 ☎020 7201 3833, ⓦdinnerbyheston.com; ⊖Knightsbridge; map pp.90–91. Blumenthal doesn't actually cook here – the head chef worked with him at the *Fat Duck* – and there is less emphasis on flashy molecular cuisine, but the creative food, using old English recipes, is as intriguing as you would expect – try the spiced pigeon and the tipsy cake. Mains from £28; the three-course weekday lunch menu (£38) is a bargain. Daily noon–2.30pm & 6.30–10.30pm.

1

**Medlar** 438 Kings Rd, SW10 ☎020 7349 1900, ⓦmedlarrestaurant.co.uk; ⊖Fulham Broadway; map pp.90–91. Lovely Michelin-starred place offering French-influenced Modern British food – duck breast and confit with puy lentils, beetroot, mustard fruits and paysanne salad, for example – in a relaxed dining room. It's all prix fixe, and good value, with three-course lunches (£27 Mon–Fri, £30 Sat, £35 Sun) and dinners (£45 Mon–Sat, £35 Sun). Daily noon–3pm & 6.30–10.30pm.

### BAYSWATER AND NOTTING HILL

**Le Café Anglais** 8 Porchester Gardens, W2 ☎020 7221 1415, ⓦlecafeanglais.co.uk; ⊖Bayswater; map pp.90–91. Splendid Modern British/European brasserie and oyster bar in an airy, vaguely Art Deco space – hard to believe you're in the bland Whiteley's shopping mall. Mains £14–28; set lunch menus (two/three courses) from £10. Mon–Thurs noon–3.30pm & 6.30–10.30pm, Fri noon–3.30pm & 6.30–11pm, Sat 11am–3.30pm & 6.30–11pm, Sun noon–3.30pm & 6.30–10pm.

**Hereford Road** 3 Hereford Rd, W2 ☎020 7727 1144, ⓦherefordroad.org; ⊖Queensway/Notting Hill Gate; map pp.90–91. St John alumni Tom Pemberton brings highly accomplished English cooking to West London, with the focus on old-fashioned excellence and the best produce. Mains from £11.50, and bargain set meals, from £9.50, on weekday lunchtimes. Mon–Sat noon–3pm & 6–10.30pm, Sun noon–4pm & 6–10pm.

### NORTH LONDON

**Jin Kichi** 73 Heath St, NW3 ☎020 7794 6158, ⓦwww .jinkichi.com; ⊖Hampstead. Tiny, homely and very busy neighbourhood Japanese diner specializing in charcoal-grilled yakitori (skewers): lots of chicken, of course, but also

quails' eggs or ox tongue, among others. Tues–Sat 12.30–2pm & 6–10.45pm, Sun 12.30–2pm & 6–10pm.

**Manna** 4 Erskine Rd, NW3 ☎020 7722 8028, ⓦmannav.com; ⊖Chalk Farm; map pp.56–57. Upscale veggie restaurant, full of Primrose Hill yoga bunnies, serving large portions of mostly organic food, much of it vegan, from around the world. Mains £12–14. Tues–Fri noon–3pm & 6.30–10pm, Sat noon–3pm & 6–10pm, Sun noon–8.30pm.

**Namaaste Kitchen** 64 Parkway ☎020 7485 5977, ⓦnamaastekitchen.co.uk; ⊖Camden Town; map pp.56–57. Superb contemporary Indian and Pakistani restaurant, presenting unusual dishes from spicy crab-and-cod cakes to wild rabbit achari, plus a gluten-free menu. Mains £9–17, set menu £10. Mon–Thurs noon–2.30pm & 5.30–11.30pm, Fri & Sat noon–11.30pm, Sun noon–11pm.

### SOUTH LONDON

**Old Brewery** Pepys Building, Old Royal Naval College, SE10 ☎0203 327 1280, ⓦoldbrewerygreenwich.com; Cutty Sark DLR. The café of the Meantime craft brewery serves light meals during the day before transforming into a more expensive Modern British brasserie in the evening. Daily 11am–11pm.

### WEST LONDON

**Chez Lindsay** 11 Hill Rise, Richmond TW10 ☎020 8948 7473, ⓦchezlindsay.co.uk; ⊖Richmond. Small, bright Breton restaurant, serving galettes, crêpes and more formal French main courses, including lots of fresh fish and shellfish. Galettes from £4, mains £11–23. Mon–Sat noon–11pm, Sun noon–10pm.

## DRINKING

### WESTMINSTER

**The Chandos** 29 St Martin's Lane, W1 ☎020 7836 1401; ⊖Charing Cross; map pp.60–61. If you can get one of the booths downstairs, or the leather sofas upstairs in the more relaxed Opera Room Bar, then you'll find it difficult to leave, especially given the cheap Sam Smith's beer. Mon–Sat 11am–11pm, Sun noon–10.30pm.

★**St Stephen's Tavern** 10 Bridge St, SW1 ☎020 7925 2286, ⓦststephenstavern.co.uk; ⊖Westminster; map pp.60–61. Opulent Victorian pub, built in 1867, wall to wall with civil servants and MPs, and serving good real ales. Mon–Fri 11am–11pm, Sat 11am–8pm, Sun noon–6pm.

### ST JAMES'S, MAYFAIR AND MARYLEBONE

**Guinea** 30 Bruton Place, W1 ☎020 7409 1728, ⓦtheguinea.co.uk; ⊖Bond Street or Oxford Circus; map pp.60–61. Pretty, old-fashioned, flower-strewn

back-lane pub, serving good Young's bitter and excellent steak-and-kidney pies. Invariably packed to its tiny rafters. There's a traditional steak restaurant attached. Mon–Fri 11am–11pm, Sat 6–11pm.

**ICA Bar** The Mall, SW1 ☎020 7930 8619, ⓦica.org.uk; ⊖Piccadilly Circus or Charing Cross; map pp.60–61. Cool drinking venue in the contemporary gallery, popular with an arty crowd. Tues evenings (6–7.30pm) see buy-one-get-one-free deals on cocktails. Tues–Sun 11am–11pm.

**Red Lion** 23 Crown Passage, SW1 ☎020 7930 4141; ⊖Green Park; map pp.60–61. Hidden away in a passageway off Pall Mall, this is a genuinely warm and cosy local, with super-friendly bar staff, well-kept beer and above-average sandwiches. Mon–Sat 11.30am–11pm.

**The Windmill** 6–8 Mill St, W1 ☎020 7491 8050, ⓦwindmillmayfair.co.uk; ⊖Oxford Circus; map pp.60–61. Convivial pub just off Regent St, a perfect retreat for exhausted shoppers. The Young's beers are good, as are the pies, for which the pub has won numerous awards. Mon–Fri 11am–11pm, Sat noon–5pm.

## SOHO

**Argyll Arms** 18 Argyll St, W1 ☎020 7734 6117, Ⓦnicholsonspubs.co.uk; ⊖Oxford Circus; map pp.60–61. Mobbed by shoppers and tourists alike, but this Nicholson's pub has preserved many features of its Victorian interior and offers a good range of real ales. Mon–Thurs 10am–11.30pm, Fri & Sat 10am–midnight, Sun 10am–11pm.

**Dog & Duck** 18 Bateman St, W1 ☎020 7494 0697, Ⓦnicholsonspubs.co.uk; ⊖Tottenham Court Road; map pp.60–61. Tiny Nicholson's corner pub that retains much of its old character, beautiful Victorian tiling and mosaics, a choice of real ales and typically mixed Soho clientele. If it gets too busy downstairs, head upstairs to the George Orwell Bar (he used to drink here). Daily 10am–11pm.

**LAB** 12 Old Compton St, W1 ☎020 7437 7820, Ⓦlabbaruk.com; ⊖Leicester Square; map pp.60–61. Two-floor bar with a clubby feel where cocktail-school graduates serve up classics and new concoctions. DJs Thurs–Sat. Mon–Sat 4pm–midnight, Sun 4–10.30pm.

★**The Social** 5 Little Portland St, W1 ☎020 7636 4992, Ⓦthesocial.com; ⊖Oxford Circus; map p.71. Retro club/bar and diner, with DJs playing everything from afro to electronica, and a genuinely hedonistic, hard-partying crowd. Mon–Wed noon–midnight, Thurs & Fri 9am–1am, Sat 6pm–1am.

## COVENT GARDEN AND STRAND

★**Cross Keys** 31 Endell St, WC2 ☎020 7836 5185, Ⓦcrosskeyscoventgarden.com; ⊖Covent Garden; map pp.60–61. Stuffed with copper pots, and memorabilia, and fronted with a profusion of flowers, this most welcoming of West End pubs attracts an appealing blend of older Covent Garden residents, young workers and tourists. Mon–Sat 11am–11pm, Sun noon–10.30pm.

★**Gordon's** 47 Villiers St, WC2 ☎020 7930 1408, Ⓦgordonswinebar.com; ⊖Charing Cross or Embankment; map pp.60–61. Cavernous, shabby, atmospheric wine bar specializing in ports, sherries and Madeiras. The genial atmosphere makes this a favourite with local office workers, who spill outdoors in the summer. Mon–Sat 11am–11pm, Sun noon–10pm.

**Lamb & Flag** 33 Rose St, WC2 ☎020 7497 9504, Ⓦlambandflagcoventgarden.co.uk; ⊖Leicester Square; map pp.60–61. Over 300 years old, this agreeably tatty Fuller's pub, tucked away down an alley between Garrick and Floral streets, is invariably packed. Mon–Thurs 11am–11pm, Fri & Sat 11am–11.30pm, Sun noon–10.30pm.

**The Salisbury** 90 St Martin's Lane, WC2 ☎020 7836 5863, Ⓦtaylor-walker.co.uk; ⊖Leicester Square; map pp.60–61. Beautifully preserved Victorian pub, run by Taylor Walker, with etched and engraved windows, bronze figurines and Art Nouveau fittings. Mon–Wed 11am–11pm, Thurs 11am–11.30pm, Fri 11am–midnight, Sat noon–midnight, Sun noon–10.30pm.

## BLOOMSBURY

**The Duke** 7 Roger St, WC1 ☎020 7242 7230, Ⓦdukepub.co.uk; ⊖Russell Square; map p.71. Lovely little neighbourhood gastropub, without the pretensions often associated with the breed, and an authentic Art Deco bent to the decor. Its discreet location keeps the crowd in the small bar manageable. Mon–Sat noon–11pm.

**The Lamb** 94 Lamb's Conduit St, WC1 ☎020 7405 0713, Ⓦyoungs.co.uk; ⊖Russell Square; map p.71. This marvellously well-preserved Victorian pub, serving Young's ales, is packed with atmosphere with its old mirrors, gleaming dark wood and etched glass "snob" screens. Check out the intriguing old sepia photos lining the walls. Mon–Wed noon–11pm, Thurs & Fri noon–midnight, Sat 11am–midnight, Sun noon–10.30pm.

**Museum Tavern** 49 Great Russell St, WC1 ☎020 7242 8987, Ⓦtaylor-walker.co.uk; ⊖Tottenham Court Road or Russell Square; map p.71. Karl Marx's erstwhile drinking hole is a handsome old Taylor Walker pub opposite the main entrance to the British Museum. Mon–Thurs 11am–11.30pm, Fri & Sat 11am–midnight, Sun 10am–10pm.

## HOLBORN

**Princess Louise** 209 High Holborn, WC1 ☎020 7405 8816, Ⓦprincesslouisepub.co.uk; ⊖Holborn; map p.71. Architecturally, one of London's most impressive Victorian pubs, featuring gold-trimmed mirrors, gorgeous mosaics and a fine moulded ceiling. Even the toilets are listed. The Sam Smith's beer is reasonably priced, too. Mon–Fri 11am–11pm, Sat noon–11pm, Sun noon–6.45pm.

**Ye Olde Mitre** 1 Ely Court, EC1 ☎020 7405 4751, Ⓦyeoldemitreholborn.co.uk; ⊖Farringdon; map pp.76–77. Hidden down a tiny alleyway off Hatton Garden, this atmospheric Fuller's pub dates back to 1546; the low-ceilinged, wood-panelled rooms are packed with history and the ales are good. Mon–Fri 11am–11pm.

## CLERKENWELL

★**Jerusalem Tavern** 55 Britton St, EC1 ☎020 7490 4281, Ⓦstpetersbrewery.co.uk; ⊖Farringdon; map pp.76–77. Something special: a tiny, converted Georgian coffee house – the frontage dates from 1810 – that has retained much of its original character. Better still, the excellent draught beers are from St Peter's Brewery in Suffolk. Mon–Fri 11am–11pm.

**1**

**The Three Kings** 7 Clerkenwell Close, EC1 ☎ 020 7253 0483; ⊖ Farringdon; map pp.76–77. This Clerkenwell favourite is tucked away just north of Clerkenwell Green, with a delightful eclectic interior and two small rooms upstairs perfect for long occupation. Right next to *The Crown*, on Clerkenwell Green itself, which is also well worth a trip. Mon–Fri noon–11pm, Sat 5.30–11pm.

### THE CITY

★**The Black Friar** 174 Queen Victoria St, EC4 ☎ 020 7236 5474, ⓦ nicholsonspubs.co.uk; ⊖ Blackfriars; map pp.76–77. Quirky old Nicholson's pub with Art Nouveau marble friezes of boozy monks and a highly decorated alcove – all original, dating from 1905. A lovely fireplace and an unhurried atmosphere make this a relaxing place to drink. Mon–Sat 10am–11pm, Sun noon–10.30pm.

**The Counting House** 50 Cornhill, EC2 ☎ 020 7283 7123, ⓦ the-counting-house.com; ⊖ Bank; map pp.76–77. Inspired Fuller's conversion, of an old bank, with a magnificent interior featuring high ceilings, marble pillars, mosaic flooring and a large, oval island bar. Mon–Fri 11am–11pm.

**The Lamb Tavern** 10–12 Leadenhall Market, EC3 ☎ 020 7626 2454, ⓦ lambtavernleadenhall.com; ⊖ Monument; map pp.76–77. In the heart of beautiful Leadenhall Market, this Young's pub offers almost exclusively standing room only (both inside and out). The tiled *Tom's Bar* downstairs can be cosier, and offers cheese and sausage platters. Mon–Fri 11am–11pm.

★**Ye Olde Cheshire Cheese** Wine Office Court, 145 Fleet St, EC4 ☎ 020 7353 6170; ⊖ Temple or Blackfriars; map pp.76–77. This seventeenth-century watering hole – the haunt of eminent historical figures including Dickens and Dr Johnson – has several snug, dark-panelled bars and real fires. Popular with tourists, but by no means exclusively so. Mon–Fri 11.30am–11pm, Sat noon–11pm.

### THE EAST END AND DOCKLANDS

**The Gun** 27 Coldharbour, E14 ☎ 020 7515 5222, ⓦ thegundocklands.com; ⊖ Canary Wharf, South Quay or Blackwall DLR. Legendary dockers' pub, once the haunt of Lord Nelson, *The Gun* is now a classy gastropub, with unrivalled views over to the O2. Mon–Sat 11am–midnight, Sun 11am–11pm.

**Loungelover** 1 Whitby St, E1 ☎ 020 7012 1234, ⓦ loungelover.co.uk; ⊖ Shoreditch High Street Overground; map pp.76–77. Behind the unprepossessing facade of this former meat-packing factory lies a opulently camp bar with a nice line in creative cocktails. It's been around a while on the Shoreditch scene and seems set to stay, despite the occasionally too-cool-for-school service. Mon–Thurs 6pm–midnight, Fri & Sat 5pm–1am.

**The Owl & Pussycat** 34 Redchurch St, E2 ☎ 020 3487 0088, ⓦ owlandpussycatshoreditch.com; ⊖ Shoreditch High Street Overground; map pp 76–77. One of many old boozers in the area to have been gussied up and hipsterfied, this backstreet pub has managed to keep a generally mellow vibe. It can get hectic at the weekends, but that comes with the territory. Sun & Mon noon–11pm, Tues–Sat noon–midnight.

**Ten Bells** 84 Commercial St, E1 ☎ 020 7366 1721, ⓦ tenbells.com; ⊖ Shoreditch High Street Overground; map pp.76–77. Historic pub, with Jack the Ripper associations, with some beautiful Victorian tiling and a fantastic Modern British restaurant upstairs (booking essential; closed Mon). Mon–Wed & Sun noon–midnight, Thurs–Sat noon–1am.

**Town of Ramsgate** 62 Wapping High St, EW1 ☎ 020 7481 8000, ⓦ townoframsgate.co.uk; ⊖ Wapping Overground. Dark, narrow, medieval pub near what used to be Execution Dock. Captain Blood was discovered here with the Crown Jewels under his cloak, "Hanging" Judge Jeffreys was arrested here trying to flee, and Captain Bligh and Fletcher Christian were regulars. The beer garden, overlooking the river, is a big draw. Daily noon–midnight.

**Worship Street Whistling Shop** 63 Worship St, EC2 ☎ 020 7247 0015, ⓦ whistlingshop.com; ⊖ Old Street; map pp.76–77. Theatrical, shabbily opulent cocktail bar that set the bar high when it spearheaded London's gin palace craze. The drinks, composed with unusual ingredients, are wildly creative. Tues 5pm–midnight, Wed & Thurs 5pm–1am, Fri & Sat 5pm–2am.

### SOUTH BANK AND SOUTHWARK

**Anchor & Hope** 36 The Cut, SE1 ☎ 020 7928 9898, ⓦ anchorandhopepub.co.uk; ⊖ Southwark; map p.82. The *Anchor* gastropub dishes up excellent, simple grub: Modern European and creative, with mouth-watering puds. Bookings are only taken for Sunday lunch. Mon 5–11pm, Tues–Sat 11am–11pm, Sun 12.30–5pm.

**The Anchor** 34 Park St, SE1 ☎ 020 7407 1577; ⊖ London Bridge; map pp.84–85. Built in 1770, this sprawling pub retains only a few vestiges of the past, but has one of the city's few riverside terraces – inevitably it's often crowded with tourists. Mon–Wed 11am–11pm, Thurs–Sat 11am–midnight, Sun noon–11pm.

**George Inn** 77 Borough High St, SE1 ☎ 020 7407 2056, ⓦ nationaltrust.org.uk/george-inn; ⊖ Borough or London Bridge; map pp.84–85. London's only surviving galleried coaching inn, dating from the seventeenth century and now owned by the National Trust; mobbed by tourists, but it does serve a good range of real ales. Daily 11am–11pm.

★**King's Arms** 25 Roupell St, SE1 ☎ 020 7207 0784, ⓦ windmilltaverns.com; ⊖ Waterloo; map p.82. Terrific

1

local divided into two sections; a traditional drinking area in the front, with a tastefully cluttered, conservatory-style dining space at the rear, where good Thai food is served at long wooden tables. Mon–Fri 11am–11pm, Sat noon–11pm, Sun noon–10.30pm.

## KENSINGTON AND CHELSEA

★**Churchill Arms** 119 Kensington Church St, W8 📞020 7727 4242, ⓦ churchillarmskensington.co.uk; ⊖ Notting Hill Gate; map pp.90–91. Justifiably popular, flower-festooned pub serving Fuller's beers, Guinness, and good Thai food. Mon–Wed 11am–11pm, Thurs–Sat 11am–midnight, Sun noon–10.30pm.

**Cooper's Arms Bar** 87 Flood St, SW3 📞020 7376 3120, ⓦ coopersarms.co.uk; ⊖ Sloane Square; map pp.90–91. Decent, spacious neighbourhood pub, which may not be more than the sum of its parts – reasonable gastropub food, a range of beers, plenty of spots to choose from – but is still a good find so close to the King's Road. Daily noon–11pm.

**The Elgin** 96 Ladbroke Grove, W11 📞020 7229 5663, ⓦ geronimo-inns.co.uk; ⊖ Ladbroke Grove; map pp.90–91. Capacious pub where the buzzy vibe, lovely original features, funky decor and fancy gastropub menu bring in the cool Portobello crowd. Mon–Thurs 11am–11pm, Fri & Sat 11am–midnight, Sun noon–10.30pm.

**Grenadier** 18 Wilton Row, SW1 📞020 7235 3074, ⓦ taylor-walker.co.uk; ⊖ Hyde Park Corner or Knightsbridge; map pp.90–91. Located in a cobbled mews, this quaint little Taylor Walker pub was Wellington's local (his horse block still stands outside) and his officers' mess; the original pewter bar survives, as does a cosy, old-fashioned ambience. Real ales and pricey bar food. Mon–Sat noon–11pm, Sun noon–10.30pm.

★**The Nag's Head** 53 Kinnerton St, SW1 📞020 7235 1135; ⊖ Hyde Park Corner or Knightsbridge; map pp.90–91. Convivial, quirky little pub in a posh mews, with eclectic, raffish memorabilia plastered over the walls, real ales, occasional live jazz and a mobile phone ban. Like going back in time – and only in a good way. Mon–Sat 11am–11pm, Sun noon–10.30pm.

**The Pig's Ear** 35 Old Church St, SW3 📞020 7352 2908, ⓦ thepigsear.info; ⊖ Sloane Square; map pp.90–91. Charming, locally adored gastropub serving the best craft ales and classy Modern British food. Daily noon–11pm.

## NORTH LONDON

**Edinboro Castle** 57 Mornington Terrace, NW1 📞020 7255 9651, ⓦ www.edinborocastlepub.co.uk; ⊖ Camden Town; map pp.56–57. A large pub with an unfussy interior and an enormous beer garden which hosts summer weekend barbecues. Above-average selection of

draught continental lagers and a couple of real ales, plus a not-bad gastro menu. Mon–Sat noon–11pm, Sun noon–10.30pm.

**The Flask** 77 Highgate West Hill, N6 📞020 8348 7346, ⓦ theflaskhighgate.com; bus #210 from ⊖ Archway. Ideally situated at the heart of Highgate village green – with a rambling, low-ceilinged interior and a summer terrace – and, as a result, very, very popular at the weekend. Mon–Sat noon–11pm, Sun noon–10.30pm.

**The Holly Bush** 22 Holly Mount, off Holly Hill, NW3 📞020 7435 2892, ⓦ hollybushhampstead.co.uk; ⊖ Hampstead. A lovely, creaky old Fuller's pub, with a real fire in winter, tucked away in the steep backstreets of Hampstead village. Some fine real ales on offer, as well as decent food (particularly the sausages and pies), though it can get mobbed at weekends. Mon–Sat noon–11pm, Sun noon–10.30pm.

**Lock Tavern** 35 Chalk Farm Rd, NW1 📞020 7482 7163, ⓦ lock-tavern.com; ⊖ Chalk Farm; map pp.56–57. Rambling pub with comfy sofas, a leafy roof terrace and a beer garden, street-food-style pub grub and DJs playing anything from punk funk and electro to avant-country. Mon–Thurs noon–midnight, Fri & Sat noon–1am, Sun noon–11pm.

**Prince Alfred** 5a Formosa St, W9 📞020 7286 3287, ⓦ theprincealfred.com; ⊖ Warwick Ave; map pp.56–57. A Victorian pub with all its original 1862 fittings intact, right down to the glazed "snob screens" that divide the bar into a series of "snugs". There's a pricey Modern European restaurant at the back. Mon–Thurs noon–11pm, Fri & Sat noon–midnight, Sun noon–10.30pm.

## SOUTH LONDON

**Crown & Greyhound** 73 Dulwich Village, SE21 📞020 8299 4976, ⓦ www.thecrownandgreyhound.co.uk; North Dulwich station from London Bridge. Large Victorian pub, convenient for the Picture Gallery, with a big beer garden. Mon–Wed 11am–11pm, Thurs–Sat 11am–midnight, Sun noon–10.30pm.

**Cutty Sark** Ballast Quay, off Lassell St, SE10 📞020 8858 3146, ⓦ cuttysarkse10.co.uk; Cutty Sark DLR or Maze Hill station from Charing Cross or London Bridge. This Georgian pub is a good place for a riverside pint and can often be less touristy than the nearby *Trafalgar Tavern*. Mon–Sat 11am–11pm, Sun noon–10.30pm.

## WEST LONDON

★**Dove** 19 Upper Mall, W6 📞020 8748 9474, ⓦ dovehammersmith.co.uk; ⊖ Ravenscourt Park. Wonderful low-beamed, old riverside pub with the smallest bar in the UK (4ft by 7ft), a terrace and very popular Sunday roasts. Mon–Sat 11am–11pm, Sun noon–10.30pm.

**White Cross Hotel** Water Lane, Richmond, TW9 ☎020 8940 6844, ⊚thewhitecrossrichmond.com; ⊖Richmond. With a longer pedigree and more character than its rivals, the *White Cross* has a very popular, large garden overlooking the river and a lounge with an open fire. Mon–Sat 11am–11pm, Sun 11am–10.30pm.

## NIGHTLIFE

### LIVE MUSIC VENUES

London's live music scene is extremely diverse, encompassing all variations of rock, blues, roots and world music, and, along with impressive homegrown talent, the city's media spotlight makes it pretty much the place for young bands to break into the global mainstream.

#### GENERAL VENUES

★**Academy Brixton** 211 Stockwell Rd, SW9 ☎0844 477 2000, ⊚o2academybrixton.co.uk; ⊖Brixton. The Academy has seen them all, from mods and rockers to Snoop Dogg. The 5000-capacity Art Deco hall doesn't always deliver perfect sound quality, but remains a cracking place to see bands.

**Cargo** 83 Rivington St, EC2 ☎020 7739 3440, ⊚cargo-london.com; ⊖Old Street or Shoreditch High Street Overground; map pp.76–77. Small, popular venue in what was once a railway arch, with a restaurant and chilled garden area. Hosts a variety of live acts, including jazz, hip-hop, indie and folk, and excellent club nights.

**Forum** 9–17 Highgate Rd, NW5 ☎020 7428 4099, ⊚mamacolive.com/theforum; ⊖Kentish Town. Decent mid-sized venue, with a large stage hosting a mix of successful and underground new acts and groups inching their way onto the nostalgia circuit.

**Hammersmith Apollo** 45 Queen Caroline St, W6 ☎020 8563 3800, ⊚eventimapollo.com; ⊖Hammersmith. The former Hammersmith Odeon is a cavernous space (downstairs is seating or standing, depending on the occasion), featuring everyone from Jack White to James Blunt, plus stand-up and popular theatre.

★**O2 Shepherds Bush Empire** Shepherd's Bush Green, W12 ☎0844 477 2000, ⊚o2shepherdsbush empire.co.uk; ⊖Shepherd's Bush. Yet another grand old theatre, the 2000-capacity Empire now hosts a fine cross-section of interesting UK and international bands. There's often a great atmosphere at the front downstairs, while the vertigo-inducing upstairs balconies provide great stage views.

★**Roundhouse** Chalk Farm Rd, NW1 ☎0844 482 8008, ⊚roundhouse.org.uk; ⊖Chalk Farm; map pp.56–57. This magnificent listed Victorian steam engine shed is one of London's premier performing arts centres; alongside circus, comedy and spoken word, its programme includes artier rock acts and world music.

#### ROCK, BLUES, INDIE AND FOLK

★**12 Bar Club** Denmark St, WC2 ☎020 7240 2622, ⊚12barclub.com; ⊖Tottenham Court Road; map pp.60–61. Tiny, atmospheric bar and venue offering up-and-coming, cheap and often pleasantly eccentric indie, blues and folk gigs.

**Borderline** Orange Yard, Manette St, W1 ☎0844 847 2465, ⊚mamacolive.com/theborderline; ⊖Tottenham Court Road; map pp.60–61. Small and slightly ramshackle basement joint with awkward pillars but good sound and a diverse musical policy.

**Green Note** 106 Parkway, NW1 ☎020 7485 9899, ⊚greennote.co.uk; ⊖Camden Town; map pp.56–57. Intimate music venue that punches way above its weight with its excellent line-up of roots, folk, acoustic and world music, and has a little veggie café to boot.

**KOKO** 1a Camden High St, NW1 ⊚koko.uk.com; ⊖Mornington Crescent; map p.56–57. An institution since its days as the Camden Palace, this venue's grand interior hosts popular club nights and gigs – and has historically been a favourite venue for superstars doing "secret" shows.

**Underworld** 174 Camden High St, NW1 ☎020 7482 1932, ⊚theunderworldcamden.co.uk; ⊖Camden Town; map pp.56–57. Shouty, scruffy warren under the *World's End* pub – a great place to check out metal, metalcore and nu-metal bands.

★**Union Chapel** Compton Terrace, N1 ☎020 7226 1686, ⊚unionchapel.org.uk; ⊖Highbury & Islington; map pp.56–57. Intimate venue in a beautiful old church (seating is on pews); the line-up ranges from contemporary folk via comedy to world music, R'n'B and indie legends.

---

## NOTTING HILL CARNIVAL

The two-day free **festival** (⊚thenottinghillcarnival.com) in Notting Hill is the longest-running, best-known and biggest street party in Europe. Dating back more than fifty years, the Caribbean carnival is a tumult of imaginatively decorated parade floats, eye-catching costumes, thumping sound systems, live bands, irresistible food and huge crowds. It takes place on the Sunday and Monday of the last weekend of August.

**1**

## JAZZ AND WORLD MUSIC

**Jazz Café** 5 Parkway, NW1 ☎020 7485 6834, ⓦmamacolive.com/thejazzcafe; ⊖Camden Town; map pp.56–57. A combination of big names (at big prices) and acts from the clubbier end of jazz – along with Latin, funk and urban – keep the dancefloor and balcony buzzing. You can dine, too, if you book in advance – though the service gets mixed reports.

**Kings Place** 90 York Way, N1 ☎020 7520 1490, ⓦkingsplace.co.uk; ⊖King's Cross; map pp.56–57. Excellent classical, jazz and world music gigs at this rather swish development, with great acoustics, beside the *Guardian* newspaper's offices.

**Ronnie Scott's** 47 Frith St, W1 ☎020 7439 0747, ⓦronniescotts.co.uk; ⊖Leicester Square; map pp.60–61. The most famous jazz club in London, this small, smart and atmospheric Soho stalwart features all the jazz greats, with some gigs from up-and-coming stars.

★**The Vortex** 11 Gillett Square, N16 ☎020 7254 4097, ⓦvortexjazz.co.uk; Dalston Kingsland or Dalston Junction Overground. This small, purpose-built venue is a serious player on the live jazz scene, combining a touch of urban style with a cosy, friendly atmosphere – it's a good place to check out free and improvised jazz.

## CLUBS

Disco tunnels, sticky-floored indie clubs and epic house nights – London has it all. Many clubs keep going until 6am or later; some are open all week, others sporadically; and very often a venue will host a different club each night of the week. Admission charges vary enormously, with small midweek nights starting at around £3–5 and large weekend events charging as much as £30; around £10–15 is the average. For the latest, check flyers in the city's record stores and bars or log on to ⓦtimeout.com and ⓦresidentadvisor.net.

★**Dalston Superstore** 177 Kingsland High St, E8 ☎020 7254 2273, ⓦdalstonsuperstore.com; Dalston Junction Overground; map pp.56–57. Starting its days as a gay club, this hedonistic Dalston stalwart brings in the hipster crowds with its savvy hipster mix of electronica, house in all its forms, old-school disco pop and indie. Good

food, too. Usually Wed–Sat; plus some Sun nights.

**Fabric** 77a Charterhouse St, EC1 ☎020 7336 8898, ⓦfabriclondon.com; ⊖Farringdon; map pp.76–77. Despite big queues (book online to speed things up) and a mazelike layout that means you may take hours to find friends, jackets and some of its numerous rooms, this huge club remains one of the world's finest, focusing on drum'n'bass and dubstep, hip-hop, techno and house, with live bands and quality DJ line-ups. Usually Fri–Sat 11pm–5.30am or 8am.

**Madame JoJo's** 8–10 Brewer St, W1 ☎020 7734 3040, ⓦmadamejojos.com; ⊖Piccadilly Circus; map pp.60–61. Louche, enjoyable and somewhat battered Soho institution. Alongside burlesque, cabaret and drag shows, you'll find electronica, disco and rock – the big club nights include funk (Fri), and indie (Tues). Usually Tues–Sun until 3am, with drag and burlesque shows earlier in the evening.

★**Notting Hill Arts Club** 21 Notting Hill Gate, W11 ☎020 7460 4459, ⓦnottinghillartsclub .com; ⊖Notting Hill Gate; map pp.90–91. Groovy, arty, dressed-down basement club/bar that's popular for everything from Latin-inspired funk, jazz and hip-hop through to disco, house and indie. Usually Tues–Sat.

**Plastic People** 147–149 Curtain Rd, EC2 ☎020 7739 6471, ⓦplasticpeople.co.uk; ⊖Old Street; map pp.76–77. Thumping basement club whose broad booking policy stretches through techno and Afro-pop to reggae and dubstep. Usually Thurs 9.30/10pm–2am, Fri & Sat until 4am.

**Proud Camden** Stables Market, Chalk Farm Rd, NW1 ☎0207 482 3867, ⓦproudcamden.com; ⊖Camden Town; map pp.56–57. Indie, rave, live bands, costume parties, exhibitions and more – *Proud Camden*, in a former horse hospital, also offers decent food during the day and an outdoor terrace in summer. Hours vary – clubs usually till 2.30am.

**XOYO** 32–37 Cowper St, EC2 ☎020 7354 9993, ⓦxoyo .co.uk; ⊖Old Street; map pp.76–77. Huge Shoreditch club whose legendary weekend club nights and regular live gigs pull in the biggest names in everything from EDM to indie rock. Usually Tues–Sat.

## GAY AND LESBIAN NIGHTLIFE

London's **lesbian and gay scene** is so huge, diverse and well established that it's easy to forget just how much – and how fast – it has grown over the last couple of decades. **Soho** remains its spiritual heart, with a mix of traditional gay pubs, designer café-bars and a range of gay-run services, while Vauxhall and Shoreditch/Dalston are also good stomping grounds. Details of most events appear at ⓦtimeout.com. The major **outdoor event** of the year is **Pride in London** (ⓦprideinlondon.org) in late June/early July, a colourful, noisy march through the city streets and various entertainment events.

### BARS AND CLUBS

London's gay club nights appear and disappear with

alarming frequency, so always check the listings to see what's happening (see p.106). Entry prices can be as low as

1

£5, but you're looking at more like £12–20 for all-nighters. Most places welcome most people, and the scene tends to be friendly.

## MIXED BARS

**The Black Cap** 171 Camden High St, NW1 ☎ 020 7485 0538, ⓦ theblackcap.com; ⊖ Camden Town; map pp.56–57. Venerable north London establishment offering cabaret, drag and dancing almost every night. The upstairs *Shufflewick* bar is quieter and more pub-like, and there's a terrace. Mon & Tues noon–12.30am, Wed & Thurs noon–2am, Fri noon–3am, Sun noon–1am.

**Freedom** 66 Wardour St, W1 ☎ 020 7734 0071, ⓦ freedombarsoho.com; ⊖ Piccadilly Circus; map pp.60–61. Established gay place, long popular with a straight/gay/metrosexual Soho crowd. The basement becomes an intimate club later on, hosting regular cabaret and club nights. Mon–Thurs 4pm–3am, Fri & Sat 2pm–3am, Sun 2–10.30pm.

**George & Dragon** 2–4 Hackney Rd, E2 ☎ 020 7012 1100; ⊖ Old Street; map pp.76–77. Dandies, fashionistas and locals meet in this lively, often rammed Shoreditch hangout. The interior setup is traditional, but the attitudes – and the club nights ("Cockabilly", anyone?) are not. Daily 6pm–midnight.

**Ku Bar** 30 Lisle St, WC2 ☎ 020 7437 4303, ⓦ ku-bar.co.uk; ⊖ Leicester Square; map pp.60–61. The Lisle Street original, with a downstairs club open late, is one of Soho's largest and best-loved gay bars, serving a scene-conscious yet low-on-attitude clientele. It has a stylish sibling bar on Frith Street. Mon–Sat noon–3am, Sun noon–midnight.

**★ Retro Bar** 2 George Court (off Strand), WC2 ☎ 020 7839 8760, ⓦ retrobarlondon.co.uk; ⊖ Charing Cross or Embankment; map pp.60–61. Indie/retro bar playing 1970s, 80s, rock, pop, rockabilly and alternative sounds, and featuring regular DJ nights. Mon–Fri noon–11pm, Sat 2–11pm, Sun 2–10.30pm.

**The Yard** 57 Rupert St, W1 ☎ 020 7437 2652, ⓦ yardbar.co.uk; ⊖ Piccadilly Circus; map pp.60–61. The courtyard often heaves with a mixed, post-work crowd at this laidback, sociable bar – in fine weather it's one of the best spots in Soho for alfresco drinking. Mon–Wed 4–11.30pm, Thurs 3–11.30pm, Fri & Sat 2pm–midnight, Sun 2–10.30pm.

## LESBIAN BARS

**She Bar** 23 Old Compton St, W1 ☎ 020 7437 4303, ⓦ she-soho.com; ⊖ Tottenham Court Road; map pp.60–61. Rather swish lesbian bar from the *Ku Bar* stable (see above) in the heart of Soho, with occasional DJ nights. Mon–Thurs 4–11.30pm, Fri & Sat 4pm–12.30am, Sun 4–10.30pm.

**Star at Night** 22 Great Chapel St, W1 ☎ 020 7494 2488, ⓦ thestaratnight.com; ⊖ Tottenham Court Road; map pp.60–61. Comfortable, mixed but female-led, venue. It's popular with a slightly older crowd who want somewhere to sit, a decent glass of wine (or gin) and good conversation. Tues–Sat 6–11.30pm.

## GAY MEN'S BARS

**★ BarCode** Arch 69, Albert Embankment, SE11 ☎ 020 7582 4180, ⓦ barcode-london.com; ⊖ Vauxhall; map pp.56–57. Slick, spacious cruisey gay men's bar in the heart of Vauxhall's clubbing quarter. Thurs 10pm–4am, Fri 8pm–8am, Sat 10pm–midnight.

**Comptons** 53 Old Compton St, W1 ☎ 0203 238 0163, ⓦ faucetinn.com; ⊖ Leicester Square or Piccadilly Circus; map pp.60–61. This large, friendly pub attracts a butch, cruising yet relaxed 25-plus crowd. DJs at weekends. Mon–Thurs noon–11.30pm, Fri & Sat noon–midnight, Sun noon–10.30pm.

**The King's Arms** 23 Poland St, W1 ☎ 020 7734 5907; ⊖ Oxford Circus; map pp.60–61. London's best-known and perennially popular bear bar, with a traditional London pub atmosphere, with a karaoke night on Sun. Mon–Thurs noon–11pm, Fri & Sat noon–midnight, Sun 1pm–10.30pm.

## CLUBS

**Area** 67–68 Albert Embankment, SE1 ☎ 020 3242 0040, ⓦ arealondon.net; ⊖ Vauxhall; map pp.56–57. With two dancefloors and impressive laser and light displays, *Area* hosts big-name international DJs and the after-hours club *Beyond* on Sunday mornings (from 3am). Nights vary.

**★ Duckie** Royal Vauxhall Tavern, 372 Kennington Lane, SE11 ☎ 020 7737 4043, ⓦ duckie.co.uk; ⊖ Vauxhall; map pp.56–57. *Duckie*'s decadent mix of performance art and skewed theme nights, as well as cult DJs The Readers Wifes playing everything from Kim Wilde to the Velvet Underground, has kept this splendid club night going strong for more than fifteen years. Sat 9pm–2am.

**★ The Eagle** 349 Kennington Lane, SE11 ☎ 020 7793 0903, ⓦ eaglelondon.com; ⊖ Vauxhall; map pp.56–57. Home to the excellent Sunday-nighter Horse Meat Disco, with a vibe that loosely evokes late 1970s New York, complete with facial hair, checked shirts and a pool table. Nightly.

**Fire** South Lambeth Rd, SW8 ☎ 020 3242 0040, ⓦ firelondon.net; ⊖ Vauxhall; map pp.56–57. *Fire* is London's superclub of choice for a mixed though mostly male crowd of disco bunnies and hardboyz. Fri, Sat & occasionally Sun.

**Heaven** Villiers St, WC2 ☎ 0844 847 2351, ⓦ heavennightclub-london.com; ⊖ Charing Cross or Embankment; map pp.60–61. Said to be the UK's most popular gay club, this 2000-capacity venue is home to G-A-Y (Thurs–Sat), the queen of London's scene nights, with big-name DJs, PAs and shows. Thurs–Sat & Mon.

**Popstarz** Various locations ⓦ popstarz.org. The unusual, long-established and winning formula of indie, pop and R&B, plus cheap beer and no attitude attracts a

mixed, studenty crowd. Usually Fri 10pm–5am.

★**Sink the Pink** Bethnal Green Working Men's Club, 42 Pollard Row, E2 ☎ 020 7739 7170, ⓦ sinkthepinklondon.com; ⊖ Bethnal Green. Theatrical, youthful and glamorous fun – attracting a decadent, mixed and inclusive crowd. Various Sat nights.

## THEATRE AND COMEDY

London has enjoyed a reputation for quality **theatre** since the time of Shakespeare and, despite the continuing dominance of blockbuster musicals and revenue-spinning star vehicles, still provides platforms for innovation and new writing. The **West End** is the heart of "Theatreland", with Shaftesbury Avenue its most congested drag, but the term is more of a conceptual pigeon-hole than a geographical term. Some of the most exciting work is performed in what have become known as the **Off-West End** theatres, while further down the financial ladder still are the **fringe** theatres, often pub venues, where ticket prices are lower, and quality more variable. As for **comedy**, you're never too far from a gig in London, whether it's a big-name stadium show, an old favourite like the Comedy Store – at the heart of the alternative comedy movement of the 1980s – or a neighbourhood pub hosting new young hopefuls. Check ⓦ chortle.co.uk and ⓦ timeout.com for listings.

### COSTS

**Prices** Tickets for £15 are restricted to the fringe; the box-office average is closer to £35–40 with £50–110 the usual top price. The cheapest way to get a ticket is to go to the theatre box office in person; you will probably be charged a booking fee if you buy over the phone or online. Keep an eye on the websites, however, for special deals including cheap Monday seats, or standby "on-the-day" tickets – even for the big musicals and well-reviewed plays. Students, senior citizens and the unemployed can get concessionary rates for most shows, and many theatres offer reductions on standbys to these groups. Whatever you do, avoid the touts and the unofficial ticket agencies that abound in the West End – there's no guarantee that the tickets are genuine.

**Discount tickets** The Society of London Theatre runs a useful booth, tkts (Mon–Sat 10am–7pm, Sun 11am–4.30pm; ⓦ tkts.co.uk), in Leicester Square, which sells on-the-day tickets for all the West End shows at discounts of up to fifty percent, though they tend to be in the top end of the price range, are limited to four per person, and carry a service charge of £3 per ticket.

### THEATRES

**Almeida** Almeida St, N1 ☎ 020 7359 4404, ⓦ almeida .co.uk; ⊖ Angel or Highbury & Islington. Popular little Islington venue that premieres excellent new plays and excitingly reworked classics, and has attracted some big Hollywood names.

**Arcola Theatre** 24 Ashwin St, E8 ☎ 020 7503 1646, ⓦ arcolatheatre.com; Dalston Kingsland or Dalston Junction Overground. Exciting fringe theatre in an old Dalston factory. Challenging plays – classics and modern works – include shows from young, international companies. Some "Pay what you can" tickets on Tuesday nights.

**Barbican Centre** Silk St, EC2 ☎ 020 7638 8891, ⓦ barbican.org.uk; ⊖ Barbican or Moorgate. A wide variety of productions from puppetry and musicals to new and classical drama.

**Battersea Arts Centre** 176 Lavender Hill, SW11 ☎ 020 7223 2223, ⓦ bac.org.uk; Clapham Junction train station from Victoria or Waterloo. A multistage building, housed in an old town hall, renowned for excellent contemporary drama, physical theatre, comedy and cabaret.

**Bush** 7 Uxbridge Rd, W12 8LJ ☎ 020 8743 5050, ⓦ bushtheatre.co.uk; ⊖ Shepherd's Bush Market. This lively local theatre is second only to the Royal Court as a reliable venue for new writing.

**Donmar Warehouse** 41 Earlham St, WC2 ☎ 0844 871 7624, ⓦ donmarwarehouse.com; ⊖ Covent Garden. A small, central performance space, noted for new writing and interesting reappraisals of the classics.

**Menier Chocolate Factory** 53 Southwark St, SE1 ☎ 020 7378 1713, ⓦ www.menierchocolatefactory .com; ⊖ London Bridge. Great fringe producing house in a former Victorian factory, with a decent bar and restaurant attached. Shows – musical revivals, old classics, new writing – are consistently good.

**National Theatre** South Bank, SE1 ☎ 020 7452 3000, ⓦ nationaltheatre.org.uk; ⊖ Waterloo. The country's top actors and directors produce shows ranging from Greek tragedies via experimental new writing to Broadway musicals in three theatres. Some productions sell out months in advance, but day tickets, for the lowest-priced seats available, go on sale on the morning of each performance – get there by 8am. Look out, too, for special "Travelex" performances, when half the seats go for £15.

**Open Air Theatre** Regent's Park, Inner Circle, NW1 ☎ 0844 826 4242, ⓦ openairtheatre.com;

Baker Street. Lovely alfresco space in Regent's Park hosting a tourist-friendly summer programme of Shakespeare, musicals, plays and concerts, many of which are geared towards children.

★ **Roundhouse** Chalk Farm Rd, NW1 ☎ 0844 482 8008, ⓦ roundhouse.org.uk; ⊖ Chalk Farm. Camden's most exciting cultural venue, in an old – round – engine repairs shed, puts on cutting-edge theatre, circus, cabaret and live gigs.

**Royal Court** Sloane Square, SW1 ☎ 020 7565 5000, ⓦ royalcourttheatre.com; ⊖ Sloane Square. The Royal Court is one of the best places in London to catch radical new writing, either in the proscenium arch Theatre Downstairs, or the smaller Theatre Upstairs.

**Sam Wanamaker Playhouse** New Globe Walk, SE1 ☎ 020 7401 9919, ⓦ shakespearesglobe.com; ⊖ London Bridge, Blackfriars or Southwark. Indoor Jacobean-style theatre, lit by candles and with bench seating, on the Globe site. Some Shakespearean plays, plus Jacobean productions and the occasional opera.

**Shakespeare's Globe** New Globe Walk, SE1 ☎ 020 7401 9919, ⓦ shakespearesglobe.com; ⊖ London Bridge, Blackfriars or Southwark. This open-roofed replica Elizabethan theatre uses only natural light and the minimum of scenery, and puts on fun Shakespearean shows – along with works from the Bard's contemporaries, including Christopher Marlowe, and modern works on Elizabethan themes – from May to September. Seats from around £15, with "Yard" tickets (standing-room only) for around a fiver.

**Soho Theatre** 21 Dean St, W1 ☎ 020 7478 0100, ⓦ sohotheatre.com; ⊖ Tottenham Court Road. Very central venue that specializes in new writing from around the globe, as well as regular comedy and cabaret.

**Tricycle Theatre** 269 Kilburn High Rd, NW6 ☎ 020 7328 1000, ⓦ tricycle.co.uk; ⊖ Kilburn. One of London's most dynamic venues, showcasing a mixed bag of new plays, often with a multicultural bent, and usually with a sharp political focus.

## CINEMA

There are a lot of cinemas in London, especially the **West End**, with the biggest on and around Leicester Square. A few classy independent chains show more offbeat screenings, in various locations – check out the **Picturehouse** (ⓦ picturehouses.co.uk), **Curzon** (ⓦ curzoncinemas.com) and **Everyman** (ⓦ everymancinema.com). **Tickets** at the major screens cost at least £13, although concessionary rates are offered for some shows at virtually all cinemas, usually at off-peak times. Anyone with an Orange phone can make use of the two-for-one "Orange Wednesday" tickets.

**BFI Southbank** Belvedere Rd, South Bank, SE1 ☎ 020 7928 3232, ⓦ bfi.org.uk; ⊖ Waterloo. Splendid themed seasons, showing between eight and fourteen films daily on four screens. The BFI also runs the IMAX (☎ 033 0333 7878), a huge glazed drum in the middle of Waterloo roundabout. The colossal screen is not recommended for anyone with vertigo.

**Electric** 191 Portobello Rd, W11 ☎ 020 7908 9696, ⓦ electriccinema.co.uk; ⊖ Notting Hill Gate or Ladbroke Grove. One of the oldest cinemas in the country (opened 1911), the Electric keeps much of its lovely old interior, but has added the requisite indie armchairs, footstools and two-seater sofas, along with a glam bar, to create a luxury experience. The programme concentrates on the quirkiest mainstream hits and offbeat offerings.

**ICA Cinema** Nash House, The Mall, SW1 ☎ 020 7930 3647, ⓦ ica.org.uk; ⊖ Piccadilly Circus or Charing Cross. One of the capital's most cutting-edge programmes – offering world, documentary and underground movies in the Institute of Contemporary Arts.

**Prince Charles** 7 Leicester Place, WC2 ☎ 020 7494 3654, ⓦ princecharlescinema.com; ⊖ Leicester Square or Piccadilly Circus. Two screens in the heart of the West End, with good prices (starting at just £5, less for members) and a daily changing programme of newish movies, classics and cult favourites, plus participatory "singalong" romps.

## CLASSICAL MUSIC

On most days you should be able to catch a concert by one of the major **orchestras** based in the capital or a more specialized ensemble. Unless a glamorous guest conductor is wielding the baton, or one of the world's high-profile orchestras is giving a performance, full houses are a rarity, so even at the biggest concert halls you should be able to pick up a ticket for around £15 (the usual range is about £12–50). During the week there are also numerous **free concerts**, often at lunchtimes, in London's churches or given by the city's two leading conservatoires, the Royal College of Music (ⓦ rcm.ac.uk) and Royal Academy of Music (ⓦ ram.ac.uk).

### CONCERT VENUES

**Barbican Centre** Silk St, EC2 ☎ 020 7638 8891, ⓦ barbican.org.uk; ⊖ Barbican or Moorgate. With the outstanding resident London Symphony Orchestra (ⓦ lso.co.uk), the BBC Symphony Orchestra (ⓦ bbc .co.uk/orchestras) as associate orchestra, and top foreign orchestras and big-name soloists in regular attendance, the Barbican is an outstanding venue for classical music.

## THE PROMS

The **London Proms** (Royal Albert Hall ☎0845 401 5040, ☻bbc.co.uk/proms; ⊖South Kensington) provide a summer-season feast of classical music, much of it at bargain-basement prices; uniquely, there are five hundred **standing places** available each night, which cost just £5, even on the famed last night. Standing tickets are made available only on the day itself and must be bought on the door. Seated **tickets** cost between £12 and £95; those for the last night are allocated by ballot and start at £57. The acoustics may not be the world's best, but the calibre of the performers is unbeatable, the atmosphere superb, and the programme a creative mix of standards and new or obscure works. And the hall is so vast that even if you turn up an hour or so before the show starts you are unlikely to be turned away.

**Southbank Centre** Belvedere Rd, South Bank, SE1 ☎020 7960 4200, ☻southbankcentre.co .uk; ⊖Waterloo or Embankment. The SBC has three spaces, none of which is exclusively used for classical music. The 2500-seat Royal Festival Hall (RFH), home to the Philharmonia (☻philharmonia.co.uk) and the London Philharmonic (☻lpo.co.uk), is tailor-made for large-scale choral and orchestral works, while the Queen Elizabeth Hall (QEH) and intimate Purcell Room are used for chamber concerts, solo recitals, opera and choirs.

**Wigmore Hall** 36 Wigmore St, W1 ☎020 7935 2141, ☻wigmore-hall.org.uk; ⊖Bond Street or Oxford Circus. With its near-perfect acoustics, the Wigmore Hall – built in 1901 as a hall for the adjacent Bechstein piano showroom – is a firm favourite, so book well in advance. Piano recitals and chamber music are superb, as are the recitals by some of the world's greatest singers.

### OPERA

**English National Opera** Coliseum, St Martin's Lane, WC2 ☎020 7845 9300, ☻eno.org; ⊖Leicester Square or Charing Cross. Operas sung in English, an adventurous repertoire, modern productions and reasonable pricing (£16–130, with standbys for concessions from £15 and various special deals available).

**Opera Up Close** King's Head, 115 Upper St, N1 ☎020 7478 0160, ☻kingsheadtheatre.com; ⊖Angel or Highbury & Islington. New writing and classics with a twist from superb resident company Opera Up Close, who sing in English with the most basic of accompaniment In this tiny pub theatre and regularly appear at other venues too.

**Royal Opera House** Bow St, WC2 ☎020 7304 4000, ☻roh.org.uk; ⊖Covent Garden. This beautiful old opera house puts on lavish operas, most of them, but not all, fairly traditonal productions. All are performed in the original language with subtitles. Ticket prices can reach £900, but the restricted-view seating (or standing room) from around £15 is perfectly good. Get in line early for one of the day seats, which are released from 10am on the day of a performance.

### DANCE

The biggest dance festival is **Dance Umbrella** (☻danceumbrella.co.uk), a season (Oct/Nov) of new and cutting-edge work. For a **roundup** of all the major dance events in town, check ☻londondance.com.

**The Place** 17 Duke's Rd, WC1 ☎020 7121 1100, ☻theplace.org.uk; ⊖Euston. A small theatre that presents the work of contemporary choreographers and student performers.

**Royal Opera House** Bow St, WC2 ☎020 7304 4000, ☻roh.org.uk; ⊖Covent Garden. Based at the Opera House, the Royal Ballet is a world-renowned classical company with some outstanding principals. Tickets for the main house are cheaper than for opera (£7–200), with more experimental, generally less expensive, productions in the smaller Linbury Studio Theatre. Sell-outs are frequent so book early.

**Sadler's Wells** Rosebery Ave, EC1 ☎0844 412 4300, ☻sadlerswells.com; ⊖Angel. Sadler's Wells hosts Britain's best contemporary dance companies and many of the finest international companies are regular visitors. The Lilian Baylis Theatre, tucked around the back, puts on smaller-scale shows, while the Peacock Theatre near Covent Garden adds some populist shows, including street dance, to the mix.

### SHOPPING

#### DEPARTMENT STORES

**Fortnum & Mason** 181 Piccadilly, W1 ☎0845 300 1707, ☻fortnumandmason.com; ⊖Green Park or Piccadilly Circus; map pp.60–61. Beautiful 300-year-old store with murals, cherubs, chandeliers and fountains as a backdrop to its perfectly English offerings. Famous for its

**1**

fabulous, pricey food, it also specializes in upmarket designer clothes, furniture, luggage and jewellery. Mon–Sat 10am–9pm, Sun noon–6pm.

**Harrods** 87–135 Brompton Rd, Knightsbridge, SW1 ☎0845 605 1234, ⓦharrods.com; ⊖Knightsbridge; map pp.90–91. Harrods has everything, including pretension in spades – a "clean and presentable" dress code is enforced, and backpacks either have to be carried or placed in the store's left luggage. Check out the life-size bronze statue of Princess Diana and Dodi Al Fayed, who was the son of previous owner Mohamed Al Fayed, dancing on a beach. Shopping-wise, it is most notable for its huge toy department, designer labels and sumptuous food hall, with exquisite Arts and Crafts tiling. Mon–Sat 10am–8pm, Sun noon–6pm.

**Harvey Nichols** 109–125 Knightsbridge, SW1 ☎020 7201 8088, ⓦharveynichols.com; ⊖Knightsbridge; map pp.90–91. "Harvey Nicks" has all the latest designer collections, luxury items and cosmetics ranges, and a food hall offering frivolous goodies at high prices. Mon–Sat 10am–8pm, Sun noon–6pm.

**John Lewis** 300 Oxford St, W1 ☎020 7629 7711, ⓦjohnlewis.co.uk; ⊖Oxford Circus; map pp.60–61. Famous for being "never knowingly undersold", this much loved institution can't be beaten for basics, including well-made clothes, furniture and household goods. Mon–Sat 10am–8pm, Sun noon–6pm.

★**Liberty** 210–220 Regent St, W1 ☎020 7734 1234, ⓦliberty.co.uk; ⊖Oxford Circus; map pp.60–61. A fabulous emporium of luxury, this exquisite store, with its mock-Tudor exterior, is most famous for its fabrics, design and accessories, but is also great for mainstream and high fashion. Mon–Sat 10am–8pm, Sun noon–6pm.

★**Selfridges** 400 Oxford St, W1 ☎0800 123 400, ⓦselfridges.com; ⊖Bond Street; map pp.90–91. This huge, airy palace of clothes, food and furnishings was London's first great department store. The vast mens- and womenswear departments offer mainstream designers and casual lines alongside hipper, younger labels. The food hall is superb, too. Hours vary; usually Mon–Sat 9.30am–9pm, Sun noon–6pm.

## BOOKS

**Daunt Books** 83 Marylebone High St, W1 ☎020 7224 2295, ⓦdauntbooks.co.uk; ⊖Bond Street or Baker Street; map pp.90–91. Inspirational range of travel literature and guidebooks, with lots of novels and nonfiction too, in a handsome, galleried interior. Other branches. Mon–Sat 9am–7.30pm, Sun 11am–6pm.

**Foyles** 107 Charing Cross Rd, WC2 ☎020 7437 5660, ⓦfoyles.co.uk ⊖Tottenham Court Road; map pp.60–61. This venerable old bookstore has moved down the road and given itself a revamp, with huge departments devoted to fiction, nonfiction, kids books and more. Mon–Sat

9.30am–9pm, Sun noon–6pm.

**Hatchards** 187 Piccadilly, W1 ☎020 7439 9921, ⓦwww.hatchards.co.uk; ⊖Piccadilly Circus; map pp.60–61. A little overshadowed by the colossal Waterstones down the road, and actually part of the Waterstones group, the venerable Hatchards holds its own when it comes to quality fiction, biography, history and travel. Mon–Sat 9.30am–7pm, Sun noon–6pm.

**London Review Bookshop** 14 Bury Place, WC1 ☎020 7269 9030, ⓦlrbshop.co.uk; ⊖Holborn; map p.71. All the books reviewed in the august literary journal and many, many more in this tranquil Bloomsbury bookstore. Mon–Sat 10am–6.30pm, Sun noon–6pm.

★**Persephone Books** 59 Lamb's Conduit St, WC1 ☎020 7242 9292, ⓦpersephonebooks.co.uk; ⊖Russell Square or Holborn; map p.71. Lovely offspring of a publishing house that specializes in neglected twentieth-century writing by women. Mon–Fri 10am–6pm, Sat noon–5pm.

## MUSIC

**Gramex** 104 Lower Marsh, SE1 ☎020 7401 3830, ⓦgramex.co.uk; ⊖Lambeth North; map pp.82. A splendid find for classical-music and jazz-lovers, this new and secondhand record store features CDs and vinyl, and comfy leather armchairs. Mon–Sat 11am–7pm.

**Honest Jon's** 278 Portobello Rd, W10 ☎020 8969 9822, ⓦhonestjons.com; ⊖Ladbroke Grove; map pp.90–91. Jazz, soul, funk, R&B, rare groove, reggae, world music and more in this West London stalwart, with current releases, secondhand finds and reissues. Mon–Sat 10am–6pm, Sun 11am–5pm.

**Rough Trade** 130 Talbot Rd, W11 ☎020 7229 8541, ⓦroughtrade.com; ⊖Ladbroke Grove; map pp.90–91. This historic indie specialist has knowledgeable, friendly staff and a dizzying array of CDs and vinyl from electronica via reggae to indie and beyond. There's another branch, Rough Trade East, in the Old Truman Brewery (91 Brick Lane, E1). Mon–Sat 10am–6.30pm, Sun 11am–5pm.

## MARKETS

★**Borough Market** 8 Southwark St, SE1 ☎020 7407 1002, ⓦboroughmarket.org.uk; ⊖London Bridge or Borough; map pp.84–85. Foodie heaven with suppliers from all over the UK converging to sell organic and artisan goodies. Wed & Thurs 10am–5pm, Fri 10am–6pm, Sat 8am–5pm.

**Brick Lane** Brick Lane, Cygnet and Sclater streets, E1; Bacon, Cheshire and Chilton streets, E2; ⊖Aldgate East or Liverpool Street; map pp.76–77. Huge, sprawling, cheap and frenzied, this famous East End market has become a fixture on the hipster circuit, with great vintage clothes and good food stalls. It would be hard to say what you *can't* find here. Sun 9am–5pm.

1

**Camden Market** Camden High St to Chalk Farm Rd, NW1 ⓦcamdenlock.net; ⊖ Camden Town or Chalk Farm; map pp.56–57. Once beloved of hippies, punks and Goths, and now a firm favourite with European tourists, Camden is actually a gaggle of markets, segueing into each other and supplemented by lively stores and restaurants in the surrounding streets. Don't miss the fantastic food stalls down by the canal. Daily 9.30am–6.30pm, but most action Thurs–Sun.

★ **Columbia Road Flower Market** Columbia Rd, E2 ⓦcolumbiaroad.info; map pp.76–77. This pretty East End street spills over in a profusion of blooms and resounds with the bellows of Cockney barrow boys during its glorious Sunday market. Come late for the best bargains, or early to enjoy a coffee and brunch in one of the groovy local cafés. It's an excellent shopping area, abounding in indie, arty and vintage stores. Sun 8am–around 3pm.

**Greenwich Market** Greenwich High Rd, SE10 ⓦgreenwichmarketlondon.com; Greenwich train station from Charing Cross or London Bridge, or Greenwich or Cutty Sark DLR; map pp.56–57. Sprawling flea markets with some 120 stalls. Tues, Wed & Fri–Sun are best for arts, crafts and food; for antiques and vintage come on Tues, Thurs and Fri. Tues–Sun 10am–5.30pm.

**Portobello Road Market** Portobello and Golborne rds, W10 and W11 ⓦshopportobello.co .uk; ⊖ Ladbroke Grove or Notting Hill Gate; map pp.56–57. Approach this enormous market, or rather markets, from the Notting Hill end, winding your way through the antiques and bric-a-brac down to the fruit and veg, and then via the fashion stalls under the Westway to the thriving vintage scene at Portobello Green. The Golborne Road market is cheaper and less crowded, with antique and retro furniture on Fri and Sat (food and bric-à-brac Mon–Thurs). Antique market: Sat 8am–6pm. Portobello Green: Fri–Sun. Golborne Rd: Mon–Sat.

**Spitalfields** Commercial St, E1 ⓦvisitspitalfields .com; ⊖ Liverpool St; map pp.76–77. The East End's historic Victorian fruit and veg hall houses a fashionable food, crafts and vintage market, with rotating themed markets each Sat. Mon–Fri 10am–5pm, Sun 9am–5pm.

## DIRECTORY

**Hospitals** For 24hr accident and emergency phone ☎999 or turn up at St Mary's Hospital, Praed St, W2 (☎020 3312 6666; ⊖ Paddington) or University College London Hospital, 235 Euston Rd, NW1 (☎020 3456 7890; ⊖ Euston Square or Warren Street).

**Left luggage** Left luggage is available at all airports and major train terminals.

**Police** Phone ☎999 in emergencies, otherwise ☎0101 (ⓦmet.police.uk). Central police stations include: Charing Cross, Agar St, WC2 (⊖ Charing Cross); Holborn, 10 Lambs Conduit St, WC1 (⊖ Holborn); Marylebone, 1–9 Seymour Street W1 (⊖ Marble Arch); and West End Central, 27 Savile Row, W1 (⊖ Oxford Circus). The City of London has its own police force, 182 Bishopsgate, EC2 (☎020 7601 2222, ⓦcityoflondon.police.uk; ⊖ Liverpool Street).

**Post offices** The only (vaguely) late-opening post office is at 24–28 William IV St, WC2N 4DL, near Trafalgar Square (Mon–Fri 8.30am–6.30pm, Tues opens 9.15am, Sat 9am–5.30pm); it's also the city's poste restante collection point. For general postal enquiries phone ☎0345 611 2970 (Mon–Fri 8.15am–6pm, Sat 8.30am–2pm), or visit ⓦroyalmail.com.

# The Southeast

SEVEN SISTERS

# The Southeast

The southeast corner of England was traditionally where London went on holiday. In the past, trainloads of East Enders were shuttled to the hop fields and orchards of Kent for a working break from the city; boats ferried people down the Thames to the beaches of north Kent; while everyone from royalty to cuckolding couples enjoyed the seaside at Brighton, a blot of decadence in the otherwise sedate county of Sussex. Although many of the old seaside resorts have struggled to keep their tourist custom in the face of ever more accessible foreign destinations, the region still has considerable charm, its narrow country lanes and verdant meadows appearing, in places, almost untouched by modern life.

The proximity of Kent and Sussex to the continent has dictated the history of this region, which has served as a gateway for an array of invaders. **Roman** remains dot the coastal area – most spectacularly at **Bignor** and **Fishbourne** in Sussex and **Lullingstone** in Kent – and many roads, including the main A2 London to Dover, follow the arrow-straight tracks laid by the legionaries. When **Christianity** spread through Europe, it arrived in Britain on the **Isle of Thanet** – the northeast tip of Kent, since rejoined to the mainland by silting. In 597 AD Augustine moved inland and established a monastery at **Canterbury**, still the home of the Church of England and the county's prime historic attraction.

The last successful invasion of England took place in 1066, when the **Normans** overran King Harold's army near **Hastings**, on a site now marked by **Battle Abbey**. The Normans left their mark all over this corner of the kingdom, and Kent remains unmatched in its profusion of medieval castles, among them **Dover**'s sprawling cliff-top fortress guarding against continental invasion and **Rochester**'s huge, box-like citadel, close to the old dockyards of **Chatham**, power base of the formerly invincible British navy.

Away from the great historic sites, you can spend unhurried days in elegant old towns such as **Royal Tunbridge Wells**, **Rye** and **Lewes**, or enjoy the less elevated charms of the traditional resorts, of which fashionable **Brighton** is by far the best, combining the buzz of a university town with a good-time atmosphere. The picturesque **South Downs Way**, which winds its way through the South Downs National Park, offers an expanse of rolling chalk uplands that, as much as anywhere can in the crowded southeast, gets you away from it all. Kent and Sussex also harbour some of the country's finest **gardens** – ranging from the lush flowerbeds of **Sissinghurst** to the great landscaped estate of **Petworth House** – and a string of excellent **art galleries**, among them the Pallant Gallery in **Chichester**, the Turner Contemporary in **Margate**, the Towner in **Eastbourne** and the tiny Ditchling Museum of Art and Craft just outside Brighton.

The portion of **Surrey** within and around the M25 orbital motorway has little for tourists, but beyond the ring road it takes on a more rural aspect, with miles of beautiful countryside and woodlands to explore.

TURNER CONTEMPORARY, MARGATE

# Highlights

**❶ Whitstable Oyster Festival** Scoff fresh oysters and quaff dark oyster ale in this week-long festival of food, music and beer by the sea. **See p.135**

**❷ Margate** With its quirky Old Town, its broad sandy beach and the fabulous Turner Contemporary art gallery, this brash old resort is an increasingly hip destination. **See p.136**

**❸ Canterbury Cathedral** The destination of the pilgrims in Chaucer's *Canterbury Tales*, with a magnificent sixteenth-century interior that includes a shrine to the murdered Thomas à Becket. **See p.139**

**❹ The White Cliffs of Dover** Immortalized in song, art and literature, the famed chalky cliffs offer walks and vistas over the Channel. **See p.147**

**❺ Rye** Ancient hilltop town of picturesque cobbled streets, with some great places to eat, shop and sleep. **See p.154**

**❻ Walking the South Downs Way** Experience the best walking in the southeast – and some fantastic views – on this national trail, which spans England's newest National Park. **See p.160**

**❼ The Lanes and North Laine, Brighton** Explore the café- and shop-crammed streets of the maze-like Lanes and the buzzy, hip North Laine: Brighton at its best. **See p.163**

**HIGHLIGHTS ARE MARKED ON THE MAP ON PP.132–133**

## GETTING AROUND

**By car** Outside of the main towns, driving is the easiest way to get around, although commuter traffic in this corner of England is very heavy. The A2, M2 and M20 link the capital with Dover and Ramsgate, while the M23/A23 provides a quick run to Brighton. The A27 runs west–east across the Sussex coast, giving access to Chichester, Arundel, Brighton, Lewes, Eastbourne and Hastings, but can be slow-going.

**By train** Southeastern (ⓦsoutheasternrailway.co.uk) covers Kent and the easternmost part of Sussex, and runs the high-speed services from London

St Pancras to the North Kent coast and Chichester. The rest of Sussex, and parts of Surrey, are served by Southern Railways (ⓦsouthernrailway.com). Surrey is mainly served by South West Trains (ⓦsouthwesttrains.co.uk).

**By bus** National Express services from London and other main towns are pretty good, though local bus services are less impressive, and tend to dry up completely on Sundays outside of the major towns. Traveline (ⓦtravelinesoutheast.org.uk) has route details and timetables.

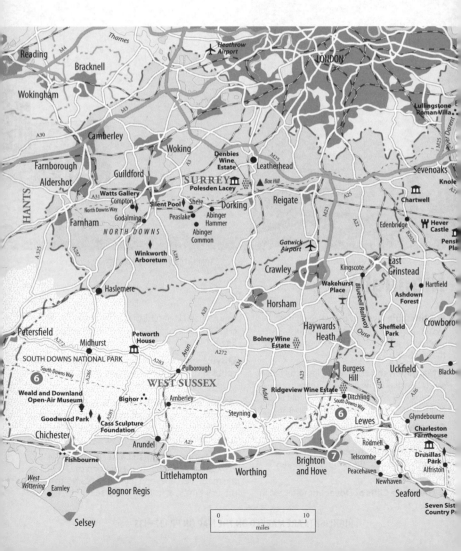

# North Kent

North Kent has a good share of appealing destinations, all easily accessible from London. The attractive town of **Rochester** boasts both historic and literary interest, while the old-fashioned seaside resorts of **Whitstable** and **Broadstairs** are favourites with weekenders from the capital. **Margate**, meanwhile, offers a dash of offbeat bucket-and-spade charm with the presence of the Tate Modern and a thriving vintage scene.

## Rochester and around

The handsome Medway town of **ROCHESTER** was first settled by the Romans, who built a fortress on the site of the present castle; some kind of fortification has remained here ever since. The town's most famous son is **Charles Dickens**, who spent his youth and

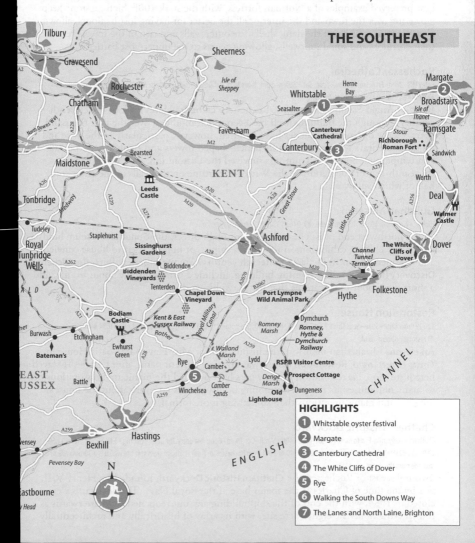

**THE SOUTHEAST**

**HIGHLIGHTS**

1. Whitstable oyster festival
2. Margate
3. Canterbury Cathedral
4. The White Cliffs of Dover
5. Rye
6. Walking the South Downs Way
7. The Lanes and North Laine, Brighton

final years near here – mischievously, it appears as "Mudfog" in *The Mudfog Papers*, and "Dullborough" in *The Uncommercial Traveller* as well as featuring in Pickwick Papers and much of his last, unfinished novel, *The Mystery of Edwin Drood*. Many of the town's buildings feature in his novels.

In neighbouring Chatham, the colossal **Chatham Historic Dockyard** records more than four hundred years of British maritime history, and is well worth a trip even if ships don't rock your boat.

**2**

### Rochester castle

Northwest end of High St • Daily: April–Sept 10am–6pm; Oct–March 10am–4pm • £6; EH • ☎ 01634 335882, ⓦ english-heritage.org.uk

In 1077, William I gave Gundulf – architect of the White Tower at the Tower of London – the job of improving defences on the River Medway's northernmost bridge on Watling Street. The resulting **Rochester castle**, now ruined, remains one of England's best-preserved examples of a Norman fortress, with the stark 100ft-high ragstone keep glowering over the town and the interior all the better for having lost its floors, allowing clear views up and down the dank shell. The outer walls and two of the towers retain their corridors and spiral stairwells, allowing access to the uppermost battlements.

### Rochester Cathedral

Boley Hill • Mon–Fri & Sun 7.30am–6pm, Sat 7.30am–5pm; tours Mon–Fri & Sun 10am–4.30pm, Sat 10am–2pm • Free; tours £4 • ☎ 01634 843366, ⓦ rochestercathedral.org

Built on Anglo-Saxon foundations, Rochester's **cathedral** dates back to the eleventh century – though the building itself has been much modified over the past thousand years. Plenty of Norman touches have endured, however, particularly in the nave and on the cathedral's west front, with its pencil-shaped towers and richly carved portal and tympanum. Some fine paintings survived the Dissolution; look out for the thirteenth-century depiction of the Wheel of Fortune on the walls of the choir (only half of which survives).

### Guildhall Museum

High St • Tues–Sun 10am–4.30pm • Free • ☎ 01634 332900, ⓦ medway.gov.uk

At the northwest end of Rochester's pleasant High Street, the **Guildhall Museum** holds a very good, chilling exhibition on the prison ships – or hulks – used to house convicts and prisoners of war in the late eighteenth century. Among other exhibits, the **Dickens Discovery Rooms**, in the adjoining building, include a wordy display about his life, and a short film about the locations that feature in his work.

### Restoration House

17–19 Crow Lane • June–Sept Thurs & Fri 10am–5pm • £7.50; pre-booked tours £8.50; gardens only £4 • ☎ 01634 848520, ⓦ restorationhouse.co.uk

An elegant Elizabethan mansion, the inspiration for Miss Havisham's Satis House in *Great Expectations*, **Restoration House** was given its current name after Charles II stayed here just before his restoration. The owners have avoided the manicured restorations of so many old houses; its ragged, crumbling beauty reveals far more about the house's long life and many alterations than something more formal.

### Chatham Historic Dockyard

Chatham • Daily: mid-Feb to March & Nov 10am–4pm; April–Oct 10am–6pm; last entry 2hr before closing • £18.50, children £11.50 • ☎ 01634 823800, ⓦ thedockyard.co.uk • Bus #140 or #141 from Rochester, or from Chatham train station, which is a 30min walk or a £7 taxi ride from the docks

Two miles east of Rochester, the **Chatham Historic Dockyard**, founded by Henry VIII, was by the time of Charles II the major base of the Royal Navy. The dockyards were closed in 1984, with the end of the shipbuilding era, but reopened soon afterwards as a tourist attraction. The eighty-acre site, with its array of historically and architecturally fascinating ships and buildings, is too big to explore in one trip. Highlights include the Victorian sloop **HMS Gannet**, the 400yd-long **Victorian Ropery**, the **No 1 Smithery** exhibition and the **Ocelot submarine**, the last warship built at the yard.

## ARRIVAL AND INFORMATION ROCHESTER

**By train** Rochester train station is at the southeastern end of High Street.

**Destinations** Canterbury (every 30–45min; 50min); Chatham (every 5–25min; 3min); London Charing Cross (Mon–Sat every 30min; 1hr 10min); London St Pancras (every 30min–hourly; 35–40min); London Victoria (every 20–40min; 45min–1hr).

**By bus** Regular local buses to and from Chatham depart from Corporation Street, which runs parallel to High Street.

**Tourist office** 95 High Street (Mon–Sat 10am–5pm, Sun 10.30am–5pm; ☎ 01634 338141, ⓦ visitmedway.org).

## ACCOMMODATION

**Salisbury House** 29 Watts Ave ☎ 01634 400182. Pleasant Victorian guesthouse with large rooms, friendly owners and a great location on a quiet leafy street, just a 10min walk up the hill behind the castle. **£70**

**Ship & Trades** Maritime Way, Chatham Maritime ☎ 01634 895200, ⓦ shipandtradeschatham.co.uk. This lively waterside pub-restaurant near the dockyards offers contemporary, nautically themed B&B rooms, some with great views. Rates include breakfast. **£80**

## EATING AND DRINKING

**The Deaf Cat** 83 High St ⓦ thedeafcat.com. Opposite the cathedral, this boho coffee shop and gallery, dedicated to the memory of Dickens' deaf cat, serves good coffee, veggie sandwiches and simple home-made cakes to a laidback crowd. Mon–Sat 9am–5pm, Sun 10am–5pm.

**Topes** 60 High St ☎ 01634 845270, ⓦ topesrestaurant .com. Rochester's nicest restaurant, around the corner from the cathedral, serves Modern British dishes such as guinea fowl, wild garlic and radicchio risotto in a wood-panelled dining room with sloping ceilings. Wed–Sat noon–2.30pm & 6.30–9pm, Sun noon–2.30pm.

# Whitstable

Fishermen, artists, yachties and foodies rub along in **WHITSTABLE**, where the sense of community, and tradition, is strong. The **oysters** for which the town is famed have been farmed here since classical times, when the Romans feasted on the region's marine delicacies, and today the annual **Oyster Festival** (end July; ⓦ whitstableoysterfestival .co.uk) sees the place come alive with a parade, performances, the "Landing of the Oysters" ceremony and raucous oyster-eating competitions.

Follow the signs from the vibrant **High Street** and **Harbour Street**, with its delis, restaurants and indie stores, to reach the **seafront**, a quiet shingle beach punctuated by weathered groynes and backed for most of its length by seaside houses and colourful beach huts in varying states of repair.

## Whitstable Harbour

The Victorian **harbour**, a mix of pretty and gritty that defines Whitstable to a tee, bustles with a fish market, whelk stalls and a couple of seafood restaurants, and offers plenty of places to sit outside and watch the activity. The handsome 1892 Thames sailing barge, **Greta** (☎ 07711 657919, ⓦ greta1892.co.uk), offers boat trips around the estuary.

## ARRIVAL AND INFORMATION WHITSTABLE

**By train** From the train station it's a 15min walk to the centre, along Cromwell Road to Harbour St, the northern continuation of High Street.

**Destinations** Broadstairs (Mon–Sat every 30min; 25min); London Victoria (every 30min–1hr; 1hr 30min); Margate (Mon–Sat every 30min; 23min); Ramsgate (Mon–Sat every 30min; 35min).

**By bus** Buses #4, #4A, #4B and #5 shuttle between Whitstable town centre and Canterbury (every 15min; 30min).

**Tourist information** The Whitstable Shop, 34 Harbour Street (Mon–Fri 10am–4pm, Sat 10am–3pm, Sun 11am–2pm; ☎ 01227 770060, ⓦ canterbury.co.uk).

**2**

## GETTING AROUND

**By bike** Local cycle routes include the picturesque Crab and Winkle Way, a disused railway line linking the town to Canterbury, 6 miles away, and the coastal Oyster Bay Trail.
**Bike rental** Kent Cycle Hire, 61 Harbour Street (book in advance; ☎01227 388058, ⓦkentcyclehire.com), rents bikes from £18/day to £77/week, with tandems and child seats available. You can also pick up here and drop off in Canterbury.

## ACCOMMODATION

**Copeland House** 4 Island Wall ☎01227 266207, ⓦcopelandhouse.co.uk. Georgian B&B in a great location, with a garden backing onto the beachside walk. The six rooms – two with sea views – are cosy and comfortable; some bathrooms are private but not en suite (gowns are provided). No credit cards. £85

★**Fishermen's Huts** Near the harbour ☎01227 280280, ⓦwhitstablefishermanshuts.com. Thirteen two-storey weatherboard cockle-farmers' huts (sleeping two to six) offering cute, characterful accommodation near the harbour. Most have sea views, and some have basic self-catering facilities. Rates include full breakfast, served at the nearby *Continental Hotel*; weekday rates soar during school holidays. Sun–Thurs £95, Fri & Sat (two-night min) £195

## EATING AND DRINKING

**Old Neptune** Marine Terrace ☎01227 272262, ⓦneppy.co.uk. Standing alone in its white weatherboards on the beach, this atmospheric pub is the perfect spot to enjoy a sundowner at a picnic table on the shingle, or to hunker down with a pint after a bracing beach walk. Some real ales, plus occasional live music. Mon–Wed & Sun noon–10.30pm, Thurs noon–11pm, Fri & Sat noon–11.30pm.

★**The Sportsman** Faversham Rd, Seasalter ☎01227 273370, ⓦthesportsmanseasalter.co.uk. The drab exterior belies the Michelin-starred experience inside this fabulous gastropub, in a lonesome spot between marshes and beach four miles west of town. The faultless, deceptively simple food takes local sourcing to the extreme: fresh seafood, marsh lamb, veg from a farm down the road, seaweed from the beach, bread and butter made right here – even the salt comes from the sea outside. Mains from £18; reservations advised. Food served Tues–Sat noon–2pm & 7–9pm, Sun noon–2.30pm.

★**Wheeler's Oyster Bar** 8 High St ☎01227 273311, ⓦwheelersoysterbar.com. A Whitstable institution dating back to 1856, this is one of the best restaurants in Kent. It's an informal, friendly little place, with just four tables in a tiny back parlour and a few stools at the fish counter, but the inventive, super-fresh seafood is stunning, whether you choose fresh oysters, a "light plate" or more substantial mains (from £16) like halibut roasted with a chorizo crust. Takeout from the counter includes tasty crab sandwiches for a couple of quid. BYO; cash only; reservations advised. Mon & Tues 10.30am–9pm, Thurs 10.15am–9pm, Fri 10.15am–9.30pm, Sat 10am–10pm, Sun 11.30am–9pm.

# Margate

The seaside town of **MARGATE** may not be the prettiest on the Kent coast, but its offbeat combination of eccentricity, nostalgia and cheery seaside fun give it a definite appeal. With the splendid **Turner Contemporary**, a cluster of funky cafés, **vintage shops** and indie galleries in the old town, and a couple of excellent places to stay – not to mention the golden sandy **beach** – a stopover in Margate has plenty to recommend it.

## Turner Contemporary

Rendezvous • Tues–Sun 10am–6pm • Free • ☎01843 233000, ⓦturnercontemporary.org

Rearing up on the east side of the harbour, the stunning, opalescent **Turner Contemporary** dominates the seafront. Named for J.M.W. Turner, who went to school in the Old Town in the 1780s, and who returned frequently as an adult to take advantage of the dazzling light, the gallery is built on the site of the lodging house where he painted some of his famous seascapes. Offering fantastic views of the ever-changing seascape through its enormous windows, the tranquil space hosts temporary exhibitions of high-profile contemporary art.

## Shell Grotto

Grotto Hill • Easter–Oct daily 10am–5pm; Nov–Easter Sat & Sun 11am–4pm • £3.50 • ☎01843 220008, ⓦshellgrotto.co.uk

Discovered, or so the story goes, in 1835, Margate's bizarre **Shell Grotto** has been captivating visitors ever since. Accessed via a damp subterranean passageway, the grotto's hallways and chambers are completely covered with mosaics made entirely from shells – more than 4.5 million of them, tinted silvery grey and black by the fumes of Victorian gas lamps. The origins of the grotto remain a mystery – some believe it to be an ancient pagan temple, others a more recent Regency folly – which only adds to its offbeat charm.

## ARRIVAL AND INFORMATION

**By train** The station is near the seafront on Station Road.
Destinations Broadstairs (every 5–30min; 5min); Canterbury (hourly; 30min); London Street Pancras (hourly; 1hr 30min); London Victoria (Mon–Sat every 30min; 1hr 50min); Ramsgate (every 5–20min; 10min); Whitstable (Mon–Sat every 30min; 23min).
**By bus** Buses pull in at the clocktower on Marine Parade.

**MARGATE**

Destinations Broadstairs (every 5–15min; 25min); Canterbury (every 20–30min; 50min); London Victoria (4 daily; 2hr 30min); Ramsgate (every 5–15min; 30min).
**Tourist office** The Droit House, Harbour Arm (April–Oct daily 10am–5pm; Nov–March Tues–Sat 10am–5pm; ☎01843 577577, ⓦvisitthanet.co.uk).

## ACCOMMODATION

**Reading Rooms** 31 Hawley Square ☎01843 225166, ⓦthereadingroomsmargate.co.uk. Stunning boutique B&B in a handsome Georgian townhouse. The three artfully distressed guest rooms have huge, luxurious bathrooms; breakfast Is served in your room. No children. **£150**
★**Walpole Bay Hotel** Fifth Ave, Cliftonville ☎01843 221703, ⓦwalpolebayhotel.co.uk. This family-run hotel

has changed little since Edwardian times, and exudes an air of shabby gentility from its pot-plant-cluttered dining room to its clanky vintage elevator. Don't miss the living museum and collection of napery art; with its eccentric charm, the *Walpole* is a favourite of many artists and writers. Rooms vary considerably, but most have sea views, and all are comfy, clean and well equipped. **£85**

## EATING AND DRINKING

**BeBeached** Harbour Arm ☎01843 226008, ⓦbebeached.co.uk. Irresistible on a sunny day, this colourful café – spot the kitsch pink parasols – offers cheery, creative comfort food. Brunches are particularly popular, and there are some great veggie options. Service can be slow when it's busy, so take your time, relax on a deckchair and drink in the sea view. Mains from £7. Wed, Thurs & Sun 11am–4.30pm, Fri & Sat 11am–4.30pm & 7.30–9.30pm.
★**GB Pizza Co** 14a Marine Drive ☎01843 297700, ⓦgreatbritishpizza.com. Phenomenally good, thin-crust

gourmet pizzas on the seafront – try the Margate-rita, or pear and blue cheese – plus fab coffee, cakes and organic wine. Gluten-free bases available. Mon–Sat noon–9pm, Sun noon–3pm.
★**The Lifeboat** 1 Market St ☎07837 024259, ⓦthelifeboat-margate.com. Cosy tavern on the Old Town's main square with a friendly, rustic interior, a great range of local drinks – ales, wines, ciders, perries and juices – and artisan cheeses, sausages and pies from Kentish producers. Live folk music, too. Daily noon–midnight or earlier.

# Broadstairs

Overlooking its golden sandy beach – Viking Bay – from its cliff-top setting, unspoiled **BROADSTAIRS** is the smallest and most immediately charming of the resort towns in northeast Kent. A fishing village turned Victorian resort, it's within walking distance of several sandy **bays** and is renowned for its excellent **folk festival**. It also has strong **Charles Dickens** connections: the author stayed in various hotels here, and eventually rented an "airy nest" overlooking the sea, where he finished writing *David Copperfield*. A small **museum** and, in June, the **Dickens Festival** (ⓦbroadstairsdickensfestival.co.uk), play up the associations.

## Dickens House Museum

2 Victoria Parade • Daily: Easter to mid-June, Sept & Oct 1–4.30pm; mid-June to Aug 10am–5pm • £3.75 • ☎01843 861232, ⓦdickensfellowship.org/broadstairs

The broad balconied cottage that now houses the **Dickens House Museum** was once the home of Miss Mary Pearson Strong, on whom Dickens based the character of Betsey Trotwood in *David Copperfield*. Inside you'll find Victorian posters, photography and costumes, Dickens' correspondence, illustrations from the original novels and a reconstruction of Betsey Trotwood's parlour.

## ARRIVAL AND DEPARTURE

**By train** Broadstairs station is on Lloyd Road, a 10min walk along the High Street to the seafront.
Destinations Canterbury (hourly; 25min); London St Pancras (hourly; 1hr 20min); London Victoria (every 30min–hourly; 1hr 55min); Margate (every 5–30min; 5min); Ramsgate (every 20min–hourly; 7min); Whitstable (Mon–Sat every 30min; 25min).

## BROADSTAIRS

**By bus** Buses stop along the High Street.
Destinations Canterbury (every 20–30min; 1hr 30min); London Victoria (4 daily; 2hr 45min); Margate (every 5–15min; 25min); Ramsgate (every 10–20min; 10min).
**Tourist information** The nearest tourist office is in Margate (see p.137); ⓦ visitbroadstairs.co.uk is a useful website.

## ACCOMMODATION

★**Belvidere Place** Belvedere Rd ☎01843 579850, ⓦ belvidereplace.co.uk. This stylish, quirky boutique B&B earns extra points for its warm, friendly management and gourmet breakfasts. The five lovely rooms feature sleek bathrooms, contemporary art and one-off vintage furniture finds. **£130**

**East Horndon Hotel** 4 Eastern Esplanade ☎01843 868306, ⓦ easthorndonhotel.com. Comfortable B&B in a spacious Victorian house overlooking Stone Bay, just a 5min seaside stroll from the centre of Broadstairs. Rooms are large, spruce and well equipped, some with sea views. **£80**

## EATING AND DRINKING

**Morelli's** 14 Victoria Parade ☎01843 862500 ⓦ morellisgelato.com/stores/broadstairs. Deliciously old-fashioned 1930s ice-cream parlour, with vintage formica, leatherette and wicker decor and a free jukebox featuring Sinatra and Rat Pack classics. Scoops of delicious home-made gelato cost from £2. Mon–Fri 8am–5.30pm, Sat & Sun 8am–6pm.

**Tartar Frigate** Harbour St ☎01843 862013, ⓦ tartarfrigate.co.uk. In an unbeatable location right on the harbour, this eighteenth-century flint pub is a relaxed, friendly place to hangout, with regular folk bands and jam sessions. There's a popular seafood restaurant upstairs, too

(for which you should book ahead). Pub Mon–Sat 11am–11pm, Sun 11am–10.30pm; restaurant Mon–Sat noon–1.45pm & 7–9.45pm, Sun seatings 12.30pm & 3.30pm.

★**Wyatt & Jones** 23–27 Harbour St ☎01843 865126, ⓦ wyattandjones.co.uk. Stylish, airy restaurant a pebble's throw from the beach, dishing up super-fresh Modern British food – smoked cod in a wild garlic and mussel chowder, duck breast with herb potato cake and braised chicory – using the best seasonal, mainly Kentish, ingredients. Mains from £12. Mon–Sat 9–11am, noon–3pm & 6–10pm, Sun 9–11am & 12.30–5pm.

# Ramsgate

**RAMSGATE**, the largest of the Thanet towns, is rich in robust Victorian red brick and elegant Georgian squares. It has a handsome location, set high on a cliff that's linked to the seafront and **Royal Harbour** by broad, sweeping ramps. Down by the bustling harbour a collection of cafés and bars overlooks the bobbing yachts, while the town's small, popular **beach** lies just a short stroll away.

## Ramsgate Maritime Museum

Clock House, Royal Harbour • May–Sept Tues–Sun 10am–5.30pm • £1.50 • ☎01843 570662, ⓦ ramsgatemaritimemuseum.org

The **Ramsgate Maritime Museum** chronicles the seafaring history of the area from Roman times. One illuminating section focuses on the Goodwin Sands sandbanks, six miles southeast of Ramsgate – the occasional playing pitch of the eccentric Goodwin Sands Cricket Club.

## ARRIVAL AND DEPARTURE

**By train** Ramsgate's station lies about a mile northwest of the centre, at the end of Wilfred Road, at the top of the High Street.
Destinations Broadstairs (every 20min–hourly; 7min); Canterbury (hourly; 22min); Faversham (Mon–Sat every 30min; 40min); London Street Pancras (hourly; 1hr 15min); London Charing Cross (every 20–40min; 2hr 15min);

## RAMSGATE

London Victoria (Mon–Sat every 30min–hourly; 2hr); Margate (every 5–20min; 10min); Whitstable (Mon–Sat every 30min; 35min).
**By bus** Buses pull in at the harbour.
Destinations Broadstairs (every 10–20min; 10min); Canterbury (Mon–Sat hourly; 45min); London Victoria (4 daily; 3hr); Margate (every 5–15min; 30min).

## ACCOMMODATION, EATING AND DRINKING

**Age & Sons** Charlotte Court ☎01843 851515, ⓦ ageandsons.co.uk. Three options, occupying a Victorian warehouse on a shady square, accessed by an alley: a relaxed ground-floor café with comfy outdoor seating, a restaurant offering creative Kentish cuisine (mains from £11), and a basement bar. Café: Tues–Sun 10am–5pm (kitchen closes 3.30pm); restaurant: Tues–Sat noon–3.30pm & 7–9.30pm, Sun noon–3.30pm; bar: Fri & Sat 7pm–late.

**Belgian Café** 98 Royal Parade ☎01843 587925, ⓦ www.belgiancafe.co.uk. Big, informal brasserie-style place near the seafront, its outside tables spilling over with an eclectic crowd enjoying great breakfasts and brunches, Belgian beers, real ales and marina views. Occasional live music. Sun–Thurs 7am–2am, Fri & Sat 7am–3am.

**Caboose Café and Bar** 18 Queen St ☎01843 570984, ⓦ caboosecafe.co.uk. Casual coffee bar that's both friendly and cool, with gourmet coffee and an inexpensive light menu – sandwiches, salads, Mediterranean-style snacks – plus big breakfasts and brunches, with a Mexican menu in the evening. Regular live events. Mon & Tues 9am–5pm, Wed–Fri 9am–11pm, Sat 10am–11pm, Sun 10am–5pm.

**Royal Harbour Hotel** 10–12 Nelson Crescent ☎01843 591514, ⓦ royalharbourhotel.co.uk. Two interconnecting Georgian townhouses with 27 quirky, nautically themed rooms, from tiny "cabins" to four-posters with sea views, and a cosy lounge with real fire, newspapers and an honesty bar. <u>£120</u>

# Canterbury

The fine old city of **CANTERBURY** offers a rich slice through two thousand years of English history, with Roman and early Christian remains, a ruined Norman castle and a famous cathedral that looms over a medieval warren of time-skewed Tudor buildings. Its compact centre, partly ringed by ancient **walls**, is virtually car-free, but this doesn't stop the High Street seizing up in high summer with the milling crowds.

### Brief history

The city that began as a Belgic settlement was known as **Durovernum Cantiacorum** to the Romans, who established a garrison and supply base here, and renamed **Cantwarabyrig** by the Saxons. In 597 the Saxon King Ethelbert welcomed the monk Augustine, despatched by the pope to convert England to Christianity; one of the two Benedictine monasteries founded by Augustine – Christ Church, raised on the site of the Roman basilica – was to become England's first cathedral.

After the Norman invasion, a power struggle ensued between the archbishops, the abbots from the nearby monastery – now **St Augustine's Abbey** – and King Henry II. This culminated in the assassination of Archbishop **Thomas à Becket** in the cathedral in 1170, a martyrdom that created one of Christendom's greatest shrines and made Canterbury one of the country's richest cities. Geoffrey Chaucer's **Canterbury Tales**, written towards the end of the fourteenth century, portrays the festive, ribald nature of medieval pilgrimages to Becket's tomb, which was later plundered and destroyed on the orders of Henry VIII.

With its pilgrimage days effectively over, the next couple of centuries saw a downturn in Canterbury's fortunes. In 1830, however, a pioneering passenger railway service, linking the city to the seaside at Whitstable, resulted in another bout of growth. Canterbury suffered extensive damage from German bombing in 1942 during one of the **"Baedeker Raids"** – a Nazi campaign to destroy Britain's most treasured historic sites as identified in the eponymous German travel guides. The cathedral survived, however, and today, along with St Augustine's Abbey and the venerable St Martin's Church (at the corner of B. Holmes Road and St Martin's Lane), has been designated by UNESCO as a **World Heritage Site**.

## Canterbury Cathedral

Buttermarket • April–Oct Mon–Sat 9am–5.30pm, Sun 12.30–2.30pm; Nov–March Mon–Sat 9am–5pm, Sun 12.30–2.30pm; last entry 30min before closing; tours Mon–Fri 10.30am (not in Jan), noon & 2pm (2.30pm in summer), Sat 10.30am, noon & 1pm • £10.50, guided tours £5, audio-tours £4 • ☎01227 762862, ⓦ www.canterbury-cathedral.org

Mother Church of the Church of England, **Canterbury Cathedral** fills the northeast

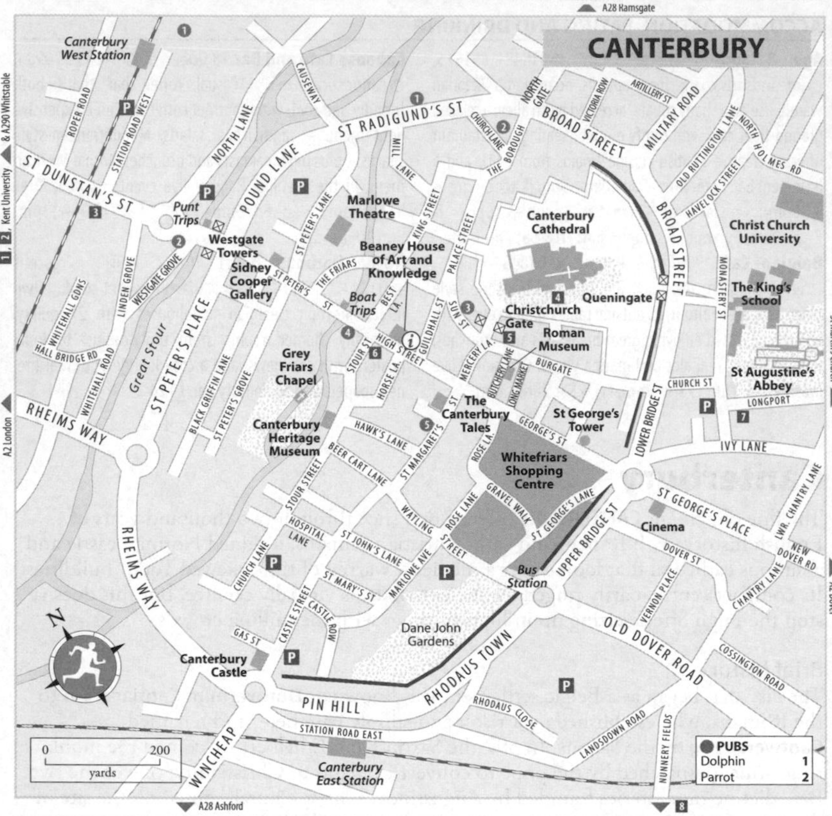

**CANTERBURY**

*Map labels (clockwise/by area):*

A28 Ramsgate · A28 Ashford · A2 London · A2 Dover · Kent University & A290 Whitstable · St Martin's Church

Canterbury West Station · ROVER ROAD · STATION ROAD WEST · NORTH LANE · CAUSEWAY · ST RADIGUND'S ST · MILL LANE · THE BOROUGH · CHURCH LANE · NORTH GATE · VICTORIA ROW · ARTILLERY ST · MILITARY ROAD · OLD RUTTINGTON LANE · NORTH HOLMES RD · HAVELOCK STREET · MONASTERY ST

ST DUNSTAN'S ST · POUND LANE · ST PETER'S LANE · NORTH LANE · THE FRIARS · KING STREET · PALACE STREET · BROAD STREET · OLD RUTTINGTON LANE

Marlowe Theatre · Beaney House of Art and Knowledge · Canterbury Cathedral · Christ Church University · The King's School

Punt Trips · Westgate Towers · Sidney Cooper Gallery · Boat Trips · Christchurch Gate · Queningate · Roman Museum · St Augustine's Abbey

WESTGATE GROVE · LINDEN GROVE · WHITEFALL GDNS · HALL BRIDGE RD · WHITEFALL ROAD · LINDEN GROVE · BLACK GRIFFIN LANE · ST PETER'S GROVE · GUILDHALL ST · THE FRIARS · HIGH STREET · MERCERY LANE · BURGATE · BUTCHERY LANE · CHURCH ST · LONGPORT · IVY LANE

Grey Friars Chapel · Canterbury Heritage Museum · The Canterbury Tales · St George's Tower · Whitefriars Shopping Centre · Cinema

RHEIMS WAY · Great Stour · ST PETER'S PLACE · HAWK'S LANE · BEER CART LANE · ST MARGARET'S ST · ROSE LANE · GEORGE'S ST · GRAVEL WALK · ST GEORGE'S LANE · LOWER BRIDGE ST · UPPER BRIDGE ST · ST GEORGE'S PLACE · LWR CHANTRY LANE · NEW DOVER RD · CHANTRY LANE

STOUR STREET · HOSPITAL LANE · ST JOHN'S LANE · WATLING STREET · ROSE LANE · MARLOWE AVE · ST MARY'S ST · DOVER ST · VERNON PLACE

CHURCH LANE · CASTLE STREET · CASTLE ROW · GAS ST · Bus Station · Dane John Gardens · OLD DOVER ROAD · COSSINGTON ROAD

N · Canterbury Castle · PIN HILL · WINCHEAP · RHODAUS TOWN · RHODAUS CLOSE · STATION ROAD EAST · LANSDOWN ROAD · NUNNERY FIELDS

Canterbury East Station

| 0 | 200 |
|---|---|
| | yards |

| ■ ACCOMMODATION | | | | |
|---|---|---|---|---|
| ABode | 6 | House of Agnes | 3 | No. 7 Longport |
| Arthouse B&B | 1 | Kipps | 8 | YHA Canterbury |
| Cathedral Gate | 5 | Neals Place Farm | 2 | |

| No. 7 Longport | 7 |
|---|---|
| YHA Canterbury | 4 |

| ● PUBS | |
|---|---|
| Dolphin | 1 |
| Parrot | 2 |

| ● CAFÉS & RESTAURANTS | | | |
|---|---|---|---|
| Boho Café | 4 | The Goods Shed | 1 |
| Café des Amis | 2 | Tiny Tim's | 5 |
| Deeson's | 3 | | |

quadrant of the city with a sense of authority, even if architecturally it's not the country's most impressive. A cathedral has stood here since 602, but the building you see today owes most to a Norman archbishop, Lanfranc, who in 1070 rebuilt the place after a huge fire. It was modified over successive centuries, and today the puritanical lines of the late medieval Perpendicular style dominate.

### The interior

In the magnificent interior, look for the tomb of Henry IV and his wife, Joan of Navarre, and for the gilt bronze effigy of Edward III's son, the Black Prince, all of them in the **Trinity Chapel** beyond the Gothic Quire. Vivid medieval **stained-glass windows** here depict the life and miraculous works of Thomas à Becket. The spot where Becket died, known as "The Martyrdom", is in the northwest transept by the **Altar of the Sword's Point**, where a jagged modern sculpture of the assassins' weapons is suspended on the wall. Steps from here descend to the low, Romanesque arches of the **crypt**, one of the few remaining relics of the Norman cathedral and considered the finest such structure in the country, with some amazingly well-preserved carvings on the capitals of the sturdy columns.

# Roman Museum

Butchery Lane • Daily 10am–5pm • £8 • ☎ 01227 785575, ⓦ canterbury.co.uk/museums

Following the devastating German bombings of 1942, excavations of the destroyed Longmarket area, off the High Street, exposed the foundations of a Roman townhouse complete with mosaic floors. These are now preserved *in situ* in the subterranean **Roman Museum**, but it's the rich haul of **artefacts**, domestic and military, that prove to be the big attraction.

**2**

# Canterbury Tales

St Margaret's St • Daily: Jan, Feb, Nov & Dec 10am–4.30pm; March–June, Sept & Oct 10am–5pm; July & Aug 9.30am–5pm • £8.75, children £6.75 • ☎ 01227 479227, ⓦ canterburytales.org.uk

Based on Geoffrey Chaucer's book, the **Canterbury Tales** is a quasi-educational, fun, attraction. Costumed guides set you on your way through odour-enhanced galleries depicting a series of fourteenth-century tableaux as you follow the progress of a group of pilgrims (or rather, suitably scrofulous mannequins) from London to Becket's fabulously ornate shrine. Each new space provides a setting for one of the famous tales.

# Beaney House of Art and Knowledge

18 High St • Mon–Wed, Fri & Sat 9am–5pm, Thurs 9am–7pm, Sun 10am–5pm • Free • ☎ 01227 378100, ⓦ thebeaney.co.uk

With its stuffed animals, pinned beetles and intriguing cases of **antiquities and archeological finds**, the **Beaney House of Art and Knowledge**, a sturdy terracotta, brick and mock-Tudor ensemble built in 1898, has the not unlikeable feel of a Victorian collection. Don't miss the **paintings**, including the Van Dyck portrait of Kent MP Sir Basil Dixwell (1638), a Walter Sickert landscape (1937), painted during his four-year stay on the Kent coast, and the vigorous images of 1930s Kentish hop-pickers and gypsies by English Impressionist Dame Laura Knight.

# Canterbury Heritage Museum

Stour St • Daily 10am–5pm • £8 • ☎ 01227 475202, ⓦ canterbury.co.uk/museums

The **Canterbury Heritage Museum** provides an excellent jaunt through local history, with particularly strong sections on the Roman city, the medieval pilgrimage era and the Tudors and Stuarts – and interesting sections on local literary figures Christopher Marlowe, Joseph Conrad and Oliver Postgate (originator, in the 1970s, of *Bagpuss* and *The Clangers*).

# St Augustine's Abbey

Monastery St • April–Sept daily 10am–6pm; Oct Wed–Sun 10am–5pm; Nov–March Sat & Sun 10am–4pm • £5.20; EH • ☎ 01227 767345, ⓦ english-heritage.org.uk

Ruined **St Augustine's Abbey**, founded as a monastery by Augustine in 598, was vastly altered and enlarged by the Normans before being destroyed in the Dissolution. Today, it is an atmospheric site, with more to see than its ruinous state might suggest. Ground plans, clearly delineated in stone on soft carpets of grass, along with scattered semi-intact chapels, altar slabs and tombstones, evoke the original buildings almost as powerfully as if they were still standing, while information panels admirably recount the abbey's changing fortunes.

**ARRIVAL AND INFORMATION**                      **CANTERBURY**

**By train** Canterbury has two train stations: Canterbury East (in the south) and Canterbury West (in the north), each a 15min walk from the cathedral. Canterbury West is used by the high-speed train from London St Pancras.

Destinations from Canterbury East Chatham (every 30min; 45min); Dover Priory (Mon–Sat every 30min, Sun hourly; 30min); London Victoria (every 30min; 1hr 35min); Rochester (every 30–45min; 50min).

**Destinations from Canterbury West** Ashford (every 10–30min; 15–25min); Broadstairs (hourly; 25min); London Bridge (Mon–Sat every 30min; 1hr 40min); London Charing Cross (Mon–Sat every 30min; 1hr 45min); London St Pancras (Mon–Sat hourly; 55min); Margate (hourly; 30min); Ramsgate (hourly; 22min).

**By bus** National Express services and local Stagecoach East Kent buses use the station just inside the city walls on St George's Lane beside the Whitefriars shopping complex.

**Destinations** Broadstairs (every 20–30min; 1hr 30min); Deal (Mon–Sat 1–3 hourly, Sun 5 daily; 1hr 5min); Dover (every 30min–6 daily; 35min); London Victoria (hourly; 1hr 50min); Margate (every 20–30min; 50min); Ramsgate (hourly; 45min); Sandwich (every 20min–5 daily; 40min); Whitstable (every 15min; 30min).

**Tourist office** In the Beaney, 18 High Street (Mon–Wed 9am–5pm, Thurs 9am–7pm, Fri & Sat 9am–5pm, Sun 10am–5pm; T 01227 861162, W canterbury.co.uk).

## ACCOMMODATION

Canterbury accommodation consists mostly of B&Bs and small hotels and can be difficult to secure in July and August, when prices increase – book well in advance if possible.

### HOTELS AND B&BS

**ABode** 30 High St T 01227 766266, W abodehotels.co.uk/canterbury. Standard rooms are rather ordinary, while the priciest suite comes with a rooftop terrace and cathedral views. Various, good-value online packages are available. *Michael Caines'* restaurant and his less expensive tavern are on site. **£130**

**Arthouse B&B** 24 London Rd T 07976 725457, W arthousebandb.com. You get a variety of options, and wonderful seclusion in this funky B&B situated in an old fire station, a 10min walk from Westgate. The main Victorian house has two doubles (each with private bathroom) sharing a lounge and kitchen – you can rent both and have the place completely to yourself. There's also a sunny self-contained double and a modern Scandinavian-style timber studio in the back garden. A DIY continental breakfast is optional. **£65**

**Cathedral Gate** 36 Burgate T 01227 464381, W cathgate.co.uk. Built in 1438 and with a fantastic location next to the cathedral, this ancient pilgrims' hostelry – all crooked, creaking floors and narrow, steep staircases – is in no way fancy, but it's comfortable, with cathedral views from many of the rooms and a simple continental breakfast. The cheapest rooms share toilets and (tiny) showers, but have basins and tea- and coffee-making facilities. **£81.50**

**House of Agnes** 71 St Dunstan's St T 01227 472185, W houseofagnes.co.uk. You can't fail but be charmed by the crooked exterior of this quirky B&B near Westgate, which has eight individually themed and designed rooms in the main fourteenth-century house (mentioned in *David Copperfield*), and another eight, less characterful, options in the large walled garden at the back. There's a guest lounge with an honesty bar. **£90**

**★No. 7 Longport** 7 Longport T 01227 455367, W 7longport.co.uk. This fabulous little hideaway – a tiny, luxuriously decorated fifteenth-century cottage with a double bedroom, wet room and lounge – is tucked away in the courtyard garden of the friendly owners' home, opposite St Augustine's Abbey. Breakfasts are wonderful, with lots of locally sourced ingredients, and can be eaten in the main house or the courtyard. **£90**

### HOSTELS

**★Kipps** 40 Nunnery Fields T 01227 786121, W kipps-hostel.com. This excellent self-catering hostel, a 10min walk from Canterbury East Station, is clean and very friendly with homely touches and a nice walled garden. Nightly events mean you can be sociable, but it's more a home from home than a party hostel. No curfew. Single-sex and mixed en-suite dorms plus single, double and triple rooms. Dorms **£19.50**, doubles **£65**

**YHA Canterbury** 54 New Dover Rd T 0845 371 9010, W yha.org.uk/hostel/canterbury. Half a mile out of town, 15min on foot from Canterbury East Station, this seventy-bed hostel is set in a Victorian villa. There's a café and self-catering facilities. It's closed during the day, with an 11pm curfew. Dorms **£19**, doubles **£52**

### CAMPSITE

**Neals Place Farm** Neals Place Rd T 01227 765632, W nealsplacefarmcampsite.co.uk. On a working farm off the A290, a mere 20min walk from the city, this is a peaceful campsite, with eighteen spacious pitches in an orchard. Closed Oct–March. Pitches **£10** (plus £2.50 per person), caravan **£20** (plus £2.50 per person)

## EATING

**Boho Café** 27 High St T 01227 458931. This funky café-bar, with its paintbox-bright, mismatched decor, has a cheerful neighbourhood feel. The menu (around £5–10) ranges from big breakfasts via tapas and coffee and cake to home-made burgers. There's seating on the street, and a pretty suntrap garden at the back. Free wi-fi. Mon–Sat 9am–6pm, Sun 10am–5pm.

**Café des Amis** 93–95 St Dunstan's St T 01227 464390,

**2**

ⓦcafedez.com. Very popular, lively Mexican/Tex-Mex place with eclectic, carnivalesque decor and delicious food. Try the paella (£26.50 for two) followed by a bubbling chocolate *fundido*. Mon–Thurs noon–10pm, Fri noon–10.30pm, Sat 10am–10.30pm, Sun 9am–9.30pm.

**Deeson's** 25–26 Sun St ☎01227 767854, ⓦdeesonsrestaurant.co.uk. With its fresh flowers, linocuts and local art, this is an appealing setting in which to enjoy creative Modern British cuisine. Based on local produce, the menu changes regularly, but mains (from £13) such as roast loin of saltmarsh lamb with salsify are typical. Good-value set lunch and early evening menus. Mon–Sat noon–3pm & 5–10pm, Sun noon–10pm.

★**The Goods Shed** Station Rd West ☎01227 459153, ⓦthegoodsshed.co.uk. It doesn't get any more locally sourced than this – a buzzing, shabby-chic Modern British restaurant in the excellent Goods Shed farmers' market, where most of the ingredients are provided by the stalls themselves. The regularly changing menu might feature dishes such as scallops with bean purée and chorizo (£8.50), or pork chop with black pudding and apple and quince purée (£14). Tues–Fri 8–10.30am, noon–2.30pm & 6–9.30pm, Sat 8–10.30am, noon–3pm & 6–9.30pm, Sun 9–10.30am & noon–3pm.

**Tiny Tim's** 34 St Margaret's St ☎01227 450793, ⓦtinytimstearoom.com. Despite the name there's nothing twee about this elegant, 1930s-inspired tearoom, which offers more than twenty blends of tea as well as luxurious afternoon teas (all day, from £16.50), breakfasts and light lunches. In good weather you can sit in the cute back garden. Tues–Sat 9.30am–5pm, Sun 10.30am–4pm.

## DRINKING

Canterbury is a nice place for a drink, with a number of pubs serving **real ales** in cosy, historic buildings. The local Shepherd Neame-owned places are in the majority, but look out, too, for beers from Canterbury's own Wantsum and Canterbury breweries.

**Dolphin** 17 St Radigund's St ☎01227 455963, ⓦthedolphincanterbury.co.uk. Likeable 1930s-built pub with a good selection of local real ales, a log fire in winter and a big, grassy beer garden in summer. Tasty food, too; the Sunday lunch (not available in summer) is a local favourite. Daily noon–late.

**Parrot** Radigund's Hall, 1–9 Church Lane ☎01227 762355, ⓦtheparrotonline.com. Ancient hostelry – one of the oldest in Canterbury – in a quiet location, with loads of character, a decent selection of ales and a not-quite-gastro gastropub menu. There's a beer terrace at the back. Daily noon–late.

## ENTERTAINMENT

Taking place over two weeks in October, the **Canterbury Festival** (ⓦcanterburyfestival.co.uk) offers an international mix of music, theatre and performance. **Lounge on the Farm** (ⓦloungeonthefarm.co.uk), meanwhile, in early July, is a family-friendly and relatively chilled contender on the music festival calendar, staging a smart range of nostalgia bands, big names and up-and-coming local artists. Its location, on a working farm 10min south of Canterbury, is due to change in 2015, so check the website for news.

**Gulbenkian Theatre** Kent University ☎01227 769075, ⓦthegulbenkian.co.uk. Various cultural events, including contemporary drama, dance, comedy and film, are hosted at this excellent theatre-cum-cinema.

**Marlowe Theatre** The Friars ☎01227 787787, ⓦmarlowetheatre.com. This modern theatre, named after the sixteenth-century Canterbury-born playwright, is the city's main venue for mainstream music, drama and shows.

# Sandwich and around

Tiny **SANDWICH**, one of the best-preserved medieval towns in the country, is a sleepy, picturesque place, with some fine half-timbered buildings lining its narrow lanes, a peaceful **quayside** and a lovely location on the willow-lined banks of the River Stour. It also boasts one of England's best golf courses, the **Royal St George's Golf Course** (ⓦroyalstgeorges.com), less than a mile east of town.

## The quayside

Sandwich's riverfront **quayside**, peaceful today, was once the heart of a great medieval port. Thanks to silting up of the estuary the sea is now miles away, but the waterfront gives the place a breezily nautical atmosphere, with small boats moored by the toll

## THE CINQUE PORTS

In 1278 Dover, Hythe, Sandwich, Romney and Hastings – already part of a long-established but unofficial confederation of defensive coastal settlements – were formalized under a charter by Edward I as the **Cinque Ports** (pronounced "sink", despite the name's French origin). In return for providing England with maritime support, the five ports were granted trading privileges and other liberties – including self-government, exemption from taxes and tolls and "possession of goods thrown overboard" – that enabled them to prosper while neighbouring ports struggled.

Rye, Winchelsea and seven other **"limb" ports** on the southeast coast were later added to the confederation. The ports' privileges were eventually revoked in 1685; their maritime services had become increasingly unnecessary after Henry VIII had founded a professional navy and, due to a shifting coastline, several of their harbours had silted up anyway, stranding some of them miles inland. Today, of all the Cinque Ports, only Dover is still a major working port.

bridge, open countryside stretching out across the river, and the cry of seagulls raking the air. **Boat trips** (£7–35; ☎ 07958 376183, ⊛ sandwichriverbus.co.uk) run from the toll bridge over the Stour up to Richborough Roman Fort and down to the estuary to spot seals and birds.

### ARRIVAL AND INFORMATION                                   SANDWICH

**By train** Sandwich station is off St George's Road, from where it's a 10min walk north to the town centre and the quay.
Destinations Deal (every 30min–1hr; 6min); Dover (every 30min–1hr; 25min); London Charing Cross (hourly; 2hr 20min); Ramsgate (hourly; 15min).
**By bus** Buses pull in and depart from outside the tourist office.

Destinations Canterbury (every 20min–1hr; 45min); Deal (Mon–Sat every 20min–1hr; 25–35min); Dover (Mon–Sat every 45min–1hr; 45min–1hr); Ramsgate (Mon–Sat hourly; 30min).
**Tourist office** In the Guildhall, Cattle Market, in the town centre (April–Oct Mon–Sat 10am–4pm; ☎ 01304 613565, ⊛ whitecliffscountry.org.uk).

### ACCOMMODATION

**Bell Hotel** The Quay ☎ 01304 613388, ⊛ bellhotel sandwich.co.uk. Rambling nineteenth-century hostelry that has stood on this site since Tudor times. Rooms are comfy, in an uncontroversial, contemporary style; the priciest have balconies overlooking the Stour. There's a good in-house restaurant, and service throughout is great. **£110**

### EATING AND DRINKING

**George and Dragon** 24 Fisher St ☎ 01304 613106, ⊛ georgeanddragon-sandwich.co.uk. A fifteenth-century inn and popular, unpretentious gastropub, with good Modern British food (mains average £13), well-kept cask ales, roaring real fires in winter and a courtyard for alfresco dining. Booking advised in the evening. Mon–Fri 11am–3pm & 6–11pm, Sat 11am–11pm, Sun 11am–4.30pm; food served Mon–Sat noon–2pm & 6–9pm, Sun noon–2pm.

**No Name** 1 No Name St ☎ 01304 612626, ⊛ nonameshop.co.uk. For picnic supplies, including hot baguettes, look no further than this excellent French deli opposite the Guildhall. During the day you can also choose from a seasonally changing menu of light French dishes – tartines, soups, quiche – and heartier mains such as baked mussels, duck confit and thyme-roasted chicken. Dishes around £5–10. Deli Mon–Sat 8am–5pm, Sun 9am–4pm; bistro daily 9am–3pm.

# Deal

The low-key seaside town of **DEAL**, six miles southeast of Sandwich, was the site of Julius Caesar's first successful landfall in Britain in 55 BC. Today it's an appealing place, with a broad, steeply shelving shingle **beach** backed by a jumble of faded Georgian townhouses, a picturesque **old town** redolent with maritime history, and a striking concrete **pier** lined with hopeful anglers casting their lines. Henry VIII's two seafront **castles**, linked by a seaside path, are the main attractions, and there are enough nice **places to eat**, drink and stay to make the town an appealing weekend destination.

## Deal Castle

Marine Rd • April–Sept daily 10am–6pm; Oct daily 10am–5pm; Nov–March Sat & Sun 10am–4pm • £5.20; EH • ☎ 01304 372762,
ⓦ english-heritage.org.uk

Diminutive **Deal Castle**, at the south end of town, is one of the most striking of Henry VIII's forts. Its distinctive shape – viewed from the air it looks like a Tudor rose – is owed less to aesthetics than to sophisticated military engineering: squat rounded walls would be better at deflecting missiles. Self-guided **audio-tours** outline every detail of the design, with the bare rooms revealing how the castle changed over the years and giving a good sense of how the soldiers lived.

## Walmer Castle

Kingsdown Rd, one mile south of Deal • April–Sept daily 10am–6pm; Oct daily 10am–5pm • £7.90; EH • ☎ 01304 364288, ⓦ english
-heritage.org.uk • Hourly Stagecoach buses from Deal; also accessible on foot along the seafront (30min)

South of Deal Castle, **Walmer Castle** is another of Henry VIII's rotund Tudor-rose-shaped defences, built to protect the coast from its enemies across the Channel. Like Deal Castle it saw little fighting, and changed use when it became the official residence of the Lords Warden of the Cinque Ports in 1708 (which it remains, though the title itself is now strictly ceremonial). Adapted over the years, today the castle resembles a heavily fortified stately home more than a military stronghold. The best-known resident was the Duke of Wellington, who was given the post of Lord Warden in 1828 and who died here in 1852; not surprisingly, the house is packed with memorabilia such as the armchair in which he expired and a pair of original Wellington boots.

### ARRIVAL AND INFORMATION                                          DEAL

**By train** The station is on Queen St, a 10min walk from the sea.
Destinations Dover (every 30min–1hr; 15min); London Charing Cross (every 30min–1hr; 2hr 10min); Ramsgate (every 30min–1hr; 20min); Sandwich (every 30min–1hr; 6min).
**By bus** Buses run from South Street in the town centre.

Destinations Canterbury (Mon–Sat 1–3 hourly, Sun 5 daily; 1hr 5min); Dover (every 20min–1hr; 50min); London Victoria (2 daily; 2hr 35min–3hr 25min); Sandwich (Mon–Sat every 20min–1hr; 25–35min).
**Tourist office** Town Hall, High Street (Mon–Fri 9.30am–1pm & 2–4.30pm, Sat 10am–2pm; ☎ 01304 369576, ⓦ whitecliffscountry.org.uk).

### ACCOMMODATION AND EATING

**81 Beach St** 81 Beach St ☎ 01304 368136, ⓦ 81beach street.co.uk. Unfussy, contemporary beachfront brasserie. Mains might include slow-cooked pork belly (£16) or baked skate with saffron rice (£15.50); weekday lunches are less expensive (two courses £12.80, three courses £15.90). Mon–Sat noon–3pm & 6–10pm, Sun noon–4pm.
★ **Black Douglas Coffee House** 82 Beach St ☎ 01304 365486, ⓦ blackdouglas.co.uk. Funky, cosily informal little spot on the blustery seafront, with scrubbed wooden tables, local art on the walls, newspapers and books for

browsing, and a focus on good, locally sourced home-made food. Mon–Thurs & Sat 9am–5pm, Fri 9am–5pm & 7–10pm, Sun 10am–4pm.
**Number 1 B&B** 1 Ranelagh Rd ☎ 01304 364459, ⓦ numberonebandb.co.uk. This friendly, popular B&B is the nicest place to stay in town. The handsome Victorian townhouse is in a great spot, near Deal Castle and the beach, and the four rooms are stylish and contemporary, with luxurious extras. Good breakfasts, too. Two-night minimum stay on summer weekends. **£87**

# Dover and around

Given its importance as a travel hub – it's the busiest ferry port in Europe – **DOVER** is surprisingly small, and, badly bombed during World War II, its town centre and seafront don't inspire many travellers to linger. The main attractions, however, are big ones: **Dover Castle**, looming proudly above town, and the iconic **White Cliffs**, flanking the town on both sides.

# Dover Castle

Castle Hill • April–July & Sept daily 10am–6pm; Aug daily 9.30am–6pm; Oct daily 10am–5pm; Nov to mid-Feb Sat & Sun 10am–4pm • £17.50; children £10.50; EH • ☎ 01304 211067, ⓦ english-heritage.org.uk

No historical stone goes unturned at **Dover Castle**, an astonishingly imposing defensive complex that has protected the English coast for more than two thousand years. In 1068 **William the Conqueror**, following the Battle of Hastings, built over the earthworks of an Iron Age hillfort here; a century later, Henry II constructed the handsome **keep**, or Great Tower, that now presides over the heart of the complex. The grounds also include a **Roman lighthouse**, a **Saxon church** – with motifs graffitied by irreverent Crusaders still visible near the pulpit – and all manner of later additions, including a network of **Secret Wartime Tunnels** dug during the Napoleonic Wars and extended during World War II.

Ideally you should allow a **full day** for a visit. If time is short, head first for the **Operation Dynamo tunnel tours**, affecting immersive experiences that, accompanied by the muffled sound of anti-aircraft guns and screaming Spitfires, shed light on the build-up to the war and the Dunkirk evacuation. From there, make your way to Henry's **Great Tower**. Here the opulent medieval royal court has been painstakingly recreated; everything from the pots and pans in the kitchen to the richly coloured furniture and wall hangings in the King's Chamber.

# The White Cliffs of Dover

Stretching sixteen miles along the coast, a towering 350ft high in places, the vast **White Cliffs of Dover** are composed of chalk – plus traces of quartz, shells and flint. Much of the cliffs lie within the Kent Downs Area of Outstanding Natural Beauty, and with their chalk grasslands home to rare plants, butterflies and migrant birds, have been designated a Site of Special Scientific Interest. A **walk** along the cliffs affords you amazing views of the Straits of Dover – and on a clear day you may well even see France.

## ARRIVAL AND INFORMATION | DOVER

**By train** Dover Priory station is off Folkestone Road, a 10min walk west of the centre.
Destinations Canterbury (every 30min–1hr; 30min); London Charing Cross (every 30min–1hr; 1hr 55min); London St Pancras (hourly; 1hr 10min); London Victoria (Mon–Sat every 20–40min; 2hr).
**By bus** Buses from London run to the ferry terminal, and then on to the town-centre bus station on Pencester Road.

Destinations Canterbury (every 30min–6 daily; 35min); Deal (every 20min–1hr; 50min); Hastings (every 1–2hr; 2hr 40min); London Victoria (every 30min–1hr; 2hr 5min–3hr); Sandwich (Mon–Sat every 45min–1hr; 45min–1hr).
**Tourist office** In the Dover Museum, Market Square (April–Sept Mon–Sat 9.30am–5pm, Sun 10am–3pm; Oct–March Mon–Sat 9.30am–5pm; ☎ 01304 201066, ⓦ whitecliffscountry.org.uk).

## ACCOMMODATION

**Maison Dieu** 89 Maison Dieu Rd ☎ 01304 204033, ⓦ maisondieu.com. Very welcoming, central guesthouse with seven spotless single, double, twin and family rooms, most of which are en suite. A few have views over the garden to Dover Castle. Good breakfasts, but they cost extra. **£70**
**Marquis at Alkham** Alkham, 5 miles west of Dover ☎ 01304 873410, ⓦ themarquisatalkham.co.uk. This

swanky restaurant-with-rooms offers luxury accommodation behind the exterior of a 200-year-old inn. The ten chic rooms have huge windows, many with picture-perfect views across the Downs, and the award-winning *Marquis* restaurant is superb. Rates include breakfast; staying during the week, when you can choose a room-only tariff, is cheaper. **£149**

## EATING AND DRINKING

★**Allotment** 9 High St ☎ 01304 214467, ⓦ theallotmentdover.co.uk. A light-filled oasis on Dover's unremarkable High Street, this simple, shabby-chic bistro is by far the best place to eat in town. The daily-changing menu concentrates on the best seasonal produce, with many

ingredients sourced from local allotments and lots of delicious veggie options (don't miss the goat's cheese and asparagus tart). Mains £8.50–16. Tues–Sat 8.30am–11pm.
**The Coastguard** St Margaret's Bay, four miles east of Dover ☎ 01304 851019,

ⓦwww.thecoastguard.co.uk. This beachside pub, at the bottom of the White Cliffs in the seaside village of St Margaret's Bay, is a great spot for a summer lunch, with a large seasalty terrace and small beer garden that stretches practically down to the shingle. Creative local dishes, with lots of fresh fish and seafood. Mains £10–20. Daily 10.30am–11pm; food 12.30–2.45pm & 6.30–8.45pm.

# Romney Marsh

In Roman times, what is now the southernmost chunk of Kent was submerged beneath the English Channel. The lowering of the sea levels in the Middle Ages and later reclamation created a hundred-square-mile area of shingle and marshland, now known as **Romney Marsh**. Once home to important Cinque and limb ports (see box, p.145), and villages made wealthy from the wool trade, this now rather forlorn expanse presents a melancholy aspect, given over to agriculture and with few sights – unless you count the sheep, the birdlife and several curious medieval **churches**. While this flat, depopulated area makes good walking and cycling country, its salt-speckled, big-skied strangeness can also be appreciated on the dinky **Romney, Hythe & Dymchurch Railway** (RH&DR; April–Oct daily; Nov–March occasional weekends, plus special events and tours; £16 Hythe–Dungeness return, less for shorter journeys; ☎01797 362353, ⓦrhdr .org.uk), a fifteen-inch-gauge line whose miniature steam trains run the 13.5 miles between the loneseome shingle spit of **Dungeness** and seaside town of **Hythe**. The latter has an eerie medieval **ossuary** in the Norman church of St Leonard's, high on a hill on the north side of town (May–Sept Mon–Sat 11am–1pm & 2–4pm, Sun 2–4pm; ☎01303 262370, ⓦstleonardschurchhythekent.org).

## Port Lympne Wild Animal Park

Lympne, 3 miles west of Hythe • Daily: April–Oct 9.30am–6.30pm, last admission 3pm; Nov–March 9.30am–5pm, last admission 2.30pm • £23.95, children £19.95 (save 20 percent by booking online); valid for a year • ☎ 0844 842 4647, ⓦ aspinallfoundation.org/port-lympne

An incongruous sight in this quiet corner of Kent, **Port Lympne Wild Animal Park** is home to more than six hundred beasts, including lemurs, gorillas, African elephants, Barbary lions (now extinct in the wild) and the largest breeding herd of black rhinos outside Africa. Visits are safari-style, on bone-rattling trucks. The best way to see the park can be outside opening hours: **dusk safaris** including dinner are available in summer (£45), while **accommodation** options range from glamping to self-catering.

## Dungeness

An end-of-the-earth eeriness pervades **DUNGENESS**, the windlashed shingle headland at the marsh's southernmost tip. Dominated by two hulking nuclear power stations (one of them disused), "the Ness" is not conventionally pretty, but there's a strange beauty to this lost-in-time spot, where a scattering of weatherboard shacks and disused railway carriages houses fishermen, artists and recluses drawn to the area's bleak, otherworldly allure. The late Derek Jarman, artist and filmmaker, made his home here, at **Prospect Cottage** – on Dungeness Road, a twenty-minute walk from the RH&DR station – and the shingle garden he created from beachcombed treasures and tough little plants remains a poignant memorial. Panoramic views over the headland can be had from the decommissioned **Old Lighthouse** (May & mid-Sept to end Oct Sat & Sun 10.30am–4.30pm; June Wed–Sun 10.30am–4.30pm; July to mid-Sept daily 10.30am–4.30pm; £3.50; ☎01797 321300, ⓦdungenesslighthouse.com), built in 1904.

The unique ecology around here attracts huge colonies of gulls, terns, smews and gadwalls; you can see them, and all manner of waterbirds, waders and wildfowl, from the excellent **RSPB visitor centre** (daily: March–Oct 10am–5pm; Nov–Feb 10am–4pm; £3; ☎01797 320558, ⓦrspb.org.uk) on the Lydd road three miles from Dungeness.

# The High Weald

The Weald stretches across a large area between the North and South Downs and includes parts of both Kent and Sussex. The central part, the High Weald, is epitomized by gentle hills, sunken country lanes and somnolent villages as well as some of England's most beautiful gardens, including **Sissinghurst**, **Wakehurst Place** and **Sheffield Park** – the last of these the southern terminus of the vintage **Bluebell Railway**. The bracken and gorse-speckled heathland that makes up nearby **Ashdown Forest** – setting for the Winnie-the-Pooh stories – is a lovely spot for longer walks. The Weald also offers a wealth of picturesque historical sites, foremost among them a trio of picture-book castles – **Leeds Castle**, **Hever Castle** and **Bodiam Castle** – as well as stately homes at **Penshurst** and **Knole**, a well-preserved Roman villa at **Lullingstone**, the fascinating home of wartime leader Winston Churchill at **Chartwell** and Rudyard Kipling's countryside retreat at **Bateman's**. **Tunbridge Wells**, set in the heart of the beautiful High Weald countryside, makes a good base.

**2**

## Royal Tunbridge Wells

The handsome spa town of **ROYAL TUNBRIDGE WELLS** was established after a bubbling ferrous **spring** discovered here in 1606 was claimed to have curative properties, and reached its height of popularity during the Regency period when restorative cures were in vogue. It remains an elegant place, with some smart places to stay and eat and three lovely urban parks: the **Grove** and, to the north, **Calverley Grounds** offer formal gardens, paths and splendid views, while the wilder **Common**, spreading out to the west, is laced with historic pathways.

### The Pantiles

Tucked off the southernmost end of the High Street, the colonnaded **Pantiles** – named for the clay tiles, shaped in wooden pans, that paved the street in the seventeenth century – is a pedestrianized parade of independent shops, delis and cafés that exudes a faded elegance. Here, at the original **Chalybeate Spring**, outside the 1804 Bath House, a costumed "dipper" will serve you a cup of the iron-rich waters (Easter–Sept Wed–Sun 10.30am–3.30pm; 50p), a tradition dating back to the eighteenth century.

### Tunbridge Wells Museum

Mount Pleasant Rd • Mon–Sat 9.30am–5pm, Sun 10am–4pm • Free • ☎ 01892 554171, ⊛ tunbridgewellsmuseum.org

Sitting above the town library, **Tunbridge Wells Museum** offers an intriguing mishmash of local history, its old glass cabinets filled with everything from fossils to dandy Georgian glad rags, fading maps and scruffy stuffed animals. Take a look at its exquisite "Tunbridge Ware", the finely crafted wooden marquetry, dating from the late eighteenth century and popular until the 1920s, that was applied to everything from boxes to book covers to furniture.

### ARRIVAL AND INFORMATION            ROYAL TUNBRIDGE WELLS

**By train** The train station stands where the High Street becomes Mount Pleasant Road.
Destinations Hastings (via Battle; every 30min–1hr; 40–50min); London Bridge (every 15–30min; 45min); London Charing Cross (every 15–30min; 55min).
**By bus** Buses set down and pick up along the High Street and Mount Pleasant Road.

Destinations Brighton (every 30min–1hr; 1hr 40min); Hever (Mon–Sat 2 daily; 35–45min); Lewes (every 30min–1hr; 1hr 10min); London Victoria (1 daily; 1hr 40min).
**Tourist office** The Corn Exchange, The Pantiles (April–Sept Mon–Sat 10am–3pm; Oct–March Tues–Sat 10am–3pm; ☎ 01892 515675, ⊛ visittunbridgewells .com).

### ACCOMMODATION

★**Hotel du Vin** Crescent Rd ☎ 0844 748 9266, ⊛ hotelduvin.com. Elegantly set in a Georgian mansion overlooking Calverley Grounds, this member of the luxe

*Hotel du Vin* chain is mellow and quietly classy with a cosy bar and lounge and a sloping old staircase leading up to the rooms. **£125**

**The Victorian B&B** 22 Lansdowne Rd ☎01892 533633, ⓦthevictorianbandb.com. Bursting with authentic High Victoriana, to the point of fabulous kitsch, this comfortable, characterful and friendly B&B offers three rooms. There's a pretty garden, where you can take the rather good breakfast in summer. **£100**

### EATING AND DRINKING

**The Black Pig** 18 Grove Hill Rd ☎01892 523030, ⓦthe blackpig.net. Excellent gastropub, where locally sourced, free-range and organic dishes on the daily changing menu might include venison bresaola or pan-roasted hake, plus snacks including delicious home-made Scotch eggs. The terrace is lovely in summer. Daily noon–11pm; food served Mon–Thurs noon–2.30pm & 7–9.30pm, Fri noon–2.30pm & 7–10pm, Sat noon–4pm & 6–10pm, Sun noon–9pm.

**Mount Edgcumbe** The Common ☎01892 618854, ⓦthemountedgcumbe.com. An offbeat place for a drink, a coffee or a Modern British meal. Hidden on the Common, this Georgian house has a deliciously rural feel, with a very nice garden. Regular live jazz and blues. Mon–Wed 11am–11pm,

Thurs–Sat 11am–11.30pm, Sun noon–10.30pm; food served Mon–Thurs noon–3pm & 6–9.30pm, Fri & Sat noon–9.30pm, Sun bar menu noon–8pm.

★**Sankey's** 39 Mount Ephraim ☎01892 511422, ⓦsankeys.co.uk. Appealing brasserie and oyster bar serving top-notch seafood from £11, along with fish and chips. You can also get food – and lots of craft beers – in the cosy pub upstairs, decked out with enamel signs and brewery mirrors. There's a sunny deck. Restaurant: Tues–Sat noon–3pm & 6–10pm; pub: Mon–Wed & Sun noon–midnight, Thurs noon–1am, Fri & Sat noon–3am; food served Mon–Thurs noon–3pm & 6–8pm, Fri noon–3pm, Sat noon–5pm, Sun noon–4pm & 6–8pm.

## Sissinghurst

Biddenden Rd, 15 miles east of Tunbridge Wells • Mid-March to mid-May & July–Oct daily 11am–5.30pm; mid-May to end June Mon, Wed & Fri 11am–7pm, Tues, Thurs, Sat & Sun 11am–5.30pm; Nov & Dec daily 11am–3pm • £11.20; NT • ☎01580 710700, ⓦnationaltrust.org.uk/sissinghurst

When she and her husband took it over in 1930, the writer Vita Sackville-West described the neglected Tudor estate of **Sissinghurst** as "a garden crying out for rescue". Over the following thirty years they transformed the five-acre plot into one of England's greatest country gardens, the romantic abundance of flowers, spilling over onto narrow brick pathways, defying the formality of the great gardens that came before. Don't miss the **White Garden**, with its pale blooms and silvery-grey foliage, and, in season, the lush, overblown **Rose Garden**. In the Tudor **tower** that Vita used as her quarters you can climb 78 steep stairs to get a bird's-eye view of the gardens and the ancient surrounding woodlands; halfway up, peep into Vita's study, which feels intensely personal still, with rugs on the floor and a photo of her lover, Virginia Woolf, on her desk.

## Bodiam Castle

Bodiam, near Robertsbridge, 20 miles southeast of Tunbridge Wells • Jan to mid-Feb Sat & Sun 11am–4pm; mid-Feb to Oct daily 10.30am–5pm • £7.20; NT • ☎01580 830196, ⓦnationaltrust.org.uk/bodiam-castle/ • Steam train from Tenterden (April–Sept up to 5 services a day; ☎01580 765155, ⓦkesr.org.uk)

One of the country's most picturesque castles, **Bodiam** is a classically stout square block with rounded corner turrets, battlements and a wide moat. When it was built in 1385 to guard what were the lower reaches of the River Rother, Bodiam was state-of-the-art military architecture, but during the Civil War, a company of Roundheads breached the fortress and removed its roof to reduce its effectiveness as a possible stronghold for the king. Over the next 250 years Bodiam fell into neglect until restoration in the last century. The extremely steep spiral staircases, leading to the crenellated battlements, will test all but the strongest of thighs.

## Bateman's

Bateman's Lane, Burwash, off the A265, 20 miles southeast of Tunbridge Wells • Daily: mid-March to Oct 11am–5pm; Nov & Dec 11.30am–3.30pm • £8.95; NT • ☎01435 882302, ⓦnationaltrust.org.uk/batemans

Half a mile south of the picturesque village of Burwash, **Bateman's** was the idyllic home of the writer and journalist Rudyard Kipling from 1902 until his death in 1936. The house was built by a local ironmaster in the seventeenth century and is set amid attractive gardens, which feature a still-working watermill converted by Kipling to generate electricity (it grinds corn most Wednesdays and Saturdays at 2pm). Inside, the house displays Kipling's letters, early editions of his work and mementos from his travels.

## Leeds Castle

30 miles northeast of Tunbridge Wells • Daily: April–Sept 10.30am–4.30pm; Oct–March 10.30am–3pm • £19, children £11 • ☎ 01622 765400, ⓦ leeds-castle.com

Its reflection shimmering in a lake, the enormous **Leeds Castle** resembles a fairy-tale palace. Beginning life around 1119, it has had a chequered history and is now run as a commercial concern, with a range of paying attractions including golf, hot-air ballooning, Segway tours and jousting, plus a branch of the zip-lining treetop adventure experience **Go Ape** (ⓦ goape.co.uk). The castle's interior fails to match the stunning exterior and the grounds, and though you can see a set of royal apartments, overall the twentieth-century renovations have tended to quash any historical charm; if you're happy to forego the paying attractions, you could simply wander around the five hundred acres of beautifully landscaped grounds for free on one of the **public footpaths**.

## Penshurst Place

Penshurst, 7 miles northwest of Tunbridge Wells • April–Oct daily noon–4pm, grounds 10.30am–6pm • £10, grounds only £8 • ☎ 01892 870307, ⓦ penshurstplace.com • Trains from London Bridge or Charing Cross to Penshurst Station, then a 2.5-mile walk)

Tudor timber-framed houses line the main street of the attractive village of **PENSHURST**. Presiding over it all is fourteenth-century **Penshurst Place**, home to the Sidney family since 1552 and birthplace of the Elizabethan soldier and poet, Sir Philip Sidney. The jaw-dropping Barons Hall is the glory of the interior, with its 60ft-high chestnut-beamed roof still in place. The 48 acres of grounds offer good parkland walks, while the eleven-acre walled **garden** is a beautiful example of Elizabethan garden design.

## Hever Castle

10 miles northwest of Tunbridge Wells • April–Oct daily 10.30am–6pm; March, Nov & Dec Wed–Sun 10.30am–4pm • £15.50, children £8.70, gardens only £13/£8.20 • ☎ 01732 865224, ⓦ hevercastle.co.uk • Trains from London Bridge or Victoria to Hever (1.5 miles from castle)

The moated **Hever Castle** was the childhood home of Anne Boleyn, second wife of Henry VIII, and where Anne of Cleves, Henry's fourth wife, lived after their divorce. In 1903, having fallen into disrepair, the castle was bought by William Waldorf Astor, American millionaire-owner of *The Observer*, who had the house assiduously restored in mock Tudor style. Today, Hever has an intimate feel, and though it does display some intriguing Elizabethan and Jacobite artefacts it tells you more overall about the aspirations of American plutocrats than the lifestyle of Tudor nobles. **Anne Boleyn's room** is the most affecting; you can see the prayer book she carried to the executioner's block, inscribed in her own writing and with references to the Pope crossed out. Outside is Waldorf Astor's beautiful **Italian Garden**, decorated with statuary, some more than two thousand years old, as well as a traditional yew-hedge maze, adventure playground, splashy water maze and boating lakes.

## Chartwell

Mapleton Rd, Westerham, 17.5 miles northwest of Tunbridge Wells • March–Oct daily 11am–5pm • £12.50; gardens and studio only £6.25; NT • ☎ 01732 868381, ⓦ nationaltrust.org.uk/chartwell

Packed with the wartime Prime Minister's possessions – including his rather contemplative

**2**

## ENGLISH WINE: A SPARKLING SUCCESS STORY

The **English wine** industry is booming. Around four hundred vineyards across the country produce about four million bottles a year (more than fifty percent of it sparkling), and the best of the harvest more than rivals the more famous names over the Channel – indeed, many sparkling wines from the southeast have beaten the best Champagnes in international blind-tasting competitions. With almost identical soil and geology to the Champagne region, and increased temperatures due to global warming, the southeast is home to many of the country's best vineyards, several of which now offer **tours and tastings**. In the southeast these include:

### KENT

**Biddenden** Gribble Bridge Lane, Biddenden ☎01580 291726, ⊛biddendenvineyards.com. Kent's oldest commercial vineyard, producing wines from eleven varieties of grape, as well as traditional ciders and juices. Free themed vineyard tours run once or twice a month, but you can take a self-guided tour any time, and there is a shop/café on site. Mon–Sat 10am–5pm, Sun 11am–5pm (Jan & Feb closed Sun).

**Chapel Down** Small Hythe, Tenterden ☎01580 763033, ⊛chapeldown.com. Multi-award-winning winemaker, suppliers to Jamie Oliver and Gordon Ramsay – they do a great lager, too – with a wine and English produce store on site, as well as a lovely terrace restaurant overlooking the vines. Guided tours and tastings (£10) daily April–Oct.

### SUSSEX

**Bolney Wine Estate** Foxhole Lane, Bolney ☎01444 881894, ⊛bolneywineestate.co.uk. This small, family-run vineyard has a lovely setting and offers a variety of tours, some finishing up at the on-site café. The vineyard has won awards for its sparkling wines, but is also known – unusually for the UK – for its red wines. Shop Mon–Sat 9am–5pm; café closed Mon. Tours £16–39.50 (Fri, Sat & Sun – see website for dates).

**Ridgeview Wine Estate** Ditchling Common, off the B2112 ☎01444 241441, ⊛ridgeview.co.uk. Long-established, multi-award-winning vineyard, known for its sparkling wines, produced using traditional Champagne grape varieties and methods. Tours (1hr 30min–2hr; pre-booking essential) run a couple of times a month, or you can just turn up at the cellar door and taste before you buy. Mon–Sat 11am–4pm, closed Sat in Jan & Feb; tours £15.

### SURREY

**Denbies Wine Estate** London Rd, Dorking ☎01306 876616, ⊛denbies.co.uk. Vast commercial vineyard specializing in sparkling wines and whites – on a good year, they can produce up to 400,000 bottles. Tours include a "train" (truck) ride through the surrounding estate, which also has public footpaths. Mon–Sat 9.30am–5.30pm, Sun 10am–5.30pm; Nov–March closes 5pm; indoor tours £9.95, £14 with sparkling wines, £16 with food; "train" tours £6, £10.50 with sparkling wine.

---

paintings – there is something touchingly intimate and rather fascinating about **Chartwell**, the country residence of **Winston Churchill** from 1924 until his death in 1965. In the rolling **grounds**, dotted with lakes and ponds and shaded by mature fruit trees, you can see his **studio**, lined ceiling to floor with more than one hundred canvases; the works are of varying quality, however, and some of the best can be seen in the house itself.

# Knole

Sevenoaks, entered from the south end of Sevenoaks High St • **House** Mid-March to Oct Tues–Sun noon–4pm • £10.40; NT **Grounds** Daily dawn–dusk • Free; NT • ☎01732 462100, ⊛nationaltrust.org.uk/knole • Trains from London Bridge or Charing Cross to Sevenoaks station, from where it is about a 20min walk to the Knole entrance

Covering a whopping four acres and designed to echo the calendar – with 365 rooms, 52 staircases, twelve entrances and seven courtyards – **Knole** palace, in the commuter town of **Sevenoaks**, is an astonishingly handsome ensemble. Built in 1456 as a residence for the archbishops of Canterbury, it was appropriated in 1538 by Henry VIII, who loved to hunt in its thousand acres of **parkland** (still today home to several hundred wild deer). Elizabeth

I gave the estate to her Lord Treasurer, Thomas Sackville, who remodelled the house in Renaissance style in 1605; it has remained in the family's hands ever since, with its Jacobean exterior preserved. Writer and gardener Vita Sackville-West was brought up here, and her lover Virginia Woolf derived inspiration for her novel *Orlando* from frequent visits. Highlights of this evocatively decaying treasure trove include the lustrous **Venetian Ambassador's Room** with its staggering carved and gilded bed, once belonging to James II; it, and its hangings of sea-green, blue and gold velvet, are literally crumbling away.

## Lullingstone Roman Villa

9 miles north of Sevenoaks • April–Sept daily 10am–6pm; Oct daily 10am–5pm; Nov–April Sat & Sun 10am–4pm• £6.40; EH • ☎ 01322 863467, ⓦ english-heritage.org.uk • From Sevenoaks there are trains to the village of Eynsford (every 30min; 15min), from where it's a 15min walk

In a rural spot alongside the trickle of the River Darent, **Lullingstone Roman Villa**, believed to have started as a farm around 100 AD, grew to become an important estate and remained occupied until the fifth century. The site is known for its brilliantly preserved mosaics, including a fine **mosaic floor** depicting Bellerophon riding Pegasus and slaying the Chimera, a fire-breathing she-beast, but displays throughout – including a couple of human skeletons – offer lively and often poignant glimpses into Roman domestic life.

## Ashdown Forest

**Information Barn** Wych Cross • April–Sept Mon–Fri 2–5pm, Sat & Sun 11am–5pm; Oct–March Sat & Sun 11am–dusk • ☎ 01342 823583, ⓦ ashdownforest.org • There are dozens of free parking sites on the main roads through the Forest; Metrobus # 291 runs between Tunbridge Wells and East Grinstead, stopping at Hartfield, Coleman's Hatch and Forest Row (Mon–Sat hourly)

Just north of Sheffield Park, the ten-square-mile expanse of **Ashdown Forest** – which is in fact almost two-thirds heathland – is best known as the home of the much-loved fictional bear **Winnie-the-Pooh**. A. A. Milne wrote his famous children's books from his weekend home at the northeastern edge of the forest, modelling the stories closely on the local area. Today you can visit Pooh Bridge and many other spots described in the stories; download a leaflet from the website; or, for Pooh Bridge, park at the dedicated car park just off the B2026.

## Sheffield Park

On the A275 East Grinstead–Lewes main road, about 2 miles north of the junction with the A272 • **Garden** Daily: Jan & Feb, Nov & Dec 10.30am–4pm; March to Oct 10.30am–5.30pm **Parkland** Dawn–dusk • £9; NT • ☎ 01825 790231, ⓦ nationaltrust.org.uk/sheffield -park-and-garden • Bluebell Railway (see below) from East Grinstead

Eighteen miles southwest of Tunbridge Wells lies the country estate of **Sheffield Park**, its centrepiece a Gothic mansion built for Lord Sheffield by James Wyatt. The house is closed to the public, but you can roam around the beautiful hundred-acre **gardens**, which were laid out by Capability Brown and are famed for their spectacular autumn colour.

## Bluebell Railway

Sheffield Park Station, on the A275 East Grinstead–Lewes main road, about 2 miles north of the junction with the A272 • April–Oct daily; Nov–March Sat, Sun & school hols • Day ticket with unlimited travel £16.50 • ☎ 01825 720800, ⓦ www.bluebell-railway.com • Regular trains from London Victoria to East Grinstead, the Bluebell Railway's northern terminus; 1hr

A mile southwest of Sheffield Park lies the southern terminus of the **Bluebell Railway**, whose vintage steam locomotives chuff eleven miles north via Horsted Keynes and Kingscote stations to the mainline station at East Grinstead. The service gets extremely crowded at weekends, especially in May, when the bluebells blossom in the woods through which the line passes. The stations have all been beautifully restored in period style, and Sheffield Park station is also home to the railway sheds and a small museum.

## Wakehurst Place

On the B2028 between Ardingly and Turners Hill • Daily: March–Oct 10am–6pm; Nov–Feb 10am–4.30pm; Millennium Seedbank closes 1hr earlier • £12.50; NT • 📞 01444 894066, 🌐 kew.org/visit-wakehurst

**Wakehurst Place**, a Jacobean mansion twenty miles west of Tunbridge Wells, is the country home of Kew Royal Botanic Gardens. The 180-acre site is given over mainly to trees and shrubs in a variety of horticultural environments, and is also home to the **Millennium Seed Bank**, whose aim is to safeguard some 24,000 plant species by freezing the seeds in underground vaults.

# Rye and around

Perched on a hill overlooking the Romney Marshes, the pretty, ancient town of **RYE** was added as a "limb" to the original Cinque Ports (see box, p.145), but was subsequently marooned two miles inland by the retreat of the sea and the silting-up of the River Rother. It is now one of the most visited places in East Sussex – half-timbered, skew-roofed and quintessentially English, with plenty of interesting independent shops to poke around in and some excellent places to eat.

Rye's most picturesque street – and the most photographed – is the sloping cobbled **Mermaid Street**, the town's main thoroughfare in the sixteenth century. At the top of Mermaid Street, just around the corner in West Street, lies **Lamb House** (end March–Oct Tues & Sat 2–6pm; £5; NT; 📞 01580 762334, 🌐 nationaltrust.org.uk/lamb-house), home of the authors Henry James and (subsequently) E.F. Benson. Just a few cobbled yards away is the peaceful oasis of Church Square, where **St Mary's Church** boasts the oldest functioning pendulum clock in the country; the ascent of the church tower (£3) offers fine views over the clay-tiled roofs.

Rye's acclaimed **literary festival** (🌐 ryefestival.co.uk) takes place over two weeks in September and also features a wide range of musical and visual arts events. The other big annual event is **Rye Bay Scallop Week** (🌐 scallop.org.uk), held at the end of February.

## Rye Castle Museum

**Ypres Tower** Church Square • Daily: April–Oct 10.30am–4.30pm; Nov–March 10.30am–3.30pm • £3 **East St Museum** 3 East St • Normally April–Oct Sat, Sun & bank hols 10.30am–4.30pm, but call ahead to check • Free • 📞 01797 227798, 🌐 ryemuseum.co.uk

In the far corner of Church Square stands the **Ypres** (pronounced "Wipers") **Tower**, built to keep watch for cross-Channel invaders and now a part of the **Rye Castle Museum**; the other museum site is on nearby East Street. Both buildings house a number of relics from Rye's past, including an eighteenth-century fire engine and plenty of paraphernalia from the town's smuggling heyday.

## Rye Art Gallery

107 High St • **Stormont Studio** Mon & Thurs–Sat 10.30am–5pm, Sun noon–4pm • **Easton Rooms** Mon–Sat 10.30am–5pm, Sun noon–4pm • Free • 📞 01797 222433, 🌐 ryeartgallery.co.uk

The excellent **Rye Art Gallery** is housed in two interlinked buildings: the Stormont Studio contains a small permanent collection, including works by artists associated with Rye, such as Edward Burra and Paul Nash, while the Easton Rooms stages changing exhibitions by contemporary artists.

## Winchelsea

Perched on a hill two miles southwest of Rye, **Winchelsea** was rebuilt by Edward I after the original settlement, Old Winchelsea – one of the Cinque Ports (see box, p.145) – was washed away in the great storm of 1287. Today the tiny town (no more than a few streets arranged around a central square) feels positively deserted, but it's well worth the trip from Rye to visit the ruined Gothic **Church of St Thomas à Becket**, with its beautiful 1930s stained-glass windows.

## Camber Sands

Around three miles east of Rye, on the other side of the River Rother estuary, **Camber Sands** is a two-mile stretch of gorgeous dune-backed sandy beach that has become a renowned centre of wind- and watersports. The nicest way to reach it from Rye is by bike, on the three-mile dedicated cycle path.

### ARRIVAL AND GETTING AROUND
RYE AND AROUND

**By train** Rye's train station is at the bottom of Station Approach, off Cinque Ports St; it's a 5min walk up to the High Street. Regular trains run to Hastings (hourly; 20min) and London St Pancras (hourly; 1hr 10min).
**By bus** Bus #100 runs into the centre of town from Hastings (Mon–Sat hourly, Sun every 2hr; 40min), passing

through Winchelsea en route. Buses #711 and #100 run from Rye station to Camber Sands (Mon–Sat hourly, Sun every 2hr; 15min).
**Bike rental** You can rent bicycles from Rye Hire, 1 Cyprus Place (Mon–Fri 8am–5pm, Sat 8am–noon; £10/half day, £15/day; ☎01797 223033, ⓦ ryehire.co.uk).

### INFORMATION

**Tourist office** 4–5 Lion Street (daily: April–Sept 10am–5pm; Oct–March 10am–4pm; ☎01797 229049, ⓦ visit1066country.com).
**Heritage and Information Centre** Strand Quay (daily:

April–Oct 10am–5pm; Nov, Feb & March 10am–4pm; Dec & Jan call to check opening hours; ☎01797 226696, ⓦ ryeheritage.co.uk). Privately run.

### ACCOMMODATION

★**The George** 98 High St ☎01797 222114, ⓦ thegeorgeinrye.com. This luxurious small hotel manages to get everything just right, from the cosy, wood-beamed bar and excellent restaurant to the tasteful, individually furnished rooms: there are 34 to choose from, ranging from an Arts and Crafts-styled room decked out in William Morris textiles to a hip Art Deco hangout with a circular bed. **£135**
**Rye Windmill** Off Ferry Rd ☎01797 224027, ⓦ rye windmill.co.uk. Great-value for Rye, this 300-year-old Grade

II-listed smock windmill contains ten spotless contemporary en-suite rooms. Splash out on the Windmill Suite (£150) at the top of the mill for panoramic views over Rye. **£85**
**Ship Inn** The Strand ☎01797 222233, ⓦ theshipinnrye .co.uk. Ten quirky rooms above an equally characterful quayside pub. Despite being on the small side, rooms are funky, cheerful and charming, featuring bright prints and wallpaper, with fun touches such as rubber ducks in the bathroom and teabags stored in retro tins. **£100**

### EATING AND DRINKING

★**Ambrette** In the White Vine House hotel, 24 High St ☎01797 222043, ⓦ theambrette.co.uk. The oak-panelled dining room of the *White Vine House hotel* provides a suitably stunning backdrop to fabulous contemporary Indian cuisine – the likes of pan-grilled steak of Kentish mutton in a Kashmiri-style sauce, or local fish served with mung lentil kedgeree (mains £11–17). For the full experience opt for the Tasting menu (£50). Mon–Thurs 11.30am–2.30pm & 6–9.30pm, Fri–Sun 11.30am–2.30pm & 5.30–10pm.
**Knoops** Tower Forge, Hilders Cliff, Landgate ☎01797 225838, ⓦ knoops.co.uk. This little place only offers one thing – hot chocolate – but it does it with style. Choose your chocolate (from 27% to 80% solids; £3), add your extras (various spices, peppers, fruits, even flowers – all 50p, or a shot of something stronger for £1) and wait to be presented with your own bowl of made-to-order

chocolatey loveliness. Daily 10am–6pm.
**Tuscan Kitchen** 8 Lion St ☎01797 223269, ⓦ tuscankitchenrye.co.uk. The delicious, authentic Tuscan cuisine on offer at this beamed, low-ceilinged restaurant has won it a lot of fans; pasta dishes are around £10–12, while mains such as *pollo alla cacciatora* or fillet steak range from £14 to £23. Book well ahead. Wed & Thurs 6–10pm, Fri & Sat noon–3pm & 6–10pm, Sun noon–3pm & 6–9.30pm.
★**Ship Inn** The Strand ☎01797 222233, ⓦ theshipinnrye.co.uk. Fabulous, laidback quayside pub, with quirky decor, well-worn sofas and plenty of cosy nooks, plus board games (including a Rye-themed Monopoly) to while away a rainy afternoon. There's a good selection of local ales on tap, and excellent seasonal food. Daily 11am–11pm; food served Mon–Fri noon–3pm & 6.30–10pm, Sat & Sun noon–3.30pm & 6.30–10.30pm.

# Hastings

Once an influential Cinque Port (see box, p.145), **HASTINGS** is a curious mixture of unpretentious fishing port, tatty seaside resort and bohemian retreat popular with artists. The town is best known, however, for the eponymous **battle** which took place nearby; in 1066, William, Duke of Normandy, landed at Pevensey Bay, a few miles west of town, and marched to meet Harold's army at nearby Battle (see opposite).

## Old Town

The pretty **Old Town**, east of the pier, is by far the nicest part of Hastings. **High Street** and pedestrianized **George Street** are the focus, both lined with antiques shops, galleries, restaurants and pubs. Running parallel to the High Street is **All Saints Street**, punctuated with the odd, rickety, timber-framed dwelling from the fifteenth century.

## West Hill

The quickest way up **West Hill**, which separates the Old Town from the less interesting modern quarter, is to hop on the **West Hill Cliff Railway**, which climbs up from George Street (April–Oct daily 10am–5.30pm; Nov–Feb Sat & Sun 11am–4pm; £2.50 return; ☎01424 451111).

### Hastings Castle

West Hill • Hours vary but generally mid-Feb to Easter Sat & Sun 10am–3pm; Easter–Oct daily 10am–4pm • £4.50 • ☎01424 422964, ⓦ smugglersadventure.co.uk & ⓦ visit1066country.com

Very little remains of **Hastings Castle**, erected by William the Conqueror in 1066: storms in the thirteenth century caused the cliffs to subside, tipping most of it into the sea. The ruins, however, offer an excellent prospect of the town, and an audiovisual show, **The 1066 Story**, describes the events of the last successful invasion of the British mainland.

## The Stade

Down by the seafront, the area known as **The Stade** is characterized by its tall, black weatherboard **net shops**, most dating from the mid-nineteenth century, and still in use today. The Stade is home to the town's fishing fleet – the largest beach-launched fleet in Europe – and many of the net shops sell fresh fish.

### Jerwood Gallery

Rock-a-Nore Rd • Tues–Fri 11am–5pm, Sat & Sun 11am–6pm; first Tues of month open until 8pm; extended hours during school holidays • £8, free on first Tues of month 4–8pm • ☎01424 728377, ⓦ jerwoodgallery.org

Adjacent to the fishing quarter, the sleek **Jerwood Gallery**, covered in shimmering dark-glazed tiles, provides a home for the Jerwood Foundation's modern art collection, which includes works by Stanley Spencer, Walter Sickert and Augustus John. A café up on the first floor overlooks the fishing boats on the beach.

---

#### HASTINGS JACK-IN-THE-GREEN

The biggest weekend of the year is the **Jack-in-the-Green Festival** (May Day weekend; ⓦ hastingsjack.co.uk), three days of festivities culminating in a riotous parade of dancers, drummers and leaf-bedecked revellers through the streets of the Old Town up to Hastings' hilltop castle, where "the Jack" – a garlanded leaf-covered figure whose origins date back to the eighteenth century – is ritually slain and the spirit of summer released.

**East Hill**

Just behind the net shops, the venerable **East Hill Cliff Railway** (April–Oct daily 10am–5.30pm; Nov–Feb Sat & Sun 11am–4pm; £2.50 return; ☎01424 451111), the steepest funicular in the country, climbs up to **East Hill**, for wonderful views over the town and access to **Hastings County Park**, a beautiful expanse of heathland, woodland and sandstone cliffs, which spreads east for three miles.

# Hastings Pier

West of The Stade, **Hastings Pier** (ⓦhpcharity.co.uk), which was burnt down in an arson attack in 2010, is due to reopen in 2015 after an ambitious multi-million pound refurbishment, with open-air film screenings, funfair rides and seasonal events planned.

## ARRIVAL AND INFORMATION HASTINGS

**By train** The train station is a 10min walk from the seafront along Havelock Road.

Destinations Battle (every 30min; 15min); Brighton (every 30min; 1hr 5min); Eastbourne (every 20min; 25min); Lewes (every 30min; 55min); London Charing Cross (every 30min; 1hr 30min–1hr 45min); London St Pancras (hourly; 1hr 45min); London Victoria (hourly; 2hr); Rye (hourly; 20min); Tunbridge Wells (every 30min; 35–50min)

**By bus** National Express coach services operate from the station at the junction of Havelock and Queen's roads.

Destinations Battle (Mon–Sat hourly, Sun every 2–3 hrs; 15min); Dover (hourly; 2hr 50min); Eastbourne (Mon–Sat every 20–30min, Sun hourly; 1hr 15min); London Victoria (1 daily; 2hr 35min); Rye (Mon–Sat hourly, Sun every 2hr; 40min).

**Tourist office** On the seafront midway between the pier and the Old Town, at Aquila House on Breeds Place (hours may change but currently April–Oct Mon–Fri 9am–5pm, Sat 9.30am–5.30pm, Sun 10.30am–4pm; Nov–March Mon–Fri 9am–5pm, Sat 10am–4pm, Sun 10.30am–1pm; ☎01424 451111, ⓦvisit1066country.com).

## ACCOMMODATION

**Senlac Guesthouse** 47 Cambridge Gardens ☎01424 435767, ⓦsenlacguesthouse.co.uk. Stylish yet affordable, this friendly guesthouse near the station is fantastic value. Smart, contemporary rooms come with i-Phone docking stations, DVD players and wi-fi. The cheapest rooms share bathrooms. Breakfast costs £8.50 extra. **£55**

★**Swan House** 1 Hill St ☎01892 430014,

ⓦswanhousehastings.co.uk. Beautiful B&B in a half-timbered fifteenth-century building on one of the Old Town's most picturesque streets. Rooms are luxurious and tasteful, and there's a pretty decked patio garden in which to enjoy the gourmet breakfast on sunny days. The owners also run the quirkier but similarly elegant *Old Rectory* nearby. **£120**

## EATING, DRINKING AND ENTERTAINMENT

There's no shortage of great **restaurants** in Hastings, many serving fresh fish from the town's fishing fleet. There's also a thriving **live music** scene; pick up the *Ultimate Alternative* listings magazine (ⓦua1066.co.uk), available in pubs and clubs throughout town, for a comprehensive guide to what's on.

**Dragon** 71 George St ☎01424 423688. Hip hangout – part restaurant, part bar – with tasty food (the locally sourced menu changes weekly), art exhibitions and a nice assortment of squishy sofas. Mon–Sat noon–11pm, Sun noon–10.30pm.

**Maggies** Above the fish market, Rock-a-Nore Rd

☎01424 430205. The best fish and chips in town can be found at this first-floor café, right on the beach. It's open for lunch only, and is very popular, so you'll need to book ahead. Mon–Sat noon–2pm.

**Porter's Wine Bar** 56 High St ☎01424 427000, ⓦporterswinebar.com. Friendly, family-run wine bar, with jazz and acoustic music on Wednesday and Thursday nights and Sunday afternoons, including a regular spot by acclaimed jazz pianist and local resident Lianne Carroll. Good, home-cooked, bistro-style food also on offer. Mon–Fri noon–3pm & 7pm–midnight, Sat noon–midnight, Sun 12.30–11pm.

# Battle Abbey and Battlefield

At the south end of High St, Battle • April–Sept daily 10am–6pm; Oct daily 10am–5pm; Nov–March Sat & Sun 10am–4pm • £8; EH • ☎01424 775705, ⓦenglish-heritage.org.uk • Buses #304 and #305 from Hastings , or regular trains from Hastings and London Charing Cross to Battle station, a 10min walk away

**2**

Six miles inland from Hastings in the small town of Battle, the remains of **Battle Abbey** claim to occupy the site of the most famous land battle in British history. Here, or hereabouts, on October 14, 1066, the invading Normans swarmed up the hillside from Senlac Moor and overcame the army of King Harold, spelling an end to Anglo-Saxon England. Before the battle took place, William vowed that, should he win, he would build a religious foundation on the very spot of Harold's slaying to atone for the bloodshed, and, true to his word, Battle Abbey was built four years later and subsequently occupied by a fraternity of Benedictines.

The abbey, once one of the richest in the country, was partially destroyed in the Dissolution and much rebuilt and revised over the centuries. The magnificent 1330s gatehouse still survives, along with the thirteenth-century rib-vaulted dormitory range, but all that remains of William's original abbey church is an outline on the grass, with the site of the high altar – the spot where Harold was supposedly killed – marked by a memorial stone. An excellent **visitor centre** shows a film about the battle and the events leading up to it.

## De La Warr Pavilion

Bexhill-on-Sea • Daily 10am–5/6pm • Free • ☎ 01424 229111, ⓦ dlwp.com

The seaside town of Bexhill-on-Sea, five miles west of Hastings, would be unremarkable were it not for the iconic **De La Warr Pavilion**, a modernist masterpiece overlooking the sea. Built in 1935 by architects Erich Mendelsohn and Serge Chermayeff, the Pavilion slid gradually into disrepair after World War II, but today it has been restored to its original glory, hosting contemporary art **exhibitions** and **live performances**. The first-floor café and restaurant offer glorious views.

# Eastbourne

Like so many of the southeast's seaside resorts, **EASTBOURNE** was kick-started into life in the 1840s, when the Brighton, Lewes and Hastings Rail Company built a branch line from Lewes to the sea. Nowadays Eastbourne has a solid reputation as a retirement town by the sea, and though the contemporary **Towner Gallery** has introduced a splash of modernity, the town's charms remain for the most part sedate and old-fashioned. The focus of the elegant seafront is the Victorian **pier**, partly destroyed by fire in 2014; just to the west is the splendid **bandstand** (ⓦ www.eastbournebandstand.co.uk), which hosts various musical events throughout the year. The real draw, however, is the town's proximity to one of the scenic highlights of the South Downs National Park: the stunning coastal scenery of **Beachy Head** and the **Seven Sisters Country Park**.

## Towner Art Gallery and Museum

Devonshire Park • Tues–Sun & bank hol Mon 10am–6pm • Tours daily at 11.30am • Free • ☎ 01323 434670, ⓦ townereastbourne.org.uk

Housed in a sleek modern edifice by Devonshire Park, the excellent **Towner Art Gallery and Museum** puts on four or five exhibitions a year, which are shown alongside rotating displays of modern and contemporary art from its own permanent collection. On the second floor there's a café-bar with a small terrace overlooking the rooftops of Eastbourne to the South Downs beyond.

### ARRIVAL AND INFORMATION            EASTBOURNE

**By train** Eastbourne's train station is a splendid Italianate terminus, just a 10min walk from the seafront up Terminus Road.
Destinations Brighton (every 20min; 35min); Hastings (every 20min; 30min); Lewes (every 20min; 30min); London Victoria (Mon–Sat every 30min, Sun hourly; 1hr 35min).
**By bus** The bus station is on Junction Road, by the train station.

Destinations Brighton (every 10–15min; 1hr 15min); Hastings (Mon–Sat every 20min, Sun hourly; 1hr 10min); London Victoria (2 daily; 3–4hr); Tunbridge Wells (Mon–Sat hourly; 50min).

**Tourist office** 3 Cornfield Road, just off Terminus Road

(March, April & Oct Mon–Fri 9.15am–5.30pm, Sat 9.15am–4pm; May–Sept Mon–Fri 9.15am–5.30pm, Sat 9.15am–5pm, Sun 10am–1pm; Nov–Feb Mon–Fri 9.15am–4.30pm, Sat 9.15am–1pm; ☎0871 663 0031, ⓦ www.visiteastbourne.com).

## ACCOMMODATION AND EATING

**Dolphin** 14 South St ☎01323 746622, ⓦthedolphin eastbourne.co.uk. One of the town's nicest pubs, this laid-back hangout has locally brewed beers on tap (including Harveys and Dark Star) and serves good home-cooked food including burgers and local fish (£7.50–9.50). Mon–Thurs 11am–11pm, Fri & Sat 11am–midnight, Sun noon–10.30pm; food served Mon–Thurs noon–2.30pm & 6–9.30pm, Fri & Sat noon–9.30pm, Sun noon–8pm.

**Fusciardi's** 30 Marine Parade ☎01323 722128 ⓦfusciardiicecreams.co.uk. This fabulous ice-cream parlour is an Eastbourne institution, with piled-high sundaes that are a work of art. Cash only. Daily 9am–7pm,

later in summer.

**Pebble Beach** 53 Royal Parade ☎01323 431240, ⓦpebblebeacheastbourne.com. Boutique B&B at the eastern end of town, with six stylish, good-value rooms set across three floors of a Victorian seafront townhouse. The nicest room is up on the first floor, with floor-to-ceiling windows and a private balcony looking out to sea. **£80**

**Urban Ground** 2a Bolton Rd ☎01323 410751, ⓦurbanground.co.uk. The best coffee shop in Eastbourne by a long chalk, with hip decor, great coffee and a range of tasty sandwiches, charcuterie boards and cakes. Mon–Sat 7.30am–6pm, Sun 9am–5pm.

# Beachy Head and the Seven Sisters Country Park

A short walk west from Eastbourne – or a short bus ride – takes you out along the most dramatic stretch of coastline in the South Downs National Park, where the chalk uplands are cut by the sea into a sequence of splendid cliffs that stretch for nine pristine miles. The most spectacular of these, **Beachy Head** (575ft high) is a two-mile uphill slog from Eastbourne. A couple of miles to the west of here the cliffs dip down to **Birling Gap**, where's there's access to the beach, and a National Trust-run café and information centre. Birling Gap marks the eastern end of a series of magnificent undulating chalk cliffs known as the **Seven Sisters**, which end three miles further west at the meandering River Cuckmere. The Seven Sisters Country Park provides some of the most impressive walks in the county, taking in the cliff-top path and the lower valley of the River Cuckmere. Head up to Seaford Head, on the western side of the Cuckmere estuary, for the iconic view of the cliffs you'll see on every postcard, with the picturesque coastguard's cottages in the foreground.

## ARRIVAL AND INFORMATION — BEACHY HEAD AND SEVEN SISTERS

**By bus** Bus #13X runs from Eastbourne and Brighton via Beachy Head, Birling Gap and the Seven Sisters Country Park Visitor Centre (late April to late June Sat & Sun only; late June to mid-Sept daily; every 30min).

**By car** There are pay-and-display car parks at Beachy Head, Birling Gap (NT) and at Exceat (access point for the Cuckmere Valley) on the A259 between Brighton and Eastbourne.

**Tourist information** Beachy Head Countryside Centre,

Beachy Head (April–Oct daily 10am–4pm; call to check winter hours; ☎01323 737273, ⓦbeachyhead.org.uk). Seven Sisters Country Park Visitor Centre, Exceat, on the A259 (April–Oct daily 10.30am–4.30pm; Nov–March Sat & Sun 11am–4pm; ☎01323 870280, ⓦwww.sevensisters.org.uk). Birling Gap Information Centre, Birling Gap (daily 10am–4pm; ☎ 01323 423197, ⓦnationaltrust.org.uk/birling-gap-and-the-seven -sisters).

## ACCOMMODATION

★**Belle Tout** Beachy Head ☎01323 423185, ⓦbelletout.co.uk. For a real treat book into this fabulous lighthouse, perched high up on the dramatic cliffs just west of Beachy Head. The cosy rooms boast

stupendous views, there's a snug residents' lounge and – best of all – there's unrestricted access to the lamproom at the top of the lighthouse, where you can sit and watch the sun go down. **£185**

> ## SOUTH DOWNS NATIONAL PARK AND THE SOUTH DOWNS WAY
>
> The fifteenth and newest member of Britain's National Park family, the **South Downs National Park** came into being in 2010. Covering over six hundred square miles, it stretches for seventy miles from eastern Hampshire to the white chalk cliffs of East Sussex. The park is located in one of the most densely populated parts of the country, and in contrast to other "wilder" National Parks, it contains a high proportion of farmland – about 85 percent of the park.
>
> There are **visitor centres** in East Sussex at the Seven Sisters Country Park, at Beachy Head and at Birling Gap (see p.159 for all). The **South Downs National Park Authority** website (ⓦ southdowns.gov.uk) is another useful source of information about the area.
>
> ### THE SOUTH DOWNS WAY
>
> One of the best ways to explore the park is to strike off into the countryside on the **South Downs Way**, which rises and dips over one hundred miles along the chalk uplands between the city of Winchester and the spectacular cliffs at Beachy Head, and offers the southeast's finest walks. The OS *Landranger* **maps** #198 and #199 cover the eastern end of the route; you'll need #185 and #197 as well to cover the lot. Several **guidebooks** are available (some covering the route in just one direction); you can also check out the **website** ⓦ nationaltrail.co.uk/southdowns.

## Alfriston

Berwick Station has hourly connections to Eastbourne, Lewes and Brighton. The Cuckmere Valley Ramblerbus operates an hourly circular service from Berwick Station via Alfriston and the Seven Sisters Country Park (April–Oct Sat, Sun & bank hols; ⓦ cuckmerebuses.org.uk)

Three miles inland from Seven Sisters Country Park is the picture-perfect village of **ALFRISTON**, with plenty of creaky old smuggling inns, a picturesque village green ("The Tye") and some lovely riverside walks. On The Tye sits the fourteenth-century timber-framed and thatched **Clergy House** (Mon–Wed, Sat & Sun: mid-March to Oct 10.30am–5pm; Nov & Dec 11am–4pm; £4.80; NT; ☎01323 871961, ⓦnationaltrust .co.uk/alfriston-clergy-house), the first property to be acquired by the National Trust in 1896. A mile or so up the valley, **Drusillas Park** (daily: March–Oct 10am–5pm; Nov–Feb 10am–4pm; adults & children over 2 £13.50–17.50 depending on season; ☎01323 874100, ⓦdrusillas.co.uk) has penguins, meerkats, lemurs and more, a miniature railway, paddling pool and an excellent adventure playground.

# Lewes

**LEWES**, the county town of East Sussex, straddles the River Ouse as it carves a gap through the South Downs on its final stretch to the sea. Though there's been some rebuilding, the core of Lewes remains remarkably good-looking: replete with crooked older dwellings, narrow lanes – or "twittens" – and Georgian houses. With numerous traces of its long history still visible (not least a medieval castle), plus a lively cultural scene, plenty of independent and antiques shops, and some of England's most appealing chalkland on its doorstep, Lewes makes a great Sussex base. Nearby, the Bloomsbury Group's country home at **Charleston** and the newly opened **Ditchling Museum of Art and Craft** are both a short hop by car.

## Lewes Castle

169 High St • March–Oct Mon & Sun 11am–5.30pm, Tues–Sat 10am–5.30pm; Nov–Feb Mon & Sun 11am–4.30pm, Tues–Sat 10am–4.30pm, closed Mon in Jan • £7, combined ticket with Anne of Cleves House £10.50 • ☎01273 486290, ⓦ sussexpast.co.uk

Both **Lewes Castle** and St Pancras Priory (see opposite) were the work of William de Warenne, who was given the land by his father-in-law, William I, following the Norman Conquest. Inside the castle complex – unusual for being built on two mottes, or mounds – the shell of the eleventh-century keep remains, and can be climbed for

## LEWES BONFIRE NIGHT

Each November 5, while the rest of Britain lights small domestic bonfires or attends municipal firework displays to commemorate the 1605 foiling of a Catholic plot to blow up the Houses of Parliament, Lewes puts on a more dramatic show, whose origins lie in the deaths of the Lewes Martyrs, the seventeen Protestants burned here in 1556 at the height of Mary Tudor's militant revival of Catholicism. The town's six tightly knit bonfire societies spend much of the year organizing the spectacular Bonfire Night extravaganza, when their members dress up in traditional costumes and parade through the narrow streets carrying flaming torches and flares, before marching off onto the outskirts of town for their society's individual bonfire and fireworks display. At each of the fires, effigies of Guy Fawkes and the pope are burned alongside contemporary reviled figures. For more information on the night's celebrations see ⓦ lewesbonfirecouncil.org.uk.

excellent views over the town to the surrounding Downs. Tickets include admission to the **museum** (same hours as castle) by the entrance, where exhibits include archeological artefacts, a town model and a tapestry of the Battle of Lewes stitched to commemorate the battle's 750th anniversary in 2014.

## Southover

From the High Street, the steep, cobbled and much photographed **Keere Street** leads to **Southover**, the southern part of town. At the foot of Keere Street, tranquil **Grange Gardens** (daily dawn–dusk; free) sprawl around Southover Grange, once the childhood home of the diarist John Evelyn. Nearby on Southover High Street is the timber-framed **Anne of Cleves House** (Feb–Nov Tues–Sat 10am–5pm, Mon & Sun 11am–5pm; £5.20, combined ticket with the castle £10.50; ☏01273 474610, ⓦsussexpast .org.uk), a fifteenth-century hall house laid out as it would have looked in Tudor times. Cross the road and head down Cockshut Lane to reach the evocative ruins of **St Pancras Priory** (open access; free); in its heyday it was one of Europe's principal Cluniac institutions, with a church the size of Westminster Abbey.

## ARRIVAL AND INFORMATION           LEWES

**By train** The train station is south of High Street down Station Road.

Destinations Brighton (every 10–20min; 15min); Eastbourne (every 20–30min; 20–30min); London Victoria (Mon–Sat every 30min, Sun hourly; 1hr 10min).

**By bus** The bus station is on Eastgate St, near the foot of School Hill.

Destinations Brighton (Mon–Sat every 15min, Sun hourly;

30min); Tunbridge Wells (Mon–Sat every 30min, Sun hourly; 1hr 10min).

**Tourist office** At the junction of High Street and Fisher Street (April–Sept Mon–Sat 9.30am–4.30pm, Sun 10am–2pm; Oct–March Mon–Fri 9.30am–4.30pm, Sat 10am–2pm; ☏01273 483448, ⓦlewes.gov.uk); they hold copies of the free monthly magazine *Viva Lewes* (ⓦvivalewes.co.uk).

## ACCOMMODATION

**The Corner House** 14 Cleve Terrace ☏01273 567138, ⓦlewescornerhouse.co.uk. Super-friendly B&B on a quiet Edwardian terrace, close to Grange Gardens. The two en-suite rooms have lovely homely touches such as patchwork quilts and plenty of books, and the owner is a great source of information on the town and area. **£90**

**Monty's** Broughton House, 16 High St ☏01273 476750, ⓦmontysaccommodation.co.uk. Stylish, contemporary open-plan room on the top floor of a townhouse on the High Street, complete with a modern four-poster, freestanding bath (and separate swish shower

room) and a small kitchenette. Breakfast isn't included, but you're right in the thick of things here, with plenty of nearby cafés to choose from. **£130**

**YHA South Downs** Itford Farm, Beddingham, 5 miles from Lewes ☏0870 371 9574. The nearest hostel to Lewes is a gem, newly renovated from a characterful old farm, and in a fabulous location right on the South Downs Way footpath, with great transport connections (Southease station – with regular connections to Lewes – is just 200yd away). There's a café and licensed bar too. Dorms **£15**, doubles **£32**

2

---

**GLYNDEBOURNE**

Founded in 1934, **Glyndebourne**, three miles east of Lewes, off the A27 (☎01273 812321, ⓦ glyndebourne.com), is Britain's only unsubsidized opera house, and the Glyndebourne season (mid-May to Aug) is an indispensable part of the high-society calendar. Tickets are pricey, but there are cheaper, standing-room-only ones available at reduced prices, and discounts for under-30s if you register first.

---

**2**

## EATING AND DRINKING

**Bill's** 56 Cliffe High St ☎01273 476918, ⓦ billsproducestore.co.uk. No visit to Lewes would be complete without a leisurely weekend brunch at this always buzzing café, which started life as a greengrocer's here in Lewes and now has branches across the country. Mon–Thurs 8am–10.30pm, Fri & Sat 8am–11pm, Sun 9am–10.30pm.

★**Buttercup Café** In Pastorale Antiques, 15 Malling St ☎01273 477664, ⓦ thebuttercupcafe.co.uk. Tucked away at the end of Cliffe High Street, this cosy, quirky café is a hidden gem, with plenty of outdoor seating in a tranquil sun-trap courtyard, and a simple daily-changing seasonal menu. The salad plates (£6.50) are fabulous. Mon–Sat 9.30am–4pm.

★**Famiglia** 17 Market St ☎01273 479539, ⓦ famiglia-lazzati.co.uk. Small family-run Italian restaurant that's a local favourite for its great home-cooked, locally sourced food (pizzas from £7, pastas £8–10, mains from £13). Make sure you leave room for the lip-smackingly good "Trio" of puds. Mon–Fri noon–2.30pm & 5–10pm, Sat & Sun noon–10pm.

**Lewes Arms** Mount Place ☎01273 473252, ⓦ lewesarms.co.uk. This characterful local is a good spot to sample a pint of Sussex Best, produced down the road at Harveys brewery. Great-value, home-cooked food too (jerk chicken, burgers, home-made pasties and more, all under £9). Mon–Thurs 11am–11pm, Fri & Sat 11am–midnight, Sun noon–11pm; food served Mon–Fri noon–8.30pm, Sat noon–9pm, Sun noon–8.30pm.

## Charleston Farmhouse

6 miles east of Lewes, signposted off the A27 • April–Oct: Sun & bank hol Mon 1–5.30pm; Wed–Sat visit by 1hr tours only 1–6pm (July, Aug & Sept from noon); last entry 1hr before closing • £11, garden only £4.50 • ☎01323 811626, ⓦ charleston.org.uk

**Charleston Farmhouse** was the country home and gathering place of the writers, intellectuals and artists known as the Bloomsbury Group. Virginia Woolf's sister Vanessa Bell, Vanessa's husband, Clive Bell, and her lover, Duncan Grant, moved here during World War I so that the men, both conscientious objectors, could work on local farms. Almost every surface of the farmhouse interior is painted and the walls are hung with paintings by Picasso, Renoir and Augustus John, alongside the work of the residents. The guided tours give a fascinating insight into the lives of the unconventional group of friends and lovers; try to visit on a day when a tour is running if you can.

## Ditchling Museum of Art and Craft

8 miles west of Lewes, Ditchling • Tues–Sat & bank hol Mon 11am–5pm, Sun noon–5pm • £6.50 • ☎01273 844744, ⓦ ditchlingmuseumartcraft.org.uk

The beautifully designed two-room **Ditching Museum of Art and Craft** houses a fascinating assortment of prints, paintings, weavings, sculptures and other artefacts from the artists and craftspeople who lived in the small village of Ditchling in the last century, among them typographer and sculptor Eric Gill, printer and writer Hilary Pepler, weaver Ethel Mairet and calligrapher Edward Johnson, who designed the iconic London Underground typeface.

# Brighton

Vibrant, quirky and cool, **BRIGHTON** (or Brighton and Hove, to give it its official name) is one of the country's most popular seaside destinations. The essence of the city's appeal is its faintly bohemian vitality, a buzz that comes from a mix of holiday-makers, foreign-language students, a thriving gay community, and an energetic local student population from the art college and two universities.

Any trip to Brighton inevitably begins with a visit to its two most famous landmarks – the exuberant **Royal Pavilion** and the wonderfully tacky **Brighton Pier** – followed by a stroll along the seafront promenade or the pebbly beach. Just as interesting, though, is an exploration of Brighton's car-free **Lanes** – the maze of narrow alleys marking the old town – or a meander through the more bohemian streets of **North Laine**. Brighton's other great draw is its **cultural life**: you're spoilt for choice when it comes to live music, theatre, comedy and concerts, especially if you coincide your visit with the **Brighton Festival** (see box, p.167), the largest arts festival in England.

## The Royal Pavilion

4/5 Pavilion Buildings • Daily: April–Sept 9.30am–5.45pm; Oct–March 10am–5.15pm; last entry 45min before closing • £11 • ☏ 03000 290900, ⓦ www.brighton-hove-rpml.org.uk

In any survey to find England's most loved building, there's always a bucketful of votes for Brighton's exotic extravaganza, the **Royal Pavilion**. The building was the south-coast pied-à-terre of the fun-loving Prince Regent (the future George IV), who first visited the seaside resort in 1783 and spent much of the next forty years partying, gambling and frolicking with his mistress here. The building you see today is the work of John Nash, architect of London's Regent Street, who in 1815 redesigned the Prince's original modest dwelling into an extraordinary confection of slender minarets, twirling domes, pagodas, balconies and miscellaneous motifs imported from India and China. The result defined a genre of its own – Oriental Gothic.

Inside, the **Banqueting Room** erupts with ornate splendour and is dominated by a one-tonne chandelier hung from the jaws of a massive dragon cowering in a plantain tree. The stunning **Music Room**, the first sight of which reduced George to tears of joy, has a huge dome lined with more than 26,000 individually gilded scales and hung with exquisite umbrella-like glass lamps. After climbing the famous cast-iron staircase with its bamboo-look banisters, you can go into Victoria's sober and seldom-used bedroom and the North Gallery where the king's portrait hangs, along with a selection of satirical cartoons. More notable, though, is the **South Gallery**, decorated in sky-blue with trompe-l'oeil bamboo trellises and a carpet that appears to be strewn with flowers.

## Brighton Museum and Art Gallery

Royal Pavilion Gardens • Tues–Sun 10am–5pm • Free • ☏ 03000 290900, ⓦ www.brighton-hove-rpml.org.uk

Across the gardens from the Pavilion stands the **Brighton Museum and Art Gallery** – once part of the royal stable block – which houses a wonderful and eclectic mix of modern fashion and design, archeology, painting and local history. Among the highlights are Dalí's famous sofa (1938) based on Mae West's lips, the 13,000-object ethnographic collection, and the mummified animals and painted coffins of the Ancient Egypt galleries.

## The Lanes

Tucked between the Pavilion and the seafront is a warren of narrow, pedestrianized alleyways known as **The Lanes** – the core of the old fishing village from which Brighton evolved. Long-established antiques shops and jewellers', designer outlets and several cafés, pubs and restaurants make this a great place to wander.

## North Laine

Vibrant, buzzy **North Laine** (ⓦ northlaine.co.uk), which spreads north of North Street along Kensington Gardens and Sydney, Gardner and Bond streets, is more offbeat than

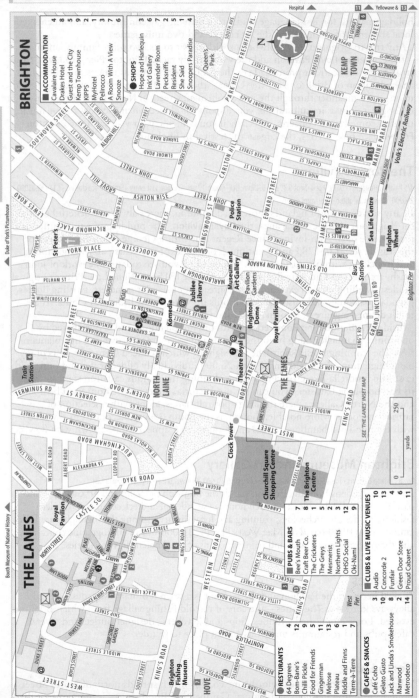

# BRIGHTON

**ACCOMMODATION**
| | |
|---|---|
| Cavalaire House | 4 |
| Drakes Hotel | 8 |
| Guest and the City | 5 |
| Kemp Townhouse | 9 |
| KIPPS | 2 |
| MyHotel | 1 |
| Pelirocco | 3 |
| A Room With A View | 7 |
| Snooze | 6 |

**SHOPS**
| | |
|---|---|
| Hope and Harlequin | 3 |
| Ink'd Gallery | 6 |
| Lavender Room | 7 |
| Pecksniffs | 2 |
| Resident | 5 |
| She Said | 1 |
| Snoopers Paradise | 4 |

**THE LANES**

**RESTURANTS**
| | |
|---|---|
| 64 Degrees | 4 |
| Bom-Bane's | 12 |
| Chilli Pickle | 5 |
| Food for Friends | 11 |
| Gingerman | 8 |
| Melrose | 13 |
| Plateau | 3 |
| Riddle and Finns | 6 |
| Terre-à-Terre | 7 |

**CAFÉS & SNACKS**
| | |
|---|---|
| Café Coho | 3 |
| Gelato Gusto | 10 |
| Jack and Linda's Smokehouse | 8 |
| Marwood | 2 |
| Metrodeco | 14 |

**PUBS & BARS**
| | |
|---|---|
| Bee's Mouth | 7 |
| Craft Beer Co. | 8 |
| The Cricketers | 1 |
| The Greys | 5 |
| Mesmerist | 2 |
| Northern Lights | 3 |
| OHSO Social | 12 |
| Oki-Nami | 9 |

**CLUBS & LIVE MUSIC VENUES**
| | |
|---|---|
| Audio | 10 |
| Concorde 2 | 13 |
| Funfair | 3 |
| Green Door Store | 6 |
| Proud Cabaret | 11 |

the Lanes. Here the eclectic shops, selling secondhand records, vintage gear, homeware, upmarket fashion and New Age objects, mingle with cool coffee shops and pavement cafés and bars.

## The seafront

To soak up the tackier side of Brighton, head down to the **seafront** and take a stroll along **Brighton Pier** (daily: April–Oct 10am–10pm; Nov–March 11am–5pm; ☏01273 609361, ⓦbrightonpier.co.uk), completed in 1899, its every inch devoted to cacophonous fun and money-making. The busiest section of the seafront lies between Brighton Pier and the derelict **West Pier**, half a mile west along the seafront; here, down at beach level underneath the old fishermen's arches, the **Lower Esplanade** is lined with cafés, gift shops, galleries (ⓦtheartistquarter.co.uk), bars and clubs. The Lower Esplanade is also home to the **Brighton Fishing Museum** (daily 9am–5pm; free; ☏01273 723064, ⓦbrightonfishingmuseum.org.uk), which displays old photos and video footage of the golden days of the local fishing industry and houses a large Sussex clinker, a boat once common on Brighton beach.

East of Brighton Pier, the 165ft **Brighton Wheel** (Mon–Thurs & Sun 10am–9pm; Fri & Sat 10am–11pm; £8 for 12–15min ride; ☏01273 722822, ⓦbrightonwheel.com), in place until 2016, offers panoramic views of the city. Opposite, on Marine Parade, the **Sea Life Centre** (daily 10am–5/6/7pm; £17.50; ☏01273 604234, ⓦvisitsealife.com/Brighton) is the world's oldest aquarium, opened in 1872; its wonderfully atmospheric Victorian aquarium hall is the main attraction. Just east of the Brighton Wheel, the antiquated locomotives of **Volk's Electric Railway** (Easter–Sept Mon & Fri 11.15am–5pm, Tues–Thurs 10.15am–5pm, Sat & Sun 10.15am–6pm; every 15min; £3.60 return; ⓦvolkselectricrailway.co.uk) – the first electric train in the country – run eastward towards **Brighton Marina** (ⓦbrightonmarina.co.uk), stopping off en route at the fabulous **Yellowave** beach sports venue (May–Sept Mon–Fri 10am–10pm, Sat & Sun 10am–8pm; Oct–April Tues–Thurs 11am–9pm, Fri 11am–5pm, Sat & Sun 10am–5pm; court rental £21/hr; ☏01273 672222, ⓦyellowave.co.uk), the perfect spot for a taster of beach volleyball on a sunny day, with six courts, plus a bouldering wall and an excellent café.

---

### A WEEKEND IN BRIGHTON

#### FRIDAY NIGHT

Start off the weekend in style with **champagne and oysters** at *Riddle and Finns* in the heart of the Lanes. Then head along to the hip Komedia theatre to catch some **comedy** or live music.

#### SATURDAY

Set aside a full morning to take in the splendours of the quirky **Pavilion**, George IV's pleasure palace by the sea. Then head down to the seafront for an **alfresco lunch** of mackerel sandwiches on the pebbles from *Jack and Linda's Smokehouse*. After an amble to the end of the garish **Brighton Pier**, spend the afternoon exploring the winding passageways of the **Lanes**, and **North Laine**'s quirky shops. Excellent cafés can be found on virtually every corner, or if it's sunny you can join the queues at *Gelato Gusto* for a *gelato* or *sorbetto*. For **dinner**, check out the excellent *Terre-à-Terre*, for vegetarian cooking like no other, or bag a stool at the counter of foodie hotspot *64 Degrees*. After dinner, head out on the town – Brighton has the best **nightlife** in the south outside of London, and is positively bursting at the seams with uber-cool bars and clubs, as well as a great collection of traditional boozers.

#### SUNDAY

There are plenty of great spots for a lazy **brunch**: try *Café Coho*, *Marwood* or *Metrodeco*. Burn off the calories afterwards with a game of **beach volleyball** at Yellowave. If it's raining you can hunker down at Brighton's independent **cinema**, the Duke of York's, or take in the exhibits at the **Brighton and Hove Art Gallery**.

## Hove

West of the city centre, **Hove** – which started life as a separate resort in the 1820s and only merged with Brighton in 1997 – is an elegant neighbourhood, with a much quieter beachfront, some beautiful Regency architecture and plenty of good shops and places to eat. The main sight is **Hove Museum**, 19 Church Street (Mon, Tues & Thurs–Sat 10am–5pm, Sun & bank hol Mon 2–5pm; free; ☎03000 290900, ⓦwww .brighton-hove-rpml.org.uk; bus #1, #1A, #6, #49 or #49A), which houses a fascinating and eclectic collection that covers everything from contemporary crafts to a 3500-year-old Bronze Age cup. A six-seater cinema shows early silent films made in Hove.

### ARRIVAL AND DEPARTURE

**BRIGHTON**

**By train** Brighton train station is at the top of Queen's Road, which descends to the Clocktower and then becomes West St, eventually leading to the seafront, a 10min walk away.
Destinations Arundel (Mon–Sat every 30min, Sun hourly; 1hr 20min); Chichester (every 30min; 45–55min); Eastbourne (every 20min; 35min); Hastings (every 30min; 1hr 5min); Lewes (every 10–20min; 15min); London Bridge (Mon–Sat 4 hourly, Sun every 30min; 1hr); London King's Cross (2–4 hourly; 1hr 15min); London Victoria (1–2 hourly; 55min–1hr 20min); Portsmouth Harbour (Mon–

Sat every 30min, Sun hourly; 1hr 30min).
**By bus** The long-distance bus station is just in from the seafront on the south side of the Old Steine.
Destinations Arundel (Mon–Fri every 30min; 2hr); Chichester (Mon–Sat every 15min, Sun every 30min; 1hr 45min); Eastbourne (every 10–15min; 1hr 15min); Lewes (Mon–Sat every 15min, Sun hourly; 30min); London Victoria (hourly; 2hr 20min); Portsmouth (Mon–Sat every 30min, Sun hourly; 3hr 30min); Tunbridge Wells (Mon–Sat every 30min, Sun hourly; 1hr 35min).

### GETTING AROUND

**By bus** A one-day CitySaver ticket (£4.70) allows you unlimited travel on the city bus network. Short-hop journeys cost £1.80. The website ⓦjourneyon.co.uk has a journey planner.
**By taxi** For a city taxi, call ☎01273 202020 or ☎01273 204060. There are central ranks at Brighton station, East St, Queens Square near the clocktower and outside St Peter's Church.
**By tour** For details of city tours, which range from ghost walks to bike tours to a "Piers and Queers" tour, see

ⓦvisitbrighton.com/things-to-do/walking-guides. The website also has downloadable PDF walking tours and podcasts.
**By bike** The website ⓦjourneyon.co.uk has a journey planner, and a downloadable cycling map of the city.
**Bike rental** Amsterdammers, Unit 8, under the station, off Trafalgar Street (£7/3hr, £10/24hr; ☎01273 571555, ⓦbrightoncyclehire.com); Brighton Beach Bike Hire, Madeira Drive, by Yellowave (£6 for 1hr, £12 for 3hr, £16 for 4+ hours; ☎07917 753794, ⓦbrightonsports.co.uk).

### INFORMATION

**Visitor information** There are ten staffed Visitor Information points (VIPs) throughout the city, including at Brighton Pier, the Royal Pavilion shop and Jubilee Library in the North Laine.
**Useful apps, magazines and websites** VisitBrighton

produces a free app for smartphones (ⓦvisitbrighton.com/ apps). The best listing magazine is *Source* (ⓦbrightonsource.co.uk), but *XYZ* (ⓦxyzmagazine.co.uk) and *BN1* (ⓦbn1magazine.co.uk) are also worth a look.

### ACCOMMODATION

Brighton's **accommodation** is pricey, with rates often rising substantially at weekends. The listings below quote weekend, high-season rates; at many places these prices will fall dramatically out of season and midweek, so it pays to check around. Note that at weekends there's generally a two-night-minimum stay. Much of the city's nicest B&B accommodation is found in **Kemp Town**, east of the city centre, either off St James's Street (the city's "Gay Village") or around Kemp Town Village, with its cool cafés, delis and antique shops.

#### HOTELS AND B&BS

**Cavalaire House** 34 Upper Rock Gardens ☎01273 696899, ⓦcavalaire.co.uk. Warm and welcoming B&B, with artwork from Brighton artists on the walls, fresh flowers in the cheery breakfast room, and a friendly resident dog. Rooms vary: the cheapest are cosy and

traditional, while the more expensive deluxe rooms have a bit more style. **£149**
**Drakes Hotel** 33–34 Marine Parade ☎01273 696934, ⓦdrakesofbrighton.com. The unbeatable seafront location is the big draw at this chic, minimalist boutique hotel. All the luxuries you'd expect are here, and the most

expensive rooms come with freestanding baths by floor-to-ceiling windows. There's an excellent in-house restaurant too. Room only £160

★**Guest and the City** 2 Broad St ☎01273 698289, ⊚guestandthecity.co.uk. Lovely B&B in a great central location a minute from the pier, with stylish rooms (the two feature rooms – £140 – come with stained-glass windows of classic Brighton scenes), and super-friendly owners who couldn't be more helpful. £90

★**Kemp Townhouse** 21 Atlingworth St ☎01273 681400, ⊚kemptownhouse.com. Stylish Regency townhouse – the city's only five-star guesthouse – with excellent service, chic rooms and great breakfasts. Seaview rooms come with binoculars for gazing out to sea, and all rooms come have a carafe of complimentary port. £115

**MyHotel** 17 Jubilee St ☎01273 900300, ⊚myhotels.com/my-hotel-brighton. Hip boutique hotel in the heart of North Laine, with rooms designed along feng shui lines, and a great bar, *Merkaba*, downstairs. Rates fluctuate with demand, so check online for last-minute bargains. £140

★**Pelirocco** 10 Regency Square ☎01273 327055, ⊚hotelpelirocco.co.uk. "England's most rock'n'roll hotel" is a real one-off, featuring extravagantly themed rooms inspired by pop culture and pin-ups. There's a Fifties-style

boudoir, a Pop Art "Modrophenia" room featuring bedside tables made from scooters, and even a twin room styled as Lord Vader's Quarters, complete with light sabre, Darth Vader costume and Star Wars DVDs. £115

**A Room With A View** 41 Marine Parade ☎01273 682885, ⊚aroomwithaviewbrighton.com. This boutique guesthouse, right on the seafront, offers some of the best views in town. All rooms come with Nespresso machines and bathrobes; some have free-standing baths, others power showers. Pick of the bunch is the first-floor balcony room (£255). £135

**Snooze** 25 St George's Terrace ☎01273 605797, ⊚snoozebrighton.com. Quirky, characterful guesthouse in Kemp Town Village, with six funky rooms that range from a 1970s-style penthouse suite to a room decked out with vintage black-and-white photos of topless pin-ups. £140

**HOSTELS**

**KIPPS** 76 Grand Parade ☎01273 604182, ⊚kipps-brighton.com. Quiet, friendly hostel in a great spot opposite the Royal Pavilion, with comfy rooms (some en suite) and dorms, a licensed bar and good-value breakfasts (£2.50 for dorms, included for rooms). Dorms £30, doubles £82

## EATING

Brighton has the greatest concentration of **restaurants** in the southeast after London – including one of the country's best vegetarian restaurants – and a thriving **café** culture, especially in the buzzy North Laine area. There are plenty of good **coffee shops** in the city, including those belonging to Brighton-based chains Ground and the Small Batch Coffee Company; the latter has its own roastery in Hove.

### CAFÉS AND SNACKS

**Café Coho** 53 Ship St ☎01273 747777, ⊚cafecoho.co.uk. Stylish café, with exposed brick walls, a counter piled high with pastries, salads and sandwiches, and tables outside for people-watching; it's a great spot for a lazy weekend brunch. The house coffee is Union's Revelation blend, and there's always a guest coffee available too. Mon–Fri 8am–6pm, Sat 8am–7pm, Sun 8.30am–6.30pm.

**Gelato Gusto** 2 Gardner St ☎01273 673402, ⊚gelatogusto.com. Fabulous *gelateria*, with regularly-changing flavours that run from Sea Salt Caramel to Syrup Sponge Pudding. Mon–Fri 11.30am–6pm, Sat & Sun 11am–6pm.

★**Jack and Linda's Smokehouse** 197 Kings Arches. This tiny beachfront smokehouse is run by a lovely couple

who've been traditionally smoking fish here for over a decade. Grab a fresh crab sandwich or hot mackerel roll (£3–4) to eat on the beach for a perfect summer lunch. April–Sept daily 10am–5pm.

★**Marwood** 52 Ship St ☎01273 382063, ⊚themarwood.com. Quirky, laidback café with great coffee and food (mains around £7) and splendidly bonkers decor that runs from stuffed animals and skateboards on the walls to Star Wars spaceships dangling from the ceiling. Mon & Tues 8am–8pm, Wed–Fri 8am–11pm, Sat 9am–11pm, Sun 10am–8pm.

**Metrodeco** 38 Upper St James St ☎01273 677243, ⊚metro-deco.com. The place to come for afternoon tea, this Parisian-style tea salon in Kemp Town serves over twenty bespoke blends of tea, dainty sandwiches, scones

---

## BRIGHTON FESTIVAL

Every May the three-week-long **Brighton Festival** (☎01273 709709, ⊚brightonfestival.org) takes over various venues around town. This arty celebration includes over two hundred events, ranging from exhibitions and street theatre to concerts and talks. Running at the same time is the **Brighton and Hove Fringe Festival** (☎01273 709709, ⊚www.brightonfestivalfringe.org.uk), which puts on over 700 events, and the **Artists' Open Houses Festival** (⊚aoh.org.uk), when hundreds of private homes fling open their doors to show the work of local artists.

2

and fancies (£16 Mon–Fri, £18 weekend), all presented on vintage crockery; splash out on a "tea cocktail" for the full experience. Great breakfasts and lunches too. Mon–Thurs & Sun 9.30am–6pm, Fri & Sat 9.30am–9pm.

## RESTAURANTS

**64 Degrees** 53 Meeting House Lane ☎ 01273 770115, ⓦ 64degrees.co.uk. The best seats in the house at this tiny restaurant in the Lanes are up at the counter of the open kitchen: the idea is that you choose several small plates of food (£5–12.50) and share them, to create your own tasting menu. The food's inventive, delicious and prepared in front of you, and the whole experience is brilliant fun. Mon–Thurs noon–2.30pm & 5–9.45pm, Fri & Sat noon–3.30pm & 6–9.45pm.

**Bom-Bane's** 24 George St ☎ 01273 606400, ⓦ bom -banes.com. Fun little café/restaurant run by musician Jane Bom-Bane. The decor is decidedly eccentric – each of the individually designed tables holds a surprise in store – and the hearty Belgium-influenced food is delicious (*stoemp* and sausage £10.25). There are weekly film nights (Wed; £5.50) and occasional live music nights. Tues, Thurs & Fri 5–11.30pm, Wed & Sat 12.30–11.30pm.

★ **Chilli Pickle** 17 Jubilee St ☎ 01273 900383, ⓦ thechillipickle.com. Stylish, buzzing restaurant in North Laine serving sophisticated, authentic Indian food – everything from masala dosas to Chennai seafood stew (mains £10–17). At lunchtimes they offer a range of thalis and "street food". Mon–Sat noon–3pm & 6–10.30pm, Sun noon–3pm & 6–10pm.

**Food for Friends** 18 Prince Albert St ☎ 01273 202310, ⓦ foodforfriends.com. Brighton's original vegetarian restaurant – on this spot for over thirty years – serves up sophisticated veggie dishes that are imaginative enough to please die-hard meat-eaters too: mains (£12–14) might include spicy Asian tofu salad, or saffron ravioli in a blue cheese sauce. Mon–Thurs & Sun

noon–10pm, Fri & Sat noon–10.30pm.

**Gingerman** 21a Norfolk Square ☎ 01273 326688, ⓦ gingermanrestaurant.com. Small but perfectly formed one-room restaurant serving up some of the best food in Brighton. The weekly-changing set menus cost £15 for 2 courses at lunch, £30 at dinner. Tues–Sun 12.30–2pm & 7–10pm.

**Melrose** 132 King's Rd ☎ 01273 326520, ⓦ melrose restaurant.co.uk. Traditional seafront establishment that's been serving up tasty, excellent-value fish and chips (£6.75), local seafood, roasts and custard-covered puddings for over forty years. The next door *Regency Restaurant* is smaller and similar. Daily 11.30am–10.30pm.

**Plateau** 1 Bartholomews ☎ 01273 733085, ⓦ plateau brighton.co.uk. Laidback little restaurant-cum-wine bar serving cocktails, organic beers and wine, and food that ranges from small "bites" (£5–9) to bigger "plats" (from £11), so you can stop by for a nibble and a drink, or a full-blown meal. Mon–Fri 11am–late, Sat & Sat 10am–late.

★ **Riddle and Finns** 12b Meeting House Lane ☎ 01273 721667, ⓦ riddleandfinns.co.uk. Bustling champagne and oyster bar in the Lanes, where you can tuck into a huge range of shellfish and fish (mains £13–19) at communal marble-topped tables in a white-tiled, candle-lit dining room with an open kitchen. It's very popular, and they don't take bookings, so expect to wait at busy times. Their sister restaurant, the beachfront *Riddle & Finns The Beach*, is equally good. Mon–Thurs & Sun noon–10pm, Fri & Sat noon–11pm, plus Sat & Sun 9.15–11.15am.

★ **Terre-à-Terre** 71 East St ☎ 01273 729051, ⓦ terreaterre.co.uk. One of the country's best vegetarian restaurants, this award-winning place serves up fabulous, inventive global veggie cuisine (mains around £15), in a modern arty setting. The taster plate for two (£23) is a good place to start if you're befuddled by the weird and wonderful creations on offer. Mon–Fri noon–10.30pm, Sat 11am–11pm, Sun 11am–10pm.

## NIGHTLIFE AND ENTERTAINMENT

As well as its mainstream **theatre** and **concert** venues, Brighton has a fantastic art-house **cinema**, myriad **clubs** and plenty of **live music venues** alongside its hip bars and traditional boozers. For up-to-date details of **what's on**, there's an array of free listings magazines available from the tourist office (see p.166).

### PUBS AND BARS

**Bee's Mouth** 10 Western Rd ☎ 01273 770083. Quirky, sumptuously decorated pub on the Brighton/Hove border, with a good range of bottled beers, and three subterranean levels hosting live music, film nights and life drawing. Mon–Thurs 4.30pm–12.30am, Fri 4.30pm–1.30am, Sat 2.30pm–1.30am, Sun 3.30pm–12.30am.

**Craft Beer Co.** 22–23 Upper North St ⓦ thecraftbeerco .com. One for beer lovers, this friendly pub has nine daily-changing cask ales and over 200 bottled varieties. The

house Craft Pale Ale is brewed for them by Kent Brewery. Mon–Wed 3–11pm, Thurs 3–11.30pm, Fri noon–midnight, Sat noon–1am, Sun noon–10.30pm.

**The Cricketers** 15 Black Lion St ☎ 01273 329472, ⓦ cricketersbrighton.co.uk. Brighton's oldest pub, immortalized by Graham Greene in *Brighton Rock*, has a traditional feel, with good daytime pub grub, real ales and a cosy courtyard bar. Mon–Thurs 11am–midnight, Fri & Sat 11am–1am, Sun noon–11pm.

**The Greys** 105 Southover St ☎ 01273 680734,

2

## LGBT BRIGHTON

Brighton has one of the longest established and most thriving **gay scenes** in Britain, centred around St James's Street in Kemp Town, and with a variety of lively clubs and bars drawing people from all over the southeast; for **listings** and events check out *Gscene magazine* (ⓦgscene.com) or Zhoosh (ⓦzhooshbrighton.co.uk). The annual **Gay Pride Festival** (date varies each summer; ⓦpridebrighton.org.uk) has loads going on, from performing arts to exhibitions, as well as the main parade and ticketed party. Information, advice and support about the LGBT scene is available from Brighton's **Lesbian and Gay Switchboard** (☎01273 234009, ⓦswitchboard.org.uk).

ⓦgreyspub.com. Friendly, laidback pub with an open fire and a great menu. Frequent live music (especially country, bluegrass and Americana), comedy and talks. Mon–Wed 4–11pm, Thurs 4–11.30pm, Fri 3pm–12.30am, Sat noon–12.30am, Sun noon–11pm.

**Mesmerist** 1–3 Prince Albert St ☎01273 328542, ⓦdrinkinbrighton.co.uk/mesmerist. Large, lively and welcoming bar inspired by 1930s gin palaces, burlesque and the steampunk movement: cheap drinks, free entry and rock'n'roll and swing tunes make this a good pre-club choice. Mon–Thurs & Sun noon–1am, Fri & Sat noon–2am.

★**Northern Lights** 6 Little East St ☎01273 747096, ⓦnorthernlightsbrighton.co.uk. Laidback, ever-popular bar with a Scandinavian theme: choose from two dozen different flavoured vodkas, aquavit, and beers from Denmark, Sweden and Finland. The Nordic menu features reindeer, Smörgåsbord and pickled herring. Mon–Thurs 5pm–midnight, Fri & Sat noon–2am, Sun noon–midnight.

**OHSO Social** 250a Kings Road Arches ☎01273 746067, ⓦohsosocial.co.uk. Get the full Brighton experience on the terrace of this late-night beachfront bar, with great cocktails and uninterrupted views of Brighton pier. Daily 9am–late.

**Oki-Nami** 6 New Rd ☎01273 773777, ⓦokinami.com. Small, one-room cocktail bar upstairs from the Japanese restaurant of the same name, co-owned by Norman Cook (aka Fatboy Slim), with a balcony overlooking New Road that's perfect for people-watching. Daily 5pm–late.

### CLUBS AND LIVE MUSIC VENUES

**Audio** 10 Marine Parade ☎01273 606 906, ⓦaudio brighton.com. Trendy seafront hangout that boasts a terrace with sea views and a large bar on the first floor. The basement club is always packed, playing everything from indie to house and drum and bass.

**Concorde 2** Madeira Shelter, Madeira Drive ☎01273

673311, ⓦconcorde2.co.uk. A Victorian tearoom in a former life, Brighton's trendiest live music venue features up-and-coming acts, big names (from The White Stripes to Jarvis Cocker) and varied club nights.

**Funfair** 12–15 King's Rd ☎01273 757447. Quirky funfair-themed club with exotic performers, a ball pit, distortion mirrors and fun music that runs from motown to disco.

★**Green Door Store** Trafalgar Arches, Lower Goods Yard ⓦthegreendoorstore.co.uk. Über-cool club and live music venue in the arches under the train station, playing anything from psych to blues, punk or powerdisco. The bar is free entry; live gig entry varies.

**Proud Cabaret Brighton** 83 St Georges Rd ☎01273 605789, ⓦproudcabaretbrighton.com. Opulent venue in a former ballroom hosting dinner and cabaret/burlesque shows, plus diverse club nights.

### ARTS CENTRES, THEATRES AND CINEMAS

**Brighton Dome** 29 New Rd ☎01273 709709, ⓦbrightondome.org. Home to three venues – Pavilion Theatre, Concert Hall and Corn Exchange – offering mainstream theatre, concerts, dance and performance.

★**Duke of Yorks Picturehouse** Preston Circus ☎0871 704 2056, ⓦpicturehouses.co.uk. Grade II-listed cinema with a licensed bar showing art-house, independent and classic films. Dukes at Komedia is its sister cinema based at the Komedia arts centre (see below).

★**Komedia** 44–47 Gardner St ☎0845 293 8480, ⓦkomedia.co.uk/brighton. A Brighton institution, this highly regarded arts venue hosts stand-up comedy, live music and cabaret, as well as fun club nights.

**Theatre Royal** New Rd ☎01273 764400, ⓦambassadortickets.com/theatreroyal. Venerable old theatre – going since 1807 – offering predominantly mainstream plays, opera and musicals.

### SHOPPING

Most of Brighton's high street chains are found in and around **Churchill Square** (ⓦchurchillsquare.co.uk). The best areas for independent shops are the **Lanes** and **North Laine** (ⓦnorthlaine.co.uk); it's also worth wandering over to **Kemp Town** for a browse around its antiques shops.

**Hope and Harlequin** 31 Sydney St ☎01273 675222, ⓦhopeandharlequin.com. Upmarket vintage shop,

stocking clothes and collectables up to the 1970s, with a special emphasis on the 1930s and 40s. Mon & Wed–Sat

10.30am–6pm, Tues noon–5pm, Sun 11am–5pm.

**Ink'd Gallery** 96 North Rd ☎ 01273 645299, ⓦ ink-d
.co.uk. Excellent contemporary art gallery, with frequent
rehangs and a great mix of artists and mediums, from
paintings and ceramics to street art. Mon–Sat
10am–6pm, Sun noon–4pm.

**Lavender Room** 16 Bond St ☎ 01273 220380,
ⓦ lavender-room.co.uk. Stylish boutique selling
fragrances, lingerie, jewellery and vintage-inspired home
accessories. Mon–Sat 10am–6pm, Sun 11am–5pm.

**Pecksniffs** 45–46 Meeting House Lane ☎ 01273
723292, ⓦ pecksniffs.com. Independent British fragrance
house in the Lanes, selling a range of perfumes, bespoke
blends and body products. Mon–Sat 10am–5pm, Sun
10.30am–4pm.

**Resident** 28 Kensington Gardens ☎ 01273 606312,
ⓦ resident-music.com. Award-winning independent
record shop in North Laine; it also sells tickets for local
venues. Mon–Sat 9am–6.30pm, Sun 10am–6pm.

**She Said** 32 Ship St ☎ 01273 777811, ⓦ shesaid
boutique.com. The city that gave rise to the "dirty
weekend" has its fair share of erotic emporiums, but this
one is the classiest – it's even been featured in *Vogue*.
Mon–Sat 10am–6pm, Sun 11am–5pm, plus occasional
late-night openings.

**Snoopers Paradise** 7–8 Kensington Gardens ☎ 01273
602558. You can't visit Brighton without popping into this
huge North Laine flea market. It contains over ninety
different stalls over two floors; Snoopers Attic
(ⓦ snoopersattic.co.uk), a "vintage makers' boutique" up
on the first floor, is worth a special mention. Mon–Sat
10am–6pm, Sun 11am–4pm.

# Arundel and around

The hilltop town of **ARUNDEL**, eighteen miles west of Brighton, has for seven centuries
been the seat of the dukes of Norfolk, whose fine **castle** looks over the valley of the
River Arun. The medieval town's well-preserved appearance and picturesque setting
draws in the crowds on summer weekends, but at any other time a visit reveals one of
West Sussex's least spoilt old towns. The two main attractions are the castle and the
towering Gothic **cathedral**, but the rest of Arundel is pleasant to wander round,
especially the antique-shop-lined Maltravers and Arun streets. North of Arundel lie a
couple more attractions: **Bignor Roman Villa**, with some outstanding Roman mosaics;
and the grand, seventeenth-century **Petworth House**, which has a notable art collection.

   At the end of August, Arundel's **festival** (ⓦ arundelfestival.co.uk) features everything
from open-air theatre to salsa bands.

## Arundel Castle

Mill Rd • April–Oct Tues–Sun & Mon in Aug & bank hol Mon: keep 10am–4.30pm; Fitzalan Chapel & grounds 10am–5pm; castle rooms
noon–5pm • Castle, keep, grounds & chapel £16; keep, grounds & chapel £11; grounds & chapel £9 • ☎ 01903 882173, ⓦ arundelcastle.org

Despite its medieval appearance, much of what you see of **Arundel Castle** is
comparatively new, the result of a series of lavish reconstructions from 1718 onwards,
after the original Norman structure was badly damaged during the Civil War. One of
the oldest parts is the twelfth-century **keep**, from which you can peer down onto the
current duke's spacious residence and the pristine castle grounds. Inside the main
castle, the highlights include the impressive **Barons Hall** and the **library**, which has
paintings by Gainsborough, Holbein and Van Dyck. On the edge of the castle grounds,
the fourteenth-century **Fitzalan Chapel** houses tombs of past dukes of Norfolk,
including twin effigies of the seventh duke – one as he looked when he died and,
underneath, one of his emaciated corpse. Nearby, the **Collector Earl's Garden** is a
playfully theatrical take on a Jacobean garden, with exotic planting, and pavilions,
obelisks and urns made from green oak rather than stone.

## Arundel Cathedral

Corner of Parson's Hill & London Rd • Daily 9am–6pm or dusk • Free • ☎ 01903 882297, ⓦ www.arundelcathedral.org

The flamboyant **Arundel Cathedral** was constructed in the 1870s by the fifteenth duke
of Norfolk over the town's former Catholic church; its spire was designed by John

Hansom, inventor of the hansom cab. Inside are the enshrined remains of St Philip Howard, the canonized thirteenth earl, who was sentenced to death in 1585, accused of Catholic conspiracy against Elizabeth I's Protestant court. He died of dysentery in the Tower of London ten years later.

## Bignor Roman Villa

6 miles north of Arundel, Bignor • March–Oct daily 10am–5pm, last entry 4pm • £6 • ☏ 01798 869259, ⓦ bignorromanvilla.co.uk

The excavated third-century ruins of the **Bignor Roman Villa** are famed for their spectacular Roman mosaics. The site is superbly situated at the base of the South Downs and features the longest extant section of mosaic in England, as well as the remains of a hypocaust, the Romans' underfloor heating system.

## Petworth House

11 miles north of Arundel • **House** Mid-March to Oct Mon–Wed, Sat & Sun 11am–5pm, also Thurs & Fri for 45min guided snapshot tours only • **Pleasure Ground** Daily: mid-Jan to mid-March 10.30am–3.30pm; mid-March to Oct 10.30am–5pm; Nov to mid-Dec 10.30am–3.30pm • **Park** Daily 8am–dusk • House £12.50, snapshot tours £5, Pleasure Ground and park free; NT • ☏ 01798 342207, ⓦ nationaltrust.org.uk/petworth • Train to Pulborough, then Stagecoach Coastline #1 bus (Mon–Sat hourly, Sun every 2hr)

**Petworth House**, adjoining the pretty little town of **PETWORTH**, is one of the southeast's most impressive stately homes. Built in the late seventeenth century, the house is stuffed with treasures – including the 1592 Molyneux globe, believed to be the earliest terrestrial globe in existence – and contains an outstanding art collection, with paintings by Van Dyck, Titian, Gainsborough, Bosch, Reynolds, Blake and Turner (the last a frequent guest here). The 700-acre **grounds**, home to a large herd of fallow deer, were landscaped by Capability Brown and are considered one of his finest achievements.

### ARRIVAL AND INFORMATION
ARUNDEL

**By train** Arundel's station is half a mile south of the town centre over the river on the A27.
Destinations Brighton (Mon–Sat every 30min, Sun hourly; 1hr 20min); Chichester (Mon–Sat every 30min, Sun hourly; 20min); London Victoria (Mon–Sat every 30min, Sun hourly; 1hr 30min); Portsmouth Harbour (every 30min; 55min).

**By bus** Buses pull in either on High Street or River Road.
Destinations Brighton (Mon–Fri every 30min; 2hr); Chichester (Mon–Sat every 2hr; 35min).
**Tourist information** There's a self-service Visitor Information Point at Arundel Museum, opposite the castle entrance on Mill Road (daily 10am–4pm; ⓦ sussexbythesea.com).

### ACCOMMODATION

**Amberley Castle** Amberley ☏ 01798 831992, ⓦ amberleycastle.co.uk. For a real splurge, indulge in an overnight stay at this 600-year-old castle, complete with portcullis, 60ft curtain walls, gardens, lakes, croquet lawn and nineteen luxurious bedrooms, many with four-poster beds. **£265**

**Swan Hotel** 27–29 High St ☏ 01903 882314, ⓦ swanarundel.co.uk. Fourteen smart rooms above a pub, decked out in shabby chic style, with shutters and bare boards or coir carpets, and seaside prints on the wall. **£115**

### EATING AND DRINKING

**Bay Tree** 21 Tarrant St ☏ 01903 883679, ⓦ thebaytreearundel.co.uk. Cosy and relaxed little restaurant squeezed into three low-beamed rooms, with a small terrace out the back. Mains such as pheasant breast wrapped in bacon cost £16–18 at dinner; lunch features simpler dishes. Mon–Fri 11.30am–2.45pm & 6.30–9.15pm, Sat 10.30am–4pm & 6.30–9.30pm, Sun 10.30am–4pm & 6.30–9.15pm.
**George and Dragon Inn** Burpham ☏ 01903 883131,

ⓦ georgeatburpham.co.uk. Three miles from Arundel (a lovely walk up the east bank of the river), this seventeenth-century pub has bags of character, real ales from the Arundel Brewery and a foodie-friendly à la carte menu (mains £11–20). Mon–Fri 10.30am–3pm & 6–11pm, Sat 10.30am–11pm, Sun 10.30am–10pm; food served Mon–Fri 10.30am–2.30pm & 6–9pm, Sat 10.30am–3pm & 6–9.30pm, Sun noon–5pm & 6–9pm.

# Chichester and around

The handsome city of **CHICHESTER** has plenty to recommend it: a splendid twelfth-century **cathedral**, a thriving cultural scene and an outstanding collection of modern British art on show at the **Pallant House Gallery**. The city began life as a Roman settlement, and its Roman cruciform street plan is still evident in the four-quadrant symmetry of the town centre. The main streets lead off from the Gothic **Market Cross**, a bulky octagonal rotunda topped by ornate finials and a crown lantern spire, built in 1501 to provide shelter for the market traders. The big attraction outside Chichester is **Fishbourne Roman Palace**, the largest excavated Roman site in Britain, though for families a day at dune-backed **West Wittering beach** will be hard to beat.

**2**

Chichester Festivities (℡ 01243 528356, ⓦ chifest.org.uk) is Chichester's annual arts festival, taking place at a range of venues over two weeks in late June, and featuring music, talks, theatre, comedy and other events.

## Chichester Cathedral

West St • Daily: mid-April to mid-Oct 7.15am–7pm; mid-Oct to mid-April 7.15am–6pm; drop-in 45min guided tours Mon–Sat 11.15am & 2.30pm • Free • ℡ 01243 782595, ⓦ chichestercathedral.org.uk

Chichester's chief attraction is its fine Gothic **Cathedral**. Building began in 1076, but the church was extensively rebuilt following a fire a century later and has been only minimally modified since about 1300, except for the slender spire and the unique, freestanding fifteenth-century bell tower. The **interior** is renowned for its modern devotional art, which includes a stained-glass window by Marc Chagall and an altar-screen tapestry by John Piper. Older treasures include a sixteenth-century painting in the north transept of the past bishops of Chichester, and the fourteenth-century Fitzalan tomb that inspired Philip Larkin to write *An Arundel Tomb*. However, the highlight is a pair of carvings created around 1140, the **Chichester Reliefs**, which show the raising of Lazarus and Christ at the gate of Bethany; originally brightly coloured, with semiprecious stones set in the figures' eyes, the reliefs are among the finest Romanesque stone carvings in England.

## Pallant House Gallery

9 North Pallant • Tues, Wed, Fri & Sat 10am–5pm, Thurs 10am–8pm, Sun & bank hols 11am–5pm; highlights tours Sat 2pm, themed tours Thurs 5.15pm • £8, Tues £4, Thurs 5–8pm free (£4 for main exhibition) • ℡ 01243 774557, ⓦ pallant.org.uk

Off South Street, in the well-preserved Georgian quadrant of the city known as the Pallants, you'll find **Pallant House Gallery**, a superlative collection of twentieth-century British art housed in a Queen Anne townhouse and award-winning contemporary extension. Artists on display from the permanent collection include Henry Moore, Lucian Freud, Walter Sickert, Barbara Hepworth and Peter Blake, and there are also excellent temporary exhibitions.

## Novium

Tower St • April–Oct Mon–Sat 10am–5pm, Sun 10am–4pm; Nov–March Tues–Sat 10am–5pm • £7 • ℡ 01243 775888, ⓦ thenovium.org

The city's museum of local history – the **Novium** – is housed in a sleek new building around the corner from the cathedral, and is centred around an excavated Roman bath house on the ground floor. The two floors above contain an eclectic assortment of local artefacts, from mammoth bones to Saxon cremation pots and a nineteenth-century mousetrap.

## Fishbourne Roman Palace

Salthill Rd, Fishbourne • Feb & Nov to mid-Dec daily 10am–4pm; March–Oct daily 10am–5pm; mid-Dec to Jan Sat & Sun 10am–4pm • £8.70 • ☎ 01243 789829, ⓦ sussexpast.co.uk • Train from Chichester to Fishbourne (hourly; 3min); turn right from the station and the palace is a few minutes' walk away

**Fishbourne**, two miles west of Chichester, is the largest and best-preserved Roman dwelling in the country. Roman relics have long been turning up hereabouts, and in 1960 a workman unearthed their source – the site of a depot constructed by the invading Romans in 43 AD, which is thought later to have become the vast, hundred-room palace of a Romanized Celtic aristocrat. The one surviving wing, the north wing, displays floor mosaics depicting Fishbourne's famous dolphin-riding cupid as well as the more usual geometric patterns. An audiovisual programme portrays the palace as it would have been in Roman times, and the extensive gardens attempt to recreate the palace grounds.

## Cass Sculpture Foundation

Goodwood, 5 miles north of Chichester • April–Nov Tues–Sun & bank hol Mon 10.30am–4.30pm • £12.50 • ☎ 01243 538449, ⓦ sculpture.org.uk

Five miles north of Chichester lies **Cass Sculpture Foundation**, an absolute must for anyone interested in contemporary art, with more than eighty large-scale works, some of which have been specially commissioned, sited in a 26-acre woodland environment. The selection of pieces on display changes from year to year as the pieces are sold; past artists have included Antony Gormley, Thomas Heatherwick, Eduardo Paolozzi, Andy Goldsworthy and Rachel Whiteread.

## Weald and Downland Open-Air Museum

7 miles north of Chichester, Singleton • Jan & Feb Wed, Sat & Sun 10.30am–4pm; March, Nov & Dec daily 10.30am–4pm; April–Oct daily 10.30am–6pm; Downland Gridshell tour daily at 1.30pm • £11.90 • ☎ 01243 811363, ⓦ www.wealddown.co.uk • Stagecoach Coastline bus #60 from Chichester or Midhurst (Mon–Sat every 30min, Sun hourly)

More than fifty old buildings – from a Tudor market hall to a medieval farmstead – have been saved from destruction and reconstructed at the fifty-acre **Weald and Downland Open-Air Museum**, with stewards on hand to bring the buildings to life. There's a daily guided tour of the Downland Gridshell building, the museum's workshop and store, and there are also numerous special events and activities throughout the year.

## West Wittering beach

8 miles south of Chichester • Daily: mid-March to mid-Oct 6.30am–8.30pm; mid-Oct to mid-March 7am–6pm • Parking £1–8 depending on season, day & time • ☎ 01243 514143 (Estate Office), ⓦ westwitteringbeach.co.uk • Buses #52 & #53 run from Chichester bus station to West Wittering village (15–25min), a 10min walk from the beach

Unspoilt **West Wittering beach** is one of the loveliest beaches in Sussex, with acres of dune-backed soft sand, and warm, shallow lagoons at low tide. A brilliant watersports outfit, X-Train (☎ 01243 513077, ⓦ x-train.co.uk), offers windsurfing, kitesurfing,

---

### GLORIOUS GOODWOOD

Four miles north of Chichester, the **Goodwood Estate** (☎ 01243 775055, ⓦ goodwood.co.uk) is most famous for its racecourse and its motor-racing circuit, and for its three big sporting events: the **Festival of Speed** (late June/early July), a long weekend of vintage and special cars; **Glorious Goodwood** (late July), one of *the* social events of the horse-racing year; and the **Goodwood Revival** (mid-Sept), a motor-racing meeting staged in the 1940s, 50s and 60s. All three events are very popular; buy tickets and book accommodation well in advance.

stand-up paddle-boarding and more. The beach gets very busy on summer weekends; come early, or be prepared for traffic jams.

## ARRIVAL AND DEPARTURE                                    CHICHESTER

**By train** Chichester's train station lies on Stockbridge Rd; it's a 10min walk north to the Market Cross.

Destinations Arundel (Mon–Sat every 30min, Sun hourly; 20–30min); Brighton (every 30min; 45–55min); London Victoria (every 30min; 1hr 35min); Portsmouth Harbour (Mon–Sat every 30min, Sun hourly; 30–50min).

**By bus** The bus station is across the road from the train station on Southgate.

Destinations Arundel (Mon–Sat hourly; 30min); Brighton (Mon–Sat every 15min, Sun every 30min; 1hr 45min); Portsmouth (hourly; 55min).

## INFORMATION AND GETTING AROUND

**Tourist office** At the Novium, Tower Street (Mon–Sat 10am–5pm, Sun 10am–4pm; ☎01243 775888, ⓦvisitchichester.org).

**By tour** Guided tours are bookable through the tourist office (April–Sept Tues & Wed at 11am, Sat at 2pm; Oct–

March Tues at 11am, Sat at 2pm; £4.50).

**Bike rental** Barreg Cycles, 2 miles from the centre in Fishbourne, rents bikes (£15/day; ☎01243 786104, ⓦbarreg.co.uk).

## ACCOMMODATION

★**Chichester Apartments** 230 Oving Rd ☎01243 771464, ⓦchichesterapartments.co.uk. Six beautiful, stylish serviced apartments, with underfloor heating, fresh flowers and quality linen. Everything you might need is provided, from top-notch toiletries to breakfast supplies and cooking essentials. Super-friendly owners too. Three-

night mini-break (per night) **£99**, weekly rate **£500**

★**Musgrove House B&B** 63 Oving Rd ☎01243 790179, ⓦmusgrovehouse.co.uk. This smart, friendly boutique B&B, a short walk for the centre, is fantastic value: the three impeccably tasteful rooms come with iPod docks, silk duvets and local art on the walls. **£80**

## EATING AND DRINKING

**Amelie and Friends** 31 North St ☎01243 771444, ⓦamelieandfriends.com. Buzzy little restaurant with a strikingly designed wood-and-white interior and a peaceful walled garden at the back, perfect for lazy alfresco lunches or afternoon tea (offered daily 3–4pm; book in advance). Mains such as sea bream or apple and cheddar potato latkes cost £10–17, with lighter dishes available at lunchtime. Mon–Fri noon–2.30pm, 3–4pm & 5.30–9pm, Sat noon–4pm & 5–9pm, Sun noon–2.30pm & 3–4pm.

**Park Tavern** 11 Priory Rd ☎01243 785057, ⓦparktavernchichester.co.uk. Fab pub overlooking Priory Park, with quirky decor and good-value home-made food (around the £10 mark), plus sandwiches and

ploughman's. Fuller's on tap, plus a guest ale. Mon–Sat 11am–11pm, Sun noon–10.30pm; food served Mon–Fri noon–3pm & 6–9pm, Sat 11am–9pm, Sun noon–4pm.

★**Richmond Arms** Mill Rd, West Ashling ☎01243 572046, ⓦtherichmondarms.co.uk. Five miles from Chichester, West Ashling's village pub is a real find, with heaps of style and great food that runs from roast duck with pomegranate molasses and pickled rhubarb, to BBQ Cornish squid with spicy coleslaw (£15–22). On Friday and Saturday evenings a pizza wagon serves up artisan-style pizzas. Wed–Sat noon–2pm & 6–9pm, Sun noon–3pm.

## ENTERTAINMENT

**Chichester Festival Theatre** Oaklands Park ☎01243 781312, ⓦcft.org.uk. Highly regarded theatre, with a

season running roughly between Easter and October; in the shorter winter season it hosts touring shows.

# Guildford and around

Prettily set near the River Wey, in rolling Surrey countryside, **GUILDFORD** is an attractive place, its cobbled high street lined with half-timbered buildings. For good views, walk up to the medieval **Guildford Castle** (April–Sept daily 10am–5pm; March & Oct Sat & Sun 11am–4pm; £3; ⓦwww.guildford.gov.uk/Castle), which has a viewing platform in the tower.

## Watts Gallery

Down Lane, Compton, 3 miles southwest of Guildford • Tues–Sun 11am–5pm • £7.50 • ☎ 01483 810235, ⓦ wattsgallery.org.uk

Surrey played a key role in the Arts and Crafts movement of the late nineteenth and early twentieth centuries, with many artists finding inspiration in its bucolic, quintessentially English countryside. Established in 1904 by influential local artists Mary and George Frederic Watts, the **Watts Gallery** displays a variety of George Watts' striking work – from light-infused metaphysical landscapes to socially conscious portraits and vigorous sculpture – and some excellent temporary exhibitions of related works from around the world.

## Winkworth Arboretum

Hascombe Rd, Godalming, 7 miles south of Guildford • Daily: Nov–Jan 10am–4pm; Feb & March 10am–5pm; April–Oct 10am–6pm • £6.50; NT • ☎ 01483 208477, ⓦ nationaltrust.org.uk/winkworth-arboretum • Godalming train station is 2 miles northwest

**Winkworth Arboretum** is a dazzling hillside ensemble of trees that is particularly spectacular in autumn, when the views down the steep wooded slopes into the valley below blaze with reds and oranges, and in spring, when the haze of bluebells, cherry blossom and azaleas bring a different aspect. The arboretum was the creation of Dr Wilfred Fox, who in the 1930s and 1940s planted more than a thousand exotic and rare trees among the existing oak and hazel woods.

## Shere and around

**SHERE**, its half-beamed and rough-plastered cottages clustered around the River Tillingbourne – more of a stream, really, populated with ducks and with a shady green alongside – must be Surrey's prettiest village. Walks and biking trails shoot off in all directions; a mile northwest, the tranquil **Silent Pool**, a clear spring-fed lake surrounded by box trees, is a lovely picnic spot.

Other appealing villages nearby include **Abinger Hammer** – once home to author E.M. Forster – and the quiet hamlet of **Peaslake**, whose surrounding woodlands and hills are perfect for rambles and mountain-biking.

### ARRIVAL AND INFORMATION                    GUILDFORD AND AROUND

**By train** Guildford station is a mile west of the centre, across the River Wey.
**Destinations** Godalming (every 15–35min; 8min); Gomshall (for Shere; every 1–2hr; 15min); London Waterloo (every 15–25min; 33min).

**Tourist office** 155 High Street (May–Oct Mon–Sat 9.30am–5pm, Sun 11am–4pm; Nov–April closed Sun; ☎ 01483 444333, ⓦ www.guildford.gov.uk /visitguildford).

### ACCOMMODATION AND EATING

★ **Rookery Nook** The Square, Shere ☎ 01483 209382, ⓦ rookerynook.info. In the centre of the village, this cute half-timbered fifteenth-century cottage offers comfortable B&B in two clean, quiet rooms, one with North Downs views, with shared bath. The friendly owners are keen walkers and cyclists. __£85__

**The White Horse** The St, Hascombe ☎ 01483 208258, ⓦ whitehorsepub.net. Historic old pub, 8 miles south of Guildford, warmed in winter by a woodburning stove and with a large garden. You can drink real ales and eat upmarket, locally sourced gastropub food (mains from £10) outside or in the smart dining room. Mon–Thurs 11am–11pm, Fri & Sat 11am–midnight, Sun noon–10.30pm; food served noon–3pm & 6–10pm.

# Dorking and around

Set at the mouth of a gap carved by the River Mole through the North Downs, the historic market town of **DORKING** (ⓦ visitdorking.com) has a profusion of **antique stores** – nearly twenty of them on sixteenth-century **West Street** alone – and is also surrounded by lovely Surrey Hills countryside. **Box Hill**, on a chalk escarpment above the Mole river north of Dorking, draws streams of walkers and cyclists; you can also take walks in the grounds of **Polesden Lacey**.

## Box Hill

Box Hill Rd, 3 miles northeast of Dorking • Daily dawn to dusk • Free • NT • ☎ 01306 885502, ⓦ nationaltrust.org.uk/box-hill • Box Hill & Westhumble train station is 0.5 mile west

**Box Hill**, a mile from the North Downs Way, offers walking trails and cycle paths through woodlands of rare wild box trees, yew, oak and beech, and across chalk grasslands scattered with wild flowers and fluttering with butterflies. Trails include an adventurous "natural play trail" for kids, a two-mile Stepping Stones walk along the River Mole, and some longer, more strenuous options. Brilliant views abound, most famously from the **Salomons' Memorial** viewpoint near the café, where on a clear day you can see across the Weald to the South Downs.

## Polesden Lacey

Near Great Bookham, 4 miles northwest of Dorking • **House** March to mid-Nov Mon–Fri 12.30–5pm, Sat & Sun 11am–5pm • £11.35 with gardens; NT **Gardens** Feb–Oct 10am–5pm; Nov–Jan daily 10am–4pm • £7; NT • ☎ 01372 452048, ⓦ nationaltrust.org.uk/polesden -lacey • Boxhill & Westhumble station is 3 miles east

Minutes from the North Downs Way, the grand Edwardian estate of **Polesden Lacey** practically begs you to while away the day with a picnic. If you're feeling more active, take a wander around the gardens, which include a hop field, orchard and an old walled rose garden, and the 1400-acre surrounding estate – in summer you can even play croquet.

The **house** itself is largely set up to appear as it might have in 1906, when owned by the wildly wealthy socialite Margaret Greville. An old-fashioned wireless burbles in the library, and in the billiards room you can take a quick shot to the accompaniment of 78s on the wind-up Vitrola.

### ARRIVAL AND DEPARTURE                    DORKING AND AROUND

**By train** Dorking's main station lies around 1.5 miles north of the centre.
**Destinations** Box Hill & Westhumble (every 30min–1hr;

2min); London Victoria (every 30min; 1hr); London Waterloo (every 30min; 50min).

### ACCOMMODATION AND EATING

**Leylands Farm** Leylands Lane, Abinger Common, 6 miles southwest of Dorking ☎ 01306 730115, ⓦ leylandsfarm.co.uk. Luxurious, peaceful B&B in a self-contained, two-storey barn conversion – complete with living/dining room with a toasty woodburner – next to a rustic farmhouse. No credit cards; reduced rates for stays of more than one night. **£90**
**Running Horses** Old London Rd, Mickleham ☎ 01372 372279, ⓦ therunninghorses.co.uk. An upmarket

sixteenth-century inn near Box Hill, serving excellent Modern British food. It's not cheap, with even the simplest dishes like posh sausage and mash or pearl barley and Somerset brie risotto at around £14, but the three-course menu for £28.50 is good value. They also offer five B&B rooms. Mon–Sat noon–11pm, Sun noon–10,30pm; food served Mon–Fri noon–2.30pm & 7–9.30pm, Sat noon–3pm & 7–9.30pm, Sun noon–6pm. **£110**

# Hampshire, Dorset and Wiltshire

NEW FOREST PONY AT LATCHMORE BOTTOM

# Hampshire, Dorset and Wiltshire

The distant past is perhaps more tangible in Hampshire (often abbreviated to "Hants"), Dorset and Wiltshire than in any other part of England. Predominantly rural, these three counties overlap substantially with the ancient kingdom of Wessex, whose most famous ruler, Alfred, repulsed the Danes in the ninth century and came close to establishing the first unified state in England. And even before Wessex came into being, many earlier civilizations had left their stamp on the region. The chalky uplands of Wiltshire boast several of Europe's greatest Neolithic sites, including Stonehenge and Avebury, while in Dorset you'll find Maiden Castle, the most striking Iron Age hill fort in the country, and the Cerne Abbas Giant, source of many a legend.

The Romans tramped all over these southern counties, leaving the most conspicuous signs of their occupation at the amphitheatre of **Dorchester** – though that town is more closely associated with the novels of Thomas Hardy and his vision of Wessex. None of the landscapes of this region could be described as grand or wild, but the countryside is consistently seductive, not least the crumbling fossil-bearing cliffs around **Lyme Regis**, the managed woodlands of the **New Forest** and the gentle, open curves of **Salisbury Plain**. Its towns are also generally modest and slow-paced, with the notable exceptions of the two great maritime bases of **Portsmouth** and **Southampton**, a fair proportion of whose visitors are simply passing through on their way to the more genteel pleasures of the **Isle of Wight**. The two great cathedral cities in these parts, **Salisbury** and **Winchester**, and the seaside resort of **Bournemouth** see most tourist traffic, and the great houses of **Wilton**, **Stourhead**, **Longleat** and **Kingston Lacy** also attract the crowds: you don't have to wander far off the beaten track, however, to find pretty medieval churches, manor houses, rolling landscapes and unspoilt country inns.

# Portsmouth

Britain's foremost naval station, **PORTSMOUTH** occupies the bulbous peninsula of Portsea Island, on the eastern flank of a huge, easily defended harbour. The ancient Romans raised a fortress on the northernmost edge of this inlet, but this strategic location wasn't fully exploited until Tudor times, when Henry VII established the world's first dry dock here and made Portsmouth a royal dockyard. It has flourished ever since and nowadays Portsmouth is a large industrialized city, its harbour clogged with naval frigates, ferries bound for the continent or the Isle of Wight, and swarms of dredgers and tugs.

KAYAKING AROUND OLD HARRY ROCKS, STUDLAND BAY

# Highlights

❶ **Osborne House** Wander around the stunning gardens and get an insight into royal family life at Queen Victoria's former seaside home. **See p.195**

❷ **The New Forest** William the Conqueror's old hunting ground, home to wild ponies and deer, is ideal for walking, biking and riding. **See p.201**

❸ **Sea kayaking in Studland** View the rugged Old Harry Rocks up close on a guided kayak tour through sea arches and below towering chalk cliffs. **See p.211**

❹ **Square and Compass, Worth Matravers** A pub straight from a Thomas Hardy novel, with

wonky rooms, a tiny hatch of a bar, real ales and stunning views. **See p.211**

❺ **Durdle Door** Famous natural arch at the end of a splendid beach, accessed by a steep cliff path – a great place for walkers and swimmers alike. **See p.212**

❻ **Hive Beach Café, Burton Bradstock** Sit right on the beach and sample some of Dorset's freshest local seafood, washed down with an ice-cold glass of wine. **See p.221**

❼ **Stonehenge** Marvel at one of Britain's most iconic sites, which is now much enhanced by an informative environmentally-friendly visitor centre. **See p.225**

HIGHLIGHTS ARE MARKED ON THE MAP ON P.182

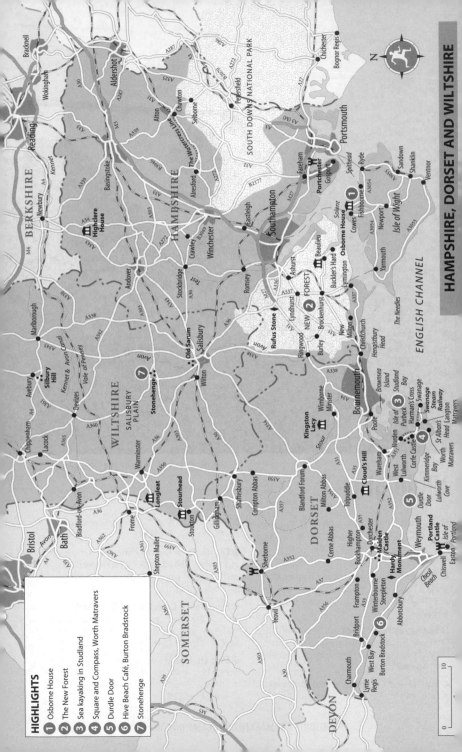

---

**TOP 5 OUTINGS FOR KIDS**

Visit **Beaulieu Motor Museum**, paradise for petrol-heads. See p.203.
Take a boat to **Brownsea Island**. See box, p.208.
Explore a 1940s schoolroom at **Tyneham** deserted village. See p.212.
Go on a **fossil-hunting tour** at Charmouth. See box, p.222.
Check out the lions, giraffes and rhino in deepest rural Wiltshire, at **Longleat Safari Park**.
  See p.227.

---

Due to its military importance, Portsmouth was heavily bombed during World War II, and bland tower blocks now give the city an ugly profile. Only **Old Portsmouth**, based around the original harbour, preserves some Georgian and a little Tudor character. East of here is **Southsea**, a residential suburb of terraces with a half-hearted resort strewn along its shingle beach, where a mass of B&Bs face stoic naval monuments and tawdry seaside amusements.

# Portsmouth Historic Dockyard

Queen St • Daily: April–Oct 10am–6pm; Nov–March 10am–5.30pm; last entry 1hr 30min before closing • All-inclusive ticket £26, for unlimited visits to all attractions; individual attraction tickets £17 except Action Stations and National Museum, £11; all tickets valid for one year • ☎ 023 9283 9766, ⓦ historicdockyard.co.uk

For most visitors, a trip to Portsmouth begins and ends at the **Historic Dockyard**, in the **Royal Naval Base** at the end of Queen Street. The complex comprises three ships and several museums, with the main attractions being HMS *Victory*, HMS *Warrior*, the National Museum of the Royal Navy, the Mary Rose Museum, and a boat tour around the harbour. In addition, the Dockyard Apprentice exhibition gives insights into the working of the docks in the early twentieth century, while Action Stations provides interactive activities and simulators, plus the UK's tallest indoor climbing tower.

## HMS Warrior

Portsmouth Historic Dockyard's youngest ship, **HMS Warrior**, dates from 1860. It was Britain's first armoured (iron-clad) battleship, complete with sails and steam engines, and was the pride of the fleet in its day. The ship displays a wealth of weaponry, including rifles, pistols and sabres, though the *Warrior* was never challenged nor even fired a cannon in her 22 years at sea.

## Mary Rose Museum

The impressive, new boat-shaped **Mary Rose Museum** was built around Henry VIII's flagship, the **Mary Rose**, and houses not only the ship itself, but also thousands of objects retrieved from or near the wreck including guns, gold and the crew's personal effects. The ship capsized before the king's eyes off Spithead in 1545 while engaging French intruders, sinking swiftly with almost all her seven-hundred-strong crew. In 1982 a massive conservation project successfully raised the remains of the hull, which silt had preserved beneath the seabed, and you can now view the world's only remaining sixteenth-century warship through protective glass windows.

## HMS Victory

**HMS Victory** was already forty years old when she set sail from Portsmouth for Trafalgar on September 14, 1805, returning in triumph three months later, but bearing the corpse of Admiral Nelson. Shot by a sniper from a French ship at the height of the battle, Nelson expired below deck three hours later, having been assured that victory was in sight. A plaque on the deck marks the spot where Nelson was fatally wounded and you can also see the wooden cask in which his body was preserved in brandy for the return trip to Britain. Although badly damaged during

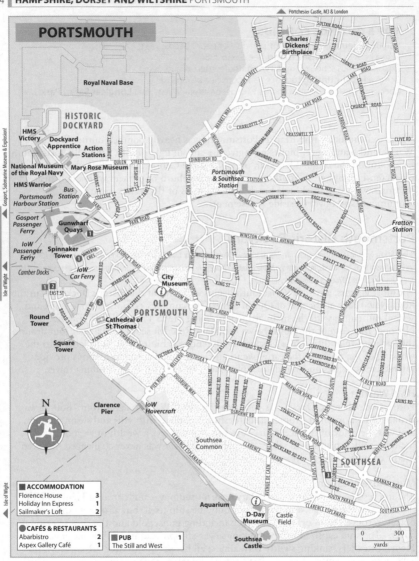

the battle, the *Victory* continued in service for a further twenty years, before being retired to the dry dock where she rests today.

### National Museum of the Royal Navy

Opposite the *Victory*, various buildings house the exhaustive **National Museum of the Royal Navy**. Tracing naval history from Alfred the Great's fleet to the present day, the collection includes some jolly figureheads, Nelson memorabilia, including the only surviving sail from HMS *Victory*, and nautical models, though coverage of more recent conflicts is scantily treated. The Trafalgar Experience is a noisy, vivid recreation of the battle itself, with gory bits to thrill the kids.

> **BOATS TO GOSPORT**
>
> Gosport can be reached by taking the **passenger ferry** from Harbour train station jetty between the historic dockyard and Gunwharf Quays (daily 5.30am–midnight every 10–15min; 5min; £2.90 return; ☎ 023 9252 4551, ⓦ gosportferry.co.uk). If you're planning to visit both Gosport's museums, however, it's worth taking the **Waterbus** (ⓦ portsmouth-boat-trips.co.uk /waterbus/portsmouth_harbour_waterbus.html), which shuttles hourly (10am–4pm) between the Historic Dockyard, Gunwharf Quays, the Submarine Museum and Explosion!, since its fare is included in the joint Gosport Museums' ticket.

## Royal Navy Submarine Museum

Haslar Jetty, Gosport • Daily: April–Oct 10am–5.30pm; Nov–March 10am–4.30pm, last tour 1hr before closing • £12.50, joint ticket with Explosion! including Waterbus £15 • ☎ 023 9251 0354, ⓦ submarine-museum.co.uk

Portsmouth's naval theme persists throughout otherwise humdrum Gosport, where the **Royal Navy Submarine Museum** displays, unsurprisingly, submarines – six in total, some of which you can enter. Allow a couple of hours to explore these slightly creepy vessels – a guided tour inside HMS *Alliance* gives you a gloomy insight into how cramped life was on board, and the museum elaborates evocatively on the history of submersible craft.

## Explosion! The Museum of Naval Firepower

Priddy's Hard, Gosport • April–Oct daily 10am–5pm; Nov–March Sat & Sun 10am–4pm, last entry 1hr before closing • £10, joint ticket with Submarine Museum including Waterbus £15 • ☎ 023 9250 5600, ⓦ explosion.org.uk

Near the Royal Submarine Museum, housed in an old armaments depot, **Explosion!** tells the story of naval warfare from the days of gunpowder to the present, with weapons of all descriptions, including mines, big guns and torpedoes, all backed up by vivid computer animations.

## The Spinnaker Tower

Gunwharf Quays • Sept–July daily 10am–5.30pm; Aug Mon–Thurs & Sun 9.30am–6pm, Fri & Sat 9.30am–5.30pm • £8.95 • ☎ 023 9285 7520, ⓦ spinnakertower.co.uk

From Portsmouth Harbour train station, it's a short walk along the historic waterfront to the sleek modern **Gunwharf Quays** development, with a multitude of cafés, restaurants, nightspots and shops. Here you'll find the **Spinnaker Tower**, an elegant, 557ft-high sail-like structure, offering **views** of up to twenty miles over land and sea. Its three viewing decks can be reached by a high-speed lift, the highest one being open to the elements, though most people stick to View Deck 1, which has one of Europe's largest glass floors.

## Old Portsmouth

It's a well-signposted fifteen-minute walk south of Gunwharf Quays to what remains of **Old Portsmouth**. Along the way, you pass the simple **Cathedral of St Thomas** on the High Street, whose original twelfth-century features have been obscured by rebuilding after the Civil War and again in the twentieth century. The High Street ends at a maze of cobbled Georgian streets huddling behind a fifteenth-century wall protecting the **Camber**, or old port, where Walter Raleigh landed the first potatoes and tobacco from the New World. Nearby, the Round and Square towers, which punctuate the Tudor fortifications, are popular vantage points for observing the comings and goings of the boats.

## D-Day Museum

Clarence Esplanade, Southsea • Daily: April–Sept 10am–5.30pm; Oct–March 10am–5pm; last entry 30min before closing • £6.50 • ☎ 023 9282 6722, ⓦ ddaymuseum.co.uk

In the suburb of **Southsea**, south and west of Old Portsmouth, the **D-Day Museum** focuses on Portsmouth's role as the principal assembly point for the Normandy beach landings in World War II, code-named "Operation Overlord". The museum's most striking exhibit is the 295ft-long Overlord Embroidery, a sort of twentieth-century equivalent of the Bayeux Tapestry, which took five years to complete.

## Southsea Castle

Clarence Esplanade, Southsea • March–Oct Tues–Sun & bank hol Mons 10am–5pm • Free • ☎ 023 9282 6722, ⊛ southseacastle.co.uk

Next door to the D-Day Museum, Southsea's most historic building, marked by a little lighthouse, is the squat **Southsea Castle**, built from the remains of Beaulieu Abbey (see p.203). You can go inside the keep and learn about Portsmouth's military history, and can climb up to the spot from where Henry VIII is said to have watched the *Mary Rose* sink in 1545 (see p.183), though in fact you can get just as good views by climbing along the adjacent seafront ramparts.

## Charles Dickens' Birthplace

393 Old Commercial Rd • April–Sept Tues–Sun & bank hol Mons 10am–5.30pm, plus sporadic days in winter; check website for details • £4 • ☎ 023 9282 6722, ⊛ charlesdickensbirthplace.co.uk

Just over a mile northeast of Old Portsmouth, **Charles Dickens' Birthplace** is set up to look much as it would have looked when the famous novelist was born here in 1812. Charles's father, John, moved to Portsmouth in 1809 to work for the Navy Pay Office before he was recalled to London in 1815, so Charles only lived here for three years, but nevertheless he is said to have returned often and set parts of *Nicholas Nickleby* in the city. The modest house not only contains period furniture but also a wealth of information about the time when Dickens lived here, and the influences on his novels.

## Portchester Castle

Church Rd, Portchester • April–Sept daily 10am–6pm; Oct daily 10am–5pm; Nov–March Sat & Sun 10am–4pm, but Feb half-term daily 10am–4pm • £5.20; EH

Six miles northwest of the city centre, just past the marina development at Port Solent, **Portchester Castle** was built by the Romans in the third century, and boasts the finest surviving example of Roman walls in northern Europe – still over 20ft high and incorporating some twenty bastions. The Normans felt no need to make any substantial alterations when they moved in, but a keep was later built within Portchester's precincts by Henry II, which Richard II extended and Henry V used as his garrison when assembling the army that was to fight the Battle of Agincourt.

### ARRIVAL AND INFORMATION                                              PORTSMOUTH

**By train** Portsmouth's main train station is in the city centre, but the line continues to Harbour Station, the most convenient stop for the dockyard sights and old town. Destinations Brighton (every 30min; 1hr 20min–1hr 30min); London Waterloo (every 15–20min; 1hr 35min–2hr 10min); Salisbury (hourly; 1hr 15min); Southampton (every 15–20min; 45min–1hr); Winchester (hourly; 1hr 10min).

**By bus** National Express buses stop at The Hard Interchange, right by Harbour Station. Destinations London Victoria (hourly; 1hr 45min–2hr 20min); Southampton (hourly; 50min–1hr).

**By ferry** Wightlink passenger catamarans leave from the jetty at Harbour Station for Ryde, on the Isle of Wight (see p.190), while car ferries depart from the ferry port off Gunwharf Road, just south of Gunwharf Quays, for Fishbourne on the Isle of Wight (see p.189). Hovercraft link Southsea with Ryde, while ferries run regularly from Harbour Station to Gosport, on the other side of Portsmouth Harbour (see box, p.185).

**Tourist offices** There are two tourist offices in Portsmouth (☎ 023 9282 6722, ⊛ visitportsmouth.co.uk), one in the City Museum, 2 Museum Road (Tues–Sun 10am–5pm), the other in the D-Day Museum on Clarence Esplanade in Southsea (April–Sept daily 10am–5pm; Oct–March daily 10am–4pm).

## ACCOMMODATION

**Florence House** 2 Malvern Rd, Southsea ☎023 9275 1666, ⓦflorencehousehotel.co.uk. Tasteful boutique B&B in an Edwardian townhouse with a range of rooms over three floors, all spick and span and with flatscreen TVs. There's a tiny downstairs bar and communal lounge, and parking permits can be provided. If it's full, the same group runs three other boutique-style hotels in the same area. __£86__

**Holiday Inn Express** The Plaza, Gunwharf Quays ☎023 9289 4240, ⓦhiexpress.co.uk. It may be part of a chain, but it's clean and contemporary, and Portsmouth's most central option. The rooms are compact, but its location, right on Gunwharf Quays, can't be faulted. There's a large, airy breakfast room and bar too. __£136__

**Sailmaker's Loft** 5 Bath Square ☎023 9282 3045, ⓦsailmakersloft.org.uk. This modern B&B is just back from the waterfront, right opposite *The Still* pub, with top-floor rooms overlooking the water. It's worth paying the extra £5 to have your own bathroom. __£65__

## EATING AND DRINKING

**Abarbistro** 58 White Hart Rd ☎023 9281 1585, ⓦabarbistro.co.uk. Lively bar/restaurant with an outside terrace on the edge of Old Portsmouth. The menu features bistro-style classics such as moules (£13) and steaks (£19), plus a daily-changing menu of fish and pasta dishes. Mon–Sat 11am–11pm, Sun noon–11pm.

**Aspex Gallery Café** The Vulcan Building, Gunwharf Quays ☎023 9277 8080, ⓦaspex.org.uk. Cosy café on the ground floor of the Aspex Gallery in a historic former naval building near the waterfront. The menu features simple dishes such as delicious home-made soups with focaccia (£4), vast ploughman's for two (£8), plus some daily specials, all eaten surrounded by installations and artworks: there's a great children's corner too. Daily 11am–4pm.

**The Still and West** 2 Bath Square, Old Portsmouth ☎023 9282 1567, ⓦstillandwest.co.uk. A waterfront terrace and cosy interior with views over the harbour make this pub worth stopping by: the food ranges from the traditional fish and chips (£10.50) to whole sea bream (£14.50) and Hampshire lamb chops (£16). Mon–Sat 10am–11pm, Sun 11am–10.30pm; food served Mon–Fri noon–9pm, Sat noon–10pm, Sun noon–8pm.

# Southampton

A glance at the map gives some idea of the strategic maritime importance of **SOUTHAMPTON**, which stands on a triangular peninsula formed at the place where the rivers Itchen and Test flow into Southampton Water, an eight-mile inlet from the Solent. Sure enough, Southampton has figured in numerous stirring events: it witnessed the exodus of Henry V's Agincourt-bound army, the Pilgrim Fathers' departure in the *Mayflower* in 1620 and the maiden voyages of such ships as the *Queen Mary* and the *Titanic*. Despite its pummelling by the Luftwaffe and some disastrous postwar urban sprawl, the thousand-year-old city has retained some of its medieval charm in parts and reinvented itself as a twenty-first century shopping centre in others, with the giant glass-and-steel **West Quay** as its focus. A short stroll north of here, Southampton's new **Cultural Quarter** is worth a visit, with its open squares, excellent art gallery and the superb Sea City Museum.

## City Art Gallery

Civic Centre, Commercial Rd • Mon–Fri 10am–3pm, Sat 10am–5pm • Free • ☎ 023 8083 3000, ⓦ southampton.gov.uk/art

Core of the modern town is the Civic Centre, a short walk east of the train station and home to the excellent **Southampton City Art Gallery**. Its collection is particularly strong on contemporary British artists with works by Gilbert and George, Anthony Gormley and Andy Goldsworthy. Older paintings are also on show, among them works by Gainsborough, Joshua Reynolds and the Impressionists – Monet and Pissarro included.

## The Sea City Museum

Civic Centre, Havelock Rd • Daily 10am–5pm • £6, children free, joint ticket with Tudor House £9.50 • ☎ 023 8083 3007, ⓦ seacitymuseum.co.uk

The purpose-built **Sea City Museum** is a triumph of design that succeeds in being both moving and fun. Opened on April 10, 2012, the hundredth anniversary of the day that the *Titanic* sailed from Southampton's Town Quay on its maiden voyage, the museum provides a fascinating insight into the history of the ship, its crew, its significance to Edwardian Southampton and, of course, an account of the fateful journey, which started in high excitement to end only four days later in tragedy. Impressive **interactive displays** give you the chance to steer the *Titanic* around the icebergs, while recreations of a second-class cabin and the boiler room allow you to imagine life as both crew and passenger. **Interviews with survivors** of the disaster are particularly moving, with tales of children being put into hessian sacks and hauled up from the lifeboats onto the rescue ship, the *Carpathia*.

Upstairs, the Gateway to the World gallery details the history of Southampton and its **maritime heritage**, from its beginnings as a small Roman port to the modern day. Exhibits as diverse as an early log boat, found in nearby Hamble, a collection of prehistoric flints, and a giant model of the *Queen Mary* are on display.

## Medieval Merchants House

58 French St • April–Sept Sun noon–5pm • £4; EH

Standing in one of Southampton's busiest streets in medieval times, the **Medieval Merchants House** was built in 1290 by John Fortin, a merchant who made his money trading with Bordeaux. The house has been restored to its fourteenth-century condition, with replica furniture such as a canopied four-poster bed that a wealthy merchant would have enjoyed languishing in during medieval times.

## The Tudor House Museum and Garden

St Michael's Square • Tues–Fri 10am–3pm, Sat & Sun 10am–5pm • £4.75 • ☎ 023 8083 4242, ⓦ www.tudorhouseandgarden.com

This excellent **Tudor House Museum and Garden** was built in 1492 by the wealthy John Dawtrey, who worked on Henry VIII's shipping fleet and who could afford to embellish his home with the best glass and oak available. The house then passed on to other city bigwigs, including artist George Rogers who added a new Georgian wing at the back. By the early 1800s, it sat in the middle of a district of slums and was earmarked for demolition until saved by philanthropist and collector William Spranger, whose collection of Victorian curios were left here when the house became a museum in 1912. Today, the museum houses an intriguing mishmash of high-tech interactive displays, historic paintings and artefacts including a Greek amphora and a recreated **Victorian kitchen**. You can also visit the recreated **Tudor garden** which contains a good café and the ruins of the Norman St John's Palace, built in the 1300s by a wealthy merchant when this part of town sat right on the quayside.

### ARRIVAL AND INFORMATION                                    SOUTHAMPTON

**By train** Southampton's central station is in Blechynden Terrace, west of the Civic Centre.

**Destinations** Bournemouth (every 15–20min; 30–50min); London Waterloo (every 15–20min; 1hr 20min–1hr 30min); Portsmouth (every 15–20min; 50min–1hr); Salisbury (every 30min; 30–40min); Weymouth (every 30min; 1hr 20min–1hr 35min); Winchester (every 15min; 15–30min).

**By bus** National Express buses run from the coach station on Harbour Parade.

**Destinations** Bournemouth (12 daily; 45min–1hr); London Victoria (15 daily; 2hr–2hr 30min); Portsmouth (13 daily; 50min–1hr); Salisbury (1 daily; 40min); Weymouth (3 daily; 2hr 40min) and Winchester (every 20–30min; 25–45min).

**Tourist information** There is no tourist office in Southampton, though *Oceans* tearoom, at 13 High St, acts

> ### TOP 5: FOOD WITH A VIEW
> **Hive Beach Café** Burton Bradstock. See p.221
> **Kuti's Royal Thai** Southampton. See opposite
> **The Salt Cellar** Shaftesbury. See p.218
> **Urban Reef** Boscombe. See p.206
> **Wheelers Crab Shed** Isle of Wight. See p.193

as a basic Information Point (Mon–Sat 9am–5pm, Sun 10am–4pm; ☎ 023 8178 1017, ⓦ discoversouthampton. co.uk), where you can pick up leaflets, maps and guides to the city.

## ACCOMMODATION

**Ennios** Town Quay Rd ☎ 023 8022 1159, ⓦ ennios -boutique-hotel.co.uk. In a former warehouse right on the waterfront, this boutique-style hotel has plush rooms with comfortable beds and smart bathrooms. The stylishly decorated rooms come with L'Occitane toiletries, and there's an excellent Italian restaurant downstairs. **£95**

★ **Pig in the Wall** 8 Western Esplanade, ☎ 0238 063 6900, ⓦ thepighotel.com. Built into the city walls, Southampton's most stylish boutique hotel has been cleverly renovated and beautifully decorated in a shabby-chic style. All the rooms have powerful showers and top-of-the range coffee machines – the large (pricier) rooms boast glamorous roll top baths in the room itself. There's a great bar/lounge/deli downstairs, or you can jump in one of the hotel Land Rovers which will take you to their sister hotel/restaurant in the New Forest for dinner (see p.205). **£130**

## EATING AND DRINKING

**The Arthouse Gallery Café** 178 Above Bar St ☎ 023 8023 8582, ⓦ thearthousesouthampton.co.uk. Friendly community-run café, which serves delicious home-made vegan and vegetarian dishes, such as a "global" hotpot and Greek meze with hummus, pitta and stuffed vine leaves (both £8), as well as organic ciders and beers. The café also hosts workshops, art exhibitions, knitting circles and live music; upstairs, there's a piano, comfy sofas and plenty of board games. Tues & Sun noon–5pm, Wed, Thurs & Fri 11am–9.30pm, Sat noon–10pm.

**Kuti's Royal Thai** Gate House, Royal Pier ☎ 023 8033 9211, ⓦ kutisroyalthaipier.co.uk. Choose from the à la carte menu or an excellent all-you-can-eat Thai buffet (Mon–Thurs £16, Fri & Sat £18) at this superbly ornate waterside restaurant that was once the terminal for ocean liners including the *Titanic*. There are fine views over the water from the upstairs restaurant, as well as an outside deck for summer evenings. Mon 6–10.30pm, Tues–Sun noon–2.30pm & 6pm–midnight.

**Red Lion** 55 High St ☎ 023 8033 3595. One of the oldest and most atmospheric pubs in Southampton, dating from the twelfth century, complete with its own minstrels' gallery. The half-timbered apartment known as Henry V's "Court Room" was used for the famous trial of a group of hapless lords who had conspired to murder Henry V, in 1415. They serve fine real ales and traditional British dishes. Mon–Sat 11am–11pm, Sun noon–10.30pm; food served daily noon–2pm & 6–9pm.

# The Isle of Wight

The lozenge-shaped **ISLE OF WIGHT** has begun to shake off its old-fashioned image and attract a younger, livelier crowd, with a couple of major annual **rock festivals** and a scattering of fashionable hotels. Despite measuring less than 23 miles at its widest point, the island packs in a surprising variety of landscapes and coastal scenery. Its **beaches** have long attracted holiday-makers, and the island was a favourite of such eminent Victorians as Tennyson, Dickens, Swinburne, Julia Margaret Cameron and Queen Victoria herself, who made **Osborne House**, near Cowes, her permanent home after Albert died.

## ARRIVAL AND DEPARTURE ISLE OF WIGHT

There are three **ferry** departure points from the mainland to the Isle of Wight – Portsmouth, Southampton and Lymington. **Wightlink** (ⓦ wightlink.co.uk) runs car ferries from Lymington to Yarmouth (40min) and from Gunwharf Terminal in Portsmouth to Fishbourne (45min), as well as a high-speed catamaran from Portsmouth Harbour to Ryde Pier (passengers only; 20min). **Hovertravel** (ⓦ hovertravel.co.uk), meanwhile, runs hovercraft from Clarence Esplanade in Southsea to Ryde (passengers only; 10min). From Southampton, **Red Funnel** (ⓦ redfunnel.co.uk) operates a high-speed catamaran to West Cowes (passengers only; 25min) and a car ferry to East Cowes (1hr). **Fare** structures and **schedules** on all routes are labyrinthine, from £16 for a day-return foot passenger ticket on the Southampton to West Cowes route in low season to over £100 for a high-season return for a car and four passengers on the Lymington to Yarmouth route: check the ferry companies' websites for full details of current fares.

## INFORMATION

**Tourist information** There are no walk-in tourist offices on the island, but general tourist information is available on ⓦ islandbreaks.co.uk or ☎ 01983 813813.

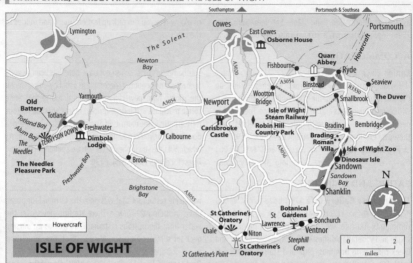

ISLE OF WIGHT

## GETTING AROUND

**By bus** Local buses are run by Southern Vectis (☎ 0871 200 2233, ⌨ islandbuses.info), who sell good-value tickets offering unlimited travel on their network (£10/day, £15/2 days, £24/week).

**By train** There are two train lines on the island: the seasonal Isle of Wight Steam Railway (☎ 01983 882204, ⌨ iwsteamrailway.co.uk) runs from Wootton Bridge to Smallbrook Junction, where it connects with the east-coast

Island line from Ryde to Shanklin (every 20–40min; 25min; ☎ 0345 600 0650, ⌨ islandlinetrains.co.uk).

**By bike** Cycling is a popular way of getting around the island, though in summer the narrow lanes can get very busy. For bike rental, contact Wight Cycle Hire (☎ 01983 761800, ⌨ wightcyclehire.co.uk): its office is in Yarmouth, but it can deliver bikes anywhere on the island (£10/half-day, £14/day).

# Ryde

As a major ferry terminal, **RYDE** is the first landfall many visitors make on the island, but one where few choose to linger, despite some grand nineteenth-century architecture and a fine sandy town beach.

## Postcard Museum

The Royal Victoria Arcade, Union St • Mon–Fri noon–5pm, Sat 11am–5pm, also Sun 11am–5pm in Aug • £3.50 • ☎ 01983 717435, ⌨ donaldmcgill.info

Ryde's quirky little **Postcard Museum** crams in a good proportion of the twelve thousand saucy postcards created by artist Donald McGill. The cards, produced throughout the first half of the twentieth century, reached their peak of popularity in the 1930s. Packed with daft double entendres, the collection here also shows how far things have moved since the Obscene Publications Act regularly tried to have McGill's cards banned.

## ARRIVAL AND DEPARTURE                                                           RYDE

The **bus station**, **Hovercraft terminal** and **Esplanade train station** are all near the base of the pier, while **catamarans** from Portsmouth dock at the Pier Head.

## ACCOMMODATION AND EATING

**The Boathouse** Springvale Rd, Seaview, 2 miles east of Ryde ☎ 01983 810616, ⌨ theboathouseiow.co.uk. It's a pleasant 2-mile walk along the coast to this classy

gastropub, whose garden boasts fantastic views across the Solent. A great spot for a drink, it also serves fish and chips (£11.50) and more upmarket fare such as lobster salad

(£18) and fresh fish of the day. It also has spacious en-suite rooms decorated in a contemporary style with iPod docks: superior rooms have sea views. Mon–Thurs & Sun 9am–10.30pm, Fri–Sat 9am–11pm; food served daily 9–11am, noon–2.30pm & 6–9.30pm. **£125**

**Kasbah** 76 Union St ☎01983 810088. Lively Moroccan-themed café-bar where you can chill out to world music and play chess. Also has a friendly, laidback B&B upstairs with clean and cosy rooms, some with sea views – it can be noisy at weekends, but is great value. Mon & Tues 11.30am–11pm, Wed–Sat 11.30am–2am, Sun noon–12.30am. **£70**

**Olivos** 32–33 Union St, Ryde ☎01983 611118, ⓦolivorestaurant.co.uk/ryde. Tasty Italian dishes in a buzzy, stylish restaurant with bare-brick walls and an open kitchen. There are decent pizzas (£9–11) and pasta dishes (£10–13), plus some less usual main courses, such as venison with meatballs (£16) and chicken drumsticks stuffed with chorizo and mozzarella (£13). Daily 8am–11pm.

★**The Priory Bay Hotel** Priory Drive, Seaview ☎01983 613146, ⓦpriorybay.com. Three miles east of Ryde, this elegant country house hotel has a wonderful setting with lawns leading down to the sands of Priory Bay. It's smart but unstuffy, child-friendly and has a great restaurant, where many of the ingredients are foraged from the grounds or caught in the local seas. There's also an outdoor pool, plus some self-catering cottages and luxurious yurts in the grounds. **£200**

# Quarr Abbey

Just outside the village of Binstead • Gardens Mon–Sat 10.30am–4.30pm, Sun 11.15–4pm • Free • ☎01983 882420, ⓦquarrabbey.co.uk • Buses #4, #9 and the seasonal Downs Breezer stop outside the Abbey

Two miles west of Ryde's centre, **Quarr Abbey** was founded in 1132 by Richard de Redvers as one of the first Cistercian monasteries in Britain. Its name derives from the nearby quarries, where stone was extracted for use in the construction of Winchester and Chichester cathedrals. Only stunted ruins survived the Dissolution and ensuing plunder of ready-cut stone. In 1907 a new Benedictine abbey was founded just west of the ruins – a striking rose-brick building with Byzantine overtones, which can be visited on guided tours (check the website for times). You can wander freely around the grounds, where you'll find a very fine tea garden and farm shop.

# Brading Roman Villa

Morton Old Road • Daily 9.30am–5pm • £6.50 • ☎01983 406223, ⓦbradingromanvilla.org.uk • Buses #2 & #3 from Ryde or Sandown

Just south of the ancient village of **Brading**, on the busy Ryde to Sandown A3055, the remains of **Brading Roman Villa** are renowned for their **mosaics**. This is the more impressive of two such villas on the island, both of which were probably sites of bacchanalian worship. The Brading site is housed in an attractive modern museum and its superbly preserved mosaics include intact images of Medusa and depictions of Orpheus.

# Sandown

The traditional seaside resort of **SANDOWN** merges with its neighbour Shanklin across the sandy reach of Sandown Bay, representing the island's holiday-making epicentre. Sandown, a traditional 1960s bucket-and-spade resort, appropriately enough possesses the island's only surviving pleasure **pier**, bedecked with various traditional amusements and a large theatre with nightly entertainment in season.

## THE ISLE OF WIGHT STEAM RAILWAY

The seasonal **Isle of Wight Steam Railway** (☎01983 882204, ⓦiwsteamrailway.co.uk) makes the delightful ten-mile return trip from Smallbrook Junction (where it connects with the main island line) to Wootton Bridge, between Ryde and Newport. Its impeccably restored carriages in traditional green livery run through lovely unspoilt countryside, stopping at Ashey and Havenstreet, where there's a small museum of railway memorabilia. The adult return fare (£12) is valid for any travel on that day.

## Isle of Wight Zoo

Yaverland Seafront • Jan to mid-Feb Thurs–Sun 11am–3pm; mid-Feb to March & Oct–Nov daily 10am–4pm; April–Sept 10am–5.30pm; closed in adverse weather • £10 • ☎ 01983 403883, ☒ isleofwightzoo.com

At the northern end of the Esplanade, and built into the walls of a Victorian fort, the **Isle of Wight Zoo** houses Britain's largest collection of tigers including some endangered species that are virtually extinct in the wild. It's also home to panthers and other big cats, as well as some frisky lemurs and monkeys, and an exhaustive selection of spiders and snakes.

## Dinosaur Isle

Culver Parade • Daily: April–Aug 10am–6pm; Sept–Oct 10am–5pm; Nov–March 10am–4pm • £5, children £3.80 • ☎ 01983 404344, ☒ www.dinosaurisle.com

On Sandown's seafront esplanade, **Dinosaur Isle** is housed in a purpose-built museum shaped like a giant pterosaur. Inside, you'll find robotic dinosaurs and life-size replicas of the various species once found on the island, while the museum's collection also showcases some of the prehistoric finds on the island, one of Europe's richest sites for dinosaur remains.

### ARRIVAL AND DEPARTURE | SANDOWN

**By train** The Island Line train station, served by trains from Ryde and Shanklin, is on Station Ave, about a 10min walk inland from the pier.

**By Bus** Buses #2, #3 & #8 between Ryde and Newport stop in Sandown.

### ACCOMMODATION AND EATING

**The Lawns** 72 Broadway ☎ 01983 402549, ☒ lawnshotel isleofwight.co.uk. Friendly, comfortable, non-smoking guesthouse with attractive gardens, a bar and free wi-fi; the plush rooms have flatscreen TVs, and the breakfasts are good. Minimum stay of three nights in the summer. **£88**

**The Reef** The Esplanade ☎ 01983 403219, ☒ thereefsan down.co.uk. A bright bar/restaurant right on the seafront with great views. It serves up a range of mid-priced dishes including pizzas, pasta, steaks and fresh fish: prices start at around £9 for a pizza, £10 for burgers, up to £20 for a 10oz fillet steak. Food served summer daily 11am–10pm; winter Sun–Thurs 11am–9pm, Fri & Sat 11am–9.30pm.

# Shanklin

**SHANKLIN**, with its auburn cliffs, Old Village and scenic Chine, has a marginally more sophisticated aura than its northern neighbour. The rose-clad, thatched **Old Village** may be syrupy, but the adjacent **Shanklin Chine** (daily: April to late May & mid-Sept to Oct 10am–5pm; late May to mid-Sept 10am–10pm; £3.90, ☎ 01983 866432, ☒ shanklinchine.co.uk), a twisting pathway descending a mossy ravine and decorated on summer nights with fairy lights, is undeniably picturesque; former local resident John Keats once drew inspiration from the environs.

### ARRIVAL AND DEPARTURE | SHANKLIN

**By train** The final stop on the Island Line from Ryde, Shanklin train station is about half a mile inland at the top of Regent Street.

**By bus** The bus station (buses #2 & #3 from Ryde and Newport) is a little south of the train station.

### ACCOMMODATION

**Rylstone Manor** Rylstone Gardens ☎ 01983 862806, ☒ rylstone-manor.co.uk. This superb Victorian pile, with period decor, sits right in the middle of the leafy public gardens at the top of the cliff. It has its own bar and dining room, though children under 16 are not allowed and in high season there is a 3-night minimum let. **£145**

### EATING AND DRINKING

**Fisherman's Cottage** Southern end of the Esplanade, at the bottom of Shanklin Chine ☎ 01983 863882, ☒ shanklinchine.co.uk/index.php/fishermans-cottage -welcome. An atmospheric nineteenth-century thatched pub right on the seafront, with outside tables: it's child-friendly and serves wholesome pub food, such as fish pie and cod and chips. Opening times vary, but generally March–Oct Mon–Sat 11am–midnight, Sun 11am–10.30pm; food served Mon–Sat noon–8pm, Sun noon–5pm.

★**Old Thatch Teashop** 4 Church Rd ☎01983 865587, ⓦoldthatchteashop.co.uk. There's a warren of rooms in

this friendly and efficient teahouse, with pretty gardens at the back. It serves lunches – soup and sandwiches – and is highly regarded for its delicious home-made scones and cakes. Mon–Sat 10am–5pm, Sun 11am–5pm, but sometimes stays open later in summer.

## Ventnor

The seaside resort of **VENTNOR** and its two village suburbs of **Bonchurch** and **St Lawrence** sit at the foot of St Boniface Down, the island's highest point at 787ft. The Down periodically disintegrates into landslides, creating the jumbled terraces known locally as the **Undercliff**, whose sheltered, south-facing aspect, mild winter temperatures and thick carpet of undergrowth have contributed to the former fishing village becoming a fashionable health spa. Thanks to these unique factors, the town possesses rather more character than the island's other resorts, its Gothic Revival buildings clinging dizzily to zigzagging bends.

3

The floral terraces of the Cascade curve down to the slender Esplanade and narrow beach, where some of the former boat-builders' cottages now house shops, cafés and restaurants. From the Esplanade, it's a pleasant mile-long stroll to Ventnor's rolling **Botanical Gardens**, filled with exotic plants and impressive glasshoues (daily 10am– 4pm, £6.75; ☎01983 855397, ⓦbotanic.co.uk).

| ACCOMMODATION | VENTNOR |
|---|---|

**Hambrough Hotel** Hambrough Rd ☎01983 856333, ⓦthehambrough.com. Small, stylish, modern hotel above the top-quality *Hambrough* restaurant. The comfortable rooms come with all the luxuries, including flatscreen TV and espresso machines; most have sea views, and some have balconies. **£170**

**The Lake Hotel** Shore Rd, Lower Bonchurch ☎01983 852613, ⓦlakehotel.co.uk. Family-run hotel in a nineteenth-century country manor with lovely grounds. It has an attractive sun lounge, a bar and terrace and twenty large, comfortable rooms, all en suite. Free wi-fi. **£98**

### EATING AND DRINKING

**El Toro Contento** 2 Pier St ☎01983 857600, ⓦeltorocontento.co.uk. A cosy restaurant dishing up home-made tapas, such as chorizo in cider, and spicy mussels, most for under a fiver. Also serves Spanish hams and cheeses and will cook paella for £10.40 a head (min 4 people) with 24hr notice. Summer daily 5–10pm; winter Thurs–Sun 4–10pm.

★**The Pond Café** Bonchurch Village Rd, Bonchurch ☎01983 855666, ⓦthehambrough.com/the-pond -cafe. Cheaper and less formal than its sister restaurant in Ventnor, *The Hambrough*, this small, smart restaurant

overlooking the village pond is nevertheless very well-regarded. It serves rustic Italian-style cuisine, with a short menu of good-value dishes, such as roast pigeon (£15) and beetroot risotto (£12.50), plus tasty stone-baked pizzas (9.50). Thurs–Mon 10.30am–3pm & 6–9.30pm.

★**Wheelers Crab Shed** Steephill Cove ☎01983 852177. Delicious home-made crab pasties, sandwiches and ciabattas served from a pretty shack on the seashore. Also tasty local lobster salads and daily fish specials. May– Sept daily except Tues (plus sunny weekends & hols in other months) 11am–3.30pm.

## The southwest coast

The western Undercliff begins to recede at the village of Niton, where a footpath continues to the most southerly tip of the island, **St Catherine's Point**, marked by a modern lighthouse. A prominent landmark on the downs behind is **St Catherine's Oratory**, known locally as the "Pepper Pot": originally a lighthouse, it reputedly dates from 1325.

Seven miles northwest along the coast, Military Road ascends the flank of Compton Down before descending into Freshwater Bay. If you're walking this way, you might stop off at the National Trust-owned **Compton Bay**, a splendid spot for a swim or a picnic, frequented by local surfers and accessed by a steep path leading down from the dark red cliffs.

## Dimbola Lodge

Terrace Lane, Freshwater Bay • Nov–March Tues–Sun plus bank hol Mons 10am–4pm; April–Oct daily 10am–5pm • £5 • ☎ 01983 756814, ⓦ dimbola.co.uk

On the coastal road at Freshwater Bay, **Dimbola Lodge** was the home of pioneer photographer Julia Margaret Cameron, who settled here after visiting local resident Tennyson in 1860. The building now houses a gallery of her work plus changing exhibitions, as well as a room devoted to memorabilia from the Isle of Wight festival. There's also a bookshop and tearoom/restaurant.

### ACCOMMODATION

**Tom's Eco Lodge** Tapnell Farm, Newport Rd ☎ 07717 666346, ⓦ tomsecolodge.com. Set on a lovely farm with stunning views over the distant Solent, these ready erected, upmarket tents are the ultimate in glamping – they come complete with fridges, electricity, private hotwater showers and flushing toilets. Great for families. **£671** (three-night weekend breaks) or £1560/week

## The Needles and Alum Bay

The breezy four-mile ridge of **Tennyson Down** running from Freshwater Bay to **The Needles** is one of the island's most satisfying walks, with vistas onto rolling downs and vales. On top of the Down, there's a monument to the eponymous poet, who lived on the island for forty years from 1853 until his death. At its western tip sits the **Needles Old Battery**, a gun emplacement built 250ft above the sea in 1863 (April–Oct daily 10.30am–5pm; fort may be closed in bad weather; £5; NT; ☎ 01983 754772, ⓦ nationaltrust.org.uk). There are fabulous views from here over the three tall chalk stacks known as **The Needles**, which jut out into the English Channel. Needles Pleasure Cruises runs **boat trips** round the Needles (April–Oct; £5.50; ☎ 01983 761587; ⓦ www .needlespleasurecruises.co.uk) from **Alum Bay**, a twenty-minute walk away. To catch the boat, you can walk down the cliff path or take the chairlift (£4 return), which descends the polychrome cliffs to ochre-hued sands.

## Yarmouth

Four miles east of the Needles and linked to Lymington in the New Forest by car ferry, the pleasant town of **YARMOUTH**, on the northern coast of the Isle of Wight, makes a lovely entrance to the island and is the best base for exploring its western tip. Although razed by the French in 1377, the port prospered after **Yarmouth Castle** (Easter–Sept Mon–Thurs & Sun 11am–4pm; £4; EH), tucked between the quay and the pier, was commissioned by Henry VIII. Inside, some of the rooms have recreated life in a sixteenth-century castle, and there's also a display on the many wrecks that floundered here in the Solent, while the battlements afford superb views over the estuary. Yarmouth's only other real sight is the Grade II listed **pier**, England's longest wooden pier still in use.

### ACCOMMODATION                 YARMOUTH

**The George Hotel** Quay St ☎ 01983 760331, ⓦ thegeorge.co.uk. In a great position right by the ferry dock, with a lovely garden overlooking the Solent, this seventeenth-century hotel has hosted the likes of Charles II in its time. The rooms are comfortable and elegantly furnished, some with balconies looking out over the water, and there's an excellent restaurant downstairs, specializing in local and organic produce. **£190**

### EATING AND DRINKING

**The Blue Crab** High St ☎ 01983 760014, ⓦ thebluecrab.co.uk. A simply decorated restaurant, with cosy booths, that offers fish and shellfish dishes such whole Cornish sole (£17). Also does top-quality fresh fish and chips to take away for £7. Tues, Wed & Sun 11am–3pm, Thurs 10am–3pm & 6–11pm, Fri & Sat 11am–3pm & 6–11pm.

**Gossips Café** The Square, on the pier ☎ 01983 760646,

ⓦthegossipscafe.co.uk. A great place for lunch or a snack – it does a huge selection of sandwiches (most around £4) and tortilla wraps, as well as hot dishes, such as pizzas (from £5) and daily specials, including seafood chowder

(£7) and Thai prawn curry (£8). The real selling point, however, is the superb view of the comings and goings of the boats. Summer Mon–Fri 8.45am–6pm, Sat & Sun 8.30am–6.30pm; winter daily 8.45am–4.30/5pm.

## Cowes

**COWES**, at the island's northern tip, is associated with sailing craft and boat building: Henry VIII installed a castle to defend the Solent's expanding naval dockyards from the French and Spanish, and in the 1950s the world's first hovercraft made its test runs here. In 1820 the Prince Regent's patronage of the yacht club gave the port its cachet with the Royal Yacht Squadron, now one of the world's most exclusive sailing clubs. The first week of August sees the international yachting festival **Cowes Week** (ⓦaamcowesweek.co.uk), where serious sailors mingle with visiting royalty; most summer weekends see some form of nautical event taking place in or around town.

The town is bisected by the River Medina, with **West Cowes** being the older, more interesting half. At the bottom of the meandering High Street, **boat trips** around the harbour and the Solent leave from Thetis Wharf, near the Parade (☏01983 564602, ⓦsolentcruises.co.uk). The more industrial **East Cowes**, where you'll find Osborne House, is connected to West Cowes by a "floating bridge", or chain ferry (every 10–15min, Mon–Sat 5.35am–12.30am, Sun 6.40am–12.30am; pedestrians free, cars £2).

**3**

### Osborne House

East Cowes • April–Sept daily 10am–6pm; Oct daily 10am–4pm; Nov–March Sat & Sun 10am–4pm • £13.40; EH • ☏01983 200022, ⓦenglishheritage.org.uk • Bus #4 from Ryde or #5 from Newport, or either from East Cowes

The only place of interest in East Cowes is Queen Victoria's family home, **Osborne House**, signposted one mile southeast of town. The house was built in the late 1840s by Prince Albert and Thomas Cubitt in the style of an Italianate villa, with balconies and large terraces overlooking the landscaped gardens towards the Solent. The **state rooms**, used for entertaining visiting dignitaries, exude formality as one would expect – the Durbar Room, clad almost entirely in ivory, is particularly impressive – while the **private apartments** feel homely in a manner appropriate to an affluent family holiday residence that Osborne was. Following Albert's death, the desolate Victoria spent much of her time here, and it's where she eventually died in 1901. Since then, according to her wishes, the house has remained virtually unaltered, allowing an intimate glimpse into Victoria's family life. In the **grounds**, you can see the remains of a barracks with its own drawbridge, built by Prince Albert as a place where the boys could play soldiers, and Queen Victoria's original bathing machine, next to her private beach.

## ACCOMMODATION

COWES

### WEST COWES

**Villa Rothsay** Baring Rd, West Cowes ☏01983 295178, ⓦvilla-rothsay.co.uk. Upmarket boutique hotel that's maintained its Victorian roots with period decor throughout – think drapes, ornate stairways and stained-glass windows. Some of the rooms have sea views and balconies (£10 extra) and there are great views from the grounds and raised patio area. **£145**

### EAST COWES AND AROUND

**Albert Cottage** York Ave, East Cowes ☏01983 299309, ⓦalbertcottagehotel.com. Adjacent to and once part of the Osborne estate, this lovely mansion, set in its own

grounds, has a country house feel to it. Rooms are very comfortable, and have flatscreen TVs; it has its own highly rated restaurant, too. **£125**

★**Into the Woods** Lower Westwood, Brocks Copse Rd, Wootton ☏07769 696464, ⓦisleofwighttreehouse .com. Lovely, luxury treehouse (sleeps 4) and shepherds' huts (sleep 6) to rent on a farm in a secluded wood, three miles south of East Cowes. Both are beautifully finished and eco-friendly complete with wood-burning stoves, en-suite showers, and even wi-fi. The location is peaceful, with chickens and geese, rope swings to play on and woods to run around in – the perfect combination of nature and home comforts. Two nights from **£300**

## EATING AND DRINKING

### WEST COWES

**The Coast Bar & Dining Room** 15 Shooters Hill ☎01983 298574, ⍟thecoastbar.co.uk. Light and airy bar/restaurant with wooden floors and a lively, informal vibe. The menu features wood-fired pizzas (£8–12), plus the likes of seafood bouillabaisse (£14.50), mushroom risotto (£11) and and a good selection of steaks (£17.50). Daily 9am–midnight.

**Lugleys** The Parade, West Cowes, ☎01983 299618, ⍟lugleysofcowes.com. In a great position facing the sea, this fashionable bar/restaurant is a good spot for a coffee, evening drink or quality meal, with a menu featuring

salmon and prawn linguine (£12) and fresh fish from around £14. There are also good-value set menus (three courses for £19). Mon–Fri 10am–3pm & 6–11pm, Sat 10am–11pm, Sun 10am–4pm.

**Moocows** 55 Cross St ☎01983 200750, ⍟moocowstuff .com. It may overlook a car park, but this lively, stylish café-bar is a great place to hangout. It hosts arts and crafts workshops, quiz and poetry evenings and serves imaginative meze, such as local wild mushrooms and goats cheese on toast (£8), stuffed courgettes (£7), chorizo with melon and mint (£9) and venison on ciabatta (£9) – and the cocktails are delicious too. Tues–Sat 10.30am–late.

## Carisbrooke Castle

Castle Hill, southwest of Newport • Daily: April–Sept 10am–4.45pm; Oct–Easter 10am–3.45pm • £7.70; EH • ☎01983 523112, ⍟englishheritage.org.uk • Buses #6, #12 or #38 from Newport

**NEWPORT**, the capital of the Isle of Wight, sits at the centre of the island at a point where the River Medina's commercial navigability ends. The town isn't particularly engaging, but is worth a visit for the hilltop fortress of **Carisbrooke Castle**. The most famous resident of this austere Norman pile was Charles I, detained here (and caught one night ignominiously jammed between his room's bars while attempting escape) before his execution in London. The **museum** features relics from his incarceration, as well as those of the last royal resident, Princess Beatrice, Queen Victoria's youngest daughter. There's also a sixteenth-century well-house, where you can watch donkeys trudge around a huge treadmill to raise a barrel 160ft up the well shaft.

# Winchester and around

Nowadays a tranquil, handsome market town, **WINCHESTER** was once one of the mightiest settlements in England. Under the Romans it was Venta Belgarum, the fifth largest town in Britain, but it was **Alfred the Great** who really put Winchester on the map when he made it the capital of his Wessex kingdom in the ninth century. For the next two hundred years or so Winchester ranked alongside London, its status affirmed by William the Conqueror's coronation in both cities and by his commissioning of the local monks to prepare the **Domesday Book**. It wasn't until after the Battle of Naseby in 1645, when Cromwell took the city, that Winchester began its decline into provinciality.

Hampshire's county town now has a scholarly and slightly anachronistic air, embodied by the ancient almshouses that still provide shelter for senior citizens of "noble poverty" – the pensioners can be seen walking round the town in medieval black or mulberry-coloured gowns with silver badges. It also makes a good base from which to explore the nearby towns of **Chawton** and **Selborne**, homes, respectively, to Jane Austen and the eminent naturalist, Gilbert White.

## Winchester Cathedral

9 The Close • Mon–Sat 9.30am–5pm, Sun 12.30–3pm • £7.50, including a guided tour (ticket valid for one year); tower tour £6 • ☎01962 857275, ⍟winchester-cathedral.org.uk

The first minster to be built in Winchester was raised by Cenwalh, the Saxon king of Wessex in the mid-seventh century, and traces of this building have been

unearthed near the present **cathedral**, which was begun in 1079 and completed some three hundred years later. The exterior is not its best feature – squat and massive, it crouches stumpily over the tidy lawns of the Cathedral Close. The interior is rich and complex, however, and its 556ft **nave** makes this Europe's longest medieval church. Outstanding features include the carved Norman font of black Tournai marble, the fourteenth-century misericords (the choir stalls are the oldest complete set in the country) and some amazing monuments – **William of Wykeham's Chantry**, halfway down the nave on the right, is one of the most ornate.

**Jane Austen**, who died in Winchester, is commemorated close to the font by a memorial brass and slab beneath which she's interred, though she's recorded simply as the daughter of a local clergyman. Above the high altar lie the mortuary chests of pre-Conquest kings, including **Canute** (though the bones were mixed up after Cromwell's Roundheads broke up the chests in 1645); **William Rufus**, killed while hunting in the New Forest in 1100, lies in the presbytery.

Behind the impressive Victorian screen at the end of the presbytery, look out for the memorial shrine to **St Swithun**. Originally buried outside in the churchyard, his remains were later interred inside where the "rain of heaven" could no longer fall on him, whereupon he took revenge and the heavens opened for forty days – hence the legend that if it rains on St Swithun's Day (July 15) it will do so for another forty. His exact burial place is unknown.

Accessible from the north transept, the Norman **crypt** – often flooded – is home to Anthony Gormley's contemplative figure *Sound II,* reflected in the waters. The cathedral's original foundations were dug in marshy ground, and at the beginning of the last century a steadfast diver, William Walker, spent five years replacing the rotten timber foundations with concrete.

## City Museum

The Square • April–Oct Mon–Sat 10am–5pm, Sun noon–5pm; Nov–March Tues–Sat 10am–4pm, Sun noon–4pm • Free • ☎ 01962 863064, ⓦ winchester.gov.uk/museums

Just off the High Street on the Square, the **City Museum** recounts Winchester's history with archeological and historical displays. Set on three floors, it is an imaginative medley of local artefacts including recreated traditional shopfronts, some impressive Roman mosaics, medieval coins and skeletons.

## Great Hall

At the top of the High St on Castle Ave • Daily 10am–5pm • Free, £3 donation requested • ☎ 01962 846476, ⓦ hants.gov.uk/greathall

The **Great Hall** is all that remains of a thirteenth-century castle destroyed by Cromwell. Sir Walter Raleigh heard his death sentence here in 1603, though he wasn't finally dispatched until 1618, and Judge Jeffreys held one of his Bloody Assizes (see p.213) in the castle after Monmouth's rebellion in 1685. The main interest now is a large, brightly painted disc slung on one wall like some curious antique dartboard. This is alleged to be King Arthur's Round Table, but the woodwork is probably fourteenth-century, later repainted as a PR exercise for the Tudor dynasty – the portrait of Arthur at the top of the table bears an uncanny resemblance to Henry VIII.

## College Street

College Street is home to the buildings of **Winchester College**, the oldest public school in England – established in 1382 by William of Wykeham for "poor scholars", it now educates few but the wealthy and privileged. You can look round the medieval college buildings, its cloisters and Gothic chapel on a **guided tour** (Mon, Wed, Fri & Sat 10.45am, noon, 2.15pm & 3.30pm; Tues & Thurs 10.45am & noon; Sun 2.15pm & 3.30pm; £6; ☎ 01962 621100, ⓦ winchestercollege.org).

At no.8 College Street stands the house where **Jane Austen** died. She moved here from Chawton in 1817 (see p.201), when she was already ill with Addison's Disease, and died later the same year, aged 42. The house is privately owned, though, so you can't look round. At the top of the street, the thirteenth-century **Kings Gate** is one of the city's original medieval gateways, housing the tiny St Swithun's Church.

### Wolvesey Castle

Entrance off College St • April–Sept daily 10am–5pm • Free • EH • ⓦ englishheritage.org.uk

East of the cathedral, the remains of Winchester's Saxon walls bracket the ruins of the twelfth-century **Wolvesey Castle** – actually the palace for the Bishops of Winchester, who once wielded great clout over England's religious and political affairs. As a result, this was once one of the most important buildings in Winchester, encompassing its own stables, prison, chapel and gardens. Today, the castle ruins remain impressive, dwarfing the current dwelling place of the Bishop of Winchester, a relatively modest house built in 1680, which sits alongside it.

## Hospital of St Cross

St Cross Rd • April–Oct Mon–Sat 9.30am–5pm, Sun 1–5pm; Nov–March Mon–Sat 10.30am–3.30pm • £4 • ☎ 01962 878218, ⓦ stcrossvillage.com

About a mile south of College Walk, reached by a pleasant stroll across the water meadows of the Itchen, lies the **Hospital of St Cross**. Founded in 1136 as a hostel for poor brethren, it boasts a fine church, begun in that year and completed a century or so later, where you can see a triptych by the Flemish painter Mabuse. Needy wayfarers may still apply for the "dole" at the porter's lodge – a tiny portion of bread and beer.

## ARRIVAL AND INFORMATION

WINCHESTER

**By train** Winchester train station is about a mile northwest of the cathedral on Stockbridge Road.

**Destinations** Bournemouth (every 15–20min; 45min–1hr); London Waterloo (every 15–20min; 1hr–1hr 10min); Portsmouth (hourly; 1hr); Southampton (every 15–20min; 15–20min).

**By bus** National Express buses pull in and depart from the conveniently located bus station on the Broadway, opposite the tourist office.

**Destinations** Bournemouth (5 daily; 1hr 15min–1hr 35min); London (8 daily; 1hr 50min–2hr); Southampton (approx every hour; 25–45min).

**Tourist office** In the imposing Guildhall (May–Sept Mon–Sat 10am–5pm, Sun & bank hols 11am–4pm; Oct–April Mon–Sat 10am–5pm; ☎01962 840500, ⓦ visitwinchester.co.uk).

## ACCOMMODATION

**29 Christchurch Rd** 29 Christchurch Rd ☎01962 868 661, ⓦ fetherstondilke.com. Well-furnished, comfortable B&B in a charming Regency house located in a quiet residential part of town. No smoking. **£95**

★**Hotel du Vin** Southgate St ☎01962 841414, ⓦ hotelduvin.com. The first in the classy hotel chain, this lovely Georgian townhouse has been given a stylish makeover and now comprises plush rooms – some cottage-style, with their own private entrances and terraces – a lovely patio garden, chic bar and great restaurant (see below). This is the first choice for accommodation in Winchester, especially if you can bag one of their periodic special offers. **£155**

**The Old Vine** 8 Great Minster St ☎01962 854616, ⓦ oldvinewinchester.com. Lovely, big rooms that combine period decor with modern touches such as widescreen TVs, above a fine bar/restaurant, and right opposite the cathedral. The street can be noisy at night. **£120**

## EATING AND DRINKING

**The Black Boy** Wharf Hill ☎01962 861754, ⓦ the blackboypub.com. Fantastic old pub with log fires in winter, walls lined with books and low ceilings hung with old coins and miniature bottles. Good cask ales from local breweries are on draught and there's reasonable pub grub from £8.50, as well as a small outdoor terrace. Mon–Thurs noon–11pm, Fri & Sat noon–midnight, Sun noon–11.30pm.

**Ginger Two For Tea** 28–29 St Thomas St ☎01962 877733, ⓦ gingertwofortea.co.uk. Small teashop tucked away in the backstreets, serving tasty lunches – the smoked salmon stack (£6) is delicious – home-made cakes, coffees and a huge array of herbal and fruit teas. Mon–Fri 7.30am–6pm, Sat 8.30am–6pm, Sun 9.30am–5pm.

★**Hotel du Vin** Southgate St ☎01962 841414, ⓦ hotelduvin.com. Buzzy bistro-style restaurant in a series of attractive dining rooms, some with open fireplaces. The food is excellent, much of it locally sourced, and reasonably priced, with main courses such as beef bourguignon (£19), and starters such as baked figs with gorgonzola and Serrano ham for £9.50. The wine list, as you would expect, is impressive, with many wines available by the half bottle. Mon–Sat noon–2.30pm & 5.30–10pm, Sun noon–4pm & 6–9pm.

**Wykeham Arms** 75 Kingsgate St ☎01962 853834, ⓦ wykehamarmswinchester.co.uk. This highly atmospheric eighteenth-century pub has a warren of cosy rooms, with open fireplaces, good bar snacks and decent beers. Daily 11am–11pm.

---

## THE REAL DOWNTON ABBEY

Tucked away in the northern reaches of Hampshire, 20 miles north of Winchester, **Highclere Castle** (castle, exhibition and gardens £20, castle and gardens £13, gardens only £5; ☎01635 253210, ⓦ highclerecastle.co.uk) will be very familiar to fans of ITV's hit period drama, **Downton Abbey**, which is filmed here. Home to Lord Carnarvon and his family, the house is approached via a long drive that winds through a stunning 5000-acre estate, and is surrounded by beautiful **gardens** designed by Capability Brown. Inside the house, *Downton Abbey* aficionados will enjoy loitering in the **Drawing Room** and the **Library**, scene of many a drama and quivering stiff-upper-lip of Lord Grantham and his family, while upstairs you can peer into the bedrooms of the Crawley girls. In the castle cellars, an **Egyptian Exhibition** celebrates the real-life fifth Earl of Carnarvon, who, in 1922, discovered the tomb of Tutankhamun with Howard Carter, and who funded many of Carter's expeditions. Since the house is still a family home and is also sometimes closed for filming, its opening hours vary from month to month and year to year; call or check the website for details.

---

**THE WATERCRESS LINE**

**ALRESFORD**, six miles east of Winchester, is the departure-point for the **Mid-Hants Watercress Line** (Aug & school hols daily; Feb–July, Sept & Oct days vary, call or check website for details; £16; ☎01962 733810, ⓦwatercressline.co.uk), a steam-powered railway so named because it passes through the former watercress beds that once flourished here. The train chuffs ten miles to **Alton**, with gourmet dinners served on board on Saturday evenings, plus real ales from local breweries and traditional Sunday lunches.

---

## Chawton

A mile southwest of Alton and sixteen miles northeast of Winchester, the village of **CHAWTON** was home to Jane Austen from 1809 to 1817, during the last and most prolific years of her life – it was here that she wrote or revised almost all of her six books, including *Sense and Sensibility* and *Pride and Prejudice*. A plain red-brick building in the centre of the village, **Jane Austen's House** (Jan to mid-Feb Sat & Sun 10.30am–4.30pm; mid-Feb to May & Dec daily 10.30am–4.30pm; June–Aug daily 10am–5pm; £7.50; ☎01420 83262, ⓦwww.jane-austens-house-museum.org.uk) contains first editions of some of her greatest works and provides a fascinating insight into the daily life of the author.

### Chawton House

**House** Tours (£7) take place Jan–March Tues at 2.30pm; April–Dec Tues & Thurs at 2.30pm; June–Sept also Wed at 10.30am; book ahead on ☎01420 541010 as places are limited • **Gardens** Mon–Fri 10am–3pm • £3.50

A short walk from Jane Austen's house is **Chawton House**, which belonged to Jane's brother, Edward Austen Knight. It remained in the Austen family until 1987, when it was bought by American IT millionairess Sandy Lerner who opened the **Chawton House Library**, containing an impressive collection of women's writing in English from 1600–1830. The house, which has now been fully restored, can be visited on a guided **tour**, or you can look round the **gardens** independently. The **library** is open by appointment only (Mon–Fri 10am–5pm).

---

**ARRIVAL AND DEPARTURE** CHAWTON

**By bus** From Winchester bus station, take the hourly #X64 to Alton Butts then it's a 12min walk.

**By train** The village is accessible on the "Watercress line" steam train (see box above).

---

# The New Forest

Covering about 220 square miles, the **NEW FOREST** is one of southern England's favourite rural playgrounds, attracting some 13.5 million day-visits annually. The land was requisitioned by William the Conqueror in 1079 as a hunting ground, and the rights of its inhabitants soon became subservient to those of his precious deer. Fences to impede their progress were forbidden and terrible punishments were meted out to those who were caught poaching – hands were lopped off, eyes put out. Later monarchs less passionate about hunting than the Normans gradually restored the commoners' rights, and today the New Forest enjoys a unique patchwork of ancient laws and privileges alongside the regulations applying to its National Park status.

The **trees** here are now much more varied than they were in pre-Norman times, with birch, holly, yew, Scots pine and other conifers interspersed with the ancient oaks and beeches. One of the most venerable trees is the much-visited **Knightwood Oak**, just a few hundred yards north of the A35, three miles southwest of Lyndhurst, which measures about 22ft in circumference at shoulder height. The most conspicuous species of **fauna** is the New Forest **pony** – you'll see them grazing nonchalantly by the roadsides and ambling through some villages. The local deer are less visible now that some of the faster roads are fenced, although several species still roam the woods, including the tiny **sika deer**, descendants of a pair that escaped from nearby Beaulieu in 1904.

### ARRIVAL AND DEPARTURE                                      THE NEW FOREST

**By train** The main London to Weymouth train line passes through the New Forest, with fast trains stopping at Brockenhurst (see p.204): slower trains also stop at Ashurst, Sway and New Milton. From Brockenhurst a branch line runs to Lymington (every 30min; 10min) to link with the Isle of Wight ferry.

### GETTING AROUND

Though the southern Forest stretches have a reasonably efficient bus network, to get the best from the New Forest, you need to walk or ride through it, avoiding the places cars can reach.

**By bus** Useful routes through the Forest include bus #6 from Southampton to Lymington via Lyndhurst and Brockenhurst; the coastal routes #X1 and #X2 from Bournemouth and Christchurch to Lymington; and in summer the hop-on hop-off open-top New Forest Tour bus which runs on three different circular routes around the Forest, taking in all the main settlements, and can carry up to four bikes free (mid-June to mid-Sept; £13 for a one-day ticket, which is valid on all three routes; ⓦthenewforesttour.info). Services are run by More Buses (☏0845 072 7093, ⓦmorebus.co.uk) and Blue Star (☏01280 618233, ⓦbluestarbus.co.uk).

**By bike** There are 150 miles of car-free gravel roads in the Forest, making cycling an appealing prospect – pick up a book of route maps from tourist offices or bike rental shops. Bikes can be rented at several places in the Forest: for details of cycle routes and bike hire outfits, check ⓦnew-forest-national-park.com/bike-hire-in-the-new-forest.html.

### INFORMATION

**Information offices** There are two information centres in the Forest, one in Lyndhurst (see below), and the other in Lymington (see p.204), in the St Barbe Museum, on New St, off the High Street (daily 10am–4pm; ☏01590 689000, ⓦlymington.org).

**Maps** The Ordnance Survey Leisure Map 22 of the New Forest is best for exploring. Shops in Lyndhurst sell specialist walking books and natural history guides.

### ACCOMMODATION

**Camping** There are ten campsites throughout the Forest run by Camping in the Forest (☏0845 130 8224, ⓦcampingintheforest.co.uk); all are open from mid-April to early Sept, and some are open year-round. Some are very simple, with few or no facilities, others have electricity and hot shower blocks, but they all have open access to the Forest, many have streams and fords running through them, with ponies and donkeys wandering freely.

# Lyndhurst

**LYNDHURST**, its town centre skewered by an agonizing one-way system, isn't a particularly interesting place, though the brick **parish church** is worth a glance for its William Morris glass and the grave of Mrs Reginald Hargreaves, better known as Alice Liddell, Lewis Carroll's model for Alice. The town is of most interest to visitors for the **New Forest Museum and Visitor Centre** in the central car park off the High Street (daily 10am–5pm; ☏023 8028 2269, ⓦnewforestcentre.org.uk), and the adjoining **museum** (£4), which focuses on the history, wildlife and industries of the Forest. The Forest's most visited site, the **Rufus Stone**, stands three miles northwest of Lyndhurst. Erected in 1745, it marks the putative spot where the Conqueror's son and heir, **William II** – aka William Rufus after his ruddy complexion – was killed by a crossbow bolt in 1100.

### ACCOMMODATION                                                  LYNDHURST

**Limewood Hotel** Beaulieu Road ☏023 8028 7177, ⓦlimewoodhotel.co.uk. About a mile outside Lyndhurst, this luxurious hotel has smart, spacious designer-style rooms in a country-house atmosphere, with its own restaurant. The grounds are beautiful and the Herb House spa with its outdoor hot tub to die for. **£315**

**Rufus House** Southampton Rd ☏023 8028 2930, ⓦrufushouse.co.uk. A couple of mins out of town on the Ashurst road, opposite some fine New Forest countryside, this good-value place has plenty of character. Its tower room has a four-poster bed, though front rooms face a busy road. **£98**

## EATING AND DRINKING

★ **The Oak Inn** Pinkney Lane, Bank ☎ 023 8028 2350, ⓦ oakinnlyndhurst.co.uk. Fantastic little country pub a mile out of Lyndhurst, with low wooden ceilings and a roaring fire in winter and a garden for the summer. It's popular with walkers and cyclists and there's decent food, featuring local ingredients – it's best to book in advance. Mon–Fri 11.30am–3pm & 5.30–11pm, Sat 11.30am–11pm, Sun noon–10.30pm; food served Mon–Fri noon–2.30pm & 6–9.30pm, Sat noon–9.30pm, Sun noon–9pm.

**La Pergola** Southampton Rd ☎ 023 8028 4184, ⓦ la-pergola.co.uk. Lively Italian restaurant in an attractive building with its own garden. Sizzling meat dishes cost around £15–18, and there's tasty pasta and pizza from £9 and superb home-made desserts, as well as daily specials. Tues–Sun & bank hols 11am–2.30pm & 6–10.30pm.

# Beaulieu

The village of **BEAULIEU** (pronounced "Bewley"), in the southeast corner of the New Forest, was the site of one of England's most influential monasteries, a Cistercian house founded in 1204 by King John – in remorse, it is said, for ordering a group of supplicating monks to be trampled to death. Built using stone ferried from Caen in northern France and Quarr on the Isle of Wight, the **abbey** managed a self-sufficient estate of ten thousand acres, but was dismantled soon after the Dissolution. Its refectory now forms the parish church, which, like everything else in Beaulieu, has been subsumed by the Montagu family who have owned a large chunk of the New Forest since one of Charles II's illegitimate progeny was created duke of the estate.

## Beaulieu Palace and the Motor Museum

Daily: June–Sept 10am–6pm; Oct–May 10am–5pm • £20 • ☎ 01590 612435, ⓦ beaulieu.co.uk

**Beaulieu** estate comprises **Palace House**, the attractive if unexceptional family home of the Montagus, a ruined Cistercian **Abbey** and the main attraction, the **National Motor Museum**, all set in fine grounds. The Motor Museum's collections of 250 vehicles includes spindly antiques, recent classics and Formula I cars rubbing shoulders with land-speed racers, vintage Rolls-Royces, Ferraris and a Sinclair C5, as well as some of *Top Gear*'s more outlandish vehicles. A monorail runs through the museum and round the grounds, towards the Palace House, formerly the abbey's gatehouse, which ccontains masses of Montagu-related memorabilia, while the undercroft of the abbey houses an exhibition depicting medieval monastic life.

## EATING AND DRINKING            BEAULIEU

**The Terrace** The Montagu Arms, Lyndhurst Rd ☎ 01590 612324, ⓦ montaguarmshotel.co.uk. The New Forest's only Michelin-starred restaurant, in an attractive dining room overlooking a pretty garden where you can eat in the summer. The menu uses local, seasonal ingredients, some grown in the hotel's own kitchen garden, and features dishes such as monkfish with asparagus or Lymington sea bass with watercress. The two-course lunch menu is good value at £22.50, while the three-course evening menu will set you back £70. Wed & Thurs noon–2.30pm & 7–9pm, Fri & Sat noon–2.30pm & 6.30–9pm.

# Buckler's Hard

The hamlet of **BUCKLER'S HARD**, a couple of miles downstream from Beaulieu, has a wonderful setting. A row of picturesque thatched shipwrights' cottages, some of which are inhabited, leads down to the Beaulieu River; it doesn't look much like a **shipyard** now, but from Elizabethan times onwards dozens of men o' war were assembled here from giant New Forest oaks. Several of Nelson's ships were launched here, to be towed carefully by rowing boats past the sandbanks and across the Solent to Portsmouth. The largest house in the hamlet, which forms part of the Montagu estate, belonged to Henry Adams, the master builder responsible for most of the Trafalgar fleet; it's now a hotel, pub and restaurant (see p.204). At the top of the village is the **Maritime Museum**, which traces the history of the great ships and incorporates buildings preserved in their eighteenth-century form. The hamlet is also the starting point for a bucolic **river cruise** down the Beaulieu River (Easter to Oct daily roughly every hour 11am–4.30pm; 30min; £4.50).

### ARRIVAL AND INFORMATION

BUCKLERS HARD

**Entry** The site is open daily: April–Sept 10am–5.30pm; Oct-March 10am–4.30pm. Tickets (£6.20) include entrance to the museum and parking.

**Tourist information** For more information call ☎01590 616203 or check ⊛bucklershard.co.uk.

### ACCOMMODATION

**The Master Builder's Hotel** ☎0844 815 3399, ⊛themasterbuilders.co.uk. Picturesque and peaceful, this wonderful quirky hotel is in a sixteenth-century building with open fires and a superb location overlooking the river; the rooms are a mixed bunch, some have oriental flourishes and individually designed furniture, and some have views of the river. There's also a decent restaurant and pub – you can take your drink outside onto the lawns in nice weather. **£140**

## Lymington

The most pleasant point of access for ferries to the Isle of Wight (see p.189) is **LYMINGTON**, a sheltered haven that's become one of the busiest leisure harbours on the south coast. Rising from the quay area, the cobbled street of the old town is lined with Georgian houses. At the top of the High Street (opposite Church Lane) is the partly thirteenth-century church of **St Thomas the Apostle**, with a cupola-topped tower built in 1670.

### ARRIVAL AND DEPARTURE

LYMINGTON

**By train** A branch line runs from the main line at Brockenhurst to Lymington (every 30min; 10min). Trains call first at Lymington Town station, a short walk from the high street, then run onto Lymington Pier to link with the

Isle of Wight ferry.
**By bus** Bus #6 runs from Southampton to Lymington via Lyndhurst and Brockenhurst; the coastal routes #X1 and #X2 run here from Christchurch and Bournemouth.

### ACCOMMODATION, EATING AND DRINKING

**Britannia House** Mill Lane ☎01590 672091, ⊛britannia-house.com. A well-kept, friendly and central B&B, right by the train station. The comfortable rooms are on the small side but there's a fine sitting room commanding views over the waterfront. **£90**
**Lanes** Ashley Lane ☎01590 672777, ⊛lanesoflymington.com. Set in an old chapel and former school, with some tables on an internal balcony, this bright buzzy restaurant and bar serves locally sourced fish and meats (£17–25) including sea bass and duck breast, and less pricey burgers and steaks (£11–19). Tues–Sat 11.30–2.30pm & 6.30–9.30pm, also open Sun 6.30–9.30pm in July & Aug.
**The Ship Inn** The Quay ☎01590 676903, ⊛theshiplymington.co.uk. With a terrace facing the water, this classy, friendly pub has a stylish nautical interior

of bleached wood and chrome. It also offers a superior restaurant menu featuring Modern British seasonal dishes such as pork belly with scallops (£18), along with pub classics like beef and Guinness pie (£12). Daily 11am–11pm; food served Mon–Sat noon–10pm, Sun noon–9pm.
**Stanwell House** High St ☎01590 677123, ⊛stanwellhouse.com. The most upmarket choice in town, this handsome boutique-style hotel has an array of individually designed rooms boasting rolltop baths, flatscreen TVs and the like. Its seafood restaurant is also the top spot to eat, in a dining room with a distinctly colonial feel (mains from around £17); there is also a less formal bistro serving modern European cuisine, and light snacks and afternoon teas are also available. Daily 7am–9pm. **£140**

## Brockenhurst

You'll frequently find New Forest ponies strolling down the high street of **BROCKENHURST**, undoubtedly the most attractive and liveliest town in the forest. Surrounded by idyllic heath and woodland and with a ford at one end of its High Street, it's a picturesque spot and a useful travel hub.

### ARRIVAL AND DEPARTURE

BROCKENHURST

**By train** The train station is on the eastern edge of town    – from here, turn left and left again into the main Brookley

Road, where you'll find the bulk of shops, banks and places to eat and drink. Mainline services run every 15–20min from/to London Waterloo (1hr 30min), Southampton (15–20min) and Winchester (30min). In addition, a branch line runs to Lymington (every 30min; 10min) to link with the Isle of Wight ferry.

## ACCOMMODATION, EATING AND DRINKING

★**New Park Manor** Lyndhurst Rd ☎ 0844 482 2152, ⓦ luxuryfamilyhotels.co.uk. This lovely family-friendly country house hotel in the middle of the New Forest pulls off the difficult trick of being both stylish and luxurious as well as relaxed and efficient. The staff are friendly and helpful and there's a fantastic spa, with an outdoor hot tub where you can sip champagne while watching the deer in the neighbouring fields. There are plenty of rooms that sleep families as well as inter-connecting rooms (childcare in the hotel crèche is free) and the hotel restaurant specializes in local produce. Family suites **£345**; doubles **£115**

★**The Pig** Beaulieu Rd ☎ 01590 622354, ⓦ thepighotel .co.uk. Brockenhurst's best restaurant by a mile is in a fabulous New Forest country house, set in stunning grounds. The innovative menu uses ingredients from its gardens or from the surrounding area – fish is smoked on site, eggs come from its own chickens, and the herbs and vegetables are all home-grown. All the ingredients are sourced from within 25 miles and the results are delicious, such as New Forest wood pigeon with locally foraged mushrooms (around £14). Daily 12.30–2.30pm & 6.30–9.30pm. **£140**

**Rose and Crown** Lyndhurst Rd ☎ 01590 622225, ⓦ rosecrownpubbrockenhurst.co.uk. A traditional Forest inn dating from the thirteenth century with a pleasant garden and a skittle alley. It serves large portions of good-value pub grub (most mains from £9–15), a selection of real ales and also has en-suite rooms (£90). Daily 11am–11pm.

**Thatched Cottage Hotel** 16 Brookley Rd ☎ 01590 623090, ⓦ thatched-cottage.co.uk. Dating from 1627, this is indeed an ancient thatched cottage, with tiny, low-beamed rooms as crammed with character as they are with furniture. There are just five rooms in the original building, along with newer "garden rooms"; the cream teas are divine, too. **£90**

# Bournemouth and around

Renowned for its pristine sandy beach (one of southern England's cleanest) and its gardens, the resort of **BOURNEMOUTH** dates from 1811, when a local squire, Louis Tregonwell, built a summerhouse on the wild, unpopulated heathland that once occupied this stretch of coast, and planted the first of the pine trees that now characterize the area. The mild climate, sheltered site and glorious beach encouraged the rapid growth of a full-scale family-holiday resort, complete with piers, cliff railways and boat trips. Today Bournemouth has a rather genteel, slightly geriatric image, counterbalanced by burgeoning numbers of language students, clubbers and a low-key surfing scene in the neighbouring suburb of **Boscombe**.

## Russell-Cotes Art Gallery and Museum

Russell-Cotes Rd, East Cliff • Tues–Sun & bank hols 10am–5pm • Oct–March free; April–Sept £5• ☎ 01202 451858, ⓦ russell-cotes .bournemouth.gov.uk

Surrounded by lovely gardens on a cliff-top, the **Russell-Cotes Art Gallery and Museum** has one of the UK's best collections of Victoriana, collected from around the world by the wealthy Russell-Cotes family. The quirky assortment of artworks, Oriental souvenirs and curios, such as the axe that allegedly beheaded Mary Queen of Scots, are displayed in an ornately decorated mansion, once the family home. Highlights of the collection are Rossetti's *Venus Verticordia* (1864) and England's most important collection of Victorian nudes, which scandalized much of society at the time.

## St Peter's Church

Hinton Rd

In the centre of town, the graveyard of **St Peter's** church is where **Mary Shelley**, author of the Gothic horror tale *Frankenstein*, is buried, together with the heart of her husband, the Romantic poet Percy Bysshe Shelley. The tombs of Mary's parents

– radical thinker William Godwin and early feminist Mary Wollstonecraft – are also in the graveyard.

## ARRIVAL AND INFORMATION BOURNEMOUTH

The **train station** and **bus station** lie opposite each other about a mile inland. They're connected to the town centre and seafront by frequent buses, or you can walk there in around 15–20min.

**By train** Destinations Brockenhurst (every 15–20min; 15–25min); Dorchester (every 30min–1hr; 45min); London Waterloo (every 30min; 2hr); Poole (every 20min; 10min); Southampton (every 15–20min; 30–50min); Weymouth (hourly; 55min); Winchester (every 15–20min; 45min–1hr).
**By bus** Destinations Direct National Express buses run to London (hourly; 2hr 30min); Salisbury (Mon–Sat every 30min, Sun 7 daily; 1hr 10min); Southampton (12 daily; 45min–1hr); Weymouth (4 daily; 1hr 15min–1hr 30min); and Winchester (5 daily; 1hr 15min–1hr 35min).
**Tourist office** Westover Road (June–Aug Mon–Sat 9.30am–5pm, Sun 11am–3pm; Sept–Oct & April–June Mon–Sat 10am–4.30pm; ☎0845 051 1700, ⓦ bournemouth.co.uk).

## ACCOMMODATION

**The Cumberland** East Overcliff Drive, East Cliff ☎01202 290722, ⓦcumberlandbournemouth.co.uk. This sumptuous Art Deco building is right on the seafront and has its own substantial outdoor pool in the front garden. It also has a leisure club and stylish bar. Rooms are more standard, though bag one with a sea view and you won't be disappointed. **£190**
★ **The Greenhouse Hotel** 4 Grove Rd ☎01202 498900, ⓦthegreenhousehotel.co.uk. Boutique-style, eco-friendly hotel in a Grade II-listed Victorian villa a short walk from the town centre. The stylish rooms come with all the latest mod cons, ultra-comfy beds, plus free home-made biscuits. The environmental standards are very high – water is solar-heated, and much of the electricity generated on site. There's also an excellent bar and restaurant. **£130**
**Urban Beach Hotel** 23 Argyll Rd, Boscombe ☎01202 301509, ⓦurbanbeachhotel.co.uk. A short (but steep) walk from Boscombe's surf beach, and close to the shops, this old Victorian townhouse has been given a boutique makeover. There are a variety of rooms, all of which are stylish with designer furniture, comfy beds and DVDs. The downstairs bar/restaurant serves great cocktails. **£100**

## EATING AND DRINKING

**Kino Lounge** 39 Bourne Ave ☎01202 552588. Small, fashionable wood-and-chrome restaurant just off Bournemouth's main square. It serves good-value and very tasty pizzas plus a Mediterranean-influenced menu which includes meze and pasta. Most mains £5–8. Mon–Thurs 11am–10pm, Fri & Sat 11am–11pm.
**Koh Thai Tapas** Daimler House, 38-40 Poole Hill ☎01202 294723, ⓦkoh-thai.co.uk. Lively restaurant done out with stylish Thai decor – all dark wood furniture, comfy sofas and fresh orchids. The Thai food is beautifully presented and can be ordered in tapas size (£5–7) or full portions. Mains (£9–17) include Thai curries, stir fries and noodles. The cocktails are great too. Mon 5.30–10pm, Tues–Thurs & Sun 12.30–3pm & 5.30–10pm, Fri & Sat 12.30–3pm & 5.30–10.30pm.
★ **Urban Reef** Undercliff Drive, Boscombe ☎01202 443960, ⓦurbanreef.com. Art Deco-style restaurant/bar/café in a fabulous position on Boscombe seafront. Designed to give great sea views from both floors, its quirky decor features a mock-up beach hut hanging on the wall, and there's a large deck for drinks on the front. Food varies from eggs Florentine (£7.25) and cooked breakfast (£7.50), through ciabattas and wraps (£8) to mains such as lamb meatballs (£8) and line-caught sea bass (£18). Mon & Tues 9am–6pm, Wed–Fri 9am–11pm, Sat 8am–11pm, Sun 8am–6pm.

## NIGHTLIFE AND ENTERTAINMENT

**Flirt** 21 The Triangle ☎01202 553999, ⓦ flirtcafebar .com. Quirky, gay-friendly café by day, serving good-value buffet lunches, which turns into a buzzy bar/restaurant at night. Sit on one of the old airline seats and enjoy a beer, and look out for various themed evenings from cabaret and quiz nights to book clubs and open mic sessions. Daily 9am–11pm.
**O2 Academy** 570 Christchurch Rd, Boscombe ☎01202 399922, ⓦo2academybournemouth.co.uk. Big name acts play in this atmospheric venue that used to be Boscombe's old Opera House. Also hosts regular club nights with top DJs.
★ **Sixty Million Postcards** 19–21 Exeter Rd ☎01202 292697, ⓦsixtymillionpostcards.com. One of Bournemouth's best bars, attracting an unpretentious but trendy student crowd. There are board games, various alcoves for cosy chats and comfy sofas. Offers a good range of beers, drinks and good-value burgers, with occasional live music. Mon–Thurs & Sun noon–midnight, Fri & Sat noon–2am.

# Wimborne Minster

An ancient town on the banks of the River Stour, just a few minutes' drive north from the suburbs of Bournemouth, **WIMBORNE MINSTER** is an attractive little town, worth an hour or two's wander around its narrow alleys, or along the riverbank. It's home to southern England's largest covered **market** (Fri–Sun; ⓦwimbornemarket.co.uk), though its main point of interest is the great church, the Minster of St Cuthberga.

## Minster of St Cuthberga

High St • Mon–Sat 9.30am–5.30pm, Sun 2.30–5.30pm; Chained Library Easter–Oct daily 10.30am–12.30pm & 2–4pm; phone for winter opening times • Free • ☎ 01202 884753, ⓦ wimborneminster.org.uk

Built on the site of an eighth-century monastery, the **Minster of St Cuthberga**'s massive twin towers of mottled grey and tawny stone dwarf the rest of town. At one time the church was even more imposing – its spire crashed down during morning service in 1602. What remains today is basically Norman with later additions, such as the Perpendicular west tower; this bears a figure dressed as a grenadier of the Napoleonic era, who strikes every quarter-hour with a hammer. The **Chained Library** above the choir vestry, dating from 1686, is Wimborne's most prized possession and one of the oldest public libraries in the country. Its collection of ancient books includes a manuscript written on lambskin dating from 1343.

# Kingston Lacy

2 miles northwest of Wimborne Minster • **House** Mid-March to Oct Wed–Sun 11am–5pm • £12.50 (includes grounds); NT • **Grounds** Daily: mid-March to Oct 10.30am–5.30pm; Nov to mid-March 10.30am–4pm • £7 • ☎ 01202 883402, ⓦ nationaltrust.org.uk/kingston-lacy

The glorious seventeenth-century mansion of **Kingston Lacy** stands in 250 acres of parkland grazed by a herd of Red Devon cattle. Designed for the Bankes family, who were exiled from Corfe Castle (see p.210) after the Roundheads reduced it to rubble, the brick building was clad in grey stone during the nineteenth century by Sir Charles Barry, co-architect of the Houses of Parliament. William Bankes, then owner of the house, was a great traveller and collector, and the **Spanish Room** is a superb scrapbook of his Grand Tour souvenirs. Kingston Lacy's **picture collection** is also outstanding, featuring Titian, Rubens, Velázquez and many other old masters.

# Christchurch

**CHRISTCHURCH**, five miles east of Bournemouth, is best known for **Christchurch Priory** (April–Oct Mon–Sat 9.30am–5pm, Sun 2.15–5.30pm; Nov–March Mon–Sat 9.30am–4pm, Sun 2.15–5.30pm; £3 donation requested; ☎ 01202 485804, ⓦ christchurchpriory.org), which, at 311ft, is England's longest parish church. The oldest parts of the current church date back to 1094, and its fan-vaulted North Porch is the country's biggest. Fine **views** can be gained from the top of the 120ft-high **tower** (£2.50; book on ☎ 01202 485804).

The area round the old town quay has a carefully preserved charm, with the **Red House Museum and Gardens** on Quay Road (Tues–Fri 10am–5pm, Sat 10am–4pm; free; ☎ 0845 603 5635, ⓦ www3.hants.gov.uk/redhouse.htm) containing an affectionate collection of local memorabilia. **Boat trips** (Easter–Oct daily; ☎ 01202 429119) leave from the grassy banks of the riverside quay east to the sandspit at Mudeford (30min; £7.50 return) or upriver to Tuckton (15min; £3 return).

## ARRIVAL AND INFORMATION — CHRISTCHURCH

**By train** Christchurch is on the main London to Weymouth line; the train station is on Stour Road, about a mile north of the town centre.

**By bus** Local buses from Bournemouth in the east, Lymington in the west and Ringwood in the north, pull up at the bus stop close to the tourist office on the high street.

**Tourist office** 49 High Street (Mon 9am–4.30pm, Tues–Sat 10am–4.30pm; ☎ 01202 471780, ⓦ visitchristchurch.info).

## ACCOMMODATION

**Captains Club Hotel** Wick Lane ☎01202 475111, ⓦcaptainsclubhotel.com. Although the modern glass exterior resembles a car showroom, things improve dramatically inside and there's a fine riverside terrace, bar, restaurant and spa. The contemporary rooms come with great river views. Check website for special offers and last-minute deals which reduce the price dramatically. **£250**

**Kings Hotel** 18 Castle St ☎01202 483434, ⓦthekings-christchurch.co.uk. A decent place in the centre of town right opposite the castle ruins. The sixteen rooms are well furnished in boutique style, with Egyptian cotton sheets, flatscreen TVs and free wi-fi, and some have views over the castle at the front. There's a good restaurant and lively bar downstairs, too. **£120**

## EATING AND DRINKING

**The Boathouse** 9 Quay Rd, ☎01202 480033, ⓦboathouse.co.uk. This modern café-bar/restaurant is in a lovely location overlooking the river with a large outdoor terrace, and a modern wood-burner inside. Main courses include the hearty New Forest game casserole with dumplings (£15) or mussels and chips (£15.50), as well as a selection of tasty stone-baked pizzas (£9–12). Mon–Thurs & Sun 9am–9pm, Fri & Sat 9am–10pm.

**The Jetty** Christchurch Harbour Hotel, 95 Mudeford ☎01202 400950, ⓦthejetty.co.uk. Michelin-starred chef Alex Aitken uses local seasonal produce in this contemporary wooden restaurant with stunning views of Christchurch harbour. Interesting main courses include a seafood cassoulet paella featuring local fish and shellfish (£21): the set lunch/early evening menu is good value at £22 for three courses. Mon–Sat noon–2.30pm & 6.30–10pm, Sun noon–8pm.

**Ye Olde George Inn** 2a Castle St ☎01202 479383, ⓦyeoldegeorgeinn.co.uk. Christchurch's oldest pub, the *George* is an attractive former coaching inn with a great courtyard garden, and a warren of small rooms inside. Serves reasonably priced pub grub and a selection of real ales. Mon–Sat 11am–11pm, Sun noon–10.30pm; food served daily 11.30am–9.30pm.

# Poole

West of Bournemouth, **POOLE** is an ancient seaport on a huge, almost landlocked harbour. The town developed in the thirteenth century and was successively colonized by pirates, fishermen and timber traders. The old quarter by the quayside contains more than one hundred historic buildings, as well as the contemporary Poole Museum.

## Poole Museum

4 Old High St • Easter–Oct Mon–Sat 10am–5pm, Sun noon–5pm; Nov–Easter Tues–Sat 10am–4pm, Sun noon–4pm • Free • ☎01202 262600, ⓦboroughofpoole.com/museums

**Poole Museum** traces the town's development through the centuries, with displays of local ceramics and tiles and a rare Iron Age log boat that was dug out of the harbour in 1964: carved out of a single tree trunk, the 33ft-long boat dates from around 300 BC. Look out, too, for the fascinating footage of the flying boats that took off from Poole harbour during the 1940s for the Far East and Australia.

## Brownsea Island

Feb & March boats from Sandbanks only (Sat & Sun 10am–4pm, every 30min); April–Oct boats from Sandbanks and Poole Quay (daily 10am–5pm, every 30min) • Boats from Sandbanks £6 return; boats from Poole Quay £10 return • Entrance to island £6.60; NT • ☎01202 707744, ⓦnationaltrust.org.uk/brownsea-island

**Brownsea Island** is famed for its red squirrels, wading birds and other **wildlife**, which you can spot along themed trails. The landscape is surprisingly diverse for such a small island – much of it is heavily wooded, though there are also areas of heath and marsh, and narrow, shingly beaches – and it's pretty easy to escape from the boat-trippers and find a peaceful corner to picnic.

## Compton Acres

164 Canford Cliffs Rd • Daily: Easter–Oct 10am–6pm; Nov–Easter 10am–4pm; last entry 1hr before closing • £7.95 • ☎01202 700778, ⓦcomptonacres.co.uk • Bus #50 from Bournemouth and #52 from Poole

One of the area's best-known gardens, **Compton Acres**, lies on the outskirts of Poole, signposted off the A35 Poole Road towards Bournemouth. Spectacularly sited over ten acres on steep slopes above Poole Harbour, each of the seven gardens here has a different international theme, including a formal Italian garden and the elegantly understated Japanese Garden, its meandering streams crossed by stone steps and wooden bridges.

## ARRIVAL AND INFORMATION                                    POOLE

**By train** Poole's train station is on Serpentine Road, about a 15min walk from the waterfront along the high street.
**Destinations** Bournemouth (every 20min; 10min); London Waterloo (every 30min; 2hr–2hr 10min); Weymouth (every 30min; 35–45min).
**By bus** The bus station is in front of the Dolphin Centre on

Kingland Road, with regular National Express services to London Victoria (13 daily; 2hr 55min–3hr 45min).
**Tourist office** Poole Quay (April–June, Sept & Oct daily 10am–5pm; July & Aug daily 10am–6pm; Nov–March Mon–Fri 10am–5pm, Sat 10am–4pm; ☎0845 234 5560, ⓦpooletourism.com).

## ACCOMMODATION

**Corkers** 1 High St ☎01202 681393, ⓦcorkers.co.uk. Above a lively café/restaurant, this B&B offers some of the best-value rooms in town – the two superb front rooms, one of which sleeps three, have harbour-facing balconies. Parking offered for a small fee. **£85**
**★Hotel du Vin** Thames St ☎01202 685666,

ⓦhotelduvin.com. Inside a fine old mansion house with a double staircase, this stylish hotel has plush, comfortable, rooms, an atmospheric restaurant and wine cellar, and a very cosy bar with its own log fire – great in winter. The location is great, in the pretty old town, a minute's walk from the Quay. **£135**

## EATING AND DRINKING

**Da Vinci's** 7 The Quay ☎01202 667528, ⓦda-vincis .co.uk. Set in an old warehouse on Poole Quay, this is an old-fashioned Italian restaurant with friendly service and harbour views. The menu features inexpensive pizza and pasta (£8–14), as well as pricier traditional dishes, such as vitello Milanese (£17), and daily fish specials. Mon–Fri noon–2pm & 5.30–10pm, Sat & Sun noon–10.30pm.
**★Deli on the Quay** D17 Dolphin Quays, The Quay ☎01202 660022, ⓦdelionthequay.com. Bright, light harbourfront café-deli stacked with delicious preserves, wines and the like. The café serves fresh croissants, sandwiches and decent coffee. Mon & Wed–Fri 9am–5pm, Tues 9am–8.30pm, Sat & Sun 10am–5pm; Nov–March closes 4pm Mon–Fri, Aug open until 10pm.

**Poole Arms** The Quay ☎01202 673450. Completely covered with green tiles, this wonderfully atmospheric historic pub is reassuringly old-fashioned, with decent beers and fresh fish daily. There's outdoor seating on the waterfront too. Mon–Sat 11am–11pm, Sun noon–11pm; food served daily noon–2.30pm & 6–8.30pm.
**Storm** 16 High St ☎01202 674970. Owned by a chef/ fisherman, this restaurant, unsurprisingly, specializes in locally caught seafood. The menu changes daily according to what is available, but expect such delights as local pollack (£18) or sea bass with curly kale (£20). Mon–Fri & Sun 6–11pm, Sat 5.30–11pm, phone for irregular lunchtime hours.

# The Isle of Purbeck

Though not actually an island, the **ISLE OF PURBECK** – a promontory of low hills and heathland jutting out beyond Poole Harbour – does have an insular and distinctive feel. Reached from the east by the ferry from Sandbanks at the narrow mouth of Poole Harbour, or by a long and congested landward journey via the bottleneck of **Wareham**, Purbeck can be a difficult destination to reach, but its villages are immensely pretty, none more so than **Corfe Castle**, with its majestic ruins. From **Swanage**, a low-key seaside resort, the Dorset Coast Path provides access to the oily shales of Kimmeridge Bay, the spectacular cove at **Lulworth** and the much-photographed natural arch of **Durdle Door**. The whole coast from Purbeck to Exmouth in Devon – dubbed the **Jurassic Coast** (ⓦjurassiccoast.com) – is a World Heritage Site on account of its geological significance and fossil remains; walkers can access it along the South West Coast Path.

## ARRIVAL AND GETTING AROUND                          ISLE OF PURBECK

**By ferry** There are regular ferries from Sandbanks (7am–11pm every 20min; pedestrians & bikes £1, cars

£3.50; ☎01929 450203, ⓦsandbanksferry.co.uk).
**By bike** Cycling is a great way to get around, though be

prepared for steep hills; bikes can be rented from Cycle Experience at Wareham Station (☎01929 556601, ⊛purbeck cyclehire.co.uk) and Charlie the Bikemonger, 5 Queen's Rd, in Swanage (☎01929 475833, ⊛charliethebikemonger.com).

**By bus** The Purbeck Breezer runs two services around the Purbecks – route #40 from Poole to Swanage via Wareham

and Corfe Castle, and route #50 from Bournemouth to Swanage via the Sandbanks ferry and Studland. In summer, some services are open-top.

**By train** Wareham is the only place served by mainline trains, though a restored steam train service also runs between Swanage and Norden (see opposite).

## Wareham

The grid pattern of its streets indicates the Saxon origins of **WAREHAM**, and the town is surrounded by even older earth ramparts known as the Walls. A riverside setting adds greatly to its charms, though the place gets fairly overrun in summer. Nearby lies an enclave of quaint houses around **Lady St Mary's Church**, which contains the marble coffin of Edward the Martyr, murdered at Corfe Castle in 978 by his stepmother, to make way for her son Ethelred. **St Martin's Church**, at the north end of town, dates from Saxon times and holds a faded twelfth-century mural of St Martin offering his cloak to a beggar. The church's most striking feature, however, is a romantic effigy of T.E. Lawrence in Arab dress, which was originally destined for Salisbury Cathedral, but was rejected by the dean there who disapproved of Lawrence's sexual proclivities. Lawrence was killed in 1935 in a motorbike accident on the road from Bovington (six miles west); his simply furnished cottage is at **Clouds Hill**, seven miles northwest of Wareham (mid-March to Oct Wed–Sun 11am–5pm or dusk; £5.50; NT; ☎01929 405616, ⊛nationaltrust .org.uk/clouds-hill). The small **museum** next to Wareham's town hall in East Street (Easter–Oct Mon–Sat 10am–4pm; free; ☎01929 553448, ⊛greenacre.info/WTM) focuses on local history and Lawrence memorabilia.

### ARRIVAL AND INFORMATION                                      WAREHAM

**By train** Wareham station, a 15min walk north of the town, sees regular trains from London (every 30min; 2hr 20min) and Weymouth (every 20–40min; 25–35min).

**Tourist office** Trinity Church, South Street (Easter–Oct Mon–Sat 9.30am–5pm; Nov–Easter Mon 10am–4pm, Tues– Sat 9.30am–4pm; ☎01929 552740, ⊛purbeck.gov.uk).

## Corfe Castle

The romantic **castle ruins** (daily: March & Oct 10am–5pm; April–Sept 10am–6pm; Nov–Feb 10am–4pm; £8; NT; ☎01929 481294, ⊛nationaltrust.org.uk/corfe-castle) crowning the hill behind the village of **CORFE CASTLE** are perhaps the most evocative in England. The family seat of Sir John Bankes, Attorney General to Charles I, this Royalist stronghold withstood a Cromwellian siege for six weeks, gallantly defended by Lady Bankes. One of her own men, Colonel Pitman, eventually betrayed the castle to the Roundheads, after which it was reduced to its present gap-toothed state by gunpowder. Apparently the victorious Roundheads were so impressed by Lady Bankes' courage that they allowed her to take the keys to the castle with her – they can still be seen in the library at the Bankes' subsequent home, Kingston Lacy (see p.207).

### ACCOMMODATION                                               CORFE CASTLE

**Mortons House** East St, Corfe Castle ☎01929 480988, ⊛mortonshouse.co.uk. A sixteenth-century manor house with a beautiful walled garden and log fires in winter, this award-winning small hotel has snug rooms, some with four-poster beds and stone fireplaces. The restaurant offers top local cuisine. **£160**

**Norden Farm** Norden ☎01929 480098, ⊛nordenfarm .com. Tucked into a tranquil valley, this working farm has

extensive fields for tents and caravans, good facilities, its own shop and a menagerie of animals. Closed Nov–Feb. Pitches from **£13**

**Norden House** Norden Farm, Norden ☎01929 480177, ⊛nordenhouse.com. If you don't fancy camping, you can stay in Norden House, a Georgian building in the grounds of the farm, which has a range of comfortable rooms, a lovely garden and its own slightly pricey restaurant. **£90**

## EATING AND DRINKING

**The Greyhound** The Square, Corfe Castle ☎ 01929 480205, ⓦ greyhoundcorfe.co.uk. One of England's oldest coaching inns, with frequent live music and a pleasant garden at the back with views of the castle. The food is good, with local specialities such as venison casserole (£14.50), as well as a good range of hearty sandwiches – the steak sandwich comes with chips and salad for £8.50. Daily 11am–11pm; food daily noon–9pm.

★ **The Scott Arms** West St, Kingston ☎ 01929 480270, ⓦ thescottarms.com. In the neighbouring village, a steep climb above Corfe Castle, this is a wonderful old inn with a warren of cosy rooms at the front and a large, modern-looking back room that doubles as its restaurant. But the biggest draw is its garden, which commands a stupendous view over Corfe Castle in the valley below. The food is substantial and varied and good value at around £9 for mains, while in summer you can also eat from the *Jerk Shak* selling fantastic Caribbean food in the garden. Daily 11am–11pm; food served Mon–Thurs noon–2.30pm & 6.30–8.30pm, Fri noon–2.30pm & 6–8.45pm, Sat noon–2.45pm & 6–8.45pm, Sun noon–3.45pm & 6–8.30pm.

# Swanage

Purbeck's largest town, **SWANAGE**, is a traditional seaside resort with a pleasant sandy beach and an ornate town hall. The town's station is the southern terminus of the **Swanage Steam Railway** (April–Oct daily; Nov– March Sat & Sun plus school hols; £11.50 return; ☎ 01929 425800, ⓦ swanagerailway.co.uk), which runs for six miles to Norden, just north of Corfe Castle. West of Swanage, you can pick up the coastal path to **Durlston Country Park**, around a mile out of town. Set in 280 acres of coastal woodland and crisscrossed with cliff-top paths, it is a great place for a picnic or for wind-blown walks.

## ACCOMMODATION SWANAGE AND AROUND

**The Swanage Haven** 3 Victoria Rd ☎ 01929 423088, ⓦ swanagehaven.com. Good-value boutique-style guesthouse: the smart rooms have flatscreen TVs and the decked garden has a great outdoor hot tub. Breakfasts are good, made from locally sourced ingredients. No children. **£150**

★ **Tom's Field Campsite** Langton Matravers, a couple of miles west of Swanage ☎ 01929 427110, ⓦ tomsfieldcamping.co.uk. Wonderfully sited and well-run, this is the best campsite in the region, with sea views from some of the pitches and direct access to the coast path. It also lets out bunks in a converted Nissen hut – The Walker's Barn – or a converted pigsty called The Stone Room. The campsite has a well-stocked shop, but only takes reservations for longer stays – for short stays, especially on sunny weekends, you'll need to turn up early to bag a pitch. Stone Room **£25**; Walker's Barn per person **£12**; camping pitches **£14**

## EATING AND DRINKING

**Gee Whites** The Old Stone Quay, 1 High St ☎ 01929 425720, ⓦ geewhites.co.uk. Completely rebuilt in 2014, this superb open-air seafood bar and ice-cream parlour is right on the quay serving local lobster, crabs, mussels and oysters. The menu changes daily according to what's been caught, but a bowl of mussels with bread or tempura prawns costs a very reasonable £6. Summer daily 9am–9.30pm; outside summer hours are weather dependent.

★ **Seventh Wave** Durlston Castle & Country Park, Lighthouse Rd ☎ 01929 421111, ⓦ 7eventhwave.com. Inside Durlston Castle with stunning views over the coast, this is an unmissable stop – either for a coffee, drink or full meal. There are tapas-like snacks from around £4, fresh fish or mains from £14–18. April–Sept Mon–Fri 10am–5pm, Sat & Sun 10am–5pm & 6–9pm; Oct–March daily 9.30am–4pm.

★ **Square and Compass** Worth Matravers, 4 miles west of Swanage ☎ 01929 439229, ⓦ squareandcompasspub.co.uk. In a quintessential Purbeck village, with stunning views over the surrounding downs and sea, this is one of England's finest pubs: the bar is a tiny hatch, the interior is a winter fug of log fires, walkers, families and dogs (and the occasional live band), while outside there's a motley collection of stone seats and wooden benches. Regularly winning CAMRA awards for its local ales and ciders, and with its own little fossil museum, it also serves delicious home-made pies and pasties. Mon–Thurs noon–3pm & 6–11pm, Fri–Sun noon–11pm.

# Studland

East of Swanage, you can follow the Southwest Coast path over Ballard Down to descend into the pretty village of **STUDLAND** at the southern end of **Studland Bay**. The most northerly stretch of the beach, **Shell Bay**, is a magnificent strand of icing-sugar sand backed by a remarkable heathland ecosystem that's home to all six British species of reptile – adders are quite common, so be careful. On Middle Beach, you can **hire kayaks** from the **Studland Sea School** (☎01929 450430, ⍵studlandseaschool.co.uk) or take one of their excellent guided kayak or snorkelling tours round Old Harry Rocks, through cliff arches and sea caves.

★**Bankes Arms** Manor Rd ☎01929 450225, ⍵bankesarms.com. Lovely location, good food, and a great range of real ales, some from local independent breweries and others from its own on-site Isle of Purbeck Brewery. The pub food costs slightly more than average,

but the portions are big, and frankly it's worth it for the joy of sitting in the grassy front garden with fantastic bay views, or by the roaring log fire in the cosy Purbeck stone interior. Daily 11am–11pm; food served noon–9.30pm (Sun to 9pm).

# Kimmeridge Bay

Towards the western half of the Isle of Purbeck the coastal geology changes as the grey-white chalk and limestone cliffs give way to darker beds of shale. **Kimmeridge Bay** may not have a sandy beach but it does have a remarkable marine wildlife reserve much appreciated by divers. The Lulworth artillery ranges west of Kimmeridge are inaccessible during weekdays but generally open at weekends and in school holidays – watch out for the red warning flags and notices and always stick to the path.

# Tyneham

Beyond Kimmeridge, the coastal path passes close to the deserted village of **Tyneham**, whose residents were summarily evicted by the army in 1943. You can wander around the abandoned stone cottages, which have an eerie fascination, while an exhibition in the church explains the history of the village. Some of the buildings, such as the **school house**, have been restored to their 1940s condition.

# Lulworth Cove and around

The quaint thatch-and-stone villages of **EAST LULWORTH** and **WEST LULWORTH** form a prelude to **Lulworth Cove**, a perfect shell-shaped bite formed when the sea broke through a weakness in the cliffs and then gnawed away at them from behind, forming a circular cave that eventually collapsed to leave a bay enclosed by sandstone cliffs. West of the cove, **Stair Hole** is a roofless sea cave riddled with arches that will eventually collapse to form another Lulworth Cove. The mysteries of local geology are explained at the **Lulworth Heritage Centre** (daily 10am–4/6pm; free) by the car park at the top of the lane leading down to the cove.

## Durdle Door

A mile west of Lulworth Cove, the iconic limestone arch of **Durdle Door** can be reached via the steep uphill path that starts from Lulworth Cove's car park. The arch itself sits at the end of a long shingle beach (which can be accessed via steep steps), a lovely place for catching the sun and swimming in fresh, clear water. There are further steps to a bay just east of Durdle Door, **St Oswald's Bay**, with another shingle beach and offshore rocks that you can swim out to.

**Castle Inn** Main Rd, West Lulworth ☎01929 400311, ⍵thecastleinn-lulworthcove.co.uk. Up in the village, this sixteenth-century thatched pub has a lovely terraced garden,

a good range of local real ales and a selection of traditional pub games. High-quality pub grub features home-made steak and ale pie and beef bourguignon. It's also very dog-friendly. Mon–Fri noon–2.30pm & 6–10.30pm, Sat & Sun noon–10.30pm; food served daily noon–9pm.

**Durdle Door Holiday Park** ☏ 01929 400200, ⓦ lulworth.com. Superbly positioned up on the cliffs above Durdle Door, this campsite has fabulous views from its touring field, while tents can be pitched in the more sheltered wooded field. It's a 20min walk across fields to Lulworth Cove and there's also a shop and café-bar on site. Pitches £33

**Lulworth Cove Inn** Main Rd, Lulworth Cove ☏ 01929

400333, ⓦ lulworth-coveinn.co.uk. With a great location right on the main street leading down to the cove and overlooking the duck pond, this is the first choice in Lulworth itself, especially if you can bag one of the front rooms that come with their own cove-view terraces (£10 extra). The pub downstairs offers local Blandford ales, real fires, a pleasant garden and decent food, including citrus salmon skewer (£10.50) and haddock smokie (£14.50) among the usual pub staples. Daily 11am–11pm; food served noon–9pm. £100

# Dorchester and around

For many, **DORCHESTER**, county town of Dorset, is essentially **Thomas Hardy**'s town; he was born at Higher Bockhampton, three miles east, his heart is buried in Stinsford, a couple of miles northeast (the rest of him is in Westminster Abbey), and he spent much of his life in Dorchester itself, where his statue now stands on High West Street. The town appears in his novels as Casterbridge, and the local countryside is evocatively depicted, notably the wild heathland of the east (Egdon Heath) and the eerie yew forest of Cranborne Chase. The real Dorchester – liveliest on Wednesday, market day – has a pleasant central core of mostly seventeenth-century and Georgian buildings, though the town's origins go back to the Romans, who founded "Durnovaria" in about 70 AD. The Roman walls were replaced in the eighteenth century by tree-lined avenues called "Walks", but some traces of the Roman period have survived. On the southeast edge of town, **Maumbury Rings** is where the Romans held vast gladiatorial combats in an amphitheatre adapted from a Stone Age site.

In addition to its Hardy connections, Dorchester is also associated with the notorious **Judge Jeffreys**, who, after the ill-fated rebellion of the Duke of Monmouth (one of Charles II's illegitimate offspring) against James II, held his "**Bloody Assizes**" in the Oak Room of the former Antelope Hotel (now offices) on Cornhill in 1685. A total of 292 men were sentenced to death, though most got away with a flogging and transportation to the West Indies, while 74 were hung, drawn and quartered, their heads stuck on pikes throughout Dorset and Somerset. Judge Jeffreys lodged just round the corner in High West Street, in what are now offices.

## Old Crown Courts

58–60 High St • Mon–Thurs 10am–4.30pm • £2 • ☏ 01305 267992

The **Old Crown Courts**, also known as Shire Hall, are of interest principally as the place where six men from the nearby village of Tolpuddle, now known as the **Tolpuddle Martyrs** (see p.125), were sentenced to transportation for forming what was in effect Britain's first trade union. Although the council buildings are still in use, the room in which the Martyrs were tried has been preserved as a memorial; you can sit behind the judge's desk and bang his gavel, or ponder their fate from the jurors' bench.

## Dorset County Museum

High West St • April–Oct Mon–Sat 10am–5pm; Nov–March Mon–Sat 10am–4pm • £6.50 • ☏ 01305 262735, ⓦ dorsetcountymuseum.org

The best place to find out about Dorchester's history is the engrossing **Dorset County Museum**, where archeological and geological displays trace Celtic and Roman history, including a section on nearby Maiden Castle (see p.214). Pride of place goes to the recreation of Thomas Hardy's study, where his pens are inscribed with the names of the books he wrote with them.

## Maiden Castle

Around 2 miles southwest of Dorchester • Open access • Free

One of southern England's finest prehistoric sites, **MAIDEN CASTLE** stands on a hill southwest of Dorchester. Covering about 115 acres, it was first developed around 3000 BC by a Stone Age farming community and then used during the Bronze Age as a funeral mound. Iron Age dwellers expanded it into a populous settlement and fortified it with a daunting series of ramparts and ditches, just in time for the arrival of Vespasian's Second Legion. The ancient Britons' slingstones were no match for the more sophisticated weapons of the Roman invaders, however, and Maiden Castle was stormed in a massacre in 43 AD. What you see today is a massive series of grassy concentric ridges about 60ft high, creasing the surface of the hill. The main finds from the site are displayed in the Dorset County Museum (see p.213).

## Cerne Abbas giant

Cerne Abbas, 7 miles north of Dorchester, just off the A352 • Open access • Free; NT • ☎ 01297 489481, ⍩ nationaltrust.org.uk/cerne-giant

The village of **CERNE ABBAS** has bags of charm, with gorgeous Tudor cottages and abbey ruins, but its main attraction is the enormously priapic **giant** carved in the chalk hillside just north of the village, standing 180ft high and brandishing a club over his disproportionately small head. The age of the monument is disputed, though it is likely that the giant originated as some primeval fertility symbol. Folklore has it that lying on the outsize member will induce conception, but the National Trust, who now own the site, do their best to stop people wandering over it and damaging the 2ft-deep trenches that form the outlines. Although you can walk round the giant, the carving itself is fenced off to avoid erosion and you don't get the full impact of the giant when you are so close – for the best view, follow signs to the car park and **viewpoint** on the hillside opposite.

## Milton Abbas

Bus #311 from Dorchester (3 daily; 45min)

The village of **MILTON ABBAS**, ten miles east of Cerne Abbas, is an unusual English rural idyll. It owes its model-like neatness to the First Earl of Dorchester who, in the eighteenth century, found the medieval squalor of former "Middleton" a blot on the landscape of his estate. He had the village razed and rebuilt in its present location as thirty semi-detached, whitewashed and thatched cottages on wide grassy verges. No trace remains of the old

---

### HARDY'S WESSEX

**Thomas Hardy** (1840–1928) resurrected the old name of **Wessex** to describe the region in which he set most of his fiction. In his books, the area stretched from Devon and Somerset ("Lower Wessex" and "Outer Wessex") to Berkshire and Oxfordshire ("North Wessex"), though its central core was Dorset ("South Wessex"), the county where Hardy spent most of his life. His books richly depict the life and appearance of the surroundings, often disguised under fictional names. Thus Salisbury makes an appearance as "Melchester", Weymouth (where he briefly lived) as "Budmouth Regis", and Bournemouth as "Sandbourne" in *Tess of the d'Urbervilles*. But it is **Dorchester**, the "Casterbridge" of his novels, that is portrayed in most detail, to the extent that many of the town's landmarks that still remain can be identified in the books (especially *The Mayor of Casterbridge* and *Far From the Madding Crowd*). Hardy was born and lived (1840–62 and 1867–70) in Higher Bockhampton, three miles northeast of the town, in what is now **Hardy's Cottage** (mid-March to Oct Wed–Sun & bank hols 11am–5pm; £5.50; NT; ☎ 01305 262366, ⍩ nationaltrust.org.uk /hardys-cottage), where a few bits of period furniture and some original manuscripts are displayed. Having worked as an architect, Hardy returned to Dorchester in 1885, and spent the rest of his life in **Max Gate**, in Alington Avenue, which he designed himself (mid-March to Oct Wed–Sun & bank hols 11am–5pm; £5.50; NT; ☎ 01305 262538, ⍩ nationaltrust.org.uk/max-gate). Here, he completed *Tess of the D'Urbervilles*, *Jude the Obscure* and much of his poetry.

village, which once surrounded the fourteenth-century **abbey church** (now part of Milton Abbey school), a mile's walk away near the lake at the bottom of the village.

## Tolpuddle Martyrs Museum

Tolpuddle, 8 miles east of Dorchester, off the A3 • April–Oct Tues–Sat 10am–5pm, Sun 11am–5pm; Nov–March Thurs–Sat 10am–4pm, Sun 11am–4pm • Free • ☎ 01305 848237, ⓦ tolpuddlemartyrs.org.uk

The delightful Dorset village of **TOLPUDDLE** is of interest principally because of the **Tolpuddle Martyrs**. In 1834, six villagers, George and James Loveless, Thomas and John Standfield, John Brine and James Hammett, were sentenced to transportation for banding together to form the Friendly Society of Agricultural Labourers, in order to petition for a small wage increase on the grounds that their families were starving. After a public outcry the men were pardoned, and the Martyrs passed into history as founders of the trade union movement. Six memorial cottages were built in 1934 to commemorate the centenary of the Martyrs' conviction. The middle one has been turned into the little **Tolpuddle Martyrs Museum**, which charts the story of the men, from their harsh rural lives before their conviction to the horrors of transportation in a convict ship and the brutal conditions of the penal colonies in Australia.

### ARRIVAL AND INFORMATION

### DORCHESTER AND AROUND

**By train** Dorchester has two train stations, Dorchester South and Dorchester West, both south of the centre.
Destinations from Dorchester South Bournemouth (every 30min; 40–45min); London (every 30min; 2hr 35min–2hr 50min); Weymouth (every 15–20min; 10–15min).
Destinations from Dorchester West Bath (7 daily; 2hr); Bristol (7 daily; 2hr 30min).
**By bus** Most local buses stop around the car park on

Acland Rd, to the east of South St, though long-distance buses pull in next to Dorchester South train station.
Destinations Bournemouth (4 daily; 1hr–1hr 40min); London (1 daily; 3hr 50min); Weymouth (roughly every 15min; 30min).
**Tourist office** 11 Antelope Walk (April–Oct Mon–Sat 9am–5pm; Nov–March Mon–Sat 9am–4pm; ☎ 01305 267992, ⓦ visit-dorset.com).

### ACCOMMODATION

**The Old Rectory** Winterbourne Steepleton, 4 miles west of Dorchester ☎ 01305 889468, ⓦ theoldrectorybandb .co.uk. A lovely former rectory in a tiny, pretty village. Dating from 1850, the B&B has four comfortable en-suite rooms, one with a four-poster, and attractive well-kept gardens. **£70**

**Westwood House** 29 High West St ☎ 01305 268018, ⓦ westwoodhouse.co.uk. Comfortable Georgian townhouse on the busy high street, with well-furnished rooms, all with wi-fi and flatscreen TVs. The breakfasts are great, and include options such as smoked haddock with poached egg. **£95**

### EATING AND DRINKING

★ **Café Jagos** 8 High West St ☎ 01305 266056, ⓦ cafejagos.com. Good-value salads and sandwiches come in large portions at this pleasant café with contemporary decor – the panninis (£5) and main courses such as local rabbit and cider stew (£8), are all tasty. On Fri and Sat nights the bar area comes into its own with frequent live music and DJs. Mon–Thurs 10am–4pm, Fri–Sat 10am–4pm & 10pm–4am.
**Potters Café** 19 Durngate St ☎ 01305 260312. Very appealing café/restaurant with a log fire in winter and a

small garden. It serves a range of inexpensive dishes such as fish soup, tiger prawns and curries from £7 to £9. Mon–Sat 9.30am–4pm, Sun 10am–2.30pm.
**Sienna** 36 High West St ☎ 01305 250022, ⓦ siennarestaurant.co.uk. Dorset's only Michelin-starred restaurant, this tiny, upmarket place specializes in locally sourced Modern British cuisine such as West Country venison with celeriac and pear. Prices start at around £26 for the two-course lunch menu, up to £65 a head for the evening tasting menu. Tues 7–9pm, Wed–Sat 12.30–2pm & 7–9.30pm.

# Sherborne

Tucked away in the northwest corner of Dorset, ten miles north of Cerne Abbas, the pretty town of **SHERBORNE** was once the capital of Wessex, its church having cathedral status until Old Sarum (see p.225) usurped the bishopric in 1075.

## Abbey Church

3 Abbey Close • Daily: April–Oct 8am–6pm; Nov–March 8am–4pm • Suggested donation £3.50 • ☎ 01935 812452, ⓦ sherborneabbey.com

Sherborne's former historical glory is embodied by the magnificent **Abbey Church** founded in 705 and later becoming a Benedictine abbey. Most of its extant parts date from a rebuilding in the fifteenth century. Among the abbey church's many tombs are those of Alfred the Great's two brothers, Ethelred and Ethelbert, and the Elizabethan poet Thomas Wyatt, all in the northeast corner.

## The castles

Sherborne boasts no fewer than two "castles", both associated with Sir Walter Raleigh. Queen Elizabeth I first leased, then gave, Raleigh the twelfth-century **Old Castle**, on Castletom (April–June, Sept & Oct daily 10am–5pm; July & Aug daily 10am–6pm; £3.70; EH; ☎ 01935 812730, ⓦ english-heritage.org.uk/daysout/properties/sherborne -old-castle) but it seems that he despaired of feudal accommodation and built himself a more comfortably domesticated house, **Sherborne Castle**, in adjacent parkland, accessed from New Road (April–Oct Tues–Thurs, Sat & Sun 11am–4.30pm; castle interior closed on Sat until 2pm; castle and gardens £11, gardens only £6; ☎ 01935 812072, ⓦ sherbornecastle.com). When Sir Walter fell from the queen's favour by seducing her maid of honour, the Digby family acquired the house and have lived here ever since. The Old Castle fared less happily, and was pulverized by Cromwellian cannon fire for the obstinately Royalist leanings of its occupants.

### ARRIVAL AND INFORMATION                                                SHERBORNE

**By train** The station is 5min south of the town centre, and is served by hourly trains between London and Exeter, with some services continuing on to Plymouth.
**By bus** Buses from Dorchester, Yeovil and Blandford Forum

pull in outside the train station.
**Tourist office** 3 Tilton Court, Digby Road (Mon–Sat: April–Oct 9am–5pm; Oct & Nov 9.30am–4pm; Dec–March 10am–3pm; ☎ 01935 815341, ⓦ sherbornetown.com).

### ACCOMMODATION AND EATING

**The Eastbury** Long St ☎ 01935 813131, ⓦ theeastbury hotel.co.uk. In a fine Georgian house, with its own highly regarded restaurant, bar and lovely walled gardens. The front rooms are on the small side and it's worth paying extra for an executive room, which are spacious and boutique in feel, overlooking the gardens. The restaurant specializes in dishes made from seasonal and locally

sourced ingredients. **£150**
★ **Oliver's** 19 Cheap St ☎ 01935 815005, ⓦ olivers coffeehouse.co.uk. With long wooden benches laid out in a former butcher's, adorned with the original tiles, this friendly café-deli serves great cakes and coffee, accompanied by oodles of atmosphere. Mon–Fri 9am–5pm, Sat 9.30am–5pm, Sun 10–4pm.

# Shaftesbury

Fifteen miles east of Sherborne on the A30, **SHAFTESBURY** perches on a spur of lumpy hills, with severe gradients on three sides of the town. On a clear day, views from the town are terrific – one of the best vantage points is **Gold Hill**, quaint, cobbled and very steep. At its crest, the **Gold Hill Museum and Garden** (April–Oct daily 10.30am–4pm; free; ☎ 01747 852157, ⓦ goldhillmuseum.org.uk) displays items ranging from locally made buttons, for which the area was once renowned, to a mummified cat.

Pilgrims used to flock to Shaftesbury to pay homage to the bones of Edward the Martyr, which were brought to the **Abbey** in 978, though now only the footings of the abbey church survive, just off the main street on Park Walk (April–Oct daily 10am–5pm; £3; ☎ 01747 852910, ⓦ shaftesburyabbey.org.uk). **St Peter's Church** on the marketplace is one of the few reminders of Shaftesbury's medieval grandeur, when it boasted a castle, twelve churches and four market crosses.

## ARRIVAL AND INFORMATION

### SHAFTESBURY

**By bus** Shaftesbury has services from Salisbury (Mon–Sat 8 daily; 1hr 15min) and Blandford Forum (Mon–Sat 7 daily; 40min).

**Tourist office** 8 Bell Street (April–Sept Mon–Sat 10am–5pm; Oct–March Mon–Sat 10am–3pm; ☎01747 853514, ⓦ shaftesburydorset.com).

## ACCOMMODATION

**The Grosvenor Arms** The Commons ☎01747 850580, ⓦ thegrosvenorarms.co.uk. This former coaching inn in the centre of town has had a successful makeover into a buzzy, boutique-style hotel. The rooms are stylish with comfy beds, coffee machines and flat-screen TVs, and the downstairs restaurant is good too, with a wood-fired pizza oven, plus local fish and meat dishes. **£150**

**La Fleur de Lys** Bleke St ☎01747 853717, ⓦ lafleurdelys.co.uk. Long-established hotel, with a range of comfortable rooms above a highly rated if pricey restaurant; the back rooms have the best views, while those at the front are on a busy through-road. **£135**

## EATING AND DRINKING

**The Mitre** 23 High St ☎01747 853002, ⓦ youngs .co.uk. A traditional pub with a terrace at the back giving lovely views; inside, there's a cosy dining room with a wood-burning stove and reasonably priced pub grub including steak and ale pie (£10). Mon–Thurs 10.30am–11pm, Fri & Sat 10.30am–midnight, Sun noon–10.30pm; food served summer noon–9pm; winter noon–3pm & 6–9pm.

★**The Salt Cellar** Gold Hill ☎01747 851838. Right at the top of the hill itself and with great views, this place serves inexpensive snacks and daily specials from around £8, including home-made pies, in the pillar-lined interior or at outdoor tables on the cobbles. Mon–Sat 9am–5pm, Sun 10am–5pm.

# Weymouth and around

Whether George III's passion for sea bathing was a symptom of his eventual madness is uncertain, but it was at **WEYMOUTH** that in 1789 he became the first reigning monarch to follow the craze. Sycophantic gentry rushed into the waves behind him, and soon the town, formerly a busy port, took on the elegant Georgian stamp that it bears today.

A lively family holiday destination in summer, Weymouth reverts to a more sedate rhythm out of season. The highlight, of course, is its long sandy beach, but there are also a number of "all-weather" attractions in town. A few buildings survive from pre-Georgian times: the restored **Tudor House** at 3 Trinity Street (May to mid-Oct Tues–Fri 1–3.45pm; Nov, Dec & Feb–April first Sun of month 2–4pm; £3.50; ☎01305 779711) and the ruins of **Sandsfoot Castle** (free access), built by Henry VIII, overlooking Portland Harbour. But Weymouth's most imposing architectural heritage stands along the **Esplanade**, a dignified range of bow-fronted and porticoed buildings gazing out across the graceful bay. At the far end of the Esplanade, the Quay juts out into the sea, housing the town's ferry terminals and its newest attraction, the 173ft-high **Sea Life Tower** (April–July & Sept–Oct daily 11am–5pm; Aug daily 11am–6pm; Nov–March Mon & Thurs–Sun 11am–3pm; from £5.40 or combined ticket with Sea Life Adventure Park £22.85, £15.50 online; ☎03333 212001, ⓦ sealifeweymouth .com), which provides stunning views over the town and coastline. Beyond here, the more intimate quayside of the **Old Harbour** is linked to the Esplanade by the pedestrianized **St Mary's Street**. At the other end of the promenade, in Lodmoor Country Park, the excellent **Sea Life Park** (daily March–Oct 10am–5pm, Nov–Feb 10am–4pm; last admission 1hr before closing; combined ticket with Sea Life Tower £22.85, £15.50 online; ☎03333 212001, ⓦ sealifeweymouth.com) is home to turtles, penguins, otters and seals, as well as a sea-horse breeding centre, and the crocodile creek log flume ride.

Just south of the town stretch the giant arms of Portland Harbour, and a long causeway links Weymouth to the **Isle of Portland**. The causeway stands on the easternmost section of the eighteen-mile bank of pebbles known as Chesil Beach (see p.220), running northwest towards the fishing port of **West Bay**.

## ARRIVAL AND INFORMATION                                                                    WEYMOUTH

**By train** Weymouth is served at least hourly by trains from London (2hr 45min), Southampton (1hr 25min–1hr 40min), Bournemouth (50min) and Poole (35–45min), with less regular services from Bristol (2hr 30min) and Bath (2hr 10min); trains arrive at the station on King St, a couple of mins' walk back from the seafront.

**By bus** Buses from Dorchester (3–4 hourly; 30min) pull in at the stops by King George III's statue.

**Tourist office** A volunteer-run information service is based in Weymouth Pavilion, The Esplanade (daily 10am–6pm; ☎ 01305 783225, ⓦ visitweymouth.co.uk).

## ACCOMMODATION

★**Bay View House** 35 The Esplanade ☎ 01305 782083, ⓦ bayview-weymouth.co.uk. Clean, friendly and well-kept guesthouse. The comfortable room at the front with a bay window overlooking the sea is great value (it's just a little bit costlier than the others). Also has family rooms and free private garage parking. **£60**

**Old Harbour View** 12 Trinity Rd ☎ 01305 774633, ⓦ oldharbourview.co.uk. Cosy guesthouse in a great location right on the harbourfront. It consists of just two

rooms in a Georgian townhouse, but it's worth paying a few pounds extra for the one at the front with a harbour view. The breakfasts are great, using locally sourced and free-range ingredients. **£86**

**The Seaham** 3 Waterloo Place ☎ 01305 782010, ⓦ the seahamweymouth.co.uk. Attractive Georgian terraced house at the quieter end of town. The rooms are comfortable and well furnished and some have sea views; breakfast includes a good choice of local free-range products. **£80**

## EATING AND DRINKING

**Enzos** 110 The Esplanade ☎ 01305 778666, ⓦ enzo -ristorante.co.uk. Traditional Italian restaurant, but with clean, contemporary decor, tiled floors and modern furnishings; it's right on the seafront, but slightly away from the hubbub of the main drag. It serves a range of pasta dishes (£8–10), as well as daily local specials, such as linguine lobster (£15). Excellent value. Daily 12.30– 2.30pm & 5.30–10.30pm.

**Floods Bistro** 19 Custom House Quay ☎ 01305 772270, ⓦ floodsrestaurant.co.uk. Small harbourfront restaurant

with a few outside tables, serving top-quality fresh fish – try the skate wing with mussels and herb sauce (£13), or they may even have lobster or John Dory depending on the catch of the day. Daily noon–2.30pm & 7–11pm.

**Phoenix Bakery Cafe** 6–7 Coburg ☎ 01305 767894, ⓦ phoenixbakery.co.uk. This artisan bakery is a great place to pick up supplies for a picnic, including warm pastries, cakes and savouries straight from the oven – or check out the delicious mushroom and cheese bruschettas for lunch, while watching the bakers at work. Daily 9am–4pm.

# Isle of Portland

Stark, wind-battered and treeless, the **Isle of Portland** is famed above all for its hard white limestone, which has been quarried here for centuries – Wren used it for St Paul's Cathedral, and it clads the UN headquarters in New York. It was also used for the 6000ft breakwater that protects Portland Harbour – the largest artificial harbour in Britain, built by convicts in the nineteenth century and the main centre for the 2012 Olympic Games sailing events. It is still surveyed by **Portland Castle** (daily: April–Sept 10am–6pm; Oct & Nov 10am–5pm; £4.90; EH; ☎ 01305 820539, ⓦ englishheritage .org.uk/daysout/properties/portland-castle), which was commissioned by Henry VIII. Southeast of here, the craggy limestone of the Isle rises to 496ft at Verne Hill. At **Portland Bill**, the southern tip of the island, you can climb the 153 steps of **Portland Lighthouse** (Easter–June Sun–Thurs 11am–5pm; July–Sept Sun–Fri 11am–5pm; £4; ☎ 01305 820495), which dates from 1906, for superb views in all directions.

## ARRIVAL AND INFORMATION                                                                      PORTLAND

**By bus** First Bus runs bus #1 every 10 min from Commercial Road in Weymouth to Portland (30–40min).

## EATING AND DRINKING

**Cove House Inn** 91 Chiswell ☎ 01305 820895, ⓦ thecovehouseinn.co.uk. A good spot for food or a quick drink, with pub staples, such as burgers (£8), as well as a daily local fish menu, featuring such treats as scallops with

chilli, garlic and cream (£11). It's cosy inside with a wood-burner and big windows with sea views, while the outside tables look over Chesil Beach. Mon–Sat 11am–11pm, Sun noon–10.30pm.

**Crab House Café** Ferrymans Way, Portland Rd at the entrance to the Portland causeway ☎ 01305 788867, ⓦ crabhousecafe.co.uk. In a great location overlooking Chesil Beach, this upmarket beach shack is renowned for its superb, locally caught fresh fish and seafood, including oysters from its own beds. The menu changes daily according to the catch, but expect dishes such as turbot steak poached in saffron cream with mussels (£22). There are tables outside, and reservations are advised for the restaurant, though you may be lucky to squeeze into the café area. Wed & Thurs noon–2pm & 6–9pm, Fri & Sat noon–2.30pm & 6–9.30pm, Sun noon–3.30pm.

## Chesil Beach

**Chesil Beach** is the strangest feature of the Dorset coast, a 200yd-wide, 50ft-high bank of pebbles that extends for eighteen miles, its component stones gradually decreasing in size from fist-like pebbles at Portland to "pea gravel" at Burton Bradstock in the west. This sorting is an effect of the powerful coastal currents, which make this one of the most dangerous beaches in Europe – churchyards in the local villages display plenty of evidence of wrecks and drownings. Though not a swimming beach, Chesil is popular with sea anglers, and its wild, uncommercialized atmosphere makes an appealing antidote to the south-coast resorts. Behind the beach, **The Fleet**, a brackish lagoon, was the setting for J. Meade Faulkner's classic smuggling tale, *Moonfleet*.

### ACCOMMODATION

★ **East Shilvinghampton Farm** Portesham ☎ 01420 80804, ⓦ featherdown.co.uk. A lovely farm in a beautiful valley, a couple of miles inland from the Fleet Lagoon. It has seven spacious, luxurious tents to rent – ready-erected, with running water, a toilet, a wood-burning stove and comfortable beds – in an idyllic field that looks down the valley, with horses, goats and chickens in the paddock next door. From **£200** for three nights

## Abbotsbury

At the point where Chesil Beach attaches itself to the shore is the pretty village of **ABBOTSBURY**, all tawny ironstone and thatch. The village has three main attractions, which can be visited individually or on a combined Passport ticket for £17.

The most absorbing is the **Swannery** (daily mid-March to Oct 10am–5pm; £10.95, ☎ 01305 871130), a wetland reserve for mute swans dating back to medieval times, when presumably it formed part of the abbot's larder. If you visit in late May or June, you'll see baby cygnets waddling around and squabbling at your feet. The eel-grass reeds through which the swans paddle were once harvested to thatch roofs throughout the region. One example can be seen on the fifteenth-century Tithe Barn, the last remnant of the abbey and today housing the **Children's Farm**, whose highlights include goat-racing and pony rides (mid-March to Aug & Oct half-term daily 10am–5pm; Sept & Oct Sat & Sun 10am–5pm; £9.50; ☎ 01305 871130). Lastly, in the **Subtropical Gardens** (daily: Nov–March 10am–4pm, April–Oct 10am–5pm; closed over Christmas period; £10.95; ☎ 01305 871387) delicate species thrive in the microclimate created by Chesil's stones, which act as a giant radiator to deter all but the worst frosts.

### INFORMATION                                                                    ABBOTSBURY

**Tourist office** West Yard Barn, West Street (☎ 01305 871130, ⓦ abbotsbury-tourism.co.uk).

# Bridport

Ten miles west of Abbotsbury is the pretty town of **BRIDPORT**, mentioned in the Domesday Book of 1086 and an important port before the rivers silted up in the early 1700s, leaving it stranded a mile or so inland today. It's a pleasant old town of solid brick buildings with very wide streets, a hangover from its days as a major rope-making centre when cords were stretched between the houses to be twisted and dyed. Today, it's a lively **market** town (Wed & Sat) with an arty, alternative vibe. The town's harbour lies a mile or so south at **West Bay**, which has a fine sandy beach sheltered below majestic red cliffs – the sheer East Cliffs are a tempting challenge for intrepid walkers – and made a suitably brooding location for the ITV murder series, *Broadchurch*.

## ACCOMMODATION, EATING AND DRINKING BRIDPORT AND AROUND

**The Bull** 34 East St ☎01308 422878, ⓦthebullhotel .co.uk. Friendly, boutique-style hotel in a former seventeenth-century coaching inn in the centre of town. The rooms are comfortable and modern, with Neal's Yard toiletries: there are some family rooms, too. The restaurant and bar are good, too: try the Lyme Bay scallops (£9.50) to start, followed by a 12oz rib-eye steak (£21). Daily noon–3pm & 6.30–9.30pm. **£100**

★ **Hive Beach Café** Beach Rd, Burton Bradstock, 3 miles east of Bridport ☎01308 897070, ⓦhivebeachcafe .co.uk. Laidback café/restaurant on the beach, serving top-quality seafood, such as baked halibut (£17) and grilled Cornish sardines (£11). If your budget can stretch to it, splash out on the fabulous seafood platter featuring local lobster, crab and scallops (£60 for two). Also delicious home-made cakes, excellent coffee, good breakfasts and very friendly service. Hours vary according to the season, but if it's a

nice day they will almost certainly be open.

★ **Norburton Hall** Shipton Lane, Burton Bradstock ☎01308 897007, ⓦnorburtonhall.com. The Edwardian *Norburton Hall* is a great place to stay, with six acres of rolling grounds close to the beach at Burton Bradstock. It has three beautifully furnished en-suite bedrooms, one with a four-poster bed: grand without being too formal, it also has several self-catering cottages to rent in the outbuildings. Cottages from **£420**/week; B&B **£130**

**The Riverside** West Bay ☎01308 422011, ⓦthefishrestaurant-westbay.co.uk. Reservations are recommended for this renowned restaurant which offers fresh, sumptuous fish and seafood and fine river views. There is a daily changing menu, but expect the likes of grilled John Dory with chargrilled peppers (£22). The two-course mid-week lunch menu is good value at around £20. Tues–Sat noon–2.30pm 6.30–9pm, Sun noon–2.30pm.

# Lyme Regis

**LYME REGIS**, Dorset's most westerly town, shelters snugly between steep, fossil-filled cliffs. Its intimate size and photogenic qualities make this a popular and congested spot in high summer, with some upmarket literary associations – Jane Austen summered in a seafront cottage and set part of *Persuasion* in Lyme (the town appears in the 1995 film version), while novelist John Fowles lived here until his death in 2005 (the film adaptation of his book, *The French Lieutenant's Woman*, was shot here).

Colourwashed cottages and elegant Regency and Victorian villas line its seafront and flanking streets, but Lyme's best-known feature is a practical reminder of its commercial origins: **the Cobb**, a curving harbour wall originally built in the thirteenth century. It has suffered many alterations since, most notably in the nineteenth century, when its massive boulders were clad in neater blocks of Portland stone.

On Bridge Street, the excellent **Lyme Regis Museum** (Easter–Oct Mon–Sat 10am–5pm, Sun 11am–5pm; Nov–Easter Wed–Sun, plus Mon & Tues in school hols 11am–4pm; £3.95; ☎01297 443370, ⓦlymeregismuseum.co.uk) displays artefacts related to the town's literary connections, including John Fowles' office chair, and provides a crash course in local history and geology, while **Dinosaurland** on Coombe Street (late Feb to late Oct daily 10am–4pm; sporadic openings at other times; £5; ☎01297 443541, ⓦdinosaurland.co.uk), fills out the story of ammonites and other local fossils. The town is also something of a foodie destination, with lots of superb fish restaurants and good pubs, plus the **Town Mill Complex** (ⓦtownmill.org.uk) in Mill Lane, just off Coombe Street, where there's a fantastic cheese shop, local brewery and café, as well as a working mill, pottery and art gallery.

## ARRIVAL AND INFORMATION LYME REGIS

**By train** Lyme's nearest station is in Axminster, 5 miles north, served by regular trains from London Waterloo and

Exeter: bus #31 runs from the station to Lyme, then on to Weymouth.

**3**

---

### LYME'S JURASSIC COAST

The cliffs around Lyme are made up of a complex layer of limestone, greensand and unstable clay, a perfect medium for preserving **fossils**, which are exposed by landslips of the waterlogged clays. In 1811, after a fierce storm caused parts of the cliffs to collapse, 12-year-old Mary Anning, a keen fossil-hunter, discovered an almost complete dinosaur skeleton, a 30ft ichthyosaurus now displayed in London's Natural History Museum.

Hands-off inspection of the area's complex **geology** can be enjoyed all around the town: as you walk along the seafront and out towards The Cobb, look for the outlines of ammonites in the walls and paving stones. To the west of Lyme, the **Undercliff** is a fascinating jumble of overgrown landslips, now a nature reserve, where a great path wends its way through the undergrowth for around seven miles to neighbouring Seaton in Devon. East of Lyme, a huge landslip in 2008 closed the Dorset Coast Path to **Charmouth** (Jane Austen's favourite resort), as well as blocking the two-mile beach route to the resort, which was previously walkable at low tide. At Charmouth, you can take the coastal path leading to the headland of **Golden Cap**, whose brilliant outcrop of auburn sandstone is crowned with gorse.

---

**By bus** First Buses (ⓦ firstgroup.com) runs a daily bus service from Exeter (1hr 40min), Bridport (35min), Weymouth (1hr 40min) and Poole every couple of hours (3hr 20min).

**Tourist office** Church Street (April–Oct Mon–Sat 10am–5am, Sun 10am–4pm; Nov–March Mon–Sat 10am–3pm; ☎ 01297 442138, ⓦ lymeregis.org).

### ACCOMMODATION

**Alexandra Hotel** Pound St ☎ 01297 442010, ⓦ hotelalexandra.co.uk. Popular with honeymooners, this is the town's top hotel, located inside an eighteenth-century manor house with bleached wood floors and lovely gardens overlooking the sea. Many of the comfortable rooms have sea views, and there is also a highly rated restaurant. **£177**

**Old Lyme** 29 Coombe St ☎ 01297 442929, ⓦ oldlymeguesthouse.co.uk. Central guesthouse right in the town centre in a lovely 300-year-old stone former post office. There are six smallish but spruce bedrooms – one is a triple room and all are en suite, or with a private bathroom. **£80**

### EATING AND DRINKING

**Hix Oyster and Fish House** Cobb Rd ☎ 01297 446910, ⓦ hixoysterandfishhouse.co.uk. In a lovely location overlooking the town and sea, this airy restaurant, owned by acclaimed chef Mark Hix, specializes in local fish and seafood: sublime main courses include Portland black bream (£20), though there are cheaper options, like fish pie (£15). April–Oct daily noon–10pm; Nov–March Tues–Sat noon–10pm, Sun noon–6pm.

**Royal Standard** 25 Marine Parade ☎ 01297 442637, ⓦ theroyalstandardlymeregis.co.uk. Beachside inn dating back four hundred years, with a log fire inside, and a great sea-facing beer garden that leads onto the beach. There are real ales on tap, brewed by Palmers in nearby Bridport, and decently priced pub grub (from £9). Daily 10am–11pm; food served noon–9pm.

**Tierra Kitchen** 1a Coombe St ☎ 01297 445189,

ⓦ tierrakitchen.co.uk. Overlooking the mill stream, *Tierra Kitchen* is a bright vegetarian restaurant serving a range of tasty seasonal dishes such as butternut squash and cheddar sausages, meze and vegetable tagine (£7–9) or evening meals like pistachio tortilla and pumpkin gnocchi (around £14). It also serves coffees, cakes and pastries. Thurs–Sat 11am–3pm & 6–10pm, Sun 11am–3pm.

**Town Mill Bakery** 2 Coombe St ☎ 01297 444754, ⓦ townmillbakery.com. A wonderful bakery/café serving a superb array of breads, cakes and muffins all freshly baked on the premises. The ingredients are mostly local and largely organic, with sublime breakfasts of home-made jam, boiled eggs and local honey – choose your bread and toast it yourself, then sit at the long wooden communal tables. Lunch includes home-made soup and pizzas (from £7). Tues–Sun 8.30am–4pm, til 8pm in summer.

# Salisbury and around

**SALISBURY**, huddled below Wiltshire's chalky plain in the converging valleys of the Avon and Nadder, sprang into existence in the early thirteenth century, when the bishopric was moved from nearby **Old Sarum** (see p.225). Today, it looks from a distance very much as it did when Constable painted his celebrated view of it, and though traffic may clog its centre, this prosperous and well-kept city is designed on a pleasantly human scale, with no sprawling suburbs or high-rise buildings to challenge the supremacy of the cathedral's immense spire. The city's inspiring silhouette is best admired by taking a twenty-minute walk through the water meadows southwest of the centre to the suburb of **Harnham**.

North of Salisbury stretches a hundred thousand acres of chalky upland, known as **Salisbury Plain**; it's managed by the Ministry of Defence whose presence has protected it from development and intensive farming, thereby preserving species that are all but extinct elsewhere in England (see box, p.225). Though largely deserted today, in previous times Salisbury Plain positively throbbed with communities. Stone Age, Bronze Age and Iron Age settlements left hundreds of burial mounds scattered over the chalklands, as well as major complexes at Danebury, Badbury, Figsbury, **Old Sarum**, and, of course, the great circle of **Stonehenge**, England's most famous historical monument. To the west, Salisbury's hinterland also includes one of Wiltshire's great country mansions, **Wilton House**, as well as Stourhead and Longleat Safari Park.

## Salisbury Cathedral

Daily Mon–Sat 9am–5pm, Sun noon–4pm • **Chapter House** April–Oct Mon–Sat 9.30am–4.30pm, Sun 12.45–3.45pm; Nov–March Mon–Sat 10am–4.30pm, Sun 12.45–3.45pm • £6.50 suggested donation • **Tower tours** April–Sept Mon–Sat at least one daily, usually at 1.15pm, up to 5 a day at busy times; advance booking recommended on ☎ 01722 555120 • £10 • ⓦ salisburycathedral.org.uk

Begun in 1220, **Salisbury Cathedral** was mostly completed within forty years and is thus unusually consistent in its style, with one prominent exception – the **spire**, which was added a century later and, at 404ft, is the highest in England. Its survival is something of a miracle, for the foundations penetrate only about 6ft into marshy ground, and when Christopher Wren surveyed it he found the spire to be leaning almost 2.5ft out of true. He added further tie rods, which finally arrested the movement.

The interior is over-austere, but there's an amazing sense of space and light in its high nave, despite the sombre pillars of grey Purbeck marble, which are visibly bowing beneath the weight they bear. Monuments and carved tombs line the walls. Don't miss the octagonal **chapter house,** which displays a rare original copy of the Magna Carta, and whose walls are decorated with a frieze of scenes from the Old Testament.

### The Close

Surrounding the cathedral is the **Close**, a peaceful precinct of lawns and mellow old buildings. Most of the houses have seemly Georgian facades, though some, like the Bishop's Palace and the deanery, date from the thirteenth century. **Mompesson House** (mid-March to Oct Mon–Wed, Sat & Sun 11am–5pm; £5.70, garden only £1; NT; ☎ 01722 420980, ⓦ nationaltrust.org.uk/mompesson-house), built by a wealthy merchant in 1701, contains some beautifully furnished eighteenth-century rooms and a superbly carved staircase. Also in the Close is the **King's House**, home to the **Salisbury and South Wiltshire Museum** (Oct–May Mon–Sat 10am–5pm; June–Sept Mon–Sat 10am–5pm & Sun noon–5pm; £5; ☎ 01722 332151, ⓦ salisburymuseum.org.uk) – an absorbing account of local history.

## Around the Market Square

The Close's **North Gate** opens onto the centre's older streets, where narrow pedestrianized alleyways bear names like Fish Row and Salt Lane, indicative of their trading origin. Many half-timbered houses and inns have survived, and the last of four market crosses, **Poultry Cross**, stands on stilts in Silver Street, near the Market Square. The market, held on Tuesdays and Saturdays, still serves a large agricultural area, as it did in earlier times when the city grew wealthy on wool. Nearby, the church of **St Thomas** – named after Thomas à Becket – is worth a look inside for its carved timber

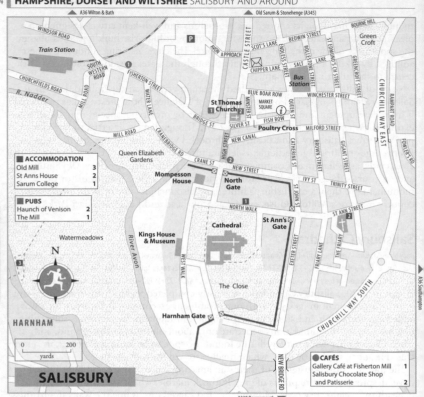

roof and "Doom painting" over the chancel arch, depicting Christ presiding over the Last Judgment. Dating from 1475, it's the largest of its kind in England.

## ARRIVAL AND DEPARTURE

SALISBURY

**By train** Trains from London arrive half a mile west of Salisbury's centre, on South Western Road.
Destinations Bath (hourly; 55min); Bristol (hourly; 1hr 10min); London Waterloo (every 30min; 1hr 30min); Portsmouth (hourly; 1hr 20min); Southampton (every 30min; 30min–50min).
**By bus** Buses stop at various sites around the city centre.
Destinations Bournemouth (Mon–Sat every 30min, Sun hourly; 1hr 15min); London (1 daily; 3hr 15min); Southampton (Mon–Sat hourly; 1hr 10min).

## INFORMATION AND TOURS

**Tourist office** Fish Row, just off Market Square (Mon–Fri 9am–5pm, Sat 10am–4pm, Sun & bank hols 10am–2pm; ☎ 01722 3428606, ⓦ visitwiltshire.co.uk) and is the starting point for informative and inexpensive guided walks of the city.

**Bus tours** Tours to Stonehenge and Old Sarum depart from the train station (bus only £14, with entry to Old Sarum and Stonehenge £28; ☎ 01722 336855, ⓦ thestonehengetour.info) every 30min in summer, and hourly in winter.

## ACCOMMODATION

★ **Old Mill** Town Path, Harnham ☎ 01722 327517, ⓦ signature-hospitality.com. The fully equipped rooms of this riverside pub have great views across the meadows to the cathedral. The location feels really rural but is just a short walk from the city centre. Real ales are on tap in the bar, and there's

an adjoining restaurant serving good local food. **£110**
**St Anns House** 32–34 St Ann St ☎ 01722 335657, ⓦ stannshouse.co.uk. A well-restored Georgian townhouse with stylish, comfortable rooms in a quiet street a short walk from the cathedral. **£90**

★**Sarum College** 19 The Close ☎01722 424800, ⓦsarum.ac.uk. By no means luxurious but in the best location in Salisbury, this friendly ecumenical college rents out simple en-suite doubles with views over The Close and cathedral, plus others without private facilities. There's also a decent common room, and breakfast is included. **£100**

### EATING AND DRINKING

★**Gallery Café at Fisherton Mill** 108 Fisherton St ☎01722 500200, ⓦfishertonmill.co.uk. Great café within a renovated mill/art gallery serving delicious soups (£4.50), sandwiches on stone-baked bread (£5.60) and main courses such as salmon with artichoke (£13). Upstairs, you can watch artists at work in their studios, weaving and making jewellery. Tues–Fri 10am–5pm, Sat 9.30am–5pm. Also open for dinner sporadically; check website.

★**Haunch of Venison** 1 Minster St ☎01722 411313. One of the city's most atmospheric and historic pubs, with a wonderful warren of rooms, and a fireplace dating from 1588. The quirky, sloping-floored restaurant serves interesting dishes such as venison and redcurrant sausages (£11) and crackled pork belly with cider mustard sauce (£17). Daily 11am–11pm.

**The Mill** 7 The Maltings ☎01722 412127, ⓦgkpubs .co.uk/pubs-in-salisbury/mill-pub. Large, lively, popular pub whose main attraction is its lovely riverside location, right in the city centre. Standard pub meals, such as sausage and mash and bbq ribs, and real ales are available, as well as tea and coffee until 9pm. Mon–Thurs & Sun 11am–11pm, Fri & Sat 11am–midnight ; food served daily 11am–9pm.

**Salisbury Chocolate Shop and Patisserie** 33 High St ☎01722 327422, ⓦchocolatesandpatisserie.com. Long-established and popular café/chocolate shop with tables outside on a pedestrianized street. It serves delicious cakes and croissants baked daily – the hot chocolate is particularly tasty, and there's a good range of coffees too. Mon–Sat 9.30am–5pm, Sun noon–5pm.

## Old Sarum

2 miles north of Salisbury • Daily: July & Aug 9am–6pm; Sept–June 10am–5pm • £4; EH • ☎01722 335398, ⓦenglish-heritage.org.uk

The ruins of **Old Sarum** occupy a bleak hilltop site. Possibly occupied up to five thousand years ago, then developed as an Iron Age fort whose double protective ditches remain, it was settled by Romans and Saxons before the Norman bishopric of Sherborne was moved here in the 1070s. Within a couple of decades a new **cathedral** had been consecrated at Old Sarum, and a large religious community was living alongside the soldiers in the central castle. Old Sarum was an uncomfortable place, parched and windswept, and in 1220 the dissatisfied clergy – additionally at loggerheads with the castle's occupants – appealed to the pope for permission to decamp to Salisbury (still known officially as New Sarum). When permission was granted, the stone from the cathedral was commandeered for Salisbury's gateways, and once the church had gone the population waned. By the nineteenth century Old Sarum was deserted, and today the dominant features of the site are huge earthworks, banks and ditches, with a broad trench encircling the rudimentary remains of the Norman palace, castle and cathedral.

## Stonehenge

9 miles north of Salisbury • Daily: mid-March to May & Sept to mid-Oct 9.30am–7pm; June–Aug 9am–8pm; mid-Oct to mid-March 9.30am–5pm; last entry 2hr before closing; advance booking of timed tickets essential • £14.90; EH • ☎0870 333 1181, ⓦenglish -heritage.org.uk/Stonehenge • Shuttle buses to the site leave every 10min from the visitor centre

No ancient structure in England arouses more controversy than **Stonehenge**, a

---

### THE GREAT BUSTARDS OF SALISBURY PLAIN

The empty expanses of Salisbury Plain are home to the country's only colony of **Great Bustards**, the world's heaviest flying bird, which became extinct in the UK in the 1840s. Chicks were reintroduced here from Russia in 2004 to a secret location, and the first Great Bustard to be born in the UK in nearly two hundred years appeared in 2009. Visits can be arranged to see the 3ft-high birds: you will be taken in a landrover to a hide, from where you can view the birds in their natural habitat (£10/person; call ☎01980 671466 or see ⓦgreatbustard.org for details).

**3**

## STONEHENGE – A BRIEF HISTORY

Some people may find **Stonehenge** underwhelming, but understanding a little of its history and ancient significance gives an insight into its mystical appeal. What exists today is only a small part of the original prehistoric complex, as many of the outlying stones were probably plundered by medieval and later farmers for building materials. The **construction** of Stonehenge is thought to have taken place in several stages. In about 3000 BC the outer circular bank and ditch were built, just inside which was dug a ring of 56 pits, which at a later date were filled with a mixture of earth and human ash. Around 2500 BC the first stones were raised within the earthworks, comprising approximately forty great blocks of dolerite (bluestone), whose ultimate source was Preseli in Wales. Some archeologists have suggested that these monoliths were found lying on Salisbury Plain, having been borne down from the Welsh mountains by a glacier in the last Ice Age, but the lack of any other glacial debris on the plain would seem to disprove this theory. It really does seem to be the case that the stones were cut from quarries in Preseli and dragged or floated here on rafts, a prodigious task that has defeated recent attempts to emulate it.

The crucial phase in the creation of the site came during the next six hundred years, when the incomplete bluestone circle was transformed by the construction of a circle of 25 **trilithons** (two uprights crossed by a lintel) and an inner horseshoe formation of five trilithons. Hewn from Marlborough Downs sandstone, these colossal stones (called sarsens), ranging from 13ft to 21ft in height and weighing up to thirty tons, were carefully dressed and worked – for example, to compensate for perspectival distortion the uprights have a slight swelling in the middle, the same trick as the builders of the Parthenon were to employ hundreds of years later. More bluestones were arranged in various patterns within the outer circle over this period. The purpose of all this work remains baffling, however. The symmetry and location of the site (a slight rise in a flat valley with even views of the horizon in all directions) as well as its alignment towards the points of sunrise and sunset on the summer and winter solstices tend to support the supposition that it was some sort of observatory or time-measuring device. The site ceased to be used at around 1600 BC, and by the Middle Ages it had become a "landmark". Recent excavations have revealed the existence of a much larger settlement here than had previously been thought – the most substantial Neolithic village of this period to be found on the British mainland in fact – covering a wide area.

mysterious ring of monoliths. While archeologists argue over whether it was a place of ritual sacrifice and sun-worship, an astronomical calculator or a royal palace, the guardians of the site have struggled for years to accommodate its year-round visitors, particularly during the summer **solstice**, when crowds of 35,000 or more gather to watch the sunrise.

Access to the stones themselves is via a **shuttle-bus service** from a smart new **visitor centre** that opened in 2013, after years of debate and planning. This low-rise, environmentally sensitive pair of buildings includes a shop, café and **exhibition** space combining archeological remains from the area with high-tech interactive displays explaining the significance and history of it all. Outside, you can look round a cluster of recreated Neolithic houses, and try your hand at pulling a life-size Preseli bluestone. Perhaps a more fitting way to approach to the site, however, is on foot – it's a pleasant, way-marked thirty-minute walk across fields to the stones.

## Wilton House

5 miles west of Salisbury • **House** Easter & May–Aug Sun–Thurs & bank hol Sat 11.30am–5pm • £14.50 (includes grounds) • **Grounds** Middle two weeks of April plus May to mid-Sept daily 11am–5.30pm • £6

The splendid **Wilton House** dominates the village of Wilton, renowned for its carpet industry. The original Tudor house, built for the first earl of Pembroke on the site of a dissolved Benedictine abbey, was ruined by fire in 1647 and rebuilt by Inigo Jones, whose classic hallmarks can be seen in the sumptuous Single Cube and Double Cube rooms, so called because of their precise dimensions.

The easel **paintings** are what makes Wilton really special, however – the collection includes works by Van Dyck, Rembrandt, two of the Brueghel family, Poussin, Andrea del Sarto and Tintoretto. In the grounds, the famous **Palladian Bridge** has been joined by various ancillary attractions including an adventure playground and an audiovisual show on the colourful earls of Pembroke.

## Stourhead

25 miles west of Salisbury • **House** Mid-Feb to mid-March Sat & Sun 11am–3pm; mid-March to Oct daily 11am–4.30pm; Nov daily 11am–3.30pm; Dec Fri–Sun 11am–3pm • £8.80, £14.70 with garden; NT • **Gardens** mid-April to Sept daily 9am–7pm; Oct to mid-April daily 9am–5pm • £8.80, £14.70 with house • **King Alfred's Tower** March–Oct Sat & Sun noon–4pm • £3.60 • ☎01747 841152, ⓦnationaltrust.org.uk/stourhead

Landscape gardening was a favoured mode of display among the grandest eighteenth-century landowners, and **Stourhead** is one of the most accomplished examples of the genre. The Stourton estate was bought in 1717 by Henry Hoare, who commissioned Colen Campbell to build a new villa in the Palladian style. Hoare's heir, another Henry, returned from his Grand Tour in 1741 with his head full of the paintings of Claude and Poussin, and determined to translate their images of well-ordered, wistful classicism into real life. He dammed the Stour to create a lake, then planted the terrain with blocks of trees, domed temples, stone bridges, grottoes and statues, all mirrored vividly in the water. The house itself is of minor interest, though it has some good Chippendale furniture, but it is the stunning **gardens** that are the highlight. At the entrance, you can pick up a map detailing a lovely two-mile walk around the lake. The estate itself is vast and includes a pub, a church, a farm shop (a good place to pick up a picnic), plus **King Alfred's Tower**, three miles or so from the main entrance (you can drive round the estate and park by the tower, if it's too far to walk). Built in 1772, it is one of England's oldest follies, and you can climb the two hundred or so steps up to the top for fine views across the estate and into neighbouring counties.

## Longleat

27 miles west of Salisbury • Opening hours and closing days vary throughout the season, but are generally 10am–5pm, 6pm or 7pm; check website for exact times and days • House and grounds only £13.95, all attractions £26.77 • ☎ 01985 844400, ⓦ longleat.co.uk

The African savanna intrudes into the bucolic Wiltshire countryside at **Longleat** safari and adventure park. In 1946 the sixth marquess of Bath became the first stately-home owner to open his house to the paying public on a regular basis, and in 1966 he caused even more amazement when Longleat's Capability Brown landscapes were turned into England's first drive-through **safari park,** with lions, tigers, giraffes and rhinos on show, plus monkeys clambering all over your car. Other attractions followed, including a large hedge maze, a *Doctor Who* exhibition, high-tech simulators, and the seventh marquess's saucy murals (children not admitted). Beyond the razzmatazz, there's an exquisitely furnished Elizabethan house, with an enormous library and a fine collection of pictures, including Titian's *Holy Family*.

# Avebury

The village of **AVEBURY** stands in the midst of a **stone circle** (free access) that rivals Stonehenge – the individual stones are generally smaller, but the circle itself is much wider and more complex. A massive earthwork 20ft high and 1400ft across encloses the main circle, which is approached by four causeways across the inner ditch, two of them leading into wide avenues stretching over a mile beyond the circle. It was probably built soon after 2500 BC, and presumably had a similar ritual or religious function to Stonehenge. The structure of Avebury's diffuse circle is quite difficult to grasp, but there are plans on the site, and the nearby museum (see p.228) has further details and background on the site.

## Alexander Keiller Museum

Daily: April–Oct 10am–6pm; Nov–March 10am–4pm • £4.90; NT • ☎ 01672 539250, ⓦ nationaltrust.org.uk/avebury

You can get an excellent overview of the Avebury stones and their significance at the nearby **Alexander Keiller Museum**, at the western entrance. The museum is housed in two separate buildings: the **Stables Gallery** houses some of Keiller's original finds, while the seventeenth-century **Barn Gallery** has exhibits on local archeology, interactive displays plus activities for children.

## Avebury Manor

Thurs–Tues: mid-Feb to March & Nov to mid-Dec 11am–4pm; March–Oct 11am–5pm • £10; NT • ☎ 01672 539250, ⓦ nationaltrust.org
.uk/avebury

Built on the site of a former priory, the pretty sixteenth-century **Avebury Manor** has been recently refurbished by BBC TV's *The Manor Reborn* programme. Unlike most National Trust properties, little of the house's original decoration remained, and almost all the furnishings here have been recreated or purchased, so as you wander round the house, you can lie on the beds, sit on the sofas and even play billiards in the Billiards Room. The gardens have been replanted too, with topiary and walled gardens, and there's a vintage-style tearoom in the former West Library.

## Silbury Hill and West Kennet Long Barrow

Just outside Avebury, the neat green mound of **Silbury Hill** is disregarded by the majority of drivers whizzing by on the A4. At 130ft it's no great height, but when you realize it's the largest prehistoric artificial mound in Europe, and was made using nothing more than primitive spades, it commands more respect. It was probably constructed around 2600 BC, and though no one knows quite what it was for, the likelihood is that it was a burial mound. You can't actually walk on the hill – having admired it briefly from the car park, cross the road to the footpath that leads half a mile to the **West Kennet Long Barrow** (free access; NT & EH). Dating from about 3250 BC, this was definitely a chamber tomb – nearly fifty burials have been discovered here.

### ACCOMMODATION AND EATING                                    AVEBURY

**Circles** Next to the Barn Gallery ☎ 01672 539250. This National Trust café is your best bet for an inexpensive lunch, offering good meals and snacks, with plenty of veggie options and, of course, tasty cakes and cream teas. There's indoor seating in a converted farm building, and outdoor tables in the courtyard. Daily: April–Oct 10am–5.30pm; Nov–March 10am–4pm.

**Manor Farm** High St ☎ 01672 539294, ⓦ manorfarmavebury.com. A comfortable B&B on a working farm right in the centre of the village. There are three rooms, two of which have views over the Avebury stones, and there's also a private guests' sitting room. **£100**

# Lacock

**LACOCK**, twelve miles west of Avebury, is the perfect English feudal village, albeit one gentrified by the National Trust and besieged by tourists all summer, partly due to its fame as a location for several films and TV series – the recent *Harry Potter* films among others. The village's most famous son is photography pioneer **Henry Fox Talbot**, a member of the dynasty that has lived in the local abbey since it passed to Sir William Sharington on the Dissolution of the Monasteries in 1539. Fox Talbot was the first person to produce a photographic negative, and the **Fox Talbot Museum**, in a sixteenth-century barn by the abbey gates (daily: mid-Feb to Oct 10.30am–5.30pm; Nov to mid-Feb 11am–4pm; £12.50 including abbey, abbey garden and cloisters; NT; ☎ 01249 73045, ⓦ nationaltrust
.org.uk/lacock), captures something of the excitement he must have experienced as the dim outline of an oriel window in the abbey imprinted itself on a piece of silver nitrate paper.

The **abbey** itself (mid-Feb to Oct daily except Tues 11am–5pm; Nov to mid-Feb Sat & Sun noon–4pm; cloisters and grounds same hours as Fox Talbot museum; £12.50 including museum; NT; ☎01249 73045, ☯nationaltrust.org.uk/lacock), preserves a few monastic fragments amid the eighteenth-century Gothic, while the church of **St Cyriac** (free access) contains the opulent tomb of Sir William Sharington himself, buried beneath a splendid barrel-vaulted roof.

## ARRIVAL AND DEPARTURE
LACOCK

**By bus** The #234 runs hourly from Chippenham and Frome, stopping outside the *George Inn* (☯firstgroup.com).

## ACCOMMODATION AND EATING

**Beechfield House Hotel** Beanacre, 2 miles south of Lacock ☎01225 703700, ☯beechfieldhouse.co.uk. This lovely country house hotel has comfortable rooms, an excellent restaurant and a heated outdoor pool all set in attractive grounds. It has family rooms and the service is friendly but professional. **£150**

**George Inn** 4 West St ☎01249 730263. A rambling, attractive pub with roaring fires and a dog-wheel (the dog powered the wheel to turn a spit over the fire). Good for a drink, with a variety of guest ales, plus decent pub food,

such as home-made pie of the day (£11.50). Mon–Thurs 11am–3pm & 6–11pm, Fri & Sat 11am–11pm, Sun 11am–10.30pm; food served noon–2.30pm & 6–9pm (closes 8.30pm on Sun).

**Lacock Pottery** The Tanyard, Church St ☎01249 730266, ☯lacockbedandbreakfast.com. Three comfortable B&B rooms in a lovely old building overlooking the church and the village. Breakfasts are good, featuring home-made bread and jams. **£90**, or **£100** at weekends

# Bradford-on-Avon

With its buildings of auburn stone and lovely river- and canalside walks, **BRADFORD-ON-AVON** is the most appealing town in Wiltshire's northwest corner. Sheltering against a steep wooded slope, it takes its name from its "broad ford" across the Avon, though the original fording place was replaced by a **bridge** dating mainly from the seventeenth century. The domed structure at one end is a quaint old jail converted from a chapel.

The local industry, based on textiles, was revolutionized with the arrival of Flemish weavers in 1659, and many of the town's handsome buildings reflect the prosperity of this period. Yet Bradford's most significant building is the tiny **Church of St Laurence** (April–Sept 10am–6pm; Oct–March 10am–4pm) on Church Street, an outstanding example of Saxon church architecture dating from 700 AD. Its distinctive feature is its carved angels over the chancel arch.

## ARRIVAL AND INFORMATION
BRADFORD-ON-AVON

**By train** The station is on St Margaret's Street, close to the town centre.
Destinations Bath (2 hourly; 15min); Bristol (2 hourly; 30min); Dorchester (every 2hr; 1hr 30min); and Salisbury (hourly; 45min).

**Tourist office** 50 St Margaret's Street (April–Oct Mon–Sat 10am–5pm, Sun 10am–4pm; Nov–March Mon–Sat 10am–4pm, Sun 11am–3pm; ☎01225 865797, ☯bradfordonavon.co.uk).

## ACCOMMODATION AND EATING

**Bradford Old Windmill** 4 Mason's Lane ☎01225 866842, ☯bradfordoldwindmill.co.uk. A characterful B&B based in a converted windmill, with a variety of quirky rooms, including a couple in the tower itself and one with a waterbed. **£100**

**Lock Inn Café** Frome Rd ☎01225 868068, ☯thelockinn.co.uk. This rambling café by the canal is the best place for an inexpensive meal at any time of the day, with interesting meals, such as feta fritters (£9) and jerk

chicken (£9) which you can eat in a series of Wendy houses or inside a moored canalboat. They also rent bikes and canoes. Mon & Sun 8.30am–6pm, Tues–Sat 8.30am–9pm.

**Priory Steps** Newtown ☎01225 862230, ☯priorysteps.co.uk. A family home converted from seventeenth-century weavers' cottages, with well-prepared dinners (by prior arrangement; £25) and excellent views from all the guest rooms over the rooftops of Bradford-on-Avon. **£92**

# Oxfordshire, the Cotswolds and around

BIBURY

# Oxfordshire, the Cotswolds and around

About sixty miles northwest of London, the small university city of Oxford is one of England's great urban set-pieces, presenting as impressive a collection of Gothic, Classical and Revival architecture as anywhere in Europe. Oxford anchors a diverse swathe of terrain that reaches across central southern England straddling the Chiltern Hills, a picturesque band of chalk uplands on the fringes of the capital. Close to the orbital M25 motorway this is commuter country, but further out a rural spirit survives from England's pre-industrial past, felt most tangibly in the Cotswolds, rolling hills between Oxford and Cheltenham that encompass some of the country's most celebrated landscapes and photogenic villages.

Covering much of **Oxfordshire** and **Gloucestershire**, the picture-postcard **Cotswolds** region is dotted with glorious honey-coloured villages, old churches and handsome stone mansions, with scenic drives galore and plenty of walking opportunities, not least on the long-distance Cotswolds Way. Highlights include the engaging market town of **Chipping Campden**, the delightful village of **Northleach** and bustling **Cirencester**. Within striking distance of Oxford are handsome **Woodstock**, a little town that lies alongside one of England's most imposing country homes, **Blenheim Palace**, and further south, **Henley-on-Thames**, an attractive spot on the river, famous for its regatta. To the west lies **Cheltenham**, an appealing Regency spa town famous for its horse-racing that serves as a base for visits to **Gloucester** cathedral.

Striking west from the Chilterns across the North Wessex Downs is the 85-mile-long **Ridgeway**, a prehistoric track – and now a national trail possessing a string of prehistoric sites, the most extraordinary being the gigantic chalk horse that gives the **Vale of White Horse** its name. Bordering south Oxfordshire, **Berkshire** has the royal residence of **Windsor Castle** as its focus, but can also offer a fine gallery in the Thames-side village of **Cookham**. Arching round to the north of London, the counties of **Buckinghamshire** and **Bedfordshire** have lower-key attractions, including a museum of the wartime codebreakers at **Bletchley**, on a looping route to the ancient town of **St Albans**.

## GETTING AROUND      OXFORDSHIRE, THE COTSWOLDS & AROUND

**By train** There are mainline train services from London's Paddington Station to Reading, Oxford, Cheltenham and Gloucester; trains from Paddington also stop at Cotswold villages including Kingham (midway between Burford and

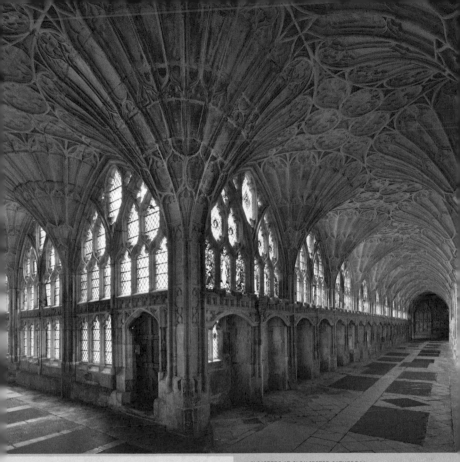

CLOISTERS AT GLOUCESTER CATHEDRAL

# Highlights

**❶ Oxford** One of Britain's most captivating cities, with dozens of historic colleges, memorable museums and an enjoyably lively undergraduate atmosphere. **See p.235**

**❷ Chipping Campden** Perfectly preserved medieval wool town, with honey-coloured houses lining its historic main street. **See p.260**

**❸ Cirencester** Self-styled "Capital of the Cotswolds", with a bustling marketplace overlooked by the superb Gothic church of St John the Baptist. **See p.263**

**❹ Festivals in Cheltenham** Cheltenham's three-day National Hunt Festival is one of the highlights of the British racing calendar, while the town also boasts lively festivals dedicated to folk, jazz, classical music, literature and science. See p.266

**❺ Gloucester Cathedral** The earliest – and one of the finest – examples of English Perpendicular architecture, topped by a magnificent tower. **See p.269**

**❻ Windsor Castle** The oldest and largest inhabited castle in the world – still an important ceremonial residence of the Queen, in the Berkshire countryside outside London **See p.272**

**HIGHLIGHTS ARE MARKED ON THE MAP ON P.234**

Stow-on-the-Wold) and Moreton-in-Marsh (between Stow-on-the-Wold and Chipping Campden). Oxford is also on the main cross-country line between Birmingham and Reading/Southampton. Chiltern line trains from London Marylebone also serve Oxford, as well as smaller stations in Buckinghamshire. Branch lines supplement the main routes.

**By bus** Long-distance buses stick mostly to the motorways, providing an efficient service to all the larger towns, but local services between the villages are patchy, sometimes nonexistent.

**By car** The Cotswolds are enclosed by the M5, M4 and M40, which, along with the M1 and AI(M) to the east, provide easy access.

# Oxford

When visitors think of **OXFORD**, they almost always imagine its **university**, revered as one of the world's great academic institutions, inhabiting honey-coloured stone buildings set around ivy-clad quadrangles. The image is accurate enough, but although the university dominates central Oxford both physically and spiritually, the wider city has an entirely different character, its economy built chiefly on the **factories** of Cowley, south of the centre. It was here that Britain's first mass-produced cars were produced in the 1920s and, although there have been more downs than ups in recent years, the plants are still vitally important to the area.

Oxford should be high on anyone's itinerary, and can keep you occupied for several days. The **colleges** include some of England's finest architecture, and the city also has some excellent **museums** and a good range of bars and restaurants.

**4**

## OXFORD'S COLLEGES

So where, exactly, is **Oxford University**? Everywhere – and nowhere. The university itself is nothing more than an administrative body, setting examinations and awarding degrees. Although it has its own offices (on Wellington Square), they are of no particular interest. What draws all the attention are the university's constituent **colleges** – 38 of them (plus another six religious foundations known as Permanent Private Halls), most occupying historic buildings scattered throughout the city centre. It is they which hold the 800-year-old history of the university, and exemplify its spirit.

The origins of the university are obscure, but it seems that the reputation of **Henry I**, the so-called "Scholar King", helped attract students in the early twelfth century. The first **colleges**, founded mostly by rich bishops, were essentially ecclesiastical institutions and this was reflected in collegiate rules and regulations – until 1877 lecturers were not allowed to marry, and women were not granted degrees until 1920.

There are common **architectural features** among the colleges, with the students' rooms and most of the communal areas – chapels, halls (dining rooms) and libraries – arranged around quadrangles (**quads**). Each, however, has its own character and often a label, whether it's the richest (St John's), most left-wing (Wadham) or most public-school-dominated (Christ Church). Collegiate rivalries are long established, usually revolving around sports, and tension between the city and the university – "Town" and "Gown" – has existed as long as the university itself.

### EXPLORING THE COLLEGES

All the more popular colleges have restricted **opening hours** – and may close totally during academic functions. Most now also impose an **admission charge**, while some (such as University and Queens) are out of bounds to outsiders. Regardless of published rules, it's always worth asking at the **porter's lodge**, at the main entrance of each college: porters have ultimate discretion and if you ask they may let you look around. One nice way to gain access is to attend choral evensong, held during term time and offering the chance to enjoy superb music in historic surroundings for free. New College Choir is generally reckoned to be the best, while Queens College and Merton are also good. Some colleges also **rent out student rooms** in the holidays (see p.246).

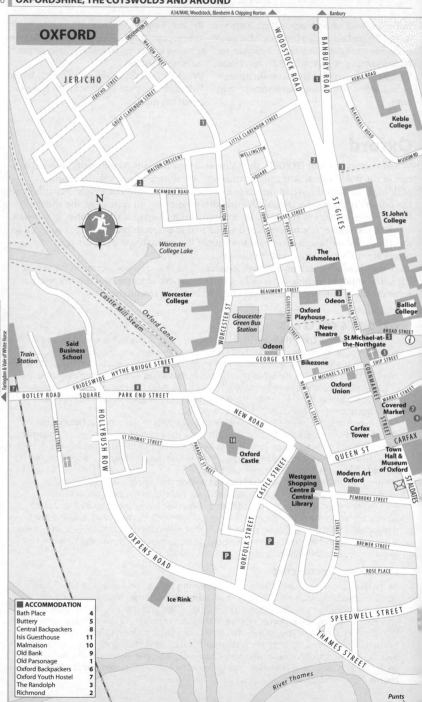

OXFORD

JERICHO

A34/M40, Woodstock, Blenheim & Chipping Norton — Banbury

OBSERVATION ST

WALTON STREET

JERICHO STREET

GREAT CLARENDON STREET

WOODSTOCK ROAD

BANBURY ROAD

KEBLE ROAD

BLACKHALL ROAD

Keble College

WALTON CRESCENT

LITTLE CLARENDON STREET

WELLINGTON SQUARE

M MUSEUM RD

RICHMOND ROAD

WALTON STREET

ST JOHN'S STREET

PUSEY STREET

PUSEY LANE

ST GILES

St John's College

Worcester College Lake

The Ashmolean

N

Worcester College

BEAUMONT STREET

GLOUCESTER STREET

Odeon

Balliol College

WORCESTER ST

Gloucester Green Bus Station

Oxford Playhouse

New Theatre

BROAD STREET

St Michael-at-the-Northgate

Train Station

Said Business School

Castle Mill Steam

Oxford Canal

Odeon

GEORGE STREET

Bikezone

SHIP STREET

CORNMARKET

HYTHE BRIDGE STREET

ST MICHAEL'S STREET

Oxford Union

FRIDESWIDE

BOTLEY ROAD

SQUARE

PARK END STREET

NEW INN HALL STREET

MARKET STREET

Covered Market

Farringdon & Vale of White Horse

BECKET STREET

HOLLYBUSH ROW

ST THOMAS' STREET

NEW ROAD

Carfax Tower

QUEEN ST

CARFAX

ST ALDATES

PARADISE STREET

Oxford Castle

CASTLE STREET

Westgate Shopping Centre & Central Library

Modern Art Oxford

Town Hall & Museum of Oxford

OXPENS ROAD

NORFOLK STREET

P

P

ST EBBE'S STREET

PEMBROKE STREET

BREWER STREET

ROSE PLACE

Ice Rink

SPEEDWELL STREET

THAMES STREET

River Thames

Punts

| ACCOMMODATION | |
|---|---|
| Bath Place | 4 |
| Buttery | 5 |
| Central Backpackers | 8 |
| Isis Guesthouse | 11 |
| Malmaison | 10 |
| Old Bank | 9 |
| Old Parsonage | 1 |
| Oxford Backpackers | 6 |
| Oxford Youth Hostel | 7 |
| The Randolph | 3 |
| Richmond | 2 |

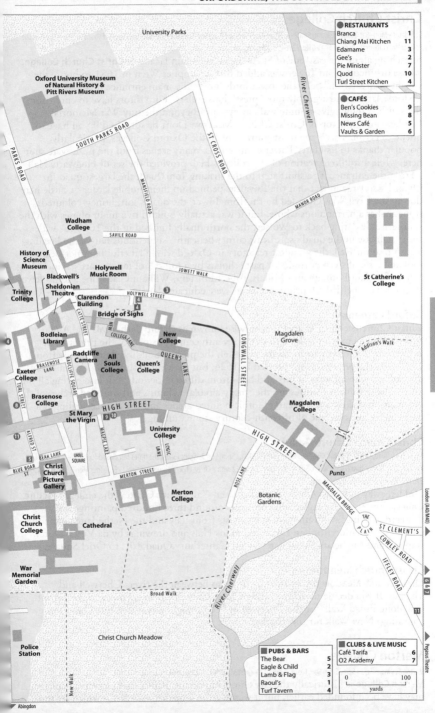

University Parks

River Cherwell

Oxford University Museum
of Natural History &
Pitt Rivers Museum

SOUTH PARKS ROAD

PARKS ROAD

ST CROSS ROAD

MANSFIELD ROAD

MANOR ROAD

Wadham
College

SAVILE ROAD

St Catherine's
College

History of
Science
Museum

Blackwell's

Holywell
Music Room

Sheldonian
Theatre

JOWETT WALK

Trinity
College

Clarendon
Building

HOLYWELL STREET

Bridge of Sighs

New
College

COLLEGE LANE

Magdalen
Grove

Addison's Walk

Bodleian
Library

Radcliffe
Camera

RADCLIFFE SQUARE

All
Souls
College

Queen's
College

QUEENS LANE

LONGWALL STREET

Exeter
College

BRASENOSE LANE

TURL STREET

Brasenose
College

HIGH STREET

St Mary
the Virgin

Magdalen
College

University
College

LOGIC LANE

ALFRED ST

BEAR LANE

ORIEL SQUARE

HIGH STREET

Christ
Church
Picture
Gallery

BLUE BOAR ST

MERTON STREET

ROSE LANE

Punts

MAGPIE LANE

Botanic
Gardens

MAGDALEN BRIDGE

Merton
College

London (A40/M40)

Christ
Church
College

Cathedral

THE PLAIN

ST CLEMENT'S

COWLEY ROAD

War
Memorial
Garden

IFFLEY ROAD

6 & 7

Broad Walk

River Cherwell

11

New Walk

Christ Church Meadow

Pegasus Theatre

Police
Station

Abingdon

● RESTAURANTS
| Branca | 1 |
| Chiang Mai Kitchen | 11 |
| Edamame | 3 |
| Gee's | 2 |
| Pie Minister | 7 |
| Quod | 10 |
| Turl Street Kitchen | 4 |

● CAFÉS
| Ben's Cookies | 9 |
| Missing Bean | 8 |
| News Café | 5 |
| Vaults & Garden | 6 |

■ PUBS & BARS
| The Bear | 5 |
| Eagle & Child | 2 |
| Lamb & Flag | 3 |
| Raoul's | 1 |
| Turf Tavern | 4 |

■ CLUBS & LIVE MUSIC
| Café Tarifa | 6 |
| O2 Academy | 7 |

| 0 | | 100 |
| yards | | |

4

## Christ Church College

St Aldates • Mon–Sat 10am–4.30pm, Sun 2–4.30pm • July & Aug £8.50, rest of year £7–8; discounts apply if you visit at times when the hall and/or cathedral are closed • ☎ 01865 276492, ⓦ chch.ox.ac.uk

Stretching along the east side of St Aldates is the main facade of **Christ Church College**, whose distinctive Tom Tower was added by Christopher Wren in 1681 to house the weighty "Great Tom" bell. The tower lords it over the main entrance of what is Oxford's largest and arguably most prestigious college, but visitors have to enter from the south, a signed five-minute walk away – just beyond the tiny War Memorial Garden and at the top of Christ Church Meadow. Don't be surprised if you have to queue to get in. This is the most touristy of all the Oxford Colleges, particularly popular thanks to its Harry Potter connections: many scenes from the films were shot here, while a studio recreation of the college's Hall provided the set of Hogwarts Hall.

From the entrance it's a short step to the striking **Tom Quad**, the largest quad in Oxford – so large in fact that the Royalists penned up their mobile larder of cattle here during the Civil War. Guarded by the Tom Tower, the quad's soft, honey-coloured stone makes a harmonious whole, but it was actually built in two main phases with the southern side dating back to Wolsey, the north finally finished in the 1660s. A wide stone staircase in the quad's southeast corner beneath a stupendous fan-vaulted ceiling leads up to the **Hall**, the grandest refectory in Oxford with a fanciful hammer-beam roof and a set of stern portraits of past scholars by a roll call of famous artists, including Reynolds, Gainsborough and Millais. Albert Einstein, William Gladstone and no fewer than twelve other British prime ministers were educated here.

### Oxford Cathedral

Christ Church's college chapel is otherwise known as **Oxford Cathedral**. The Anglo-Saxons built a church on this site in the seventh century as part of the priory of St Frideswide (Oxford's patron saint), although the present building dates mainly from 1120–80. The priory was suppressed in 1524, but the church survived. It's unusually discordant, with all sorts of bits and bobs from different periods, but fascinating all the same. The dominant features are the sturdy circular columns and rounded arches of the Normans, but there are also early Gothic pointed arches and the chancel ceiling is a particularly fine example of fifteenth-century stone vaulting.

### Christ Church Picture Gallery

Canterbury Quad, Christ Church • July–Sept Mon–Sat 10.30am–5pm, Sun 2–5pm; June same times but closed Tues; Oct–May Mon & Wed–Sat 10.30am–1pm & 2–4.30pm, Sun 2–4.30pm • £4, or £2 with a Christ Church admission ticket • Free tour Mon 2.30pm • ☎ 01865 276172, ⓦ www.chch.ox.ac.uk/gallery

Hidden away in Christ Church's pocket-sized Canterbury Quad is the college's **Picture Gallery**. The extensive collection comprises around three hundred paintings and two thousand drawings, with fine works by artists from Italy and the Netherlands including paintings by Tintoretto, Van Dyck and Frans Hals and drawings by da Vinci, Dürer, Raphael and Michelangelo. A gateway off Canterbury Quad exits to Oriel Square.

### Christ Church Meadow

**Christ Church Meadow** fills in the tapering gap between the rivers Cherwell and Thames. If you decide to delay visiting Christ Church College, you can take a stroll east along Broad Walk for the Cherwell or keep straight down tree-lined (and more appealing) New Walk for the Thames.

## Merton College

Merton St • Mon–Fri 2–5pm, Sat & Sun 10am–5pm • £3 • ☎ 01865 276310, ⓦ merton.ox.ac.uk

**Merton College** is historically the city's most important. Balliol and University colleges may have been founded earlier, but it was Merton – opened in 1264 – which set the model for colleges in both Oxford and Cambridge, being the first to gather its students and tutors together in one place. Furthermore, unlike the other two, Merton retains some of its original medieval buildings, with the best of the thirteenth-century architecture clustered around **Mob Quad**, a charming courtyard with mullioned windows and Gothic doorways to the right of the Front Quad. From the Mob Quad, an archway leads through to the **Chapel**, dating from 1290, inside which you'll find the funerary plaque of Thomas Bodley, founder of Oxford's famous Bodleian Library (see p.240).

## Magdalen College

High St • Daily: July–Sept noon–7pm, rest of year 1–6pm or dusk • £5 • ☎ 01865 276000, ⓦ magd.ox.ac.uk

At the east end of the High Street stands **Magdalen College** (pronounced mawdlin), whose gaggle of stone buildings is overshadowed by its chunky medieval bell tower. Steer right from the entrance and you reach the **Chapel**, which has a handsome reredos, though you have to admire it through the windows of an ungainly stone screen. The adjacent **cloisters** are adorned by standing figures, some biblical and others folkloric, most notably a tribe of grotesques. Magdalen also boasts better **grounds** than most other colleges, with a bridge – at the back of the cloisters – spanning the River Cherwell to join **Addison's Walk**. You can hire punts from beneath **Magdalen Bridge**, beside the college.

## Botanic Garden

Rose Lane • Daily 9am–6pm; March, April, Sept & Oct closes 5pm; Nov–Feb closes 4pm • £4.50 • ⓦ www.botanic-garden.ox.ac.uk

Bounded by a curve of the River Cherwell, Oxford's **Botanic Garden** is the oldest of its kind in England, established in 1621. Still enclosed by its original high wall, it comprises several different zones, from a lily pond, a bog garden and a rock garden through to borders of bearded irises and variegated plants. There are also six large **glasshouses** housing tropical and carnivorous species.

## New College

New College Lane • Daily: Easter–Oct 11am–5pm, rest of year 2–4pm • Easter–Oct £3, rest of year free • ☎ 01865 279555, ⓦ new.ox.ac.uk

Founded in 1379, **New College** is entered via the large but rather plain **Front Quad**. On the left side of the quad rises the magnificent Perpendicular **Chapel**, arguably the finest in Oxford. The ante-chapel contains some superb fourteenth-century stained glass and

---

### TAKING TO THE WATER

**Punting** is a favourite summer pastime among both students and visitors, but handling a punt – a flat-bottomed boat ideal for the shallow waters of the Thames and Cherwell rivers – requires some practice. The punt is propelled and steered with a long pole, which beginners inevitably get stuck in riverbed mud: if this happens, let go of it and paddle back, or you're likely to be dragged overboard.

There are two central **boat rental** places: Magdalen Bridge Boathouse (☎ 01865 202643, ⓦ oxfordpunting.co.uk), beside the Cherwell at the east end of the High Street; and Salter's Steamers (☎ 01865 243421, ⓦ salterssteamers.co.uk) at Folly Bridge, south of Christ Church. Opening times vary: call for details, or try and arrive early (around 10am) to avoid the queues which build up on sunny summer afternoons. At either expect to **pay** £20 per hour plus a deposit of about £50; ID is required. Punts can take a maximum of five people: four sitting and one punting.

Salters Steamers also runs **passenger boats** along the Thames from Folly Bridge downstream to Abingdon, about eight miles south, between late May and mid-September. There are two boats daily (4hr return; £20). Oxford River Cruises (☎ 01865 987147, ⓦ oxfordrivercruises.com) also sets sail from Folly Bridge (April–Oct): details of their half-dozen cruises – including a "lunchtime picnic" trip – are online.

the west window – of 1778 – holds an intriguing Nativity scene based on a design by Sir Joshua Reynolds. Beneath it stands the wonderful 1951 sculpture *Lazarus* by Jacob Epstein. Immediately past the chapel lies the college's peaceful **cloisters**.

An archway on the east side of the Front Quad leads through to the modest **Garden Quad**, with the thick flowerbeds of the **College Garden** beckoning beyond. The north side of the garden is flanked by the largest and best-preserved section of Oxford's medieval **city wall**. The conspicuous earthen **mound** in the middle is a later decorative addition, not medieval.

## Bridge of Sighs

Spanning **New College Lane** a few paces off Catte Street, you can't miss the iconic **Bridge of Sighs**, an archway completed in 1914 to link two buildings of Hertford College. In truth it bears little resemblance to its Venetian namesake but nonetheless has a certain Italianate elegance. It was designed, so the story goes, to give residents of Hertford's older buildings to the south a way to reach the newfangled flushing toilets being installed across the road without having to venture outdoors.

## New College Lane

Under the Bridge of Sighs, atmospheric, traffic-free **New College Lane**, a favourite cyclists' rat-run, extends east, flanked for the most part by high, medieval stone walls. Squeeze down narrow **St Helen's Passage** – decorously renamed from its original title, Hell's Passage – on the left to reach the famed *Turf Tavern* (see p.247) and the seventeenth-century cottages on Bath Place, insinuated into kinks of the medieval city walls. Just past St Helen's Passage, the modest house on the left, topped by a mini-observatory, was the home of astronomer Edmund Halley (1656–1742), discoverer of the comet which bears his name.

## Bodleian Library

Broad St · Closed to the public; some rooms accessible on tours (see below) · ☎ 01865 287400, ⓦ bodley.ox.ac.uk

Christopher Wren's pupil Nicholas Hawksmoor designed the **Clarendon Building**, a domineering, solidly symmetrical edifice at the east end of Broad Street, completed in 1713. It now forms part of the **Bodleian Library**. Founded by scholar Sir Thomas Bodley in 1602, the Bodleian is the UK's largest library after the British Library in London, with an estimated 117 miles of shelving. It includes the modernist 1930s **New Bodleian** (now known as the **Weston Library** after extensive renovation) directly opposite the Clarendon, designed by Sir Giles Gilbert Scott and linked to the main building by tunnels. As one of the UK and Ireland's six copyright libraries, the Bodleian must find room for a copy of every book, pamphlet, magazine and newspaper published in Britain.

---

**TOURS**                                                  **BODLEIAN LIBRARY**

An **audio-guide** is available for self-guided tours of the quad and Divinity School (40min; £2.50) – or there's a host of **guided tours** to those few areas of the Bodleian open to the public. It's always advisable to **book in advance** with the tours office (Mon–Sat 9am–4pm, Sun 11am–4pm; ☎ 01865 287400, ⓦ www.bodley.ox.ac.uk), located inside the Great Gate on Catte Street.

**Mini tour** 30min; £5. Divinity School and Duke Humfrey's Library. Mon–Sat 3.30pm, 4pm & 4.40pm, Sun 12.45pm, 2.15pm, 3.15pm, 4pm & 4.40pm.
**Standard tour** 1hr; £7. Divinity School, Duke Humfrey's Library and Convocation House. Mon–Sat 10.30am, 11.30am, 1pm & 2pm, Sun 11.30am, 2pm & 3pm.
**Extended tour "Upstairs Downstairs"** 1hr 30min;

£13. Divinity School, Duke Humfrey's Library, Convocation House, Gladstone Link, Radcliffe Camera. Wed & Sat 9.15am; booking essential.
**Extended tour "Reading rooms"** 1hr 30min; £13. Divinity School, Duke Humfrey's Library, Convocation House, Upper Reading Room. Sun 11.15am & 1.15pm; booking essential.

## Old Schools Quadrangle

Mon–Fri 9am–5pm, Sat 9am–4.30pm, Sun 11am–5pm • Free

Behind the Clarendon Building you enter the Bodleian's beautifully proportioned **Old Schools Quadrangle**, completed in 1619 in an ornate Jacobean-Gothic style and offering access to all of the university's academic faculties, or schools: the name of each is lettered in gold above the doorways which ring the quad. On the east side rises the handsome **Tower of the Five Orders**, its tiers of columns in ascending order Tuscan, Doric, Ionic, Corinthian and Composite.

## The Divinity School

Mon–Fri 9am–5pm, Sat 9am–4.30pm, Sun 11am–5pm • £1

Entered from the quad, the **Divinity School** is a highlight. Begun in 1424, this exceptional room is a masterpiece of late Gothic architecture, featuring an extravagant vaulted ceiling adorned with a riot of pendants and 455 decorative bosses. Built to house the university's theology faculty, it was, until the nineteenth century, also where degree candidates were questioned about their subject by two interlocutors, with a professor acting as umpire. Few interiors in Oxford are as impressive.

## Duke Humfrey's Library

Only accessible on guided tours

Above the Divinity School stands the atmospheric **Duke Humfrey's Library**, in working use as a reading room from its completion in 1487 right through to 2014, when its collections were transferred to the new Weston Library building. The room, extensively added to during the early seventeenth century, is distinguished by its superb beamed ceiling and carved corbels.

## Convocation House

Only accessible on guided tours

Alongside the Divinity School is the **Convocation House**, a sombre wood-panelled chamber where parliament sat during the Civil War, which now sports a fancy fan-vaulted ceiling completed in 1759.

# The Sheldonian Theatre

Broad St • Feb–Nov Mon–Sat 10am–4.30pm, July & Aug also Sun 10.30am–4pm; Dec & Jan Mon–Fri 10am–3.30pm • £3.50 •
ⓦ www.sheldon.ox.ac.uk

At the east end of Broad Street, the **Sheldonian Theatre** is ringed by railings topped with a line of glum-looking, pop-eyed classical busts. The Sheldonian was Christopher Wren's first major work, a reworking of the Theatre of Marcellus in Rome, semicircular at the back and rectangular at the front. It was conceived in 1663, when the 31-year-old Wren's main job was as professor of astronomy. Designed as a stage for university ceremonies, nowadays it also functions as a concert hall, but the interior lacks much sense of drama, and even the views from the cupola are disappointing.

# Museum of the History of Science

Broad St • Tues–Fri noon–5pm, Sat 10am–5pm, Sun 2–5pm • Free • ⓦ mhs.ox.ac.uk

The classical heads that shield the Sheldonian Theatre (see above) continue along the front of the fascinating **Museum of the History of Science**, whose two floors display an amazing clutter of antique microscopes and astrolabes, sundials, quadrants and sextants. The highlights are Elizabeth I's own astrolabe and a blackboard used by Einstein in 1931, still covered with his scribbled equations.

## Trinity College

Broad St • Not set hours, usually Mon–Fri 9am–12.15pm & 1.30–4pm, Sat & Sun 1–4pm • £2 • ☎ 01865 279900, ⓦ trinity.ox.ac.uk

**Trinity College** is fronted by three dinky lodge-cottages. Behind them the manicured lawn of the Front Quad stretches back to the richly decorated **Chapel**, awash with Baroque stucco work. Its high altar is flanked by an exquisite example of the work of Grinling Gibbons – a distinctive performance, with cherubs' heads peering out from delicate foliage. Behind the chapel stands **Durham Quad**, an attractive ensemble of old stone buildings begun at the end of the seventeenth century.

## Exeter College

Turl St • Daily 2–5pm • Free • ☎ 01865 279600, ⓦ exeter.ox.ac.uk

In medieval **Exeter College** aim for the elaborate Gothic Revival chapel, conceived by Gilbert Scott in the 1850s. It contains a fine set of **stained-glass windows** illustrating biblical stories – St Paul on the road to Damascus, Samson bringing down the pillars of the Philistine temple – as well as a superb Pre-Raphaelite tapestry, the *Adoration of the Magi*, a collaboration between William Morris and Edward Burne-Jones, both former students.

## The Radcliffe Camera

Radcliffe Sq • Closed to the public; accessible only on Bodleian Library's extended tour: Wed & Sat 9.15am • £13 • booking essential • ☎ 01865 287400, ⓦ bodley.ox.ac.uk

The mighty rotunda of the **Radcliffe Camera**, built between 1737 and 1748 by James Gibbs, architect of London's St Martin's-in-the-Fields church, displays no false modesty. Dr John Radcliffe, royal physician (to William III), was, according to a contemporary diarist, "very ambitious of glory": when he died in 1714 he bequeathed a mountain of money for the construction of a library. Gibbs was one of the few British architects of the period to have trained in Rome and his design is thoroughly Italian in style, its limestone columns ascending to a delicate balustrade, decorated with pin-prick urns and encircling a lead-sheathed dome. Taken over by the Bodleian Library in 1860, it now houses a reading-room, accessible to the public only on the Bodleian's "extended tour" (see p.240).

## All Souls College

High St • Mon–Fri 2–4pm, closed Aug • Free • ☎ 01865 279379, ⓦ all-souls.ox.ac.uk

Running the entire east side of Radcliffe Square, its immense chapel windows the epitome of the Perpendicular Gothic style, **All Souls College** is one of the quietest places in central Oxford: it has no undergraduates. Uniquely, it admits only "fellows" – that is, distinguished scholars – either by election of existing fellows, or by an exam reputed to be the hardest in the world. The result is that All Souls is generally silent. Sightseers gather at the elaborate gates on Radcliffe Square, wondering how to gain access to the lovely quad beyond: turn right and walk around the corner onto High Street to reach the **college entrance**. This gives onto the modest Front Quad, location of the spectacular fifteenth-century **chapel**, with its gilded hammerbeam roof and neck-cricking reredos (though all its figures are Victorian replacements). Move through to the spacious **North Quad**, the object of all that admiration: Hawksmoor's soaring Gothic twin towers face the Radcliffe Square gates, while ahead, the Codrington Library – also Hawksmoor – sports a conspicuous, brightly decorated sundial designed by Wren.

## Church of St Mary the Virgin

High St • Daily 9am–5pm, July & Aug until 6pm • Free; tower £3 • ⓦ www.university-church.ox.ac.uk

On the High Street behind Radcliffe Square, **St Mary the Virgin** is a hotchpotch of architectural styles, but mostly dates from the fifteenth century. The church's saving

## FIRST FOR COFFEE

East of St Mary's two cafés face each other across the High Street, both claiming to be **England's oldest coffee house**. To the south, the *Grand Café* occupies the site of a coffee house opened by a Lebanese Jew named Jacob in or just after 1650. Opposite, the *Queen's Lane Coffee House* stands where a Syrian Jew named Cirques Jobson launched a competing enterprise at roughly the same time. Whichever was first, Oxford's gentlefolk were drinking coffee – and also hot chocolate – several years ahead of London.

graces are its elaborate, thirteenth-century pinnacled spire and its distinctive Baroque **porch**, flanked by chunky corkscrewed pillars. The interior is disappointingly mundane, though the carved poppy heads on the choir stalls are of some historical interest: the tips were brusquely squared off when a platform was installed here in 1555 to stage the heresy trial of Cranmer, Latimer and Ridley, leading Protestants who had run foul of Queen Mary. The church's other diversion is the **tower**, with wonderful views.

## Covered Market

High St • Mon–Sat 9am–5.30pm, Sun 10am–4pm • ⓦ oxford-coveredmarket.co.uk

For refreshment on the hoof – as well as a fascinating glimpse into the everyday life of Oxford away from the colleges – drop into the **Covered Market**, wedged between the High Street and Market Street. Opened in 1774, it remains full of atmosphere, home to butchers, bakers, fishmongers, greengrocers and cheese sellers as well as cafés, clothes boutiques and shoe shops.

## Carfax Tower

Carfax • Daily 10am–5.30pm, Oct closes 4.30pm, March closes 4pm, Nov–Feb closes 3pm • £2.20

The busy **Carfax** crossroads is a fulcrum, where chiefly "gown" architecture along the High Street to the east is balanced by the distinctly "town" atmosphere of Cornmarket and Queen Street to the west. This has been a crossroads for more than a thousand years: roads met here in Saxon times, and the name "Carfax" derives from the Latin *quadrifurcus* ("four-forked"). The junction is overlooked by a square thirteenth-century **tower**, adorned by a pair of clocktower jacks. You can **climb** it for wide views over the centre, though other vantage points – principally St Mary's (see opposite) – have the edge.

## St Michael-at-the-Northgate

Cornmarket • Daily 10.30am–5pm, Nov–March closes 4pm • Church free; tower £2.50 • ⓦ www.smng.org.uk

Storming north of Carfax, **Cornmarket** is now a busy pedestrianized shopping strip lined with familiar high-street stores. There's precious little here to fire the imagination until you reach **St Michael-at-the-Northgate**, a church recorded in the Domesday Book, with a late fourteenth-century font where Shakespeare's godson was baptized in 1606. The church's Saxon **tower**, built in 1050, is Oxford's oldest surviving building; enter for rooftop views and to see an eleventh-century sheela-na-gig.

## Ashmolean Museum

Beaumont St • Tues–Sun 10am–5pm • Free • ☎ 01865 278000, ⓦ www.ashmolean.org

Second only to the British Museum in London, the **Ashmolean Museum** occupies a mammoth Neoclassical building on the corner of Beaumont Street and St Giles. It grew from the collections of the magpie-like **John Tradescant**, gardener to Charles I and an energetic traveller, and today it possesses a vast and far-reaching collection covering everything from Minoan vases to Stradivarius violins.

Light and airy modern galleries cover four floors (pick up a **plan** at reception). The "orientation" gallery in the basement provides a thematic overview of the museum, while the ground floor houses the museum's "ancient world" exhibits, including its superb Egyptology collection and an imposing room full of Greek sculptures. Floor 1 is dedicated to Mediterranean, Indian and Islamic artefacts (Hindu bronzes, Iranian pottery and so on) while floor 2 is mainly European, including the museum's wide-ranging collection of Dutch, Flemish and Italian paintings. Floor 3 focuses on European art since 1800, including works by Sickert, Pissarro and the Pre-Raphaelites.

## Oxford University Museum of Natural History

Parks Road • Daily 10am–5pm • Free • ☎ 01865 272950, ⓦ www.oum.ox.ac.uk

From the Ashmolean, it's a brief walk north up St Giles to the *Lamb & Flag* pub, beside which an alley cuts east through to the **Oxford University Museum of Natural History**. The building, constructed under the guidance of John Ruskin, looks like a cross between a railway station and a church – and the same applies inside, where a High Victorian-Gothic fusion of cast iron and glass features soaring columns and capitals decorated with animal and plant motifs. Exhibits include some impressive dinosaur skeletons, models of exotic beasties, a four-billion-year-old meteorite, and so on.

## Pitt Rivers Museum

Parks Road • Mon noon–4.30pm, Tues–Sun 10am–4.30pm • Free • ☎ 01865 270927, ⓦ www.prm.ox.ac.uk

Oxford's eye-popping **Pitt Rivers Museum** is housed in the same building as the University Museum of Natural History, accessed via a door at the rear of the ground-floor level. Founded in 1884, this is one of the world's finest ethnographic museums and an extraordinary relic of the Victorian age, arranged like an exotic junk shop with each intricately crammed cabinet labelled meticulously by hand. The exhibits – brought to England by, among others, Captain Cook – range from totem poles and mummified crocodiles to African fetishes and gruesome shrunken heads.

## Modern Art Oxford

30 Pembroke St • Tues–Sat 11am–6pm, Sun noon–5pm • Free • ☎ 01865 722733, ⓦ www.modernartoxford.org.uk

Just south of Carfax, narrow Pembroke Street heads west to the outstanding **Modern Art Oxford** gallery, founded in 1965 and hosting an excellent changing programme of temporary exhibitions. It's worth stopping by, whatever happens to be showing.

## Oxford Castle Unlocked

New Road • Daily 10am–5pm; tours every 20min, last at 4.20pm • £9.95; discount for booking online • ☎ 01865 260666, ⓦ oxfordcastleunlocked.co.uk

West of Carfax is the site of what was **Oxford Castle**, built in 1071. Only the motte (mound) survives: the buildings atop it were demolished after the Civil War. In later centuries a cluster of stern Victorian edifices beside the mound served chiefly as Oxford's prison, decommissioned in 1996 and now a luxury hotel, around which cluster shops, bars and restaurants. To one side, the excellent heritage centre **Oxford Castle Unlocked** offers memorable forty-minute **guided tours**, during which costumed warders lead you up the Saxon-era **St George's Tower**, show you medieval prison cells and take you down into the Romanesque crypt beneath **St George's Chapel**, telling tales of wars, executions and hauntings along the way.

| ARRIVAL AND DEPARTURE | OXFORD |
|---|---|

**By train** Oxford station is on the west side of the city centre, a 10min walk from the centre along Hythe Bridge Street. Don't mix it up with the new Oxford Parkway station in the northern outskirts, served by direct buses into the centre.

Destinations Bath (2 hourly; 1hr 20min–1hr 40min); Birmingham (2 hourly; 1hr 10min); Bristol (hourly; 1hr 40min); Cheltenham (every 30min; 2hr–2hr 15min); Gloucester (every 30min; 1hr 40min–2hr 20min); London (2–3 hourly; 1hr); Winchester (2 hourly; 1hr 10min–1hr 30min); Worcester (2 hourly; 1hr 15min–1hr 35min).

**By bus** Most buses are operated by Oxford Bus (☎01865 785400, ⓦoxfordbus.co.uk) or Stagecoach (☎01865 772250, ⓦwww.stagecoachbus.com/oxfordshire). Long-distance routes terminate at Gloucester Green bus station, in the city centre adjoining George Street; most county buses terminate on Magdalen Street, St Giles or St Aldates.

Destinations London Victoria coach station (Oxford Tube and X90 express coaches daily every 10–30min; 1hr 40min); Heathrow airport (Airline coach daily every 20–30min; 1hr 30min); Gatwick airport (Airline coach daily hourly; 2hr). Burford (45min), Northleach (1hr) and Cheltenham (1hr 30min) are served by the #853 (Mon–Sat 2–4 daily, Sun daily).

**By car** Five big park-and-ride sites (ⓦparkandride.net) are signposted around the ring road. All offer cheap parking (around £2 a day) as well as frequent buses into the centre (usually every 8–15min: Mon–Sat 6am–11pm, Sun 8am–7pm; £2.70 return). Central Oxford is not car-friendly: many streets are pedestrianized and parking is limited. The largest car park is at the Westgate shopping mall, accessed off Thames Street (around £28 for up to 24hrs).

## GETTING AROUND

**On foot** From the rail station to Magdalen Bridge is roughly a mile and a quarter, and passes almost everything of interest on the way.

**By bike** Bainton Bikes at Walton Street Cycles, 78 Walton Street (☎01865 311610, ⓦbaintonbikes.com) rents bikes from £10/day.

**By taxi** There are taxi ranks at Carfax, Gloucester Green, St Giles and the railway station. Otherwise call Radio Taxis (☎01865 242424, ⓦradiotaxisoxford.co.uk).

## INFORMATION AND TOURS

**Tourist office** 15 Broad Street (Mon–Sat 9.30am–5.30pm, Sun 10am–4pm; Oct–March closes 30min earlier; ☎01865 252200, ⓦvisitoxfordand oxfordshire.com). Staff also sell discounted tickets for a range of nearby attractions, including Blenheim Palace, as well as tickets for coaches to London.

**Listings information** *Daily Info* (ⓦdailyinfo.co.uk) is the continually updated online version of Oxford's student newssheet. You'll spot the paper version (printed twice a week) pinned up in colleges and cafés around town.

**Guided tours** The tourist office offers excellent guided walking tours of the city centre (daily 10.45am & 2pm; extra slots if there's sufficient demand; 2hr; £8.50). Many walking guides tout for business along Broad Street, offering daytime walks and evening ghost tours, and Blackwell's bookshop, 48–53 Broad Street (☎01865 792792) also runs several literary-themed walking tours each week (April–Oct; £8).

**4**

---

## A WEEKEND IN OXFORD

### FRIDAY NIGHT

Toast your weekend with a **champagne cocktail** in the *Randolph's Morse Bar* and a slap-up **dinner** at, say, *Al Shami*, *Gee's* or *Jamie's Italian*.

### SATURDAY

Start the day with a visit to the **Covered Market**, to relax with a coffee while getting a flavour of town life and watch the butchers and fishmongers lay out the new day's wares, then join a **walking tour** offered by the tourist office. Grab a bite to eat and devote the afternoon to "gown" life: choose two or three of the **colleges** (such as Christ Church, Merton and New) and pick up the atmosphere of the old city-centre streets (Broad, Merton, Turl) as you go. End the day with a **punt**, before setting off down the **Cowley Road** to sample Oxford's lounge bars and ethnic restaurants, and perhaps find some live music.

### SUNDAY

Begin with a lazy brunch in one of **Jericho**'s taverns and cafés – or, if you prefer, a genteel 11.15am "coffee concert" at the Holywell Music Room – before tackling the wonder that is the **Ashmolean Museum**. Sample more history at **Oxford Castle Unlocked**, or opt for a country walk in the park behind **Magdalen College** – then settle in at *Quod* for early-evening jazz followed by dinner.

## ACCOMMODATION

As well as the places listed below, another good source of accommodation is the **university**. Outside term time, many colleges let out rooms on a B&B basis at often bargain rates. Expect little or no hotel-style service, but you are free to soak up the college ambience and may score with a view over a historic quad. For more information, visit ⓦ oxfordrooms.co.uk.

### HOTELS

★**Bath Place** 4 Bath Place ☎ 01865 791812, ⓦ bath place.co.uk. This unusual hotel is tucked away down an old cobbled courtyard flanked by ancient buildings in an unbeatable central location. The sixteen creaky rooms are each individually decorated in attractive antique style with canopied beds and bare stone walls. **£120**

★**Malmaison** Oxford Castle, 3 New Rd ☎ 01865 268400, ⓦ malmaison.com. Classy designer hotel in what was a Victorian prison, part of the Oxford Castle complex. Rooms – which take up three cells, knocked through – are nothing short of glamorous, featuring contemporary bathrooms and hi-tech gadgets. Head through to C wing for bigger mezzanine suites. **£210**

**Old Bank** 92 High St ☎ 01865 799599, ⓦ oldbank -hotel.co.uk. Great location for a slick hotel in a shiny conversion of an old bank. All 42 bedrooms are decorated in crisp, modern style, some with great views over All Souls College opposite. **£220**

**Old Parsonage** 1 Banbury Rd ☎ 01865 310210, ⓦ oldparsonage-hotel.co.uk. Completely refurbished in 2014, this lovely hotel occupies a charming, wisteria-clad old building of 1660, with 35 tasteful, modern rooms. Free parking, and free walking tours for guests on request. **£235**

**The Randolph** 1 Beaumont St ☎ 01865 256400, ⓦ randolph-hotel.com. Oxford's most famous hotel, long the favoured choice of the well-heeled visitor, occupying a neo-Gothic brick building with a distinctive, nineteenth-century interior. Now part of the *Macdonald* chain, still with traditional service, well-appointed bedrooms and a distinguished club atmosphere. **£224**

### GUESTHOUSES AND B&BS

**Buttery** 11 Broad St ☎ 01865 811950, ⓦ thebutteryhotel.co.uk. Slap-bang central location for this friendly sixteen-room guesthouse-cum-hotel, with modest rooms, plain but decent. Choose a back room to avoid the noise of carousing students. **£115**

**Isis Guesthouse** 45–53 Iffley Rd ☎ 01865 613700, ⓦ isisguesthouse.com. From July to September, this college hall – within easy walking distance of Magdalen Bridge – becomes a guesthouse with 37 single and double rooms (about half en suite), decorated in a brisk if frugal modern style. **£90**

**Richmond** 25 Walton Crescent ☎ 01865 311777, ⓦ the -richmond-oxford.co.uk. Quiet B&B attached to the excellent *Al-Shami* Lebanese restaurant. Rooms are simple but prices are remarkably low – and you can opt for a delicious Lebanese breakfast (hummus, olives, white cheese, pitta bread etc). **£65**

### HOSTELS

**Central Backpackers** 13 Park End St ☎ 01865 242288, ⓦ centralbackpackers.co.uk. Independent hostel with fifty beds (including female-only dorms), 24-hour access and a friendly attitude. On a busy street: expect noise from nearby bars. Dorms **£22–28**

**Oxford Backpackers** 9a Hythe Bridge St ☎ 01865 721761, ⓦ hostels.co.uk. Independent hostel with 120 beds in bright, modern dorms (including female-only) and 24-hour access – but just a touch scruffy. Dorms **£20–26**

**Oxford Youth Hostel** 2a Botley Rd ☎ 0845 371 9131, ⓦ yha.org.uk. In a modern block behind the train station, this popular YHA hostel has 187 beds in four- and six-bedded dorms, plus nine doubles, some en suite. There's 24-hour access, with good facilities and a decent café. Dorms **£18-23**, doubles **£45**

## EATING

With so many students and tourists, Oxford has a wide choice of places to eat. Lunchtimes tend to be very busy, though there's no shortage of options. The **restaurant** scene ranges from fine dining to more affordable outlets offering seasonal cooking. The best choice lies on the edge of the centre, along Walton Street and Little Clarendon Street in easygoing Jericho, or southeast on the grungier Cowley Road, buzzing with after-work lounge bars.

### CAFÉS

★**Ben's Cookies** 108 Covered Market ☎ 01865 247407, ⓦ benscookies.com. This hole in the wall – the first outlet in the Ben's Cookies chain – has been churning out the best cookies in Oxford, perhaps England (and some say the world) since 1984, from ginger to peanut butter to triple chocolate chunk. Mon–Sat 9.15am–5.30pm, Sun 10am–4pm.

**Missing Bean** 14 Turl St ☎ 01865 794886, ⓦ www.themissingbean.co.uk. Plate-glass windows look out onto this pleasant old street, as conversation swirls and reputedly the best coffee in Oxford goes down. Mon–Fri 8am–6.30pm, Sat 9am–6.30pm, Sun 10am–5.30pm.

**News Café** 1 Ship St ☎ 01865 242317. Breakfasts, bagels and daily specials, plus beer and wine in this brisk and efficient café. Plenty of local and international newspapers are on hand too. Sun–Thurs 9am–5pm, Fri & Sat 9am–6pm.

★**Vaults & Garden** Radcliffe Sq ☎01865 279112, ⊛thevaultsandgarden.com. Occupying atmospheric stone-vaulted chambers attached to St Mary's church, this always-busy café serves up good-quality organic, locally sourced wholefood, as well as coffee and cake. A small outside terrace area gazes up at the Radcliffe Camera. Cash only. Daily 8.30am–6pm.

### RESTAURANTS

**Branca** 111 Walton St ☎01865 556111, ⊛branca -restaurants.com. Large, buzzy bar-brasserie dishing up well-prepared Italian food, from simple pastas, pizzas and risottos through to more elaborate meat and fish mains (£10–16). Daily noon–11pm.

**Chiang Mai Kitchen** 130a High St ☎01865 202233, ⊛chiangmaikitchen.co.uk. An authentically spicy blast of Thai cooking in a homely little timber-framed medieval building tucked down an alleyway off the High Street. All the traditional classics are done well, including a good vegetarian selection. Mains around £9. Reservations advised. Mon–Sat noon–10.30pm, Sun noon–10pm.

**Edamame** 15 Holywell St ☎01865 246916, ⊛edamame .co.uk. Voted one of the best Japanese restaurants in Britain, this tiny canteen-style place enjoys a flawless reputation. No bookings are taken, so you may have to queue (and then share a table). Tuck into ramen noodle soup with pork, chicken or tofu, for instance, or salmon *teriyaki*. There's plenty for vegetarians. Thursday night is sushi night. Mains £6–9. Cards not accepted at lunchtime. Wed 11.30am–2.30pm, Thurs–Sat 11.30am–2.30pm & 5–8.30pm, Sun noon–3.30pm.

**Gee's** 61 Banbury Rd ☎01865 553540, ⊛gees -restaurant.co.uk. Formal restaurant occupying chic Victorian conservatory premises. The inventive menu takes in British seasonal dishes such as asparagus and locally reared spring lamb, aided by steaks, fish dishes and more Continental cuisine – lobster linguine, bouillabaisse, duck confit. Mains £14–24; two-course early supper menu (Mon–Fri until 6pm) £13. Book ahead. Sun–Thurs 10am–10.30pm, Fri & Sat 10am–11pm.

★**Pie Minister** 56 Covered Market ☎01865 241613, ⊛pieminister.co.uk. Your nose will lead you to this pie shop inside the Covered Market. The wide choice includes deerstalker pie (venison and red wine), moo pie (beef and ale), heidi pie (goat's cheese and spinach), and so on, all accompanied by mashed potato, gravy and minty peas for around £5–6. Mon–Sat 10am–5pm, Sun 11am–4pm.

**Quod** 92 High St ☎01865 202505, ⊛quod.co.uk. Landmark brasserie in a central location. Once the solemn hall of a bank, the spacious interior now offers picture windows and contemporary art. Plump for the two-course set lunch (£13) – think devilled kidneys on toast or minty courgette soup, followed by steak *béarnaise* or mushroom tagliatelle. À la carte mains are £12–17. There's a nice bar, and live jazz on Sunday (5–7pm). Mon–Sat 7am–11pm, Sun 7am–10.30pm.

★**Turl Street Kitchen** 16 Turl St ☎01865 264171, ⊛turlstreetkitchen.co.uk. Much-loved hideaway on a charming backstreet, one of Oxford's top spots for a quiet battery-recharge over coffee and cake. Food is seasonal and hearty – parsnip soup, braised free-range chicken with chickpeas, fennel and wild garlic gratin – served in a cosy setting of sofas and grained wood. Mains £8–14. All profits support a local charity. Sun–Thurs 8am–midnight, Fri & Sat 8am–1am.

### DRINKING

**The Bear** 6 Alfred St ☎01865 728164, ⊛bearoxford .co.uk. Tucked away down a narrow side street, this tiny old pub (the oldest in Oxford, founded roughly 800 years ago) offers a wide range of beers amid its traditional decor, which includes a collection of ties. Mon–Thurs 11am–11pm, Fri & Sat 11am–midnight, Sun 11.30am–10.30pm.

**Eagle & Child** 49 St Giles ☎01865 302925, ⊛nicholsonspubs.co.uk. Dubbed the "Bird & Baby", this was once the haunt of J.R.R. Tolkien and C.S. Lewis. The beer is still good and the old wood-panelled rooms at the front are great, but the pub is no longer independently owned – and feels a bit corporate. Mon–Thurs 11am–11pm, Fri & Sat 11am–midnight, Sun noon–10.30pm.

★**Lamb & Flag** 12 St Giles ☎01865 515787. Generations of university types have relished this quiet old tavern, which comes with low-beamed ceilings and cramped but cosy rooms in which to enjoy hand-drawn ale and genuine pork scratchings. Cash only. Mon–Sat noon–11pm, Sun noon–10.30pm.

**Raoul's** 32 Walton St ☎01865 553732, ⊛raoulsbar .com. Famed Jericho cocktail bar, with a retro 70s theme, great tunes and a devoted clientele. Navigate the mammoth menu of cocktails to choose a fave or three. Sun–Tues 4pm–midnight, Wed–Sat 4pm–1am.

★**Turf Tavern** 4 Bath Place ☎01865 243235, ⊛theturftavern.co.uk. Small, atmospheric medieval pub, reached via narrow passageways off Holywell Street, with a fine range of beers, and mulled wine in winter. Mon–Sat 11am–11.15pm, Sun 11am–10.30pm.

---

### TOP 5 PUBS

**The Angel** Henley-on-Thames. See p.250
**Eight Bells** Chipping Campden. See p.261
**Falkland Arms** Great Tew. See p.256
**Queen's Head** Stow-on-the-Wold. See p.258
**Turf Tavern** Oxford. See above

## ENTERTAINMENT AND NIGHTLIFE

### CLUBS AND LIVE MUSIC

**Café Tarifa** 56 Cowley Rd ☏01865 256091, ⓦfacebook.com/cafetarifaoxford. Atmospheric lounge bar decked out in Moorish/Arabian style, with cocktails and cushions, also hosting a variety of generally chilled live music and DJ nights and cult movie screenings. Mon–Thurs 5pm–midnight, Fri 5pm–12.30am, Sat noon–12.30am, Sun 5–11pm.

**O2 Academy** 190 Cowley Rd ☏01865 813500, ⓦo2academyoxford.co.uk. Oxford's liveliest indie and dance venue, with a fast-moving programme of live bands and guest DJs.

### CLASSICAL MUSIC AND THEATRE

**Holywell Music Room** 32 Holywell St ☏01865 766266, ⓦwww.music.ox.ac.uk. This small, plain, Georgian building was opened in 1748 as the first public music hall in England. It offers a varied programme, from straight classical to experimental, with occasional bouts of jazz. Popular Sunday morning "coffee concerts" (ⓦcoffeeconcerts.co.uk) run year-round.

**North Wall** South Parade ☏01865 319450, ⓦthenorthwall.com. This much-loved arts centre located in posh Summertown, a mile or so north of the centre, hosts small-scale theatre, comedy and workshops.

**Sheldonian Theatre** Broad St ☏01865 277299, ⓦwww.sheldon.ox.ac.uk. Seventeenth-century edifice that is Oxford's top concert hall, despite rather dodgy acoustics, with the Oxford Philomusica symphony orchestra in residence (ⓦoxfordphil.com).

## DIRECTORY

**Bookshops** The leading university bookshop is Blackwell, 48 Broad Street (☏01865 792792, ⓦblackwell.co.uk). The Albion Beatnik Bookstore, 34a Walton Street (☏07737 876213, ⓦalbionbeatnikbookstore.blogspot.com) stocks "interesting twentieth-century books", and hosts readings and jazz evenings.

**Markets** Gloucester Green hosts a food market (Wed 9am–5pm) and arts and crafts market (Thurs 9am–5pm), as well as a great local farmers' market (1st & 3rd Thurs of month 9am–3pm).

# Around Oxford

From Oxford, a short journey west brings you into the Cotswolds; your first stop could be Burford (see p.253) or Moreton-in-Marsh (see p.257). Even nearer to Oxford lie the charming little town of **Woodstock** and its imperious country-house neighbour **Blenheim Palace**, birthplace of Winston Churchill, while further south, at the edges of Oxfordshire, you could make for the pleasantly old-fashioned riverside haunt of **Henley-on-Thames** or the open walking country around the **Vale of White Horse**.

## Woodstock

**WOODSTOCK**, eight miles northwest of Oxford, has royal associations going back to Saxon times, with a string of kings attracted by its excellent hunting. The Royalists used Woodstock as a base during the Civil War, but, after their defeat, Cromwell never got round to destroying either the town or its manor house: the latter was ultimately given to the Duke of Marlborough in 1704, who razed it to build Blenheim Palace (see p.249). Long dependent on royal and then ducal patronage, Woodstock is now both a well-heeled commuter town for Oxford and a base for visitors to Blenheim. It is also an extremely pretty little place, its handsome stone buildings gathered around the main square, at the junction of Market and High streets.

### Oxfordshire Museum

Park St • Tues–Sat 10am–5pm, Sun 2–5pm • Free • ☏01993 811456, ⓦwww.tomocc.org.uk

Occupying an eighteenth-century house in the centre of Woodstock, the rather good **Oxfordshire Museum** offers an engaging take on the county's archeology, social history and industry. Part of the rear garden shelters original megalosaurus footprints, recovered from a local quarry and displayed amid a Jurassic garden of ferns, pines and redwoods.

## ARRIVAL AND INFORMATION                                      WOODSTOCK

**By bus** #S3 (hourly) to/from Oxford (30min) and Chipping Norton (20min); #233 (Mon–Sat hourly) to/from Burford (45min).

**Useful websites** ⓦ wakeuptowoodstock.com & ⓦ oxfordshirecotswolds.org

## ACCOMMODATION AND EATING

**The Bear** Park St ☎ 01993 811124, ⓦ bearhotelwoodstock.co.uk. Behind the ivy-clad walls of this thirteenth-century coaching inn lurks a stylish, modern chain hotel – oak-carved four-poster beds, roaring log fires and all. Grab a table by the bay window for upscale, country-house food: Gressingham duck, Scottish beef and the like. Two-course menu £32. Food served Mon–Thurs noon–2.30pm & 7–9.30pm, Fri & Sat noon–2.30pm & 6.45–10pm, Sun noon–2.30pm & 7–9pm. **£100**

**King's Arms** Market St ☎ 01993 813636, ⓦ www .kingshotelwoodstock.co.uk. Chic little hotel, with fifteen contemporary-styled rooms. The fine restaurant (mains £12–17) specializes in Modern British cuisine – leg of lamb or organic salmon. The bar/restaurant can remain busy until after 11pm: if you want an early night, choose a room at the back. Food served Mon–Fri noon–2.30pm & 6.30–9.30pm, Sat & Sun noon–9pm. **£150**

# Blenheim Palace

Woodstock • **Palace** Mid-Feb to end Oct daily 10.30am–5.30pm; Nov to mid-Dec Wed–Sun same times **Park** Daily 9am–6pm or dusk • Palace, park and gardens £22; park and gardens £13 • ☎ 01993 810530, ⓦ blenheimpalace.com

In 1704, as a thank-you for his victory over the French at the Battle of Blenheim, Queen Anne gave John Churchill, **Duke of Marlborough** (1650–1722) the royal estate of Woodstock, along with the promise of enough cash to build himself a gargantuan palace.

Work started promptly on **Blenheim Palace** with Sir John Vanbrugh, who was also responsible for Castle Howard in Yorkshire (see p.617), as principal architect. However, the duke's formidable wife, Sarah Jennings, who had wanted Christopher Wren, was soon at loggerheads with Vanbrugh, while Queen Anne had second thoughts, stifling the flow of money. Construction work was halted and the house was only finished after the duke's death at the instigation of his widow, who ended up paying most of the bills and designing much of the interior herself. The end result is England's grandest example of Baroque civic architecture, an Italianate palace of finely worked yellow stone that is more a monument than a house – just as Vanbrugh intended.

The **interior** of the house is stuffed with paintings and tapestries, plus all manner of objets d'art, including furniture from Versailles and carvings by Grinling Gibbons. The **Churchill Exhibition** on the ground floor provides a fascinating introduction to Winston (1874–1965), born at Blenheim as grandson of the seventh Duke of Marlborough, and buried alongside his wife in the graveyard of Bladon church just outside the estate.

## The gardens and park

Miniature train: March–Oct every 30min • 50p

Start your exploration of Blenheim's **gardens** by riding the narrow-gauge **miniature train** on a looping journey to the **Pleasure Gardens** a few hundred yards to the east (also an easy walk). Here, as well as a café, you'll find a butterfly house, lavender garden, maze and other diversions. On the west side of the house, fountains spout beside the terrace of the palace café and paths lead down to the lake past the vivid **Rose Garden**. A path from the front of the house leads you across Blenheim's open **park** down to Vanbrugh's **Grand Bridge** and up to the hilltop **Column of Victory**, topped by a heroic statue of the 1st Duke.

## ARRIVAL AND DEPARTURE                                         BLENHEIM PALACE

**Entrances** The Blenheim Palace estate has two entrances: the Hensington Gate lies just south of Woodstock on the A44 Oxford Road, a few minutes' walk from the town centre, while the quieter Woodstock Gate is in the centre of

Woodstock, at the far end of Park Street.
**By bus** #S3 (hourly) stops at the Hensington Gate, on its route to/from Chipping Norton (20min) and Oxford (30min), as does #233 (Mon–Sat hourly) to/from Burford (45min).

## TOURS

**Blenheim Palace tours** Free guided tours (35min) inside the palace depart about every quarter-hour, though you're free to opt out and stroll at your own pace. On Sundays or when the palace is very busy, the tours are replaced by guides stationed in every room, who give details as you move through.

# Henley-on-Thames

Three counties – Oxfordshire, Berkshire and Buckinghamshire – meet at **HENLEY-ON-THAMES**, long a favourite stopping place for travellers between London and Oxford. Nowadays, Henley is a good-looking, affluent commuter town at its prettiest among the old brick and stone buildings that flank the short main drag, **Hart Street**. At one end of Hart Street is the Market Place and its fetching **Town Hall**, at the other stand the easy Georgian curves of **Henley Bridge**. Overlooking the bridge is the parish church of **St Mary**, whose square tower sports a set of little turrets worked in chequerboard flint and stone.

## River and Rowing Museum

Mill Meadows • Daily 10am–5.30pm; Sept–April closes 5pm • £8.50 • ☎01491 415600, ⓦ rrm.co.uk

A five-minute walk south along the riverbank from the foot of Hart Street lies Henley's imaginative **River and Rowing Museum**. Three galleries explore the wildlife and ecology of the Thames along with the history of rowing and the regatta, from ancient triremes to the modern Olympics. A fourth gallery is devoted to models illustrating scenes from the children's classic *Wind in the Willows* by Kenneth Grahame (1859–1932), set near Henley.

## ARRIVAL AND DEPARTURE

### HENLEY-ON-THAMES

**By train** Trains serve Henley (1–2 hourly, with 1 or 2 changes) from London Paddington (1hr) and Reading (30min). From the station, it's a 5min walk north to Hart Street.

**By bus** Buses, including services from Oxford (hourly; 50min) and London (every 30min; 45min direct or 1hr, changing at Twyford) stop on Hart Street or Bell Street in the centre.

## INFORMATION AND TOURS

**Tourist office** In the Town Hall (Mon–Sat 10am–4pm; Oct–March 10.30am–3.30pm; ☎01491 578034, ⓦsouthernoxfordshire.com and ⓦvisitoxfordandoxfordshire.com).

**Boat trips** Just south of the bridge, Hobbs of Henley offers boat trips along the Thames (Easter–Sept; 1hr; £8.75; ☎01491 572035, ⓦhobbsofhenley.com), and has rowing boats and motor-launches for rent.

## ACCOMMODATION AND EATING

★**The Angel** Thameside ☎01491 410678, ⓦtheangelhenley.com. Of Henley's many pubs, this one stands out for its prime riverside location, with a fine outside deck overlooking the water. Decent food, too: light bites £5–8, mains £10–14. Food served Mon–Fri noon–10pm, Sat 11.30am–10pm, Sun 11.30am–7pm.

**Hotel du Vin** New St ☎0844 736 4258, ⓦhotelduvin.com. This slick central hotel occupies the creatively revamped old Brakspear Brewery. Rooms are in contemporary boutique style; a few on the top floor have river views. The restaurant serves sumptuous modern European cuisine using local produce. Mains £13–19. Food served Mon–Sat noon–2.30pm & 5.30–10pm, Sun noon–4pm & 6–9.30pm. **£135**

**Maison Blanc** 1 Duke St ☎01491 577294, ⓦmaisonblanc.co.uk. Part of local celebrity chef Raymond Blanc's culinary empire, this busy little café does good coffee along with fancy cakes, sandwiches and freshly baked bread – perfect for a picnic. Mon–Sat 8am–6pm, Sun 9am–5.30pm.

---

## HENLEY ROYAL REGATTA

Henley is best known for its **Royal Regatta**, established in 1839 and now the world's top amateur rowing tournament. The regatta, featuring past and potential Olympic rowers, begins on the Wednesday before the first weekend in July and runs for five days. Contact the Regatta Headquarters on the east side of Henley Bridge for ticket details (☎01491 572153, ⓦhrr.co.uk).

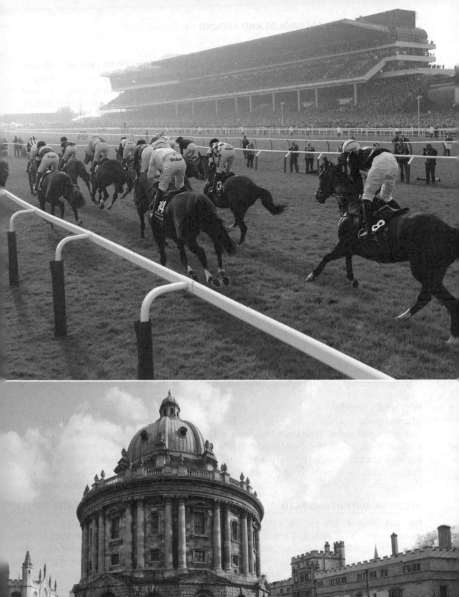

## Vale of White Horse

In the southwestern corner of Oxfordshire lies the pretty **Vale of White Horse**, a shallow valley whose fertile farmland is studded with tiny villages and dotted with a striking collection of prehistoric remains. The **Ridgeway National Trail**, running along – or near – the top of the downs, links several of these ancient sites and offers wonderful, breezy views. The Vale is easily visited as a day-trip from Oxford or elsewhere, but you might opt to stay locally in one of the Vale's quaint villages – tiny **Woolstone** is perhaps the most appealing.

### The Uffington White Horse

Dawn to dusk • Free • ☎ 01793 762209, ⓦ nationaltrust.org.uk • 10mins walk from signposted car park • From Oxford, take a bus to Wantage (45mins), then change for a Swindon-bound bus to Woolstone (35mins), 15mins walk away

**White Horse Hill**, overlooking the B4507 six miles west of the unexciting market town of Wantage, follows close behind Stonehenge (see p.225) and Avebury (see p.227) in the hierarchy of Britain's ancient sites, though it attracts nothing like the same number of visitors. Carved into the north-facing slope of the downs, the 374ft-long **Uffington White Horse** looks like something created with a few swift strokes of an immense brush. The first written record of the horse's existence dates from the time of Henry II, but it was cut much earlier, probably in the first century BC, making it one of the oldest chalk figures in Britain. There's no lack of weird and wonderful theories concerning its origins, but burial sites excavated in the surrounding area point to the horse having some kind of sacred function, though no one knows quite what.

Just below the horse is **Dragon Hill**, a small flat-topped hillock that has its own legend. Locals long asserted that this was where St George killed and buried the dragon, a theory proved, so they argued, by the bare patch at the top and the channel down the side, where blood trickled from the creature's wounds. Here also, at the top of the hill, is the Iron Age earthwork of **Uffington Castle**, which provides wonderful views over the Vale.

### Wayland's Smithy

The Ridgeway trail runs alongside the white horse and continues west to reach, after one and a half miles, **Wayland's Smithy**, a 5000-year-old burial mound encircled by trees. It is one of the best Neolithic remains in the area, though heavy restoration has rather detracted from its mystery. In ignorance of its original function, the invading Saxons named it after Weland (hence Wayland), an invisible smith who, according to their legends, made impenetrable armour and shod horses without ever being seen.

**ACCOMMODATION AND EATING**　　　　　　　　　　　　　　**VALE OF WHITE HORSE**

**Fox and Hounds** Uffington ☎ 01367 820680, ⓦ uffingtonpub.co.uk. Friendly local pub in this quiet village a mile and a half north of White Horse Hill, with two house-proud en-suite rooms for B&B and decent food (mains around £11). Food served Mon–Fri noon–2pm & 6–9pm, Sat noon–3pm & 6–9pm, Sun noon–3pm. **£75**

**White Horse Inn** Woolstone ☎ 01367 820726, ⓦ whitehorsewoolstone.co.uk. A mile north of White Horse Hill, this half-timbered, partly thatched old inn offers swanky accommodation, mostly in a modern annexe, and upmarket pub food (mains £13–20). Food served daily noon–2.30pm & 6–9pm. **£80**

# The Cotswolds

The limestone hills that make up the **Cotswolds** are preposterously photogenic, dotted with a string of picture-book villages, many of them built by wealthy cloth merchants between the fourteenth and sixteenth centuries. Largely bypassed by the Industrial Revolution, which heralded the area's commercial decline, the Cotswolds is characterised by beautifully preserved traditional architecture. Numerous churches are decorated with beautiful carving, for which the local limestone was ideal: soft and easy to carve when first quarried, but hardening after long exposure to the sunlight.

## THE RIDGEWAY NATIONAL TRAIL

The Iron Age inhabitants of Britain developed the **Ridgeway** (Ⓦ nationaltrail.co.uk/ridgeway) as a major thoroughfare, a fast route that beetled across the chalky downs of modern-day Berkshire and Oxfordshire, negotiated the Thames and then traversed the Chiltern Hills. It was probably once part of a longer route extending from the Dorset coast to the Wash in Norfolk. Today, the Ridgeway is a National Trail, running from **Overton Hill**, near Avebury in Wiltshire, to **Ivinghoe Beacon**, 87 miles to the northeast near Tring. Crossing five counties, it keeps to the hills and avoids densely populated areas, except where the Thames slices through the trail at **Goring Gap**, marking the transition from the open Berkshire–Oxfordshire downs to the wooded valleys of the Chilterns.

It's fairly easy hiking, and most of the route is accessible to cyclists. The prevailing winds mean that it is best walked in a northeasterly direction. The trail is strewn with prehistoric monuments, though the finest archeological remains are on the downs edging the **Vale of White Horse** (see opposite) and around **Avebury** (see p.227).

For their beauty and ease of access the Cotswolds are a major tourist attraction, with many towns afflicted by plagues of tearooms, antiques shops and coach parties. To see the region at its best, avoid the main towns and instead escape into the countryside. If you have a car, almost any minor road between Oxford and Cheltenham will deliver views, thatched cottages and oodles of rural atmosphere; otherwise, plan day-walks from one of the more attractive centres – **Chipping Campden** is the number one choice, or opt for **Northleach**, foodie hub **Kingham** or the walkers' haven of **Winchcombe**.

This might be a tamed landscape, but there's good scope for exploring the byways, either in the gentler valleys that are most typical of the Cotswolds or along the dramatic escarpment that marks the western boundary with the Severn Valley. The **Cotswold Way** national trail runs for a hundred miles along the edge of the Cotswold escarpment from Chipping Campden in the northeast to Bath in the southwest, with a number of prehistoric sites providing added interest along the route. The section around **Belas Knap** is particularly rewarding, offering superb views over Cheltenham and the Severn Valley to the distant Malvern Hills.

4

### GETTING AROUND
### THE COTSWOLDS

**By train** Hourly trains from London Paddington (via Oxford) stop at Kingham (1hr 25min) and Moreton-in-Marsh (1hr 35min), access points for the central and northern Cotswolds between Stow and Chipping Campden. On a different line from Paddington via Swindon, hourly trains serve Kemble (1hr 15min), near Tetbury and Cirencester.

**By bus** Local buses do a reasonable job connecting the larger towns and villages, but few buses run on Sundays. Smaller villages are rarely served more than once a week, if at all. Local tourist offices will be able to advise on travel plans – or check the public transport info at Ⓦ escapetothecotswolds.org.uk.

**On foot** The Cotswolds is prime walking country: at any point there's likely to be a marked trail nearby for anything from an hour's rural stroll to a multi-day epic. Loads of routes are downloadable for free (see below), with full descriptions and maps.

### INFORMATION

**Useful websites** Ⓦ cotswolds.com, Ⓦ oxfordshirecotswolds.org & Ⓦ escapetothecotswolds.org.uk

# Burford

Twenty miles west of Oxford you get your first real taste of the Cotswolds at **BURFORD**, where the long and wide High Street, which slopes down to the bridge over the River Windrush, is simply magnificent, despite the traffic. The street is flanked by a remarkable line of old buildings that exhibit

## FIVE COTSWOLDS CHURCHES

**St James** Chipping Campden. See p.260
**St John the Baptist** Burford. See p.254
**St John the Baptist** Cirencester. See p.263
**St Mary** Tetbury. See p.264
**St Peter and St Paul** Northleach. See p.259

---

**FIVE COTSWOLDS RESTAURANTS**

**Angel, Burford** Splendid Cotswold inn-restaurant with a creative, innovative approach that blends a wide range of styles and flavours. See p.below.

**Eight Bells, Chipping Campden** Fine traditional inn on the edge of one of the Cotswolds' most beautiful villages, serving posh pub grub to remember. See p.261.

**Horse and Groom, Bourton-on-the-Hill** Highly acclaimed free house with a flawless local reputation for great service and quality seasonal ingredients. See p.257.

**Jesse's Bistro, Cirencester** Classy, much-loved little hideaway specialising in fresh Cornish fish and seafood, alongside classic Modern British favourites as well. See p.264.

**Kingham Plough, Kingham** Outstanding rural gastropub, using locally sourced ingredients and state-of-the-art methods to encapsulate the best of the region's flavours. See p.256.

---

almost every type of classic Cotswolds feature, from wonky mullioned windows and half-timbered facades with bendy beams, through to spiky brick chimneys, fancy bow-fronted, stone houses and grand horse-and-carriage gateways.

## Church of St John the Baptist

Church Green, near the river • ⑩ burfordchurch.org

Of all the Cotswold churches, **St John the Baptist** has the most historical resonance, with architectural bits and pieces surviving from every phase of its construction, beginning with the Normans and ending in the wool boom of the seventeenth century – the soaring Gothic spire built atop the old Norman tower is particularly eye-catching. Thereafter, it was pretty much left alone and, most unusually, its clutter of mausoleums, chapels and chantries survived the Reformation. A plaque outside commemorates three "Levellers" – a loose coalition of free-thinking radicals that blossomed during the English Civil War – who were executed here in 1649 and whose aims are commemorated on **Levellers Day** in May (⑩ levellersday.wordpress.com).

### ARRIVAL AND INFORMATION                                         BURFORD

**By bus** #853 (Mon–Sat 2–4 daily, Sun daily) stops by the A40 at the top of Burford from Northleach (15min), Cheltenham (45min) and Oxford (45min). Also #233 (Mon–Sat hourly) from Woodstock (50min) and #X10 from Chipping Norton (Mon–Sat hourly; 30min) stop on the High Street.

**Tourist office** 33a High Street (Mon–Sat 9.30am–5pm, Sun 10am–4pm; ☎ 01993 823558, ⑩ www.oxford shirecotswolds.org).

### ACCOMMODATION AND EATING

★**Angel** 14 Witney St ☎ 01993 822714, ⑩ theangelatburford.co.uk. This sixteenth-century inn is highly regarded for its lively, creative menu – a madeira *jus* enlivening roast chicken, coriander and chilli adding zip to crab linguine, and so on. Mains £14–18, or two-course menu £18. Also three ensuite rooms, tasteful and traditional. Food served Mon–Sat noon–3pm & 6–9.30pm, Sun noon–4pm & 6–8.30pm. £90

**Bay Tree** Sheep St ☎ 01993 822791, ⑩ cotswold-inns -hotels.co.uk. First-class hotel in a lovely location off the High Street, occupying a wisteria-clad stone house dating from the sixteenth century. Its twenty-odd rooms, in the main house and a couple of annexes, are done up in a distinctly lavish rendition of period character. Bar meals are excellent (from £12) featuring anything from oriental-style duck confit to local pork sausages. Food served daily noon–2pm & 7–9.30pm. £180

**Bull** 105 High St ☎ 01993 822220, ⑩ bullatburford .co.uk. This venerable old inn has been hosting guests for more than three hundred years – Charles II dallied here with Nell Gwynne, as did Lord Nelson with Lady Hamilton. Traditionally styled rooms feature panelling and four-poster beds. The restaurant grafts French and Mediterranean influences onto local ingredients, with emphasis on fish and seafood. Mains £16–21. Food served Mon–Sat noon–3pm & 6–9.30pm, Sun noon–4pm & 6–9pm. £100

## Kelmscott Manor

Kelmscott • April–Oct Wed & Sat 11am–5pm • £9 • Timed tickets: call ahead to confirm arrangements • ☎ 01367 252486, ⑩ kelmscottmanor.org.uk • No public transport • The car park is a 10min walk from the house

**Kelmscott Manor**, amid the Thames-side water-meadows about eight miles south of Burford off the A361, is a place of pilgrimage for devotees of **William Morris** (see box below), who used this Tudor house as a summer home from 1871 to his death in 1896. The simple beauty of the house is enhanced by the furniture, fabrics and wallpapers created by Morris and his Pre-Raphaelite friends, including Burne-Jones and Rossetti.

# Kingham

When *Country Life* magazine calls you "England's favourite village", it could easily prompt a downward spiral. But for **KINGHAM**, set in the Evenlode Valley between Chipping Norton (the highest town in Oxfordshire) and Stow-on-the-Wold (the highest town in the Cotswolds), everything's looking up. There's still nothing to do in this cheery, noticeably upmarket village, other than eat well, walk well and sleep well… but that's the point. The stroll in from the railway station – served by mainline trains from London and Oxford – is lovely, marked by the Perpendicular tower of **St Andrew's Church**.

## Daylesford Organic

Daylesford • Mon–Wed 9am–5pm, Thurs–Sat 9am–6pm, Sun 10am–4pm • ☎ 01608 731700, Ⓦ daylesfordorganic.com

A mile north of Kingham in **DAYLESFORD** village, *Daylesford Organic* was founded in the 1980s when a local landowning family converted their farm to organic. Fashions caught up, and now Daylesford not only markets its own-brand produce but has a village **shop** – more like the smartest London food hall, vast, immaculate and expensive. It's a rather absorbing glimpse of Chelsea in the Cotswolds.

**4**

### ARRIVAL AND DEPARTURE

### KINGHAM

**By train** Kingham has hourly trains from London Paddington (1hr 25min), Oxford (25min), Moreton (10min) and Worcester (50min). The station is a mile west of the village.
**By bus** The only buses are sporadic local services.

---

### WILLIAM MORRIS AND THE PRE-RAPHAELITES

Socialist, artist, writer and craftsman **William Morris** (1834–1896) had a profound influence on his contemporaries and on subsequent generations. In some respects he was an ally of Karl Marx, railing against the iniquities of private property and the squalor of industrialized society, but – in contrast to Marx – he believed machines enslave the individual, and that people would be liberated only through a sort of communistic, crafts-based economy. His prose/poem story *News from Nowhere* vaguely described his Utopian society, but his main legacy turned out to be the **Arts and Crafts Movement**.

Morris's career as an artist began at Oxford, where he met **Edward Burne-Jones**, who shared his admiration for the arts of the Middle Ages. After graduating they both ended up in London, painting under the direction of Dante Gabriel Rossetti, the leading light of the **Pre-Raphaelites** – a loose grouping of artists intent on regaining the spiritual purity characteristic of art before Raphael and the Renaissance "tainted" the world with humanism. In 1861 Morris founded **Morris & Co** ("The Firm"), whose designs came to embody the ideas of the Arts and Crafts Movement, one of whose basic tenets was formulated by its founder: "Have nothing in your houses that you do not know to be useful or believe to be beautiful." Rossetti and Burne-Jones were among the designers, though Morris's own designs for fabrics, wallpapers and numerous other products were to prove a massive influence in Britain. The Laura Ashley aesthetic is a lineal descendant of Morris's rustic nostalgia.

Not content with his artistic endeavours, in 1890 Morris set up the **Kelmscott Press**, named after (but not located at) his summer home, whose masterpiece was the so-called *Kelmscott Chaucer*, the collected poems of one of the Pre-Raphaelites' greatest heroes, with woodcuts by Burne-Jones. Morris also pioneered interest in the architecture of the Cotswolds and, in response to the Victorian penchant for modernizing churches and cottages, he instigated the **Society for the Protection of Ancient Buildings** (Ⓦ spab.org.uk), still an active force in preserving the country's architectural heritage.

## WALKS AROUND KINGHAM

Kingham has loads of **walking** possibilities – not least within the **Foxholes Nature Reserve** (ⓦbbowt.org.uk), an ancient woodland famed for its spring bluebells. Download maps for longer trails at ⓦwww.oxfordshirecotswolds.org, including Walk 1, a **circular route** to/from Kingham Station (3.5 miles; 2hr 30min), exploring the fields around Bledington.

### ACCOMMODATION AND EATING

**Daylesford Organic** Daylesford ☎01608 731700, ⓦdaylesford.com. This super-sleek farm complex includes a spectacularly well-stocked deli and café, where light lunches (£10–14) are filled out by cream teas and informal suppers (Fri & Sat only; booking essential). Absurdly expensive, but very good. Mon–Wed 9am–5pm, Thurs–Sat 9am–6pm, Sun 10am–4pm, also Fri & Sat 7–9pm.

★**Kingham Plough** Kingham ☎01608 658327, ⓦthekinghamplough.co.uk. The epitome of a Cotswold gastropub, book ahead for one of Oxfordshire's most atmospheric, upmarket and welcoming restaurants. Local, seasonal produce of all kinds, expertly prepared, is served off a short, daily-changing menu (mains £16–25). They

also have seven country-style rooms. Food served Mon–Thurs noon–9pm, Fri & Sat noon–9.30pm, Sun noon–3pm & 6–8pm. **£95**

**Kings Head** Bledington ☎01608 658365, ⓦthekingsheadinn.net. Just west of Kingham, this sixteenth-century inn hosts regulars supping pints at the bar, and also serves local, ethically sourced food – potted shrimps, steak-and-ale pie, Cotswold lamb – alongside Modern British fusion dishes (mains £13–15). The rooms, some floral, some designer-chic, are a snip. Food served Mon–Thurs noon–2pm & 6.30–9pm, Fri noon–2pm & 6.30–9.30pm, Sat noon–2.30pm & 6.30–9.30pm, Sun noon–2.30pm & 7–9pm. **£95**

## 4  Great Tew

In a region which has beautiful villages and fine old pubs coming out of its ears, **GREAT TEW**, about five miles east of Chipping Norton via the A361 and B4022, takes the biscuit. It has Cotswold character aplenty, its thatched cottages and honey-coloured stone houses weaving around grassy hillocks, flanked on all sides by rolling woodland.

### ACCOMMODATION AND EATING                     GREAT TEW

★**Falkland Arms** 19-21 The Green ☎01608 683653, ⓦfalklandarms.co.uk. Idyllic, locally renowned country pub, which rotates guest beers in addition to its Wadworth cask ales, and sells a fine selection of single malts, herbal wines, snuff and clay pipes you can fill with tobacco for a smoke in the

flower-filled garden. Little has changed in the flagstone-floored bar since the sixteenth century, although the snug is now a small dining room serving home-made food (mains £9–17). Also with six sympathetically renovated rooms. Food served daily noon–2.30pm & 6–9.30pm. **£120**

## The Rollright Stones

Five miles north of Kingham, off the A3400 • Always open • Free, but £1 donation in honesty box requested • ⓦrollrightstones.co.uk

A signed country lane off the A44 leads to the **Rollright Stones**, a scattering of megalithic monuments in the fields either side of the lane. The eerie array consists of large natural stones moved here – no one is sure why – plus several burial chambers and barrows. The largest group is the **King's Men**, comprising over seventy irregularly spaced stones forming a circle one hundred feet in diameter, one of the most important such monuments in the country. The circle gets its name from a legend about a witch who turned a king and his army (of unknown identity) into these gnarled rocks to stop them invading England. Across the lane stands the **King's Stone** monolith, offering pensive views, with the **Whispering Knights** in sight on the field margin.

## Chastleton House

Four miles east of Moreton-in-Marsh off the A44 • April–Sept Wed–Sun 1–5pm; March & Oct Wed–Sun 1–4pm • £8.50; NT • Timed tickets, pre-bookable on ☎01494 755560, ⓦnationaltrust.org.uk • No public transport

Built between 1605 and 1612 by Walter Jones, a Welsh wool merchant, **Chastleton House** ranks among England's most splendid Jacobean properties, set amid ornamental gardens that include the country's first-ever croquet lawn. Inside, the house looks stuck in time, with unwashed upholstery, unpolished wood panelling and miscellaneous clutter: the National Trust, who took it on in 1991, wisely decided to stick to the "lived-in" look. Among the highlights are the barrel-vaulted long gallery and, in the beer cellar, the longest ladder (dated 1805) you're ever likely to see. There's also a wonderful topiary garden.

## Moreton-in-Marsh

A key transport hub and one of the Cotswolds' more sensible towns, **MORETON-IN-MARSH** is named for a now-vanished wetland nearby. It has always been an important access point for the countryside and remains so with its **railway station**, on the line between London, Oxford and Worcester. It also sits astride the A429 Fosse Way, the former Roman road that linked Exeter with Lincoln. On the broad, handsome **High Street**, enhanced with Jacobean and Georgian facades, stands the nineteenth-century **Redesdale Hall**, named for Lord Redesdale, father of the infamous Mitford sisters (among them Diana, wife of British wartime fascist leader Oswald Mosley; and Unity, a close companion of Adolf Hitler), who as children lived at Batsford House near the town.

### ARRIVAL AND INFORMATION

MORETON-IN-MARSH

**By train** Moreton has hourly trains from London Paddington (1hr 35min), Oxford (35min), Kingham (10min) and Worcester (40min). The station is a two-minute walk from the High Street.

**By bus** #21 (Mon–Sat 3 daily) from Broadway (25min), Chipping Campden (45min) and Stratford-upon-Avon (1hr 15min); #22 (Mon–Sat 5 daily) from Chipping Campden (30min) and Stratford-upon-Avon (1hr); #23 (Mon–Sat 2 daily) from Stratford-upon-Avon (1hr

5min); #801 (Mon–Sat hourly; June–Sept also 2 on Sun) from Stow-on-the-Wold (15min), Lower Slaughter (20min), Bourton-on-the-Water (25min), Northleach (40min) and Cheltenham (1hr 15min).

**Tourist office** High Street (Mon 8.45am–4pm, Tues–Thurs 8.45am–5.15pm, Fri 8.45am–4.45pm, Sat 10am–1pm; Nov–March Sat closes 12.30pm; ☎01608 650881, ⓦcotswold.gov.uk & ⓦcotswolds.com).

### ACCOMMODATION AND EATING

**Acacia Guest House** 2 New Rd ☎01608 650130, ⓦacaciainthecotswolds.co.uk. Decent little B&B on the short street connecting the station to the High Street – very handy for arrivals and departures by train or bus. **£60**

★**Horse and Groom** Bourton-on-the-Hill ☎01386 700413, ⓦhorseandgroom.info. Occupying a Georgian building of honey-coloured Cotswold stone two miles west of Moreton, this free house has a reputation for good beer and excellent food. The menu changes frequently, focused on meat sourced from local farmers and seasonal veg. It's popular: book ahead. Mains

£10–20. Also five appealing rooms, one with French doors opening onto the garden. Mon–Fri 11am–2.30pm & 6–11pm, Sat 11am–3pm & 6–11pm, Sun noon–3.30pm. **£120**

**Manor House** High St ☎01608 650501, ⓦcotswold-inns-hotels.co.uk. Pleasant four-star hotel occupying a sixteenth-century former coaching inn, with a nice garden and stylish rooms. Its posh restaurant, with muted contemporary styling, serves Modern British cuisine (three courses £39), with good vegetarian options available. Daily noon–2.30pm & 7–9.30pm. **£120**

## Stow-on-the-Wold

Ambling over a steep hill seven hundred feet above sea level, **STOW-ON-THE-WOLD**, five miles south of Moreton, draws in a number of visitors disproportionate to its size and attractions, which essentially comprise an old **marketplace** surrounded by pubs, antique and souvenir shops, and an inordinate number of tearooms. The narrow walled alleyways, or "tchures", running into the square were designed for funnelling sheep into the market, which is itself dominated by an imposing Victorian hall. **St Edward's church** has a photogenic north porch, where two yew trees flanking the door appear to have grown into the stonework.

---

### WALKS AROUND STOW-ON-THE-WOLD

"Meadows and Mills" is an easy **walk** (4 miles; 2hr 30min) downloadable at
ⓦ escapetothecotswolds.org.uk which heads downhill from Stow across fields to Lower
Slaughter and Bourton-on-the-Water. The high wolds west of Stow are horse country: aim for
the *Plough Inn* at Ford, on the B4077, bedecked in equestrian memorabilia. A pleasant **circular
walk** (6 miles; 3hr) starts at the pub, heads to Cutsdean village and follows a back lane to skirt
Jackdaw's Castle, ex-jockey Jonjo O'Neill's training yard, returning to Ford alongside the "gallops".

---

## Cotswold Cricket Museum

Brewery Yard • Tues–Sat 9.30am–5pm, Sun 9.30am–3.30pm • £3.50 • ☎ 01451 870083, ⓦ cotswoldcricketmuseum.co.uk

Just off the square, the small **Cotswold Cricket Museum** is a labour of love: the owner
Andy Collier has built up memorabilia over 25 years, from blazers to signed bats and
photos galore. He's always around for a chat: cricket buffs could lose a day to this place.

### ARRIVAL AND INFORMATION

**By bus** Buses stop just off the main square, including #801
(Mon–Sat every 1–2hrs; May–Sept also twice on Sun)
from Bourton-on-the-Water (10min), Lower Slaughter
(5min), Moreton (15min), Northleach (30min) and
Cheltenham (1hr).

**Tourist office** In the cricket museum, Brewery Yard
(Tues–Sat 9.30am–5pm, Sun 9.30am–3.30pm; ☎ 01451
830341, ⓦ stowinfo.co.uk & ⓦ cotswolds.com).

### ACCOMMODATION AND EATING

**Number Nine** 9 Park St ☎ 01451 870333, ⓦ number
-nine.info. Pleasant old house offering quality B&B just
down from the town square. The three bedrooms feature
low beams but contemporary styling – and the rates are a
bargain. £65

**Porch House** Digbeth St ☎ 01451 870048, ⓦ porch
-house.co.uk. Purportedly the oldest inn in Britain, with
parts of the building dated at 947 AD (though the interiors
have been freshly modernized). The 13 hessian-floored
rooms look good, but are on the small side. The restaurant
is a comfortably posh affair (mains £12–17), with cheaper
nosh in the wonky-beamed pub. Food served – pub
Mon–Sat noon–9.30pm, Sun noon–8.30pm;
restaurant Mon–Sat 6.30–9.30pm. £100

★**Queen's Head** The Square ☎ 01451 830563
ⓦ donnington-brewery.com. Traditional old pub that
provides good beer, good service and a pleasant chatty
atmosphere. Food is a level above standard pub grub
(mains roughly £9–11). Mon–Sat 11am–11pm, Sun
noon–10.30pm.

★**YHA hostel** The Square ☎ 0845 371 9540, ⓦ yha
.org.uk. This good-looking Georgian townhouse is the
Cotswolds' only youth hostel – an excellent choice for a
budget stay, with small dorms and a choice of family rooms
(4–6 beds) as well as kitchen facilities, a garden and a little
café. Dorms £19–23, doubles £50

---

## Bourton-on-the-Water

**BOURTON-ON-THE-WATER** is the epicentre of Cotswold tourism. Beside the village
green – flanked by photogenic Jacobean and Georgian facades in yellow Cotswold
stone – five picturesque little **bridges** span the shallow River Windrush, dappled
by shade from overhanging trees. It looks lovely, but its proximity to main roads
means that it's invariably packed with people: tourist coaches cram in all summer
long and the little **High Street** now concentrates on souvenirs and teashops,
interspersed with everything from a Model Village and Motoring Museum to a
Dragonfly Maze and Bird Park.

## Lower Slaughter

A mile outside Bourton-on-the-Water, **LOWER SLAUGHTER** (as in *slohtre*, Old English
for a marshy place, cognate with "slough") is a more enticing prospect, though still on
the day-trippers' circuit. Pop by to take in some of the most celebrated village scenery
in the Cotswolds, as the River Eye snakes its way between immaculate honeystone
cottages. There is a small **museum** (and souvenir shop) signposted in a former mill, but

the main attraction of the stroll through the village is to stop in for a little something at one of the grand hotels occupying gated mansions on both sides of the street.

# Northleach

Secluded in a shallow depression, **NORTHLEACH** is one of the most appealing and atmospheric villages in the Cotswolds – a great base to explore the area. Despite the fact that the A40 Oxford–Cheltenham road and A429 Fosse Way cross at a large roundabout nearby, virtually no tourist traffic makes its way into the centre. Rows of immaculate late medieval cottages cluster around the **Market Place** and adjoining **Green**.

## The Old Prison

A429 • Daily 9.30am–4.30pm • Free • ☎ 01451 861563, ⓦ escapetothecotswolds.org.uk

Just outside town the old Georgian **prison** has interesting displays on the history of crime and punishment, along with "**Escape to the Cotswolds**", a visitor centre explaining the work of the Cotswolds Conservation Board in maintaining the Cotswolds Area of Outstanding Natural Beauty.

## Church of St Peter and St Paul

Mill End • Daily 9am–5pm • Free • ☎ 01451 861432, ⓦ northleach.org

One of the finest of the Cotswolds wool churches, **St Peter and St Paul** is a classic example of the fifteenth-century Perpendicular style, with a soaring tower and beautifully proportioned nave lit by wide clerestory windows. The floors of the aisles are inlaid with an exceptional collection of memorial brasses, marking the tombs of the merchants whose endowments paid for the church. On several, you can make out the woolsacks laid out beneath the owner's feet – a symbol of wealth and power that survives today in the House of Lords in London, where a woolsack is placed on the Lord Chancellor's seat.

## Keith Harding's World of Mechanical Music

High St • Daily 10am–5pm • £8 • ☎ 01451 860181, ⓦ mechanicalmusic.co.uk

Two minutes' walk along the High Street from the Market Place, **Keith Harding's World of Mechanical Music** holds a bewildering collection of antique musical boxes, automata, barrel organs and mechanical instruments, all stuffed into one room. The entrance fee includes an hour-long tour.

| **ARRIVAL AND DEPARTURE** | **NORTHLEACH** |
|---|---|
| **By bus** Buses stop by the Green. | Moreton-in-Marsh (45min); #853 (Mon–Sat 2–4 daily, Sun |
| Destinations #801 (Mon–Sat every 2hrs) to Cheltenham | daily) to Burford (15min), Oxford (1hr) and Cheltenham |
| (35min), Bourton-on-the-Water (15min), Lower | (30min); #855 (Mon–Sat 5–6 daily) to Cirencester (20– |
| Slaughter (20min), Stow-on-the-Wold (30min) and | 40min) and Bibury (20min). |

## ACCOMMODATION AND EATING

**Cotswold Lion Café** Old Prison ☎ 01451 861563, ⓦ escapetothecotswolds.org.uk. Friendly daytime café on the edge of the town, serving up teas, coffees, cakes and light lunches (under £10). Daily 9.30am–4.30pm.

**Wheatsheaf** West End ☎ 01451 860244, ⓦ cotswoldswheatsheaf.com. Excellent former coaching inn, remodelled in a bright modern style softened by period furniture, bookcases and etchings. Its restaurant has upscale Mediterranean-influenced cuisine – lamb shank with polenta, aubergine and apricot tagine, and so forth. Mains £13–18. Also 14 comfortable, en-suite guest rooms. Food served daily noon–3pm (Sun 3.30pm) & 6–9pm. **£140**

# Bibury

A detour between Northleach and Cirencester passes through **BIBURY**, dubbed "the most beautiful village in England" by Victorian designer William Morris (see box, p.225). Bibury draws attention for **Arlington Row**, originally built around 1380 as a wool store and converted in the seventeenth century into a line of cottages to house weavers. Their hound's-tooth gables, warm yellow stone and wonky windows stole William Morris's heart – and are now immortalised in the British passport as an image of England.

### ARRIVAL AND DEPARTURE                                                BIBURY

**By bus** #855 (Mon–Sat 5 daily) from Northleach (20min) and Cirencester (20min)

## Chipping Campden

On the northern edge of the Cotswolds near Stratford-upon-Avon (see p.425), **CHIPPING CAMPDEN** gives a better idea than anywhere else in the area as to how a prosperous wool town might have looked in the Middle Ages. Its name derives from the Saxon term *campadene*, meaning cultivated valley, and the Old English *ceapen*, or market. The elegant **High Street** is hemmed in by mostly Tudor and Jacobean facades – an undulating line of weather-beaten roofs above twisted beams and mullioned windows. The evocative seventeenth-century **Market Hall** has survived too, an open-sided pavilion propped up on sturdy stone piers in the middle of the High Street, where farmers once gathered to sell their produce.

### The Old Silk Mill

Sheep St • Daily 10am–5pm • **Hart Silversmiths** Mon–Fri 9am–5pm, Sat 9am–noon • ☎ 01386 841100, ⓦ hartsilversmiths.co.uk

Just off the High Street is the **Old Silk Mill**, where designer Charles Ashbee relocated the London Guild of Handicraft in 1902, introducing the Arts and Crafts movement (see box, p.255) to the Cotswolds. Today, as well as housing galleries of local art, the building rings with the noise of chisels from the resident stone carvers. Upstairs, you're free to wander into the workshop of **Hart**, a silversmith firm – like stepping into an old photograph, with metalworking tools strewn everywhere under low ceilings, and staff perched by the windows working by hand on decorative pieces.

### Court Barn Museum

Church St • Tues–Sun 10am–5pm; Oct–March closes 4pm • £4 • ☎ 01386 841951, ⓦ courtbarn.org.uk

The history of the Guild of Handicraft, and its leading exponents, is explained at the superb **Court Barn museum**. Sited opposite a magnificent row of seventeenth-century Cotswold stone **almshouses**, the museum displays the work of Charles Ashbee and eight Arts and Crafts cohorts, placing it all in context with informative displays and short videos. Featured works include the bookbinding of Katharine Adams, stained-glass design of Paul Woodroffe and furniture by Gordon Russell.

### St James' Church

Church St • March–Oct Mon–Sat 10am–5pm, Sun 2–6pm; Nov–Feb Mon–Sat 11am–4pm, Sun 2–4pm; closes 3pm in Dec & Jan • Free • ⓦ stjameschurchcampden.co.uk

At the top of the village rises **St James' Church**. Built in the fifteenth century, the zenith of Campden's wool-trading days, this is the archetypal Cotswold wool church, beneath a magnificent 120ft tower. Inside, the airy nave is bathed in light from the clerestory windows. The South Chapel holds the ostentatious **funerary memorial** of the Hicks family, with fancily carved marble effigies lying on a table-tomb.

### Dover's Hill

Panoramic views crown the short but severe hike up the first stage of the Cotswold Way, north from Chipping Campden to **Dover's Hill** (which is also accessible by car). The highest point, 740ft above sea level, affords breathtaking vistas to the Malvern Hills and beyond. This is where, in 1612, local lawyer Robert Dover organised competitions of running, jumping, wrestling and shin-kicking that rapidly became known as the **Cotswold Olimpicks**, still staged here annually (see ⓦ olimpickgames.com).

## ARRIVAL AND INFORMATION

**By train** Moreton-in-Marsh station (see p.257) is eight miles away, connected by bus #21 or #22 (Mon–Sat every 1–2hrs; 45min).

**By bus** Buses stop on the High Street, including the linked buses #21 & #22.

Destinations Broadway (Mon–Sat 3 daily; 20min),

### CHIPPING CAMPDEN

Moreton-in-Marsh (Mon–Sat every 1–2hrs; 45min) and Stratford-upon-Avon (Mon–Sat every 1–2hrs; 35min).

**Tourist office** High Street (March–Oct daily 9.30am–5pm; Nov–Feb Mon–Thurs 9.30am–1pm, Fri–Sun 9.30am–4pm; ☎01386 841206, ⓦcampdenonline .org & ⓦcotswolds.com).

## ACCOMMODATION AND EATING

★ **Badgers Hall** High St ☎01386 840839, ⓦbadgershall. com. This tearoom in an old stone house has won awards for its inch-perfect take on traditional English tea and cakes, all freshly made daily. Also light lunches (under £10). En-suite guest rooms upstairs feature period detail – beamed ceilings and antique pine furniture. Tearoom Mon–Sat 10am–4.30pm, Sun 11am–4.30pm. **£110**

★ **Eight Bells** Church St ☎01386 840371, ⓦeightbellsinn.co.uk. Much-loved old inn with a first-rate restaurant – pheasant with mushrooms, pork with apricots and chestnuts, lamb's liver on bubble and squeak. Mains

£13–17. Also with seven individually done-up bedrooms, smartly modern without boutique pretension. Food served Mon–Thurs noon–2pm & 6.30–9pm, Fri & Sat noon–2.30pm & 6.30–9.30pm, Sun noon–9pm. **£115**

**Volunteer Inn** Lower High St ☎01386 840688, ⓦthe volunteerinn.net. Nine budget rooms at this lively pub, often used by walkers and cyclists (you can rent bikes here from £12/day; see ⓦcyclecotswolds.co.uk). The onsite *Maharaja* restaurant serves unusual Bangladeshi fish and chicken curries and fruity Kashmiri dishes (mains £8–17). Food served Sun–Thurs 5–10.30pm, Fri & Sat 5–11pm. **£60**

# Broadway

BROADWAY, five miles west of Chipping Campden, is a particularly handsome little village at the foot of the steep escarpment that rolls along the western edge of the Cotswolds. It seems likely that the Romans were the first to settle here, but Broadway's high times were as a stagecoach stop on the route from London to Worcester. Its long, broad main street, framed by honeystone cottages and shaded by chestnut trees, attracts more visitors than is comfortable, but things do quieten down in the evening.

## Gordon Russell Design Museum

Russell Sq • Tues–Sun 11am–5pm; Nov–Feb closes 4pm; closed Jan • £5 • ☎01386 854695, ⓦgordonrussellmuseum.org

Just off the village green, the absorbing **Gordon Russell Design Museum** is dedicated to the work of this local furniture-maker (1892–1980), whose factory formerly stood next door. Influenced both by the Arts and Crafts movement but also by modern technology, Russell's stated aim was to "make decent furniture for ordinary people" through "a blend of hand and machine". The museum showcases many of his classic furniture designs, alongside other period artefacts ranging from metalware to mirrors.

## Ashmolean Museum Broadway

65 High St • Tues–Sun 10am–5pm • £6 • ☎01386 859047, ⓦwww.ashmoleanbroadway.org

A former coaching inn now holds an annexe of Oxford's **Ashmolean Museum**. Objects across four floors of displays include embroidered tapestries and furniture in the panelled ground floor rooms, Worcester porcelain, glass, examples of William Morris tiles, and Cotswold pottery on the upper levels, as well as paintings by Gainsborough and Reynolds.

## Broadway Tower

Fish Hill • Daily 10am–5pm; shorter hours in bad weather • £4.80 • ☎01386 852390, ⓦbroadwaytower.co.uk

A mile southeast of the village, **Broadway Tower**, a turreted folly built in 1798, has become an icon of the Cotswolds, perched at more than 1,000 feet above sea level with stupendous views that purportedly encompass thirteen counties. Now privately owned, it stands alongside a family activity park with an adventure playground, snack bar and picnic area. The historical displays inside are a bit limp: visit to climb the 71 steps to the roof, for those views. A circular **walk** (4 miles; 3hr) heads up to the tower.

**4**

## ARRIVAL AND INFORMATION

**By bus** #21 (Mon–Sat 3 daily) from Chipping Campden (20min), Moreton-in-Marsh (25min) and Stratford-upon-Avon (50min); #606 (Mon–Sat 4 daily) from Winchcombe (35min) and Cheltenham (1hr).

## BROADWAY

**Tourist office** Russell Sq (April–Oct Mon–Sat 10am–5pm, Sun 11am–3pm; Feb, March, Nov & Dec closes 4pm; Jan closed; ☎ 01386 852937, ⓦ beautifulbroadway .com).

## ACCOMMODATION AND EATING

**Crown and Trumpet** 14 Church St ☎ 01386 853202, ⓦ cotswoldholidays.co.uk. This cheery, historic local tavern has decent beers, a lively atmosphere, quality Sunday roasts and regular sessions of live blues and jazz. Mains £6–12. Also five simple en-suite rooms. Food served Mon–Fri 11am–3pm & 5–11pm, Sat 11am–11pm, Sun noon–4pm & 6–10.30pm. **£70**
**Olive Branch** 78 High St ☎ 01386 853440, ⓦ theolivebranch-broadway.com.   Award-winning guesthouse in an old stone house – a touch

pastel-and-chintz, but cosy and well run. Some rooms have king-size beds and access to the garden. **£102**
**Russell's** 20 High St ☎ 01386 853555, ⓦ russellsofbroad way.co.uk. This relaxed, stylish restaurant serves Modern British cooking: Cotswold lamb chops with honey-roasted figs, lamb and sweetbreads, monkfish with bulghur wheat and pomegranate. Mains £17–24, or two-course set menu £17. Seven boutique rooms feature mood-lighting, designer furniture and huge stand-alone bathtubs and showers-for-two. Food served daily noon–2.30pm & 6–9.30pm. **£115**

# Winchcombe and around

About eight miles southwest of Broadway – and nine miles northeast of Cheltenham – **WINCHCOMBE** has a long main street flanked by a fetching medley of stone and half-timbered buildings. Placid today, it was an important Saxon town and one-time capital of the kingdom of Mercia, and flourished during the medieval cloth boom, one of the results being **St Peter's** church, a mainly fifteenth-century structure distinguished by forty alarming gargoyles that ring the exterior.

## Sudeley Castle

Winchcombe • April–Oct daily 10am–5pm • £14 • ☎ 01242 604244, ⓦ sudeleycastle.co.uk

Rising amid a magnificent estate on Winchcombe's southern edge, **Sudeley Castle** combines ravishing good looks with a fascinating history. **Richard III** lived at Sudeley for several years, and in 1535 **Henry VIII** spent a week here with Anne Boleyn. **Katherine Parr**, Henry's sixth wife, died at Sudeley in 1548. During the **Civil War** Sudeley acted as a Royalist garrison, coming under repeated attack. The ruins mouldered grandly, attracting the attention of **George III**, who fell down a crumbling flight of stairs on a visit in 1788. Restored in the nineteenth century, battlemented Sudeley now stands amid exquisite **grounds**: explore the towering ruins of the Elizabethan **Banqueting Hall** – left romantically untouched –and stroll through a grove of mulberry trees to reach the spectacular **Queen's Garden**, surrounded by yews and filled with summer roses. Alongside stands the Perpendicular Gothic **St Mary's Church**, housing a beautiful Victorian tomb that marks the final resting-place of Katherine Parr.

## Belas Knap

2 miles south of Winchcombe • Always open • Free; EH • ⓦ english-heritage.org.uk • On foot from Winchcombe, the path strikes off to the right near the entrance to Sudeley Castle. When you reach the country lane at the top, turn right and then left for the 10min hike to the barrow

The Neolithic long barrow of **Belas Knap** occupies one of the Cotswolds' wildest summits. Dating from around 3000 BC, this is the best-preserved burial chamber in England, stretched out like a strange sleeping beast cloaked in green velvet, more than fifty metres long. The best way to get there is to **walk**.

## ARRIVAL AND INFORMATION

**By bus** #606 (Mon–Sat 4 daily) from Broadway (35min) and Cheltenham (25min).

## WINCHCOMBE AND AROUND

**Tourist office** High Street (April–Oct daily 10am–4pm; ☎ 01242 602925, ⓦ winchcombe.co.uk & ⓦ cotswolds.com).

**ACCOMMODATION AND EATING**

**Lion Inn** 37 North St ☎01242 603300, ⓦthelionwinchcombe.co.uk. This fifteenth-century coaching inn is now a family-run bolt hole, with seven modern ensuite rooms. The menu relies on seasonal local produce, but also ventures into light European styles for tagines or seafood dishes. Mains £13–17. Food served daily noon–3pm & 6–9.30pm. **£100**

**White Hart** High St ☎01242 602359, ⓦwhitehart winchcombe.co.uk. A good-looking old tavern with wooden floors and benches. Eight en-suite rooms are decorated in traditional-meets-folksy manner, and there are also three cheaper "ramblers" rooms with shared bath. The restaurant is a great place to eat, focusing on hearty British cooking – especially gourmet sausages (venison and red wine, pork and stilton) and other meaty mains (£10–20). Two-course lunch £10. Food served daily 8am–9pm. **£70**

# Cirencester

Self-styled "Capital of the Cotswolds", the affluent town of **CIRENCESTER** lies on the southern fringes of the region, midway between Oxford and Bristol. As Corinium, it became a provincial capital and a centre of trade under the **Romans**, in Britannia second in size and importance only to "Londinium" (London). The Saxons destroyed almost all of the Roman city, and the town only revived with the wool boom of the Middle Ages. Few medieval buildings have survived, however, and the houses along the town's most handsome streets – Park, Thomas and Coxwell – date mostly from the seventeenth and eighteenth centuries. Cirencester's heart is the delightful **Market Place**, packed with traders' stalls every Monday and Friday, and for the fortnightly Saturday farmers' market.

## Church of St John the Baptist

Market Place • Daily 10am–5pm; Oct–March closes 4pm • Free • ☎01285 659317, ⓦcirenparish.co.uk

The magnificent parish church of **St John the Baptist**, built during the fifteenth century, dominates the market place. The church's most notable feature is its huge **porch**, so big that it once served as the local town hall. The flying buttresses that support the tower had to be added when it transpired that the church had been built over the filled-in Roman ditch that ran beside the Gloucester–Silchester road, which passed this way. Inside the church is a colourful wineglass **pulpit**, carved in stone around 1450, and the **Boleyn Cup**, a gilded silver goblet made in 1535 for Anne Boleyn.

## Corinium Museum

Park St • Mon–Sat 10am–5pm, Sun 2–5pm; Nov–March closes 4pm • £4.95 • ☎01285 655611, ⓦcoriniummuseum.org

West of the Market Place, the sleek **Corinium Museum** is devoted to the history of the town from Roman to Victorian times. The collection of Romano-British antiquities is particularly fine, including wonderful **mosaic pavements**. Other highlights include a trove of Bronze Age gold and an excellent video on Cotswold life in the Iron Age.

## New Brewery Arts Centre

Brewery Court, off Cricklade St • Mon–Sat 9am–5pm, April–Dec also Sun 10am–4pm • Free • ☎01285 657181, ⓦnewbreweryarts.org.uk

Just south of the Market Place, the **New Brewery Arts Centre** is occupied by more than a dozen resident artists whose studios you can visit and whose work you can buy in the shop. It's worth popping by to see who is working and exhibiting – and, perhaps, to catch some live music.

---

**WALKS AROUND WINCHCOMBE**

Winchcombe sets itself up as the **walking** capital of the Cotswolds. Aside from the **Cotswold Way** there's the **Gloucestershire Way** to Stow or Tewkesbury, and two long-distance routes heading north into Worcestershire, the **Wychavon Way** and **St Kenelm's Way**. The website ⓦwinchcombewelcomeswalkers.com has full information, including details of a scenic loop (5 miles; 3hr) through **Spoonley Wood**, two miles southeast of town. It starts by the war memorial opposite Winchcombe's church.

## ARRIVAL AND INFORMATION

### CIRENCESTER

**By train** From Kemble station, about 5 miles southwest – served by hourly trains from London Paddington (1hr 15min) and Cheltenham (1hr) – take bus #881 (Mon–Sat every 2hrs; 15min) or a taxi (about £10).

**By bus** National Express coaches from London and Heathrow Airport stop on London Rd, while local buses stop in or near Market Place.

Destinations #51 to Cheltenham (Mon–Sat hourly; 40min); #852 to Gloucester (Mon–Sat 4 daily; 1hr 10min);

#855 to Bibury (Mon–Sat 4 daily; 15min), Moreton-in-Marsh (Mon–Sat daily, Northleach (Mon–Sat 5–6 daily, 20–40min); 1hr 20min), Stow-on-the-Wold (Mon–Sat daily; 1hr 10min); and #881 to Tetbury (Mon–Sat 5 daily; 40min); National Express to Heathrow airport (5 daily; 1hr 30min) and London Victoria (5–8 daily; 2hr 20min).

**Tourist office** At the Corinium Museum, Park Street (Mon–Sat 10am–5pm, Sun 2–5pm; Nov–March closes 4pm; ☎01285 654180, ⓦ cotswolds.com & ⓦ cotswold.gov.uk).

## ACCOMMODATION

**Corinium** 12 Gloucester St ☎01285 659711, ⓦ coriniumhotel.com. Decent three-star family-run hotel in a historic property a short walk northwest of the centre. Only fifteen rooms, modestly priced and adequately furnished. **£105**

**Fleece** Market Place ☎01285 658507, ⓦ thefleececirencester.co.uk. This old town-centre inn

has been freshly updated to a smart, contemporary look. The 28 rooms, all beams and low ceilings, feature swanky en-suite bathrooms. **£94**

**Ivy House** 2 Victoria Rd ☎01285 656626, ⓦ ivyhousecotswolds.com. One of the more attractive of a string of B&Bs along this road, a high-gabled Victorian house with four en-suite rooms. **£80**

## EATING AND DRINKING

**Graze** 3 Gosditch St ☎01285 658957, ⓦ bathales.com. Across from the church, this splendid old building – its neo-Gothic facade concealing what was a thirteenth-century tithe barn – is now a rather good gastropub, turning out locally sourced pork and lamb chops, steaks and burgers. Mon–Thurs 11am–11pm, Fri 11am–midnight, Sat 9am–midnight, Sun 9am–11pm.

★**Jesse's Bistro** The Stableyard, 14 Black Jack St ☎01285 641497, ⓦ jessesbistro.co.uk. Wonderful little hideaway, in a courtyard near the museum. The speciality here is fish and seafood, freshly caught and whisked over direct from Cornwall. Expect crab salad or *moules marinière*, oven-roasted mackerel or pepper-crusted bream alongside

meaty favourites such as rump steak or calves' liver. Mains roughly £12–14. Mon noon–2.30pm, Tues–Sat noon–2.30pm & 7–9.30pm.

**Made By Bob** The Corn Hall, 26 Market Place ☎01285 641818, ⓦ foodmadebybob.com. Buzzy, hip daytime café/restaurant. Opens for breakfast (Bircher muesli, kippers, eggs Benedict, full English; £5–10), and stays open after lunch for posh tea. Watch the chefs prepare anything from fish soup with gruyère or red pepper tart to grilled squid or ribeye steak (mains £9–18) – or visit the deli section for swanky sandwiches (£5–6). Mon–Wed 7.30am–5.30pm, Thurs & Fri 7.30am–5.30pm & 7–9pm, Sat 8am–5.30pm.

# Tetbury and around

With Prince Charles's Highgrove estate and Princess Anne's Gatcombe Park nearby, **TETBURY** is the Cotswolds' most royal town – but this attractive, engaging place has plenty going for it with or without the Windsors. Scenic countryside, good shopping and excellent food make a fine combination. Just down from the central crossroads, marked by the seventeenth-century **Market House**, Tetbury's **church** (daily 10am–4pm) – curiously dedicated to both St Mary the Virgin and St Mary Magdalene – is one of England's finest examples of **Georgian Gothic**: the view along the eighteenth-century nave, with its dark box pews, candle chandeliers, slender wooden columns and enormous windows, is breathtaking.

## Highgrove

Doughton • Garden tours: April–Oct selected days & times • From £24.50 • Booking essential: ☎020 7766 7310, ⓦ highgrovegardens.com

**Highgrove**, home of Prince Charles and Camilla, Duchess of Cornwall, lies about a mile southwest in **DOUGHTON**. Two-hour tours of the **gardens** – led, needless to say, by a guide rather than HRH himself – operate in the summer. There's a waiting list of several weeks.

## Westonbirt: the National Arboretum

3 miles southwest of Tetbury • Daily 9am–8pm; Sept–March closes 5pm • Guided walks March–Oct Wed 11am, Sat & Sun 2pm • £5–9 depending on season; guided walks free • ☎ 01666 880220, ⓦ forestry.gov.uk/westonbirt • Bus #27 (Mon–Fri 5 daily, 3 on Sat; 8min from Tetbury)

Everything about **Westonbirt: The National Arboretum** relies on superlatives, from its role as protector of some of the oldest, biggest and rarest trees in the world to the display of natural colours it puts on in autumn. With seventeen miles of paths to roam, across six hundred acres, the best advice is to make a day of it. There are guided walks, **self-guided trails** and lots for kids and families.

### ARRIVAL AND INFORMATION
### TETBURY

**By train** From Kemble station, about seven miles northeast – served by hourly trains from London Paddington (1hr 15min) and Cheltenham (1hr) – take bus #881 (Mon–Sat every 2hrs; 25min) or a taxi (about £18).

**By bus** Buses drop off in the centre, including #881 from

Cirencester (Mon–Sat every 2hrs; 40min).

**Tourist office** 33 Church Street (March–Oct Mon–Sat 10am–4pm; Nov–Feb Mon–Sat 11am–2pm; ☎ 01666 503552, ⓦ visittetbury.co.uk & ⓦ cotswolds.com).

### ACCOMMODATION AND EATING

**The Ormond** 23 Long St ☎ 01666 505690, ⓦ theormondattetbury.co.uk. This inn-restaurant focuses on local suppliers – think honey-roast ham, steak and ale pie or juniper duck with sausage – served in a cheery, informal setting. Mains £11–18. Doubles as a three-star hotel, with tasteful, wittily done-up rooms. Food served Mon–Sat noon–2.30pm & 6.30–9.30pm, Sun noon–3pm & 7–9pm. **£120**

★ **Priory Inn** London Rd ☎ 01666 502251, ⓦ theprioryinn.co.uk. Although the mains of Gloucester pork or Bibury trout are excellent (£12–18), the speciality

at this family-friendly spot is wood-fired pizza (£8–12). Also with fourteen neutral, unfussy rooms. Food served Mon–Fri noon–3pm & 5–10pm, Sat & Sun noon–10pm. **£99**

**Snooty Fox** Market Place ☎ 01666 502436, ⓦ snooty-fox.co.uk. Traditional coaching inn, renamed by a former owner who was snubbed by the local hunt, now thoroughly updated. Rooms feature a nod to the traditional here, a touch of playfulness there, and the food is uncomplicated, presented decently and charged moderately. Mains £11–21. Mon–Fri 7.30am–9.30pm, Sat 8am–9.30pm, Sun 8am–9pm. **£80**

# Painswick

**PAINSWICK** is a beautiful old Cotswolds wool town easily accessible from Cheltenham. The fame of Painswick's **church** stems not so much from the building itself as from the surrounding **graveyard**, where 99 yew trees, trimmed into bulbous lollipops, surround a collection of eighteenth-century table tombs unrivalled in the Cotswolds.

## Rococo Garden

Half a mile north of Painswick, off Gloucester Rd (B4073) • Mid-Jan to Oct daily 11am–5pm • £6.50 • ☎ 01452 813204, ⓦ rococogarden.org.uk

Created in the early eighteenth century, the **Rococo Garden** has been restored to its original form with the aid of a painting from 1748. This is England's only example of Rococo garden design, a short-lived fashion typified by a mix of formal geometrical shapes and

---

### THAMES HEAD

Between Cirencester and Tetbury, **Kemble** is surrounded by water meadows regarded as the **source of the River Thames**. From Kemble station – served by hourly trains from London Paddington (1hr 15min) and Cheltenham (1hr) – walk half a mile north to the *Thames Head Inn* (☎ 01285 770259, ⓦ thamesheadinn.co.uk), by the railway bridge on the A433. At the pub, bar staff and a sketch-map hanging in the porch can point you onto the stroll of about fifteen minutes to **Thames Head**, a point by a copse in open fields, where a stone marker declares a shallow depression to be the river's source. However, the Thames is fed by groundwater, and since the water table rises and falls, the river's source shifts: don't be disappointed if Thames Head is dry when you visit. The **Thames Path** (ⓦ nationaltrail.co.uk) starts here: walk it direct to Greenwich in southeast London, 184 miles away.

more naturalistic, curving lines. With a vegetable patch as an unusual centrepiece, it spreads across a sheltered gully – for the best views, walk around anticlockwise.

### ARRIVAL AND INFORMATION                                    PAINSWICK

**By bus** #46 runs from Cheltenham (hourly; 30min).
**Tourist office** Painswick's summer-only tourist office (April–Oct Mon–Wed 10am–1pm, Thurs & Fri 10am–4pm, Sat 10am–1pm; ☏ 07503 516924, ⓦ visitthecotswolds.

org.uk & ⓦ cotswolds.com) was, at the time of writing, temporarily housed in St Mary's Church ahead of a relocation to the gravedigger's hut in the churchyard.

### ACCOMMODATION AND EATING

**Cardynham House** Tibbiwell St ☏ 01452 814006, ⓦ cardynham.co.uk. Lovely guesthouse with nine modern themed rooms, most with four-poster beds, all en suite. The bistro (closed Sun eve & Mon) has simple, well-cooked nosh – cod loin, lamb cutlets, beef stroganoff and the like (mains £12–16). **£90**

★**Olivas** Friday St ☏ 01452 814774, ⓦ olivas .moonfruit.com. Brilliant deli and café that does delicious Mediterranean-style lunches – Spanish soups and stews of chicken, chickpeas and chorizo, stuffed aubergines, loads of tapas including calamari, whitebait, olives, and more, all around £10. Daily 10am–5pm.

# Cheltenham

Until the eighteenth century **CHELTENHAM** was a modest Cotswold town like any other, but the discovery of a spring in 1716 transformed it into Britain's most popular **spa**. During Cheltenham's heyday, a century or so later, royalty and nobility descended in droves to take the waters, which were said to cure anything from constipation to worms. These days, the town – still lively, still posh – has lots of good restaurants and some of England's best-preserved Regency architecture.

Cheltenham also has excellent **arts festivals** (ⓦ cheltenhamfestivals.com) – **jazz** (April), **science** (June), **classical music** (July) and **literature** (Oct), plus a separately run **folk** festival (Feb) – as well as world-class **horse-racing** (see box, p.268).

## Promenade

Cheltenham's main street, **Promenade**, sweeps majestically south from the High Street, lined with some of the town's grandest houses and smartest shops. It leads into Imperial Square, whose greenery is surrounded by proud Regency terraces that herald the handsome terraces and squares of the Montpellier district, which stretches south in a narrow block to Suffolk Road, making for a pleasant urban stroll.

## The Wilson (Cheltenham Art Gallery and Museum)

Clarence St · Daily 9.30am–5.15pm · Free · ☏ 01242 237431, ⓦ thewilson.org.uk

Just off the Promenade stands **The Wilson**, formerly known as the **Cheltenham Art Gallery and Museum**, now housing the tourist office, a shop selling beautiful work by the Gloucestershire Guild of Craftsmen (ⓦ guildcrafts.org.uk) and four floors of exhibitions. The rebranding honours Edward Wilson, a Cheltonian who was on Scott's ill-fated Antarctic expedition of 1912. Photographs and some of his Antarctic gear are displayed alongside a collection focused on the Arts and Crafts movement (see box, p.255), ranging from superb furniture to ceramics, jewellery, pottery and exquisitely hand-illustrated books.

## Holst Birthplace Museum

4 Clarence Rd · June–Sept Tues–Sat 10am–5pm, Sun 1.30–5pm; rest of year Tues–Sat 10am–4pm; closed Jan · £5 · ☏ 01242 524846, ⓦ holstmuseum.org.uk

Housed in a refined Regency terrace house, the **Holst Birthplace Museum** was where the composer of *The Planets* was born, in 1874. Its intimate rooms hold plenty of Holst memorabilia – including his piano in the ground-floor music room – and give a good insight into Victorian family life.

## Pittville Pump Room

Pittville Park • Daily 10am–4pm • ☎ 01242 523852, ⓦ pittvillepumproom.org.uk

About ten minutes' walk north along handsome Evesham Road brings you into the **Pittville** district, where local chancer Joseph Pitt began work on a grand spa in the 1820s, soon afterwards running out of cash, though he did manage to complete the domed **Pump Room** before he hit the skids. A lovely Classical structure with an imposing colonnaded facade, it is now used mainly as a concert hall, but you can still sample the pungent **spa waters** from the marble fountain in the main auditorium for free.

### ARRIVAL AND INFORMATION

### CHELTENHAM

**By train** Cheltenham Spa station is on Queen's Rd, southwest of the centre; local buses run into town every 10min, otherwise it's a 20min walk.

Destinations Birmingham New Street (2–3 hourly; 40min); Bristol (every 30min; 40min); London Paddington (hourly, some change at Swindon; 2hr 15min).

**By bus** National Express coaches to and from London and

Heathrow Airport stop on Royal Well Road. Local buses stop on Promenade.

Destinations #46 to Painswick (hourly; 30min); #51 to Cirencester (Mon–Sat hourly; 40min); #94 to Gloucester (every 10min; 35min); #606 to Winchcombe (Mon–Sat approx hourly; 20min) and Broadway (Mon–Sat 2–3 daily; 45min); #801 to Northleach (Mon–Sat

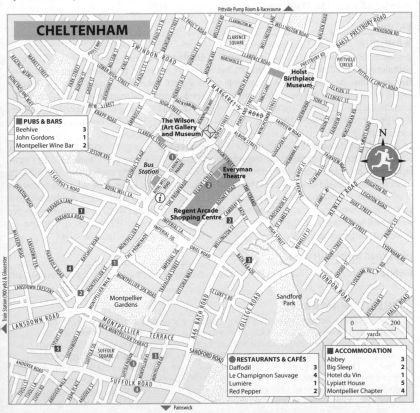

**CHELTENHAM**

**PUBS & BARS**
Beehive 3
John Gordons 1
Montpellier Wine Bar 2

**RESTAURANTS & CAFÉS**
Daffodil 3
Le Champignon Sauvage 4
Lumière 1
Red Pepper 2

**ACCOMMODATION**
Abbey 3
Big Sleep 2
Hotel du Vin 1
Lypiatt House 5
Montpellier Chapter 4

every 1–2hrs; 35min), Stow-on-the-Wold (Mon–Sat hourly; June–Sept also 2 on Sun; 1hr) and Moreton-in-Marsh (Mon–Sat hourly; June–Sept also 2 on Sun; 1hr 15min); #853 to Northleach (Mon–Sat 3 daily, Sun daily; 30min), Burford (Mon–Sat 3 daily, Sun daily;

45min) and Oxford (Mon–Sat 3 daily, Sun daily; 1hr 30min).

**Tourist office** In The Wilson gallery, Clarence Street (daily 9.30am–5.15pm; ☎01242 237431, ⓦvisitcheltenham .com & ⓦcotswolds.com).

## ACCOMMODATION

Cheltenham has plenty of **hotels** and **guesthouses**, many of them in fine Regency houses, but you should book well in advance during the races and festivals.

**Abbey** 14 Bath Parade ☎01242 516053, ⓦabbeyhotel -cheltenham.com. Thirteen individually furnished rooms at this centrally located B&B, with wholesome breakfasts taken overlooking the garden. **£87**

**Big Sleep** Wellington St ☎01242 696999, ⓦthebigsleephotel.com. Contemporary budget hotel with 59 rooms including family rooms and suites, all with a retro designer feel and hi-tech gadgetry but no frills – and unusually low prices. **£55**

**Hotel du Vin** Parabola Rd ☎01242 588450, ⓦhotelduvin.com. Occupying a splendid old Regency mansion, this glam boutique-style hotel in the sought-after Montpellier district has 49 stylish rooms and suites

and a reputation for excellence. **£105**

**Lypiatt House** Lypiatt Rd ☎01242 224994, ⓦlypiatt .co.uk. Splendid, four-square Victorian villa set in its own grounds a short walk from the centre, with spacious rooms, open fires and a conservatory with a small bar. **£98**

**Montpellier Chapter** Bayshill Rd ☎01242 527788, ⓦthemontpellierchapterhotel.com. Gloriously grand villa hotel in the classy Montpellier neighbourhood. The restaurant is super-stylish, with its open kitchen and glassed terrace, and the same contemporary flair extends to the rooms, with their monsoon showers, feature walls, hi-tech gadgetry and some with in-room bathtubs and/or balconies. **£125**

## EATING

★**Daffodil** 18–20 Suffolk Parade ☎01242 700055, ⓦwww.thedaffodil.com. Eat in the circle bar or auditorium of this breathtakingly designed 1920s Art Deco ex-cinema, where the screen has been replaced with a hubbub of chefs. Great atmosphere and first-class British cuisine (mains £14–22), as well as cocktails and a swish of style. Live jazz Sat lunchtime & Mon night. Mon–Sat noon–11pm.

**Le Champignon Sauvage** 24 Suffolk Rd ☎01242 573449, ⓦlechampignonsauvage.co.uk. Cheltenham's highest-rated restaurant, its sensitively updated classic French cuisine awarded two Michelin stars among a welter of other awards. The ambience is chic and intimate, the presentation immaculately artistic. The full menu is £48 (two courses) or £59 (three courses), or opt for the smaller set menu at £26 (two courses). Book well ahead. Tues–Sat

12.30–1.15pm & 7.30–8.30pm.

**Lumière** Clarence Parade ☎01242 222200, ⓦwww .lumiere.cc. Upscale, contemporary, seasonal British food in a genial ambience of informality. Cornish scallops or sexed-up corned beef prelude mains such as Gloucester Old Spot pork done two ways, partridge or local venison. Three-course menu £55 (or £28 at lunch). Tues 7–9pm, Wed–Sat noon–1.30pm & 7–9pm.

**Red Pepper** 13 Regent St ☎01242 253900, ⓦwww .redpeppercheltenham.co.uk. Family-run deli, coffee lounge and bistro in the centre of town, with a friendly, informal vibe. Light lunches of pie and mash or fishcake and salad (£7–9), through to rack of lamb, gnocchi or sea bass in the evenings (mains £11–15). Downstairs coffee lounge daily 9am–6pm; upstairs bistro Tues–Fri 6–9.30pm, Sat noon–3pm & 6–9.30pm, Sun noon–3pm.

## DRINKING AND NIGHTLIFE

**Beehive** 1–3 Montpellier Villas ☎01242 702270, ⓦthebeehivemontpellier.com. Popular, easygoing pub

---

### CHELTENHAM RACES

**Cheltenham racecourse** (☎01242 513014, ⓦcheltenham.co.uk), on the north side of town, is Britain's main venue for National Hunt racing, also known as "steeplechase" – where the horses jump hurdles or fences. The principal events are the four-day **Festival** in March, which attracts sixty thousand people each day, culminating in the famous **Cheltenham Gold Cup**, and the three-day **Open** in November, but there are smaller meetings throughout the season, which runs from late October to early May. For what many say is the best view, book ahead for entry to the pen opposite the main stand, known as Best Mate Enclosure (about £10–50, depending on event).

in Montpellier, under new management in 2014, with good beer, a friendly ambience and decent pub grub in the atmospheric restaurant upstairs. Mon–Sat 11am–11pm, Sun noon–10pm.

★**John Gordons** 11 Montpellier Arcade ☏01242 245985, ⓦjohngordons.co.uk. Lovely little independent wine bar, hidden off Montpellier's fanciest street. Take a seat in the shop or outside in the old Victorian covered arcade to watch the world go by while sampling a glass or two of wine, alongside a plate of

charcuterie, cheeses and/or antipasti (£6–14). Mon–Wed 9.30am–11pm, Thurs–Sat 9.30am–midnight, Sun 11am–10pm.

**Montpellier Wine Bar** Bayshill Lodge, Montpellier St ☏01242 527774, ⓦmontpellierwinebar.co.uk. Stylish wine bar and restaurant with lovely bow-fronted windows on a busy little corner. Hangout at the bar with glass of something smooth, or drop in mid-morning for brunch. Mon–Thurs 10am–3pm & 6–9.30pm, Fri–Sun 10am–9.30pm.

# Gloucester and around

For centuries life was good for **GLOUCESTER**, ten miles west of Cheltenham. The Romans chose this spot for a garrison to guard the River Severn, while in Saxon and Norman times the Severn developed into one of Europe's busiest trade routes. The city became a major religious centre too, but from the fifteenth century onwards a combination of fire, plague, civil war and increasing competition from rival towns sent Gloucester into a decline from which it never recovered – even the opening of a new canal in 1827 between Gloucester and Sharpness to the south failed to revive the town's dwindling fortunes.

Today, the **canal** is busy once again, though this time with pleasure boats, and the Victorian **docks** have undergone a facelift, offering a fascinating glimpse into the region's industrial past. The main reason for a visit, however, remains Gloucester's magnificent **cathedral**, one of the finest in the country.

**4**

## Gloucester Cathedral

College Green • Daily 7.30am–6pm • Free • ⓦ gloucestercathedral.org.uk

The superb condition of **Gloucester Cathedral** is striking in a city that has lost so much of its history. The Saxons founded an abbey here, but four centuries later Benedictine monks arrived intent on building their own church; work began in 1089. As a place of worship it shot to importance after the murder of King Edward II in 1327 at Berkeley Castle (see p.271): Gloucester took his body, and the king's shrine became a major place of pilgrimage. The money generated helped finance the conversion of the church into the country's first and greatest example of the **Perpendicular style**: the magnificent 225ft tower crowns the achievement.

Beneath the reconstructions of the fourteenth and fifteenth centuries, some Norman aspects remain, best seen in the **nave**, which is flanked by sturdy pillars and arches adorned with immaculate zigzag carvings. The **choir** provides the best vantage point for admiring the **east window** completed in around 1350 and – at almost 80ft tall – the largest medieval window in Britain, a stunning cliff face of stained glass. Beneath it, to the left (as you're facing the east window) is the **tomb of Edward II**, immortalized in alabaster and marble. Below the east window lies the **Lady Chapel**, whose delicate carved tracery holds a staggering patchwork of windows. The innovative nature of the cathedral's design can also be appreciated in the beautiful **cloisters**, completed in 1367 and featuring the first fan vaulting in the country – used to represent the corridors of Hogwart's School in the *Harry Potter* films.

## Gloucester Waterways Museum

Gloucester Docks • Daily: July & Aug 10.30am–5pm; rest of year 11am–4pm; boat trips May–Aug daily on the hour noon–3pm; April, Sept & Oct Sat & Sun only; 45min • £5.50; boat trip £6 • ☏ 01452 318200, ⓦ canalrivertrust.org.uk/gloucester-waterways-museum

Less than half a mile southwest of the city centre, **Gloucester Docks** holds fourteen warehouses built for storing grain following the opening of the Sharpness canal to the River Severn in 1827. Most have been turned into offices and shops, but the southernmost Llanthony Warehouse is now occupied by the **Gloucester Waterways Museum**, which delves into every nook and cranny of the area's watery history, from the engineering of the locks to the lives of the horses that trod the towpaths, along with plenty of interactive displays. The museum runs regular **boat trips** out onto the Sharpness canal, with commentary.

## ARRIVAL AND INFORMATION
GLOUCESTER

**By train** Gloucester station is on Bruton Way, a 5min walk east of the centre.

Destinations Birmingham New Street (hourly; 50min); Bristol (hourly; 40min); London Paddington (hourly, some change at Swindon; 1hr 55min).

**By bus** National Express coaches to and from London and Heathrow Airport stop opposite the train station, as do local buses.

Destinations #94 to Cheltenham (every 10min; 35min), #852 to Cirencester (Mon–Sat 4 daily; 1hr 10min), #853 to Northleach (Mon–Sat 2 daily, Sun daily; 55min), Burford (Mon–Sat 2 daily, Sun daily; 1hr 20min) and Oxford (Mon–Sat 2 daily, Sun daily; 2hr).

**Tourist office** 28 Southgate Street (Mon 10am–5pm, Tues–Sat 9.30am–5pm; ☎01452 396572, ⓦthecityofgloucester.co.uk & ⓦcotswolds.com).

## ACCOMMODATION AND EATING

**Café René** 31 Southgate St ☎01452 309340, ⓦcaferene.co.uk. This lively, fancifully decorated central pub serves decent burgers and steaks, with plenty for vegetarians (mains £9–14) and lighter lunches, as well as great Sunday barbecues in summer, and live blues, jazz and acoustic music twice a week. After 11pm on weekend nights, the cellar bar turns into a club (£2 admission), for loud local DJs. Sun–Thurs 11am–midnight, Fri & Sat 11am–4am.

**Mulberry House** 2a Heathville Rd ☎01452 720079, ⓦthe-mulberry-house.co.uk. Decent B&B in a modern family home roughly ten minutes' walk northeast. Two en-suite doubles are enhanced with quality breakfasts. Cash only. **£55**

**New Inn** 16 Northgate St ☎01452 522177, ⓦnewinn-hotel.co.uk. Pop into this fourteenth-century pub in the city centre to sup a pint of one of their several cask ales and have a gander at the preserved interior – this is Britain's most complete surviving medieval courtyard tavern, ringed by galleries (and, reputedly, haunted). Also 33 fairly basic rooms, with corporate furniture and swirly carpets. Mon–Thurs 11am–11pm,

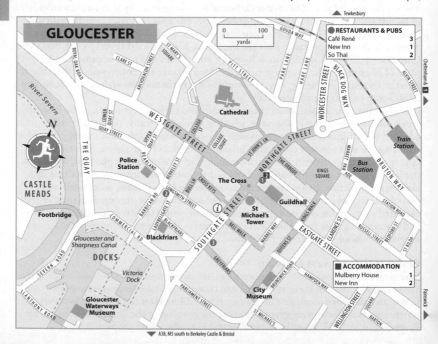

Fri & Sat 11am–midnight, Sun noon–10.30pm. **£54**
**So Thai** Longsmith St ☎01452 535185, ⓦso-thai
.co.uk. This Thai restaurant has rapidly gained a reputation
for quality and authenticity. The decor takes in vaulted

brickwork, service is attentive and the food – including
unusual northern Thai pork curry with pineapple and lamb
*massaman curry* – expertly prepared. Mains £9–16, two-
course lunch menu £9. Tues–Sun 11am–10pm.

## Berkeley Castle

Berkeley, 15 miles south of Gloucester • April–Oct Sun–Wed 11am–5pm • £10 • ☎01453 810303, ⓦberkeley-castle.com

Secluded within an enclave swathe of meadows and gardens, **Berkeley Castle** dominates
the Vale of Berkeley, a low-lying strip tucked between the Cotswold Edge and the River
Severn. The stronghold has a turreted medieval appearance, its twelfth-century austerity
softened by its gradual transformation into a family home (the Berkeleys have been in
residence here for almost 900 years). The interior is packed with mementoes of its long
history, including its grisliest moment when, in 1327, **Edward II** was murdered here
– purportedly by a red-hot poker thrust into his backside. You can view the cell where
the event took place, along with dungeons, dining room, kitchen, picture gallery and
the Great Hall.

# Berkshire

One of the "Home Counties" that ring London, **Berkshire** covers a diverse swathe of
terrain immediately west of the capital. It is known as a royal county for the
presence of **Windsor Castle**, one of the Queen's residences and by far the most
important attraction in the area. All around Windsor, the county boundary is
formed by the River Thames, on its route into London: a little upstream, at the
riverside village of **Cookham**, a gallery displaying works by the local twentieth-
century artist Stanley Spencer gives bucolic insight into a now-lost rural idyll. To
the north stretch the Chiltern Hills of Buckinghamshire (see p.273), while to the
south and west, past Henley-on-Thames (see p.250), rise the Berkshire Downs
above humdrum Newbury. The largest town hereabouts is **Reading** – missable, but
an important rail crossroads.

## Reading

**READING**, 35 miles west of London, sprawls to a population above 300,000, making
it a city in all but name. Prosperous and modern, it is prominent today as a rail
crossroads: the huge train station is the third-busiest in the country outside London,
standing at the junction of lines from London, Cornwall, South Wales, the West
Midlands and the south coast, also with direct links to Heathrow and Gatwick
airports. Reading itself is light on attractions, but boasts a couple of curiosities.
First is the **prison** (no public access), a severe-looking structure on Forbury Road,
where Oscar Wilde was incarcerated in the 1890s and wrote his poignant *Ballad of
Reading Gaol*. The other is a Victorian **replica of the Bayeux Tapestry** recording
William the Conqueror's invasion of England in 1066, seventy metres long and now
displayed at the **Museum of Reading**, in the town hall on Blagrave Street, two
minutes' walk from the station (Tues–Sat 10am–4pm, Sun 11am–4pm; free;
ⓦreadingmuseum.org.uk).

### ARRIVAL AND DEPARTURE                                                    READING

**By train** The train station is on the north side of town, five
minutes' walk from the centre.
Destinations Birmingham New Street (every 30min; 1hr
35min); Bristol (every 30min; 1hr 15min); Gatwick Airport

(hourly; 1hr 15min); Heathrow Airport (every 30min;
55min); London Paddington (every 10min; 25min); Oxford
(every 15min; 25min); Southampton (every 30min;
45min); Winchester (every 30min; 30min).

# Windsor

Every weekend trains from London Waterloo and Paddington are packed with people heading for **WINDSOR**, the royal enclave 21 miles west of London, where they join the human conveyor belt round **Windsor Castle**. If you've got the energy or inclination, it's also possible to cross the river to visit **Eton College**, which grew from a fifteenth-century free school for impoverished scholars and choristers to become one of the most elitist schools in the world (for guided tours contact ☎01752 671000, ⓦetoncollege.com).

## Windsor Castle

Daily: March–Oct 9.45am–5.15pm; Nov–Feb 9.45am–4.15pm • £18.50 • ☎ 020 7766 7304, ⓦ royalcollection.org.uk

Towering above the town on a steep chalk bluff, **Windsor Castle** is an undeniably imposing sight, its chilly grey walls, punctuated by mighty medieval bastions, continuing as far as the eye can see. Inside, most visitors just gape in awe at the monotonous, gilded grandeur of the **State Apartments**, while the real highlights – the paintings from the Royal Collection that line the walls – are rarely given a second glance. More impressive is **St George's Chapel**, a glorious Perpendicular structure ranking with Henry VII's chapel in Westminster Abbey (see p.62), and the second most important resting place for royal corpses after the Abbey. On a fine day, put aside some time for exploring **Windsor Great Park**, which stretches for several miles to the south of the castle.

### ARRIVAL AND DEPARTURE                                        WINDSOR

**By train** London Paddington to Windsor & Eton Central station via Slough (every 30min; 40min) or London Waterloo to Windsor & Eton Riverside station (every 30min; 55min). From Oxford and Reading, change at Slough.

# Cookham and around

Tiny **COOKHAM**, a prosperous Berkshire village five miles northwest of Windsor on the border with Buckinghamshire, was the former home of **Stanley Spencer** (1891–1959), one of Britain's greatest – and most eccentric – artists. Cliveden (see opposite) is on the doorstep.

## Stanley Spencer Gallery

High St • April–Oct daily 10.30am–5.30pm; Nov–March Thurs–Sun 11am–4.30pm • £5 • ☎01628 471885, ⓦ stanleyspencer.org.uk • 15min walk from Cookham station

The son of a local music teacher, Stanley Spencer spent much of his life in Cookham, which he once famously described as "a village in Heaven". Much of his work was inspired by the Bible, and many of his paintings depict biblical tales transposed into his Cookham surroundings. Much of Spencer's most acclaimed work is displayed in London's Tate Britain, but there's a fine sample here at the **Stanley Spencer Gallery**, which occupies the old Methodist Chapel on the High Street. Three prime exhibits are *View from Cookham Bridge*, the unsettling *Sarah Tubb and the Heavenly Visitors*, and the wonderful (unfinished) *Christ Preaching at Cookham Regatta*. The permanent collection is enhanced by regular exhibitions of Spencer's paintings and the gallery also contains incidental Spencer letters, documents and memorabilia. Download details of an hour-long walk round Cookham, visiting places with which Spencer is associated, from the gallery website.

## Bray

About three miles south of Cookham, on the banks of the Thames south of Maidenhead, the even smaller village of **BRAY** has the unlikely distinction of hosting two of Britain's four triple-Michelin-starred restaurants (the other two are in London) – including, famously, Heston Blumenthal's *Fat Duck*.

## ARRIVAL AND DEPARTURE

**By train** First get to Maidenhead, served by trains every 15min from London Paddington (40min) and Reading

## COOKHAM AND AROUND

(15min). Change at Maidenhead for hourly trains to Cookham (7min). Bray is a mile or so from Maidenhead station.

## EATING AND DRINKING

### COOKHAM

**Bel & The Dragon** High St ☏ 01628 521263, ⓦ belandthedragon-cookham.co.uk. Just across the street from the Spencer Gallery, this historic half-timbered pub is a nice place for a pint, while the airy modern restaurant offers excellent upmarket international cuisine (mains £10–27), with a more affordable bar menu, backed by an extensive wine list. Also five comfortable rustic-style rooms. Food served Mon–Fri noon–3pm & 6–10pm, Sat 10.30am–3pm & 6–10pm, Sun noon–9pm. **£114**

### BRAY

**Fat Duck** High St ☏ 01628 580333, ⓦ thefatduck .co.uk. Regularly voted one of the world's top restaurants, showcasing chef Heston Blumenthal's uniquely inventive

culinary style, with tasting menus (f195) featuring classic creations like snail porridge and egg-and-bacon ice cream, with whiskey wine gums to finish. Reservations (bookable up to two months in advance) are like gold dust. Tues–Sat noon–2pm & 7–9pm.

**Waterside Inn** Ferry Rd ☏ 01628 620691, ⓦ waterside -inn.co.uk. Part of the Roux family's culinary empire, this lovely restaurant has been wowing diners with its idiosyncratic take on classical French cuisine since 1972. Signature dishes include the sumptuous soufflé Suissesse (cheese soufflé with double cream) and *tronçonnette de homard* (pan-fried lobster with white port sauce). Lunchtime menus are £50–80, while the main six-course tasting menu is £160. Reserve well in advance. Wed–Sun noon–2pm & 7–10pm.

# Bucks and Beds

**4**

The muddled landscapes of **Buckinghamshire** (abbreviated to "Bucks") and **Bedfordshire** ("Beds") mark the transition between London's satellite towns and the Midlands; suburbs now encircle many of what were once small country towns. The **Chiltern Hills** extend across the region southwest from the workaday Bedfordshire town of Luton, bumping across Bucks as far as the River Thames – this is handsome countryside, characterised by steep forested ridges and deep valleys interrupted by rolling farmland. North Bucks offers a couple of fine attractions: **Stowe Gardens**, dotted with outdoor sculptures and follies, and the World War II code-breaking centre of **Bletchley Park**. Meanwhile, Bedfordshire's most distinctive attraction is whopping **Woburn Abbey** and its nearby safari park.

## Cliveden

Taplow, 1 mile east of Cookham **Grounds** Daily: mid-Feb to Oct 10am–5.30pm; Nov & Dec 10am–4pm • £9 (free with NT) **House** 30min tours run April–Oct Thurs & Sun 3–5.30pm • £1.50 extra (free with NT) • ☏ 01628 605069, ⓦ nationaltrust.org.uk/cliveden

Perched on a ridge overlooking the Thames, **Cliveden** (pronounced cliv-dun) is a grand Victorian mansion, designed with sweeping Neoclassical lines by Sir Charles Barry, architect of the Houses of Parliament. Its most famous occupant was **Nancy Astor**, the first woman MP, though the house remains best known for the scandalous **Profumo Affair**. Conservative cabinet minister John Profumo met 19-year-old model Christine Keeler at a party at Cliveden in 1961 and had a brief affair with her. Keeler, meanwhile, was also involved with a number of other men, including a Soviet intelligence officer. Profumo was forced to resign in 1963 after having lied to parliament, and Prime Minister Harold Macmillan resigned shortly afterwards.

The National Trust now owns Cliveden. Visits focus on the **grounds**, where a large slice of broadleaf woodland is intercepted by several themed gardens and a maze. The house is now a luxury **hotel** (ⓦ clivedenhouse.co.uk), with non-guests admitted only on guided tours. Its lavish interiors feature acres of wood panelling and portraits of past owners, culminating in the French Dining Room, containing the fittings and furnishings of Madame de Pompadour's eighteenth-century dining room.

## Roald Dahl Museum and Story Centre

81 High St • Tues–Fri 10am–5pm, Sat & Sun 11am–5pm • £6.60 • ☎ 01494 892192, ⓦ roalddahlmuseum.org • Train from London Marylebone to Great Missenden (every 30min; 45min), then 5min walk from the station down the hill to the museum

A leafy Chiltern commuter town 35 miles northwest of London, **GREAT MISSENDEN** was home for many years to **Roald Dahl** (1916–1990), one of the world's greatest children's storywriters. His house remains in private hands, but nearby is the **Roald Dahl Museum and Story Centre**, an unmissable treat for Dahl fans. As well as chronicling the author's life, it explores the nature of creative writing, supported by hints from contemporary writers and interactive games.

## Stowe Gardens

3 miles northwest of Buckingham • Daily 10am–6pm; Nov–Feb closes 4pm • £8.50, joint ticket with Stowe House £13.70; NT • ☎ 01280 817156, ⓦ nationaltrust.org.uk/stowe & ⓦ stowehouse.org

The extensive **Stowe Landscape Gardens** contain an extraordinary collection of outdoor sculptures, monuments and decorative buildings by some of the eighteenth century's greatest designers and architects. The thirty-odd structures are spread over a sequence of separate, carefully planned landscapes, from the lake views of the Western and Eastern gardens to the wooded delights of the Elysian Fields and the gentle folds of the Grecian Valley, **Capability Brown**'s first large-scale design. Many buildings are of interest, most memorably the Neo-Romanesque **Hermitage**, the eccentric **Gothic Temple**, the magnificent **Grecian Temple** (Temple of Concord and Victory) and the beautifully composed **Palladian Bridge**, one of only three such bridges in the country. **Stowe House**, with its Neoclassical facade, is used by Stowe School, which offers regular guided tours.

## Bletchley Park

Sherwood Drive, Bletchley, 2 miles south of Milton Keynes • Daily 9.30am–5pm; Nov–Feb closes 4pm • £15 including audioguide • ☎ 01908 640404, ⓦ bletchleypark.org.uk • 5min walk from Bletchley station, served by trains from London Euston (every 15min; 50min) and Birmingham New St (hourly; 1hr; change at Milton Keynes or Northampton).

**Bletchley Park** – now on the edge of Milton Keynes – was the headquarters of Britain's leading code-breakers during World War II, known as "Station X". This was where the British built the first programmable digital computer, Colossus, in 1943, and it was here that they famously broke the German "**Enigma**" code which was encrypting communications within Hitler's armed forces. Much of Station X has survived, its Nissen huts spread over a leafy parcel of land that surrounds the original Victorian mansion. Inside are displays exploring the workings of Station X as well as the stolen Enigma machine that was crucial in deciphering the German code.

## Woburn Abbey and Safari Park

Woburn, 5 miles east of Milton Keynes **Abbey** April–Oct daily 11am–5pm • £14.50 • ☎ 01525 290333, ⓦ woburnabbey.co.uk **Safari park** March–Oct daily 10am–6pm, may close in bad weather • £22 • ☎ 01525 290407, ⓦ woburnsafari.co.uk • No public transport

The grandiloquent Georgian facade of **Woburn Abbey** overlooks a chunk of landscaped parkland on the eastern edge of Woburn village, 35 miles north of London. Called an abbey because it was built on the site of a Cistercian foundation, the house is the ancestral pile of the dukes of Bedford. The lavish state rooms contain some fine paintings, including an exquisite set of **Tudor portraits**, most notably the famous *Armada Portrait* of Elizabeth I by George Gower. Elsewhere are works by Van Dyck, Velázquez, Gainsborough, Rembrandt, Reynolds and Canaletto.

Another part of the duke's enormous estate is home to **Woburn Safari Park**, Britain's largest drive-through wildlife reserve. The animals include endangered species such as the African white rhino and bongo antelope. In high season traffic can achieve rush-hour congestion; arrive early for a quieter experience.

# St Albans

Just beyond the M25 orbital motorway north of London, **ST ALBANS** in Hertfordshire is one of the most appealing towns on the peripheries of the capital, its blend of medieval and modern features grafted onto the site of **Verulamium**, a town founded by the Romans soon after their successful invasion of 43 AD. After Boudica burned it to the ground eighteen years later, reconstruction was swift and the town grew into a major administrative base. It was here, in 209 AD, that a Roman soldier by the name of Alban became the country's first Christian martyr, when he was beheaded for giving shelter to a priest. Pilgrims later flocked to the town, with the place of execution marked by a hill-top cathedral that was once one of the largest churches in the Christian world.

## The cathedral

Off High St • Daily 8.30am–5.45pm • Free • ☎ 01727 860780, ⓦ stalbanscathedral.org

An abbey was constructed here in 1077 on the site of a Saxon monastery founded by King Offa of Mercia; despite subsequent alterations, the legacy of the Normans remains the most impressive aspect of the vast brick-and-flint **cathedral**. The sheer scale of their design is breathtaking: the **nave**, almost 300 feet long, is the longest medieval nave in Britain. Behind the high altar a stone **reredos** hides the fourteenth-century **shrine of St Alban**. The tomb was smashed up during the Reformation, but the Victorians discovered the pieces and gamely put them all together again.

4

## Verulamium

St Michael's St **Museum** Mon–Sat 10am–5.30pm, Sun 2–5.30pm • £5 • ☎ 01727 751810, ⓦ stalbansmuseums.org.uk **Hypocaust** Mon–Sat 10am–4.30pm, Sun 2–4.30pm; Oct–March closes 3.45pm • Free **Theatre** Daily 10am–5pm; Nov–Feb closes 4pm • £2.50 • ☎ 01727 835035, ⓦ romantheatre.co.uk

**Verulamium Museum** holds a series of well-conceived displays illustrating life in Roman Britain, but these are eclipsed by the wonderful floor **mosaics** unearthed hereabouts in the 1930s and 1950s. Dating from about 200 AD, the Sea God Mosaic has created its share of academic debate, with some arguing it depicts a god of nature with stag antler horns rather than a sea god with lobster claws — but there's no disputing the subject of the Lion Mosaic, in which a lion carries the bloodied head of a stag in its jaws. The most beautiful is the Shell Mosaic, whose semicircular design depicts a beautifully crafted scallop shell within a border made up of rolling waves.

The adjacent **Verulamium Park** holds a scattering of Roman remains, including fragments of the old city wall and a building sheltering the **Hypocaust**, comprising the foundations of a townhouse complete with the original underfloor heating system of the bath suite. Just to the west, across busy Bluehouse Hill, the **Roman Theatre of Verulamium** was built around 140 AD, but was reduced to the status of a municipal rubbish dump by the fifth century and is little more than a small hollow now.

### ARRIVAL AND INFORMATION                                    ST ALBANS

**By train** St Albans City station – served by frequent trains from London St Pancras (every 10min; 20min) – is off Victoria St, 10min walk east of the centre.

**Tourist office** In the town hall on Market Place (Mon–Sat 10am–4.30pm; ☎ 01727 864511, ⓦ enjoystalbans.com).

### EATING AND DRINKING

**Ye Olde Fighting Cocks** 16 Abbey Mill Lane ☎ 01727 869152, ⓦ yeoldefightingcocks.co.uk. St Albans hosts the headquarters of CAMRA, the Campaign for Real Ale: excellent, hand-pumped beers are available in many a local pub. This antique hostelry is a good choice – crowded on sunny summer days, but still with lots of enjoyable nooks and crannies in which to nurse a pint. Mon–Thurs 11am–11.30pm, Fri & Sat 11am–midnight, Sun noon–11.30pm.

# Bristol, Bath and Somerset

GLASTONBURY FESTIVAL

**5**

# Bristol, Bath and Somerset

The soft, undulating green swards of Somerset encapsulate rural England at its best. The scenery is always varied, with tidy cricket greens and well-kept country pubs contrasting with its wilder, more dramatic landscapes, from limestone gorges to windswept marshland. A world away from all of this, the main city hereabouts is Bristol, one of the most dynamic and cosmopolitan centres outside London. Its medieval old quarter and revitalized waterfront are supplemented by a superb range of pubs, clubs and restaurants. Just a few miles away, the graceful, Georgian, honey-toned terraces of Bath combine with beautifully preserved Roman baths, a clutch of first-class museums and a mellow café culture to make it an unmissable stop.

Within easy reach to the south lie the exquisite cathedral city of **Wells** and the ancient town of **Glastonbury**, a site steeped in Christian lore, Arthurian legend and New Age mysticism. The nearby **Mendip Hills** are fine walking territory and are pocked by cave systems, as at **Wookey Hole** and **Cheddar Gorge**. Beyond here, verdant **South Somerset**, with its pretty little hamstone villages and traditional cider farms, matches the county's bucolic ideal more than any other region. The county town of **Taunton** makes a useful base for exploring the **Quantocks**, while further west, straddling the border with Devon, the heathery slopes and wide-open spaces of **Exmoor** offer a range of hikes, with wonderful views from its cliffy seaboard.

## Bristol

On the borders of Gloucestershire and Somerset, **BRISTOL** has harmoniously blended its mercantile roots with an innovative, modern culture, fuelled by technology-based industries, a large student population and a lively arts and music scene. As well as its vibrant **nightlife**, the city's sights range from medieval churches to cutting-edge attractions highlighting its maritime and scientific achievements.

Weaving through its centre, the River Avon forms part of a system of waterways that made Bristol a great inland port, in later years booming on the transatlantic trafficking of rum, tobacco and slaves. In the nineteenth century, the illustrious **Isambard Kingdom Brunel** laid the foundations of a tradition of engineering, creating two of Bristol's greatest monuments: the *ss Great Britain* and the lofty Clifton Suspension Bridge.

THERMAE BATH SPA

# Highlights

**❶ ss Great Britain, Bristol** Moored in the dock in which she was built, the iconic ship is now an iconic museum, an interactive insight into life aboard a nineteenth-century steamer. **See p.285**

**❷ Thermae Bath Spa** Take the purifying waters at this cutting-edge facility in the UK's original spa town. **See p.291**

**❸ Royal Crescent, Bath** In a city famous for its graceful arcs of Georgian terraces, this is the granddaddy of them all, an architectural tour de force with a magnificent vista. **See p.292**

**❹ Wells Cathedral** A gem of medieval masonry, this richly ornamented Gothic masterpiece is the centrepiece of England's smallest city. **See p.295**

**❺ Cheddar Gorge** Impressive rockscape with a network of illuminated caves at its base; it's an excellent starting point for wild walks in the Mendip Hills. **See p.297**

**❻ Glastonbury Festival** Pack your tent, dust off your welllies and enjoy the ride that is simply Britain's biggest, boldest and best music festival. **See p.301**

**❼ Exmoor** Whether you ride it, bike it or hike it, the rolling wilderness of Exmoor offers fine opportunities to experience the great outdoors. **See p.308**

**HIGHLIGHTS ARE MARKED ON THE MAP ON P.280**

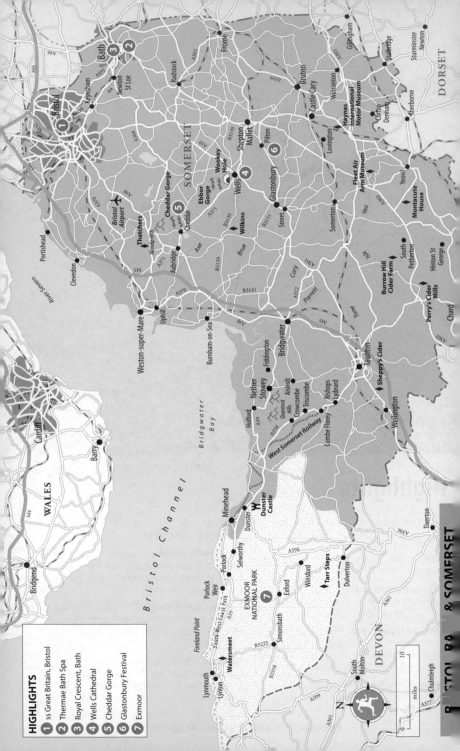

## HIGHLIGHTS

1. ss Great Britain, Bristol
2. Thermae Bath Spa
3. Royal Crescent, Bath
4. Wells Cathedral
5. Cheddar Gorge
6. Glastonbury Festival
7. Exmoor

BRISTOL BA & SOMERSET

# Bristol Cathedral

College Green • Mon–Fri 8am–6pm, Sat & Sun 8am–5pm • **Evensong** Mon–Fri 5.15pm, Sat & Sun 3.30pm • Free **Guided tours** usually Sat 11.30am, sometimes also 1.30pm • Free • ⓦ bristol-cathedral.co.uk

Founded as an abbey around 1140 on the supposed spot of St Augustine's convocation with Celtic Christians in 603, venerable **Bristol Cathedral** became a cathedral church with the Dissolution of the Monasteries in the mid-sixteenth century. The two towers on the west front were erected in the nineteenth century in a faithful act of homage to Edmund Knowle, architect and abbot at the start of the fourteenth century. The interior offers a unique example among Britain's cathedrals of a German-style "hall church", in which the aisles, nave and choir rise to the same height. Abbot Knowle's immense **choir** offers one of the country's most exquisite illustrations of the early Decorated style of Gothic, while the adjoining thirteenth-century **Elder Lady Chapel** contains some fine tombs and eccentric carvings of animals, including (between the arches on the right) a monkey playing the bagpipes accompanied by a ram on the violin. The **Eastern Lady Chapel** has some of England's finest examples of heraldic glass. From the south transept, a door leads to the **Chapter House**, a richly carved piece of late Norman architecture.

# Georgian House

7 Great George St • Easter–Oct Wed, Thurs, Sat & Sun 10.30am–4pm, July & Aug also Tues & Fri • Free • ☎ 0117 921 1362, ⓦ bristolmuseums.org.uk/georgian-house-museum

Built in 1791, the deceptively large **Georgian House** is the former home of a local sugar merchant, its spacious and faithfully restored rooms filled with sumptuous examples of period furniture. The basement gives particular insight into domestic times past, while upstairs, illustrated panels tell the story of the family's dealings in the West Indies, including their involvement in slavery.

# City Museum and Art Gallery

Queen's Rd, at the top of Park St • Daily 10am–5pm, Sat & Sun till 6pm • Free • ☎ 0117 922 3571, ⓦ bristolmuseums.org.uk/bristol -museum-and-art-gallery

Housed in a grandiose Edwardian-Baroque building, the **City Museum and Art Gallery** has sections on local archeology, geology and natural history, as well as an important collection of Chinese porcelain and some magnificent Assyrian reliefs carved in the eighth century BC. Art works by Banksy, the Bristol School and French Impressionists are mixed in with some choice older pieces, including a portrait of Martin Luther by Cranach the Elder and Giovanni Bellini's unusual *Descent into Limbo*.

---

### BANKSY AND THE BRISTOL STREET-ART SCENE

An integral part of Bristol's cultural profile, the street artist known as **Banksy** has managed to maintain his anonymity despite his global celebrity, with exhibitions pulling crowds from London to Los Angeles. It was in Bristol, though, a city known since the 1980s for its **graffiti art**, that he first made his mark, leaving his stencilled daubs and freehand murals on walls throughout the inner city. Websites such as ⓦ bristol-street-art.co.uk will allow you to track down his surviving murals, though it's easy enough to locate his more iconic works such as *The Mild Mild West* (1999) on Stokes Croft and *The Naked Man* (2006) off the bottom of Park Street.

The sly wit that undercuts Banky's social satire has led to his works becoming accepted and even protected by the city supremos, culminating in a wildly successful exhibition in the City Museum in 2009. And in further proof of the council's changing attitudes, in August 2011 over 35 graffiti artists from around the globe descended on **Nelson Street**, just off The Centre, to turn its run-down office blocks into a gallery of stunning street art: look out for Nick Walker's eleven-storey-high banker, Aryz's wolf in a lumberjack shirt and El Mac's huge photo-realistic mural of a woman and her baby.

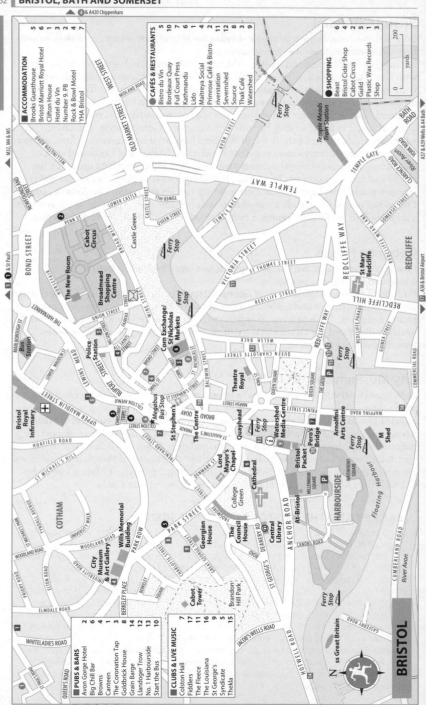

**ACCOMMODATION**
| | |
|---|---|
| Brooks Guesthouse | 5 |
| Bristol Marriott Royal Hotel | 6 |
| Clifton House | 1 |
| Hotel du Vin | 3 |
| Number 9, PB | 2 |
| Rock & Bowl Motel | 4 |
| YHA Bristol | 7 |

**CAFÉS & RESTAURANTS**
| | |
|---|---|
| Bistro du Vin | 5 |
| Bordeaux Quay | 10 |
| Full Court Press | 6 |
| Kathmandu | 1 |
| Lido | 4 |
| Maitreya Social | 2 |
| Primrose Café & Bistro | 11 |
| riverstation | 12 |
| Severnshed | 7 |
| Source | 8 |
| Thali Café | 3 |
| Watershed | 9 |

**SHOPPING**
| | |
|---|---|
| Beast | 6 |
| Bristol Cider Shop | 4 |
| Cabot Circus | 2 |
| Guild | 5 |
| Plastic Wax Records | 1 |
| Shop | 3 |

**PUBS & BARS**
| | |
|---|---|
| Avon Gorge Hotel | 2 |
| Big Chill Bar | 6 |
| Browns | 4 |
| Canteen | 1 |
| The Coronation Tap | 3 |
| Goldbrick House | 8 |
| Grain Barge | 14 |
| Llandoger Trow | 12 |
| No. 1 Harbourside | 13 |
| Start the Bus | 10 |

**CLUBS & LIVE MUSIC**
| | |
|---|---|
| Colston Hall | 7 |
| Fiddlers | 11 |
| The Fleece | 16 |
| The Louisiana | 9 |
| St George's | 5 |
| Syndicate | 15 |
| Thekla | 13 |

BRISTOL

## St Stephen's

21 Stephen's St, off Corn St • Mon–Fri & Sun 8.45am–4pm • Free • ☎ 0117 927 7977, ⓦ saint-stephens.com

Surrounded by characterless modern buildings just east of The Centre, **St Stephen's** is one of Bristol's oldest and most graceful churches. It dates from the thirteenth century, was rebuilt in the fifteenth, and was thoroughly restored with plenty of neo-Gothic trimmings in 1875. The church has some flamboyant tombs inside, mainly of various members of the merchant class who were the church's main patrons.

## Corn Exchange

The Georgian **Corn Exchange** was designed by John Wood of Bath and now contains the covered **St Nicholas Markets**, a lively spot for a wander or a bite to eat. The four engraved brass pillars outside the entrance date from the sixteenth and seventeenth centuries and originally served as trading tables – thought to be the "nails" that gave rise to the expression "pay on the nail".

## The New Room

36 The Horsefair, Broadmead • Mon–Sat 10am–4pm • Free • ☎ 0117 926 4740, ⓦ newroombristol.org.uk

Hidden inside **Broadmead** shopping centre is England's first Methodist chapel, **the New Room**. Established by John Wesley in 1739, it looks very much as he left it, with a double-deck pulpit in the chapel, beneath a hidden upstairs window from which the evangelist could observe the progress of his trainee preachers.

## King Street and around

**King Street**, a short walk southeast from The Centre, was laid out on marshland in 1663 and still holds a cluster of historic buildings, among them the **Theatre Royal**, the oldest working theatre in the country, opened in 1766 and preserving many of its original Georgian features. Further down, and in a very different architectural style, stands the timber-framed **Llandoger Trow** pub (see p.288), once the haunt of seafarers, and reputed to have been the meeting place of Daniel Defoe and Alexander Selkirk, the model for Robinson Crusoe. South of King Street is the elegant, grassy **Queen Square**.

## St Mary Redcliffe

Redcliffe Way, Redcliffe • Mon–Sat 8.30am–5pm, Sun 8am–8pm • Free • ☎ 0117 929 1487, ⓦ stmaryredcliffe.co.uk

Described by Elizabeth I as "the fairest, goodliest and most famous parish church in England", the richly decorated church of **St Mary Redcliffe**, across Redcliffe Bridge from The Centre, was largely paid for and used by merchants and mariners. The present building was begun at the end of the thirteenth century, though it was added to in subsequent centuries and its tall spire – a distinctive feature on the city's skyline – dates from 1872. Inside, memorials and tombs recall figures associated with the building, including the Handel Window, installed in 1859 on the centenary of the death of Handel, who composed on the magnificent organ here.

Above the church's north porch is the muniment room, where **Thomas Chatterton** claimed to have found a trove of medieval manuscripts; the poems, distributed as the work of a fifteenth-century monk named Thomas Rowley, were in fact dazzling fakes. The young poet committed suicide after his forgery was exposed, supplying English literature with one of its most glamorous stories of self-destructive genius. The "Marvellous Boy" (according to William Wordsworth) is remembered by a memorial stone in the south transept.

**5**

## THE SLAVE TRADE IN BRISTOL

Over two hundred years after the abolition of the **British slave trade**, Bristol is still haunted by the instrumental part it played in the trafficking of African men, women and children to the New World – indeed, it was Bristol-born Sir John Yeamans, a Barbados planter, who effectively introduced slavery to North America.

The slave trade in Britain was monopolized by the London-based **Royal African Company** until 1698, when the market was opened to all. For the next hundred years, the city's merchants were able to participate in the "**triangular trade**" whereby brass pots, glass beads and other manufactured goods were traded for slaves on the coast of West Africa, who were then shipped to plantations in the Americas, the vessels returning to Europe with cargoes of sugar, cotton, tobacco and other slave-labour-produced commodities. By the 1730s, Bristol had become – along with London and Liverpool – one of the main beneficiaries of the trade; in 1750 alone, Bristol ships transported some eight thousand of the twenty thousand slaves sent that year to colonies in the Caribbean and America. The direct profits, together with the numerous spin-offs, helped to finance some of the city's finest Georgian architecture.

Bristol's primacy in the trade had been long supplanted by Liverpool by the time opposition to slavery began to gather force: first the Quakers and Methodists, then more powerful forces, voiced their discontent. By the 1780s, the Anglican Dean Josiah Tucker and the Evangelical writer Hannah More had become active abolitionists, and Samuel Taylor Coleridge made a famous anti-slavery speech in Bristol in 1795.

The British slave trade was finally abolished in 1807, but its legacy is still felt strongly in the city, particularly in the divisive figure of **Edward Colston**. The eighteenth-century sugar magnate is revered by many as a great philanthropist – his name given to numerous buildings, streets and schools in Bristol – but reviled by more as a leading light in the Royal African Company. His statue in The Centre has more than once been the subject of graffiti attacks and calls for its removal, and Massive Attack still refuse to play the Colston Hall because of the connotations of its name.

## At-Bristol

Anchor Rd • Daily 10am–5pm, Sat, Sun & hols till 6pm • £12.05, under-15s £7.70, under-3s free • ☎ 0845 345 1235, ⊛ at-bristol.org.uk

Occupying a corner of Harbourside's sleekly modern **Millennium Square**, marked out by the spherical, stainless-steel planetarium attached to one side, **At-Bristol** deals with all things science. It's chiefly aimed at children, but there's enough interactive wizardry here to entertain and inform everyone, with opportunities to view the blood in your veins, freeze your shadow and create your own short films (with input from Aardman Animations). The planetarium has up to eight shows daily, which should be booked when you buy your entry ticket (from £1 extra).

## M-Shed

Princes Wharf, Wapping Rd • Tues–Fri 10am–5pm, Sat, Sun & bank hols 10am–6pm • Free, £2 donation suggested • Guided tours Tues & Thurs–Sat 11.30am, Wed 2.30pm; 1hr; £2 • Boat and railway rides on selected days throughout the year; £1–5 • ☎ 0117 352 6600, ⊛ bristolmuseums.org.uk/m-shed

Opened in 2011, the superb **M-Shed**, housed in an old harbourside transit shed, is Bristol's first museum dedicated to itself, past and present, and offers the best official insight into what makes the city tick. It's an enjoyable, unashamedly populist survey, full of memorabilia and anecdotes and casting light on everything from the city's mercantile history and its role in the transatlantic slave trade to its festivals and street-life. On the ground floor, Bristol Places charts the city's changing face, from the Bristol Dinosaur through its development as a port and the hardships of World War II. Bristol People, on the floor above, and the adjoining Bristol Life, look at the (often ordinary) folk who have shaped the city, whilst the latter includes an excellent – and long overdue – display on the slave trade in Bristol. Afetrwards, head out to the long terrace for fantastic harbour views.

# ss Great Britain

Great Western Dockyard • Daily 10am–5.30pm, Nov–March till 4.30pm • £13.75 • ☎ 0117 926 0680, ⓦ ssgreatbritain.org

Harbourside's major draw, and one of Bristol's iconic sights, the **ss Great Britain** was the first propeller-driven, ocean-going iron ship in the world, built by **Isambard Kingdom Brunel** in 1843. She initially ran between Liverpool and New York, then between Liverpool and Melbourne, circumnavigating the globe 32 times and chalking up over a million miles at sea. Her ocean-going days ended in 1886 when she was caught in a storm off Cape Horn, and she was eventually recovered and returned to Bristol in 1970. On board, you can see restored cabins and peer into the immense engine room, whilst the adjoining museum gives the background of the vessel and of Bristol's long shipbuilding history.

# Clifton

On the western side of the city, **Clifton**, once an aloof spa resort, is now Bristol's stateliest neighbourhood. At the top of Blackboy Hill, the wide green expanses of **Durdham Down** and **Clifton Downs** stretch right up to the edge of the Avon Gorge, a popular spot for picnickers, joggers and kite-flyers. On the southern edge of the Downs is the select enclave of Clifton Village, centred on the Mall, where **Royal York Crescent**, the longest Georgian crescent in the country, offers splendid views over the steep drop to the River Avon below.

## Clifton Suspension Bridge

Free, £1 for vehicles **Visitor Centre** Daily 10am–5pm • Free **Guided tours** Easter–Oct Sat & Sun 3pm • 45min • Free • ⓦ cliftonbridge.org.uk

A few minutes' walk from Clifton Village is Bristol's most famous symbol, **Clifton Suspension Bridge**, 702ft long and poised 245ft above high water. Money was first put forward for a bridge to span the Avon Gorge by a Bristol wine merchant in 1754, though it wasn't until 1829 that a competition was held for a design, won by **Isambard Kingdom Brunel** on a second round, and not until 1864 that the bridge was completed, five years after Brunel's death. Hampered by financial difficulties, the bridge never quite matched the engineer's original ambitious design, which included Egyptian-style towers topped by sphinxes at each end. You can see copies of his plans in the **Visitor Centre** at the far side of the bridge, alongside designs proposed by Brunel's rivals, some of them frankly bizarre.

### ARRIVAL AND DEPARTURE                                          BRISTOL

**By train** Temple Meads train station is a 20min walk east of the city centre.

Destinations Bath (every 15–30min; 15min); Birmingham (every 30min–1hr; 1hr 25min); Bridgwater (every 30min–1hr; 50min); Cheltenham (every 30min–1hr; 40min–1hr); Exeter (every 30min–1hr; 1hr); Gloucester (every 30min–1hr; 50min); London Paddington (every 30min–1hr; 1hr 40min); Taunton (every 15–50min; 30min); Yeovil (7 daily; 1hr 10min).

**By bus** Bristol's bus station (ⓦ firstgroup.com) is centrally located off Marlborough Street; Megabus services to and from London stop opposite Colston Hall, off The Centre, the traffic-ridden nucleus of the city.

Destinations Bath (Mon–Sat every 15min, Sun every 30min; 50min); Glastonbury (every 30min; 1hr 30min); London (every 30min–1hr; 2hr 30min); Wells (every 30min; 1hr).

### INFORMATION AND TOURS

**Tourist office** E-Shed, Canon's Road (Daily 11am–4pm, Sat from 10am; ☎ 0906 711 2191, ⓦ visitbristol.co.uk).

**Tours** City Sightseeing Bristol (☎ 07425 788123, ⓦ citysightseeingbristol.co.uk) runs a hop-on, hop-off,

open-top bus tour of the city's key sights (£13), while Bristol Packet (☎ 0117 926 8157, ⓦ bristolpacket.co.uk) offers cruises around the harbour and along the river to Bath (from £5.75).

### GETTING AROUND

**By ferry** A ferry, setting off from the Quayhead, just south of The Centre, connects various parts of the Floating Harbour, including Temple Meads station and the ss Great Britain (every 20min; 10am–6.15pm; from £1.50 single;

£2.50 return; £6 all-day ticket; ⓦ bristolferry.com).

**By bus** Local buses are useful for getting to Clifton's upper reaches; take #8 or #9 from Temple Meads station or The Centre, which also connects the city's train and bus stations.

**5**

## BRISTOL'S FESTIVALS

Try to coincide your visit to Bristol with one of its numerous festivals, mostly held during the summer. Highlights are **St Paul's Carnival** (Ⓦstpaulscarnival.co.uk) on the first Saturday of July, a celebration of the city's Afro-Caribbean culture with floats, stalls and live music; the **Bristol Harbour Festival** (Ⓦbristolharbourfestival.co.uk), a weekend of live music, waterside festivities and fireworks over a weekend in late July; and the **Bristol International Balloon Fiesta** (Ⓦbristolballoonfiesta.co.uk), at Ashton Court, featuring mass hot-air balloon launches and "night glows" over four days in mid-August.

## ACCOMMODATION

With a few notable exceptions, good accommodation in Bristol is surprisingly thin on the ground. Hotels and B&Bs in the centre can suffer from traffic noise and the sound of late-night drinkers; for quieter and more traditional lodgings, choose Clifton, with a range of pubs and restaurants on the main axis of Whiteladies Road.

★**Brooks Guesthouse** St Nicholas St, entrance on Exchange Ave ☎0117 930 0066, Ⓦbrooksguesthouse bristol.com. Set in the midst of bustling St Nicholas Markets, this boutique B&B has small but comfortable rooms that come with iPod docks, DVD players and free wi-fi. The airy modern breakfast room gives onto a spacious courtyard for relaxing with a book or a drink. You can also stay in an airstream trailer on the roof (from £110). **£65**

**Bristol Marriott** Royal Hotel College Green ☎0117 925 5100, Ⓦbristolmarriottroyal.co.uk. Right next to Bristol Cathedral, this Italianate-style Victorian hotel is by far the more attractive of the city's two *Marriotts*, with spacious rooms, two restaurants and a Champagne bar, and a lovely swimming pool. **£105**

**Clifton House** 4 Tyndall's Park Rd ☎0117 973 5407, Ⓦcliftonhousebristol.com. This handily sited B&B at the bottom of Clifton and near the centre offers fairly plush rooms with big windows, modern bathrooms and plenty of space – superior rooms, costing £20 extra, are huge. There's free wi-fi and parking. **£75**

**Hotel du Vin** The Sugar House, Narrow Lewins Mead ☎0117 925 5577, Ⓦhotelduvin.co.uk. Chic conversion of an old dockside sugar factory, centrally located, with dark, contemporary decor. Rooms have big beds and grand bathrooms, and there's an excellent restaurant to boot (see below). **£149**

★**Number 9. PB** 9 Prince's Buildings ☎0117 973 4615, Ⓦ9pb.co.uk. A short walk from the Clifton Suspension Bridge and within staggering distance of several real-ale pubs, this five-storey Georgian B&B, lovingly cared for by its easy-going owners, enjoys a grand vista over the Avon Gorge from its antique-filled rooms. Great breakfasts, too. Singles from £60. No credit cards. **£85**

**Rock & Bowl Motel** 22 Nelson St ☎0117 325 1980, Ⓦrocknbowlmotel.com. Clean and efficiently run hostel in an ex-dole office above a busy bowling alley. Single- and mixed-sex dorms (4- to 12-person) and a few en-suite doubles and twins, plus a self-catering kitchen. Laundry and wi-fi. Dorms **£16**, doubles **£49**

**YHA Bristol** 14 Narrow Quay ☎0845 371 9726, Ⓦyha .org.uk. In a refurbished warehouse on the quayside, this warm and friendly hostel has mostly four-bed dorms, plus (smallish) private doubles. There's a decent kitchen, and prices include an abundant breakfast. Dorms **£20.50**, doubles **£49**

## EATING

### CAFÉS

**Full Court Press** 59 Broad St ☎07794 808552, Ⓦfcpcoffee.com. The select menu of superb speciality coffees at this dinky joint near St Nicks Markets have made it an instant hit with local connoisseurs. Try your single coffee served four ways (£8). Mon–Fri 7.30am–5pm, Sat 9am–5pm, Sun 10am–4pm.

**Primrose Café & Bistro** 1 Clifton Arcade, Boyces Ave ☎0117 946 6577, Ⓦprimrosecafe.co.uk. Homely café in Clifton Village serving a good range of teas and organic fruit juices. Light-hearted lunchtime sandwiches include onion bhaji and mango chutney; evening fare (from £13.95) is more elaborate. Café Mon–Sat 9am–5pm, Sun 9.30am–3pm; bistro Tues–Thurs 6pm–late, Fri 7pm–late.

**Watershed** 1 Canon's Rd ☎0117 927 5101, Ⓦwatershed.co.uk. Cool café-bar overlooking the boats in one of Bristol's longest-established arts complexes. Good coffee and local beers are supplemented by an appetizing menu, and there's free wi-fi and a small (non-smoking) terrace. Mon & Sat 10am–11pm, Tues–Fri 9.30am–11pm, Sun 10am–10.30pm.

### RESTAURANTS

**Bistro du Vin** Hotel du Vin, The Sugar House, Narrow Lewins Mead ☎0117 925 5577, Ⓦhotelduvin.com. Fine French bistro-style dining in a former sugar factory, using good seasonal West Country produce in its Modern European menu; mains from £14. Mon–Sat noon–2.30pm & 5.30–10pm, Fri & Sat till 10.30pm, Sun noon–4pm & 6–9.30pm.

**Bordeaux Quay** V-Shed, Harbourside ☎0117 943 1200, ⓦbordeaux-quay.co.uk. Housed in a former warehouse, with an elegantly minimalist restaurant upstairs offering harbour views (mains from £13), and a less formal downstairs brasserie (main dishes from £10.50). The food in both is mainly Mediterranean, and is steadfastly organic. There's also a bar and an excellent deli. Restaurant Tues–Sat 6–10pm, Sun noon–3pm; brasserie and bar Mon–Fri 8am–10.30pm, Sat 9am–10.30pm, Sun 9am–9pm.

**Kathmandu** Colston Tower, Colston St ☎0117 929 4455, ⓦkathmandu-curry.com. This smart, family-run restaurant is a bastion of quality Nepalese cooking, though the menu also ventures south of the border as well. Tasty dishes, including *momo* (£7.95) and *chhoyla* (lamb cooked in a Tandoori oven with ginger and garlic; £9.95), are pepped up by spices imported from the owners' home village just outside Kathmandu. Mon–Thurs 5.45–11pm, Fri & Sat 5.45pm–midnight.

★ **Lido** Oakfield Place, Clifton; restaurant entrance on Southleigh Rd ☎0117 933 9533, ⓦlidobristol.com. Set-piece venue given a stylish new lease of life as a restaurant/bar and pool/spa complex. The glass-walled restaurant overlooks the outdoor pool, which makes dining on dishes like wood-roast chicken and chickpeas (£17.50) while others exercise a deliciously guilty affair. Restaurant daily noon–3pm & Mon–Sat 6–10pm, poolside bar Mon–Sat 8am–11pm, Sun 9am–6pm.

**Maitreya Social** 89 St Mark's Rd ☎0117 951 0100, ⓦcafemaitreya.co.uk. Tucked away in the multicultural but rundown neighbourhood of Easton, this easy-going place serves delicious, inventive vegetarian dishes – smoky roasted parsnip and cashew roulade (£10.95), for example,

or warm samphire salad. Tues–Thurs 6–11.30pm, Fri & Sat 10am–11.30pm, Sun 10am–4pm.

**riverstation** The Grove ☎0117 914 4434, ⓦriverstation.co.uk. Two-storey former river-police station, with all-day brunches at the relaxed ground-floor bar and kitchen and more refined Modern European dining upstairs. Set lunches here cost around £13, while main courses in the evening start at £15.50. Try to bag a table by the window for the dockside views. Restaurant Mon–Sat noon–2.30pm & 6–10.30pm, Fri & Sat till 11pm, Sun noon–3pm; bar and kitchen Mon–Wed 9am–11pm, Thurs–Sat 9am–midnight, Sun 10am–5pm.

**Severnshed** The Grove ☎0117 925 1212, ⓦsevernshed restaurant.co.uk. With a waterside terrace, *Severnshed* serves pastas and pizzas (from £7) and grills, including firesticks – meat or fish kebabs (£17–21). DJs provide the soundtrack on Fri and Sat evenings. Daily 9am–11pm, Fri & Sat till 2am.

★ **Source** 1–3 Exchange Ave, off St Nicholas St ☎0117 927 2998, ⓦsource-food.co.uk. Almost all the food in this airy canteen next to St Nick's Markets is from the West Country, and much of it is organic and can be bought to take away – Cornish crab cakes, salt-marsh lamb, Somerset rosé veal (from £8), for example. Mon–Fri 8am–5pm, Sat 8am–6pm, first Sun of month 9am–4pm.

**Thali Café** 1 Regent St, Clifton ☎0117 974 3793, ⓦthethalicafe.co.uk. *Dhaba*-style South Asian food in vibrant surroundings. This Clifton branch – there are four others across Bristol – has the trademark deep-pink decor and range of tasty *thalis*, a balanced selection of dishes served on a stainless-steel platter (from £8.95). Daily noon–10pm, Sat & Sun from 10am.

## DRINKING

**Avon Gorge Hotel** Sion Hill ☎0117 973 8955, ⓦtheavongorge.com. Perched on the edge of the Gorge in Clifton Village, the hotel's modern bar draws in the crowds thanks to the magnificent views of the Suspension Bridge from its broad terrace. Daily 11am–11pm, Sun till 10.30pm.

**Big Chill Bar** 15 Small St ☎0117 930 4217, ⓦbigchill .net/bristol. Cool lounge and club for late-night drinking and dancing, connected to the festival of the same name. North American soul food comes courtesy of Mi Casa Cantina pop-up, but it's the quality live music and DJs (Wed–Sat) that make this place. Mon 5pm–1am, Tues & Wed noon–1am, Thurs noon–2am, Fri & Sat noon–3am.

**Browns** 38 Queen's Rd ☎0117 930 4777, ⓦbrowns -restaurants.com. Spacious and relaxed place for an evening drink, housed in the Venetian-style former university refectory. Wide choice of tipples includes 45 wines and Champagnes by the glass and some fine cocktails. Mon–Sat 8am–midnight, Mon & Tues till 11pm, Wed till 11.30pm, Sun 9am–11pm.

**Canteen** Hamilton House, 80 Stokes Croft ☎0117 923

2017, ⓦcanteenbristol.co.uk. Overlooked by one of Banksy's most famous murals, a drab 1960s office block now accommodates this incredibly popular collective-style bar. Take a seat at a graffitied table for a coffee or a pint, or try something from the cheap, sustainable menu. Live music from 9.30pm most nights (from 4pm on Sun). Daily 10am–midnight, Fri & Sat till 1am.

★ **The Coronation Tap** 8 Sion Place, Clifton ☎0117 973 9617, ⓦthecoronationtap.com. A proper cider house, The *Cori Tap* produces its own Exhibition "apple juice", which is sold by the half-pint only, and stocks a wide range of locally produced ciders. Excellent live music, too. Daily 5.30pm–11.30pm, Sat & Sun from 7pm.

**Goldbrick House** 69 Park St ☎0117 945 1950, ⓦgoldbrickhouse.co.uk. Stylish multi-level concept – café, restaurant (think cauliflower, hazelnut and gruyere pearl barley risotto; £13.25) and choice cocktail bar – housed in an old Georgian building, with original fireplaces and dark leather armchairs. Mon–Thurs 9am–midnight, Fri & Sat 9am–1am.

**5**

**Grain Barge** Mardyke Wharf, Hotwell Rd ☎0117 929 9347, ⓦgrainbarge.com. Floating pub, café and restaurant near the mouth of the harbour, with a tranquil ambience and half a dozen real ales brewed at the Bristol Beer Factory. Interesting calendar of events, including live music on Fri evenings. Daily noon–11pm, Fri & Sat till 11.30pm.

**Llandoger Trow** 1–3 King St ☎0117 926 1650, ⓦbrewersfayre.co.uk. Seventeenth-century drinking den full of historical associations (see p.283), with cosy nooks and armchairs, benches outside and a separate restaurant upstairs. Snacks and full meals available. Gets very busy on summer evenings. Mon–Sat 11am–11pm, Sun noon–10.30pm.

**No.1 Harbourside** 1 Canon's Rd ☎0117 929 1100, ⓦno1harbourside.co.uk. Laidback lounge bar for drinks and snacks all day until late, and live music (Wed–Sat). Meals (beetroot salad, ox-cheek ragu) are accompanied by free soup. Daily 10am–midnight, Mon & Sun till 11pm, Fri & Sat till 2am.

**Start the Bus** 7–9 Baldwin St ☎0117 930 4370, ⓦstartthebus.tv. Mellow, slightly grungy bar/restaurant by day, buzzing music venue at night, with live bands most evenings. Food (including pulled-pork burgers and fishfinger sandwiches) served until 10pm. Daily noon–1am, Thurs till 2am, Fri & Sat till 3am.

## NIGHTLIFE AND ENTERTAINMENT

**Colston Hall** Colston St ☎0844 887 1500, ⓦcolstonhall.org. Major names in the classical, jazz, rock and world genres appear in this stalwart mainstream venue. Hosts various Bristol music festivals throughout the year.

**Fiddlers** Willway St, Bedminster ☎0117 987 3403, ⓦfiddlers.co.uk. Mainly live folk, world music and Afrobeat at this relaxed, family-run venue (formerly a prison) south of the river.

**The Fleece** 12 St Thomas St ☎0117 945 0996, ⓦthefleece.co.uk. Stone-flagged ex-wool warehouse, now a loud, sweaty pub staging everything from acoustic blues and alt-country to punk and deathcore.

**The Louisiana** Wapping Rd ☎0117 926 5978, ⓦthelouisiana.net. Established music pub with a well-earned reputation for helping break bands (The White Stripes, Florence and the Machine) and promoting local

artists. It's a mite cramped, but the acoustics and atmosphere are excellent.

★**St George's** Great George St ☎0845 402 4001, ⓦstgeorgesbristol.co.uk. Elegant Georgian church with superb acoustics, staging a packed programme of lunchtime and evening concerts covering classical, world, folk and jazz music.

**Syndicate** 15 Nelson St ☎0117 945 0325, ⓦthesyndicate.com. A real super-club, the largest in Bristol, and home to various club nights dealing in house, garage, electro and R&B.

**Thekla** East Mud Dock, The Grove ☎0117 929 3301, ⓦtheklabristol.co.uk. Much-loved studenty riverboat venue, staging a varied line-up of live bands plus indie, house and pop club nights. Look out for the Banksy stencil of the Grim Reaper on its hull.

## SHOPPING

**Beast** St Nicholas Market & 224 Cheltenham Rd ⓦbeast-clothing.com. Amusing T-shirts, hoodies and hats emblazoned with snippets of the local lingo – choose from "Ark At Ee" and "Gert Lush" among others. The Cheltenham Road branch closes an hour later. Mon–Sat 9.30am–5pm.

**Bristol Cider Shop** 7 Christmas Steps ⓦbristolcidershop.co.uk. Welcoming store stocking over fifty varieties of local cider and perry, with six on tap, including Perry's and the legendary Wilkins. Tues–Sat 10am–6pm.

**Cabot Circus** ⓦcabotcircus.com. Ultra-contemporary shopping precinct filled with the usual big-name brands such as Hollister, Apple, Sony and a three-floor House of Fraser, plus the only Harvey Nichols in the South West. Mon–Sat 10am–8pm, Sun 11am–5pm.

**Guild** 68–70 Park St ⓦbristolguild.co.uk. Quality

independent retailer operating at the top of Park Street for over a hundred years. Various departments, from designer kitchen goods to a gourmet food hall, plus an outside terrace for a quick coffee break. Mon–Sat 10am–6pm.

**Plastic Wax Records** 222 Cheltenham Rd ⓦplasticwaxrecords.com. Bristol's largest record dealer, with wall-to-wall vinyl across all genres (some 10,000 LPs, allegedly). Mon & Sun noon–4.30pm, Tues–Fri 9.30am–7pm, Sat 9am–6pm.

**Shop** 19 Christmas Steps ⓦshoptheshop.co.uk. Charming "Social Enterprise" that specializes in retro clothing at retro prices, plus vintage homeware, books and records. It's all non-profit, so any extras go towards community art events, and the friendly staff provide free coffee to boot. Mon–Sat 11am–6pm.

# Bath

Just twelve miles from Bristol, **BATH** has a very different feel from its neighbour – more harmonious, compact, leisurely and complacent. The city's elegant crescents and Georgian buildings are studded with plaques naming Bath's eminent inhabitants from its heyday as a spa resort; it was here that Jane Austen set *Persuasion* and *Northanger Abbey*, and where Gainsborough established himself as a portraitist and landscape painter.

Bath owes its name and fame to its **hot springs** – the only ones in the country – which made it a place of reverence for the local Celtic population, though it took Roman technology to turn it into a fully fledged bathing establishment. The baths fell into decline with the departure of the Romans, but the town later regained its importance under the Saxons, its abbey seeing the coronation of the **first king of all England**, Edgar, in 973. A new bathing complex was built in the sixteenth century, popularized by the visit of Elizabeth I in 1574, and the city reached its fashionable zenith in the eighteenth century, when **Beau Nash** ruled the town's social scene (see box below). It was at this time, Bath's "Golden Age", that the city acquired its ranks of Palladian mansions and Regency townhouses, all of them built in the local **Bath stone**. The legacy is a city whose greatest enjoyment comes simply from wandering its streets, with their pale gold architecture and sweeping vistas.

## The Roman Baths

Abbey Churchyard • Daily: March–June, Sept & Oct 9am–6pm; July & Aug 9am–10pm; Nov–Feb 9.30am–5.30pm; last entry 1hr before closing • £13.50, £14 in July & Aug, £17 combined ticket with Fashion Museum • Free audioguides and hourly guided tours • ☎ 0225 477785, ⓦ romanbaths.co.uk

There are hours of entertainment in Bath's premier attraction, the **Roman Baths**, comprising the baths themselves and an informative museum – highlights include the Sacred Spring, part of the temple of the local deity Sulis Minerva, where water still bubbles up at a constant 46.5ºC; the open-air (but originally covered) Great Bath, its vaporous waters surrounded by nineteenth-century pillars, terraces and statues of famous Romans; the Circular Bath, where bathers cooled off; and the Norman King's Bath, where people were taking a restorative dip right up until 1978.

Among a quantity of coins, jewellery and sculpture exhibited are the bronze head of Sulis Minerva and a grand, Celtic-inspired gorgon's head from the temple's pediment. Models of the complex at its greatest extent give some idea of the awe which it must have inspired, while the graffiti salvaged from the Roman era – mainly curses and boasts – offer a personal slant on this antique leisure centre.

You can get a free glimpse into the baths from the next-door **Pump Room**, the social hub of the Georgian spa community and still redolent of that era, which houses a formal tearoom and restaurant (see p.294).

---

### BEAU NASH

Bath's social renaissance in the eighteenth century was largely due to one man: **Richard "Beau" Nash** (1674–1761), an ex-army officer, ex-lawyer, dandy and gambler, who became Bath's Master of Ceremonies in 1704, conducting public balls of an unprecedented splendour. Wielding dictatorial powers over dress and behaviour, Nash orchestrated the social manners of the city and even extended his influence to cover road improvements and the design of buildings. In an early example of health awareness, he banned smoking in Bath's public rooms at a time when pipe-smoking was generally enjoyed among men, women and children. Less philanthropically, he also encouraged gambling and even took a percentage of the bank's takings. According to his rules, balls were always to begin at 6pm and end at 11pm and each one had to open with a minuet "danced by two persons of the highest distinction present". White aprons were banned, gossipers and scandalmongers were shunned, and, most radical of all, the wearing of swords in public places was forbidden. Nash's fortunes changed when gambling restrictions were introduced in 1739, greatly reducing his influence; he died in poverty aged 87, but was treated to a suitably lavish send-off.

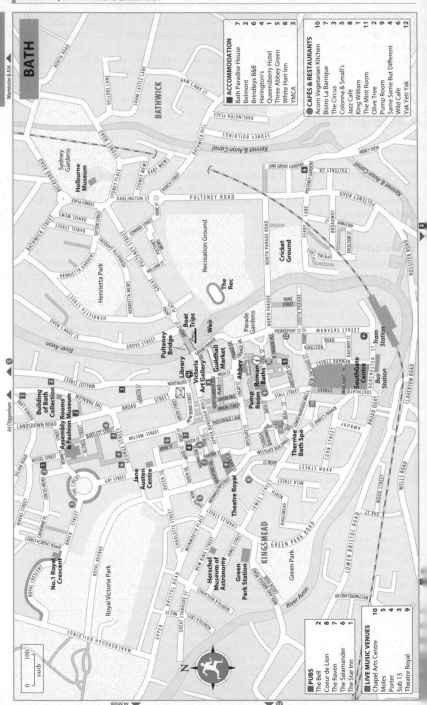

**BATH**

Warminster & A36

BATHWICK

M4 Chippenham

M4 Bristol

A4 Bristol

■ **ACCOMMODATION**
| | |
|---|---|
| Bath Paradise House | 7 |
| Belmont | 2 |
| Brindleys B&B | 6 |
| Harrington's | 4 |
| Queensberry Hotel | 1 |
| Three Abbey Green | 5 |
| White Hart Inn | 8 |
| YMCA | 3 |

● **CAFÉS & RESTAURANTS**
| | |
|---|---|
| Acorn Vegetarian Kitchen | 10 |
| Bistro La Barrique | 7 |
| The Circus | 3 |
| Colonna & Small's | 5 |
| Jazz Café | 8 |
| King William | 1 |
| The Mint Room | 11 |
| Olive Tree | 2 |
| Pump Room | 9 |
| Same Same But Different | 4 |
| Wild Café | 6 |
| Yak Yeti Yak | 12 |

■ **PUBS**
| | |
|---|---|
| The Bell | 2 |
| Coeur de Lion | 8 |
| The Raven | 7 |
| The Salamander | 6 |
| The Star Inn | 1 |

■ **LIVE MUSIC VENUES**
| | |
|---|---|
| Chapel Arts Centre | 10 |
| Moles | 4 |
| Porter | 3 |
| Sub 13 | 9 |
| Theatre Royal | 1 |

0 — 100 yards

N

# Bath Abbey

**5**

Abbey Churchyard • April–Oct Mon 9.30am–5.30pm, Tues–Fri 9am–5.30pm, Sat 9am–6pm, Sun 1–2.30pm & 4.30–5.30pm (till 6pm in Aug); Nov–March Mon–Sat 9am–4.30pm, Sun 1–2.30pm & 4.30–5.30pm • Requested donation £2.50 • ⓦ bathabbey.org

Although there has been a church on the site since the seventh century, **Bath Abbey** did not take its present form until the end of the fifteenth century, when Bishop Oliver King began work on the ruins of the previous Norman building, some of which were incorporated into the new church. The bishop was said to have been inspired by a vision of angels ascending and descending a ladder to heaven, which the present facade recalls on the turrets flanking the central window. The west front also features the founder's signature in the form of carvings of olive trees surmounted by crowns, a play on his name.

The **interior** is in a restrained Perpendicular style, although it does boast splendid fan vaulting on the ceiling, which was not completed until the nineteenth century. The floor and walls are crammed with elaborate monuments and memorials, and traces of the grander Norman building are visible in the Gethsemane Chapel.

On most days, you can join a 45-minute tower tour (£6) to see the massive bells, clock and bell-pulling machinery, and can enjoy a bird's-eye view of Bath – but be prepared for the 212 spiral steps.

# Thermae Bath Spa

Hot Bath St • **Baths** Daily: New Royal Bath 9am–9.30pm, last entry 7pm; Cross Bath 10am–8pm, last entry 6pm • £17 (1hr 30min) to £57 (full day) **Visitor centre** April–Sept Mon–Sat 10am–5pm, Sun 11am–4pm • Free • ☎ 0844 888 0844, ⓦ thermaebathspa.com

At the bottom of the elegantly colonnaded Bath Street, the fantastic **Thermae Bath Spa** allows you to take the waters in much the same way that visitors to Bath have done throughout the ages, but with state-of-the-art spa facilities. Heated by the city's thermal waters, the spa includes two open-air pools, one on the roof of its centrepiece, the New Royal Bath, Sir Nicholas Grimshaw's sleekly futuristic "glass cube". Various treatments are offered, from massages to hot-stone therapies and a small **visitor centre** has displays relating to Bath's thermal waters.

# Queen Square and around

North of Hot Bath Street, Sawclose is presided over by the **Theatre Royal**, opened in 1805 and one of the country's finest surviving Georgian theatres; Beau Nash had his first house in Bath here from 1743, in what is now the theatre's foyer. Barton Street leads north of Sawclose to **Queen Square**, the first Bath venture of the architect **John Wood the Elder** (1704–54), champion of Neoclassical Palladianism, who lived at no. 15 (not no. 24 as a tablet there asserts). East of the square, the wide shopping strand of **Milsom Street** was designed by Wood as the main thoroughfare of Georgian Bath.

# Herschel Museum of Astronomy

19 New King St • Mid-Jan to mid-Dec Daily 1–5pm, Sat & Sun from 11am • £6 • ☎ 01225 446865, ⓦ bath-preservation-trust.org.uk

A few minutes west of the centre is the small **Herschel Museum of Astronomy**, the former home of the musician and astronomer Sir William Herschel and his sister Caroline, who together discovered the planet Uranus here in 1781. Among the furnishings, musical instruments and knick-knacks from the Herschels' era, you can see a replica of the telescope with which Uranus was identified.

# Jane Austen Centre

40 Gay St • April–Oct daily 9.45am–5.30pm, July & Aug 9.30am–6pm; Nov–March Mon–Fri & Sun 11am–4.30pm, Sat 9.45am–5.30pm • £8 • ☎ 01225 443000, ⓦ janeausten.co.uk

The **Jane Austen Centre** provides a superficial overview of the author's connections with

**5**

Bath, illustrated by extracts from her writings, contemporary costumes, furnishings and household items; visits start with a talk every twenty minutes. Austen herself, who wasn't entirely enamoured of the city, lived just down the road at 25 Gay Street – one of a number of places the author inhabited while in Bath.

## The Royal Crescent and around

**No. 1 Royal Crescent** Mid-Feb to Dec daily 10.30–5.30pm, Mon from noon • £8.50, or £10.50 with Building of Bath Collection • ☎ 01225 428126, ⓦ no1royalcrescent.org.uk

At the top of Gay Street, the elder John Wood's masterpiece, **The Circus**, consists of three crescents arranged in a tight circle of three-storey houses, with a carved frieze running round the entire circle. Wood died soon after laying the foundation stone, and the job was finished by his son, **John Wood the Younger** (1728–1782), who was as instrumental as his father in defining Bath's elegant Georgian appearance. The painter Thomas Gainsborough lived at no. 17 from 1760 to 1774.

The Circus is connected by Brock Street to the **Royal Crescent**, grandest of Bath's crescents, begun by the younger John Wood in 1767. The stately arc of thirty houses – said to be the country's first – is set off by a spacious sloping lawn from which a magnificent vista extends to green hills and distant ribbons of honey-coloured stone. The interior of **No. 1 Royal Crescent**, on the corner with Brock Street, has been restored to reflect as nearly as possible its original Georgian appearance at the end of the eighteenth century.

At the bottom of the Crescent, Royal Avenue leads onto **Royal Victoria Park**, the city's largest open space, containing an aviary and nine acres of botanical gardens.

## The Fashion Museum

Assembly Rooms, Bennett St • Daily 10.30am–6pm, Nov–Feb till 5pm; last admission 1hr before closing • £8, or £17 with the Roman Baths; NT • ☎ 01225 477789, ⓦ fashionmuseum.co.uk

The younger John Wood's **Assembly Rooms**, east of the Circus, were, with the Pump Room, the centre of Bath's social scene. The building was virtually destroyed by bombing during World War II, but it has since been perfectly restored and houses the **Fashion Museum**, an entertaining collection of clothing from the Stuart era to the latest Milanese designs.

## Building of Bath Collection

The Vineyards, The Paragon • Mid-Feb to Nov Tues–Fri 10am–5pm, Sat & Sun 10.30am–5pm • £5, or £10.50 with No. 1 Royal Crescent • ☎ 01225 333895, ⓦ buildingofbathcollection.org.uk

The Georgian-Gothic Countess of Huntingdon's Chapel houses the **Building of Bath Collection**, a fascinating exploration of the construction and architecture of the city and a great place to start your visit. Everything is covered, from the kind of facades associated with the two John Woods to balustrades, door designs and such aspects of interior ornamentation as marbling, stencilling and japanning.

## Holburne Museum

Great Pulteney St • Daily 10am–5pm, Sun from 11am • Free • ☎ 01225 388569, ⓦ holburne.org

The River Avon is crossed by the graceful, shop-lined **Pulteney Bridge**, an Italianate structure designed by Robert Adam, from the other side of which a lengthy vista stretches along Great Pulteney Street to the imposing classical facade of the **Holburne Museum**. The building, with a startlingly modern extension at the back, holds an impressive range of decorative and fine art, mostly furniture, silverware, porcelain and paintings, including several works by Gainsborough, notably the famous *Byam Family*, his largest portrait. Look out, too, for works by Constable, Stubbs and Angelika Kauffman.

## ARRIVAL AND INFORMATION

**BATH**

**By train** Bath Spa train station is a short walk south of the centre at the bottom of Manvers Street.

Destinations Bristol (every 15–30min; 15min); London Paddington (every 30min–1hr; 1hr 30min); Salisbury (every 30min–1hr; 1hr).

**By bus** The bus station (ⓦ firstgroup.com) lies next to the train station on Dorchester Street.

Destinations Bristol (Mon–Sat every 15min, Sun every 30min; 50min); London (12 daily; 2hr 30min–3hr 15min);

Salisbury (Mon–Sat every 30min with change; 2hr 35min–2hr 50min); Wells (Mon–Sat hourly, Sun 7 daily; 1hr 20min).

**By bike** If you're coming from Bristol, you can cycle all the way along a cycle-path that follows the route of a disused railway line and the course of the River Avon.

**Tourist office** Next to the abbey in Abbey Churchyard (Mon–Sat 9.30am–5.30pm, Sun 10am–4pm; ☎ 0906 711 2000, ⓦ visitbath.co.uk).

## GETTING AROUND AND TOURS

Walking or biking are the best ways to enjoy Bath's Georgian terraces – cars are a hindrance and parking is expensive; drivers should use one of the Park-and-Ride car parks on the periphery of town.

**Bike rental** Bath Bike Hire, Sydney Wharf, Bathwick Hill (£10/day; ☎ 01225 447276, ⓦ bathbikehire.com). They also rent narrowboats (from £60/half-day).

**Boat tours** Hour-long river trips can be made from Pulteney Bridge; operators include Pulteney Cruisers (March–Nov 1–3 hourly; £8; ☎ 01225 312900, ⓦ bathboating.com) and Avon Cruising (April–Oct 5–7 daily; £8; ☎ 07791 910650, ⓦ pulteneyprincess.co.uk).

**Walking tours** Mayor's Guides run free 2hr walking tours, starting outside the Pump Room in Abbey Churchyard (ⓦ bathguides.org.uk; Mon–Fri & Sun 10.30am & 2pm, Sat 10.30am, May–Sept also Tues & Thurs 7pm), while the Jane Austen Centre arranges 1hr 30min walks in the author's footsteps, also leaving from Abbey Churchyard (☎ 01225 443000, ⓦ janeausten .co.uk; Sat & Sun 11am; £12).

## ACCOMMODATION

Bath is chock-full of hotels and B&Bs, but most of the latter are small, and it's always worth booking early, especially at weekends, when most places demand a two-night minimum and prices rise; rates quoted below are midweek. There are also good-value, central hostels, though the nearest campsites are some distance outside town. Note that the centre can get noisy at night, so choose a room away from the street for an undisturbed sleep.

**Bath Paradise House** 86–88 Holloway ☎ 01225 317723, ⓦ paradise-house.co.uk. Georgian villa an uphill trudge from the centre, but with wonderful views. Open fires in winter, elegant four-posters in some of the rooms, and three rooms opening straight onto the award-winning gardens. **£130**

**Belmont** 7 Belmont, Lansdown Rd ☎ 01225 423082, ⓦ belmontbath.co.uk. Large doubles, some with tiny, clean, modern en-suite bathrooms, in a centrally located B&B in a house designed by John Wood. No credit cards. **£50**

**Brindleys B&B** 14 Pulteney Gardens ☎ 01225 461728, ⓦ brindleysbath.co.uk. Half a dozen light, airy and elegantly decorated bijou en-suite rooms that have more than a hint of a French country manor house about them, a feeling that extends to the stylish communal areas. It's set in a quiet residential area but is just a 5min walk from the centre of town. **£130**

**Harington's** Queen St ☎ 01225 461728, ⓦ haringtonshotel.co.uk. Central hotel in a converted townhouse with friendly service and modern, well-equipped rooms, mostly quite small, and some at the top of steep steps. Breakfasts are superlative, food is available throughout the day and there's wi-fi. **£148**

**Queensberry Hotel** Russel St ☎ 01225 447928, ⓦ thequeensberry.co.uk. Spread across four Georgian townhouses at the top end of town, the *Queensberry* has got quirky cool down to a "T", with tastefully minimalist rooms – each one different and each one with a fabulous bathroom – stylish communal areas, a lovely walled garden, and a superb basement restaurant (see p.294) that means dinner-and-room offers can often prove to be a good deal. **£140**

★**Three Abbey Green** 3 Abbey Green ☎ 01225 428558, ⓦ threeabbeygreen.com. Top-notch B&B in a superbly renovated Georgian house just steps from the abbey. The airy, spotless rooms are beautifully done; the larger ones overlooking a peaceful square are more expensive. **£120**

★**White Hart Inn** Widcombe Hill ☎ 01225 313985, ⓦ whitehartbath.co.uk. The comfiest of Bath's hostels has a kitchen, a first-class bar/restaurant and a spacious courtyard. There are clean doubles and twins available, some en suite. Midnight curfew. Dorms **£15**, doubles **£50**

**YMCA** International House, Broad St ☎ 01225 325900, ⓦ bathymca.co.uk. Clean, central and spacious, this friendly place has dorms, singles and doubles. No curfew, but no kitchen, either. All rates include breakfast (cooked breakfast £3.50 extra). Dorms **£21**, doubles **£60**

**5**

## EATING

### CAFÉS

**Colonna & Small's** 6 Chapel Row ☎07766 808067, ⊛colonnaandsmalls.co.uk. The high-browed but helpful brewmasters at this stripped-back coffee specialists serve a serious cup of Joe. Choose from a range of weekly changing single-origin espresso beans and filter coffees. Just don't ask for milk. Or sugar. Mon–Fri 8am–5.30pm, Sat 8.30am–5.30pm, Sun 10am–4pm.

**Jazz Café** 1 Kingsmead Square ☎01225 329002, ⊛bathjazzcafe.co.uk. Big breakfasts, snack fodder and dishes such as shredded slow-cooked chilli beef (£8.75) are served at this boho hangout. There are beers and wines, newspapers are on hand, and outside seating to boot. Mon–Sat 8.30am–5pm, Sun10.30am–4pm.

★**Wild Café** 10a Queen St ☎01225 448673, ⊛wildcafe.co.uk. Tucked away down a cobbled sidestreet behind Queen Square, the open kitchen at this incredibly popular whitewashed café – look out for the blue bicycle outside – does a roaring trade in crispy risotto balls, rabbit pies (mains from £9.95), salads and sandwiches (including an excellent BLT; £5.75). Mon–Fri 8am–5pm, Sat 9am–6pm, Sun 10am–5pm.

### RESTAURANTS

★**Acorn Vegetarian Kitchen** 2 North Parade Passage ☎01225 446059, ⊛acornvegetariankitchen.co.uk. Bath's favourite veggie and vegan restaurant offers original and delicious dishes in an unruffled, arty environment: think truffled broccoli and curried cauliflower fritter (mains from £15.75, £9.75 at lunch; "Little Plates" from £2.95). Beers and wines are organic. Mon–Fri & Sun noon–3pm & 5.30–9.30pm, Sat noon–3.30pm & 5.30–10pm.

**Bistro La Barrique** 31 Barton St ☎01225 463861, ⊛bistrolabarique.co.uk. This place has cornered the market in "French tapas", or *petits plats*, ideal for grazing on such dishes as mushroom flan, gratinated duck confit and boeuf bourguignon, most costing £6.50. The room is nothing special, but there's a nice walled garden where you can eat alfresco. Daily noon–2.30pm & 5pm–late.

**The Circus** 34 Brock St ☎01225 466020, ⊛thecircuscafeandrestaurant.co.uk. There's a refined but relaxed atmosphere at this little family-run brasserie, just a stroll from the Royal Crescent, which specializes in well-prepared Modern British dishes such as West Country rabbit (£16.90, £5 cheaper at lunch). Mon–Sat 10am–midnight.

★**King William** 36 Thomas St ☎01225 428096, ⊛kingwilliampub.com. North of the centre, beyond The Paragon/Bathwick Street but well worth the walk, the *King William* regularly receives accolades for its excellent, locally sourced food, such as slow-cooked pork belly (£15) and butterbean and leek crumble (£13), but the beer and wine list is top-drawer, too. Bar Mon–Fri noon–3pm & 5–11pm, Sat noon–midnight, Sun noon–11pm; restaurant Wed–Fri 6–9pm, Sat 6–10pm, Sun noon–3pm.

**The Mint Room** Longmead Gospel Hall, Lower Bristol Rd ☎01225 446656, ⊛themintroom.co.uk. Indian food but not as you know it: innovative yet authentic regional cuisine ranging from *murgh palak paneer* (chicken breast stuffed with spinach and home-made cheese) to a South Indian seafood *moilee* (mains from £7.95). Daily noon–2.30pm & 6–11pm, Fri & Sat till 11.30pm.

**Olive Tree** Queensberry Hotel, Russel St ☎01225 447928, ⊛olivetreebath.co.uk. This is one of Bath's top restaurants, offering French-inspired dishes, a contemporary ambience and discreetly attentive service. The menu might feature crab lasagne (£12.95) or beetroot and tarragon risotto (£18), and the desserts are delectable. Set-price lunches from £18.50. Mon–Thurs 7–9.30pm, Fri & Sat 12.30–2pm & 6.30–10pm, Sun 12.30–2pm & 7–9.30pm.

**Pump Room** Abbey Churchyard ☎01225 444477, ⊛romanbaths.co.uk. Splash out on a Champagne breakfast, sample the excellent lunchtime menu (mains from £12.95) or succumb to a Bath bun or a range of cream teas, all accompanied by a classical trio. It's a bit hammy and overpriced, and you may have to queue, but you get a good view of the Baths. Daily 9.30am–4.30pm; July, Aug & Dec and during major festivals 9.30am–9pm.

**Same Same But Different** 7a Prince's Buildings, Bartlett St ☎01225 466856, ⊛samesame.co.uk. Excellent café/restaurant that manages to mix a laidback ambience with quality food – unusual tapas dishes start at £4.50, or go for something a bit more substantial, such as finger-licking sticky pork with triple-cooked chips (£10.95). Mon 8am–6pm, Tues–Fri 8am–11pm, Sat 9am–11pm, Sun 10am–5pm.

**Yak Yeti Yak** 12 Pierrepont St ☎01225 442299, ⊛yakyetiyak.co.uk. Quality Nepalese restaurant in a series of cellar rooms with a choice of chairs or floor cushions. Meat dishes are stir-fried or spicily marinated, and there's a good vegetarian selection (dishes all £5.60–8.90). Daily noon–2pm & 6–10.30pm, Fri & Sat from 5pm.

## DRINKING

★**The Bell** 103 Walcot St ☎01225 460426, ⊛thebellinnbath.co.uk. Easy-going, slightly grungy tavern with a great jukebox, live music (Mon & Wed eve, plus Sun lunchtime) and DJs (Fri, Sat & Sun). There's bar billiards and a beer garden with table footy. Mon–Sat 11.30am–11pm, Sun noon–10.30pm.

**Coeur de Lion** 17 Northumberland Place ☎01225 463568, ⊛coeur-de-lion.co.uk. Centrally located tavern on a flagstoned shopping alley, with a few tables outside (and more upstairs). It's Bath's smallest boozer (it serves local Abbey Ales) and a regular tourist stop, but has good lunchtime food (baguettes from £4.75). Daily 10am–11.30pm.

## BATH'S FESTIVALS

Bath hosts a great range of festivals throughout the year, notably the **Bath International Music Festival** (w bathfestivals.org.uk/music), held between mid-May and June and featuring jazz, classical and world music; the **Bath Fringe Festival** (late May to early June; w bathfringe.co.uk), with the accent on art and performance; and **Bath Literature Festival** (ten days in Feb/March; w bathfestivals.org.uk/literature). For further information on these and other festivals, contact the festivals office at Abbey Chambers, Kingston Buildings (☎ 01225 462231, w bathfestivals.org.uk).

**The Raven** 6–7 Queen St ☎ 01225 425045, w theravenof bath.co.uk. Civilized watering hole with first-rate local ales – it was CAMRA Pub of the Year in 2013 – served both downstairs and in the less crowded upstairs room (unless one of the storytelling nights is being held there). Food available, including renowned pies (£8.80). Mon–Thurs 11.30am–11pm, Fri & Sat 11.30am–midnight, Sun noon–10.30pm.
**The Salamander** 3 John St ☎ 01225 428889. Local brewer Bath Ales pub with a traditional, dark-wood interior, a relaxed atmosphere and tasty dishes available at the bar or in the upstairs restaurant (mains from £11.95). Daily 10am–11.30pm.
★**The Star Inn** 23 The Vineyards, The Paragon ☎ 01225 425071. First licensed in 1760, this Abbey Ales pub has a classic Victorian interior, and beers that include the award-winning Bellringer and draught Bass served from a jug. Mon–Thurs noon–2.30pm & 5.30pm–midnight, Fri & Sat noon–1am, Sun noon–midnight.

### NIGHTLIFE AND ENTERTAINMENT

The **theatres** in town often stage productions before or after their London run, but most are fairly mainstream. Bath's **music** scene is lively, especially during the festival (see box above), while its small (and relaxed) clubbing scene, overshadowed by the proximity of Bristol, takes place mostly in unventilated basements.

**Chapel Arts Centre** St James' Memorial Hall, Lower Borough Walls ☎ 01225 461700, w chapelarts.org. Nice little venue for all kinds of performing arts, with an emphasis on jazz, blues and folk. Arrive early to get one of the cabaret-style tables.
★**Moles** 14 George St ☎ 01225 404445, w moles .co.uk. Currently being renovated following a fire in March 2014, this Bath institution should be up and running soon and featuring its much-loved mix of good live music, DJs and club nights. The cramped basement can get pretty hot and sweaty, though – not for claustrophobes. Normally Mon & Sun 11am–midnight, Tues & Wed 11am–2am, Thurs 11am–3am, Fri & Sat 11am–4am.
**Porter** 15A George St ☎ 01225 585100, w theporter .co.uk. This multifaceted Georgian townhouse is home to a mellow lounge-bar on the first floor, with over half a dozen craft beers, and a late-night basement bar, with live jazz every Thurs, DJs at the weekend, and a monthly comedy club (£3). Lounge bar daily 10am–midnight, Fri & Sat till 2am; basement bar Thurs 6pm–midnight, Fri & Sat 6pm–2am.
**Sub 13** 144 Edgar Buildings, George St ☎ 01225 466667, w sub13.net. Settle into a white leather booth in the Champagne lounge or chill out in the backyard terrace at this edgy basement bar, boasting the best drinks list in town Mon–Sat 5pm–midnight, Fri till 2am, Sat till 3am.
**Theatre Royal** Sawclose ☎ 01225 448844, w theatre royal.org.uk. Theatre and ballet fans should check out what's showing at this historic venue, if only for the atmosphere. More experimental productions are staged in its Ustinov Studio, with family shows at the egg.

# Wells

The miniature cathedral city of **WELLS**, 21 miles south of Bristol and the same distance southwest from Bath, has not significantly altered in eight hundred years. Charming and compact, it is eminently walkable, and a stroll around its tightly knit streets reveals a cluster of medieval buildings, archways and almshouses.

## Wells Cathedral

Cathedral Green • Daily 7am–7pm, Oct–March till 6pm; tours Mon–Sat 10am, 11am, 1pm, 2pm & 3pm (Nov–March 11am, noon & 2pm); 1hr; free • Suggested donation £6 • ☎ 01749 674483, w wellscathedral.org.uk

Hidden from sight until you pass into its spacious close from central Market Place, **Wells Cathedral** presents a majestic spectacle, the broad lawn of the former graveyard providing a perfect foreground. The west front teems with some three hundred thirteenth-century figures of saints and kings, once brightly painted and gilded, though their present honey tint has a subtle splendour of its own. The sensational facade was constructed about fifty years after work on the main building was begun in 1180.

The **interior** is a supreme example of early English Gothic, the long nave punctuated by a dramatic and very modern-looking "scissor arch", one of three that were constructed in 1338 to take the extra weight of the newly built tower. Beyond the arches, there are some gnarled old tombs to be seen in the aisles of the **Quire**, at the end of which is the richly coloured stained glass of the fourteenth-century **Lady Chapel**. The **capitals and corbels** of the transepts hold some amusing narrative carvings, and in the north transept there's a 24-hour astronomical **clock** dating from 1390. Opposite the clock, a well-worn flight of steps leads to the **Chapter House**, an octagonal room elaborately ribbed in the Decorated style.

## Wells & Mendip Museum

8 Cathedral Green • Easter–Oct Mon–Sat 10am–5pm; Nov–Easter Mon–Sat 11am–4pm • £3 • ☏ 01749 673477, ⓦ wellsmuseum.org.uk

The row of clerical houses on the north side of Cathedral Green mainly dates from the seventeenth and eighteenth centuries. The chancellor's house is now the **Wells & Mendip Museum**, displaying some of the cathedral's original statuary as well as a good geological section with fossils from the Mendip area and, until 2018, changing exhibitions on World War I – the Somme battlefield, a military field hospital – using artefacts donated by local residents.

## Vicars' Close

The cottages that constitute picturesque **Vicars' Close**, linked to the cathedral by the Chain Gate, were built in the mid-fourteenth century to house the men of the choir, and its members still make up most of their inhabitants today. The cobbled close is the oldest continuously habited medieval street in Europe but has undergone various alterations over the years – you can get a good idea of its initial appearance at no. 22, which was restored to its original proportions in 1863.

## Bishop's Palace

Daily: Mid-Feb–March, Nov & Dec 10am–4pm; April–Oct 10am–6pm; tours daily 11.30am, April–Oct also 2.30pm • £7.70 • ☏ 01749 988111, ⓦ bishopspalace.org.uk

The tranquil grounds of the **Bishop's Palace**, residence of the Bishop of Bath and Wells since 1206, are reachable through the Bishop's Eye archway from Market Place. The palace was walled and moated as a result of a rift with the borough in the fourteenth century, and the imposing gatehouse still features the grooves of the portcullis and a chute for pouring oil and molten lead on would-be assailants. The gardens contain the springs from which the city takes its name and the scant but impressive remains of the **Great Hall**, built at the end of the thirteenth century and despoiled during the Reformation. Across the lawn stand the square **Bishop's Chapel** and **Bishop Jocelyn's Hall**, a few state rooms holding displays relating to the history of the site and the Undercroft café.

**By bus** Buses (☏ 0845 602 0156, ⓦ firstgroup.com or ⓦ webberbus.com) pull in at the station off Market Street. Destinations Bath (Mon–Sat hourly, Sun 7 daily; 1hr 20min); Bridgwater (Mon–Sat 1–3 hourly; 1hr 20min); Bristol (every 30min–1hr; 1hr 5min); Glastonbury (Mon–Sat every 15min, Sun hourly; 15min); Taunton (Mon–Sat 8 daily; 1hr 20min); Wookey Hole (Mon–Sat every 30min–1hr; 15min); Yeovil (1–3 hourly; 1hr 20min).

**Tourist office** There's an info desk in the Wells & Mendip Museum, 8 Cathedral Green (Easter–Oct Mon–Sat 10am–5pm; Nov–Easter Mon–Sat 11am–4pm; ☏ 01749 671770, ⓔ visitwellsinfo@gmail.com).

## ACCOMMODATION

**Beryl** Hawkers Lane, 1 mile northeast of Wells ☎01749 678738, ⓦberyl-wells.co.uk. Luxury country-house B&B, a former hunting lodge, set in lovely gardens with a children's play area and pool (May–Sept). Decor varies between the 14 rooms – some are quite twee, others stylishly understated – though all enjoy views. __£100__

**The Crown** Market Place ☎01749 673457, ⓦwww .crownatwells.co.uk. Fifteenth-century coaching inn where William Penn was arrested in 1695 for illegal preaching; it's got a suitably old-fashioned flavour that verges on the fusty and faded. Rooms can be noisy from the bar and bistro below and/or the Saturday market. __£95__

**Swan Hotel** Sadler St ☎01749 836300, ⓦswanhotelwells.co.uk. A swankier choice than *The Crown*, this rambling inn has plenty of antique character, plus friendly service and a rated restaurant (for which booking is essential). Pricier rooms have cathedral views. __£122__

## EATING AND DRINKING

**The Fountain Inn** 1 St Thomas St ☎01749 672317, ⓦthefountaininn.co.uk. Leave the touristy pubs of High Street Wells behind and head under the Chain Gate and beyond Vicar's Close to this rustic-chic gastropub northeast of the cathedral. Good food, with an interesting menu that includes an excellent confit of duck, halloumi burger and chargrilled Priddy rib-eye (£18.50). Mon 6–11pm, Tues–Thurs noon–3.30pm & 6–10pm, Fri & Sat noon–3.30pm & 6–11pm, Sun noon–3.30pm & 7–11pm.

★ **The Good Earth** 4 Priory Rd ☎01749 678600. Lovely wholefood restaurant that was making a name for itself with its delicious home-made quiches long before eco food was in vogue. Soups, salads, veggie pizzas and other organic goodies (mains from £4.95) available to eat in or take away. Mon–Fri 9am–4.30pm, Sat 9am–6pm.

**Old Spot** 12 Sadler St ☎01749 689099, ⓦtheoldspot .co.uk. Spacious, easy-going place with Old Spot pork among other appetising items on the eclectic set-price two- and three-course lunches (£15.50/£18.50) and à la carte dinners (mains from £12.50). Wed–Sat 12.30–2.30pm & 7–9.30pm, Sun 12.30–2.30pm.

# The Mendips

Northwest of Wells, the ancient woodland, exposed heaths and limestone crags of the **Mendip Hills** are chiefly famous for **Wookey Hole** – the most impressive of many caves in this narrow limestone chain – and for **Cheddar Gorge**, where a walk through the narrow cleft makes a starting point for more adventurous hikes across the Mendips.

## Wookey Hole

Two miles northwest of Wells • Daily 10am–5pm, Nov–March till 4pm • £18, online £15.30 • ☎01749 672243, ⓦwookey.co.uk

It's folklore rather than geology that takes precedence at **Wookey Hole**, a stunning cave complex of deep pools and intricate rock formations hollowed out by the River Axe. Highlight of the hour-long tour is the alleged petrified remains of the Witch of Wookey, a "blear-eyed hag" who was said to turn her evil eye on crops, young lovers and local farmers. To finish off, there's a functioning Victorian paper mill and rooms containing speleological exhibits, plus a melange of family "attractions" that range from King Kong to a Clown Museum.

## Cheddar Gorge

Six miles west of Wookey on the A371, the nondescript village of **Cheddar** has given its name to Britain's best-known cheese – most of it now mass-produced far from here – and is also renowned for the **Cheddar Gorge**, lying about a mile to the north.

Cutting a jagged gash across the Mendip Hills, the limestone gorge is an amazing geological phenomenon, though its natural beauty is rather compromised by Lower Gorge's mile of trinket shops and parking areas. Few trippers venture further than the first few curves of the gorge, which holds its most dramatic scenery – at its narrowest, the road squeezes between cliffs towering almost 500ft above – though each turn of the two-mile length presents new, sometimes startling vistas.

**5**

Those fit enough can climb the 274 steps of **Jacob's Ladder** to a cliff-top tower with views towards Glastonbury Tor, with occasional glimpses of Exmoor and the sea (spring/autumn half-terms & Easter–Sept daily, also Feb–Easter & Oct weekends only: Easter, May, July & Aug 10am–5pm, other times from 10.30am; free to Cheddar Caves ticket-holders). From the tower, there's a circular three-mile cliff-top Gorge Walk, and you can branch off along marked paths to such secluded spots as **Black Rock** reserve, just two miles from Cheddar, or **Black Down** and Beacon Batch, at 1068ft the Mendips' highest point.

### Cheddar Caves

Daily: Easter, May, July & Aug 10am–5pm, rest of year from 10.30am • £18.95, online £16.11 • ☎ 01934 742343, ⓦ cheddargorge.co.uk

Beneath the towering Cheddar Gorge, the **Cheddar Caves** were scooped out by underground rivers in the wake of the Ice Age, and subsequently occupied by primitive communities. Today, the caves are floodlit to pick out the subtle tones of the rock, and the array of rock formations that resemble organ pipes, waterfalls and giant birds.

#### ARRIVAL AND INFORMATION

**By bus** The Mendip Hills are most easily explored with your own wheels. Public transport (ⓦ firstgroup.com or ⓦ webberbus.com) is essentially limited to First Group's #126 (Mon–Sat hourly, 4 on Sun; 25min) and Webber Bus #67 (Mon–Sat every 30min–1hr; 15min), both from Wells.

#### THE MENDIPS

**Tourist information** There's a National Trust information centre in Cheddar Gorge (11am–5pm: mid-March–Oct daily except Thurs, mid-July to mid-Sept daily; ☎ 01934 844518, ⓦ nationaltrust.org.uk).

#### ACCOMMODATION AND EATING

**Chedwell Cottage** 59 Redcliffe St, Cheddar ☎ 01934 743268, ⓔ info@chedwellcottage.co.uk. In a quiet lane a 10min walk from the gorge, the charming owners of this homely B&B provide three simply furnished en-suite rooms and delicious breakfasts including home-made bread. No credit cards. <u>£65</u>

**The Wookey Hole Inn** Wookey Hole ☎ 01749 676677, ⓦ wookeyholeinn.com. Very close to the caves, this is a great place to stay the night, with funky, fully equipped

guest rooms and a restaurant (booking essential) that offers a range of expensive but memorable dishes (mains from £12.95). Mon–Sat noon–2.30pm & 7–9.30pm, Sun noon–3pm. <u>£100</u>

**YHA** Cheddar Hillfield, Cheddar ☎ 0845 371 9730, ⓦ yha.org.uk. Clinically refurbished Victorian house with clean, spacious rooms – four- to six-bed dorms, en-suite doubles and family rooms – and a decent kitchen. Dorms <u>£19</u>, doubles <u>£39</u>

# Glastonbury

On the southern edge of the Mendips and six miles south of Wells, **GLASTONBURY**, famed for its annual music festival, is built around the evocative set of ruins belonging to its former abbey. The town lies at the heart of the so-called **Isle of Avalon**, a region rich with mystical associations, and for centuries it has been one of the main Arthurian sites of the West Country – today, it's an enthusiastic centre for all manner of New Age cults.

## Glastonbury Abbey

Abbey Gatehouse, Magdalene St • Daily 9am–6pm, June–Aug till 8pm, Nov–Feb till 4pm • £6 • ☎ 01458 832267, ⓦ glastonburyabbey.com

Aside from its mythological origins, **Glastonbury Abbey** can claim to be the country's oldest Christian foundation, dating back to the seventh century and possibly earlier. Enlarged by St Dunstan in the tenth century, it became the richest Benedictine abbey in the country; three Anglo-Saxon kings (Edmund, Edgar and Edmund Ironside) were buried here, and the library had a far-reaching fame. Further expansion took place under the Normans, though most of the additions were destroyed by fire in 1184. Rebuilt, the abbey was the longest in Europe when it was destroyed during the

**CLOCKWISE FROM TOP** EXMOOR NATIONAL PARK (P.308); BANKSY MURAL, BRISTOL (P.281); BURROW HILL CIDER FARM (P.303) >

**5**

> ### GLASTONBURY TALES
>
> At the heart of the complex web of **myths surrounding Glastonbury** is the early Christian legend that the young Jesus once visited this site, a story that is not as far-fetched as it sounds. The Romans had a heavy presence in the area, mining lead in the Mendips, and one of these mines was owned by **Joseph of Arimathea**, a well-to-do tin merchant said to have been related to Mary. It's not completely unfeasible that the merchant took his kinsman on one of his many visits to his property, in a period of Christ's life of which nothing is recorded – it was this possibility to which William Blake referred in his *Glastonbury Hymn*, better known as *Jerusalem*: "And did those feet in ancient times/Walk upon England's mountains green?"
>
> Another legend relates how Joseph was imprisoned for twelve years after the Crucifixion, miraculously kept alive by the **Holy Grail**, the chalice of the Last Supper, in which the blood was gathered from the wound in Christ's side. The Grail, along with the spear that had caused the wound, were later taken by Joseph to Glastonbury, where he built the "First Church", around which the abbey later grew, and commenced the conversion of Britain.
>
> Glastonbury is also popularly identified with the mythical **Avalon**; the story goes that King Arthur, having been mortally wounded in battle, sailed to Avalon where he was buried in the abbey's choir, alongside his queen – somehow Glastonbury was taken to be the best candidate for the place.

Dissolution of the Monasteries in 1539, and the ruins, now hidden behind walls and nestled among grassy parkland, can only hint at its former extent. The most complete set of remains is the shell of the Lady Chapel, with its carved figures of the Annunciation, the Magi and Herod.

The abbey's **choir**, announced by the half-worn but striking transept piers, holds what is alleged to be the tomb of **Arthur and Guinevere**. The discovery of two bodies in an ancient cemetery outside the abbey in 1191 was taken to confirm that here was, indeed, the mystical Avalon; they were transferred here in 1278 but disappeared in the mid-sixteenth century. Elsewhere in the grounds, the fourteenth-century **abbot's kitchen** is the only monastic building to survive intact, with four huge corner fireplaces and a great central lantern above. Behind the main entrance to the grounds, look out for the thorn tree that is supposedly a descendant of the original **Glastonbury Thorn** on Wearyall Hill, said to have sprouted from the staff of Joseph of Arimathea. Big-name **concerts and drama productions** take place in the abbey grounds in summer – check the website for details.

## Glastonbury Lake Villages Museum

9 High St • Mon–Sat 10am–4pm • £3; EH • ☎ 01458 832954, ⓦ english-heritage.org.uk

The fifteenth-century **Glastonbury Tribunal** provides an atmospheric setting for the small but interesting **Glastonbury Lake Villages Museum**, with displays from the Iron Age settlements that fringed the former marshland below the Tor. The villages' wattle houses were consistently rebuilt on layers of clay as they slowly submerged into the marshes, and the perfectly preserved finds include jewellery made from animal bones and a 3000-year-old wooden canoe.

## Somerset Rural Life Museum

Abbey Farm, Chilkwell St • Previously Tues–Sat 10am–5pm • Free • ☎ 01823 2788057, ⓦ somersetrurallifemuseum.org.uk

Centred round the fourteenth-century Abbey Barn, the engaging **Somerset Rural Life Museum** has historically focused on a range of local rural occupations, from cider-making and peat-digging to the unusual practice of mud-horse fishing, named after the sledge shrimpers used to navigate the mud flats of Bridgwater Bay. It was closed for refurbishment at the time of writing but is expected to reopen in early 2016.

# Chalice Well

Chilkwell St • Daily 10am–6pm, Nov–March till 4.30pm • £4 • ☎ 01458 831154, ⓦ chalicewell.org.uk

The **Chalice Well** stands amid a lush garden intended for quiet contemplation at the foot of Glastonbury Tor. The iron-red waters of the well – which is fondly supposed to be the hiding place of the Holy Grail – were considered to have curative properties, making the town a spa for a brief period in the eighteenth century, and they are still prized (there's a tap in Well House Lane).

# Glastonbury Tor

From Chilkwell St, turn left into Well House Lane and immediately right for the footpath that leads up to the Tor; the shorter, steeper path is accessed from the top of Well House Lane and is served by the Tor Bus (see below) • Free; NT • ⓦ nationaltrust.org.uk

Towering over the Somerset Levels, the 521ft-high conical hill of **Glastonbury Tor** commands stupendous views as far as the Welsh mountains on very clear days. It is topped by the dilapidated **St Michael's Tower**, sole remnant of a fourteenth-century church, and pilgrims once embarked on the stiff climb up here with hard peas in their shoes as penance – nowadays, people come to picnic, fly kites or feel the vibrations of crossing ley-lines.

## ARRIVAL AND INFORMATION                                    GLASTONBURY

**By bus** Frequent buses (ⓦ firstgroup.com) #29, #375, #376 and #377 connect Glastonbury with Wells; #376 also goes to Bristol and #29 to Taunton.

Destinations Bristol (Mon–Sat every 30min, Sun hourly; 1hr 35min); Taunton (Mon–Sat 8 daily 1hr 5min); Wells (Mon–Sat every 15min, Sun hourly; 15min).

**Tourist office** The Tribunal, 9 High Street (Mon–Sat 10am–4pm; ☎ 01458 832954, ⓦ glastonburytic.co.uk).

**Internet** There's internet access in the tourist office, and a relaxed internet café in Glastonbury's Assembly Rooms (Tues–Sat noon–6pm; ⓦ assemblyrooms.org.uk), reached through a courtyard off the High Street.

## GETTING AROUND

**By bus** The Glastonbury Tor Bus runs from the abbey car park to the base of the Tor every 30min, and stops at the Somerset Rural Life Museum (when open) and Chalice Well (April–Sept daily 10am–5pm; £3, valid all day).

**By bike** Glastonbury Cycles, 67 High Street (☎ 01458 830639, ✉ glastonburycycles@live.co.uk) rents bikes for £10/15 per half-/full-day.

## ACCOMMODATION

**George & Pilgrim Hotel** 1 High St ☎ 01458 831146, ⓦ relaxinnz.co.uk. This fifteenth-century oak-panelled inn with mullioned windows brims with medieval atmosphere. It's tired and worn in parts and some of the rooms are a bit ordinary – go for one of the older ones, which include frilly four-posters. **£85**

**Glastonbury Backpackers** 4 Market Place ☎ 01458 833353, ⓦ glastonburybackpackers.com. Centrally located former coaching inn (it's in *The Crown*), a bit scuffed, but clean enough, with a kitchen, a games room, wi-fi access and no curfew. Also private 3-, 4- and 5-person rooms available (£22pp). Can get noisy from the lively bar (closes 2.30am at weekends). Dorms **£15**

**Mapleleaf Middlewick Cottages** Wick Lane, 1.5 miles

---

### GLASTONBURY FESTIVAL

**Glastonbury Festival of Contemporary and Performing Arts** (ⓦ glastonburyfestivals .co.uk) takes place most years over four days in late June, with happy campers braving the predictable mudfest at Worthy Farm, outside Pilton, six miles east of Glastonbury itself. Having started as a small hippy affair in the 1970s, "Glastonbury" has become the biggest and best-organized festival in the country, without shedding too much of its alternative feel. Much more than just a music festival, large parts of the sprawling site are given over to themed "lifestyle" areas, from the meditation marquees of Green Fields to campfire-filled Strummerville and futuristic Arcadia. Bands cover all musical spectrums, from up-and-coming indie groups to international superstars – recent headliners have included Arcade Fire, Metallica and Kasabian. Despite the steep price (£210), tickets are invariably snapped up within hours of going on sale around October of the previous year.

**5**

north of Glastonbury ☎01458 832351, ⓦmiddlewick holidaycottages.co.uk. A dozen self-catering cottages plus glamping cabins in rural surroundings, the former with stone walls, oak floors and, in some, cosy wood burners. There's a steam room, indoor pool, BBQ and pizza oven. **£92.50**

★**White House** 21 Manor House Rd ☎01458 830886, ⓦtheglastonburywhitehouse.com. Lovely B&B with two en-suite rooms. Everything is eco-friendly and organic, including the optional veggie breakfast (from £5), which can be served in your room. **£75**

### EATING AND DRINKING

**Blue Note Café** 4a High St ☎01458 832907. A relaxed place to hangout over coffees and cakes with some courtyard seating. It's vegetarian and mostly organic, with nourishing soups, salads and halloumi burgers (mains from £5.50). Daily 9am–5pm.

**Hawthorns** 8–12 Northload St ☎01458 831255. Homely bar and restaurant whose main draw is its eclectic menu: daily ethnic specials (from £12.50) and a variety of award-winning curries chalked up on the blackboard. Tues & Wed 6–11pm, Thurs noon–3pm & 6–11pm, Fri & Sat noon–11pm, Sun noon–10pm.

★**Hundred Monkeys** 52 High St ☎01458 833386, ⓦhundredmonkeyscafe.com. Mellow contemporary café/restaurant whose wholesome snacks include a renowned seafood soup, as well as gourmet sarnies (from £6) and varied salads (from £7). Take-away available. Mon–Thurs 8am–8pm, Fri & Sat 8am–9pm, Sun 9am–5pm.

**King Arthur** 31–33 Benedict St ☎01458 831442. Wood-floored freehouse near St Benedict's Church, serving pricey salads (£10) and pies (£13) and with live music most nights. Drinks are reassuringly local: beer from Glastonbury Ales, cider from Wilkins. Mon 5pm–midnight, Tues–Sat noon–midnight, Sun noon–11pm.

# South Somerset

Verdant South Somerset matches the county's rural image more so than any other region: rolling fields are broken by the occasional isolated farm, while the backcountry lanes that link them are plied by tractors loaded with hay. Majestic **Montacute House** – like many of the villages hereabouts, made in soft honeyed hamstone – is one of the finest stately homes in Somerset, whilst the region's two destination **museums** provide more adrenalin-fuelled thrills and spills.

## Montacute House

Montacute • **House** Mid-March to Oct daily except Tues 11am–5pm; Nov to mid-March Sat & Sun noon–3pm by guided tour only **Gardens** Mid-March to Oct daily 10am–5pm; Nov to mid-March Wed–Sun 11am–4pm • £11.20, gardens only (Tues only) £5.40; NT • ☎01935 823289, ⓦnationaltrust.org.uk/montacutehouse • South West Coaches #81 from Yeovil to South Petherton

Dominating the picture-postcard hamlet of the same name, **Montacute House** still makes the striking statement that Sir Edward Phelips intended when he built it in the late sixteenth century. The beautifully designed mansion, set in formal gardens and surrounded by parkland, is today stuffed with fine furniture and tapestries, whilst its Long Gallery is host to sixty or so of the National Portrait Gallery's vast collection of Tudor and Elizabethan portraits.

## Fleet Air Arm Museum

RNAS Yeovilton • April–Oct & school hols daily 10am–5.30pm; Nov–March Wed–Sun 10am–4.30pm • £14 • ☎01935 840565, ⓦfleetairarm.com • Nippy Bus N11 from Yeovil

Occupying part of Europe's busiest military air base, the brilliantly interactive **Fleet Air Arm Museum** boasts one of the largest collections of naval aircraft in the world. After working your way through exhibitions that deal with British naval aviation and span World War II and Korea, you're treated to a noisy Phantom fighter launch from the flight deck of an "aircraft carrier" and, in the final hall, the chance to nose around the first Concorde built in Britain.

## SOMERSET CIDER FARMS

Nothing is quite so synonymous with Somerset as **cider**, a drink ingrained in the regional identity. Most pubs across the region stock one or two local ciders, but for the real deal it's hard to beat a visit to a working cider farm itself, where you can sample traditional ciders (around £3.70 for 2l) and learn more about the cider-making process.

**Burrow Hill Cider Farm** Pass Vale Farm, Burrow Hill ☎01460 240782, ⊛ciderbrandy.co.uk. Tastings are done in an old, dark ciderhouse dripping with atmosphere – try one of their single-variety, bottle-fermented sparkling ciders (developed in the same way as Champagne) or their highly regarded cider brandy. Mon–Sat 9am–5.30pm, tours by arrangement.

**Perry's Cider Mills** Dowlish Wake ☎01460 55195, ⊛perryscider.co.uk. Archetypal cider farm and orchards, with a dozen farmhouse and single-variety ciders, plus a small free rural museum. Mon–Fri 9am–5.30pm, Sat 9.30am–4.30pm, Sun 10am–1pm.

**Sheppy's Cider** Three Bridges, Bradford-on-Tone ☎01823 461233, ⊛sheppyscider.com.

Complex combining a shop, tea rooms, museum (£3), and orchards complete with resident herd of longhorn cattle. Mon–Sat 8.30am–6pm, July & Aug also Sun 11am–4pm.

**Thatchers** Myrtle Farm Sandford ☎01934 822862, ⊛thatcherscider.co.uk. Producers of the famous Thatchers Gold, plus eleven other ciders. It's a big operation, but you can still taste their cider straight from the barrel at their shop, or take a walk through their orchards nearby. Mon–Sat 9am–6pm, Sun 10am–1pm.

**Wilkins** Lands End Farm Wedmore ☎01934 712385, ⊛wilkinscider.com. Legendary cider-maker Roger Wilkins offers generous tastings in his Banksy-decorated barn up on the Isle of Wedmore. Daily 10am–8pm, Sun till 1pm.

# Haynes International Motor Museum

Sparkford • Daily: March–Oct 9.30am–5.30pm; Nov–Feb 10am–4.30pm • £13.50 • ☎01963 440804, ⊛haynesmotormuseum.com • South West Coaches #1/1A/1B/1C from Castle Cary to Yeovil

Every petrol-head's dream, the **Haynes International Motor Museum** opened in 1985 with the private collection of John Haynes and now houses over four hundred gleaming automobiles. Some of the classiest cars in history are here, but it's worth seeking out the 1905 Daimler Limousine, whose one careful owner was King Edward VII, and the rare 1931 Duesenberg, which takes pride of place on a pedestal in the final hall and is now worth a cool $10 million.

## ARRIVAL AND INFORMATION                                    SOUTH SOMERSET

Most people visit South Somerset in their car, which is by far the easiest way to see the region once you're here. The main gateway on public transport is workaday **Yeovil**, though there are also train stations at **Castle Cary** and **Bruton**. Local buses connect these three, and other towns and villages in the region, but are infrequent and slow.

**By train** The "Heart of Wessex" line runs from Bath and Bristol to Bruton, Castle Cary and Yeovil (8 daily, 3–5 on Sun). Destinations Bath (50min–1hr 10min); Bristol (1hr 10min–1hr 30min); Taunton (8 daily; 25min; from Castle Cary only).
**By bus** National Express runs a daily service from Bristol to Yeovil (1hr 35min). Numerous but sporadic services are run by

South West Coaches (⊛southwestcoaches.co.uk); Nippy Bus (⊛www.nippybus.co.uk) will probably prove more useful.
**Tourist information** There's a regional information centre at Cartgate Picnic Site, off the A303/A3088 six miles west of Yeovil (April–Oct daily 9.30am–4.30pm; Nov–March Mon & Fri 10am–3pm; ☎01935 829333).

## ACCOMMODATION AND EATING

South Somerset is blessed with some exceptional places to eat, from converted chapels to award-winning gastropubs. Many of the best places are in the smaller towns and villages, such as **Bruton** and gorgeous little **Hinton St George**, or between them, meaning you'll need your own wheels to get to them.

★**At The Chapel** High St, Bruton ☎01749 814070, ⊛atthechapel.co.uk. Contemporary gem in sleepy Bruton, home to a buzzing restaurant (mains from

£11.50; wood-fired pizzas served all day), an artisan bakery, and a cocktail bar where the altar used to be. The eight stripped-back and stylish rooms all

5

have king-sized beds. Daily 8am–9.30pm, Sun till 8pm. **£100**

★ **Lord Poulett Arms** Hinton St George ☎ 01460 73149, ⓦ lordpoulettarms.com. Award-winning pub-restaurant in a beautiful hamstone village, serving game from Exmoor and fish from Dorset (mains from £14.95), plus local ales and cider. Rooms are classy but comfortable. Daily noon–2pm & 7–9pm; bar noon–3pm & 6.30–11pm. **£85**

**The Masons Arms** 41 Lower Odcombe ☎ 01935 862591, ⓦ masonsarmsodcombe.co.uk. Lovely looking thatch-roofed inn whose friendly owners offer a blend of classic pub grub and à la carte dishes (from £13.75), served in generous portions. Rooms overlook the garden; camping available. Daily noon–2pm & 6.30–9.30pm, bar till midnight. **£90**, pitches **£10** (plus £2 per person)

★ **The Pilgrims at Lovington** Lovington ☎ 01963 240600, ⓦ thepilgrimsatlovington.co.uk. This fantastic place combines the relaxed atmosphere of a country pub

with the elegant cooking of a fine-dining restaurant (locally leaning mains from £15). There are also five modern rooms in the old cider barn (no under-14s). Tues 7–11pm, Wed–Sat noon–3pm & 7–11pm, plus last Sun of the month noon–3pm. **£95**

**Provender** 3 Market Square, South Petherton ☎ 01460 240681, ⓦ provender.co.uk. Chic spot on a pretty square, with a deli stocking farmhouse cheeses, smoked meats and speciality breads, and a light-filled café at the back selling soups and savoury tartlets. Mon 10am–4pm, Tues, Thurs & Fri 9.30am–5pm, Wed 9.30am–3pm, Sat 9am–3pm.

**The Queens Arms** Corton Denham ☎ 01963 220317, ⓦ thequeensarms.com. Attractive former AA Pub of the Year with a range of classy twins and doubles and solid but sophisticated food (spit-roast hog, roasted tomato and mozzarella arancini; mains from £9.95). Excellent selection of bottled beers and ciders. Daily noon–3pm & 6–10pm, Sun till 9pm. **£110**

# Taunton

West of Glastonbury, the county town of **Taunton** makes a handy starting point for excursions into the Quantock Hills, and, as home to the worthwhile **Museum of Somerset**, is of more interest than nearby Bridgwater. While in town, take a look at the pinnacled and battlemented towers of its two most important churches – **St James** on Coal Orchard and **St Mary Magdalene** on Church Square – both fifteenth-century structures remodelled by the Victorians.

## Museum of Somerset

Taunton Castle, Castle Green • Tues–Sat 10am–5pm • Free • ☎ 01823 255088, ⓦ www.somerset.gov.uk/museums

Started in the twelfth century, **Taunton Castle** staged the trial of royal claimant Perkin Warbeck, who in 1490 declared himself to be the Duke of York, the younger of the "Princes in the Tower" – the sons of Edward IV, who had been murdered seven years earlier. Parts of the structure were pulled down in 1662 and much of the rest has been altered, and it now houses the **Museum of Somerset**, a wide-ranging display that includes finds from Somerset's Lake Villages; the "Frome Hoard", the second largest collection of Roman coins ever discovered in Britain; and a superb fragment of Roman mosaic found near Langport in the Somerset Levels. Part of the castle houses the Great Hall where Judge Jeffreys held one of his "Bloody Assizes" following the Monmouth Rebellion of 1685, at which 144 prisoners were sentenced to be hanged, drawn and quartered.

### ARRIVAL AND INFORMATION                                     TAUNTON

**By train** The train station lies a 20min walk north of town. There's also the West Somerset Railway (see box, p.307), which terminates at Bishops Lydeard.

Destinations Bridgwater (1–2 hourly; 10min); Bristol (every 15–30min; 35min–1hr 5min).

**By bus** Taunton's bus station (ⓦ firstgroup.com) is off Castle Green.

Destinations Bishops Lydeard (Mon–Sat every 30min, Sun hourly; 30min); Bridgwater (Mon–Sat every 30min, Sun hourly; 45min); Combe Florey (Mon–Sat every 30min,

Sun hourly; 35min); Dulverton (Mon–Sat hourly; 1hr 20min); Dunster (Mon–Sat every 30min, Sun hourly; 1hr 20min); Glastonbury (Mon–Sat 8 daily; 1hr 5min); London (9–10 daily; 3–4hr); Minehead (Mon–Sat every 30min, Sun hourly; 1hr 25min); Wells (Mon–Sat 8 daily; 1hr 20min); Yeovil (Mon–Sat hourly; 1hr 15min).

**Tourist office** In the library building, Paul Street (Mon–Sat 9.30am–4.30pm; ☎ 01823 336344, ⓦ tauntondeane .gov.uk). Provides information and publications on the whole area, including the Quantocks.

## ACCOMMODATION AND EATING

**The Castle** Castle Green ☎01823 272671, ⓦthe-castle-hotel.com. The town's most atmospheric hotel is an upmarket choice, a wisteria-clad, three-hundred-year-old mansion next to Taunton Castle, exuding an appropriately old-fashioned baronial style. Breakfast costs from £6.50 on top of room rates. **£139**

**The Cosy Club** Hunts Court, Corporation St ☎01823 253476, ⓦcosyclub.co.uk. In a converted Victorian arts college, this bar has several rooms across two floors, with comfy chairs and quirky decor. Coffees, teas and meals are available; tapas are £11.50 for three, burgers from £7.95. Daily 9am–10pm.

**The Old Mill** Netherclay, Bishop's Hull, 2 miles west of Taunton ☎01823 289732, ⓦbandbtaunton.co.uk. Right on the River Tone, this peaceful B&B set in a former corn mill only has a couple of rooms, the larger one worth the slightly higher price for its river views. Restored pieces of the old mill machinery lend the place the air of a small museum. No credit cards. **£65**

# Bridgwater

Sedate **BRIDGWATER** has seen little excitement since it was embroiled in the Civil War and its aftermath, in particular the events surrounding the **Monmouth Rebellion** of 1685. Having landed from his base in Holland, the Protestant Duke of Monmouth, an illegitimate son of Charles II, led his rebel army against the Catholic James II, but his disorganized band were mown down by the king's troops at the **Battle of Sedgemoor** in nearby Westonzoyland. Monmouth himself was captured and later beheaded, and a period of repression was unleashed under the infamous Judge Jeffreys, whose "Bloody Assizes" resulted in gibbets and gutted corpses displayed around Somerset.

## Blake Museum

5 Blake St • April–Oct Tues–Sat 10am–4pm • Free • ☎01278 456127, ⓦblakemuseumfriends.org.uk

The sixteenth-century building housing the **Blake Museum**, by the River Parrett, is reputedly the birthplace of local hero Robert Blake, admiral under Oliver Cromwell, and as such it suitably chronicles his swashbuckling career against Royalists, the Dutch and the Spanish. Other areas covered include the Monmouth Rebellion and the Battle of Sedgemoor, as well as the local brick and tile industry.

### ARRIVAL AND DEPARTURE

### BRIDGWATER

**By train** The train station is on Wellington Road, a 15min walk east of the Blake Museum.
Destinations Taunton (1–2 hourly; 10min).
**By bus** The bus station is on Watsons Lane, on the eastern side of the River Parrett.

Destinations Glastonbury (Mon–Sat 7 daily; 1hr); Taunton (Mon–Sat every 30min, Sun hourly; 45min); and Wells (Mon–Sat 1–3 hourly; 1hr 20min). For the northern Quantocks, bus #14 stops at Nether Stowey (Mon–Sat 6 daily; 50min).

### ACCOMMODATION AND EATING

**The Old Vicarage Hotel** 45–51 St Mary St ☎01278 458891, ⓦtheoldvicaragebridgwater.com. Opposite St Mary's Church, the *Old Vicarage* occupies one of Bridgwater's oldest buildings and offers small and differing doubles, plus a rather grand four-poster (£120). The café-bistro does classic English dishes (mains from £12.95).

---

#### BRIDGWATER CARNIVAL

A good time to be in Bridgwater is for the **carnival** celebrations (ⓦbridgwatercarnival.org.uk), said to be the largest illuminated procession in Europe, attracting up to 150,000 people. The festivities usually take place on the first Saturday in November, near Bonfire Night (one of the Catholic conspirators of the Gunpowder Plot hailed from nearby Nether Stowey). Grandly festooned floats belonging to Somerset's seventy-odd carnival clubs roll through town, before heading off to do the same in various other local towns and villages, including Glastonbury and Wells.

**5**

Mon–Sat: café 10.30am–3pm, restaurant 6.30–8.30pm (residents only on Mon), bar 6–10pm. **£77** **Tudor Hotel** 21 St Mary St ☎01278 422093, ⓦ tudorhotel.co.uk. Modernized business hotel in a former bakery, whose rooms are furnished in a low-key, traditional style. There's a little more atmosphere in the restaurant and bar. Free wi-fi. Restaurant Mon–Sat noon–2pm & 6.30–10pm, Sun noon–2.30pm. **£70**

# The Quantock Hills

Extending for some twelve miles north of Taunton, the **Quantock Hills** are fairly off the beaten track, enclosed by a triangle of roads leading coastwards from Bridgwater and Taunton. Its snug villages, many of them boasting beautifully preserved churches, are connected by steep, narrow lanes and set in scenic wooded valleys or "combes" that are watered by clear streams and grazed by red deer.

## Nether Stowey and around

Eight miles west of Bridgwater on the A39, on the edge of the hills, the pretty village of **NETHER STOWEY** is best known for its association with **Samuel Taylor Coleridge**, who in 1796 walked here from Bristol to join his wife and child at their new home. Coleridge drew inspiration for some of his best-known works whilst rambling through the surrounding countryside, and you can pick up a leaflet at his former abode for the **Coleridge Way** (ⓦcoleridgeway.co.uk), a walking route that supposedly follows the poet's footsteps between Nether Stowey and Lynmouth (see p.310) on the Exmoor coast; waymarked with quill signs, the 51-mile hike passes through some of the most scenic parts of the Quantocks and Exmoor.

### Coleridge Cottage

35 Lime St • March–Oct Mon & Thurs–Sun 11am–5pm • £5.20; NT • ☎ 01278 732662, ⓦ nationaltrust.org.uk/coleridgecottage

At this "miserable cottage", as Sara Coleridge rather harshly called what is now **Coleridge Cottage**, you can see the poet's parlour and reading room, and, upstairs, his bedroom and an exhibition room containing various letters and first editions. Rooms, including the kitchen, are laid out as they would have been in the eighteenth century, filled with the family's personal belongings and mementos.

## The western Quantocks

On the southwestern edge of the Quantocks, the village of **BISHOPS LYDEARD**, terminus of the West Somerset Railway, is worth a wander, not least for **St Mary's** church, with a splendid tower and carved bench-ends inside. A couple of miles north, pretty **COMBE**

---

### COLERIDGE AND WORDSWORTH IN THE QUANTOCKS

Shortly after moving into their new home in **Nether Stowey**, the **Coleridges** were visited by **William Wordsworth** and his sister Dorothy, who soon afterwards moved into the somewhat grander Alfoxden House, near Holford, a couple of miles down the road. The year that Coleridge and Wordsworth spent as neighbours was extraordinarily productive – Coleridge composed some of his best poetry at this time, including **The Rime of the Ancient Mariner** and **Kubla Khan**, and the two poets in collaboration produced the **Lyrical Ballads**, the poetic manifesto of early English Romanticism. Many of the greatest figures of the age made the trek down to visit the pair, among them Charles Lamb, Thomas De Quincey, Robert Southey, Humphry Davy and William Hazlitt, and it was the coming and going of these intellectuals that stirred the suspicions of the local authorities in a period when England was at war with France. Spies were sent to track them and Wordsworth was finally given notice to leave in June 1798, shortly before Lyrical Ballads rolled off the press.

## THE WEST SOMERSET RAILWAY

Fringing the western side of the Quantocks, the **West Somerset Railway** (☎01643 704996, ⓦ west-somerset-railway.co.uk) is a restored branch line that runs twenty miles between the station outside the village of Bishops Lydeard, five miles northwest of Taunton, to Minehead on the Somerset coast (see p.308; 1hr 15min; £11.40 one-way, £17 return). Between late March and October (plus some weekend and winter dates), up to seven steam and diesel trains depart daily from Bishops Lydeard, stopping at renovated stations on the way. Rover tickets, allowing multiple journeys, cost £17/day, £32/two days, £68/week, and bikes cost £2 extra. Bus #28 goes to Bishops Lydeard station from Taunton town centre and train station.

**FLOREY** is almost exclusively built of the pink-red sandstone characteristic of Quantock villages. For over fifteen years (1829–45), the local rector was the unconventional cleric Sydney Smith, called "the greatest master of ridicule since Swift" by the essayist Macaulay; more recently it was home to Evelyn Waugh.

A little over three miles further north along the A358, **CROWCOMBE** is another typical cob-and-thatch Quantock village, with a well-preserved Church House from 1515 and a lovely old church with a superb collection of pagan-looking carved bench-ends. A minor road from here winds up to **Triscombe Stone**, in the heart of the Quantocks, from where a footpath leads for about a mile to the range's highest point at **Wills Neck** (1260ft).

Stretching between Wills Neck and the village of Aisholt, the moorland plateau of **Aisholt Common** is best explored from **West Bagborough**, where a five-mile path starts at Birches Corner. Lower down the slopes, outside Aisholt, the banks of **Hawkridge Reservoir** make a lovely picnic stop.

| GETTING AROUND | THE QUANTOCK HILLS |
|---|---|

**By public transport** The West Somerset Railway (see box above) stops near some of the villages along the west flank of the range, though you'll need your own transport or foot-power to reach the best spots, as public transport in the Quantocks is minimal.

## ACCOMMODATION AND EATING

★**The Blue Ball Inn** Triscombe ☎01984 618242, ⓦ blueballinn.info. This secluded inn below Wills Neck has two tastefully decorated B&B rooms, plus meals sourced from neighbouring farms (mains from £11), good local ales and a nice pub garden. Tues–Sat noon–3pm & 6–11pm (Sat noon–11pm in summer), Sun noon–6pm. **£75**

**Carew Arms** Crowcombe ☎01984 618631, ⓦ thecarewarms.co.uk. Don't be put off by the stags' heads covering the walls and the riding boots by the fire – this is a delightful rustic pub with a skittles alley and a spacious garden. Local ales complement the top-notch nosh (from £12.95). Half a dozen rooms also available. Daily noon–2pm, Tues–Sat also 7–9pm. **£64**

**Farmers Arms** Combe Florey ☎01823 432267, ⓦ farmersarmsatcombeflorey.co.uk. Signposted off the A358 just north of the village, this tidily thatched old pub has log fires, an attractive garden and a menu strong on lamb and poultry (mains from £8.50 at lunch, £15 at dinner). Booking advisable at peak times. Mon–Sat noon–2pm & 7–9pm, Sun noon–2.30pm.

**Mill Farm Caravan and Camping Park** Fiddington, a couple of miles east of Nether Stowey ☎01278 732286, ⓦ millfarm.biz. This family-friendly site has indoor and outdoor pools, a boating lake, a gym and pony rides. Advance booking essential at peak times. There are cottages that can be rented by the week (£490). Closed Dec–Feb. Camping pitches **£20.50**

**The Old House** Castle St, Nether Stowey ☎01278 732392, ⓦ theoldhouse-quantocks.co.uk. This large house in the centre of the village once accommodated Samuel Coleridge. The two rooms – Sarah's Room and the huge Coleridge Suite – are period-furnished, and there's an acre of garden. Self-catering cottages also available (from £495/week). **£80**

★**Parsonage Farm** Over Stowey, a mile south of Nether Stowey ☎01278 733237, ⓦ parsonfarm.co.uk. In the shadow of a lovely old Quantock church, this homely B&B with its own orchard and walled kitchen garden has stone floors, brick fireplaces and heaps of character. Run organically and sustainably by a native of Vermont, it offers a Vermont breakfast among other options, and simple candle-lit suppers (£11). **£65**

**5**

# Exmoor

A high, bare plateau sliced by wooded combes and gurgling streams, **EXMOOR** (ⓦexmoor-nationalpark.gov.uk) can present one of the most forbidding landscapes in England, especially when shrouded in a sea mist. On clear days, though, the moorland of this National Park reveals rich bursts of colour and an amazing diversity of wildlife, from buzzards to the unique **Exmoor ponies**, a breed closely related to prehistoric horses and now on the endangered list; in the treeless heartland of the moor in particular, it's not difficult to spot these short and stocky animals. Much more elusive are the **red deer**, England's largest native wild animal, of which Exmoor supports the country's only wild population, currently around three thousand.

Endless **walking routes** are possible along a network of some six hundred miles of footpaths and bridleways, and **horseriding** is another option for getting the most out of Exmoor's desolate beauty. Inland, there are four obvious bases for walks, all on the Somerset side of the county border: **Dulverton** in the southeast, site of the main information facilities; **Simonsbath** in the centre; **Exford**, near Exmoor's highest point at Dunkery Beacon; and the attractive village of **Winsford**, close to the A396 on the east of the moor.

Exmoor's coastline offers an alluring alternative to the open moorland, all of it accessible via the **South West Coast Path**, which embarks on its long coastal journey at **Minehead**, though there is more charm to be found further west at the sister villages of **Lynton** and **Lynmouth**, just over the Devon border.

## Dulverton and the eastern moor

The village of **DULVERTON**, on the southern edge of the National Park, is the Park Authority's headquarters and, with its cafés and shops, makes a good entry point to Exmoor. Five miles north, just west of the A396, **WINSFORD** lays justified claim to being the moor's prettiest hamlet. A scattering of thatched cottages ranged around a sleepy green, it is watered by a confluence of streams and rivers, giving it no fewer than seven bridges, and makes a good stopover on the way to nearby **Tarr Steps**, a seventeen-span clapper bridge that is one of the Moor's most famous beauty spots.

Four miles northwest of Winsford, the village of **EXFORD**, an ancient crossing point on the River Exe, is popular with hunting folk as well as with walkers for the four-mile hike to **Dunkery Beacon**, Exmoor's highest point at 1704ft.

## Exmoor Forest and Simonsbath

At the heart of the National Park lies **Exmoor Forest**, the barest (and wettest) part of the moor, scarcely populated except by roaming sheep and a few red deer – the word "forest" denotes simply that it was a king's hunting reserve. In the middle of it stands the village of **SIMONSBATH** (pronounced "Simmonsbath"), once home to the Knight family, who bought the forest in 1819 and, by introducing tenant farmers, building roads and importing sheep, brought systematic agriculture to an area that had never before produced any income.

## Minehead

The Somerset port of **MINEHEAD** quickly became a favourite Victorian watering hole with the arrival of the railway, and it has preserved an upbeat holiday-town atmosphere ever since. Steep lanes link the two quarters of **Higher Town**, on the slopes of North Hill, containing some of the oldest houses, and **Quay Town**, the harbour area. Minehead is a terminus for the **West Somerset Railway**, which curves eastwards into the

---

**THE SOUTH WEST COAST PATH**

Britain's longest national trail, the **South West Coast Path** (ⓦ southwestcoastpath.com) starts at Minehead and tracks the coastline along the northern seaboard of Somerset and Devon, round Cornwall, back into Devon and on to Dorset, where it finishes close to the entrance to Poole Harbour. Much of the **630-mile route** runs on land owned by the National Trust, and all of it is well signposted.

The relevant Ordnance Survey **maps** can be found at most village shops en route, while Aurum Press (ⓦ aurumpress.co.uk) produces four *National Trail Guides* covering the route and the **South West Coast Path Association** (ⓞ 01752 896237, ⓦ swp.org.uk) publishes an annual guide to the whole path, including accommodation lists, ferry timetables, tide times and transport details.

---

Quantocks as far as Bishops Lydeard (see p.306), and also for the South West Coast Path (see box above), signposted beyond the harbour.

# Dunster

Three miles southeast of Minehead, the old village of **DUNSTER** is the area's major attraction. Its impressive castle rears above its well-preserved High Street, where the octagonal **Yarn Market**, dating from 1609, recalls Dunster's wool-making heyday.

## Dunster Castle

Castle and watermill early March to Oct daily 11am–5pm; Dec 6–21 Sat & Sun 11am–3pm; grounds early March to Oct daily 10am–5pm; Nov & Dec 11am–4pm • £9.30, grounds only £5.60; NT • ⓞ 01643 821314, ⓦ nationaltrust.org.uk/dunstercastle

A landmark for miles around with its towers and turrets, **Dunster Castle** has parts dating back to the thirteenth century, but most of its fortifications were demolished following the Civil War. The structure was subjected to a thorough Victorian restoration in 1868–72, from which it emerged as something of an architectural showpiece, though its interior preserves much from its earlier incarnations. Tours take in a bedroom once occupied by Charles II, a fine seventeenth-century carved staircase, a richly decorated banqueting hall and various portraits of the Luttrells, owners of the house for six hundred years. The grounds include terraced gardens and riverside walks, all overlooked by a hilltop folly, **Conygar Tower**, dating from 1775.

Tickets to the castle also include entry to three-hundred-year-old **Dunster Water Mill**, on the River Anvill at the southern end of the village. The mill is still used commercially, grinding the various grains that go into making the flour sold in the shop.

# Porlock

Six miles west of Minehead and cupped on three sides by the hogbacked hills of Exmoor, the thatch-and-cob houses and distinctive charm of **PORLOCK** draw armies of tourists. Many come in search of the village's literary links: according to Coleridge's own less-than-reliable testimony, it was a "man from Porlock" who broke the opium trance in which he was composing *Kubla Khan*, while the High Street's fourteenth-century *Ship Inn* features prominently in the Exmoor romance *Lorna Doone* and, in real life, sheltered the poet Robert Southey. Just two miles west yet feeling refreshingly remote, the tiny harbour of **PORLOCK WEIR** is a tranquil spot for a breath of sea air and a drink.

# Lynton

Eleven miles west of Porlock, just inside Devon, the Victorian resort of **LYNTON** perches above a lofty gorge with splendid views over the sea. Almost completely cut off from the rest of the country for most of its history, the village struck lucky during the Napoleonic Wars, when frustrated Grand Tourists – unable to visit their usual continental haunts

**5**

– discovered in Lynton a domestic piece of alpine landscape, nicknaming the area "Little Switzerland". Samuel Taylor Coleridge and William Hazlitt trudged over to Lynton from the Quantocks, but the greatest spur to the village's popularity came with the publication in 1869 of R.D. Blackmore's Exmoor melodrama *Lorna Doone*, based on the outlaw clans who inhabited these parts in the seventeenth century.

## Lynmouth and around

Some 500ft below Lynton, at the junction and estuary of the East and West Lyn rivers, **LYNMOUTH** – joined to Lynton by an ingenious **cliff railway** (mid-Feb to mid-Nov daily generally 10am–7pm, though closing times vary; £3.50 return; ⓦcliffrailwaylynton .co.uk), or walkable along an adjacent zigzagging path – was where the poet Percy Shelley spent his nine-week honeymoon with his 16-year-old bride Harriet Westbrook, writing his polemical *Queen Mab*. At the top of the village, you can explore the walks and waterfalls and an exhibition on the uses of waterpower in the wooded **Glen Lyn Gorge** (daily 10am–6pm, Nov–Easter till 3pm; £5), all the more poignant given that the village was almost washed away by flooding in August 1952, when 34 people lost their lives. **Boat trips** (Easter–Sept; £10; ☏01598 753207) depart from the harbour for Woody Bay and back – a great opportunity to view the cliffs and the birdlife that thrives on them.

A beautiful mile-and-a-half walk follows the river east from Lynmouth to where the East Lyn River joins Hoar Oak Water at the aptly named **Watersmeet**, one of Exmoor's most celebrated beauty spots, overlooked by two slender bridges.

### ARRIVAL AND DEPARTURE
### EXMOOR

**By bus** In addition to the bus services (ⓦfilers.co.uk, ⓦfirstgroup.com, ⓦquantockheritage.com & ⓦweb berbus.com) listed below, the Moor Rover provides a service to and from anywhere within the National Park (and along the Coleridge Way; see p.306) for walkers and bikers – bikes are hitched on the back; call to book a ride at least 24hr in advance (☏01643 709701, ⓦatwest.org.uk).
**Destinations from Dulverton** Taunton (Mon–Sat hourly; 1hr 20min).
**Destinations from Dunster** Bishops Lydeard (Mon–Sat every 30min, Sun hourly; 50min); Minehead (Mon–Sat every 30min, Sun hourly; 10min); Taunton (Mon–Sat every 30min, Sun hourly; 1hr 20min).

**Destinations from Lynton/Lynmouth** Barnstaple (Mon–Sat 4–9 daily; 55min–1hr 5min); Ilfracombe (April–Oct 3 daily, Nov–March weekends only; 55min–1hr); Minehead (Mon–Sat 2 daily; 55min); Porlock (3 daily; 40min).
**Destinations from Minehead** Bishops Lydeard (Mon–Sat every 30min, Sun hourly; 55min); Bridgwater (Mon–Fri daily; 1hr 25min); Dunster (Mon–Sat every 30min, Sun hourly; 10min); Lynmouth (Mon–Sat 2 daily; 55min); Nether Stowey (Mon–Sat 6 daily; 1hr 5min); Porlock (Mon–Sat 11 daily; 15min); Porlock Weir (Mon–Sat 9 daily; 25min); Taunton (Mon–Sat every 30min, Sun hourly; 1hr 25min); Wells (Mon–Sat 8 daily; 1hr 20min).

### INFORMATION

#### NATIONAL PARK VISITOR CENTRES
**Dulverton** 7–9 Fore Street (daily: April–Oct 10am–5pm; Nov–March 10.30am–3pm; ☏01398 323841).
**Dunster** At the top of Dunster Steep, by the main car park (Easter–Oct daily 10am–5pm; Nov & Feb half-term to Easter Sat & Sun 10.30am–3pm; ☏01643 821835).
**Lynmouth** Lynmouth Pavilion, The Esplanade (daily 10am–5pm; ☏01598 752509).

#### TOURIST OFFICES
**Minehead** The Beach Hotel, The Avenue (☏01643 702624, ⓦminehead.co.uk).
**Porlock** The Old School Centre, West End, High Street (summer Mon–Fri 10am–1pm & 2–5pm, Sat 10am–5pm, Sun 10am–1pm; winter Tues–Fri 10am–1pm, Sat 10am–2pm; ☏01643 863150, ⓦporlock.co.uk).
**Lynton** In the town hall, Lee Road (daily 10am–5pm, Sun till 2pm; ☏01598 752225, ⓦlynton-lynmouth-tourism.co.uk).

### TOURS AND ACTIVITIES

Check the website ⓦactiveexmoor.com for adventure-activity operators. Whether walking or riding, bear in mind that over seventy percent of the National Park is privately owned and that access is theoretically restricted to public rights of way; special permission should certainly be sought before camping, canoeing, fishing or similar.

**Exmoor Adventures** (☎01643 863536, ⓦexmooradventures.co.uk). Rock-climbing, kayaking and other group activities (from £35pp).

**Red Stag Safaris** (☎01643 841831, ⓦredstagsafari .co.uk). Small-group 4WD trips taking in wildlife and local history (from £25pp).

## ACCOMMODATION AND EATING

**Baytree** 29 Blenheim Rd, Minehead ☎01643 703374, ⓦbaytreebandbminehead.co.uk. Victorian B&B offering roomy en-suites, including a family unit. The science fiction author Arthur C. Clarke was born a few doors along at no. 13. No credit cards. No children under-10. Closed Nov–March. **£60**

★**Glen Lodge** Hawkcombe ☎01643 863371, ⓦglenlodge.net. Beautifully furnished Victorian B&B offering perfect seclusion, comfort and character. There are distant sea views from the rooms and access to the moor right behind. No credit cards. **£90**

**Hillside House** 22 Watersmeet Rd, Lynmouth ☎01598 753836, ⓦhillside-lynmouth.co.uk. Apart from the teddy bears, this simple but cosy B&B is refreshingly free of the tweeness that affects most of the guesthouses hereabouts. Most rooms are spacious, and all but one enjoy views over the East Lyn River. **£56**

**Lorna Doone Hotel** High St, Porlock ☎01643 862404, ⓦlornadoonehotel.co.uk. This thoroughly Victorian lodging offers rooms of varying sizes (and prices), all clean, comfortable and en suite, with wi-fi access. The restaurant is equally varied, ranging from cream teas to Thai food (mains from £7.95). Daily noon–8pm. **£55**

**Luttrell Arms** 36 High St, Dunster ☎01643 821555, ⓦluttrellarms.co.uk. Traditional, atmospheric fifteenth-century inn with open fires and beamed rooms, some with four-posters. The bar and more formal restaurant (mains £14–19) offer decent food, and there's a pleasant garden. Bar daily 10am–11pm; restaurant daily 7–9.30pm. **£133**

★**Miller's at the Anchor** Porlock Weir ☎01643 862753, ⓦmillersattheanchor.co.uk. This wonderfully unique, curio-stuffed hotel, accurately pitched as a "hunting lodge by the sea", enjoys a superb setting on tranquil Porlock Weir's miniature harbourfront. The rooms – it's worth paying more for the lovely harbour views – are great, the staff courteous, and there's even a quirky mini-cinema. Light lunches and à la carte dinners are available in the equally atmospheric restaurant. Daily noon–3pm Wed–Sun also 7–8.30pm. **£88**

★**North Walk House** North Walk, Lynton ☎01598 753372, ⓦnorthwalkhouse.co.uk. Top-quality B&B in a stunning position overlooking the sea, and convenient for the coast path. The spacious, stylish rooms have wooden floors bedecked in rugs, and most have wrought-iron beds. Breakfasts are filling and delicious, and great organic dinners are available to guests for £28 per person. Garden studio (from £175 for 3nts) also available. **£120**

**Rising Sun** Harbourside, Lynmouth ☎01598 753223, ⓦrisingsunlynmouth.co.uk. The stylish rooms in this fourteenth-century harbourfront inn all have the requisite beams and sloping floors. The pub and restaurant are equally atmospheric, and attract crowds for their classic English dishes of steak and lamb, plus plenty of seafood (from £12.25) – there are few vegetarian options. Bar daily 11am–11pm, Sun till 10.30pm; food served daily noon–2.30pm & 6–9pm in bar, 7–8.30pm in restaurant. **£150**

**Royal Oak** Winsford ☎01643 851455, ⓦroyaloakexmoor.co.uk. This thatched and rambling old inn dominates the centre of charming Winsford and offers Exmoor ales, snacks and an extensive restaurant menu (mains from £11). The accommodation is plush (some rooms have four-posters) but does vary, so check first. Daily noon–2pm & 6.30–9pm. **£100**

**Shelley's** 8 Watersmeet Rd, Lynmouth ☎01598 753219, ⓦshelleyshotel.co.uk. Right next to the Glen Lyn Gorge, this traditional hotel/B&B has friendly owners, a great location and literary credentials. You can sleep in the room supposed to have been occupied by the poet Shelley when he honeymooned here. No under-12s. **£89**

★**Simonsbath House** Simonsbath ☎01643 831259, ⓦsimonsbathhouse.co.uk. Cosy bolt hole offering spacious and swanky rooms with glorious moorland views and a quality restaurant (three-course meals £22). Self-catering cottages in a converted barn are also available (from £200 for 2nts). **£120**

**Tongdam** 26 High St, Dulverton ☎01398 323397, ⓦtongdam.com. Take a break from English country cooking at this quality Thai outpost (most dishes £12.50–16.50). There's also excellent, modern and tastefully furnished accommodation: two doubles with shared bathroom and a suite with a separate sitting room and a balcony. Daily noon–3pm & 6–10.30pm. **£56**

**Vanilla Pod** 10–12 Queens St, Lynton ☎01598 753706. Good wholesome meals are served at this friendly place, which morphs from a café-bar by day into a Modern British restaurant come nightfall. Evening mains such as pork in cider start at £7.50. Daily 10am–9.30pm.

**Woods** 4 Bank Square, Dulverton ☎01398 324007, ⓦwoodsdulverton.co.uk. Decorated with a scattering of antlers, boots and riding whips, this gastropub offers Gallic-inspired dishes such as chicken liver and foie gras parfait and confit of duck leg (mains from £11). Excellent wine list, too. Daily noon–2pm & 6–9.30pm (Sun from 7pm).

# Devon and Cornwall

EDEN PROJECT

# Devon and Cornwall

At the western extremity of England, the counties of Devon and Cornwall encompass everything from genteel, cosy villages to vast Atlantic-facing strands of golden sand and wild expanses of granite moorland. The winning combination of rural peace and first-class beaches lends the peninsula a particular appeal to outdoors enthusiasts, and the local galleries, museums and restaurants provide plenty of rainy-day diversions. Together, these attractions have made the region perennially popular, so much so that tourism has replaced the traditional occupations of fishing and farming as the main source of employment and income. The authentic character of Devon and Cornwall may be obscured during the summer season, but avoid the peak periods and you can't fail to be seduced by their considerable charms.

If it's wilderness you're after, nothing can beat the remoter tracts of **Dartmoor**, the greatest of the West Country's granite massifs, much of which retains its solitude despite its proximity to the region's two major cities. Of these, **Exeter** is by far the more interesting, dominated by the twin towers of its medieval cathedral and offering a rich selection of restaurants and nightlife. As for **Plymouth**, much of this great naval port was destroyed by bombing during World War II, though some of the city's Elizabethan core has survived.

The coastline on either side of Exeter and Plymouth enjoys more hours of sunshine than anywhere else on the British mainland, and there is some justification in Devon's principal resort, **Torquay**, styling itself the capital of the "English Riviera". St Tropez it ain't, but there's no denying a certain glamour, alloyed with an old-fashioned charm that the seaside towns of **East Devon** and the cliff-backed resorts of the county's northern littoral share.

Cornwall too has its pockets of concentrated tourist development – chiefly at **Falmouth** and **Newquay**, the first of these a sailing centre, the second a major draw for surfers due to its fine west-facing beaches. **St Ives** is another crowd-puller, though the town has a separate identity as an arts centre. Further up Cornwall's long northern coast, the fortified site of **Tintagel** and the rock-walled harbour of **Boscastle** have an almost embattled character in the face of the turbulent Atlantic. However, the full elemental power of the ocean can best be appreciated on the western headlands of **Lizard Point** and **Land's End**, where the cliffs resound to the constant thunder of the waves, or, offshore, on **Lundy Island**, in the Bristol Channel, and the **Isles of Scilly**, 28 miles west of Land's End.

Inland, the mild climate has enabled a slew of gardens to flourish, none quirkier than the **Eden Project**, which imaginatively highlights the diversity of the earth's plant systems with the help of science-fiction-style "biomes".

DARTMOOR NATIONAL PARK

# Highlights

**❶ Hiking on Dartmoor** Experience this bleakly beautiful landscape along a good network of paths. **See p.332**

**❷ Surfing in North Devon** The endless ranks of rollers pounding Devon's west-facing northern coast – above all at Woolacombe, Croyde and Saunton – draw surfers of every ability. **See p.341**

**❸ Eden Project, Cornwall** Embark on a voyage of discovery around the planet's ecosystems at this disused clay pit, now home to a fantastic array of exotic plants and crops. **See p.346**

**❹ Cornish beaches** Cornwall has some of the country's best beaches, most of them in fabulous settings. Beauties include Newquay, Whitesand Bay, the Isles of Scilly and Bude; and Porthcurno, overlooked by dramatic black crags. **See p.355**

**❺ St Ives** Fine-sand beaches, a brace of renowned galleries and a maze of tiny lanes give this bustling harbour town a feel-good vibe. **See p.358**

**❻ Seafood in Padstow** The local catch goes straight into the excellent restaurants of the southwestern peninsula. Padstow, where celebrity chef Rick Stein owns a number of places, is a great culinary hotspot. **See p.364**

HIGHLIGHTS ARE MARKED ON THE MAP ON P.316

# DEVON & CORNWALL

## HIGHLIGHTS

1. Hiking on Dartmoor
2. Surfing in North Devon
3. Eden Project, Cornwall
4. Cornish beaches
5. St Ives
6. Seafood in Padstow

Weston-super-Mare

SOMERSET

Minehead

EXMOOR NATIONAL PARK

Dulverton

Bridgwater

Taunton

Lynton

Lyme Regis

Seaton

Beer

Honiton

Sidmouth

Budleigh Salterton

A La Ronde

Topsham

Exmouth

Teignmouth

Torquay

Paignton

Paignton & Dartmouth Steam Railway

Brixham

Dartmouth

Kingsbridge

Salcombe

SOUTH HAMS

Saltram House

ENGLISH CHANNEL

Credton

Exeter

Tiverton

Eggesford

Barnstaple

Ilfracombe

Woolacombe

Croyde

Saunton

Appledore

Bideford

Clovelly

Great Torrington

Meeth

DEVON

Okehampton

DARTMOOR NATIONAL PARK

Princetown

Buckfastleigh

Totnes

Newton Abbot

Lydford

Tavistock

Buckland Abbey

Mount Edgcumbe

Plymouth

R.Tamar

Launceston

Calstock

Looe

Polperro

Fowey

Par

St Austell

Lanhydrock

Liskeard

St Neot

Bolventor

BODMIN MOOR

Camelford

Bodmin

Wadebridge

Rock

Padstow

Polzeath

Port Isaac

Tintagel

Boscastle

Morwenstow

Hartland

Hartland Point

Bude

South West Coast Path

Lundy Island

Hartland Point

R.Torridge

Eden Project

Mevagissey

Lost Gardens of Heligan

Gorran Haven

Veryan

St Mawes

Falmouth

Lizard Peninsula

Coverack

Lizard Point

Lizard

Helston

Penzance

St Ives

Camborne

Redruth

St Agnes

Perranporth

Newquay

Newquay Airport

Truro

CORNWALL

St Just

Land's End

Porthcurno

Penwith Peninsula

ATLANTIC OCEAN

Isles of Scilly

Bryher

Tresco

St Martin's

St Mary's

N

0    10    miles

**GETTING AROUND**                                        **DEVON AND CORNWALL**

Getting around the West Country by public transport can be a convoluted and lengthy process, especially in remoter areas.

**By train** You can reach Exeter, Plymouth, Bodmin, Truro and Penzance by train on the main rail lines from London and the Midlands, with branch lines linking Falmouth (from Truro), Newquay (from Par) and St Ives (from St Erth). The frequent London Waterloo–Exeter service makes several useful stops in Devon, at Axminster, Feniton, Honiton and Pinhoe.

**By bus** Buses from the chief towns fan out along the coasts and into the interior, though the service can be rudimentary (or completely non-existent) for the smaller villages.

**South West Coast Path** The best way of exploring the coast of Devon and Cornwall is on foot along the South West Coast Path (⟨w⟩ southwestcoastpath.com), England's longest waymarked trail.

# Devon

With its verdant meadows, winding country lanes and cosy thatched cottages, **Devon** has long been idealized as a vision of a pre-industrial, "authentic" England. In fact much of the county is now inhabited largely by retired folk and urban refugees, but there is still tranquillity and sugar-free charm to be found here, from moorland villages to quiet coves on the cliff-hung coastline.

Reminders of Devon's leading role in the country's **maritime history** are never far away, particularly in the two cities of **Exeter** and **Plymouth**. These days it's the yachties who take advantage of the numerous creeks and bays, especially on Devon's southern coast, where ports such as **Dartmouth** and **Salcombe** are awash with amateur sailors. Landlubbers flock to the sandy beaches and seaside resorts, of which **Torquay**, on the south coast, and **Ilfracombe**, on the north, are the busiest. The most attractive are those that have preserved traces of their nineteenth-century elegance, such as **Sidmouth**, in east Devon. Inland, the county is characterized by swards of lush pasture and a scattering of sheltered villages, the population dropping to almost zero on **Dartmoor**, the wildest and bleakest of the West's moors.

## Exeter

**EXETER** has more historical sights than any other town in Devon or Cornwall, legacies of an eventful existence dating from its Celtic foundation and the establishment here of the most westerly Roman outpost. After the Roman withdrawal, Exeter was refounded by Alfred the Great and by the time of the Norman Conquest had become one of the largest towns in England, profiting from its position on the banks of the River Exe. The expansion of the wool trade in the Tudor period sustained the city until the eighteenth century. Since then, Exeter has maintained its status as Devon's commercial and cultural hub, despite having much of its ancient centre gutted by World War II bombing.

### Exeter Cathedral

The Cloisters, south of Cathedral Close • Mon–Sat 9am–4.45pm, Sun 11.30am–3.30pm • £6, or £8 including access to the North Tower; tours of the roof (1hr 30min) cost an additional £5 • ☎ 01392 255573, ⟨w⟩ exeter-cathedral.org.uk

The most distinctive feature of the city's skyline, **Exeter Cathedral** is a stately monument with two great Norman towers flanking the nave. Close up, it's the facade's ornate Gothic screen that commands attention: its three tiers of sculpted (and very weathered) figures – including Alfred, Athelstan, Canute, William the Conqueror and Richard II – were begun around 1360, part of a rebuilding programme which left only the towers from the original construction.

Entering the cathedral, you're confronted by the longest unbroken **Gothic ceiling** in the world, its **bosses** vividly painted – one, towards the west front, shows the murder of Thomas à Becket. The **Lady Chapel** and **Chapter House** – at the far end of the building and off the right transept respectively – are thirteenth-century, but the main part of the

6

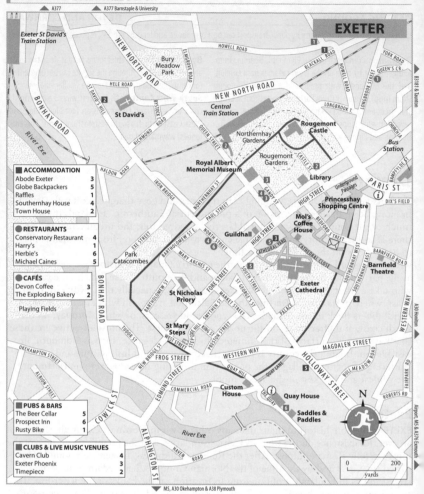

**EXETER**

nave, including the lavish rib vaulting, dates from a century later. There are many fine examples of sculpture from this period, including, in the minstrels' gallery high up on the left side, angels playing musical instruments, and, below them, figures of Edward III and Queen Philippa. In the **Choir** don't miss the 60ft **bishop's throne** or the **misericords** – decorated with mythological figures and dating from around 1260, they are thought to be the oldest in the country. Outside, a graceful statue of the theologian Richard Hooker surveys the **Cathedral Close**, a motley mixture of architectural styles from Tudor to Regency, though most display Exeter's trademark red brickwork. For a glimpse of the cathedral's clock mechanism and spectacular views across the city, consider joining one of the guided tours of the roof.

## The Guildhall

High St • Generally Mon–Fri 10.30am–1pm & 1.30–4pm, Sat 10.30am–12.30pm, but subject to change at short notice and sometimes closed for functions; call ahead • Free • ☎ 01392 665500

Some older structures still stand amid the banal concrete of the modern town centre, including, on the pedestrianized High Street, Exeter's finest civic building, the

**6**

fourteenth-century **Guildhall**, claimed to be England's oldest municipal building in regular use. It's fronted by an elegant Renaissance portico, and merits a glance inside for its main chamber, whose arched roof timbers rest on carved bears holding staves, symbols of the Yorkist cause during the Wars of the Roses.

## Royal Albert Memorial Museum

Queen St • Tues–Sun 10am–5pm • Free • ☎ 01392 265858, Ⓦ rammuseum.org.uk

The **Royal Albert Memorial Museum** is the closest thing in Devon to a county museum. Exuding the Victorian spirit of wide-ranging curiosity, it includes everything from a menagerie of stuffed animals to mock-ups of the various building styles used at different periods in the city. The collections of silverware, watches and clocks contrast nicely with the colourful ethnography section, and the picture gallery has some good specimens of West Country art.

## Underground passages

Paris St • June–Sept & school hols Mon–Sat 9.30am–5.30pm, Sun 10.30am–4pm; Oct–May Tues–Fri 11.30am–5.30pm, Sat 9.30am–5.30pm, Sun 11.30am–4pm • £6 • ☎ 01392 665887, Ⓦ exeter.gov.uk/passages

Off the top end of the High Street, the Princesshay shopping precinct holds the entrance to a network of **underground passages**, first excavated in the fourteenth century to bring water to the cathedral precincts, and now visitable on a guided **tour** – not recommended for claustrophobes.

## Around the River Exe

The **River Exe** marks the old city's southwestern boundary; today, the **Quayside** is mostly devoted to leisure activities. Pubs, shops and cafés share space with handsomely restored nineteenth-century warehouses and the smart **Custom House**, built in 1681, its opulence reflecting the former importance of the cloth trade. The area comes into its own at night, but is worth a wander at any time; you can rent bikes and canoes here, too (see p.320).

### ARRIVAL AND DEPARTURE                                          EXETER

**By plane** Exeter's airport is around 6 miles east of the centre, just off the A30. Stagecoach buses #56A and #56B connect the airport with the bus station on Paris Street (roughly hourly; 20min).
Destinations London City (1–3 daily; 1hr 15min); Manchester (1–3 daily; 1hr 10min); St Mary's, Isles of Scilly (late April to Oct Mon–Sat 1–5 daily; 1hr).

**By train** Exeter has two main train stations, Exeter Central and St David's, the latter a 15min uphill walk or 10min bus ride from the city centre. South West trains from Salisbury stop at both, as do trains on the branch lines to Barnstaple and Exmouth, but most long-distance trains stop at St David's only.
Destinations Barnstaple (Mon–Sat hourly, Sun 7 daily;

1hr–1hr 30min); Bodmin (every 30min–1hr; 2hr–2hr 30min); Liskeard (every 1–2hr; 1hr 30min–2hr); London (every 30min–1hr; 2–3hr); Par (roughly hourly; 2hr); Penzance (roughly hourly; 3hr–3hr 10min); Plymouth (every 30min–1hr; 1hr); Torquay (every 30min–1hr; 35–55min); Totnes (every 30min–1hr; 35min); Truro (every 30min–1hr; 2hr 20min–2hr 40min).

**By bus** The bus station is on Paris St, one block north of the tourist office.

Destinations Newquay (2 daily; 3hr 30min); Penzance (2 daily; 4hr–4hr 40min); Plymouth (every 1–2hr; 50min–1hr 45min); Sidmouth (Mon–Sat every 20–30min, Sun every 30min–1hr; 40–50min); Torquay (roughly hourly; 1hr–1hr 10min); Truro (2 daily; 3hr 20min).

## INFORMATION AND ACTIVITIES

**Tourist office** Dix's Field, off Princesshay (Mon–Sat 9.30am–4.30pm; ☎01392 665700, ⓦheartofdevon .com).

**Saddles & Paddles** On the quayside (☎01392 424241,

ⓦsadpad.com). You can rent bikes here (£15/day); they also have canoes (£10 for the first hour and £5/hr thereafter), should you wish to explore the Exeter Canal, which runs 5 miles to Topsham and beyond.

## ACCOMMODATION

**Abode Exeter** Cathedral Yard ☎01392 319955, ⓦabodehotels.co.uk. Built in 1769 and reputedly the first inn in England to be described as a "hotel", the former *Royal Clarence* is now part of a smart national chain. It's in a superb location near the cathedral, with contemporary bedrooms (some small) and a swanky restaurant (see below). **£85**

**Globe Backpackers** 71 Holloway St ☎01392 215521, ⓦexeterbackpackers.co.uk. Clean and central (though a bit of a hike from the stations), this hostel has a kitchen and free wi-fi. Dorms have six to ten beds and there are a few private rooms too. Closed noon–3.30pm. Dorms **£17.50**; doubles **£45**

**Raffles** 11 Blackall Rd ☎01392 270200, ⓦraffles -exeter.co.uk. The rooms in this elegant Victorian B&B are

furnished with Pre-Raphaelite etchings and other items from the owners' antiques business. Breakfasts make use of the organic garden produce. Free wi-fi. **£78**

★**Southernhay House** 36 Southernhay East ☎01392 435324, ⓦsouthernhayhouse.com. Attractive, individually themed rooms in a renovated nineteenth-century townhouse, with plush carpets and – in the best rooms – freestanding bathtubs. Breakfast is included as standard, but cheaper rates are available if you stay on a room-only basis. **£150**

**Town House** 54 St David's Hill ☎01392 494994, ⓦtownhouseexeter.co.uk. This Edwardian guesthouse midway between the train stations backs onto a churchyard and has a garden, wi-fi access and abundant breakfasts. Rooms are modern but some bathrooms are small. **£79**

## EATING

**Conservatory Restaurant** 18 North St ☎01392 273858, ⓦtheconservatoryrestaurant.co.uk. Centrally located restaurant popular for its fresh fish dishes (including grilled sole from Cornwall) and wine from Devon. The two-course lunch is good value at £16.95. Tues–Sat noon–2pm & 5.30–9pm.

★**Devon Coffee** 88 Queen St ☎07796 678559, ⓦfacebook.com/devoncoffeeshop. Relaxed, independent coffee shop, where the decor is all stressed wood and chalkboards. The brownies here (£2.20) are exceedingly good and the coffee – as you'd expect from the name – isn't bad either. Mon–Sat 8am–6pm, Sun 10am–4pm.

★**The Exploding Bakery** 1b Central Crescent, Queen St ☎01392 427900, ⓦexplodingbakery .com. Slurp top-quality coffee (just £2 a cup) as you watch sweet-smelling cakes being pulled out of the ovens at this busy little wholesale bakery. If people-watching gets boring, there's plenty of art on the walls.

Mon–Fri 8am–4pm, Sat 9am–4pm.

**Harry's** 86 Longbrook St ☎01392 202234, ⓦharrys -exeter.co.uk. In a converted Victorian stonemason's workshop, this place attracts a cheery crowd with its good-value Mexican, Italian and American staples (most mains around £10). Daily 10am–2pm & 6–11pm.

★**Herbie's** 15 North St ☎01392 258473. Friendly, dimly lit place serving up great vegan, vegetarian and wholefood dishes (most mains under £10) plus organic beers, wines and ice cream. Mon 11am–2.30pm, Tues–Fri 11am–2.30pm & 6–9.30pm, Sat 10.30am–3.30pm & 6–9.30pm.

**Michael Caines** Abode Exeter Hotel, Cathedral Yard ☎01392 319955, ⓦmichaelcaines.com. Exeter's classiest restaurant offers sophisticated modern European cuisine in sleek surroundings. Prices are fairly high, but there are cheaper, two-course menus on offer at lunchtime and during the early evening (£14.95 and £16.95 respectively). Mon–Sat noon–2.30pm & 6–9pm (last orders).

## DRINKING

**The Beer Cellar** 2 South St ☎01392 757570, ⓦbeer -cellar.co.uk. This friendly corner bar near the cathedral does great craft beer on tap and in bottles to take away.

Look out for beers from the local Branscombe Vale Brewery. Daily 10am–10.30pm.

**Prospect Inn** The Quay ☎01392 273152,

Ⓦ heavitreebrewery.co.uk. You can eat and drink sitting outside at this seventeenth-century riverside pub, which was the setting for TV drama *The Onedin Line*. Mon–Thurs & Sun 10am–11pm, Fri & Sat 10am–midnight.

★**Rusty Bike** 67 Howell Rd ☏ 01392 214440,

Ⓦ rustybike-exeter.co.uk. There's an excellent vibe at this pub with vintage table-football and a range of malt whiskies and tequilas as well as local beers and ciders. Also offers good bar meals, a garden and occasional live music. Mon–Fri 5–11pm, Sat noon–midnight, Sun noon–11pm.

### NIGHTLIFE AND ENTERTAINMENT

**Cavern Club** 83–84 Queen St ☏ 01392 495370, Ⓦ exetercavern.com. A long-established hub of Exeter's music scene, this subterranean haunt is best known for its live bands (think indie, punk and metal) but it also has more diverse club nights and is open for daytime snacks. Daily 11.30am–5pm & 8pm–late.

**Exeter Phoenix** Bradlynch Place, Gandy St ☏ 01392 667080, Ⓦ exeterphoenix.org.uk. Live music and comedy are among the cultural offerings at this arts centre, which also hosts films, exhibitions and readings and has a

nice café-bar. Mon–Sat 10am–11pm (and sometimes Sun for events).

**Timepiece** Little Castle St ☏ 01392 493096, Ⓦ timepiecenightclub.co.uk. Occupying a former prison, this bar, club and performance venue hosts student nights (Mon in term time), salsa parties (Tues) and world music sessions (Sun in term time), plus big indie, chart and house nights on Fri and Sat. Tues–Sat 7.30pm–1.30/2am, also Sun & Mon in term time.

6

# A La Ronde

5 miles south of Exeter off the A376 • Mid-Feb to Oct daily 11am–5pm; Nov to mid-Feb Sat & Sun noon–4pm • £7.80; NT • ☏ 01395 265514, Ⓦ nationaltrust.org.uk/a-la-ronde • Take bus #56 from Exeter's bus station and get off at the Courtlands Cross stop

The Gothic folly of **A La Ronde** was the creation of two spinster cousins, Jane and Mary Parminter, who in the 1790s were inspired by their European Grand Tour to build a **sixteen-sided house**, possibly based on the Byzantine basilica of San Vitale in Ravenna. The end product is filled with mementos of the Parminters' travels as well as a number of their more offbeat creations, such as a frieze made of feathers culled from game birds and chickens. In the upper rooms are a gallery and staircase completely covered in shells, too fragile to be visited, though part can be glimpsed from the completely enclosed octagonal room on the first floor. Superb views over the Exe estuary extend from the dormer windows on the second floor.

# Exmouth

**EXMOUTH**, ten miles south of Exeter, started as a Roman port and went on to become the first of the county's resorts to be popularized by holiday-makers in the late eighteenth century. Overlooking lawns, rock pools and a respectable two miles of beach, Exmouth's Georgian terraced houses once accommodated the wives of Nelson and Byron – installed at nos. 6 and 19 The Beacon respectively (on a rise overlooking the seafront, above the public gardens). Today it's a relaxed spot that attracts a steady stream of visitors – both from Exeter and, in the summer, from other beach resorts along the south coast.

### ARRIVAL AND DEPARTURE                                                    EXMOUTH

**By train** The train station is on Imperial Road, on the western edge of town.

Destinations Barnstaple (hourly; 1hr 45min); Exeter St David's (every 30min; 30min); Paignton (hourly; 1hr 30min).

**By bus and ferry** Buses from/to Exeter (Stagecoach bus #57;

every 15min; 40min) and Budleigh Salterton (Stagecoach bus #357; roughly every 15min; 20min) arrive at and depart from the bus station, just next to the railway station. In addition, from Easter to Oct, Exmouth is linked by an hourly ferry to Starcross, on the other side of the Exe estuary (£4.50 one way), served by buses from/to Torquay (see p.324).

# Budleigh Salterton

Bounded on each side by red sandstone cliffs, **BUDLEIGH SALTERTON** has a more genteel air than Exmouth – its thatched and whitewashed cottages inspired Noël Coward to write about the place, and John Millais painted his famous *Boyhood of Raleigh* on the shingle beach here (Sir Walter Raleigh was born in pretty East Budleigh, a couple of miles inland).

### ARRIVAL AND DEPARTURE BUDLEIGH SALTERTON

**By bus** Stagecoach runs a frequent service between Exeter and Budleigh Salterton (#357; roughly every 15min; 20min).

## 6 Sidmouth

Set amid a shelf of crumbling red sandstone, **SIDMOUTH** is the stately queen of east Devon's resorts. The cream-and-white town boasts nearly five hundred buildings listed as having special historic or architectural interest, among them the grand Georgian homes of **York Terrace** behind the Esplanade. Both the mile-long main town beach and **Jacob's Ladder**, a cliff-backed shingle and sand strip to the west of town, are easily accessible and well tended. To the east, the coast path climbs steep Salcombe Hill to follow cliffs that give sanctuary to a range of birdlife including yellowhammers, green woodpeckers and the rarer grasshopper warbler. Further on, the path descends to meet one of the most isolated and attractive beaches in the area, **Weston Mouth**.

### ARRIVAL AND INFORMATION SIDMOUTH

**By bus** Sidmouth can be reached on bus #52A or #52B from Exeter's bus station (every 15–30min; 50min).
**Tourist office** The tourist office is on Ham Lane, off the eastern end of the Esplanade (Feb–March & Nov–Dec

Mon–Sat 10am–1.30pm; April & Oct Mon–Sat 10am–4pm, Sun 10am–1.30pm; May–Sept daily 10am–5pm; ☎01395 516441, ⓦ visitsidmouth.co.uk). Head here for information on bay cruises and free guided walks around the area.

### ACCOMMODATION

**The Hollies** Salcombe Rd ☎01395 514580, ⓦ holliesguesthouse.co.uk. Rooms in this Regency building blend contemporary and traditional styles, with the owner's watercolours on the walls. The seafront is less than a 10min walk away. **£70**
**The Longhouse** Salcombe Hill Rd ☎01395 577973,

ⓦ holidaysinsidmouth.co.uk. It's about a mile from the seafront, but the hilltop views from this B&B – once part of the Norman Lockyer Observatory – compensate. The two rooms are large and comfortable, and there's a nice patio-garden. No credit cards. **£85**

### EATING AND DRINKING

**The Dairy Shop** 5 Church St ☎01395 513018. Stacked wall to wall with chutneys, gooseberry wine, biscuits and the like, this café-cum-shop is a good spot for soups (£4.95), savoury crêpes (£5.25) or an ice cream – try the knickerbocker glory. Mon–Sat 9am–5pm.

**Swan Inn** 37 York St ☎01395 512849, ⓦ youngs.co.uk. Close to the tourist office, this convivial but slightly run-down pub with a garden serves real ales, baguettes, plus meat and fish dishes (rump steak £11.25). Mon–Sat 11am–11pm, Sun noon–11pm; food served Mon–Sat noon–9.30pm, Sun noon–8pm.

## Beer

Eight miles east of Sidmouth, the largely unspoiled fishing village of **BEER** lies huddled within a small sheltered cove between gleaming white headlands. A stream

---

### SIDMOUTH FOLK WEEK

Sidmouth hosts what many consider to be the country's best **folk festival** over eight days in early August. It's an upbeat affair: folk and roots artists from around the country perform in marquees, pubs and hotels around town, and there are numerous ceilidhs and pavement buskers. Accommodation during this period is at a premium but campsites are laid on outside town with shuttle buses to the centre. Tickets can be bought for specific days, for the weekend or the entire week. For detailed information, see ⓦ sidmouthfolkweek.co.uk. Book early for the main acts.

rushes along a deep channel dug into Beer's main street, and if you can ignore the crowds in high summer much of the village looks unchanged since the time when it was a smugglers' haven. While away a sunny afternoon here fishing for mackerel in the bay (around £6/person), or pull up a deckchair and tuck into a couple of fresh crab sandwiches on the beach.

## Beer Quarry Caves
Quarry Lane, about a mile west of the village • Mid-April to Sept 10am–5.30pm; last tour 1hr before closing • £7 • ☏ 01297 680282, ⓦ beerquarrycaves.co.uk.

The area around Beer is best known for its quarries, which were worked from Roman times until the nineteenth century: **Beer stone** was used in many of Devon's churches and houses, and as far afield as London. You can visit the underground **Beer Quarry Caves**, which includes an exhibition of pieces carved by medieval masons.

### ARRIVAL AND DEPARTURE                                                          BEER

**By bus** Beer is connected to Sidmouth by bus #899 (Mon–Sat 3–5 daily; 25–50min), which departs from Sidmouth Triangle.

### ACCOMMODATION AND EATING

**Bay View** Fore St ☏ 01297 20489, ⓦ bayviewbeer.com. Close to the beach and harbour, most of the rooms in this bright B&B overlook the sea. Abundant breakfasts in the attached café, which does crab sandwiches to take away (£6.50 with tea or coffee), include smoked haddock and waffles with maple syrup. Closed Nov–Easter. **£80**

**Steamers** New Cut ☏ 01297 22922, ⓦ steamersrestaurant.co.uk. Attractive, family-run restaurant on a quiet alley just up from the harbour. The fresh fish dishes are the main reason to come here, with locally caught hake, sole and sea bass (£15–20) all featuring on the menu. Tues–Sat 10.30am–2pm and 6.45–9pm, Sun 11.45am–2.15pm.

# Torquay

Sporting a mini-corniche and promenades landscaped with flowerbeds, **TORQUAY** comes closest to living up to the self-styled "English Riviera" sobriquet. The much-vaunted palm trees and the coloured lights that festoon the harbour by night contribute to the town's unique flavour, a blend of the mildly exotic with classic English provincialism. Torquay's transformation from a fishing village began with its establishment as a fashionable haven for invalids, among them the consumptive Elizabeth Barrett Browning, who spent three years here.

The town centres on the small **harbour** and marina, separated by limestone cliffs from Torquay's main beach, **Abbey Sands**, which takes its name from Torre Abbey, behind the beachside road.

## Torre Abbey
The King's Drive • Wed–Sun 10am–5pm • £7.50 • ☏ 01803 293593, ⓦ torre-abbey.org.uk

The Norman church that once stood here was razed by Henry VIII, though a gatehouse, tithe barn, chapter house and tower escaped demolition. **Torre Abbey** now contains a good museum, set in pretty ornamental gardens, with collections of silver and glass, window designs by Edward Burne-Jones, illustrations by William Blake, and nineteenth-century and contemporary works of art.

## Torquay Museum
529 Babbacombe Rd • Mon–Thurs 10am–4pm • £5.50 • ☏ 01803 293975, ⓦ torquaymuseum.org

**Torquay Museum**, a short walk up from the harbour, includes a section devoted to **Agatha Christie**, who was born and raised in Torquay, though most of the space here is given over to local and natural history displays, including a collection of more than 150,000 plants, birds, insects, shells and reptiles.

## Living Coasts

Beacon Quay • Daily: Easter–Sept 10am–5pm; Oct–Easter 10am–4pm; last entry 1hr before closing • £10.50, or £21.50 with Paignton Zoo (see below) • ☎01803 202470, ⊛ livingcoasts.org.uk

At the northern end of Torquay harbour, **Living Coasts** is home to a variety of fauna and flora found on British shores, including puffins, penguins and seals. There are reconstructed beaches, cliff faces and an estuary, as well as underwater viewing areas and a huge meshed aviary. The rooftop café and restaurant have splendid panoramic views.

**6**

## The beaches

East of Torquay's harbour, you can follow the shore round to some good sand beaches. **Meadfoot Beach**, one of the busiest, is reached by crossing Daddyhole Plain, named after a large chasm in the adjacent cliff caused by a landslide, but locally attributed to the devil ("Daddy"). North of the Hope's Nose promontory, the coast path leads to a string of less crowded beaches, including **Babbacombe Beach** and, beyond, **Watcombe** and **Maidencombe**.

### ARRIVAL AND INFORMATION                                      TORQUAY

**By train** Torquay's main train station is off Rathmore Road, southwest of Torre Abbey Gardens. There are regular trains from/to Exeter (every 15–55min; 35–55min).

**By bus** Most buses stop on Lymington Road (a short walk north of the centre), or on The Strand, close to the marina.

Destinations Exeter (at least 12 daily; 1hr); Plymouth (Mon–Sat 9 daily, Sun 6 daily; 2hr–2hr 50min).

**Tourist office** The English Riviera Visitor Information Centre is on Vaughan Parade, by the harbour (daily 9.30am–5pm; ☎0844 474 2233, ⊛ englishriviera.co.uk).

### ACCOMMODATION

**Allerdale Hotel** 21 Croft Rd ☎01803 292667, ⊛ allerdale hotel.co.uk. For glorious views and stately surroundings, head for this Victorian villa, a pleasingly old-fashioned place with a long garden and spacious rooms. Meals are available, and there's a bar, snooker and free wi-fi. **£80**

**Exton House** 12 Bridge Rd ☎01803 293561, ⊛ extonhotel.co.uk. Small, clean and quiet B&B a 10min walk from the train station (free pick-up is usually offered),

and just 15min from the centre. The guests' lounge has a balcony, and there's free wi-fi. Book direct for the best rates. **£60**

**Torquay Backpackers** 119 Abbey Rd ☎01803 299924, ⊛ torquaybackpackers.co.uk. Friendly hostel a 15min walk northeast of the train station, with free wi-fi, free tea and coffee, and nice common areas (including space outside for barbecues). Weekly rates available. Dorms **£17**; doubles **£38**

### EATING AND DRINKING

**Hole in the Wall** Park Lane ☎01803 200755. This pub is supposed to be one of Torquay's oldest, and was Irish playwright Sean O'Casey's boozer when he lived here. There's a good range of beers, a separate restaurant (with mains around £10) and live music on Tues, Thurs and Sun. Daily noon–midnight; food served Mon–Sat noon–2.30pm & 5.30–9.30pm, Sun 12.30–2.30pm & 6–9.30pm.

**Number 7 Fish Bistro** Beacon Terrace ☎01803 295055, ⊛ no7-fish.com. Just above the harbour, this place is a must for seafood fans, covering everything from fresh whole crab to grilled turbot – or whatever else the boats have brought in. Most mains cost around £18. June–Oct Mon–Sat 12.15–1.45pm & 6–9.45pm; Nov–May Tues–Sat same hours.

# Paignton

Lacking Torquay's gloss, **PAIGNTON** is the least attractive of the Riviera's resorts, though it is home to **Paignton Zoo** (daily: summer 10am–6pm; winter 10am–4.30pm or dusk; £14.45, or £21.50 with Living Coasts in Torquay; ⊛ paigntonzoo.org.uk), a mile out on Totnes Road. Near the seafront, Paignton's main train station is also the terminus of the **Dartmouth Steam Railway** (April–Oct daily, plus selected dates Nov–March; ☎01803 555872, ⊛ dartmouthrailriver.co.uk), which connects with **Goodrington Sands** beach before following the Dart to Kingswear, seven miles south. You could make a day of it by taking the ferry from Kingswear to Dartmouth (see p.327), then taking a riverboat up the Dart to Totnes, from where you can take any bus back to Paignton – a "Round Robin" ticket (£23.50) lets you do this.

## ARRIVAL AND DEPARTURE                                    PAIGNTON

**By train** Trains from Exeter (every 30min–1hr; 40min–1hr 10min) and Torquay (every 30min–1hr; 5min) arrive at the main train station off Sands Road, 5mins from the harbour.
**By bus** The bus station is next to the train station,

off Sands Road.
Destinations Brixham (every 10–20min; 20min); Exeter (every 30min–1hr; 1hr 15min–1hr 30min); Torquay (every 5–10min; 20–35min).

# Brixham

**6**

BRIXHAM is a major fishing port and the prettiest of the Torbay towns. Among the trawlers on the quayside is moored a full-size reconstruction of the **Golden Hind** (March–Oct daily 10am–4pm, £4; ☎01803 856223, ⓦgoldenhind.co.uk), the surprisingly small vessel in which Francis Drake circumnavigated the world. The harbour is overlooked by an unflattering statue of William III, who landed in Brixham to claim the crown of England in 1688.

From the harbour, climb King Street and follow Berry Head Road to reach the promontory at the southern limit of Torbay, **Berry Head**, now a conservation area attracting colonies of nesting seabirds. There are fabulous views, and you can see the remains of fortifications built during the Napoleonic Wars.

## ARRIVAL AND INFORMATION                                    BRIXHAM

**By bus** Most buses arrive at and depart from Town Square and Bank Lane, in the upper town.
Destinations Exeter (2 daily; 1hr 40min); Paignton (every 10–20min; 25min); Torquay (every 10–20min; 40–50min).

**Tourist office** The tourist office (daily 10am–5pm; ☎0844 474 2233, ⓦenglishriviera.co.uk) is inside Hobb Nobs Gift Shop at 19 The Quay.

## ACCOMMODATION

**Harbour View** King St ☎01803 853052, ⓦharbourview brixhambandb.co.uk. As the name implies, its position is the best asset of this B&B, which has small but clean and modern en-suite rooms. The owners also take care of some self-catering accommodation; call for details. **£80**

**Quayside Hotel** King St ☎01803 855751, ⓦquaysidehotel.co.uk. Handsome 29-room hotel with superb harbour views, two bars and a good restaurant where meat and seafood dishes are £15–17. It's worth paying extra for a harbour-facing room. **£102**

## EATING AND DRINKING

**Blue Anchor** 83 Fore St ☎01803 859373. A great spot for a relaxed pint of local ale, with open fires and low beams. They also offer a full menu of (rather mediocre) bar food. Mon–Sat 11am–midnight, Sun 11am–11.30pm; food served daily noon–2.30pm & 6–9.30pm.
**Poopdeck** 14 The Quay ☎01803 858681, ⓦpoopdeck

restaurant.com. You'll find all manner of cockles, whelks and crab sticks at Brixham's harbourside stalls, but for a top-class seafood feast try this place, where a plate of grilled local fish costs £17.50 and a hot shellfish platter is £24.95 – book early for a table overlooking the harbour. Tues–Thurs 6–9.30pm, Fri & Sat noon–2.30pm & 6–10pm, Sun noon–2.30pm.

# Greenway

4 miles west of Brixham, outside Galmpton • Early March to Oct Wed–Sun 10.30am–5pm, also Tues same hours during Easter and summer school hols • £9.40; NT • ☎01803 842382, ⓦnationaltrust.org/greenway • Greenway Ferry (☎01803 882811, ⓦgreenwayferry.co.uk) offers services from Dartmouth (6–8/day; £8 return) and Totnes (1 daily; £8 return), as well as from Torquay (11am) and Brixham (11.30am) for £22/person including return journey by vintage bus; steam trains run from Paignton to Greenway Halt (up to 10 daily; 20min; £7.50), from where it's a 30min walk through woodland to the house; coming by car, parking is free but must be booked a day in advance

The birthplace of Walter Raleigh's three seafaring half-brothers, the Gilberts, and later rebuilt for Agatha Christie, **Greenway** stands high above the Dart amid steep wooded grounds (the ascent from the river landing is challenging). As well as arriving by ferry or steam train (see above), you can reach the house on foot on the waymarked "**Greenway walk**" from Brixham (around 1hr 30min) or via the Dart Valley Trail from Dartmouth or Kingswear (both around 1hr 20min) – Dartmouth's tourist office can supply route maps (see p.328). Once here, you'll find a low-key collection of memorabilia belonging to the Christie family, including archeological scraps, silverware, ceramics and books, while the grounds afford lovely views over the river.

## Totnes

On the west bank of the River Dart, **TOTNES** has an ancient pedigree, its period of greatest prosperity occurring in the sixteenth century when this inland port exported cloth to France and brought back wine. Some handsome sixteenth-century buildings survive from that era, and there is still a working port down on the river, but these days Totnes has mellowed into a residential market town, popular with the alternative and New Age crowd.

The town centres on the long main street that changes its name from Fore Street to the High Street at the **East Gate**, a much retouched medieval arch. On Fore Street, the town **museum**, occupying a four-storey Elizabethan house, illustrates how wealthy clothiers lived at the peak of Totnes's fortunes (April–Sept Mon–Sat 10.30am–4.30pm; last admission 3.30pm; £3; ☎01803 863821, ⓦtotnesmuseum.org). From the East Gate, **Ramparts Walk** trails off along the old city walls, curving round the fifteenth-century church of **St Mary**, a red sandstone building containing an exquisitely carved rood screen. Looming over the High Street, the town's oldest monument, **Totnes Castle**, is a classic Norman structure of the motte and bailey design (daily: April–Sept 10am–6pm; Oct 10am–5pm; £3.70; EH; ☎1803 864406, ⓦenglish-heritage.org.uk).

### ARRIVAL AND INFORMATION                                            TOTNES

**By train** Totnes train station lies just off Station Road, a 10min walk north from the centre; it's served by trains from/to Exeter (every 10–40min; 30min) and Plymouth (every 10min–1hr; 30min).

**By bus** Most buses stop on or around two central streets: The Plains and Coronation Road.

Destinations Exeter (up to 12 daily; 1hr 15min–1hr 35min);

Paignton (every 20min; 15–50min); Plymouth (Mon–Sat every 10min–1hr, Sun 8 daily; 1hr–1hr 15min); Torquay (Mon–Sat every 30min, Sun every 20min–1hr; 50min).

**Tourist office** At The Town Mill, near the Morrisons car park (April–Oct Mon–Fri 9.30am–5pm, Sat 10am–4pm; Nov–March Mon–Fri 10am–4pm, Sat 10am–1pm; ☎01803 863168, ⓦtotnesinformation.co.uk)

### ACCOMMODATION

**Alison Fenwick's B&B** 3 Plymouth Rd, off the High St ☎01803 866917, ⓦtotnes-accommodation.co.uk. Central, great-value B&B run by a former tourist guide, with three simple rooms, one of them en suite. Wi-fi available. No credit cards. Closed Nov–Feb. **£50**

**Great Grubb** Fallowfields, Plymouth Rd ☎01803 849071, ⓦthegreatgrubb.co.uk. Leather sofas, restful colours, healthy breakfasts and a patio are the main appeal of this friendly B&B a short walk from the centre,

where work by local artists is displayed in the rooms. Free wi-fi. **£70**

**Royal Seven Stars Hotel** The Plains ☎01803 862125, ⓦroyalsevenstars.co.uk. This seventeenth-century coaching inn has had a modern makeover, giving it contemporary bedrooms and a stylish bar alongside the traditional *Saloon Bar* and brasserie. The Sunday-night deal, including a carvery meal and breakfast for two, is great value at £80. **£118.75**

### EATING AND DRINKING

**The Barrel House** 59 High St ☎01803 863000, ⓦbarrel housetotnes.co.uk. There's a café at street level and a former

ballroom upstairs where you can eat salads, burgers and more for around £10. Occasional DJs, live music and comedy nights.

---

### EXCURSIONS FROM TOTNES

The highest navigable point on the **River Dart** for seagoing vessels, Totnes is the starting point for **cruises to Dartmouth**, leaving from Steamer Quay (Feb–Oct 1–4 daily; 1hr 15min; £14 return; ☎01803 555872, ⓦdartmouthrailriver.co.uk). **Riverside walks** in either direction pass some congenial pubs and, near the railway bridge at Littlehempston, the station of the **South Devon Railway**, where you can board a steam train running along the Dart to Buckfastleigh, on the edge of Dartmoor (late March to Oct 4–9 daily; 30min; £12.40 return; ☎08453 451420, ⓦsouthdevonrailway.co.uk).

Food served Mon–Sat 9am–11.30am & noon–4pm, Sun noon–3pm; shows usually Wed–Sat from 8pm.

**Steam Packet Inn** St Peter's Quay ☎01803 863880, ⓦ steampacketinn.co.uk. This family-friendly inn reached by walking south along The Plains makes an excellent spot for a riverside drink or bite to eat. There's a range of local ales, bar snacks and meals in the conservatory restaurant (most mains £11–13). Also has double rooms available on a bed and breakfast basis (£105). Mon–Sat 11am–11pm, Sun noon–10.30pm.

**Willow** 87 High St ☎01803 862605. Inexpensive vegetarian snacks, evening meals and organic drinks are served at this mellow café/restaurant. Main dishes are less than £10. There's a courtyard, and live acoustic music on Fri. No credit cards. Mon, Tues & Thurs 10am–5pm, Wed, Fri & Sat 10am–5pm & 6.30–9pm.

**6**

# Dartmouth and around

South of Torbay, and eight miles downstream from Totnes, **DARTMOUTH** has thrived since the Normans recognized the trading potential of this deep-water port. Today its activities embrace fishing, freight and a booming leisure industry, as well as the education of the senior service's officer class at the Royal Naval College, on a hill overlooking the port.

Regular ferries shuttle across the River Dart between Dartmouth and **Kingswear**, terminus of the Dartmouth Steam Railway (see p.324). **Boat cruises** from Dartmouth are the best way to view the deep creeks and grand houses overlooking the river, among them Greenway (see p.325).

## Dartmouth Museum

Duke St • April–Oct Mon & Sun 1–4pm, Tues–Sat 10am–4pm; Nov–March daily noon–3pm • £2 • ☎01803 832923, ⓦ dartmouthmuseum.org

Behind the enclosed boat basin at the heart of town, the four-storey **Butterwalk** at the top of Duke Street was built in the seventeenth century for a local merchant. The timber-framed construction, richly decorated with woodcarvings, was restored after bombing in World War II though still looks precarious as it overhangs the street on eleven granite columns. This arcade now holds shops and Dartmouth's small **museum**, mainly devoted to maritime curios, including old maps, prints and models of ships.

## Dartmouth Castle

A mile southeast of town off Castle Rd • April–Sept daily 10am–6pm; Oct daily 10am–5pm; Nov–March Sat & Sun 10am–4pm • £5.50; FH • ☎01803 833588, ⓦ english-heritage.org.uk

A twenty-minute riverside walk southeast from **Bayard's Cove** – a short cobbled quay lined with eighteenth-century houses, where the Pilgrim Fathers stopped en route to the New World – brings you to **Dartmouth Castle**, one of two fortifications on opposite sides of the estuary dating from the fifteenth century. The castle was the first in England to be constructed specifically to withstand artillery, though was never tested in action, and consequently is excellently preserved.

If you don't fancy the walk back, you can take a **ferry** back to Dartmouth Quay (Easter–Oct continuous service 10am–4/5pm; £2; ⓦ dartmouthcastleferry.co.uk).

## Blackpool Sands

Roughly two miles southwest of Dartmouth Castle, the coastal path brings you through the pretty hilltop village of **Stoke Fleming** to **Blackpool Sands**, the best beach in the area. The unspoilt cove, flanked by steep, wooded cliffs, was the site of a battle in 1404 in which Devon archers repulsed a Breton invasion force sent to punish the privateers of Dartmouth for their cross-Channel raiding.

### ARRIVAL AND INFORMATION
### DARTMOUTH

**By ferry** Coming from Torbay, visitors to Dartmouth can save time and a long detour through Totnes by using the frequent Higher Ferry (ⓦ dartmouthhigherferry.com) or Lower Ferry (southhams.gov.uk/DartmouthLowerFerry) across the Dart from Kingswear (50p–£1.50 foot passengers; £4.50–4.70 for cars); the last ones are at around 10.45pm.

**Tourist office** The Discover Dartmouth tourist office is on Mayor's Ave (March Mon–Sat 10am–4pm; April–Oct Mon–Sat 9.30am–4.30pm, Sun 10am–2pm; Nov–Feb Mon, Tues & Thurs–Sat 10am–4pm; ☏01803 834224, ⓦdiscoverdartmouth.com).

## ACCOMMODATION, EATING AND DRINKING

**Avondale** 5 Vicarage Hill ☏07968 026449, ⓦavondaledartmouth.co.uk. On a steep hill west of the quay, this is a friendly, spacious and simply furnished B&B with terrific views over the town and river. Free wi-fi. **£88**

**Browns** 27–29 Victoria Rd ☏01803 832572, ⓦbrownshoteldartmouth.co.uk. Boutique-style hotel, with small, stylish rooms decorated with contemporary paintings. Good Mediterranean dishes are served in the bar and restaurant. Mon–Thurs & Sun 10am–7/8pm, Fri & Sat 11am–11.30pm. **£145**

**Café Alf Resco** Lower St ☏01803 835880, ⓦcafealfresco.co.uk. Funky snack bar that's good for all-day breakfasts, steaming coffees and occasional live music in summer. There's decent accommodation available above the café. Daily 7am–2pm. **£90**

**The Seahorse** 5 South Embankment ☏01803 835147, ⓦseahorserestaurant.co.uk. Seafood restaurant facing the river, offering such Italian-inspired dishes as spaghetti with clams and flame-grilled sea bass. It's pricey, with mains costing £19 and up, but there's a two-course lunch menu (£20), and the same team also runs *Rockfish*, a couple of doors down, which serves first-class fish and chips (daily noon–9.30pm). Tues–Sat noon–3pm & 6–10pm, Sun 12.30–2.30pm.

# Salcombe

The area between the Dart and Plym estuaries, the **South Hams**, holds some of Devon's comeliest villages and most striking coastline. The "capital" of the region, **Kingsbridge**, is a useful transport hub but lacks the appeal of **SALCOMBE**, reachable on a summer ferry from Kingsbridge. Once a nondescript fishing village, Devon's southernmost resort is now a full-blown sailing and holiday centre, its calm waters strewn with small pleasure craft.

You can swot up on boating and local history at **Salcombe Maritime Museum** on Market Street, off the north end of the central Fore Street (April–Oct daily 10.30am–12.30pm & 2.30–4.30pm; £1.50; ☏01548 843080, ⓦsalcombemuseum.org.uk) or take a ferry down to South Sands and climb up to the intriguing **Overbeck's Museum** at Sharpitor (mid-Feb to Oct daily 11am–5pm; £7.80; NT; ☏01548 842893, ⓦnationaltrust.org.uk/overbecks), which focuses on the area's natural history and nineteenth-century curiosities.

## ARRIVAL AND INFORMATION SALCOMBE

**By bus** Salcombe is served by regular buses from Kingsbridge (hourly; 30min), which is where you'll have to change if you're coming from Dartmouth and further afield.

**Tourist office** Market Street (late March to mid-July & Sept–Nov daily 10am–5pm; late July to Aug Mon–Sat 9am–6pm, Sun 10am–5pm; Nov to mid-March Mon–Sat 10am–3pm; ☏01548 843927, ⓦsalcombeinformation. co.uk).

## ACCOMMODATION AND EATING

**Higher Rew Caravan and Camping Park** 2 miles west of town, near Kingsbridge ☏01548 842681, ⓦhigherrew.co.uk. Large, grassy campsite on a slope near town, surrounded by attractive farmland. The on-site facilities are good, and there are plenty of places for kids to play. Closed Nov–March. Pitches **£20**

**Waverley** Devon Rd ☏01548 842633, ⓦwaverley bandb.co.uk. Rooms in this B&B are clean and the breakfasts are excellent, with lots of choice. It's less than a 10min walk to the centre. Self-catering also available. **£80**

**Winking Prawn** North Sands ☏01548 842326, ⓦwinkingprawn.co.uk. Right on the beach, this is an alluring stop for a cappuccino, baguette or ice cream by day, or a chargrilled steak or Cajun chicken salad in the evening, from around 6pm, when booking is advised (mains £15–20). You don't need to book for the summer barbecues (May–Sept 4–8.30pm; £16.95). Daily 8.45am–8.30pm.

# Plymouth and around

**PLYMOUTH**'s predominantly bland and modern face belies its great historic role as a naval base and, in the sixteenth century, the stamping ground of such national heroes as John Hawkins and Francis Drake. It was from here that Drake sailed to defeat the

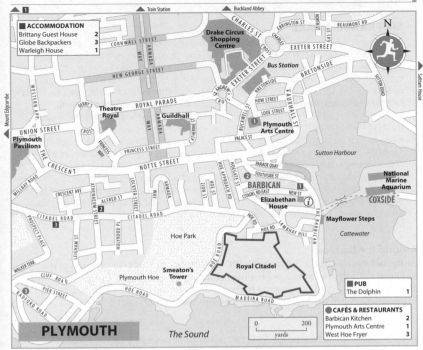

**6**

One of the best local excursions from Plymouth is to **Mount Edgcumbe**, where woods and meadows provide a welcome antidote to the urban bustle. East of Plymouth, the aristocratic opulence of **Saltram House** includes fine art and furniture, while to the north you can visit Francis Drake's old home at **Buckland Abbey**.

Spanish Armada in 1588, and 32 years later the port was the last embarkation point for the Pilgrim Fathers, whose New Plymouth colony became the nucleus for the English settlement of North America. The importance of the city's Devonport dockyards made the city a target in World War II, when the Luftwaffe reduced most of the old centre to rubble. Subsequent reconstruction has done little to improve the place, though it would be difficult to spoil the glorious vista over **Plymouth Sound**, the basin of calm water at the mouth of the combined Plym, Tavy and Tamar estuaries, largely unchanged since Drake played his famous game of bowls on the Hoe before joining battle with the Armada.

One of the best local excursions from Plymouth is to **Mount Edgcumbe**, where woods and meadows provide a welcome antidote to the urban bustle. East of Plymouth, the aristocratic opulence of **Saltram House** includes fine art and furniture, while to the north you can visit Francis Drake's old home at **Buckland Abbey**.

## Plymouth Hoe

A good place to start a tour of the city is **Plymouth Hoe**, an immense esplanade with glorious views over the water. Here, alongside various war memorials stands a rather portly statue of Sir Francis Drake, gazing grandly out to the sea. Appropriately, there's a bowling green back from the brow.

### Smeaton's Tower

Plymouth Hoe • Jan & Dec Sat 10am–3pm; Feb–March Tues–Sun 10am–3pm; April–Sept Tues–Sun 10am–4.30pm; Oct & Nov Tues–Sat 10am–3pm • £2.60 • ☎ 01752 304774, ⊕ plymouth.gov.uk

One of the city's best-known landmarks, the red-and-white-striped **Smeaton's Tower** was erected in 1759 by John Smeaton on the treacherous Eddystone Rocks, fourteen miles out to sea. When replaced by a larger lighthouse in 1882, it was reassembled here, where it gives lofty views across Plymouth Sound.

**6**

---

### SIR FRANCIS DRAKE

Born around 1540 near Tavistock, **Francis Drake** worked in the domestic coastal trade from the age of 13, but was soon taking part in the first English slaving expeditions between Africa and the West Indies, led by his Plymouth kinsman John Hawkins. Later, Drake was active in the secret war against Spain, raiding and looting merchant ships in actions unofficially sanctioned by Elizabeth I. In 1572 he became the first Englishman to sight the Pacific, and soon afterwards, on board the *Golden Hinde* (see p.85), became the first to **circumnavigate the world**, for which he received a knighthood on his return in 1580. The following year Drake was made mayor of Plymouth, settling in Buckland Abbey (see opposite), but was back in action before long – in 1587 he "singed the king of Spain's beard" by entering Cadiz harbour and destroying 33 vessels that were to have formed part of Philip II's **armada**. When the replacement invasion fleet appeared in the English Channel in 1588, Drake – along with Raleigh, Hawkins and Frobisher – played a leading role in wrecking it. The following year he set off on an unsuccessful expedition to help the Portuguese against Spain, but otherwise most of the next decade was spent in relative inactivity in Plymouth, Exeter and London. Finally, in 1596 Drake left with Hawkins for a raid on Panama, a venture that cost the lives of both captains.

---

## Around the Barbican

At the old town's quay at **Sutton Harbour**, the **Mayflower Steps** commemorate the sailing of the Pilgrim Fathers, with a plaque listing the names and professions of the 102 Puritans on board. Edging the harbour, the **Barbican** district is the heart of old Plymouth: most of the buildings are now shops and restaurants.

### Elizabethan House

32 New St • April–Sept Tues–Sat 10am–noon & 1–5pm • £2.60 • ☎ 01752 304774, ⓦ plymouth.gov.uk

New Street holds some of Plymouth's oldest buildings, among them the **Elizabethan House**, a captain's dwelling retaining most of the original architectural features, including a spiral staircase around what was probably a disused ship's mast. The three floors are crammed with fine sixteenth- and seventeenth-century furniture and textiles.

### National Marine Aquarium

Rope Walk • Daily: April–Sept 10am–6pm; Oct–March 10am–5pm; last entry 1hr before closing • £13.75 • ☎ 0844 893 7938, ⓦ national-aquarium.co.uk

Across the footbridge from Sutton Harbour, the **National Marine Aquarium** has recreated a range of marine environments, from moorland stream to coral reef and deep-sea ocean. The most popular exhibits are the seahorses, the colourful reefs and the sharks, though some of the smaller tanks hold equally compelling exhibits – the anemones, for example.

## Mount Edgcumbe

2 miles southwest of the city, across the River Tamar • **House** April–Sept Sun–Thurs 11am–4.30pm (last admission 4pm) • £7.20 • **Park** daily 8am–dusk • Free • ☎ 01752 822236, ⓦ mountedgcumbe.gov.uk • Bus #34 from Royal Parade to Stonehouse, then passenger ferry to Cremyll from Admiral's Hard (at least hourly; ⓦ cremyll-ferry.co.uk); alternatively, in summer take the direct motor-launch from the Mayflower Steps to Cawsand (ⓦ cawsandferry.co.uk), then 2hr walk to house

Lying on the Cornish side of Plymouth Sound and visible from the Hoe is **Mount Edgcumbe house**, a reconstruction of the bomb-damaged Tudor original, though inside the predominant note is eighteenth-century, the rooms elegantly restored with authentic Regency furniture. Far more enticing are the impeccable **gardens** divided into French, Italian and English sections – the first two a blaze of flowerbeds adorned with classical statuary, the last an acre of sweeping lawn shaded by exotic trees. The **park**, which is open all year, gives access to the coastal path and the huge **Whitsand Bay**, the best bathing beach for miles around, though subject to dangerous shifting sands and fierce currents.

## Saltram House

Near Plympton, 2 miles east of Plymouth off the A38 • **House** Mid-March to Oct daily except Fri noon–4.30pm • £10 (includes garden); NT • **Garden** Jan to mid-March & Nov–Dec daily 10am–4pm; mid-March to Oct daily 10am–5pm • £5.10 (or £10 with house) • Buses #19 or #21 from Royal Parade to Cot Hill, from where it's a walk of a mile or so (signposted) • ☎ 01752 333500, ⓦ nationaltrust.org.uk/saltram

The remodelled Tudor **Saltram House** is Devon's largest country house, featuring work by architect Robert Adam and fourteen portraits by **Joshua Reynolds**, who was born in nearby Plympton. The showpiece is the Saloon, a fussy but exquisitely furnished room dripping with gilt and plaster, and set off by a huge Axminster carpet especially woven for it in 1770. Saltram's landscaped **garden** provides a breather from this riot of interior design.

6

## Buckland Abbey

9 miles north of Plymouth • Mid-Feb to mid-March & early Dec to late Dec daily 11.30am–4.30pm; mid-March to Oct daily 10.30am–5.30pm; Nov Fri–Sun 11.30am–4.30pm • £9.05, grounds only £5; NT • From Plymouth, take #83 or "Blue Flash" service #12 to Tavistock, changing at Yelverton for #55 • ☎ 01822 853607, ⓦ nationaltrust.org.uk/buckland-abbey

Close to the River Tavy and on the edge of Dartmoor, **Buckland Abbey** was once the most westerly of England's Cistercian abbeys. After its dissolution, Buckland was converted to a family home by the privateer Richard Grenville (cousin of Walter Raleigh), from whom the estate was acquired by Francis Drake in 1582, the year after he became mayor of Plymouth. It remained Drake's home until his death, though the house reveals few traces of his residence. There are, however, numerous maps, portraits and mementos of his buccaneering exploits on show, most famous of which is Drake's Drum, which was said to beat a supernatural warning of impending danger to the country. More eye-catching are the oak-panelled **Great Hall**, previously the nave of the abbey, and, in the majestic grounds, a fine fourteenth-century **monastic barn**.

### ARRIVAL AND INFORMATION

### PLYMOUTH

**By train** Plymouth's train station is a mile north of the Hoe off Saltash Road. Frequent buses run between the station and the city centre.

Destinations Bodmin (every 30min–1hr; 45min); Exeter (every 20min–1hr; 1hr); Liskeard (every 30min–1hr; 30min); Par (every 30min–1hr; 50min); Penzance (every 30min–1hr; 2hr); Truro (every 30min–1hr; 1hr 20min).

**By bus** Buses pull in at the Bretonside bus station, just over St Andrew's Cross from Royal Parade.

Destinations Bodmin (hourly; 1hr 25min); Exeter (every

1–2hr; 1hr 15min–1hr 50min); Falmouth (2 daily; 2hr 30min); Newquay (hourly; 2hr); Penzance (5–6 daily; 3hr–3hr 30min); St Austell (4 daily; 1hr 20min); St Ives (3 daily; 3hr–3hr 30min); Torquay (Mon–Sat hourly, Sun 8 daily; 1hr 20min–2hr); Truro (5 daily; 2hr).

**Tourist office** The tourist office is off Sutton Harbour at 3–5 The Barbican (April–Oct Mon–Sat 9am–5pm, Sun 10am–4pm; Nov–March Mon–Fri 9am–5pm, Sat 10am–4pm; ☎ 01752 306330, ⓦ visitplymouth.co.uk).

### ACCOMMODATION

**Brittany Guest House** 28 Athenaeum St ☎ 01752 262247, ⓦ brittanyguesthouse.co.uk. A good choice on this row close to the Barbican, with all rooms en suite. The easy-going owners offer a choice of breakfasts, and there's even a car park (a definite bonus in these parts). **£60**

**Globe Backpackers** 172 Citadel Rd ☎ 01752 225158, ⓦ plymouthbackpackers.co.uk. Relaxed hostel west of the Hoe, with kitchen, free tea and coffee, free wi-fi and a courtyard garden. It's a bit run-down, but clean enough.

Book ahead during the summer. Dorms **£16.50**; doubles **£38**

**Warleigh House** 5 miles northwest of the centre on Horsham Lane ☎ 07971 220152, ⓦ warleighhouse.co.uk. Beautifully furnished country house on the banks of the River Tavy, parts of which date back to the twelfth century, offering top-quality bed and breakfast accommodation. Two of the three rooms have four-poster beds, and all come with their own flatscreen TV and iPod dock. **£168**

### EATING AND DRINKING

**Barbican Kitchen** 60 Southside St ☎ 01752 604448, ⓦ barbicankitchen.com. Modern decor, tasty food and a casual ambience draw the crowds at this bistro, housed in the ancient Black Friars Distillery. Choose from a varied

menu that runs from sausage and mash to steak medallions (£10–19). There are some decent veggie options too. Mon–Thurs noon–2.30pm & 5–9.30pm, Fri & Sat noon–2.30pm & 5–10pm, Sun noon–3pm & 6–9pm.

**The Dolphin** 14 The Barbican ☎01752 660876. A local institution, this harbourside pub has an authentic atmosphere and Tribute and Bass ales straight from the barrel. Look out for the pictures by Beryl Cook, who used to drink here. Mon–Thurs 10am–11pm, Fri & Sat 10am–midnight, Sun 11am–11.30pm.

**Plymouth Arts Centre** 38 Looe St ☎01752 206114, ⓦplymouthartscentre.org. Exhibitions, films and performances are held here, and there's a very good restaurant run by one of Jamie Oliver's students, serving home-made burgers and fish dishes (from £10). Restaurant Tues–Sat 10am–11pm.

**West Hoe Fryer** 7 Radford Rd ☎01752 221409. It doesn't get much simpler than this: an old-style fish shop with a queue for takeaway orders on one side and tables on the other. Locals flock here for the chips (from £1.80), wrapped up with extras like pickled eggs and cockles. Mon–Sat noon–2pm & 5–9pm.

# Dartmoor

Occupying the main part of the county between Exeter and Plymouth, **DARTMOOR** is southern England's greatest expanse of wilderness, some 368 square miles of raw granite, barren bogland, sparse grass and heather-grown moor. It was not always so desolate, as testified by the remnants of scattered Stone Age settlements and the ruined relics of the area's nineteenth-century tin-mining industry. Today desultory flocks of sheep and groups of ponies are virtually the only living creatures to be seen wandering over the central fastnesses of the National Park, with solitary birds – buzzards, kestrels, pipits, stonechats and wagtails – wheeling and hovering high above.

The core of Dartmoor, characterized by tumbling streams and high tors chiselled by the elements, is **Dartmoor Forest**, which has belonged to the Duchy of Cornwall since 1307, though there is almost unlimited public access. Networks of signposts or painted stones exist to guide **walkers**, but map-reading abilities are a prerequisite for any but the shortest walks, and considerable experience is essential for longer distances. Overnight parking is only allowed in authorized places, and no vehicles are permitted beyond fifteen yards from the road; camping should be out of sight of houses and roads, and fires are strictly forbidden. Information on **guided walks** and riding facilities is available from National Park visitor centres and tourist offices in Dartmoor's major towns and villages.

## Princetown

**PRINCETOWN** owes its growth to the presence of Dartmoor Prison, a high-security jail originally constructed for POWs captured in the Napoleonic Wars. The grim presence seeps into the village, some of whose functional grey stone houses – as well as the parish church of St Michael – were built by French and American prisoners. The best of the surrounding countryside lies immediately to the north.

---

### WALKING ON DARTMOOR

**Walking** is the best way to experience the moor. Broadly speaking, the gentler contours of the southern moor provide less strenuous rambles, while the harsher northern tracts require more skill and stamina. The web of paths links up with some of Devon's long-distance trails, such as the **Dartmoor Way**, **Tarka Trail**, **Templer Way** and the **Two Moors Way**. Information on these and a range of shorter hikes can be found at ⓦdartmoor-npa.gov.uk and ⓦdevon.gov .uk, while more detailed itineraries are available from local bookshops and tourist offices. An extensive programme of **guided walks**, varying from two to six hours (£5), is listed in the *Dartmoor Visitor Guide* and on the National Park's website.

Few walks are signposted or waymarked, so **map-reading** abilities and a compass are prerequisites for all but the shortest of strolls – the 1:25,000 Ordnance Survey *Explorer* map OL28 should suffice. Waterproof clothing is also essential.

Beware of **firing schedules** in the northwest quadrant of the moor (see box, p.337).

---

6

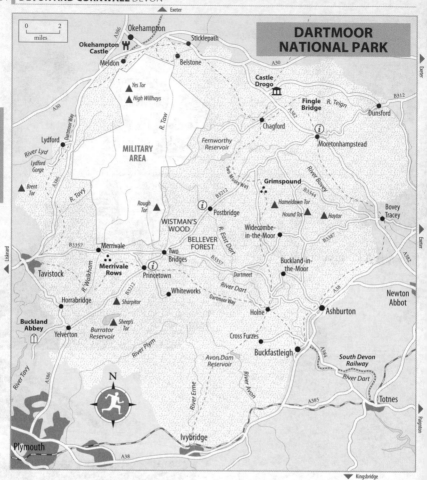

## Postbridge and around

Northeast of Princetown, two miles north of the crossroads at **Two Bridges**, you can see one of Dartmoor's **clapper bridges**: used by tin miners and farmers since medieval times, these simple structures consist of huge slabs of granite supported by piers of the same material. The largest and best preserved of these is three miles northeast at **POSTBRIDGE**. From here, you can head south through **Bellever Forest** to the open moor, where **Bellever Tor** (1453ft) affords outstanding views. North of Two Bridges, the dwarfed and misshapen oaks of **Wistman's Wood** are an evocative relic of the original Dartmoor Forest, cluttered with lichen-covered boulders and a dense undergrowth of ferns. The gnarled old trees are alleged to have been the site of druidic gatherings, a story unsupported by any evidence but quite plausible in this solitary spot.

## Grimspound

3 miles northeast of Postbridge, off the B3212 • Open access • Free

The Bronze Age village of **Grimspound** lies below Hameldown Tor, about a mile off the road. Inhabited some three thousand years ago, this is the most complete example of Dartmoor's prehistoric settlements, consisting of 24 circular huts scattered within a four-acre enclosure. The site is thought to have been the model for the Stone Age settlement in which Sherlock Holmes camped in *The Hound of the Baskervilles*; while **Hound Tor**, an outcrop three miles to the southwest, provided inspiration for Conan Doyle's tale – according to local legend, phantom hounds were sighted racing across the moor to hurl themselves on the tomb of a hated squire following his death in 1677.

## The southeastern moor

Four miles east of the crossroads at Two Bridges, crowds home in on the beauty spot of **Dartmeet**, where the valley is memorably lush and you don't need to walk far to leave the car park and ice-cream vans behind. From here the Dart pursues a leisurely course, joined by the River Webburn near the pretty moorland village of **BUCKLAND-IN-THE-MOOR**, one of a cluster of moorstone-and-thatched hamlets on this southeastern side of the moor. South of Buckland, the village of **HOLNE** is another rustic idyll surrounded on three sides by wooded valleys. Two and a half miles north of Buckland, **WIDECOMBE-IN-THE-MOOR** is set in a hollow amid high granite-strewn ridges. Its church of **St Pancras** provides a famous local landmark, its pinnacled tower dwarfing the fourteenth-century main building, whose interior includes a beautiful painted rood screen.

## The northeastern moor

On Dartmoor's northeastern edge, the market town of **MORETONHAMPSTEAD** makes an attractive entry point from Exeter. Moretonhampstead has a historic rivalry with neighbouring **CHAGFORD**, a Stannary town (a chartered centre of the tin trade) that also flourished from the local wool industry. It stands on a hillside overlooking the River Teign, and has a fine fifteenth-century church and some good accommodation and eating options. Numerous **walks** can be made along the Teign and elsewhere in the vicinity.

### Castle Drogo

2.5 miles northeast of Chagford across the A382, near Drewsteignton • **House** Late Feb to mid-March daily 11am–4pm; mid-March to Oct daily 11am–5pm; Nov to mid-Dec Sat & Sun noon–4pm • £8.70 (includes grounds); NT • **Grounds** Daily: Jan to mid-March 11am–4.30pm; mid-March to Oct 9am–5.30pm; Nov & Dec 11am–4.30pm • £5.50 • Bus #173 from Exeter's bus station stops outside the castle (Mon–Sat only; 50min) • ☎ 01647 433306, ⊕ nationaltrust.org.uk/castle-drogo

The twentieth-century extravaganza of **Castle Drogo** is stupendously sited above the Teign gorge northeast of Chagford. Having retired at the age of 33, grocery magnate Julius Drewe unearthed a link that suggested his descent from a Norman baron, and set about creating a castle befitting his pedigree. Begun in 1910, to a design by **Edwin Lutyens**, it was not completed until 1930, but the result was an unsurpassed synthesis of medieval and modern elements. Paths lead from Drogo east to **Fingle Bridge**, a lovely spot, where shaded green pools shelter trout and the occasional salmon. At the time of writing, the castle was undergoing extensive renovation work but remained open to the public, giving visitors a rare chance to see rooms that had long been hidden from view.

## Okehampton

The main centre on the northern fringes of Dartmoor, **OKEHAMPTON** grew prosperous as a market town for the medieval wool trade, and some fine old buildings survive between the two branches of the River Okement that meet here, among them the prominent fifteenth-century tower of the **Chapel of St James**. Across the road from the seventeenth-century town hall, a granite archway leads into the **Museum of Dartmoor Life** (April–Oct Mon–Fri 10.15am–4.15pm, Sat 10.15am–1pm; £2.50; ☎ 01837 52295, ⊕ museumofdartmoorlife.org.uk), which offers an excellent overview of habitation on the moor since earliest times.

**6**

## Okehampton Castle

A mile southwest of Okehampton · Daily: April–June & Sept–Oct 10am–5pm; July & Aug 10am–6pm · £4; EH · ☎ 01837 52844, ⓦ english-heritage.org.uk

Perched above the West Okement, **Okehampton Castle** is the shattered hulk of a stronghold laid waste by Henry VIII. The tottering ruins include a gatehouse, Norman keep, and the remains of the Great Hall, buttery and kitchens. Woodland walks and riverside picnic tables invite a gentle exploration of what was once the deer park of the earls of Devon.

## The western moor

Southwest from Princetown, walkers can trace the grassy path of the defunct rail line to **Burrator Reservoir**, four miles away; flooded in the 1890s to provide water for Plymouth, this is the biggest stretch of water on Dartmoor. The wooded lakeside teems with wildlife, and the boulder-strewn slopes are overlooked by the craggy peaks of **Sharpitor** (1312ft) and **Sheep's Tor** (1150ft). From here, the best walk is to strike northwest to meet the valley of the **River Walkham**, which rises in a peat bog at Walkham Head, five miles north of Princetown, then scurries through moorland and woods to join the River Tavy at Double Waters, two miles south of Tavistock.

### Merrivale

The River Tavy crosses the B3357 Tavistock road four miles west of Princetown at **MERRIVALE**, a tiny settlement amounting to little more than a pub. Merrivale makes another good starting point for moorland walks – it's only half a mile west of one of Dartmoor's most important prehistoric sites, the **Merrivale Rows**. These upright stones form a stately procession, stretching 850ft across the bare landscape. Dating from between 2500 BC and 750 BC, they are probably connected with burial rites.

## Lydford

Five miles southwest of Okehampton, the village of **LYDFORD** preserves the sturdy but small-scale **Lydford Castle** (daylight hours; free), a Saxon outpost, then a Norman keep and later used as a prison. The chief attraction here, though – apart from the hotels and restaurants – is the one-and-a-half-mile **Lydford Gorge** (March–Oct daily 10am–5pm; £6.90; NT; ☎ 01822 820320, ⓦ nationaltrust.org.uk/lydford-gorge), overgrown with thick woods and alive with butterflies, spotted woodpeckers, dippers and herons.

## Tavistock and around

The main town of the western moor, **TAVISTOCK** owes its distinctive Victorian appearance to the building boom that followed the discovery of copper deposits here in 1844. Originally, however, this market and Stannary town on the River Tavy grew around what was once the West Country's most important Benedictine abbey, established in the eleventh century. Some scant remnants survive in the churchyard of **St Eustace**, a mainly fifteenth-century building with stained glass from William Morris's studio in the south aisle.

North of Tavistock, a four-mile lane wanders up to **Brent Tor**, 1130ft high and dominating Dartmoor's western fringes. Access to its conical summit is easiest along a path gently ascending through gorse on its southwestern side, leading to the small church of St Michael at the top.

---

| ARRIVAL AND DEPARTURE | DARTMOOR |
|---|---|

**BY TRAIN**

Between mid-May and mid-Sept, Okehampton has a useful Sunday rail connection with Exeter (Sun 5 daily; 45min). The station is south of the centre, a 15min walk up Station Road from Fore Street.

**BY BUS**

Destinations from Princetown Exeter (late-May to mid-Sept Sat & Sun 1 daily; 1hr 30min); Moretonhampstead (late May to mid-Sept Sat & Sun 1 daily; 45min); Tavistock (Mon–Sat 1–3 daily; 30min).

Destinations from Moretonhampstead Chagford (Mon–Sat 3 daily; 15min); Exeter (5–7 daily; 50min); Okehampton (Mon–Sat 1 daily; 1hr); Princetown (late May to mid-Sept Sat & Sun 1 daily; 45min).

Destinations from Chagford Exeter (Mon–Sat 5 daily; 1hr); Moretonhampstead (Mon–Sat 3 daily; 15min); Okehampton (Mon–Sat 5 daily; 50min).

Destinations from Okehampton Exeter (every 30min–1hr; 50min–1hr 15min); Okehampton (Mon–Sat 1 daily; 1hr); Tavistock (7–9 daily; 45–55min).

Destinations from Tavistock Okehampton (7–9 daily; 45–55min); Plymouth (Mon–Sat every 15–30min, hourly on Sun; 1hr) and Princetown (Mon–Sat 1 3 daily; 30min).

**6**

## GETTING AROUND

**By bus** Public transport is good to the main centres on the periphery of the moor – Okehampton, Tavistock, Moretonhampstead – but extremely sketchy for the heart of the moor. The best bets are the #82 "Transmoor Link" (late May to mid-Sept weekends only), between Tavistock and Exeter, taking in Princetown, Two Bridges, Postbridge and Moretonhampstead en route, and the #98 connecting Tavistock, Princetown, Two Bridges and Postbridge (Mon–Sat only).

## INFORMATION

**Princetown National Park Visitor Centre** Tavistock Road (March & Oct daily 10am–4pm; April–Sept daily 10am–5pm; Nov–Feb Thurs–Sun 10.30am–3.30pm; ☎01822 890414, ⓦdartmoor-npa.gov.uk).

**Postbridge National Park Visitor Centre** The Postbridge information centre is in the car park off the B3212. (March & Oct Thurs–Sun 10am–4pm; April–Sept 10am–5pm; Nov–Feb Thurs–Sun 10.30am–3.30pm; ☎01822 880272, ⓦdartmoor-npa.gov.uk).

**Moretonhampstead tourist office** New Street (Easter–Oct daily 9.30am–5pm; Nov–Easter Thurs–Sat 10am–4.30pm, Sun 11am–3pm; ☎01647 440043, ⓦmoretonhampstead.com)

## ACCOMMODATION AND EATING

Scattered **accommodation** options include several **camping barns**, which it's always wise to book ahead, particularly at weekends: call the numbers given in our reviews, or else the YHA, which administers them (☎0800 019 1700, ⓦyha.org.uk).

**22 Mill Street** Chagford ☎01647 432244, ⓦ22millst.com. This smart country restaurant offers top-quality modern European cuisine: two- and three-course menus cost £19/£24 for lunch, £36/£42 for dinner. They also have two luxury guestrooms. Wed Sat noon–2.30pm & 7–10pm. **£129**

**Castle Inn** Next to Lydford Castle ☎01822 820241, ⓦcastleinndartmoor.co.uk. Sixteenth-century inn where one of the en-suite rooms has its own roof terrace looking onto the castle (£95); there are also little cottage rooms and one with a four-poster. Free wi-fi. The oak-beamed, fire-lit bar provides good drinks and there's a beer garden and a restaurant. Daily noon–11pm; food served noon–9pm. **£70**

**Cyprian's Cot** 47 New St Chagford ☎01647 432256, ⓦcyprianscot.co.uk. Comfy, sixteenth-century cottage where you can warm your bones by an inglenook fireplace and in fine weather breakfast and take tea in the garden. Worth booking ahead during summer. **£70**

★**Dartmoor Inn** A386, opposite Lydford turning ☎01822 820221, ⓦdartmoorinn.com. Three spacious guest rooms available above a popular gastropub, each furnished with antiques from France and England. The restaurant menu features tasty options like beetroot risotto and slow-roasted pork belly (mains £11–23) and there's a set menu for Sun lunch (£24 for three courses). Booking advised. Tues–Sat noon–3pm & 6–9pm; Sun noon–3pm. **£100**

**Duchy House** Tavistock Rd, Princetown ☎01822 890552, ⓦduchyhouse.co.uk. Some 300yd from the centre of Princetown, this Victorian B&B offers staid but reliable accommodation in traditionally furnished rooms – one with its own bathroom – and a guests' lounge. **£70**

---

### FIRING RANGES ON DARTMOOR

A significant portion of northern Dartmoor, containing the moor's highest tors and some of its most famous beauty spots, is run by the **Ministry of Defence**, whose **firing ranges** are marked by red-and-white posts; when firing is in progress, red flags or red lights signify that entry is prohibited. Generally, if no warning flags are flying by 9am between April and Sept, or by 10am from Oct to March, there will be no firing on that day; alternatively, check at ☎0800 458 4868 or ⓦmod.uk/access.

**6**

**Great Houndtor camping barn** Near Manaton ☎08000 191700, ⓦyha.org.uk. This YHA-managed former farmhouse on the eastern edge of Dartmoor offers a cooking area and hot water for showers, and there's a wood burner – but be sure to bring your sleeping bag and other useful camping gear. Per person £7

**Higher Venton Farm** Half a mile south of Widecombe ☎01364 621235, ⓦventonfarm.com. A peaceful sixteenth-century thatched longhouse that was once home to the Dartmoor writer Beatrice Chase. The bedrooms are fine (the cheapest double shares a bathroom), and it's close to a couple of good pubs. £66

**Kestor Inn** Manaton ☎01647 221626, ⓦwww.kestorinn.com. A popular pub with walkers, serving hot food as well as local ales and ciders, and selling maps, provisions and walking guides. There are en-suite rooms available here too, some with good views. Daily 11am–11pm; food served noon–2pm (Sun till 4pm) & 6.30–9pm. £85

**Meadowlea** 65 Station Rd, Okehampton ☎01837 53200, ⓦmeadowleaguesthouse.co.uk. A short walk south of the centre, below the train station and within 550yd of the Granite Way cycling route, this bike-friendly B&B has seven rooms (four en suite), wi-fi access and cycle storage. £65

★**Mount Tavy Cottage** Half a mile east of Tavistock on the B3357 (Princetown road) ☎01822 614253, ⓦmounttavy.co.uk. Set on a beautiful plot with its own lake, this B&B in a former gardener's cottage has comfortable rooms, organic breakfasts, evening meals and a few self-catering options. £75

**Plume of Feathers** The Square, Princetown ☎01822 890240, ⓦtheplumeoffeathersdartmoor.co.uk. B&B, bunkhouse dorms and a campsite right in the centre of Princetown. Reasonably priced meals are available here, with most mains going for around a tenner. Dorms £18; doubles £75; camping per person £7

**Sparrowhawk Backpackers** 45 Ford St, Moretonhampstead ☎01647 440318, ⓦsparrowhawkbackpackers.co.uk. Excellent, eco-minded hostel with fourteen beds in a light and spacious bunkroom and a private room sleeping up to four. Good kitchen for self-catering. Dorms £17; double £38

**Warren House Inn** 2 miles northeast of Postbridge ☎01822 880208, ⓦwarrenhouseinn.co.uk. Set in a bleak tract of moorland, this solitary pub offers fire-lit comfort and very basic meals, including a steak and ale pie with chips and veg (£12). Easter–Nov Mon–Sat 11am–11pm, Sun 11am–10.30pm; Nov–Easter Mon & Tues 11am–3pm, Wed & Thurs 11am–10pm, Fri & Sat 10am–11pm, Sun noon–10pm.

**YHA Dartmoor** Bellever, near Postbridge ☎0845 371 9622, ⓦyha.org.uk. One of Dartmoor's two YHA hostels lies a mile or so south of Postbridge on the edge of the forest and on the banks of the East Dart River. By bus, take the daily #98 from Tavistock or Princetown (not Sun) or #82 from Princetown or Exeter (summer Sat & Sun only) to Postbridge and walk a mile. Dorms £21.50

**YHA Okehampton** Klondyke Rd, Okehampton ☎01837 53916, ⓦyha.org.uk. Housed in a converted goods shed at the station, this well-run hostel offers a range of outdoor activities as well as bike rental. Camping also available. Dorms £25; doubles £63; camping per person £6

# Barnstaple

**BARNSTAPLE**, at the head of the Taw estuary, makes an excellent North Devon base, well connected to the resorts of Bideford Bay, Ilfracombe and Woolacombe, as well as to the western fringes of Exmoor. The town's centuries-old role as a marketplace is perpetuated in the daily bustle around the huge timber-framed **Pannier Market** off the High Street, alongside which runs **Butchers Row**, its 33 archways now converted to a variety of uses. At the end of Boutport Street, the **Museum of Barnstaple and North Devon** (Nov to mid-March Mon–Sat 10am–4pm, mid-March to Oct Mon–Sat 10am–5pm; free; ☎01271 346747) holds a lively miscellany that includes a collection of the eighteenth-century pottery for which the region was famous. The museum lies alongside the Taw, where footpaths make for a pleasant riverside stroll, with the colonnaded eighteenth-century **Queen Anne's Walk** – built as a merchants' exchange – providing some architectural interest. It houses the **Barnstaple Heritage Centre** (April–Oct Tues–Sat 9.30am–4.30pm; Nov–March Tues–Fri 9.30am–4pm, Sat 10am–3.30pm; £3.50; ☎01271 373003), which traces the town's social history by means of reconstructions and touch-screen computers.

## ARRIVAL AND INFORMATION

**By train** Barnstaple's train station is on the south side of the Taw, a 5min walk from the centre. There are good connections with Exeter on the Tarka Line (Mon–Sat hourly, Sun 7 daily; 1hr 10min).

**6**

## THE TARKA LINE AND THE TARKA TRAIL

North Devon is closely associated with Henry Williamson's **Tarka the Otter** (1927), which relates the travels and travails of a young otter, and is one of the finest pieces of nature writing in the English language. With parts of the book set in the Taw valley, it was perhaps inevitable that the Exeter to Barnstaple rail route – which follows the Taw for half of its length – should be dubbed the **Tarka Line**. Barnstaple itself forms the centre of the figure-of-eight traced by the **Tarka Trail**, which tracks the otter's wanderings for a distance of more than 180 miles. To the north, the trail penetrates Exmoor (see p.308) then follows the coast back, passing through Williamson's home village of **Georgeham** on its return to Barnstaple. South, the path takes in Bideford (see p.341), and continues as far as Okehampton (see p.335).

Twenty-three miles of the trail follow a former rail line that's ideally suited to **bicycles**, and there are bike rental shops at Barnstaple and Bideford. You can pick up a *Tarka Trail* booklet and free leaflets on individual sections of the trail from tourist offices.

**By bus** The bus station is centrally located between Silver Street and Belle Meadow Road.
Destinations Bideford (every 10–20min; 30min); Croyde (every 30min; 30min); Exeter (up to 8 daily; 2hr);

Ilfracombe (every 20min; 40min).
**Tourist office** The local tourist office is inside the Museum of North Devon on The Square (Mon–Sat 10am–5pm; ☎01271 375000, ⍟staynorthdevon.co.uk)

### ACCOMMODATION

**Broomhill Art Hotel** Muddiford, 2 miles north of Barnstaple off the A39 ☎01271 850262, ⍟broomhillart.co.uk. Striking combination of gallery, restaurant and hotel where the rooms look onto a sculpture garden. Half-board only at weekends. __£75__
**The Old Vicarage** Barbican Terrace ☎01271 328504, ⍟oldvicaragebarnstaple.co.uk. This well-kept Victorian house has modern double and twin rooms, some with

freestanding bathtubs and all with good-sized beds. Handily, there's on-site parking too. __£82__
**Yeo Dale Hotel** Pilton Bridge ☎01271 342954, ⍟yeodalehotel.co.uk. Clean rooms in a converted Georgian merchant's house, just a short walk from the centre. The best ones (£125) are on the first floor, and there are cheaper doubles higher up – though taller visitors should beware the steeply sloping ceilings in these rooms. __£85__

### EATING AND DRINKING

**Old School Coffee House** 6 Church Lane ☎01271 372793. This well-preserved building from 1659 now houses a no-frills café/restaurant – nothing fancy, but brimming with atmosphere. The meals are a bit hit and miss but the coffee and cakes are good value (try a slice of the chocolate and raisin cake for 85p). Mon–Sat 9.15am–3pm.

**Terra Madre** Broomhill Art Hotel, Muddiford ☎01271 850262, ⍟broomhillart.co.uk. Bar meals, delicious, Mediterranean-style fixed-price lunches (Wed–Sun; £16) and dinners (usually Wed–Sat; £25) and high teas are served at this restaurant attached to a hotel and gallery (see above). Lunch Wed–Sun 12.30–1.30pm; dinner Wed–Sat 7.30–8.30pm; high tea Wed–Fri 2–4pm.

## Ilfracombe and around

The most popular resort on Devon's northern coast, **ILFRACOMBE** is essentially little changed since its evolution into a Victorian and Edwardian tourist centre. In summer, if the crowds of holiday-makers become oppressive, you can escape on a coastal tour, a fishing trip or the fifteen-mile cruise to Lundy Island (see box, p.342), all available at the small harbour. On foot, you can explore the attractive stretch of coast running east out of Ilfracombe and beyond the grassy cliffs of Hillsborough, where a succession of undeveloped coves and inlets is surrounded by jagged slanting rocks and heather-covered hills.

There are sandy **beaches** here, though many prefer those beyond **Morte Point**, five miles west of Ilfracombe, from where the view takes in Lundy. Below the promontory, the pocket-sized **Barricane Beach**, famous for the tropical shells washed up by Atlantic currents from the Caribbean, is a popular swimming spot.

**6**

## ARRIVAL AND INFORMATION

**By bus** Stagecoach bus #21 runs every 20–30min from/to Barnstaple (40min), Bideford (1hr 30min) and Braunton (30min) stopping at the St James Place Gardens in Ilfracombe, a short walk west of The Quay.

**Tourist office** The tourist office is at the Landmark

### ILFRACOMBE AND AROUND

Theatre, on the seafront (April–Sept Mon–Thurs 9am–5pm, Fri 10am–5pm, Sat & Sun 10.30am–4.30pm; Oct–March Mon–Fri 9.30am–4.30pm, Sat 10.30am–4.30pm; ☎01271 863001, ⓦvisitilfracombe .co.uk).

## ACCOMMODATION

**Collingdale** 29 St James Place ☎01271 867835, ⓦoceanbackpackers.co.uk. Attractive Victorian house with friendly owners, where six of the nine rooms look out over the harbour. There's also a small bar and a lounge to relax in. **£82**

**Ocean Backpackers** 29 St James Place ☎01271 867835, ⓦoceanbackpackers.co.uk. Excellent, central hostel that's popular with surfers. Dorms are mostly five- or

six-bed, there are doubles available, and there's a well-equipped kitchen and free wi-fi. Dorms **£17.50**; doubles **£45**

★**Westwood** Torrs Park ☎01271 867443, ⓦwest -wood.co.uk. In a quiet area a 10min walk from the centre (and just 5min from the coast path), this B&B is more like a boutique hotel, with original floors and ceilings, boldly decorated rooms and terrific views. **£95**

## EATING AND DRINKING

**Combe Cottage** 63 High St ☎01271 862605, ⓦcombecottage.co.uk. Along a busy part of the High Street, this dimly lit restaurant is a good choice for lunch during the day (cottage pie £7.85), or a tasty dinner in the evening, with bistro-style mains for around £13. There are only eight tables, so booking is advised. Tues–Thurs 9.30am–2.30pm, Fri & Sat 9.30am–2.30pm & 6pm to around 11pm, Sun 6pm to around 11pm.

**The Quay** 11 The Quay ☎01271 868090,

ⓦ11thequay.co.uk. By the harbour and with great sea views, Ilfracombe's most famous restaurant (co-owned by artist Damien Hirst, whose works are displayed) offers European-inspired dishes using local ingredients – deep-fried feta cheese fingers, for example, or roasted fillet of cod with pancetta. Most mains are around £16–22. Drinks and snacks are available daily in the relaxed ground-floor bar. Daily noon–2.30pm & 6–9.30pm; reduced hours in winter.

# Woolacombe and around

**Woolacombe Sands** is a broad, west-facing beach much favoured by surfers and families alike. At the more crowded northern end of the beach, a cluster of hotels, villas and retirement homes makes up the summer resort of **WOOLACOMBE**. At the quieter southern end lies the choice swimming and surfing spot of **Putsborough Sands**, whose flat, golden sands are often washed by sets of powerful waves, and the promontory of **Baggy Point**, where gannets, shags, cormorants and shearwaters gather from September to November.

South of here is **Croyde Bay**, another surfers' delight, more compact than Woolacombe, with stalls on the sand renting surfboards and wet suits. South again around the headland is **Saunton Sands**, a magnificent long stretch of wind-blown coast pummelled by seemingly endless ranks of classic breakers.

## ARRIVAL AND INFORMATION

**By bus** Bus #303 runs between Barnstaple and Woolacombe Sands, half a mile east of town (Mon–Sat 4–6 daily; 45min), whie bus #31 makes the 40min run between Woolacombe and Ilfracombe (Mon–Sat roughly hourly).

### WOOLACOMBE AND AROUND

**Tourist office** The Esplanade, Woolacombe (April–Oct Mon–Sat 10am–5pm, Sun 10am–3pm; Nov–March Mon–Sat 10am–1pm; ☎01271 870553, ⓦwoolacombetourism.co.uk).

## ACCOMMODATION

**North Morte Farm** Mortehoe, a mile north of Woolacombe ☎01271 870381, ⓦnorthmortefarm .co.uk. More peaceful than many of the campsites around here, this has panoramic sea views and access to Rockham Beach, though not much shelter. Mortehoe's pubs are a short walk away. Closed Nov–March. Per person **£9.25**

**Rocks Hotel** Beach Rd, Woolacombe ☎01271 870361, ⓦtherockshotel.co.uk. Woolacombe's best-value accommodation choice is this surfer-friendly place close to the beach, with smallish but smart, high-spec bedrooms and bathrooms, and a breakfast room styled like a 1950s American diner. Sea-view rooms cost an extra £10. **£79**

## SURFING IN NORTH DEVON

Devon's premier **surfing** sites are on the west-facing coast between Morte Point and the Taw estuary. The two extensive fine-sand beaches of **Woolacombe Sands**, to the north, and **Saunton Sands**, south, are long enough to accommodate masses of surfers (and they often do), but smaller **Croyde Bay**, sandwiched between them, does get congested in summer. **Equipment** is available to rent from numerous places in the villages of Woolacombe and Croyde or from stalls on the beach (around £8–12 for 4hr or £10–15/day for a board, £8 for 4hr or £10/day for a wet suit). You can see local surf reports and live webcams at ⓦ magicseaweed .com. If you find yourself without any waves, you can while away half an hour at the tiny **Museum of British Surfing** in Braunton, four miles east of Croyde (Mon & Wed–Sat 10am–4pm, Sun 10am–3pm; £4; ☏ 01271 815155, ⓦ museumofbritishsurfing.org.uk), which uses interactive exhibits and old boards to tell the story of British board riding – from the early "surf bathers" of the 1920s to today's fearless big-wave surfers.

**6**

**Woolacombe Bay Hotel** South St, Woolacombe ☏ 01271 870388, ⓦ woolacombe-bay-hotel.co.uk. This grand building just up from the beach once housed American troops training for the Normandy landings, and is now a tidy hotel with comfortable rooms, good leisure facilities (including an indoor pool) and a restaurant overlooking the water. **£97**

### EATING AND DRINKING

**Bar Electric** Beach Rd, Woolacombe ☏ 01271 870429. Friendly hangout that stays buzzing until late, with themed food nights and a long list of drinks and meals, including pizzas and pastas (all £10–12). Wed–Fri 5pm–midnight, Sat noon–midnight, Sun noon–3pm; food served Wed–Fri 5–9pm, Sat noon–3pm & 5–9pm, Sun noon–3pm.

**Blue Groove** Hobbs Hill, Croyde ☏ 01271 890111, ⓦ blue-groove.co.uk. As well as burgers, steaks and seafood, this modern village restaurant/bar offers a good range of international food, from Thai mussels to Greek sharing plates (most mains £10–13). Easter–Nov daily 9am–late, Dec Fri & Sat 9am–late.

★ **The Thatch** Hobbs Hill, Croyde ☏ 01271 890349, ⓦ thethatchcroyde.com. Perennially popular thatched pub in the centre of Croyde, worth visiting for its ice-cold local cider and enormous stacks of nachos (from £8.95). There's often live music on Fri nights, when the pub and its two big beer gardens get especially busy. Mon–Thurs 8.30am–11pm, Fri–Sun 8.30am–midnight.

# Bideford and around

Like Barnstaple, nine miles to the east, the handsome estuary town of **BIDEFORD** formed an important link in north Devon's trade network in the Middle Ages, mainly due to its **bridge**, which still straddles the River Torridge. Just northwest is the seafront village of Westward Ho!, which faces a broad, sandy beach blessed with fairly consistent swell. A couple of miles downstream from Bideford, the old shipbuilding port of **APPLEDORE**, lined with pastel-coloured Georgian houses, is worth visiting for a wander and a drink in one of its cosy **pubs**.

### ARRIVAL AND INFORMATION
### BIDEFORD AND AROUND

**By bus** One of the handiest bus routes here is #5B (Mon–Sat roughly every 2hr) which links Bideford with Barnstaple (30min) and Exeter (2hr 10min). Buses #21 and #21A (Mon–Sat roughly every 20min; hourly on Sun) make trips to Westward Ho! (20min) and Appledore (15min) respectively.

**Tourist office** In the Burton Art Gallery and Museum, Kingsley Road (Mon–Sat 10am–4pm, Sun 11am–4pm; ☏ 01237 477676, ⓦ burtonartgallery.co.uk).

### ACCOMMODATION AND EATING

**Hoops Inn** 5 miles west of Bideford along the A39 ☏ 01237 451222, ⓦ hoopsinn.co.uk. The building dates back to the thirteenth entury, but the food at this well-run pub is modern, with inventive dishes like sea bass with saffron potatoes and cockle sauce (£13.95). Mon–Sat 10am–11pm, Sun noon–10.30pm; food served all day.

**Westward Living** Cornborough Road, Westward Ho! ☏ 01237 238967, ⓦ themountbideford.co.uk. Ten top-notch self-catering properties set amid serene farmland, each sleeping two to six people. Several of the rentals come with their own private hot tub and one – a single-storey cottage – is specially adapted for wheelchair users. **£140**

**6**

## LUNDY

There are fewer than thirty full-time residents on **Lundy**, a tiny windswept island twelve miles north of Hartland Point. Now a refuge for thousands of marine birds, Lundy has no cars, just one pub and one shop – indeed little has changed since the Marisco family established itself here in the twelfth century, making use of the shingle beaches and coves to terrorize shipping along the Bristol Channel. The family's fortunes only fell in 1242 when one of their number, William de Marisco, was found to be plotting against the king, whereupon he was hung, drawn and quartered at Tower Hill in London. The castle erected by Henry III on Lundy's southern end dates from this time.

Today the island is managed by the Landmark Trust. Unless you're on a specially arranged diving or climbing expedition, **walking** along the interweaving tracks and footpaths is really the only thing to do here. The shores – mainly cliffy on the west, softer and undulating on the east – shelter a rich variety of **birdlife**, including kittiwakes, fulmars, shags and Manx shearwaters, which often nest in rabbit burrows. The most famous birds, though, are the **puffins** after which Lundy is named – from the Norse *Lunde* (puffin) and *ey* (island). They can only be sighted in April and May, when they come ashore to mate. Offshore, **grey seals** can be seen all the year round.

### ARRIVAL AND INFORMATION

**By boat** Between April and Oct, the *MS Oldenburg* sails to Lundy up to four times a week from Ilfracombe, less frequently from Bideford (around 2hr from both places; day returns £35, child £18, open returns £62). To reserve a place, call ☎ 01271 863636 or visit ⓦ lundyisland.co.uk (day returns are also booked from local tourist offices).

### ACCOMMODATION

**Self-catering** A number of idiosyncratic Landmark Trust properties are available for self-catering by the week. These range from eighteenth-century hideaways for two in a castle keep to weathered fishermen's cottages. They're hugely popular, so book well in advance through the Landmark Trust (☎ 01628 825925, ⓦ landmarktrust.org.uk).

**B&B** The Landmark Trust can occasionally organise accommodation on a bed and breakfast basis, with meals at the island's pub. £95

**Camping** Lundy has a small campsite (closed Nov–March; book two weeks ahead). Per person £12

## Clovelly

West along Bideford Bay, picturesque **CLOVELLY** was put on the map in the second half of the nineteenth century by two books: Charles Dickens' *A Message From the Sea* and *Westward Ho!* by Charles Kingsley, whose father was rector here for six years. The picture-postcard tone of the village has been preserved by strict regulations, but its excessive quaintness and the streams of visitors on summer days can make it hard to see beyond the artifice.

Beyond the **visitor centre**, where an entrance fee to the village is charged, the cobbled, traffic-free main street plunges down past neat, flower-smothered cottages. The tethered sledges here are used for transporting goods, the only way to carry supplies up and down the hill since they stopped using donkeys. At the bottom, Clovelly's stony beach and tiny harbour snuggle under a cleft in the cliff wall.

### ARRIVAL AND GETTING AROUND — CLOVELLY

**By bus** Bus #319 from Bideford Quay (Mon–Sat at least 2 daily; 35min) stops outside the visitor centre. The same buses then continue on to Hartland (15min).

**Land Rover service** If you can't face the return climb to the top of the village, make use of the Land Rover service that leaves from behind the *Red Lion* on the quayside (Easter–Oct 10am–5.30pm, roughly every 15min; £2.50).

### INFORMATION

**Tourist office** There's a visitor centre at the top of the village (daily 10am–4pm, summer school hols 9am–6pm; ⓦ clovelly.co.uk); an entrance fee to the village is payable here (£6.75).

### ACCOMMODATION AND EATING

**East Dyke Farmhouse** Higher Clovelly, near the A39 junction ☎ 01237 431216, ⓦ bedbreakfastclovelly .co.uk. Away from the old village, this 200-year-old building with a beamed and flagstoned dining room has guest rooms

with fridges and private bathrooms. No credit cards. **£70**
**Red Lion** The Quay ☎ 01237 431237, ⓦ clovelly.co.uk.
Of the village's two luxurious and pricey hotels, this one
enjoys the best position, right on the harbourside. It's got a
congenial bar and a formal restaurant specializing in super-
fresh seafood. **£150**

## Hartland and around

Three miles west of Clovelly, the inland village of **HARTLAND** holds little appeal, but the
surrounding coastline is spectacular. You could arrive at **Hartland Point** along minor
roads, but the best approach is on foot along the coast path. The jagged black rocks of
the dramatic headland are battered by the sea and overlooked by a solitary lighthouse
350ft up. South of Hartland Point, the saw-toothed rocks and near-vertical escarpments
defiantly confront the waves, with spectacular waterfalls tumbling over the cliffs.

### Hartland Abbey

1.5 miles west of Hartland • **Mansion** Easter to early Oct Sun–Thurs 2–5pm • £11 (includes grounds) • **Grounds** Easter–early Oct Sun–
Thurs 11.30am–5pm • £7 • ☎ 01237 441496, ⓦ hartlandabbey.com

Surrounded by gardens and lush woodland, **Hartland Abbey** is an eighteenth-century
mansion incorporating the ruins of an abbey dissolved in 1539. The Regency library has
portraits by Gainsborough and Reynolds, George Gilbert Scott designed the vaulted
Alhambra Corridor and outer hall, and fine furniture, old photographs and frescoes are
everywhere. A path leads a mile from the house to cliffs and a small, sandy bay.

#### ARRIVAL AND DEPARTURE                                    HARTLAND AND AROUND

**By bus** Stagecoach service #319 (Mon–Sat at least two
daily) links Hartland with Clovelly (15min), Bideford
(55min) and Barnstaple (1hr 25min).

#### ACCOMMODATION AND EATING

**2 Harton Manor** The Square, off Fore St ☎ 01237
441670, ⓦ twohartonmanor.co.uk. Small, friendly B&B
offering two rooms above an artist's studio — one en suite
with a four-poster. Organic, locally sourced and Aga-
cooked breakfasts are eaten in the flagstoned kitchen. **£80**
**Stoke Barton Farm** Stoke, half a mile west of Hartland
Abbey ☎ 01237 441238, ⓦ westcountry camping
.co.uk. Right by the fourteenth-century church of
St Nectan's, this working farm offers basic camping during

the summer. Closed Nov–Feb. Per person **£6.50**
**Woodview Campsite** 8 miles south of Hartland at
Little Youlstone ☎ 01288 331492, ⓦ woodview
campsite.co.uk. Although it's tough to reach along skinny
single-track roads, this very tidy campsite rewards with
great countryside views and a chance for some proper
peace and quiet. The toilets and showers are immaculately
clean, and there's free wi-fi onsite. Per person **£6**

# Cornwall

When D.H. Lawrence wrote that being in **Cornwall** was "like being at a window and
looking out of England", he wasn't just thinking of its geographical extremity. Virtually
unaffected by the Roman conquest, Cornwall was for centuries the last haven for a **Celtic
culture** elsewhere eradicated by the Saxons. Primitive granite crosses and a crop of Celtic
saints remain as traces of this formative period, and the Cornish language is present in
place names that in many cases have grown more exotic as they have mutated over time.

Cornwall's formerly thriving **industrial economy** is far more conspicuous than in
neighbouring Devon. Its more westerly stretches in particular are littered with the
derelict stacks and castle-like ruins of the engine houses that once powered the region's
**copper** and **tin mines**, while deposits of **china clay** continue to be mined in the area
around St Austell, as witnessed by the conical spoil heaps thereabouts. Also prominent
throughout the county are the grey nonconformist chapels that reflect the impact of
Methodism on Cornwall's mining communities. Nowadays, of course, Cornwall's most
flourishing industry is tourism. The impact of the holiday business has been uneven,

for instance cluttering **Land's End** with a tacky leisure complex but leaving Cornwall's other great headland, **Lizard Point**, undeveloped. The thronged resorts of **Falmouth**, site of the National Maritime Museum, and **Newquay**, the West's chief surfing and partying centre, have adapted to the demands of mass tourism, but its effects have been more destructive in smaller, quainter places, such as **Mevagissey**, **Polperro** and **Padstow**, whose genuine charms can be hard to make out in full season. Other villages, such as **Fowey** and **Boscastle**, still preserve an authentic feel, however, while you couldn't wish for anything more remote than **Bodmin Moor**, a tract of wilderness in the heart of Cornwall, or the **Isles of Scilly**, idyllically free of development. It would be hard to compromise the sense of desolation surrounding **Tintagel**, site of what is fondly known as King Arthur's Castle, or the appeal of the seaside resorts of **St Ives** and **Bude** – both with great surfing beaches – while, near **St Austell**, the spectacular **Eden Project** celebrates environmental diversity with visionary style.

## Looe

The southeast strip of the Cornish coast holds a string of compact harbour towns interspersed with long stretches of magnificent coastline. The first of these towns, **LOOE**, was drawing crowds as early as 1800, when the first "bathing-machines" were wheeled out; it was the arrival of the railway in 1879, though, that really packed its beaches. Though the river-divided town now touts itself as something of a shark-fishing centre, most people come here for the sand, the handiest stretch being the beach in front of East Looe. Away from the river mouth, you'll find cleaner water a mile eastwards at **Millendreath**.

### ARRIVAL AND INFORMATION                                    LOOE

**By train** Looe's train station is on the east bank of the river, on Station Road. There's a rail link from Liskeard to Looe (roughly hourly, not Sun in winter; 30min).
**By bus** Most buses to and from Looe stop on the eastern side of the bridge joining East Looe with West Looe.
Destinations Liskeard (Mon–Sat hourly, Sun every 2hr;

30min); Plymouth (Mon–Sat hourly, Sun 2 daily; 1hr 10min–1hr 35min); Polperro (Mon–Sat every 20min–1hr, Sun hourly; 30min).
**Tourist office** New Guildhall, Fore Street (April–Oct daily 10am–5pm; Nov–March daily 10am–3pm; ☎01503 262072, ⓦ visit-southeastcornwall.co.uk).

### ACCOMMODATION AND EATING

**Old Sail Loft** The Quay ☎01503 262131, ⓦ theoldsailloftrestaurant.com. This oak-beamed former warehouse offers the freshest seafood as well as meat-based dishes, such as lemon sole with crab and shellfish butter (£19) or a lamb shank with red wine and shallot sauce (£17). Mon & Wed–Sat noon–2pm & 6–8.45pm (last orders), Tues & Sun 6–8.45pm.
**Schooner Point** 1 Trelawney Terrace, West Looe ☎01503 262670, ⓦ schoonerpoint.co.uk. Just 100yd

from Looe Bridge, this family-run guesthouse has great river views from most of its good-value rooms, which include a single with a private shower. **£80**
**Shutta House** Shutta Rd ☎01503 264233, ⓦ shuttahouse.co.uk. A short walk outside the centre and just across from the station, this neo-Gothic ex-vicarage has clean, airy en-suite rooms, some with garden views, and free wi-fi. **£68**

## Polperro

Linked to Looe by frequent buses, **POLPERRO** is smaller and quainter than its neighbour, but has a similar feel. From the bus stop and car park at the top of the village, it's a five- or ten-minute walk alongside the River Pol to the pretty harbour. The surrounding cliffs and the tightly packed houses rising on each side of the stream have an undeniable charm, and the tangle of lanes is little changed since the village's heyday of pilchard fishing and smuggling. However, the influx of tourists has inevitably taken its toll, and the straggling main street – the Coombes – is now an unbroken row of tacky shops and food outlets.

## ARRIVAL AND DEPARTURE

**By bus** Polperro is served by frequent buses from Looe (Mon–Sat every 20min–1hr, Sun hourly; 30min) and Plymouth (Mon–Sat hourly; Sun 2 daily; 2hr).

## ACCOMMODATION, EATING AND DRINKING

**The House on the Props** Talland St ☎01503 272310, ⓦhouseontheprops.co.uk. Staying at this quirky B&B right on the harbour is a bit like being on a boat, with snug rooms, wonky floors and awesome views; there's also a tearoom and restaurant on board. One-night stays at weekends cost £10 extra. **£80**

**Penryn House** The Coombes ☎01503 272157, ⓦpenrynhouse.co.uk. Relaxed and friendly B&B with a country-house feel. The immaculately clean rooms are small but cosy – those at the back are quietest, but have no view. Parking available. **£75**

## EATING AND DRINKING

**Blue Peter** The Quay ☎01503 272743, ⓦthebluepeter .co.uk. Welcoming harbourside pub serving real ales and local scrumpy. The bar food is good (around £10 for fish and chips) and there's live music at weekends. Daily 11am–11pm; food served noon–3pm & 6–9pm.

# Fowey

The ten miles from Polperro west to Polruan are among south Cornwall's finest stretches of the coastal path, giving access to some beautiful secluded **sand beaches**. There are frequent ferries across the River Fowey from Polruan, affording a fine prospect of **FOWEY** (pronounced "Foy"), a cascade of neat, pale terraces at the mouth of one of the peninsula's greatest rivers. The major port on the county's south coast in the fourteenth century, Fowey finally became so ambitious that it provoked Edward IV to strip the town of its military capability, though it continued to thrive commercially, becoming the leading port for china-clay shipments in the nineteenth century.

Fowey's steep layout centres on the distinctive fifteenth-century church of **St Fimbarrus**. Below the church, the **Ship Inn**, which sports some fine Elizabethan panelling and plaster ceilings, held the local Roundhead HQ during the Civil War. From here, Fore Street, Lostwithiel Street and the Esplanade fan out, the **Esplanade** leading to a footpath that gives access to some splendid **coastal walks**. One of these passes Menabilly House, where **Daphne Du Maurier** lived for 24 years – it was the model for the "Manderley" of her novel *Rebecca*. The house is not open to the public, but the path takes you down to the twin coves of **Polridmouth**, where Rebecca met her watery end. The tourist office (see below) houses a small exhibition of Du Maurier's life and work, and can provide information on the eight-day **Fowey Festival** (☎01726 879500, ⓦfoweyfestival.com), which takes place each May, with literary workshops, comedy shows and concerts.

## ARRIVAL AND INFORMATION

**By bus** Fowey is easily accessible from the west, with buses #524 and #525 running from Par (Mon–Sat every 20–30min, Sun 5 daily; 20min) and St Austell (Mon–Sat every 20–30min, Sun 8 daily; 45min).

**By ferry** Fowey can be reached by ferry across the river every 10–15min daily from Bodinnick (foot passengers and vehicles) and Polruan (foot passengers only); tickets cost £1.70 for a foot passenger, £3.60–4.60 for a car and passengers (☎01726 870232, ⓦctomsandson.co.uk).

**Tourist office** 5 South Street (Mon–Sat 9.30am–5pm, Sun 10am–4pm; ☎01726 833616, ⓦfowey.co.uk).

## ACCOMMODATION AND EATING

**Coombe Farm** A mile southwest of town, off the B3269 ☎01726 833123, ⓦcoombefarmbb.co.uk. A 20min walk from town, this place provides perfect rural isolation – and there's a bathing area just 300yd away. Free parking. **£70**

**Old Quay House** 28 Fore St ☎01726 833302, ⓦtheoldquayhouse.com. Pricey harbourside hotel with eleven compact yet fresh-feeling rooms, some of which have balconies. The restaurant here, *Q*, serves plenty of fresh seafood. Daily 12.30–2.30pm & 7–9pm; **£180**

6

**Sam's** 20 Fore St ☎ 01726 832273, ⓦ samsfowey.co.uk. With a menu ranging from burgers (£8–14) to seafood (£11–15), this place has 1960s rock'n'roll decor and friendly service. It doesn't take bookings, so arrive early or be prepared to wait. There's a late-closing lounge bar upstairs. Daily noon–9pm (last orders).

## St Austell Bay

It was the discovery of china clay, or kaolin, in the downs to the north of **St Austell Bay** that spurred the area's growth in the eighteenth century. An essential ingredient in the production of porcelain, kaolin had until then only been produced in northern China. Still a vital part of Cornwall's economy, the clay is now mostly exported for use in the manufacture of paper, as well as paint and medicines. The conical spoil heaps left by the mines are a feature of the local landscape, the great green and white mounds making an eerie sight.

The town of **ST AUSTELL** itself is fairly unexciting, but makes a useful stop for trips in the surrounding area. Its nearest link to the sea is at **CHARLESTOWN**, an easy downhill walk from the centre of town. This unspoilt port is still used for china clay shipments, and provides a backdrop for the location filming that frequently takes place here. Behind the harbour, the **Shipwreck & Heritage Centre** (March–Oct daily 10am–5pm; £5.95; ☎ 01726 69897, ⓦ shipwreckcharlestown.com) is entered through tunnels once used to convey the clay to the docks, and shows a good collection of photos and relics as well as tableaux of historical scenes.

On either side of the dock, the coarse sand and stone **beaches** have small rock pools, above which cliff walks lead around the bay.

### ARRIVAL AND DEPARTURE                     ST AUSTELL BAY

**By train** St Austell is the main rail stop in southeast Cornwall, with regular services from/to Bodmin (every 30min–1hr; 20min) and Truro (every 30min–1hr; 20min); the station is off High Cross Street.

**By bus** Buses pull in next to St Austell's train station, off High Cross Street.

Destinations Bodmin (Mon–Sat hourly, Sun 4 daily; 50min); Charlestown (Mon–Sat roughly every 15min, Sun every 30min–1hr; 15–30min); Falmouth (2 daily; 1hr); Newquay (hourly; 50min); Plymouth (4 daily; 1hr 20min); Truro (Mon–Sat every 30min–1hr, Sun every 1–2hr; 1hr).

### ACCOMMODATION

**T'Gallants** Harbour Front, Charlestown ☎ 01726 70203, ⓦ t-gallants.co.uk. Elegantly furnished Georgian B&B at the back of the harbour with a variety of en-suite rooms. Those at the front, including one with a four-poster, have sea views and cost more than the others. **£75**

## The Eden Project

4 miles northeast of St Austell • Daily: April–Oct 9.30am–6pm; Nov–March 9.30am–3pm; last entry 1hr 30min before closing • £23.50, or £19.95 online, £19.50 if arriving by bus, by bike or on foot; tickets are valid for a year when registered as a donation • ☎ 01726 811911, ⓦ edenproject.com • Arriving by bus, the most useful services are #101 from St Austell train station (20min) and the #527 from Newquay (1hr 15min) and St Austell (25min)

Occupying a 160ft-deep crater whose awesome scale only reveals itself once you have passed the entrance at its lip, the **Eden Project** showcases the diversity of the planet's plant life in an imaginative style. Centre stage are the geodesic "**biomes**" – vast conservatories made up of eco-friendly Teflon-coated, hexagonal panels. One holds groves of olive and citrus trees, cacti and other plants usually found in the warm, temperate zones of the Mediterranean, southern Africa and southwestern USA, while the larger one contains plants from the tropics, including teak and mahogany trees, with a waterfall and river gushing through. Equally impressive are the **grounds**, where plantations of bamboo, tea, hops, hemp and tobacco are interspersed with brilliant displays of flowers. In summer, the grassy arena sees **performances** of a range of music – from Peter Gabriel to Ellie Goulding – and in winter they set up a skating rink.

# Mevagissey and around

**MEVAGISSEY** was once known for the construction of fast vessels, used for carrying contraband as well as pilchards. Today the tiny port might display a few stacks of lobster pots, but the real business is tourism, and in summer the maze of backstreets is saturated with day-trippers, converging on the inner harbour and overflowing onto the large sand beach at **Pentewan** a mile to the north.

Four miles south of Mevagissey juts the striking headland of **Dodman Point**, cause of many a wreck and topped by a stark granite cross built by a local parson as a seamark in 1896. The promontory holds the substantial remains of an Iron Age fort, with an earthwork bulwark cutting right across the point. Curving away to the west, elegant **Veryan Bay** holds a string of exquisite inlets and coves, such as **Hemmick Beach**, a fine place for a dip with rocky outcrops affording a measure of privacy, and **Porthluney Cove**, a crescent of sand whose centrepiece is the battlemented **Caerhays Castle** (mid-March to mid-June Mon–Fri noon–4pm, tours at 11am, 12.30pm and 2pm; gardens mid-Feb to mid-June daily 10am–5pm; last entry 1hr before closing; house £8, garden £8, combined ticket £13; ☎01872 501310, ⓦwww.caerhays.co.uk), built in 1808 by John Nash and surrounded by beautiful gardens. A little further on is the minuscule and whitewashed village of **Portloe**, fronted by jagged black rocks that throw up fountains of seaspray, giving it a good, end-of-the-road feel.

### Lost Gardens of Heligan

2 miles northwest of Mevagissey, near Pentewan • April–Sept daily 10am–6pm; Oct–March Mon–Fri 10am–5pm, Sun 11am–5pm; last entry 1hr 30min before closing • £11 • ☎01726 845100, ⓦheligan.com • Served by regular buses (#525 and #524) from Mevagissey (20min) and St Austell (35min)

A couple of miles north of Mevagissey lie the **Lost Gardens of Heligan**, a fascinating Victorian garden which had fallen into neglect and was resurrected by Tim Smit, the visionary instigator of the Eden Project (see opposite). A boardwalk takes you through a jungle and under a canopy of bamboo and ferns down to the Lost Valley, where there are lakes, woods and wild-flower meadows.

### ARRIVAL AND DEPARTURE                    MEVAGISSEY AND AROUND

**By bus** From St Austell's bus and train station, the #525 and #524 services leave for Mevagissey (Mon–Sat every 30min, Sun hourly; 25min), continuing to the Lost Gardens of Heligan (20min).

### ACCOMMODATION AND EATING

**Alvorada** 17 Church St ☎01726 842055. Small, family-run Portuguese restaurant with dishes such as *caldeirada* (fish stew) and *rojoes* (pork stew) costing around £16.50. Choose a fish dish and there's a chance it'll have been caught by the chef. Usually open from around 6.30pm until late: July & Aug daily; March–June & Sept Tues–Sat; Oct–Feb Thurs–Sat.

**Wild Air** Polkirt Hill, Mevagissey ☎01726 843302, ⓦwildair.co.uk. Away from the harbour crowds, this wi-fi-enabled B&B has three tastefully furnished rooms, all with en-suite or private bathrooms, and all enjoying lofty views over the harbour and coast. No children. **£80**

**YHA Boswinger** Boswinger, half a mile from Hemmick Beach and 3.5 miles southwest of Mevagissey ☎0845 371 9107, ⓦyha.org.uk. Set in a former farmhouse, this is a remote spot a mile from the bus stop at Gorran Churchtown (#G1 from St Austell and Mevagissey; Mon–Fri only). Kitchen and meals available. Groups only Nov–March. Dorms **£20.50**; doubles **£58**

# Truro

Cornwall's capital, **TRURO**, presents a mixture of different styles, from the graceful Georgian architecture that came with the tin-mining boom of the 1800s to its neo-Gothic cathedral and its modern shopping centre. It's an attractive place, not overwhelmed by tourism and with a range of good-value facilities.

## Truro Cathedral

St Mary's St • Mon–Sat 7.30am–6pm, Sun 9am–5pm • Free (£5 suggested donation) • Tours take place April–Oct Mon–Thurs 11am, Fri 11.30am; free • ☎ 01872 276782, ⓦ trurocathedral.org.uk

Truro's dominant feature is its faux-medieval **cathedral**, completed in 1910 and incorporating part of the fabric of the old parish church that previously occupied the site. In the airy interior, the neo-Gothic baptistry commands attention, complete with emphatically pointed arches and elaborate roof vaulting.

**6**

## Royal Cornwall Museum

River St • Mon–Sat 10am–4.45pm, last admission 45min before closing • £4.50 • ☎ 01872 272205, ⓦ www.royalcornwallmuseum.org.uk

Truro's **Royal Cornwall Museum** offers a rich and wide-ranging hoard that takes in everything from the region's natural history to Celtic inscriptions. If time is tight you could confine yourself to the renowned collection of minerals on the ground floor and the upstairs galleries holding works by Cornish artists including members of the Newlyn School.

### ARRIVAL AND INFORMATION                                    TRURO

**By train** The train station is just off Richmond Hill, a 10min walk west of the centre.

Destinations Exeter (at least hourly; 2hr 20min); Falmouth (every 30min; 20min); Liskeard (every 30min–1hr; 50min); Penzance (every 30min–1hr; 45min); Plymouth (every 30min–1hr; 1hr 20min).

**By bus** Buses stop centrally at Lemon Quay or near the train station.

Destinations Falmouth (Mon–Sat every 30min, Sun hourly; 35–50min); Newquay (Mon–Sat every 15min, Sun every 30min; 55min–1hr 25min); Penzance (Mon–Sat every 30min–1hr, Sun 9 daily; 1hr 45min); Plymouth (4–5 daily; 2hr 15min); St Austell (Mon–Sat every 30min–1hr, Sun every 1–2hr; 50min–1hr 15min); St Ives (Mon–Sat every 30min, Sun 1 daily; 1hr–1hr 35min); St Mawes (Mon–Sat 7 daily, Sun 3 daily; 1hr).

**Tourist office** Municipal Buildings, Boscawen Street (Mon–Sat 9am–5pm ☎ 01872 274555, ⓦ tourism .truro.gov.uk).

### ACCOMMODATION

**Bay Tree** 28 Ferris Town ☎ 01872 240274, ⓦ baytree -guesthouse.co.uk. Homely, restored Georgian house halfway between the train station and the town centre, with a friendly owner and shared bathrooms (one room has its own shower). Singles available. Advance booking recommended. No credit cards. **£60**

**Truro Lodge** 10 The Parade ☎ 07813 755210, ⓦ trurobackpackers.co.uk. Relaxed hostel in a large Georgian terrace house near the centre. There's a self-catering kitchen, a lounge and a nice veranda, plus free wi-fi. Dorms **£18**; singles **£30**; doubles **£45**

### EATING AND DRINKING

**One Eyed Cat** 116 Kenwyn St ☎ 01872 222122, ⓦ oneeyedcat.co.uk. In a converted chapel, this bar and brasserie has an incongruous setting, but the food, either tapas or more substantial meat and seafood dishes (*moules frites* £12.95), is good. Reservations essential at weekends. Mon–Fri noon–late, Sat & Sun 11.30am–late.

**Secret Garden Café** 15 Kenwyn St ☎ 01872 271540. Veggie, vegan and gluten-free delights await at this chilled daytime-only café. Super-healthy snacks include salads (from £4.95), and burgers made from beetroot and beans (£9.75). Cornish ciders and beers are available too. Mon–Sat 10.30am–4.30pm.

**Wig & Pen** 1 Frances St ☎ 01872 273208, ⓦ stauste llbrewery.co.uk. The pick of Truro's pubs serves St Austell ales and bar food, as well as brunches and cream teas, with some tables outside. Simple bar meals such as stuffed red peppers and seafood pancakes cost around £10. Smarter food is served at *Quills*, in the basement, with mains for £11–20. Mon–Thurs 11am–11pm, Fri & Sat 11am–midnight, Sun 11am–8pm; restaurant Tues–Sat 7–9pm.

# Falmouth

Amid the lush tranquillity of the **Carrick Roads** estuary basin, the major resort of **FALMOUTH** is the site of one of Cornwall's mightiest castles, **Pendennis Castle**, and of one of the country's foremost collections of boats in the **National Maritime Museum Cornwall**. The town sits at the mouth of the Fal estuary, at the end of a rail branch line from Truro and connected by ferry to Truro and St Mawes. Round Pendennis Point, south of the centre, a long sandy bay holds a succession of sheltered **beaches**: from the popular **Gyllyngvase Beach**, you can reach the more attractive **Swanpool Beach** by cliff path, or walk a couple of miles further on to **Maenporth**, from where there are some fine cliff-top walks.

## National Maritime Museum Cornwall

Discovery Quay • Daily 10am–5pm • £11.50 • ☎ 01326 313388, ⓦ nmmc.co.uk

Vessels from all around the world are exhibited in Falmouth's **National Maritime Museum Cornwall**. Of every size and shape, the craft are arranged on three levels, many of them suspended in mid-air in the cavernous Flotilla Gallery. Smaller galleries examine specific aspects of boat-building, seafaring history and Falmouth's packet ships, and a lighthouse-like lookout tower offers excellent views over the harbour and estuary.

## Pendennis Castle

Pendennis Head • April–Sept daily 10am–6pm; Oct daily 10am–5pm; Nov–Feb Sat & Sun 10am–4pm • £7; EH • ☎ 01326 316594, ⓦ english-heritage.org.uk

A few minutes' walk west of the National Maritime Museum, **Pendennis Castle** stands sentinel at the tip of the promontory that separates the Carrick Roads estuary from Falmouth Bay. The extensive fortification shows little evidence of its five-month siege by the Parliamentarians during the Civil War, which ended only when half its defenders had died and the rest had been starved into submission. Though this is a less-refined contemporary of the castle at St Mawes (see p.350), its site wins hands down, the stout ramparts offering the best all-round views of Carrick Roads and Falmouth Bay.

## ARRIVAL AND INFORMATION                                    FALMOUTH

**By train** The branch rail line from Truro (Mon–Sat every 30min, Sun 10 daily; 30min) stops at Falmouth Town, best for the centre, and Falmouth Docks, 2min away, near Pendennis Castle.
**By bus** Most buses stop on The Moor, close to the Prince of Wales Pier and just east of the High Street.
Destinations Helston (Mon–Sat hourly, Sun 2–4 daily;

50min); Penzance (Mon–Sat hourly, Sun 1 daily; 1–2hr); St Austell (2 daily; 1hr 10min); Truro (Mon–Sat every 30min, Sun hourly; 40–50min).
**Tourist office** Prince of Wales Pier (April–Oct Mon–Sat 9.30am–6pm, Sun 9.30am–5pm; Nov–March Mon, Tues & Thurs–Sat 10am–3pm; ☎ 01326 741194, ⓦ discoverfalmouth.co.uk).

## ACCOMMODATION

**Falmouth Lodge** 9 Gyllyngvase Terrace ☎ 01326 319996, ⓦ falmouthbackpackers.co.uk. Clean and friendly backpackers' hostel located a couple of mins' walk from the beach, with a sociable lounge and kitchen and free wi-fi. Dorms **£19**; doubles **£56**
**Falmouth Townhouse** Grove Place ☎ 01326 312009, ⓦ falmouthtownhouse.co.uk. Chic boutique hotel in a Georgian building just across from the Maritime Museum.

It's all highly designed, with a buzzing bar, spacious guestrooms and quirky bathrooms, though some rooms suffer from street noise at night. **£75**
**Royal Duchy Hotel** Cliff Rd ☎ 01326 313042, ⓦ royalduchy.co.uk. Big, seafront hotel with everything from fairly plain doubles and singles to a suite with sea views and its own luxurious lounge area. There are two bars here, along with a restaurant and a spa. **£194**

## EATING AND DRINKING

**Café Cinnamon** Old Brewery Yard ☎ 01326 211457. Wholefood, vegetarian and vegan café that offers lunchtime snacks and organic wines. Try the special salads and burgers, which change regularly, and leave room for tasty cakes (£3 a slice). Tues–Sat 10am–4pm.
**Chain Locker** Quay St ☎ 01326 311085. This harbourside drinker festooned with nautical bits and pieces offers real

ales and standard bar meals (£7–10), but its main asset is the outdoor seating – the perfect spot to while away an evening. Mon–Thurs & Sun 11am–11pm, Fri & Sat 11am–midnight; food served noon–9pm.
★**Espressini** 39 Killigrew St ☎ 07580 590248, ⓦ espressini.co.uk. Deliciously fresh croissants and sourdough sandwiches (£3.60) are available at this little

**6**

independent café, but it's really the coffee that makes it worth a visit: tasty, single-origin stuff from countries as diverse as Ethiopia, Nicaragua and Papua New Guinea. Mon–Sat 8am–6pm, Sun 10am–4pm.

**Gylly Beach Café** Gyllyngvase Beach ☎ 01326 312884, ⓦ gyllybeach.com. Cool beachside hangout serving everything from fish finger sandwiches to slow-braised lamb. Breakfast is served until 11.30am, lunch dishes cost £5–10, evening mains upwards of £13. Check the website for events and special meal deals. Daily 9am–late, reduced hours in winter.

## 6 St Mawes and around

Situated on the east side of the Carrick Roads estuary, the two-pronged **Roseland peninsula** is a luxuriant backwater of woods and sheltered creeks. The main settlement is **ST MAWES**, a tranquil old fishing port easily reached on ferries from Falmouth. Moving east from St Mawes, you could spend a pleasant afternoon poking around the southern arm of the peninsula, which holds the twelfth- to thirteenth-century church of **ST ANTHONY-IN-ROSELAND** and the **lighthouse** on St Anthony's Head, marking the entry into Carrick Roads. Two and a half miles north of St Mawes, the scattered hamlet of **ST JUST-IN-ROSELAND** holds the strikingly picturesque church of St Just, right next to the creek and surrounded by palms and subtropical shrubbery, its gravestones tumbling down to the water's edge.

### St Mawes Castle

Half a mile west of the quay • April–Sept daily 10am–6pm; Oct daily 10am–5pm; Nov–March Sat & Sun 10am–4pm • £4.60; EH • ☎ 01326 270526, ⓦ english-heritage.org.uk

At the end of the walled seafront of St Mawes stands the sister fort of Pendennis Castle, the small and pristine **St Mawes Castle**, built during the reign of Henry VIII to a clover-leaf design. The castle owes its excellent condition to its early surrender to Parliamentary forces during the Civil War in 1646. The dungeons and gun installations contain various artillery exhibits as well as some background on local social history.

### Trelissick Garden

6 miles north of St Mawes near the village of Feock • Daily: Jan to mid-Feb 10.30am–4pm; mid-Feb to Oct 10.30am–5.30pm; Nov & Dec 11am–4pm • £8.60; NT • The King Harry Ferry from the opposite side of the river (daily; every 20min) stops near here, as do ferries from Falmouth, St Mawes and Truro (in summer), and the #493 bus from Truro (not Sun) • ☎ 01872 862090, ⓦ nationaltrust .org.uk/trelissick-garden

On a spectacular site that was first settled in the Iron Age, **Trelissick Garden** is today celebrated for its hydrangeas and other Mediterranean species, and has a splendid woodland walk along the River Fal. There's also a café here, as well as a shop selling secondhand books.

### ARRIVAL AND GETTING AROUND
ST MAWES AND AROUND

**By bus** There are regular buses (#550 and #551) between Truro and St Mawes (Mon–Sat 7 daily, Sun 3 daily; 1hr 10min), stopping off at St Just-in-Roseland (7min from St Mawes) en route.

**By ferry** St Mawes can be reached on frequent ferries from Falmouth's Prince of Wales Pier and Custom House Quay (£8.10 return). Between March and Nov, passenger ferries from St Mawes also cross to the southern arm of the peninsula (daily 9am–5.30pm every 30min; £5.85 return).

**By car** By road, the fastest route from Truro, Falmouth and west Cornwall involves crossing the River Fal on the chain-driven King Harry Ferry (every 20min: April–Sept Mon–Sat 7.20am–9.20pm, Sun 9am–9.20pm; Oct–March Mon–Sat 7.20am–7.20pm, Sun 9am–7.20pm; £8 return per car; foot passengers and bicycles are transported free in exchange for a charity donation; ☎ 01872 862312 ⓦ falriver.co.uk).

> **TOP 5 DEVON AND CORNWALL RESTAURANTS**
>
> **Dartmoor Inn, Lydford** See p.337.
> **Tresanton Hotel, St Mawes** See opposite.
> **Porthminster Café, St Ives** See p.359.
> **Fifteen Cornwall, Newquay** See p.363.
> **The Seafood Restaurant, Padstow** See p.365.

## ACCOMMODATION AND EATING

**Nearwater** Polvarth Road, St Mawes ☏ 01326 279278. There's a subtle nautical theme running through this elegantly furnished B&B, which has three good-sized rooms. The shared lounge has an open fireplace, and when it's warmer, guests can relax in the garden. **£110**

★**Tresanton Hotel** St Mawes ☏ 01326 270055, ⓦ tresanton.com. Cornwall doesn't get much ritzier than this, a slice of Mediterranean-style luxury with bright, sunny colours and a yacht and speedboat available to guests in summer. There's a fabulous restaurant too, where you can have a snack lunch or full meal (mains £20–£35). Daily 12.30–2.30pm & 7.30–9.30pm. **£260**

6

# The Lizard peninsula

The **Lizard peninsula** – from the Celtic *lys ardh*, or "high point" – is mercifully undeveloped. If this flat and treeless expanse can be said to have a centre, it's **Helston**, a junction for **buses** running from Falmouth and Truro and for services to the spartan villages of the peninsula's interior and coast.

## Helston

**HELSTON** is best known for its **Furry Dance** (or Flora Dance), which dates from the seventeenth century. Held on May 8 (unless this falls on Sun or Mon, when the procession takes place on the preceding Sat), it's a stately procession of top-hatted men and summer-frocked women performing a solemn dance through the town's streets and gardens. You can learn something about it and absorb plenty of other local history in the eclectic **Helston Folk Museum** (Mon–Sat 10am–4pm; free; ☏ 1326 564027), housed in former market buildings behind the Guildhall on Church Street.

## Porthleven and around

Two and a half miles southwest of Helston, tin ore from inland mines was once shipped from **PORTHLEVEN**. Good **beaches** lie to either side: the best for swimming are around **Rinsey Head**, three miles north along the coast, including the sheltered **Praa Sands**. One and a quarter miles south of Porthleven, strong currents make it unsafe to swim at **Loe Bar**, a strip of shingle which separates the freshwater **Loe Pool** from the sea. The elongated Pool is one of two sites which claim to be the place where the sword Excalibur was restored to its watery source (the other is on Bodmin Moor). The path

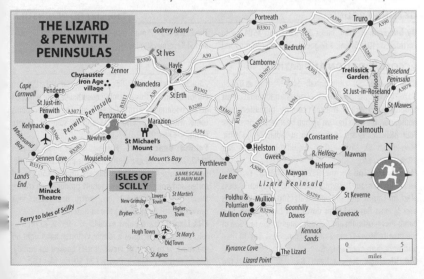

THE LIZARD & PENWITH PENINSULAS

running along the western edge of Loe Pool makes a fine walking route between here and Helston.

## Mullion and around

The inland village of **MULLION**, five miles south of Porthleven, has a fifteenth- to sixteenth-century church dedicated to the Breton **St Mellane** (or Malo), with a dog-door for canine churchgoers. A lane leads a mile and a quarter west to **Mullion Cove**, where a tiny beach is sheltered behind harbour walls and rock stacks, though the neighbouring sands at **Polurrian** and **Poldhu**, to the north, are better and attract surfers.

## Lizard Point and around

Four miles south of Mullion, the peninsula's best-known beach, **Kynance Cove**, has sheer 100ft cliffs, stacks and arches of serpentine rock and offshore outcrops. The water quality here is excellent – but take care not to be stranded by the tide. A little more than a mile southeast, **Lizard Point**, the southern tip of the promontory and mainland Britain's southernmost point, is marked by a plain lighthouse above a tiny cove and a restless, churning sea. If you're not following the coast path, you can reach the point via the road and footpath leading a mile south from the nondescript village called simply **THE LIZARD**, where you'll find several places to stay and eat.

## The east coast

In the north of the peninsula, the snug hamlets dotted around the **River Helford** are a complete contrast to the rugged character of most of the Lizard. On the river's south side, **Frenchman's Creek**, one of a splay of serene inlets, was the inspiration for Daphne Du Maurier's novel of the same name. From Helford Passage you can take a ferry (April–Oct, on demand; £6 return) to reach **Helford**, an agreeable old smugglers' haunt on the south bank.

South of here, on the B3293, the broad, windswept plateau of Goonhilly Downs is interrupted by the futuristic saucers of Goonhilly Satellite Station and the nearby ranks of wind turbines. Heading east, the road splits: left to **ST KEVERNE**, an inland village whose tidy square is flanked by two inns and a church, right to **COVERACK**, a fishing port in a sheltered bay. Following the coast path or negotiating minor roads south will bring you to the safe and clean swimming spot of **Kennack Sands**.

| GETTING AROUND | THE LIZARD PENINSULA |
|---|---|

**By bus** From Helston, buses #2, #251 and #504 go to Porthleven (10–15min), #37 goes to Mullion (30min) and The Lizard (45–55min), and #36 goes to Coverack (25min) and St Keverne (30min).

## ACCOMMODATION AND EATING

**Blue Anchor** 50 Coinagehall St, Helston ☎ 01326 562821, ⓦ spingoales.com. Deeply traditional West Country pub, once a fifteenth-century monastery rest house, now brewing its own Spingo beer on the premises. Four B&B rooms are available in an adjacent building. Mon–Thurs & Sun 10am–midnight, Fri & Sat 10am–1am. **£65**

**Mounts Bay Inn** On the B3296 in Mullion ☎ 01326 240221, ⓦ mountsbaymullion.co.uk. Mullion's best place for Cornish ales and pub meals (£10–15) with views over Mounts Bay and steps down to a beer garden. Live bands every fortnight and Cornish songs on the last Sun of the month. Mon–Thurs 11am–11pm, Fri & Sat 11am–midnight, Sun noon–11pm.

**Old Vicarage** Nansmellyon Rd, Mullion ☎ 01326 240898, ⓔ bandbmullion@hotmail.com. Facing an enclosed garden, this charming guesthouse once provided accommodation to Arthur Conan Doyle. The elegant rooms come with period furnishings and en-suite or private facilities. **£86**

**Poldhu Beach Café** Poldhu Cove, near Mullion ☎ 01326 240530, ⓦ poldhu.net. The perfect beach café, with energizing breakfasts, burgers (from £3.50), good coffee and hot chocolate, and locally produced ice cream. Daily 9.30am–4.30/5.30pm, with occasional late opening until 8pm during the summer.

**YHA Lizard** Lizard Point ☎ 0845 371 9550, ⓦ yha.org .uk. This hostel occupies a former Victorian hotel right on the coast, with majestic views. It gets booked up quickly. Groups only Nov–March. Dorms **£22.50**; doubles **£52**

# The Penwith peninsula

Though more densely populated than the Lizard, the **Penwith peninsula** is a more rugged landscape, with a raw appeal that is still encapsulated by **Land's End**, despite the commercialization of that headland. The seascapes, the quality of the light and the slow tempo of the local fishing communities made this area a hotbed of artistic activity from the late nineteenth century onwards, when the painters of Newlyn, near **Penzance**, established a distinctive school of painting. More innovative figures – among them Ben Nicholson, Barbara Hepworth and Naum Gabo – were soon afterwards to make **St Ives** one of England's liveliest cultural communities, and their enduring influence is illustrated in the St Ives branch of the **Tate Gallery**, which showcases the modern artists associated with the locality.

**6**

## Penzance

Occupying a sheltered position at the northwest corner of Mount's Bay, **PENZANCE** has always been a major port, but most traces of the medieval town were obliterated at the end of the sixteenth century by a Spanish raiding party. From the top of **Market Jew Street** (from *Marghas Jew*, meaning "Thursday Market"), which climbs from the harbour and the train and bus stations, turn left into **Chapel Street** to see some of the town's finest buildings, including the flamboyant **Egyptian House**, built in 1835 to contain a geological museum but subsequently abandoned until its restoration thirty years ago. Across the street, the seventeenth-century **Union Hotel** originally held the town's assembly rooms, where news of Admiral Nelson's victory at Trafalgar and the death of Nelson himself was first announced in 1805.

### Penlee House Gallery and Museum

Morrab Rd, west of Chapel St • Mon–Sat: Easter–Sept 10am–5pm; Oct–April 10.30am–4.30pm; last admission 30min before closing • £4.50, free on Sat • ☎ 01736 363625, ⓦ penleehouse.org.uk

Long a centre of the local art movements, **Penlee House Gallery and Museum** holds an important collection of **Cornish art**, notably works of the Newlyn School – impressionistic harbour scenes, frequently sentimentalized but often bathed in an evocatively luminous light. There are also displays on local archeology and history, and frequent exhibitions.

### Jubilee Pool

Seafront • Normally late May to early Sept daily 10.30am–6pm, but closed at the time of writing • ⓦ jubileepool.co.uk

On the seafront, bulging out of the Promenade into Mount's Bay, the Art Deco **Jubilee Pool** is a tidal, saltwater (though chlorinated) open-air swimming pool, built to mark the Silver Jubilee of George V in 1935. It was badly damaged by stormy weather in February 2014, and at the time of writing had still not been fully repaired – apparently due to a lack of funding.

### Newlyn Art Gallery

24 New Rd, Newlyn • April–Oct Mon–Sat 10am–5pm; Nov–March Tues–Sat 10am–5pm • Free • ☎ 01736 363715, ⓦ newlynartgallery .co.uk

From the Promenade, it's an easy 15–20min walk to **Newlyn**, Cornwall's biggest fishing port, lying immediately south of Penzance. The **art gallery**, near the harbour, merits a visit for its exhibitions of contemporary work, often curated by Cornish artists. Originally opened in 1895 and remodelled several times since, the gallery has a pleasant top-floor café with sea views.

---

**ARRIVAL AND DEPARTURE** | **PENZANCE**

**By train** Penzance's train station lies on the seafront, on Station Road.
**Destinations** Bodmin (at least hourly; 1hr 10min); Exeter (at least hourly; 3hr); Plymouth (at least hourly; 2hr); St Ives (most via St Erth; hourly; 25–45min); Truro (at least hourly; 40min).

**6**

**By bus** The bus station is next to the train station on the seafront.

Destinations Falmouth (every 1–2hr; 1hr–1hr 45min); Helston (Mon–Sat hourly, Sun 7 daily; 1hr); Plymouth (7 daily; 2hr 50min–4hr); St Austell (2–3 daily; 1hr 50min–2hr 20min); St Ives (Mon–Sat every 15–20min, Sun every 30min–1hr; 35–50min); Truro (Mon–Fri every 30min–1hr; Sun 8 daily; 40min).

**By boat** From Easter to Oct boats depart from Penzance Quay for St Mary's on the Isles of Scilly (Mon–Sat 4–6 weekly; 2hr 40min; ☎01736 334220, ⓦislesofscilly -travel.co.uk).

## ACCOMMODATION

**Abbey Hotel** Abbey St, off Chapel St ☎01736 366906, ⓦtheabbeyonline.co.uk. Pamper yourself at this homely, seventeenth-century hotel owned by 1960s model Jean Shrimpton and now run by her son. Lashings of old-fashioned comfort, books and antiques everywhere, and great views. **£130**

**Penzance Backpackers** Alexandra Rd, parallel to Morrab Rd ☎01736 363836, ⓦpzbackpack.com. One of the region's tidiest and most welcoming hostels, with en-suite dorms, a kitchen, lounge and laundry, and wi-fi. Dorms **£16**; doubles **£36**

**Warwick House** 17 Regent Terrace ☎01736 363881, ⓦwarwickhousepenzance.co.uk. Handily located near the centre of town and a short stroll up from the promenade, this popular B&B has clean rooms decorated in blue and white – the best ones have views of the water. **£92**

## EATING AND DRINKING

**Admiral Benbow** 46 Chapel St ☎01736 363448. Characterful pub crammed with gaudy ships' figureheads and other nautical items. The bar meals are pretty standard, but this is a drinking pub, and the atmosphere more than compensates. Daily 11am–11pm; food served noon–3pm & 6–9.30pm.

**Archie Browns** Bread St ☎01736 362828, ⓦarchiebrowns.co.uk. Vegans, vegetarians and wholefoodies will be happy in this café above a health shop, with its relaxed, friendly vibe and local art on the walls. Dishes include quiches, curries, stews and homity pie (£5–8). Mon–Sat 9am–5pm.

★ **Lost and Found** 16 Chapel St ☎07792 358110. Part antique shop, part café, *Lost and Found* is spread across several rooms, each brightened by old maps, instruments and other assorted curios. Sweet-toothed shoppers will love the cupcakes and tray bakes, which go for around £2.75 a pop. Tues–Fri 9.30am–5.30pm, Sat 10am–5.30pm.

**Harris's** 46 New St ☎01736 364408, ⓦharrissrestaurant.co.uk. Traditional fine dining at this formal restaurant, with the accent on seafood. Mains such as roast monkfish and grilled sole cost around £20. Be sure to leave room for one of the memorably good desserts. Mon 6.30–8.30pm, Tues–Sat noon–8.30pm.

## St Michael's Mount

Off Marazion, 5 miles east of Penzance • **House** April–June & Sept–Oct Mon–Fri & Sun 10.30am–5pm; July & Aug Mon–Fri & Sun 10.30am–5.30pm • £8, £10.50 with garden; NT • **Garden** Mid-April to June Mon–Fri 10.30am–5pm; July to late Aug Thurs & Fri 10.30am–5.30pm; Sept Thurs & Fri 10.30am–5pm • £5, £10.50 with house • At low tide the promontory can be approached on foot via a cobbled causeway (daily tide times on the website); at high tide there are boats from Marazion (£2) • ☎01736 710507, ⓦstmichaelsmount.co.uk

Frequent buses from Penzance leave for Marazion, five miles east, the access point to **St Michael's Mount**, a couple of hundred yards offshore. A vision of the archangel Michael led to the building of a church on this granite pile around the fifth century, and within three centuries a Celtic monastery had been founded here. The present building derives from a **chapel** raised in the eleventh century by Edward the Confessor, who handed it over to the Benedictine monks of Brittany's Mont St Michel, whose island abbey was the model for this one. Following the Civil War, it became the residence of the St Aubyn family, who still inhabit the castle. Some of the buildings date from the twelfth century, but the later additions are more interesting, such as the battlemented **chapel** and the seventeenth-century decorations of the **Chevy Chase Room**, the former refectory.

## Mousehole

Accounts vary as to the derivation of the name of **MOUSEHOLE** (pronounced "Mowzle"), though it may be from a smugglers' cave just to the south. In any case, the name evokes perfectly this minuscule fishing port cradled in the arms of a granite breakwater, three miles south of Penzance. The village attracts more visitors than it can handle, so hang around until the crowds have departed before exploring its tight tangle of lanes, where you'll come across Mousehole's oldest house, the fourteenth-century **Keigwin House**, a survivor of the sacking of the village by Spaniards in 1595.

## ARRIVAL AND DEPARTURE     MOUSEHOLE

**By bus** The #6 bus (Mon–Sat every 30min; hourly on Sun) connects Mousehole's harbour with Newlyn (10min) and Penzance (15min).

## ACCOMMODATION AND EATING

**6**

**Ship Inn** Harbourside ☎ 01736 731234, ⓦ shipmousehole.co.uk. Overlooking the boats, this is a perfect spot for a pint or a Ploughman's Lunch (£7.95) or Cornish fish pie (£12). Accommodation is available in surprisingly modern en-suite rooms, some in an annexe (those with a view cost extra). Mon–Sat 11am–11pm, Sun 11am–10.30pm; food served noon–2.30pm & 6–8.30pm. **£95**

## Porthcurno

Eight miles west of Mousehole, one of Penwith's best **beaches** lies at **PORTHCURNO**, sandwiched between cliffs. On the shore to the east, a white pyramid marks the spot where the first transatlantic cables were laid in 1880. On the headland beyond lies an Iron Age fort, **Treryn Dinas**, close to the famous rocking stone called **Logan Rock**, a seventy-ton monster that was knocked off its perch in 1824 by a gang of sailors, among them a nephew of writer and poet Oliver Goldsmith. Somehow they replaced the stone, but it never rocked again.

### Minack Theatre

South end of village • Exhibition Centre daily: April–Sept generally 9.30am–5.30pm, but may close at noon on Tues and Thurs when performances take place; Oct–March 10am–4pm; last entry 30min before closing • £4.50 • Theatre performances cost £9–11.50 • ☎ 01736 810181, ⓦ minack.com

Steep steps lead up from the beach of tiny white shells to the **Minack Theatre**, hewn out of the cliff in the 1930s and since enlarged to hold 750 seats, though retaining the basic Greek-inspired design. The spectacular backdrop of Porthcurno Bay makes this one of the country's most inspiring theatres (providing the weather holds) from mid-April to September, when a range of plays, operas and musicals are presented – bring a cushion and a rug. The attached **Exhibition Centre** gives access to the theatre during the day and explains the story of its creation.

## ARRIVAL AND DEPARTURE     PORTHCURNO

**By bus** Only one bus service – #1A – runs to and from Porthcurno, making up to three trips per day to Land's End (15min), Newlyn (25min) and Penzance (35min).

## Land's End

The extreme western tip of England, **Land's End**, lies four miles west of Porthcurno. Best approached on foot along the coastal path, the 60ft turf-covered cliffs provide a platform to view the Irish Lady, the Armed Knight, Dr Syntax Head and the rest of the Land's End outcrops. Beyond, look out for the Longships lighthouse, a mile and a half out to sea, and you can sometimes spot the Wolf Rock lighthouse, nine miles southwest, or even the Isles of Scilly, 28 miles away (see p.359).

## ARRIVAL AND DEPARTURE     LAND'S END

**By bus** Hourly buses run to and from the car park at Land's End, providing easy connections to Newlyn (40min) and Penzance (50min).

## Whitesand Bay

To the north of Land's End the rounded granite cliffs fall away at **Whitesand Bay** to reveal a glistening mile-long shelf of beach that offers the best swimming on the

Penwith peninsula. The rollers make for good surfing and boards can be rented at **Sennen Cove**, the more popular southern end of the beach.

## ARRIVAL AND DEPARTURE WHITESAND BAY

**By bus** Bus #1, which connects Penzance with Land's End, stops at Sennen Cove (3 daily Mon–Sat, 2 on Sun).

## ACCOMMODATION AND EATING

**Pengelly House** Sennen Cove ☎01736 871866, ⓦpengellyhouse.com. Guesthouse near the beach, offering three rooms (including a single) with mini-fridges, a large shared bathroom and wi-fi access, but no breakfast (nearby breakfast places are plentiful). **£70**

**Trevedra Farm** 2 miles northeast of Sennen, off the

A30 ☎01736 871818, ⓦtrevedrafarm.co.uk. Popular but spacious campsite with sea views stretching off into the distance. There's a modern block within easy walking distance of the pitches providing good facilities, including a shop and a restaurant serving buffet breakfasts. Per person **£5.50**

## St Just-in-Penwith and around

Three miles north of Sennen Cove, the highly scenic headland of **Cape Cornwall** is dominated by the chimney of the Cape Cornwall Mine, which closed in 1870. Half a mile inland is the grimly grey village of **ST JUST-IN-PENWITH**, formerly a centre of the tin and copper industry, with rows of cottages radiating out from Bank Square. The tone is somewhat lightened by **Plen-an-Gwary**, a grassy open-air theatre where miracle plays were once staged, later used by Methodist preachers and Cornish wrestlers.

## ARRIVAL AND DEPARTURE ST JUST-IN-PENWITH

**By bus** From the bus station in Penzance, bus #10 runs to the centre of St Just (hourly; 25min).

**By plane** Land's End Airport, around 1.5 miles south of St Just, handles flights to and from St Mary's on the Isles of

Scilly (April–Oct Mon–Sat 4–11 daily; 15–20min). For exact times call ☎01736 334220 or see ⓦislesofscilly -travel.co.uk.

## ACCOMMODATION AND EATING

**Dog & Rabbit** North Row, just off Market Square ☎01736 449811. Tucked away on a narrow alley, this quirky café does good soups to eat in or take away (£4) plus a good selection of teas and coffees. The walls are covered in art, and there's a noticeboard giving details of local exhibitions, concerts and yoga classes. Thurs–Sat 9am–5pm.

**Kegen Teg** 12 Market Square ☎01736 788562. Organic, local and mainly vegetarian food – try the home-made falafel or Welsh rarebit (both £8.20) – with tasty breakfasts, cakes, smoothies and organic ice cream. Daily 10am–5pm.

**Kelynack Caravan and Camping Park** Kelynack ☎01736 787633, ⓦkelynackcaravans.co.uk. Secluded

campsite, one of the few sheltered ones on Penwith, about a mile south of St Just. There are also B&B rooms and self-catering options. Camping per person **£7.50**; doubles **£80**

**Old Fire Station** Nancherrow Terrace, near Market Square ☎01736 786463, ⓦoldfirestationstjust.co.uk. Central, modern B&B with an open-plan lounge and breakfast room, and three smallish but airy en-suite bedrooms, the top two with distant sea views. **£70**

**YHA Land's End** ☎0845 371 9643, ⓦyha.org.uk. Less than a mile south of St Just and a convenient half-mile from the coast path, this hostel has camping facilities and a kitchen, and also sells cooked meals. Take the left fork past the post office to find it. Dorms **£21**; doubles **£50**

## Zennor and around

Eight miles northeast of St Just, set in a landscape of rolling granite moorland, **ZENNOR** is where D.H. Lawrence came to live with his wife Frieda in 1916. "It is a most beautiful place," he wrote, "lovelier even than the Mediterranean". The Lawrences stayed a year and a half in the village – long enough for him to write *Women in Love* – before being given notice to quit by the local constabulary, who suspected them of unpatriotic sympathies (their Cornish experiences were later described in *Kangaroo*). Zennor's fascinating **Wayside Museum** is dedicated to Cornish life from prehistoric times (daily: April & Oct 10.30am–4.30pm; May–Sept 10am–5.30pm; £3.95; ☎01736 796945). At the top of the lane, the church of **St Sennen** displays a

**6**

sixteenth-century bench-carving of a mermaid who, according to local legend, was so entranced by the singing of a chorister that she lured him down to the sea, from where he never returned – though his song can still occasionally be heard.

## Chysauster

2 miles inland from Zennor • Daily: April–June & Sept 10am–5pm; July & Aug 10am–6pm; Oct 10am–4pm • £3.70; EH • ☎ 07831 757934, ⓦ english-heritage.org.uk

On a windy hillside a couple of miles inland from Zennor, the Iron Age village of **Chysauster** is the best-preserved ancient settlement in the Southwest. Dating from about the first century BC, it contains two rows of four buildings, each consisting of a courtyard with small chambers leading off it, and a garden that was presumably used for growing vegetables.

### ARRIVAL AND DEPARTURE                                    ZENNOR AND AROUND

**By bus** The #16 and #16A buses from St Ives to Penzance (hourly Mon–Sat) stop near the turn-off for Zennor. From here it's a short stroll into the village.

### ACCOMMODATION AND EATING

**Gurnard's Head** Treen, a mile or so west of Zennor ☎ 01736 796928, ⓦ gurnardshead.co.uk. This relaxed gastropub serves delicious Mediterranean-inspired meals (mains around £16–17; booking advised). Smallish B&B rooms are also available. Daily noon/12.30–11pm; food served noon/12.30–2.30pm & 6/6.30–9pm. **£105**

**Zennor Chapel** ☎ 01736 798307, ⓦ zennorchapel guesthouse.com. Newly refreshed, this guesthouse in a former Wesleyan chapel has five rooms, each with space for two to four people, and all with en-suite bathrooms. The café downstairs turns out breakfasts 8–10am (not included in rate), and sells coffee and cakes throughout the day. Doubles **£80**; family room **£90**

## St Ives

East of Zennor, the road runs four hilly miles on to the steeply built town of **ST IVES**. By the time the pilchard reserves dried up around the early 1900s, the town was beginning to attract a vibrant **artists' colony**, precursors of the wave later headed by Ben Nicholson, Barbara Hepworth, Naum Gabo and the potter Bernard Leach, who in the 1960s were followed by a third wave including Peter Lanyon and Patrick Heron.

### Tate St Ives

Porthmeor Beach • March–Oct daily 10am–5.20pm; Nov–Feb Tues–Sun 10am–4.20pm; closes two or three times a year for about ten days, so check ahead • £7, £11 with Hepworth Museum • ☎ 01736 796226, ⓦ tate.org.uk

The place to view the best work created in St Ives is the **Tate St Ives**, overlooking Porthmeor Beach on the north side of town. Most of the paintings, sculptures and ceramics displayed within the airy, gleaming-white building date from 1925 to 1975, with specially commissioned contemporary works also on view as well as exhibitions. The gallery's rooftop **café** is a splendid spot for a coffee.

### Barbara Hepworth Museum

Barnoon Hill • March–Oct daily 10am–5.20pm; Nov–Feb Tues–Sun 10am–4.20pm • £6.60 or £11 with the Tate • ☎ 01924 247360, ⓦ tate.org.uk

Not far from the Tate St Ives, the **Barbara Hepworth Museum** provides further insight into the local arts scene. One of the foremost nonfigurative sculptors of her time, Hepworth lived in the building from 1949 until her death in a studio fire in 1975. Apart from the sculptures, which are arranged in positions chosen by Hepworth in the house and garden, the museum has background on her art, from photos and letters to catalogues and reviews.

### The beaches

**Porthmeor Beach** dominates the northern side of St Ives, its excellent water quality and surfer-friendly rollers drawing a regular crowd, while the broader **Porthminster Beach**, south of the station, is usually less busy. A third town beach, the small and sheltered **Porthgwidden**, lies in the lee of the prong of land separating Porthmeor and Porthminster, while east of town a string of magnificent golden beaches lines **St Ives Bay** on either side of the Hayle estuary.

## ARRIVAL AND INFORMATION

ST IVES

**By train** Trains from Penzance (most via St Erth; every 30min–1hr; 30–50min) arrive at the train station on Trelyon Ave, off Porthminster Beach.

**By bus** The bus station is on Station Hill, just off The Terrace.

Destinations Penzance (Mon–Sat 3–5 hourly, Sun hourly; 50min); Plymouth (3 daily; 3hr 20min–3hr 45min); Truro

(Mon–Sat every 30min, Sun 1 daily; 1hr 10min–1hr 40min).

**Tourist office** Inside the Guildhall on Street-an-Pol, a 5min walk northwest from the bus station (April Mon–Sat 10am–3pm, May Mon–Sat 10am–4pm, Sun 10am–3pm, June daily 10am–4pm, July–Sept daily 9.30am–5pm, Oct–March Mon–Fri 10am–3pm; ☎09052 522250, ⓦ stivestic.co.uk).

## ACCOMMODATION

**Cornerways** 1 Bethesda Place ☎01736 796706, ⓦ cornerwaysstives.com. Daphne du Maurier once stayed here; it's now a modern cottage conversion with friendly management and small, bright rooms. Ask about complimentary tickets for the Tate and Hepworth galleries. **£80**

★**Little Leaf** 16 Park Ave ☎01736 795427, ⓦ littleleafguesthouse.co.uk. With friendly young hosts and local art on the walls, this guesthouse has six en-suite rooms, two with fantastic views. Breakfasts are fresh and use locally sourced ingredients. Free wi-fi and use of iPad in

the communal lounge. **£70**

**Atlantic Heights** 11 Ocean View Terrace ☎01872 858 726, ⓦ atlanticheights.net. It's a steep hike away from the centre, but this guesthouse rewards with cracking views from two of its en-suite rooms. Friendly staff. **£70**

**St Ives Backpackers** The Gallery ☎01736 799444, ⓦ backpackers.co.uk/st-ives. Centrally located hostel in an old Wesleyan chapel school from 1845. Dorms have 4–8 beds, and guests can make use of a kitchen, games and free wi-fi. Dorms **£17.95**; double **£40**

## EATING

**Alba** Wharf Rd ☎01736 797222, ⓦ thealbarestaurant .com. Sleekly modern harbourfront restaurant with top-class seafood, including a superb fish soup (£7.25). Set-price menus (£16.95 & £19.95) are available 6–7.30pm, otherwise mains are £12–23. Sit upstairs for the best view. Daily noon–2pm & 5.30–10pm.

**Blas Burgerworks** The Warren ☎01736 797272, ⓦ blasburgerworks.co.uk. This "alternative burger bar" doles out extremely good burgers (£9–11), using local ingredients. There's just one small room with four communal tables made from found or reclaimed wood. No reservations. Daily 5–10pm.

**The Cornish Deli** 3 Chapel St ☎01736 795100 ⓦ cornishdeli.com. The tables fill up quickly at this cosy

deli-cum-café, which sells excellent sandwiches (using meat from the local butcher's shop), as well as wine, Cornish chocolate, West Country cheeses and the like. In summer, proper bistro-style meals (£16.95 for two courses) are served in the evenings from 6pm. No credit cards. July–Sept daily 9.30am–9.30pm, Oct–June Mon–Sat 9.30am–4pm.

★**Porthminster Café** Porthminster Beach ☎01736 795352, ⓦ porthminstercafe.co.uk. With its sun deck and beach location, this is an appealing venue for coffees, snack lunches and sophisticated seafood dinners (mains around £20; book ahead). April–Sept daily 9.30am–9.30pm; Nov–March Tues, Wed & Sun 9.30am–4pm, Thurs–Sat 9.30am–9.30pm.

# The Isles of Scilly

The **Isles of Scilly** are a compact archipelago of about a hundred islands, 28 miles southwest of Land's End. None is bigger than three miles across, and only five of them are inhabited – **St Mary's**, **Tresco**, **Bryher**, **St Martin's** and **St Agnes**. In the annals of folklore, the Scillies are the peaks of the submerged land of Lyonnesse, a fertile plain that extended west from Penwith before the ocean broke in, drowning the land and leaving only one survivor to tell the tale. In fact they form part of the same granite mass as Land's End, Bodmin Moor and Dartmoor, and despite rarely rising above 100ft, they possess a remarkable variety of landscape. Points of interest include irresistible **beaches**, such as Par Beach on St Martin's; the Southwest's greatest concentration of **prehistoric remains**; some fabulous **rock formations**, and the impressive **Tresco Abbey Gardens**. Along with tourism, the main source of income is flower-growing, for which the equable climate and the long hours of sunshine – their name means "Sun Isles" – make the islands ideal. The profusion of **wild flowers** is even more noticeable than the fields of narcissi and daffodils, and the heaths and pathways are often dense with marigolds, gorse, sea thrift, trefoil and poppies, not to mention a host of more exotic varieties introduced by visiting foreign vessels. The waters hereabouts are held to be among the country's best for **diving**, while between May and September, on a Wednesday or Friday evening, islanders gather for **gig races**, performed by six-oared vessels – some of them more than a hundred years old and 30ft long.



Free of traffic, theme parks and amusement arcades, the islands are a welcome respite from the tourist trail, the main drawbacks being the high cost of reaching them and the shortage of **accommodation**, most of which is on the main isle of St Mary's.

## St Mary's

The majority of the resident population of just over two thousand is concentrated on the biggest island, **St Mary's**, which has the lion's share of facilities in its capital, **Hugh Town**, and the richest trove of prehistoric sites. The cove-fringed island is also home to **Star Castle**, a huge eight-pointed fortress that was originally built to deter Spanish invasions, and is now a four-star hotel.

## Tresco

The second-largest island, **Tresco**, presents an appealing contrast between the orderly landscape around the remains of its ancient abbey and the bleak, untended northern half. The exuberant **Tresco Abbey Gardens** (daily 10am–4pm; £12; Ⓣ01720 424108, Ⓦtresco.co.uk), hosting an impressive collection of subtropical plants in the southern part of the island, is the archipelago's most popular visitor attraction.

## Bryher

West of Tresco, **Bryher** has the smallest population, the slow routines of island life quickening only in the tourist season. The bracing, back-to-nature feel here is nowhere more evident than on the exposed western shore, where **Hell Bay** sees some formidable Atlantic storms.

## St Martin's

East of Tresco, **St Martin's** has a reputation as the least striking of the Scillies with the most introverted population, but its white-sand beaches are as majestically wild as any. **Par Beach** deserves a special mention – there are stunning views from its cliffy northeastern end, and the surrounding waters are much favoured by scuba enthusiasts.

## St Agnes

On the southwest rim of the main group, the tidy lanes and picturesque cottages of **St Agnes** are nicely complemented by the weathered boulders and craggy headlands of its indented shoreline. The year-round population here is small (many of the islanders still make their living by farming flowers) and even in summer there are plenty of tranquil spots.

## The uninhabited islands

A visit to the isles would be incomplete without a sortie to the **uninhabited islands**, sanctuaries for seals, puffins and other marine birdlife. On the largest, **Samson**, you can poke around prehistoric and more recent remains that testify to former settlement. Some of the smaller islets are worth visiting for their delightfully deserted beaches, though the majority amount to no more than bare rocks. This chaotic profusion of rocks of all shapes and sizes, each bearing a name, is densest at the archipelago's extremities – the **Western Rocks**, lashed by ferocious seas and the cause of innumerable wrecks over the years, and the milder **Eastern Isles**.

## ARRIVAL AND DEPARTURE                    THE ISLES OF SCILLY

Transport to the Isles of Scilly – by plane and by boat – is operated by **Isles of Scilly Travel** (☎01736 334220, ⓦislesofscilly-travel.co.uk).

**6**

**By plane** For most of the year, the main departure points for flights are Land's End Airport, near St Just; Newquay; Exeter; Bristol and Southampton. In winter there are departures only from Land's End and Newquay. For a one-

way flight from Land's End, expect to pay around £70.
**By boat** Boats to St Mary's depart from Penzance's South Pier between Easter and Oct (2hr 45min). A one-way fare from Penzance will cost in the region of £42.

## GETTING AROUND AND INFORMATION

**By boat** Boats link each of the inhabited islands, though services are sporadic in winter. The St Mary's Boatmen's Association (☎1720 423999, ⓦscillyboating.co.uk) publishes up-to-date timetables and fares online.
**By bike** Cycling is the ideal way to get around (bikes can be taken on ferries from the mainland for £13 each way). Alternatively, you can rent bikes from St Mary's Bike Hire on The Strand, Hugh Town (☎07796 638506; £10/day).

**Tourist office** Schiller Shelter, Porthcressa beachfront, St Mary's (mid-March to mid-April Mon–Sat 9am–4pm; mid-April to mid-May Mon–Sat 9am–5pm, Sun 9am–2pm; mid-May to mid-Sept Mon–Sat 9am–6.30pm, Sun 9am–2pm; mid-Sept to mid-Oct Mon–Sat 9am–5pm; mid-Oct to mid-March Mon–Fri 10am–2pm; ☎01720 424031, ⓦsimplyscilly.co.uk).

## ACCOMMODATION AND EATING

St Mary's has the great majority of the **accommodation** on the islands; the smaller isles (excepting Tresco) each have two or three B&Bs only, and these are booked up early. Two of the islands – Tresco and St Martin's – have luxury hotels, and all the islands except Tresco have **campsites**, which usually close in winter (camping rough is not allowed). See ⓦsimplyscilly.co.uk for complete accommodation lists. St Mary's also has most of the **restaurants** and **pubs**. Each of the other inhabited islands has a pub serving food and one or two cafés, while all hotels and some B&Bs also provide meals.

# Cornwall's Atlantic coast

The north Cornish coast is punctuated by some of the finest beaches in England, the most popular of which are to be found around **Newquay**, the surfers' capital, and **Padstow**, also renowned for its gourmet seafood restaurants. North of the Camel estuary, the coast features an almost unbroken line of cliffs as far as the Devon border; this gaunt, exposed terrain makes a melodramatic setting for **Tintagel Castle**. There are more good beaches at **Bude, St Agnes** and **Polzeath**.

## Newquay

In a superb position on a knuckle of cliffs overlooking fine golden sands and Atlantic rollers, its glorious natural advantages have made **NEWQUAY** the premier resort of north Cornwall. The "new quay" in question was built in the fifteenth century in what was already a long-established fishing port, up to then more colourfully known as Towan Blistra. The town was given a boost in the nineteenth century when a railway was constructed across the peninsula for china clay shipments; with the trains came a swelling stream of seasonal visitors.

Today, the town centre is a tacky parade of shops, bars and restaurants from which lanes lead to ornamental gardens and cliff-top lawns. The main attraction is the **beaches**. A number of **surfing competitions** and festivals run through the summer, when Newquay can get very crowded – it's also popular with stag and hen parties.

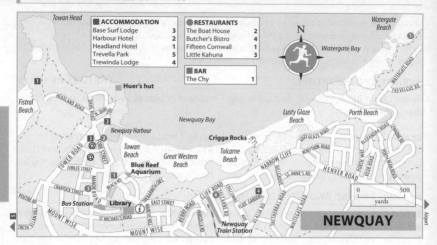

## The beaches

All Newquay's beaches can be reached fairly easily on foot from the centre, otherwise take bus #556 for Porth Beach and Watergate Bay,
#585 and #587 for Crantock and #587 for Holywell Bay

In the crook of Towan Head, **Towan Beach** is the most central of the seven miles of firm
sandy beaches that line the coast around Newquay. Town beaches such as this and
**Porth Beach**, with its grassy headland, can get very busy with families in high season,
and are popular with surfers all year, though the latter are more partial to **Watergate
Bay** to the north, and **Fistral Bay**, west of Towan Head.

On the other side of East Pentire Head from Fistral, **Crantock Beach** – reachable over
the Gannel River by ferry or upstream footbridge – is usually less crowded, and has a
lovely backdrop of dunes and undulating grassland. South of Crantock, **Holywell Bay**
and the three-mile expanse of **Perran Beach**, enhanced by caves and natural rock arches,
are also very popular with surfers.

### ARRIVAL AND DEPARTURE

NEWQUAY

**By plane** Newquay's airport is at St Mawgan, 5 miles
northeast of town, with connections to major British and
Irish cities, and linked to town by local buses.
Destinations St Mary's, Isles of Scilly (Mon–Sat 2–4 daily,
1 on Sat in winter; 30min); London Gatwick (2–3 daily;
1hr); Manchester (1 daily; 1hr 20min).
**By train** Newquay is served by trains from Par (3–8 daily,
not Sun in winter; 50min); the train station is off Cliff Road,

a short walk east of the centre.
**By bus** The bus station is on Manor Road, near the tourist
office.
Destinations Bodmin (hourly; 55min); Padstow (Mon–Sat
hourly, Sun 5 daily; 1hr 20min); Plymouth (every 30min–
1hr; 1hr 50min–2hr 20min); St Austell (Mon–Sat every
30min–1hr, Sun 3 daily; 50min); Truro (every 20–30min;
50min–1hr 25min).

### INFORMATION

**Tourist office** Marcus Hill (April–Oct Mon–Fri
9am–5.30pm, Sat & Sun 10am–4pm; Nov–March

Mon–Fri 10am–4pm, Sat & Sun 10am–3pm; ☎ 01637
854020, ⓦ visitnewquay.org).

### ACCOMMODATION

**Base Surf Lodge** 20 Tower Rd ☎ 07766 132124,
ⓦ basesurflodge.co.uk. A good central option for small
groups, with fresh, private bunk rooms sleeping 2–6
people. The whole place is geared up for surfers, with board
storage facilities and free hot drinks to warm you up post-
surf. Beginners should ask about their surf and stay

packages, which include lessons. Dorms __£25__.
**Harbour Hotel** North Quay Hill ☎ 01637 873040,
ⓦ theharbour.uk.com. Small, luxurious hotel with
stunning views from its stylish rooms, all of which have
balconies. Some rooms are tiny, so check first. __£80__
**Headland Hotel** Fistral Beach ☎ 01637 872211,

Ⓦ headlandhotel.co.uk. Opened atop a craggy headland in 1900 and still going strong, the hotel that starred in *The Witches* has nearly a hundred rooms and suites to choose from – many with ocean views – plus self-catering cottages. **£165**

**Trevella Park** Near Crantock, 1.5 miles southwest of town ☎ 01637 830308, Ⓦ trevella.co.uk. It can feel crowded at peak times, but this remains one of the better holiday parks near Newquay, with good, clean facilities for campers and a heated outdoor pool. Per person **£9.35**

**Trewinda Lodge** 17 Eliot Gardens ☎ 01637 877533, Ⓦ trewinda-lodge.co.uk. The owners of this B&B, close to

---

**TOP 5 DEVON AND CORNWALL SURF SPOTS**

**Croyde Bay** See p.340
**Fistral** See opposite
**Polzeath** See p.365
**Watergate Bay** See opposite
**Whitesand Bay** See p.355

---

Tolcarne Beach, can give informed advice to surfers (they also run Dolphin Surf School). Rooms are on the small side, but clean and comfortable, and there's wi-fi. **£60**

## EATING AND DRINKING

**The Boat House** Newquay Harbour ☎ 01637 874062, Ⓦ theboathousenewquay.co.uk. The most atmospheric place in town, this restaurant sits right by the old harbour. Inevitably, seafood is the main event: locally caught monkfish, plaice and crab (£11–17), and whatever else appears on the daily specials board. March–Dec daily 10am–11pm; food served noon–3pm & 6.30–9.30pm.

★**Butcher's Bistro** 26 Cliff Rd ☎ 01637 874470. Tucked away beside a fast food joint, this small, maritime-themed bistro does very good steaks and seafood, including fish line-caught by the chef. For a real treat try the seafood feast – a big, steaming bowl of prawns, crab claws, mussels and boneless fish (£19.95) Mon, Tues & Thurs–Sat 6–9.30pm.

**The Chy** 12 Beach Rd ☎ 01637 873415, Ⓦ thekoola .com. Contemporary bar/restaurant with a spacious terrace and upper deck where you can order everything from breakfasts and sandwiches to burgers and seafood

dishes (around £10). In the evening, you can sip cocktails and listen to DJs. Mon, Fri & Sat 10am–4am, Tues–Thurs 10.30am–2am, Sun 11am–midnight; food served all day.

★**Fifteen Cornwall** Watergate Bay ☎ 01637 861000, Ⓦ fifteencornwall.co.uk. Overlooking the beach, this contemporary restaurant set up by TV chef Jamie Oliver showcases the culinary talents of trainee chefs. The Italian-inspired but locally sourced dishes are inventive and delicious; set menus are £28 at lunchtime, £60 in the evening, and breakfasts are also worth tucking into. Daily 8.30–10am, noon–2.30pm & 6.15–9.15pm.

**Little Kahuna** 4–6 Crantock St ☎ 01637 850440, Ⓦ littlekahuna.co.uk. Mouthwatering Asian dishes from Goan fish curries to spicy *som tam* salads are presented beautifully at this intimate (and extremely popular) little restaurant. Mains are around £15, and you'd be wise to book ahead. Daily 5.30pm–late.

## St Agnes

Though surrounded by ruined engine houses, the village of **ST AGNES** gives little hint of the conditions in which its population once lived, the uniform grey ex-miners' cottages now fronted by immaculate flower-filled gardens, and its steep, straggling streets busy in summer with troops of holiday-makers.

At the end of a steep valley below St Agnes, **Trevaunance Cove** is the site of several failed attempts to create a harbour for the town, and now has a fine sandy beach. West of the village lies one of Cornwall's most famous vantage points, **St Agnes Beacon**, 630ft high, from which views extend inland to Bodmin Moor and even across the peninsula to St Michael's Mount. To the northwest, the headland of **St Agnes Head** has the area's largest colony of breeding kittiwakes, and the nearby cliffs also shelter fulmars and guillemots, while grey seals are a common sight offshore.

### ARRIVAL AND DEPARTURE         ST AGNES

**By bus** Take bus #587 from Newquay's bus station (hourly) for the 1hr ride to the village.

## Perranporth

Three miles north of St Agnes, **PERRANPORTH** lies at the southern end of **Perran Beach**, a three-mile expanse of sand enhanced by caves and natural rock arches. It's very popular with surfers – boards and equipment are available to rent in summer.

**6**

## Padstow and around

PADSTOW attracts nearly as many holiday-makers as Newquay, but has a very different feel. Enclosed within the estuary of the Camel – the only river outlet of any size on Cornwall's north coast – the town has long retained its position as North Cornwall's principal fishing port, and can boast some of the county's best seafood **restaurants**. The **harbour** is jammed with launches and boats offering cruises in the bay, while a **ferry** (see below) carries people across the river to **ROCK** – close to the isolated church of **St Enodoc** (John Betjeman's burial place) and to the good beaches around Polzeath. Padstow is also known for its annual **Obby Oss** festival, a May Day romp when a local in horse costume prances through the town preceded by a masked and club-wielding "teaser", in a spirited re-enactment of an old fertility rite.

### Church of St Petroc

Church Lane • Usually open for visitors 9am–5pm

On the hill overlooking Padstow, the **Church of St Petroc** is dedicated to Cornwall's most important saint, a Welsh or Irish monk who landed here in the sixth century, died in the area and gave his name to the town – "Petrock's Stow". The building has a fine fifteenth-century font, an Elizabethan pulpit and some amusing carved bench ends – seek out the one to the right of the altar depicting a fox preaching to a congregation of geese.

### Prideaux Place

Half a mile west of the quay • Easter–Sept Mon–Thurs & Sun 1.30–4pm; grounds open from 12.30pm • £8.50, grounds only £4 • ☎01841 532411, ⓦ prideauxplace.co.uk

Padstow's ancient Prideaux family – whose Cornish origins date back to the Normans – still occupy **Prideaux Place**, an Elizabethan manor house with grand staircases, richly furnished rooms full of portraits, fantastically ornate ceilings and formal gardens. You might recognize some parts of the house, which is used extensively for location filming and has appeared in a plethora of films, including *Oscar and Lucinda* (1997).

### The Beaches

The area immediately west of Padstow has some fine **beaches** – all within a short walk or drive of the town. On the **west side** of the estuary, round **Stepper Point**, you can reach the sandy and secluded **Harlyn Bay** and, turning the corner southwards, **Constantine Bay**, the best surfing beach hereabouts. The dunes backing the beach and the rock pools skirting it make this one of the most appealing bays on this coast, though the tides can be treacherous and bathing hazardous near the rocks. Three or four miles further south, the slate outcrops of **Bedruthan Steps** were traditionally held to be the stepping-stones of a giant; they can be readily viewed from the cliff-top path and the B3276, with steps descending to the broad beach below (not safe for swimming).

### ARRIVAL AND DEPARTURE                         PADSTOW AND AROUND

**By bus** Buses #556 from Newquay (Mon–Sat hourly, Sun 4 daily; 1hr 15min) and #555 from Bodmin (Mon–Sat hourly, Sun 6 daily; 55min) pull in on Station Road, above the harbour.

### GETTING AROUND AND INFORMATION

**By ferry** The ferry across the river to Rock operates daily year-round, roughly every 20min during the day (£3 return).

**By bus** Bus #556 (hourly) connects Padstow with Harlyn Bay (5min) and Constantine Bay (10min). Every 2hr, the same bus calls at Bedruthan (30min).

**Tourist office** North Quay, by the harbour (Easter–Oct Mon–Fri 9am–5.30pm, Sat & Sun 10am–5pm; Nov–Easter Mon–Fri 10am–4pm, Sat 10am–3pm, Sun 11am–2pm; ☎01841 533449, ⓦ padstowlive.com).

### ACCOMMODATION

**St Petroc's Hotel** Treverbyn Rd ☎01841 532700, ⓦ rickstein.com. Restaurateur Rick Stein has extended his Padstow empire to include classy accommodation, including this chic little lodging away from the harbour, with modernist decor and outstanding breakfasts. But even the very small rooms (described as snug in marketing materials) are pricey. **£160**

**Treverbyn House** Treverbyn Rd ☎01841 532855, ⓦtreverbynhouse.com. A short walk up from the harbour, this elegant Edwardian B&B has large, beautifully furnished rooms with wi-fi. Breakfast is served in the dining room or on a terrace in the garden with views over the river. **£120**

**YHA Treyarnon** Treyarnon Bay, 4.5 miles west of Padstow ☎0845 371 9664, ⓦyha.org.uk. Perfectly sited hostel in a 1930s summer villa right by the beach. Take bus #556 from Padstow or Newquay to Constantine, then walk half a mile. Surf packages available. Camping pitches **£13**; dorms **£21**; doubles **£63**

## EATING AND DRINKING

Foodies know Padstow for its high-class **restaurants**, particularly those associated with star chef **Rick Stein**; the waiting list for a table at one of his establishments can be months long, though a weekday reservation out of season can mean booking only a day or two ahead. For something a little cheaper, try Stein's fish and chip shop or his deli, both on South Quay.

★**Margot's Bistro** 11 Duke St ☎01841 533441, ⓦmargotsbistro.co.uk. The tables at this small, unassuming restaurant are booked up for weeks in advance, which is testament to the quality of the food: think Cornish rib-eye steaks, fillets of grey mullet and pan-fried sardines. Most mains are £13.50, which makes this place better value than the town's other top restaurants.

Tues 7–8.30pm, Wed–Sat noon–1.30pm & 7–8.30pm.

★**The Seafood Restaurant** Riverside ☎01841 532700, ⓦrickstein.com. The core of Rick Stein's culinary empire, this is one of Britain's top places for fish, with most mains – Singapore chilli crab, Padstow lobster, Newlyn fish pie – costing £25–35. Daily noon–2.30pm & 6.30–10pm.

## Polzeath and around

Facing west into Padstow Bay, the beaches around **POLZEATH** are the finest in the vicinity, pelted by rollers that make **Hayle Bay**, in particular, one of the most popular **surfing** venues in the West Country. A mile south of Polzeath, **Daymer Bay** is more favoured by the windsurfing crowd. All the gear can be rented from shops on the beach, where you can get information on tuition, and there are campsites and bars in the vicinity.

Heading east, the coastal path brings you through cliff-top growths of feathery tamarisk, which flower spectacularly in July and August. From the headland of **Pentire Point**, views unfold for miles over the offshore islets of **The Mouls** and **Newland**, which foster populations of grey seals and puffins. Half a mile east, the scanty remains of an Iron Age fort stand on **Rump's Point**, from where the path descends a mile or so to **Lundy Bay**, a pleasant sandy cove surrounded by green fields. Climbing again, you pass the shafts of an old antimony mine on the way to **Doyden Point**, which is picturesquely ornamented with a nineteenth-century castle folly once used for gambling parties.

### Port Isaac

Beyond the inlet of **Port Quin**, the next settlement of any size is **PORT ISAAC**, wedged in a gap in the precipitous cliff wall and dedicated to the crab and lobster trade. The cramped village, whose narrow lanes lead down to a pebble beach where rock pools are exposed at low tide, has become increasingly popular with tourists in recent years thanks to its role in the British TV series *Doc Martin*.

## ARRIVAL AND GETTING AROUND

POLZEATH AND AROUND

**By bus** The area's most useful bus service is #584 (Mon–Fri 4 daily; Sat 3 daily), which connects Polzeath with Wadebridge (35min), Rock (10min), Camelford (40min) and Port Isaac (15min). Bus #213 (Mon–Fri 1 daily) also connects Polzeath with Rock (8min) and Wadebridge (35min). Coming from further afield (eg Newquay or Bodmin) involves a change at Wadebridge.

## ACCOMMODATION AND EATING

### POLZEATH

**Valley Caravan Park** 200m south of Polzeath beach, signposted up the lane behind the shop ☎01208 862391. Accommodation around Polzeath is scarce, but

6

this is a useful campsite, with a stream running through that attracts ducks and geese. Closed Oct–Easter. Pitches £23

★**The Waterfront** Beach Rd ☎01208 869655. A relaxed café/restaurant just back from the beach, with a first-floor terrace and an eclectic menu (mains around £14–16) taking inspiration from as far afield as Morocco and Sri Lanka. Daily 10am–12.30am (last food orders at 9pm).

**PORT ISAAC**

**The Old School Hotel** Fore St, above the eastern end of the beach ☎01208 880721, ⓦtheoldschoolhotel .co.uk. Right in the centre of Port Isaac, this place comes

with stylish, contemporary rooms, a garden, free parking, wi-fi and great views. £114

**The Slipway** Harbour Front ☎01208 880264, ⓦportisaachotel.com. Port Isaac is famous for crab, and the restaurant at this quayside hotel is a good place to enjoy it (£9.50). There are good en-suite rooms here too, some with views over the harbour. Daily 11am–3pm & 6.30–9pm (until 9.30pm in summer). £110

**Stowaways Tea Shoppe** 76A Fore St ☎01208 881083, ⓦstowawaysportisaac.co.uk. Welcoming, old-fashioned teashop selling sandwiches, a wide range of cakes (for a couple of pounds per slice) and a whole load of *Doc Martin* merchandise. Daily 10.30am–5pm.

# Tintagel

Despite its romantic name and its famous **castle** standing aloof on a promontory to the north, the village of **TINTAGEL** is for the most part a dreary collection of cafés and B&Bs. Apart from the castle, Tintagel has one other item of genuine interest: the **Old Post Office** on Fore Street (daily: mid-Feb to early April & Oct 11am–4pm; early April to late May 10.30am–5pm; late May to Sept 10.30am–5.30pm; £3.70; NT; ☎01840 770024, ⓦnationaltrust.org.uk/tintagel-old-post-office), a slate-built, rickety-roofed construction dating from the fourteenth century, now restored to its appearance in the Victorian era.

### Tintagel Castle

Half a mile northwest of the village • April–Sept daily 10am–6pm; Oct daily 10am–5pm; Nov–March Sat & Sun 10am–4pm • £6.10; EH • ☎01840 770328, ⓦtintagelcastle.co.uk

The wild and unspoiled coast around Tintagel provides an appropriate backdrop for the forsaken ruins of **Tintagel Castle**. It was the twelfth-century chronicler Geoffrey of Monmouth who first popularized the notion that this was the **birthplace of King Arthur**, son of Uther Pendragon and Ygrayne, though the visible ruins in fact belong to a Norman stronghold occupied by the earls of Cornwall. After sporadic spurts of rebuilding, the castle was allowed to decay, and most of it had been washed into the sea by the sixteenth century. The remains of a sixth-century **Celtic monastery** on the headland have provided important insights into how the country's earliest monastic houses were organized.

---

### THE CAMEL TRAIL AND THE SAINTS' WAY

The old railway line between Padstow and Wadebridge has been converted into an excellent **cycle track** that forms part of the **Camel Trail**, a fifteen-mile traffic-free path that follows the river up as far as Wenfordbridge, on the edge of Bodmin Moor, with a turn-off for Bodmin. The five-mile Padstow–Wadebridge stretch offers glimpses of a variety of birdlife, especially around the small **Pinkson Creek**, habitat of terns, herons, curlews and egrets.

You can **rent bikes** from Trail Bike Hire (☎01841 532594, ⓦtrailbikehire.co.uk; £12/day; daily 9am–6pm) and Padstow Cycle Hire (☎01841 533533, ⓦpadstowcyclehire.com; £14/day; daily 9am–5pm with late opening until 9pm in summer), both on South Quay, by the start of the Camel Trail. Further up the Trail at Wadebridge, Bridge Bike Hire (☎01208 813050, ⓦbridgebikehire.co.uk; £12/day has a greater stock, though it's still advisable to reserve.

Padstow also marks one end of the thirty-mile cross-peninsula **Saints' Way**, linking up with Fowey on Cornwall's south coast (see p.345). Leaflets and books detailing the walk are available from the tourist offices at Padstow, Bodmin and Fowey.

## ARRIVAL AND INFORMATION

**By bus** Buses pull in on Bossiney Road, opposite the tourist office.

Destinations Boscastle (Mon–Sat 6 daily; 10min); Bude (Mon–Sat 5–6 daily; 40min); Camelford (Mon–Sat every 1–2hr; 15min).

**Tourist office** The tourist office is in the car park off Bossiney Road (daily: April–Oct 10am–4pm; Nov–March 10am–12.30pm; ☎01840 779084, ⓦvisitboscastleandtintagel.com), and has a small exhibition about the region's cultural heritage.

## ACCOMMODATION AND EATING

**The Avalon** Atlantic Road ☎01840 770116, ⓦtintagelbedbreakfast.co.uk. The rooms are nothing special but if you just want a clean and central place to lay your head, you could do worse than this welcoming B&B. The most expensive bedrooms have views of the sea and castle, while the cheaper ones look out over the village and countryside. **£84**

**Bosayne** Atlantic Rd ☎01840 770514, ⓦbosayne .co.uk. In a quiet spot a few mins' walk from Tintagel's centre, this good-value B&B has en-suite doubles and singles with shared bathrooms, all with an iPod dock and access to free wi-fi. Some rooms have sea views. **£67**

★**Charlie's** Fore St ☎01840 779500, ⓦonline-deli .co.uk. There's a lot to like about this family-friendly deli-restaurant, not least the excellent home-made cakes and Cornish cream teas (gluten-free scones are available). The staff are friendly, and there's a good selection of pickles and relishes to take home. Mon–Sat 10am–5pm.

**YHA Tintagel** Dunderhole Point ☎0845 371 9145, ⓦyha.org.uk. Three-quarters of a mile south of Tintagel, the offices of a former slate quarry now house this hostel with great coastal views. There's a kitchen and BBQ area but no restaurant. Dorms **£21.50**

# Boscastle

Three miles east of Tintagel, the port of **BOSCASTLE** lies compressed within a narrow ravine drilled by the rivers Jordan and Valency, and ending in a twisty harbour. The tidy riverfront bordered by thatched and lime-washed cottages was the scene of a devastating flash flood in 2004, but the damage has now been repaired. Above and behind, you can see more seventeenth- and eighteenth-century cottages on a circular walk that traces the valley of the Valency for about a mile to reach Boscastle's graceful parish church of **St Juliot**, tucked away in a peaceful glen, where Thomas Hardy once worked as a young architect.

## ARRIVAL AND INFORMATION

**By bus** There are bus stops at the car park and Boscastle Bridge, at the top of the harbour.

Destinations Bude (Mon–Sat 6 daily; 40min); Camelford (Mon–Sat 6 daily, 25min); Tintagel (Mon–Sat

6 daily; 10min).

**Tourist office** The Harbour (Mon–Sat: April–Sept 10am–5pm; Oct–March 10.30am–4pm; ☎01840 250010, ⓦvisitboscastleandtintagel.com).

## ACCOMMODATION

**Boscastle House** Doctors Hill ☎01840 250654, ⓦboscastlehouse.co.uk. Six spacious rooms with high ceilings in a tranquil nineteenth-century house that was built for a local doctor. The interiors are fresh and modern, and a couple of the rooms have decent views. **£80**

**Old Rectory** St Juliot, 1.5 miles east of Boscastle ☎01840 250225, ⓦstjuliot.com. For a real Thomas Hardy experience, head for this luxurious Victorian B&B,

where you can stay in the author's bedroom and roam the extensive grounds. **£110**

★**YHA Boscastle** Palace Stables, Harbourside ☎0845 371 9006, ⓦyha.org.uk. Fine old hostel in a former stables right by the river. Rooms have two to six beds and there's a self-catering kitchen and a comfy lounge. Groups only Dec–March. Dorms **£22.50**; doubles **£75**

## EATING AND DRINKING

**Boscastle Farm Shop** Hillsborough Farm, a mile east of Boscastle along the B3263 ☎01840 250827, ⓦboscastlefarmshop.co.uk. Busy farm shop just a short stroll off the coastal path, selling fresh fruit and veg, cuts of local meat and locally made biscuits. The café at the back does good breakfast baps (£3.75) and has views over the

sea and countryside. Daily 9am–5pm.

**Napoleon Inn** High St ☎01840 250204, ⓦnapoleoninn .co.uk. Among Boscastle's excellent pubs, this one in the upper town has tankards hanging off the ceiling, real ale, great food (mains around £12) and live music evenings every Fri. Daily noon–11pm; food served 12.30–8.30pm.

**6**

## Bude and around

Just four miles from the Devon border, Cornwall's northernmost town of **BUDE** is built around an estuary surrounded by a fine expanse of sands. The town has sprouted a crop of hotels and holiday homes, though these have not unduly spoilt the place nor the magnificent cliffy coast surrounding it.

Of the excellent beaches hereabouts, the central **Summerleaze** is clean and spacious, but the mile-long **Widemouth Bay**, south of town, is the main focus of the holiday crowds (though bathing can be dangerous near the rocks at low tide). Surfers also congregate five miles down the coast at **Crackington Haven**, wonderfully situated between 430ft crags at the mouth of a lush valley. To the **north** of Bude, acres-wide **Crooklets** is the scene of **surfing** and life-saving demonstrations and competitions. A couple of miles further on, **Sandy Mouth** holds a pristine expanse of sand with rock pools beneath the encircling cliffs. It's a short walk from here to another surfers' delight, **Duckpool**, a tiny sandy cove flanked by jagged reefs at low tide, and dominated by the three-hundred-foot **Steeple Point**.

### ARRIVAL AND INFORMATION

### BUDE AND AROUND

**By bus** Buses stop on The Strand.
Destinations Boscastle (Mon–Sat 6 daily; 40min); Exeter (Mon–Sat 8 daily, Sun 2 daily; 2hr); Hartland (Mon–Sat 5 daily; 45min).

**Tourist office** In the car park off the Crescent (April–Sept Mon–Sat 10am–5/6pm, Sun 10am–4pm; Oct–March daily 10am–4pm; ☏ 01288 354240, ⓦ visitbude.info).

### ACCOMMODATION AND EATING

**Brendon Arms** Falcon Terrace ☏ 01288 354542, ⓦ brendonarms.co.uk. Large, agreeable old inn with tables on the front lawn, good for a pint of real ale and a snack or bar meal for around £10. Accommodation available. Daily 11am/noon–midnight; food served noon–2pm & 6–9pm. £80

★**Cerenety** A mile south of Bude on Lynstone Lane ☏ 01288 356778 or ☏ 07429 016962, ⓦ cerenetycampsite.co.uk. Back-to-basics, eco-friendly camping just outside Bude, with handsome grassy areas to pitch up on, plus solar-powered showers and composting toilets. In the mornings, hot drinks and breakfast baps can be bought from a little caravan on the site. Pitches £14

**Life's a Beach** Summerleaze Beach ☏ 01288 355222, ⓦ lifesabeach.info. Right on the beach, this is a café by

day, offering baguettes, burgers and drinks, and a romantic bistro strong on seafood in the evening (mains £16.50–20). Mon–Sat 10.30am–3.30pm & 7–8.45pm, Sun 10.30am–3.30pm.

**North Shore** 57 Killerton Rd ☏ 01288 354256, ⓦ northshorebude.com. Friendly backpackers' hostel 5min from the centre of town, with clean and spacious rooms – including en-suite doubles – a large garden, a kitchen and internet access. Dorms £20; doubles £48

**Upper Lynstone** Lynstone ☏ 01288 352017, ⓦ upperlynstone.co.uk. This clean, basic campsite lies some three-quarters of a mile south of town, linked by a panoramic cliff-top walk. There's a shop on site, and electric hook-ups. Closed Oct–Easter. Pitches £21

## Bodmin Moor

**Bodmin Moor**, the smallest of the West Country's great moors, has some beautiful tors, torrents and rock formations, but much of its fascination lies in the strong human imprint, particularly the wealth of relics left behind by its **Bronze Age** population. Separated from these by some three millennia, the churches in the villages of **St Neot**, **Blisland** and **Altarnun** are among the region's finest examples of fifteenth-century art and architecture.

### Bodmin

**BODMIN**'s position on the western edge of Bodmin Moor, equidistant from the north and south Cornish coasts and the Fowey and Camel rivers, encouraged its growth as a trading town. It was also an important ecclesiastical centre after the establishment of a priory by St Petroc, who moved here from Padstow in the sixth century.

**KING ARTHUR IN CORNWALL**

Did **King Arthur** really exist? If he did, it's likely that he was an amalgam of two people: a sixth-century Celtic warlord who united the local tribes in a series of successful battles against the invading Anglo-Saxons, and a local Cornish saint. Whatever his origins, his role was recounted and inflated by poets and troubadours in later centuries. The Arthurian legends were elaborated by the medieval chroniclers Geoffrey of Monmouth and William of Malmesbury and in Thomas Malory's epic, *Morte d'Arthur* (1485), further romanticized in Tennyson's *Idylls of the King* (1859) and resurrected in T.H. White's saga, *The Once and Future King* (1958).

Although there are places throughout Britain and Europe that claim some association with Arthur, it's England's West Country, and **Cornwall** in particular, that has the greatest concentration of places boasting a link. Here, the myths, enriched by fellow Celts from Brittany and Wales, have established deep roots, so that, for example, the spirit of Arthur is said to be embodied in the Cornish chough – a bird now almost extinct. Cornwall's most famous Arthurian site is his supposed birthplace, **Tintagel**, where Merlin apparently lived in a cave under the castle (he also resided on a rock near Mousehole, south of Penzance, according to some sources). Nearby **Bodmin Moor** is littered with places with names such as "King Arthur's Bed" and "King Arthur's Downs", while Camlan, the battlefield where Arthur was mortally wounded fighting against his nephew Mordred, is associated with Slaughterbridge, on the northern reaches of the moor near **Camelford** (which is also sometimes identified as Camelot itself). At **Dozmary Pool**, the knight Bedivere was dispatched by the dying Arthur to return the sword Excalibur to the mysterious hand emerging from the water – though Loe Pool in Mount's Bay also claims this honour. Arthur's body, it is claimed, was carried after the battle to **Boscastle**, on Cornwall's northern coast, from where a funeral barge transported it to Avalon, identified with Glastonbury in Somerset (see p.298).

### Church of St Petroc

Priory Rd • Open for services April–Sept Mon–Sat 11am–3pm; at other times call to check • Free • ☎ 01208 73867

After Bodmin's priory had disappeared, the town retained its prestige through its **church of St Petroc**, built in the fifteenth century and still Cornwall's largest parish church. Inside, there's an extravagantly carved twelfth-century font and an ivory casket that once held the bones of the saint. The southwest corner of the churchyard holds a sacred well.

### Bodmin Jail

Berrycoombe Rd • Daily 10am–5pm • £7.50 ; entry to grounds and café is free • ☎ 01208 76292, ⓦ bodminjail.org

The notorious **Bodmin Jail** is redolent of the public executions that were guaranteed crowd-pullers until 1862, though it didn't finally close until 1927. You can visit part of the original eighteenth-century structure, including the condemned cell and "execution pit", and some grisly exhibits chronicling the lives of the inmates. *The Warder's Room*, a café/restaurant, stays open until late.

### Lanhydrock

3 miles southeast of Bodmin; less than 2 miles from Bodmin Parkway station • **House** Tues–Sun: March & Oct 11am–5pm; April–Sept 11am–5.30pm; also open Mon in school hols • £11.30 (includes grounds and gardens); NT • **Gardens** Feb–Nov 10am–6pm • £7 • ☎ 01208 265950, ⓦ nationaltrust.org.uk/lanhydrock

One of Cornwall's most celebrated country houses, **Lanhydrock** originally dates from the seventeenth century but was totally rebuilt after a fire in 1881. Much remains of its Jacobean past within the granite exterior, however; the fifty rooms include a long picture gallery with a plaster ceiling depicting scenes from the Old Testament, while the servants' quarters fascinatingly reveal the daily workings of a Victorian manor house. The grounds have magnificent **gardens** with lush beds of magnolias, azaleas and rhododendrons, and a huge area of wooded parkland bordering onto the River Fowey.

## Blisland

**BLISLAND** stands in the Camel valley on the western slopes of Bodmin Moor, three miles northeast of Bodmin. Georgian and Victorian houses cluster around a village green and a church whose well-restored interior has an Italianate altar and a startlingly painted screen.

## The western moor

On **Pendrift Common** above Blisland, the gigantic **Jubilee Rock** is inscribed with various patriotic insignia commemorating the jubilee of George III's coronation in 1809. From this 700ft vantage point you look eastward over the De Lank gorge and the boulder-crowned knoll of **Hawk's Tor**, three miles away. On the shoulder of the tor stand the Neolithic **Stripple Stones**, a circular platform once holding 28 standing stones, of which just four are still upright.

## The northern tors

The northern half of Bodmin Moor is dominated by its two highest tors, both of them easily accessible from **CAMELFORD**, an unassuming local centre known for its slate industry. Four miles southeast, **Rough Tor** is the second highest peak on Bodmin Moor at 1311ft. A short distance to the east stand **Little Rough Tor**, where there are the remains of an Iron Age camp, and **Showery Tor**, capped by a prominent formation of piled rocks. Easily visible to the southeast, **Brown Willy** is, at 1378ft, the highest peak in Cornwall, as its original name signified – Bronewhella, or "highest hill". Like Rough Tor, Brown Willy shows various faces, its sugarloaf appearance from the north sharpening into a long multi-peaked crest as you approach. The tor is accessible by continuing from the summit of Rough Tor across the valley of the De Lank, or, from the south, by footpath from Bolventor.

## Bolventor and around

The village of **BOLVENTOR**, lying at the centre of the moor midway between Bodmin and Launceston, is an uninspiring place close to one of the moor's chief focuses for walkers and literary sightseers alike – **Jamaica Inn**.

### Jamaica Inn

10 miles northeast of Bodmin along the A30 • Museum open daily: mid-March to Oct 10am–5pm (until 6pm during school summer hols) • £3.95 • ☏ 01566 86250, ⓦ jamaicainn.co.uk

A staging post even before the precursor of the A30 road was laid here in 1769, the inn was described as being "alone in glory, four square to the winds" by **Daphne Du Maurier**, who stayed here in 1930, soaking up inspiration for her smugglers' yarn, *Jamaica Inn*. There's a room inside devoted to the author, and the hotel also has an attached **Smugglers Museum**, illustrating the diverse ruses used for concealing contraband.

### Dozmary Pool

A mile south of Bolventor

The car park at *Jamaica Inn* makes a useful place to leave your vehicle and venture forth on foot. Just a mile south, **Dozmary Pool** is another link in the West Country's Arthurian mythologies – after Arthur's death Sir Bedivere hurled Excalibur, the king's sword, into the pool, where it was seized by an arm raised from the depths. Despite its proximity to the A30, the diamond-shaped lake usually preserves an ethereal air, though it's been known to run dry in summer, dealing a bit of a blow to the legend that it is bottomless.

## Altarnun

Four miles northeast of Bolventor, **ALTARNUN** is a pleasant, granite-grey village snugly sheltered beneath the eastern heights of the moor. Its prominent **church**, St Nonna's, contains a fine Norman font and 79 bench ends carved at the beginning of the sixteenth century, depicting saints, musicians and clowns.

## St Neot and the southeastern moor

Approached through a lush wooded valley, **ST NEOT** is one of the moor's prettiest villages. Its fifteenth-century **church** contains some of the most impressive stained-glass windows of any parish church in the country, the oldest glass being the fifteenth-century **Creation Window**, at the east end of the south aisle.

### Golitha Falls

One of the moor's most attractive spots lies a couple of miles east of St Neot, below Draynes Bridge, where the Fowey tumbles through the **Golitha Falls**, less a waterfall than a series of rapids. Dippers and wagtails flit through the trees, and there's a pleasant woodland walk to Siblyback Lake reservoir just over a mile away.

**6**

### Kilmar and Stowe's Hill

North and east of Siblyback Lake are some of Bodmin Moor's grandest landscapes. The quite modest elevations of Hawk's Tor (1079ft) and the lower Trewartha Tor appear enormous from the north, though they are overtopped by **Kilmar**, highest of the hills on the moor's eastern flank at 1280ft. **Stowe's Hill** is the site of the moor's most famous stone pile, **The Cheesewring**, a precarious pillar of balancing granite slabs, marvellously eroded by the wind. A mile or so south down Stowe's Hill stands an artificial rock phenomenon, **The Hurlers**, a wide complex of three circles dating from about 1500 BC. The purpose of these stark upright stones is not known, though they owe their name to the legend that they were men turned to stone for playing the Celtic game of hurling on the Sabbath.

### Minions and Trethevy

The Hurlers are easily accessible just outside **MINIONS**, Cornwall's highest village, three miles south of which stands another Stone Age survival, **Trethevy Quoit**, a chamber tomb nearly nine feet high, surmounted by a massive capstone. Originally enclosed in earth, the stones have been stripped by centuries of weathering to create Cornwall's most impressive megalithic monument.

| ARRIVAL AND INFORMATION | BODMIN MOOR |

**By train** 3 miles outside Bodmin itself, Bodmin Parkway train station has a regular bus connection (hourly; 15min) to the centre of Bodmin.
Destinations Exeter (every 30min–1hr; 1hr 40min); Penzance (every 30min–1hr; 1hr 20min); Plymouth (every 30min–1hr; 45min).
**By bus** Most buses to and from Bodmin stop on Mount Folly, near the tourist office.

Destinations Newquay (hourly; 50min); Padstow (Mon–Sat hourly, Sun 6 daily; 50min); Plymouth (9 daily; 1hr 10min–1hr 30min); St Austell (Mon–Sat hourly, Sun 5 daily; 50min).
**Tourist office** Mount Folly, Bodmin (March–May & Oct Mon–Fri 8.45am–4pm plus some Sats 10am–5pm; June–Sept Mon–Fri 8.45am–5pm, Sat 10am–5pm; Nov–Feb Mon–Fri 8.45am–2pm; ☎01208 76616, ⍟bodminlive.com).

## ACCOMMODATION AND EATING

★**Bedknobs** Polgwyn, Castle St, Bodmin ☎01208 77553, ⍟bedknobs.co.uk. Victorian villa in an acre of wooded garden, with three spacious and luxurious rooms, the priciest with its own en-suite Airbath and the cheapest with a separate bathroom that includes a spa bath. Friendly, eco-aware hosts and lots of extras. No under-12s. **£85**

**Jamaica Inn** Bolventor ☎01566 86250, ⍟jamaicainn .co.uk. Despite its fame, this inn immortalized by Daphne du Maurier has lost any trace of romance since its development into a bland hotel and restaurant complex. It occupies a grand site, though, ideal for excursions onto the moor. Mon–Sat 7.30am–midnight, Sun 7.30am–10.30pm; food served 7.30am–11am, noon–3.30pm & 5–9.30pm. **£79**

**Mason's Arms** Fore St, Camelford ☎01840 213309, ⍟masonsarmscamelford.co.uk. Traditional, rather poky pub with St Austell ales and some of the best nosh around (mains around £10). Daily 11am–11pm; food served noon–2.30pm & 6–9pm.

**Roscrea** 18 St Nicholas Rd, Bodmin ☎01208 74400, ⍟roscrea.co.uk. Central, friendly B&B with tasteful Victorian rooms. Breakfasts include eggs laid in the garden, and you can request a great two-course dinner for £18.50 – a good option. **£85**

# East Anglia

KING'S COLLEGE CHAPEL, CAMBRIDGE

# East Anglia

Strictly speaking, East Anglia is made up of just three counties – Suffolk, Norfolk and Cambridgeshire, which were settled in the fifth century by Angles from today's Schleswig-Holstein – but it has come to be loosely applied to parts of Essex too. As a region it's renowned for its wide skies and flat landscapes – if you're looking for mountains, you've come to the wrong place. East Anglia can surprise, nonetheless: parts of Suffolk and Norfolk are decidedly hilly, with steep coastal cliffs; broad rivers cut through the fenlands; and Norfolk also boasts some wonderful sandy beaches. Fine medieval churches abound, built in the days when this was England's most progressive and prosperous region.

**7**

Heading into East Anglia from the south takes you through **Essex**, whose proximity to London has turned much of the county into an unappetizing commuter strip. Amid the suburban gloom, there are, however, several worthwhile destinations, most notably **Colchester**, once a major Roman town and now a busy place with an imposing castle, and the handsome hamlets of the bucolic **Stour River Valley** on the Essex–Suffolk border. Essex's **Dedham** is one of the prettiest of these villages, but the prime attraction hereabouts is Suffolk's **Flatford Mill**, famous for its associations with the painter John Constable.

**Suffolk** boasts a string of pretty little towns – **Lavenham** is the prime example – that enjoyed immense prosperity from the thirteenth to the sixteenth century, the heyday of the wool trade. The county town of **Ipswich** has more to offer than it's given credit for, but really it's the Suffolk coast that holds the main appeal, especially the delightful seaside resort of **Southwold** and neighbouring **Aldeburgh** with its prestigious music festival.

**Norfolk**, as everyone knows thanks to Noël Coward, is very flat. It's also one of the most sparsely populated and tranquil counties in England, a remarkable turnaround from the days when it was an economic and political powerhouse – until, that is, the Industrial Revolution simply passed it by. Its capital, **Norwich**, is East Anglia's largest city, renowned for its Norman cathedral and castle; nearby are the **Broads**, a unique landscape of reed-ridden waterways that have been intensively mined by boat-rental companies. Similarly popular, the **Norfolk coast** holds a string of busy, very English seaside resorts – **Cromer** and **Sheringham** to name but two – but for the most part it's charmingly unspoilt, its marshes, creeks and tidal flats studded with tiny flintstone villages, most enjoyably **Blakeney** and **Cley**.

SOUTHWOLD

# Highlights

**❶ Orford** Solitary hamlet with a splendid coastal setting that makes for a wonderful weekend away. **See p.387**

**❷ The Aldeburgh Festival** The region's prime classical music festival takes place every summer. **See p.388**

**❸ Southwold** Handsome and genteel seaside town, which is perfect for walking and bathing – with the added incentive of the most inventive Under the Pier Show in the country. **See p.390**

**❹ Norwich Market** This open-air market is the region's biggest and best for everything from whelks to wellies. **See p.394**

**❺ Holkham Bay and beach** Wide bay holding Norfolk's finest beach – acres of golden sand set against pine-dusted dunes. **See p.404**

**❻ Ely** Isolated Cambridgeshire town, with a true fenland flavour and a magnificent cathedral. **See p.409**

**❼ Cambridge** With some of the finest late medieval architecture in Europe, Cambridge is a must-see, its compact centre graced by dignified old colleges and their neatly manicured quadrangles. **See p.412**

HIGHLIGHTS ARE MARKED ON THE MAP ON P.376

## LONG-DISTANCE FOOTPATHS

Given the prevailing flatness of the terrain, hiking in East Anglia is less strenuous than in most other English regions, and there are several **long-distance footpaths**. The main one is the **Peddars Way**, which runs north from Knettishall Heath, near Thetford, to the coast at Holme, near Hunstanton, where it continues east as the **Norfolk Coast Path** to Cromer – 93 miles in total (Ⓦ nationaltrail.co.uk for both). At Cromer, you can pick up the 62-mile **Weavers' Way** (Ⓦ ldwa.org.uk), which wends its way through the Broads to the coast at Great Yarmouth.

**Cambridge** is much visited, principally because of its world-renowned university, whose ancient colleges boast some of the finest medieval and early-modern architecture in the country. The rest of Cambridgeshire is pancake-flat **fenland**, for centuries an inhospitable marshland, but now rich alluvial farming land. The cathedral town of **Ely**, settled on one of the few areas of raised ground in the fens, is an easy and popular day-trip from Cambridge.

**HIGHLIGHTS**

1. Orford
2. The Aldeburgh Festival
3. Southwold
4. Norwich Market
5. Holkham Bay and beach
6. Ely
7. Cambridge

EAST ANGLIA

---

**TOP 5 GREAT PLACES TO STAY**

**Cley Mill B&B** Cley. See p.402
**Crown & Castle** Orford. See p. 388
**Gothic House** Norwich. See p. 396

**The Great House** Lavenham. See p.383
**Ocean House B&B** Aldeburgh. See p.389

---

**GETTING AROUND**                                         **EAST ANGLIA**

**By train** Trains from London are fast and frequent: one main line links Colchester, Ipswich and Norwich, another Cambridge and Ely. Among several cross-country services, there are trains between Peterborough, Ely, Norwich and Ipswich.

**By bus** Beyond the major towns you'll have to rely on local buses. Services are patchy, except on the north Norfolk coast, which is well served by the Norfolk Coasthopper bus (ⓦ coasthopper.co.uk).

# Colchester

If you visit only one place in Essex, it should be **COLCHESTER**, a lively, medium-sized town with a **castle**, a university and an army base, just fifty miles or so northeast of London. Colchester prides itself on being England's oldest town, and there is indeed documentary evidence of a settlement here as early as the fifth century BC. Today, Colchester makes a potential base for explorations of the surrounding countryside – particularly the **Stour valley** towns of Constable country, within easy reach a few miles to the north.

### Brief history

By the first century AD, the town was the region's capital under **King Cunobelin** – better known as Shakespeare's Cymbeline – and when the **Romans** invaded Britain in 43 AD they chose Colchester (Camulodunum) as their new capital, though it was soon eclipsed by London. Later, the conquering Normans built one of their mightiest strongholds here, but the conflict that most marked the town was the **Civil War**. In 1648, Colchester was subjected to a gruelling siege by the Parliamentarian army; after three months, during which the population ate every living creature within the walls and then some, the town finally surrendered and the Royalist leaders were promptly executed for their pains.

## Colchester castle

Castle Park · Mon–Sat 10am–5pm, Sun 11–5pm · £7.50 · Guided tours 45min; £2.80 · ☎ 01206 282939, ⓦ www.cimuseums.org.uk/castle

At the heart of Colchester are the remains of its **castle**, a ruggedly imposing, honey-coloured keep, set in attractive parkland stretching down to the River Colne. Begun less than ten years after the Battle of Hastings, the keep was the largest in Europe at the time, built on the site of the Temple of Claudius. Inside the keep, a **museum** holds an excellent collection of Romano-British archeological finds, notably a miscellany of coins and tombstones. The museum also runs regular **guided tours**, giving access to the Roman vaults and the castle roof, which are otherwise out of bounds. Outside, down towards the river in Castle Park, is a section of the old **Roman walls**, whose battered remains are still visible around much of the town centre. They were erected after Boudica had sacked the city and, as such, are a case of too little too late.

## Firstsite Contemporary Visual Arts Centre

Lewis Gardens, High St · Daily 10am–5pm · Free · ☎ 01206 577067, ⓦ firstsite.uk.net

In a new and stunningly handsome modern building near the castle, the **Firstsite Contemporary Visual Arts Centre** offers a varied and often challenging programme of

**7**

---

**BETRAYED AND ABUSED: BOUDICA OF THE ICENI**

**Boudica** – aka Boadicea – was the wife of Prasutagus, chief of the Iceni tribe of Norfolk, who allied himself to the Romans during their conquest of Britain in 43 AD. Five years later, when the Iceni were no longer useful, the Romans attempted to disarm them and, although the Iceni rebelled, they were soon brought to heel. On Prasutagus's death, the Romans confiscated his property and when Boudica protested, they flogged her and raped her daughters. Enraged, Boudica determined to take her revenge, quickly rallying the Iceni and their allies before setting off on a rampage across southern Britain in 60 AD.

As the ultimate symbol of Roman oppression, the **Temple of Claudius** in **Colchester** was the initial focus of hatred, but, once Colchester had been razed, Boudica turned her sights elsewhere. She laid waste to London and St Albans, massacring over seventy thousand citizens and inflicting crushing defeats on the Roman units stationed there. She was far from squeamish, ripping traitors' arms out of their sockets and torturing every Roman and Roman collaborator in sight. The Roman governor Suetonius Paulinus eventually defeated her in a pitched battle, which cost the Romans just four hundred lives and the Britons untold thousands. Boudica knew what to expect from the Romans, so she opted for **suicide**, thereby ensuring her later reputation as a patriotic Englishwoman, who died fighting for liberty and freedom – claims that Boudica would have found incomprehensible.

---

temporary exhibitions. Recent exhibitors have included Roger Hiorns and Bruce McLean. The building itself has a lustrous metallic gold sheen and was designed by the Uruguayan architect Rafael Viñoly.

## The Town Hall

High St

Colchester's wide and largely pedestrianized **High Street** follows pretty much the same route as it did in Roman times. The most arresting building here is the flamboyant **Town Hall**, built in 1902 and topped by a statue of St Helena, mother of Constantine the Great and daughter of "Old King Cole" of nursery-rhyme fame – after whom, some say, the town was named.

## Balkerne Gate

High St

Looming above the western end of the High Street is the town landmark, "**Jumbo**", a disused nineteenth-century water tower, considerably more imposing than the nearby **Balkerne Gate**, which marked the western entrance to Roman Colchester. Built in 50 AD, this is the largest surviving Roman gateway in the country, though with the remains at only a touch over 6ft high, it's far from spectacular.

### ARRIVAL AND INFORMATION                                    COLCHESTER

**By train** Colchester has two train stations, Colchester North for mainline services and Colchester Town for local services to the Tendring peninsula. From Colchester North, it's a 15min walk south into town – follow the signs – whilst Colchester Town station is on the southeast corner of the town centre, about 500yds from the High Street.
Colchester North to: Ipswich (every 30min; 20min); London Liverpool Street (every 20min; 1hr); Norwich (every 30min; 1hr); Sudbury (change at Marks Tey; hourly; 40min).
Colchester Town to: Walton-on-the-Naze (hourly; 50min).
**By bus** The bus station is on Osborne St, a short walk south

of the castle and the High St, with some services leaving from neighbouring Standwell and Queen streets.
Destinations Chambers bus #753 (ⓦchambersbus.co.uk) links Colchester with Bury St Edmunds (Mon–Sat hourly; 2hr); Lavenham (Mon–Sat hourly; 1hr 30min) and Sudbury (Mon–Sat hourly; 50min). There is also a reasonably frequent bus to Dedham (Mon–Sat 3–4 daily; 40min). Timetable details on ⓦsuffolkonboard.com.
**Tourist office** On the ground floor of the Hollytrees Museum, on the High Street near the castle (Mon–Sat 10am–5pm; ☎01206 282920, ⓦvisitcolchester.com).

## A DAY BY THE SEASIDE: ESSEX'S SUNSHINE COAST

Jutting out into the North Sea to the east of Colchester is the wide and chunky **Tendring peninsula**, aka Essex's **"Sunshine Coast"**, though the name has as much to do with tourist flannel as the Essex climate. Nonetheless, seaside resorts do line up along the Tendring's south coast. Biggest and brassiest is **Clacton-on-Sea**, though the most agreeable is **Walton-on-the-Naze**, a pleasant little place with an enjoyable seafront promenade and a wide sandy beach. There's an hourly train service to Walton from Colchester Town Station (see opposite).

## ACCOMMODATION

**Four Sevens Guesthouse** 28 Inglis Road ☎ 01206 546093, ⊛ foursevens.co.uk. One of the best of the town's B&Bs, in an attractively remodelled Victorian house with six bright and breezy guest rooms decorated in an uncluttered modern style. Two of the rooms are en suite, which cost an extra £10. On a leafy residential street, a brief walk southwest from the centre. **£65**

**North Hill Hotel** 51 North Hill ☎ 01206 574001, ⊛ northhillhotel.com. In an intelligently revamped older building, this appealing, mid-range hotel has seventeen guest rooms with lots of original features – especially the exposed half-timbered walls and beams. Handy central location too, just north of the High St, but North Hill can be noisy, so you may prefer a room at the back. **£70**

## EATING

Colchester's **oysters** have been highly prized since Roman times and today are at their best among the oyster fisheries of **Mersea Island**, about 6 miles south of Colchester; the season runs from September to May.

**The Company Shed** 129 Coast Rd, West Mersea ☎ 01206 382700, ⊛ the-company-shed.co.uk. The freshest of oysters served simply at rickety tables in, to quote their own PR, a "romantically weatherbeaten shed". Romantic or not, the oysters are indeed delicious. Tues–Sat 9am–5pm, Sun 10am–5pm. Last orders for eating-in 4pm.

**Il Padrino** 11 Church St ☎ 01206 366699, ⊛ ilpadrinocolchester.co.uk. Opened in 2013, this

excellent Italian café-cum-restaurant serves all the classics for lunch and dinner and even offers breakfast too. The daily specials, chalked up on a blackboard, are a real feature and prices are very reasonable with mains averaging £13 (£9 for pasta dishes). Cosy premises and attentive service. Narrow Church Street is a few yards from the west end of the High Street. Mon 9am–2pm, Tues–Sat 9am–2pm & 6–10pm.

# The Stour Valley

Six miles or so north of Colchester, the **Stour River Valley** forms the border between Essex and Suffolk, and signals the beginning of East Anglia proper. The valley is dotted with lovely little villages, where rickety, half-timbered Tudor houses and elegant Georgian dwellings cluster around medieval churches, proud buildings with square, self-confident towers. The Stour's prettiest villages are concentrated along its lower reaches – to the east of the A134 – in Dedham Vale, with **Dedham** the most appealing of them all. The vale is also known as **"Constable Country"**, as it was the home of John Constable, one of England's greatest artists, and the subject of his most famous paintings. Inevitably, there's a Constable shrine – the much-visited complex of old buildings down by the river at **Flatford Mill**. Elsewhere, the best-preserved of the old south Suffolk wool towns is **Lavenham**, whilst neighbouring **Sudbury** has a fine museum, devoted to the work of another outstanding English artist, Thomas Gainsborough.

## Brief history

The villages along the River Stour and its tributaries were once busy little places at the heart of East Anglia's medieval **weaving trade**. By the 1480s, the region produced more cloth than any other part of the country, but in Tudor times production shifted to Colchester, Ipswich and Norwich and, although most of the smaller settlements continued spinning cloth for the next three hundred years or so, their importance slowly dwindled. Bypassed by the Industrial Revolution, **south Suffolk** had, by the late nineteenth century, become a remote rural backwater, an impoverished area whose decline had one unforeseen consequence: with few exceptions, the towns and villages were never prosperous enough to modernize, so the architectural legacy of medieval and Tudor times survived and now pulls in second-home owners and tourists alike.

| GETTING AROUND | THE STOUR VALLEY |
|---|---|

**By public transport** Seeing the Stour Valley by public transport can be problematic – distances are small (Dedham Vale is only about ten miles long), but buses between the villages are patchy, especially on the weekend. The only local rail service is the short branch line between Sudbury and Marks Tey on the London Liverpool Street to Colchester line.

## Flatford Mill

"I associate my careless boyhood with all that lies on the banks of the Stour," wrote **John Constable**, who was born in **East Bergholt**, nine miles northeast of Colchester, in 1776. The house in which he was born has long since disappeared, so it has been left to **FLATFORD MILL**, a mile or so to the south, to take up the painter's cause. The mill was owned by his father and was where Constable painted his most celebrated canvas, *The Hay Wain* (now in London's National Gallery), which created a sensation when it was exhibited in Paris in 1824. To the chagrin of many of his contemporaries, Constable turned away from the landscape painting conventions of the day, rendering his scenery with a realistic directness that harked back to the Dutch landscape painters of the seventeenth century.

The mill itself – not the one he painted, but a Victorian replacement – is not open to the public and neither is neighbouring **Willy Lott's Cottage**, which does actually feature in *The Hay Wain*, but the National Trust has colonized several local buildings, principally **Bridge Cottage**.

### Bridge Cottage

Flatford Mill • Jan & Feb Sat & Sun 10.30am–3.30pm; March Wed–Sun 11am–4pm; April daily 10.30am–5pm; May–Sept daily 10.30am–5.30pm; Oct daily 10.30am–5pm; Nov & Dec Wed–Sun 10.30am–3.30pm • NT • Free, except for parking • ☎ 01206 298260 • The nearest train station is at Manningtree, 2 miles away

Neat and trim and tidily thatched, **Bridge Cottage** was familiar to Constable and, although none of the artist's paintings is displayed here, it is packed with Constabilia alongside a small exhibition on the artist's life and times. The cottage also has a very pleasant riverside tearoom where you can take in the view.

| ACCOMMODATION | FLATFORD MILL |
|---|---|

**The Granary B&B** Flatford Mill ☎ 01206 298111, ⓦ granaryflatford.co.uk. In the annexe of the old granary that was once owned by Constable's father, this appealing B&B has a real cottage feel with its beamed ceilings and antique furniture. There are two ground-floor guest rooms, both en suite. **£62**

## Dedham

Constable went to school just upriver from Flatford Mill in **DEDHAM**, a pretty little village whose wide and lazy main street is graced by a handsome medley of old

---

### GUIDED WALKS AROUND FLATFORD MILL

Many visitors to Flatford Mill are keen to see the sites associated with Constable's paintings and, although there is something a tad futile about this – so much has changed – the National Trust does organize volunteer-led **guided walks** to several key locations; the nearest are the remains of the Dry Dock next to Bridge Cottage and the *Hay Wain* view itself. For more details, call ☎ 01206 298260 or consult ⓦ nationaltrust.org.uk.

timber-framed houses and Georgian villas. The main sight as such is the **Church of St Mary** (daily 9am–dusk; free; ⓦ dedham-parishchurch.org.uk), a large, well-proportioned structure with a sweeping, sixteenth-century nave that is adorned by some attractive Victorian stained glass. Constable painted the church on several occasions, and today it holds one of the artist's rare religious paintings, *The Ascension* – though frankly, it's a good job Constable concentrated on landscapes. Be aware that day-trippers arrive here by the coachload throughout the summer.

### Sir Alfred Munnings Art Museum

Castle House, on the road to Ardleigh • April–July & Sept–Oct Wed–Sun 2–5pm; Aug Wed–Sun 11am–5pm • £6.50 • ☎ 01206 322127
ⓦ siralfredmunnings.co.uk

The **Sir Alfred Munnings Art Museum**, in a substantial country villa about a mile south of Dedham, exhibits the work of the eponymous artist, who, though barely remembered today, was President of the Royal Academy in the 1940s. Munnings (1875–1959) made a name for himself as an official war artist attached to the Canadian cavalry in 1918 and it was then that he discovered his penchant for painting horses, a skill that was to bring him scores of aristocratic commissions. It was Modernism that did for Munnings: he savaged almost every form of modern art there was, creating enemies by the score and ensuring he was soon ridiculed as old-fashioned and out-of-touch. The museum displays a comprehensive range of Munnings' paintings and posters and although few would say they were inspiring, seeing them is a pleasant way to fill a (rainy) afternoon.

### ARRIVAL AND DEPARTURE                                    DEDHAM

**By bus** There is a reasonably frequent bus service to Dedham from Colchester (Mon–Sat 3–4 daily; 40min), but there are no buses between Dedham and Stoke-by-Nayland. See ⓦ suffolkonboard.com.

### ACCOMMODATION AND EATING

**The Sun Inn** High St ☎01206 323351, ⓦ thesuninndedham.com. Among Dedham's several pubs, the pick is *The Sun*, an ancient place that has been sympathetically modernized. The menu is strong on local ingredients and offers tasty Italian and British dishes, all washed down by real ales; mains average around £13. They also have several attractive en-suite rooms; rates increase £30 or so on the weekend. Daily: 11am–11pm; food served noon–2.30pm & 6.30–9.30pm. **£120**

## Stoke-by-Nayland

West of Dedham, **STOKE-BY-NAYLAND** is the most picturesque of villages, where a knot of half-timbered and pastel-painted cottages cuddle up to one of Constable's favourite subjects, **St Mary's Church** (daily 9am–5pm; free), with its pretty brick-and-stone-trimmed tower. The doors of the south porch are covered by the beautifully carved if badly weathered figures of a medieval **Jesse Tree**.

### ARRIVAL AND DEPARTURE                          STOKE-BY-NAYLAND

**By bus** There is a good service to Stoke-by-Nayland from both Colchester (Mon–Sat hourly; 30min) and Sudbury (Mon–Sat hourly; 30min). There are no buses between Dedham and Stoke-by-Nayland. Timetable details on ⓦ suffolkonboard.com.

### ACCOMMODATION AND EATING

**The Angel Inn** Polstead St ☎01206 263245, ⓦ angelinnsuffolk.co.uk. Things are on the move at this agreeable country pub with its bare-brick walls and rustic beams. The menu is firmly British – steak-and-ale pie, fish and chips – with mains averaging around £12. *The Angel* also has half-a-dozen en-suite guest rooms, each of which is kitted out in a bright and cheerful modern style. Kitchen: Mon–Sat noon–2.30pm & 6–9.30pm; Sun noon–4pm & 6–9pm. Bar: daily 10am–11pm. **£120**

**The Crown** Polstead St ☎01206 262001, ⓦ crowninn .net. *The Crown* may fancy itself just a little too much, but there's no disputing the quality of the food or the

7

inventiveness of the menu, which features such delights as venison chop with horseradish and mustard butter, watercress and chips. Mains start at £15. The decor is appealing too, with the open-plan restaurant spreading over several separate areas and decorated in a sort of low-key, country-house style with pastel shades to the fore. The same decorative approach has been followed in the eleven bedrooms, which are all kept in tip-top condition. **£130**

# Sudbury

By far the most important town in this part of the Stour Valley, **SUDBURY** holds a handful of timber-framed houses that recall its days of wool-trade prosperity, though in fact its salad days were underwritten by another local industry, **silk weaving**. The town's most famous export, however, is **Thomas Gainsborough** (1727–88), the leading English portraitist of the eighteenth century. Although he left Sudbury when he was just 13, moving to London where he was apprenticed to an engraver, the artist is still very much identified with the town: his statue, with brush and palette, stands on Market Hill, the predominantly Victorian marketplace, while a superb collection of his work is on display a few yards away inside the house where he was born, now **Gainsborough's House**.

## Gainsborough's House

46 Gainsborough St • Mon–Sat 10am–5pm & Sun 11am–5pm • £6.50 • ☎ 01787 372958, ⓦ gainsborough.org.

On display in **Gainsborough's House** is the earliest of the artist's surviving portrait paintings, *Boy and Girl*, a remarkably self-assured work dated to 1744, though it comes in two pieces as someone, somewhere chopped up the original. Later, during stints in Ipswich, Bath and London, Gainsborough developed a fluid, flatteringly easy style that was ideal for his well-heeled subjects, who posed in becoming postures painted in soft, evanescent colours. Examples of Gainsborough's later work include the particularly striking *Portrait of Abel Moysey, MP* (1771). Look out also for one of Gainsborough's specialities, his wonderful "**conversation pieces**", so called because the sitters engage in polite chitchat – or genteel activity – with a landscape as the backdrop.

### ARRIVAL AND INFORMATION

### SUDBURY

**By train** Sudbury train station is a 5–10min walk from the centre via Station Road.
Destinations Marks Tey, on the London to Colchester line (hourly; 20min).
**By bus** Sudbury bus station is on Hamilton Rd, just south of Market Hill. The main local bus company is H.C. Chambers (☎ 01787 375360, ⓦ chambersbus.co.uk).

Destinations Bury St Edmunds (Mon–Sat hourly; 1hr 10min); Colchester (Mon–Sat hourly; 50min); Lavenham (Mon–Sat hourly; 35min); Stoke-by-Nayland (Mon–Sat hourly; 30min).
**Tourist office** Inside the library, on Market Hill (April–Sept Mon–Fri 9am–5pm, Sat 10am–4.45pm; Oct–March Mon–Fri 9am–5pm, Sat 10am–2.45pm; ☎ 01787 881320, ⓦ sudburytowncouncil.co.uk).

### EATING AND DRINKING

**Black Adder Brewery Tap** 21 East St ☎ 01787 370876, ⓦ blackaddertap.co.uk. Enjoyable neighbourhood pub where the big deal is the beer – a rotating selection of real ales on draught, but always including something from Mauldons, a local brewer. There's a courtyard patio and pub grub. Mon–Thurs 11am–11pm, Fri & Sat 11am–midnight, Sun noon–10.30pm.

**The Secret Garden** 21 Friars St ☎ 01787 372030, ⓦ tsg .uk.net. Cosy local tearoom in a very old building, where the sophisticated menu has lots of French flourishes and they do their best to source locally. For lunch, try their ham, spinach and cheddar cheese on focaccia for around £10; dinner might include a seared sea bass fillet or grilled duck breast. Mon–Sat 9am–5pm, plus Fri & Sat 7–9.30pm.

# Lavenham

**LAVENHAM**, eight miles northeast of Sudbury, was once a centre of the region's wool trade and is now one of the most visited villages in Suffolk, thanks to its unrivalled ensemble of perfectly preserved half-timbered houses. In outward appearance at least, the whole place has changed little since the demise of the wool industry, owing in part to a zealous local preservation society, which has carefully maintained the village's antique appearance. Lavenham is at its most beguiling in the triangular **Market Place**, an airy spot flanked by pastel-painted, medieval dwellings whose beams have been warped into all sorts of wonky angles by the passing of the years.

## Guildhall of Corpus Christi

Market Place • Jan to early March Sat & Sun 11am–4pm; mid- to late March Wed–Sun 11am–4pm; April–Oct daily 11am–5pm; Nov & Dec Thurs–Sun 11am–4pm • NT • £5.35 • ☎ 01787 247646, ⓦ nationaltrust.org.uk/lavenham-guildhall

On the Market Place you'll find the village's most celebrated building, the lime-washed, timber-framed **Guildhall of Corpus Christi**, erected in the sixteenth century as the headquarters of one of Lavenham's four guilds. In the much-altered interior (used successively as a prison and workhouse), there are modest exhibitions on timber-framed buildings, medieval guilds, village life and the wool industry, though most visitors soon end up in the walled garden or the teashop next door.

## Church of St Peter and St Paul

Church St • Daily 8.30am–4pm • Free • ☎ 01787 247244, ⓦ lavenhamchurch.wordpress.com

The Perpendicular **church of St Peter and St Paul**, located a short walk southwest of the centre, features gargoyle water-spouts and carved boars above the entrance. Local merchants endowed the church with a nave of majestic proportions and a mighty flint tower, at 141ft the highest for miles around, partly to celebrate the Tudor victory at the Battle of Bosworth in 1485 (see p.682), but mainly to show just how wealthy they had become.

### ARRIVAL AND INFORMATION                                     LAVENHAM

**By bus** Buses pull in at the corner of Water and Church streets, a 5min walk from Market Place. Among several services, perhaps the most useful is Chambers bus #753 (ⓦ chambersbus.co.uk), which links Lavenham with Sudbury, Bury St Edmunds and Colchester.
Destinations Bury St Edmunds (Mon–Sat hourly; 40min);

Colchester (Mon–Sat hourly; 1hr 30min); Sudbury (Mon–Sat hourly, 35min).
**Tourist office** Lady St, just south of Market Place (mid-March to Oct daily 10am–4.45pm; Nov to mid-Dec daily 11am–3pm; Jan to mid-March Sat & Sun 11am–3pm; ☎ 01787 248207, ⓦ heartofsuffolk.co.uk).

### ACCOMMODATION AND EATING

★**The Great House** Market Place ☎ 01787 247431, ⓦ greathouse.co.uk. Delightful, family-run hotel bang in the centre of the village. Each of the five guest rooms is decorated in a thoughtful and tasteful manner, amalgamating the original features of the old – very old – house with the new. Deeply comfortable beds and a great breakfast round it all off. The hotel restaurant specializes in classic French cuisine, with both set meals and à la carte. Main courses start at £20. Food served Wed–Sun noon–2.30pm, Tues–Sat 7–10.30pm. **£125**
★**Swan Hotel** High St ☎ 01787 247477,

ⓦ theswanatlavenham.co.uk. This excellent hotel is a veritable rabbit warren of a place, its nooks and crannies dating back several hundred years. There's a lovely, very traditional, lounge to snooze in, a courtyard garden, an authentic Elizabethan Wool Hall and a wood-panelled bar. Just as appealing, most of the comfy guest rooms abound in original features and the restaurant is first-rate too, serving imaginative British-based cuisine – roasted wood pigeon and puy lentils for example – with mains starting at around £16. Restaurant daily 7–9pm; brasserie daily noon–2.30pm & 5.30–9pm. **£180**

# Bury St Edmunds

An amiable, eminently likeable place, **BURY ST EDMUNDS**, ten miles north of Lavenham, is one of the prettiest towns in Suffolk. It started out as a Benedictine monastery, founded to accommodate the remains of Edmund, the last Saxon king of East Anglia, who was tortured and beheaded by the marauding Danes in 869. Almost two centuries later, England was briefly ruled by the kings of Denmark and the shrewdest of them, **King Canute**, granted the monastery a generous endowment and built the monks a brand-new church. It was a popular move and the abbey prospered:

7

by the time of its dissolution in 1539, it had become the richest religious house in the country. Most of the abbey disappeared long ago, and nowadays Bury is better known for its graceful Georgian streets, its flower gardens and its gargantuan sugar-beet plant.

## Angel Hill

At the heart of the town is **Angel Hill**, a broad, spacious square partly framed by Georgian buildings, the most distinguished being the ivy-covered **Angel Hotel**, which features in Dickens' *The Pickwick Papers*. Dickens also gave readings of his work in the **Athenaeum**, the Georgian assembly rooms at the far end of the square. A twelfth-century wall runs along the east side of Angel Hill, with the bulky fourteenth-century **Abbey Gate** forming the entrance to the abbey gardens and ruins beyond.

## Abbey Gardens and ruins

Mustow St & Angel Hill • Mon–Sat 7.30am–dusk, Sun 9am–dusk • Free; EH • ⓦ english-heritage.org.uk

Ensconced within the immaculate greenery of the **Abbey Gardens**, the abbey **ruins** are themselves like nothing so much as petrified porridge, with little to remind you of the grandiose Norman complex that once dominated the town. Thousands of medieval pilgrims once sought solace at St Edmund's altar and the cult was of such significance that the barons of England gathered here to swear that they would make King John sign their petition – the Magna Carta of 1215. A plaque marks the spot where they met beside what was once the high altar of the old abbey church, whose crumbly remains are on the far (right) side of the abbey gardens behind the Cathedral.

## St Edmundsbury cathedral

Angel Hill • Daily 8.30am–6pm • Free, but £3 donation requested • Sat 7.30am–dusk, Sun 9am–dusk • Free • ☎ 01284 748720, ⓦ stedscathedral.co.uk

Abutting the gardens, the Anglican **St Edmundsbury Cathedral** is a hangar-like affair with a beautiful painted roof whose chancel and transepts were added as recently as the 1960s. It was a toss-up between this church and **St Mary's** (Mon–Sat 10am–4pm, 3pm in winter; free), further down the street, as to which would be given cathedral status in 1914. The presence of the tomb of the resolutely Catholic Mary Tudor in the latter was the clinching factor.

## Corn Exchange

Bury's main commercial area lies just to the west of Angel Hill up along Abbeygate. There's been some intrusive modern planning here, but sterling Victorian buildings flank both the L-shaped **Cornhill** and the **Buttermarket**, the two short main streets, as well as the narrower streets in between. The dominant edifice is the **Corn Exchange**, whose portico is all Neoclassical extravagance with a whopping set of stone columns and a carved tympanum up above. Perhaps the Victorian merchants who footed the bill decided it was too showy after all, for they had a Biblical quote inscribed above the columns in an apparent flash of modesty – "The Earth is the Lord's and the Fulness Thereof".

### ARRIVAL AND DEPARTURE

BURY ST EDMUNDS

**By train** Bury St Edmunds' train station is on the northern edge of the centre, a 10min walk from Angel Hill via Northgate Street.

Destinations Cambridge (hourly; 45min); Ely (every 2hr; 30min); Ipswich (hourly; 40min).

**By bus** The bus station is on St Andrew Street North, a 5min walk northwest of Angel Hill.

Destinations Lavenham (Mon–Sat hourly; 40min).

**Tourist office** 6 Angel Hill (Easter–Oct Mon–Fri 9.30am–5pm, plus May–Sept Sat 9.30am–5pm & Sun 10am–3pm; Nov–Easter Mon–Fri 10am–4pm, Sat 10am–1pm; ☎ 01284 764667, ⓦ visit-burystedmunds.co.uk).

## ACCOMMODATION

**Chantry Hotel** 8 Sparhawk St ☎01284 767427, ⓦchantryhotel.com. There are fourteen guest rooms here in this privately-owned hotel and they occupy the Georgian house at the front and the annexe behind. The decor is retro with big wooden beds and even the odd four-poster. A handy, central location too. **£110**

★**The Old Cannon B&B** 86 Cannon St ☎01284 768769, ⓦoldcannonbrewery.co.uk. Bury's most distinctive B&B; there are a handful of neat and trim modern guest rooms here, all en suite, in an intelligently recycled brewhouse, which is itself attached to a micro-brewery, restaurant and bar (see below). Cannon Street is on the north side of town, a 5min walk from the centre. **£120**

## EATING AND DRINKING

**Baileys 2** 5 Whiting St ☎01284 706198, ⓦbaileys2 .co.uk. This cosy, modern place just off Abbeygate is the best teashop in town. The food is fresh and the menu extensive, but look no further than the toasties (£5). Mon–Sat 9am–4pm.

**Maison Bleue** 31 Churchgate St ☎01284 760623, ⓦwww.maisonbleue.co.uk. Slick and sleek seafood restaurant noted for its outstanding (French-influenced) menu, covering everything from crab and cod through to sardines and skate. Main courses average £22. Tues–Sat noon–2pm & 7–9.30pm.

★**The Nutshell** 17 The Traverse ☎01284 764867, ⓦthenutshellpub.co.uk. At the top of Abbeygate, The *Nutshell* claims to be Britain's smallest pub and it certainly is small – it's only sixteen feet by seven, big enough for twelve customers or maybe fifteen, provided they can raise a pint without raising their elbows. The pub is owned by the excellent Greene King brewery, which provides some sterling beers. Daily 11am–11pm.

**The Old Cannon** 86 Cannon St ☎01284 768769, ⓦoldcannonbrewery.co.uk. With a B&B (see above) in the adjoining brewhouse, the *Old Cannon's* restaurant-bar offers an excellent range of daily specials with due prominence given to local ingredients. Main courses are competitively priced at around £14. Kitchen: Mon–Sat noon–9pm & Sun noon–3pm; Bar: Mon–Sat noon–11pm & Sun noon–10.30pm.

7

# Ipswich

**IPSWICH**, situated at the head of the Orwell estuary, was a rich trading port in the Middle Ages, but its appearance today is mainly the result of a revival of fortunes in the Victorian era – give or take some clumsy postwar development. The two surviving reminders of old Ipswich – **Christchurch Mansion** and the splendid **Ancient House** – plus the recently renovated **quayside** are all reason enough to spend at least an afternoon here, and there's also the **Cornhill**, the ancient Saxon marketplace and still the town's focal point, an agreeable urban space flanked by a bevy of imposing Victorian edifices – the Italianate town hall, the old Neoclassical Post Office and the grandiose pseudo-Jacobean Lloyds building.

## Ancient House

30 Buttermarket, at corner of St Stephen's Lane • Lakeland store: Mon–Sat 9am–5.30pm

From Cornhill, it's just a couple of minutes' walk southeast to Ipswich's most famous building, the **Ancient House**, whose exterior was decorated around 1670 in extravagant style, a riot of pargeting and stucco work that together make it one of the finest examples of Restoration artistry in the country. The house is now a branch of the Lakeland housewares chain, and as such you're free to take a peek inside to view yet more of the decor, including its hammerbeam roof.

## Christchurch Mansion

Soane St • Tues–Sun 10am–5pm • Free • ☎01473 433554, ⓦwww.cimuseums.org.uk

**Christchurch Mansion** is a handsome, if much-restored Tudor building, sporting seventeenth-century Dutch-style gables and set in 65 acres of parkland – an area larger than the town centre itself. The labyrinthine interior is worth exploring, with period furnishings and a good assortment of paintings by Constable and Gainsborough, both inside the main building and in the attached **Wolsey Art Gallery**.

## The Wet Dock

Neptune Quay, half a mile south of Cornhill

The **Wet Dock** was the largest dock in Europe when it opened in 1845. Today, after an imaginative refurbishment, it's flanked by apartments and offices, pubs, hotels and restaurants, many converted from the old marine warehouses. Walking around the Wet Dock is a pleasant way to pass an hour or so – look out, in particular, for the proud Neoclassical **Customs House**.

### ARRIVAL AND INFORMATION                                        IPSWICH

**By train** Ipswich train station is on the south bank of the River Orwell, about 10min walk from Cornhill along Princes Street.

Destinations Bury St Edmunds (hourly; 35min); Cambridge (hourly; 1hr 20min); Colchester (every 30min; 20min); Ely (every 2hr; 1hr); London Liverpool Street (every 30min; 1hr); Norwich (every 30min; 40min).

**By bus** There are two bus stations: the Cattle Market bus station, a 5min walk south of Cornhill on Turret Lane, has long-distance and regional services (ⓦ suffolkonboard .com) and the second, Tower Ramparts, immediately north of Cornhill, has local services.

Destinations Aldeburgh (Mon–Sat hourly; 1hr 30min); Orford (Mon–Sat every 1–2hr; 1hr 50min; change at Rendlesham).

**Tourist office** St Stephen's Church, St Stephens Lane (Mon–Sat 9am–5pm; ☏ 01473 258070, ⓦ allaboutipswich.com).

### ACCOMMODATION

**Salthouse Harbour Hotel** Neptune Quay ☏ 01473 226789, ⓦ salthouseharbour.co.uk. Housed in an imaginatively converted old warehouse down on the quayside, this is the city's best choice, with 70 large, modern and minimalist-style rooms whose floor-to-ceiling windows look out over Ipswich's harbour. Depending on demand, rates can go up to more than £200. **£140**

### EATING AND DRINKING

**Aqua Eight** 8 Lion St ☏ 01473 218989, ⓦ aquaeight .com. Cool Asian fusion restaurant right in the heart of town. Most mains go for £10–12, but you can't go wrong with the superb steamed silver cod with ginger and scallions in soya sauce for £18.50. It also has a great bar serving good oriental-style meze and finger food. Tues–Thurs noon–2.30pm & 7–10pm, Fri & Sat noon–2.30pm & 5.30–11pm, Sun 5.30–10pm.

**The Eaterie** Salthouse Harbour Hotel ☏ 01473 226789, ⓦ salthouseharbour.co.uk. The restaurant lives up to the hotel's high standards (see above), with curvy banquettes and a low-lit, warehousey feel. The food is hearty rather than healthy, but served with a flourish and a good eye to detail. There are usually a few specials on the board too; generally starters are £5.95–8.95, mains £12.95–16.95. Daily noon–10pm.

# The Suffolk coast

The **Suffolk coast** feels detached from the rest of the county: the main road and rail lines from Ipswich to the seaport of Lowestoft funnel traffic a few miles inland for most of the way, and patches of marsh and woodland make the separation still more complete. The coast has long been plagued by erosion and this has contributed to the virtual extinction of the local fishing industry, and, in the case of **Dunwich**, almost destroyed the whole town. What is left, however, is undoubtedly one of the most unspoilt shorelines in the country – if, that is, you set aside the Sizewell nuclear power station. Highlights include the sleepy isolation of minuscule **Orford** and several genteel resorts, most notably **Southwold** and **Aldeburgh**, which have both evaded the lurid fate of so many English seaside towns. There are scores of delightful **walks** around here too, easy routes along the coast that are best followed with either the appropriate *OS Explorer Map* or the simplified footpath maps available at most tourist offices. The

Suffolk coast is also host to East Anglia's most compelling cultural gathering, the three-week-long **Aldeburgh Festival**, which takes place every June.

## GETTING AROUND                                THE SUFFOLK COAST

**By public transport** Getting around the Suffolk coast requires planning; work out your route in advance on ⓦtravelineeastanglia.org.uk or ⓦsuffolkonboard.com. Some journeys are straightforward – there is, for example, a regular bus from Ipswich to Aldeburgh – but some are more complicated: to get from Southwold to Aldeburgh, for instance, you catch the bus to Halesworth, the train from Halesworth to Saxmundham and then another bus to Aldeburgh, which all in all takes at least a couple of hours.

# Sutton Hoo

Tranmer House • Beside the B1083, to the southeast of Woodbridge: follow the signs from the A12 • Exhibition Hall: Jan to early March, Nov & Dec Sat & Sun 11am–4pm, plus additional opening during school holidays; mid-March to Oct daily 10.30am–5pm • £7.50; NT • ⓣ01394 389700, ⓦnationaltrust.org.uk/Sutton-hoo • No public transport

In 1939, a local farmer-cum-archeologist by the name of Basil Brown investigated one of a group of burial mounds on a sandy ridge at **Sutton Hoo**, on a remote part of the Suffolk coast between Ipswich and Orford. Much to everyone's amazement, including his own, he unearthed the forty-oar burial ship of an Anglo-Saxon warrior king, packed with his most valuable possessions, from a splendid iron and tinted-bronze helmet through to his intricately worked gold and jewelled ornaments. Much of the Sutton Hoo treasure is now in London's British Museum (see p.70), but a scattering of artefacts can be seen in the **Sutton Hoo exhibition hall**, which explains the history and significance of the finds. Afterwards, you can wander out onto the burial site itself, about 500 yards away.

**7**

# Orford

On the far side of the Tunstall Forest, some twenty miles from Ipswich, two medieval buildings dominate the tiny, eminently appealing village of **ORFORD**. The more impressive is the twelfth-century **castle** (April–Oct daily 10am–5pm; Nov–March Sat & Sun 10am–4pm; £6; EH; ⓦenglish-heritage.org.uk), built on high ground by Henry II, and under siege within months of its completion from Henry's rebellious sons. Most of the castle disappeared centuries ago, but the lofty keep remains, its striking stature hinting at the scale of the original fortifications. Orford's other medieval edifice is **St Bartholomew's church**, where Benjamin Britten premiered his most successful children's work, *Noye's Fludde*, as part of the 1958 Aldeburgh Festival.

## Orford Ness National Nature Reserve

Boat trips Mid-April to late June & Oct Sat only; July to Sept Tues–Sat; outward boats 10am–2pm, last boat back 5pm • £9; NT • ⓣ01728 648024, ⓦnationaltrust.org.uk/orford-ness

From the top of the castle keep, there's a great view across **Orford Ness National Nature Reserve**, a six-mile-long shingle spit that has all but blocked Orford from the sea since Tudor times. The National Trust offers **boat trips** across to the Ness from Orford Quay, 400yds down the road from the church – and a five-mile hiking trail threads its way along the spit. En route, the trail passes a string of abandoned military buildings, where some of the pioneer research on radar and atomic weapons testing was carried out.

## ARRIVAL AND DEPARTURE                                ORFORD

**By bus** There's a long-winded bus service between Orford and Ipswich (Mon–Sat every 1–2hr; 1hr 50min; change at Rendlesham) and a speedier bus service to Aldeburgh (Mon–Sat hourly; 1hr; change at Rendlesham).

## ACCOMMODATION AND EATING

**Butley Orford Oysterage** Market Hill ⓣ01394 450277, ⓦpinneysoforford.co.uk. A local institution, dishing up great fish and seafood, much of it caught and smoked locally and served in this simple café/restaurant.

Hours vary, but usually Mon–Fri 10am–4.30pm, Sat 9am–4.30pm & Sun 10am–4pm.

★**Crown & Castle** Market Hill ☎01394 450205, ⓦcrownandcastle.co.uk. Orford's gentle, unhurried air is best experienced by staying overnight at this outstanding hotel, with eighteen stylish guest rooms (breakfast included), and an excellent restaurant. Local, seasonal ingredients are the focus – rump of Suffolk lamb with broad-bean cream sauce for example – with mains around £20. Food served 12.15–2pm & 6.45–9pm. **£205**

## Aldeburgh

Well-heeled **ALDEBURGH**, a small seaside town just along the coast from Orford, is best known for its annual **arts festival**, the brainchild of composer **Benjamin Britten** (1913–76), who is buried in the village churchyard alongside the tenor Peter Pears, his lover and musical collaborator. They lived by the seafront in Crag House on Crabbe Street – named after the poet, George Crabbe, who provided Britten with his greatest inspiration (see box, below) – before moving to a large house a few miles away.

Outside of June, Aldeburgh is a relaxed and low-key coastal resort, with a small fishing fleet selling its daily catch from wooden shacks along the pebbled shore. Aldeburgh's slightly old-fashioned/local shop appearance is fiercely defended by its citizens, who caused an almighty rumpus – Barbours at dawn – when Maggi Hambling's 13ft-high *Scallop* sculpture appeared on the beach in 2003. Hambling described the sculpture as a conversation with the sea and a suitable memorial to Britten; many disgruntled locals compare it to a mantelpiece ornament gone wrong.

Aldeburgh's wide **High Street** and its narrow side streets run close to the beach, but this was not always the case – hence their quixotic appearance. The sea swallowed much of what was once an extensive medieval town long ago and today Aldeburgh's oldest remaining building, the sixteenth-century, red-brick, flint and timber **Moot Hall**, which began its days in the centre of town, now finds itself on the seashore. Several **footpaths** radiate out from Aldeburgh, with the most obvious trail leading

---

### BENJAMIN BRITTEN AND THE ALDEBURGH FESTIVAL

Born in Lowestoft in 1913, **Benjamin Britten** was closely associated with Suffolk for most of his life. The main break was during World War II when, as a conscientious objector, Britten exiled himself to the USA. Ironically enough, it was here that Britten first read the work of the nineteenth-century Suffolk poet, George Crabbe, whose *The Borough*, a grisly portrait of the life of the fishermen of Aldeburgh, was the basis of the libretto of Britten's best-known opera, *Peter Grimes*, which was premiered in London in 1945 to great acclaim. In 1948, Britten launched the **Aldeburgh Festival** as a showpiece for his own works and those of his contemporaries. He lived in the village for the next ten years, during which time he completed much of his finest work as a conductor and pianist. For the rest of his life he composed many works specifically for the festival, including his masterpiece for children, *Noye's Fludde*, and the last of his fifteen operas, *Death in Venice*.

By the mid-1960s, the festival had outgrown the parish churches in which it began, and moved into a collection of disused malthouses, five miles west of Aldeburgh on the River Alde, just south of the small village of **Snape**. The complex, the **Snape Maltings** (ⓦsnapemaltings .co.uk), was subsequently converted into one of the finest concert venues in the country and, in addition to the concert hall, there are now recording studios, galleries, a tearoom, and a pub, the *Plough & Sail*. The Aldeburgh Festival takes place every June for two and a half weeks. Core performances are still held at the Maltings, but a string of other local venues are pressed into service as well. Throughout the rest of the year, the Maltings hosts a wide-ranging programme of musical and theatrical events.

For more information, contact **Aldeburgh Music** (☎01728 687110, ⓦaldeburgh.co.uk), which operates two box offices, one at Snape Maltings, the other in Aldeburgh, at 152 High Street. **Tickets** for the Aldeburgh Festival usually go on sale to the public towards the end of March, and sell out fast for the big-name recitals.

north along the coast to Thorpeness, and others going southwest to the winding estuary of the **River Alde.**

## ARRIVAL AND INFORMATION ALDEBURGH

**By bus** Buses to Aldeburgh pull in along the High Street. Destinations Ipswich (Mon–Sat hourly; 1hr 30min); Saxmundham train station (Mon–Sat hourly; 30min). **Tourist office** 48 High Street (April–Oct Mon–Sat

10am–5pm & Sun noon–4pm; Nov–March Mon–Sat 10am–3pm; ☎01728 453637, ⓦsuffolkcoastal.gov .uk/tourism).

## ACCOMMODATION

**Brudenell** The Parade ☎01728 452071, ⓦbrudenellhotel.co.uk. This bright and smart seafront hotel has something of a New England feel that sits very comfortably here in Aldeburgh. There's a pleasant sitting room downstairs with sea views and the bedrooms are thoughtfully furnished in a contemporary style. **£190**

★**Ocean House B&B** 25 Crag Path ☎01728 452094, ⓦoceanhousealdeburgh.co.uk. In an immaculately maintained Victorian dwelling right on the seafront in the centre of town, *Ocean House* has just three traditional, en-suite guest rooms including a top-floor suite. The English breakfasts, with home-made bread, are delicious. **£100**

## EATING AND DRINKING

★**Aldeburgh Fish & Chip Shop** 226 High St ☎01728 454685, ⓦaldeburghfishandchips.co.uk. One of Aldeburgh's two outstanding chippies – this is the original, doing takeaway only; most people wander down to the seafront to nibble away there. Tues & Wed noon–2pm, Thurs noon–2pm & 5–8pm, Fri & Sat noon–2pm & 5–9pm, Sun noon–2.30pm.

**The Golden Galleon** 137 High St ☎01728 454685, ⓦaldeburghfishandchips.co.uk. Sit-down fish-and-chip restaurant, sister to the *Fish & Chip Shop* down the road.

Mon–Wed & Fri noon–2pm & 5–8pm; Thurs noon–2pm; Sat noon–2.30pm & 5.30–8pm; Sun noon–7pm.

★**The Lighthouse** 77 High St ☎01728 453377, ⓦlighthouserestaurant.co.uk. Aldeburgh's best restaurant, a relaxed, informal and always busy place in cosy premises. The menu favours locally sourced ingredients, featuring everything from burgers and fish and chips to the likes of venison tagine with couscous. Mains average around £12 at lunchtimes, more in the evening. Daily: coffee: 10am–noon; lunch: noon–2pm; dinner: 6.30–10pm.

# Dunwich

Tiny **DUNWICH**, about twelve miles up the coast from Aldeburgh, is probably the strangest and certainly the eeriest place on the Suffolk coast. The one-time seat of the kings of East Anglia, a bishopric and formerly a large port, Dunwich peaked in the twelfth century since when it's all been downhill: over the last millennium something like a mile of land has been lost to the sea, a process that continues at the rate of about a yard a year. As a result, the whole of the medieval city now lies under water, including all twelve churches, the last of which toppled over the cliffs in 1919. All that survives today are fragments of the Greyfriars monastery, which originally lay to the west of the city and now dangles near the sea's edge. For a potted history of the lost city, head for the **museum** (daily: April–Sept 11.30am–4.30pm; Oct noon–4pm; donation; ☎01728 648796, ⓦdunwichmuseum.org.uk) in what's left of Dunwich – little more than one small street of terraced houses built by the local landowner in the nineteenth century.

## Dunwich Heath & Beach

**Heath:** daily 9am–9pm or dusk **NT shop & tearoom** April–Sept daily 10am–5pm; March & Oct Wed–Sun 10am–4pm; Nov–Feb Sat & Sun 10am–4pm • £4.50 for parking; NT • ☎01728 648501, ⓦnationaltrust.org.uk/dunwich-heath-and-beach

From Dunwich's seashore car park, it's possible to walk south along the coast and then cut inland up and over the dunes to **Dunwich Heath**, where heather and gorse spread over a slab of upland that is now owned by the National Trust. You can also drive here – the turning is clearly signed on the more southerly of the two byroads to Dunwich. The parcel of heath at the end of this byroad offers wonderful views over the coast and here also are a set of old coastguard cottages, which now accommodate a National Trust shop and tearoom.

## Minsmere RSPB Nature Reserve

**Reserve** Daily 9am–9pm or dusk **Visitor centre** Daily 9am–5pm, 4pm in the depths of winter • £8 • ☎ 01728 648281, ⓦ rspb.org.uk

From the coastguard cottages at Dunwich Heath, it's a twenty-minute walk south along the dunes and then inland to the **Minsmere RSPB Nature Reserve visitor centre**, though there's a road here too – just watch for the sign on the more southerly of the two byroads into Dunwich. The reserve covers a varied terrain of marsh, scrub and beach, and in the autumn it's a gathering place for wading birds and waterfowl, which arrive here by the hundred. The reserve is also home to a small population of bitterns, one of England's rarest birds. You can rent binoculars from the visitor centre and strike out on the trails to the birdwatching hides.

### ARRIVAL AND DEPARTURE                                          DUNWICH

**By bus** Buses to Dunwich pull in beside the *Ship Inn*, just back from the coast.

**Destination** Aldeburgh (Mon–Sat every 1–2hr; 40min).

### ACCOMMODATION

**Dunwich Coastguard Cottages** IP17 3DJ ☎ 0844 3351287, ⓦ nationaltrustcottages.co.uk. The former coastguard cottages at Dunwich Heath now hold several

very comfortable one- and two-bedroom apartments. These are available for rent, with a minimum two-night stay. Average weekly cost **£650**

### EATING AND DRINKING

**Flora Tea Rooms** Dunwich beach ☎ 01728 648433. Right on the beach, this extremely popular café is a large hut-like affair, where they serve steaming cups of tea and

piping hot fish and chips to an assortment of birdwatchers, hikers and anglers. Daily 11am–4pm.

# Southwold

Perched on robust cliffs just to the north of the River Blyth, by the sixteenth century **SOUTHWOLD** had become Suffolk's busiest fishing port. Eventually, however, it lost most of its fishery to neighbouring Lowestoft and today, although a small fleet still brings in herring, sprats and cod, the town is primarily a seaside resort, a genteel and eminently appealing little place with none of the crassness of many of its competitors. There are fine Georgian buildings, a long sandy beach, open heathland, a dinky harbour and even a little industry – in the shape of the Adnams brewery – but no burger bars and certainly no amusement arcades. This gentility was not to the liking of **George Orwell**, who lived for a time at his parents' house at 36 High Street (a plaque marks the spot), but he might well have taken a liking to Southwold's major music festival, **Latitude** (ⓦ latitudefestival.co.uk), which spreads over four days in the middle of July with happy campers grubbing down in Henham Park beside the A12 about five miles west of town.

## Market Place and around

The centre of Southwold is its triangular, pocket-sized **Market Place**, sitting at one end of the town's busy High Street and framed by attractive, mostly Georgian buildings. From here, it's a couple of hundred yards north along Church Street to **East Green**, one of the several greens that were left as firebreaks after the town was gutted by fire in 1659. On one side of East Green is **Adnams Brewery**, on the other a stumpy old lighthouse. Close by is Southwold's architectural pride and joy, the **Church of St Edmund**, a handsome fifteenth-century structure whose solid symmetries are balanced by its long and elegantly carved windows.

## The Sailors' Reading Room

East Cliff • Daily 9am–dusk • Free • No phone, ⓦ southwoldsailorsreadingroom.co.uk

From Market Place, it's a short stroll along East Street to a cliff-top vantage point, which offers a grand view over the beach. Also on the cliff is the curious **Sailors' Reading Room**, where pensioners gather to shoot the breeze in the mornings amid a room full of model ships, seafaring texts and vintage photos of local tars, all beards and sea boots.

## Under the Pier Show

Southwold pier • Daily 9am–7pm, 5pm in winter • Free • ☎ 01502 7221055, ⓦ underthepier.com & ⓦ southwoldpier.co.uk

Jutting out from the beach, **Southwold pier** is the latest incarnation of a structure that dates back to 1899. Revamped and renovated a decade ago, the pier houses the usual – if rather more polite than usual – cafés and souvenir shops, but its star turn is the **Under the Pier Show**, where a series of knowingly playful machines, handmade by Tim Hunkin, provide all sorts of arcade-style sensory surprises, from the "Autofrisk" to the "Rent-a-Dog" and the mischievous (and emotionally rewarding) "Whack-a-banker".

## The harbour

The **harbour**, at the mouth of the River Blyth, is an idyllic spot, where fishing smacks rest against old wooden jetties and nets are spread out along the banks to dry. From the mouth of the river, a footpath leads west to a tiny passenger **ferry** (April–Oct Mon–Fri 10am–12.30pm & 2–5pm, Sat & Sun 10am–5pm, but weekends only in early May & early Oct; 90p; ⓦ explorewalberswick.co.uk), which shuffles across the river to Walberswick. If you're heading back towards Southwold, however, keep going along the river until you pass the *Harbour Inn* and then take the path that leads back into town across **Southwold Common**. The whole circular walk takes about thirty minutes.

7

### ARRIVAL AND INFORMATION

### SOUTHWOLD

**By bus** Buses to Southwold pull in on the High Street just to the west of the town centre.

Destinations Halesworth train station, on the Ipswich to Lowestoft line (Mon–Sat hourly; 30min); Norwich (Mon–Fri 1 daily; 1hr).

**Tourist office** 7 Child's Yard, off High Street (April–Oct Mon–Fri 10am–5pm, Sat 10am–5.30pm, Sun 11am–4pm; Nov–March Mon–Fri 10.30am–3pm, Sat 10am–4.30pm; ☎ 01502 724729, ⓦ visit-sunrisecoast.co.uk).

### ACCOMMODATION

**The Crown** 90 High St ☎ 01502 722275, ⓦ adnams .co.uk. The less upmarket (and less expensive) of Adnams' two hotels in Southwold, with a dozen or so rooms above a bar/restaurant. Most of the rooms are large and have been recently refurbished with each decorated in a pleasant, contemporary style. **£150**

★ **Home@21** 21 North Parade ☎ 01502 722573, ⓦ homeat21.co.uk. Near the pier, this seafront guesthouse occupies a well-maintained Victorian terrace house. There are three sympathetically updated guest rooms, two of which are en suite and two sea-facing. **£90**

**The Swan** Market Place ☎ 01502 722186, ⓦ adnams .co.uk. Delightful if pricey hotel occupying a splendid Georgian building right at the heart of Southwold. The main building is a real period piece, its nooks and crannies holding all manner of Georgian details. Some of the guest rooms are here, others (the "Lighthouse Rooms") are in the more modern garden annexe at the back. **£185**

### EATING AND DRINKING

★ **The Crown** 90 High St ☎ 01502 722275, ⓦ hotels .adnams.co.uk. Deluxe bar food featuring local, seasonal ingredients, all washed down with Adnams ales. Mains average around £16 and tables are allocated on a first-come, first-served basis. Food daily noon–2pm & 6–9pm, drinks till 11pm.

**Lord Nelson** East St ☎ 01502 722079, ⓦ thelordnelson southwold.co.uk. This lively neighbourhood pub, with its low, beamed ceilings, has a first-rate locally inspired menu. Try, for example, the herring, Nelson smokes (smoked haddock and cod in sauce) or the dressed crab. Food daily noon–2pm & 7–9pm.

★ **Tilly's** 51 High St ☎ 01502 725677. The pick of Southwold's several teashops, serving a great line in sandwiches and home-made cakes both inside and outside in the walled garden. Daily 9am–7pm.

# Norwich

One of the five largest cities in Norman England, **NORWICH** once served a vast hinterland of East Anglian **cloth producers**, whose work was brought here by river and then exported to the Continent. Its isolated position beyond the Fens meant that it enjoyed closer links with the Low Countries than with the rest of England and, by 1700, Norwich was the second-richest city in the country after London. With the onset of the Industrial Revolution, however, Norwich lost ground to the northern manufacturing towns – the city's famous mustard company, Colman's, is one of its few industrial success stories – and this has helped preserve much of the ancient street plan and many of the city's older buildings. Pride of place goes to the beautiful **cathedral** and the sterling **castle**, but the city's hallmark is its medieval **churches**, thirty or so squat flintstone structures with sturdy towers and sinuous stone tracery round the windows. Many are no longer in regular use and are now in the care of the **Norwich Historic Churches Trust** (ⓦnorwich-churches.org), whose website describes each church in precise detail.

Norwich's relative isolation has also meant that the population has never swelled to any great extent and today, with just 230,000 inhabitants, it remains an easy and enjoyable city to negotiate. Yet Norwich is no provincial backwater. In the 1960s, the foundation of the **University of East Anglia** (UEA) made it much more cosmopolitan and bolstered its arts scene, while in the 1980s it attracted new high-tech companies, who created something of a mini-boom, making the city one of England's wealthiest.

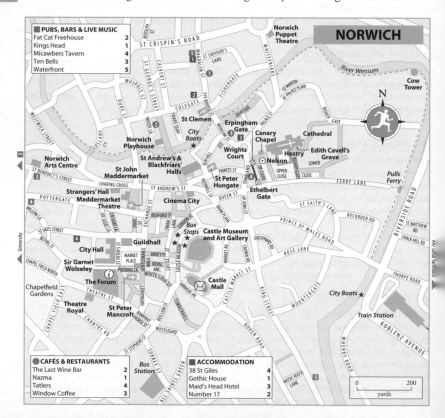

**NORWICH**

**PUBS, BARS & LIVE MUSIC**
| | |
|---|---|
| Fat Cat Freehouse | 2 |
| Kings Head | 1 |
| Micawbers Tavern | 4 |
| Ten Bells | 3 |
| Waterfront | 5 |

**CAFÉS & RESTAURANTS**
| | |
|---|---|
| The Last Wine Bar | 2 |
| Nazma | 1 |
| Tatlers | 4 |
| Window Coffee | 3 |

**ACCOMMODATION**
| | |
|---|---|
| 38 St Giles | 4 |
| Gothic House | 1 |
| Maid's Head Hotel | 3 |
| Number 17 | 2 |

0 · · · 200
yards

As East Anglia's unofficial capital, Norwich also lies at the hub of the region's **transport** network, serving as a useful base for visiting the Broads and as a springboard for the north Norfolk coast.

## Cathedral

Tombland • Daily 7.30am–6pm • Free, but donation requested • ☎ 01603 218300, ⓦ cathedral.org.uk

Of all the medieval buildings in Norwich, it's the **Cathedral** that fires the imagination: a mighty, sand-coloured structure finessed by its prickly octagonal spire, it rises to a height of 315ft, second only to Salisbury Cathedral in Wiltshire. Entered via the Hostry, a glassy, well-proportioned visitor centre, the **interior** is pleasantly light thanks to a creamy tint in the stone and the clear glass windows of much of the **nave**, where the thick pillars are a powerful legacy of the Norman builders who began the cathedral in 1096. The nave's architectural highlight is the ceiling, a finely crafted affair whose delicate and geometrically precise fan vaulting is adorned by several dozen roof **bosses**. Pushing on down the south (right) side of the ambulatory, you soon reach **St Luke's Chapel** and the cathedral's finest work of art, the *Despenser Reredos*, a superb painted panel commissioned to celebrate the crushing of the Peasants' Revolt of 1381. Accessible from the south aisle of the nave are the cathedral's unique **cloisters**. Built between 1297 and 1450, and the only two-storey cloisters left standing in England, they contain a remarkable set of sculpted **bosses**, similar to the ones in the main nave, but here they are close enough to be scrutinized without binoculars. The dominant theme of the fabulously intricate carving is the **Apocalypse**, but look out also for the bosses depicting green men, originally pagan fertility symbols.

### Cathedral precincts

Outside, in front of the main entrance, stands the medieval **Canary Chapel**. This is the original building of Norwich School, whose blue-blazered pupils are often visible during term time – the rambling school buildings are adjacent. A statue of the school's most famous boy, **Horatio Nelson**, faces the chapel, standing on the green of the **Upper Close**, which is guarded by two ornate and imposing medieval gates, **Erpingham** and, a few yards to the south, **Ethelbert**. Beside the Erpingham gate is a memorial to **Edith Cavell**, a local woman who was a nurse in occupied Brussels during World War I. She was shot by the Germans in 1915 for helping Allied prisoners to escape, a fate that made her an instant folk hero; her grave is outside the cathedral ambulatory. Both gates lead onto the old Saxon marketplace, **Tombland**, a wide and busy thoroughfare whose name derives from the Saxon word for an open space.

## Elm Hill

Near the north end of Tombland is Elm Hill, a dinky cobbled street – more a gentle slope than a hill – where the quirky half-timbered houses still appeal despite the tourist crowds; **Wright's Court**, down a passageway at no. 43, is one of the few remaining enclosed courtyards that were once a feature of the city.

## Strangers' Hall

Charing Cross • Mid-Feb to Sept Wed–Sat 10am–4pm • £4.50 • ☎ 01603 667229, ⓦ museums.norfolk.gov.uk

**Strangers' Hall** is the city's most unusual attraction. Dating back to the fourteenth century, it's a veritable rabbit warren of a place stuffed with all manner of bygones including ancient fireplaces, oodles of wood panelling, a Regency music room and a Georgian dining room. Allow an hour or so to explore its nooks and crannies, though the most impressive room, the Great Hall, with its church-like Gothic windows, comes right at the beginning. The hall is named after the Protestant refugees who fled here from the Spanish Netherlands to avoid the tender mercies of the Inquisition in the 1560s; at the peak of the migration, these "Strangers" accounted for around a third of the local population.

## St John Maddermarket

Pottergate • April–Oct Tues–Sat 11am–3pm; Nov–March Wed & Fri 11am–2pm • Free • ☎ 01223 324 442, ⓦ visitchurches.org.uk

**St John Maddermarket** is one of the thirty medieval churches standing within the boundaries of the old city walls. Apart from the stone trimmings, the church – which is named after madder, the yellow flower the weavers used to make red vegetable dye – is almost entirely composed of flint rubble, the traditional building material of east Norfolk. The exterior is in the Perpendicular style, characterized by vertical lines and large windows framed by flowing, but plain, tracery. By comparison, the interior is a disappointment, though there's compensation in a trio of finely carved Jacobean tombstones.

## Market Place

The city's **Market Place** is the site of one of the country's largest open-air **markets** (closed Sun), with stalls selling everything from bargain-basement clothes to local mussels and whelks. Four very different but equally distinctive buildings oversee the market's stripy awnings, the oldest of them being the fifteenth-century **Guildhall**, a capacious flint and stone structure begun in 1407. Opposite, commanding the heights of the marketplace, are the austere **City Hall**, a lumbering brick pile with a landmark clocktower that was built in the 1930s in a Scandinavian style, and **The Forum**, a large and flashy, glassy structure completed in 2001. The latter is home to the city's main library and tourist office (see p.396). On the south side of Market Place is the finest of the four buildings, **St Peter Mancroft** (Mon–Sat 10am–3pm), whose long and graceful nave leads to a mighty stone tower, an intricately carved affair surmounted by a spiky little spire, whilst inside slender columns reach up to the delicate groining of the roof.

Back outside and just below the church is **Gentlemen's Walk**, the town's main promenade, which runs along the bottom of the marketplace and abuts the **Royal Arcade**, an Art Nouveau extravagance from 1899. The arcade has been beautifully restored to reveal the swirling tiling, ironwork and stained glass.

## Castle Museum and Art Gallery

Castle Hill • Oct–June Mon–Sat 10am–4.30pm, Sun 1–4.30pm; July–Sept Mon–Sat 10am–5pm, Sun 1–5pm • £7.95 • ☎ 01603 493625, ⓦ museums.norfolk.gov.uk

Perched high on a grassy mound in the centre of town – and with a modern shopping mall drilled into its side – stern **Norwich Castle** dates from the twelfth century. Formerly a reminder of Norman power and then a prison, the castle now holds the **Castle Museum and Art Gallery**, where pride of place goes to the art galleries. These score well with their temporary displays and the outstanding selection of work by the **Norwich School**. Founded in 1803, and in existence for just thirty years, this school of landscape painters produced – for the most part – richly coloured, formally composed land- and seascapes in oil and watercolour, paintings whose realism harked back to the Dutch landscape painters of the seventeenth century. The leading figures were **John Crome** (1768–1821) – aka "Old Crome" – and **John Sell Cotman** (1782–1842), each of whom has a gallery devoted to their work.

The **castle keep** itself is no more than a shell, its gloomy walls towering above a scattering of local archeological finds and some gory examples of traditional forms of punishment. More unusual is a bloated model **dragon**, known as Snap, which was paraded round town on the annual guilds' day procession – a folkloric

**CLOCKWISE FROM TOP LEFT** NORFOLK BROADS (P.398); NORWICH MARKET; ALDEBURGH (P.388); LAVENHAM (P.382) >

hand-me-down from the dragon St George had so much trouble finishing off. To see more of the keep, join one of the regular **guided tours** that explore the battlements and the dungeons.

## University of East Anglia

**UEA Campus** Earlham Rd • Open access • Free • ☎ 01603 456161, ⓦ uea.ac.uk **Sainsbury Centre for Visual Arts** Tues–Fri 10am–6pm, Sat & Sun 10am–5pm • Free, but admission charged for some exhibitions • ☎ 01603 593199, ⓦ scva.org.uk • To get to the UEA campus by bus from the city centre, take #25 or #35 from Castle Meadow, or #25 from the train station

The **University of East Anglia** (UEA) occupies a sprawling campus on the western outskirts of the city beside the B1108. Its buildings are resolutely modern, an assortment of concrete-and-glass blocks of varying designs, some quite ordinary, others like the prize-winning "ziggurat" halls of residence, designed by Denys Lasdun, eminently memorable. The main reason to visit is the **Sainsbury Centre for Visual Arts**, which occupies a large, shed-like building designed by Norman Foster. Well-lit and beautifully presented, the body of the permanent collection spreads out over the main floor, beginning with a substantial selection of non-European – particularly Asian and African – artefacts positioned close to some of the European paintings and sculptures they influenced and/or inspired.

### ARRIVAL AND INFORMATION

NORWICH

**By plane** Norwich Airport (ⓦ norwichairport.co.uk) serves national and international destinations and is about 4 miles northwest of the city centre along the A140. There are regular buses to the city centre (20min) from the airport's Park and Ride.

**By train** Norwich train station is on the east bank of the River Wensum, a 10min walk from the city centre along Prince of Wales Road.

Destinations Cambridge (hourly; 1hr 20min); Cromer (hourly; 45min); Colchester (every 30min; 1hr); Ely (every 30min; 1hr); Ipswich (every 30min; 40min); London Liverpool Street (every 30min; 1hr 50min).

**By bus** Long-distance buses mostly terminate at the

Surrey Street Station, from where it's around 10min walk north to the town centre. Some services also stop in the centre on Castle Meadow.

Destinations: Blakeney (hourly; 2hr); Cromer (2–3 hourly; 1hr 10min); Holt (hourly; 1hr 20min); King's Lynn (2 hourly; 1hr 50min); London Victoria (every 2hr; 3hr 30min–4hr 15min; Sheringham (hourly; 1hr 30min).

**Tourist office** In the glassy Forum building overlooking Market Place (April–Oct Mon–Sat 9.30am–5.30pm, plus mid-July to mid-Sept Sun 10.30am–3.30pm; Nov–March Mon–Sat 9.30am–5.30pm; ☎ 01603 213999, ⓦ visitnorwich.co.uk).

### ACCOMMODATION

**38 St Giles** 38 St Giles St ☎ 01603 662944, ⓦ 38stgiles .co.uk. Billing itself as a cross between a B&B and a hotel, this deluxe establishment has five en-suite guest rooms of varying size and description, but all top quality. Great home-made breakfasts too. It's in a handy location, just a few yards from the Market Place. **£130**

★**Gothic House** King's Head Yard, Magdalen St ☎ 01603 631879, ⓦ gothic-house-norwich.com. This particularly charming B&B occupies a slender, three-storey Georgian house down a little courtyard off Magdalen

Street. The interior has been meticulously renovated in a period style and the two salon-style bedrooms are reached via the most charming of spiral staircases. The guest rooms are not attached to their bathrooms, but this really is no inconvenience. **£95**

**Maid's Head Hotel** Tombland ☎ 01603 209955, ⓦ maidsheadhotel.co.uk. Not everyone's cup of tea perhaps, but this chain hotel is delightfully idiosyncratic – a rabbit warren of a place with all sorts of architectural bits and pieces, from the mock-Tudor facade to the ancient,

---

### NORWICH ARTS CENTRE

Housed in a redundant church, the inventive and creative **Norwich Arts Centre**, 51 St Benedict's Street (☎ 01603 660352, ⓦ norwichartscentre.co.uk), covers many bases, including a wide range of performing and media arts plus an enterprising programme of participatory workshops and activities with an arts bias. Some of the kids' workshops are really first-rate, like "Revamp Pirates" in which household objects are turned into piratical paraphernalia.

wood-panelled bar, though there is also a clumpy modern extension. The rooms are mostly large and very comfortable in a standard-issue sort of way, and the location, bang in the centre opposite the cathedral, can't be beat. If you are a light sleeper, you should avoid those rooms that overlook the street especially on the weekend. **£90**

**Number 17** 17 Colegate ☎01603 764486, ⓦ number17norwich.co.uk. Family-run guesthouse with eight en-suite guest rooms decorated in a brisk, modern style with solid oak flooring; there are two larger family rooms as well. Good location, in one of the nicest parts of the centre. **£85**

## EATING

**The Last Wine Bar** 76 St George's St ☎01603 626626, ⓦ lastwinebar.co.uk. Imaginatively converted old shoe factory, a couple of minutes' walk north of the river, holding an unpretentious wine bar in one section and an excellent restaurant in the other. The food is firmly Modern British, with the likes of braised lamb shank with carrots and parsnips in a rosemary jus (around £15). Mon–Fri noon–2.30pm & 5pm–12.30am, Sat noon–2.30pm & 6pm–12.30am; kitchen closes 10.30pm.

**Nazma** 15 Magdalen St ☎01603 618701, ⓦ nazmabrasseries.co.uk. The menu at this splendid and modern Indian restaurant covers all the classics, each prepared from scratch with the freshest of ingredients. Particularly strong on Bangladeshi cuisine. Eat in or

takeaway. Mains around £9. Daily noon–2.30pm & 6pm–midnight.

**Tatlers** 21 Tombland ☎01603 766670, ⓦ tatlersrestaurant.co.uk. Enticing contemporary restaurant, where they stick to local, seasonal ingredients when they can. The portions are a tad nouvelle, but there's a good wine cellar to compensate. Try the wood pigeon. Mains around £16. Tues–Sat noon–2pm & 6-9pm.

**Window Coffee** 25 Wensum St ☎07913 672491, ⓦ thewindowcoffee.com. Odd little place – "little" being the operative word as it's billed as the smallest coffee shop in the world. It occupies the window of what was once a shop, and sells excellent coffee and cakes with a smile. Tues–Fri 8am–3pm & Sat 9am–3pm.

## DRINKING

**Fat Cat Freehouse** 49 West End St ☎01603 624364, ⓦ fatcatpub.co.uk. Award-winning pub with a friendly atmosphere and a fantastic range of well-kept, top-quality draught ales. Also a great range of bottled beers, ciders and perries. It's northwest of the city centre off the Dereham Road. Mon–Wed & Sun noon–11pm, Thurs–Sat noon–midnight.

★**Kings Head** 42 Magdalen St ⓦ kingsheadnorwich .com. The perfect drinkers' pub with precious little in the way of distraction – there are certainly no one-armed bandits here. The outstanding selection of real ales is supplemented by an equally impressive range of bottled beers, most notably Belgian. The pub has just two smallish rooms, so you may need to be assertive to get served. Daily 11am–11pm.

**Micawbers Tavern** 92 Pottergate ☎01603 626627. Lodged in an old beamed building on one of the city's prettiest streets, this friendly, busy pub is a local par excellence, featuring an outstanding range of guest ales on draught. There's home-cooked food and Sports TV too. Daily 4pm till late.

**Ten Bells** 74 St Benedict's St at Ten Bells Lane ☎01603 920292, ⓦ tenbellsnorwich.co.uk. Weird and wonderful place that attracts a weird and wonderful clientele, who hunker down among the old sofas and the rickety chairs with barely a light to illuminate proceedings. Lots of students and great cocktails. Mon–Thurs noon–midnight, Fri & Sat noon–1am & Sun noon–11.30pm.

## NIGHTLIFE AND ENTERTAINMENT

**Cinema City** Suckling House, St Andrew's St ☎0871 902 5724, ⓦ picturehouses.co.uk. Easily the best cinema in town, featuring prime new releases plus themed evenings and cult and classic films. Also live feeds, a Kids' Club and regular late-night horror films.

**Norwich Arts Centre** 51 St Benedict's St ☎01603 660352, ⓦ norwichartscentre.co.uk. Popular rendezvous featuring everything from kids' theatre to world music (see box opposite).

**Norwich Puppet Theatre** Church of St James, Whitefriars ☎01603 629921, ⓦ puppettheatre.co.uk. Housed in a deconsecrated medieval church beside the busy Whitefriars roundabout, this long-established puppet theatre company has an outstanding reputation for the

quality of its puppets and the excellence of its shows. Some performances are aimed at young children – who are simply enraptured – others are for adults.

**Theatre Royal** Theatre St ☎01603 630000, ⓦ theatreroyalnorwich.co.uk. This is the city's major performance venue, located in a clunky modern building with a capacious auditorium. It casts its artistic net wide, from World Music to opera.

**Waterfront** 139–141 King St ☎01603 508050, ⓦ waterfrontnorwich.com. This happening club and alternative music venue, which occupies what was once an old beer bottling plant, showcases some great bands, both big names and local talent, and offers club and DJ nights too. Schedule as per website.

**7**

**7**

## THE NORFOLK BROADS

Three **rivers** – the Yare, Waveney and Bure – meander across the flatlands to the east of Norwich, converging on Breydon Water before flowing into the sea at Great Yarmouth. In places these rivers swell into wide expanses of water known as **"broads"**, which for years were thought to be natural lakes. In fact they're the result of extensive peat cutting – several centuries of accumulated diggings made in a region where wood was scarce and peat a valuable source of energy. The pits flooded when sea levels rose in the thirteenth and fourteenth centuries to create these **Norfolk Broads** (W enjoythebroads.com), now one of the most important wetlands in Europe – a haven for many birds such as kingfishers, grebes and warblers – and one of the county's major tourist attractions. Looking after the Broads, the **Broads Authority** (W broads-authority.gov.uk) maintains a series of information centres throughout the region.

The Norfolk Broads are crisscrossed by roads and rail lines, but the best – really the only – way to see them is **by boat**, and you could happily spend a week or so exploring the 125 miles of lock-free navigable waterways, visiting the various churches, pubs and windmills en route. Of the many **boat rental** companies, Blakes (T 0844 8567060, W blakes.co.uk) and Norfolk Broads Boating Holidays (T 01603 782207, W broads.co.uk), are both well established and have rental outlets at **Wroxham**, seven miles northeast of Norwich – and easy to reach by train, bus and car. Prices for cruisers start at around £700 a week for four people in peak season, but less expensive, short-term rentals are widely available too. **Houseboats** are much cheaper than cruisers, but they are, of course, static, or you can opt for a short **boat trip** at a string of Broads locations.

Trying to explore the Broads by car is pretty much a waste of time, but cyclists and walkers can take advantage of the region's network of footpaths and cycle trails. There are **bike rental** points dotted around the region and **walkers** might consider the 62-mile Weavers' Way, a long-distance footpath that winds through the best parts of the Broads on its way from Cromer to Great Yarmouth.

# North Norfolk coast

About forty miles from one end to the other, the **north Norfolk coast** is one of the UK's top tourist destinations, attracting a wide cross-section of the population to its long sandy beaches and seaside resorts. This stretch of coast begins (or ends) at **Cromer**, perhaps the most appealing of the larger resorts on account of its handsome setting, perched on the edge of blustery cliffs. A few miles to the west is another well-established resort, **Sheringham**, but thereafter the shoreline becomes a ragged patchwork of salt marshes, dunes and shingle spits trimmed by a string of charming villages, principally **Cley**, **Blakeney**, **Burnham Market** and **Wells-next-the-Sea**, all of which are prime targets for an overnight stay.

**GETTING AROUND**                                                 **NORTH NORFOLK COAST**

Public transport along the north Norfolk coast is reasonable – no more. Without a car you'll be reliant on local buses to fill in the gaps between train stations.

**By train** There are hourly trains on the Bittern Line (T 08457 484950, W bitternline.com) from Norwich to Cromer and Sheringham.

**By bus** Easily the most useful bus is the Norfolk Coasthopper (T 01553 776980 or T 0871 200 2233, W coasthopper.co.uk), which runs along the coast between Cromer and King's Lynn via a whole gaggle of coastal towns and villages, including Blakeney, Sheringham, Wells and Burnham Market. Frequencies vary on different stretches of the route and there are more services in the summer than in the winter, but on the more popular stretches buses appear every 30min or hourly, less frequently on Sundays. There are lots of different tickets and discounts; perhaps the most useful is the Coasthopper Rover, which provides unlimited travel on the whole of the route for either one-day (£9), three days (£18) or seven days (£32); tickets can be bought from the driver.

# Cromer

Dramatically poised on a high bluff, **CROMER** should be the most memorable of the Norfolk coastal resorts, but its fine aspect has long been undermined by a certain shabbiness in its narrow streets and alleys. Things are at last on the mend, with new businesses arriving to add a touch of flair, and the town council keeps a string of cliff-top mini-parks and gardens in immaculate condition.

It's no more than the place deserves: Cromer has a long history, first as a prosperous medieval port – witness the tower of **St Peter and St Paul**, at 160ft the tallest in Norfolk – and then as a fashionable watering hole after the advent of the railway in the 1880s. There are three things you must do here: take a walk on the beach, stroll out onto the **pier**, and, of course, grab a **crab:** Cromer crabs are famous right across England and several places sell them, reliably fresh, and cooked and stuffed every which way.

## ARRIVAL AND INFORMATION

**By train** Cromer has managed to retain its rail link with Norwich; from Cromer station, it's a 5min walk into the centre. Destinations Norwich (hourly; 45min); Sheringham (hourly; 10min).

**By bus** Buses to Cromer, including the Norfolk Coasthopper (see p.398), stop on Cadogan Rd, on the western side of the town centre.

**Tourist office** North Norfolk Information Centre is on the south side of the town centre on Louden Road (Jan to late May & Sept–Dec daily 10am–4pm; late May to Aug Mon–Sat 10am–5pm, Sun 10am–4pm; ☎01263 512497, ⓦ visitnorfolk.co.uk).

## ACCOMMODATION

**Cliftonville Hotel** 29 Runton Rd ☎01263 512543, ⓦ cliftonvillehotel.co.uk. Among the big old mansions that line Runton Road just west of the town centre facing out to sea, this is the smartest, its grand Edwardian foyer equipped with an impressive double staircase and oodles of wood panelling. After the foyer, the rooms beyond can't help but seem a tad mundane, but they are large and most have sea views. **£120**

**Virginia Court Hotel** Cliff Ave ☎01263 512398, ⓦ virginiacourt.co.uk. The new owners of this medium-sized hotel are in the process of a major upgrade – and have started with what's most important: the beds are super comfy, the towels super thick, the duvets super warm and there's free wi-fi. The hotel dates back to Edwardian times, hence the capacious foyer with its wide, sweeping staircase, and the atmosphere is very much that of a traditional seaside hotel, friendly and relaxed. **£140**

## EATING AND DRINKING

**Mary Jane's Fish & Chip Shop** 27 Garden St ☎01263 511208. Many Norfolk tourists are fastidious about their fish and chips, with allegiances strongly argued and felt. This basic, family-owned place is especially popular, for the lightness of the batter and the freshness of the fish. Eat in or take away. Daily from 11am.

**Rocket House Café** RNLI building, The Gangway ☎01263 519126, ⓦ rockethousecafe.co.uk. Offering sparkling views over the beach, pier and ocean from its giant windows – and from its blustery terrace – this café has the best location in town, though the food lacks subtlety – stick to the crabs and the salads (which start at just £4.50). Mon–Fri 9am–5pm, Sat & Sun 10am–5pm.

**Virginia Court Hotel** Cliff Ave ☎01263 512398, ⓦ virginiacourt.co.uk. Excellent hotel restaurant, where the emphasis is on local, seasonal ingredients – try, for example, the roast duckling with an orange and redcurrant jus. Mains average £14. Accommodation and dinner deals available. Daily: afternoon teas 2–5pm & dinner 6–8.30pm.

# Felbrigg Hall

Felbrigg • **House** March–Oct Mon–Wed, Sat & Sun 11am–5pm **Gardens** March–Oct daily 11am–5pm; Nov to mid-Dec Thurs–Sun 11am–4pm **Park** Daily dawn to dusk • House & gardens £9.45; garden only £4.45; park only free; NT • ☎01263 837444, ⓦ nationaltrust .org.uk/felbrigg-hall • 2 miles southwest of Cromer off the A148 • No public transport

A charming Jacobean mansion, **Felbrigg Hall** boasts an appealing main facade, the soft hues of the ageing limestone and brick intercepted by three bay windows, which together sport a large inscription – "Gloria Deo in Excelsis" – in celebration of the reviving fortunes of the family who then owned the place, the Windhams. The interior is splendid too, with the studied informality of both the dining and drawing rooms enlivened by their magnificent seventeenth-century plasterwork ceilings. The surrounding **parkland** divides into two, with woods to the north and open pasture to the south. A popular spot to head for is the medieval **church of St Margaret's**, which contains a fancy memorial to William Windham I and his wife by Grinling Gibbons. Nearer the house, the **walled garden** features flowering borders, while the stables have been converted into pleasant tearooms.

## Blickling Hall

Blickling · **House & garden** Early March Sat & Sun 11am–3pm; late March to Oct Wed–Mon noon–5pm; Nov Sat & Sun 11am–2pm; Dec Sat & Sun 11am–5pm · £12.15; NT **Park** Daily dawn to dusk · Free · ☎ 01263 738030, ⓦ nationaltrust.org.uk/blickling-estate · 10 miles south of Cromer via the A140, No public transport

Set in a sheltered, wooded valley, **Blickling Hall** is a grand Jacobean pile dating from the 1620s. It was built for Sir Henry Hobart, a Lord Chief Justice, and although it was extensively remodelled over a century later, the integrity of the earlier design was respected and as a result, the long facade, with its slender chimneys, high gables and towers, remains the apotheosis of Jacobean design. Inside, highlights include a superb plasterwork ceiling in the Long Gallery and a grand main staircase. There's also a gargantuan tapestry depicting Peter the Great defeating the Swedes, given to one of the family by no less than Catherine the Great. The remains of the last of the male Hobarts are stashed away in a weird pyramidal mausoleum in the **parkland** that encircles the house.

## Sheringham

**SHERINGHAM**, just four miles west of Cromer, is a popular seaside town with an amiable, easy-going air – though frankly you're still only marking time until you hit the more appealing places further to the west. One of the distinctive features of the town is the smooth beach pebbles that face and decorate the houses, a **flinting technique** used frequently in this part of Norfolk: the best examples are on and around the High Street. Apart from the shingle **beach**, the main sight as such is the local museum, **The Mo** (March–Oct Tues–Sat 10am–4.30pm, Sun noon–4pm; £3.70; ⓦ sheringhammuseum.co.uk), which focuses on the town's nautical history.

An enjoyable out-of-town jaunt is on the **North Norfolk Railway**, whose steam and diesel trains shuttle along the five miles of track southwest from Sheringham to the modest market town of **Holt** (April & Oct most days; May–Sept daily; Nov–March limited service; all-day ticket £11.50; ☎01263 820800, ⓦwww.nnrailway.co.uk).

### Sheringham Park

Upper Sheringham · Daily dawn to dusk · Free, but parking £4.80; NT · ☎ 01263 820550, ⓦ nationaltrust.org.uk/sheringham-park · Reached from Sheringham along the B1157, or from Cromer along the A148 · Buses from Cromer and Sheringham train stations

Stretching over a large and distinctly hilly chunk of land just a couple of miles to the southwest of town, Sheringham Park was laid out to a design by **Humphry Repton** (1752–1818), one of England's most celebrated landscape gardeners. Repton's original design has been modified on several occasions, but the broad principles have survived, most memorably in the several **lookout points** that dot the wooded ridge running across the southern half of the park. There is also an area of heathland and a magnificent, 50-acre **rhododendron garden**, seen at its best from late May to early June.

### ARRIVAL AND INFORMATION

SHERINGHAM

**By train** Sheringham has two train stations, standing opposite each other on either side of Station Road. One is the terminus of the privately-run North Norfolk Railway (see above), the other is the terminus of the Bittern Line from Norwich.

Destinations Cromer (hourly; 10min); Norwich (hourly; 1hr).

**By bus** Buses to Sheringham, including the Coasthopper (see p.398), pull in on Station Approach, by the train stations.

**Tourist office** Station Approach, next to the train stations (June–Aug Mon–Sat 10am–5pm, Sun 10am–4pm; April–May & Sept–Oct daily 10am–2pm; ☎01263 824329, ✆visitnorthnorfolk.com).

### ACCOMMODATION AND EATING

★**Dales Country House Hotel** Lodge Hill, Upper Sheringham ☎01263 824555, ✆dalescountry house.co.uk. In a superb location on the edge of Sheringham Park, this splendid hotel occupies a rambling Edwardian mansion. The pick of the guest rooms come complete with mini-terrace, four-posters, oak furniture and open fireplaces. The hotel also possesses a smashing restaurant with a menu that exhibits both flair and imagination; mains start at £15. Daily noon–2pm & 6.30–9.30pm. **£170**

**No. 10 Restaurant** 10 Augusta St ☎01263 824400, ✆no10sheringham.com. This is the best restaurant in Sheringham – and in the prettiest of premises. The menu is well-considered – the cod fillet with spring onion risotto and red pepper sauce (£16) is a good example – and they serve snacks too. Meals: Wed–Sat noon–2pm & 6.30–9.30pm; teas, coffees and snacks: Wed–Sat 10am–noon.

## Salthouse

The tiny hamlet of **SALTHOUSE** may look inconsequential today, but the flocks of sheep that once grazed here provided a rich living for the lord of the manor. Today, the main evidence of this past wealth is the **church of St Nicholas,** an imposing and strikingly beautiful edifice stuck on top of a grassy knoll, its prominent position both a reminder to the faithful and a landmark for those at sea.

### ARRIVAL AND DEPARTURE                                                SALTHOUSE

**By bus** The Norfolk Coasthopper bus (see p.398) pulls in beside The Green, a small triangular piece of grass beside the A149.

### EATING AND DRINKING

**Cookie's Crab Shack** The Green ☎01263 740352, ✆salthouse.org.uk. *Cookie's* has something of a cult following, not for the decor, which is simple in the extreme, but for the freshness and variety of the seafood. Crabs, prawns and smoked fish lead the maritime way, but there's lots more to choose from including samphire, a local delicacy harvested from the surrounding mud flats and salt marshes from late June to mid-September. Daily: Oct–March 10am–4pm; April–Sept 9am–7pm.

## Cley Marshes Nature Reserve

A149 • **Reserve** dawn to dusk • **Visitor Centre** daily: April–Oct 10am–5pm; Nov–March 10am–4pm • £4 • ☎01263 740008, ✆norfolkwildlifetrust.org.uk

Beside the A149, between Salthouse and Cley (see p.402), **Cley Marshes Nature Reserve**, with its conspicuous, roadside visitor centre, attracts birdwatchers like bees to a honey-pot. Owned and operated by the Norfolk Wildlife Trust (NWT), the visitor centre issues permits for entering the reserve, whose saltwater and freshwater marshes, reed beds and coastal shingle ridge are accessed on several footpaths and overseen by half a dozen hides.

## Cley beach and Blakeney Point

**Blakeney Point National Trust information centre** April–Sept dawn to dusk • Free; NT • No phone, ✆nationaltrust.org.uk/blakeney

On the west side of the Cley Marshes Nature Reserve – and about 400 yards east of Cley village – is the mile-long byroad that leads to the shingle mounds of **Cley beach.** This is the starting point for the four-mile hike west out along the spit to **Blakeney Point,** a nature reserve famed for its colonies of terns and seals. The seal colony is made up of several hundred common and grey seals, and the old lifeboat house, at the end of the spit, is now a National Trust **information centre.** The shifting shingle can make walking difficult, so keep to the low-water mark. The easier alternative is to take one of the **boat trips** to the point from Blakeney or Morston (see box opposite).

## Cley

Once a busy wool port, **CLEY** (more formally **Cley-next-the-Sea** and pronounced "cly") is today little more than a row of flint cottages and Georgian mansions set beside a narrow, marshy inlet that (just) gives access to the sea. The sea once dipped further inland, which explains why Cley's fine medieval **church of St Margaret** is located half a mile to the south, at the very edge of the current village, overlooking the green. You're near a couple of splendid **nature reserves** here, both excellent destinations for birdwatchers – and don't miss the **Cley Smokehouse** for superb locally smoked fish.

### ARRIVAL AND DEPARTURE CLEY

**By bus** The Norfolk Coasthopper bus (see p.398) stops outside the Picnic Fayre deli on Cley's main street (which is also the A149).

### ACCOMMODATION AND EATING

★**Cley Mill B&B** Cley ☎01263 740209, ⓦcleywindmill.co.uk. This outstanding B&B occupies a converted windmill that offers wonderful views over the surrounding marshes. The guest rooms, both in the windmill and the adjoining outhouses, are decorated in attractive period style and the best have splendid beamed ceilings; self-catering arrangements are possible as well. At peak times, there's a minimum two-night stay. The *Mill's* smart and very agreeable restaurant specializes in traditional, home-made English cooking. Dinner is served at 7.30pm and a three-course set meal costs £32.50 per person. Advance reservations – by 10am of the same day – are required. **£159**

**Cley Smokehouse** High St, Cley ☎01263 740282, ⓦcleysmokehouse.com. Excellent, famed little place in an old forge on the main street, where they prepare delicious local oak-smoked fish – among other delicacies – to take away. Mon–Sat 9am–5pm, Sun 9.30am–4.30pm.

## Blakeney and around

Delightful **BLAKENEY**, a mile or so west of Cley, was once a bustling port, but that was long before its harbour silted up and nowadays it's a lovely little place of pebble-covered cottages with a laidback nautical air. Crab sandwiches are sold from stalls at the quayside, the meandering high street is flanked by family-run shops, and footpaths stretch out along the sea wall to east and west, allowing long, lingering views over the salt marshes.

Blakeney **harbour** is linked to the sea by a narrow channel that wriggles its way through the salt marshes and is only navigable for a few hours at high tide. At low tide the harbour is no more than a muddy creek (ideal for a bit of quayside crabbing and mud sliding). Blakeney is also close to the charming ruins of **Binham Priory**.

### Binham Priory

Binham NR21 0DQ • Priory ruins: dawn to dusk; Priory church: April–Sept daily 9am–6pm, Oct–March daily 9am–4pm • Free; EH • ☎01328 830 362, ⓦenglish-heritage.org.uk • No public transport

The substantial remains of **Binham Priory** boast a handsome rural setting about four miles southwest of Blakeney. The Benedictines established a priory here in the late eleventh century, which was suppressed in 1540. Today, the ruins focus on the **priory church**, whose nave was turned into the parish church during the Reformation. Inside, the nave arcades are a handsome illustration of the transition between the Norman and Early English styles, a triple bank of windows that sheds light on the spartan interior. Look out for the remains of the former rood-screen at the back of the church. The Protestants whitewashed the screen and then covered it with biblical texts, but the paint is wearing thin and the saints they were keen to conceal have started to pop out again.

### BOAT TRIPS TO BLAKENEY POINT

Depending on the tides, there are **boat trips** to **Blakeney Point** (see p.401) from either Blakeney or **Morston quay**, a mile or so to the west. Passengers have a couple of hours at the point before being ferried back and also get the chance to have a close-up look at the seal colony just off the point. Some boat trips just offer the seal colony. The main **operators** advertise departure times on blackboards by Blakeney quayside; you can reserve in advance with Beans Boats (T 01263 740505, W beansboattrips.co.uk) or Bishop's Boats (T 01263 740753, W bishopsboats.co.uk). All boat trips cost £10.

### ARRIVAL AND DEPARTURE — BLAKENEY

**By bus** Buses to Blakeney, including the Norfolk Coasthopper (see p.398) pull in at the Westgate bus shelter, a couple of minutes' walk from the harbour.

### ACCOMMODATION AND EATING

**Blakeney White Horse** 4 High St T 01263 740574, W blakeneywhitehorse.co.uk. This well-regarded inn holds nine guest rooms kitted out in a bright and cheerful version of country-house style. The *White Horse* is also noted for its food. Great play is made of local ingredients, the bread is baked here daily, and they offer lunchtime snacks and à la carte suppers. Mains average £15. Food served daily noon–2pm & 6–9.30pm. **£80**

**King's Arms** Westgate St T 01263 740341, W blakeneykingsarms.co.uk. The best pub in Blakeney by far, this traditional boozer, with its low, beamed ceilings and rabbit-warren rooms, offers top-ranking bar food (mains average £12), largely English but with an international zip. They also have seven, modest en-suite bedrooms. Food served daily, lunch and dinner. **£80**

**The Moorings** High St T 01263 740054, W blakeney-moorings.co.uk. Informal, cheerful little bistro where the creative menu is particularly strong on Norfolk meat, fish and shellfish. A typical main course might be sautéed lamb kidneys with pancetta and rosemary with a white bean ragout (£16.50). Tues–Sat 10.30am–9.30pm, Sun 10.30am–4.30pm.

7

## Wells-next-the-Sea

Despite its name, **WELLS-NEXT-THE-SEA**, some eight miles west of Blakeney, is actually a good mile or so from open water. In Tudor times, before the harbour silted up, this was one of the great ports of eastern England, a major player in the trade with the Netherlands. Today, the port is a shadow of itself, but Wells is a popular coastal resort.

The town divides into three areas, starting with the **Buttlands**, a broad rectangular green on the south side of town, lined with oak and beech trees and framed by a string of fine Georgian houses. North from here, across Station Road, lie the narrow lanes of the town centre with **Staithe Street**, the minuscule main drag. Staithe Street leads down to the **quay**, a somewhat forlorn affair inhabited by a couple of amusement arcades and fish-and-chip shops, and the mile-long byroad that scuttles north to the **beach**, a handsome sandy tract backed by pine-clad dunes. The beach road is shadowed by a high flood defence and a tiny narrow-gauge **railway** that scoots down to the beach (Easter to October every twenty minutes or so from 10.30am; £1.30 each way).

### ARRIVAL AND INFORMATION — WELLS-NEXT-THE-SEA

**By bus** Buses stop on Station Road, in between Staithe Street and the Buttlands; some also travel towards the quay. The town is on route of the Norfolk Coasthopper bus (see p.398).

**Tourist office** The volunteer-run tourist office is a few yards from the quay on Staithe Street (T 01328 710885, W visitnorthnorfolk.com).

### ACCOMMODATION

★**The Crown** The Buttlands T 01328 710209, W crownhotelnorfolk.co.uk. This enjoyable hotel occupies an especially attractive, three-storey former coaching inn with a handsome Georgian facade. Inside, the first batch of public rooms is cosy and quaint, all low ceilings and stone-flagged floors, and upstairs the dozen guest rooms are decorated in an imaginative and especially soothing style. **£140**

**The Merchant's House** 47 Freeman St T 01328 711877, W the-merchants-house.co.uk. Occupying one of the oldest houses in Wells, parts of which date back to the fifteenth century, this deluxe B&B has just two cosy, en-suite guest rooms. It's handily located, just a couple of minutes' walk from the quayside. **£85**

**Pinewoods Holiday Park** Beach Rd; ☎ 01328 710439, ⓦ pinewoods.co.uk. Behind a long line of pine-clad sand dunes that abut a splendid sandy beach, *Pinewoods* has been welcoming holiday-makers for over sixty years. It's a sprawling complex that holds touring and static caravans, beach huts, camping pitches and cosy wooden lodges. It is located about 15min walk from the quay and accessible on the narrow-gauge railway (see p.403). The camp and caravan pitches are open from mid-March to late October, the lodges from mid-March to December. Tariffs vary widely, but in high season a three-bed (six berth) lodge for a week costs around **£750**

### EATING

**The Crown** The Buttlands ☎ 01328 710209, ⓦ crownhotelnorfolk.co.uk. *The Crown* hotel (see p.403) prides itself on its food, with splendid takes on traditional British dishes. Mains average around £16. Mon–Sat noon–2.30pm & 6.30–9.30pm, Sun noon–9pm.

## 7 Holkham Hall

Three miles west of Wells on the A149 • **Hall** April–Oct Sun, Mon & Thurs noon–4pm • **Park** April–Oct daily 9am–5pm; Nov–March pedestrians & cyclists only daily 9am–5pm or dusk • Hall £13, plus £2.50 parking (April–Sept) for hall & park • ☎ 01328 713111, ⓦ holkham.co.uk

One of the most popular outings from Wells is to neighbouring **Holkham Hall**, a grand and self-assured (or vainglorious) stately home designed by the eighteenth-century architect William Kent for the first earl of Leicester – and still owned by the family. The severe sandy-coloured Palladian exterior belies the warmth and richness of the interior, which retains much of its original decoration, notably the much-admired marble hall, with its fluted columns and intricate reliefs. The rich colours of the state rooms are an appropriate backdrop for a fabulous selection of **paintings**, including canvases by Van Dyck, Rubens, Gainsborough and Gaspar Poussin.

The **grounds** are laid out on sandy, saline land, much of it originally salt marsh. The focal point is an 80ft-high **obelisk**, atop a grassy knoll, from where you can view both the hall to the north and the triumphal arch to the south. In common with the rest of the north Norfolk coast, there's plenty of **birdlife** – Holkham's lake attracts Canada geese, herons and grebes, and several hundred deer graze the open pastures.

### Holkham Bay

The **footpaths** latticing the Holkham estate stretch as far as the A149, from where a half-mile byroad – **Lady Anne's Drive** – leads north across the marshes from opposite the *Victoria Hotel* to **Holkham Bay**, which boasts one of the finest beaches on this stretch of coast, with golden sand and pine-studded sand dunes flanking a tidal lagoon. Warblers, flycatchers and redstarts inhabit the drier coastal reaches, while waders paddle about the mud and salt flats.

### ARRIVAL AND DEPARTURE HOLKHAM HALL AND BAY

**By bus** The Norfolk Coasthopper (see p.398) stops beside the *Victoria Hotel* at the north entrance of the Holkham estate (about a mile from the house) and at the south end of Lady Anne's Drive, which leads (in about 5min) to Holkham Bay.

## Little Walsingham

For centuries, **LITTLE WALSINGHAM**, five miles south of Wells, rivalled Bury Street Edmunds and Canterbury as the foremost **pilgrimage site** in England. It all began in 1061 when the Lady of the Manor, a certain Richeldis de Faverches, built a replica of the **Santa Casa** (Mary's home in Nazareth) here in this remote part of Norfolk – inspired, it is said, by visions of the Virgin Mary. It brought instant fame and fortune to Little Walsingham and every medieval king from Henry III onwards made at least one trip, walking the last mile barefoot – though this didn't stop Henry VIII from destroying the shrine in the Dissolution of the 1530s. Pilgrimages resumed in earnest after 1922, an Anglo–Catholic prelude to the building of an **Anglican shrine** in the 1930s – much to the initial chagrin of the diocesan authorities. Nowadays, the village does good business out of its holy connections as well as from the **Wells & Walsingham Light Railway (WWLR)** steam railway, which links it with Wells (April–Oct 3–5 daily; 30min; £9 return; ☎01328 711630, ⓦwellswalsinghamrailway.co.uk).

### Common Place and Walsingham Abbey Grounds

Shirehall Museum & Walsingham Abbey, Common Place • April to late Oct daily 11am–4pm • £4 • ☎01328 820510, ⓦwalsinghamabbey.com

Little Walsingham has an attractive and singularly old-fashioned centre, beginning with **Common Place**, the main square, whose half-timbered buildings surround a quaint octagonal structure built to protect the village pump in the sixteenth century. Also on Common Place is the mildly diverting **Shirehall Museum** through which you gain access to the **Walsingham abbey grounds**, whose lovely landscaped gardens stretch down to the River Stiffkey enclosing the scant ruins of the abbey.

### Anglican shrine

Common Place • Daily all reasonable hours • Free • ☎01328 820255, ⓦwalsinghamanglican.org.uk

Dotted around Little Walsingham are a number of shrines catering to a variety of denominations, but the main event is the **Anglican shrine**. Flanked by attractive gardens as well as a visitor centre, where there's a small exhibition on the history of the cult, the shrine is a strange-looking building, rather like a cross between an English village hall and an Orthodox church. The interior holds a series of small chapels and a Holy Well with healing waters as well as the idiosyncratic Holy House – **Santa Casa** – which contains the much revered **statue** of Our Lady of Walsingham.

| ARRIVAL AND DEPARTURE | LITTLE WALSINGHAM |
|---|---|
| **By bus** Norfolk Green's (☎01553 776980 or ☎0871 2002233, ⓦnorfolkgreen.co.uk) bus service #29 runs south from Wells to Fakenham via Little Walsingham, pausing outside the Anglican Shrine (Mon–Sat hourly, Sun every 2hr).<br>**By train** From the train station (for the steam train from | Wells, see above), it's a 5min walk south to Common Place: from the station, turn left along Egmere Road and take the second major right down Bridewell Street.<br>**Tourist office** Shares its premises with the Shirehall Museum (April to late Oct daily 11am–4pm; ☎01328 820510, ⓦvisitnorthnorfolk.com). |

| EATING | |
|---|---|
| **Old Bakehouse Tea Room** 33 High St ☎01328 820454, ⓦoldbakehousewalsingham.co.uk. In the centre of the village, this long-established tearoom offers a | tasty range of home-made cakes, scones and soups plus top-ranking cream teas. Wed–Sun 10.30am–4.30pm. |

## Burnham Market and around

As you head west from Wells, it's about five miles along the coast to the pretty little village of **BURNHAM MARKET**, where a medley of Georgian and Victorian houses surrounds a dinky little green. The village attracts a well-heeled, north London crowd, most of them here to enjoy the assorted comforts of the *Hoste Arms* (see p.406) and/or hunker down in their second homes.

### Burnham Thorpe

Straggling **BURNHAM THORPE**, a mile or so to the southeast of Burnham Market, was the birthplace of **Horatio Nelson** (see box, p.406), who was born in the village parsonage on September 29, 1758. The parsonage was demolished years ago, but the great man is still celebrated in the village's **All Saints Church**, where the lectern is made out of timbers taken from Nelson's last ship, the *Victory*, the chancel sports a Nelson bust, and the south aisle has a small exhibition on his life and times. The

---

### SHOT TO BITS: THE LIFE AND TIMES OF NELSON

**Horatio Nelson** (1758–1805) joined the navy at the tender age of 12, and was soon sent to the West Indies, where he met and married Frances Nisbet, retiring to Burnham Thorpe in 1787. Back in action by 1793, his bravery cost him first the sight of his right eye, and shortly afterwards his right arm. His personal life was equally eventful – famously, his infatuation with Emma Hamilton, wife of the ambassador to Naples, caused the eventual break-up of his marriage. His finest hour was during the **Battle of Trafalgar** in 1805, when he led the British navy to victory against the combined French and Spanish fleets, a crucial engagement that set the scene for Britain's century-long domination of the high seas. The victory didn't do Nelson much good – he was shot in the chest during the battle and died shortly afterwards. Subsequently, Nelson was placed in a barrel of brandy and the pickled body shipped back to England, where he was buried at St Paul's. In all the naval hullabaloo, Nelson's far-from-positive attitude to the landowners of his home village was soon glossed over: in 1797, he sent a batch of blankets back to Norfolk to keep the poor warm, railing that an average farm labourer received "Not quite two pence a day for each person; and to drink nothing but water, for beer our poor labourers never taste…"

---

other place to head for is the village pub (see below), where Nelson held a farewell party for the locals in 1793.

### ARRIVAL AND DEPARTURE

**By bus** The Norfolk Coasthopper bus (see p.398) stops beside the green on the Market Place in Burnham Market,

### BURNHAM MARKET AND AROUND

but it does not pass through Burnham Thorpe.

### ACCOMMODATION, EATING AND DRINKING

**Hoste Arms** Market Place, Burnham Market ☎ 01328 738777, ⓦ thehoste.com. One of the most fashionable spots on the Norfolk coast, this former coaching inn has been sympathetically modernized. The hotel's guest rooms are round the back and range from the small (verging on the cramped) to the much more expansive (and expensive). At the front, the *Hoste's* antique bar, complete with its wooden beams and stone-flagged floor, is merely a foretaste of the several, chi-chi dining areas beyond. Throughout, the menu is a well-balanced mixture of "land and sea", anything from wood pigeon with strawberries to

cod in beer batter. Main courses average around £16 in the evening, slightly less at lunch. Daily noon–9.15pm. **£120**

**Lord Nelson** Walsingham Road, Burnham Thorpe ☎ 01328 738241, ⓦ nelsonslocal.co.uk. They have kept modernity at bay here at this ancient village pub, from the old wooden benches through to the serving hatch and tiled floor. There's a good range of real ales plus above-average bar food – try, for instance, the Norfolk chicken breast wrapped in ham with a green-herb filling (£14). Mon–Sat noon–3pm & 6–11pm, Sun noon–10.30pm; food served: daily noon–2.30pm & 6–9pm.

## Brancaster and around

From Burnham Market, it's a couple of miles west to **BURNHAM DEEPDALE**, which leads seamlessly into **BRANCASTER STAITHE** and then **BRANCASTER**, all three of which spread along the main coastal road, the A149. Behind them, to the north, lies pristine coastline, a tract of lagoon, sandspit and creek that pokes its head out into the ocean, attracting an extravagant range of wildfowl. This is prime **walking** territory and it's best explored along the Norfolk Coast Path (see box, p.376) as it nudges its way through the marshes which back up towards the ocean. Pushing on west from Brancaster, it's a mile or so more to minuscule **TITCHWELL**, with its handful of flint-walled houses, old stone cross and bird reserve.

### Titchwell Marsh RSPB Nature Reserve

Titchwell • Daily dawn to dusk • Free, but £5 parking • **Information centre** Daily: March–Oct 9.30am–5pm; Nov–Feb 9.30am–4pm • ☎ 01485 210779, ⓦ rspb.org.uk

The old sea approaches to Titchwell harbour have now become the RSPB's **Titchwell**

**Marsh Nature Reserve**, whose mix of marsh, reed-bed, mud-flat, lagoon and sandy beach attracts a wide variety of birds, including marsh harriers, bearded tits, avocets, gulls and terns. A series of footpaths explore this varied terrain, there are several well-positioned bird hides, including a super-duper Parrinder hide, and a very helpful shop-cum-information centre.

| ARRIVAL AND DEPARTURE | BRANCASTER AND AROUND |
|---|---|
| **By bus** The Norfolk Coasthopper bus (see p.398) sticks to the main coastal road, the A149, as it travels through | Burnham Deepdale, Brancaster Staithe, Brancaster and Titchwell. |

### ACCOMMODATION, EATING AND DRINKING

★**Titchwell Manor Hotel** Titchwell (A149) ☎ 01485 210221, ⓦ titchwellmanor.com. Facing out towards the salt marshes that roll down towards the sea, this large Victorian hotel is one of the most enjoyable on the Norfolk coast. There are nine guest rooms in the main building with more in the contemporary-style, courtyard complex round the back. Everything is high spec, from the top-quality duvets to the bespoke furniture. The menu is very British with traditional dishes superbly prepared – anything from fish and chips with mushy peas (£13) through to lobster thermidor with new potatoes. Food served daily noon–2.30pm & 6.30-9.30pm, plus snacks and light meals in-between times. **£180**

**White Horse** Brancaster Staithe ☎ 01485 210262, ⓦ whitehorsebrancaster.co.uk. This combined hotel, pub and restaurant backs straight onto the marshes, lagoons and creeks of the coast – and, even better, the North Norfolk Coast Path runs along the bottom of the car park. The hotel divides into two sections: there are seven en-suite rooms in the main building and eight more at the back with grass roofs. Brancaster is famous for its mussels and oysters, which you can try in the restaurant, or choose the local duck or beef (main courses average £16). Food served: daily noon–2pm & 6.30–9pm; also bar menu daily 11am–9pm. **£140**

## Holme-next-the-Sea

**HOLME-NEXT-THE-SEA**, some three miles west of Titchwell, is the quietest of villages, its gentle ramble of old flint cottages and farm buildings nudging up towards the sand dunes of the coast. It's here at Holme that the Norfolk Coast Path (see box, p.376) intersects with the Peddars Way (see box, p.376), which follows the route of an old Roman road for most of its course, though it's likely the Romans simply enhanced what was there before: any doubts on the matter were surely quashed when, in 1998, gales uncovered a fascinating prehistoric site in the sands just off Holme, comprising a circle of timber posts surrounding a sort of inverted tree stump. Dated to around 2050 BC, "**Seahenge**", as it soon became known, attracted hundreds of visitors, but fears for its safety, prompted its removal to the Lynn Museum in King's Lynn (see p.408) and there's nothing to see here today. From Holme, it's just three miles or so to Hunstanton, a kiss-me-quick resort at the west end of the north Norfolk coast.

### Holme Dunes National Nature Reserve

**Reserve** Daily 10am–5pm, or dusk if earlier **Visitor centre** April–Oct daily 10am–5pm • Parking £5 • £4 for the reserve's footpaths and bird hides, but you can walk through the reserve on the Norfolk Coast Path for free • ☎ 01485 525240, ⓦ norfolkwildlifetrust.org.uk • 40min walk to the visitor centre from the nearest Coasthopper bus stop on the A149 at Holme

The **Holme Dunes National Nature Reserve** stretches along the coast at the point where The Wash meets the North Sea. The extensive sand and mud flats here have long protected the coast and allowed for the formation of a band of sand dunes, which have, in their turn, created areas of salt- and freshwater marsh, reed-beds, and Corsican pine woodland. This varied terrain attracts all sorts of **birds**, both migrants and residents. The reserve's **visitor centre** can be reached on foot from Thornham via the Norfolk Coast Path (3 miles) and by car from Holme-next-the-Sea: from the A149, turn down Beach Road just to the west of Holme-next-the-Sea and, near the end of the road, turn right down the signed gravel track.

7

**By bus** The Norfolk Coasthopper bus (see p.398) sticks to the main coastal road, the A149, as it travels along the edge of Holme-next-the-Sea.

# King's Lynn

Straddling the canalized River Great Ouse just before it slides into The Wash, **King's Lynn** is an ancient port whose merchants grew rich importing fish from Scandinavia, timber from the Baltic and wine from France, while exporting wool, salt and corn. The good times came to an end when the focus of maritime trade moved to the Atlantic seaboard, but its port struggled on until it was reinvigorated in the 1970s by the burgeoning trade between the UK and the EU. Much of the old centre was demolished during the 1960s and as a result most of Lynn – as it's known locally – is not especially enticing, but it does have a cluster of especially handsome old **riverside buildings**, and its lively, open-air **markets** attract large fenland crowds.

## Saturday Market Place and around

Behind the King's Lynn waterfront, the **Saturday Market Place**, the older and smaller of the town's two marketplaces, is a focal point of the old town. In addition to the Saturday market, it's home to Lynn's main parish church, **St Margaret's**, and the striking **Trinity Guildhall**, which has a wonderful, chequered flint-and-stone facade dating to 1421. Just across from the church is the former **Hanseatic Warehouse**, the most evocative of the medieval warehouses that survive along the quayside. Built around 1475, its half-timbered upper floor juts unevenly over the cobbles of St Margaret's Lane.

### Custom House

A couple of minutes' walk north of the Saturday Market Place along Georgian Queen Street stands Lynn's finest building, the **Custom House**, which was erected beside Purfleet Quay in 1683. It's in a style that was clearly influenced by the Dutch, with classical pilasters, petite dormer windows and a rooftop balustrade, but it's the dinky little cupola that catches the eye. The tourist office (see opposite) is inside.

## King Street and around

Beyond the Custom House, **King Street** continues where Queen Street leaves off, and is perhaps the town's most elegant thoroughfare, lined with beautifully proportioned Georgian buildings. On the left, just after Ferry Lane, **St George's Guildhall** is one of the oldest surviving guildhalls in England. It was a theatre in Elizabethan times and is now part of the popular King's Lynn Arts Centre (see opposite). At the end of King Street, the **Tuesday Market Place** is a handsome square surrounded by Georgian buildings and the plodding Neoclassical **Corn Exchange** (now a theatre); it hosts King's Lynn's main market on Fridays and, yes, Tuesdays.

## Lynn Museum

Market St • Tues–Sat 10am–5pm • £3.95 • ☎ 01553 775001, ⓦ museums.norfolk.gov.uk

Located in the old Union Chapel by the bus station, right in the centre of town, much of the refurbished Lynn Museum is given over to "Seahenge", a circle of 556 oak timbers, preserved in peat, that were found on the Norfolk coast in 1998 (see p.407). The timber circle is reckoned to be around 4000 years old and is now housed in an atmospheric gallery that showcases both the timbers themselves, their original position and possible purpose. The rest of the museum has displays on every aspect of life in Lynn from medieval times onwards.

## ARRIVAL AND INFORMATION
KING'S LYNN

**By train** King's Lynn train station is about 500yds east of the town centre.

Destinations Ely (hourly; 30min); London King's Cross (hourly; 1hr 40min); Cambridge (hourly; 45min).

**By bus** The bus station is right in the centre just to the west of Railway Road. The Norfolk Coasthopper (see p.398) begins (and ends) its journey at King's Lynn, putting a string of Norfolk destinations within easy reach.

**Tourist office** In the centre, down by the river at Custom House, Purfleet Quay (Mon–Sat 10am–5pm, Sun noon–5pm; Oct–March closes 4pm; ☎ 01553 763044, ⓦ visitwestnorfolk.com).

## ACCOMMODATION

**Bank House Hotel** King's Staithe Square ☎ 01553 660492, ⓦ thebankhouse.co.uk. A riverside boutique hotel in a fantastic Georgian house in the heart of King's Lynn's historic district. The eleven rooms are lovely, and its great bar and restaurant (see below) make it almost a destination in itself. Rooms and rates vary, but almost all rooms enjoy river views. **£110**

**The Old Rectory** 33 Goodwins Rd, east off London Rd, a southerly extension of Railway Rd ☎ 01553 768544, ⓦ www.theoldrectory-kingslynn.com. Small, agreeable B&B in a substantial Victorian house on the southern side of town; bedrooms are decorated in a reassuringly modern/cosy style. **£65**

## EATING, DRINKING & ENTERTAINMENT

**Bank House Hotel** King's Staithe Square ☎ 01553 660492, ⓦ thebankhouse.co.uk. Wonderfully inviting bar and restaurant, whose Modern British menu features such dishes as Lowestoft plaice and guinea fowl with bacon and cabbage. Mains average £12. Mon–Fri noon–2.30pm & 6.30–9pm; Sat noon–5.30pm & 6.30–9.30pm & Sun noon–3pm & 7–9pm.

**King's Lynn Arts Centre** 29 King St ☎ 01553 764864, ⓦ kingslynnarts.co.uk. Stages a wide range of performances and exhibitions both here and in several other downtown venues, including the old Corn Exchange on Tuesday Market Place.

# Ely

Perched on a mound of clay above the River Great Ouse about thirty miles south of King's Lynn, the attractive little town of **ELY** – literally "eel island" – was to all intents and purposes a true island until the draining of the fens in the seventeenth century. Until then, the town was encircled by treacherous marshland, which could only be crossed with the help of the local "fen-slodgers" who knew the firm tussock paths. In 1070, **Hereward the Wake** turned this inaccessibility to military advantage, holding out against the Normans and forcing William the Conqueror to undertake a prolonged siege – and finally to build an improvised road floated on bundles of sticks. Centuries later, the Victorian writer Charles Kingsley resurrected this obscure conflict in his novel *Hereward the Wake*. He presented the protagonist as the Last of the English who "never really bent their necks to the Norman yoke and ... kept alive those free institutions which were the germs of our British liberty" – a heady mixture of nationalism and historical poppycock that went down a storm.

Since then, Ely has been associated with Hereward, which is more than a little ridiculous as Ely is, above all else, a Norman town: it was the Normans who built the **cathedral**, a towering structure visible for miles across the flat fenland landscape and Ely's principal sight. The rest of Ely is at its busiest to the immediate north of the cathedral on the **High Street**, a slender thoroughfare lined with old-fashioned shops, and at its prettiest down by the **river**, a relaxing spot with a riverside footpath and a tearoom or two. Ely is also within easy driving distance of an undrained and unmolested chunk of fenland, the National Trust's **Wicken Fen**.

## Ely Cathedral

June–Sept daily 7am–7pm; Oct–May Mon–Sat 7am–6.30pm, Sun 7am–5pm • Mon–Sat £6.50, Sun free; Mon–Sat fee includes a ground-floor tour, but octagon tours cost an extra £7.50, £9 on Sun (reserve ahead) • ☎ 01353 667735, ⓦ elycathedral .org

**Ely Cathedral** is one of the most impressive churches in England, but the west facade, where visitors enter, has been an oddly lopsided affair ever since one of the transepts collapsed in a storm in 1701. Nonetheless, the remaining transept, which was completed in the 1180s, is an imposing structure, its dog-tooth windows, castellated towers and blind arcading possessing all the rough, almost brutal charm of the Normans.

The first things to strike you as you enter the **nave** are the sheer length of the building and the lively nineteenth-century painted ceiling, largely the work of amateur volunteers. The nave's procession of plain late Norman arches leads to the architectural feature that makes Ely so special, the **octagon** – the only one of its kind in England – built in 1322 to replace the collapsed central tower. Its construction, employing the largest oaks available in England to support some four hundred tons of glass and lead, remains one of the wonders of the medieval world, and the effect, as you look up into this Gothic dome, is simply breathtaking. When the central tower collapsed, it fell eastwards onto the **choir**, the first three bays of which were rebuilt at the same time as the octagon in the Decorated style – in contrast to the plainer Early English of the choir bays beyond. The other marvel is the **Lady Chapel**, a separate building accessible via the north transept. It lost its sculpture and its stained glass during the Reformation, but its fan vaulting remains, an exquisite example of English Gothic. The south triforium near the main entrance holds the **Stained Glass Museum** (Mon–Sat 10.30am–5pm, Sun noon–4.30pm; £4.50; ⓦ stainedglassmuseum.com), an Anglican money-spinner that exhibits examples of this applied art from 1200 to the 1970s.

## Oliver Cromwell's House

29 St Mary's St • April–Oct daily 10am–5pm; Nov–March Mon–Fri & Sun 11am–4pm, Sat 10am–5pm • £4.90 • ☎ 01353 662062, ⓦ visitely.org.uk

Near the cathedral is **Oliver Cromwell's House**, a timber-framed former vicarage that holds a small exhibition on the Protector's ten-year sojourn in Ely, when he was employed as a tithe collector. The tourist office (see opposite) is here as well.

### THE FENS

One of the strangest of all English landscapes, **the Fens** cover a vast area of eastern England from just north of Cambridge right up to Boston in Lincolnshire. For centuries, they were an inhospitable wilderness of quaking bogs and marshland, punctuated by clay islands on which small communities eked out a livelihood cutting peat for fuel, using reeds for thatching and living on a diet of fish and wildfowl. Piecemeal land reclamation took place throughout the Middle Ages, but it wasn't until the seventeenth century that the systematic draining of the Fens was undertaken – amid fierce local opposition – by the Dutch engineer **Cornelius Vermuyden**. This wholesale draining had unforeseen consequences: as it dried out, the peaty soil shrank to below the level of the rivers, causing frequent flooding, and the region's **windmills**, which had previously been vital in keeping the waters at bay, now compounded the problem by causing further shrinkage. The engineers had to do some rapid backtracking and the task of draining the Fens was only completed in the 1820s following the introduction of **steam-driven pumps**, leviathans which could control water levels with much greater precision than their windmill predecessors. Drained, the Fens now comprise some of the most fertile agricultural land in Europe – though at least **Wicken Fen** (see opposite) gives the flavour of what went before.

## ARRIVAL AND INFORMATION

**ELY**

**By train** Ely lies on a major rail intersection, receiving direct trains from as far afield as Liverpool, Norwich and London, as well as from Cambridge. From the train station, it's a 10min walk to the cathedral, straight up Station Road and then Back Hill before veering right along The Gallery. Destinations Cambridge (every 30min; 20min); Ipswich (every 2hr; 1hr); King's Lynn (hourly; 30min); London King's Cross (every 30min; 1hr); Norwich (every 30min; 1hr).

**By bus** Buses stop on Market Street immediately north of the cathedral.
Destinations Cambridge (hourly; 1hr)
**Tourist office** In Oliver Cromwell's House, 29 St Mary's Street (April–Oct daily 10am–5pm; Nov–March Mon–Fri & Sun 11am–4pm, Sat 10am–5pm; ☎01353 662062, ⓦ visitely.org.uk).

## ACCOMMODATION

**Peacocks Tearoom** 65 Waterside ☎01353 661100, ⓦ peacockstearoom.co.uk. After the success of their tearoom (see below), the owners of *Peacocks* have ventured into B&B, offering two comfortably furnished suites in the same riverside premises. The suites are kitted out in antique style – and very pleasant they are too. **£125**
**29 Waterside B&B** 29 Waterside ☎01353 614329, ⓔinfo@29waterside.org.uk. Ely is short of places to stay, but this cosy B&B, in a pair of pretty little brick cottages dating back to the 1750s, helps remedy things. Several original features have been preserved, including the beamed ceilings, and the remainder has been sympathetically modernized. If the sun is out, breakfast can be taken in the garden. **£70**

## EATING AND DRINKING

**Peacocks Tearoom** 65 Waterside ☎01353 661100, ⓦ peacockstearoom.co.uk. Down by the river, this popular tearoom – easily the best in town – serves a delicious range of cream teas, salads, sandwiches, soups and lunches with the odd surprise: try, for example, the chocolate zucchini cake. Also an enormous choice of teas from around the world. Wed–Sun 10.30am–5pm.

# Wicken Fen National Nature Reserve

Lode Lane, Wicken • **Nature Reserve** Daily 10am–5pm or dusk **Dragonfly Centre** End May to end Sept Sat & Sun 11am–4pm • £6.15; NT • ☎01353 7202734 • ⓦ nationaltrust.org.uk/wicken-fen • No public transport

**Wicken Fen National Nature Reserve**, nine miles south of Ely, is one of the few remaining areas of undrained fenland and as such is an important wetland habitat. It owes its survival to a group of Victorian entomologists who donated the land to the National Trust in 1899. The seven hundred acres are undrained but not uncultivated – sedge and reed cutting are still carried out to preserve the landscape as it is – and the reserve is easily explored by means of several clearly marked **footpaths**. The reserve holds about ten birdwatching hides and is also one of the best places in the UK to see dragonflies.

---

## PETERBOROUGH CATHEDRAL

Burgeoning **Peterborough**, some thirty miles northwest of Ely, has just one distinct – but unmissable – attraction – its superb Norman **cathedral** (Mon–Fri 9am–5pm, Sat 9am–3pm, Sun noon–3pm; donation requested; ☎01733 355315, ⓦ peterborough-cathedral.org.uk). Work on the present church began a year after the great fire of 1116 and was largely completed within the century. The one significant later addition is the thirteenth-century west facade, one of the most magnificent in England, made up of three deeply recessed arches, though the purity of the design is marred slightly by an incongruous central porch added in 1370.

The interior is a wonderful example of Norman architecture. Round-arched rib vaults and shallow blind arcades line the nave, while up above the painted wooden ceiling, dating from 1220, is an exquisite example of medieval art, one of the most important in Europe. There are several notable tombs in the cathedral, too, beginning with that of Henry VIII's first wife, **Catherine of Aragon**, who is buried in the north aisle of the presbytery under a slab of black Irish marble.

Peterborough **train station** is a short, signposted walk across the pedestrianized town centre from the cathedral.

# Cambridge

On the whole, **CAMBRIDGE** is a much quieter and more secluded place than Oxford, though for the visitor what really sets it apart from its scholarly rival is "**The Backs**" – the green sward of land that straddles the languid River Cam, providing exquisite views over the backs of the old colleges. At the front, the handsome facades of these same colleges dominate the layout of the town centre, lining up along the main streets. Most of the older colleges date back to the late thirteenth and early fourteenth centuries and are designed to a **similar plan**, with the main gate leading through to a series of "courts," typically a carefully manicured slab of lawn surrounded on all four sides by college residences or offices. Many of the buildings are extraordinarily beautiful, but the most famous is **King's College**, whose magnificent **King's College Chapel** is one of the great statements of late Gothic architecture. There are 31 university colleges in total, each an independent, self-governing body, proud of its achievements and attracting – for the most part at least – a close loyalty from its students.

Note that most colleges have restricted **opening times** and some impose admission charges; during the exam period (late April to early June) most of them close their doors to the public at least some of the time.

## King's College

King's Parade • Term time: Mon–Fri 9.30am–3.30pm, Sat 9.30am–3.15pm, Sun 1.15–2.30pm; rest of year: daily 9.30am–4.30pm • £7.50 including chapel • ☎ 01223 331100, ⓦ www.kings.cam.ac.uk

Henry VI founded **King's College** in 1441, but he was disappointed with his initial efforts. So, four years later, he cleared away half of the town to make room for a much grander foundation. His plans were ambitious, but the Wars of the Roses – and bouts of royal insanity – intervened and by the time of his death in 1471 very little had been finished and work on what was intended to be Henry's **Great Court** hadn't even started. This part of the site remained empty for no less than three hundred years and the Great Court complex of today – facing King's Parade from behind a long stone screen – is largely neo-Gothic, built in the 1820s to a design by William Wilkins. Henry's workmen did, however, start on the college's finest building, the much-celebrated **King's College Chapel**, on the north side of today's Great Court.

King's College once enjoyed an exclusive supply of students from Eton and until 1851 claimed the right to award its students degrees without taking any examinations. The first non-Etonians were only accepted in 1873. Times have changed, however, and, if anything, King's is now one of the more progressive colleges, having been one of the first to admit women in 1972.

### King's College Chapel

Opening times as for King's College • Entrance either via the main gatehouse on King's Parade or the North Gate, at the end of Senate House Passage

Committed to canvas by Turner and Canaletto, and eulogized in no fewer than three sonnets by Wordsworth, **King's College Chapel** is now internationally famous for its **boys' choir**, whose members process across the college grounds during term time in their antiquated garb to sing **evensong** (Mon–Sat at 5.30pm & Sun 3.30pm) and carols on Christmas Eve. The setting for the choristers is supreme, the chapel impossibly slender, its streamlined buttresses channelling up to a dainty balustrade and four spiky turrets, though the exterior was, in a sense at least, a happy accident – its design predicated by the carefully composed interior. Here, the high and handsome **nave** has an exquisite ceiling, whose fantail tracery is a complex geometry of extraordinary complexity and delicacy. The nave is flooded with

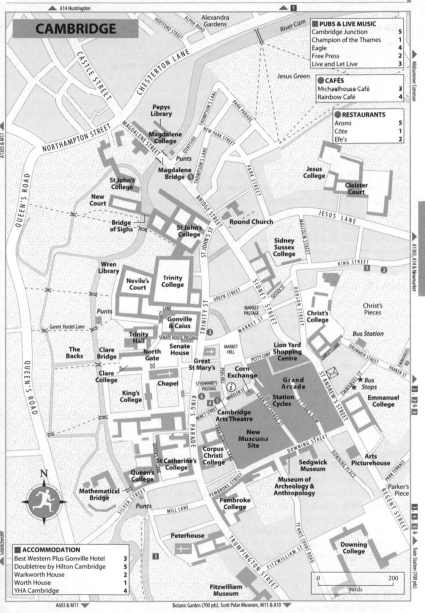

kaleidoscopic patterns of light that filter in through copious stained-glass windows. Paid for by Henry VIII, the **stained glass** was largely the work of Flemish glaziers, with the lower windows portraying scenes from the New Testament and the Apocrypha, and the upper windows the Old Testament. Above the **altar** hangs Rubens' tender *Adoration of the Magi* and an exhibition in the side **chantries** puts more historical flesh on Henry's grand plans.

> ### CAMBRIDGE: TAKING A PUNT
> **Punting** is the quintessential Cambridge activity, though it is, in fact, a good deal harder than it looks. First-timers find themselves zigzagging across the water and "punt jams" are very common on the stretch of the River Cam beside The Backs in summer. **Punt rental** is available at several points, including the boatyard at Mill Lane (beside the Silver Street bridge), at Magdalene Bridge, and at the Garret Hostel Lane bridge at the back of Trinity College. It costs around £25/hr to hire a punt (and most places charge a deposit), with up to six people in each punt. Alternatively, you can embark on a **chauffeured punt** from any of the rental places for about £18/hr per person.

## King's Parade

King's College dominates **King's Parade**, the town's medieval High Street, but the higgledy-piggledy shops and cafés opposite are an attractive foil to Wilkins' architectural screen. At the northern end of King's Parade is **Great St Mary's** (May–Aug Mon–Sat 9am–5pm, Sun 12.30–5pm; Sept–April closes 4pm; free; ☎01223 462914, ⓦwww.gsm.cam.ac.uk), the university's pet church, a sturdy Gothic structure whose **tower** (£3.50) offers a good view of the surrounding colleges. Opposite the church stands **Senate House**, an exercise in Palladian classicism by James Gibbs, and the scene of graduation ceremonies on the last Saturday in June, when champagne corks fly around the rabbit-fur collars and black gowns.

## Gonville and Caius College

Trinity St • No set opening hours • Free • ☎ 01223 332400, ⓦ cai.cam.ac.uk

The northern continuation of King's Parade is Trinity Street, a short way along which, on the left, is the cramped main entrance to **Gonville and Caius College**, known simply as Caius (pronounced "keys"), after the sixteenth-century co-founder John Keys, who latinized his name as was then the custom with men of learning. The design of the college owes much to Keys, who placed three gates on two adjoining courts, each representing a different stage on the path to academic enlightenment: at the main entrance is the **Gate of Humility**, through which the student entered the college; the **Gate of Virtue**, sporting the female figures of Fame and Wealth, marks the entrance to Caius Court; and the exquisite **Gate of Honour**, capped with sundials and decorated with classical motifs, leads onto Senate House Passage.

## Clare College

Trinity Lane • Daily 10.45am–4.30pm • Summer £2; winter free • ☎ 01223 333200, ⓦ www.clare.cam.ac.uk

Senate House Passage continues west beyond Caius College's Gate of Honour en route to **Clare College**. Clare's plain period-piece courtyards, completed in the early eighteenth century, lead to one of the most picturesque of all the bridges over the Cam, **Clare Bridge**. Beyond lies the **Fellows' Garden**, one of the loveliest college gardens open to the public (times as college). Back at the entrance to Clare, it's a few steps more to the North Gate of King's College, beside King's College Chapel (see p.412).

## Trinity College

Trinity St • **College** Daily 10am–4.30pm • £1 • ☎ 01223 338400, ⓦ trin.cam.ac.uk **Wren Library** Mon–Fri noon–2pm, plus Sat during term 10.30am–12.30pm • Free

**Trinity College** is the largest of the Cambridge colleges and its very long list of famous alumni includes John Dryden and Vladimir Nabokov; the Cambridge spies Blunt, Burgess and Philby; Aleister Crowley and Enoch Powell; Pandit Nehru, Bertrand Russell and Prince Charles.

A statue of Henry VIII, who founded the college in 1546, sits in majesty over Trinity's **Great Gate**, his sceptre replaced long ago with a chair leg by a student wag.

Beyond lies the vast asymmetrical expanse of **Great Court**, which displays a superb range of Tudor buildings, the oldest of which is the fifteenth-century clocktower. The centrepiece of the court is a delicate fountain, in which, legend has it, Lord Byron used to bathe naked with his pet bear – the college forbade students from keeping dogs.

On the far side of the Great Court, walk through "**the screens**" – the narrow passage separating the Hall from the kitchens – to reach **Nevile's Court**, where Newton first calculated the speed of sound. The west end of Nevile's Court is enclosed by one of the university's most famous buildings, the **Wren Library**. Viewed from the outside, it's impossible to appreciate the scale of the interior thanks to Wren's clever device of concealing the internal floor level by means of two rows of stone columns. Natural light pours into the white stuccoed interior, which contrasts wonderfully with the dark lime-wood bookcases, also Wren-designed.

## St John's College

St John's St • Daily: March–Oct 10am–5.30pm; Nov–Feb 10am–3.30pm • £5 • ☎ 01223 338600, ⓦ www.joh.cam.ac.uk

Next door to Trinity, **St John's College** sports a grandiloquent Tudor gatehouse, which is distinguished by the coat of arms of the founder, Lady Margaret Beaufort, the mother of Henry VII. Beyond, three successive courts lead to the river, but there's an excess of dull reddish brickwork here – enough for Wordsworth, who lived above the kitchens on F staircase, to describe the place as "gloomy". The arcade on the far side of Third Court leads through to the **Bridge of Sighs**, a chunky, covered bridge built in 1831 but in most respects very unlike its Venetian namesake. The bridge is best viewed from the much older – and much more stylish – Wren-designed bridge a few yards to the south. The Bridge of Sighs links the old college with the fanciful nineteenth-century **New Court**, a crenellated neo-Gothic extravaganza topped by a feast of dinky stone chimneys and pinnacles.

## Magdalene College

Magdalene St • **College** Daily 10am–6pm • Free • ☎ 01223 332100, ⓦ www.magd.cam.ac.uk **Pepys Library** Jan to late March, Oct to mid-Dec Mon–Sat 2–4pm; late April to mid-Sept Mon–Fri 2–4pm & 11.30am–12.30pm & 1.30–2.30pm • Free

Founded as a hostel by the Benedictines, **Magdalene College** – pronounced "maudlin" – became a university college in 1542; it was also the last of the colleges to admit women, finally surrendering in 1988. The main focus of attention here is the **Pepys Library**, in the second of the college's ancient courtyards. Samuel Pepys, a Magdalene student, bequeathed his entire library to the college, where it has been displayed ever since in its original red-oak bookshelves. His famous diary is also parked here.

## Jesus College

Jesus Lane • Daily 10am–5pm • Free • ☎ 01223 339339, ⓦ www.jesus.cam.ac.uk

The intimate cloisters of **Jesus College** are reminiscent of a monastery – appropriately, as the Bishop of Ely founded the college on the grounds of a suppressed Benedictine nunnery in 1496. Beyond the main red-brick gateway, much of the ground plan of the nunnery has been preserved, especially around **Cloister Court**, the first court on the right after the entrance and the prettiest part of the college, dripping with ivy and, in summer, overflowing with hanging baskets. Entered from the Cloister Court, the college **chapel** occupies the former priory chancel and looks like a medieval parish church, though in fact it was imaginatively restored in the nineteenth century, using ceiling designs by William Morris and Pre-Raphaelite stained glass. The poet Samuel Taylor Coleridge was the college's most famously bad student, absconding in his first year to join the Light Dragoons, and returning only to be kicked out for a combination of bad debts and unconventional opinions.

## Sidney Sussex College

Sidney St • No set opening times • Free • ☎ 01223 338800, ⓦ www.sid.cam.ac.uk

The sombre, mostly mock-Gothic facade of **Sidney Sussex College** glowers over Sidney Street. The interior is fairly unexciting too, though the long, slender **chapel** is noteworthy for its fancy marble floor, hooped roof and Baroque wood panelling, as well as for being the last resting place of the skull of its most famous alumnus, Oliver Cromwell – though the exact location remains a closely guarded secret. Incidentally, neighbouring **Hobson Street** is named after the owner of a Cambridge livery stable, who would only allow customers to take the horse nearest the door, hence "Hobson's choice".

## Christ's College

St Andrew's St • Daily 9.30am–4.30pm • Free • ☎ 01223 334900, ⓦ www.christs.cam.ac.uk

Close to Cambridge's central shopping area, the turreted gateway of **Christ's College** features the coat of arms of the founder, Lady Margaret Beaufort, who also founded St John's. Passing through First Court you come to the Fellows' Building, attributed to Inigo Jones, whose central arch gives access to the **Fellows' Garden**. The poet John Milton is said to have either painted or composed here, though there's no definite proof that he did either; another of Christ's famous undergraduates was Charles Darwin, who showed little academic promise and spent most of his time hunting.

## University museums

To either side of Downing Street, in a rambling assortment of large, mostly Victorian buildings, is a cluster of scientific and specialist museums with university affiliations. On the south side of the street are the **Sedgwick Museum of Earth Sciences** (Mon–Fri 10am–1pm & 2–5pm, Sat 10am–4pm; free; ⓦ sedgwickmuseum.org), which displays fossils and skeletons of dinosaurs, reptiles and mammals, plus one of the oldest geological collections in the world; and the **Museum of Archeology and Anthropology** (Tues–Sat 10.30am–4.30pm & Sun noon–4.30pm; free; ⓦ maa.cam.ac.uk), where a wide-ranging assortment of archeological finds is supplemented by an anthropological collection, whose prime exhibits are derived from the "cabinets of curiosities" collected by eighteenth-century explorers. On the north side of Downing, incorporated within a larger complex known as the **New Museums Site**, are the **Whipple Museum of the History of Science** (Mon–Fri 12.30–4.30pm; free; ⓦ www.hps.cam.ac.uk/whipple), crammed with antique scientific instruments and entered on Free School Lane; and the **Museum of Zoology** (ⓦ museum.zoo.cam.ac.uk), though this is closed for refurbishment until 2016.

## Queens' College

Silver St, but visitors' gate on Queens' Lane • Mid-March to mid-May & late June to Sept daily 10am–4.30pm; Oct Mon–Fri 2–4pm, Sat & Sun 10am–4.30pm; Nov to mid-March daily 10am–4pm • £3 in summer, otherwise free • ☎ 01223 335511, ⓦ www.queens.cam.ac.uk

**Queens' College** is particularly beautiful, boasting, in the **Old Court** and the **Cloister Court**, two dream-like, fairytale Tudor courtyards: the first of the two is a perfect illustration of the original collegiate ideal, with kitchens, library, chapel, hall and rooms all set around a tiny green. Flanking Cloister Court is the Long Gallery of the President's Lodge, the last remaining half-timbered building in the university, and the tower where Erasmus is thought to have beavered away during his four years here, probably from 1510 to 1514. Equally eye-catching is the wooden **Mathematical Bridge** over the River Cam (visible for free from the Silver Street Bridge), a copy of the mid-eighteenth-century original, which – so it was claimed – would stay in place even if the nuts and bolts were removed.

# Pembroke College

Trumpington St • No set opening times • Free • ☎ 01223 338100, ⓦ www.pem.cam.ac.uk

**Pembroke College** holds Wren's first-ever commission, the **college chapel**, paid for by his Royalist uncle, the erstwhile Bishop of Ely, in thanks for his deliverance from the Tower of London after seventeen years' imprisonment. It holds a particularly fine, though modern, stained-glass east window and a delicate fifteenth-century marble relief of St Michael and the Virgin. Close by, outside the Victorian library, is a statue of a toga-clad William Pitt the Younger, who entered Pembroke at fifteen and was prime minister ten years later.

# The Fitzwilliam Museum

Trumpington St • Tues–Sat 10am–5pm, Sun noon–5pm • Free • ☎ 01223 332900, ⓦ www.fitzmuseum.cam.ac.uk

The **Fitzwilliam Museum** displays the city's premier fine and applied art collection in an imposing Neoclassical edifice, which was built to house the vast hoard bequeathed by Viscount Fitzwilliam in 1816. Since then, the museum has been gifted a string of private collections, most of which follow a particular specialism. The **Lower Galleries**, on the ground floor, contain a wealth of antiquities including Egyptian sarcophagi and mummies, fifth-century BC Greek vases, plus a bewildering display of early European and Asian ceramics and sections dedicated to armour, glass and pewterware. Temporary exhibitions are held on the ground floor too. The **Upper Galleries** contain an eclectic assortment of mostly eighteenth, nineteenth- and early twentieth-century European paintings and sculptures, with more modern pieces by Lucian Freud, David Hockney, Henry Moore, Ben Nicholson, Jacob Epstein and Barbara Hepworth.

# Scott Polar Museum

Lensfield Rd • Tues–Sat 10am–4pm • Free • ☎ 01223 336540, ⓦ www.spri.cam.ac.uk

The pocket-sized **Scott Polar Museum** begins with a section devoted to the native peoples of the Arctic with an especially enjoyable collection of Inuit soapstone sculptures. It continues with pen sketches of the European explorers who ventured to both poles with varying degrees of success and it's here you'll find a substantial set of documents – original letters and incidental artefacts, etc – relating to the fateful expedition to the South Pole led by Captain Robert Falcon Scott (1868–1912), after whom the museum is named.

# Cambridge University Botanic Garden

Main entrance: the Brookside Gate, corner of Trumpington Rd and Bateman St • Daily: Feb, March & Oct 10am–5pm; April–Sept 10am–6pm; Nov–Jan 10am–4pm • £4.50 • ☎ 01223 336265, ⓦ www.botanic.cam.ac.uk

Opened in 1846 and covering forty acres, the **Cambridge University Botanic Garden** has several glasshouses as well as bountiful outdoor displays. The outdoor beds are mostly arranged by natural order, but there's also a particularly interesting series of chronological beds, showing when different plants were introduced into Britain.

## ARRIVAL AND INFORMATION                                                    CAMBRIDGE

**By plane** Cambridge is just 30 miles north of London Stansted Airport; there are hourly trains between the two (30min).

**By train** Cambridge train station, in the middle of a redevelopment zone with tower blocks sprouting up all around it, is a mile or so southeast of the city centre, off Hills Road. From here, it's an easy if tedious 20min walk into the centre or take any one of several local (Citi) buses to Emmanuel Street.

Destinations Bury St Edmunds (hourly; 40min); Ely (every 30min; 15min); Ipswich (hourly; 1hr 20min); King's Lynn (hourly; 45min); London King's Cross (every 30min; 50min); London Stansted Airport (hourly; 30min); Norwich (hourly; 1hr 20min).

**By bus** The long-distance bus station is on the east side of the city centre on Drummer Street.

Destinations London Victoria (every 2hr; 2hr).

**By car** Arriving by car, you'll find much of the city centre closed to traffic and on-street parking well-nigh impossible to find, so most visitors plump for a park-and-ride car park; these are signposted on all major approaches.

**Tourist office** Handily located on Peas Hill, just off King's Parade (April–Oct Mon–Sat 10am–5pm, Sun 11am–3pm; Nov–March Mon–Sat 10am–5pm; ☎0871 226 8006, ⓦvisitcambridge.org).

## GETTING AROUND

**By bike** Popular with locals and students alike, cycling is an enjoyable way to get around the city. Among a small army of bike rental outlets, one of the biggest is Station Cycles (ⓦstationcycles.co.uk), which has three local stores including one in the city centre beneath the Grand Arcade shopping centre on Corn Exchange Street (☎01223 307655). Wherever you leave your bike, padlock it securely as bike theft is not infrequent.

## ACCOMMODATION

Cambridge is light on central accommodation and those few **hotels** and **guesthouses** that do occupy prime locations tend to be expensive. That said, there is a cluster of less pricey places, including a YHA hostel, near the train station and another on Chesterton Lane and its continuation, Chesterton Rd, the busy street running east from the top of Magdalene St. In high season, when vacant rooms are often thin on the ground, the **accommodation-booking service** run by the tourist office can be very useful.

**Best Western Plus Gonville Hotel** Gonville Place ☎01223 366611, ⓦgonvillehotel.co.uk. One of the better mid-range hotel choices in Cambridge, this recently refurbished 84-room establishment occupies a long and somewhat undistinguished building just set back off a busy main road. Proficient and efficient lodgings. **£180**

★**Doubletree by Hilton Cambridge** Granta Place, Mill Lane ☎01223 259988, ⓦdoubletree3.hilton.com. This is the city's most appealing hotel by a long chalk, occupying a stylishly designed 1960s building a couple of minutes' walk from the centre. The best rooms have balconies overlooking the river (though the views are hardly riveting); breakfasts are first-rate as you would expect at this price. The hotel is also home to a Marco Pierre White steakhouse. **£250**

**Warkworth House** Warkworth Terrace ☎01223 363682, ⓦwarkworthhouse.co.uk. Welcoming, family-run B&B with a handful of straightforward, bright and unfussy en suite rooms. In a substantial Victorian property a shortish walk southeast of the bus station off Parkside. **£85**

**Worth House** 152 Chesterton Rd ☎01223 316074, ⓦworth-house.co.uk. Very recommendable B&B in a pleasantly upgraded Victorian house a 20min walk from the centre. All the bedrooms are decorated in a bright modern style and have generous en-suite bathrooms. Great breakfasts too. **£70**

**YHA Cambridge** 97 Tenison Rd ☎0845 3719728, ⓦyha.org.uk/hostel/cambridge. This long-established but recently revamped hostel occupies a rambling Victorian house near the train station – Tenison Road is a right turn a couple of hundred yards down Station Road. Facilities include a laundry and self-catering, a cycle store, a games room and a small courtyard garden. There are just over one hundred beds in two- to six-bedded rooms and advance reservations are advised. Dorms **£16**, doubles **£45**

## EATING

With most Cambridge students eating at their college dining halls, good-quality restaurants are comparatively thin on the ground, whereas the **takeaway** and **café** scene is on a roll.

★**Aromi** 1 Bene't St ☎01223 300117, ⓦaromi.co.uk. The furnishings and fittings may be standard–issue modern, but, oh my word, the food here at this little café is absolutely superb: they offer authentic Sicilian food – pizza slices, focaccia and cannolis, plus a hatful of other delights. Eat in or takeaway. Expect queues at peak times. Mon–Thurs 9am–5pm, Fri–Sun 9am–8pm.

**Côte** 21 Bridge St ☎01223 311053, ⓦcote-restaurants.co.uk. One of a medium-sized but burgeoning chain, this informal, bistro–style restaurant has a justified reputation for the excellence of its French-based cuisine, featuring the likes of beef bourguignon and fish parmentier. Breakfast, lunch and dinner, where main courses average a very reasonable £14. Mon–Fri 8am–11pm, Sat 9am–11pm & Sun 9am–10.30pm.

**Efe's** 78 King St ☎01223 500005, ⓦefesrestaurant-cambridge.co.uk. Long-established Turkish restaurant, where the decor may be uninspiring, but the chargrilled meats – the house speciality – are extremely tasty. Mains around £10. Mon–Fri noon–2.30pm & 6–11pm; Sat & Sun noon–11pm.

**Michaelhouse Café** Trinity St ☎01223 309147 ⓦmichaelhouse.org.uk. Good-quality café food – snacks, salads and so forth – in an attractively renovated medieval church. Great, central location too. Mon–Sat 8am–5pm.

**Rainbow Café** 9a King's Parade ☎01223 321551,

ⓦrainbowcafe.co.uk. Cramped but agreeable vegetarian restaurant with main courses – ranging from Jamaican roti cups to North African tagine – for around £10. Specializes in vegan and gluten-free food plus organic wines. Handy location, down an alley opposite King's College. Tues–Sat 10am–10pm, Sun 10am–4pm.

## DRINKING

**Champion of the Thames** 68 King St ☎01223 351464. Gratifyingly old-fashioned central pub with decent beer and a student/academic crowd. Sun–Thurs noon–11pm, Fri & Sat 11am–11pm.

**Eagle** 8 Bene't St ☎01223 505020, ⓦgkpubs.co.uk. Owned and operated by Greene King, this ancient city-centre inn, with its antique appearance and cobbled courtyard, is associated with Crick and Watson who discovered DNA in 1953. It gets horribly crowded, but is still worth a pint of anyone's time – Greene King ales are reliably good. Mon–Sat 10am–11pm, Sun 11am–10.30pm.

★**Free Press** 7 Prospect Row ☎01223 368337, ⓦfreepresspub.com. Classic, traditional and superbly maintained backstreet local with a great selection of real ales and single malts. Walled garden too. Just off Parkside. Mon–Thurs noon–2pm & 6–11pm; Fri & Sat noon–11pm; Sun noon–2.30pm & 7–10.30pm.

**Live and Let Live** 40 Mawson Rd ☎01223 460261. This smashing pub, in an old corner building among a battery of terrace houses, is the epitome of the traditional local – from the pot-pourri furnishings and fittings through to the wood-panelled alcoves. Mawson Road leads off Mill Road in between Parker's Piece and the train station. Mon–Fri 11.30am–2.30pm & 5.30–11pm; Sat 11.30am–2.30pm & 6–11pm; Sun noon–2pm & 7–10.30pm.

## NIGHTLIFE AND ENTERTAINMENT

The **performing arts** scene is at its busiest and best during term time with numerous student drama productions, classical concerts and gigs culminating in the traditional whizzerama of excess following the exam season. The most celebrated concerts are those given by **King's College choir** (see p.412), though the choral scholars who perform at the chapels of St John's College and Trinity are also exceptionally good. The four-day **Cambridge Folk Festival** (ⓦcambridgefolkfestival.co.uk), one of the longest-running folk festivals in the world, takes place in neighbouring Cherry Hinton at the back end of July to early August. For upcoming events, the tourist office (see opposite) issues various free **listings** leaflets and brochures.

**Arts Picturehouse** 38–39 St Andrew's St ☎0871 902 5720, ⓦpicturehouses.co.uk. Art-house cinema with an excellent, wide-ranging programme.

**Cambridge Arts Theatre** 6 St Edward's Passage, off King's Parade ☎01223 503333, ⓦcambridge artstheatre.com. The city's main rep theatre, founded by John Maynard Keynes, and launch pad of a thousand-and-one famous careers; offers a top-notch range of cutting-edge and classic productions.

**Cambridge Corn Exchange** Wheeler St ☎01223 357851, ⓦwww.cornex.co.uk. Revamped nineteenth-century trading hall, now the main city-centre venue for opera, ballet, musicals and comedy as well as regular rock and folk gigs.

**Cambridge Junction** Clifton Way ☎01223 511511, ⓦjunction.co.uk. Rock, indie, jazz, reggae or soul gigs, plus theatre, comedy and dance at this popular arts venue. Out near the train station.

# Duxford Imperial War Museum

Duxford, Jct 10 off the M11 • Daily: mid-March to late Oct 10am–6pm; late Oct to mid-March 10am–4pm • £17.50 • ☎01223 835000, ⓦiwm.org.uk

Eight miles south of Cambridge, the giant hangars of the **Duxford Imperial War Museum** dominate the eponymous airfield. Throughout World War II, East Anglia was a centre of operations for the RAF and the USAF, with the region's flat, unobstructed landscape dotted by dozens of airfields, among which Duxford was one of the more important. In total, the museum holds more than 150 historic aircraft, a wide-ranging collection of civil and military planes from the Sunderland flying boat to Concorde and the Vulcan B2 bombers, which were used for the first and last time in the 1982 Falklands conflict; the Spitfires, however, remain the most enduringly popular. Most of the planes are kept in full working order and are taken out for a spin several times a year at **Duxford Air Shows**, which attract thousands of visitors. There are usually half a dozen air shows a year (as well as temporary exhibitions) and advance bookings are strongly recommended – call ahead or consult the museum website.

# The West Midlands and the Peak District

IRONBRIDGE GORGE

# The West Midlands and the Peak District

Birmingham, the urban epicentre of the West Midlands, is Britain's second city and was once the world's greatest industrial metropolis, its slew of factories powering the Industrial Revolution. Long saddled with a reputation as an ugly, unappealing city, Birmingham has broken free, redeveloping its central core with vim and architectural verve, its prestige buildings – especially Selfridges and the Symphony hall – helping to redefine and reshape its image. Within easy striking distance is Stratford-upon-Avon, famous as the birthplace of William Shakespeare and for the exemplary Royal Shakespeare Company, the RSC. Beyond are the rural shires that stretch out towards Wales, with the bumpy Malvern Hills, one of the region's scenic highlights in between; you could also drift north to the rugged scenery of the Peak District, whose surly, stirring landscapes enclose the attractive little spa town of Buxton.

**8**

Change was forced on Birmingham by the drastic decline in its manufacturing base during the 1970s; things were even worse in the **Black Country**, that knot of industrial towns clinging to the western side of the city, where de-industrialization has proved particularly painful. The counties to the south and west of Birmingham and beyond the Black Country – **Warwickshire**, **Worcestershire**, **Herefordshire** and **Shropshire** – comprise a rural stronghold that maintains an emotional and political distance from the conurbation. Of the four counties, **Warwickshire** is the least obviously scenic, but draws by far the largest number of visitors, for – as the road signs declare at every entry point – this is "Shakespeare Country". The prime target is, of course, **Stratford-upon-Avon**, with its handful of Shakespeare-related sites and world-class theatre, but spare time also for the town of **Warwick**, which has a superb church and a whopping castle.

Neighbouring **Worcestershire**, which stretches southwest from the urban fringes of the West Midlands, holds two principal places of interest: **Worcester**, which is graced by a mighty cathedral, and **Great Malvern**, a mannered inland resort spread along the rolling contours of the **Malvern Hills** – prime walking territory. From here, it's west again for **Herefordshire**, a large and sparsely populated county that's home to several amenable market towns, most notably **Hereford**, where the remarkable medieval Mappa Mundi map is displayed in the cathedral, and pocket-sized **Ross-on-Wye**, which is within easy striking distance of an especially scenic stretch of the **Wye River Valley**. Next door, to the north, is rural **Shropshire** which has one of the region's prettiest towns, **Ludlow**, awash with antique half-timbered buildings, and the slow-paced county town of **Shrewsbury**, which is also close to the hiking trails of the **Long Mynd**. Shropshire has a fascinating industrial history, too, for it was here in the **Ironbridge Gorge** that British industrialists built the world's first iron bridge and pioneered the use of coal as a smelting fuel.

ROYAL SHAKESPEARE THEATRE, STRATFORD-UPON-AVON

# Highlights

**❶ RSC theatres, Stratford-upon-Avon**
Shakespeare's birthplace is quite simply the best place in the world to see the great man's plays, performed by the pre-eminent Royal Shakespeare Company. **See p.425 & p.429**

**❷ Mappa Mundi, Hereford Cathedral** This glorious antique map, dating to around 1000 AD, provides a riveting insight into the medieval mind with all its quirks and superstitions. **See p.436**

**❸ Ironbridge Gorge** The first iron bridge ever constructed arches high above the River Severn – industrial poetry in motion. **See p.442**

**❹ Ludlow** A postcard-pretty country town with a collection of half-timbered houses and a sprawling castle – and some wonderful restaurants, too. **See p.448**

**❺ Staying Cool, Birmingham** Stay Cool and be cool by renting an apartment at the top of the Rotunda, one of Birmingham's landmark buildings. Enjoy the views – they are simply fabulous. **See p.456**

**❻ Buxton** Good-looking and relaxed former spa town with good hotels and restaurants – an ideal base for exploring the Peak District. **See p.463**

**❼ Hiking in the Peak District** The wonderful wilds of the Peak District are crisscrossed by hiking trails – start with an amiable stroll or two near Bakewell. **See p.471**

**HIGHLIGHTS ARE MARKED ON THE MAP ON P.424**

To the north of the sprawling Birmingham conurbation is **Derbyshire**, whose northern reaches incorporate the region's finest scenery in the rough landscapes of the **Peak District National Park**. The park's many hiking trails attract visitors by the thousand and one of the best bases is the appealing former spa town of **Buxton**. The Peak District is also home to the limestone caverns of **Castleton**, the so-called "Plague Village" of **Eyam** and the grandiose stately pile of **Chatsworth House**, a real favourite hereabouts.

**HIGHLIGHTS**

1. RSC theatres, Stratford-upon-Avon
2. Mappa Mundi, Hereford Cathedral
3. Ironbridge Gorge
4. Ludlow
5. Staying Cool, Birmingham
6. Buxton
7. Hiking in the Peak District

**THE WEST MIDLANDS AND THE PEAK DISTRICT**

**Birmingham** has a major international **airport** and is readily accessible by **train** from London, Liverpool, Manchester, Leeds, York and a score of other towns. It is also well served by the National Express **bus** network, with dozens of buses leaving every hour for destinations all over Britain. Furthermore, Birmingham acts as a public transport hub for the whole of the West Midlands with trains fanning out into the surrounding counties. However, once you leave the rail network behind you'll find local buses thin on the ground, especially in the quieter parts of Worcestershire, Herefordshire and Shropshire. In the Peak District, local buses rule the roost with a dense (if occasionally complicated) network of services that will take you most places on most days.

# Stratford-upon-Avon

Despite its worldwide fame, **STRATFORD-UPON-AVON** is at heart an unassuming market town with an unexceptional pedigree. A charter for Stratford's weekly market was granted in the twelfth century and the town later became an important stopping-off point for stagecoaches between London, Oxford and the north. Like all such places, Stratford had its clearly defined class system and within this typical milieu John and Mary **Shakespeare** occupied the middle rank, and would have been forgotten long ago had their first son, William, not turned out to be the greatest writer ever to use the English language. A consequence of their good fortune is that this pleasant little town is all but smothered by package-tourist hype and, in the summer at least, its central streets groan under the weight of thousands of visitors. Don't let that deter you: the **Royal Shakespeare Company** offers superb theatre and if you are willing to forgo the

**8**

## SHAKESPEARE: WHAT'S IN A NAME?

Over the past hundred years or so, the deification of **William Shakespeare** (1564–1616) has been dogged by a backlash among a fringe of revisionist scholars and literary figures sometimes known as "**Anti-Stratfordians**". According to these revisionists, the famous plays and sonnets were not written by a glover's son from Stratford, but by someone else, and William Shakespeare was merely a nom de plume. A variety of candidates has been proposed for the authorship of Shakespeare's works, and they range from the faintly plausible (Christopher Marlowe, Francis Bacon, Ben Jonson, and the Earls of Rutland, Southampton and Oxford) to the manifestly whacko (Queen Elizabeth I, King James I and Daniel Defoe, author of *Robinson Crusoe*, who was born six years after publication of the first Folio).

Lying at the root of the authorship debate are several **unresolved questions** that have puzzled scholars for years. How could a man of modest background have such an intimate knowledge of royal protocol? How could he know so much about Italy without ever having travelled there? Why did he not leave a library in his will, when the author of the plays clearly possessed an intimate knowledge of classical literature? And why, given that Shakespeare was supposedly a well-known dramatist, did no death notice or obituary appear in publications of the day?

The speculation surrounding Shakespeare's work stems from the lack of **definite information** about his life. The few details that have been preserved come mostly from official archives – birth, marriage and death certificates and court records. However, we do know that in around 1587 the young Shakespeare was forced to flee Stratford after being caught poaching. Five companies of players passed through Stratford on tour that year, and it is believed he **absconded** with one of them to London, where a theatre boom was in full swing. *Henry VI*, Shakespeare's first play, appeared soon after, followed by the hugely successful *Richard III*. Over the next decade, Shakespeare's output was prodigious. Thirty-eight plays appeared and most were performed by his own theatre troupes based in London's **Globe** theatre (see p.85).

Success secured Shakespeare the **patronage** of London's fashionable set and the ageing Queen Elizabeth I regularly attended the Globe, as did her successor, James I, whose Scottish ancestry and fascination with the occult partly explain the subject matter of *Macbeth* – Shakespeare knew the commercial value of appealing to the rich and powerful. This, as much as his extraordinary talent, ensured his plays were the most acclaimed of the day, earning him enough money **to retire** comfortably to Stratford, where he abandoned literature in the last years of his life to concentrate on business and family affairs.

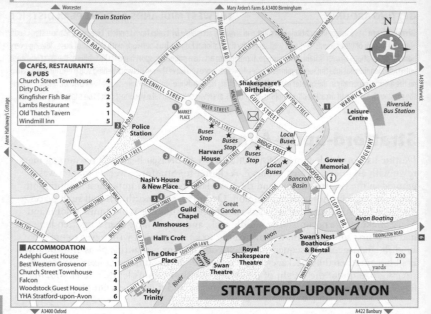

STRATFORD-UPON-AVON

**● CAFÉS, RESTAURANTS & PUBS**

| | |
|---|---|
| Church Street Townhouse | 4 |
| Dirty Duck | 6 |
| Kingfisher Fish Bar | 2 |
| Lambs Restaurant | 3 |
| Old Thatch Tavern | 1 |
| Windmill Inn | 5 |

**■ ACCOMMODATION**

| | |
|---|---|
| Adelphi Guest House | 2 |
| Best Western Grosvenor | 1 |
| Church Street Townhouse | 5 |
| Falcon | 4 |
| Woodstock Guest House | 3 |
| YHA Stratford-upon-Avon | 6 |

busiest attractions – principally **Shakespeare's Birthplace** – you can avoid the crush. All of Stratford's key attractions – many of them owned and run by the **Shakespeare Birthplace Trust** (see p.428) – are dotted around the centre, a flat and compact slice of land spreading back from the River Avon.

## Shakespeare's Birthplace

Henley St • Daily: April–June & Sept–Oct 9am–5pm; July–Aug 9am–5.30pm; Nov–March 10am–4pm • Shakespeare Birthplace Trust combination ticket £15.90/£23.90 (see p.428) • ☎ 01789 204016, ⓦ shakespeare.org.uk

Top of everyone's bardic itinerary is **Shakespeare's Birthplace**, comprising a modern visitor centre – the Shakespeare Centre – and the heavily restored, half-timbered building where the great man was born, or rather, where it is generally believed he was born. The visitor centre pokes into every corner of Shakespeare's life and times, making the most of what little hard evidence there is. Next door, the half-timbered birthplace dwelling is actually two buildings knocked into one. The northern, much smaller and later part was the house of Joan, Shakespeare's sister; adjoining it is the main family home, bought by John Shakespeare in 1556 and now returned to something like its original appearance. It includes a glover's workshop, where Shakespeare's father beavered away, though some argue that he was a wool merchant or a butcher. Despite the many historical uncertainties, the house has been attracting visitors for centuries and upstairs one of the old mullioned windows, now displayed in a glass cabinet, bears the scratch-mark signatures of some of them, including Thomas Carlyle and Walter Scott.

## Nash's House and New Place

Chapel St • Daily: mid-March to Oct 10am–5pm, Nov to mid-March 11am–4pm, but closed till 2015/16 & exhibits temporarily moved to Harvard House, 26 High St (same hours) • Shakespeare Birthplace Trust combination ticket £15.90/£23.90 (see p.428) • ☎ 01789 204016, ⓦ shakespeare.org.uk

An attractive Tudor building – and also a Birthplace Trust property – **Nash's House** was once owned by Thomas Nash, the first husband of Shakespeare's granddaughter,

Elizabeth Hall. The house is kitted out with a pleasant assortment of period furnishings and has a cabinet of woodcarvings made from the **mulberry tree** that once stood outside and was reputedly planted by Shakespeare himself. It also has displays featuring the archeological bits and pieces retrieved during a recent excavation of the adjacent garden, which contains the foundations of **New Place**, Shakespeare's last residence, though this was demolished long ago. Note, however, that Nash's House will be closed for refurbishment until around 2015/16, its exhibits temporarily relocated to **Harvard House**.

## Hall's Croft

Old Town • Daily: mid-March to Oct 10am–5pm, Nov to mid-March 11am–4pm • Shakespeare Birthplace Trust combination ticket £15.90/£23.90 (see p.428) • ☎ 01789 204016, ⌂ shakespeare.org.uk

Stratford's most impressive medieval house is **Hall's Croft**, the former home of Shakespeare's elder daughter, Susanna, and her doctor husband, John Hall. This immaculately maintained house, with its beamed ceilings and rickety rooms, holds a good-looking medley of period furniture and – mostly upstairs – a fascinating display on **Elizabethan medicine**. Hall established something of a reputation for his medical know-how and after his death some of his case notes were published in a volume entitled *Select Observations on English Bodies*.

## Holy Trinity Church

Old Town • March & Oct Mon–Sat 9am–5pm, Sun 12.30–5pm; April–Sept Mon–Sat 8.30am–6pm & Sun 12.30–5pm; Nov–Feb Mon–Sat 9am–4pm & Sun 12.30–5pm • Free, but chancel £2 • ☎ 01789 266316, ⌂ stratford-upon-avon.org

The mellow, honey-coloured stonework of **Holy Trinity Church** dates from the thirteenth century. Enhanced by its riverside setting, the dignified proportions of this quintessentially English church are the result, however, of several centuries of chopping and changing, culminating in the replacement of the original wooden spire with today's stone version in 1763. Inside, the nave is flanked by a fine set of stained-glass windows, some of which are medieval, and bathed in light from the clerestory windows up above. Quite unusually, you'll see that the nave is built on a slight skew from the line of the chancel – supposedly to represent Christ's inclined head on the cross. William Shakespeare lies buried in the **chancel**, his remains overseen by a sedate and studious memorial plaque and effigy added just seven years after his death.

## Bancroft Basin

In front of the recently remodelled **Royal Shakespeare Theatre**, the manicured lawns of

8

---

### STRATFORD'S THEATRES

Sitting pretty beside the River Avon are the **Royal Shakespeare Company**'s two main **theatres**, the Swan and the Royal Shakespeare. There was no theatre in Stratford in Shakespeare's day and indeed the first hometown festival in his honour was only held in 1769 at the behest of London-based David Garrick. Thereafter, the idea of building a permanent home in which to perform Shakespeare's works slowly gained momentum, and finally, in 1879, the first Memorial Theatre was opened on land donated by local beer baron Charles Flower. A fire in 1926 necessitated the construction of a new theatre, and the ensuing architectural competition, won by Elisabeth Scott, produced the **Royal Shakespeare Theatre**, a red-brick edifice that has recently been remodelled and extended, its proscenium stage replaced by a thrust stage – to the horror of many and the delight of some. Attached to the main theatre is the **Swan Theatre**, a replica "in-the-round" Elizabethan stage that has also been refurbished, whilst close by is the RSC's third theatre, formerly the Courtyard Theatre and now closed pending its conversion into a more modern auditorium and its renaming as **The Other Place**.

a small riverside park stretch north as far as **Bancroft Basin**, where the Stratford Canal meets the river. This is one of the prettiest parts of Stratford with brightly-painted narrowboats bobbing in the water and a fancy pedestrian bridge leading over to the finely sculpted **Gower Memorial** of 1888, where Shakespeare sits surrounded by characters from his plays.

## Anne Hathaway's Cottage

Cottage Lane, Shottery • Daily: mid-March to Oct 9am–5pm; Nov to mid–March 10am–4pm • £9.50, or Shakespeare Birthplace Trust combination ticket £23.90 (see below) • ☎ 01789 204016, ⊕ shakespeare.org.uk

**Anne Hathaway's Cottage**, a Birthplace Trust property, is just over a mile west of the centre in the well-heeled suburb of **Shottery**. The cottage – actually an old farmhouse – is an immaculately maintained, half-timbered affair with a thatched roof and dinky little chimneys. This was the home of Anne Hathaway before she married Shakespeare in 1582, and the interior holds a comely combination of period furniture, including a superb, finely carved four-poster bed. The garden is splendid too, bursting with blooms in the summertime. The adjacent orchard features more than forty types of tree, shrub and rose mentioned in the plays, with each bearing the appropriate quotation inscribed on a plaque. The nicest way to get to the cottage from the centre is on the signposted **footpath** from Evesham Place, at the south end of Rother Street.

## Mary Arden's Farm

Station Rd, Wilmcote CV37 9UN, 3 miles northwest of Stratford, • Mid–March to Oct daily 9am–5pm • £12.50, or Shakespeare Birthplace Trust combination ticket £23.90 (see below) • ☎ 01789 204016, ⊕ shakespeare.org.uk

**Mary Arden's Farm**, a further Birthplace Trust property, takes its name from Shakespeare's mother, the only unmarried daughter of her father, Robert, at the time of his death in 1556. Unusually for the period, Mary inherited the house and land, thus becoming one of the neighbourhood's most eligible women – John Shakespeare, eager for self-improvement, married her within a year. The house is a well-furnished example of an Elizabethan farmhouse and a platoon of guides fills in the details of family life and traditions with assorted farmyard activities too.

### ARRIVAL AND DEPARTURE

STRATFORD-UPON-AVON

**By train** Stratford's main train station is on the northwest edge of town, a 10min walk from the centre.
Destinations Birmingham Moor Street & Snow Hill stations (hourly; 1hr 10min/55min); London Marylebone (direct every 3hr; 2hr; with one change, hourly 2hr 20min).

**By bus** Local buses arrive and depart from Bridge/Wood streets; National Express services and most other long-distance buses pull into the Riverside bus station on the east side of the town centre, off Bridgeway.

### INFORMATION

**Tourist office** Handily located by the bridge at the junction of Bridgeway and Bridgefoot (March–Oct Mon–Sat 9am–5.30pm & Sun 10am–4pm; Nov–Feb Mon–Sat 9am–5.30pm but may close Sun; ☎01789 264293, ⊕ discover-stratford.com). Among many other useful things, they offer a last-minute accommodation booking service that can be especially handy at the height of the summer.
**Shakespeare Birthplace Trust** (☎01789 204016,

⊕ shakespeare.org.uk) owns five properties – three in the town centre (Shakespeare's Birthplace, Nash's House and Hall's Croft) and two on the outskirts (Anne Hathaway's Cottage and Mary Arden's Farm). Tickets are not available for the three individual properties in the town centre – instead you have to buy a combined ticket for £15.90 or a ticket for all five at £23.90; you can also purchase an individual ticket at the two outlying attractions. Tickets are on sale at all five and online.

### ACCOMMODATION

In peak months and during the **Shakespeare birthday celebrations** around April 23, it's pretty much essential to book accommodation well ahead. The town has a dozen or so **hotels**, the pick of which occupy old half-timbered buildings right in the centre, but most visitors choose to stay in a **B&B**; there's a particular concentration to the west of the centre around Grove Road and Evesham Place.

**Adelphi Guest House** 39 Grove Rd ☎01789 204469, ⓦadelphi-guesthouse.com. Extremely cosy B&B in a good-looking Victorian townhouse a short walk from the centre. The owners have accumulated all sorts of interesting curios – from vintage theatrical posters to ornate chandeliers – and the five double guest rooms are all en suite. The best room, which has a four-poster, is in the attic and offers pleasing views. Top-ranking, home-cooked breakfasts too. £70

**Best Western Grosvenor** Warwick Rd ☎01789 269213, ⓦbwgh.co.uk. Close to the canal, just a couple of minutes' walk from the town centre, the *Grosvenor* occupies a row of pleasant, two-storey Georgian houses. The interior is humdrum-modern but perfectly adequate and there's ample parking at the back. £80

**Church Street Townhouse** 16 Church St ☎01789 262222, ⓦchurchstreettownhouse.com. Twelve deluxe guest rooms decorated in a smart and neat modern manner and equipped with king-size beds. Two nights' minimum stay on the weekend. Convenient, central location and first-rate breakfasts. It's a popular spot, so advance reservations are recommended. £110

**Falcon** Chapel St ☎0844 411 9005, ⓦlegacy-hotels .co.uk. Handily situated in the middle of town, this chain hotel is a rambling affair whose front section, with its half-timbered facade and stone-flagged bar, dates from the sixteenth century. A corridor connects this part of the hotel to the modern block behind, where the rooms are neat, trim and really rather well designed; the rooms in other parts of the hotel, however, are not nearly as appealing. £95

**Woodstock Guest House** 30 Grove Rd ☎01789 299881, ⓦwoodstock-house.co.uk. A smart, neatly kept B&B just a 5min walk from the centre, by the start of the path to Anne Hathaway's Cottage (see opposite). The five extremely comfortable bedrooms are all en suite, decorated in a fetching modern style. £78

**YHA Stratford-upon-Avon** Hemmingford House, Wellesbourne Road, Alveston, 2 miles east on the B4086 ☎0845 371 9661, ⓦyha.org.uk. Occupying a rambling Georgian mansion on the edge of the village of Alveston, this medium-sized hostel has dorms, double and family rooms, some of which are en suite, plus wi-fi, car parking and self-catering facilities. Breakfasts and evening meals are on offer, too. Advance reservations advised. Local bus from Wood Street in Stratford. Dorms £18, doubles £34

## EATING AND DRINKING

**Church Street Townhouse** 16 Church St ☎01789 262222, ⓦchurchstreettownhouse.com. Smart, appealing bar and restaurant in one of the town's oldest premises. The menu is creative with due emphasis on local ingredients – try, for example, the vegetable risotto (£11.50) or the pan-roasted turbot with braised oxtail (£20). Daily 8am–10pm.

**Dirty Duck** 53 Waterside ☎01789 297312, ⓦoldenglishinns.co.uk. The archetypal actors' pub, stuffed to the gunwales every night with a vocal entourage of RSC thesps and admirers. Traditional beers in somewhat spartan premises plus a terrace for hot-weather drinking. Now one of a large pub chain. Daily 11am–11pm.

**Kingfisher Fish Bar** 13 Ely St ☎01789 292513. The best fish-and-chip shop in town, a 5min walk from the theatres. Takeaway and sit-down. Mon–Sat

11.30am–1.45pm & 5–9.30pm.

★**Lambs Restaurant** 12 Sheep St ☎01789 292554, ⓦlambsrestaurant.co.uk. A mouthwatering range of stylish English and continental dishes – slow-roasted lamb shank, for example – dished up in a smart restaurant with lots of period features including beamed ceilings and modern art on the walls. Daily specials around £11, other main courses £13–18. Mon & Tues 5–9pm, Wed–Sat noon–2pm & 5–9pm, Sun noon–2pm & 6–9pm.

**Old Thatch Tavern** Market Place ☎01789 295216. Ancient pub with a convivial atmosphere and a good range of beers attracting a mixed bag of tourists and locals. Daily 11am–11pm.

**Windmill Inn** Church St ☎01789 297687. Popular pub with a rabbit-warren of rooms and low-beamed ceilings. Flowers beers too. Daily 11am–11pm.

## NIGHTLIFE AND ENTERTAINMENT: THE RSC

**The Royal Shakespeare Company** ☎0844 800 1110, ⓦrsc.org.uk. The RSC works on a repertory system, which means you could stay in Stratford for a few days and see three or four different plays, and not necessarily by Shakespeare: though the RSC does indeed focus on the Bard's plays, it offers other productions too, from new modern writing through to works by Shakespeare's contemporaries. With the Courtyard Theatre/The Other Place closed for a revamp, the RSC is currently confined to two venues – the Royal Shakespeare and the Swan. Tickets start from as little as £14 and can be bought online, by phone (Mon–Sat 10am–6pm), and in person at the Royal Shakespeare box office. Note that some performances are sold out months in advance and although there's always the off-chance of a last-minute return or stand-by ticket (for unsold seats), don't bet on it.

8

# Warwick

Pocket-sized **WARWICK**, just eight miles northeast of Stratford, is famous for its massive **castle**, but it also possesses several charming streetscapes erected in the aftermath of a great fire in 1694. An hour or two is quite enough time to nose around the town centre, though you'll need the whole day if, braving the crowds and the medieval musicians, you're also set on exploring the castle and its extensive grounds: either way, Warwick is the perfect day-trip from Stratford.

## Warwick Castle

Daily: Core hours April–Sept 10am–6pm; Oct–March 10am–5pm • Various ticketing options from £18 in advance (£24 on the day); parking £6–10 • ☎ 01926 495421; recorded info ☎ 0871 265 2000, ⓦ warwick-castle.com

Towering above the River Avon at the foot of the town centre, **Warwick Castle** is often proclaimed the "greatest medieval castle in Britain". This claim is valid enough if bulk equals greatness, but actually much of the existing structure is the result of extensive nineteenth-century tinkering. It's likely that the Saxons raised the first fortress on this site, though things really took off with the Normans, who built a large motte and bailey here towards the end of the eleventh century. Almost three hundred years later, the eleventh Earl of Warwick turned the stronghold into a formidable stone castle, complete with elaborate gatehouses, multiple turrets and a keep.

The **entrance** to the castle is through the old stable block at the foot of Castle Street. Beyond, a footpath leads round to the imposing moated and mounded **East Gate**. Over the footbridge – and beyond the protective towers – is the main **courtyard**. You can stroll along the ramparts and climb the towers, but most visitors head straight for one or other of the special, very touristy displays installed inside the castle's many chambers and towers. The **grounds** are perhaps much more enjoyable, acres of woodland and lawn inhabited by peacocks and including a large glass **conservatory**. A footbridge leads over the River Avon to **River Island**, the site of jousting tournaments and other such medieval hoopla.

## Lord Leycester Hospital

60 High St • Tues–Sun plus Bank Holiday Mon: April–Oct 10am–5pm; Nov–March 10am–4.30pm • £5.90 • ☎ 01926 491422, ⓦ lordleycester.com

The remarkable **Lord Leycester Hospital**, a tangle of half-timbered buildings leaning at fairy-tale angles against the old West Gate, represents one of Britain's best-preserved examples of domestic Elizabethan architecture. It was established as a hostel for old soldiers by Robert Dudley, Earl of Leicester – a favourite of Queen Elizabeth I – and incorporates several beamed buildings, principally the Great Hall and the Guildhall, as well as a wonderful galleried courtyard and an intimate chantry chapel. There's a tearoom too, plus a modest regimental museum (Tue–Sat only) – appropriately enough as retired servicemen (and their wives) still live here.

## St Mary's Church

Old Square • Daily: April–Sept 10am–6pm; Oct–March 10am–4.30pm • £2 donation suggested • ☎ 01926 403940, ⓦ stmaryswarwick .org.uk

Rebuilt in a weird Gothic-Renaissance amalgam after the fire of 1694, **St Mary's Church** may not look too exciting from the outside, but inside the chancel, which survived the fire untouched, is a simply glorious illustration of the Perpendicular style with a splendid vaulted ceiling of flying and fronded ribs. On the right-hand side of the chancel is the **Beauchamp Chantry Chapel**, which contains the equally beautiful tomb of Richard Beauchamp, Earl of Warwick, who is depicted in an elaborate,

---

## COVENTRY CATHEDRAL

At the outbreak of World War II, **COVENTRY**, eleven miles north of Warwick, was a major engineering centre and its factories attracted the attentions of the Luftwaffe, who well-nigh levelled the town in a huge bombing raid on November 14, 1940. Out of the ashes arose what is now Coventry's one sight of note, Basil Spence's **St Michael's Cathedral** (Mon–Sat 10am–5pm, Sun noon–4pm; £8; ☎024 7652 1210, ⓦcoventrycathedral.org.uk), raised alongside the burnt-out shell of the old cathedral right in the centre of town and dedicated with a performance of Benjamin Britten's specially written *War Requiem* in 1962. One of the country's most successful postwar buildings, the cathedral's pink sandstone is light and graceful, the main entrance adorned by a stunningly forceful *St Michael Defeating the Devil* by Jacob Epstein. Inside, Spence's high and slender nave is bathed in light from the soaring stained-glass windows, a perfect setting for the magnificent and immense **tapestry** of *Christ in Glory* by **Graham Sutherland**. The choice of artist could not have been more appropriate. A painter, graphic artist and designer, Sutherland (1903–80) had been one of Britain's official war artists, his particular job being to record the effects of German bombing. A canopied walkway links the new cathedral with the old, whose shattered nave flanks the church tower and spire that somehow eluded the bombs.

---

gilded-bronze suit of armour of Italian design from the tip of his swan helmet down to his mailed feet. A griffin and a bear guard Richard, who lies with his hands half-joined in prayer so that, on the Resurrection, his first sight would be of Christ Triumphant at the Second Coming. The adjacent tomb of Ambrose Dudley is of finely carved and painted alabaster, as is that of Robert Dudley and his wife – the same Dudley who founded the Lord Leycester Hospital (see opposite).

### ARRIVAL AND INFORMATION WARWICK

**By train** Warwick train station is at the northern edge of town, a 15min walk from the centre via Station and Coventry roads.
**Destinations** Birmingham Snow Hill (every 30min to 1hr; 30min); Stratford-upon-Avon (every 2hr; 30min).

**By bus** Buses stop on Market St, in the town centre close to Market Place.
**Tourist office** The old Courthouse, on the corner of Castle and Jury streets (Mon–Fri 9.30am–4.30pm, Sat 10am–4.30pm; ☎01926 492212, ⓦvisitwarwick.co.uk).

### ACCOMMODATION AND EATING

**Catalan** 6 Jury St ☎01926 498930, ⓦcatalantapas .co.uk. This rustic-looking, café/restaurant has a wide-ranging, Mediterranean-inspired menu, but the tasty tapas are its speciality – try, for example, the sardines or the white beans, shallots and leeks in a tomato sauce. Tapas average around £4.50, à la carte mains £15, less at lunch times. Mon–Fri noon–3pm & 6–9.30pm.

**Rose and Crown** 30 Market Place ☎01926 411117, ⓦroseandcrownwarwick.co.uk. Self-proclaimed as one of

a "group of enthusiasts" rather than a chain, this centrally located pub offers thirteen attractive, competitively priced guest rooms, all en suite, five above the pub and eight just across the street. Each is decorated in a bright and breezy contemporary style. The first rate pub-cum-restaurant offers a lively, creative menu from breakfast through to dinner. Try, for example, the Cornish lamb with green bean and caper beurre noisette. A prime selection of guest beers and house wines, too. Mains average £16. Daily 8am–11pm. **£85**

# Worcester and around

In geographical terms, **Worcestershire** can be compared to a huge saucer, with the low-lying plains of the Severn Valley and the Vale of Evesham, Britain's foremost fruit-growing area, rising to a lip of hills, principally the Malverns in the west and the Cotswolds (see p.252) to the south. In character, the county divides into two broad belts. To the north lie the industrial and overspill towns – Droitwich and Redditch for instance – that have much in common with the Birmingham conurbation, while the south is predominantly rural. Bang at the geographical heart of the county is

**WORCESTER**, an amenable county town where a liberal helping of half-timbered Tudor and handsome Georgian buildings stand cheek by jowl with some fairly charmless modern developments. The biggest single influence on the city has always been the **River Severn**, which flows along Worcester's west flank. It was the river that made the city an important settlement as early as Saxon times, though its propensity to breach its banks has prompted the construction of a battery of defences which tumble down the slope from the mighty bulk of the **cathedral**, easily the town's star turn. Worcester's centre is small and compact, and handily, all the key sights plus the best restaurants are clustered within the immediate vicinity of the cathedral.

## Worcester Cathedral

Daily 7.30am–6pm • Free • ☎ 01905 732900, ⓦ worcestercathedral.co.uk

Towering above the River Severn, the soaring sandstone of **Worcester Cathedral** comprises a rich stew of architectural styles dating from 1084. The bulk of the church is firmly medieval, from the Norman transepts through to the late Gothic cloister, though the Victorians did have a good old hack at the exterior. Inside, the highlight is the thirteenth-century **choir**, a beautiful illustration of the Early English style, with a forest of slender pillars rising above the intricately worked choir stalls. Here also, in front of the high altar, is the **table tomb** of England's most reviled monarch, **King John** (1167–1216), who certainly would not have appreciated the lion that lies at his feet biting the end of his sword – a reference to the curbing of his power by the barons when they obliged him to sign the Magna Carta. Just beyond the tomb – on the right – is **Prince Arthur's Chantry**, a delicate lacy confection of carved stonework erected in 1504 to commemorate Arthur, King Henry VII's son, who died at the age of 15. He was on his honeymoon with Catherine of Aragon, who was soon passed on – with such momentous consequences – to his younger brother, the future Henry VIII. A doorway on the south side of the nave leads to the **cloisters**, with their delightful roof bosses, and the circular, largely Norman **chapter house**, which has the distinction of being the first such building constructed with the use of a central supporting pillar.

## Worcester Porcelain Museum

Severn St • Easter to Oct Mon–Sat 10am–5pm; Oct–Easter Tues–Sat 10.30am–4pm • £6 • ☎ 01905 21247, ⓦ worcesterporcelainmuseum.org

There was a time when Severn Street, tucked away just to the south of the cathedral, hummed with the activity of one of England's largest porcelain factories, **Royal Worcester**. Those days ended, however, when the company hit the skids and was finally rolled up in 2008 after more than one hundred and fifty years in production. The old factory complex is currently being turned into apartments, but the **Worcester Porcelain Museum** has survived, exhibiting a comprehensive collection of the ornate, indeed fancifully ornate, porcelain for which Royal Worcester was famous.

## The Commandery

Sidbury • Easter–Oct Mon–Sat 10am–5pm, Sun 1.30–5pm; Nov to Easter reduced hours – call for details • £5.50 • ☎ 01905 361 821, ⓦ www.whub.org.uk/cms/

Occupying Worcester's oldest building, a rambling, half-timbered structure dating from the early sixteenth century, the **Commandery**, on the far side of the busy Sidbury dual carriageway, holds six different displays tracking through the history of the Commandery and its assorted occupants. The building itself is historically important: **King Charles II** used it as his headquarters during the battle-cum-siege of Worcester in 1651, the end game of his unsuccessful attempt to regain the throne from Cromwell and the Parliamentarians, who had executed his father – King Charles I – in 1649. The high point inside is the medieval **painted chamber**, whose walls are covered with intriguing cameos recalling the building's original use as a monastery hospital. Each relates to a saint with healing powers – for example St Thomas à Becket is shown being stabbed in the head by a group of knights, which was enough to make him the patron saint for headaches.

## Greyfriars

Friar St • Late Feb to late Dec Tues–Sat 1–5pm• £4.70; NT • ☎ 01905 23571, ⓦ nationaltrust.org.uk/greyfriars

From the Commandery, it's a short step northwest along Sidbury to narrow **Friar Street**, whose hotchpotch of half-timbered houses and small, independent shops make it Worcester's prettiest thoroughfare. Among the buildings is **Greyfriars**, a largely fifteenth-century townhouse whose wonky timbers and dark-stained panelling shelter a charming collection of antiques. There's an attractive walled garden here too. From Greyfriars, it's a couple of minutes' walk west to the High Street, a couple more back to the cathedral.

## Elgar Birthplace Museum

Crown East Lane, Lower Broadheath, 3 miles west of Worcester off the A44 • Daily 11am–5pm, last admission 4.15pm • £7.50 • ☎ 01905 333224, ⓦ elgarmuseum.org

One of Worcestershire's most famous sons was **Sir Edward Elgar** (1857–1934), the first internationally acclaimed English composer for almost two hundred years. Elgar built his reputation on a series of lyrical works celebrating his abiding love of the Worcestershire countryside, quintessentially English pieces among which the most famous is the *Enigma Variations*. The **Elgar Birthplace Museum**, in Lower Broadheath, comprises a modern visitor centre exploring Elgar's life and times and the substantial brick cottage where he was born; the cramped rooms contain several scores, personal correspondence in his spidery handwriting, photographs and mementos. The museum also organizes special events, from illustrated talks to concerts. Lower Broadheath is not, however, of any scenic interest – if you want to see the green, quilted landscapes beloved of Elgar you'll have to push on to the Malverns.

### ARRIVAL AND INFORMATION                                    WORCESTER

**By train** Worcester has two main train stations. The handiest for the city centre is Foregate Street, from where it's about 800yds south to the cathedral along Foregate Street and its continuation The Cross and then High Street. The other train station, Shrub Hill, is further out, about a mile to the northeast of the cathedral.
Destinations Worcester Foregate to: Birmingham Moor Street (every 30min; 1hr); Hereford (hourly; 50min).

**By bus** The bus station is at the back of the sprawling Crowngate shopping about 600yds northwest of the cathedral.
Destinations Great Malvern (2 hourly; 50min); Hereford (Mon–Sat 2 daily; 1hr 20min)
**Tourist office** Guildhall, towards the cathedral end of the High Street (Mon–Sat 9.30am–5pm; ☎ 01905 726311, ⓦ visitworcestershire.org).

### ACCOMMODATION

**Barrington House B&B** 204 Henwick Rd ☎ 01905 422965, ⓦ barringtonhouse.eu. Occupying an immaculately restored Georgian property right by the river about a mile north of the centre along the A443 – and across the river from Worcester Racecourse – this is the best B&B in town. It comes with a large garden and has three en-suite guest rooms decorated in a broadly period style. Tasty breakfasts too. **£80**

**Diglis House Hotel** Severn St ☎ 01905 353518, ⓦ diglishousehotel.co.uk. Medium-sized hotel in an attractive Georgian villa beside the river, about 5min walk south of the cathedral at the end of Severn Street. Some of the guest rooms are in the main building, others in the modern annexe, and all are decorated in a pleasant if somewhat staid version of country-house style. The hotel's prime feature is the large conservatory overlooking the river. **£110**

### EATING AND DRINKING

**Mac & Jac's Café** 44 Friar St ☎ 01905 731331, ⓦ macandjacs.co.uk. With a sister café in Great Malvern

(see p.435), this attractive little place occupies an old, half-timbered building near the Cathedral. Offers a delicious range of home-made snacks and meals – try, for example, the pollack and salmon fishcake with green beans, anchovy and caper mayonnaise (£11). Mon–Sat 9am–5pm, plus occasional supper evenings.

**Saffrons Bistro** 15 New St (a northerly continuation of Friar St) ☎01905 610505, ⓦsaffronsbistro.co.uk. Undoubtedly one of Worcester's best restaurants, this cheerfully decorated little place is strong on locally sourced ingredients – and the proof is in the eating. Try, for example, the delicious slow-braised blade of beef with green beans, mushrooms and shallots in a red wine sauce. Reservations advised in the evening. Mains hover around £15. Mon–Fri noon–2.15pm & 5.30–9.30pm, Sat noon–2.15pm & 5.30–10.30pm.

# The Malvern Hills

One of the more prosperous parts of the West Midlands, **The Malverns** is the generic name for a string of towns and villages stretched along the eastern lower slopes of the **MALVERN HILLS**, which rise spectacularly out of the flatlands a few miles to the southwest of Worcester. About nine miles from north to south – between the A44 and the M50 – and never more than five miles wide, the hills straddle the Worcestershire–Herefordshire boundary. Of ancient granite rock, they are punctuated by over twenty summits, mostly around 1000ft high, and in between lie innumerable dips and hollows. It's easy, if energetic, walking country, with great views, and there's an excellent network of **hiking trails**, most of which can be completed in a day or half-day with **Great Malvern** being the obvious base.

## Great Malvern

Of all the towns in the Malverns, it's **GREAT MALVERN** that grabs the attention, its pocket-sized centre clambering up the hillside with the crags of North Hill beckoning beyond. The grand old houses, which congregate on and around the top of the main drag, **Church Street**, mostly date from Great Malvern's nineteenth-century heyday as a spa town when the local **spring waters** drew the Victorians here by the train load. You can still sample the waters today (see box opposite), but the town's principal sight is its splendid **Priory Church**, close to the top of Church Street (daily 9am–5pm; free; ⓦgreatmalvernpriory.org.uk). The Benedictines built one of their abbeys here at Great Malvern and, although Henry VIII closed the place down in 1538, the church's elaborate decoration and fabulous late medieval **stained-glass windows** proclaim the priory's former wealth.

### Malvern Museum

Priory Gatehouse, Abbey Road · Easter–Oct daily 10.30am–5pm · £2 · ☎01684 567811, ⓦmalvernmuseum.co.uk

Behind the Priory Church is the delicately proportioned **Priory Gatehouse**, which now holds the tiny **Malvern Museum** of local history. One of the most interesting rooms explores what life was like here in medieval times, another looks at Great Malvern's days as a spa town with old promotional cartoons showing patients packed into soaked sheets before, their ailments cured, they hop gaily away from their crutches.

---

### HIKING THE MALVERN HILLS

Great Malvern tourist office (see opposite) sells hiking maps and issues half a dozen free **Trail Guide leaflets**, which describe circular routes up to and along the hills that rise behind the town. The shortest trail is just one and a half miles, the longest four. One of the most appealing is the 2.5-mile hoof up to the top – and back – of **North Hill** (1307ft), from where there are panoramic views over the surrounding countryside; this hike also takes in *St Ann's Well Café*, where you can taste the local spring water (see box opposite).

## TAKING THE GREAT MALVERN WATERS

The gushing **Malvhina spring** in the mini-park at the top of Church Street is the obvious and certainly the most convenient way to taste Great Malvern's waters. There's also a spring at **St Ann's Well Café**, a sweet little café in an attractive Georgian building a stiff 25-minute walk up the wooded hillside from town (normally Easter to June & Sept Tues–Sun 11am–3.30pm; July & Aug daily 10am–4pm; Oct to Easter Fri 11.30am–3.30pm, Sat & Sun 10am–4pm; but check times on ☎01684 560285 or ⓦstannswell.co.uk); the signposted path begins beside the *Mount Pleasant Hotel*, on Belle Vue Terrace, just to the left (south) of the top of Church Street.

### ARRIVAL AND INFORMATION

### GREAT MALVERN

**By train** From Great Malvern's rustic train station, with its dainty ironwork and quaint chimneys, it's about 800yd to the town centre – take Avenue Road, which leads to Church St, the steeply sloping main drag.

Destinations Birmingham (hourly; 1hr); Hereford (hourly; 35min); Ledbury (hourly; 15min); Worcester Foregate (hourly; 15min).

**Tourist office** At the top of Church St, just up and across from the Priory Church (daily 10am–5pm; ☎01684 892289, ⓦvisitthemalverns.org).

### ACCOMMODATION

**Abbey Hotel** Abbey Rd ☎01684 892332, ⓦsarova -abbeyhotel.com. Easily the most conspicuous hotel in Great Malvern, a few yards from the tourist office, much of it occupying a rambling, creeper-clad Victorian building executed in a sort of neo-Baronial style. It's part of a small chain, and the guest rooms, especially in the hotel's lumpy modern wing, can be a little characterless – but they are comfortable enough and some have attractive views back over town. **£90**

**Amazing View in The Malverns** 8 Hanley Terrace, Malvern Wells, a short drive south along (and just off) the A449 (Wells Rd). ☎01684 565808, ⓦamazingview .info. Deluxe B&B with three, commodious, en-suite guest rooms in a tastefully modernised Victorian house. Has a superb location perched on the hill with panoramic views across the plain below. Tasty breakfasts, too. **£75**

**The Cottage in the Wood** Holywell Rd, Malvern Wells, WR14 4LG ☎01684 588860, ⓦcottageinthewood .co.uk. Family-run hotel with a dozen or so cheery, comfortable guest rooms in the main house and a brace of small annexes. The main house is not so much a cottage as a spacious villa built as a dower house to a neigbhbouring estate in the late 1700s. Wooded grounds surround the hotel and there are fine views. The rooms vary considerably in size and comfort, but start at **£99**

### EATING AND DRINKING

**Mac & Jac's Café** 23 Abbey Rd ☎01684 573300, ⓦmacandjacs.co.uk. This bright and cheery café does its level best to source things locally (with the exception of its teas, the house speciality). Offers a particularly good range of salads with a typical dish being crispy duck salad with soy and sesame (£7). Takeaway, too. Next door to the Malvern Museum. Tues–Sat 9am–6pm, Sun 10am–4pm.

**The Morgan** 52 Clarence Rd ☎01684 578575, ⓦwyevalleybrewery.co.uk. Near the train station, this is the best pub in town, where you can sample the assorted brews of Herefordshire's much-praised Wye Valley Brewery. Drink outside on the terrace if the sun is out, or inside in the wood-panelled bar. Mon–Thurs noon–3pm & 5–11pm, Fri & Sat noon–11pm & Sun noon–10.30pm.

# Herefordshire

Over the Malvern Hills from Worcestershire, the rolling agricultural landscapes of **HEREFORDSHIRE** have an easy-going charm, but the finest scenery hereabouts is along the banks of the **River Wye**, which wriggles and worms its way across the county. Plonked in the middle of Herefordshire on the Wye is the county town, **Hereford**, a sleepy, rather old-fashioned place whose proudest possession, the cathedral's remarkable **Mappa Mundi** map, was almost flogged off in a round of ecclesiastical budget cuts back in the 1980s. Beyond Hereford, the southeast corner of the county has one especially attractive town, **Ross-on-Wye**, a genial little place with a picturesque setting that also serves as a convenient gateway to one of the wilder portions of the **Wye River Valley**, around **Symonds Yat**, where canoeists gather in their droves.

**GETTING AROUND**                                                    **HEREFORDSHIRE**

**By train** Herefordshire possesses one rail line, linking Ledbury and Hereford with points north to Shrewsbury and east to Great Malvern and Worcester.

**By bus** Local buses provide a reasonable service between

the county's villages and towns, except on Sundays when there's very little at all. For timetable details, consult ⓦ travelinemidlands.co.uk or pop into the nearest tourist office.

# Hereford

A low-key county town with a spacious feel, **HEREFORD** was long a border garrison held against the Welsh, its military importance guaranteed by its strategic position beside the River Wye. It also became a religious centre after the Welsh murdered the Saxon king **Ethelbert** near here in 794. Today, with the fortifications that once girdled the city all but vanished, it's the **cathedral** – and its extraordinary medieval **Mappa Mundi** – which forms the focus of interest. The cathedral lies just to the north of the river at the heart of the city centre, whose compact tangle of narrow streets and squares is clumsily boxed in by the ring road. Taken as a whole, Hereford makes for a pleasant overnight stay, especially as it possesses a particularly fine hotel; also don't leave town without sampling the favourite local tipple, **cider**.

## Hereford Cathedral

Daily 9.15am–5.30pm • Free • ☎ 01432 374202, ⓦ herefordcathedral.org

**Hereford Cathedral** is a curious building, an uncomfortable amalgamation of styles, with bits and pieces added to the eleventh-century church by a string of bishops and culminating in an extensive – and not especially sympathetic – Victorian refit. From the outside, the sandstone **tower** is the dominant feature, constructed in the early fourteenth century to eclipse the Norman western tower, which collapsed under its own weight in 1786. The crashing masonry mauled the **nave** and its replacement lacks some of the grandeur of most other English cathedrals, though the forceful symmetries of the long rank of surviving Norman arches and piers more than hint at what went before. The **north transept** is, however, a flawless exercise in thirteenth-century taste, its soaring windows a classic example of Early English architecture.

### The Mappa Mundi

April–Oct Mon–Sat 10am–5pm; Nov–Easter Mon–Sat 10am–4pm, but some closures for maintenance in Jan • £6 • ⓦ themappamundi .co.uk

In the 1980s, the cathedral's finances were so parlous that a plan was drawn up to sell its most treasured possession, the **Mappa Mundi**. Luckily, the government and John Paul Getty Jr. rode to the rescue, with the oil tycoon stumping up a million pounds to keep the map here and install it in a new building, the New Library, which blends in seamlessly with the older buildings it adjoins at the west end of the cloisters.

The Mappa Mundi exhibit begins with a series of interpretative panels explaining the historical background to – and the composition of – the Mappa. Included is a copy of the Mappa in English, which is particularly helpful as the original, which is displayed in a dimly lit room just beyond, is in Latin. Measuring 64 by 52 inches and dating to about 1300, the Mappa provides an extraordinary insight into medieval society. It is indeed a map (as we know it) in so far as it suggests the general geography of the world – with Asia at the top and Europe and Africa below, to left and right respectively – but it also squeezes in history, mythology and theology.

In the same building as the Mappa Mundi is the **Chained Library**, a remarkably extensive collection of books and manuscripts dating from the eighth to the eighteenth century. A selection is always open on display.

DOVEDALE, PEAK DISTRICT NATIONAL PARK, DERBYSHIRE (P.462) >

## Hereford Museum and Art Gallery

Broad St • Wed–Sat 11am–4pm • Free • ☎ 01432 260692, ⓦ herefordshire.gov.uk

After the Mappa, Hereford's other attractions can't help but seem rather pedestrian. Nonetheless, the **Hereford Museum and Art Gallery**, in a flamboyant Victorian building opposite the cathedral, does hold a mildly diverting collection of geological remains and local memorabilia spruced up by temporary art exhibitions.

### ARRIVAL AND INFORMATION HEREFORD

**By train** Hereford train station is about 800yd northeast of the main square, High Town, via Station Approach, Commercial Road and its continuation Commercial Street. Destinations Birmingham (hourly; 1hr 30min); Great Malvern (hourly; 30min); Ledbury (every 30min; 20min); Ludlow (every 30min; 30min); Shrewsbury (every 30min; 1hr); Worcester (hourly; 40min).

**By bus** The long-distance bus station is on the northeast side of the town centre, just off Commercial Rd; local and regional buses stop in the centre on High Town.

Destinations Ledbury (4 daily; 40min); Ross-on-Wye (Mon–Sat hourly, Sun 5 every 2hr; 1hr); Worcester (Mon–Sat 2 daily; 1hr 20min).

**Tourist office** 1 King St, opposite the cathedral (April–Sept daily 10am–4pm, Oct–March Mon–Fri 10am–4pm; ☎ 01432 268430, ⓦ visitherefordshire.co.uk).

### ACCOMMODATION, EATING AND DRINKING

**The Barrels** 69 St Owen's St ☎ 01432 274968, ⓦ wyevalleybrewery.co.uk. A popular local just five minutes' walk southeast of High Town, *The Barrels* is the home pub of the local Wye Valley Brewery, whose trademark bitters are much acclaimed. Mon–Thurs 11am–11.30pm, Fri & Sat 11am–midnight, Sun noon–11.30pm.

**Cafe@allsaints** All Saints Church, Broad St ☎ 01432 370415, ⓦ cafeatallsaints.co.uk. Near the cathedral, in the old church at the top of Broad Street, this excellent café has become something of a local institution since it was founded by a local foodie in the late 1990s. Serves a range of well-conceived and tasty dishes – ricotta pie with salad leaves for instance – at around £6. Mon–Sat 8am–5pm.

★**Castle House** Castle St ☎ 01432 356321, ⓦ castlehse.co.uk. Occupying an immaculately refurbished Georgian mansion and a neighbouring townhouse not far from the cathedral, it's hard to praise this 24-room hotel too highly: the staff are obliging; the better/bigger rooms are simply delightful, with all sorts of period details; and the breakfast room has a lovely outside terrace. There are two first-rate restaurants – one formal, the other casual – and both emphasise local ingredients with Hereford beef and Gloucestershire pork being prime examples. Main courses start at £10. Food served daily noon–2pm & 6.30–9.30pm (9pm on Sun). **£150**

**No. 21** 21 Aylestone Hill, HR1 1HR ☎ 01432 279897, ⓦ 21aylestonehill.co.uk. In a substantial, half-timbered Edwardian house just northeast of the centre on the Malvern Road (A4103), this comfortable B&B has four, en-suite guest rooms decorated in soothing shades and complete with period flourishes. It's located within easy walking distance of the centre, near the train station and beside the A465 (Aylestone Hill). **£70**

# Ledbury

Heading east from Hereford, it's an easy fifteen miles along the A438 to **LEDBURY**, an amenable little town glued to the western edge of the Malvern Hills. The focus of the town is the short and wide **High Street**, whose tiny **Market Place** is home to the dinky **Market House**, a Tudor beamed building raised on oak columns and with herringbone-pattern beams. From beside it, narrow **Church Lane** runs up the slope framed by an especially fine ensemble of half-timbered Tudor and Stuart buildings, sometimes called "Black and Whites". Among them, at the foot of the lane in the town council offices, is the so-called **Painted Room** (guided tours: March–May Mon–Fri 11.30am–3pm; June–Sept Mon–Sat 11am–4pm; plus mid-July to mid-Sept Sun 2–5pm; free; 15min; ⓦ visitledbury.co.uk), featuring bold symmetrical floral frescoes painted on wattle-and-daub walls sometime in the sixteenth century. Just beyond, at the end of the lane, is **St Michael's parish church**, whose strong and angular detached spire pokes high into the sky.

### ARRIVAL AND DEPARTURE LEDBURY

**By train** Ledbury train station is on the northern edge of town, about three-quarters of a mile from the High Street

– straight along The Homend.

Destinations Birmingham (hourly; 1hr 15min); Great

Malvern (hourly; 15min); Hereford (every 30min; 20min); Worcester Foregate (hourly; 25min).

**By bus** What few buses there are, pull in beside the Market House and across the street at the war memorial.

Destinations Hereford (4 daily; 40min); Ross-on-Wye

(1 weekly; 40min).

**Tourist information** Currently at the Ice Bytes Ice Cream Parlour, just north of the Market House at 38 Homend (Mon–Sat 10am–5pm; ☎0844 567 8650, ⓦvisitledbury .info).

## ACCOMMODATION AND EATING

**Feathers Hotel** 25 High St ⓦ01531 635266, ⓦfeathers -ledbury.co.uk. In a superb "Black and White" building on the High Street, this ancient hotel, with its creaky wooden floors and exposed beams, has shed its somewhat fusty image to become the best hotel in the area, the pick of this twenty-odd guest rooms benefiting from oodles of period details. The brasserie (*Fuggles*) is the more relaxing of the two on-site restaurants, its menu featuring a range of tasty British dishes – try, for example, the guinea fowl with asparagus and garlic mashed potato. Mains average £18, less at lunch times. Daily noon–2pm & 7–9.30pm, 9pm on Sunday. **£145**

**Little Acre B&B** Little Acre, Much Marcle, 8 miles

southwest of Ledbury ☎01989 740600, ⓦlittleacre .co.uk. Rural B&B with three en-suite guest rooms skilfully shoehorned into a sympathetically and tastefully modernised old cottage. Supremely quiet location just west of Much Marcle, friendly hosts and great breakfasts. **£85**

**Market House Café** 1 Homend ☎01989 740600, ⓦmarkethousecafe.co.uk. Cosy little café (and separate deli) next to the Market House, where they serve up a delicious range of home-made food from scones and breads to soups and sandwiches. Delicious full-English breakfasts, too. They source from local suppliers whenever they can. Mon–Fri 9am–4pm, Sat 9am–5pm.

# Ross-on-Wye

Nestling above a loop in the river sixteen miles southeast of Hereford, **ROSS-ON-WYE** is a relaxed and easy-going market town with an artsy/New Age undertow. Ross's jumble of narrow streets converges on **Market Place**, which is shadowed by the seventeenth-century **Market House**, a sturdy two-storey sandstone structure that sports a medallion bust of a bewigged Charles II. Veer right at the top of Market Place, then turn left up Church Street to reach Ross's other noteworthy building, the mostly thirteenth-century **St Mary's Church**, whose sturdy stonework culminates in a slender, tapering spire. In front of the church, at the foot of the graveyard, is a plain but rare **Plague Cross**, commemorating the three hundred or so townsfolk who were buried here by night without coffins during a savage outbreak of the plague in 1637.

**8**

## ARRIVAL AND INFORMATION

ROSS-ON-WYE

**By bus** Ross bus station is on Cantilupe Rd, a 4min-walk from Market Place; there are no trains.

Destinations Goodrich (Mon–Sat every 2hrs, Sun 5 daily;

20min); Hereford (Mon–Sat hourly, Sun every 2hr; 50min); Ledbury (1 weekly; 40min).

## ACCOMMODATION

★**Linden House** 14 Church St ☎01989 565373, ⓦlindenguesthouse.com. In a fetching Georgian building opposite St Mary's Church, this B&B has three en-suite guest rooms, each of which is cosily decorated, and a self-catering holiday apartment on the top floor. The breakfasts are delicious too – both traditional and vegetarian. **£70**

**Old Court House B&B** 53 High St ☎01989 762275, ⓦtheoldcourthousebandb.co.uk. An unusual B&B in so far as it occupies a rabbit warren of an old stone building, complete with open fires and exposed wooden beams. Has four en-suite guest rooms of varying size, two with four posters. Handily located in the centre of the town. **£80**

## EATING AND DRINKING

**Pots and Pieces Teashop** 40 High St ☎01989 566123, ⓦpotsandpieces.com. This appealing little café and gift shop immediately behind the Market House sells a tasty range of snacks and light meals. The toasted tea-cakes are the best for miles around – and don't avoid the home-made cakes. Mon–Fri 9am–5pm & Sat 10am–5pm, plus June–Aug Sun 11am–4pm.

**Yaks N Yetis** 1 Brookend St ☎01989 564963. Not the prettiest of restaurants perhaps, but this is genuine Nepalese (Gurkha) cuisine – and the staff are more than willing to help explain its intricacies. It's delicious and, with mains from around £7, economically priced too. Brookend is a continuation of Broad Street, which runs north from Market Place. Tues–Sun noon–2.30pm & 6–11pm.

## The Wye River Valley

Travelling south from Ross along the B4234, it's just five miles to the sullen sandstone mass of **Goodrich Castle** (April–June, Sept & Oct daily 10am–5pm; July & Aug daily 10am–6pm; Nov–March Sat & Sun 10am–4pm; £6.20; EH; ⍟english-heritage.org.uk), which commands wide views over the hills and woods of the **Wye River Valley**. The castle's strategic location guaranteed its importance as a border stronghold from the twelfth century onwards and today the substantial ruins incorporate a Norman keep, a maze of later rooms and passageways and walkable ramparts. The castle stands next to the tiny village of **GOODRICH**, from where it's around a mile and half southeast along narrow country lanes to the solitary *YHA Wye Valley Hostel* (see below), which, with the **Wye Valley Walk** running past the front door, makes a great base (in a no-frills sort of way) for **hikers**.

From Goodrich, it's a couple of miles south along narrow country lanes to a fork in the road – veer right for Symonds Yat East, or keep straight for the wriggly road up to the top of **Symonds Yat Rock**, one of the region's most celebrated viewpoints, rising high above a wooded loop in the River Wye. Down below is **SYMONDS YAT EAST**, a pretty little hamlet that straggles along the east bank of the river. It's a popular spot and one that offers canoe rental and regular **river trips** (40min) – and there's a good hotel here too (see below). The road to the village is a dead end, so you have to double back to regain Goodrich (or Symonds Yat Rock), though you can cross the river to **Symonds Yat West** by means of a hand-pulled rope **ferry**, which leaves from outside the *Saracens Head Inn* (see below).

**ACCOMMODATION AND EATING**      **WYE RIVER VALLEY AT SYMONDS YAT**

**Doward Park Campsite** Great Doward, Symonds Yat West ☎01600 890438, ⍟dowardpark.co.uk. Pleasant, partly wooded campsite in a remote location a couple of miles west of Symonds Yat West. Pitches **£16**

**Saracens Head Inn** Symonds Yat East ☎01600 890345, ⍟saracensheadinn.co.uk. There are ten en-suite guest rooms in this village hotel beside the River Wye, each decorated in pleasant modern style with wooden floors and pastel-painted walls. You can eat well both in the restaurant and in the bar, with the menu featuring mostly English favourites – though there are

international dishes as well - with mains averaging £12. Food served daily noon–2.30pm & 6.30–9pm. **£89**

**YHA Wye Valley Hostel** Near Goodrich HR9 6JJ ☎0845 371 9666, ⍟yha.org.uk. If you're after a remote location, this is the hostel to head for – in a Victorian rectory in its own grounds above the River Wye. There are 78 beds, in anything from two- to ten-bed dorms, as well as camping and self-catering facilities; evening meals are also provided on request. Formerly the *Welsh Bicknor YHA Hostel*. Dorms **£19**, doubles **£39**

## Hay-on-Wye

Straddling the Anglo-Welsh border some twenty miles west of Hereford, the hilly little town of **HAY-ON-WYE** has an attractive riverside **setting** and narrow, winding streets lined with an engaging assortment of old stone houses, but is known to most people for one thing – **books**. Hay saw its first bookshop open in 1961; today just about every inch of the town is given over to the trade, including the old cinema. The prestigious **Hay Festival of literature and the arts** (⍟hayfestival.com), is held over ten days at the end of May, when London's literary world decamps here en masse.

**ARRIVAL AND INFORMATION**      **HAY-ON-WYE**

**By bus** Buses stop on Oxford Rd, just along from the tourist office.
Destinations Brecon (6 daily; 45min); Hereford (5 daily; 1hr).
**Tourist office** In the craft centre on Oxford Road (daily:

Easter–Oct 10am–1pm & 2–5pm; Nov–Easter 11am–1pm & 2–4pm; ☎01497 820144, ⍟hay-on-wye.co.uk). The useful free booklet (*Hay-on-Wye Booksellers, Printsellers & Bookbinders*) details the town's bookshops, galleries, restaurants and bars.

**ACCOMMODATION**

Hay has plenty of accommodation, though prices are a little higher here than in places nearby, and there are no hostels. Everywhere gets booked up months in advance for the Festival.

★**Old Black Lion** Lion St ☎01497 820841, ⓦoldblacklion.co.uk. Very well-regarded thirteenth-century inn which has charming en-suite rooms both above the pub and in the neighbouring annexe, which are slightly more appealing. **£99**

**Radnors End** A 10min walk from town across the Hay Bridge on the road to Clyro ☎01497 820780, ⓦhay-on-wye.co.uk/radnorsend. Small but neat camping field in a beautiful setting overlooking Hay, with on-site showers and laundry facilities. Closed Nov–Feb. Pitches **£5**

**Seven Stars** 11 Broad St ☎ 01497 820886, ⓦtheseven-stars.co.uk. Former town pub near the clocktower, with eight modestly sized but cosy rooms, some with original oak beams and window frames. There's also an indoor swimming pool and sauna. **£84**

**The Start** Hay Bridge ☎01497 821391, ⓦthe-start.net. Neatly renovated Georgian house on the riverbank, with three rooms boasting antique furnishings and handmade quilts. The vegetable garden provides many of the ingredients for the scrumptious breakfast. **£75**

★**Tinto House** 13 Broad St ☎01497 821556, ⓦtinto-house.co.uk. Charming old house with three large, sumptuous rooms, each different, and a self-contained unit in the old stable block which has splendid garden views. **£90**

## EATING AND DRINKING

**Blue Boar** Castle St ☎01497 820884. Tasteful, wood-panelled real ale pub centred around a gently curving bar and two stone fireplaces, with a separate dining area to one side. Daily 9am–11pm; food served 11.30am–2pm & 6–9.30pm.

**The Granary** Broad St ☎01497 820790. This unpretentious café-bistro offers a wide range of excellent meals, with good veggie options. Save space for the wonderful desserts and espresso. Mains £10. Daily 9am–5.30pm, school holidays until 9pm.

**The Old Stables Tearooms** Bear St ☎07796 484766. Barely half a dozen tables are crammed into this delightful place, with chalked-up boards offering superb Welsh produce and a fantastic array of teas and home-made tarts.

On a warm day, eat in the flower-filled yard. Tues–Fri 10.30am–3pm, Sat 10.30am–4.30pm.

**Shepherd's Ice Cream** 9 High Town ☎01497 821898. Popular Georgian-style café/ice-cream parlour doling out local ice cream made from sheep's milk; flavours include raspberry cheesecake and banana toffee crunch. Mon–Fri 9.30am–5.30pm, Sat 9.30am–6pm, Sun 10.30am–5.30pm.

★**Three Tuns** Broad St ☎ 01497 821855, ⓦthree-tuns.com. Set in Hay's second-oldest building (after the castle), the ancient stonework, outdoor terrace and crackling open fires make for an atmospheric dining spot. Food includes creations such as seared scallops with truffle cauliflower puree and fennel dressing (£15). Daily 11am–11pm.

## SHOPPING

Hay has more than thirty **bookshops**, many of which are highly specialized, focusing on areas like travel, poetry or murder mystery.

**Richard Booth's Bookshop** 44 Lion St ☎01497 820322, ⓦboothbooks.co.uk. Just beyond the main square, High Town, this slicked-up, three-floored emporium (despite the name, no longer owned by Booth) offers unlimited browsing potential. Superb stock of first edition, rare and antiquarian books, mostly at a price. Incorporated into the rear of the bookshop is the wonderful little Bookshop Cinema, screening arthouse movies at weekends. Bookshop Mon–Sat 9am–5.30pm, Sun 11am–5pm.

**Rose's Books** 14 Broad St ☎01497 8200130, ⓦstellabooks.com. Opposite the clocktower, Rose's Books has a wonderful stock of rare and collectable children's and illustrated books. Mon–Fri 10am–5.30pm, Sat & Sun 9.30am–5.30pm.

**8**

---

### CANOEING AND HIKING AROUND HAY-ON-WYE

Hay-on-Wye's environs are readily and pleasantly explored by **kayak or canoe** along the River Wye. In four to six days, it's possible to paddle your way downriver from Hay to Ross-on-Wye (see p.439), overnighting in tents on isolated stretches of riverbank, or holing up in comfortable B&Bs and pubs along the way. Hay's **Paddles & Pedals**, down by the river on the far side of the Clyro bridge (☎01497 820604, ⓦpaddlesandpedals.co.uk), is a reputable outfit for **kayak and canoe rental**, full of good ideas and advice. Rental of life jackets and other essential equipment (such as waterproof canisters to carry your gear) is included in the price, which works out at around £35 per canoe for 24 hours, with discounts for longer trips. In addition, Paddles & Pedals will transport their customers to and from the departure and finishing points by minibus; advance reservations are essential.

# Shropshire

One of England's largest and least populated counties, **SHROPSHIRE** (ⓦshropshiretourism
.co.uk) stretches from its long and winding border with Wales to the very edge of the
urban Black Country. The Industrial Revolution made a huge stride forward here, with the
spanning of the River Severn by the very first **iron bridge** and, although the assorted
industries that subsequently squeezed into the **Ironbridge Gorge** are long gone, a series of
**museums** celebrates their craftsmanship – from tiles through to iron. The River Severn also
flows through the county town of **Shrewsbury**, whose antique centre holds dozens of old
half-timbered buildings, though **Ludlow**, further south, has the edge when it comes to
handsome Tudor and Jacobean architecture. In between the two lie some of the most
beautiful parts of Shropshire, primarily the **Long Mynd**, a prime hiking area that is readily
explored from the attractive little town of **Church Stretton**.

## GETTING AROUND
SHROPSHIRE

**By train** There are frequent trains from Birmingham to
Telford and Shrewsbury, which is also linked to Church
Stretton and Ludlow on the Hereford line.
**By bus** Bus services are patchy, but one small step forward
has been the creation of the Shropshire Hills Shuttle bus
service (mid-April to Sept Sat & Sun only; every 1–2hr;

ⓦ shropshirehillsaonb.co.uk) aimed at the tourist market.
The shuttle noses round the Long Mynd as well as the
Stiperstones and drops by Church Stretton. An adult Day
Rover ticket, valid on the whole route, costs just £7.
Timetables are available at most Shropshire tourist offices
and on the website.

## Ironbridge Gorge

**IRONBRIDGE GORGE**, the collective title for a cluster of small villages huddled in the
Severn Valley to the south of new-town Telford, was the crucible of the Industrial
Revolution, a process encapsulated by its famous span across the Severn – the world's
first **iron bridge**, engineered by **Abraham Darby** and opened on New Year's Day, 1781.
Darby was the third innovative industrialist of that name – the first Abraham Darby
started iron-smelting here back in 1709 and the second invented the forging process
that made it possible to produce massive single beams in iron. Under the guidance of
such creative figures as the Darbys and Thomas Telford, the area's factories once

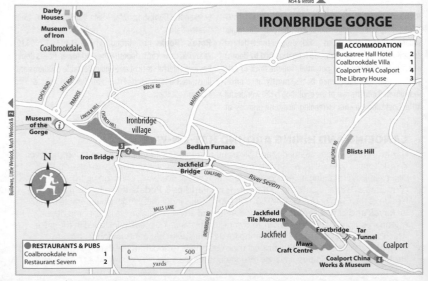

churned out engines, rails, wheels and other heavy-duty iron pieces in quantities unmatched anywhere else in the world. Manufacturing has now all but vanished, but the surviving monuments make the Gorge the most extensive **industrial heritage site** in England – and one that has been granted World Heritage Site status by UNESCO.

The Gorge contains several museums and an assortment of other industrial attractions spread along a five-mile stretch of the Severn Valley. A thorough exploration takes a couple of days, but the highlights – the **Iron Bridge** itself, the **Museum of Iron** and the **Jackfield Tile Museum** – are easily manageable on a day-trip.

## Ironbridge village

There must have been an awful lot of nail-biting during the construction of the **Iron Bridge** over the River Severn in the late 1770s. No one was quite sure how the new material would wear and although the single-span design looked sound, many feared the bridge would simply tumble into the river. To compensate, Abraham Darby used more iron than was strictly necessary, but the end result still manages to appear stunningly graceful, arching between the steep banks with the river far below. The settlement at the north end of the span was promptly renamed **IRONBRIDGE**, and today its brown-brick houses climb prettily up the hill from the bridge.

### Museum of the Gorge

Wharfage · Daily 10am–5pm · £4.15, but covered by Passport Ticket (see p.444) · ☎ 01952 433424, ⓦ ironbridge.org.uk

Ironbridge village is also home to the **Museum of the Gorge**, in a church-like, neo-Gothic old riverside warehouse about seven hundred yards west of the bridge along the main road. This provides an introduction to the Gorge's industrial history and gives a few environmental pointers too; it also houses the main visitor centre (see p.444).

## Coalbrookdale Museum of Iron

Wellington Rd, Coalbrookdale · Daily 10am–5pm · £9.25, but covered by Passport Ticket (see p.444) · ☎ 01952 433424, ⓦ ironbridge.org.uk

At the roundabout just to the west of the Museum of the Gorge, turn right for the half-mile trip up to what was once the Gorge's big industrial deal, the **Coalbrookdale iron foundry**, which boomed throughout the eighteenth and early nineteenth century, employing up to four thousand men and boys. The foundry has been imaginatively converted into the **Museum of Iron**, with a wide range of displays on iron-making in general and the history of the company in particular. There are superb examples of Victorian and Edwardian ironwork here, including the intricate castings – stags, dogs and even camels – that became the house speciality. Also in the complex, across from the foundry beneath a protective canopy, are the ruins of the **furnace** where Abraham Darby pioneered the use of coke as a smelting fuel in place of charcoal.

## Bedlam Furnace

B4373, about 600 yards east of Ironbridge Village · Open access · Free

Heading **east** from the Iron Bridge along the north bank of the river, you soon pass the battered brick-and-stone remains of the **Bedlam furnace** (open access; free), one of the first furnaces to use coke rather than charcoal. It was kept alight around the clock, and at night its fiery silhouette was said to have scared passers-by out of their wits – hence the name.

## Blists Hill Victorian Town

Coalport Rd · About 1m north of the River Severn – take the signed turning between the Bedlam Furnace and Coalport · Daily 10am–5pm · £16.50, but covered by Passport Ticket (see p.444) · ☎ 01952 433424, ⓦ ironbridge.org.uk

The rambling **Blists Hill Victorian Town** is the Gorge's most popular attraction, enclosing a substantial number of reconstructed Victorian buildings, most notably a school, a candle-maker's, a doctor's surgery, a pub and wrought-iron works. Jam-packed on most summer days, it's especially popular with school parties, who keep the period-dressed employees busy.

## Tar Tunnel

Coalport High St, Coalport • On the north bank of the river, 500 yards east of the turning to Blists Hill & on the west edge of Coalport • April–Oct daily 10.30am–4pm • £3.25, but covered by Passport Ticket (see p.444) • ☎ 01952 433424, ⓦ ironbridge.org.uk

Built to transport coal from one part of the Gorge to another, but named for the bitumen that oozes naturally from its walls, the **Tar Tunnel** may not be long, but it's certainly more than a tad spooky and you'll be issued with a hard hat for reassurance.

## Coalport China Museum

Coalport • Daily 10am–5pm • £8.50, but covered by Passport Ticket (see p.444) • ☎ 01952 433424, ⓦ ironbridge.org.uk

The most easterly of the industrial sites on the north bank of the River Severn (and yards from the Tar Tunnel), the former **Coalport China works** occupies a sprawling brick complex, which incorporates the **Coalport China Museum**, packed with gaudy Coalport wares. There's also a workshop, where potters demonstrate their skills, and two **bottle-kilns**, those distinctive conical structures that were long the hallmark of the pottery industry.

## Jackfield

There are two ways to reach Jackfield from the north bank of the Severn: the Jackfield Bridge just east of Bedlam Furnace and the footbridge beside the Tar Tunnel.

Now a sleepy little village of pretty brown-brick cottages that string along the south bank of the River Severn, **JACKFIELD** was once a sooty, grimy place that hummed to the tune of two large tile factories, Maws and Craven Dunnill. Both were built in the middle of the nineteenth century to the latest industrial design, a fully integrated manufacturing system that produced literally thousands of tiles at breakneck speed. The more easterly of the two has been turned into the **Maws Craft Centre** (ⓦ mawscraftcentre.co.uk), which holds more than twenty arts, craft and specialist shops, while the other, about half a mile away, boasts the Jackfield Tile Museum.

### Jackfield Tile Museum

Jackfield • Daily 10am–5pm • £8.50, but covered by Passport Ticket (see p.444) • ☎ 01952 433424, ⓦ ironbridge.org.uk

A small part of the expansive Craven Dunnill factory still produces Craven Dunnill tiles (ⓦ cravendunnill-jackfield.co.uk), but mostly it's home to the outstanding **Jackfield Tile Museum**. The exhibits here include the superb "Style Gallery" and "Tiles Everywhere Galleries", where room after room illustrates many different types of tile, by style – Art Deco and Art Nouveau through to Arts and Crafts and the Aesthetic Movement – and location, from a London underground station to a butcher's shop.

---

| **ARRIVAL AND DEPARTURE** | **IRONBRIDGE GORGE** |
|---|---|

**By bus** Arriva bus #96 (ⓦ arrivabus.co.uk) connects both Shrewsbury (35min) and Telford (30min) bus stations with Ironbridge village (Mon–Sat every 2hr). There's also an Arriva service to Much Wenlock (Mon–Sat every 2hr; 30min).

---

**GETTING AROUND**

**By bus** Bus services along the Gorge are limited to the Gorge Connect (late July to late Aug daily 9am–5pm; every 30min; ⓦ arrivabus.co.uk), which links Coalbrookdale in the west with Coalport in the east, taking in Ironbridge village and Blists Hill on the way. A day ticket costs £7; Passport Ticket holders (see below) travel free.

---

**INFORMATION**

**Tourist information** Ironbridge Gorge tourist information (Mon–Fri 9am–5pm, Sat & Sun 10am–5pm; ☎ 01952 433424, ⓦ ironbridge.org.uk) is in the Museum of the Gorge, approximately 700 yards west of Ironbridge village along the main road. In addition to local maps and information, they sell attraction passes.

**Admissions and passes** Each museum and attraction charges its own admission fee, but if you're intending to visit several, then buy a Passport Ticket (£27.50), which allows access to all ten of them once in any calendar year. Passport Tickets are available at all the main sights and at tourist information. An extra £1.50 covers parking at all the sites, except in Ironbridge village, where metered charges apply.

## ACCOMMODATION

**Buckatree Hall Hotel** The Wrekin, Telford, just south of the M54 and Wellington ☎01952 641821, ⓦbuckatreehallhotel.co.uk. In a pleasant rural setting near the wooded slopes of The Wrekin, the distinctive 1334ft peak that rises high above its surroundings, the *Buckatree* comprises the original Edwardian house and a modern annexe-wing. Most of the rooms have balconies. **£70**

**Coalbrookdale Villa** 17 Paradise, Coalbrookdale ☎01952 433450, ⓦcoalbrookdalevilla.co.uk. This B&B occupies an attractive Victorian ironmaster's house set in its own grounds about half a mile up the hill from Ironbridge village in the tiny hamlet of Paradise. Sedately decorated,

country-house-style, en-suite bedrooms. **£75**

**The Library House** 11 Severn Bank, Ironbridge village ☎01952 432299, ⓦlibraryhouse.com. Enjoyable B&B, the best in the village, in a charming Georgian villa just yards from the Iron Bridge. Four doubles, decorated in a modern rendition of period style. **£90**

**YHA Coalport** Coalport ☎0845 371 9325, ⓦyha.org.uk. At the east end of the Gorge in the former Coalport China factory, this YHA hostel has 80 beds in two- to ten-bedded rooms, self-catering facilities, laundry, a shop and a café. Popular with school groups and for activity breaks. Dorms **£18**, doubles **£27.50**

## EATING AND DRINKING

**Coalbrookdale Inn** 12 Wellington Rd, Coalbrookdale ☎01952 432166, ⓦthecoalbrookdaleinn.co.uk. On the main road across from the Coalbrookdale iron foundry, this traditional pub offers a top-notch selection of real ales plus filling pub grub, including locally made pork pies. Live music too. Mon–Thurs noon–2pm & 5–11.30pm, Fri–Sun noon–11.30pm.

**Restaurant Severn** 33 High St, Ironbridge village ☎01952 432233, ⓦrestaurantseven.co.uk. This smart little place, just a few yards from the bridge, offers an inventive menu with main courses such as venison in a cognac and cranberry sauce. In the evening, a two-course set meal costs around £26. Wed–Sat 6.30–8.30pm, plus occasional Sun noon–1.30pm.

# Much Wenlock and around

Heading west from Ironbridge village along the northern bank of the River Severn, it's only a couple of miles to the A4169 and three more to **MUCH WENLOCK**, a tiny town where a medley of Tudor, Jacobean and Georgian buildings dot the High Street – and pull in day-trippers by the score. At the foot of the High Street is the **Guildhall**, sitting pretty on sturdy oak columns, but the town's architectural high point is Wenlock Priory.

## Wenlock Priory

Sheinton St • April–Sept daily 10am–6pm; Oct daily 10am–5pm; Nov–Feb Sat & Sun 10am–4pm • £4.20; EH • ☎01952 727466, ⓦenglish-heritage.org.uk

The Saxons built a monastery at Much Wenlock, but the remains of today's **Wenlock Priory** mostly stem from the thirteenth and fourteenth centuries when its successor, a Cluniac monastery founded here in the 1080s, reached the height of its wealth and power. Set amid immaculate gardens and fringed by woodland, the ruins are particularly picturesque, from the peeling stonework of the old priory church's transepts to the shattered bulk of **St Michael's chapel**.

## Wenlock Edge

Attracting hikers from all over the region, the beautiful and deeply rural **Wenlock Edge** is a limestone escarpment that runs twenty-odd miles southwest from Much Wenlock. The south side of the escarpment is a gently shelving slope of open farmland, while the thickly wooded north side scarps steeply down to the Shropshire plains. Much of the Edge is owned by the National Trust, which maintains a network of waymarked **trails** that wind through the woodland from a string of car parks along the B4371 – and are graded by colour according to length and difficulty.

## ARRIVAL AND DEPARTURE

## MUCH WENLOCK AND AROUND

**By bus** Buses to Much Wenlock (ⓦarrivabus.co.uk) stop on Queen St, in the centre of town; there are no buses along the length of the B4371 (Wenlock Edge).

**Destinations** Ironbridge village (Mon–Sat every 2hr; 30min); Shrewsbury (Mon–Sat hourly; 30min).

## ACCOMMODATION AND EATING

**George & Dragon Inn** 2 High St, Much Wenlock ☎ 01952 727312, ⊕ thegeorgedragon.co.uk. Cask ales and a friendly atmosphere are the trade marks of this traditional pub, where they also serve good-quality pub food – try the fish and chips. Daily 11am–11pm.

**YHA Wilderhope Manor** Longville-in-the-Dale, 1 mile south of the B4371 ☎ 0845 371 9149, ⊕ yha.org.uk.

One of the YHA's most distinctive hostels, the recently upgraded *Wilderhope Manor* occupies a remote Elizabethan mansion next to a farm – the turning is clearly signed on the edge of Longville-in-the-Dale. Facilities include a self-catering kitchen, a café, a laundry and a cycle store; open all year. Dorms **£16**, doubles **£48**

# Shrewsbury

**SHREWSBURY**, the county town of Shropshire, sits in a tight and narrow loop of the River Severn. It would be difficult to design a better defensive site and predictably the Normans built a stone castle here, one which Edward I decided to strengthen and expand in the thirteenth century, though by then the local economy owed as much to the Welsh wool trade as it did to the town's military importance. In Georgian times, Shrewsbury became a fashionable staging post on the busy London to Holyhead/ Ireland route and has since evolved into a laidback, middling market town. It's the overall feel of the place that is its main appeal, rather than any specific sight, though to celebrate its associations with **Charles Darwin**, the town is now the possessor of a 40ft-high sculpture entitled **Quantum Leap**: it cost nigh-on half a million pounds, so many locals are rueing the cost rather than celebrating the artistic vision.

The obvious place to start an exploration of Shrewsbury is the **train station** (see below), built in a fetching combination of styles, neo-Baronial meets country house, in the 1840s. Poking up above the train station are the battered ramparts of the **castle**, a pale reminder of the mighty medieval fortress that once dominated the town – the illustrious Thomas Telford turned the castle into the private home of a local bigwig in the 1780s. **Castle Gates** and its continuation **Castle Street/Pride Hill** cuts up from the station into the heart of the river loop where the medieval town took root. Turn left off Castle Street onto St Mary's Street and you soon reach Shrewsbury's most interesting church, **St Mary's**, whose architecturally jumbled interior is redeemed by a magnificent east window. From St Mary's, it's a couple of minutes' walk to **St Alkmund's Church**, from where there's a charming view of the fine old buildings of **Fish Street**, which cuts its way down to the High Street. Turn right here to get to **The Square** which is at the very heart of the town; its narrow confines are inhabited by the **Old Market Hall**, a heavy-duty stone structure dating from 1596.

## Abbey Church

Abbey Foregate • April–Oct daily 10am–4pm, Nov–March daily 10.30am–3pm • Free • ☎ 01743 232723, ⊕ shrewsburyabbey.com

From The Square, High Street snakes down the hill to become **Wyle Cop**, lined with higgledy-piggledy ancient buildings and leading to the **English Bridge**, which sweeps across the Severn in grand Georgian style. Beyond the bridge is the stumpy red-stone mass of the **Abbey Church**, all that remains of the Benedictine abbey that was a major political and religious force hereabouts until the Dissolution. The church is still in use as a place of worship; its best feature is the doughty Norman columns of the nave.

## ARRIVAL AND INFORMATION
## SHREWSBURY

**By train** Shrewsbury train station stands at the northeast tip of the town centre.

Destinations Birmingham (every 30min; 1hr); Church Stretton (hourly; 15min); Hereford (every 30min; 1hr); Ludlow (hourly; 30min); Telford (every 30min; 20min).

**By bus** Most buses pull into the Raven Meadows bus station, off Smithfield Rd, a 5min walk north of The Square.

Destinations Ironbridge village (Mon–Sat every 2hr; 35min; ⊕ arrivabus.co.uk); Much Wenlock (Mon–Sat hourly; 30min).

**Tourist office** In The Square (Easter–Sept daily 10am–5pm; Oct–Easter Tues–Sun 10am–5pm; ☎ 01743 258888, ⊕ shropshiretourism.co.uk); shares premises with the Shrewsbury Museum & Art Gallery.

## ACCOMMODATION

★ **Lion and Pheasant** 50 Wyle Cop ☎01743 770345, ⓦlionandpheasant.co.uk. Excellent, medium-sized, town-centre hotel in the shell of a former coaching inn; rooms are in pastel shades with lots of period details. Delicious breakfasts too. **£100**

**Old House Suites** The Old House, 20 Dogpole ☎0781 3610904, ⓦtheoldhousesuites.com. Cannily restored ancient merchant's house offering three suites kitted out in immaculate period style – down to the heavy drapes and wood panelling. An up-market B&B, whose owner will give you the low-down on the house's history. **£85**

**Prince Rupert Hotel** Butcher Row, off Pride Hill ☎01743 499955, ⓦprinceruperthotel.co.uk. A smart and popular hotel, the *Rupert* occupies a cannily converted old building in the middle of the town centre. There are seventy comfortable guest rooms – including twelve suites – and the pick have a platoon of period details, from wood panelling through to exposed wooden beams. **£100**

## EATING AND DRINKING

**Admiral Benbow** 24 Swan Hill ☎01743 244423, ⓦtheadmiralbenbowpub.co.uk/wp. Popular and enterprising, town-centre pub with a beer garden and a fine selection of real ales and Hereford farmhouse ciders and perry. Mon–Fri 5–11pm, Sat noon–11pm & Sun 7–10.30pm.

**Golden Cross** 14 Princess St ☎01743 362507, ⓦgoldencrosshotel.co.uk. This must be the best restaurant in Shrewsbury, a cosy, intimate kind of place (don't be deterred by the mullion windows) that offers a select international menu – try, for example, the pan-roasted, oriental crusted fillet of sea bass. In the city centre, a 2min walk from The Square. Mains average a very reasonable £13. Daily noon–2.30pm & 5.30–9.30pm.

**Good Life Coffee Shop & Restaurant** Barracks Passage, just off 73 Wyle Cop ☎01743 350455, ⓦgoodlife-shrewsbury.co.uk. Something of a local institution, this excellent café specializes in salads and vegetarian dishes from a daily menu. Locals swear by the quiches. Mains around £7. Mon–Sat 9am–4pm.

# Long Mynd

Beginning about nine miles south of Shrewsbury, the upland heaths of the **Long Mynd**, some ten miles long and between two and four miles wide, run parallel to and just to the west of the A49. This is prime **walking** territory and the heathlands are latticed with footpaths, the pick of which offer sweeping views over the border to the Black Mountains of Wales. Also popular with hikers, if even more remote, are the **Stiperstones**, a clot of boggy heather dotted with ancient cairns and earthworks that lies to the west of the Long Mynd.

## Church Stretton

Nestled at the foot of the Mynd is **CHURCH STRETTON**, a tidy little village that makes an ideal base for hiking the area. The village also possesses the dinky parish **church of St Laurence**, parts of which – especially the nave and transepts – are Norman. Look out also for the (badly weathered) fertility symbol over the side door, just to the left of the entrance – it's a genital-splaying **sheela-na-gig**, whose sheer explicitness is eye-watering.

## ARRIVAL AND INFORMATION                    CHURCH STRETTON

**By train** The train station is beside the A49 about 600 yards east of High St, which forms the heart of the village. Destinations Hereford (every 1hr–1hr 30min; 40min); Ludlow (every 1hr–1hr 30min; 15min); Shrewsbury (hourly; 15min).

**By bus** Most buses pull in beside the train station, but some also continue on to High Street. There's a useful Shropshire Hills Shuttle bus service (see p.442).

**Tourist office** The library, Church Street (Mon–Sat 9.30am–1pm & 2–5pm; ☎01694 723133, ⓦchurchstretton .co.uk).

## ACCOMMODATION

**Victoria House** 48 High St ☎01694 723823, ⓦvictoriahouse-shropshire.co.uk. The most central of several excellent B&Bs in the area, this extraordinarily cosy little place has six guest rooms above the owner's teashop (see p.448). The rooms are kitted out with heavy drapes, thick carpets and iron beds; breakfast is delicious. **£55**

**YHA Bridges** 5 miles west of Church Stretton on the edge of Ratlinghope SY5 0SP ☎01588 650656, ⓦyha.org.uk. On the edge of a tiny village, this hostel occupies a converted village school, has 38 beds in four- to twelve-bedded rooms, a café, camping and a self-catering kitchen. It's an ideal base for hiking to the Long Mynd or the Stiperstones. Dorms **£16**

8

## EATING

**Berry's Coffee House** 17 High St ☎ 01694 7224452, ⓦ berryscoffeehouse.co.uk. This is the dinkiest of (licensed) cafés, squeezed into antique premises in the centre of the village. They serve delicious snacks and light meals, but their salads are especially tasty – locally-smoked salmon with Berry's dill sauce salad gives the

flavour. Reckon on £8 per salad. Daily 9am–5pm.

**Jemima's Kitchen** 48 High St ☎ 01694 723823, ⓦ victoriahouse-shropshire.co.uk. Delicious home-made and home-baked snacks and light meals here at this cosy café. Specialist teas and mouth-watering scones, too. Thurs–Sun 9.30am–4pm.

# Ludlow

Perched on a hill in a loop of the River Teme, **LUDLOW**, thirty miles from Shrewsbury, is one of the most picturesque towns in the West Midlands, if not in England – a gaggle of beautifully preserved Georgian and black-and-white half-timbered buildings packed around a craggy stone castle, with rural Shropshire forming a drowsy backdrop. These are strong recommendations in themselves, but Ludlow earns bonus points by being something of a gastronomic hidey-hole with a clutch of outstanding **restaurants**, whose chefs and sous-chefs gather at the much-vaunted **Ludlow Food & Drink Festival** (ⓦ foodfestival.co.uk), held over three days every September. The other notable knees-up is the Ludlow Arts & Shakespeare Festival (ⓦ ludlowartsfestival.co.uk), ten days of musical and theatrical fun held in June or July.

## Ludlow Castle

Castle Square • April–July & Sept daily 10am–5pm; Aug daily 10am–6pm; Oct–Dec & mid-Feb to March daily 10am–4pm; Jan to mid-Feb Sat & Sun 10am–4pm • £5 • ☎ 01584 873355, ⓦ ludlowcastle.com

Ludlow's large and imposing **castle** dates mostly from Norman times, its rambling ruins incorporating towers and turrets, gatehouses and concentric walls as well as the remains of the 110ft Norman **keep** and an unusual **Round Chapel** built in 1120. With its spectacular setting high above the river, the castle also offers grand views over the surrounding countryside.

## Castle Square and around

The castle entrance abuts **Castle Square**, an airy rectangle whose eastern side breaks into several short and narrow lanes, with the one on the left leading through to the gracefully proportioned **Church of St Laurence**, whose interior is distinguished by its stained-glass windows and exquisite misericords in the choir. From the church, it's a few paces to the **Butter Cross**, a Neoclassical extravagance from 1744, and a few more to the **Bull Ring**, home of the **Feathers Hotel**, a fine Jacobean building with the fanciest wooden facade imaginable.

## Broad Street

To the south of Castle Square, the gridiron of streets laid out by the Normans has survived intact, though most of the buildings date from the eighteenth century. Steeply sloping **Broad Street** is particularly attractive, flanked by many of Ludlow's five hundred half-timbered Tudor and red-brick Georgian listed buildings. At the foot of Broad Street is Ludlow's only surviving **medieval gate**, which was turned into a house in the eighteenth century.

## ARRIVAL AND INFORMATION                                     LUDLOW

**By train** Ludlow train station is a 15min walk from the castle – just follow the signs.

Destinations Church Stretton (every 1hr–1hr 30min; 15min); Hereford (every 30min; 30min); Shrewsbury (hourly; 30min).

**By bus** Most buses stop at the top of Mill Street, just

off Castle Square.

Destinations Church Stretton (every 2hr; 30min); Hereford (every 2hr; 1hr 20min); Shrewsbury (every 2hr; 1hr 15min).

**Tourist office** Castle Square (Mon–Sat 10am–4.45pm, plus April–Oct Sun 10.30am–5pm; ☎ 01584 875053, ⓦ ludlow.org.uk).

## ACCOMMODATION

**Dinham Hall Hotel** Dinham ☎01584 876464, ⓦdinhamhall.co.uk. Handily located close to the castle, this deluxe, medium-sized hotel, with its thirteen appealing guest rooms, occupies a rambling, bow-windowed eighteenth-century stone mansion, which has previously seen service as a boarding house for Ludlow School. **£145**

**Ludlow Bed & Breakfast** 35 Lower Broad St ☎01584 876912, ⓦludlowbedandbreakfast.blogspot.co.uk. Near the bridge, a 5–10min walk from the castle, this cosy B&B has just two doubles in a pair of Georgian terrace cottages, which have been carefully knocked into one. Great breakfasts. **£75**

## EATING

**★La Bécasse** 17 Corve St ☎01584 872325, ⓦlabecasse.co.uk. Top-ranking restaurant with a strong French influence, where a two-course lunch menu du jour costs a reasonable £32. Try, for example, the boned and rolled local rabbit saddle with smoked bacon and caramelized celery. Reservations essential. Tues–Sat noon–2.30pm & 7–10pm.

**The Fish House** 51 Bullring ☎01584 879790, ⓦthefishhouseludlow.co.uk. First-class fishmongers with a few tables where they serve sparkling wine and fresh seafood – anything from a plate of smoked mackerel (£4.50) through to dressed crabs, oysters and prawns. Wed–Sat 9am–4pm.

**Mr Underhill's** Dinham Weir ☎01584 874431, ⓦmr-underhills.co.uk. One of the very best of Ludlow's top-flight restaurants, with a menu skilfully crafted from local ingredients, and some superb, creative vegetarian options (try the asparagus, cep-scented pasta and garden herbs). The eight-course daily market menu costs £70 per person. Reservations essential. Wed–Sun evenings only.

# Birmingham

If anywhere can be described as the first purely industrial conurbation, it has to be **BIRMINGHAM**. Unlike the more specialist industrial towns that grew up across the north and the Midlands, "Brum" – and its "Brummies" – turned its hand to every kind of manufacturing, gaining the epithet "the city of 1001 trades". It was here also that the pioneers of the Industrial Revolution – James Watt, Matthew Boulton, Josiah Wedgwood, Joseph Priestley and Erasmus Darwin (grandfather of Charles) – formed the **Lunar Society**, an extraordinary melting-pot of scientific and industrial ideas. They conceived the world's first purpose-built factory, invented gas lighting and pioneered both the distillation of oxygen and the mass production of the steam engine. Thus, a modest Midlands market town mushroomed into the nation's economic dynamo with the population to match: in 1841 there were 180,000 inhabitants; just fifty years later that number had trebled.

Now Britain's second-largest city, with a population of over one million, Birmingham has long outgrown the squalor and misery of its boom years and today its industrial supremacy is recalled – but only recalled – by a crop of **recycled buildings**, from warehouses to an old custard factory, and an extensive network of **canals**. This recent (and enforced) shift to a post-manufacturing economy has also been trumped by an intelligent and far-reaching revamp of the city centre that has included the construction of a glitzy **Convention Centre**, a talented reconstruction of the **Bull Ring**, the reinvigoration of the excellent **Birmingham Museum & Art Gallery**, and, at a time when other councils are nervously biting their nails, the building of a lavish, state-of-the-art **Library**. Birmingham has also launched a whole range of cultural initiatives – including the provision of a fabulous new concert hall for the **City of Birmingham Symphony Orchestra** – and boasts both a first-rate restaurant scene and a boisterous nightlife. While Birmingham doesn't have the density of attractions of a capital city, it's well worth at least a couple of days of anyone's time.

## The Bull Ring

A few steps from New Street Station, Rotunda Square, at the intersection of New and High streets, takes its name from the soaring **Rotunda**, a handsome and distinctive cylindrical tower that is the sole survivor of the notorious **Bull Ring** shopping centre, which fulfilled every miserable cliché of 1960s town planning until its demolition in

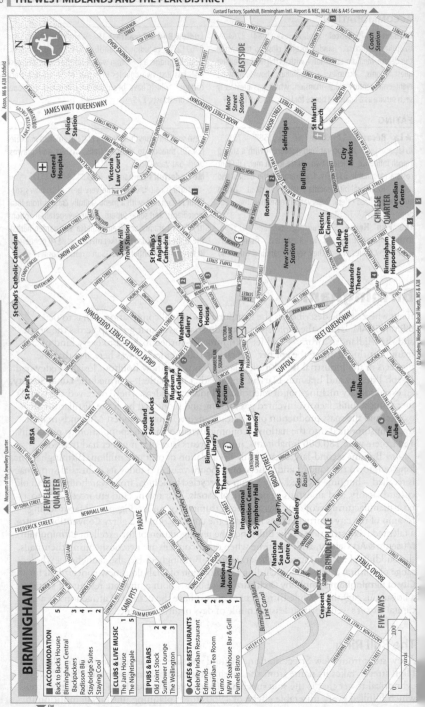

8

BIRMINGHAM

■ ACCOMMODATION
Back to Backs Houses        5
Birmingham Central         3
Backpackers                4
Radisson Blu               1
Staybridge Suites          2
Staying Cool

■ CLUBS & LIVE MUSIC
The Jam House              1
The Nightingale            2

■ PUBS & BARS
Old Joint Stock            2
Sunflower Lounge           4
The Wellington             3

● CAFÉS & RESTAURANTS
Celebrity Indian Restaurant    5
Edmunds                        4
Edwardian Tea Room             2
Fumo                           3
MPW Steakhouse Bar & Grill     6
Purnells Bistro                1

2001. The new Bull Ring shopping centre, which replaced it, has two strokes of real invention. Firstly, the architects split the shops into two separate sections, providing an uninterrupted view of the medieval spire of St Martin's in between – an obvious contrast between the old and the new perhaps, but still extraordinarily effective. The second coup was the design of **Selfridges'** store.

### Selfridges

Bull Ring · Core hours: Mon–Fri 10am–8pm, Sat 9am–8pm, Sun 11am–5.30pm · ☎ 0800 123400, ⓦ style.selfridges.com/store/birmingham

Birmingham's **Selfridges** is an extraordinary sight – a billowing organic swell protruding from the Bull Ring's east side, and seen to best advantage from the wide stone stairway that descends from Rotunda Square to St Martin's. Reminiscent of an inside-out octopus, Selfridges shimmers with an architectural chain mail of thousands of spun aluminium discs, an altogether bold and hugely successful attempt to create a popular city landmark.

### St Martin's Church

St Martin's Square · Daily 10am–5pm · Free · ☎ 0121 600 6020, ⓦ bullring.org

Nestling at the foot of the Bull Ring, the newly scrubbed and polished **St Martin's Church** is a fetching amalgamation of the Gothic and the neo-Gothic, its mighty spire poking high into the sky. The church has had some hard times, attacked by the Victorians and bombed by the Luftwaffe, but the interior, with its capacious three-aisled nave, is saved from mediocrity by a delightful **Burne-Jones stained-glass window**, a richly coloured, finely detailed affair whose panes sport angels, saints, biblical figures and scenes.

### The city markets

Edgbaston St

Across from St Martin's Church are Birmingham's three main **markets** – two selling fresh produce, one indoor (Mon–Sat 9am–5.30pm), the other outdoor (Tues–Sat 9am–5pm), with the **Rag Market** (Tues, Thurs, Fri & Sat 9am–5pm) in between. There was a time when the Rag Market was crammed with every sort of material you could imagine and then some; its heyday is gone but it still musters up all sorts of knick-knacks, always sold at bargain-basement prices.

## Victoria Square

Busy **New Street** stretches west from the Bull Ring en route to the handsomely refurbished **Victoria Square**, whose centrepiece is a large and particularly engaging **water fountain** designed by Dhruva Mistry. The waterfall outdoes poor old Queen Victoria, whose statue is glum and uninspired, though the thrusting self-confidence of her bourgeoisie is very apparent in the flamboyant **Council House** behind her, its gables and cupolas, columns and towers completed in 1879. Across the square, and very different, is the **Town Hall** of 1834, whose classical design – by Joseph Hansom, who went on to design Hansom cabs – was based on the Roman temple in Nîmes. The building's simple, flowing lines contrast with much of its surroundings, but it's an appealing structure all the same, and now houses a performing arts venue.

## The Birmingham Museum and Art Gallery

Chamberlain Square · Daily 10am–5pm, Fri from 10.30am · Free · ☎ 0121 348 8007, ⓦ bmag.org.uk

The **Birmingham Museum and Art Gallery** (BM&AG), which occupies a grand, rambling, Edwardian building and one of its neighbours, possesses a multifaceted collection running from fine and applied art through to archeological finds. The key paintings, including the BM&AG's prime collection of Pre-Raphaelites, are spread over one long floor – Floor 2 – which is where you'll also find the **Staffordshire Hoard**, the largest collection of Anglo-Saxon gold ever discovered, with more than 1500 pieces mostly related to warfare. The museum's collection is too large for it all to be exhibited at any one time, and artworks are regularly rotated, so be sure to pick up a **plan** at reception. There's also a good **café** here (see p.457).

### The Pre-Raphaelites

The BM&AG holds a significant sample of **European** paintings and an excellent collection of eighteenth- and nineteenth-century British art, most notably a supreme muster of **Pre-Raphaelite** work. Founded in 1848, the Pre-Raphaelite Brotherhood consisted of seven young artists, of whom Rossetti, Holman Hunt, Millais and Madox Brown are the best known. The name of the group was selected to express their commitment to honest observation, which they thought had been lost with the Renaissance. Two seminal Pre-Raphaelite paintings on display are **Dante Gabriel Rossetti**'s stirring *Beata Beatrix* (1870) and **Ford Madox Brown**'s powerful image of emigration, *The Last of England* (1855). The Brotherhood disbanded in the 1850s, but a second wave of artists carried on in its footsteps, most notably **Edward Burne-Jones**, whose *Star of Bethlehem* – in Room 14 – is one of the largest watercolours ever painted, a mysterious, almost magical piece with earnest Magi and a film-star-like Virgin Mary.

### The Industrial Gallery, Gas Hall and the Waterhall Gallery

Sharing Floor 2 is the **Industrial Gallery**, which is set around an expansive atrium whose wrought-iron columns and balconies clamber up towards fancy skylights. The gallery holds a choice selection of ceramics, jewellery and stained glass retrieved from defunct churches all over Birmingham. Here also is the *Edwardian Tea Room*, one of the city's more pleasant places for a cuppa (see p.457). Elsewhere, the cavernous **Gas Hall** is an impressive venue for touring art exhibitions, while the **Waterhall Gallery**, inside the Council House, just across Edmund Street from the main museum building, showcases temporary exhibitions of modern and contemporary art.

## Hall of Memory and around

Centenary Square • Mon–Sat 10am–4pm • Free • ⓦ hallofmemory.co.uk

Erected in the 1920s to commemorate the thirteen thousand from Birmingham who died in World War I, the distinctive **Hall of Memory** is an architectural hybrid, a delightful mix of Art Deco and Neoclassical features, whose centrepiece is a domed Remembrance chamber. From the memorial, it's a brief walk to the newly constructed Library and the showpiece **International Convention Centre** (ICC) and **Symphony Hall** with the **Birmingham Repertory Theatre** on the right.

## Birmingham Library

Centenary Square • Mon–Fri 8am–8pm, Sat 9am–5pm & Sun 11am–4pm • Free • ☎ 0121 242 4242, ⓦ libraryofbirmingham.com

At a time when many British libraries were under threat, it was a brave move for the City Council to fund the construction of a new **Library**, a prestige structure that was completed in 2013 to a striking design, its cubic superstructure clad with a shimmering filigree of overlapping metal rings. Local opinion seems to be divided as to whether it was a sound investment, but it's certainly a city landmark and the interior has all mod cons plus outside terraces with views over the city centre.

## Gas Street Basin

**Gas Street Basin** is the hub of Birmingham's intricate canal system. There are eight canals within the city's boundaries, comprising 32 miles of canal, with most dug in the late eighteenth century before the railways made them uneconomic. Much of the surviving canal network slices through the city's grimy, industrial bowels, but certain sections have been immaculately restored with Gas Street Basin leading the way. The Basin, which is edged by a delightful medley of old brick buildings, lies at the junction of the Worcester and Birmingham and Birmingham Main Line canals and its dark waters almost invariably bob with a fleet of brightly painted narrowboats.

## The Mailbox

Following the towpath along the canal southeast from Gas Street Basin soon brings you to **The Mailbox**, a striking reinvention of Birmingham's old postal sorting office complete with restaurants, hotels, and some of the snazziest shops in the city – including Harvey Nichols – and recently emerging from a thorough refit.

## Brindleyplace

Also near Gas Street Basin is the waterside **Brindleyplace**, which is named after James Brindley, the eighteenth-century engineer responsible for many of Britain's early canals. It's an aesthetically pleasing development, even though many of its cafés, restaurants and shops are multinational chains, with an attractive central plaza popular with office staff at lunch times. Just off the central square is the city's much-lauded Ikon Gallery.

### Ikon Gallery

1 Oozells Square • Tues–Sun 11am–6pm • Free • ☎ 0121 248 0708, ⓦ ikon-gallery.org

Housed in a substantial Victorian building in the Brindleyplace complex, the splendid **Ikon Gallery** is one of the country's most imaginative venues for touring exhibitions of contemporary art, with recent exhibitions by the likes of Cornelia Parker and Pakistan's Imran Qureshi. Perhaps even better, the gallery organises all sorts of workshops, family days and special events – from 'Art Explorer' days for children to 'Plastic Fantastic' and guided tours of the gallery itself.

## Birmingham & Fazeley Canal

Just beyond Brindleyplace, in front of the massive dome of the National Indoor Arena (NIA), the canal forks: the Birmingham Main Line Canal cuts west (to the left) and the more interesting **Birmingham & Fazeley Canal** leads northeast (to the right), running past a sequence of antique brick buildings en route to the quaint **Scotland Street Locks**. Further on, the canal slices past a string of new apartment blocks as well as the (signed) flight of steps that clambers up to Newhall Street, about half a mile beyond the main canal junction – and a few minutes' walk from **St Paul's Square**, where an attractive ensemble of old houses flank the charming Neoclassical **St Paul's church** (ⓦ saintpaulbrum.org).

## St Philip's Cathedral

Colmore Row • Mon–Fri 7.30am–6.30pm, 5pm in August; Sat & Sun 8.30am–5pm • Free • ☎ 0121 262 1840, ⓦ birminghamcathedral.com

The string of fancily carved, High Victorian stone buildings on Colmore Row provides a suitable backdrop for **St Philip's Anglican Cathedral**, a bijou example of English Baroque. Consecrated in 1715, the church is a handsome affair, its graceful, galleried interior all balance and poise, its harmonies unruffled by the Victorians, who enlarged the original church in the 1880s, when four stained-glass windows were commissioned from local boy **Edward Burne-Jones**, a leading light of the Pre-Raphaelite movement. The windows are typical of his style – intensely coloured, fastidiously detailed and distinctly sentimental. Three – the *Nativity*, *Crucifixion* and *Ascension* – are at the east end of the church beyond the high altar, the fourth – the *Last Judgement* – is directly opposite.

8

## Jewellery Quarter

Ⓦ the-quarter.com • Jewellery Quarter train station & metro stop are on the Snow Hill line

Birmingham's long-established **Jewellery Quarter** lies to the northwest of the city centre. Buckle-makers and toy-makers first colonized this area in the 1750s, opening the way for hundreds of silversmiths, jewellers and goldsmiths, and today there are still several hundred jewellery-related companies in the district with most of the **jewellery shops** concentrated along Vittoria Street and its northerly continuation, Vyse Street.

### Museum of the Jewellery Quarter

75 Vyse St • Tues–Sat 10.30am–5pm • £5 • Ⓣ 0121 348 8140, Ⓦ bmag.org.uk/museum-of-the-jewellery-quarter • A brief walk from the Jewellery Quarter train station and metro stop

The engrossing **Museum of the Jewellery Quarter** occupies a former jewellery-maker's that closed down in the early 1980s. What makes it so distinctive is that the owners just shut up shop, leaving everything intact and untouched, down to the dirty teacups. The museum details the rise and fall of the jewellery trade in Birmingham, but it's the old building that steals the show.

## The Custard Factory

Gibb St • Ⓣ 0121 224 7777, Ⓦ custardfactory.co.uk

Below the Bull Ring, **Digbeth** falls away to the southeast. Jammed with traffic and jostled by decrepit industrial buildings, it's hardly enticing, but there are two reasons to venture out here. The first is the bus station on the right; the second – on the left just along and off Gibb Street – is the arts complex that occupies **The Custard Factory**, a handsome, homely affair set around a friendly little courtyard. The complex offers a fascinating variety of workshops and, among much else, has gallery space for temporary exhibitions of modern art.

## Back to Backs

55–63 Hurst St • Feb–Dec Tues–Sun 10am–5pm • 1hr guided tours; advance reservations required • £7.25; NT • Booking line Ⓣ 0121 666 7671, Ⓣ 0121 622 2442, Ⓦ nationaltrust.org.uk/birmingham-back-to-backs

The sheer scale of the industrial boom that gripped nineteenth-century Birmingham is hard to grasp, but the raw statistics speak for themselves: in 1811, there were just 85,000 Brummies, a century later there were literally ten times more. The demand for cheap **housing** spawned the **back-to-back**, quickly erected dwellings that were one room deep and two, sometimes three storeys high, built in groups ("courts") around a courtyard where the communal privies were located. Even by the standards of the time, this was pretty grim stuff and as early as the 1870s Birmingham council banned the construction of any more. The last Birmingham courts were bulldozed in the 1970s, but one set survived and this, the **Birmingham Back to Backs**, has been restored by the National Trust. The tour wends its way through four separate homes, each of which represents a different period from the early nineteenth century onwards, with titbits about the families who lived here and lots of period bygones to touch and feel; you can stay here too (see p.456).

### ARRIVAL AND DEPARTURE
BIRMINGHAM

**By plane** Birmingham's International Airport is 8 miles east of the city centre off the A45 – and near the M42 (Junction 6); the terminal is beside Birmingham International train station, from where there are regular services into New Street train station (every 10–15min; 12min).

**By train** Most inter-city trains and many local services use New Street train station, which is right in the heart of the city – and is currently undergoing a long-term (and long overdue) refurbishment. There are, however, two other mainline stations in the city centre. These are Snow Hill and Moor Street, respectively a (signed) 10min-walk north and a 5-minute walk east of New Street station. Moor Street, the prettiest of the three – with much of its Edwardian

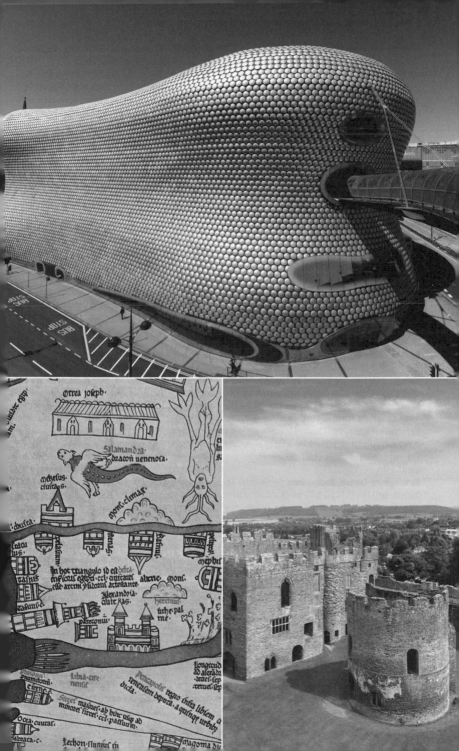

fabric intact – is used primarily by Chiltern Railways.
Destinations (New St) Birmingham International (every 10–15min; 12min); Coventry (3–5 hourly; 25min); Derby (every 30min; 45min); Great Malvern (hourly; 1hr); Hereford (hourly; 1hr 30min); Ledbury (hourly; 1hr 15min); London Euston (every 30min; 1hr 25min); Shrewsbury (every 30min; 1hr); Telford (Mon–Sat every 30min, Sun hourly; 40min).
Destinations (Moor St) London Marylebone (every 30min;

1hr 50min); Stratford-upon-Avon (hourly; 1hr 10min); Worcester Foregate (every 30min; 1hr).
Destinations (Snow Hill Station) Stratford-upon-Avon (hourly; 1hr); Warwick (every 30min to 1hr; 30min).
**By bus** National Express long-distance buses arrive at the Birmingham bus station, in Digbeth, from where it's a 10min walk northwest to the Bull Ring.
Destinations London (every 45min; 2hr 45min); Manchester (4–5 daily; 2hr 20min).

## GETTING AROUND

Birmingham has an excellent public transport system, whose trains, metro and buses delve into almost every urban nook and cranny. Various companies provide these services, but they are all co-ordinated by Centro (☎0121 200 2787, ⌨ centro.org.uk).

## INFORMATION

**Tourist office** In the Library, on Centenary Square (Mon–Fri 10am–6pm, Sat 9am–5pm; ☎0844 888 3883, ⌨ visitbirmingham.com). There's also a tourist information kiosk in front of New Street station, at the junction of New Street and Corporation Street (Mon–Sat 9am–5pm, Sun 10am–4pm; same details).

## ACCOMMODATION

To see Birmingham at its best, you really need to stay in the centre, preferably in the vicinity of **Centenary Square**, though chain hotels do monopolize the downtown core. Visit Birmingham (⌨ visitbirmingham.com) operates a free **room-booking** service.

**Back to Backs Houses** 52 Inge St ☎0344 335 1287, ⌨ nationaltrustcottages.co.uk. The most distinctive place to stay in town: the National Trust has refurbished a small block of nineteenth-century back-to-back workers' houses conveniently located just to the south of the city centre along Hurst Street. Part of the complex now holds two small "cottages" – really terraced houses – kitted out in Victorian period style, but with the addition of en-suite and self-catering facilities. Each accommodates two guests. **£100**
**Birmingham Central Backpackers** 58 Coventry St, Digbeth ☎0121 643 0033, ⌨ birminghambackpackers .com. Welcoming hostel with self-catering facilities, free wi-fi, a large sociable lounge, a small garden and a café-bar. Dorms have four to twelve bunks per room. A short walk from Digbeth bus station. Dorms from **£16**, Doubles **£40**
**Radisson Blu** 12 Holloway Circus ☎0121 654 6000, ⌨ radissonblu.co.uk. Smart hotel in a tall, sleek skyrise

within a few minutes' walk of the centre. The interior is designed in routine modern-minimalist style, but the floor-to-ceiling windows of many of the bedrooms add more than a dash of élan. **£80**
**Staybridge Suites** One Martineau Place, Corporation St ☎0871 423 4948, ⌨ staybridgesuites.com /Birmingham. Classic, 1960s, city-centre office block that has been skilfully converted into a hotel, holding 179 smart, modern suites with fitted kitchenettes. Capacious breakfast area, too. Double rooms from as little as **£50**
★**Staying Cool** The Rotunda, New St ☎0121 285 1290, ⌨ stayingcool.com. The top three floors of the Rotunda, right at the heart of the city, have been converted into fully furnished, serviced apartments. All the apartments are modern and spotless, and those on the top floor – Floor 20 – come with a balcony from where there are panoramic views over the city. The apartments can be rented for one night – no problem. **£140**

## EATING

Central Birmingham has a bevy of first-rate restaurants with a string of smart new venues springing up in the slipstream of the burgeoning conference and trade-fair business. Birmingham's gastronomic speciality is the **balti**, a delicious Kashmiri stew cooked and served in a small wok-like dish called a *karahi*, with naan bread instead of cutlery. The original balti houses are concentrated out in the suburbs of Balsall Heath, Moseley and Sparkhill to the south of the centre, but there are now prime balti houses in the centre too.

**Celebrity Indian Restaurant** 44 Broad St ☎0121 643 8969, ⌨ celebrityrestaurant.co.uk. Locals swear that the best baltis are served out in the city's suburbs, but this smart, city-centre restaurant runs them close – and saves

the journey out. A wide-ranging menu covers all the classics and a 'traditional Brummy balti' will rush you about £10. Daily 5.30pm–midnight.
**Edmunds** 6 Central Square, Brindleyplace ☎0121 633

4944, ⓦedmundsrestaurant.co.uk. High-style dining in smart, contemporary premises. An inventive menu features seasonal ingredients – venison with dauphine potato, duck liver, parsnip mousseline and hazelnut crumble is typical. A two-course, lunchtime set meal is £15, but will set you back more than twice that in the evenings. Reservations well nigh essential. Tues–Fri noon–2pm & 5.30–10.30pm, plus Sat 5.30–10pm.

**Edwardian Tea Room** (BM&AG), Chamberlain Square ⓣ0121 348 8007, ⓦbmag.org.uk. Recently upgraded, this relaxing café has a great setting in one of the large and fancily decorated halls of the museum's industrial section – check out all those handsome cast-iron columns. The food doesn't quite match up to the surroundings – but stick to the simpler dishes and you won't go wrong. Mon–Sat 11am–4.30pm & Sun 12.30–4.30pm.

★**Fumo** 1 Waterloo St ⓣ0121 643 8979, ⓦsancarlofumo.co.uk. In smart modern premises, this fast-paced Italian restaurant serves up excellent and authentic Italian cuisine – from the basics (pizzas and pastas) through to more elaborate concoctions like monkfish and prawns marinated in garlic, parsley and lemon. Mains are a snip at around £9. Daily 11.30am–11.30pm.

**MPW Steakhouse Bar & Grill** The Cube, 200 Wharfside St ⓣ0121 634 3433, ⓦmpwsteakhouse birmingham.co.uk. Amazingly popular cocktail bar and restaurant, the inspiration of Marco Pierre White. A no-nonsense menu features steaks (as you would expect), but there are other offerings too – for example pork belly, bramley apple with bubble and squeak and mustard sauce (£16.65). One of the reasons for its popularity is the location – on the top-floor of The Cube, a high-rise office block that has been creatively reconfigured, including the addition of a sculpture-like external casing/screen. Mon–Fri noon–2.30pm & 5–10pm; Sat & Sun noon–10pm.

★**Purnells Bistro** 11 Newhall St ⓣ0121 200 1588, ⓦpurnellsbistro-gingers.com. A new venture by Michelin-starred chef Glynn Purnell, who already operates one of the city's best restaurants – *Purnell's* – this combined cocktail bar and up-market bistro offers "honest portions of food, inspired by rustic home cooking". Quite. A la carte mains average £14 and include such delights as mackerel pastilla with a tomato and olive salsa. Reservations recommended. Food served daily noon–2.30pm & 5–10pm, closed Sun eve.

## DRINKING

★**Old Joint Stock** 4 Temple Row West ⓣ0121 200 1892, ⓦoldjointstocktheatre.co.uk. This charming pub has the fanciest decor in town – with busts and a balustrade, a balcony and chandeliers, all dating from its days as a bank. There's a medium-sized theatre studio upstairs mostly featuring improv comedy and musical theatre. Daily 11am–11pm.

**Sunflower Lounge** 76 Smallbrook Queensway ⓣ0121 632 6756, ⓦthesunflowerlounge.com. Quirky pub-cum-bar in modern premises on the inner ring road near

New Street station. Attracts an indie/student crowd and covers many bases, with quizzes and big-screen TV plus resident DJs and live gigs. It really is cool without being pretentious – just as they say on their website. Daily hours vary depending on event.

**The Wellington** 37 Bennetts Hill ⓣ0121 200 3115, ⓦthewellingtonrealale.co.uk. Specialist real ale pub with a top-notch range of local brews, including those of the much-proclaimed Black Country Brewery, and a good selection of ciders, too. Daily 10am–midnight.

## NIGHTLIFE AND ENTERTAINMENT

Birmingham's **club scene** is one of Britain's best, spanning everything from word-of-mouth underground parties to meat-market mainstream clubs. **Live music** is strong, too, with big-name concerts at several major venues and other (often local) bands appearing at some clubs and pubs. Birmingham's showpiece **Symphony Orchestra** and **Royal Ballet** are the spearheads of the city's **classical scene**. The city also lines up a string of top-ranking **festivals** - including the **Jazz Festival** (ⓦbirminghamjazzfestival.com) held for two weeks in July. For details of all upcoming events, performances and exhibitions, ask at the tourist office (see opposite) or consult either ⓦbirminghammail.co.uk or ⓦlivebrum.co.uk.

### LIVE MUSIC AND CLUBS

★**The Jam House** 3 St Paul's Square ⓣ0121 200 3030, ⓦthejamhouse.com. Jazz, funk, blues and swing club/pub pulling in artists from every corner of the globe. Great vibe; great gigs. Tues–Sat from 6pm.

**The Nightingale** 18 Kent St ⓣ0121 622 1718, ⓦnightingaleclub.co.uk. The king/queen of Brum's gay clubs, popular with straights as well. Five bars, three levels, two discos, a café-bar and even a garden. Just south of the Hippodrome (see opposite). Thurs–Sat from 9pm.

**O2 Academy** 16–18 Horsefair, Bristol St Ticket line: ⓣ0844 477 2000, ⓦo2academybirmingham.co.uk. State-of-the-art venue with three rooms hosting either gigs or club nights, though the big deal are the top-ranking artists – Katey P, Paloma Faith, The Kooks and so forth.

### CLASSICAL MUSIC, THEATRE, DANCE AND CINEMA

**Birmingham Hippodrome** Hurst St ⓣ0844 338 5000, ⓦbirminghamhippodrome.com. Lavishly refurbished, the Hippodrome is home to the Birmingham Royal Ballet. Also features touring plays and big pre- and post-West End productions, plus a splendiferous Christmas pantomime.

**Birmingham Repertory Theatre** Centenary Square, Broad St ☎0121 236 4455, ⓦbirmingham-rep.co.uk. Mixed diet of classics and new work featuring local and experimental writing.

**Electric Cinema** 47 Station St ☎0121 643 7879, ⓦtheelectric.co.uk. Britain's oldest working cinema, housed in a handsome Art Deco building, with an inventive programme of mainstream and art-house films. Sofas and waiter service also.

**Symphony Hall** International Convention Centre, Broad St ☎0121 345 0600, ⓦthsh.co.uk. Acoustically one of the most advanced concert halls in Europe, home of the acclaimed City of Birmingham Symphony Orchestra (CBSO; ⓦcbso.co.uk), as well as a venue for touring music and opera.

**Town Hall** Broad St ☎0121 345 0600, ⓦthsh.co.uk. Recently refitted and refurbished, the old Town Hall offers a varied programme of pop, classical and jazz music through to modern dance and ballet.

# Lichfield

Spreading north from the Birmingham conurbation, the county of **Staffordshire** has one especially interesting town, **LICHFIELD**, a slow-moving, amenable kind of place that pulls in the tourists for two reasons – its magnificent sandstone **Cathedral** and as the birthplace of **Samuel Johnson**, whose considerable achievements are remembered at the **Samuel Johnson Birthplace Museum**.

## The Cathedral

The Close • Mon–Sat 8.30am–6pm, Sun 7.30am–6pm • Free, but donation requested • ☎01543 306100, ⓦlichfield-cathedral.org

Begun in 1085, but substantially rebuilt on several subsequent occasions, **Lichfield Cathedral** is unique in possessing three spires – an appropriate distinction for a bishopric that once extended over virtually all of the Midlands. Approaching the cathedral, the magnificent **west front** is adorned by over one hundred statues of biblical figures, English kings and the supposed ancestors of Christ. Inside, the soaring **vaulted roof** extends without interruption into the choir, looking like the ribcage of a giant beast – a distinctly eerie experience. Most impressive of all, however, is the **Lady Chapel**, at the far end of the choir, which boasts a set of magnificent sixteenth-century windows, purchased from a Cistercian abbey in Belgium in 1802. The cathedral's greatest treasure, the **Chad Gospels**, is displayed in the **chapter house**, off the north side of the choir. A rare and exquisite example of Anglo-Saxon artistry dating to the eighth century, this illuminated manuscript contains the gospels of Matthew and Mark, and a fragment of the gospel of Luke.

## Samuel Johnson Birthplace Museum

Breadmarket St, Market Square • Daily: April–Sept 10.30am–4.30pm; Oct–March 11am–3.30pm • Free • ☎01543 264972, ⓦsamueljohnsonbirthplace.org.uk

Samuel Johnson's father was a bookseller and the **Samuel Johnson Birthplace Museum** was both the family home and his place of work. The museum's ground floor still serves as a **bookshop**, while up above, a series of displays explore the life and times of eighteenth-century England's most celebrated wit and critic, best known for compiling the first Dictionary of the English language. The top floor holds a collection of personal memorabilia, including Johnson's favourite armchair, his chocolate pot (chocolate was a delicacy in Georgian times) and ivory writing tablets.

### ARRIVAL AND INFORMATION                                    LICHFIELD

**By train** Lichfield has two train stations: Lichfield City, about 5min walk south of the centre, and Lichfield Trent Valley on the eastern fringe of the city, about 20min walk from the centre.

**Destinations** Birmingham New Street (from both Lichfield stations: every 30min; 40min).

**By bus** The bus station is on Birmingham Road, opposite Lichfield City Station.

Destinations Derby (every 30min, change at Burton; 1hr 30min).

**Tourist information** in St Mary's Church, Breadmarket St, on the Market Square (Mon–Sat 9.30am–4pm; ☎01543 256611, ⓦvisitlichfield.com).

## ACCOMMODATION AND EATING

**The Bogey Hole** 23 Dam St ☎01543 264303, ⓦthebogeyhole.co.uk. Cosy B&B in an old and well-kept terrace house with four en-suite guest rooms decorated in traditional style. In a great location – on a pedestrianised street a few yards from the Cathedral. **£60**

**Chapters** 19 The Close ☎01543 306125, ⓦlichfield -cathedral.org. Next door to the cathedral, this old-fashioned café has a pleasant atmosphere and offers inexpensive

home-made food from soups and sandwiches to cakes and quiches. Mon–Sat 9am–4pm & Sun 10am–4pm.

**Siam Corner Ma Ma Thai** 17 Bird St ☎01543 411911, ⓦsiamcornermamathai.co.uk. Two short blocks southwest of the Market Square, this is a smart and modern Thai place serving all the classics; main courses average £15. Mon 5–10.30pm, Tues–Sun noon–2.30pm & 5–10.30pm.

# Derby

Resurgent **DERBY** may be close to the wilds of the Peak District (see p.460), but it has more in common with its big-city neighbours, Nottingham and Leicester, except that here the industrial base is thriving with **Rolls-Royce** leading the way. Furthermore, recent attempts to spruce up the town have proved particularly successful and there's one prime attraction in the centre too, the **Derby Museum and Art Gallery**. The gallery is located just west of the central **Market Place** and southwest of the city's most impressive building, the **cathedral**, whose ponderous medieval tower rises high above its modest Victorian surroundings. An hour or two will do to see the sights before you hightail it off to the Peak District.

8

## Derby Museum and Art Gallery

The Strand • Tues–Sun 10am–5pm • Free • ☎01332 641901, ⓦderbymuseums.org

Among much else, **Derby Museum and Art Gallery** exhibits a splendid collection of Derby **porcelain**, several hundred pieces tracking through its different phases and styles from the mid-eighteenth century until today. The museum's star turn, however, is its prime collection of the work of **Joseph Wright** (1734–97), a local artist generally regarded as one of the most talented English painters of his generation. Wright was one of the few artists of his period to find inspiration in technology and his depictions of the scientific world were hugely influential – as in his *The Alchemist Discovering Phosphorus* and *A Philosopher Lecturing on the Orrery*.

## ARRIVAL AND INFORMATION                                                          DERBY

**By train** Derby train station is a mile to the southeast of the city centre – just follow the signs – but it's a dreary walk, so you might as well take a taxi.

Destinations Birmingham New Street (every 20min; 40min); Leicester (every 20min; 30min); London St Pancras (every 30min; 1hr 30min); Nottingham (every 20min; 25min).

**By bus** The bus station is on Morledge on the southeast side of the city centre. One useful service beginning here is

High Peak Buses' (ⓦhighpeakbuses.com) TransPeak service across the Peak District to Manchester.

Destinations Ashbourne (hourly; 40min); Bakewell (hourly; 1hr); Buxton (hourly; 1hr 35min); Manchester (5 daily; 3hr).

**Tourist office** For the moment at least, Derby tourist information centre remains in a part of the Assembly Rooms, on Market Place, that escaped the recent fire (Mon–Sat 9.30am–4.30pm; ☎01332 643411, ⓦvisitderby.co.uk).

## EATING AND DRINKING

**Brunswick Inn** 1 Railway Terrace ☎01332 290677, ⓦbrunswickderby.co.uk. In a good-looking Georgian terrace building just a couple of minutes' walk from the train station, this traditional pub, with its leather

banquettes and garden, offers an impressive range of ciders and real ales, some of which are brewed on the premises. Daily 11am–11pm, Sun from noon.

**The European** 22 Irongate ☎01332 368732,

ⓦtheeuropeanrestaurant.co.uk. Friendly, family-run restaurant-cum-bistro offering a tasty range of Italian dishes – all the classics and then some. Above a shop in an attractive old building, just across the street from the cathedral. Mains average £10, a tad less at lunch times. Mon 6–10pm, Tues–Sat noon–2pm & 6–10pm.

**The Kitchen** 47 Sadler Gate ⓣ01332 608619, ⓦthekitchenderby.com. Bright and breezy, independent café with an imaginative range of sandwiches, salads and light bites – and featuring their own home-grown produce. A few yards from Derby Museum. Mon–Sat 8am–5pm.

# The Peak District

In 1951, the hills and dales of the **PEAK DISTRICT**, at the southern tip of the Pennine range, became Britain's first National Park. Wedged between Derby, Manchester and Sheffield, it is effectively the back garden for the fifteen million people who live within an hour's drive of its boundaries, though somehow it accommodates the huge influx with minimum fuss.

Landscapes in the Peak District come in two forms. The brooding high moorland tops of **Dark Peak**, to the east of Manchester, take their name from the underlying gritstone, known as millstone grit for its former use – a function commemorated in the millstones demarcating the park boundary. Windswept, mist-shrouded and inhospitable, the flat tops of these peaks are nevertheless a firm favourite with walkers on the **Pennine Way**, which meanders north from the tiny village of **Edale** to the Scottish border. Altogether more forgiving, the southern limestone hills of the **White Peak** have been eroded into deep forested dales populated by small stone villages and often threaded by walking trails, some of which follow former rail routes. The limestone is riddled with complex cave systems around **Castleton** and on the periphery of **Buxton**, a pleasant former spa town lying just outside the park's boundaries and at the end of an industrialized corridor that reaches out from Manchester. Elsewhere, one of the country's most distinctive manorial piles, **Chatsworth House**, stands near **Bakewell**, a town famed locally not just for its cakes but also for its **well-dressing**, a possibly pagan ritual of thanksgiving for fresh water that takes place in about thirty local villages each summer. The well-dressing season starts in May and continues through to mid-September; get exact dates and details on ⓦwelldressing.com.

As for a **base**, Buxton is your best bet by a (fairly) long chalk, though if you're after hiking and cycling you'll probably prefer one of the area's villages – Edale or Castleton will do very nicely.

## ARRIVAL AND DEPARTURE
## THE PEAK DISTRICT

**By train** Frequent trains run south from Manchester to end-of-the-line Buxton, and Manchester/Sheffield trains stop at Edale.

**By bus** The main bus access is on High Peak Buses' (ⓦhighpeakbuses.com) TransPeak service from Derby to Manchester via Bakewell and Buxton (5 daily; 3hr). Otherwise, First (ⓦfirstgroup.com) bus #272 runs from Sheffield to Castleton, via Hathersage and Hope, and TM Travel (ⓦtmtravel.co.uk) bus #65 connects Sheffield to Buxton. See ⓦtravelineeastmidlands.co.uk. for detailed route planning.

## GETTING AROUND

**By bus** Within the Peak District, you'll find local bus services are reasonably frequent, though less so on Sundays and in winter. Local tourist offices almost always have bus and train timetables or see ⓦ travelineeastmidlands.co.uk.
**By bike** The Peak District has a good network of dedicated

cycle lanes and trails, sometimes along former railway lines, and the Peak District National Park Authority (see below) operates three cycle rental outlets: at Ashbourne (ⓣ01335 343156); Derwent, Bamford (ⓣ01433 651261); and Parsley Hay, Buxton (ⓣ01298 84493).

## INFORMATION

**Visitor centres** The Peak District National Park Authority (ⓣ01629 816200) operates four visitor centres, including those at Bakewell and Castleton; these supplement a host of town and village tourist information offices.

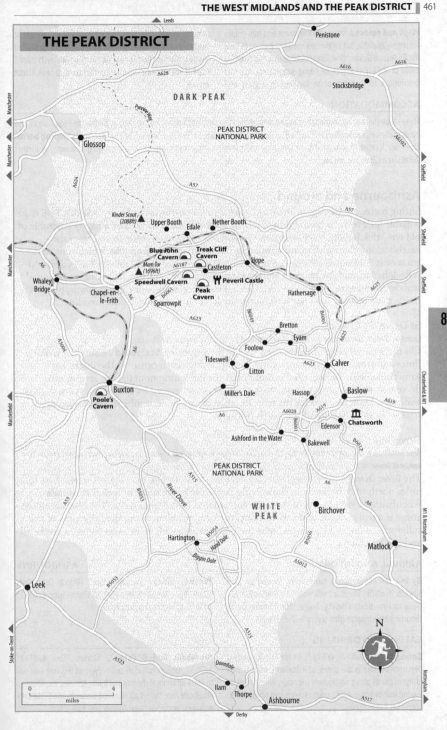

**THE PEAK DISTRICT**

**Maps and guides** A variety of Peaks maps and trail guides are widely available, but for the non-specialist it's hard to beat the *Grate Little Guides* (ⓦ walksaboutthepeakdistrict.co.uk), a series of leaflets that provide hiking suggestions and trail descriptions for a dozen or so localities in a clear and straightforward style. They cost £3 each and are on sale at most tourist information centres. Note that the maps printed on the leaflets are best used in conjunction with an OS map. **Useful websites** ⓦ visitpeakdistrict.com; ⓦ peakdistrict .gov.uk

## ACCOMMODATION

There's a plethora of accommodation in and around the Peak District National Park, mostly in **B&Bs**. The Peak District also holds numerous **campsites** and half a dozen or so **YHA hostels** as well as a network of YHA-operated **camping barns**. These are located in converted farm buildings and provide simple and inexpensive self-catering facilities. For further details, consult ⓦ yha.org.uk.

# Ashbourne and around

Sitting pretty on the edge of the Peaks twelve miles northwest of Derby, **ASHBOURNE** is an amiable little town, whose stubby, cobbled **Market Place** is flanked by a happy ensemble of old red-brick buildings. Hikers tramp in and out of town en route to and from the neighbouring dales with many wandering the popular **Tissington Trail**, which runs north from near Ashbourne for thirteen miles along the route of an old railway line. Cafés and pubs loiter around Ashbourne's **Market Place** and nearby, just down the hill, a suspended wooden beam spans St John's Street. Once a common feature of English towns, but now a rarity, these **gallows** were not warnings to malcontents, but advertising hoardings.

## St Oswald's Church

Church St · Daily 9am–4pm, 5pm in summer · Free · ☎ 01335 343052, ⓦ derbyshirechurches.org

On the western edge of Ashbourne stands the imposing **St Oswald's Church**, a striking lime- and ironstone structure dating from the thirteenth century. The interior is something of an architectural muddle, but it's intriguing nonetheless, its columns decorated with all sorts of miniature sculptures and graced by handsome stained-glass windows. Look out also for the five superbly carved table-tombs in the Cockayne Chapel in the east aisle of the north transept.

## Dovedale

Head north from Ashbourne along the A515 and then follow the signs to the car park, which is on a narrow country road just beyond the hamlet of Thorpe

The **River Dove**, which wriggles its way across the Peak District, is at its scenic best four miles north of Ashbourne in the stirring two-mile gorge that comprises **Dovedale** – confusingly, other parts of the river are situated in different dales. The **hike** along the gorge is a real pleasure and easy to boot, the only problem being the bogginess of the valley after rain, but be warned that the place heaves with visitors on summer weekends and bank holidays.

## ARRIVAL AND INFORMATION                                          ASHBOURNE

**By bus** The bus station is conveniently located on King Edward St, off Dig Street, a 2min walk from Market Place. Destinations Buxton (every 1–2hr; 1hr 15min); Derby (hourly; 40min); Hartington (every 1–2hr; 35min).

**Tourist office** Market Place (March–Oct daily 10am–5pm; Nov–Feb Mon–Sat 10.30am–4pm; ☎ 01335 343666, ⓦ visitpeakdistrict.com).

## EATING AND DRINKING

**Bennetts** 19 St John St ☎ 01335 342982. Independent department store in the centre of Ashbourne with a wide range of goods plus a particularly cosy café, where they do a good line in home-made cakes, scones and sandwiches. Mon–Sat 9am–4pm.

**Bramhalls Deli & Café** 22 Market Place ☎ 01335 342631, ⓦ bramhallsdeli.co.uk. Pop into this first-rate deli to stock up on local cheeses and hams, terrines, etc. There's a small café here too – tuck into local sausages and Derbyshire oatcakes. Mon–Sat 8am–5pm & Sun 9am–5pm.

# Hartington

Best approached from the east, through the boisterous scenery of Hand Dale, **HARTINGTON**, 11 miles north of Ashbourne, is one of the prettiest villages in the Peaks, with an easy ramble of stone houses zeroing in on a tiny duck pond. The village is also within easy walking distance of the River Dove as well as a sequence of handsome limestone dales – **Biggin Dale** is perhaps the pick. The other excitement is cheese – the village has its own specialist **cheese shop** (ⓦhartingtoncheeseshop.co.uk) with a raft of local and international cheeses and a selection of chutneys to lighten the gastronomic load.

## ARRIVAL AND DEPARTURE HARTINGTON

**By bus** Buses stop on Mill Lane in the centre of the village, a few yards from the duck pond.

Destinations Ashbourne (every 1–2hr; 35min); Buxton (every 1–2hr; 45min).

## ACCOMMODATION

**The Hayloft** Church St ☎01298 84358, ⓦhartingtonhayloft.co.uk. Perhaps the best of Hartington's several B&Bs, in a sympathetically converted barn a few yards from the duck pond and part of a working farm. There are just four guest rooms – each of which is decorated in a straightforward modern style. **£60**

**YHA Hartington** Hall Bank ☎0845 371 9740, ⓦyha.org .uk. Well-equipped hostel whose 130 beds – in one- to eight-bed dorms – are squeezed into a seventeenth-century manor house, Hartington Hall, about 300 yards from the centre of the village. Facilities include a self-catering kitchen, a café and internet access. Dorms **£19**, doubles **£39**

# Buxton

**BUXTON**, twelve miles north of Hartington, has had more than its fair share of ups and downs, but with its centre revamped and reconfigured, it is without doubt the most agreeable town in the Peak District and its string of excellent B&Bs make it a perfect base for further explorations. Buxton has a long history as a **spa**, beginning with the Romans, who happened upon a spring from which 1500 gallons of pure water gushed every hour at a constant 28°C. Impressed by the recuperative qualities of the water, the Romans came here by the chariot load, setting a trend that was to last hundreds of years. The spa's heyday came at the end of the eighteenth century with the **fifth Duke of Devonshire**'s grand design to create a northern answer to Bath or Cheltenham, a plan ultimately thwarted by the climate, but not before some distinguished buildings had been erected. Victorian Buxton may not have had quite the élan of its more southerly rivals but it still flourished, creating the rows of handsome stone houses that inhabit the town centre today. The town's **thermal baths** were closed for lack of custom in 1972, but Buxton has hung on not least because of its splendid **festival** (see box, p.464).

**8**

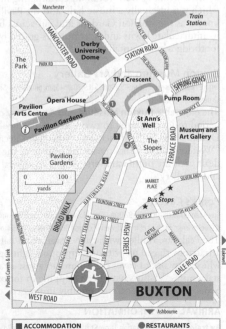

| ■ ACCOMMODATION | | ● RESTAURANTS | |
|---|---|---|---|
| Buxton's Victorian Guest House | 2 | Columbine | 2 |
| Grosvenor House | 1 | Old Hall Hotel | 1 |
| Roseleigh | 3 | Old Sun Inn | 3 |

## BUXTON FESTIVAL

Buxton boasts the outstanding **Buxton Festival** (box office ☎ 0845 127 2190, ⓦ buxtonfestival
.co.uk), which runs for two and a half weeks in July and features a full programme of classical
music, opera and literary readings. This has spawned the first-rate **Buxton Festival Fringe**
(ⓦ buxtonfringe.org.uk), also in July, which focuses on contemporary music, theatre and film.

### The Crescent

The centrepiece of Buxton's hilly, compact centre is **The Crescent**, a broad sweep of
Georgian stonework commissioned by the fifth Duke of Devonshire in 1780 and modelled
on the Royal Crescent in Bath. It was cleaned and scrubbed a few years ago, but has lain
idle ever since and plans to turn it into a five-star hotel complete with thermal baths have
yet to materialise. Facing The Crescent, and also currently empty, is the old **Pump Room**,
an attractive Victorian building where visitors once sampled the local waters; next to it is a
**water fountain**, supplied by St Ann's Well and still used to fill many a local water bottle.
For a better view of The Crescent and the town centre, clamber up **The Slopes**, a narrow
slice of park that rises behind the Pump Room dotted with decorative urns. From here, it's
impossible to miss the enormous **dome** of what was originally the Duke of Devonshire's
stables and riding school, erected in 1789 and now part of Derby University.

### Pavilion Gardens and around

Next to The Crescent, the appealing old stone buildings of **The Square** – though square
it isn't – nudge up to the grandly refurbished **Buxton Opera House**, an Edwardian
extravagance whose twin towers date from 1903. Stretching back from the Opera
House are the **Pavilion Gardens**, a slender string of connected buildings distinguished
by their wrought-iron work and culminating in a large and glassy dome, the **Octagon**,
which was originally a music hall, and the **Pavilion Arts Centre**. The adjoining **park**, also
known as the Pavilion Gardens and cut across by the River Wye, is especially pleasant,
its immaculate lawns and neat borders graced by a bandstand, ponds, dinky little
footbridges and fountains.

### Buxton Museum and Art Gallery

Terrace Road • Tues–Fri 9.30am–5.30pm, Sat 9.30am–5pm, plus Easter–Sept Sun 10.30am–5pm • Free • ☎ 01629 533540,
ⓦ derbyshire.gov.uk

The enjoyable **Buxton Museum and Art Gallery** delves into all things local, including a
period room dedicated to two Victorian archeologist-cum-geologists – William Boyd
Dawkins and Wilfred Jackson – who spent decades exploring the Peaks. Upstairs,
"Wonders of the Peak" tracks the history of the region. The most diverting section
deals with the **petrifactioners**, who turned local semi-precious stones into ornaments
and jewellery.

### Poole's Cavern

Green Lane • March–Oct daily 9.30am–5pm; Nov–Feb Sat & Sun 10am–4pm, plus weekday tours at fixed times • £9 • ☎ 01298 26978,
ⓦ poolescavern.co.uk • 1 mile southwest of central Buxton: take the A53 towards Macclesfield/Leek and watch for the sign

The Peaks are riddled with cave systems and half a dozen have become popular tourist
attractions rigged up with underground lighting. One of the best is **Poole's Cavern**,
whose network of caves culminates in a vast-chamber dripping with stalactites and
stalagmites. Visitors have been popping in for centuries – apparently, Mary, Queen of
Scots, dropped by and was suitably impressed.

### ARRIVAL AND INFORMATION                                                        BUXTON

**By train** Buxton train station is on Station Road, a 3min
walk from the town centre.
Destinations Manchester Piccadilly or Manchester Oxford

Road Station (hourly; 1hr).
**By bus** Buses stop on Market Place, a 4min walk from the
Opera House.

**Destinations** Ashbourne (every 1–2hr; 1hr 15min); Bakewell (hourly; 30min); Derby (hourly; 1hr 35min); Hartington (every 1–2hr; 45min).

**Tourist office** Pavilion Gardens, behind the Opera House (daily: April–Oct 9.30am–5pm; Nov–March 10am–4pm; ☎ 01298 25106, ⓦ visitbuxton.co.uk).

## ACCOMMODATION

Buxton town centre is liberally sprinkled with **B&Bs** and finding somewhere to stay is rarely a problem, except during the Buxton Festival (see box opposite), when advance reservations are essential.

**Buxton's Victorian Guest House** 3a Broad Walk ☎ 01298 78759, ⓦ buxtonvictorian.co.uk. Cosy B&B in a grand Victorian house with a handful of well-appointed, frilly rooms featuring four-posters and Indian-print cushions. Local produce is served up at breakfast whenever feasible. **£94**

★**Grosvenor House** 1 Broad Walk ☎ 01298 72439, ⓦ grosvenorbuxton.co.uk. There are eight unfussy, en-suite guest rooms – seven doubles and one single – in this attractive B&B, which is located in a handsome Victorian

townhouse. The best rooms offer gentle views over the gardens. Delicious home-made breakfasts, too. **£70**

**Roseleigh** 19 Broad Walk ☎ 01298 24904, ⓦ roseleighhotel.co.uk. This classic, three-storey gritstone Victorian townhouse, overlooking Pavilion Gardens, is an excellent place to stay. The trim public rooms are decorated in attractive Victorian style, and the en-suite bedrooms are well appointed. Family-run and competitively priced. **£80**

## EATING AND DRINKING

**Columbine** 7 Hall Bank ☎ 01298 78752, ⓦ columbinerestaurant.co.uk. The menu at this small and intimate restaurant, right in the centre of Buxton, is short but imaginative, with main courses – such as saddle of monkfish with crab risotto – averaging £17. Pre-theatre dinners, from about 5pm, can be reserved in advance. May–Oct Mon–Sat 7–10pm; Nov–April Mon & Wed–Sat 7–10pm.

**Old Hall Hotel** The Square ☎ 01298 22841, ⓦ oldhallhotelbuxton.co.uk. A few steps from the Opera House and occupying a building that dates back to the

1570s, the *Old Hall* offers good quality food in both its (fairly formal) restaurant and in the bar. The menu is Modern British with due prominence given to local/ seasonal ingredients. Mains average £16, less at lunch times. Daily noon–2pm & 6–9.30pm.

**Old Sun Inn** 33 High St ☎ 01298 23452, ⓦ theoldsuninnbuxton.com. This fine old pub, with its maze of antique beamed rooms, is just south of Market Place. It's a good spot for a fine range of real ales and above-average bar food. Daily noon–11pm.

# Castleton and around

A hikers' heaven and haven, pocket-sized **CASTLETON**, a scenic ten miles northeast of Buxton via Sparrowpit and the dramatic **Winnats Pass**, lies on the northern edge of the White Peak, its huddle of old stone cottages ringed by hills and set beside a babbling brook. It's s distinctly unpretentious place – and none the worse for that – and the hikers are joined by platoons of cyclists and cavers, with all gathering together to prepare for the off on **Market Place**, yards from the main drag, just behind the church.

## Peveril Castle

Off Market Place • April–Oct daily 10am–5pm; Nov–March Sat & Sun 10am–4pm • EH • £4.60 • ☎ 01433 620613, ⓦ english-heritage.org.uk

Overseeing Castleton is **Peveril Castle**, from which the village takes its name. William the Conqueror's illegitimate son William Peveril raised the first fortifications here to protect the king's rights to the forest that then covered the district, but most of the remains – principally the ruinous square keep – date to the 1170s. After a stiff climb up to the keep, you can trace much of the surviving curtain wall, which commands great views over the Hope Valley down below.

## Caves around Castleton

The limestone hills pressing in on Castleton are riddled with water-worn **cave systems**, four of which have been developed as tourist attractions complete with subterranean lighting. Each can be reached by car or on foot, though most visitors settle for just one set of caves – the Peak Cavern and the Treak Cliff Cavern are particularly recommended.

## Peak Cavern

Off Goosehill • April–Oct daily 10am–5pm; Nov–March Sat & Sun 10am–5pm, plus additional weekday tours (see website for times) • £9.25; joint ticket with Speedwell Cavern £15.50 • ☎ 01433 620285, ⓦ peakcavern.co.uk

**Peak Cavern** is the handiest of Castleton's four cave systems, tucked into a gully at the back of the village, its gaping mouth once providing shelter for a rope factory and a small village. Daniel Defoe, visiting in the eighteenth century, noted the cavern's colourful local name, the **Devil's Arse**, a reference to the fiendish fashion in which its interior contours twisted and turned.

## Speedwell Cavern

Winnats Rd • April–Oct daily 10am–5pm; Nov–March daily 10am–4pm • £10, joint ticket with Peak Cavern £15.50 • ☎ 01433 623018, ⓦ speedwellcavern.co.uk

Some 700 yards or so west from Castleton along the main road is **Speedwell Cavern**. At 600 feet below ground, this is the deepest of the cave systems, but the main drama comes with the means of access – down a hundred dripping steps and then by boat through a quarter-mile-long claustrophobic tunnel that was blasted out in search of lead. At the end lies the Bottomless Pit, a pool where forty thousand tonnes of mining rubble were once dumped without raising the water level one iota.

## Treak Cliff Cavern

Buxton Rd • Daily 10am–5pm • £8.95 • ☎ 01433 620571, ⓦ bluejohnstone.com • About 800 yards west of Castleton up off a minor road (and signed from the A6187)

**Treak Cliff Cavern** is a major source of a rare sparkling fluorspar known as **Blue John**. Highly prized for ornaments and jewellery since Georgian times, this semi-precious stone comes in a multitude of hues from blue through deep red to yellow, depending on its hydrocarbon impurities. The Treak Cliff contains the best examples of the stone *in situ* and is also the best cave to visit in its own right, dripping – literally – with ancient stalactites, flowstone and bizarre rock formations, all visible on an entertaining forty-minute walking tour through the main cave system.

## Blue John Cavern

Mam Tor • Daily: April–Oct 9.30am–5pm; Nov–March 9.30am–dusk • £10 • ☎ 01433 620638, ⓦ bluejohn-cavern.co.uk • About 3 miles west of Castleton (and signed off Winnats Rd)

Tours of the **Blue John Cavern** dive deep into the rock, with narrow steps and sloping paths following an ancient watercourse. The tour leads through whirlpool-hollowed chambers to Lord Mulgrave's Dining Room, a cavern where the eponymous lord and owner once put on a banquet for his miners (heaven knows what they made of his 'generosity'). A goodly sample of Blue John is on sale at the cavern gift shop.

## ARRIVAL AND INFORMATION                                    CASTLETON

**By train** There are no trains to Castleton – the nearest you'll get is Hope, a couple of miles or so to the east along the valley on the Manchester–Sheffield line. Regular buses run from near Hope train station to Castleton (every 1–2hr; 10min).
Destinations (from Hope) Edale (hourly; 6min); Hathersage (hourly; 10min); Manchester Piccadilly (hourly; 50min); Sheffield (hourly; 30min).

**By bus** Castleton's main bus stop is yards from the centre of the village on How Lane (the A6187). The principal bus service is the South Yorkshire First bus #272.

Destinations Bakewell (3 daily; 50min); Hathersage (hourly; 20min); Hope (hourly; 10min); Sheffield (hourly; 1hr).

**Tourist office** A combined museum, community centre and tourist office on Buxton Road (daily: April–Oct 10am–5pm; Nov–March 10.30am–4.30pm; ☎ 01629 816572, ⓦ peakdistrict.gov.uk) stands beside the car park on the west side of the village, just off the main street (the A6187).

**Maps** The tourist office sells hiking leaflets and maps, which are invaluable for a string of walking routes that take you up to the bulging hilltops that rise in every direction.

## ACCOMMODATION AND EATING

You should book accommodation in advance at holiday times when Castleton heaves with visitors. The restaurant scene is a tad patchy, but at least things are beginning to improve.

**1530 The Restaurant** Cruck Barn, Cross St ☎01433 621870, ⓦ1530therestaurant.co.uk. In an old stone building near the centre of the village, this bright and breezy restaurant specialises in Italian cuisine – from pizzas and pastas through to more ambitious dishes, like the sea bass with artichokes and sun-dried tomatoes. Mains average £12, less at lunch times. Daily except Tues noon–2pm & 6–10pm.

**Bargate Cottage** Market Place ☎01433 620201, ⓦbargatecottage.co.uk. In an old cottage at the heart of the village, this friendly B&B has a handful of en-suite rooms decorated in a cosy, traditional style. The home-made breakfasts are delicious. **£70**

**Causeway House** Back St ☎01433 623291, ⓦcausewayhouse.co.uk. The cream of the crop, this B&B occupies an old and well-tended stone cottage just north of Market Place. There are five guest rooms, three en suite, all tastefully kitted out to make the most of the cottage's original features. **£75**

**YHA Castleton Losehill Hall** Castleton Road, signed off the A6187 ☎0845 371 9628, ⓦyha.org.uk. The YHA has spent a bucket refurbishing this Victorian Neo-Gothic mansion set in its own grounds to the north of the village. It's a well-equipped hostel with a self-catering kitchen, a café, laundry, wi-fi, cycle store and drying room, and its 144 beds are parcelled up into two- to six-bedded rooms, most of which are en suite. Dorms **£18**, doubles **£30**

# Edale village

There's almost nothing to **EDALE VILLAGE**, about five miles northwest of Castleton, except for a slender, half-mile trail of stone houses, which march up the main street from the train station with a couple of pubs, an old stone church and a scattering of B&Bs on the way – and it's this somnambulant air that is its immediate appeal. The village is also extremely popular with walkers, who arrive in droves throughout the year to set off on the **Pennine Way** (see box below) – the route's starting point is signposted from outside the *Old Nag's Head* at the head of the village. If that sounds too daunting, note that there are lots of more manageable alternatives, including an excellent **circular walk** (9 miles; 5hr) that takes in the first part of the Pennine Way, leading up onto the bleak gritstone, table-top of **Kinder Scout** (2088ft), below which Edale cowers.

**8**

## ARRIVAL AND INFORMATION

EDALE VILLAGE

**By train** At the southern end of the village, Edale train station is on the Sheffield–Manchester line.
Destinations Hope – for Castleton (hourly; 6min); Hathersage (hourly; 15min); Manchester Piccadilly (hourly; 45min); Sheffield (hourly; 35min).
**Moorland Centre** From Edale train station, it's 400 yards

or so up the road to the Moorland Centre (April–Sept daily 9.30am–5pm; Oct & March Mon–Fri 10am–3.30pm, Sat & Sun 9.30am–4.30pm; Nov & Jan–Feb Sat & Sun 9.30am–3.30pm; closed Dec; ☎01433 670207, ⓦpeakdistrict.gov.uk), who sell all manner of trail leaflets and hiking guides and can advise on local accommodation.

## ACCOMMODATION AND EATING

**Cheshire Cheese Inn** Edale Rd, Hope S33 6ZF between Castleton and Hope ☎01433 623313, ⓦthecheshire

cheeseinn.co.uk. Two attractively renovated old stone cottages with a cosy/folksy bar downstairs and four extremely

---

### THE PENNINE WAY

The 268-mile-long **Pennine Way** (ⓦnationaltrail.co.uk) was the country's first official long-distance footpath, opened in 1965. It stretches north from the boggy plateau of the Peak District's Kinder Scout near **Edale village**, proceeds through the Yorkshire Dales and Teesdale, and then crosses Hadrian's Wall and the Northumberland National Park, before entering Scotland to fizzle out at the village of Kirk Yetholm. One of the most popular walks in the country, either taken in sections or completed in two to three weeks, the Pennine Way is a challenge in the best of weather, since it passes through some of the wildest countryside in Britain. You must certainly be properly equipped and able to use a map and compass. The **National Trail Guides** *Pennine Way: South* and *Pennine Way: North*, are essential, though some still prefer to stick to Wainwright's *Pennine Way Companion*. Information centres along the route – like the one at Edale village (see above) – stock a selection of guides and associated trail leaflets and can offer advice.

pleasant en-suite guest rooms up above. The good-quality bar food features local, seasonal ingredients. Food served: Tues–Fri noon–2pm & 6–9pm; Sat noon–9pm & Sun noon–7.30pm. Bar: Tues–Fri noon–3pm & 6–10pm; Sat noon–11.30pm & Sun noon–10pm. **£80**

**Stonecroft** Edale ☎01433 670262, ⊛stonecroft guesthouse.co.uk. The pick of several B&Bs in Edale village, this detached Edwardian house offers two comfortable guest rooms decorated in an unfussy traditional style. **£80**

**Upper Booth Camping** West of Edale village on the way to Kinder Scout ☎01433 670250, ⊛upperboothcamping.co.uk. This conveniently located campsite and camping barn is a popular spot for walkers on the Pennine Way. Car parking extra. Camping barn per person **£8**, camping per person **£6**

**YHA Edale** Rowland Cote, Nether Booth, 2 miles east of Edale train station ☎0845 371 9514, ⊛yha.org.uk. With 157 beds in two- to ten-bedded rooms, plus good facilities including a laundry, café and self-catering kitchen, this YHA also offers an extensive range of outdoor activities. These must be booked in advance – as must accommodation. The hostel is signed from the road into Edale, or you can hike across the fields from the nearby Moorland Centre (see p.467). Dorms **£18**, doubles **£40**

# Hathersage

Hilly **HATHERSAGE**, six miles east of Castleton, has a hard time persuading people not to shoot straight past on their way to the heart of the Peaks. This little town is, however, worth at least an hour of anyone's time, the prime target being the much-restored **Church of St Michael and All Angels**, a good-looking stone structure perched up on the hill on its eastern edge. The views out over the surrounding countryside are delightful and, enclosed within a miniature iron fence in the churchyard, is the **grave** – or at least what legend asserts to be the grave – of Robin Hood's old sparring partner, **Little John**.

In the 1800s, Hathersage became a **needle-making centre** with a string of factories billowing out dust and dirt. The metalworking tradition has been revived by the Sheffield designer **David Mellor**, whose cutlery factory is in the distinctive **Round Building**, a gritstone edifice with a sweeping lead roof about half a mile south of town on the B6001. There's a **Design Museum** (Mon–Sat 9.30am–5pm, Sun 11am–5pm; ☎01433 650220, ⊛davidmellordesign.com) here too, as well as a shop (same times).

## ARRIVAL AND DEPARTURE                    HATHERSAGE

**By train** Hathersage train station, which is on the Manchester–Sheffield line, is about 500 yards south of the village's main street (also the A6187).
Destinations Hope – for Castleton (hourly; 7min); Edale (hourly; 15min); Manchester Piccadilly (hourly; 1hr); Sheffield (hourly; 20min).

**By bus** Buses to Hathersage pull into the centre of the village near the *George Hotel*. The principal bus service, South Yorkshire First bus #272, links Hathersage with Castleton and Sheffield.
Destinations Bakewell (3 daily; 45min); Castleton (hourly; 20min); Hope (hourly; 10min); Sheffield (hourly; 50min).

## ACCOMMODATION AND EATING

**George Hotel** Castleton Rd ☎01433 650436, ⊛george-hotel.net. In an immaculately maintained former coaching inn, this first–rate hotel offers twenty-or-so comfortable bedrooms decorated in plush, country-house style. The *George* also has a very good restaurant featuring Modern British cuisine with mains averaging £16. Daily noon–2.30pm & 6.30–10pm, from 7pm on the weekend. **£100**

**YHA Hathersage** Castleton Rd ☎0845 371 9021, ⊛yha.org.uk. This relatively frugal hostel occupies a rambling Victorian house on the main road just to the west of the *George*. It has forty beds, in two- to six-bed rooms, and a good range of facilities, including a café and a self-catering kitchen. Dorms **£13**, doubles **£20**

# Eyam

Within a year of September 7, 1665, the lonely lead-mining settlement of **EYAM** (pronounced "Eem"), five miles south of Hathersage, had lost almost half of its population of 750 to the bubonic plague, a calamity that earned it the enduring epithet "**The Plague Village**". The first victim was one George Vicars, a journeyman tailor who is said to have released some infected fleas into his lodgings from a package of cloth he

---

## RING A RING O' ROSES: EYAM AND THE PLAGUE

As the people of Eyam began to drop like flies from the **plague** in the autumn of 1665, they resorted to **folkloric remedies** to stave off the inevitable. Some, thinking it to be a miasma, kept coal braziers alight day and night in the hope that the smoke would push the infection back into the sky from where it was thought to have come. Others tried herb infusions and draughts of brine or lemon juice; yet more applied poultices and bleeding by leeches. When all else failed, **charms and spells** were wheeled out – the plucked tail of a pigeon laid against the sore supposedly drew out the poison. All, of course, had no effect and the death toll mounted. The horrors of a plague-ridden England were recorded in the *Ring o'roses* nursery rhyme that remains in use today:

---

had brought here from London. Acutely conscious of the danger to neighbouring villages, **William Mompesson**, the village rector, speedily organized a self-imposed quarantine, arranging for food to be left at places on the parish boundary. Payment was made with coins left in pools of disinfecting vinegar in holes chiselled into the old boundary stones – and these can still be seen at **Mompesson's Well**, half a mile up the hill to the north of the village and accessible by footpath.

### Church of St Lawrence

Church St • Easter–Sept Mon–Sat 9am–6pm, Sun 1–5.30pm; Oct–Easter Mon–Sat 9am–4pm, Sun 1–5.30pm • Free • ☎ 01433 630930, ⓦ eyam-church.org

In the **graveyard** of the **church of St Lawrence** – of medieval foundation but revamped in the nineteenth century – stands a conspicuous, eighth-century carved Celtic cross, and close by is the distinctive table-tomb of Mompesson's wife, whose sterling work nursing sick villagers caused her early death. Rather more cheerful is the grave of one **Harry Bagshawe** (d. 1927), a local cricketer whose tombstone shows a ball breaking his wicket with the umpire's finger raised above, presumably – on this occasion – to heaven. Inside the church, informative panels reveal more of the village's plague history.

### Eyam Museum

Hawkhill Rd • April–Oct Tues–Sun 10am–4.30pm • £2.50 • ☎ 01433 631371, ⓦ eyam-museum.org.uk

It's a few minutes' walk along Main Street and up Hawkhill Road – follow the signs – to the modest Methodist chapel that now houses the **Eyam Museum**, which tracks the village's history and has a good section on the bubonic plague – its transmission, symptoms and social aftermath.

### ARRIVAL AND DEPARTURE                                                         EYAM

**By bus** Buses to Eyam stop on The Square, at the east end of the village, with most then proceeding west along the lengthy main street, Church St/Main Road.

**Destinations** Baslow (every 2hr; 10min); Hathersage (every 2hr; 20min); Sheffield (3–5 daily; 1hr).

### ACCOMMODATION AND EATING

**Crown Cottage** Main Rd ☎ 01433 630858, ⓦ crown -cottage.co.uk. This cosy B&B occupies an old stone house on the west side of the village. There are four, pleasantly turned out, en-suite guest rooms here as well as an outside terrace to catch the Derbyshire sun. **£70**

**Miner's Arms** Water Lane ☎ 01433 630853, ⓦ theminersarmseyam.co.uk. It's true that there isn't too much choice, but the best place to eat in Eyam is the *Miner's Arms*, in ancient, beamed premises at the east end of the village, just off The Square. They serve traditional British food in both the bar and the restaurant. Mon noon–2pm

& 6–8pm; Tues–Sat noon–2pm & 6–9pm; Sun noon–3pm.

**YHA Eyam** Hawkhill Rd ☎ 0845 371 9738, ⓦ yha.org .uk. This well-equipped hostel occupies an idiosyncratic Victorian house, whose ersatz medieval towers and turrets overlook Eyam from amid wooded grounds on Hawkhill Road, a stiff, half-mile ramble up from Eyam Museum (see above). The hostel has a café, self-catering facilities, a cycle store and a lounge, and its sixty beds are parcelled up into two- to ten-bed rooms; advance reservations are recommended. Dorms **£16**, doubles **£39**

**8**

## Baslow

**BASLOW**, beside the busy junction of the A623/A619 four miles southeast of Eyam, is an unassuming little village, whose oldest stone cottages string prettily along the River Derwent. The only building of any real note is **St Anne's Church**, a medieval structure whose chunky stone spire pokes up above the Victorian castellations of its nave. Baslow may be inconsequential, but it is handy for the nearby Chatsworth estate (see opposite) and it also possesses one of the Peaks' finest hotels, *Fischer's Baslow Hall* (see below).

### ARRIVAL AND DEPARTURE                                          BASLOW

**By bus** Buses pull in by St Anne's church in the village centre. Destinations Bakewell (hourly; 15min); Buxton (4 daily; 50min); Chesterfield (hourly; 30min); Eyam (every 2hr; 10min); Sheffield (3–5 daily; 45min).

### ACCOMMODATION AND EATING

★ **Fischer's Baslow Hall** Calver Road (A623) ☎ 01246 583259, ⓦ fischers-baslowhall.co.uk. In its own grounds, *Fischer's* is picture-postcard perfect, a handsome Edwardian building made of local stone with matching gables and a dinky canopy over the front door. The interior is suitably lavish and the service attentive, while rooms occupy both the main building and the Garden House annexe next door. The restaurant is superb too, and has won several awards for its imaginative cuisine – Modern British at its best – with a three-course set meal costing £72. Daily noon–2pm & 7–10pm. **£150**

## Bakewell and around

**BAKEWELL**, flanking the banks of the River Wye about thirty miles north of Derby, is famous for both its **Bakewell Pudding** and its **Bakewell Tart**. The former is much more distinctive (and less commonplace), being a sweet and slippery, almond-flavoured confection – now with a dab of jam – invented here around 1860 when a cook botched a recipe for strawberry tart. Almost a century before this fortuitous mishap, the Duke of Rutland set out to turn what was then a remote village into a prestigious spa, thereby trumping the work of his rival, the Duke of Devonshire, in Buxton. The frigidity of the water made failure inevitable, leaving only the prettiness of **Bath Gardens** at the heart of the town centre as a reminder of the venture. Bakewell is within easy striking distance of the big tourist attraction hereabouts, **Chatsworth House** (see opposite).

### Ashford in the Water

Minuscule **ASHFORD IN THE WATER**, just over a mile to the west of Bakewell along the River Wye, is one of the prettiest and wealthiest villages in the Peaks, its old stone cottages nuzzling up to a quaint medieval church. It was not always so. Ashford was once a poor lead-mining settlement with sidelines in milling and agriculture, hence the name of the (impossibly picturesque) Sheepwash Bridge. There was, however, a bit of a boom when locals took to polishing the dark limestone found on the edge of the village (and nowhere else), turning it into so-called **Ashford black marble** – much to the delight of Buxton's petrifactioners (see p.464).

### ARRIVAL AND INFORMATION                          BAKEWELL AND AROUND

**By bus** Buses to Bakewell stop on – or very close to – central Rutland Square; there are no trains. Destinations Baslow (hourly; 15min); Buxton (hourly; 30min); Chesterfield (hourly; 1hr); Derby (hourly; 1hr 20min); Hathersage (3 daily; 45min); Sheffield (hourly; 1hr 30min). **Tourist office** Old Market Hall, Bridge St, right in the centre of town (daily: April–Oct 9.30am–5pm; Nov–Easter 10.30am–4.30pm; ☎ 01629 816558, ⓦ peakdistrict .gov.uk).

### ACCOMMODATION AND EATING

★ **Hassop Hall** Hassop, 3 miles north of Bakewell on the B6001 ☎ 01629 640488, ⓦ hassophall.co.uk. Hidden away in the heart of the Peaks, the rugged, solitary hamlet of Hassop is home to the wonderful *Hassop Hall*, a handsome stone manor house. The interior has kept faith with the Georgian architecture – modernization has been kept to a subtle minimum – and the views out over the surrounding parkland are delightful. The hotel restaurant (reservations required) is also first-class with a two-course set meal costing £28. **£100**

**Old Original Bakewell Pudding Shop** The Square ☎01629 812193, ⊛bakewellpuddingshop.co.uk. Bakeries all over town claim to make Bakewell Pudding to the original recipe, but the most authentic are served up here. They sell the pudding in several sizes, from the small and handy to the gargantuan, enough to keep the average

family going for a whole day. Mon–Sat 8.30am–6pm, Sun 9am–6pm.

**Riverside House Hotel** Fennel St, Ashford in the Water ☎01629 814275, ⊛riversidehousehotel.co.uk. The plush and lush *Riverside House* occupies a handsome Georgian building by the banks of the Wye. There are a dozen or so extremely well-appointed rooms here, each decorated in a full-blown country-house style, and the hotel takes justifiable pride in both its gardens and its restaurant (reservations required). **£145**

# Chatsworth House

4 miles east of Bakewell • Mid-March to late Dec daily 11am–5.30pm, last admission 4.30pm; gardens till 6pm, last admission 5pm • House & gardens £18, gardens only £12 • ☎ 01246 565300, ⊛ chatsworth.org

Fantastically popular, and certainly one of the finest stately homes in Britain, **Chatsworth House** was built in the seventeenth century by the first Duke of Devonshire. It has been owned by the family ever since and although several of them have done a fair bit of tinkering – the sixth duke, for instance, added the north wing in the 1820s – the end result is remarkably harmonious. The property is seen to best advantage from the B6012, which meanders across the estate to the west of the house, giving a full view of its vast Palladian frontage, whose clean lines are perfectly balanced by the undulating partly wooded **parkland**, which rolls in from the south and west.

Many visitors forgo the **house** altogether, concentrating on the gardens – an understandable decision given the predictability of the assorted baubles accumulated by the family over the centuries. Nonetheless, among the maze of grandiose rooms and staircases, there are several noteworthy highlights, including the ornate ceilings of the **State Apartments** and, in the State Bedroom, the four-poster bed in which George II breathed his last. And then there are the **paintings**. Among many, Frans Hals, Tintoretto, Veronese and Van Dyck all have a showing, and there's even a Rembrandt.

Back outside, the **gardens** are a real treat and owe much to the combined efforts of Capability Brown, who designed them in the 1750s, and Joseph Paxton (designer of London's Crystal Palace), who had a bash seventy years later. Among all sorts of fripperies, there are water fountains, a rock garden, an artificial waterfall, a grotto and a folly as well as a nursery and greenhouses. Afterwards, you can wend your way to the **café** in the handsomely converted former stables.

**8**

## ARRIVAL AND DEPARTURE

## CHATSWORTH HOUSE

**By bus** Buses pull into the bus stop a short walk from Chatsworth House – and at the end of a byroad leading off the B6012.

Destinations Bakewell (hourly; 17min); Baslow (hourly; 12min); Sheffield (hourly; 1hr 10min).

**On foot** The best way to get to Chatsworth is by walking one of the footpaths that network the estate with the most obvious departure point being Baslow. *The Grate Little Guide to Chatsworth* (see p.462) describes a pleasant 4-mile loop from the village, that takes in the house on the way.

## HIKING AROUND BAKEWELL

Bakewell is a popular starting point for short hikes out into the easy landscapes that make up the town's surroundings, with one of the most relaxing excursions being a four-mile loop along the banks of the **River Wye** to the south of the centre. Chatsworth (see above) is within easy hiking distance, too – about seven miles there and back – or you could venture out onto one of the best-known hikes in the National Park – the **Monsal Trail**, which cuts eight miles north and then west through some of Derbyshire's finest limestone dales using part of the old Midland Railway line. The trail begins at Coombs viaduct, one mile southeast of Bakewell, and ends at Blackwell Mill Junction, three miles east of Buxton.

# The East Midlands

VIEW DOWN BARN HILL, STAMFORD

**9**

# The East Midlands

Many tourists bypass the four major counties of the East Midlands – Nottinghamshire, Leicestershire, Northamptonshire and Lincolnshire – on their way to more obvious destinations, an understandable mistake given that the region seems, at first sight, to be short on star attractions. Nevertheless, the county towns of Nottingham and Leicester, though undeniably bruised by postwar town planning and industrial development, do have enough sights and character to give them appeal, and Lincoln, with its fine cathedral, is in parts at least a dignified old city. What's more, the countryside hereabouts is sprinkled with prestigious country homes, pretty villages and historic market towns.

In **Nottinghamshire**, Byron's **Newstead Abbey** is intriguing; the Elizabethan **Hardwick Hall** (just over the border in Derbyshire but covered in this chapter) is even better. **Leicestershire** offers Market Bosworth, an amiable country town famous as the site of the battle of Bosworth Field, and a particularly intriguing church at Breedon-on-the-Hill. The county also lies adjacent to the easy countryside of **Rutland**, the region's smallest county, where you'll find another pleasant country town, **Oakham**. Rutland and **Northamptonshire** benefit from the use of limestone as the traditional building material and rural Northamptonshire is studded with handsome stone villages and towns – most notably **Fotheringhay** – as well as a battery of country estates.

   **Lincolnshire** is very different in character from the rest of the region, an agricultural hidey-hole that remains surprisingly remote – locals sometimes call it the "forgotten county". This was not always the case: throughout medieval times the county flourished as a centre of the wool trade with Flanders, its merchants and landowners becoming some of the wealthiest in England. Reminders of the high times are legion, beginning with the majestic cathedral that graces the county town of **Lincoln**. Equally enticing is the splendidly intact stone town of **Stamford**, while out in the sticks, Lincolnshire's most distinctive feature is **The Fens**, whose pancake-flat fields, filling out much of the south of the county and extending deep into Cambridgeshire, have been reclaimed from the marshes and the sea. Fenland villages are generally short of charm, but their **parish churches**, whose spires regularly interrupt the wide-skied landscape, are simply stunning; two of the finest – at Gedney and Long Sutton – are set beside the A17 as it slices across the fens on its way to Norfolk. Very different again is the Lincolnshire **coast**, whose long sandy beach extends, with a few marshy interruptions, from Mablethorpe to **Skegness**, the region's main resort. The coast has long attracted thousands of holiday-makers from the big cities of the East Midlands and Yorkshire, hence its trail of bungalows, campsites and caravan parks, though significant chunks of the seashore are now protected as **nature reserves**, with the Gibraltar Point National Nature Reserve being the pick.

| | |
|---|---|
| **Top 5 East Midlands hotels** p.483 | **The Gunpowder Plot** p.497 |
| **Leicester festivals** p.487 | **Guided tours of Lincoln Cathedral** p.499 |
| **Pork Pies** p.490 | **The Lincoln imp** p.502 |
| **Outdoors at Rutland Water** p.494 | **Shakespeare in the Park** p.509 |
| **The Nene Way** p.496 | |

LINCOLN CATHEDRAL

# Highlights

❶ **Newstead Abbey** One-time lair of Lord Byron, this intriguing old mansion has superb period rooms, with lots of Byron memorabilia, and lovely gardens. **See p.482**

❷ **Hardwick Hall** A beautifully preserved Elizabethan mansion that was home to the formidable Bess of Hardwick, one of the leading figures of her age. The gardens and surrounding parkland are wonderful, too. **See p.484**

❸ **Lincoln Cathedral** One of the finest medieval cathedrals in the land, dominating this

fine old city and seen to best advantage on a guided tour. **See p.499**

❹ **Gibraltar Point National Nature Reserve** Escape the crowds and enjoy the wonderful birdlife at this first-class nature reserve on the coast. **See p.505**

❺ **Stamford** Lincolnshire's prettiest town, with its cobbled lanes, lovely old churches, and ancient limestone buildings, well deserves an overnight stay – and you can eat in style here too. **See p.507**

**HIGHLIGHTS ARE MARKED ON THE MAP ON P.476**

# THE EAST MIDLANDS

**By train and bus** Travelling between the cities of the East Midlands by train or bus is simple and most of the larger towns have good regional links, too. Things are very different in the country, however, where bus services are distinctly patchy.

**By plane** The region has one international airport, East Midlands (ⓦeastmidlandsairport.com), just off the M1 between Derby, Nottingham and Leicester.

# Nottingham

With a population of around 305,000, **NOTTINGHAM** is one of England's big cities. A one-time lace manufacturing and pharmaceutical centre (the Boots chain is from here), today it is still famous for its association with **Robin Hood**, the legendary thirteenth-century outlaw. Hood's bitter enemy was, of course, the **Sheriff of Nottingham**, but unfortunately his home and lair – the city's imposing medieval castle – is long gone, replaced by a handsome Palladian mansion that is still called, somewhat confusingly, Nottingham Castle. Nowadays, Nottingham is at its most diverting in and around both the castle and the handsome **Market Square**, which is also the centre of a heaving, teeming weekend nightlife. Within easy striking distance of the city is the former coal-mining village of **Eastwood**, home of the **D.H. Lawrence Birthplace Museum**.

### Brief history

Controlling a strategic crossing point over the River Trent, the Saxon town of **Nottingham** was built on one of a pair of sandstone hills whose 130ft cliffs looked out over the river valley. In 1068, William the Conqueror built a castle on the other hill, and the Saxons and Normans traded on the low ground in between, the Market Square. The castle was a military stronghold and royal palace, the equal of the great castles of Windsor and Dover, and every medieval king of England paid regular visits. In August 1642, Charles I stayed here too, riding out of the castle to raise his standard and start the Civil War – not that the locals were overly sympathetic. Hardly anyone joined up, even though the king had the ceremony repeated on the next three days.

After the Civil War, the Parliamentarians slighted the castle and, in the 1670s, the ruins were cleared by the Duke of Newcastle to make way for a palace, whose continental – and, in English terms, novel – design he chose from a pattern book, probably by Rubens. Beneath the castle lay a handsome, well-kept market town until the second half of the eighteenth century, when the city was transformed by the expansion of the lace and hosiery industries. Within the space of fifty years, Nottingham's population increased from ten thousand to fifty thousand, the resulting slum becoming a hotbed of radicalism.

The worst of Nottingham's slums were cleared in the early twentieth century, when the city centre assumed its present structure, with the main commercial area ringed by alternating industrial and residential districts. Thereafter, crass postwar development, adding tower blocks, shopping centres and a ring road, ensconced and embalmed the remnants of the city's past.

## The Market Square

One of the best-looking central squares in England, Nottingham's **Market Square** is still the heart of the city, an airy open plaza whose shops, offices and fountains are overseen and overlooked by the grand neo-Baroque **Council House**, completed as part of a make-work scheme in 1928. Just off the square there's also a statue honouring one of the city's heroes, the former manager of Nottingham Forest FC, **Brian Clough** (1935–2004), shown in his characteristic trainers and tracksuit. Clough won two European cups with Forest, a remarkable achievement by any standards, but his popularity came as much from his forthright personality and idiosyncratic utterances.

## NOTTINGHAM

Tram Stop
Tram Line —

D.H. Lawrence Birthplace Museum & 1

DERBY ROAD
CLARENDON STREET
NORTH CIRCUS STREET
E CIRCUS STREET
REGENT STREET
PARK ROW
PARK TERRACE
CUMBERLAND PLACE
MOUNT STREET
MAID MARIAN WAY
ST JAMES STREET
FRIAR LANE
HOUNDS GATE
CASTLE GATE
LISTER GATE
CASTLE ROAD
CARRINGTON STREET

TALBOT STREET
WOLLATON STREET
UPPER PARLIAMENT STREET
CHAPEL BAR
LONG ROW
WHEELER GATE
ST PETER'S GATE
BOTTLE LANE
ALBERT ST
LOW PAVEMENT
MIDDLE HILL

GOLDSMITH STREET
SOUTH SHERWOOD STREET
SHAKESPEARE STREET
BURTON STREET
TRINITY SQUARE
FOREMAN ST
KINGS WALK
MARKET STREET
QUEEN STREET
KING STREET
MILTON STREET
N. CHURCH STREET
MANSFIELD ROAD
LOWER PARLIAMENT STREET
CLUMBER STREET
LINCOLN STREET
GEORGE STREET
BROAD STREET
HEATHCOAT STREET
CRANBROOK STREET
HUNTINGDON ST
PELHAM STREET
VICTORIA STREET
CARLTON STREET
GOOSEGATE
WARSER GATE
WOOLPACK LANE
STONEY STREET
BARKER GATE
BELAR GATE
SMITHY ROW
ST MARY'S GATE
HIGH PAVEMENT
BROADWAY
CLIFF ROAD
COLIN STREET
BRIDLESMITH GATE
FLETCHER GATE
BYARD LANE
PLUMPTRE STREET

Victoria Bus Station
Royal Centre & Concert Hall
Victoria Shopping Centre
Playhouse
Library
Brian Clough Statue
MARKET SQUARE
Council House
Broadway Cinema
LACE MARKET
Adams Building
Paul Smith
Paul Smith
Nottingham Contemporary
St Mary's Church
National Ice Centre
Nottingham Castle
Broad Marsh Shopping Centre
Bus Station
Shire Hall & Galleries of Justice

0    200
yards

N

▼ Train Station (100m)    ▼ Tram Stop (50m)

Two quotes suffice to show the mettle of the man: "I wouldn't say I was the best manager in the business, but I was in the top one", and, on the subject of hoofing the football into the air, "If God had wanted us to play football in the sky, He'd have put grass up there."

## Nottingham Castle

Friar Lane • Mid-Feb to Oct daily 10am–5pm; Nov to mid-Feb Wed–Sun 10am–4pm • £5.50 • ⓦ nottinghamcity.gov.uk/castle
**Caves** 4 daily 1hr guided tours except Mon & Tues in winter • £3 • ☎ 0115 876 1400

From the Market Square, it's a five-minute walk west up Friar Lane to **Nottingham Castle**, whose heavily restored medieval gateway leads into the immaculately maintained gardens, which slope up to the squat, seventeenth-century ducal **palace**.

Inside, in the **Castle Museum and Art Gallery**, a particular highlight is the "Story of Nottingham", a lively, well-presented account of the city's development, which is currently undergoing a revamp. Here you will find a small but exquisite collection of late medieval **alabaster carvings**, an art form for which Nottingham once had an international reputation. It's worth walking up to the top floor for a turn around the main **picture gallery**, a handsome and spacious room, which displays a curious assortment of mostly English nineteenth-century Romantic paintings.

Just outside the main entrance to the palace, two sets of steps lead down into the maze of ancient **caves** that honeycomb the cliff beneath. Both are open for guided tours with one set leading into **Mortimer's Hole**, a 300ft shaft along which, so the story goes, the young Edward III and his accomplices crept in October 1330 to capture his mother, Isabella, and her lover, Roger Mortimer. The couple had already murdered Edward III's father, the hapless Edward II, and were intent on usurping the crown, but the young Edward proved too shrewd for them and Mortimer came to a grisly end.

## The Lace Market

The narrow lanes and alleys of the **Lace Market**, beginning a couple of minutes' walk east of the Market Square, are flanked by large and imposing Victorian factories and warehouses. **Stoney Street** is the Lace Market at its most striking, its star turn being the **Adams Building**, whose handsome stone-and-brick facade combines both neo-Georgian and neo-Renaissance features. Neighbouring **Broadway** doesn't lag far behind, with a line of neat red-brick and sandstone-trimmed buildings performing a neat swerve halfway along the street. At the heart of the Lace Market is the **church of St Mary's** (Ⓦstmarysnottingham.org), a good-looking mostly fifteenth-century Gothic structure with a cavernous nave. Sitting ugly on the edge of the Lace Market, there's also the spaceship-like **National Ice Centre** skating rink (Ⓦnational-ice-centre.com).

## Galleries of Justice

High Pavement • Mon–Fri 9am–5pm, tours 10am–4pm; Sat & Sun 10am–5pm, tours 10.30am–4pm • £9.50 • ☎ 0115 952 0555, Ⓦ galleriesofjustice.org.uk

The Lace Market abuts **High Pavement**, the administrative centre of Nottingham in Georgian times, and it's here you'll find **Shire Hall**, whose Neoclassical columns, pilasters and dome date from 1770. The facade also bears the marks of a real Georgian cock-up: to the left of the entrance, just below street level, the mason carved the word "Goal" onto an arch and then had to have a second bash, turning it into "Gaol"; both versions are clearly visible. The hall now houses the **Galleries of Justice**, whose child-friendly "Crime and Punishment" tour involves lots of role play. The building is actually much more interesting than the hoopla, incorporating two superbly preserved Victorian courtrooms, an Edwardian police station, some spectacularly unpleasant old cells, a women's prison with bath house and a prisoners' exercise yard.

## Nottingham Contemporary

Weekday Cross • Tues–Fri 10am–7pm, Sat 10am–6pm, Sun 11am–5pm • Free • ☎ 0115 948 9750, Ⓦ nottinghamcontemporary.org

Just along the street from the Galleries of Justice is the city's premier art gallery, **Nottingham Contemporary**, which – despite the grand assurances of the architects – looks like something assembled from a giant IKEA flat pack. That said, the gallery's temporary exhibitions are consistently strong; hit shows have included the early paintings of David Hockney and a wonderful, all-encompassing display on Haitian voodoo.

## Paul Smith

**10 Byard Lane** Mon–Sat 10am–6pm, Sun 11am–5pm • ☎ 0115 950 6712 • **20 Low Pavement** Mon–Sat 10am–6pm, Sun 11am–5pm • ☎ 0115 968 5990, Ⓦ paulsmith.co.uk

Local lad Paul Smith (b.1946) worked in a clothing factory as a young man and only developed a passion for art and design after a bike accident left him incapacitated for six months. He opened his first small shop here on Byard Lane in 1970, since when he has gone on to become one of the major success stories of contemporary British fashion, his trademark multicoloured stripes proving popular on every continent. He also has a much larger, flagship store just around the corner at 20 Low Pavement, though it's his first shop that has become something of a fashion shrine.

## ARRIVAL AND INFORMATION

**By plane** East Midlands Airport is 18 miles southwest of the city; Skylink buses (ⓦ eastmidlandsairport.com) take a circuitous route into the city centre – allow an hour; buses pull in at the Broad Marsh bus station and terminate at the bus stop on Friar Lane.

**By train** Nottingham train station is on the south side of the city centre, a 5- to 10min walk (just follow the signs), or a tram ride, from Market Square.

Destinations Birmingham (every 20–30min; 1hr 20min); Leicester (every 30min; 20min); Lincoln (hourly; 1hr 10min); London (hourly; 1hr 45min); Newark (hourly;

30min); Oakham (hourly; 1hr, change at Leicester).

**By bus** Most long-distance buses arrive at the Broad Marsh bus station, down the street from the train station on the way to the centre, but some – including services to north Nottinghamshire (see p.482) – pull in at the Victoria bus station, a 5min walk north of Market Square.

**Tourist office** Market Square, on the ground floor of Council House, 1 Smithy Row (Mon–Sat 9am–5.30pm, plus selected Sun 11am–5pm; ☎0844 477 5678, ⓦ experiencenottinghamshire.com).

## ACCOMMODATION

★**Harts Hotel** Standard Hill, Park Row ☎0115 988 1900, ⓦ hartsnottingham.co.uk. Nottingham may be short of good places to stay, but this chic, privately-owned, hotel does much to fill the gap. The 30 stylish guest rooms have ultramodern fixtures and fittings, Egyptian cotton bed linen and modern paintings on the wall. Completed in 2002, the hotel is the work of the city's leading architect, Julian Marsh, whose inventive use of space is his special hallmark. Handy central location too, plus a delightful bar

and a smashing restaurant next door (see below). **£125**

**The Walton Hotel** 2 North Road, The Park ☎0115 947 5215, ⓦ thewaltonhotel.com. Tends to garner mixed reviews, but this privately owned, small hotel does occupy a good-looking, nineteenth-century building on the edge of the city centre – a 15min walk from Market Square and overlooking busy Derby Road. There are 16 guest rooms here and they do vary considerably, though all have more than a smattering of period furnishings and fittings. **£110**

## EATING

**Annie's Burger Shack** 5 Broadway, Lace Market ⓦ anniesburgershack.com. This large and extremely busy burger joint has been a real hit in Nottingham, attracting a groovy crowd, who chomp away at a wide range of top-ranking burgers from "The German" (with grilled sauerkraut) to the "Deathray" (with jalapeños, peppers and chilli paste). There is a first-rate range of craft ales, stouts and ciders too – but come early or expect to queue. Burgers average £10. Daily 8am–10.30am & noon–9.30pm, Fri & Sat till 10.30pm.

**Edin's** 15 Broad St ☎0115 924 1112, ⓦ edinsnotting ham.co.uk. This city centre café-bar has an engaging laidback vibe with its pocket-sized open kitchen, boho furniture and jazzy, bluesy soundtrack. The menu is short, unpretentious and inexpensive or you can settle for a snack, for example the bread and cheese board. Look out for the specials chalked up on the blackboard. Mains cost as little as £6. Daily 9.30am–11.30pm, Sun till 10.30pm.

**French Living** 27 King St ☎0115 958 5885, ⓦ frenchliving.co.uk. Authentic and extremely tasty French cuisine served in an intimate, candlelit basement. Daytime snacks and baguettes in the ground-floor café too. Evening main courses from £12. Tues–Fri noon–2.30pm & 5–10.30pm, Sat noon–10.30pm.

**Harts Restaurant** Standard Hill, Park Row ☎0115 988 1900, ⓦ hartsnottingham.co.uk. One of the city's most acclaimed restaurants, occupying part of the old

general hospital and serving an international menu of carefully presented meals. Attractive modernist decor and attentive service; reservations are recommended. Mains from about £15. For something rather less expensive, go next door to the bar of *Harts Hotel* (see above), where – among much else – they serve great fish and chips with mushy peas. Restaurant daily noon–2pm & 7–10.30pm, Sun till 9pm.

★**MemSaab** 12 Maid Marian Way ☎0115 957 0009, ⓦ mem-saab.co.uk. Arguably the best Indian restaurant in Nottingham with crisp modern decor and bags of space. The food – canny amalgamations of different Indian cooking styles from different regions – is exquisite. The large and imaginative menu has main courses starting from as little as £11. Try the fried cod, Goan fish curry or the slow-cooked lamb flavoured with cardamom. Mon–Thurs 5.30–10.30pm, Fri & Sat 5.30–11pm & Sun 5–10pm.

★**World Service** Newdigate House, Castle Gate ☎0115 847 5587, ⓦ worldservicerestaurant.com. Chic restaurant with bags of decorative flair in charming premises up near the castle. A Modern British menu, featuring such offerings as pork cutlets with onion marmalade and rack of lamb with butternut squash *tarte tatin*, is prepared with imagination and close attention to detail. In the evenings, main courses start at around £17, but there are great deals at lunchtimes with two-course set meals costing £15, or £20 for three courses. Daily noon–2pm & 7–10pm, Sun noon–3.30pm.

**9**

## DRINKING

Central Nottingham's **pubs** literally heave on the weekend and are not for the faint-hearted – and indeed anyone over thirty years old (or even twenty) may well feel marooned. That said, there are one or two more relaxing places among the hullabaloo.

**Broadway Cinema Bar** Broadway Cinema, 14 Broad St in the Lace Market ☎ 0115 952 6611, ⓦ broadway.org.uk. Informal, fashionable (in an arty sort of way) bar serving an eclectic assortment of bottled beers to a cinema-keen clientele. Filling, inexpensive bar food too. Mon–Wed 9am–11pm, Thurs 9am–midnight, Fri & Sat 9am–1am & Sun 10am–11pm; food served daily 10am–9pm.

**Cast** Nottingham Playhouse, Wellington Circus ☎ 0115 941 9419, ⓦ nottinghamplayhouse.co.uk. The bar of the Nottingham Playhouse is a popular, easy-going spot with courtyard seating on summer nights. Patrons have the advantage of being able to gaze at a piece of modern art too – Anish Kapoor's whopping, reflective *Sky Mirror*. Daily noon–late.

★ **Lincolnshire Poacher** 161 Mansfield Rd ☎ 0115 941 1584, ⓦ castlerockbrewery.co.uk. Very popular and relaxed pub, where the decor is pleasantly traditional and the customers take their (real) ales fairly seriously. Attracts an older clientele. About half a mile from the Market Square. Mon–Wed 11am–11pm, Thurs–Fri 11am–midnight, Sat 10am–midnight & Sun noon–11pm.

★ **Ye Olde Trip to Jerusalem** Brewhouse Yard, below the castle ☎ 0115 947 3171, ⓦ triptojerusalem.com. Carved into the castle rock, this ancient inn – said to be the oldest in England – may well have been a meeting point for soldiers gathering for the Third Crusade. Its cave-like bars, with their rough sandstone ceilings, are delightfully secretive and there's a good range of ales too. Sun–Thurs 11am–11pm, Fri & Sat 11am–midnight.

## NIGHTLIFE

**Cookie Club** 22 St James St ☎ 0115 950 5892, ⓦ cookieclub.co.uk. Central nightspot casting a wide musical net, from indie/student favourites to goth and retro. Mon, Wed, Fri & Sat 10.30pm–3am.

**Stealth** Masonic Place, Goldsmith St ☎ 0115 828 3173, ⓦ stealthattack.co.uk. The biggest club in Nottingham hosts live music, wild club nights and a battery of leading DJs.

## ENTERTAINMENT

**Broadway** 14 Broad St in the Lace Market ☎ 0115 9526611, ⓦ broadway.org.uk. The best cinema in the city, featuring a mixed bag of mainstream and avant-garde films.

**Nottingham Playhouse** Wellington Circus ☎ 0115 941 9419, ⓦ nottinghamplayhouse.co.uk. Long-established theatre offering a wide-ranging programme of plays – Shakespeare through to Ayckbourn – plus dance,

music and comedy, often with a local twist or theme.

**Theatre Royal & Royal Concert Hall** Theatre Square ☎ 0115 989 5555, ⓦ trch.co.uk. Two venues with one set of contact details: the Theatre Royal is an attractive, well-maintained Victorian theatre and the nearby Concert Hall dates from the 1980s. All the big names in live music, both popular and classical, play at one or the other.

# D.H. Lawrence Birthplace Museum

8a Victoria St, Eastwood, off Nottingham Rd • Guided tours by advance booking only • £5 • ☎ 01773 717353, ⓦ nottingham.ac.uk /dhlheritage • There is a good bus service from Nottingham's Victoria bus station to Eastwood (every 20min; 30min); ask the driver to put you off at the nearest stop

D.H. Lawrence (1885–1930) was born in the pit village of **Eastwood**, about six miles west of Nottingham. The mine closed years ago, and Eastwood is something of a post-industrial eyesore, but Lawrence's childhood home has survived, a tiny, red-brick terraced house refurbished as the **D.H. Lawrence Birthplace Museum**. None of the furnishings and fittings are Lawrence originals, which isn't too surprising considering the family moved out when he was two, but it's an appealing evocation of the period, interlaced with biographical insights into the author's early life. Afterwards, enthusiasts can follow the three-mile Blue Line Walk round those parts of Eastwood with Lawrence associations: the walk takes an hour or so, and a brochure is available at the museum. Interestingly, few locals thought well of Lawrence – and the sexual scandals hardly helped. Famously, he ran off with Frieda, the wife of a Nottingham professor, and then there was the *Lady Chatterley's Lover* obscenity trial, but much of his local unpopularity was caused by the author's move to the political right until, eventually, he espoused a cranky and unpleasant form of (Nietzschean) elitism.

**9**

# Northern Nottinghamshire

Rural **northern Nottinghamshire**, with its gentle rolling landscapes and large ducal estates, was transformed in the nineteenth century by **coal** – deep, wide seams of the stuff that spawned dozens of collieries, and colliery towns, stretching north across the county and on into Yorkshire. Almost without exception, the mines have closed, their passing marked only by the occasional pithead winding wheel, left, bleak and solitary, to commemorate the thousands of men who laboured here. The suddenness of the pit closure programme imposed by Thatcher and her Conservative cronies in the 1980s knocked the stuffing out of the area, but one prop of its slow revival has been the tourist industry: the countryside in between these former mining communities holds several enjoyable attractions, the best-known of which is **Sherwood Forest** – or at least the patchy remains of it – with one chunk of woodland preserved in the Sherwood Forest National Nature Reserve, supposedly where Robin Hood did his canoodling with Maid Marian. Byron is a pipsqueak in the celebrity stakes by comparison, but his family home – **Newstead Abbey** – is here too, as is **Hardwick Hall**, a handsome Elizabethan mansion built at the behest of one of the most powerful women of her day, Bess of Hardwick (1521–1608).

With the exception of Hardwick Hall, all these attractions are easy to reach by **bus** from Nottingham.

## Newstead Abbey

10 miles north of Nottingham on the A60 • **Gardens & Grounds** Daily 9am–5pm or dusk; Vehicles with driver & passengers £6; pedestrians & cyclists £1 • **House** Sat & Sun noon–4pm; £5. • ☎ 01623 455900, ⓦ newsteadabbey.org.uk • A fast and frequent Pronto bus (every 20min; 25min; ☎ 01773 712265, ⓦ trentbarton.co.uk) leaves Nottingham's Victoria bus station bound for Mansfield; it stops at the gates of Newstead Abbey, a mile from the house

In 1539, **Newstead Abbey** was granted by Henry VIII to Sir John Byron, who demolished most of the church and converted the monastic buildings into a family home. **Lord Byron** (1788–1824) inherited the estate, which was by then little more than a ruin, in 1798; he restored part of the complex during his six-year residence (1808–14), but most of the present structure actually dates from later renovations, which maintained much of the shape and feel of the medieval original while creating the warren-like mansion that exists today. Inside, a string of intriguing period rooms begins with the neo-Gothic Great Hall and Byron's bedroom, one of the few rooms to look pretty much like it did when he lived here, and then continues on into the Library, which holds a collection of the poet's possessions, from letters and an inkstand through to his pistols and boxing gloves. A further room contains a set of satirical, cartoon-like watercolours entitled *The Wonderful History of Lord Byron & His Dog* by his friend Elizabeth Pigot – there's a portrait of the self-same dog, Boatswain, in the south gallery, and a conspicuous memorial bearing an absurdly extravagant inscription to the mutt in the delightful walled garden at the back of the house. Beyond lie the main **gardens**, a secretive and subtle combination of lake, Gothic waterfalls, yew tunnels and Japanese-style rockeries, complete with idiosyncratic pagodas.

## Sherwood Forest

Edwinstowe • Daily dawn–dusk • Free, but parking fee of £3 during school holidays & on weekends (April–Dec) • ☎ 01623 823202, ⓦ nottinghamshire.gov.uk

Most of **Sherwood Forest**, once a vast royal woodland of oak, birch and bracken covering all of northern Nottinghamshire, was cleared in the eighteenth century. It's difficult today to imagine the protection all the greenery provided for generations of outlaws, the most famous of whom was of course **Robin Hood**. There's no "true story" of Robin's life – the earliest reference to him, in Langland's *Piers Plowman* of 1377, treats him as a fiction – but to the balladeers of fifteenth-century England, who invented most of Hood's folklore, this was hardly the point. For them, Robin was a symbol of yeoman decency, a semi-mythological opponent of corrupt clergymen and evil officers of the law; in the early tales, Robin may show sympathy for the peasant, but he has rather more respect for the decent nobleman, and he's never credited with robbing the rich to give to the poor. This

> **TOP 5 EAST MIDLANDS HOTELS**
> **Harts Hotel** Nottingham. See p.480
> **Maiyango** Leicester. See p.489
> **Hambleton Hall** Rutland. See p.494
> **The Old Palace** Lincoln. See p.501
> **The George Hotel** Stamford. See p.509

and other parts of the legend, such as Maid Marian and Friar Tuck, were added later. Robin Hood may lack historical authenticity, but it hasn't discouraged the county council from spending thousands of pounds sustaining the **Major Oak**, the creaky tree where Maid Marian and Robin are supposed to have plighted their troth. The Major Oak is on a pleasant one-mile woodland walk that begins beside the visitor centre at the main entrance to **Sherwood Forest National Nature Reserve**, which comprises 450 acres of oak and silver birch crisscrossed with footpaths.

### ARRIVAL AND INFORMATION                                    SHERWOOD FOREST

**Tourist information** The Sherwood Forest National Nature Reserve visitor centre is half a mile north of the village of Edwinstowe, which is itself about 20 miles north of Nottingham via the A614.

**By bus** Stagecoach's Sherwood Arrow bus (ⓦstagecoachbus.com) links Nottingham's Victoria bus station with Worksop via the visitor centre (hourly; 1hr).

## Clumber Park

East entrance is 4 miles north along the A614 from Ollerton • Daily dawn–dusk; chapel & NT office daily: April–Oct 10am–5pm; Nov– March 10am–4pm • Free, but £6.50 entry per vehicle for non-NT members • ☎ 01909 544900, ⓦ nationaltrust.org.uk • Stagecoach's Sherwood Arrow bus (ⓦ stagecoachbus.com) runs up the west side of Clumber Park en route to Worksop every 2hr; ask the driver to stop at Carburton for the 2.5-mile walk to the Clumber Park NT office

Four thousand acres of park and woodland lying to the south of industrial Worksop, the **Clumber Park** estate was once the country seat of the dukes of Newcastle, and it was here in the 1770s that they constructed a grand mansion overlooking Clumber Lake. The house was dismantled in 1938, when the duke sold the estate, and today the most interesting survivor of the lakeside buildings – located about two miles west of the A614 – is the Gothic Revival **chapel**, an imposing edifice with a soaring spire and an intricately carved interior built for the seventh duke in the 1880s. Close by, the old **stable block** now houses a National Trust shop and café (same hours as chapel), and there's **bike rental** (April–Oct & winter weekends) too. The woods around the lake offer some delightful strolls and bike rides.

## Welbeck Abbey's Harley Gallery

On the A60, 2 miles north of the hamlet of Cuckney • Mon–Sat 10am–5pm, Sun 10am–4.30pm • Free • ☎ 01909 501700, ⓦ harleygallery.co.uk

Immediately to the west of Clumber Park lies **Welbeck Abbey estate**, which remains firmly in ducal hands. Here, the estate's old gas works, built on the edge of the duke's property in the 1870s, has been imaginatively turned into the **Harley Gallery**. The gallery is mainly devoted to temporary exhibitions featuring the work of local living artists, but there's also a permanent exhibition on the ducal family, variously named Cavendish, Portland and Newcastle. The one-room display includes an appealing assortment of family knick-knacks, from portraits, cameos and rare books through to silverware and paintings – and a new extension is planned to exhibit more of the family's baubles. Locally at least, the most famous of the line was the **Fifth Duke of Portland** (1800–1879), known as the "burrowing duke" for the maze of gas-lit tunnels he built underneath his estate – they are still there, but are not open to the public.

**9**

Naturally enough, many thought he was bonkers, but the truth may well be far more complex – an issue explored in Mick Jackson's novel *The Underground Man*, wherein the duke is portrayed as a shy man haunted by his obsessions. There's also a café and a first-rate **farm shop**, which attracts happy eaters from far and wide – the steak pies are especially tasty.

## Hardwick Hall

Doe Lea, Chesterfield, Derbyshire • **Hardwick Hall & gardens** Mid-Feb to Oct Wed–Sun noon–4.30pm, early Dec Wed–Sun 11am–3pm • Hall & gardens £12; gardens only £6; NT **Parkland** Daily 9am–6pm or dusk • Free • Parking per vehicle £3 for non-NT members • ☎ 01246 850430 , ⓦ nationaltrust.org • **Hardwick Old Hall** April–Oct Wed–Sun 10am–5pm • £5.40; EH • Discounted combined tickets with Hardwick Hall available • ☎ 01246 850431 • No public transport; by car via the M1: come off at Junction 29 and follow the signs from the roundabout at the top of the slip road ; it's a 3-mile trip.

Born the daughter of a minor Derbyshire squire, Elizabeth, Countess of Shrewsbury (1527–1608) – aka **Bess of Hardwick** – became one of the leading figures of Elizabethan England, renowned for her political and business acumen. She also had a penchant for building and her major achievement, **Hardwick Hall**, begun when she was 62, has survived in amazingly good condition. The house was the epitome of fashionable taste, a balance of symmetry and ingenious detail in which the rectangular lines of the building are offset by line upon line of windows – there's actually more glass than stone – while up above, her giant-sized initials (E.S.) hog every roof line. Inside on the top floor, the **High Great Chamber**, where Bess received her most distinguished guests, boasts an extraordinary plaster frieze, a brightly painted, finely worked affair celebrating the goddess Diana, the virgin huntress – it was, of course, designed to please the Virgin Queen herself. Next door, the breathtaking **Long Gallery** features exquisite furnishings and fittings from splendid chimneypieces and tapestries through to a set of portraits, including one each of the queen and Bess. Bess could exercise here while keeping out of the sun – at a time when any hint of a tan was considered decidedly plebeian.

Outside, the **garden** makes for a pleasant wander and, beyond the ha-ha (the animal-excluding low wall and ditch), rare breeds of cattle and sheep graze the surrounding **parkland**. Finally – and rather confusingly – Hardwick Hall is next to **Hardwick Old Hall**, Bess's previous home, but now little more than a broken-down if substantial ruin.

## Southwell

**SOUTHWELL**, some fourteen miles northeast of Nottingham, is a sedate and well-heeled backwater distinguished by Southwell Minster, whose perky twin towers are visible for miles around, and by the fine Georgian mansions facing it along Church Street.

### Southwell Minster

Church St • Daily 7am–6.30pm or dusk, Sun hours depend on services • ☎ 01636 812649 • ⓦ southwellminster.org

The Normans built **Southwell Minster** at the beginning of the twelfth century and, although some elements were added later, their design predominates, from the imposing west towers through to the dog-tooth decoration and the bull's-eye windows of the clerestory. Inside, in the north transept, there's a remarkably fine alabaster tomb of a long forgotten churchman, one Archbishop Sandys, who died in 1588. The red-flecked alabaster effigy of Sandys is so precise that you can see the furrows on his brow and the crow's feet round his eyes; his children are depicted kneeling below and it's assumed that Sandys was one of the first bishops to marry – and beget – after the break with Rome changed the rules. The nave's Norman stonework ends abruptly at the transepts and beyond lies the extraordinary **chapter house**, embellished with naturalistic foliage dating from the late thirteenth century – some of the earliest carving of its type in England.

## Southwell Workhouse

Upton Road, Southwell • March–Oct Wed–Sun noon–5pm • £7.70; NT • ☎ 01636 817260, ⬤ nationaltrust.org.uk

About a mile from the minster, on the edge of town out on the road to Newark, stands **Southwell Workhouse**, a substantial three-storey brick building that looks like a prison, but is in fact a rare survivor of the Victorian workhouses that once dotted every corner of the country. They were built as a result of the New Poor Law of 1834, which made a laudable attempt to provide shelter for the destitute. However, the middle classes were concerned that the workers would take advantage of free shelter, so conditions were made hard – as a matter of policy – and the "workhouses" were much feared. Most were knocked down or redeveloped years ago, but this one remained almost untouched, though its bare rooms and barred windows make the whole experience rather depressing.

### ARRIVAL AND DEPARTURE
SOUTHWELL

**By bus** There are regular NCT (Nottingham City Transport; ⬤ nctx.co.uk) buses to Southwell from King Street in central Nottingham. Buses stop near the Minster.

### EATING

**Saracen's Head** Market Place ☎ 01636 812701, ⬤ saracensheadhotel.com. Sitting pretty opposite the Minster, the *Saracen's Head* dates back to the fourteenth century and has one major claim to historical fame – for it was here that the hapless Charles I spent a sleepless night before being handed over to his enemies in Newark (see below). Since then, the place has had many ups and downs, but now – with new owners – rooms downstairs have been restored to their original half–panelled appearance with furniture and fittings to match. The afternoon teas here are first-rate or you can eat at the restaurant, which is just as good and offers a standard British menu with flourishes. Tea: Fri–Sun 2–5pm; Restaurant: Mon–Thurs noon–2.30pm & 5–9pm; Fri & Sat noon–9pm; Sun noon–3pm.

# Newark

From Nottingham, it's about twenty miles northeast to **NEWARK**, an amiable old river port and market town that was once a major staging point on the Great North Road. Fronting the town as you approach from the west are the gaunt riverside ruins of **Newark Castle** (daily dawn–dusk; free), all that's left of the mighty medieval fortress that was pounded to pieces during the Civil War by the Parliamentarians. Opposite, just across the street to the north, is **The Ossington**, a flashy structure whose Tudor appearance is entirely fraudulent – it was built in the 1880s as a temperance hotel by a local bigwig, in an effort to save drinkers from themselves. From here, it's just a couple of minutes' walk east through a network of narrow lanes and alleys to **Market Place**, an expansive square framed by attractive Georgian and Victorian facades.

## Church of St Mary Magdalene

Church Walk • Mon–Sat 8.30am–noon & 1.30–4pm, May–Sept also Sun noon–4pm • ☎ 01636 706473

Just off Market Place stands the mostly thirteenth-century **church of St Mary Magdalene**, a handsome if badly weathered structure with a massive spire (236ft) that soars high above the town centre. Inside, look out for the pair of medieval *Dance of Death* panel paintings, behind the reredos in the choir's Markham Chantry Chapel. One panel has a well-to-do man slipping his hand into his purse, the other shows a carnation-carrying skeleton pointing to the grave – an obvious reminder to the observer of his or her mortality.

### ARRIVAL AND INFORMATION
NEWARK

**By train** Newark has two train stations: Newark Castle on the Nottingham–Lincoln line is on the west side of the River Trent, a 5min walk from the castle, while the larger Newark North Gate Station, on the main London–Edinburgh line, is on Appleton Gate, from where it's a good 10min walk southwest to the castle.
Destinations Lincoln (1–2 hourly; 30min); London (every 30min; 1hr 30min); Nottingham (hourly; 30min).
**By bus** Newark bus station is on Lombard Street, from where it's a 5min walk north along Castlegate to the castle.

**9**

Destinations Nottingham (every 30min; 1hr); Southwell (1–2 hourly; 30min).

**Tourist office** In front of the castle on Castlegate (daily 9am–5pm, Oct–March till 4pm; ☎01636 655765).

### EATING AND DRINKING

**Gannets** 35 Castlegate ☎01636 702066, ⓦgannetsinnewark.co.uk. This bustling and modern café/restaurant has been popular with local townsfolk for the last few decades. It's an informal sort of place with shared tables and a wide-ranging menu, in which the pies, salads and bakes are the special highlights. Look out also for *Gannets's* programme of special events. Mon–Fri 9am–4pm, Sat 9am–5pm & Sun 9.30am–3pm.

# Leicester

At first glance, **LEICESTER**, some 25 miles south of Nottingham, seems a resolutely modern city, but further inspection reveals traces of its medieval and Roman past, situated immediately to the west of the downtown shopping area near the River Soar.

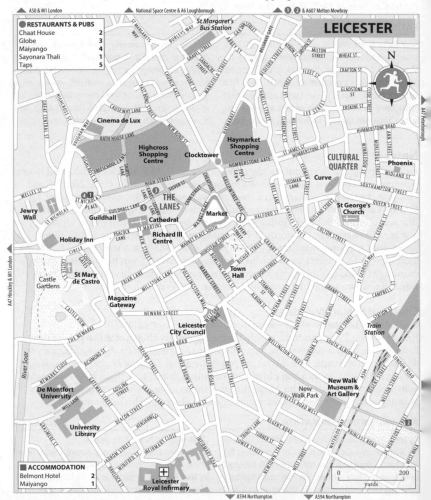

**LEICESTER**

| RESTAURANTS & PUBS | |
|---|---|
| Chaat House | 2 |
| Globe | 3 |
| Maiyango | 4 |
| Sayonara Thali | 1 |
| Taps | 5 |

| ACCOMMODATION | |
|---|---|
| Belmont Hotel | 2 |
| Maiyango | 1 |

**LEICESTER FESTIVALS**

The crowded terraced streets of the Belgrave district, on the northeastern periphery of the centre, are the hub for two major Hindu festivals – **Diwali** (ⓦ whatson.leicester.gov.uk), the Festival of Light, held in October or November, when six thousand lamps are strung out along Belgrave Road, and **Navratri** (ⓦ whatson.leicester.gov.uk), a nine-day celebration in October held in honour of the goddess Durga. In addition, the city's sizeable Afro-Caribbean community holds England's second biggest street festival after the Notting Hill Carnival (see box, p.120). It's called the **Leicester Caribbean Carnival** (ⓦ leicestercarnival.com) and it's held on the first weekend in August. ⓦ leicester.gov.uk

In 2012, its national profile was boosted by the discovery of the remains of **Richard III** beneath a council car park in the centre – the body was originally brought here after the Battle of Bosworth Field (see p.491). There followed a prolonged legal battle with York as to who should keep the king's skeleton, but Leicester won and the body will be ceremonially reinterred in Leicester Cathedral in 2015.

It's probably fair to say that Leicester has a longstanding reputation for looking rather glum, but the centre is very much on the move, with the addition of Highcross, a brand-new shopping centre, and the creation of a Cultural Quarter equipped with a flashy performance venue, **Curve Theatre**. The star turns, however, are the **New Walk Museum and Art Gallery**, which includes an exemplary collection of German Expressionist paintings, and the brand-new **King Richard III Visitor Centre**. More than a third of Leicester's population is **Asian** – the city elected England's first Asian MP, Keith Vaz, in 1987. The focus of the Asian community is the **Belgrave Road** and its environs, an area of terraced houses about a mile to the northeast of the city centre beyond the flyover, where people come from miles around to eat at the splendid **Indian restaurants**.

### Brief history

The **Romans** chose this site to keep an eye on the rebellious Corieltauvi, constructing a fortified town beside the Fosse Way (now the A46), the military road running from Lincoln to Cirencester. Later, the Emperor Hadrian kitted the place out with huge public buildings, though the Danes, who overran the area in the eighth century, were not overly impressed and didn't even bother to pilfer much of the stone. Later still, the town's medieval castle became the base of the earls of Leicester, the most distinguished of whom was **Simon de Montfort**, who forced Henry III to convene the first English Parliament in 1265. Since the late seventeenth century, Leicester has been a centre of the **hosiery trade** and it was this industry that attracted a stream of Asian immigrants to settle here from the 1950s onwards.

## The city centre

The most conspicuous buildings in Leicester's crowded centre are two large shopping centres, the ultramodern Highcross and the clumpy **Haymarket**, but the proper landmark is the Victorian **clocktower** of 1868, standing in front of the Haymarket and marking the spot where seven streets meet. One of the seven is Cheapside, which leads to Leicester's open-air **market** (Mon–Sat), one of the best of its type in the country and the place where the young **Gary Lineker**, now the UK's best-known football pundit, worked on the family stall. Good-hearted Gary remains a popular figure hereabouts and has been made a freeman of the city, which, among other things, gives him the right to graze his sheep in front of the town hall. East of the clocktower is Leicester's nascent **Cultural Quarter**, whose two main attractions are the **Curve Theatre** (see p.490) and the **Phoenix cinema** (see p.490). One of the seven streets beginning at Leicester's clocktower is Silver Street (subsequently Guildhall Lane), which passes through **The Lanes**, where a medley of small, independent shops gives this part of the centre real character.

**9**

## Leicester Cathedral

St Martin's • Mon–Sat 8am–6pm, Sun 7am–4pm • Free • ⓦ leicestercathedral.org

Abutting Guildhall Lane is **Leicester Cathedral**, a much-modified eleventh-century structure incorporating two finely carved porches – a stone one at the front and an earlier timber version at the rear. The interior, with its clutch of Gothic arches, holds a whopping big organ and several interesting side chapels, in one of which is a splendid wooden tabernacle.

## King Richard III Visitor Centre

St Martin's • Mon–Fri 10am–4pm, Sat & Sun 10am–5pm • £7.95 • ☎ 0300 300 0900, ⓦ kriii.com

Across the street from the Cathedral, Leicester's old Grammar School is a substantial Victorian red-brick that has been turned into the lavish **King Richard III Visitor Centre** after the royal body was discovered beneath the adjoining car park where the greyfriars friary church had once stood. The Centre has three distinct sections. The first examines Richard's reign and the battle of Bosworth Field that ended it; a second gives visitors the chance to peer down into the makeshift grave where the body was found; and the third relates the story of how the body was discovered – a remarkable tale in itself. This third section also reveals what detailed analysis has discovered about Richard: he suffered from curvature of the spine, enjoyed a high-protein diet and was killed by several blows to the head. It really is intriguing stuff – and it's all immaculately presented.

## Guildhall

Guildhall Lane • Daily 11am–4.30pm, but times subject to change • Free • ☎ 0116 253 2569, ⓦ leicester.gov.uk

Next door to the Cathedral is the **Guildhall**, a half-timbered building that has served, variously, as the town hall, prison and police station. The most interesting part of a visit is the rickety Great Hall, its beams bent with age, but there are a couple of old cells too, plus the town gibbet on which the bodies of the hanged were publicly displayed until the 1840s.

## The Jewry Wall

Near the Guildhall, beside the large St Nicholas Circle roundabout, you'll spot the conspicuous **church of St Nicholas**; beside that, in a little dell, lie the foundations of the Emperor Hadrian's public baths, which culminate in the **Jewry Wall**, a substantial chunk of Roman masonry some 18ft high and 73ft long. The baths were a real irritation to the emperor: the grand scheme was spoilt by the engineers, who miscalculated the line of the aqueduct that was to pipe in the water, and so bathers had to rely on a hand-filled cistern replenished from the river – which wasn't what he had in mind at all.

## Castle Gardens and St Mary de Castro

**Castle Gardens**, a narrow strip of a park that runs alongside a canalized portion of the River Soar, is a pleasant spot, incorporating the overgrown mound where Leicester's Norman castle motte once stood. At the far end of Castle Gardens, you emerge on The Newarke; turn left and follow the road round, and in a jiffy you'll reach **Castle View**, a narrow lane spanned by the Turret Gateway, a rare survivor of the city's medieval castle. Just beyond the gateway is **St Mary de Castro**, a dignified old church with a dainty crocketed spire where Chaucer may well have got married.

## New Walk Museum and Art Gallery

55 New Walk • Mon–Sat 10am–5pm, Sun 11am–5pm • Free • ☎ 0116 225 4900, ⓦ leicester.gov.uk

The **New Walk** is a long and pleasant pedestrianized promenade that's home to the city's best museum, the **New Walk Museum and Art Gallery**. The museum covers a lot of ground, from the natural world to geology and beyond, but one highlight is its extensive collection of Ancient Egyptian artefacts, featuring mummies and hieroglyphic tablets brought back to Leicester in the 1880s. The museum also holds an enjoyable collection of paintings and, although these are rotated regularly, you're likely to see a good range of works by British artists as well as an outstanding collection of German Expressionist works, mostly sketches, woodcuts and lithographs by artists such as Otto Dix and George Grosz.

## The National Space Centre

Exploration Drive, off the A6, 2 miles north of the city centre • Term time: Tues–Fri 10am–4pm, Sat & Sun 10am–5pm; school hols: daily 10am–5pm • £13, children (5–16) £11• ☎ 0116 261 0261, Ⓦ spacecentre.co.uk • Bus #54 links the train station with Abbey Lane, a 5min walk from the Space Centre

Just north of Leicester city centre, the **National Space Centre** is devoted to space, science and astronomy, with a string of themed galleries exploring everything from the planets to orbiting earth. The emphasis is on the interactive, which makes the place very popular with kids.

### ARRIVAL AND INFORMATION

### LEICESTER

**By train** Leicester train station is on London Rd, from where it's a 10min walk northwest to the city centre.
Destinations Birmingham (every 30min; 1hr); Lincoln (hourly; 1hr 40min); London (every 30min; 1hr 15min); Nottingham (every 30min; 30min); Oakham (hourly; 30min); Stamford (hourly; 50min).
**By bus** St Margaret's bus station is on the north side of the centre, just off Gravel Street – to get to the Haymarket, just

follow the signs.
Destinations Ashby-de-la-Zouch (hourly; 1hr 20min); Market Bosworth (hourly; 1hr). Both services provided by Arriva (Ⓦ arrivabus.co.uk).
**Tourist office** In the centre, a short walk south of the Haymarket at 51 Gallowtree Gate (Mon–Sat 9.30am–5.30pm, Sun 11am–5pm, ☎ 0116 299 4444, Ⓦ visitleicester.info).

### ACCOMMODATION

Leicester has a good crop of business **hotels**, mostly within walking distance of the train station. The tourist office (see above) will help find you somewhere to stay, but things rarely get tight except during the Navrati and Diwali festivals (see box, p.487).

**Belmont Hotel** De Montfort St ☎ 0116 254 4773, Ⓦ belmonthotel.co.uk. A pleasant and proficient hotel in an attractively modernized and extended Victorian property about 300 yards south of the train station via London Road. It's popular with business folk and tourists alike. **£100**
★**Maiyango** 13–21 St Nicholas Place ☎ 0116 251 8898, Ⓦ malyango.com. This small, independent hotel – the best

in town – has fourteen slick modern rooms, each with bespoke art work and handmade furniture. Their "superior" rooms have rain showers and king-size beds, whereas the larger deluxe rooms have walk-in wet rooms and bath tubs. The hotel also has a handy location, a brief walk from the principal sights and Leicester's main shopping centres. There's a first-rate restaurant on site too (see below). **£80**

### EATING AND DRINKING

Visitors come from miles around to eat at the excellent **Indian restaurants** that line up along **Belgrave Road**, which begins a mile or so northeast of the centre. There are top-notch restaurants in the city centre too and a battery of **bars**, though most of these are chains.

★**Chaat House** 108 Belgrave Rd ☎ 0116 266 0513. In operation for more than thirty years, *Chaat House* is something of a local institution, its simple decor entirely appropriate for an unpretentious, family-run place, where they serve satisfying mounds of vegetarian food in capacious aluminium dishes. Try, for example, the *matar paneer* (peas and cheese in a tomato sauce), with *gulab jamin* for dessert. £20 will cover a meal for two. Near the junction with Roberts Road. Daily noon–10pm.
**Globe** 43 Silver St ☎ 0116 253 9492, Ⓦ www .eversosensible.com/globe/. Traditional pub in an attractive old building at the heart of the city. Smashing range of real ales and good quality bar food too. Sun–Thurs 11am–11pm, Fri & Sat 11am–1am; food served

Mon–Sat noon–7pm, Sun noon–5pm.
★**Maiyango** 13–21 St Nicholas Place ☎ 0116 251 8898, Ⓦ maiyango.com. Chi-chi lounge-bar and restaurant beneath the hotel of the same name (see above). The restaurant mostly uses local, seasonal ingredients and the menu is wide-ranging – try the soy-scented guinea fowl breast in a sweet and sour plum jus, for example, or the courgette flowers with crab and lobster. Afterwards, you can relax in the charming rooftop terrace bar. Set menus and à la carte with mains averaging £16. Mon & Tues 6.30–11pm, Wed & Thurs 12.30–4pm & 6.30–11.30pm, Fri 12.30–4pm & 5–11.30pm, Sat 12.30pm–1am, Sun 6–10.30pm.
**Sayonara Thali** 49 Belgrave Road ☎ 0116 266 5888.

**9**

Flamboyantly decorated vegetarian restaurant that specializes in set thali meals, with several different dishes, breads and pickles served together on large steel plates. Full thalis from £5. Daily noon–9.30pm.

**Taps** 10 Guildhall Lane ☎0116 253 0904, ⊛taps -leicester.com. Inventive bar and restaurant, whose claim to fame is the beer taps at many of the tables – help yourself and pay later (yes, the taps are monitored as they dispense). Excellent range of bottled beers too, plus vaulted cellars that date back yonks, and an above-average menu – chicken breast stuffed with apples and stilton in a creamy leek sauce, for example, for just £15. Mon–Sat noon–11.30pm.

## ENTERTAINMENT

**Curve** 60 Rutland St ☎0116 242 3595, ⊛curveonline .co.uk. At the heart of the Cultural Quarter, Curve is Leicester's leading performing arts venue, offering a varied programme from within its startlingly dramatic glass facade.

**Phoenix** 4 Midland St ☎0116 242 2800, ⊛phoenix .org.uk. Just a couple of minutes' walk from Curve, the Phoenix is an outstanding art-house cinema, one of the best in the Midlands.

# Western Leicestershire

**Leicestershire** is arguably one of the more anonymous of the English shires, its undulating landscapes comprising an apparently haphazard mix of the industrial, post-industrial and the rural. The county's highlights are dotted across **western Leicestershire**, beginning with the well-manicured charms of **Market Bosworth**, near **Bosworth Field**, where Richard III met a sticky end in 1485. Here too is the amenable little town of **Ashby-de-la-Zouch**, home to the substantial remains of a medieval castle, **Breedon-on-the-Hill** and its fine hilltop church, and **Calke Abbey**, technically over the boundary in Derbyshire and not an abbey at all, but an intriguing country house whose faded charms witness the declining fortunes of the landed gentry.

## Market Bosworth and around

The thatched cottages and Georgian houses of tiny **MARKET BOSWORTH**, some eleven miles west of Leicester, fan out from a dinky **Market Place**, which was an important trading centre throughout the Middle Ages. From the sixteenth to the nineteenth century, the dominant family hereabouts were the Dixies, merchant-landlords who mostly ended up at the **church of St Peter**. The Dixies were not universally admired, however, and the young Samuel Johnson, who taught at the **Dixie Grammar School** – its elongated facade still abuts the Market Place – disliked the founder, Sir Wolstan Dixie, so much that he recalled his time there "with the strongest aversion and even a sense of horror".

### Church of St Peter

Church St • Daily 8.30am–dusk • Free • ☎07949 232123, ⊛marketbosworthbenefice.co.uk

The **church of St Peter**, a three-minute walk north of Market Place, is a good-looking

---

### PORK PIES

**Melton Mowbray**, some fifteen miles northeast of Leicester, is famous for its **pork pies**, an extremely popular English delicacy made of compressed balls of meat and gristle encased in wobbly jelly and thick pastry. Many may find the pie's appeal unaccountable, but in 2009 it was accorded Protected Geographical Status by the EU, a coveted designation if ever there was one. Pork pies were the traditional repast of the foxhunting fraternity, for whom Melton Mowbray was long a favourite haunt. The antics of some of the aristocratic huntsmen are legend – in 1837 the Marquis of Waterford literally painted the town's buildings red, hence the saying. Today, connoisseurs swear by the pork pies of **Dickinson & Morris** and, although their products are widely distributed, you may want to go to their shop at 10 Nottingham St, just off the Market Place in Melton Mowbray (Mon–Sat 8am–5pm; ⊛porkpie.co.uk), to sample (or gawp at) the full range, from the tiny to the enormous.

edifice with a castellated nave and a sturdy square tower. Heavily revamped by the Victorians, the church's interior is fairly routine, but the chancel does hold the early eighteenth-century **tomb** of John Dixie, one-time rector, who is honoured by a long hagiographic plaque and the effigy of his weeping sister.

## Bosworth Field

Sutton Cheney, a couple of miles south of Market Bosworth • **Heritage Centre** Daily: April–Oct 10am–5pm; Nov–March 10am–4pm • £7.95, plus £2.50 parking • ☏ 01455 290429, ⊚ bosworthbattlefield.com • No public transport

Market Bosworth is best known for the **Battle of Bosworth Field**, which was fought on hilly countryside near the village in 1485. This was the last and most decisive battle of the Wars of the Roses, an interminably long-winded and bitterly violent conflict among the nobility for control of the English Crown. The victor was Henry Tudor, subsequently Henry VII; he defeated Richard III, who famously died on the battlefield. In desperation, Shakespeare's villainous Richard cried out "A horse, a horse, my kingdom for a horse," but in fact the defeated king seems to have been a much more phlegmatic character. Taking a glass of water before the fighting started, he actually said, "I live a king: if I die, I die a king". What happened to Richard's body after the battle was long a matter of conjecture, but in 2012 his skeleton was unearthed in the centre of Leicester beneath a council car park (see p.488).

### Bosworth Battlefield Heritage Centre

The **Bosworth Battlefield Heritage Centre** features a workmanlike description of the battle and explains its historical context, though the less said about the ersatz medieval village that has taken shape next door the better. The Heritage Centre also has a section on recent archeological efforts to find the actual site of the battle: unfortunately, it turns out that the battlefield was a couple of miles further west on what is now private land, which leaves the centre, never mind the adjoining circular two-mile **Battle Trail**, which identifies where tradition had the protagonists meet, somewhat marooned. Nevertheless, the ramble along the trail is pleasant enough and on the way you'll pass **King Richard's Well**, a rough cairn where the king was supposed to have had his final drink, and there are views over to the actual battlefield too. Pick up a map at the Heritage Centre before you set out.

| **ARRIVAL AND DEPARTURE** | **MARKET BOSWORTH** |
|---|---|

**By bus** There are regular Arriva (⊚ arrivabus.co.uk) buses from Leicester to Market Bosworth's Market Place (hourly; 1hr).

**ACCOMMODATION AND EATING**

**Softleys** 2 Market Place ☏ 01455 290464, ⊚ softleys .com. Right in the centre of the village, this first-rate, family-run hotel has three well-appointed bedrooms decorated in a homely version of country-house style. The rooms are really run as an adjunct to a smart restaurant, where the menu is lively, creative and locally sourced wherever possible – the lamb is especially good. Mains average around £17. Lunch: Tues–Sat noon–2pm, last orders 1.45pm, & Sun noon–3.30pm, last orders 3pm; Dinner: Tues–Thurs 6.30–9.30pm, last orders 9pm, Fri & Sat 6.30–10pm, last orders 9.30pm. **£90**

# Ashby-de-la-Zouch and around

**ASHBY-DE-LA-ZOUCH**, fifteen miles northwest of Leicester, takes its fanciful name from two sources – the town's first Norman overlord was Alain de Parrhoet la Souche and the rest means "place by the ash trees". Nowadays, Ashby is far from rustic, but it's still an amiable little place with one main attraction, its **castle**. It's also within easy striking distance of an especially interesting country house, **Calke Abbey**, and two fascinating churches – **Staunton Harold** and the hilltop Church of St Mary and St Hardulph, at **Breedon-on-the-Hill**, which is noted for its stunning Anglo-Saxon carvings. Note, however, that there is no public transport to these three surrounding attractions.

**9**

# Ashby Castle

South St, just off the town's main St, Market St • April–June & Sept–Oct Wed–Sun 10am–5pm; July–Aug daily 10am–5pm; Nov–March Sat & Sun 10am–4pm • £4.60; EH

Originally a Norman manor house, Ashby's **castle** was the work of Edward IV's chancellor, Lord Hastings, who received his "licence to crenellate" in 1474. The rambling ruins include substantial leftovers from the old fortifications, as well as the shattered remains of the great hall, solar and chapel, but the star turn is the 100ft-high **Hastings Tower**, a self-contained four-storey stronghold which has survived in good nick. This tower house represented the latest thinking in castle design. It provided much better accommodation than was previously available; living quarters that reflected the power and pride of a burgeoning landowning class. By all accounts, Hastings was very proud of his tower, but he didn't enjoy it for long: in 1483, he was dragged from a Privy Council meeting to have his head hacked off on a log by the order of Richard III, his crime being his lacklustre support for the Yorkist cause.

### ARRIVAL AND DEPARTURE                    ASHBY-DE-LA-ZOUCH

**By bus** Arriva (ⓦ arrivabus.co.uk) operates the main bus service from Leicester bus station to Ashby's Market Street (every 30min to 1hr; 1hr 10min).

# Calke Abbey

Ticknall, 5 miles north of Ashby-de-la-Zouch • House: late Feb to Oct Mon–Wed, Sat & Sun 12.30–5pm; gardens & stables: mid-Feb to Oct daily 10am–5pm; park: daily 8am–8.30pm or dusk • £8.40 all inclusive, garden only £4.50, park & stables only £3; NT • ☎ 01332 863822, ⓦ nationaltrust.org.uk • No public transport; from Ashby, take the B587 Melbourne Road and follow the signs – the entrance is at the village of Ticknall to the north of the house; the exit is to the south • Sat Nav: DE73 7JF

The eighteenth-century facade of **Calke Abbey**, set deep in the countryside a few miles north of Ashby, is all self-confidence, its acres of dressed stone and three long lines of windows polished off with an imposing Greek Revival portico. This all cost oodles of money and the Harpurs, and then the Harpur-Crewes, who owned the estate, were doing very well until the finances of the English country estate changed after World War I. Then, the Harpur-Crewes simply hung on, becoming the epitome of faded gentility and refusing to make all but the smallest of changes – though they did finally plump for electricity in 1962. In 1981 the estate was passed in its entirety to the National Trust, who decided not to bring in the restorers and have kept the house in its dishevelled state – and this is its real charm.

In the **house**, the entrance hall adroitly sets the scene, its walls decorated with ancient, moth-eaten stuffed heads from the family's herd of prize cattle. Beyond is the Caricature Room, whose walls are lined with satirical cartoons, some by the leading cartoonists of their day. Further on, there are more animal heads and glass cabinets of stuffed birds in the capacious Saloon; an intensely cluttered Miss Havisham-like Drawing Room; and a chaotic at-home School Room. After you've finished in the house, you can stroll out into the **gardens**, pop into the Victorian estate **church**, and wander through wooded **parkland**.

# Staunton Harold Church

Staunton Harold Estate • April, May, Sept & Oct Sat & Sun 1–4.30pm; June–Aug Wed–Sun 1–4.30pm • Free; NT • ☎ 01332 863822, ⓦ nationaltrust.org.uk • No public transport, but signed off the B587 ; the church is behind the Ferrers Arts and Craft Centre • Sat Nav LE651RW

When you leave Calke Abbey, spare a little time for neighbouring **Staunton Harold Church**, a distinctly odd political rant of a building in which the local lord, the reactionary Robert Shirley, expressed his hatred of Oliver Cromwell. There's no missing Shirley's intentions as he carved them above the church door: "In the year 1653 when all things sacred were throughout the nation either demolished or profaned..." and so he goes on. Whatever the politics, it was certainly an audacious – probably foolhardy

– gesture, and sure enough Cromwell had the last laugh when an unrepentant Shirley died in prison three years later. The church itself is a good-looking affair, largely in the Perpendicular style with delightful painted ceilings and wood panelling.

## Breedon-on-the-Hill

It's five miles northeast from Ashby to the unassuming village of **BREEDON-ON-THE-HILL**, which sits in the shadow of the large, partly quarried hill from which it takes its name. A steep footpath and a winding, half-mile by-road lead up from the village to the summit, from where there are smashing views over the surrounding countryside.

### Church of St Mary and St Hardulph

Breedon-on-the-Hill • Daily 9.30am–4pm, sometimes later in summer • Free • Ⓦ benefice.org.uk/breedon_church • There are no buses to the church and the village is poorly served by bus too.

The fascinating **church of St Mary and St Hardulph** occupies the site of an Iron Age hill fort and an eighth-century Anglo-Saxon monastery. Mostly dating from the thirteenth century, the church is kitted out with a Georgian pulpit and pews as well as a large and distinctly rickety box pew. Much more rare are a number of **Anglo-Saxon carvings** that include individual saints and prophets and wall friezes, where a dense foliage of vines is inhabited by a tangle of animals and humans. The friezes are quite extraordinary, and the fact that the figures look Byzantine rather than Anglo-Saxon has fuelled much academic debate.

# Rutland

To the east of Leicestershire lies England's smallest county, **Rutland**, reinstated in its own right in 1997 following 23 unpopular years of merger with its larger neighbour. Rutland has three places of note: **Oakham**, the pocket-sized county town, and **Uppingham** – both rural centres with some elegant Georgian architecture – and the prettier, much smaller stone hamlet of **Lyddington**.

## Oakham

The prosperity of well-heeled **OAKHAM**, 24 miles east of Leicester, is bolstered by Oakham School, one of the region's more exclusive private schools, and by its proximity to **Rutland Water**, a large reservoir whose assorted facilities attract cyclists, ramblers, sailors and birdwatchers by the hundred. Oakham's stone terraces and Georgian villas are too often interrupted to assume much grace, but the town does have its architectural moments, particularly in the L-shaped **Market Place**, where a brace of sturdy awnings shelter the old water pump and town stocks, and where **Oakham School** is housed in a series of impressive ironstone buildings.

### Oakham Castle

Market Place • Mon 10am–4pm, Wed–Sat 10am–4pm • Free • ☎ 01572 758440, Ⓦ rutland.gov.uk

A few steps from the north side of the Market Place stands **Oakham Castle**, a large banqueting hall that was once part of a twelfth-century fortified house. The hall is a good example of Norman domestic architecture and surrounding the building are the grassy banks that once served to protect it. Inside, the whitewashed walls are covered with **horseshoes**, the result of an ancient custom by which every lord or lady, king or queen, is obliged to present an ornamental horseshoe when they first set foot in the town.

### All Saints' Church

Church St • Daily dawn to dusk • Free • ☎ 01572 724007, Ⓦ oakham.oakhamteam.org.uk

From Oakham Market Place, a narrow lane leads along the right-hand side of Oakham

**9**

> ### OUTDOORS AT RUTLAND WATER
>
> The gentle waters and easy, green hills of **Rutland Water** (⊛rutlandwater.org.uk) have made it a major centre for outdoor pursuits. There's sailing at Rutland Sailing Club (⊛rutlandsc.co.uk); cycle hire with Rutland Water Cycling (⊛rutlandcycling.com); and a Watersports Centre at Whitwell on the north shore (⊛anglianwater.co.uk/leisure). Rutland Water also attracts a wide range of waterfowl, which prompted the establishment of a **nature reserve** with no fewer than 31 hides and two visitor centres at its west end. The reserve is home to a successful Osprey breeding project (⊛ospreys.org.uk).

School to **All Saints' Church**, whose heavy tower and spire rise high above the town. Dating from the thirteenth century, the church is an architectural hybrid, but the airy interior is distinguished by the intense medieval carvings along the columns of the nave and choir, with Christian scenes and symbols set alongside dragons, grotesques, devils and demons.

### ARRIVAL AND DEPARTURE                                                                OAKHAM

**By train** The only place in Rutland to have a rail connection is Oakham, where the train station is on Station Road, on the northwest side of town, a 10min walk from Market Place.

Destinations Birmingham (hourly; 1hr 30min); Leicester (hourly; 30min); Melton Mowbray (hourly; 10min); Peterborough (hourly; 30min); Stamford (hourly; 15min)).

**By bus** Monday through Saturday, there is a good bus service between Oakham, Uppingham and Lyddington. In Oakham, the main bus stops are in John St, a 5min walk west of Market Place.

Destinations Lyddington (Mon–Sat hourly; 30min); Nottingham (Mon–Sat hourly; 1hr 20min); Uppingham (Mon–Sat hourly; 15min).

## Uppingham

The narrow main street of **UPPINGHAM**, six miles south of Oakham, has the uniformity of architectural style Oakham lacks, its course flanked by bow-fronted shops and ironstone houses, mostly dating from the eighteenth century. It's the general appearance that pleases, rather than any individual sight, but the town is famous as the home of **Uppingham School**, founded in 1587 and a bastion of privilege whose imposing, fortress-like building stands on the west side of the High Street.

## Lyddington

**LYDDINGTON**, some two miles south of Uppingham, is a sleepy little village of honey-coloured cottages straggling along a meandering main street, all backed by plump hills and broadleaf woodland. Early in the twelfth century, the Bishop of Lincoln chose this as the site of a small palace. Confiscated during the Reformation, **Lyddington Bede House**, on Church Lane (April–Oct Wed–Sun 10am–5pm; £4.40; EH), was later converted into almshouses by Lord Burghley and has since been beautifully restored. The highlight is the light and airy Great Chamber, with its exquisitely carved oak cornices, but look out also for the tiny ground-floor rooms, which were occupied by impoverished locals for centuries.

### ACCOMMODATION AND EATING                                                              RUTLAND

**OAKHAM**

**Castle Cottage Café** Church Passage, Market Place ☎01572 757952, ⊛castlecottagecafe.co.uk. Cosy little café featuring a tempting range of moderately-priced home-made dishes with a particularly good line in cakes and salads – try, for example, the salmon and prawn tian. Mon–Sat 8.30am–4.30pm & Sun 10am–4pm.

**Hambleton Hall** Hambleton ☎01572 756991,

⊛hambletonhall.com. Just a couple of miles southeast of Oakham, overlooking Rutland Water in the tiny hamlet of Hambleton, this opulent hotel occupies an imposing Baronial-Gothic mansion set in its own immaculate grounds. It's seriously expensive – and seriously luxurious. **£285**

**UPPINGHAM**

**Lake Isle** 16 High St East ☎01572 822951,

ⓦ lakeisle.co.uk. In a tastefully modernized eighteenth-century townhouse, the rooms here are decorated in a pleasant rendition of traditional style. The restaurant is first-rate too, offering a superb and varied menu from guinea fowl to local venison, with main courses averaging around £16. **£85**

**LYDDINGTON**
**The Old White Hart** 51 Main St ☎ 01572 821703,

ⓦ oldwhitehart.co.uk. This most convivial of village pubs, with its wooden floors and beamed ceilings, occupies a handsome stone building in the centre of Lyddington. It has ten bright and breezily decorated rooms, two in the inn and eight in the adjoining cottage, and serves delicious food, both in the bar and in the restaurant, where main courses average around £12 – try the local venison. Reservations advised. Food served Mon–Sat noon–2pm & 6.30–9pm, Sun noon–2pm. **£90**

# Northampton

Spreading north from the banks of the River Nene, **NORTHAMPTON** is a workaday town whose modern appearance largely belies its ancient past. Throughout the Middle Ages, this was one of central England's most important towns, a flourishing commercial hub whose now demolished castle was a popular stopping-off point for travelling royalty. A fire in 1675 burnt most of the medieval city to a cinder, and the Georgian town that grew up in its stead was itself swamped by the Industrial Revolution, when Northampton swarmed with **boot- and shoemakers**, whose products shod almost everyone in the British Empire. Errol Flynn kitted himself out with several pairs of Northampton shoes and boots when he was in repertory here in 1933, but he annoyed his suppliers no end by hightailing it out of town after a year, leaving a whopping debt behind him – thereby partly justifying David Niven's cryptic comment "You can count on Errol Flynn, he will always let you down".

## Church of All Saints

George Row • Mon–Sat 10am–5pm • Free • ☎ 01604 632845, ⓦ allsaintsnorthampton.co.uk
From Northampton's expansive Market Square, it's just a short walk through to the town's ecclesiastical pride and joy, the **Church of All Saints**, whose unusually secular appearance stems from its finely proportioned, pillared portico and towered cupola. A statue of a bewigged Charles II in Roman attire surmounts the portico, a (flattering) thank you for his donation of a thousand tonnes of timber after the Great Fire of 1675 had incinerated the earlier church. Inside, the handsome interior holds a sweeping timber gallery and a batch of Neoclassical pillars, which lead the eye up to the fancy plasterwork that decorates the ceiling.

## Northampton Museum and Art Gallery

4–6 Guildhall Rd • Tues–Sat 10am–5pm, Sun 2–5pm • Free • ☎ 01604 838111, ⓦ northampton.gov.uk
The **Northampton Museum and Art Gallery**, just a couple of minutes' walk from the church of All Saints, celebrates the town's industrial heritage with a wonderful collection of **shoes and boots**. Along with silk slippers, clogs and high-heeled nineteenth-century court shoes, there's one of the four boots worn by an elephant during the British Expedition of 1959, which retraced Hannibal's putative route over the Alps into Italy. There's celebrity footwear too, such as the giant DMs Elton John wore in *Tommy*, plus whole cabinets of heavy-duty riding boots, pearl-inlaid raised wooden sandals from Ottoman Turkey, and a couple of cabinets showing just how long high heels have been in fashion.

## Charles Rennie Mackintosh House

78 Derngate • Feb to mid-Dec Tues–Sun 10am–5pm, last entry 4pm • £6.70 • ☎ 01604 603407, ⓦ 78derngate.org.uk • The house is a 5–10min walk southeast of All Saints' church

**9**

In 1916–17, the Scottish architect **Charles Rennie Mackintosh** (1868–1928), the most celebrated proponent of Art Nouveau in the UK, played a key role in the remodelling of this Northampton house on behalf of two, well-heeled newly-weds, Florence and Wenman Bassett-Lowke. Since the Mackintosh redesign, **78 Derngate** has had a chequered history, but in recent years it has been painstakingly restored and now shows to fine effect many of Mackintosh's stylistic hallmarks, most notably the strong, almost stern, right angles that are set against the flowing lines of floral-influenced decorative motifs. The adjacent building, number 80, has been turned into a combined visitor centre, restaurant and exhibition space.

## ARRIVAL AND INFORMATION                                         NORTHAMPTON

**By train** Northampton train station is on the western edge of the city centre, a 10min walk from Market Square. Destinations Birmingham (every 30min; 1hr); London Euston (every 30min; 1hr).

**By bus** Buses pull into the new North Gate bus station in between Greyfriars and Bradshaw Street, a couple of minutes' walk from the Market Square.

Destinations Stoke Bruerne (every 2hr; 30min); Leicester (hourly; 2hr).

**Tourist office** In the former county courthouse across from All Saints on George Row (Mon–Fri 8am–5.30pm, plus April–Sept Sat 10am–2pm; ☎01604 367997, ⊛lovenorthampton.co.uk or ⊛visitnorthamptonshire .co.uk).

## EATING

**Sophia's** 54 Bridge St ☎01604 250654, ⊛sophias -restaurant.co.uk. This pleasantly turned-out restaurant, a short walk south of All Saints, has an excellent

Mediterranean menu with Italian dishes to the fore. Mains from as little as £12. Mon–Sat 5.30–10.30pm.

# Around Northampton

Within easy striking distance of Northampton are several pleasant attractions, including **Stoke Bruerne**, with its splendid set of canal locks, the postcard-pretty hamlet of **Ashby St Ledgers**, and the delightful village of **Fotheringhay**, where Mary, Queen of Scots was imprisoned and executed.

## Stoke Bruerne

Heading south out of Northampton on the A508, it's about eight miles to the village of **STOKE BRUERNE**, which sits beside a flight of seven locks on the Grand Union Canal. By water at least, the village is very close to England's second longest navigable tunnel, the one-and-three-quarter-miles-long **Blisworth Tunnel**, constructed at the beginning of the nineteenth century. Before the advent of steam tugs in the 1870s, boats were pushed through the tunnel by "legging" – two or more men would push with their legs against the tunnel walls until they emerged to hand over to waiting teams of horses.

To get out on the water, stroll over the canal bridge to the *Boat Inn* **pub**, jam-packed with narrowboat trinkets, where they operate **narrowboat cruises** to the tunnel (Easter–Sept most days; 30min; £3) as well as longer canal trips (call to book, as sailings don't take place every day; ☎01604 862428, ⊛boatinn.co.uk).

---

### THE NENE WAY

Northamptonshire has one notable long-distance footpath, **The Nene Way**, which follows the looping course of the river right across the county from Badby in the west to Wansford in the east, passing through Oundle and Fotheringhay on the way; beyond Wansford it continues east, following the river to its mouth at Sutton Bridge (see p.507) on the Lincolnshire coast, a total distance of 110 miles. For the most part it's easy, if sometimes muddy, going. Brochures are available from Northampton's tourist office or consult the Long Distance Walkers Association ⊛ldwa.org.uk.

### THE GUNPOWDER PLOT

Many of England's Catholics were delighted when the Protestant **Queen Elizabeth I** died in 1603, but when her successor, **James I** (1603–25), proved equally unsympathetic to their cause, a small group, under the leadership of a certain **Robert Catesby**, began to plot against the king. The conspirators met here at Ashby St Ledgers, where they hatched the simplest of plans: first they rented a cellar under Parliament and then they filled it with barrels of gunpowder – enough to blow Parliament sky high. The preparations were in the hands of **Guy Fawkes**, an ardent Catholic and experienced soldier, but the authorities discovered this so-called **Gunpowder Plot** on the eve of the attack, November 4, 1605, and the conspirators were soon rounded up and dispatched. It's quite possible that James's men knew of the plot long before November and allowed it to develop for political (anti-Catholic) reasons. Fawkes himself was tortured, tried and executed and he is still burnt in effigy across the UK on **Bonfire Night** (November 5).

## Stoke Bruerne Canal Museum

Bridge Road • April–Oct daily 10am–5pm; Nov–March Wed–Fri 11am–3pm, Sat & Sun 11am–4pm • £4.75 • ☎ 01604 862229, ⓦ stokebruernecanalmuseum.org.uk • Buses run from Northampton bus station to Bridge Road in Stoke Bruerne (every 2hr; 30min).

The exhausting task of "legging" (see opposite) is fully explained in the village's folksy **canal museum**, which is housed in a converted canalside corn mill. The museum delves into two hundred years of canal history with models, exhibits of canal art and spit-and-polish engines.

## Ashby St Ledgers

The **Gunpowder Plot** (see box above), which failed to blow the Houses of Parliament to smithereens in 1605, was hatched in **ASHBY ST LEDGERS**, immediately to the west of the M1 off the A361, about fourteen miles northwest of Northampton. Since those heated conversations, nothing much seems to have happened here and the village's one and only street, flanked by handsome limestone cottages and a patch of ancient grazing land, still leads to the conspiratorial **manor house** (no access), a beautiful Elizabethan complex set around a wide courtyard. Also of interest is the village church, **St Mary and St Leodegarius** (hence "Ledgers"; no fixed opening times), which holds some wonderful, if faded, medieval murals: the clearest is the large painting in the nave of St Christopher carrying the infant Jesus.

## Fotheringhay

Hard to believe today, but **FOTHERINGHAY**, a delightful hamlet nestling by the River Nene about thirty miles northeast of Northampton, was once an important centre of feudal power with both a weekly market and a castle. The castle was demolished long ago, but the magnificent **church of St Mary and All Saints**, rising mirage-like above the green riverine meadows, recalls Fotheringhay's medieval heyday.

### Fotheringhay Castle ruins

Signposted down a short and narrow lane on the bend of the road as you come into the village from Oundle • Open access • Free

Precious little remains of **Fotheringhay Castle**, but the fortress witnessed two key events – the birth of Richard III in 1452 and the beheading of Mary, Queen of Scots, in 1587. On the orders of Elizabeth I, Mary – who had been imprisoned for nearly twenty years – was beheaded in the castle's Great Hall with no one to stand in her support, apart, that is, from her dog, which is said to have rushed from beneath her skirts as her head hit the deck. Thereafter, the castle fell into disrepair and nowadays only a grassy mound and ditch remain to mark where it once stood.

**9**

### Church of St Mary and All Saints
Fotheringhay • Daily 9am–5pm, 4pm in winter • Free • ⓦ friends-of-fotheringhay-church.co.uk/

Begun in 1411 and 150 years in the making, Fotheringay's **church of St Mary and All Saints** is a paradigm of the Perpendicular, its exterior sporting wonderful arching buttresses, its nave lit by soaring windows and the whole caboodle topped by a splendid octagonal lantern tower. The interior is a tad bare, but there are two fancily carved medieval pieces to inspect – a painted pulpit and a sturdy stone font.

#### EATING AND DRINKING                                                    FOTHERINGHAY

**The Falcon** ⓣ 01832 226254, ⓦ thefalcon-inn.co.uk. This excellent pub-restaurant, which occupies a neat stone building with a modern patio, offers an imaginative menu – lamb shank and artichoke for example – with delicious main courses costing around £14. Food served: Mon–Sat noon–2pm & 6–9pm, Sun noon–3pm & 6–8.30pm.

# Lincoln

Reaching high into the sky from the top of a steep hill, the triple towers of **LINCOLN**'s mighty **cathedral** are visible for miles across the surrounding flatlands. The cathedral, along with the neighbouring **castle**, are the city's main tourist draws – although, for a smallish place, Lincoln also packs in several good places to eat and one outstanding hotel.

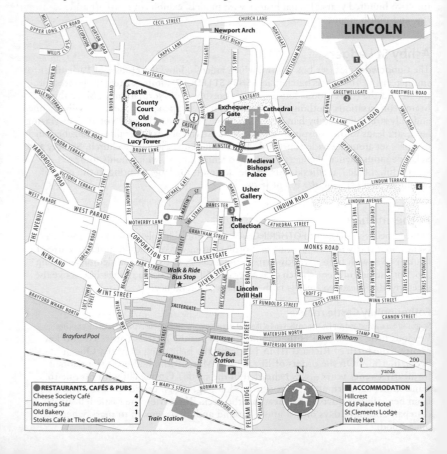

| ● RESTAURANTS, CAFÉS & PUBS | |
| --- | --- |
| Cheese Society Café | 4 |
| Morning Star | 2 |
| Old Bakery | 1 |
| Stokes Café at The Collection | 3 |

| ■ ACCOMMODATION | |
| --- | --- |
| Hillcrest | 4 |
| Old Palace Hotel | 3 |
| St Clements Lodge | 1 |
| White Hart | 2 |

Almost everything of interest is confined to the **Uphill** part of town, within easy walking distance of both castle and cathedral. In addition to the two major sights, this part of town also features a number of historic remains, notably several chunks of Roman wall, the most prominent of which is the second-century **Newport Arch** straddling Bailgate and once the main north gate into the city. There are also several well-preserved medieval stone houses, notably on and around the aptly named **Steep Hill** as it cuts down from the cathedral to the city centre.

The key sights can be seen in about half a day, though Lincoln does make for a pleasant overnight stop, particularly in December during its lively open-air **Christmas market**.

### Brief history

High ground is in short supply in Lincolnshire, so it's no surprise that the steep hill which is today surmounted by Lincoln Cathedral was fortified early, firstly by the **Celts**, who called their settlement Lindon, "hillfort by the lake", a reference to the pools formed by the River Witham in the marshy ground below. In 47 AD the **Romans** occupied Lindon and built a fortified town, which subsequently became **Lindum Colonia**, one of the four regional capitals of Roman Britain. During the reign of William the Conqueror the construction of the **castle** and **cathedral** initiated Lincoln's medieval heyday – the town boomed, first as a Norman power base and then as a centre of the wool trade with Flanders, until 1369 when the wool market was transferred to neighbouring Boston. It was almost five hundred years before Lincoln could revive, its recovery based upon the manufacture of agricultural machinery and drainage equipment for the neighbouring fenlands. As the nineteenth-century town spread south down the hill and out along the old Roman road – the Fosse Way – so Lincoln became a place of precise class distinctions: the **Uphill** area, spreading north from the cathedral, became synonymous with middle-class respectability, **Downhill** with the proletariat.

## Lincoln Cathedral

Minster Yard • July & Aug Mon–Fri 7.15am–8pm, Sat & Sun 7.15am–6pm; Sept–June Mon–Sat 7.15am–6pm, Sun 7.15am–5pm; access restricted during services • £6 including guided tour (see box below), free Sunday • ☎ 01522 561600, ⓦ lincolncathedral.com

Not a hill at all, **Castle Hill** is in fact a wide, short and level cobbled street that links Lincoln's castle and cathedral. It's a charming spot and its east end is marked by the arches of the medieval **Exchequergate**, beyond which soars the glorious west front of **Lincoln Cathedral**, a veritable cliff-face of blind arcading mobbed by decorative carving. The west front's apparent homogeneity is, however, deceptive, and further inspection reveals two phases of construction – the small stones and thick mortar of much of the facade belong to the original church, completed in 1092, whereas the longer stones and finer courses date from the early thirteenth century. These were enforced works: in 1185, an earthquake shattered much of the Norman church, which was then rebuilt under the auspices of **Bishop Hugh of Avalon**, the man responsible for most of the present cathedral, with the notable exception of the (largely) fourteenth-century central tower.

The cavernous **interior** is a fine example of Early English architecture, with the nave's pillars conforming to the same general design yet differing slightly, their varied columns and bands of dark Purbeck marble contrasting with the oolitic limestone that is the building's main material. Looking back up the nave from beneath the **central tower**, you

---

#### GUIDED TOURS OF LINCOLN CATHEDRAL

The cathedral offers two **guided tours**, both free with the price of admission. The first – the **Floor Tour** (Mon–Sat 2–3 daily) – is a quick trot around the cathedral's defining features, while the second, the **Roof Tour** (Mon–Sat 1–2 daily; 90min), takes in parts of the church otherwise out of bounds. Both are very popular, so it's a good idea to book in advance on ☎ 01522 561600.

9

can also observe a major medieval miscalculation: Bishop Hugh's roof is out of alignment with the earlier west front, and the point where they meet has all the wrong angles. It's possible to pick out other irregularities, too – the pillars have bases of different heights, and there are ten windows in the nave's north wall and nine in the south – but these are deliberate features, reflecting a medieval aversion to the vanity of symmetry.

Beyond the nave lies **St Hugh's Choir**, whose fourteenth-century misericords carry an eccentric range of carvings, with scenes from the life of Alexander the Great and King Arthur mixed up with biblical characters and folkloric parables. Further on is the open and airy **Angel Choir**, completed in 1280 and famous for the tiny, finely carved **Lincoln Imp** (see box, p.502), which embellishes one of its columns. Finally, a corridor off the choir's north aisle leads to the wooden-roofed **cloisters** and the polygonal **chapter house**, where Edward I and Edward II convened gatherings that pre-figured the creation of the English Parliament.

## Medieval Bishops' Palace

Minster Yard • April–Oct Wed–Sun 10am–5pm; Nov–March Sat & Sun 10am–4pm • £4.60; EH • ⓦ english-heritage.org.uk

Hidden behind a gated wall immediately to the south of the cathedral are the ruins of what would, in its day, have been the city's most impressive building. This, the **Medieval Bishop's Palace**, once consisted of two grand halls, a lavish chapel, kitchens and ritzy private chambers, but today the most coherent survivor is the battered and bruised **Alnwick Tower** – where the entrance is. The damage was done during the Civil War when a troop of Roundheads occupied the palace until they themselves had to evacuate the place after a fierce fire. Nonetheless, the ruins are suitably fetching, with wide views over the surrounding flatlands.

## Lincoln Castle

Castle Hill • Daily: April & Sept 10am–5pm; May–Aug 10am–6pm; Oct–March 10am–4pm • £2 • ☎ 01522 782040, ⓦ lincolnshire.gov.uk

From the west front of the cathedral, it's a quick stroll across Castle Hill to **Lincoln Castle**. Intact and forbidding, the castle walls incorporate bits and pieces from the twelfth to the nineteenth centuries with the wall walkway offering great views over town. The wall encloses a large central courtyard dotted around which are law courts, a new heritage skills centre and two former Victorian prisons, dour red-brick structures with one for debtors, the other, adjoining it to the rear, for felons. The former debtors' prison is currently being revamped to exhibit several rare documents, most notably one of the four surviving copies of the **Magna Carta**, all in time for the eight-hundred-year-anniversary of its signing – in 2015. Meanwhile, the old felons' prison contains a truly remarkable **prison chapel**. Here, the prisoners were locked in high-sided cubicles, where they could see the preacher and his pulpit but not their fellow inmates. This approach was not just applied to chapel visits: the prisoners were kept in perpetual solitary confinement, and were compelled to wear masks when they took to the exercise yard. This system was founded on the pseudo-scientific theory that defined crime as a contagious disease, but unfortunately for the theorists, their so-called Pentonville System of "Separation and Silence", which was introduced here in 1846, drove so many prisoners crazy that it had to be abandoned thirty years later; nobody ever bothered to dismantle the chapel.

## The Collection

Danes Terrace • Daily 10am–4pm • Free • ☎ 01522 782040, ⓦ thecollectionmuseum.com

Occupying two contrasting buildings – a striking modern structure and a really rather grand 1920s edifice close by – **The Collection** is Lincoln's prime museum. Pride of place in the more modern building is the city's extensive collection of archeological artefacts, from prehistoric times onwards; the older building, aka the **Usher Gallery**, focuses on temporary displays of fine art. The Usher's permanent collection includes an eclectic collection of coins, porcelain, watches and clocks. The timepieces were given to the gallery by its benefactor, James Ward Usher, a local jeweller and watchmaker who made a fortune on the back of the **Lincoln Imp** (see box, p.502).

## ARRIVAL AND INFORMATION — LINCOLN

From both the train and bus stations, it's a steep, 15min walk up to the cathedral, or you can take the Walk & Ride minibus (see below).

**By train** Lincoln train station is on St Mary's Street, right in the city centre.

Destinations Leicester (hourly; 2hr); Newark (hourly; 25min); Nottingham (hourly; 1hr); Peterborough (every 2hr; 1hr); Stamford (hourly; 2hr–2hr 30min, min of 1 change).

**By bus** The bus station is just north of the train station on Melville Street.

**Tourist office** 9 Castle Hill, between the cathedral and the castle (Mon–Sat April–Sept 10am–5pm & Sun 10.30am–4pm; Oct–March 11am–3pm; ⊕01522 545458, ⓦvisitlincoln.com). They have lots of local information and can book accommodation.

## GETTING AROUND

**By Walk & Ride minibus** Alights from St Mary's Street, near the train & bus stations, as well as from the designated bus stop on Silver Street, just off High Street, and from outside The Collection (Mon–Sat 9am–5pm; every 20min; £1.50 single fare, £3 all-day ticket).

## ACCOMMODATION

**Hillcrest** 15 Lindum Terrace ⊕01522 510182, ⓦhillcrest-hotel.com. Traditional, very English hotel in a large red-brick house that was originally a Victorian rectory. Sixteen comfortable rooms with all mod cons plus a large, sloping garden. About a 10min walk from the cathedral. **£95**

★**The Old Palace** Minster Yard ⊕01522 580000, ⓦtheoldpalace.org. Easily the best place to stay in Lincoln, this excellent hotel occupies the one-time bishop's palace, a rambling largely nineteenth-century mansion within earshot of the cathedral. The hotel has 32 rooms, half in the main building, including a tower suite, and the remainder in an immaculately reconfigured 1920s chapel. The hotel's grand drawing room is in the former library and much of the furniture has been made by local carpenters. Smashing views too. **£90**

**St Clements Lodge** 21 Langworthgate ⊕01522 521532, ⓦstclementslodge.co.uk. In a smart, modern house a short walk from the cathedral, this comfortable, very friendly B&B has three cosy, en-suite rooms. Home-made breakfasts too – try the haddock or the kippers. **£75**

**White Hart** Bailgate ⊕01522 526222, ⓦwhitehart-lincoln.co.uk. Antique former coaching inn, whose public rooms still have all sorts of hidden nooks and crannies despite a fairly humdrum modern revamp. The bedrooms are in a more traditional, country-house style and the pick overlook the cathedral. Curiously, it was here in an upstairs room during World War I that a local engineering firm set about designing the first 'tanks' at the behest of the government. To camouflage their intentions, the new behemoths were called water carriers – hence "tanks" – and the name stuck. **£95**

## EATING AND DRINKING

**Cheese Society Café** 1 St Martin's Lane ⊕01522 511003, ⓦthecheesesociety.co.uk. This bright and breezy little café has become something of a gastronomic landmark hereabouts, its tasty creations featuring all things cheesy, from rarebits, raclettes and baked halloumi dishes through to an especially delicious stilton, red wine and walnut pâté. There are non-cheesy options, too, including a good steak-frites, plus an excellent range of local beers and ciders. The owners run a specialist cheese shop nearby as well at 28 The Strait. Mon–Sat 10am–4.30pm.

**Morning Star** 11 Greetwellgate ⊕01522 527079, ⓦmorningstarlincoln.co.uk. Traditional and friendly locals' pub with a good range of ales. Bar food too. Located a couple of minutes' walk from the cathedral – if you want something livelier, head for the bars on Bailgate. Daily noon–2.30pm & 6–11pm.

**Old Bakery** 26 Burton Rd ⊕01522 576057, ⓦtheold-bakery.co.uk. Cosy, rural-chic, award-winning restaurant, where the menu is both well considered and inventive – try, for example, the grilled corn polenta and cherry tomatoes with Gorgonzola and green olive purée. Has an excellent cellar and prides itself on the quality of its cheeseboards too. Reservations recommended. Mains average £19. Tues–Sat noon–1.30pm & 6.30–9pm, Sun noon–1.30pm.

**Stokes Café at The Collection** Danesgate ⊕01522 523548, ⓦstokes-coffee.co.uk. Attached to Lincoln's principal museum, this cheerful modern café is a self–service affair where they do a tasty line in crepes,

> ## THE LINCOLN IMP
>
> The **Lincoln imp**, carved high on a column in Lincoln cathedral, had long been a source of legend, but it was the entrepreneurial James Ward Usher who turned the wee beastie into a tidy profit in the 1880s, selling Lincoln imp tie-pins, cuff-links, spoons, brooches and beads. Usher also popularized the traditional legend of the imp, a tall tale in which a couple of imps are blown to Lincoln by a playful wind. They then proceed to hop around the cathedral, until one of them is turned to stone for trying to talk to the angels carved into the roof of the Angel Choir. His chum makes a hasty exit on the back of a witch, but the wind is still supposed to haunt the cathedral, awaiting its opportunity to be mischievous again.

sandwiches and salads. They also have a line-up of special musical events, mainly jazz and classical. The owners, the Stokes family, have been roasting coffee and blending tea in Lincoln for several generations. Daily 10am–4pm.

### ENTERTAINMENT

**Lincoln Drill Hall** Free School Lane ☎ 01522 873891, ⓦ lincolndrillhall.com. Lincoln's prime arts and entertainment venue, featuring everything from stand-up and theatre to classical concerts, rock and pop.

# The Lincolnshire Wolds and the coast

Northeast and east of Lincoln, the Lincolnshire Wolds are a narrow band of chalky land whose rolling hills and gentle valleys are particularly appealing in the vicinity of **Louth**, a trim little place where conscientious objectors were sent to dig potatoes during World War II. South of Louth, the Wolds dip down to both **Woodhall Spa**, a one-time Victorian spa that served as the HQ of the Dambusters as they prepared for their celebrated Ruhr raid in 1943, and then the imposing remains of **Tattershall Castle**. East of the Wolds lies the coast, with its bungalows, campsites and caravans parked behind a sandy beach that extends, with a few marshy interruptions, north from **Skegness**, the main resort, to Mablethorpe and ultimately Cleethorpes. All this bucket-and-spade and amusement-arcade commercialism is not to everyone's taste, but small portions of the coast have been preserved and protected, most notably in the **Gibraltar Point Natural Nature Reserve** south of Skegness.

## Louth

Henry VIII didn't much care for Lincolnshire, describing it as "one of the most brutal and beestlie counties of the whole realm", his contempt based on the events of 1536, when thousands of northern peasants rebelled against his religious reforms. In Lincolnshire, this insurrection, the **Pilgrimage of Grace**, began in the northeast of the county at **LOUTH**, 25 miles from Lincoln, under the leadership of the local vicar, who was subsequently hanged, drawn and quartered for his pains. There's a commemorative **plaque** in honour of the rebels at the **church of St James** (Easter–Christmas Mon–Sat 10.30am–4pm; Christmas–Easter Mon, Wed, Fri & Sat 8am–noon; free), which is the town's one outstanding building, its soaring Perpendicular spire, buttresses, battlements and pinnacles set on a grassy knoll on the west side of the centre. The interior is delightful too, illuminated by slender windows and capped by a handsome Georgian timber roof decorated with dinky little angels. The roof of the tower vault is even finer, its intricate stonework an exercise in geometrical precision.

### ARRIVAL AND DEPARTURE
LOUTH

**By bus** Louth bus station is on the east side of the centre, a 5min walk from the Cornmarket at the east end of Queen St.

Destinations Lincoln (Mon–Sat 6 daily; 1hr); Skegness (hourly; 2hr).

**CLOCKWISE FROM TOP** ROBIN HOOD STATUE (P.482); PAUL SMITH FLAGSHIP STORE (P.479); GIBRALTAR POINT (P.505) >

**The Coffee Shop at St James's** St James's Church, Westgate ☎01507 603118. This modest, volunteer-run café has a few table and chairs inside the church, but the home-made cakes are delicious – locals set out early to get a slice of the lemon-drizzle. April to mid-Dec Mon–Sat 10.30am–4pm.

**Larders Coffee House** Little Butcher's Lane, off Mercer Row ☎01507 602888, ⓦbaristow.co.uk. In the centre of town, this cosy, family-run place does a good line in sandwiches, home-made cakes and freshly ground coffee. Mon–Sat 8am–4.30pm & Sun 10am–3pm.

## Woodhall Spa and around

Charming **WOODHALL SPA**, about twenty miles south of Louth, is an elongated village surrounded by a generous chunk of woodland. The village fans out from its main street, **The Broadway**, which is dotted with Victorian/Edwardian houses and shops, reminders of the time when the spring water of this isolated place, rich in iodine and bromine, was a popular tipple, though nowadays the village is kept afloat by its **golf course**, generally reckoned to be one of the best in England.

The tiny **Cottage Museum** (Easter–Oct daily 10.30am–4.30pm; £2; ☎01526 353775, ⓦcottagemuseum.co.uk), on Iddesleigh Road off The Broadway, outlines the development of Woodhall Spa and also has a section on the **Dambusters**, who were based at a nearby mansion, **Petwood**, on Stixwould Road, now a hotel (see below). The mansion was requisitioned by the RAF during World War II, and turned into the Officers' Mess of 617 Squadron, better known as the Dambusters, famous for their bombing raid of May 16, 1943. The raid was planned to deprive German industry of water and electricity by breaching several Ruhrland dams, a mission made possible by Barnes Wallis's famous bouncing bomb. The old **Officers' Bar** is kitted out with memorabilia from bits of aircraft engines to newspaper cuttings.

### Kinema in the Woods

Coronation Road • Tickets £6.50 • ☎01526 352166, ⓦthekinemainthewoods.co.uk

An unexpected delight, **Kinema in the Woods** is set deep in the forest, yet is only five minutes' walk from The Broadway – just follow the signs. Opened in 1922, the Kinema is one of England's few remaining picture houses where the film is projected from behind the screen, and at weekends a 1930s organ rises in front of the screen to play you through the ice-cream break. It's all very delightful – and very nostalgic too.

### Tattershall Castle

Sleaford Road, Tattershall • Mid-Feb to Oct daily 11am–5pm; Nov to mid-Dec Sat & Sun 11am–3pm • £5.70; NT • ☎01526 342543

From Woodhall Spa, it's about four miles southeast to **Tattershall Castle**, a massive, moated, red-brick keep that towers above the surrounding flatlands. There's been a castle here since Norman times, but it was Ralph Cromwell, the Lord High Treasurer, who built the present quadrangled tower in the 1440s. A veteran of Agincourt, Cromwell was familiar with contemporary French architecture and it was to France that he looked for his basic design – in England, keeps had been out of fashion since the thirteenth century. Cromwell's quest for style explains Tattershall's contradictions: the castle walls are sixteen feet thick, but there are lots of lower level windows and three doorways. In fact, it's a medieval keep as fashion accessory, a theatricality that continues with the grand chimneypieces inside the castle, though otherwise the interior is almost entirely bare.

**By bus** Most buses pull in either on or within easy walking distance of The Broadway.
Destinations Boston (Mon–Sat every 1–2hr; 1hr); Lincoln

(Mon–Sat every 1–2hr; 40min).
**Tourist office** Inside the Cottage Museum (same times; ☎01526 353775).

★**Petwood Hotel** Stixwould Road ☎01526 352411, ⓦpetwood.co.uk. The most appealing hotel hereabouts, set in immaculate gardens, *Petwood*'s handsome half-timbered gables shelter a fine panelled interior and fifty large, well-appointed bedrooms decorated in unfussy, modern style. The all-English breakfasts are excellent and so are the dinners with main courses from £14 and often featuring local, seasonal ingredients. **£125**

## Skegness and around

**SKEGNESS** has been a busy resort ever since the railways reached the Lincolnshire coast in 1875. Its heyday was pre-1960s, before the Brits began to take themselves off to sunnier climes, but it still attracts tens of thousands of city-dwellers who come for the wide, sandy beaches and for a host of attractions ranging from nightclubs to bowling greens. Every inch the traditional English seaside town, Skegness outdoes its rivals by keeping its beaches sparklingly clean and its parks spick-and-span. That said, the seafront, with its rows of souvenir shops and amusement arcades, can be dismal, especially on a rainy day, and you may well decide to sidestep the whole caboodle by heading south along the coastal road to the **Gibraltar Point National Nature Reserve**.

### Gibraltar Point National Nature Reserve

Gibraltar Rd, 3 miles south of Skegness • **Reserve** Daily dawn−dusk • Free, but parking from £1; Refreshments available April−Oct daily 10am−4pm; Nov−March Mon−Fri 11am−3pm, Sat & Sun 11am−4pm • ☎ 01754 898057, ⓦ lincstrust.org.uk/gibraltar-point

At the **Gibraltar Point National Nature Reserve**, a network of clearly signed footpaths patterns a narrow strip of salt- and freshwater marsh, sand dune and beach that attracts an inordinate number of birds, both resident and migratory. There are numerous hides dotted about, but at the time of writing the reserve's **Visitor Centre** is being repaired after extensive flood damage in late 2013; for now, refreshments are available in the car park.

### ARRIVAL AND INFORMATION                                             SKEGNESS

**By bus and train** Skegness bus and train stations are next door to each other, about 10min walk from the seashore – cut across Lumley Square and head straight up the main street to the landmark clocktower.
**Destinations by bus** Lincoln (Express bus Mon−Sat 4 daily; 1hr 20min).

**Destinations by train** Boston (hourly; 30min); Grantham (hourly; 1hr 30min); Nottingham (hourly; 2hr).
**Tourist office** By the seashore, a few yards from the clocktower on Grand Parade and in the Embassy Theatre (core hours Mon−Fri 9.30am−4pm; ☎ 0845 674 0505, ⓦ visitlincolnshire.com).

### ACCOMMODATION

**Best Western Vine Hotel** Vine Rd, Seacroft ☎ 01754 610611, ⓦ bw-vinehotel.co.uk. Skegness has scores of bargain-basement hotels, B&Bs and guesthouses, but this pleasant hotel is a cut above its rivals and has benefited from a recent upgrade. It occupies a rambling old house, which is partly clad in ivy, and the decor is resolutely modern. On a quiet residential street about three-quarters of a mile from the resort's main landmark, the clocktower, and on the road to Gibraltar Point. **£75**

# The Lincolnshire Fens

**The Fens**, that great chunk of eastern England extending from Boston in Lincolnshire right down to Cambridge, encompass some of the most productive farmland in Europe. Give or take the occasional hillock, this pancake-flat, treeless terrain has been painstakingly reclaimed from the marshes and swamps which once drained into the intrusive stump of **The Wash**, a process that has taken almost two thousand years. In earlier times, outsiders were often amazed by the dreadful conditions hereabouts, but they did spawn the distinctive culture of the so-called **fen-slodgers**, who embanked small portions of marsh to create pastureland and fields, supplementing their diets by catching fish and fowl and gathering reed and sedge for thatching and fuel. This local economy was threatened by the large-scale land reclamation schemes of the late fifteenth and sixteenth centuries, and time and again the fenlanders sabotaged progress

**9**

by breaking down new banks and dams. But the odds were stacked against the saboteurs, and a succession of great landowners eventually drained huge tracts of the fenland – and by the 1790s the fen slodgers' way of life had all but disappeared. Nonetheless, the **Lincolnshire Fens** remain a distinctive area, with a scattering of introverted little villages spread across the flatlands within easy striking distance of the A17. Several of these villages are distinguished by their imposing **medieval churches** – St Mary Magdalene's in **Gedney** and St Mary's in **Long Sutton** for example – and their soaring spires are seen to best advantage in the pale, watery sunlight and wide skies of the fenland evening. The most impressive church of all, however, looms above the area's largest town, the rough-edged old port of **Boston**, which, with a population of around sixty thousand, is Lincolnshire's second largest settlement.

## Boston

As it approaches The Wash, the muddy River Witham weaves its way through **BOSTON**, which is named after St Botolf, the Anglo-Saxon monk-saint who first established a monastery here in 645 AD. In the fourteenth century, Boston expanded to become England's second largest seaport, its flourishing economy dependent on the wool trade with Flanders. Local merchants, revelling in their success, built a church that demonstrated their wealth – the magnificent church of **St Botolph**, whose 272ft-tower still presides over the town and its environs. The church was completed in the early sixteenth century, but by then Boston was in decline. The town's fortunes only revived in the late eighteenth century when, after the nearby fens had been drained, it became a minor agricultural centre. A singular mix of fenland town and seaport, Boston is an unusual little place that is at its liveliest on **market days** – Wednesday and Saturday – when you'll hear lots of Polish voices: in recent years, Eastern Europeans have come here in their hundreds to work in food processing and agriculture.

### St Botolph's Church

Wormgate • Daily 8.30am–4.30pm; tower Mon–Sat 10am–3.30pm • Free; tower £3 • ☎ 01205 354670, ⓦ parish-of-boston.org.uk

The massive bulk of **St Botolph's** looms over the river, its exterior embellished by the high-pointed windows and elaborate tracery of the Decorated style. Most of the church dates from the fourteenth century, but the huge and distinctive tower, whose lack of a spire earned the church the nickname the "Boston Stump", is of later construction and the octagonal lantern is later still. A tortuous 365-step spiral **staircase** leads to a balcony near the top, from where the panoramic views over Boston and the fens amply repay both the price of the ticket and the effort of the climb. Down below, St Botolph's light and airy nave is an exercise in the Perpendicular, all soaring columns and high windows, a purity of design that is simply stunning. Look out also for the misericords in the chancel, which bear a lively mixture of vernacular scenes such as organ-playing bears, a pair of medieval jesters squeezing cats in imitation of bagpipes and a schoolmaster birching a boy, watched by three more awaiting the same fate. The church's most famous vicar was **John Cotton** (1584–1652), who helped stir the Puritan stew during his twenty-year tenure, encouraging a stream of Lincolnshire dissidents to head off to the colonies of New England to found their "New Jerusalem"; Cotton emigrated himself in 1633.

### The Guildhall

South St • Wed–Sat 10.30am–3.30pm • Free • ☎ 01205 365954, ⓦ www.bostonguildhall.co.uk

A creaky affair, the **Guildhall** incorporates a series of period rooms, including an antique Council Chamber, several old prison cells and the court room where, in 1607, several of the Pilgrim Fathers were (probably) tried and sentenced: they got 30 days for their failed attempt to escape religious persecution by slipping across to Holland. They may have been imprisoned here too – but no one is really sure. The Guildhall also exhibits a fascinating hotchpotch of historical artefacts, notably some ferocious anti-poacher traps and a copy of the *Book of Martyrs*, an inflammatory anti-Catholic text written by Boston's own John Foxe (1517–87).

**ARRIVAL AND INFORMATION** BOSTON

**By train** It's a 15min walk east from Boston train station to the town centre – head straight out of the station along Station Approach, turn left onto Sleaford Road at the end and then take a left down West Street at the first roundabout. Keep going and then turn left along Bridge Street for the river and the bridge over to the centre.
Destinations Grantham (hourly 50min); Skegness

(hourly; 30min).
**By bus** The bus station is also to the west of the river, just north of West Street on St George's Road and a 5min walk away from Market Place.
Destinations Lincoln (every 1–2hr; 1hr 45min).
**Tourist office** In the Guildhall, on South Street (Wed–Sat 10.30am–3.30pm; ☎01205 365954, ⊛ boston.gov.uk).

## Gedney

The A17 runs east across the Lincolnshire Fens from Sleaford to King's Lynn (see p.408). En route, it slips past the scattered hamlet of **GEDNEY**, where the massive tower of **St Mary Magdalene** (daily dawn–dusk; free) intercepts the fenland landscape. Seen from a distance, the church seems almost magical, or at least mystical, its imposing lines so much in contrast with its fen-flat surroundings. Close up, the three-aisled nave is beautiful, its battery of windows lighting the exquisite Renaissance alabaster effigies of Adlard and Cassandra Welby, who, in death, face each other on the south wall near the chancel.

## Long Sutton

There's more ecclesiastical excitement just a mile or two to the east of Gedney in **LONG SUTTON**, a modest farming centre that limps along the road until it reaches its trim Market Place. Here, the **church of St Mary** (daily dawn–dusk; free) has preserved many of its Norman features, with its arcaded tower supporting the oldest lead spire in the country, dating from around 1200. Look out also for the striking stained-glass windows. Long Sutton once lay on the edge of the five-mile-wide mouth of the **River Nene**, where it emptied into The Wash. This was the most treacherous part of the road from Lincoln to Norfolk, and locals had to guide travellers across the mud flats and marshes on horseback. In 1831, the River Nene was embanked and then spanned with a wooden bridge at **Sutton Bridge**, a hamlet just two miles east of Long Sutton – and a few miles from King's Lynn (see p.408). The present swing bridge, with its nifty central tower, was completed in 1894.

# Stamford

**STAMFORD**, in the southwest corner of Lincolnshire, is delightful, a handsome little limestone town of yellow-grey seventeenth- and eighteenth-century buildings edging narrow streets that slope up from the River Welland. The town's salad days were as a centre of the medieval wool and cloth trade, when wealthy merchants built its medley of stone churches and houses. Stamford was also the home of **William Cecil**, Elizabeth I's chief minister, who built his splendid mansion, **Burghley House**, close by.

The town survived the collapse of the wool trade, prospering as an inland port after the Welland was made navigable to the sea in 1570, and, in the eighteenth century, as a staging point on the Great North Road from London. More recently, Stamford escaped the three main threats to old English towns – the Industrial Revolution, wartime bombing and postwar development – and was designated the country's first

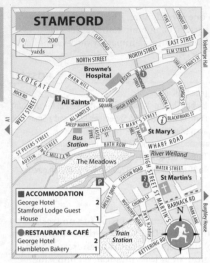

Conservation Area in 1967. Thanks to this, its unspoilt streets readily lend themselves to period drama and filmmaking, and although it's the harmony of Stamford's architecture that pleases, rather than any specific sight, there are still a handful of buildings of some special interest as well as an especially charming **High Street**.

## Church of St Mary

St Mary's St • No regular opening hours • Free

A convenient place to start an exploration of Stamford is the **Church of St Mary**, sitting pretty just above the main bridge on St Mary's Street. The church has a splendid spire and a small but airy interior, which incorporates the **Corpus Christi** (or north) chapel whose intricately embossed, painted and panelled ceiling dates from the 1480s.

## Browne's Hospital

Broad St • Late May–Sept Mon–Sat 11am–4pm, Sun 2–4.30pm • £3 • ⓦ stamfordcivicsociety.org.uk

A short stroll north of St Mary's, wide and handsome Broad Street is home to **Browne's Hospital**, the most extensive of the town's almshouses, dating from the late fifteenth century. Not all of the complex is open to the public, but it's still worth visiting with the first room – the old dormitory – capped by a splendid wood-panelled ceiling. The adjacent chapel holds some delightfully folksy misericords and then it's upstairs for the audit room, which is illuminated by a handsome set of stained-glass windows.

## Church of All Saints

All Saints' Place • Daily dawn–dusk • Free • ☏ 01780 756942, ⓦ stamfordallsaints.org.uk

Entry to the **Church of All Saints**, a stone's throw from Browne's Hospital, is via the south porch, an ornate structure with a fine – if badly weathered – crocketted gable. Inside, much of the interior is routinely Victorian, but the carved capitals are of great delicacy and there's also an engaging folkloric carving of the Last Supper behind the high altar.

## High Street St Martin's

Down the slope from St Mary's, across the reedy River Welland on **High Street St Martin's**, is *The George Hotel* (see p.509), a splendid old coaching inn whose Georgian facade supports one end of the gallows that span the street – not a warning to criminals, but a traditional advertising hoarding.

### Church of St Martin

23 High St St Martin's • Daily 9.30am–4pm • Free

The sombre, late fifteenth-century **Church of St Martin** shelters the magnificent tombs of the lords Burghley, beginning with a recumbent William Cecil (1520–1598) carved beneath twin canopies, holding his rod of office and with a lion at his feet. Immediately behind are the early eighteenth-century effigies of John Cecil and his wife, with the couple depicted as Roman aristocrats, propped up on their elbows, she to gaze at him, John to stare across the nave commandingly.

**9**

## SHAKESPEARE IN THE PARK

One of the most enjoyable of Stamford's several festivals is the **Stamford Shakespeare Company**'s (☎01780 756133, ⓦstamfordshakespeare.co.uk) open-air performances of the great man's works set in the grounds of **Tolethorpe Hall**, an Elizabethan mansion just outside Stamford. The season lasts from June to August with the audience protected from the elements by a vast canopy.

# Burghley House

Barnack Rd • House & gardens: mid-March to late Oct Sat–Thurs 11am–5pm • £13 • ☎01780 752451, ⓦburghley.co.uk. The main entrance is located about mile and a half southeast of Stamford – just follow the signs

Now famous for the prestigious Burghley Horse Trials (ⓦburghley-horse.co.uk), held over four days in late August and/or early September, Stamford's **Burghley House** is an extravagant Elizabethan mansion standing in parkland landscaped by Capability Brown. Completed in 1587 after 22 years' work, the house sports a mellow yellow ragstone exterior, embellished by dainty cupolas, a pyramidal clocktower and skeletal balustrading, all to a plan by **William Cecil**, the long-serving adviser to Elizabeth I. However, with the notable exception of the Tudor kitchen, little remains of Burghley's Elizabethan interior and, instead, the house bears the heavy hand of John, fifth Lord Burghley, who toured France and Italy in the late seventeenth century, buying paintings and commissioning furniture, statuary and tapestries. To provide a suitable setting for his old masters, John brought in Antonio Verrio and his assistant Louis Laguerre, who between them covered many of Burghley's walls and ceilings with frolicking gods and goddesses. These gaudy and gargantuan murals are at their most engulfing in the **Heaven Room**, an artfully painted classical temple that adjoins the **Hell Staircase**, where the entrance to the inferno is through the gaping mouth of a cat.

## ARRIVAL AND INFORMATION                                   STAMFORD

**By train** Stamford train station is on the south side of the River Welland, a 5- to 10min walk from the town centre.
Destinations Cambridge (hourly; 1hr 10min); Leicester (hourly; 40min); Oakham (hourly; 15min).
**By bus** The bus station is in the town centre, on

Sheepmarket, off All Saints' Street.
**Tourist office** Right in the centre of town, in the Stamford Arts Centre, 27 St Mary's Street (Mon–Sat 9.30am–5pm; Nov–March Mon–Sat 9.30am–5pm; ☎01780 755611, ⓦsouthwestlincs.com).

## ACCOMMODATION

★**The George Hotel** 71 High St St Martin's ☎01780 750750, ⓦgeorgehotelofstamford.com. Stamford's most celebrated hotel by a mile, *The George* is a sympathetically renovated old coaching inn, which comes complete with flagstone floors and antique furnishings; the most appealing of the plush rooms overlook a cobbled courtyard. There's a good restaurant, too (see below). **£165**

**Stamford Lodge Guest House** 66 Scotgate ☎01780 482932, ⓦstamfordlodge.co.uk. In an attractive, Georgian stone house on the north side of the town centre, this smartly turned-out establishment has five, en-suite guest rooms decorated in a warm and cosy version of period style. **£85**

## EATING

**The George Hotel** 71 High St St Martin's ☎01780 750750, ⓦgeorgehotelofstamford.com. The food at this excellent hotel (see above) is as classy as the rooms. There are several eating areas, but perhaps the best is the moderately priced and informal *Garden Room* where the emphasis is on British ingredients served in imaginative ways. Main courses here average around £18; you'll pay less

if you eat in the hotel's delightfully antiquated *York Bar*. Garden Room daily noon–10.30pm.
**Hambleton Bakery** 1 Ironmonger St ☎01780 754327, ⓦhambletonbakery.co.uk. If you're after a sandwich, this is the best spot in town, selling a wide range of freshly baked breads with a suitably wide selection of fillings. Mon–Sat 8.30am–5pm.

# The Northwest

SUNSET ACROSS MORECAMBE BAY

# The Northwest

Ask most Brits about northwest England and they'll probably mention football and rain. Beyond the stereotypes, however, this is one of the most exciting corners of the country, its dynamic urban centres, pretty countryside, iconic seaside resorts and historic towns offering considerable appeal. One of the world's great industrial cities, Manchester has transformed its cityscape in recent decades to place itself firmly in the vanguard of modern British urban design, and complements its top-class visitor attractions with lively cafés and an exciting music scene. Just thirty miles west, revitalized Liverpool has kept apace of the "northern renaissance", too, and is a city of great energy and charm.

The southern suburbs of Manchester bump into the steep hills of the **Pennine range**, and to the southwest the city slides into pastoral **Cheshire**, a county of rolling green countryside whose dairy farms churn out the famed crumbly white cheese. The county town, **Chester**, with its complete circuit of town walls and partly Tudor centre, is as alluring as any of the country's northern towns, capturing the essence of one of England's wealthiest counties.

The historical county of **Lancashire** reached industrial prominence in the nineteenth century primarily due to the cotton-mill towns around Manchester and the thriving port of Liverpool. Today, neither city is part of the county, but along the coast to the west and north of the major cities stretches a line of **resorts** – from Southport to **Morecambe** – which once formed the mainstay of the northern British holiday. Only **Blackpool** is really worth visiting for its own sake, a rip-roaring resort which has stayed at the top of its game by supplying undemanding entertainment with more panache than its neighbours. For anything more culturally invigorating you'll have to continue north to the historically important city of **Lancaster**, with its Tudor castle. Finally, the Crown Dependency of the **Isle of Man**, just 25 miles off the coast, provides a rugged terrain almost as rewarding as that of the Lake District, but without the seasonal overcrowding.

## GETTING AROUND
## THE NORTHWEST

**By train** Both Manchester and Liverpool are well served by trains, with regular high-speed connections to the Midlands and London, and up the west coast to Scotland. The major east–west rail lines in the region are the direct routes between Manchester, Leeds and York, and between Blackpool, Bradford, Leeds and York. The Lancaster–Leeds line slips through the Yorkshire Dales and further south, the Manchester–Sheffield line provides a rail approach to the Peak District.

**By bus** The major cities, as well as Chester, are connected by frequent bus services.

GIANT SPECTACULAR, LIVERPOOL

# Highlights

**❶ People's History Museum** Manchester's national museum tells the story behind the forces that have shaped human history and the modern world. **See p.518**

**❷ Manchester's Northern Quarter** Lose yourself in chic shops, café-bars and happening music venues in this vibrant warehouse district. **See p.520**

**❸ City walls, Chester** The handsome old town of Chester is best surveyed from the heights of its Roman walls. **See p.529**

**❹ Culture in Liverpool** From the artistic hub of the Baltic Triangle to Antony Gormley's Crosby Beach statues, this dynamic city pulses with creative energy. **See p.531**

**❺ Blackpool Pleasure Beach** Bright, bawdy and brash, Britain's cheekiest resort is constantly reinventing itself. **See p.541**

**❻ Lancaster Castle** From the dungeons to the ornate courtrooms, the castle is a historical tour-de-force. **See p.544**

**❼ Sunset across Morecambe Bay** Drink in one of the country's finest sunsets at the bar in the Art Deco *Midland Hotel*. **See p.546**

**❽ Sea-kayaking, the Calf of Man** Taking to the water in a kayak allows you to view local seal colonies, seabirds, and the Isle of Man's stunning rugged coast from a unique perspective. **See p.551**

**HIGHLIGHTS ARE MARKED ON THE MAP ON P.514**

# Manchester

**MANCHESTER** has had a global profile for more than 150 years, since the dawn of the industrial revolution. But today's elegant core of converted warehouses and glass skyscrapers is a far cry from the smoke-covered sprawl George Orwell once described as "the belly and guts of the nation". Its renewed pre-eminence expresses itself in various ways, most swaggeringly in its **football**, as home to the world's most famous and

**HIGHLIGHTS**

1. People's History Museum
2. Manchester's Northern Quarter
3. City walls, Chester
4. Culture in Liverpool
5. Blackpool Pleasure Beach
6. Lancaster Castle
7. Sunset across Morecambe Bay
8. Sea-kayaking, the Calf of Man

**THE NORTHWEST**

## MANCHESTER ORIENTATION

If Manchester can be said to have a centre, it's **Albert Square** and the cluster of buildings surrounding it – the Town Hall, the Central Library and the *Midland Hotel*, originally built in the railway age to host visitors to Britain's greatest industrial city. South of here, the former Central Station now functions as the **Manchester Central** convention centre, with the Hallé Orchestra's home, **Bridgewater Hall**, just opposite. **Chinatown** and the **Gay Village** are just a short walk to the east, while to the northeast, the revamped **Piccadilly Gardens** provides access to the hip **Northern Quarter**. To the southwest is the **Castlefield** district, site of the **Museum of Science and Industry**, and flashy **Spinningfields**, incongruous home of the People's History Museum. The central spine of the city is **Deansgate**, which runs from Castlefield to the cathedral and, in its northern environs, displays the most dramatic core of urban regeneration in the country, centred on the unalloyed modernity of **Exchange Square**.

wealthiest clubs – Manchester United and Manchester City, respectively – but also in a thriving **music scene** that has given birth to world-beaters as diverse as the Hallé Orchestra and Oasis. Moreover, the city's celebrated concert halls, theatres, clubs and cafés feed off the cosmopolitan drive provided by the country's largest **student** population outside London and a high-profile **gay** community.

There are plenty of sights, too: the centre possesses the **Manchester Art Gallery**, the **National Football Museum** and the fantastic **People's History Museum** as well as the **Museum of Science and Industry**, while further out, to the west, the revamped **Salford Quays** are home to the prestigious **Lowry arts centre**, complete with a handsome selection of L.S. Lowry paintings, the stirring and stunning **Imperial War Museum North**, and **MediaCityUK**, the new northern base of the BBC.

### Brief history

Despite a **history** stretching back to Roman times, and pockets of surviving medieval and Georgian architecture, Manchester is first and foremost a **Victorian manufacturing city**. Its rapid growth set the pace for the flowering of the Industrial Revolution elsewhere – transforming itself in just a hundred years from little more than a village to the world's major cotton centre. The spectacular rise of **Cottonopolis**, as it became known, arose from the manufacture of vast quantities of competitively priced imitations of expensive Indian calicoes, using water and then steam-driven machines developed in the late eighteenth and nineteenth centuries. This rapid industrialization brought immense wealth for a few but a life of misery for the majority. The discontent came to a head in 1819 when eleven people were killed at **Peterloo**, in what began as a peaceful demonstration against the oppressive **Corn Laws**. Things were, however, even worse when the 23-year-old Friedrich Engels came here in 1842 to work in his father's cotton plant: the grinding poverty he recorded in his *Condition of the Working Class in England* was a seminal influence on his later collaboration with **Karl Marx** in the *Communist Manifesto*.

The **Manchester Ship Canal**, constructed in 1894 to entice ocean-going vessels into Manchester and away from burgeoning Liverpool, played a crucial part in sustaining Manchester's competitiveness. From the late 1950s, however, the docks, mills, warehouses and canals were in dangerous decline. The main engine of change turned out to be the devastating **IRA bomb**, which exploded outside the Arndale shopping centre in June 1996, wiping out a fair slice of the city's commercial infrastructure. Rather than simply patching things up, the city council embarked on an ambitious rebuilding scheme, which transformed the face of the city forever.

## Albert Square

Most of Manchester's panoply of **neo-Gothic** buildings and monuments date from the city's heyday in the second half of the nineteenth century. One of the more fanciful is the

10

| ● RESTAURANTS | | ● CAFÉS & CAFÉ BARS | | ■ PUBS & BARS | | ■ CLUBS & LIVE MUSIC | |
|---|---|---|---|---|---|---|---|
| Australasia | 7 | Eighth Day | 15 | Big Hands | 16 | Albert Hall | 7 |
| Damson | 10 | Home Sweet | | Britons Protection | 12 | Band on the Wall | 1 |
| Dimitri's | 14 | Home | 1 | Circus Tavern | 8 | The Castle Hotel | 3 |
| I Am Pho | 8 | The Koffee Pot | 4 | Cloud 23 | 10 | The Deaf Institute | 15 |
| Lime Tree | 17 | Odd | 3 | Corbières | 5 | Manchester | |
| Little Yang Sing | 9 | Richmond Tea | | Mr Thomas' Chop | | Academy | 17 |
| Punjab Tandoori | 16 | Rooms | 13 | House | 6 | Matt and Phreds | 2 |
| Sam's Chop | | Takk | 6 | Sand Bar | 14 | O2 Apollo | 18 |
| House | 5 | Trof NQ | 2 | The Temple | 11 | The Ritz | 13 |
| Yang Sing | 12 | | | | | Soup Kitchen | 4 |
| Yuzu | 11 | | | | | Warehouse Project | 9 |

shrine-like, canopied **monument** to Prince Albert, Queen Victoria's husband, perched prettily in the middle of the trim little square that bears his name – **Albert Square**. The monument was erected in 1867, six years after Albert's death, supposedly because the prince had always shown an interest in industry, but perhaps more to curry favour with the grieving queen. Overlooking the prince is Alfred Waterhouse's magnificent, neo-Gothic **Town Hall** (Mon–Fri 9am–5pm; free), whose mighty clocktower, completed in 1877, pokes a sturdy finger into the sky, soaring high above its gables, columns and arcaded windows.

## St Peter's Square and around

Just south of the Town Hall is **St Peter's Square**, home to the newly reopened **Central Library** and undergoing further redevelopment. Footsteps away, over on Peter Street, the **Free Trade Hall** was the home of the city's Hallé Orchestra for more than a century – until Bridgewater Hall was completed in 1996. The Italianate facade survived intense wartime bombing and is now a protected part of the *Radisson Blu Edwardian Hotel*, whose modern tower block rises up behind at a (fairly) discreet distance.

## Central Library

St Peter's Square • Mon–Thurs 9am–8pm, Fri & Sat 9am–5pm • Free • ☎ 0161 234 1983, ⓦ manchester.gov.uk/centrallibrary • St Peter's Square Metrolink

The circular **Central Library** was built in 1934 as the world's largest municipal library, a self-consciously elegant, classical construction. After a four-year closure, it reopened, beautifully refurbished and extended, in 2014, with its showpiece domed **reading room** restored; check out the display case of sweet wrappers, found stuffed down the desks here over the last eighty years. The **children's library** is modelled on *The Secret Garden* by local author Frances Hodgson Burnett.

**10**

## Manchester Art Gallery

Mosley St • Daily 10am–5pm, till 9pm Thurs • Free • ☎ 0161 235 8888, ⓦ manchestergalleries.org • St Peter's Square Metrolink

**Manchester Art Gallery**, as well as attracting big-name exhibitions by contemporary artists, holds an invigorating collection of eighteenth- and nineteenth-century art. Spread across **Floor 1**, these works are divided by theme – Face and Place, Expressing Passions and so on – rather than by artist (or indeed school of artists), which makes it difficult to appreciate the strength of the collection, especially when it comes to its forte, the Pre-Raphaelites. There's much else – views of Victorian Manchester, a Turner or two, a pair of Gainsboroughs, and Stubbs' famous *Cheetah and Stag with Two Indians* to name but a few. **Floor 2** features temporary exhibitions and crafts, while the **Ground Floor**'s Manchester Gallery is devoted to a visual history of the city. The **Clore Art Studio** is fun for kids.

# Deansgate Locks and around

South of St Peter's Square, on **Lower Mosley Street**, stands Britain's finest concert hall, **Bridgewater Hall**, balanced on shock-absorbing springs to guarantee the clarity of the sound. The apartment block at the corner of Lower Mosley Street and Whitworth Street West bears the name of the site's previous occupant, the infamous **Hacienda Club**, the spiritual home of Factory Records, an independent label that defined a generation of music through such bands as Joy Division, New Order and the Happy Mondays before closing down in 1997.

Turn right along Whitworth Street West and you'll spot the string of café-bars and restaurants that have been shoehorned along the Rochdale canal's **Deansgate Locks**, a pattern repeated along and across the street in the old railway arches abutting Deansgate Station. Look up and you'll see the striking **Beetham Tower**, easily the tallest skyscraper in Manchester and home to a glitzy hotel.

# Castlefield

Just west of Deansgate Station, the tangle of railway viaducts and canals that lie sandwiched between Water Street, Liverpool Road and Deansgate make up pocket-sized **Castlefield**. It was here that the country's first man-made canal, the Bridgewater Canal, brought coal and other raw materials to the city's warehouses throughout the eighteenth century. By the early 1960s, the district was an eyesore, but an influx of money cleaned it up, and it now boasts cobbled canalside walks, attractive café-bars and the **Castlefield Urban Heritage Park** (always open; free), centred on an excavated and partially reconstructed Roman fort.

## MOSI: The Museum of Science and Industry

Liverpool Rd • Daily 10am–5pm • Free, but admission charge for special exhibitions • ☎ 0161 832 2244, ⓦ mosi.org.uk • Deansgate Metrolink

One of the most impressive museums of its type in the country, the **Museum of Science and Industry** mixes technological displays and blockbuster exhibitions with trenchant analysis of the social impact of industrialization. Key points of interest include the

**10**

**Power Hall**, which trumpets the region's remarkable technological contribution to the Industrial Revolution by means of a hall full of steam engines, some of which are fired up daily. There's more steam in the shape of a working replica of Robert Stephenson's *Planet*, whose original design was based on the *Rocket*, the work of Robert's father George. Built in 1830, the *Planet* reliably attained a scorching 30mph but had no brakes; the museum's version does, however, and it's used at weekends (noon–4pm; £2, children £1), dropping passengers a couple of hundred yards away at the **Station Building**, the world's oldest passenger railway station. On a rainy September 15, 1830, this was the final stop of the *Rocket*'s infamous inaugural passenger journey from Liverpool, when Liverpool MP William Huskisson was struck and fatally injured.

The **1830 Warehouse** features a sound-and-light show that delves into the history of the city's immense warehouses, and the **Air and Space Hall**, which barely touches on Manchester at all, features vintage planes, cutaway engines and space exploration displays.

## Spinningfields

From the old to the über-new, Castlefield blends into **Spinningfields**, a glitzy, corporate district that's home to law courts, financial HQs, designer shops and a crop of see-and-be-seen bars and restaurants, with one standout attraction incongruously perched on its edge.

### People's History Museum

Left Bank • Daily 10am–5pm • Free • ☎ 0161 838 9190, ⓦ phm.org.uk • Deansgate Metrolink

The superb **People's History Museum** explores Britain's rich history of radicalism and the struggles of marginalized people to acquire rights and extend suffrage – ideas that developed out of the workers' associations and religious movements of the industrial city and which helped to shape the modern world. Housed in a former pump house and an ultramodern, four-storey extension, the galleries use interactive displays – including coffins and top hats – to trace a compelling narrative from the Peterloo Massacre of 1819 onwards. As the gallery shows, this moment became the catalyst for agitation that led to the 1832 Reform Act, and subsequent rise of the egalitarian Chartist movement. The galleries go on to explore the struggle for female suffrage, the Communist party in Britain, Oswald Mosley's fascists, and the working-class origins of football and pop music, and include the finest collection of trade union banners in the country.

## Deansgate and around

**Deansgate** cuts through the city centre from the Rochdale canal to the cathedral, its architectural reference points ranging from Victorian industrialism to post-millennium posturing. One landmark is the **Great Northern** mall, flanking Deansgate between Great Bridgewater and Peter streets. This was once the **Great Northern Railway Company's Goods Warehouse**, a great sweep of brickwork dating back to the 1890s, originally an integral part of a large and ambitious trading depot with road and rail links on street level and subterranean canals down below.

### John Rylands Library

Deansgate • **Library** Mon & Sun noon–5pm, Tues–Sat 10am–5pm **Tour and treasures** Rare books can be seen close up every third Thurs of month 3–4pm (booking required) • Free • ☎ 0161 306 0555, ⓦ library.manchester.ac.uk/rylands • Deansgate Metrolink

Nestling between Spinningfields and the north end of Deansgate, **John Rylands Library** is the city's supreme example of Victorian Gothic – notwithstanding the presence of an unbecoming modern entrance wing. The architect who won the original commission, Basil Champneys, opted for a cloistered neo-Gothicism of narrow stone corridors, delicately crafted stonework, stained-glass windows and burnished wooden panelling. The library, which has survived in superb condition, now houses specialist collections of rare books and manuscripts.

### St Ann's Square

Slender **St Ann's Square** is tucked away off the eastern side of Deansgate, a couple of blocks up from the Rylands Library. Flanking the square's southern side is **St Ann's Church** (Tues–Sat 10am–5pm; free), a trim sandstone structure whose Neoclassical symmetries date from 1709, though the stained-glass windows are firmly Victorian. At the other end of the square is the **Royal Exchange**, which houses the much-lauded **Royal Exchange Theatre**. Formerly the Cotton Exchange, this building employed seven thousand people until trading finished on December 31, 1968 – the old trading board still shows the last day's prices for American and Egyptian cotton.

**10**

### Exchange Square

A pedestrian high street – **New Cathedral Street** – runs north from St Ann's Square to **Exchange Square**, with its water features, public sculptures and massive department stores (primarily Selfridges and Harvey Nichols). On the southeast side of the square stands the whopping **Arndale Centre**, once a real Sixties eyesore, but now a modern shopping precinct, clad in glass.

## Manchester Cathedral and around

Exchange Station Approach, Victoria St • Mon–Sat 8.30am–6.30pm, Sun 8.30am–7pm • Guided tours Mon–Fri 11am & 2.30pm, Sat 1pm, Sun 2.30pm • Free • ⓦ manchestercathedral.org • Victoria Metrolink

Manchester's **Cathedral** dates back to the fifteenth century, though its Gothic lines have been hacked about too much to have any real architectural coherence. Actually, it's surprising it's still here at all: in 1940, a 1000lb bomb all but destroyed the interior, knocking out most of the stained glass, which is why it's so light inside today.

### Chetham's School of Music

Long Millgate • Library Mon–Fri 9am–12.30pm & 1.30–4.30pm • Free • ⓣ 0161 834 7961, ⓦ chethams.org.uk • Victoria Metrolink

The choristers in Manchester cathedral are trained at **Chetham's School of Music**. This fifteenth-century manor house became a school and a free public library in 1653 and was turned into a music school in 1969. There are free recitals during term time and, although there's no public access to most of the complex, you can visit the oak-panelled **Library** with its handsome carved eighteenth-century bookcases. Along the side corridor is the main **Reading Room**, where Marx and Engels beavered away on the square table that still stands in the windowed alcove.

### National Football Museum

Urbis Building, Cathedral Gardens • Mon–Sat 10am–5pm, Sun 11am–5pm • Free except for special exhibitions • ⓣ 0161 605 8200, ⓦ nationalfootballmuseum.com • Victoria Metrolink

Manchester's **National Football Museum**, housed in a suitably spectacular structure – the sloping, six-storey glass Urbis building near Victoria train station – houses some true treasures of the world's most popular game. Here you can see the 1966 World Cup Final ball, Maradona's "Hand of God" shirt, and the only surviving version of the Jules Rimet world cup trophy. They also display the personal collection of Sir Stanley Matthews (1915–2000), considered one of the greatest English footballers of all time.

## Piccadilly Gardens

Off Portland St and Oldham St • Piccadilly Gardens Metrolink

**Piccadilly Gardens,** historically the largest green space in the city, was relandscaped in 2002 as a family-friendly space with shady trees, a fountain and water jets, and a pavilion at one end to screen off the traffic. The 200ft **Wheel of Manchester** (Mon–Thurs 10am–9pm, Fri 10am–11pm, Sat 9am–11pm, Sun 9am–8pm; £7) offers far-reaching views. Regular events, including weekend food **markets**, keep the gardens lively.

## The Northern Quarter

**Oldham Street**, which shoots off northeast from Piccadilly Gardens, is the shabby gateway to the hip **Northern Quarter.** Traditionally, this is Manchester's garment district and you'll still find old-fashioned shops and wholesalers selling clothes, shop fittings, mannequins and hosiery alongside the more recent designer shops, music stores and trendy café-bars. The side wall of iconic indie emporium Afflecks (see p.527) sports a colourful series of **mosaics** depicting Manchester legends – from Morrissey to Danger Mouse.

**10**

## Chinatown

From Piccadilly Gardens, it's a short walk south to **Chinatown**, whose grid of narrow streets stretch north–south from Charlotte to Princess Street between Portland and Mosley streets, with the inevitable **Dragon Arch**, at Faulkner and Nicolas, providing the focus for the annual Chinese New Year celebrations.

## Along Oxford Road

A couple of blocks out of the Gay Village, you'll come to the junction of Whitworth Street and **Oxford Road**, the latter cutting a direct route south through a string of impressive Manchester University buildings and served by an endless stream of **buses**.

### Cornerhouse

Junction of Oxford Rd and Whitworth St • ☎ 0161 200 1500, ⓦ cornerhouse.org • St Peter's Square Metrolink

One block west of the Gay Village, **Cornerhouse** is the dynamo of the Manchester arts scene. In addition to screening art-house films, it has three floors of gallery space, along with a popular café and bar (see p.526). It's due to close in spring 2015, when it will become incorporated into the major new HOME arts centre (see box opposite).

### The Manchester Museum

Oxford Rd • Daily 10am–5pm • Free • ☎ 0161 275 2648, ⓦ museum.manchester.ac.uk

The university's Gothic Revival **Manchester Museum** boasts a diverse collection spread over five floors, with displays on rocks, minerals and prehistoric life, meteorites, animal life, the human body and biomedical research. It also boasts one of the country's finest collections on **Ancient Egypt** outside of the British Museum. The redeveloped **Vivarium** is dedicated to the conservation of reptiles and amphibians, with plenty of frogs, snakes and lizards to handle.

### The Whitworth Art Gallery

Corner of Oxford Rd and Denmark Rd • See website for new opening times • Free • ☎ 0161 275 7450, ⓦ whitworth.manchester.ac.uk

The university's **Whitworth Art Gallery** was, at time of writing, closed for a £15 million renovation to double and extend its public space into the surrounding Whitworth Park. Alongside its fine collection of pre-1880s and modern art, the gallery contains

---

### MANCHESTER'S GAY VILLAGE AND GAY PRIDE

The side roads off Portland Street lead down to the Rochdale canal, where **Canal Street** forms the heart of Manchester's thriving **Gay Village**: the pink pound has filled this area of the city with canalside cafés, clubs, bars and businesses, though these days it's as busy with hooting hen-nighters as with lesbian and gay punters. Always lively, the village is packed to bursting point during Manchester's huge **Gay Pride** festival (ⓦ manchesterpride.com), which usually occurs on the last weekend of August. The village is closed off as thousands of revellers descend for music – big-name performers have included Beth Ditto and Boy George – comedy, theatre and exhibitions, all celebrating lesbian, gay, bi and transgendered sexuality (weekend tickets £22, day tickets £12.50; book online).

> **A PLACE TO CALL HOME**
>
> Due to open in 2015 on the First Street North site, just behind Whitworth Street West and roughly opposite the old Hacienda apartments (see p.517), **HOME** will be Manchester's new cultural hub, a merger between Manchester heavyweights Cornerhouse (see opposite) and the former Library Theatre Company. It will comprise two theatres, five cinema screens, gallery space, production and broadcast facilities, a kitchen and more. Keep up to date on ⓦ homemcr.org.

the country's widest range of textiles outside London's Victoria and Albert Museum. It's due to reopen in October 2015.

**10**

# Salford Quays

After the Manchester Ship Canal opened in 1894, **Salford docks** played a pivotal role in turning the city into one of Britain's busiest seaports. Following their closure in 1982, which left a post-industrial mess just a couple of miles to the west of the city centre, an extraordinarily ambitious redevelopment transformed **Salford Quays**, as it was rebranded, into a hugely popular waterfront complex with its own gleaming apartment blocks, shopping mall and arts centre, **The Lowry**. Also here is the splendid **Imperial War Museum North** and the glitzy new **MediaCityUK** site.

### The Lowry

Pier 8, Salford Quays • **Galleries** Mon–Fri & Sun 11am–5pm, Sat 10am–5pm • Free • ☎ 0843 208 6000, ⓦ thelowry.com • Harbour City Metrolink

Perched on the water's edge, **The Lowry** is the quays' shiny steel arts centre. The **Galleries**, which host sixteen different exhibitions each year, are largely devoted to the paintings of **Lawrence Stephen Lowry** (1887–1976), the artist most closely associated with Salford. The earlier paintings – those somewhat desolate, melancholic portrayals of Manchester mill workers – are the most familiar, while later works, repeating earlier paintings but changing the greys and sullen browns for lively reds and pinks, can come as a surprise.

### Imperial War Museum North

The Quays, Trafford Wharf North • Daily 10am–5pm • Free • ☎ 0161 836 4000, ⓦ iwm.org.uk • Harbour City Metrolink

A footbridge across the Manchester Ship Canal links The Lowry with the startling **Imperial War Museum North**, which raises a giant steel fin into the air, in a building designed by the architect Daniel Libeskind. The interior is just as striking, its angular lines serving as a dramatic backdrop to the displays, which kick off with the Big Picture, when the walls of the main hall are transformed into giant screens to show regularly rotated, fifteen-minute, surround-sound films. Superb themed displays fill six separate exhibition areas – the "Silos" – focusing on everything from women's work in the World Wars to the 9/11 attacks (with a 23ft section of crumpled steel recovered from the World Trade Center wreckage).

### MediaCityUK

BBC Tours • 90min tours Mon, Tues & Wed 10.30am, 12.30pm & 3pm (also Thurs & Fri in school holidays), Sat & Sun times vary • £10, children £6.50 • Book in advance on ⓦ bbc.co.uk/showsandtours • MediaCityUK Metrolink

In 2011, the BBC moved 26 of its London-based departments up north to **MediaCityUK**, a vast, purpose-built workspace for creative and digital businesses. ITV followed suit in 2013, the *Coronation Street* set arrived in 2014, and the whole place has a certain pizzazz, with telly types buzzing about on Segway scooters and the BBC offering insanely popular though mildly underwhelming **tours** (the highpoint of which is the sound studio and its semi-anechoic chamber). You don't have to join a tour, though, to wander around the piazza and visit the **Blue Peter garden**, transplanted here from London complete with Shep's paw print. The site is gradually finding its feet as an after-hours destination too.

# The National Cycling Centre

Stuart St, 2 miles east of the city centre ☎ 0161 223 2244 option 3, ⓦ nationalcyclingcentre.com • Daily 7.30am–10pm • Track taster sessions £12 (£9 concessions); BMX starter sessions from £7 (£5 concessions) • From Piccadilly Gardens (Stop D) take bus #216 to Sport City; or Velopark Metrolink

Opposite Man City's football ground (see box opposite), the **National Cycling Centre** is the home of British Cycling and one of the fastest and busiest velodromes in the world. Its stunning, Olympic-standard loop of Siberian pine track, angled at 42.5°, is in constant use, with hour-long taster sessions (bikes and coach provided) available to anyone aged 9 and over; arrive early and you might well catch the end of a Team GB training session. Also on site is a thrilling, international-standard indoor **BMX track** and the start of 7.5miles of **mountain bike** trails. Elsewhere in the city, the centre's facilities include an outdoor BMX track and a mountain-bike skills zone.

## ARRIVAL AND DEPARTURE        MANCHESTER

**By plane** Manchester Airport (☎0161 489 3000, ⓦ manchesterairport.co.uk) is 10 miles south of the city centre. There's an excellent train service to Manchester Piccadilly (£4.10 single); the taxi fare is around £25; by the time you read this, there should be a Metrolink service (ⓦ metrolink.co.uk) into the city.

**By train** Of Manchester's three stations, Piccadilly, on the east side of the centre, sees the largest number of long-distance services, some of which continue on to Oxford Road, just south of the centre. On the city's north side, Victoria Station mainly sees services to Lancashire and Yorkshire. All three stations are connected to the centre via the free Metroshuttle bus service (see below); Piccadilly and Victoria are also on the Metrolink tram line (see below).

Destinations from Manchester Piccadilly Barrow-in-Furness (Mon–Sat 7 daily, Sun 3 daily; 2hr 15min); Birmingham (hourly; 1hr 30min); Blackpool (hourly; 1hr 10min); Buxton (hourly; 1hr); Carlisle (8 daily; 1hr 50min); Chester (every 30min; 1hr–1hr 20min); Lancaster (hourly; 1hr); Leeds (hourly; 1hr); Liverpool (every 30min; 50min); London (hourly; 2hr 20min); Newcastle (10 daily; 3hr); Oxenholme (4–6 daily; 40min–1hr 10min); Sheffield (hourly;

1hr); York (every 30min; 1hr 30min).

Destinations from Manchester Oxford Road Blackpool (hourly; 1hr 15min); Carlisle (8 daily; 1hr 50min); Chester (hourly; 1hr); Lancaster (8 daily; 1hr); Leeds (10 daily; 1hr); Liverpool (every 30min; 50min); Oxenholme (8 daily; 1hr 10min); Penrith (8 daily; 1hr 40min); Sheffield (hourly; 1hr); York (hourly; 1hr 30min).

Destinations from Manchester Victoria Blackpool (6 daily; 1hr 30min); Leeds (every 30min; 1hr 20min); Liverpool (10 daily; 1hr).

**By bus** Most long-distance buses use Chorlton Street Coach Station, about half-way between Piccadilly train station and Albert Square, though some regional buses also leave from Shudehill Interchange, between the Arndale Centre and the Northern Quarter.

Destinations Birmingham (6 daily; 3hr); Blackpool (5 daily; 1hr 40min); Chester (3 daily; 1hr); Leeds (6 daily; 2hr); Liverpool (hourly; 40min); London (every 1–2hr; 4hr 30min–6hr 45min); Newcastle (6 daily; 5hr); Sheffield (4 daily; 2hr 40min).

**Travel information** For information on train and bus services, contact TFGM (☎0871 200 2233, ⓦ tfgm.com).

## GETTING AROUND

**On foot** About a 30min walk from top to bottom, central Manchester is compact enough to cover on foot.

**By bus** Three free Metroshuttle bus services (ⓦ tfgm.com) weave across the centre of town, linking the city's train stations and NCP car parks with all the major points of interest; Metroshuttle #1 runs Mon–Fri every 6min 7am–6pm then every 10min until 7pm, Sat every 6min 8am–7pm, Sun & public hols every 10min 10am–6pm; Metroshuttle #2 runs every 10min Mon–Fri 7am–7pm, Sat 8am–7pm, Sun & public hols 10am–6pm; Metroshuttle #3 runs every 10min Mon–Fri 7am–7pm, Sat 8am–7pm, no

service Sun & public hols.

**By taxi** Mantax (☎0161 230 3333) and Streetcars (☎0161 228 7878) are two reliable taxi firms.

**By tram** Metrolink trams (ⓦ metrolink.co.uk) whisk through the city centre bound for the suburbs, along an ever-expanding network of routes. Services run from approximately 6am–12.30am (Mon–Thurs), with last trams running later on Fridays and Saturdays, and Sunday services between around 7am–10.30pm. Ticket machines are on the platform; single journeys cost from £1.20, while day and weekend Travelcards (from £5 off-peak) are good value.

## INFORMATION AND TOURS

**Tourist information** Manchester Visitor Centre, 45–50 Piccadilly Plaza, on the corner of Portland Street (Mon–Sat 9.30am–5.30pm, Sun 10.30am–4.30pm; ☎0871 222 8223,

ⓦ visitmanchester.com); it does a useful blog on Fridays.

**Listings information** In print, Thursday's *City Life* supplement in the *Manchester Evening News*

## MANCHESTER FOOTBALL TOURS

Manchester is, of course, home to two mega Premier League football teams. It's tough to get tickets for matches if you're not a season-ticket holder, but **guided tours** placate out-of-town fans who want to gawp at the silverware and sit in the dug-out. You'll need to book in advance.

**Old Trafford** Sir Matt Busby Way, off Warwick Rd ✆ 0161 868 8000, ⓦ manutd.com; Old Trafford Metrolink. The self-styled "Theatre of Dreams" is the home of Manchester United, arguably the most famous football team in the world. Stadium tours include a visit to the club museum. Tours daily (except match days) 9.40am–6pm; £18, children £12.

**Etihad Stadium** Sport City, off Alan Turing Way ✆ 0161 444 1894, ⓦ mcfc.co.uk; Etihad Campus Metrolink. United's formerly long-suffering local rivals, Manchester City, became the world's richest club in 2008 after being bought by the royal family of Abu Dhabi. They play at the Etihad Stadium, east of the city centre. Tours daily 9am–5pm; £15, children £10.

**10**

(ⓦ manchestereveningnews.co.uk) covers popular events, while *The Skinny*, widely available in the Northern Quarter, is a hip and independent monthly freebie. Online, there's intelligent and incisive guidance on ⓦ creativetourist.com,

while ⓦ manchesterconfidential.com has informative restaurant reviews.

**Walking tours** The visitor centre has details of the city's many walking tours (from £7).

## ACCOMMODATION

There are many city-centre **hotels**, especially budget chains, which means you have a good chance of finding a smart, albeit formulaic, en-suite room in central Manchester for around £60–70 at almost any time of the year – except when City or United are playing at home. Less expensive **guesthouses** and **B&Bs** are concentrated some way out of the centre, mainly on the southern routes into the city. Prices often halve midweek.

### HOTELS

**ABode** 107 Piccadilly ✆ 0161 247 7744, ⓦ abode manchester.co.uk; Piccadilly Gardens Metrolink. Part of a small chain of boutique hotels, this gem occupies a former cotton warehouse a stone's throw from Piccadilly Station. Rooms are light and elegant, with high ceilings and polished wooden floors. **£210**

**Arora** 18–24 Princess St ✆ 0161 236 8999, ⓦ manchester.arorahotels.com; Piccadilly Gardens/St Peter's Square Metrolink. Four-star with more than 100 neat, modern rooms in a listed building in a great central location opposite the Manchester Art Gallery. The convivial, obliging staff pride themselves on offering a "real Manchester welcome". Good online discounts. **£99**

**Castlefield** Liverpool Rd ✆ 0161 832 7073, ⓦ castlefield-hotel.co.uk; Deansgate-Castlefield Metrolink. Large, modern, red-brick, warehouse-style hotel handily located opposite MOSI, with nicely appointed rooms, a gym and a pool (free to guests). **£110**

★ **Great John Street** Great John St ✆ 0161 831 3211, ⓦ eclectichotels.co.uk/great-john-street; Deansgate-Castlefield Metrolink. Deluxe hotel in an imaginatively refurbished old school building not far from Deansgate, with thirty individual, spacious and comfortable suites, some split-level. The on-site bar-cum-restaurant has an open fire and deep sofas, with a gallery breakfast room up above. Nice rooftop garden, too. **£240**

**Midland** Peter St ✆ 0161 236 3333, ⓦ qhotels.co.uk; St Peter's Square Metrolink. Once the terminus hotel for

the old Central Station – and where Mr Rolls first met Mr Royce – this building was the apotheosis of Edwardian style and is still arguably Manchester's most iconic hotel. The public areas today are returned to their former glory, with bedrooms in immaculate chain style. *Mr Cooper's House and Garden*, attached to the hotel, is wonderful for pre-theatre cocktails. Discounted rates if booked online. **£250**

**Radisson Blu Edwardian** Peter St ✆ 0161 835 9929, ⓦ radissonblu-edwardian.com; St Peter's Square Metrolink. The Neoclassical facade is all that's left of the Free Trade Hall; inside, this five-star hotel has a sleek modern interior full of natural light, tasteful rooms, and all the extras you'd expect – spa, gym and the trendy *Opus One* bar. **£120**

### HOSTELS

**Hilton Chambers** 15 Hilton St ✆ 0161 236 4414 ⓦ hattersgroup.com/Hilton; Piccadilly Gardens Metrolink. Part of a small chain operating in the northwest, this newish hostel is right in the heart of the Northern Quarter, and a great location for exploring the city's nightlife. A range of different rooms (room rates reduce considerably midweek) and some great communal spaces, including an outdoor deck. Dorms **£21**, doubles **£82**

**YHA Manchester** Potato Wharf, Castlefield ✆ 0845 371 9647, ⓦ yha.org.uk; Deansgate-Castlefield Metrolink. Excellent hostel overlooking the canal that runs close to the Museum of Science and Industry, with 35 rooms (thirty four-bunk, two five-bunk and three doubles). Facilities include laundry, self-catering and a café. Dorms **£20**, doubles **£40**

## EATING

Rivalling London in the breadth and scope of its **cafés** and **restaurants**, Manchester has something to suit everyone. Most options are in the city centre, but the **Rusholme** district, a couple of miles south, boasts the widest and best selection of Asian restaurants along its "Curry Mile". From Rusholme it's another couple of miles along Wilmslow Road to **Didsbury**, a leafy suburb with several excellent places to eat.

### CAFÉS AND CAFÉ-BARS

**Eighth Day** 107–111 Oxford Rd ☎0161 273 1850, ⊛8thday.coop; Metroshuttle #2. Manchester's oldest organic vegetarian café has a shop, takeaway and juice bar upstairs, with a great-value café/restaurant downstairs. Mon–Fri 9am–7pm, Sat 10am–5pm.

**Home Sweet Home** 49–51 Edge St, Northern Quarter ☎0161 224 9424, ⊛homesweethomenq.com; Shudehill Metrolink. Queues snake round the block for this gem, with huge portions of American/Tex Mex-influenced mains (from £8), luscious milkshakes and generous slices of the most extravagantly decorated cakes you will ever have seen. Mon–Thurs 9am–10pm, Fri & Sat 9am–11pm, Sun 9am–9pm.

**The Koffee Pot** 21 Hilton St, Northern Quarter ⊛thekoffeepot.co.uk; Shudehill Metrolink. Beloved by hungover hipsters, this is *the* place for a Full English (£5.80) or Veggie (£5.60) brekkie (served until 2pm) amid much Formica and red leatherette. Often packed. Mon–Fri 7.30am-onwards, Sat 9am–onwards, Sun 10am–onwards.

**Odd** 30–32 Thomas St, Northern Quarter ☎0161 833 0070, ⊛oddbar.co.uk; Shudehill Metrolink. Oozes Manchester's cosmopolitan pride in kitsch surroundings. Menus in LP sleeves list great food following the quirky theme – the NYPD (New York Pastrami Doorstep; £6.95), for instance – and there's a fab vegan breakfast (£6.75). DJ nights most weekends, and a three-page drinks menu. Mon–Wed & Sun 11am–midnight, Thurs 11am–1am, Fri & Sat 11am–1.30am.

**★ Richmond Tea Rooms** Richmond St, Gay Village ☎0161 237 9667, ⊛richmondtearooms.com; Metroshuttle #1. Without question the most brilliantly conceived tearoom in Manchester, with an amazing Tim Burton-esque *Alice in Wonderland* theme. The sumptuous afternoon teas (£6.50–23.50) are the stuff of local legend, while the adjoining cocktail lounge is a super-stylish place to kick off an evening. Mon–Thurs 11am–10pm, Fri 11am–11pm, Sat 10am–11pm, Sun 10am–10pm.

**Takk** 6 Tariff St, Northern Quarter ⊛takkmcr.com; Shudehill Metrolink. Cool yet cosy Icelandic coffee bar with a living-room feel, home-made cakes, a changing roster of sandwiches (£4), Nordic art and, of course, superior coffee – try the Red Eye (£2.60) if you never want to sleep again. Mon–Fri 8.30am–5pm, Sat 10am–6pm, Sun 11am–5pm.

**Trof NQ** 8 Thomas St, Northern Quarter ☎0161 833 3197, ⊛trofnq.co.uk; Shudehill Metrolink. Three storeys of cool, relaxed café-bar populated by trendy young things. It's ideal for a late breakfast or early afternoon drink, and hosts open-mic nights, poetry readings and DJ sets. Mon & Tues 10am–midnight, Wed & Thurs 10am–1am, Fri 10am–3am, Sat 9am–3am, Sun 9am–midnight.

### RESTAURANTS

**Australasia** 1 The Ave, Spinningfields ☎0161 831 0288, ⊛australasia.uk.com; Metroshuttle #1 or #2. A remarkable glass pyramid on street level leads down under (get it?) to Australasia, a buzzing, white-tiled restaurant that's arguably the star of the Spinningfield dining scene. Food is Modern Oz meets Pacific Rim and pricey but well regarded (mains from £15, with the Australian Wagyu steak fillet a whopping £60). Daily noon–midnight.

**Damson** Orange Building, MediaCityUK ☎0161 751 7020, ⊛damsonrestaurant.co.uk; MediaCityUK Metrolink. The first independent restaurant in TV Land, with well-cooked dishes such as roasted loin of cod and lamb rump served in an elegant dining room with great views over the piazza. Mains average £20, but there's a well-priced set menu at lunchtime and early evening (two courses £16.95, three £19.95). Mon–Thurs noon–2.45pm & 5–9.30pm, Fri & Sat noon–2.45pm & 5–10pm, Sun noon–5.30pm.

**★ Dimitri's** 1 Campfield Arcade, Deansgate ☎0161 839 3319, ⊛dimitris.co.uk; Metroshuttle #1 or #2. Long-established Manchester favourite: pick and mix from the Greek/Spanish/Italian menu (particularly good for vegetarians) and enjoy it at a semi-alfresco arcade table with a Greek coffee or Lebanese wine; you'll think you're in the Med. Mon–Thurs & Sun 11am–midnight, Fri & Sat 11am–2am.

**I Am Pho** 44 George St ☎0161 236 1230; St Peter's Square Metrolink. Very cheap, very good Vietnamese in Chinatown serving big bowls of *pho* (noodle soup); try the raw beef one, in which the meat cooks in the broth. Mon–Thurs noon–10pm, Fri & Sat noon–11pm.

**★ Lime Tree** 8 Lapwing Lane, West Didsbury ☎0161 445 1217, ⊛thelimetreerestaurant.co.uk; West Didsbury Metrolink. The finest local food, with a menu that chargrills and oven-roasts as if its life depended on it, using produce from its own smallholding. Main courses cost £14 and up, less at lunchtime. Reservations recommended. Mon & Sat 5.30–10pm, Tues–Fri noon–2.30pm & 5.30–10pm, Sun noon–8pm.

**Punjab Tandoori** 177 Wilmslow Rd, Rusholme ☎0161 225 2960. Despite the name, this is the only distinctively southern Indian – as opposed to Pakistani – restaurant on Rusholme's "Curry Mile" strip. The special *dosa* starters are great, and prices very reasonable – a full meal should cost no more than £15. A local favourite without pretensions. Daily 3pm–late.

★**Sam's Chop House** Chapel Walks, off Cross St ☎0161 834 3210, ⓦsamschophouse.co.uk; Market St Metrolink. The restaurant attached to this wonderful old-world pub is a hidden gem. It has a Victorian gas-lit feel and a delightful menu of English food (mains £14–16) – and they really know their wine, too. Mon–Sat noon–3pm & 5.30–11pm, Sun noon–8pm.

★**Yang Sing** 34 Princess St ☎0161 236 2200, ⓦyang-sing.com; St Peter's Square Metrolink. One of the best Cantonese restaurants in the country, with authentic dishes ranging from a quick fried noodle plate to the full works. For the most interesting food, stray from the printed menu; ask the friendly staff for advice. Sister restaurant, the *Little Yang Sing* on George St, slightly cheaper, is also worth stopping by. Mains from £12. Mon–Sat noon–11.30pm, Sun noon–10.30pm.

★**Yuzu** 39 Faulkner St, Chinatown ☎0161 236 4159, ⓦyuzumanchester.co.uk; St Peter's Square Metrolink. Outstanding Japanese in Chinatown with a shortish menu of exceptionally executed sashimi (from £10.50), tempura (from £5.90) dishes and more, plus a tempting range of sake. Tues–Sat noon–2pm & 5.30–10pm.

## DRINKING, NIGHTLIFE AND ENTERTAINMENT

From Victorian boozers to designer cocktail bars, Manchester does **drinking** in style, while its musical heritage and whopping student population keep things lively and interesting. There's an excellent **live music** scene, of course, and a mercurial roster of **clubs**; note too that many of the city's hip **café-bars** (see opposite) host regular club nights. See print and online listings (see p.522) for information. The bi-annual artist-led **Manchester International Festival** (ⓦmif .co.uk; next taking place in 2015) has included upwards of twenty world premieres of shows by names such as Damon Albarn and Björk, while the city hosted the inaugural **6 Music Festival** in 2014. As for **classical music**, the city is blessed with the North's most highly prized **orchestra**, the Hallé, which is resident at Bridgewater Hall. Other acclaimed names include the **BBC Philharmonic** and the **Manchester Camerata** chamber orchestra (ⓦmanchestercamerata.com), who perform at a variety of venues. A range of mainstream and fringe **theatres** produce a lively, year-round programme.

### PUBS AND BARS

★**Big Hands** 296 Oxford Rd ☎0161 272 7779. Right by the Academy venues, this intimate, über-cool bar is popular with students, usually post-gig as it has a late licence. Mon–Fri 10am–2am, Sat noon–3am, Sun 6pm–1am.

**Britons Protection** 50 Great Bridgewater St ☎0161 236 5895, ⓦbritons-protection.com. Cosy old pub with a couple of small rooms, a backyard beer garden and all sorts of Victorian detail – most splendidly the tiles and the open fires in winter. Boasts over 300 whiskies and a large mural depicting the Peterloo Massacre. Mon–Thurs 11am–11.30pm, Fri noon–12.30am, Sat 11am–midnight, Sun noon–11pm.

**Circus Tavern** 86 Portland St ☎0161 236 5818. Manchester's smallest pub, this Victorian drinking hole is a favourite city-centre pit-stop. You may have to knock to get in; when you do, you're confronted by the landlord in the corridor pulling pints. Daily 11am–11pm.

**Cloud 23** Beetham Tower, 301 Deansgate ☎0161 870 1670, ⓦcloud23bar.com. Manchester's highest and most popular cocktail bar, with a 23rd-floor glass overhang. Expensive, but worth it for the view of the city and Pennines beyond. Mon–Thurs & Sun 11am–1am, Fri & Sat 11am–2am.

**Corbières** 2 Half Moon St, just off St Ann's Square ☎0161 834 3381. Look for the Gaudí-esque wall art flanking the door of this longstanding subterranean, slightly dank drinking cellar with arguably the best jukebox in Manchester. Mon–Thurs 11am–11pm, Fri & Sat 11am–midnight, Sun 2–10.30pm.

★**Mr Thomas' Chop House** 52 Cross St ☎0161 832 2245, ⓦtomschophouse.com. Victorian classic with Dickensian nooks and crannies. Office workers, daytime drinkers, old goats and students all call it home, and there's good-value, traditional food too. Mon–Thurs 11am–11pm, Fri & Sat 11am–midnight, Sun noon–10.30pm.

**Sand Bar** 120 Grosvenor St ☎0161 273 1552, ⓦwww .sandbarmanchester.co.uk. Between the university and the city centre, this is a brilliant modern take on the traditional pub, where students, lecturers and workers shoot the breeze. There's a great selection of beers and wines. Mon–Wed & Sun noon–midnight, Thurs noon–1am, Fri & Sat noon–2am.

**The Temple** 100 Great Bridgewater St ☎0161 228 9834. Teeny-tiny subterranean boozer in an old public toilet, with an amazing jukebox and bags of atmosphere, if not much elbow room. It's run by the same people as *Big Hands* (see above) and shares its nonchalant, fun-time vibe. Mon–Thurs & Sun noon–midnight, Fri & Sat noon–1am.

> ## TOP 5 FOR MUSIC
> **Cavern Club** Liverpool. See p.540
> **The Deaf Institute** Manchester. See p.526
> **Liverpool Philharmonic** Liverpool. See p.540
> **Matt and Phreds** Manchester. See p.526
> **Warehouse Project** Manchester. See p.526

**10**

## CLUBS AND LIVE MUSIC

**Albert Hall** 27 Peter St ☎0844 858 8521, ⓦalberthall manchester.com. Former Wesleyan chapel that's now an atmospheric live-music venue hosting a select programme of high-quality, slightly leftfield artists. Hours vary.

★**Band on the Wall** 25 Swan St, Northern Quarter ☎0161 834 1786, ⓦbandonthewall.org. This legendary Northern Quarter joint remains true to its commitment to "real music": it's one of the city's best venues to see live bands – from world and folk to jazz and reggae – and it hosts club nights to boot. Box office Mon–Sat 5–9pm. Mon–Thurs 9am–1am, Fri & Sat 9am–3am, Sun noon–5pm.

★**The Castle Hotel** 66 Oldham St, Northern Quarter ☎0161 237 9485, ⓦthecastlehotel.info. Genuinely good 200-year-old pub with cask and craft ales and an extremely intimate backroom gig space. Jake Bugg played to just seventy-odd people here months before hitting the big time. Hosts regular spoken word nights too. Mon–Thurs noon–1am, Fri noon–2am, Sun noon–midnight.

★**The Deaf Institute** 135 Grosvenor St ☎0161 276 9350 ⓦthedeafinstitute.co.uk. A mile down Oxford Rd, this bar and music hall sits in a funky makeover of the elegant Victorian former deaf institute. Mostly folk, indie and r'n'b, with lots of up-and-coming talent, and a raft of great club nights. Sister venue *Gorilla* (ⓦthisisgorilla.com) on Whitworth Street is also excellent. Mon–Thurs & Sun 10am–midnight, Fri & Sat 10am–3am.

**Manchester Academy** Oxford Rd ☎0161 275 2930, ⓦmanchesteracademy.net. All three locations – Academy 1 is on the university campus, opposite the medical school; Academy 2 & 3 are inside the Students' Union building on Oxford Road – are popular student venues featuring new and established bands. Hours vary.

**Matt and Phreds** 64 Tib St, Northern Quarter ☎0161 831 7002, ⓦmattandphreds.com. The city's finest jazz bar, offering everything from swing to gritty New Orleans blues. Mon–Thurs & Sat 6pm–late, Fri 5pm–late.

**O2 Apollo Manchester** Stockport Rd, Ardwick Green ☎0844 477 7667, ⓦalive.co.uk/O2apollomanchester .co.uk. Medium-sized theatre auditorium for all kinds of concerts; a brilliant place to see big names up close, with bags of atmosphere. Hours vary.

★**The Ritz** Whitworth St West ☎0161 236 3234, ⓦmamacolive.com/theritz. This legendary dancehall has been around for decades (it's where The Smiths first played) and has a sprung dancefloor that really boings when things get going. Jumping live music and plenty of fun club nights, including a roller disco. Hours vary.

**Soup Kitchen** 31–33 Spear St, Northern Quarter ☎0161 236 5100, ⓦsoup-kitchen.co.uk. Soup-specializing canteen

with a basement club/live-music venue that's among Manchester's finest. Mon–Wed & Sun noon–11pm, Thurs noon–1am, Fri & Sat noon–4pm.

★**Warehouse Project** Underneath Piccadilly Station ⓦthewarehouseproject.com. An internationally acclaimed three-month season of the country's best dance and house acts – 2manydjs, Annie Mac, La Roux – smashing out sessions in a warehouse below the station. Tickets (£25) are like gold dust, so book well in advance. Oct–Dec Fri & Sat.

## CLASSICAL MUSIC

**Bridgewater Hall** Lower Mosley St ☎0844 907 9000, ⓦbridgewater-hall.co.uk. Home of the Hallé Orchestra, the BBC Philharmonic and the Manchester Camerata; also a full programme of chamber, pop, classical and jazz concerts.

**Royal Northern College of Music (RNCM)** 124 Oxford Rd ☎0161 907 5200, ⓦrncm.ac.uk; Metroshuttle #2. Top-quality classical and modern jazz concerts.

## THEATRE, CINEMA AND DANCE

★**Cornerhouse** 70 Oxford St ☎0161 200 1500, ⓦcornerhouse.org; St Peter's Square Metrolink. Engaging centre for contemporary arts, with three cinema screens, changing art exhibitions, recitals and talks, plus a bookshop, café and bar. Will close and be incorporated into HOME (see box, p.521) in Spring 2015.

**Dancehouse Theatre** 10 Oxford Rd ☎0161 237 9753, ⓦthedancehouse.co.uk; Metroshuttle #2. Home to the Northern Ballet School and the eponymous theatre troupe; venue for dance, drama and comedy.

**The Lowry** Pier 8, Salford Quays ☎0843 208 6000, ⓦthelowry.com; Harbour City Metrolink. This quayside venue hosts many of the biggest shows, including major National Theatre touring productions, most recently *War Horse*.

**Opera House** 3 Quay St ☎0844 871 3018, ⓦmanchesteroperahouse.org.uk; Deansgate-Castlefield Metrolink. Major venue for touring West End musicals, drama, comedy and concerts.

**Royal Exchange Theatre** St Ann's Square ☎0161 833 9833, ⓦroyalexchange.co.uk; Market St Metrolink. The theatre-in-the-round in the Royal Exchange is the most famous stage in the city, with a Studio Theatre (for works by new writers) alongside.

**Screenfields** The Lawns, Spinningfields ⓦspinning fieldsonline.com/events/screenfields. Seasonal screenings (most Thursdays May–Sept; 7pm) of feel-good summer movies for £3, with deckchairs to rent for a little extra. Enjoyable alfresco viewing and you can bring a picnic (no booze or glass bottles).

## SHOPPING

Aside from the high-end boutiques on **King Street**, and the **department stores** around Market Street and Exchange Square, the Northern Quarter has a plethora of smaller independent stores catering for all tastes. If you're around between mid-November and the week before Christmas, make for the **German Christmas Market**, which sees Albert Square transformed into a Bavarian picture postcard.

**Afflecks** 52 Church St, Northern Quarter ☎0161 839 0718, ⓦafflecks.com; Piccadilly Gardens Metrolink. A Manchester institution, where more than fifty independent stalls are spread over four floors mixing everything from goth outfits to retro cocktail dresses and quirky footwear. Mon–Fri 10.30am–6pm, Sat 10am–6pm, Sun 11am–5pm (ground and first floors only).

**Craft & Design Centre** 17 Oak St, Northern Quarter ☎0161 832 4274, ⓦcraftanddesign.com; Shudehill Metrolink. The city's best place to pick up ceramics, fabrics, earthenware, jewellery and decorative art – there's also a good little café. Mon–Sat 10am–5.30pm.

**Oklahoma** 74–76 High St, Northern Quarter ☎0161 834 1136, ⓦoklahomacafe.co.uk; Shudehill Metrolink. Hidden behind large wooden doors, this charming gift shop-cum-veggie-café is packed with fun knick-knacks and fripperies, with some pretty jewellery too. Mon–Sat 10am–7pm, Sun 10am–6pm.

**Piccadilly Records** 53 Oldham St, Northern Quarter ☎0161 839 8008, ⓦpiccadillyrecords.com; Piccadilly Gardens Metrolink. The enthusiastic staff, many of them DJs themselves, are more than willing to navigate you through the shelves of collectibles and vinyl towards some special gem, whatever your taste. Mon–Sat 10am–6pm, Sun 11am–5pm.

**Retro Rehab** 91 Oldham St, Northern Quarter ☎0161 839 2050, ⓦretro-rehab.co.uk; Piccadilly Gardens Metrolink. Gorgeously feminine dresses abound, be they reworked vintage styles or genuine 1950s pieces, in this wonderful little boutique that prides itself on the range of its fashions from across several decades. Mon–Sat 10am–6pm, Sun noon–4pm.

### DIRECTORY

**Hospital** Manchester Royal Infirmary, Oxford Road ☎0161 276 1234.

**Internet** Free at the Central Library, Street Peter's Square (see p.517) and the Visitor Centre (see p.522), plus 30min free wi-fi in the city centre (accessed on _FreebeeMcr Wi-Fi).

**Left luggage** Facilities at Piccadilly train station (Mon–Sat 7am–11pm, Sun 8am–11pm; £4 per item for 24hr; ☎0161 236 8667).

**Police** 31 Bootle Street ☎0161 872 5050.

**Post office** 26 Spring Gardens.

# Chester

CHESTER, forty miles southwest of Manchester across the Cheshire Plain, is home to a glorious two-mile ring of medieval and Roman **walls** that encircles a kernel of Tudor and Victorian buildings, all overhanging eaves, mini-courtyards, and narrow cobbled lanes, which culminate in the raised arcades called the "**Rows**". The centre of the city is full of easy charms that can be explored on foot, and taken altogether Chester has enough in the way of sights, restaurants and atmosphere to make it an enjoyable base for a day or two. Though traditionally viewed as rather staid compared to near neighbours Manchester and Liverpool, it's gradually acquiring a bit of an edge, and with a new arts centre due to open in 2015, it's one to watch.

## The Rows

Intersecting at **The Cross**, the four main thoroughfares of central Chester are lined by **The Rows**, galleried shopping arcades that run along the first floor of a wonderful set of half-timbered buildings with another set of shops down below at street level. This engaging tableau, which extends for the first 200 or 300 yards of each of the four main streets, is a blend of genuine Tudor houses and Victorian imitations. There's no clear explanation of the origin of The Rows – they were first recorded shortly after a fire wrecked Chester in 1278 – but it seems likely that the hard bedrock that lies underneath the town centre prevented its shopkeepers and merchants from constructing the cellars they required, so they built upwards instead. The finest Tudor buildings are on **Watergate Street**, though **Bridge Street** is perhaps more picturesque. From The Cross, it's also a brief walk along **Eastgate Street** to one of the old town gates, above which is perched the filigree **Eastgate Clock**, raised in honour of Queen Victoria's Diamond Jubilee.

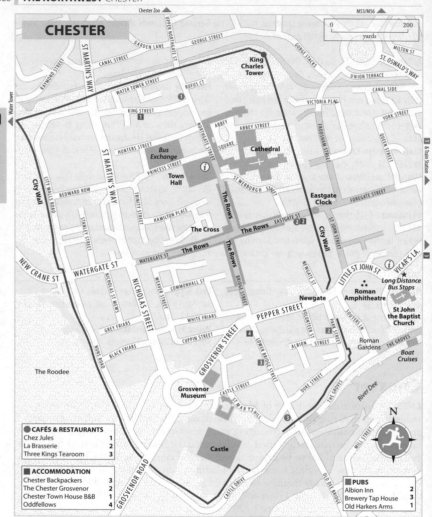

## The Cathedral

St Werburgh St, off Northgate St • Mon–Sat 9am–5pm, Sun 12.30–4pm • Free; £3 donation suggested • Cathedral at Height tours Mon–Sat 10am, 11am, 12.30pm, 1.30pm, 3pm & 4pm; 1hr; £8, children (over 8s only) £6 • ☎ 01244 324756, ⓦ chestercathedral.com

North of The Cross, along **Northgate Street**, rises the neo-Gothic **Town Hall**, whose acres of red and grey sandstone look over to the **Cathedral**, a much modified red sandstone structure dating back to the Normans. The **nave**, with its massive medieval pillars, is suitably imposing, and on one side it sports a splendid sequence of Victorian Pre-Raphaelite mosaic panels that illustrate Old Testament stories in melodramatic style. Close by, the **north transept** is the oldest and most Norman part of the church – hence the round-headed arch and arcade – and the adjoining **choir** holds an intricately carved set of fourteenth-century choir stalls with some especially beastly misericords. The atmospheric East Cloister leads to a gorgeously tranquil **garden**.

The new **Cathedral at Height** tour, an enjoyable hour-long rootle around the building's previously hidden spaces, takes you up onto the roof for panoramic views over five counties – you'll even spot Liverpool's cathedrals.

## Around the city walls

East of the cathedral, steps provide access to the top of the **city walls** – a two-mile girdle of medieval and Roman handiwork that's the most complete in Britain, though in places the wall is barely above street level. You can walk past all its towers, turrets and gateways in an hour or so, and most have a tale or two to tell. The fifteenth-century **King Charles Tower** in the northeast corner is so named because Charles I stood here in 1645 watching his troops being beaten on Rowton Moor, two miles to the southeast, while the earlier **Water Tower** at the northwest corner once stood in the river – evidence of the changes brought about by the gradual silting of the River Dee. South from the Water Tower you'll see the **Roodee**, England's oldest racecourse, laid out on a silted tidal pool where Roman ships once unloaded wine, figs and olive oil from the Mediterranean and slate, lead and silver from their mines in North Wales. Races are still held here throughout the year.

## The Grosvenor Museum

27 Grosvenor St • Mon–Sat 10.30am–5pm, Sun 1–4pm • Free • ☎ 01244 972197, ⓦ grosvenormuseum.co.uk

Scores of sculpted tomb panels and engraved headstones once propped up the wall to either side of the Water Tower, evidence of some nervous repair work undertaken when the Roman Empire was in retreat. Much of this stonework was retrieved by the Victorians and is now on display at the **Grosvenor Museum**, which also has interesting background displays on the Roman Empire in general and Roman Chester in particular. At the rear of the museum is **20 Castle Street**, a period house with nine rooms tricked out to represent domestic scenes from 1680 to 1925.

## The Roman Gardens and around

Immediately to the east of one of the old city gates, **Newgate**, a footpath leads into the **Roman Gardens** (open access), where a miscellany of Roman stonework – odd bits of pillar, coping stones and incidental statuary – is on display. Footsteps away, along Little St John Street, is the shallow, partly excavated bowl that marks the site of the **Roman Amphitheatre** (open access); it is estimated to have held seven thousand spectators, making it the largest amphitheatre in Britain, but frankly it's not much to look at today.

## Chester Zoo

Signposted off the A41 2 miles north of Chester • Daily: April–Sept 10am–5/6pm; Oct–March 10am–4/4.30pm; last admission 1hr before closing • £20, £16 in winter; children aged 3–15 £16/£13 • ⓦ chesterzoo.org • Bus #1 (daily every 20min) from the Bus Exchange

Chester's most popular attraction is **Chester Zoo**, one of the best in Europe. It is also the second largest in Britain (after London's), with over eleven thousand animals spread over a hundred landscaped acres. The zoo is well known for its **conservation projects** and has had notable success with its Asiatic lions and giant Komodo dragons. Animals are grouped by region in large paddocks viewed from a maze of pathways, from the monorail or the waterbus, with main attractions including the baby animals, the Tropical Realm and the Chimpanzee Forest with the biggest climbing frame in the country.

### ARRIVAL AND INFORMATION                                          CHESTER

**By train** The train station is a 10min walk northeast of the centre, down City Road and Foregate Street from the central Eastgate Clock. A shuttle bus (Mon–Sat 8am–6pm, free with rail ticket; every 15min) links the station with the Bus Exchange.

**Destinations** Birmingham (5 daily; 2hr); Liverpool (every

**10**

30min; 45min); London (every 20min; 3hr 30min); Manchester (every 30min; 1hr–1hr 20min).

**By bus** Long-distance buses pull in on Vicar's Lane, opposite one of the town's two tourist offices (see opposite) and a 5min walk from the city centre, while local buses use the Bus Exchange right in the centre of town, between Princess and Hunter streets, off Northgate Street.

Destinations Liverpool (every 20min; 1hr 20min); Manchester (3 daily; 1hr).

**Tourist information** Chester has two information offices: one bang in the centre, in the Town Hall, Northgate Street (April–Sept Mon–Sat 9.30am–5.30pm, Sun 10am–4pm; Oct–March Mon–Fri 10am–4pm, Sat 10am–5pm) and the other on Vicar's Lane (same hours, plus Oct–March Sun 10am–4pm). They share the same telephone number and website (☎01244 351609, ⓦvisitchester.com).

## ACCOMMODATION

Chester is a popular tourist destination and although most of its visitors are day-trippers, enough of them stay overnight to sustain dozens of **B&Bs** and a slew of **hotels**. At the height of the summer and on high days and holidays – like Chester Races – advance booking is strongly recommended, either direct or via the tourist office.

**Chester Backpackers** 67 Boughton ☎01244 400185, ⓦchesterbackpackers.co.uk. Close to the city walls and a 5min walk from the train station, in a typically Chester mock-Tudor building. En-suite doubles and two dorms (8- and 18-bed). Dorms £25, doubles £38

**The Chester Grosvenor** Eastgate St ☎01244 324024, ⓦchestergrosvenor.co.uk. Superb luxury hotel in an immaculately maintained Victorian building in the centre of town. Extremely comfortable bedrooms and a whole host of facilities, not least a full-blown spa (charges apply) and posh chocolatier Rococo onsite. Continental breakfast is included, but it's an extra £7.50 for a cooked breakfast. Rack rates are vertiginous, but look for special offers online. £300

**Chester Town House B&B** 23 King St ☎01244 350021, ⓦchestertownhouse.co.uk. Old-fashioned B&B in a comfortable seventeenth-century townhouse on a cobbled central street off Northgate Street. Five en-suite rooms and private parking. £75

★**Oddfellows** 20 Lower Bridge St ☎01244 895700, ⓦoddfellowschester.com. Quirky boutique hotel packed with look-at-me touches – from the typewriters climbing the reception walls, to the set table-for-two affixed to the ceiling, to the neon "Good Night" sign en route to the eighteen comfortable, individually styled bedrooms. There's a buzzy bar scene – including the *Secret Garden* – and popular restaurant on site too. £162

## EATING

★**Chez Jules** 71 Northgate St ☎01244 400014, ⓦchezjules.com. There's a classic brasserie menu – salade nicoise to rib-eye steak – at this popular spot in an attractive half-timbered building. In the evenings, main courses begin at around £10, with a terrific-value, two-course prix fixe menu (Mon–Sat 5–7pm, Sun all day) for £11.95 and a two-course lunch for £9.95. Mon–Sat noon–3pm & 5–10.30pm, Sun noon–4.30pm.

★**La Brasserie** Chester Grosvenor, Eastgate St ☎01244 324024, ⓦchestergrosvenor.com/chester-brasserie. In the same hotel as the Michelin-starred

*Simon Radley's*, where the à la carte menu sits at a cool £75, this is a much more affordable yet smart brasserie that serves inventive French and fusion cooking. Main courses average £20, and it's also a great place for a coffee and pastry. Mon–Fri 7am–9.30pm, Sat 11am–10pm, Sun 11am–9pm.

**Three Kings Tearoom** 90–92 Lower Bridge St ☎01244 317717, ⓦthreekingstearooms.com. An amenable little tearoom with pleasantly fuddy-duddy decor and tasty food – a filling salad and sandwich combo costs about £5. Afternoon tea (£12.50) is popular. Daily 10am–5pm.

## DRINKING

**Albion Inn** Corner of Albion and Park streets ☎01244 340345, ⓦalbioninnchester.co.uk. A Victorian terraced pub in the shadow of the city wall – no fruit machines, no muzak, just good old-fashioned decor (and a World War I theme), tasty bar food and a great range of ales. Hilariously unwelcoming signs outside – basically, if you're on a hen or stag do, or have a child in tow, forget it. Mon–Thurs & Sat noon–3pm & 5–11pm, Fri noon–11pm, Sun noon–2.30pm & 7–10.30pm.

**Brewery Tap House** 52–54 Lower Bridge St ☎01244 340999, ⓦthe-tap.co.uk. Up the cobbled ramp, this

converted medieval hall, once owned by the royalist Gamul family and confiscated by Parliament after the English Civil War, serves a good selection of ales from local brewery Spitting Feathers in a tall barn-like room with whitewashed walls. Mon–Sat noon–11pm, Sun noon–10.30pm.

★**Old Harkers Arms** 1 Russell St, below the City Rd bridge ☎01244 344525, ⓦbrunningandprice.co.uk/harkers. Canalside real-ale pub imaginatively sited in a former warehouse about 500 yards northeast of Foregate Street. Quality bar food too. Mon–Sat 11.30am–11pm, Sun noon–10.30pm.

# Liverpool

Standing proud in the 1700s as the empire's second city, **LIVERPOOL** faced a dramatic change in fortune in the twentieth century, suffering a series of harsh economic blows and ongoing urban deprivation. The postwar years were particularly tough, but the outlook changed again at the turn of the millennium, as economic and social regeneration brightened the centre and old docks, and the city's stint as European Capital of Culture in 2008 transformed the view from outside. Today Liverpool is a dynamic, exciting place with a Tate Gallery of its own, a series of innovative museums and a fascinating social history. And of course it also makes great play of its musical heritage – as well it should, considering that this is the place that gave the world The Beatles.

10

The main sights are scattered throughout the centre of town, but you can easily walk between most of them. The **River Mersey** provides one focus, whether crossing on the famous ferry to the **Wirral** peninsula or taking a tour of the Albert Dock. **Beatles** sights could easily occupy another day. If you want a cathedral, they've "got one to spare" as the song goes; plus there's a fine showing of British art in the celebrated **Walker Art Gallery** and **Tate Liverpool**, a multitude of exhibits in the terrific **World Museum Liverpool**, a revitalized arts and nightlife urban quarter centred on **FACT**, Liverpool's showcase for film and the media arts, and a whole new cutting-edge creative district known as the **Baltic Triangle**.

### Brief history

Liverpool gained its charter from King John in 1207, but remained a humble fishing village for half a millennium until the booming slave trade prompted the building of the first dock in 1715. From then until the abolition of slavery in Britain in 1807, Liverpool was the apex of the **slaving triangle** in which firearms, alcohol and textiles were traded for African slaves, who were then shipped to the Caribbean and America where they were in turn exchanged for tobacco, raw cotton and sugar. After the abolition of the trade, the port continued to grow into a seven-mile chain of docks, not only for freight but also to cope with wholesale European emigration, which saw nine million people leave for the Americas and Australasia between 1830 and 1930. During the 1970s and 1980s Liverpool became a byword for British economic malaise, but the waterfront area of the city was granted **UNESCO World Heritage** status in 2004, spurring major refurbishment of the city's magnificent municipal and industrial buildings.

## St George's Hall

St George's Place, off Lime St • Daily 10am–5pm• Free • ☎ 0151 233 3020, ⓦ liverpoolcityhalls.co.uk

Emerging from Lime Street Station, you can't miss **St George's Hall**, one of Britain's finest Greek Revival buildings and a testament to the wealth generated from transatlantic trade. Now primarily an exhibition venue, but once Liverpool's premier concert hall and crown court, its vaulted Great Hall features a floor tiled with thirty thousand precious Minton tiles (usually covered over, but open for a week or two in Aug), while the Willis organ is the third largest in Europe. You can take a self-guided tour, or call for details of the guided tours.

## Walker Art Gallery

William Brown St • Daily10am–5pm • Free; audio tour £1.95 • ⓦ liverpoolmuseums.org.uk/Walker

Liverpool's **Walker Art Gallery** houses one of the country's best provincial art collections. The paintings are up on the first floor, but don't miss the ground-floor Sculpture Gallery, nor the Craft and Design Gallery, which displays changing exhibits from a

10

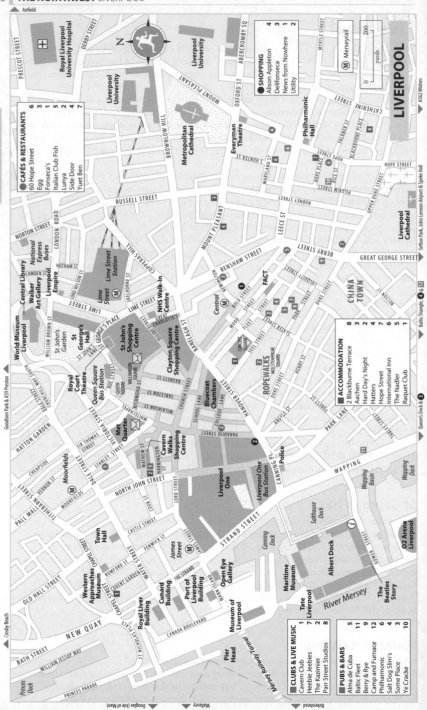

# LIVERPOOL

● SHOPPING
Alison Appleton 4
Delfonseca 3
News from Nowhere 1
Utility 2

Ⓜ Merseyrail

0    200
yards

● CAFÉS & RESTAURANTS
60 Hope Street 6
Egg 3
Fonseca's 1
Italian Club Fish 5
Lunya 2
Side Door 4
Yuet Ben 7

■ ACCOMMODATION
2 Blackburne Terrace 8
Aachen 3
Hard Day's Night 2
Hatters 4
Hope Street 7
International Inn 6
The Nadler 5
Raquet Club 1

■ CLUBS & LIVE MUSIC
Cavern Club 5
Heebie Jeebies 7
The Kazimier 1
Parr Street Studios 8

■ PUBS & BARS
Alma de Cuba 5
Baltic Fleet 11
Berry & Rye 9
Camp and Furnace 12
Philharmonic 6
Salt Dog Slim's 4
Some Place 3
Ye Cracke 10

large applied arts collection – glassware, ceramics, fabrics, precious metals and furniture, largely retrieved from the homes of the city's early industrial businessmen. Liverpool's explosive economic growth in the eighteenth and nineteenth centuries is reflected in much of the Walker's collection, as British painting begins to occupy centre stage – notably works by native Liverpudlian George Stubbs, England's greatest animal painter. Impressionists and Post-Impressionists, including Degas, Sickert, Cézanne and Monet, take the collection into more modern times and tastes, before the final round of galleries of contemporary British art. Paul Nash, Lucian Freud, Ben Nicholson, David Hockney and John Hoyland all have work here, much of it first displayed in the Walker's biennial John Moores Exhibition.

10

Children up to 8 years old will love the excellent **Big Art for Little Artists** gallery on the ground floor.

## Central Library

William Brown St • Mon–Fri 9am–8pm, Sat 9am–5pm, Sun 10am–5pm • Free • ☎ 0151 233 3069

Next to the Walker Gallery, the city's spectacular **Central Library** was reopened in May 2013 after a three-year, £50 million facelift. Approached via a "Literary Pavement" celebrating the city's considerable contribution to the written word, it centres on a stunning atrium crowned by an elliptical dome made of around 150 pieces of glass. Don't miss the beautiful circular **Picton Reading Room** and, in the **Oak Room**, a copy of John James Audubon's huge *Birds of America*.

## World Museum Liverpool

William Brown St • Daily 10am–5pm • Free • ☎ 0151 478 4393, ⓦ liverpoolmuseums.org.uk/WML

The **World Museum Liverpool** is a great family attraction. The dramatic six-storey atrium provides access to an eclectic series of themed exhibits of broad appeal – from natural history to ethnography, insects to antiquities, dinosaurs to space rockets. Excellent sections for children include the Bug House (no explanation required), plus excellent hands-on natural history and archeology discovery centres. The planetarium and theatre have free daily shows, with times posted at the information desk.

## Metropolitan Cathedral

On the hill behind Lime St, off Mount Pleasant • Daily 7.30am–6pm • Free; £3 admission to crypt • ⓦ liverpoolmetrocathedral.org.uk

The idiosyncratically shaped Catholic **Metropolitan Cathedral** of Christ the King is denigratingly known as "Paddy's Wigwam" or the "Mersey Funnel". Built in the wake of the revitalizing Second Vatican Council, it was raised on top of the tentative beginnings of Sir Edwin Lutyens' grandiose project to outdo St Peter's in Rome. The present building, to Sir Frederick Gibberd's spectacular Modernist design, is anchored by sixteen concrete ribs supporting the landmark stained-glass lantern, and was consecrated in 1967. Ceremonial steps mark the approach from Mount Pleasant/Hope Street, with a café-bar at the bottom and four huge bells at the top.

## Everyman Theatre

Hope St • Tours April–Aug Tues, Thurs & Sat 11.30am (subject to the stage programme) • Free • ☎ 0151 709 4776, ⓦ everymanplayhouse .com

At the foot of the Metropolitan Cathedral is Liverpool's iconic **Everyman Theatre**, reopened in March 2014 to citywide jubilation after a two-year rebuilding programme. Explore it on a tour or just admire its stunning **Portrait Wall** – 105 aluminium shutters featuring life-size photographs of everyday people: a celebration of the theatre's inclusive ethos.

## Liverpool Cathedral

Hope St • Daily 8am–6pm • Donation requested • Tower and audiotour Mon–Wed, Fri & Sat 10am–4.30pm, Thurs 10.30am–7.30pm, Sun 11.45am–3.30pm • £5 • Ⓦ liverpoolcathedral.org.uk

The Anglican **Liverpool Cathedral** looks much more ancient than the Metropolitan Cathedral, but was actually completed eleven years later, in 1978, after 74 years in construction. The last of the great British neo-Gothic structures, Sir Giles Gilbert Scott's masterwork claims a smattering of superlatives: Britain's largest and the world's fifth-largest cathedral, the world's tallest Gothic arches and the highest and heaviest bells. On a clear day, a trip up the 330ft tower is rewarded by views to the Welsh hills.

## Ropewalks and around

At the heart of Liverpool's regenerating city centre, **Ropewalks**, the former warehouse and factory district between Bold Street and Duke Street, is anchored by **FACT**, 88 Wood Street (Ⓦfact.co.uk) – that's Film, Art and Creative Technology – with its galleries for art, video and new media exhibitions (Tues–Sun 11am–6pm; free), community projects, cinema screens, café and bar. The beautifully proportioned Bluecoat Chambers, built in 1717 as an Anglican boarding school for orphans, is in nearby School Lane. An integral part of Liverpool's cultural life for years, **The Bluecoat** (Ⓦthebluecoat.org.uk) includes artists' studios, exhibitions, courses and performances, as well as a fantastic **Display Centre** (Ⓦwww.bluecoatdisplaycentre.com) where contemporary crafts are for sale. Further southwest is the massive new development of the **Liverpool One** shopping precinct.

In Wolstenholme Square, in the middle of Ropewalks, is *Penelope*, a huge modern sculpture of coloured plexiglass spheres on giant interwoven stalks, created by sculptor Jorge Pardo for the 2006 Biennial; it's especially striking when illuminated at night.

## Western Approaches Museum

1–3 Rumford St, off Chapel St • Mon–Thurs & Sat 10.30am–4.30pm • £6 • Ⓦ www.liverpoolwarmuseum.co.uk

En route to Pier Head, the **Western Approaches Museum** reveals an underground labyrinth of rooms, formerly headquarters for the Battle of the Atlantic during World War II. The massive Operations Room vividly displays all the technology of a 1940s nerve centre – wooden pushers and model boats, chalkboards and ladders.

## The waterfront

Dominating the waterfront are the so-called **Three Graces** – namely the Port of Liverpool Building (1907), Cunard Building (1913) and, most prominently, the 322ft-high Royal Liver Building (1910), topped by the "Liver Birds", a couple of cormorants that have become the symbol of the city. As the waterfront has developed in the last decade or so, it has sprouted a number of attractions, including **Tate Liverpool**, the excellent **Maritime Museum**, the **Beatles Story**, the impressive **Museum of Liverpool** and the marvellous **Open Eye** gallery.

### Museum of Liverpool

Pier Head • Daily 10am–5pm • Free • ☎0151 478 4545, Ⓦ liverpoolmuseums.org.uk/mol

Huge and flashy, in a show-stopping Danish-designed building, the brilliant **Museum of Liverpool** opened in 2011. Spread over three floors, the galleries play on Liverpool's historic status as the "second city of Empire", exploring the complex political and life histories that have unfolded in a community whose wealth and social fabric were built on international trade. Children will enjoy "Little Liverpool", a gallery where they can design and build their own city, while anyone with any interest in popular culture will

**10**

---

### FERRY ACROSS THE MERSEY

Though the tumult of shipping which once fought the current in Liverpool has gone, the **Pier Head** landing stage remains the embarkation point for the Mersey Ferry (☎0151 330 1444, ⓦmerseyferries.co.uk) to Woodside (for Birkenhead) and Seacombe (Wallasey). Straightforward ferry-shuttles (£2.80 return) operate during the morning and evening rush hours. At other times the boats run circular fifty-minute "river explorer" **cruises** (hourly: Mon–Fri 10am–4pm, Sat & Sun 10am–6pm; £8.50), which you can combine with a visit to the **Spaceport** space exploration visitor attraction at Seacombe (Mon–Fri 10am–3pm, Sat & Sun & Bank Hols 10am–5pm ; £9, with ferry £13; ☎0151 330 1444, ⓦspaceport.org.uk).

---

have an absolute ball at "Wondrous Place", a memorabilia-rich celebration of sports and music.

## Open Eye Gallery

19 Mann Island • Tues–Sun 10.30am–5.30pm; closed during exhibition takeovers, which take place four times a year and last approximately 12 days • Free • ☎ 0151 236 6768, ⓦ openeye.org.uk

On the new Mann Island development just by the Museum of Liverpool sits the **Open Eye Gallery**, the Northwest's only gallery dedicated to photography and related media. As well as presenting an impressive programme of international exhibitions, it contains a permanent archive of around 1600 prints from the 1930s onwards.

## Albert Dock

Five minutes' walk south of Pier Head is **Albert Dock,** built in 1846 when Liverpool's port was a world leader. Its decline began at the beginning of the twentieth century, as the new deep-draught ships were unable to berth here, and the dock last saw service in 1972. A decade later the site was given a refit, and it is now one of the city's most popular areas, full of **attractions** – including the **Beatles Story** (see box opposite) – and bars and restaurants.

## Merseyside Maritime Museum

Albert Dock • Daily 10am–5pm • Free • ⓦ liverpoolmuseums.org.uk

The **Merseyside Maritime Museum** fills one wing of the Dock; allow at least two hours to see it all. The basement houses **Seized!**, giving the lowdown on smuggling and revenue collection, along with **Emigrants to a New World**, an illuminating display detailing Liverpool's pivotal role as a springboard for more than nine million emigrants. Other galleries tell the story of the Battle of the Atlantic and of the three ill-fated liners – the *Titanic*, *Lusitania* and *Empress of Ireland*. Finally, the unmissable **International Slavery Museum** on the third floor manages to be both challenging and chilling, as it tells dehumanizing stories of slavery while examining contemporary issues of equality, freedom and racial injustice.

## Tate Liverpool

Albert Dock • June–Aug daily 10am–5.50pm; Sept–May Tues–Sun 10am–5.50pm • Free, except for special exhibitions • ⓦ tate.org.uk/liverpool

The country's national collection of modern art from the north, **Tate Liverpool** holds popular retrospectives of artists such as Mondrian, Dalí, Magritte and Calder, along with an ever-changing display from its vast collection, and temporary exhibitions of artists of international standing. There's also a full programme of events, talks and tours.

## Crosby Beach

Cambridge Rd or Mariners Rd/Hall Rd West, Crosby • Trains from Lime St to Hall Road Station; every 30min; 20min

Seven miles north of Liverpool city centre, **Crosby Beach** was an innocuous, if picturesque, spot until the arrival in 2005 of Antony Gormley's haunting **Another Place**

## THE BEATLES TRAIL

**Mathew Street**, ten minutes' walk west of Lime Street Station, is now a little enclave of Beatles nostalgia, most of it bogus and typified by the **Cavern Walks Shopping Centre**, with a bronze statue of the boys in the atrium. **The Cavern** club where the band was first spotted by Brian Epstein, saw 275 Beatles' gigs between 1961 and 1963; it closed in 1966 and was partly demolished in 1973, though a latter-day successor, the *Cavern Club* at 10 Mathew St, complete with souvenir shop, was rebuilt on the original site. The *Cavern Pub*, across the way, boasts a coiffed Lennon mannequin lounging against the wall and an exterior "Wall of Fame" highlighting the names of all the bands who appeared at the club between 1957 and 1973 as well as brass discs commemorating every Liverpool chart-topper since 1952 – the city has produced more UK No. 1 singles than any other. There's more Beatlemania at **The Beatles Shop**, 31 Mathew Street (ⓦ thebeatleshop.co.uk), which claims to have the largest range of Beatles gear in the world.

For a personal and social history, head to the Albert Dock for **The Beatles Story** (daily: April–Oct 9am–5pm, Nov–March 10am–5pm; £12.95; ⓦ beatlesstory.com), which traces the band's rise from the early days to their disparate solo careers. Then it's on to the two houses where John Lennon and Paul McCartney grew up. Both **20 Forthlin Rd**, home to the McCartney family from 1955 to 1964, and the rather more genteel **Mendips**, where Lennon lived with his Aunt Mimi and Uncle George between 1945 and 1963, are only accessible on pre-booked **National Trust** minibus tours (£20, NT members £8.30; ☎0151 427 7231 or ☎0844 800 4791), which run from both the city centre (mid-March to Oct Wed–Sun 10am & 10.50am; Feb to mid-March & Nov 10am, 12.30pm & 3pm) and Speke Hall, seven miles south (mid-March to Oct 2.30pm & 3.20pm). The experience is disarmingly intimate, whether you're sitting in John Lennon's bedroom – which has its original wallpaper – on a replica bed looking out, as he would have done, onto his front lawn, or simply entering Paul's tiny room and gazing at pictures of his childhood.

### BEATLES TOURS

**Phil Hughes** ☎0151 228 4565 or ☎07961 511223, ⓦ tourliverpool.co.uk. Small (8-seater) minibus tours run daily on demand with a Blue Badge guide well versed in The Beatles and Liverpool life (4hr; 1–4 people pay £100 in total, 5–8 £20 each). Includes city-centre pick-ups/drop-offs and refreshments.

**Magical Mystery Tour** ☎0151 236 9091, ⓦ cavernclub.org; or book at tourist offices. Tours on the multicoloured Mystery Bus (daily; 2hr; £16.95) leave from Albert Dock.

installation, spread along more than 1000 yards of the shore. An eerie set of a hundred life-size cast-iron statues, each cast from Gormley's own body, are buried at different levels in the sand, all gazing out to sea and slowly becoming submerged as high tide rolls in.

### ARRIVAL AND DEPARTURE

### LIVERPOOL

**By plane** Liverpool John Lennon Airport (☎0870 129 8484, ⓦ liverpoolairport.com) is 8 miles southeast of the city centre; it has an information desk (daily 8am–6pm). The Airlink #500 bus (5.45am–11.45pm; every 30min; £3) runs from the entrance into the city. A taxi to Lime Street costs around £15.

**By train** Mainline trains pull in to Lime Street Station, northeast of the city centre.

Destinations from Lime St Birmingham (hourly; 1hr 40min); Chester (every 30min; 45min); Leeds (hourly; 1hr 40min); London Euston (hourly; 2hr 20min); Manchester (hourly; 50min); Sheffield (hourly; 1hr 45min); York (11 daily; 2hr 15min).

**By bus** National Express buses use the station on Norton St, just northeast of Lime Street train station.

Destinations Chester (12 daily; 1hr); London (9 daily; 5hr 10min–6hr 40min); Manchester (hourly; 1hr).

**By ferry** Ferries to and from the Isle of Man, run by the Isle of Man Steam Packet Company (☎0872 299 2992, ⓦ steam -packet.com), dock at the terminals just north of Pier Head, not far from James Street Merseyrail station. From Belfast, Lagan Seaways and Mersey Seaways (☎0870 609 9299, ⓦ dfdsseaways.com) dock over the water on the Wirral at Twelve Quays, near Woodside ferry terminal (ferry or Merseyrail to Liverpool).

### GETTING AROUND

**By bus** Local buses depart from Queen Square and Liverpool One bus station. The circular CityLink service is a perfect way to see the sights (every 12min; day tickets from £3)

**By train** The suburban Merseyrail system (trains from Chester) calls at four underground stations, including Lime Street and James Street (for Pier Head and the Albert Dock).

**By bike** The largest public bicycle scheme outside of London, Citybike (☎0151 374 2034, ⓦcitybikeliverpool .co.uk) has bikes from £3 a day, with stations citywide. You can also rent from Liverpool Bicycle Ltd, 29 Parliament Street (☎0151 707 6116, ⓦliverpool-bicycle.co.uk; £10/half-day, £15/day).

## INFORMATION AND TOURS

**Tourist information** The best online source of information is ⓦvisitliverpool.com. There are visitor centres at Albert Dock, Anchor Courtyard (daily: April–Sept 10am–5.30pm, Oct–March 10am–5pm; ☎0151 233 2008, ⓦalbertdock.com) and Platform 7, Liverpool Lime Street station (daily 9.30am–5pm). Merseytravel (☎0151 236 7676, ⓦmerseytravel.gov.uk) has travel centres at Queen Square and the Liverpool One Interchange.
**Listings** The *Liverpool Echo*'s website (ⓦliverpoolecho .co.uk/whats-on) is always current; while the hip ⓦthe doublenegative.co.uk and ⓦcreativetourist.com will see you right. *The Skinny* is a useful, widely available monthly freebie.
**Beatles tours** Among the most popular jaunts in the city are those around the Fab Four's former haunts (see box, p.537).
**Football tours** You're unlikely to get a ticket for a Liverpool game, but there are daily tours around the museum, trophy room and dressing rooms (£16.50; museum only £8.50; ⓦliverpoolfc.com). Everton, the city's other Premiership side, also offers tours (Mon, Wed, Fri & Sun 11am & 1pm; ☎0151 530 5212; £10; ⓦevertonfc.com).
**Walking tours** ⓦvisitliverpool.com has details of local guides (most Easter–Sept; from £5).

## ACCOMMODATION

Budget chains are well represented in Liverpool, with *Premier, Travel Inn, Ibis, Express by Holiday Inn* and others all with convenient city-centre locations, including down by Albert Dock and near Mount Pleasant.

★ **2 Blackburne Terrace** 2 Blackburne Terrace ☎0151 702 4840, ⓦ2blackburneterrace.com. Unspeakably beautiful B&B in a grand Georgian house set back from Blackburne Place, with just four elegant and individually designed rooms boasting high thread-count linens, original artworks and cutting-edge technology. With welcoming hosts and a sumptuous breakfast, this is a hidden, high-end gem. You'll save around £40 by staying midweek. £180
**Aachen** 89–91 Mount Pleasant ☎0151 709 3477, ⓦaachenhotel.co.uk. The best of the Mount Pleasant budget choices, with a range of good-value rooms (with and without en-suite showers), big "eat-as-much-as-you-like" breakfasts, and a bar. £95
**Hard Day's Night** North John St ☎0151 236 1964, ⓦharddaysnighthotel.com. Up-to-the-minute four-star close to Mathew Street. Splashes of vibrant colour and artful lighting enhance the elegant decor. The Lennon and McCartney suites (£950/750 respectively) are the tops. Breakfast not included. £160
**Hatters** 56–60 Mount Pleasant ☎0151 709 5570, ⓦhattersgroup.com/Liverpool. Though it's housed in the former YMCA building – with an institutional feel and gymnasium-size dining hall – *Hatters* has clean rooms, friendly staff and a great location. Standard facilities, including internet. Prices fluctuate wildly according to what's on. Dorms £30, doubles £100
★ **Hope Street** 40 Hope St (entrance on Hope Place) ☎0151 709 3000, ⓦhopestreethotel.co.uk. In an unbeatable location between the cathedrals, this former Victorian warehouse retains its original elegant brickwork and cast-iron columns but now comes with hardwood floors, huge beds and luxurious bathrooms. Fabulous breakfasts, too, served in the highly rated *London Carriage Works* restaurant. Flash sales, held three times a year, offer bargain rooms; register for the email newsletter to snap one up. £152
★ **International Inn** 4 South Hunter St, off Hardman St ☎0151 709 8135, ⓦinternationalinn.co.uk. Converted Victorian warehouse in a great location, with modern en-suite rooms sleeping two to ten people, and 32 new double and twin "Cocoon Pods". Dorms £20, doubles £45, pods £55
**The Nadler** Formerly Base2Stay, 29 Seel St ☎0151 705 2626, ⓦthenadler.com/liverpool. Smack in the heart of the Ropewalks is this converted warehouse, with more than 100 minimalist rooms that complement the building's original brickwork and well-appointed modern art pieces. Rooms include a "mini-kitchen". Prices are almost halved midweek. £119
**Racquet Club** 5 Chapel St ☎0151 236 6676, ⓦracquetclub.org.uk. Boutique-style townhouse hotel with just eight rooms, each mixing fine linens and traditional furniture with contemporary art and modern fittings. Breakfast is not in the price, but is available courtesy of *Ziba*, the hotel's restaurant. £110

## EATING AND DRINKING

Many Liverpool venues morph from breakfast hangout to dinner spot to late-night live music space, making categorization increasingly futile. Most **eating** choices are in three distinct areas – at Albert Dock, around Hardman and Hope streets, and along Berry and Nelson streets, the heart of Liverpool's Chinatown. You'll enjoy a perfect evening's **bar-hopping** along Seel Street, while the blossoming **Baltic Triangle**, the old industrial warehouse district south of Chinatown, has become the city's most creative and cutting-edge quarter. Alternatively, take a short taxi ride out to Lark Lane in Aigburth, close to Sefton Park, where a dozen eating and drinking spots pack into one short street.

## CAFÉS AND RESTAURANTS

★**60 Hope Street** 60 Hope St ☎0151 707 6060, ⓦ60hopestreet.com. The star of the Liverpool gastronomic scene, set in a Georgian terrace, serves British cuisine (mains around £22) with creative flourishes – roast rump of Cumbrian lamb with broccoli purée, for example – and an extensive wine list. It takes some nerve to offer, as a dessert, deep-fried jam sandwich with Carnation milk ice cream (£8.50), but the confidence is justified. Mon–Fri noon–2.30pm & 5–10.30pm, Sat noon–3pm & 5–10.30pm, Sun noon–8pm.

**Egg** 16 Newington ☎0151 707 2755, ⓦeggcafe.co.uk. Up on the third floor, this plant-strewn bohemian café serves excellent vegan and vegetarian food with good set-meal deals. Also a nice place for a chai. Mon–Fri 9am–10.30pm, Sat & Sun 10am–10.30pm.

★**Fonseca's** 12 Stanley St ☎0151 255 0808, ⓦdelifonseca.co.uk. Bistro with a changing blackboard menu of Italian and British delights, including Welsh black beef braised in local Wapping ale, and crayfish and chicken pie (mains around £13). The small deli counter downstairs offers a sample of the wares at the newer *Delifonseca*, 30min away on the dockside (see p.540). Mon–Thurs noon–2.30 & 5–9pm, Fri & Sat noon–10pm.

**Italian Club Fish** 128 Bold St ☎0151 707 2110, ⓦtheitalianclubfish.co.uk. Proper Italian seafood place with a menu that adapts to what's fresh – try the *Sauté Di Maurizio* (£16.95) There are also a few token meat and vegetarian dishes, all around £13. Mon–Sat 10am–10pm, Sun noon–9pm.

**Lunya** 18–20 College Lane ☎0151 706 9770, ⓦlunya .co.uk. Gorgeous Catalan and Spanish deli-restaurant in the heart of Liverpool ONE, with a vast tapas selection (from around £5) and menus running the gamut from suckling pig banquet to vegan. Mon & Tues 10am–9pm, Wed & Thurs 10am–9.30pm, Fri 10am–10pm, Sat 9am–10pm, Sun 10am–8.30pm.

**Side Door** 29a Hope St ☎0151 707 7888, ⓦthesidedoor.co.uk. The intimate Georgian townhouse bistro has a winning combination of Mediterranean food and reasonable prices – with bargain pre-theatre menus from £16.95. Does a great £5 lunch, too. Mon–Wed noon–2pm & 5–9.30pm, Thurs–Sat noon–2pm & 5–10pm.

**Yuet Ben** 1 Upper Duke St ☎0151 709 5772. In business since 1968, *Yuet Ben* is widely held to be the best Chinese restaurant in Liverpool, with dishes from around £8, great set menus and a fantastic vegetarian choice. Tues–Thurs & Sun 5–11pm, Fri & Sat 5pm–midnight.

## PUBS AND BARS

**Alma de Cuba** St Peter's Church, Seel St ☎0151 702 7394, ⓦalma-de-cuba.com. It may have far more candles now than when it was a church – and even more in the mezzanine restaurant – but the mirrored altar is still the focus of this bar's rich, dark Cuban-themed interior. Daily 11am–2am.

**Baltic Fleet** 33a Wapping ☎0151 709 3116, ⓦbalticfleet publiverpool.com. Restored, no-nonsense, quiet pub with age-old shipping connections and an open fire, just south of the Albert Dock. Beer brewed on site and good pub grub on offer. Mon–Fri & Sun noon–midnight, Sat 11am–midnight.

★**Berry & Rye** 48 Berry St ⓔberryandrye@gmail .com. You'll have to hunt hard – or ask a likely local – to find this unmarked bar, but once you're in it's a delight. An intimate, bare-brick gin and whiskey joint with knowledgeable bartenders, turn-of-the-twentieth-century music – often live – and well-crafted cocktails (from £6.50). Highly recommended. Mon–Sat 5pm–2am, Sun 7pm–1am.

★**Camp and Furnace** 67 Greenland St, Baltic Triangle ☎0151 708 2890, ⓦcampandfurnace.com. The most creative and exhilarating venue in a city not short on contenders, its huge warehouses spaces – one boasting the city's biggest public screen, one with a mighty furnace at one end, a cosier bar area – host festival-style food slams (Fri), massive, communal Sunday roasts, all sorts of parties and pop-ups, art installations, live performances, the lot. Do not miss it. Mon–Thurs 9am–10pm, Fri & Sat 10am–2am, Sun 10am–midnight/1am.

★**Philharmonic** 36 Hope St ☎0151 707 2837 ⓦnicholsonspubs.co.uk. Liverpool's finest traditional watering hole where the main attractions – beer aside – are the mosaic floors, tiling, gilded wrought-iron gates and the marble decor in the gents. Daily 11am–midnight.

**Salt Dog Slim's** 79 Seel St ☎0151 709 7172. American-style bar that's a lot of fun, with a young, friendly crowd wolfing delicious hot dogs (from £3.50) washed down with plenty of beers, backed by a solidly indie soundtrack. Upstairs is the supposedly secret *81 Ltd*, which rocks a Prohibition-era speakeasy vibe, though perhaps a tad self-consciously. Daily 5pm–2am.

★**Some Place** 43 Seel St. A green light above an unmarked doorway hints at what lies up the incense-heavy staircase – an utterly gorgeous absinthe bar that is every inch a bohemian fantasy. Savour an absinthe cocktail (from £4.50), drink in the meticulous decor and channel your inner Oscar Wilde. Wed & Thurs 9pm–late, Fri & Sat 8pm–late.

**Ye Cracke** 13 Rice St ☎0151 709 4171. Crusty backstreet pub off Hope St, much loved by the young Lennon, and with a great jukebox, and cheap-as-chips food (daytime only). Mon–Thurs & Sun noon–11.30pm, Fri & Sat noon–midnight.

**10**

## NIGHTLIFE AND ENTERTAINMENT

Liverpool's **club scene** is famously unpretentious, with posing playing second fiddle to drinking and dancing, while particularly rich in home-grown live music. Popular annual **festivals** include Beatles Week (last week of Aug; Ⓦ cavernclub.org/beatleweek) and the Liverpool International Music Festival (Aug Bank Hol; Ⓦ limfestival.co.uk), with big-name acts playing across the city; while there are plenty of one-off cultural events, such as the jaw-dropping Giants Spectacular (2012 & 2014; Ⓦ giantspectacular.com). As for the classical music scene, the **Royal Liverpool Philharmonic Orchestra**, ranked with Manchester's Hallé as the Northwest's best, dominates.

**10**

### CLUBS AND LIVE MUSIC

**Cavern Club** 10 Mathew St ☎0151 236 1965, Ⓦ cavernclub.org. The self-styled "most famous club in the world" has live bands, from Beatles tribute acts to indie pop and rock, at the weekends, along with occasional backstage tours and special events. The atmosphere is always high-spirited, and even though this is not the very same *Cavern* club of the Beatles' days (see box, p.537), there's a certain thrill to it all. Open daily from 10am.

**Heebie Jeebies** 80–82 Seel St ☎0151 708 7001. Student favourite in a huge brick-vaulted room. Mainly indie and soul, with some live bands. Thurs–Sat 10pm–2am.

**★ The Kazimier** 4–5 Wolstenholme Square ☎0151 324 1723, Ⓦ thekazimier.co.uk. A super-creative, split-level place with a magical garden space (entrance at 32 Seel St); *the* place to come for cabaret-style club nights, gigs and eclectic events. Hours vary but generally noon–midnight.

**Parr Street Studios** Parr St ☎0151 707 1050, Ⓦ parrstreet.co.uk. Dynamic working recording studios – the UK's biggest outside London – hosting a long list of big names and home to bars/performance spaces Studio 2 and The Attic. Check website for details of what's on when.

### CLASSICAL MUSIC, THEATRE AND CINEMA

**Everyman Theatre** Hope St ☎0151 709 4776, Ⓦ everymanplayhouse.com. Iconic, newly reopened theatre (see p.533), staging a mix of classics with a twist, blockbusters and new writing.

**Liverpool Empire** Lime St ☎0870 606 3536, Ⓦ liverpooltheatres.com/empire.htm. The city's largest theatre, a venue for touring West End shows and large-scale opera and ballet productions.

**Philharmonic Hall** Hope St ☎0151 709 3789, Ⓦ liverpoolphil.com. Home to the Royal Liverpool Philharmonic Orchestra, and with a full programme of other concerts.

**Picturehouse at FACT** Wood St ☎0871 704 2063, Ⓦ picturehouses.co.uk. The city's only independent cinema screens new films, re-runs, cult classics and festivals.

**Playhouse** Williamson Square ☎0151 709 4776, Ⓦ everymanplayhouse.com. Sister theatre to the Everyman, staging bold productions of great plays in the three-tier main house and new plays in the 70-seat Studio.

**Royal Court Theatre** Roe St ☎0870 787 1866, Ⓦ royalcourtliverpool.co.uk. Art Deco theatre and concert hall, which sees regular plays, music and comedy acts.

## SHOPPING

Liverpool is fabulous for shopping, with the brilliantly designed Liverpool ONE shopping complex holding pretty much all the names, a stretch of independent stores on Bold Street and arty originals in the Baltic Triangle.

**Alison Appleton** 46B Jamaica St, Baltic Triangle ☎0151 709 1188, Ⓦ alisonappleton.com. Delicate, beautiful handmade teapots, cups and more in a tiny outlet in the heart of Liverpool's most dynamic quarter. Mon–Fri 9am–5pm, Sat 11am–4pm.

**Delifonseca** Brunswick Dock Ⓦ delifonseca.co.uk /delis/dockside. The new food hall of this acclaimed, two-site bistro offers a vast array of fine deli foods and wines. Daily 8am–9pm.

**News From Nowhere** 96 Bold St ☎0151 708 7270, Ⓦ newsfromnowhere.co.uk. Proper radical bookshop in the heart of Bold Street, packed to the rafters with left-leaning literature, music and more, and with an informative noticeboard. Mon–Sat 10am–5.45pm, Sun (Dec only) 11am–5pm.

**Utility** 8 Paradise Place ☎0151 702 9116, Ⓦ utilitydesign.co.uk. Stylish, design-led Liverpool store with three outlets across the city, two of them on Bold Street. This one, in Liverpool ONE, has the longest hours. Make a beeline for the quality Scouse souvenirs, particularly the brilliant wheelie bin desk tidy. Mon–Fri 9.30am–8pm, Sat 9am–7pm, Sun 11am–5pm.

# Blackpool

Shamelessly brash **BLACKPOOL** is the archetypal British seaside resort, its "Golden Mile" of piers, amusement arcades, tram and donkey rides, fish-and-chip shops, candyfloss stalls, fun pubs and bingo halls making no concessions to anything but lowbrow fun of the finest kind. It was the coming of the railway in 1846 that made Blackpool what it is today:

Blackpool's own "Eiffel Tower" on the seafront and other refined diversions were built to cater to the tastes of the first influx of visitors, but it was the Central Pier's "open-air dancing for the working classes" that heralded the crucial change of accent. Suddenly Blackpool was favoured destination for the "Wakes Weeks", when whole Lancashire mill towns descended for their annual holiday.

With seven miles of beach – the tide ebb is half a mile, leaving plenty of sand at low tide – a revamped **prom** and an increasingly attractive, gentrified centre, there is more to Blackpool than just amusements. Where other British holiday resorts have suffered from the rivalry of cheap foreign packages, Blackpool has gone from strength to strength. Underneath the populist veneer there's a sophisticated marketing approach, which balances ever more elaborate rides and public art installations with well-grounded traditional entertainment. And when other resorts begin to close up for the winter, Blackpool's main season is just beginning, as more than half a million light bulbs create the **Illuminations** that decorate the prom from late August to early November.

## Blackpool Tower

**Tower** Mon–Fri 10am–4.45pm, Sat & Sun 10am–6.15pm • Free entry to tower, but charges for attractions; for multi-attraction all-day tickets from £20 book online 24hr in advance **Circus** 1–3 shows daily; 2hr • £16.95, or included in package • ☎01253 622242, ⦾theblackpooltower.com

Between Central and North piers stands the 518ft-high **Blackpool Tower**, erected in 1894 when it was thought that the northwest really ought not to be outdone by Paris. Ride up to the top for the stunning view and an unnerving walk on the see-through glass floor. The all-day ticket covers all the other tower attractions, including the gilt Edwardian ballroom (otherwise £2.95), with its Wurlitzer organ tea dances and big band evenings, plus dungeon, children's entertainers, adventure playground, cafés and amusements. From the earliest days, there's also been a Moorish-inspired **circus** held between the tower's legs.

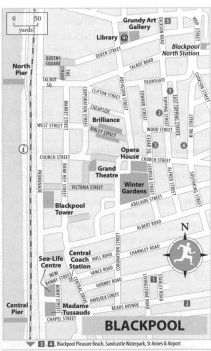

## The Comedy Carpet

Right outside Blackpool Tower, **The Comedy Carpet** is one of the country's most engaging pieces of public art – a 2200m-square, cross-shaped pavement comprising jokes and catchphrases from around a thousand comedians and writers, both old-school and new, in a dazzling typographic display that recalls a music hall playbill. Opened in 2011 by end-of-the-pier stalwart Ken Dodd, it's a unique celebration of British comedy and a marvellous way to spend an hour.

## Blackpool Pleasure Beach

March–Oct daily from 10am • Free, though rides cost; wristband £29.99, cheaper if booked online • ⦾blackpoolpleasurebeach.com

The major draw in town is **Blackpool Pleasure Beach** on the South Promenade, just south of South Pier. Entrance to the

**BLACKPOOL**

▼ **3** , **4** , Blackpool Pleasure Beach, Sandcastle Waterpark, St Annes & Airport

| ● CAFÉS & RESTAURANTS | | ■ ACCOMMODATION | | ■ CABARET | |
|---|---|---|---|---|---|
| AJ's | 2 | The Big Blue | 3 | Funny Girls | 1 |
| Kwizeen | 4 | FouRooms | 2 | | |
| The Lounge | 3 | Number One | 4 | | |
| Yorkshire Fisheries | 1 | Raffles | 1 | | |

**10**

## BLACKPOOL – BEHIND THE SCENES

There is, after all, an alternative Blackpool – one of history, heritage and even a spot of culture. Scene of party political conferences over the decades, the **Winter Gardens** (Coronation Street) opened to fanfares in 1878. Among the motley array of cafés, bars and amusements, seek out the extraordinary **Spanish Hall Suite** (in the form of a carved galleon), and the **Opera House** honours board – Lillie Langtry, George Formby and Vera Lynn are all present. From in front of the Opera House, follow Abingdon Street to Queen Street and the porticoed Central Library, next to which the **Grundy Art Gallery** (Mon–Sat 10am–5pm; free) might tempt you in to see its Victorian oils and watercolours, contemporary art and special exhibitions. **North Pier**, the first pier to be opened (1863) on the Blackpool seafront, is now a listed building. Head northbound from here on the tram to the **Imperial Hotel**, whose wood-panelled No. 10 Bar is covered with photographs and mementos of every British prime minister since Lloyd George.

amusement park is free, but you'll have to fork out for the superb array of white-knuckle rides including the 235ft-high "Big One". The wonderful antique wooden roller coasters ("woodies" to aficionados) may seem like kids' stuff, but each is unique – the original "Big Dipper" was invented at Blackpool in 1923 and still thrills, as does the "Grand National" (1935). Caution: do not disregard the warning at the thrilling "Valhalla" ride – you will indeed get (very) wet, so maybe save this one until the end of the day. Recuperate in the park's champagne and oyster bar, which adds a bit of class to the otherwise relentless barrage of fairground noise, shrieking, jangling and fast food.

## Great Promenade Show

South from the Pleasure Beach, from the Sandcastle Waterpark down to Squire's Gate • Free

Perhaps nowhere sums up the "new" Blackpool better than the **Great Promenade Show**, a set of ambitious outdoor sculptures, installations and soundscapes set along a mile or so of the new promenade. All relating to some aspect of Blackpool's history or its natural environment, these include the mighty **High Tide Organ**, which gives off haunting music when "played" by the swell of the waves, a set of sculptures of circus characters by **Sir Peter Blake**, and the world's largest **disco ball**, named "They Shoot Horses, Don't They?"

### ARRIVAL AND INFORMATION
BLACKPOOL

**By plane** Blackpool's airport (ⓦ blackpoolinternational .com) lies 2.5 miles south of the centre; however it hit financial difficulties in 2014 and was closed at the time of writing.
**By train** The town's main train station, Blackpool North, is a few minutes' walk west of the town centre on Talbot Road, with a smaller terminus, Blackpool South, just north of the Pleasure Beach on Waterloo Road.
Destinations Manchester (hourly; 1hr 10min).

**By bus** Buses pull in at the new Blackpool Central Coach Station, behind the Coral Island arcade at the junction of Central Drive and New Bonny Street.
**Tourist office** Festival House, on the Promenade (Mon & Tues 9am–6pm, Wed–Sat 9am–5pm, Sun 10am–4pm; ☎ 01253 478222, ⓦ visitblackpool.com). Brand-new, purpose-built information centre; it sells discounted admission tickets for all major Blackpool attractions (except the Pleasure Beach), and travel passes.

### GETTING AROUND

**By tram** Electric trams (ⓦ blackpooltransport.com) cover the length of the promenade, from Fleetwood, north of Blackpool, to Starr Gate, south of the Pleasure Beach. Prices vary, but the cheapest option is to buy a Blackpool1 travel

card online or from the tourist office (see above) valid for local buses and trams (1/3/7-day, £3.50/10.50/13.50); you'll pay more if you buy on board.

### ACCOMMODATION

Bed-and-breakfast **prices** are generally low (from £25/person, even less on a room-only basis or out of season), but rise at weekends and during the Illuminations. To avoid the noisy crowds in peak season, make for the North Shore, beyond North Pier (the grid west of Warbreck Hill Road has hundreds of options).

**The Big Blue** Ocean Blvd, Pleasure Beach ☎0871 222 4000, ⓦbigbluehotel.com. Spacious family rooms with games consoles and separate children's area, plus boutique-style, dark-wood executive rooms. There's a bar and brasserie, parking and a gym. It's next to the Pleasure Beach (and Blackpool South train station), and most rooms look out on the rides. Parking available. **£135**

★**FouRooms** 60 Reads Ave ☎01253 752171, ⓦfouroomsblackpool.co.uk. One of Blackpool's best boutique hotels, a tastefully converted Victorian townhouse with airy rooms and original dark wood fittings. The four suites are individually furnished, and staff are keen to help. **£120**

★**Number One** 1 St Luke's Rd ☎01253 343901, ⓦnumberoneblackpool.com. There's no other B&B quite like this – an extraordinarily lavish boutique experience hosted by the ultra-amiable Mark and Claire. There are just three extravagantly appointed rooms here, with more at *Number One South Beach* nearby. Single occupancy starts at £70. Parking available. **£100**

**Raffles** 73–77 Hornby Rd ☎01253 294713, ⓦraffleshotelblackpool.co.uk. Nice place back from Central Pier and away from the bustle, with well-kept rooms, a bar, and traditional tearooms attached. Winter rates are a good deal. **£78**

## EATING

**AJ's** 65 Topping St ☎01253 626111, ⓦajs-bistro.co.uk. A festival of meat, this unpretentious restaurant is at its best with steaks and grills, though there's a good range of seafood and poultry. Non-steak mains around £14. Tues–Fri & Sun 5.30pm–late, Sat 5pm–late.

★**Kwizeen** 49 King St ☎01253 290045, ⓦkwizeenrestaurant.co.uk. This friendly, contemporary bistro is the best restaurant in town, with a seasonally changing menu that emphasizes local produce, from Blackpool tomatoes and Lancashire cheese to Fylde farm ostriches. Mains around £15, though there's a bargain two- or three-course weekday lunch. Mon–Fri

11.45am–1.45pm & 6–9pm, Sat 6–9pm; occasionally open on Sun.

**The Lounge** 10a Cedar Square ☎01253 291112. Tapas restaurant-cum-café on cobbled Cedar Square, with friendly staff serving a selection of light lunches. Mon–Wed 11am–5pm, Thurs–Sat 11am–11pm, Sun noon–5pm.

**Yorkshire Fisheries** 14–16 Topping St ☎01253 627739, ⓦyorkshirefisheries.co.uk. Behind the Winter Gardens, this sit-down and takeaway fish and chip shop is commonly agreed to be the best in the centre of town. Mon–Sat 11.30am–7pm, Sun noon–6pm.

## NIGHTLIFE AND ENTERTAINMENT

Blackpool has a plethora of **theme bars** and any number of places for **karaoke** or **dancing**. Family-oriented fun revolves around musicals, veteran TV comedians, magicians, ice dance, tribute bands, crooners and stage spectaculars put on at a variety of end-of-pier and historic venues.

**Funny Girls** 5 Dickson Rd, off Talbot Rd ☎01253 649194, ⓦfunnygirlsonline.co.uk. A Blackpool institution – a transvestite-run bar with nightly cabaret shows that attract long (gay and straight) queues. It's a hen party favourite and not to everyone's tastes, but the best place in town if you fancy some unabashedly bawdy Blackpool fun.

**The Grand Theatre** Church St ☎01253 290190, ⓦblackpoolgrand.co.uk. Built in 1894 for the town's more refined audiences, the Grand has a tradition of distinguishing itself from other amusements, putting on performances of Shakespeare as well as more popular variety shows.

**Opera House** Winter Gardens, Church St ☎01253 625252, ⓦblackpoollive.com. Set in the Winter Gardens, the Opera House has a star-studded history that includes such populist greats as Charlie Chaplin, George Formby and Vera Lynn. These days you'll find a variety of shows on offer, including West End hits. Also in the Winter Gardens, the Empress Ballroom is a majestic gig venue (same contact details).

**Pleasure Beach Theatre** Pleasure Beach ☎0871 222 9090, ⓦblackpoolpleasurebeach.com. Spectacular stuff: huge choreographed dance shows, dramatic stunts and blood-pumping musical accompaniment.

# Lancaster

**LANCASTER**, Lancashire's county town, dates back at least as long ago as the Roman occupation, though only scant remains survive from that period. A Saxon church was later built within the ruined Roman walls as Lancaster became a strategic trading centre, and by medieval times a **castle** had been built on the heights above the river. Lancaster became an important port on the slave trade triangle, and it's the **Georgian buildings** from that time – especially those around the castle – that give the town much of its character. Many

**10**

people choose to stay here on the way to the Lakes or Dales to the north; and it's an easy side-trip the few miles west to the resort of **Morecambe** and to neighbouring **Heysham village**, with its ancient churches, or east through the **Forest of Bowland**.

## Lancaster Castle

Daily: tours every 30min 10am–4pm • £8 • ⓦ lancastercastle.com

The site of **Lancaster Castle** has been the city's focal point since Roman times. The Normans built the first defences here, at the end of the eleventh century – two hundred years later it became a **crown court**, a role it maintains today, and until 2011 it was a working prison. Currently, about a third of the battlemented building can be visited on an entertaining hour-and-a quarter-long tour, though court sittings sometimes affect the schedules.

## Judges' Lodgings

15 Castle Hill • Easter–June & Oct Mon–Fri 1–4pm, Sat & Sun noon–4pm; July–Sept Mon–Fri 10am–4pm, Sat & Sun noon–4pm • £3 • ⓣ 01524 32808

A two-minute walk down the steps between the castle and the neighbouring **Priory Church of St Mary** brings you to the seventeenth-century **Judges' Lodgings**, once used by visiting magistrates. The top floor is given over to a Museum of Childhood, with memory-jogging displays of toys and games, and a period (1900) schoolroom.

## Maritime Museum

Custom House, St George's Quay • Daily: April–Oct 11am–5pm; Nov–March 12.30–4pm • £3 • ⓣ 01524 382264

Down on the banks of the River Lune – which lent Lancaster its name – one of the eighteenth-century quayside warehouses is taken up by part of the **Maritime Museum**. The museum amply covers life on the sea and inland waterways of Lancashire, including the role of Lancaster's residents in the highly profitable slave trade.

## Williamson Park

Daily: April–Sept 10am–5pm; Oct–March 10am–4pm • Free

For a panorama of the town, Morecambe Bay and the Cumbrian fells, take a steep 25-minute walk up Moor Lane (or a taxi from the bus station) to **Williamson Park**, Lancaster's highest point. Funded by local statesman and lino magnate Lord Ashton, the park's centrepiece is the 220ft-high Ashton Memorial, a Baroque folly raised by his son in memory of his second wife.

### ARRIVAL AND DEPARTURE
LANCASTER

**By train** Trains pull in at Meeting House Lane, a 5min walk from the town centre.

Destinations Carlisle (every 30min–1hr; 50min); Manchester (every 30min–1hr; 1hr); Morecambe (every 30min–1hr; 10min).

**By bus** The bus station is on Cable St, a 5min walk from the tourist office.

Destinations Carlisle (4–5 daily; 1hr 20min); Kendal (hourly; 1hr); Manchester (2 daily; 2hr); Windermere (hourly; 1hr 45min).

---

#### ON YOUR BIKE

Lancaster promotes itself as a **cycling centre**, and miles of canal towpaths, old railway tracks and riverside paths provide excellent traffic-free routes around the Lune estuary, Lancaster Canal and Ribble Valley, southeast of Lancaster. Typical is the easy riverside path to the **Crook O'Lune** beauty spot, where you can reward yourself with a bacon buttie and an Eccles cake at *Woodie's* famous snack bar.

## INFORMATION AND TOURS

**Tourist office** The Storey, Meeting House Lane, off Castle Hill (Mon–Sat 10am–5pm; ☎01524 582394, ⓦ citycoastcountryside.co.uk).

**Canal cruises** For canal cruises, contact Lancaster Canal Boats (☎01524 389410, ⓦ budgietransport.co.uk).

## ACCOMMODATION

**Penny Street Bridge** Penny St ☎01524 599900, ⓦ pennystreetbridge.co.uk. This elegantly restored listed townhouse has 28 oddly shaped rooms, all with airy high ceilings and flat screen TVs. It's worth popping in the bar for a pint of good local ale too. **£79**

**★Sun** 63 Church St ☎01524 66006, ⓦ thesunhotelandbar.co.uk. The city centre's only four-star hotel has sixteen handsome rooms (some with king-sized beds, all with fine bathrooms) above a contemporary bar fashioned from a 300-year-old building. **£88**

## EATING AND DRINKING

**★The Borough** 3 Dalton Square ☎01524 64170, ⓦ theboroughlancaster.co.uk. Great for informal dining, this roomy gastropub – in a refurbished 1824 building – has a rigorously sourced local and organic menu. Moderately priced tapas-style platters offer smoked fish, Lancashire cheese and the like, while mains range from ostrich to salmon. Nine smart new rooms upstairs too (£95). Food served Mon–Thurs & Sun 8–11am & noon–9pm, Fri & Sat 8–11am & noon–9.30pm.

**The Music Room** Sun St ⓦ themusicroomcafe.com. A quirky, stylish little place with a marvellous glass frontage, serving top-quality coffees (it has its own roaster), teas and melt-in-the-mouth cake. The best place

in town to take a break. Mon–Sat 10am–5pm.

**Water Witch** Canal towpath, Aldcliffe Lane ☎01524 63828, ⓦ thewaterwitch.co.uk. Relaxing canalside pub named after an old canal packet boat. A youthful crowd munches burgers, shoots pool and hogs the canalside tables, and there is an impressive range of real ales and continental lagers. Food served Mon–Fri noon–9pm, Sat noon–9.30pm, Sun noon–8pm.

**Whale Tail** 78a Penny St ☎01524 845133, ⓦ whaletailcafe.co.uk. Tucked away in a yard and up on the first floor, this cheery veggie and wholefood café serves good breakfasts, quiche, moussaka and baked potatoes. Mon–Fri 10am–4pm, Sat 10am–5pm, Sun 10am–3pm.

## NIGHTLIFE AND ENTERTAINMENT

**Dukes** Moor Lane ☎01524 598500, ⓦ dukes-lancaster.org. Lancaster's arts centre is the main cultural destination in town, with cinemas and stages for all manner of theatre and dance performances, exhibition space and a café-bar.

**Yorkshire House** 2 Parliament St ☎01524 64679. Down-to-earth real ale boozer that's also a cracking alternative live-music venue, pulling in a young crowd. Mon–Wed 7pm–midnight, Sat 7pm–1am, Sat 2pm–1am, Sun 2–11.30pm.

# Morecambe and around

The seaside resort of **MORECAMBE** lies five miles west of Lancaster – there's a pleasant cycle path between the two, and bus and train services that can whizz you there in ten minutes. The sweep of the bay is the major attraction, with the Lake District fells visible beyond, while the **Stone Jetty** features bird motifs and sculptures – recognizing Morecambe Bay as Britain's most important wintering site for wildfowl and wading birds. A little way along the prom stands the statue of one of Britain's most treasured

---

### THE FOREST OF BOWLAND

The remote **Forest of Bowland** (ⓦ forestofbowland.com), designated an Area of Outstanding Natural Beauty, is a picturesque drive east from Lancaster. The name forest is used here in its traditional sense of "a royal hunting ground" – it's a captivating landscape of remote fells and farmland with plenty of walks and populated by rare birds like the golden plover, short-eared owl, snipe and merlin. Head east on the A683, turning off towards High Bentham; once at the village turn right at the sign for the station and you begin the fifteen-mile slog down an old drovers' track (now a very minor road) known as the **Trough of Bowland**. This winds through heather- and bracken-clad hills before ending up at the compact village of Slaidburn. If you've got time, it's worth pushing ahead to **Clitheroe**, a tidy little market town overlooked by a Norman keep.

comedians – Eric Bartholomew, who took the stage name **Eric Morecambe** when he met his comedy partner, Ernie Wise.

## Heysham Village
Three miles southwest of Morecambe – you can walk here along the promenade – the shoreside **HEYSHAM VILLAGE** is centred on a group of charming seventeenth-century cottages and barns. Proudest relic is the well-preserved Viking hog's-back tombstone in Saxon **St Peter's Church**, set in a romantic churchyard below the headland. Don't miss the local **nettle beer**, dating from Victorian times, and served in the village tearooms.

### ARRIVAL AND DEPARTURE            MORECAMBE

**By bus and train** The bus and train stations are close together near Central Drive; both receive regular services from Lancaster (10min).

### ACCOMMODATION

**Midland Hotel** The Promenade, Marine Road West ☎ 0845 850 3502, ⓦ elh.co.uk/hotels/midland. Lovely four-star Art Deco hotel whose comfortable rooms extend the modernist theme. Even if you're not staying it's worth popping into the electric-blue bar, and taking a drink onto the terrace to watch the sunset. **£94**

# The Isle of Man
The **Isle of Man**, almost equidistant from Ireland, England, Wales and Scotland, is one of the most beautiful spots in Britain, a mountainous, cliff-fringed island just 33 miles by 13. There's peace and quiet in abundance, walks around the unspoilt hundred-mile coastline, rural villages and steam trains straight out of a 1950s picture book – a yesteryear ensemble if ever there was one.

Many true Manx inhabitants, who comprise a shade under fifty percent of its 84,500 population, insist that the Isle of Man is not part of England, nor even of the UK. Indeed, although a Crown dependency, the island has its own government, **Tynwald**, arguably the world's oldest democratic parliament, which has run continuously since 979 AD. To further complicate matters, the island maintains a unique associate status in the EU, and also has its own sterling currency (worth the same as the mainland currency), its own laws, an independent postal service, and a Gaelic-based language which is taught in schools and seen on dual-language road signs.

All roads lead to the capital, **Douglas**, the only town of any size. From the summit of **Snaefell**, the island's highest peak, you get an idea of the island's varied scenery, the finest parts of which are to be found in the seventeen officially designated National Glens. Most of these are linked by the 95-mile **Raad Ny Foillan** (Road of the Gull) coastal footpath, which passes several of the island's numerous hill forts, Viking ship burials and Celtic crosses. Scenery aside, the main tourist draw is the **TT (Tourist Trophy) motorcycle races** (held in the two weeks around the late May bank holiday), a frenzy of speed and burning rubber that's shattered the island's peace annually since 1907.

### ARRIVAL AND DEPARTURE          THE ISLE OF MAN

**By plane** The cheapest way to get to the Isle is by air, with several budget airlines – among them Stobart Air (ⓦ aerarann.com at the time of writing), Flybe (ⓦ flybe .com); and easyJet (ⓦ easyjet.com) – offering flights from many British and Irish regional airports.

**By ferry** Ferries or the quicker fastcraft (Manannan), both run by the Isle of Man Steam Packet Company (☎ 0872 299 2992, ⓦ steam-packet.com), leave from Heysham (ferries; 1 or 2 daily; 3hr 30min) and Liverpool (fastcraft; 1 or 2 daily between March–Nov; 2hr 30min).

### GETTING AROUND

**Travel passes** "Island Explorer" tickets – sold at Douglas' Welcome Centre (see opposite) – give 1 (£16), 3 (£32), or 7 (£47) days' unlimited travel on all buses and trains. **Useful website** ⓦ gov.im/publictransport.

## INFORMATION

**Manx National Heritage** (ⓦ manxnationalheritage.im) run thirteen heritage sites and museums around the Isle of Man including the Old House of Keys, the House of Manannan, Castle Rushen and the Laxey Wheel. They also offer money-saving passes including a 10-Day Holiday pass (£20, available from any attraction).

# Douglas

Dubbed "the Naples of the North" by John Betjeman, **DOUGLAS** has developed since its 1950s heyday of seaside holiday-making into a major offshore financial centre. The seafront vista has changed little since Victorian times, and is still trodden by heavy-footed carthorses pulling trams (May–Sept, from 9am–5.30pm; £5.70 return). On Harris Promenade the opulent Edwardian **Gaiety Theatre** sports a lush interior that can be seen on fascinating tours (May–Oct, Sat 10am–12.30pm; £7.50, call ahead; ☎01624 600555, ⓦ cfvg.gov.im).

Further up Harris Promenade, approaching Broadway, the **Villa Marina gardens** display classic Victorian elegance with their colonnade walk, lawns and bandstand. The main sight, however, is the **Manx Museum**, on the corner of Kingswood Grove and Crellin's Hill (Mon–Sat 10am–5pm; free), which helps the visitor get to grips with Manx culture and heritage. Finally, out on **Douglas Head** – the point looming above the southern bay – the town's Victorian camera obscura has been restored for visits (Easter week, plus May–Sept Sat 1–4pm, Sun & bank hols 11am–4pm, weather permitting; £2).

10

## ARRIVAL AND DEPARTURE                                                          DOUGLAS

**By plane** Ronaldsway Airport (☎01624 821600, ⓦ iom-airport.com) is 10 miles south of Douglas, close to Castletown. A regular bus runs into town, while a taxi costs around £20.

**By ferry** The Isle of Man Steam Packet Company (ⓦ steam-packet.com) ferries from Liverpool, Heysham, Dublin, and Belfast arrive at the 1960s Sea Terminal (April–Oct 7am–8pm; Nov–March 8am–6/8pm), close to the centre of town, at the south end of the promenade.

**By train** The Steam Railway (March–Nov 9.50am–4.50pm; £5.20–13 return) extends for 15 miles and connects Douglas to Port Soderick, Santon, Castletown, Port St Mary and Port Erin. The Douglas station is alongside the river and fishing port, at the top end of the North Quay. Meanwhile, the Manx Electric Railway (April–Oct daily 9.40am–4.40pm; some later departures in summer; £5.40–13 return), which runs for 17.5 miles from Douglas to Snaefell, departs from the northern end of the seafront at Derby Castle Station.

**By bus** The Lord Street terminal, the hub of the island's dozen or so bus routes, is 50 yards west of the Sea Terminal's forecourt taxi rank.

## GETTING AROUND

**By bus** Buses #1, #1a, #2, #10, #11, #11a, #12 and #12a run along Douglas' promenade from North Quay; you can also take a horse-drawn tram.

**Bike rental** Eurocycles, 8a Victoria Rd, off Broadway (Mon–Sat; ☎01624 624909, ⓦ eurocycles.co.im) rents bikes.

**Car rental** Most rental outfits have offices at the airport or can deliver cars to the Sea Terminal. Contact Athol (☎01624 820092, ⓦ athol.co.im); Mylchreests (☎0800 019 0335, ⓦ mylchreests.com); or Ocean Ford (☎01624 820820, ⓦ oceanford.com).

## INFORMATION AND TOURS

**Cruises** Seasonal pleasure cruises on the *MV Karina* head out to Port Soderick or Laxey from Villier steps by the Sea Terminal (daily April–Oct, weather permitting; ☎01624 861724 or ☎07624 493592).

**Tourist information** The Welcome Centre in the Sea Terminal building (Mon–Sat 8am–6pm, plus Sun 10am–2pm May–Sept only); ☎01624 686766, is a great starting point and the best place for island-wide information. **Useful websites** ⓦ gov.im, ⓦ visitisleofman.com and ⓦ iomguide.com.

## ACCOMMODATION

**Admiral House** Loch Promenade ☎01624 629551, ⓦ admiralhouse.com. At the ferry terminal end of the prom, this retreat features rooms in bold colours and equipped with elegant bathrooms. The restaurant on the ground floor offers modern European cuisine. __£65__

**The Claremont Hotel** Loch Promenade ☎01624

**10**

617068, ⓦclaremonthoteldouglas.com. Centrally located and boasting sea views, complimentary wi-fi and gym access for all guests, The Claremont offers 56 well-appointed rooms. **£105**

**The Mereside** 1 Empire Terrace, just off the Central Promenade ☎01624 676355, ⓦhqbar.im. Small, family-owned B&B with elegant modern fittings and very well maintained modern rooms. There's a good bar/restaurant downstairs. **£70**

**The Sefton** Harris Promenade ☎01624 645500, ⓦseftonhotel.co.im. Next to the Gaiety Theatre, this four-star has sleek, spacious rooms offering either a sea view or

a balcony overlooking the impressive internal water garden. Facilities include gym, internet access, free bikes, a bar and restaurant. **£125**

**The Town House** Loch Promenade ☎01624 626125, ⓦthetownhouse.im. This apart-hotel is set over three floors and offers 6 individually designed suites with complimentary wi-fi and telephone calls. **£85**

**Welbeck Hotel** Mona Drive, off Central Promenade ☎01624 675663, ⓦwelbeckhotel.com. A traditional mid-sized family-run seaside hotel, with comfortable rooms and friendly service. It lies 100yd from the seafront, up the hill. **£90**

### EATING

★**The Bay Room** Manx Museum, Kingswood Grove ☎01624 612211. Enclosed by the Manx National Heritage Sculpture collection with wonderful views across the bay, this café serves a selection of soups, sandwiches and cakes. Mon–Sat 10am–5pm.

★**Café Tanroagan** 9 Ridgeway St ☎01624 612355, ⓦtanroagan.co.uk. The best fish and seafood on the island, straight off the boat, served simply or with an assured Mediterranean twist in a relaxed, contemporary setting. Dinner reservations essential. Mains around £20. Mon–Fri noon–2pm & 6.30–9.30pm, Sat 6.30–9.30pm.

**L'Experience** Queen's Promenade ☎01624 623103, ⓦlex.co.im. This seemingly innocuous whitewashed shack is in fact a long-standing French bistro that serves up

meat dishes as well as daily caught fish specials, and good lunchtime dishes. £18 average for a main. Mon & Wed–Sat noon–2pm & 7–11pm.

**Little Fish Café** 31 North Quay ☎01624 622518, ⓦlittlefishcafe.com. This stylish quayside eatery offers freshly brewed coffee and a breakfast, brunch and evening menu featuring locally-sourced ingredients. Tues–Sat 8am–9pm.

**The Ticket Hall** Douglas Station, North Quay. A very handy and pleasantly traditional café in the former ticket office at Douglas Station. Serving drinks and snacks until 6pm, with hot lunches and daily specials between noon and 2.30pm. Mon–Thurs 8am–6pm, Fri & Sat 8am–10pm.

### DRINKING

**Bar George** Hill St ☎01624 617799, ⓦbargeorge.im. A fashionable haunt housed in a converted Sunday School, opposite St George's church. Mon–Sat till late.

**Queen's Hotel** Queen's Promenade ☎01624 674438. This old seafront pub at the top end of the promenade is

the best place for alfresco drinks, with picnic tables looking out over the sweeping bay. Daily noon–1am.

**Rovers Return** 11 Church St ☎01624 611101. Cosy old local where you can try the local Manx beers, including "Old Bushy Tail". Daily 11am–11pm.

## Laxey

Filling a narrow valley, the straggling village of **LAXEY**, seven miles north of Douglas, spills down from its train station to a small harbour and long, pebbly beach, squeezed between two bulky headlands. The Manx Electric Railway from Douglas drops you at the station used by the Snaefell Mountain Railway (see below). Passengers disembark and then head inland and uphill to Laxey's pride, the **"Lady Isabella" Great Laxey Wheel** (March–Nov daily 9.30am–4pm; £4.50; ⓦlaxeywheel.co.uk), smartly painted in red and white. With a diameter of more than 72ft it's said to be the largest working water wheel in the world. In **Old Laxey**, around the harbour, half a mile below the station, large car parks attest to the popularity of the beach and river.

## Snaefell

Every thirty minutes, the tramcars of the **Snaefell Mountain Railway** (April–Oct daily 10.15am–3.45pm; £11 return) begin their thirty-minute climb from Laxey through increasingly denuded moorland to the island's highest point, the top of **Snaefell** (2036ft) – the Vikings' "Snow Mountain" – from where, on a clear day, you can see

England, Wales, Scotland and Ireland. At the summit, most people are content to pop into the café and bar and then soak up the views for the few minutes until the return journey. But with a decent map and good weather, you could walk back instead, following trails down to Laxey (the easiest and most direct route), Sulby Glen or the Peel–Ramsey road.

## Maughold

Bus #16 direct from Ramsey (Mon–Fri only)

The Manx Electric Railway trains stop within a mile and a half of **MAUGHOLD**, seven miles northeast of Laxey, a tiny hamlet just inland from the cliff-side lighthouse at Maughold Head. The isolation adds to the attraction of its **parish church**, with its outstanding collection of early Christian and Norse carved crosses – 44 pieces, dating from the sixth to the thirteenth century, and ranging from fragments of runic carving to a 6ft-high rectangular slab.

## Peel

The main settlement on the west coast, **PEEL** (bus #5 or #6 hourly from Douglas) is one of the most Manx of all the island's towns, with an imposing medieval **castle** rising across the harbour and a popular sandy **beach** running the length of its eastern promenade.

### Peel Castle

March–Nov daily 10am–5pm • £5, combined ticket with House of Manannan £9

What probably started out as a flint-working village on a naturally protected spot gained significance with the foundation of a **monastery** in the seventh or eighth century, parts of which remain inside the ramparts of the red sandstone **Peel Castle**. The site became the residence of the Kings of Mann until the mid-thirteenth century, when they moved to Castle Rushen in Castletown. It's a fifteen-minute walk from the town around the river harbour and over the bridge to the castle.

### House of Manannan

Daily 10am–5pm • £6, combined ticket with Peel Castle £9

On the way to the castle, you'll pass the excellent harbourside **House of Manannan** heritage centre named after the island's ancient sea god. You should allow at least two hours to get around this splendid participatory museum, where you can listen to Celtic legends in a replica roundhouse, wander through a replica kipper factory and even examine the contents and occupants of a life-sized Viking ship.

---

### TYNWALD DAY

The trans-island A1 (hourly buses #5 or #6 from Douglas) follows a deep twelve-mile-long furrow between the northern and southern ranges from Douglas to Peel. A hill at the crossroads settlement of **ST JOHN'S**, nine miles along, is the original site of **Tynwald**, the ancient Manx government, which derives its name from the Norse *Thing Völlr*, meaning "Assembly Field". Nowadays the word refers to the Douglas-based House of Keys and Legislative Council, but acts passed in the capital only become law once they have been proclaimed here on **July 5** (ancient Midsummer's Day) in an annual open-air parliament that also hears the grievances of the islanders.

Until the nineteenth century the local people arrived with their livestock and stayed a week or more – in true Viking fashion – to thrash out local issues, play sports, make marriages and hold a fair. Now **Tynwald Day** begins with a service in the chapel, followed by a procession, a fair and concerts.

---

10

**Creek Inn** The Quayside ☎ 01624 842216, ⓦ thecreekinn
.co.uk. Popular quayside pub opposite the House of
Manannan, serving real ale, with monthly guest beers, and a
delicious array of specials. Live music at the weekends. Daily
from 10am–midnight; food served noon–10pm.

**Marine Hotel** Shore Rd ☎ 01624 842337, ⓦ marine
hotelpeel.co.uk. Seafront pub, popular with locals,
serving Manx ales, guest beers and bar meals. Daily noon–
midnight; food served Mon–Sat noon–9pm, Sun
noon–6pm.

# 10 Port Erin

The small, time-warped resort of **PORT ERIN**, at the southwestern tip of the island, a
one-hour train ride from Douglas, has a wide, fine sand beach backing a deeply
indented bay sitting beneath green hills. To stretch your legs, head up the promenade
past the golf club to the entrance of Bradda Glen, where you can follow the path out
along the headland to Bradda Head.

**By bus** Buses #1 and #2 from Douglas/Castletown, and #8
from Peel/St John's, stop on Bridson St, across Station Road
and opposite the *Cherry Orchard* aparthotel.

**By train** Trains pull in on Station Rd, a couple of hundred
yards above and back from the beach.

**ACCOMMODATION**

**Rowany Cottier** Spaldrick ☎ 01624 832287,
ⓦ rowanycottier.com. Port Erin's best B&B, in a detached

house overlooking the bay, opposite the entrance to
Bradda Glen. No credit cards. **£80**

## Port St Mary and around

Two miles east of Port Erin, the fishing harbour still dominates little **PORT ST MARY**,
with its houses strung out in a chain above the busy dockside. The best beach is away
to the northeast, reached from the harbour along a well-worked Victorian path that
clings to the bay's rocky edge.

From Port St Mary, a minor road runs out along the Meayll peninsula towards
**CREGNEASH**, the oldest village on the island. The **Cregneash Village Folk Museum**
(March–Nov daily 10am–4pm; £5) is a picturesque cluster of nineteenth-century
thatched crofts populated by craftspeople in period costume; there's a tearoom and
information centre. Local views are stunning, and it's just a short walk south to **The
Chasms**, a headland of gaping rock cliffs swarming with gulls and razorbills.

The footpath continues around Spanish Head to the turf-roofed **Sound Visitor
Centre** (daily 10am–4/5pm; free), which also marks the end of the road from Port
St Mary. There's an excellent café, with windows looking out across The Sound to
the **Calf of Man**.

**By train** Regular steam trains run to Port Erin or back
to Douglas from Port St Mary. The station is a 10min
walk from the harbour along High St, Bay View Road

and Station Road.
**By bus** Hourly buses from the harbour serve Port Erin and
Douglas.

**ACCOMMODATION AND EATING**

★**Aaron House** The Promenade ☎ 01624 835702,
ⓦ aaronhouse.co.uk. High up on The Promenade, this
guesthouse lovingly recreates a Victorian experience and
features brass beds and clawfoot baths in some of the
rooms, with home-made scones and jam in the parlour and
splendid breakfasts. The bay views from the front are
superb. **£40**

**Harbour Lights** 1 Queen St ☎ 01624 832064,
ⓦ harbour-lights.net. In a sea-salty old boathouse next
to the harbour, this cheery restaurant serves fresh fish and
local produce, as well as cream teas, hot toasted crumpets
and light snacks. Thurs–Sat 10am–late, Sun
10am–4pm.

## THE CALF OF MAN

It is worth making the effort to visit the **Calf of Man**, a craggy, heath-lined nature reserve lying off the southwest tip of the Isle of Man, where resident wardens monitor the seasonal populations of kittiwakes, puffins, choughs, razorbills, shags, guillemots and others, and grey seals can be seen all year round basking on the rocks.

   **Charter boats** leave from Port St Mary, but the most reliable scheduled service (weather permitting) is from Port Erin pier (May–Sept daily; £20; 10am; ☎01624 832339); call in advance as numbers are limited and weather conditions affect schedules. You can also **sea kayak** around this spectacular coast. **Adventurous Experiences** (☎01624 843034, ⓦadventurousexperiences.com) runs trips from evening paddles (£55) to full-day excursions (from £85) – no experience is required.

**10**

# Castletown and around

From the twelfth century until 1869, **CASTLETOWN** was the island's capital, but then the influx of tourists and the increase in trade required a bigger harbour and Douglas took over. Its sleepy harbour and low-roofed cottages are dominated by **Castle Rushen** (March–Nov, daily 10am–4/5pm; £5.80), formerly home to the island's legislature and still the site of the investiture of new lieutenant-governors.

## Old House of Keys

Parliament Square • March–Nov daily 11am & 3pm • £5.50 • ☎01624 648017

Across the central Market Square and down Castle Street in tiny Parliament Square you'll find the **Old House of Keys**. Built in 1821, this was the site of the Manx parliament, the Keys, until 1874 when it was moved to Douglas. The frock-coated Secretary of the House meets you at the door and shows you into the restored debating chamber, where visitors are included in a highly entertaining participatory session of the House, guided by a hologram Speaker.

## Rushen Abbey

Ballasalla, 2 miles north of Castletown • Daily: March–Nov, 10am–4pm; May–Sept, 10am–4pm • £5 • Buses #1, #1C, #2, #8 or #X2 from Castletown or steam railway

The island's most important medieval religious site, **Rushen Abbey** lies two miles north of Castletown at Ballasalla ("place of the willows"). A Cistercian foundation of 1134, it was abandoned by its "White Monks" in the 1540s and was subsequently used as a school. The excavated remains themselves – low walls, grass-covered banks and a sole church tower from the fifteenth century – would hold only specialist appeal were it not for the excellent interpretation centre, which explains much about daily life in a Cistercian abbey.

### ARRIVAL AND DEPARTURE                                   CASTLETOWN

**By bus** Buses #8 (from Peel/Port Erin) and #1 (from Douglas) stop in the main square.

**By train** Castletown Station is a 5min walk from the centre, out along Victoria Road from the harbour.

**Destinations** include Ballabeg, Colby, Port St Mary and Port Erin to the south and Ballasalla, Santon, Port Soderick and Douglas to the north.

### EATING AND DRINKING

**The Abbey Restaurant** Ballasalla, 2 miles north of Castletown ☎01624 822393 ⓦtheabbeyrestaurant .co.im. Sat next to Rushen Abbey, this restaurant and café serves up modern European cuisine complemented by a predominately Southern European wine list. The venue is child-friendly and also boasts a spacious outdoor garden and a private dining room. Tues–Sat 10am–late.

# Cumbria and the Lakes

SUNRISE OVER WINDERMERE

# Cumbria and the Lakes

The Lake District is England's most hyped scenic area, and for good reasons. Within an area a mere thirty miles across, sixteen major lakes are squeezed between the country's highest mountains – an almost alpine landscape of glistening water, dramatic valleys and picturesque stone-built villages. Most of what people refer to as the Lake District lies within the Lake District National Park, which, in turn, falls entirely within the county of Cumbria. The county capital is Carlisle, a place that bears traces of a pedigree that stretches back to Roman times, while both the isolated western coast and eastern market towns like Kendal and Penrith counter the notion that Cumbria is all about its lakes.

**11**

Given a week you could easily see most of the famous settlements and lakes – a circuit taking in the towns of Ambleside, Windermere and Bowness, all on **Windermere**, the Wordsworth houses in **Grasmere**, and the more dramatic northern scenery near **Keswick** and **Ullswater** would give you a fair sample of the whole. But it's away from the crowds that the Lakes really begin to pay dividends, in the dramatic valleys of **Langdale** and **Eskdale**, for example, while over on the coast are more off-the-beaten-track destinations, like the estuary village of **Ravenglass** – access point for the **Ravenglass and Eskdale Railway** – and the attractive Georgian port of **Whitehaven**.

## GETTING AROUND AND INFORMATION
CUMBRIA AND THE LAKES

**By bus** National Express coaches connect London and Manchester with Windermere, Ambleside, Grasmere and Keswick. The North West Explorer Ticket (1-day £10.50, family £25; ⓦ stagecoachbus.com/northwest) is valid on the entire regional bus network.

**By train** Trains leave the West Coast main line at Oxenholme, north of Lancaster, for the branch line service to Kendal and Windermere. The only other places directly accessible by train are Penrith, further north on the West Coast line, and the towns along the Cumbrian coast.

**Useful websites** ⓦ golakes.co.uk and, for the National Park, ⓦ www.lake-district.gov.uk.

# Kendal and around

The self-billed "Gateway to the Lakes" (though nearly ten miles from Windermere), **KENDAL** is the largest of the southern Cumbrian towns. It offers rewarding rambles around the "yards" and "ginnels" on both sides of Highgate and Stricklandgate, the main streets, and while the old Market Place long since succumbed to development, traditional stalls still do business outside the Westmorland Shopping Centre every Wednesday and Saturday. Outside Kendal, the main trips are to the stately homes of **Sizergh Castle** and **Levens Hall**, just a few miles to the south, both of which have beautifully kept gardens.

WRAY CASTLE

# Highlights

**❶ Windermere** Enjoy the changing seasons and serene views with a cruise on England's largest lake. **See p.560**

**❷ Wray Castle** Picnic in the grounds of this extraordinary Victorian holiday home on the shores of Windermere. **See p.563**

**❸ Old Dungeon Ghyll Hotel, Langdale** The hikers' favourite inn – cosy rooms, stone-flagged floors and open fires – has England's most famous mountains on the doorstep. **See p.565**

**❹ Brantwood, Coniston Water** John Ruskin's elegant home and inspiring garden is beautifully sited on Coniston Water. **See p.568**

**❺ Via Ferrata, Honister Pass** The Lake District's biggest thrill sees you scrambling, climbing and hanging on for dear life along the old miners' route up Fleetwith Pike. **See p.573**

**❻ Ravenglass and Eskdale Railway** It's a great day out on the narrow-gauge railway from coast to mountains. **See p.575**

**❼ Wordsworth House, Cockermouth** Costumed staff and authentic surroundings bring the eighteenth century back to life at the birthplace of William Wordsworth. **See p.576**

**❽ Carlisle Castle** Cumbria's mightiest castle dominates the county town. **See p.580**

**HIGHLIGHTS ARE MARKED ON THE MAP ON P.556**

# Kendal Museum

Station Rd • Tues–Sat 10.30am–5pm; closed Christmas week • Free • ☎ 01539 815597, ⓦ kendalmuseum.org.uk

The **Kendal Museum** holds the district's natural history and archeological finds, and town history displays. You'll also find collections related to **Alfred Wainwright** (1907–91), Kendal's former borough treasurer (and honorary clerk at the museum). Wainwright moved to Kendal in 1941, and in 1952, dissatisfied with the accuracy of existing maps, he embarked on his series of painstakingly handwritten walking guides, with mapped routes and delicately drawn views. They have been hugely popular guidebooks ever since, which many treat as gospel in their attempts to "bag" ascents of the 214 fells he recorded.

**CUMBRIA & THE LAKES**

0 — 5
miles

**HIGHLIGHTS**

1 Windermere

2 Wray Castle

3 Old Dungeon Ghyll Hotel, Langdale

4 Brantwood, Coniston Water

5 Via Ferrata, Honister Pass

6 Ravenglass and Eskdale Railway

7 Wordsworth House, Cockermouth

8 Carlisle Castle

> **CLIMB EVERY MOUNTAIN**
>
> **Kendal mint cake**, a tooth-challenging, energy-giving, solid block of sugar and peppermint oil, was apparently invented by accident in the mid-nineteenth century. The familiar retro-packaged Romney's brand (from Kendal) is on sale throughout the Lakes, and its proudest boast is still that Kendal mint cake was carried to the top of Everest during Hillary's ascent of 1953.

## Abbot Hall

Mon–Sat 10.30am–5pm (Nov–March closes at 4pm), plus July & Aug Sun noon–4pm; closed mid-Dec to mid-Jan **Abbot Hall Art Gallery** £7, under 16s free • ☎ 01539 722464, ⓦ abbothall.org.uk **Museum of Lakeland Life and Industry** £5, under 16s free • ☎ 01539 722464, ⓦ lakelandmuseum.org.uk

The town's two main museums are at the Georgian **Abbot Hall**, by the river near the parish church. The principal hall houses the **Art Gallery**, concentrating in particular on the works of the eighteenth-century "Kendal School" of portrait painters, most famously George Romney. Across the way, the former stables contain the **Museum of Lakeland Life and Industry**, where reconstructed house interiors and workshops exhibit rural trades and crafts, from spinning and weaving to shoe-making and tanning.

11

## Sizergh Castle

Off A591, 3 miles south of Kendal • Easter–Oct Mon–Thurs & Sun 1–5pm; guided tours noon–1pm; gardens Easter–Oct daily 10am–5pm, Nov & Dec 11am–4pm • £9.45, gardens only £5.85; NT • ⓦ nationaltrust.org.uk/sizergh, ☎ 01539 560951 • Bus #555 from Kendal

**Sizergh Castle** owes its "castle" epithet to the fourteenth-century peel tower at its core, one of the best examples of the towers built as safe havens during the region's medieval border raids. There are guided tours of the rooms – largely Elizabethan – between noon and 1pm; thereafter, you can wander around at will.

## Levens Hall

Off A6, 6 miles south of Kendal • Easter to mid-Oct Mon–Thurs & Sun noon–4.30pm, last entry at 4pm; gardens Easter to mid-Oct Mon–Thurs & Sun 10am–5pm • £12.50, gardens only £8.50, under 16s free • ☎ 01539 560321, ⓦ levenshall.co.uk • Bus #555 from Kendal

Levens Hall was refurbished in the classic Elizabethan manner between 1570 and 1640. House stewards are on hand to point out the oddities and curios – for example, the dining room is panelled not with oak but with goat's leather, printed with a deep-green floral design. Outside are beautifully trimmed topiary gardens, featuring yews in the shape of pyramids, peacocks and top hats.

### ARRIVAL AND DEPARTURE | KENDAL

**By train** From Oxenholme on the West Coast main line, there's an hourly branch-line service to Kendal (5min). Kendal's train station is a 10min walk from the centre.

Destinations Oxenholme (for Carlisle, Lancaster or Manchester) (hourly; 5min); Windermere (hourly; 20min).

**By bus** The bus station is on Blackhall Road (off Stramongate), with main routes including the #599 (to Windermere, Ambleside and Grasmere) or #555 (to Keswick or Lancaster).

Destinations Ambleside (hourly; 40min); Grasmere (hourly; 1hr); Keswick (hourly; 1hr 30min); Lancaster (hourly; 1hr); Windermere/Bowness (hourly; 30min).

### ACCOMMODATION

**Beech House** 40 Greenside ☎ 01539 720385, ⓦ beechhouse-kendal.co.uk. Boutique B&B with a keen sense of decorative design – think swagged curtains, plumped pillows, richly coloured fabrics, and black-and-white bathrooms with gleaming roll-top baths. **£80**

★ **Punch Bowl Inn** Crosthwaite, 5 miles west of Kendal ☎ 015395 68237, ⓦ the-punchbowl.co.uk. A super-stylish country inn – the earth-toned rooms have exposed beams and superb bathrooms, while the restaurant serves locally sourced food (from pot-roast wood-pigeon to local lamb). Rooms are individually priced, up to £235, and are more expensive still at weekends and holidays. **£120**

## EATING AND DRINKING

★**Grainstore** Brewery Arts Centre, 122 Highgate ☎ 01539 725133, ⓦ breweryarts.co.uk. The arts centre bistro has a mix-and-match menu of Mediterranean dishes – anything from local pork-and-chilli bangers to salmon skewers – plus a range of gourmet pizzas (dishes £4.50– 9.50, pizzas £6.50–8.50). You can also get pizza, tapas and real ales in the adjacent *Vats Bar*, and there's often a weekday lunch service in holiday periods. Mon–Thurs 5–9pm, Fri 5–9.30pm, Sat noon–9.30pm, Sun 12.30–8pm.

**Waterside Wholefood** Gulfs Rd, bottom of Lowther St ☎ 01539 729743, ⓦ watersidewholefood.co.uk. A handy place by the river for veggie and vegan wholefood snacks or meals (£3.50–7), such as a lentil cottage pie or buckwheat burgers. Mon–Sat 8.30am–4.30pm.

## NIGHTLIFE AND ENTERTAINMENT

**Brewery Arts Centre** 122 Highgate ☎ 01539 725133, ⓦ breweryarts.co.uk. Hub of everything that's happening in town, with cinema, theatre, galleries and concert hall, not to mention all-day café (closed Sun), bistro (see above) and the lively *Vats Bar*.

# Cartmel

Around eighteen miles southwest of Kendal, the pretty village of **CARTMEL** is something of an upmarket getaway, with its Michelin-starred restaurant-with-rooms, winding country lanes and cobbled market square brimming with inns and antique shops. You're in luck if you're looking to buy a handmade dolls' house or embroidered footstool, while in the **Cartmel Village Shop** on the square they sell the finest sticky-toffee pudding known to humanity. Quite what the original monks of Cartmel would have made of all this is anyone's guess – the village first grew up around its twelfth-century Augustinian priory and is still dominated by the proud **Church of St Mary and St Michael**.

## Holker Hall

Cark-in-Cartmel, 2 miles west of Cartmel · Easter–Oct Mon–Fri & Sun, house 11am–4pm, gardens 10.30am–4.30pm, July & Aug until 5.30pm · £12, gardens only £8, under 16s free · ☎ 01539 558328, ⓦ holker.co.uk

A couple of miles west of Cartmel lies **Holker Hall**, one of Cumbria's most glorious country estates. The impressive 23-acre **gardens**, both formal and woodland, are the highlight for many, and a celebrated annual garden festival (June) is held here, as well as spring and winter markets. You don't have to pay the entrance fee to visit the excellent Food Hall and Courtyard Café, both of which are also open on Saturdays and in winter (when the hall is otherwise closed).

## ACCOMMODATION AND EATING                                                                                                CARTMEL

**L'Enclume** Cavendish St ☎ 01539 536362, ⓦ lenclume .co.uk/sr. One of England's most critically acclaimed dining experiences, overseen by the masterful Simon Rogan – expect a succession of artfully constructed dishes, accompanied by intensely flavoured jellied cubes, mousses or foams, or suffused with wild herbs, hedgerow flowers and exotic roots. Lunch is £45, dinner £120, while a dozen highly individual rooms and suites (up to £199, depending on location and size) mix French antique furniture and designer fabrics. Closed first two weeks Jan. Meals served Mon & Tues 6.30–9pm, Wed–Sun noon–1.30pm & 6.30–9pm. **£99**

# Ulverston

The railway line winds westwards to **ULVERSTON**, an attractive place of dappled grey limestone cottages, a jumble of cobbled alleys and traditional shops zigzagging off the central **Market Place**. Stalls are still set up here and in the surrounding streets every Thursday and Saturday. On other days (not Wed or Sun), the **market hall** on New Market Street is the centre of commercial life.

## Laurel and Hardy Museum

Brogden St • Tues & Thurs–Sun 10am–5pm, closed Jan • £4.50, family ticket £9 • ☎ 01229 582292, ⓦ laurel-and-hardy-museum.co.uk

Ulverston's most famous son is Stan Laurel (born Arthur Stanley Jefferson), the whimpering, head-scratching half of the comic duo, celebrated in a mind-boggling collection of memorabilia at the **Laurel and Hardy Museum** inside a rear entrance of the Roxy Cinema behind Coronation Hall.

### ARRIVAL AND DEPARTURE                                                    ULVERSTON

**By train** Ulverston train station is a few minutes' walk from the town centre – head down Prince's Street and turn right at the main road for County Square. Destinations Lancaster/Manchester (hourly; 40min/2hr); Barrow-in-Furness/Carlisle (hourly; 20min/2hr 20min).
**By bus** Buses arrive on Victoria Road, near the library. Destinations Kendal (Mon–Sat hourly, Sun 3 daily; 1hr); Windermere (Mon–Sat 5 daily; 45min)

### ACCOMMODATION AND EATING

**Bay Horse Hotel** Canal Foot, 1.5 miles east of Ulverston ☎ 01229 583972, ⓦ thebayhorsehotel.co.uk. A cosy old inn on the Leven estuary, with gorgeous views and fine Cumbrian cuisine. Six of the nine rooms open onto a river-view terrace, while dining in the olde-worlde bar or candlelit conservatory focuses on steaks, lamb, fresh fish, and game in season (lunch dishes £5–15, dinner mains £20–23). Lunch served Tues–Sun noon–2pm, dinner daily at 8pm. **£120**
**Gillam's** 64 Market St ☎ 01229 587564, ⓦ gillams-tearoom.co.uk. An excellent tearoom – with summer terrace garden – that's wholly organic, Fair Trade and veggie. Mon–Sat 9am–5pm, Sun 10am–4pm.
**Sefton House** 34 Queen St ☎ 01229 582190, ⓦ seftonhouse.co.uk. Amiable B&B in an attractive Georgian house that also holds Ulverston's best café, the rather wonderful *Natterjacks*, which is an afternoon-evening hangout for the local arts and music crowd. Café open Mon–Fri 3–10pm. **£65**

# Windermere town

**WINDERMERE** town was all but non-existent until 1847 when a railway terminal was built here, making England's longest lake (after which the town is named) an easily accessible resort. Windermere remains the transport hub for the southern lakes, but there's precious little else to keep you in the slate-grey streets. All the traffic pours a mile downhill to Windermere's older twin town, Bowness, actually on the lake, but you should stay long enough to make the twenty-minute stroll up through the woods to **Orrest Head** (784ft), from where you get a 360-degree panorama from the Yorkshire fells to Morecambe Bay. The path begins by the *Windermere Hotel* on the A591, across from Windermere train station.

## Lake District Visitor Centre at Brockhole

Brockhole, A591, 3 miles northwest of Windermere town • Easter–Oct daily 10am–5pm; Nov–Easter daily 10am–4pm • Free, parking fee charged • ☎ 01539 446601, ⓦ brockhole.co.uk • Buses between Windermere and Ambleside run past the visitor centre, or you can take the cruise launch from Waterhead, near Ambleside (see box below)

The Lake District National Park Authority has its main visitor centre at **Brockhole**, a

---

### WINDERMERE CRUISES

**Windermere Lake Cruises** (ⓦ windermere-lakecruises.co.uk) operates services to Lakeside at the southern tip (£10.50 return, family £20) or to Waterhead (for Ambleside) at the northern end (£10 return, family £29). There's also a direct service from Ambleside to the Lake District Visitor Centre at Brockhole (£7.50 return, family £20), and a shuttle service across the lake between Pier 3 at Bowness and Ferry House, Sawrey (£2.70 each way). An enjoyable circular **cruise around the islands** departs several times daily from Bowness (£7.50, family £20; 45min), while a 24-hour **Freedom-of-the-Lake** ticket costs £18.50, family £50. Services on all routes are frequent between Easter and October (every 30min–1hr at peak times), and reduced during the winter – but there are sailings daily except Christmas Day.

**11**

late Victorian mansion set in lush grounds on the shores of Windermere, northwest of Windermere town. It's the single best place to get to grips with what there is to see and do in the Lakes, with some excellent natural history and geological displays, lovely gardens and a big range of activities, including bike hire, adventure playground, watersports and high-ropes tree-top adventures.

## ARRIVAL AND INFORMATION

**By train** Windermere is as far into the Lakes as you can get by train, on the branch line from Oxenholme, via Kendal. Destinations Kendal (hourly; 15min) and Oxenholme (for London, Carlisle, Lancaster Manchester or Penrith hourly; 20min).

**By bus** All buses (including National Express coaches from London and Manchester) stop outside Windermere train station.

### WINDERMERE TOWN

Destinations Ambleside (hourly; 15min); Bowness (every 20–30min; 15min); Brockhole Visitor Centre (every 20–30min; 7min); Carlisle (3 daily; 2hr 20min); Grasmere (every 20–30min; 30min); Kendal (hourly; 25min); Keswick (hourly; 1hr).

**Tourist office** Victoria Street (Mon–Sat 9am–5pm, Sun 10am–5pm; ☎01539 446499, ⓦlakelandgateway.info), 100 yards from the train station.

## GETTING AROUND

**Bike rental** Country Lanes at the train station (☎01539 444544, ⓦcountrylaneslakedistrict.co.uk) provides bikes

(£23–29/day), plus route maps for local rides.

## ACCOMMODATION

★**Archway** 13 College Rd ☎01539 445613, ⓦarchwayguesthouse.co.uk. Four trim rooms in a Victorian house known for its breakfasts – either the traditional Full English or American, pancakes, kippers, home-made yoghurt and granola, smoked haddock and the like. **£66**

**Brendan Chase** 1–3 College Rd ☎01539 445638, ⓦbrendanchase.co.uk. Popular place with overseas travellers, providing a friendly welcome, a good breakfast and eight comfortable rooms (some en suite). **£60**

**Holbeck Ghyll** Holbeck Lane, off A591, 3 miles north of Windermere town ☎01539 432375, ⓦholbeckghyll .com. Luxurious rooms either in the main house or in the lodge or suites in the grounds (with room-and-dinner

prices up to £490 a night). There's a sherry decanter in every room, seven acres of gardens, and Michelin-starred food (dinner included in the price). **£250**

**Lake District Backpackers** High St, across from the tourist office ☎01539 446374, ⓦlakedistrict backpackers.co.uk. Fourteen basic backpackers' beds in three small dorms, with a couple of two-plus-one private rooms available on request. The price includes a tea-and-toast breakfast. No credit cards. **£15**

**YHA Windermere** High Cross, Bridge Lane, 1 mile north of Troutbeck Bridge ☎0845 371 9352, ⓦyha.org .uk. The local YHA hostel is a revamped old mansion with magnificent lake views. Dorms **£19**, rooms **£29**

## EATING

**Francine's** 27 Main Rd ☎01539 444088, ⓦfrancines restaurantwindermere.co.uk. Drop in during the day for anything from a *pain au chocolat* or a sandwich to a big bowl of mussels (lunch dishes mostly £6–10). Dinner sees the lights dimmed for a wide-ranging continental menu, pork belly confit to seafood casserole, with mains from £12 to £16. Tues–Sun 10am–3pm & 6–11pm.

**Hooked** Ellerthwaite Square ☎01539 448443, ⓦhookedwindermere.co.uk. Fabulous contemporary seafood place serving fish straight from the Fleetwood boats. Typical dishes include hake with chorizo, fava beans and garlic, or Thai-style sea bass. Starters are £6–7, mains £17–21. Tues–Sun 5.30–10pm; closed Dec & Jan.

# Bowness and Windermere

**BOWNESS-ON-WINDERMERE** spills back from its lakeside piers in a series of terraces lined with guesthouses and hotels. There's been a village here since the fifteenth century and a ferry service across the lake for almost as long – these days, however, you could be forgiven for thinking that Bowness begins and ends with its best-known attraction, the **World of Beatrix Potter**. At ten and a half miles long, a mile wide in parts and a shade over 200ft deep, the **lake** itself – **Windermere**, incidentally, never "Lake"

Windermere – is the heavyweight of Lake District waters. On a busy summer's day, crowds swirl around the trinket shops, cafés, ice-cream stalls and lakeside seats, but you can easily escape out on to the water or into the hills, and there are lots of attractions around town to fill a rainy day.

## The World of Beatrix Potter

Old Laundry, Crag Brow • Daily: Easter–Sept 10am–5.30pm; Oct–Easter 10am–4.30pm; closed 2 weeks in Jan • £6.95, all-year family Freedom Pass £30 • ☎ 0844 504 1233, ⊛ hop-skip-jump.com

You either like Beatrix Potter or you don't, but it's safe to say that the elaborate 3D story scenes, audiovisual "virtual walks", themed tearoom and gift shop here at the interactive **World of Beatrix Potter** find more favour with children than the more formal Potter attractions at Hill Top and Hawkshead.

## Blackwell

1.5 miles south of Bowness, off A5074 • Daily: March–Oct 10.30am–5pm; Nov–Feb 10.30am–4pm; closed 2 weeks Jan • £7.25, under 16s free • ☎ 01539 446139, ⊛ blackwell.org.uk

Mackay Hugh Baillie Scott's **Blackwell** was built in 1900 as a lakeside holiday home, and boasts a superbly restored Arts and Crafts interior. Lakeland motifs – trees, flowers, birds and berries – abound, while temporary exhibits focus on furniture and decorative art. There's an informative introductory talk (usually weekdays at 2.30pm), plus a tearoom, craft shop and gardens. Parking is available; alternatively, you can walk from Bowness in about 25 minutes (although along a busy road).

## Lakeside and Haverthwaite Railway

Easter–Oct 6–7 departures daily • £6.50 return, family £18, or £15.20 (family £42.25) including cruise boat from Bowness • ☎ 01539 531594, ⊛ lakesiderailway.co.uk

From Bowness piers, boats head to the southern reaches of Windermere at Lakeside. This is the terminus of the **Lakeside and Haverthwaite Railway**, whose steam-powered engines puff gently over four miles of track along the River Leven and through the woods of Backbarrow Gorge. Boat arrivals from Bowness connect with train departures throughout the day and, as well as the boat-and-train combination, there are also joint tickets for the Lakes Aquarium and the nearby Lakeland Motor Museum.

## Lakeland Motor Museum

Backbarrow, near Newby Bridge • Daily 9.30am–5.30pm • £8, family ticket £23; combo tickets available with lake cruise (£15.20, family £42.50) and steam railway (£13.50, family £37.50) • ⊛ lakelandmotormuseum.co.uk

The **Lakeland Motor Museum** has a smashing landmark riverside home to show off its 30,000-plus motoring history exhibits. It's a dream for petrol heads and nostalgia buffs alike, as it's simply stuffed with vintage vehicles and memorabilia, from boneshaker bikes and Bentleys to DeLoreans and Dinky toys.

## Lakes Aquarium

On the quay at Lakeside, Newby Bridge • April–Oct daily 9am–6pm, Nov–March daily 9am–5pm • £6.95, family £18.95, cheaper if bought online; joint ticket with the boat ride from Bowness, £16.45, family £49.80 • ☎ 01539 530153, ⊛ lakesaquarium.co.uk

The **Lakes Aquarium** is centred on the fish and animals found along a lakeland river. There's a pair of frisky otters (fed daily at 10.30am and 3pm), plus rays from Morecambe Bay, not to mention a walk-through tunnel aquarium containing huge carp and diving ducks. Enthusiastic staff are on hand to explain what's going on.

## ARRIVAL AND DEPARTURE

**By bus** The open-top #599 bus from Windermere train station stops at the lakeside piers (every 20–30min; 15min). For onward routes to Ambleside and Grasmere you have to return first to Windermere station.

**By ferry** The traditional ferry service is the chain-guided contraption from Ferry Nab on the Bowness side (10min walk from the cruise piers) to Ferry House, Sawrey (every

**BOWNESS**

20min; Mon–Sat 7am–10pm, Sun 9am–10pm; 50p, bike and cyclist £1, cars £4.30), providing access to Beatrix Potter's former home at Hill Top and to Hawkshead beyond. There's also a useful pedestrian launch service between Bowness piers and Ferry House, Sawrey (see box, p.559), saving you the walk down to the car ferry.

## GETTING AROUND

**Cross Lakes Experience** A connecting boat-and-minibus shuttle service (service operates Easter–Oct, up to 10 departures daily; ☎01539 448600, ⓦlake-district.gov .uk/crosslakes) runs from Bowness pier 3 to Beatrix Potter's

house at Hill Top (£10 return, family £27.85), and then to Hawkshead (£11.50, family £31.35) and Coniston Water (£20.20, family £54.85).

## ACCOMMODATION

**Angel Inn** Helm Rd ☎01539 444080, ⓦtheangelinnbowness.com. A dozen chic rooms – all burnished wood and black leather – bring a bit of metropolitan style to Bowness. Snacks, wraps and sandwiches and posh pub food are served in the contemporary bar downstairs, back restaurant or terraced garden. **£90**

**Linthwaite House** Crook Rd, B5284, 1 mile south of Bowness ☎01539 488600, ⓦlinthwaite.com. Contemporary boutique style grafted on to an ivy-covered

country house set high above Windermere. A conservatory and terrace offer fabulous lake and fell views, and you can work up an appetite for dinner with a walk in the gardens to the hotel's private tarn. Rates run up to £450, suites up to £650, dinner included. **£290**

**★Number 80** 80 Craig Walk ☎01539 443584, ⓦnumber80bed.co.uk. Colin and Mandy's quiet townhouse offers quirky, stylish B&B in four rather dramatic, earth-toned double rooms – a grown-up space for couples (no pets, no children). **£90**

## EATING AND DRINKING

Bowness has plenty of places offering pizza, fish and chips, a Chinese stir-fry or a budget café meal – a stroll along pedestrianized **Ash Street** and up **Lake Road** shows you most of the possibilities.

**★Hole in't Wall** Fallbarrow Rd ☎01539 443488. For a drink and a bar meal (£9–12) you can't beat the town's oldest hostelry, with stone-flagged floors, open fires and

real ales, plus a terrace-style beer garden that's a popular spot on summer evenings. Mon–Sat 11am–11pm, Sun noon–11pm.

# Ambleside and around

Five miles northwest of Windermere, **AMBLESIDE** town centre consists of a cluster of grey-green stone houses, shops, pubs and B&Bs hugging a circular one-way system, which loops round just south of the narrow gully of stony Stock Ghyll. Huge car parks soak up the day-trip trade, but actually Ambleside improves the longer you spend here, with some enjoyable local walks and also the best selection of accommodation and restaurants in the area. The rest of town lies a mile south at **Waterhead**, where the cruise boats dock, overlooked by the grass banks and spreading trees of Borrans Park. Four miles away, Victorian neo-Gothic **Wray Castle** is a great place to visit for the day.

---

### TOP 5 LAKE DISTRICT VIEWS

**Castlerigg Stone Circle** Keswick. See p.571
**Cat Bells** Derwent Water. See p.571
**Hardknott Roman Fort** Eskdale. See p.574

**Loughrigg Terrace** Grasmere. See p.565
**Orrest Head** Windermere. See p.559

# Armitt Collection

Rydal Rd • Mon–Sat 10am–5pm • £3.50 • ☎ 01539 431212, ⓦ armitt.com

For some background on Ambleside's history, stroll a couple of minutes from the centre along Rydal Road to the **Armitt Collection**, which catalogues the very distinct contribution to Lakeland society made by writers and artists from John Ruskin to Beatrix Potter.

# Wray Castle

Low Wray, 4 miles south of Ambleside, signposted off B5286 • Easter–Oct daily 10am–5pm, last admission at 4pm • £7.20, family ticket £18; NT • ⓦ nationaltrust.org.uk/wray-castle • Free parking at the castle, but car park usually very busy; either take bus #505 to Low Wray turn-off and 1 mile walk, or take Windermere Lake Cruises service from Waterhead or Brockhole (see box, p.559)

Take the boat across to Wray and walk up through the grounds to magnificent **Wray Castle**, a castellated, mock-Gothic mansion built in the 1840s by a wealthy couple as their retirement home. Rather appealingly, it's not presented as a period-piece but rather a family-friendly attraction where you are positively begged to walk on the grass and sit on the chairs. House tours (every hour or so) are available to explain the finer points of the architecture and history, but in the end it's the freedom to play and picnic in lovely surroundings that's the real draw.

11

## ARRIVAL AND INFORMATION
AMBLESIDE

**By bus** All buses in town stop on Kelsick Rd, opposite the library, with regular local services on the #555/599 to Windermere or Grasmere and Keswick, plus #505 services to Hawkshead/Coniston, and the #516 to Elterwater/Langdale.

Destinations Windermere (every 30–60min, 14min); Grasmere (every 30–60min, 13min); Keswick (hourly; 45min); Hawkshead/Coniston (every 1–2hr; 20min/30min); and Elterwater/Langdale (5–6 daily; 17min/30min).

**By ferry** There are ferry services from Bowness and Lakeside; it's a 15min walk into Ambleside from the piers at Waterhead.

**Tourist office** Central Buildings, Market Cross (Mon–Sat 9am–5.30pm, Sun 10am–5pm; ☎ 01539 432582, ⓦ exploresouthlakeland.co.uk.

## GETTING AROUND

**Bike rental** Ghyllside Cycles, The Slack (Mon–Sat 9.30am–5.30pm; ☎ 01539 433592, ⓦ ghyllside.co.uk) rents out bikes at £20/day.

## ACCOMMODATION

Lake Rd, running between Waterhead and Ambleside, is lined with **B&Bs**, as are Church St and Compston Road. Fancier places lie out of town, especially a mile to the south at Waterhead by the lake, which is also where you'll find Ambleside YHA. The nearest **campsite**, Low Wray, is three miles south and also right by the lake.

**Compston House** Compston Rd ☎ 01539 432305, ⓦ compstonhouse.co.uk. There's a breezy New York vibe in this traditional Lakeland house, where the American style extends from the rooms to the breakfasts

---

### WALKS FROM AMBLESIDE

A couple of good walks are accessible straight from the town centre. First, from the footbridge across the river in Rothay Park you can strike up across **Loughrigg Fell** (1099ft). Dropping down to Loughrigg Terrace (2hr), overlooking Grasmere, you then cut south at Rydal on the A591 and follow the minor road back along the River Rothay to Ambleside – a total of 6 miles (4hr).

The walk over **Wansfell to Troutbeck** and back (6 miles; around 4hr) is a little tougher. Stock Ghyll Lane runs up the left bank of the tumbling stream to **Stock Ghyll Force** waterfall. The path then rises steeply to **Wansfell Pike** (1581ft) and down into Troutbeck village, where you can have lunch either at the Mortal Man or the nearby Queen's Head, both just a short walk from the village centre. The return cuts west onto the flanks of Wansfell and back to Ambleside.

11

– home-made pancakes and maple syrup, fluffy omelettes and the like. **£80**

**Low Wray Campsite** Low Wray, off B5286 (Hawkshead road), 3 miles south; bus #505 ☎01539 463862, ⓦntlakescampsites.org.uk or ⓦ4windslakelandtipis .co.uk or ⓦlong-valley-yurts.co.uk. The beautiful National Trust site on the western shore of the lake is a glampers' haven. As well as tent pitches (prices vary according to location – some sites are bang on the water's edge), there are wooden camping pods for couples and families (£35–55), tipis (part-week rental from £245, full week from £460) and bell tents (part-week from £165, full week from £355). Bike and kayak hire make it great for families too. Closed Nov–Easter. Pitches **£8.50**

★**Randy Pike** B5286 (Hawkshead road), 3 miles south, just past Low Wray turn-off ☎01539 436088, ⓦrandypike.co.uk. Two amazing, boutique B&B suites open out on to the gardens of what was once a Victorian gentleman's hunting lodge. It's a grown-up, romantic retreat, and you can either stay put with the snack larder, terrace and gardens, or be whizzed down to the owners' *Jumble Room* restaurant in Grasmere (see p.566) for dinner. Prices are £25 higher at weekends. **£200**

**Riverside** Under Loughrigg ☎01539 432395, ⓦwww .riverside-at-ambleside.co.uk. Charming guesthouse, half a mile (10min walk) from Ambleside across Rothay Park. Six large, light country-pine-style rooms available, including a river-facing four-poster (£128) with an en-suite spa bath. **£108**

**YHA Ambleside** Waterhead, A591, 1 mile south ☎0845 371 9620, ⓦyha.org.uk. The YHA's flagship regional hostel has an impressive lakeside location (most rooms have a water view), and 260 beds divided among neatly furnished small dorms, twins, doubles and family rooms (including 11 en-suites). Tour- and activity-bookings, and licensed bar and restaurant. Dorms **£20**, rooms **£32**

## EATING AND DRINKING

★**Lucy's On A Plate** Church St ☎01539 431191, ⓦlucysofambleside.co.uk. Quirky, hugely enjoyable, informal bistro – if they know you're coming, you'll probably find yourself name-checked on the menu. Daytime café dishes (brunch, dips, pastas, salads, soup and sandwiches, £5–10) give way to a dinner menu (mains £14–19) that is "sourced locally, cooked globally". Daily noon–9pm.

**Zeffirelli's** Compston Rd ☎01539 433845, ⓦzeffirellis.com. *Zeffirelli's* independent cinema has five screens at three locations in town. The restaurant attached to the Compston Road screens is famous for its wholemeal-base pizzas, plus Italian-with-a-twist pastas and salads, all vegetarian (pizzas and mains £9–11). The menu's available at lunch and dinner, but *Zeff's* is also open from 10am as a café. There's a great music-bar upstairs, plus an associated fine-dining veggie restaurant (*Fellini's*) elsewhere in town. Daily 10am–10pm.

# Great Langdale

Three miles west of Ambleside along the A593, Skelwith Bridge marks the start of **Great Langdale**, a U-shaped glacial valley overlooked by the rocky summits of the **Langdale Pikes**, the most popular of the central Lakeland fells. You can get to the pretty village of **Elterwater** – where there's a tiny village green overlooked by the excellent *Britannia Inn* (see below) – by bus, which then continues on to the **Old Dungeon Ghyll Hotel** (see opposite) at the head of the valley. Three miles from Elterwater, at **Stickle Ghyll** car park, Harrison Stickle (2414ft), Pike of Stickle (2326ft) and Pavey Ark (2297ft) form a dramatic backdrop, though many walkers go no further than the hour-long climb to **Stickle Tarn** from Stickle Ghyll. Another car park, a mile further west up the valley road by the *Old Dungeon Ghyll Hotel*, is the starting point for a series of more hardcore hikes to resonant Lakeland peaks like Crinkle Crags (2816ft) or Bowfell (2960ft).

## ARRIVAL AND DEPARTURE                       GREAT LANGDALE

**By bus** The #516 Langdale Rambler bus from Ambleside runs to Elterwater (5–6 daily; 17min) and the *Old Dungeon Ghyll* (5–6 daily; 30min).

## ACCOMMODATION AND EATING

**Britannia Inn** Elterwater ☎01539 437210, ⓦthebritanniainn.com. The popular pub on Elterwater's green has nine cosy rooms – cosy being the operative word, since there's not a lot of space in a 500-year-old inn. Rates are £30 higher at weekends. A wide range of beers and good-value food – home-made pies and Cumberland sausage to grilled seabass and Hawkshead trout (mains £10–14) – is served either in the dining room (booking advised) or front bar. Food served daily noon–2pm & 6–9pm. **£99**

**Great Langdale** ☎ 01539 463862, ⓦ ntlakescampsites .org.uk or ⓦ long-valley-yurts.co.uk. The National Trust's stupendously-sited Langdale campsite has gone stellar since camping pods (£35–55 per night) and yurts (part-week from £285/full week £385, school and bank hols

£365/560) were added into the mix. The bar at the *Old Dungeon Ghyll* is a 5min walk away. Pitches **£8.50**

★ **Old Dungeon Ghyll** ☎ 01539 437272, ⓦ odg .co.uk. The Lakes' most famous inn is decidedly old-school – well-worn oak, floral decor, vintage furniture – but walkers can't resist its unrivalled location. Dinner (£25, reservations essential) is served at 7.30pm in the dining room, though all the action is in the stone-flagged *Hikers' Bar*, which has real ales and hearty meals (from £9). Food served noon–2pm & 6–9pm. **£116**

# Grasmere and around

Four miles northwest of Ambleside, **GRASMERE** consists of an intimate cluster of grey-stone houses on the old packhorse road that runs beside the babbling River Rothay. Pretty it certainly is, but it loses some of its charm in high summer thanks to the hordes who descend on the trail of the village's most famous former resident, **William Wordsworth** (1770–1850). The poet, his wife Mary, sister Dorothy and other members of his family are buried beneath the yews in **St Oswald's churchyard**, around which the river makes a sinuous curl. There's little else to the village, save its gift shops, galleries, tearooms and hotels, though the **lake** is just a ten-minute walk away; tremendous views unfold from **Loughrigg Terrace**, on its southern reaches. A four-mile circuit of Grasmere and adjacent **Rydal Water** takes around two hours, with the route passing Wordsworth haunts **Rydal Mount** and **Dove Cottage**.

## Dove Cottage

Town End, just outside Grasmere on A591 • Daily: March–Oct 9.30am–5.30pm; Nov–early Jan & Feb 9.30am–4.30pm • £7.75, family £17.20 • ☎ 01539 435544, ⓦ wordsworth.org.uk • Buses #555 and #599

**Dove Cottage**, home to William and Dorothy Wordsworth from 1799 to 1808, was the place where Wordsworth wrote some of his best poetry. Guides, bursting with anecdotes, lead you around the cottage rooms, little changed now but for the addition of electricity and internal plumbing. In the adjacent **museum** are paintings, manuscripts (including that of "Daffodils") and mementos of the so-called "Lake Poets" (see box, p.566), Robert Southey and Samuel Taylor Coleridge, as well as "opium-eater" Thomas De Quincey who also lived in the cottage for several years.

## Rydal Mount

2 miles southeast of Grasmere, A591 • March–Oct daily 9.30am–5pm; Nov–Feb Wed–Sun 11am–4pm; closed for 3 weeks in Jan • £7, gardens only £4, family ticket £16 • ☎ 01539 433002, ⓦ rydalmount.co.uk • Buses #555 and #599

At Dove Cottage Wordsworth had been a largely unknown poet of straitened means, but by 1813 he'd written several of his greatest works (though not all had yet been published) and had been appointed Westmorland's Distributor of Stamps, a salaried position which allowed him to take up the rent of a comfortable family house. **Rydal Mount** remained Wordsworth's home from 1813 until his death in 1850, and the house is still owned by descendants of the poet. You're free to wander around what is essentially still a family home, as well as explore Wordsworth's cherished garden.

**ARRIVAL AND DEPARTURE** **GRASMERE**

**By bus** The #555 (between Kendal and Keswick) and the #599 (from Kendal, Bowness, Windermere and Ambleside) stop on the village green.

## ACCOMMODATION AND EATING

★**Cote How Organic** Rydal, 3 miles southeast, off A591, ☎01539 432765, ⓦcotehow.co.uk. The three characterful rooms at this exclusive, romantic retreat, retain their original fireplaces and antique beds. Eco-credentials are unimpeachable, from rare-breed bacon and organic bread at breakfast to home-made candles and wind-up torches. Lovely organic café too, for great home-made scones. **£150**

★**Grasmere Independent Hostel** Broadrayne Farm, A591, 0.5 miles north ☎01539 435055, ⓦgrasmerehostel.co.uk. A stylish gem of a backpackers' hostel, with 24 beds in carpeted en-suite rooms – the price goes up a quid at weekends and two on bank holidays. There's an impressively equipped kitchen, and even a sauna, with the local pub just a few hundred yards away. Dorms **£21**

**How Foot Lodge** Town End, 0.5 miles southeast ☎01539 435366, ⓦhowfootlodge.co.uk. You won't get a better deal on good-quality B&B accommodation than in this light-filled Victorian villa just a few yards from Dove Cottage. **£75**

★**Jumble Room** Langdale Rd ☎01539 435188, ⓦthejumbleroom.co.uk. Funky, relaxed dining spot, where the menu roams the world – blue swimmer crab risotto, Thai salmon salad, or fish in organic beer batter – and, once ensconced, no one's in any hurry to leave. Most mains £14–21. Wed–Sun 5.30–10pm, plus Mon nights & weekend lunches in summer; closed 2 weeks in Dec.

**Moss Grove Organic** Grasmere ☎01539 435251, ⓦmossgrove.com. Stunning, revamped Victorian-era hotel that's been designed along organic, low-impact lines – thus, handmade beds of reclaimed timber, wallpaper coloured with natural inks, and windows screened by natural wood blinds. **£129**

**Thorney How Independent Hostel** Off Easedale Rd, 0.75 miles north ☎01539 435597, ⓦthorneyhow.co.uk. The first-ever hostel bought by the YHA (back in 1931) now trades as an indie backpackers, overseen by friendly owners. Facilities are being upgraded, but a café-bar, film nights and electric bike hire already make it a great night's stay. Dorms **£25**

# Coniston and around

**Coniston Water** is not one of the most immediately imposing of the lakes, yet it has a quiet beauty that sets it apart from the more popular destinations. The nineteenth-century art critic and social reformer John Ruskin made the lake his home, and today his isolated house, **Brantwood**, on the northeastern shore, provides the most obvious target for a day-trip. **Arthur Ransome** was also a frequent visitor, his local memories and experiences providing much of the detail in his *Swallows and Amazons* children's books.

## Coniston village

The small, slate-grey village of **CONISTON** hunkers below the craggy and coppermine-riddled bulk of **The Old Man of Coniston** (2628ft), which most fit walkers can climb in

---

### THE LAKE POETS

**William Wordsworth** dominates the literary landscape of the Lakes like no other. Born in Cockermouth in 1770, he was sent to school in Hawkshead before a stint at Cambridge, a year in France and two in Somerset. In 1799 he returned to the Lake District, settling in Grasmere, where he spent the last two-thirds of his life with his wife Mary and sister Dorothy, who not only transcribed his poems but was an accomplished diarist as well.

Wordsworth and fellow poets **Samuel Taylor Coleridge** and **Robert Southey** formed a clique that became known as the "Lake Poets", a label based more on their fluctuating friendships and their shared passion for the region than on any common subject matter in their writings. A fourth member of the Cumbrian literary elite was the critic and essayist **Thomas De Quincey**, chiefly known today for his *Confessions of an English Opium-Eater*. One of the first to fully appreciate the revolutionary nature of Wordsworth's and Coleridge's collaborative *Lyrical Ballads*, De Quincey became a long-term guest of the Wordsworths in 1807, taking over Dove Cottage from them in 1809.

**CLOCKWISE FROM TOP LEFT** RAVENGLASS & ESKDALE RAILWAY (P.575); CAT BELLS (P.571); HONISTER PASS (P.573); HILL TOP (P.569) >

**11**

> ## CONISTON'S SPEED KING
>
> On January 4, 1967, **Donald Campbell** set out to better his own world water-speed record (276mph, set three years earlier in Australia) on the glass-like surface of Coniston Water. Just as his jet-powered *Bluebird* hit an estimated 320mph, however, a patch of turbulence sent it into a somersault. Campbell was killed immediately and his body and boat lay undisturbed at the bottom of the lake until both were retrieved in 2001. Campbell's grave is in the small village cemetery behind the *Crown Hotel*, while the *Bluebird* tailfin is displayed in a purpose-built gallery at the local museum, where you can find out more about Campbell and that fateful day.

under two hours. In the village itself, **John Ruskin's grave** lies in St Andrew's original churchyard beneath a beautifully worked Celtic cross.

### Ruskin Museum

Yewdale Rd • Easter to mid-Nov daily 10am–5.30pm; mid-Nov to Easter Wed–Sun 10.30am–3.30pm • £6, family £16 • ☎ 01539 441164, ⓦ ruskinmuseum.com

The highly entertaining local museum is named after Coniston's most famous resident but is devoted to all aspects of local life and work, from pre-history to the exploits of Donald Campbell (see box above). Ruskin's fascinating ideas and theories are also given an airing – not to mention his socks, matriculation certificate from Oxford, and letters, manuscripts, sketchbooks and watercolours.

## Coniston Water

Steam Yacht Gondola Easter–Oct, 4–5 times daily from 11am, weather permitting • £11, family £27.50; NT • ☎ 01539 432733, ⓦ nationaltrust.org.uk/gondola Coniston Launch Easter–Oct hourly 10.45am–5pm; Nov–Easter up to 5 daily • £10.50/family £24 (north route) or £17.15/family £37.30 (south) • ☎ 01768 775753, ⓦ conistonlaunch.co.uk

**Coniston Water** is hidden out of sight, half a mile southeast of the village. As well as boat and kayak rental from the pier, there are two lake cruise services, which both call at Ruskin's Brantwood as well as various other points around the lake. The National Trust's restored **Steam Yacht Gondola** is the historic choice, while the **Coniston Launch** runs the solar-powered wooden vessels "Ruskin" and "Ransome" on two routes around the lake, north and south. You can stop off at any pier en route, and local walking leaflets are available, as well as special cruises throughout the year.

## Brantwood

2.5 miles southeast of Coniston, off B5285 • Mid-March to Nov daily 10.30am–5pm; Dec to mid-March Wed–Sun 10.30am–4pm • £7.20, gardens only £4.95, under 16s free • ☎ 01539 441396, ⓦ brantwood.org.uk

Sited on a hillside above the eastern shore of Coniston Water, **Brantwood** was home to John Ruskin from 1872 until his death in 1900. Ruskin was the champion of J.M.W. Turner and the Pre-Raphaelites and foremost Victorian proponent of the supremacy of Gothic architecture. His **study** and **dining room** boast superlative lake views, bettered only by those from the **Turret Room** where he used to sit in later life in his bathchair. Exhibition rooms and galleries display Ruskin-related arts and crafts, while the excellent *Jumping Jenny Tearooms* has an outdoor terrace with lake views.

### ARRIVAL AND GETTING AROUND                                    CONISTON

**By bus** The #505 "Coniston Rambler" bus (from Kendal, Windermere, Ambleside or Hawkshead) stops on the main road through Coniston village. The "Ruskin Explorer" ticket (available on the bus) includes return travel on the #505 from Windermere, a return trip on the Coniston Launch to Brantwood and entry to Brantwood itself (from £17.90).

**Cross Lakes Experience** The boat-and-minibus service from Bowness (Easter–Oct daily; ☎ 01539 448600, ⓦ lake-district.gov.uk/crosslakes) runs as far as the *Waterhead Hotel* pier (for Brantwood and lake services), at the head of Coniston Water, half a mile out of the village.

## ACCOMMODATION AND EATING

**Bank Ground Farm** Coniston Water, east side, north of Brantwood ☎01539 441264, ⓦbankground.com. The lakeside farmhouse was the original model for Holly Howe Farm in *Swallows and Amazons* and later used in the 1970s film. Seven traditionally furnished rooms have oak beams and carved beds, and there's also a farmhouse tearoom. Tearoom Easter–Oct Thurs–Sun noon–5pm, or Thurs–Tues in school summer holidays. **£90**

**Black Bull Inn** Coppermines Rd, by the bridge ☎01539 441335, ⓦblackbullconiston.co.uk. The village's best pub has a variety of reasonable B&B rooms (£10 more expensive at the weekends). It also brews its own beer, while local lamb, sausage and trout are menu mainstays (bar meals £9–16). Food served daily noon–9pm. **£100**

**Meadowdore Café** Hawkshead Old Road, ☎01539 441638, ⓦmeadowdore.com. The café B&B is of a high quality and excellent value. There are two en-suite rooms and one with a private bathroom, all tastefully furnished. The café downstairs has a conservatory and slate patio, so summer mornings start with an alfresco brekkie. **£60**

# Hawkshead and around

**HAWKSHEAD**, midway between Coniston and Ambleside, wears its beauty well, its patchwork of cottages and cobbles backed by woods and fells and barely affected by modern intrusions. Huge car parks at the village edge take the strain, and when the crowds of day-trippers leave, Hawkshead regains its natural tranquillity. It's a major stop on both the **Beatrix Potter** and **Wordsworth** trails (Potter's house, Hill Top, is nearby, while William and his brother went to school here), and makes a handy base for days out in **Grizedale Forest**.

## Beatrix Potter Gallery

Main St • Feb half-term to Easter Sat–Thurs 11am–3.30pm; Easter–May Sat–Thurs 10.30am–5pm, June–Aug daily 10.30am–5pm, Oct Sat–Thurs 10.30am–5pm • £5, family £12.50, discount available for Hill Top visitors; NT • ☎01539 436355, ⓦnationaltrust.org.uk /beatrix-potter-gallery

Hawkshead's **Beatrix Potter Gallery** occupies rooms once used by Potter's solicitor husband, William Heelis, and contains an annually changing selection of her original sketchbooks, drawings, watercolours, letters and manuscripts. Those less devoted to the "Tales" will find displays on Potter's life as a keen naturalist, conservationist and early supporter of the National Trust more diverting.

## Tarn Hows

Admission free, though drivers have to pay to use the National Trust car park • Seasonal buses sometimes run to the tarn

Beatrix Potter bequeathed her farms and land in the Lake District to the Trust on her death, including the local beauty spot **Tarn Hows** whose glistening waters are circled by woodland, paths and picnic spots. Tarn Hows is a two-mile walk from Hawkshead (or Coniston) on country lanes and paths; it takes about an hour to walk around the tarn.

## Hill Top

Near Sawrey, 2 miles southeast of Hawkshead • Sat–Thurs: Feb half-term to Easter 10.30am–3.30pm; Easter–May & Sept–Oct 10.30am–4.30pm, June–Aug 10am–5.30pm • £9, family £22.50; garden free during opening hours; NT • ☎01539 436269, ⓦnationaltrust.org .uk/hill-top

Beatrix Potter's beloved house, **Hill Top**, lies close to Hawkshead in the gorgeous hamlet of Near Sawrey. A Londoner by birth, Potter bought the farmhouse here with the proceeds from her first book, *The Tale of Peter Rabbit*, and retained it as her study long after she moved out following her marriage in 1913. Bear in mind that entry is by timed ticket, you'll probably have to wait in line to enter the small house, and sell-outs are possible, especially in school holidays (and you can't book in advance).

## Grizedale Forest

2.5 miles southwest of Hawkshead • Free, parking fee charged • Cross Lakes Experience bus from Hawkshead **Grizedale Forest Centre** Daily: Easter–Oct 10am–5pm; Nov–Easter 10am–4pm • ☎ 01229 860010, ⓦ forestry.gov.uk/grizedale

**Grizedale Forest** extends over the fells separating Coniston Water and Hawkshead from Windermere, and the picnic spots, open-air sculptures, children's activities, cycle trails and tree-top adventure course make for a great day out away from the main lakes. The best starting point is the **Grizedale Forest Centre**, where there's a café and information point.

## Go Ape

Sessions daily at Feb half-term and Easter–Oct, otherwise weekends only and closed certain other days in season • Adults £30, kids £24, advance booking essential, online or by phone • ☎ 0843 770 4785, ⓦ goape.co.uk

**Go Ape**, a high-ropes adventure course in the thick of Grizedale Forest, has you frolicking in the tree canopy for a couple of hours. You get a quick safety briefing and then make your own way around the fixed-ropes course – fantastic fun involving zip-wires, Tarzan-swings and aerial walkways.

### ARRIVAL                                                                        HAWKSHEAD

**By bus** The main bus service to Hawkshead is the #505 Coniston Rambler between Windermere, Ambleside and Coniston.

### GETTING AROUND

**Cross Lakes Experience** The bus shuttle service (Easter–Oct daily; ☎ 01539 448600, ⓦ lake-district.gov.uk /crosslakes) runs from Hawkshead to Grizedale and to the Beatrix Potter house at Hill Top, and on to Sawrey for boat connections back to Bowness.

**By bike** 4hr rental from £18, full day £25, based at Grizedale Forest Centre (ⓦ grizedalemountainbikes.co.uk, ☎ 01229 860369).

### ACCOMMODATION AND EATING

**Ann Tyson's Cottage** Wordsworth St ☎ 01539 436405, ⓦ anntysons.co.uk. Wordsworth briefly boarded here, on this quaint cobbled street, and now you can too. There are three B&B rooms in the main house (one with an antique carved bed from Ruskin's house at Brantwood), and three slightly more spacious ones to the side. £74

★**Drunken Duck Inn** Barngates crossroads, 2 miles north, off B5285 ☎ 01539 436347, ⓦ drunkenduckinn .co.uk. Stylish restaurant-with-rooms in a beautifully located 400-year-old inn. Smallish standard rooms (midweek rates) in the inn itself are cheapest, weekend stays cost at least £140, and there's more deluxe accommodation too (up to £325 a night). Bar meals at lunch (sandwiches, or dishes from belly pork to roast cod, £5–16) give way to more modish dining in the evening, with local sourcing a priority (mains £14–25; reservations essential). Daily noon–4pm & 6–9pm. £95

**Yewfield** Hawkshead Hill, 2 miles northwest off B5285 ☎ 01539 436765, ⓦ yewfield.co.uk. Splendid vegetarian guesthouse set among organic vegetable gardens and wild-flower meadows. The house is a Victorian Gothic beauty, filled with Oriental artefacts and art from the owners' travels. Closed Dec & Jan. £98

# Keswick and around

Standing on the shores of **Derwent Water**, the market town of **KESWICK** makes a good base for exploring the northern Lake District, particularly delightful **Borrowdale** to the south of town or the heights of Skiddaw (3053ft) and Blencathra (2847ft), which loom over Keswick to the north. Granted its market charter by Edward I in 1276 – **market day** is Saturday, held in the main Market Place – Keswick was an important wool and leather centre until around 1500, when these trades were supplanted by the discovery of local graphite. Keswick went on to become an important pencil-making town; the entertaining **Cumberland Pencil Museum**, across the river (daily 9.30am–5pm; £4.25; ⓦ pencilmuseum.co.uk) tells the whole story.

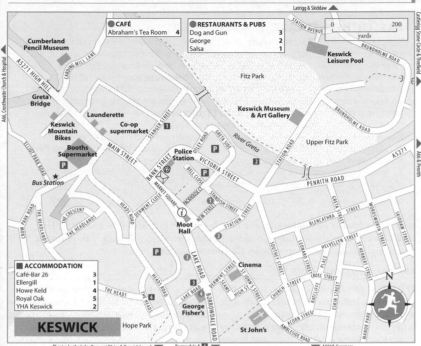

**KESWICK**

## Castlerigg Stone Circle

Don't miss Keswick's most mysterious landmark, **Castlerigg Stone Circle**, where 38 hunks of volcanic stone, the largest almost 8ft tall, form a circle 100ft in diameter, set against a magnificent mountain backdrop. Take the Threlkeld rail line path ( signposted by the *Keswick Country House Hotel*) and follow the signs for around a mile and a half all told.

## Derwent Water

Keswick Launch departures: Easter–Oct daily, Nov–Easter Sat & Sun only • £9.75 return, £2.10 per stage; 1hr summer evening cruise £9.95, family ticket £23.50 • ☎ 01768 772263, ⓦ keswick-launch.co.uk

The shores of **Derwent Water** lie five minutes' walk south of the town centre. It's ringed by crags and studded with islets, and is most easily seen by hopping on the **Keswick Launch**, which runs around the lake calling at several points en route. You can jump off the launch at any of the half a dozen piers on Derwent Water for a stroll, but if you've only got time for one hike, make it up **Cat Bells** (take the launch to Hawes End), a superb vantage point (1481ft) above the lake's western shore – allow two and a half hours for the scramble to the top and a return to the pier along the wooded shore.

## Borrowdale

It is difficult to overstate the beauty of **Borrowdale**, with its river flats and yew trees, lying at the head of Derwent Water and overshadowed by Scafell Pike, the highest mountain in England, and Great Gable, reckoned as one of the finest looking. At the straggling hamlet of **Rosthwaite**, seven miles south of Keswick, there are a couple of hotels with public bars, while another mile up the valley, eight from Keswick, there's a café and a car park at Seatoller. From here, it's twenty minutes' walk down the minor

## BASSENTHWAITE LAKE

Keswick's other lake is **Bassenthwaite**, a couple of miles northwest of town – there are regular buses along its eastern shore, including the #554 and the #73. You'll win any pub quiz if you know that Bassenthwaite is actually the only lake in the Lake District (all the others are known as waters or meres). Families will enjoy both **Mirehouse** stately home (Ⓦ www .mirehouse.com) and the **Lake District Wildlife Park** (Ⓦ www.lakedistrictwildlifepark.co.uk) – formerly Trotters World of Animals – the latter a pioneering wildlife conservation project. There's also the unique attraction of the **Lake District ospreys** (Ⓦ ospreywatch.co.uk), which nest and breed each year on the Bassenthwaite shore below Dodd Wood. From a viewing platform at the wood you'll get to see the ospreys fishing and feeding (usually April to late Aug/Sept), or you can get even closer with the nest-cam at nearby **Whinlatter Forest Park**, west of Keswick along the B5292 (the Cockermouth–Buttermere road – take bus #77 from Keswick). This is a great place for mountain-bikers (rental available), and there's a forest high-ropes Go Ape adventure course here too.

**11**

road to the hamlet of **Seathwaite**, the base for walks up **Scafell Pike** (3205ft). The classic ascent is up the thrilling Corridor Route, then descending via Esk Hause, a tough, eight-mile (6hr) loop walk in all from Seathwaite.

### ARRIVAL AND DEPARTURE
KESWICK

**By bus** Buses (including National Express services from Manchester and London) use the terminal in front of the large Booths supermarket, off Main Street.
Destinations Ambleside (hourly; 45min); Buttermere (2 daily; 30min); Carlisle (3 daily; 1hr 10min); Cockermouth (every 30min–1hr; 30min); Grasmere (hourly; 40min); Honister (Easter–Oct 4 daily; 40min); Kendal (hourly; 1hr 30min); Rosthwaite (every 30min–1hr; 25min); Seatoller (every 30min–1hr; 30min); Windermere (hourly; 1hr).

### GETTING AROUND

**By bus** Local services include the #77A (down the west side of Derwent Water, via the access point for Cat Bells) and the scenic #78 "Borrowdale Rambler", which runs south down the B5289 to Seatoller. You can use either service all day with the "Honister Rambler" ticket (from £8).
**Bike rental** Keswick Bikes, 133 Main Street (daily 9am–5pm; ☎ 01768 775202, Ⓦ keswickbikes.co.uk), rents out bikes from £25/day.

### INFORMATION AND TOURS

**Tourist office** National Park Information Centre, Moot Hall, Market Square (daily: April–Oct 9.30am–5.30pm; Nov–March 9.30am–4.30pm; ☎ 01768 772645, Ⓦ lakedistrict.gov.uk).

**Guided walks** For a good walk in good company – lakeside rambles to mountain climbs – contact Keswick Rambles (regular, sometimes daily, walks from Easter–Oct; £20; Ⓦ keswickrambles.org.uk).

### ACCOMMODATION

**B&Bs** and **guesthouses** cluster around Southey, Blencathra, Church and Eskin streets, in the grid off the A591 (Penrith road). Smarter guesthouses and **hotels** line The Heads, overlooking Hope Park, a couple of minutes south of the centre on the way to the lake, while nearby **Borrowdale** has several fine old inns and country-house hotels.

**Café-Bar 26** 26 Lake Rd ☎ 01768 780863, Ⓦ cafebar26 .co.uk. Four stylishly decorated rooms on the first floor offer a chintz-free base right in the town centre, while downstairs is a funky café-bar. It's £80 at the weekend. **£64**
★**Ellergill** 22 Stanger St ☎ 01768 773347, Ⓦ ellergill .co.uk. Owners Robin and Clare have grafted a chic European feel onto their restored Victorian house, and offer classy B&B with five rooms. **£65**
★**Howe Keld** 5–7 The Heads ☎ 01768 772417, Ⓦ howekeld.co.uk. The Fishers' boutique guesthouse puts

local crafts and materials centre stage, with furniture and floors handcrafted from Lake District trees, plus green-slate bathrooms and carpets of Herdwick wool. Breakfast is terrific, from the daily home-baked organic bread to veggie rissoles and other specialities. **£110**
**Royal Oak** Rosthwaite, on the B5289, 7 miles south ☎ 01768 777214, Ⓦ royaloakhotel.co.uk. The Borrowdale hikers' favourite – B&B rooms in a traditional inn with stone-flagged bar, where a hearty lakeland dinner (you get no choice, but a vegetarian alternative is always

available) is served promptly at 7pm, and a bacon-and-eggs breakfast at 8.30am. Rates include dinner. £124

**YHA Keswick** Station Rd ☎0845 371 9746, ☻yha.org.uk. Once a riverside woollen mill, Keswick's YHA is more budget hotel than hostel these days, but still good value. It's big (84 beds in 21 rooms) but you're still advised to book, especially for a twin-bedded or family room. Dorms £13, rooms £25

## EATING AND DRINKING

**Abraham's Tea Room** George Fisher's, 2 Borrowdale Rd ☎01768 772178, ☻georgefisher.co.uk. Keswick's celebrated outdoors store has a top-floor tearoom for home-made soups, big breakfasts, open sandwiches and other daily specials (£5–7.50). Mon–Fri 10am–5pm, Sat 9.30am–5pm, Sun 10.30am–4.30pm.

★**Dog and Gun** 2 Lake Rd ☎01768 773463. The most welcoming pub in town is a real ale, open fire, dog-friendly kind of place. Local beers aside, the food is a big draw – hearty honest stuff (nothing deep-fried, no chips, dishes £8–10), with house special, Hungarian goulash, made every day to a recipe handed down over the years. Daily noon–11pm.

**George** St John St ☎017687 72076, ☻georgehotel keswick.co.uk. Keswick's oldest inn has bags of character. There's a good bistro menu (mains £11–16), available in the restaurant or bar – slow-roast lamb to venison casserole, local trout to fish and chips. Daily 11am–11pm (Fri & Sat until midnight); food served Mon–Thurs noon–2.30pm & 5.30–9pm, Fri–Sun noon–4.30pm & 5.30–9.30pm.

**Salsa** 1 New St ☎01768 775222, ☻salsabistro.co.uk. On the right night *Salsa* can be a real buzz (it's best to book at weekends in summer) – have a drink in the downstairs bar, munch a few nachos and then move upstairs for hearty portions of fajitas, tacos, ribs, wraps, grilled fish or steak (mains £10–17). Mon–Thurs & Sun 5.30–9.30pm, Fri & Sat 5.30–10pm.

## ENTERTAINMENT

There's a fair amount going on in Keswick throughout the year, including the **jazz festival** (☻keswick.org) and **mountain festival** (☻keswickmountainfestival.co.uk), both in May, a **beer festival** in June (☻keswickbeerfestival .co.uk), and the **Keswick Agricultural Show** (Aug bank holiday, ☻keswickshow.co.uk).

**Theatre by the Lake** Lake Rd ☎017687 74411, ☻theatrebythelake.com. England's loveliest theatre hosts a full programme of drama, concerts, exhibitions, readings and talks. "Words By The Water", a literature festival, takes place here in the spring.

# Honister Pass

Near the head of Borrowdale at Seatoller, the B5289 road cuts west, snaking up and over the dramatic Honister Pass, en route to Buttermere. At the top lie the unassuming buildings of Honister Slate Mine – an unexpectedly great place for daredevil adventurers with its deep mine tours and mountain activities. Come suitably clothed – it's wet or windy up here at the best of times.

## Honister Slate Mine

Honister Pass · **Visitor centre, shop and café** Daily 9am–5pm · Free **Tours** Daily 10.30am, 12.30pm & 3.30pm · £12.50, reservations essential · ☎01768 777230, ☻honister-slate-mine.co.uk · Bus #77A from Keswick

Slate has been quarried on Honister since the eighteenth century. Honister Slate Mine, the last remaining working slate mine in England, was rescued by local entrepreneurs in 1996 and is now operating again as a sustainable, commercial enterprise. To get an idea of what traditional mining entailed, you can don a hard hat and lamp to join one of the hugely informative guided tours, which lead you through narrow tunnels into illuminated, dripping caverns.

## Via Ferrata

Daily departures from Honister Slate Mine, reservations essential · Classic £35, family £115, Extreme £39.50, family £135 · ☎01768 777714, ☻honister-slate-mine.co.uk · Bus #77A from Keswick

Honister features England's first **Via Ferrata** – a dramatic Alpine-style three-hour

11

mountain climb using a fixed cableway and harness, which allows visitors to follow the old miners' route up the exposed face of Fleetwith Pike (2126ft), the peak that's right above the mines. There are two options, labelled 'Classic' and 'Extreme', and both are terrifying and exhilarating in equal measure. Although you don't need climbing experience, you should check out the photos and videos on the website first to see what you're in for.

# Buttermere

Ringed by peaks and crags, the tranquil waters and lakeside paths of **Buttermere** make a popular day-trip from Keswick, with the best approach being the sweeping descent into the valley from Honister Pass. There's no real village here – just a few houses and farms, a couple of hotels and a youth hostel, a café and large car park. The four-mile, round-lake stroll circling Buttermere shouldn't take more than a couple of hours. You can always detour up Scarth Gap to the peak known as **Haystacks** (1900ft) if you want more of a climb and views.

## ARRIVAL AND DEPARTURE                                                 BUTTERMERE

**By bus** The direct bus is the #77 from Keswick via Whinlatter Pass; the #77A comes the long way around through Borrowdale via Honister Pass.

# Eskdale

**Eskdale** is perhaps the prettiest of the unsung Lake District valleys, reached on a long and twisting drive from Ambleside, over the dramatic Hardknott Pass. It can also be accessed from the Cumbrian coast by the Ravenglass and Eskdale Railway (see opposite) – either route ends up in the heart of superb walking country around the hamlet of **BOOT**. Here, there's an old mill to explore and several local hikes, not to mention the three-mile walk or drive back out of the valley to the superbly sited **Hardknott Roman Fort** (always open; free), which commands a strategic and panoramic position.

## ARRIVAL AND DEPARTURE                                                    ESKDALE

**By car** There's parking at Dalegarth station and at a couple of other designated areas in Eskdale, but the valley road is very narrow and side-of-the-road parking is well-nigh impossible. Come by train if you can for a hassle-free day out.

**By train** There are year-round services on the Ravenglass and Eskdale Railway (see opposite), with stops at Eskdale Green (for Stanley House) and Dalegarth station, the latter a short walk from Boot and around 1.5 miles from the *Woolpack Inn* (see below).

## ACCOMMODATION AND EATING

**Eskdale Campsite** Eskdale, Hardknott Pass road, 200 yards east of Boot ☎01946 723253, ⓦhollinsfarmcampsite.co.uk. Small, beautifully sited campsite, just a short walk from the railway and the valley's pubs. For camping without canvas they also have ten heated "pods" per night (£44). Closed 2 weeks Jan, & Feb. Pitches **£11.30**

★**Stanley House** Eskdale Green ☎01946 723327, ⓦstanleyghyll-eskdale.co.uk. B&B with a home-from-home feel and contemporary air. Accommodation is in a dozen spacious rooms, while downstairs is a huge open-plan kitchen-diner, plus lounge with woodburner.

The genial owners – who also run the *Woolpack Inn* up the valley – can arrange a lift to the pub for the night. **£110**

★**Woolpack Inn** Eskdale, Hardknott Pass road, 1 mile east of Boot ☎01946 723230, ⓦwoolpack.co.uk. Friendly country inn that's had a real facelift – eight assorted B&B rooms are slowly being freshened up, while downstairs the bar has a classy urban feel, complete with leather sofas and wood-fired pizza oven. It's also strong on Cumbrian real ales, and the beer garden has spectacular fell views. **£90**

# Ravenglass and around

A sleepy coastal village at the estuary of three rivers, the Esk, Mite and Irt, **RAVENGLASS** is the starting point for the wonderful narrow-gauge **Ravenglass and Eskdale Railway**. It's worth taking some time to look around, though, before hopping on the train or heading out to **Muncaster Castle**, the other main local attraction. The single main street preserves a row of characterful nineteenth-century cottages facing out across the estuarine mud flats and dunes – the northern section, across the Esk, is a **nature reserve** where black-headed gulls and terns are often seen (get there by crossing over the mainline railway footbridge).

## Ravenglass and Eskdale Railway

March–Oct, at least 5 trains daily (up to 15 daily in school summer hols); trains also most winter weekends, plus Christmas, New Year and Feb half-term hols · £13 return, family ticket £35 · ☎ 01229 717171, ⓦ ravenglass-railway.co.uk

Opened in 1875 to carry ore from the Eskdale mines to the coastal railway, the 15-inch-gauge track of the **Ravenglass and Eskdale Railway** winds seven miles up through the Eskdale Valley to Dalegarth Station near Boot. The ticket lets you break your journey and get off and take a walk from one of the half-dozen stations en route; the full return journey, without a break, takes an hour and forty minutes. Alternatively, take your bike up on the train (pre-booking essential, £3.50 per bike) and cycle back from Dalegarth down the traffic-free **Eskdale Trail** (8.5 miles, 2hr; route guide available from Ravenglass and Dalegarth stations).

11

## Muncaster Castle

A595, 1 mile east of Ravenglass · Feb half-term hols to first week of Nov; castle Mon–Fri & Sun noon–4.30pm; gardens and owl centre daily 10.30am–5pm or dusk; bird displays daily 2.30pm · £13, £10 without castle entrance · ☎ 01229 717614, ⓦ muncaster.co.uk · There's a footpath (30min) from Ravenglass and free parking at the castle

The **Muncaster Castle** estate, a mile east of Ravenglass, provides one of the region's best days out. Apart from the ghost-ridden rooms of the castle itself, there are also seventy acres of well-kept **grounds and gardens**, at their best in spring and autumn, as well as an entertaining **owl centre** where they breed endangered species (including England's own barn owl).

# Whitehaven

Around twenty miles up the coast from Ravenglass, some fine Georgian houses mark out the centre of **WHITEHAVEN** – one of the few grid-planned towns in England and easily the most interesting destination on Cumbria's west coast. Whitehaven had long had a trade in coal, but its rapid economic expansion was largely due to the booming slave trade – the town spent a brief period during the eighteenth century as one of Britain's busiest ports, importing sugar, rum, spices, tea, timber and tobacco.

## The Beacon Museum

West Strand, on the harbour · Tues–Sun 10am–4.30pm, plus school and bank hol Mons, last admission 3.45pm · £5.50, family ticket £10 · ☎ 01946 592302, ⓦ thebeacon-whitehaven.co.uk

The best place to swot up on Whitehaven's local history is the enterprising museum on the harbour with interactive exhibitions covering a variety of themes from slaving and smuggling to the history of the nuclear industry at nearby Sellafield. You could easily spend a couple of hours here, teaching yourself how to build a ship, tie a sailor's knot or dress like a Roman centurion.

## Rum Story

Lowther St • Daily 10am–4.30pm; closed 3rd week in Jan • £5.45, family ticket £16.45 • ☎ 01946 592933, ⓦ rumstory.co.uk

Housed in the eighteenth-century shop, courtyard and warehouses of the Jefferson family, the **Rum Story** museum is where you can learn about rum, the Navy, temperance and the hideousness of the slaves' Middle Passage, among other matters.

### ARRIVAL AND DEPARTURE                                      WHITEHAVEN

**By train** From Whitehaven's train station (services to St Bees and Ravenglass, or north to Carlisle) you can walk around the harbour to The Beacon in less than 10min.

**By bike** Whitehaven is the start of the 140-mile C2C cycle route to Sunderland/Newcastle – a metal cut-out at the harbour marks the spot.

### ACCOMMODATION

★**Lowther House** 13 Inkerman Terrace ☎ 01946 63169, ⓦ lowtherhouse-whitehaven.com. A highly personal, period restoration of an old Whitehaven house – there are three charming rooms (one with harbour and sea views); you're welcomed with tea and cake, and breakfast is a chatty affair around your host's kitchen table. **£90**

## St Bees

Five miles south of Whitehaven (and easily reached by train or bus), long sands lie a few hundred yards west of the coastal village of **St Bees**. The steep, sandstone cliffs of **St Bees Head** to the north are good for windy walks and birdwatching, while the headland's lighthouse marks the start of Alfred Wainwright's 190-mile **Coast-to-Coast Walk** to Robin Hood's Bay.

# Cockermouth

There's a lot to admire about the attractive small town and market centre of **COCKERMOUTH** – impressive Georgian facades, tree-lined streets and riverside setting – and there's no shortage of local attractions, not least the logical first stop on the **Wordsworth** trail, namely the house where the future poet was born. In the smartened-up Market Place (with monthly farmers' **markets**) there are more reminders of bygone days, including a pavement plaque teaching you the basics of talking Cumbrian.

## Wordsworth House

Main St • Easter–Oct Sat–Thurs 11am–5pm • £6.70, family ticket £16.75, admission by timed ticket on busy days; NT • ☎ 01900 824805, ⓦ nationaltrust.org.uk/wordsworthhouse

The **Wordsworth House**, where William and sister Dorothy spent their first few years, is presented as a functioning eighteenth-century home – with a costumed cook sharing recipes in the kitchen and a clerk completing the ledger with quill and ink.

## Jennings Brewery

Brewery Lane • Tours, March, Nov & Dec Mon–Sat 1–2 daily, April–Oct Mon–Sat 2 daily • £8, children over 12 only £4.50 • ☎ 0845 129 7190, ⓦ www.jenningsbrewery.co.uk

Follow your nose in town, after the heady smell of hops, and you're likely to stumble upon **Jennings Brewery**, near the river. Jennings have been brewers in Cockermouth since 1874 and you don't have to step far to sample their product, available in any local pub. Or you can take the ninety-minute brewery tour, which ends with a free tasting in the bar.

### ARRIVAL AND DEPARTURE                                      COCKERMOUTH

**By bus** All buses stop on Main Street, with the most useful service the #X4/X5 (hourly, Sun every 2hr) from Penrith (1hr 30min) and Keswick (35min).

## ACCOMMODATION AND EATING

★**Bitter End** 15 Kirkgate ☎01900 828993, ⓦbitterend.co.uk. The cosiest pub in town also contains Cumbria's smallest brewery, producing ales like "Farmers'", "Cockersnoot" and "Cuddy Lugs". Food ranges from bangers and mash to peppered tuna (most dishes £10–13, steaks up to £19). Mon–Fri 4–11pm, Sat & Sun 11am–11pm; food served Mon–Fri 4–9pm, Sat & Sun 11am–9pm.

**Merienda** 7a Station St ☎01900 822790, ⓦmerienda .co.uk. Bright and breezy café-bar offering breakfasts, soups, sandwiches, meze plates and cheese platters (£2–7.50). Also open Friday nights for tapas and music. Mon–Thurs & Sat 8am–5pm, Fri 8am–midnight, Sun 10am–4pm.

★**Six Castlegate** 6 Castlegate ☎01900 826786, ⓦsixcastlegate.co.uk. Period-piece house that retains its lofty Georgian proportions, impressive carved staircase and oak panelling, though the half-dozen B&B rooms are contemporary country in style. **£70**

# Ullswater

Wordsworth declared **Ullswater** "the happiest combination of beauty and grandeur, which any of the Lakes affords", a judgement that still holds good. At almost eight miles, it's the second longest lake in the National Park, with a dramatic serpentine shape that's overlooked by soaring fells, none higher than **Helvellyn** (3114ft), the most popular of the four 3000ft mountains in Cumbria. Cruises depart from the tiny village of **Glenridding**, at the southern foot of the lake, and also call at lovely **Pooley Bridge**, the hamlet at the head of the lake. Meanwhile, at **Gowbarrow Park**, three miles north of Glenridding, the hillside still blazes green and gold in spring, as it was doing when the Wordsworths visited in April 1802; it's thought that Dorothy's recollections of the visit in her diary inspired William to write his famous "Daffodils" poem. The car park and tearooms here mark the start of a walk up to the seventy-foot falls of **Aira Force** (40min return).

### ARRIVAL AND INFORMATION ULLSWATER

**By bus** Buses from Penrith, Keswick and Bowness/ Windermere) stop on the main road in Glenridding.

**By boat** The Glenridding steamer pier is a 5min walk from the centre, on the lakeside. There's pay-and-display parking by the pier.

**By car** Parking along the lake is difficult, especially in summer, but it's easy to park in Glenridding and use the bus or boat to visit local attractions. Use the large pay-and-display car park by the visitor centre.

**Tourist office** National Park Information Centre, in the main car park at Glenridding (Easter–Oct daily 9.30am–5.30pm; Nov–Easter Sat & Sun only 9.30am–3.30pm, weather dependent; ☎01768 482414, ⓦlakedistrict.gov.uk).

### ACCOMMODATION AND EATING

★**The Quiet Site** Watermillock ☎07768 727016, ⓦthequietsite.co.uk. The eco-friendly choice for cool campers is this hilltop site with sweeping views. Grassy camping pitches, a dozen camping pods (from £35) and a bar-in-a-barn (open most summer evenings) offer a bit of glamping comfort. Pitches **£16**

**Sharrow Bay** 2 miles south of Pooley Bridge, on the Howtown road ☎01768 486301, ⓦsharrowbay.co.uk. *Sharrow Bay* offers a breathtaking setting and highly refined Michelin-starred food. Needless to say, it's London prices in the country (rooms up to £400 a night, suites up to £700) but there are few places anywhere in England that

---

## ULLSWATER LAKE SERVICES

Ullswater steamer services started in 1859, and the lake still has a year-round ferry and cruise service. The **Ullswater Navigation & Transit Company** (☎01768 482229, ⓦullswater -steamers.co.uk) runs boats from Glenridding to Howtown on the eastern shore (40min) and on to Pooley Bridge (20min) at the northern tip, and back again. Any one stage costs £6.30 one-way, £10 return, though there's also a one-day, hop-on-hop-off "Round the Lake Pass" (£13.40). In school and summer holidays there are up to nine **daily departures** from Glenridding (basically an hourly service), down to between three and six a day at other times of the year – only Christmas Eve and Christmas Day have no sailings.

11

> **CLIMBING HELVELLYN**
>
> The climb to the summit of **Helvellyn** (3114ft) forms part of a day-long circuit from Glenridding. The most frequently chosen approach is via the infamous **Striding Edge**, an undulating rocky ridge offering the most direct access to the summit. The classic return is via the less demanding and less exposed **Swirral Edge**, where a route leads down to **Red Tarn** – the highest Lake District tarn – then follows the beck down to Glenridding past Helvellyn youth hostel. The Swirral Edge route is also the best way *up* Helvellyn if you don't fancy Striding Edge. Either approach makes for around a seven-mile (5–6hr) round walk.

compare. The dining room is open to nonresidents (reservations essential); afternoon tea here (£25) is famous, while lunch (from £30) and dinner (£75) are classy, formal affairs – desserts are renowned, notably the "icky sticky toffee pudding", which the hotel claims as its own invention. Lunch at 12.30pm for 1pm, afternoon tea at 4pm, dinner 7.30pm for 8pm. **£200**

**YHA Helvellyn** Greenside ☏0845 371 9742, ⓦyha .org.uk. Walkers wanting an early start on Helvellyn stay at this dramatically sited hostel, 900ft and a mile and a half up the valley road from Glenridding. There are lots of beds (and private rooms available for families), while the nearest pub, the *Travellers Rest*, is only a mile away. Dorms **£13**

# Penrith and around

The nearest town to Ullswater – just four miles from the head of the lake – is **PENRITH**, whose deep-red buildings are constructed from the same rust-red sandstone used to build **Penrith Castle** in the fourteenth century; this is now a romantic, crumbling ruin, opposite the train station. The town itself is at its best in the narrow streets, arcades and alleys off **Market Square**, and around **St Andrew's churchyard**, where the so-called "Giant's Grave" is actually a collection of pre-Norman crosses and "hogback" tombstones.

## Dalemain

A592, 2 miles north of Pooley Bridge, or 3 miles southwest of Penrith • Mon–Thurs & Sun: Easter–Oct 11.15am–4pm, gardens & tearoom 10.30am–5pm; Nov to mid-Dec & Feb–Easter gardens & tearoom only 11am–3pm • £10.50, gardens only £7.50, children free • ☏01768 486450, ⓦdalemain.com • No public transport

Residence to the same family since 1679, the country house of **Dalemain** started life in the twelfth century as a fortified tower, but has been added to by successive generations, culminating with a Georgian facade grafted on to a largely Elizabethan house. Its grounds are gorgeous and, while there's a guided tour of the house in the morning at 11.15am, for the rest of the time (from 11.45am, though house closed for lunch 1–1.30pm), rather remarkably, you're given the run of the public rooms, which the Hasell family still use.

## Rheged

Redhills, A66, 1.5 miles southwest of Penrith, and half a mile west of the M6 (junction 40) • Daily 10am–5.30pm • General admission and parking free; admission to one film £6.50, family £19, each extra film £5, family £14.50 • ☏01768 868000, ⓦrheged.com • Bus #X4/X5 from Penrith or Keswick/Cockermouth

**Rheged** – a Cumbrian "visitor experience", just outside Penrith – is billed as Europe's largest earth-covered building, and blends in admirably with the surrounding fells – from the main road you wouldn't know it was there. An impressive atrium-lit underground visitor centre fills you in on the region's history, and you'll also find souvenir shops, food outlets, galleries, workshops, demonstrations and play areas. The staple visit, though, is for the big-screen 3D cinema, showing family-friendly movies.

---

**POTTY PENRITH**

Potfest (W potfest.co.uk), Europe's biggest ceramics show, takes place in Penrith over two consecutive weekends (late July/early Aug). The first is **Potfest in the Park**, with ceramics on display in marquees in front of Hutton-in-the-Forest country house, as well as larger sculptural works laid out in the grounds. This is followed by the highly unusual **Potfest in the Pens**, which sees potters displaying their creations in the unlikely setting of the covered pens at Penrith's cattle market, just outside town on the A66. Here, the public can talk to the artists, learn about what inspires them and sign up for free classes.

---

### ARRIVAL AND DEPARTURE | PENRITH

**By train** Penrith train station is 5min walk south of Market Square and the main street, Middlegate.

Destinations Carlisle (and onward services to Glasgow/ Edinburgh, every 30min; 20min); Lancaster (and onward services to London, every 30min; 40min); Manchester (hourly; 1hr 40min).

**By bus** The bus station is on Albert St, behind Middlegate, and has regular services to Ullswater, Keswick, Cockermouth and Carlisle.

### ACCOMMODATION

**Askham Hall** Askham, 5 miles south of Penrith ☎ 01931 712350, W askhamhall.co.uk. Country-house living at its most gracious – the Lowther family's *Askham Hall* boasts stunning rooms (up to £320), a heated outdoor pool and gorgeous gardens to provide a touch of luxury in the Cumbrian countryside. There's both elegant restaurant dining and the *Kitchen Garden Café*, which has an outdoor wood-fired oven for pizzas. It's just as chic, but cheaper, at their nearby pub, the *George and Dragon* (see opposite). __£170__

**Brooklands** 2 Portland Place ☎ 01768 863395, W brooklandsguesthouse.com. Handsome 1870s townhouse whose colour-coordinated B&B rooms have country pine furniture and small but snazzy bathrooms. __£80__

**Crake Trees Manor** Crosby Ravensworth, 15 miles southeast of Penrith, A6 via Shap or M6 junction 39 ☎ 01931 715205, W craketreesmanor.co.uk. A gorgeous barn conversion B&B in the nearby Eden Valley. Rooms boast slate floors, antique beds, serious showers and fluffy wrap-me-up towels; or consider a night in the cosy Shepherds' Hut (£75–90, depending on season) in the grounds. __£95__

★**George and Dragon Clifton** A6, 3 miles northeast of Askham or 3 miles south of Penrith ☎ 01768 865381, W georgeanddragonclifton.co.uk. This revamped eighteenth-century inn is a class act – country-chic rooms (some up to £155) feature big beds with brocade headboards and slate-floor bathrooms, while the informal downstairs bar and restaurant (around £30 for 3 courses) sources pretty much everything from the adjacent Lowther Estate. Food served daily noon–2.30pm & 6–9pm. __£95__

# Carlisle

The county capital of Cumbria, **CARLISLE** has been fought over for more than 2000 years, ever since the construction of Hadrian's Wall – part of which survives at nearby **Birdoswald Fort**. The later struggle with the Scots defined the very nature of Carlisle as a border city: William Wallace was repelled in 1297 and Robert the Bruce eighteen years later, but Bonnie Prince Charlie's troops took Carlisle in 1745 after a six-day siege, holding it for six weeks before surrendering to the Duke of Cumberland. It's not surprising, then, that the city trumpets itself as "historic Carlisle", and is well worth a night's stop.

## Carlisle Cathedral

Castle St • Mon–Sat 7.30am–6.15pm, Sun 7.30am–5pm • Free, donation requested • ☎ 01228 548151, W carlislecathedral.org.uk

**Carlisle Cathedral** was founded in 1122 but embraces a considerably older heritage. Christianity was established in sixth-century Carlisle by St Kentigern (often known as St Mungo), who became the first bishop and patron saint of Glasgow. Parliamentarian troops during the Civil War caused much destruction, but there's still much to admire

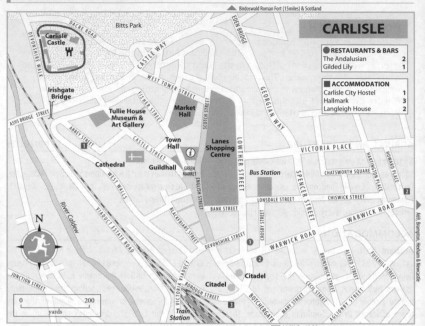

in the ornate fifteenth-century choir stalls and the glorious **East Window**, which features some of the finest pieces of fourteenth-century stained glass in the country.

## Tullie House Museum and Art Gallery

Castle St • Mon–Sat 10am–5pm, Sun 11am–5pm (Nov–March Sun noon–5pm) • £7, under 18s free • ☎ 01228 618718, ⓦ tullie house.co.uk

Among other wide-ranging attractions, the wonderful **Tullie House Museum and Art Gallery** takes an imaginative approach to Carlisle's turbulent past, with special emphasis put on life on the edge of the Roman Empire. Climbing a reconstruction of part of Hadrian's Wall, you learn about catapults and stone-throwers, while other sections elaborate on domestic life, work and burial practices.

## Carlisle Castle

Bridge St • April–Sept daily 10am–6pm; Oct daily 10am–5pm; Nov–March Sat & Sun 10am–4pm • £5.90; EH • Guided tours Easter–Oct daily; ask at the entrance • ☎ 01228 591922, ⓦ english-heritage.org.uk

With a thousand years of military occupation of the site, **Carlisle Castle** is loaded with significance – not least as the place where, in 1568, Elizabeth I kept Mary Queen of Scots as her "guest". Guided tours help bring the history to life; don't leave without climbing to the battlements for a view of the Carlisle rooftops.

### ARRIVAL AND INFORMATION                                    CARLISLE

**By train** Carlisle is on the West Coast mainline (for London–Manchester–Scotland services). There are also Cumbrian coastal services to Whitehaven, and cross-country trains to Newcastle. The Settle to Carlisle Railway, the magnificent scenic railway through the Yorkshire Dales (ⓦ settle-carlisle.co.uk), also ends its run at Carlisle (see box, p.605).

Destinations Lancaster (every 30min–1hr; 1hr); Newcastle (hourly; 1hr 20min–1hr 40min); Whitehaven (hourly; 1hr 10min).

**Hadrian's Wall Bus** The seasonal Hadrian's Wall Bus, #AD122 (see p.664) connects Carlisle with Birdoswald Fort (40min), before running on to the rest of the Hadrian's Wall sights.

**Tourist office** Old Town Hall, Green Market (March, April, Sept & Oct Mon–Sat 9.30am–5pm; May–Aug Mon–Sat 9.30am–5pm, Sun 10.30am–4pm; Nov–Feb Mon–Sat 10am–4pm; ☎01228 598596, ⓦ discovercarlisle.co.uk).

## ACCOMMODATION

**Carlisle City Hostel** 36 Abbey St ☎01228 545637, ⓦ carlislecityhostel.com. Carlisle's indie hostel makes a great townhouse budget base, with four bright bunk rooms offering flexible accommodation for friends, groups, families or solo travellers. One of the rooms is available as a private double/triple – there's also a kitchen, free tea and coffee, bike storage and secure lockers, and the location is excellent. Dorms **£15**

**Hallmark** Court Square ☎01228 531951, ⓦ hallmarkhotels.co.uk. Right outside the train station, the boutique-style *Hallmark* has a chic look, sleek rooms with big beds, and a contemporary bar and brasserie. **£89**
**Langleigh House** 6 Howard Place ☎01228 530440, ⓦ langleighhouse.co.uk. Nicely presented Victorian townhouse B&B – furnishings reflect the period, and original features abound. **£75**

## EATING AND DRINKING

**The Andalusian** Warwick Rd ☎01228 539665, ⓦ theandalusianbar.co.uk. The gorgeous tile work, carved oak bar, squishy sofas and big fireplaces make for a relaxed meet-and-greet bar, with tapas (£3–8) to share over drinks. Daily noon–midnight.
**Gilded Lily** 6 Lowther St ☎01228 593600, ⓦ gildedlily.info. Fabulous-looking restaurant and lounge bar serving cosmopolitan food at lunch and dinner, noodles to local lamb, burgers to piri-piri prawns (mains £10–22). Mon–Thurs 9am–midnight, Fri & Sat 9am–1am, Sun noon–midnight.

**11**

# Birdoswald Roman Fort

Gilsland, Brampton, 15 miles northeast of Carlisle, signposted from A69 • April–Sept daily 10am–6pm; Oct daily 10am–5pm; Nov–March Sat & Sun 10am–4pm • £5.60; EH • ☎01697 747602, ⓦ english-heritage.org.uk

One of sixteen major fortifications along Hadrian's Wall, **Birdoswald Fort** has all tiers of the Roman structure intact, while a drill hall and other buildings have been excavated. There's a tearoom and picnic area at the fort.

# Yorkshire

WHITBY

# Yorkshire

It's easy to be glib about Yorkshire – to outsiders it's the archetypal "up North" with all the clichés that implies, from flat caps to grim factories. For their part, many Yorkshire locals are happy to play up to these prejudices, while nursing a secret conviction that there really is no better place in the world to live. In some respects, it's a world apart, its most distinctive characteristics – from the broad dialect to the breathtaking landscapes – deriving from a long history of settlement, invention and independence. It's hard to argue with Yorkshire's boasts that the beer's better, the air's cleaner and the people are friendlier.

The number-one destination is undoubtedly **York**, for centuries England's second city, until the Industrial Revolution created new centres of power and influence. York's mixture of medieval, Georgian and Victorian architecture is repeated in towns such as **Beverley**, **Ripon** and **Richmond**, while the Yorkshire coast, too, retains something of its erstwhile grandeur – **Bridlington** and **Scarborough** boomed in the nineteenth century and again in the postwar period, though it's in smaller resorts like **Whitby** and **Robin Hood's Bay** that the best of the coast is to be found today.

The engine of growth during the Industrial Revolution was not in the north of the county, but in the south and west, where Leeds, Bradford, Sheffield and their satellites were once the world's mightiest producers of textiles and steel. A renewed vigour has infused South and West Yorkshire during the last decade; the city-centre transformations of **Leeds** and **Sheffield** in particular have been remarkable, while **Bradford** is a fine diversion on the way to **Haworth**, home of the Brontë sisters.

The **Yorkshire Dales**, to the northwest, form a patchwork of stone-built villages, limestone hills, serene valleys and majestic heights. The county's other National Park, the **North York Moors**, is divided into bleak upland moors and a tremendous rugged coastline between Robin Hood's Bay and Staithes.

## GETTING AROUND YORKSHIRE

**By train** Fast trains on the East Coast main line link York to London, Newcastle and Edinburgh. Leeds is served by trains from London, and is at the centre of the integrated Metro bus and train system that covers most of West and South Yorkshire. There are services to Scarborough (from York) and Whitby (from Middlesbrough), while the Settle to Carlisle line, to the southern and western Dales, can be accessed from Leeds.

**Transport passes** The North Country Rover ticket (£84 for four days in eight) covers train travel north of Leeds, Bradford and Hull and south of Newcastle and Carlisle.

# Sheffield and around

Yorkshire's second city, **SHEFFIELD** remains linked with its steel industry, in particular the production of high-quality cutlery. As early as the fourteenth century the carefully fashioned, hard-wearing knives of hardworking Sheffield enjoyed national repute, while technological advances later turned the city into one of the country's foremost centres

12

AKBAR'S RESTAURANT, BRADFORD

# Highlights

**❶ National Coal Mining Museum** A working coal mine until the mid-1980s, now a museum; you can even head underground, if you're brave enough. **See p.594**

**❷ Bradford curry houses** Bradford's Indian restaurants provide wonderful opportunities for gastronomic exploration. **See p.598**

**❸ Haworth** Visiting the moorland home of the talented and ultimately tragic Brontë sisters is an affecting experience, despite the crowds. See p.599

**❹ Malham** It's a breathtaking hike from Malham village to the glorious natural amphitheatre of Malham Cove. **See p.603**

**❺ Fountains Abbey** Enjoy views of the atmospheric ruins of Fountains Abbey set in spectacular Studley Water Gardens. **See p.609**

**❻ Harrogate Turkish Baths** The late Victorian opulence of Harrogate's magnificently restored Turkish baths is a great place to get pampered. See p.610

**❼ Jorvik/Dig!, York** Travel through time to Viking York, then seek out new discoveries at Dig! **See p.614 & p.616**

**❽ Whitby** Follow in the footsteps of Count Dracula and Captain James Cook in this spectacularly pretty former whaling port. See p.630

**HIGHLIGHTS ARE MARKED ON THE MAP ON PP.586–587**

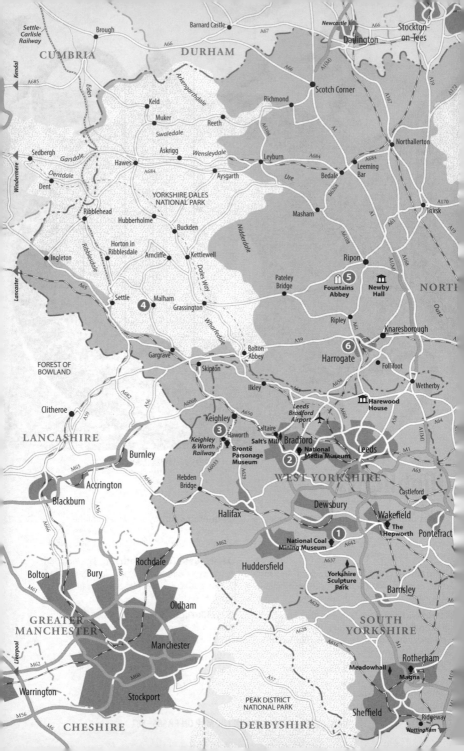

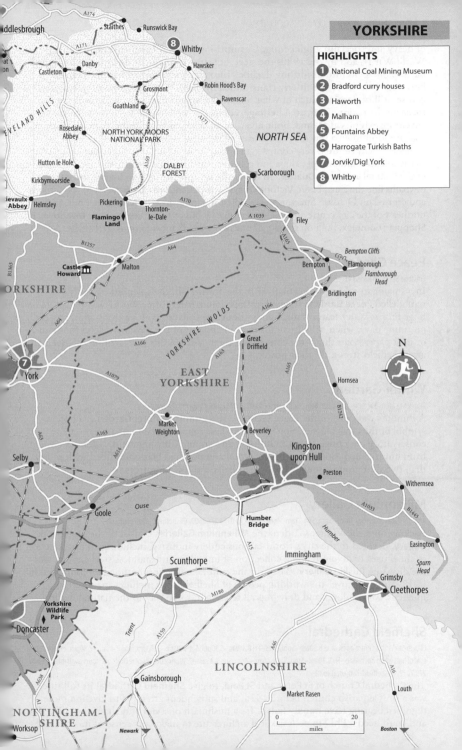

of heavy and specialist engineering. Unsurprisingly, it was bombed heavily during World War II, and by the 1980s the steel industry's subsequent downturn had tipped parts of Sheffield into dispiriting decline. The subsequent revival has been rapid, however, with the centre utterly transformed by flagship architectural projects. Steel, of course, still underpins much of what Sheffield is about: museum collections tend to focus on the region's industrial heritage, complemented by the startling science-and-adventure exhibits at **Magna**, built in a disused steel works at **Rotherham**, the former coal and iron town a few miles northeast of the city.

Sheffield's **city centre** is very compact and easily explored on foot. Southeast of the **Winter Garden/Peace Gardens** hub, clubs and galleries exist alongside the arts and media businesses of the **Cultural Industries Quarter**. To the northeast, spruced-up warehouses and cobbled towpaths line the canal basin, **Victoria Quays**. The **Devonshire Quarter**, east of the gardens and centred on Division Street, is the trendiest shopping area. A little further out, to the northeast of the city centre and easily accessible by bus or tram, lies the huge **Meadowhall Shopping Complex**, built on the site of one of Sheffield's most famous steelworks.

## Peace Gardens

Pinstone St • Open access • Free

In a small natural amphitheatre next to the Town Hall, the splendid, recently remodelled **Peace Gardens** (named in hope immediately after World War II) centre on huge bronze water features inspired by Bessemer converters. It's a lively spot, especially on sunny days, when delighted kids dash in and out of the pavement-level fountains, or float paper boats down the converging ceramic-lined rills representing the rivers that gave Sheffield steel mills their power.

## Winter Garden

Surrey St • Mon–Sat 8am–8pm, Sun 8am–6pm • Free • ☎ 0114 273 6895, ⓦ sheffield.gov.uk

A minute's walk east of the Peace Gardens, the stunning **Winter Garden** is a potent symbol of the city's regeneration. A twenty-first-century version of a Victorian conservatory on a huge scale (230ft long, and around 70ft high and wide), it's created from unvarnished, slowly weathering wood and polished glass, and filled with more than two thousand seasonally changing plants and towering trees.

## Millennium Gallery

Arundel Gate • Mon–Sat 10am–5pm, Sun 11am–4pm • Free • ☎ 0114 278 2600, ⓦ sheffieldgalleries.org.uk

Backing onto the Winter Garden, the **Millennium Galleries** consist of the **Metalwork Gallery**, devoted to the city's world-famous cutlery industry, including an introduction to the processes involved and a collection of fine silver and stainless steel cutlery, and the diverting **Ruskin Gallery**. Based on the cultural collection founded by John Ruskin in 1875 to "improve" the working people of Sheffield, this includes manuscripts, minerals, watercolours and drawings all relating in some way to the natural world.

## Sheffield Cathedral

Church St • Visitor Centre open Mon 8.30am–5pm, Tues–Fri 8.30am–6.30pm, Sat 9.30am–3.30pm, Sun 7.45am–7.30pm, except during school hols when open Mon–Fri 8.30am–5pm, Sat 9.30am–4pm, Sun 7.45am–7.30pm • Details of recitals and tours available on ☎ 0114 279 7412, ⓦ sheffield-cathedral.co.uk

The **Cathedral Church of St Peter and St Paul**, to give **Sheffield Cathedral** its full title, was a simple parish church before 1914, and subsequent attempts to give it a more dignified bearing have frankly failed. It's a mishmash of styles and changes of direction, and you'd need a PhD in ecclesiastical architecture to make any sense of it. That said,

**12**

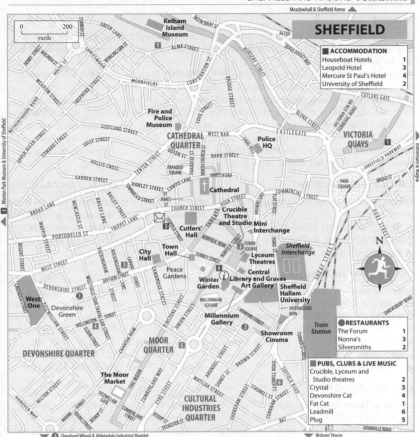

the magnificent **Shrewsbury Chapel**, at the east end of the south aisle, is worth a look. Built around 1520, it contains the tombs of the fourth and sixth Earls of Shrewsbury, whose alabaster effigies adorn their tombs.

## Kelham Island Museum

Alma St • Mon–Thurs 10am–4pm, Sun 11am–4.45pm • £5 • ☎ 0114 272 2106, ⓦ simt.co.uk

Fifteen minutes' walk north of the cathedral, the **Kelham Island Museum** reveals the breadth of the city's **industrial output** – cutlery, of course, but also Barnes Wallis's 22ft-long Grand Slam bomb, the Sheffield Simplex roadster, and the gigantic River Don steam engine. Many of the old machines are still working, arranged in period workshops where craftspeople show how they were used.

## Weston Park Museum

Weston Bank • Mon–Fri 10am–4pm, Sat 11am–5pm, Sun 11pm–4pm • Free • ☎ 0114 278 2600, ⓦ museums-sheffield.org.uk • Bus #51 or #52 from city centre, or Sheffield University tram

You can put the city's life and times into perspective a mile or so west of the centre at the **Weston Park Museum**. Here the imaginatively themed and family-friendly galleries draw together the city's extensive archeology, natural history, art and social history collections.

## Magna

Sheffield Rd (A6178), Templeborough, Rotherham, just off the M1 a mile from the Meadowhall Shopping Complex • Daily 10am–5pm • £9.85, family ticket from £25.15 • ☎ 01709 720002, ⊛ visitmagna.co.uk • Bus #69 from either Sheffield or Rotherham Interchanges, or a 15min taxi ride from Sheffield

Housed in a former steelworks building in **ROTHERHAM**, about six miles northeast of Sheffield, **Magna** is the UK's best science adventure centre. The vast internal space comfortably holds four gadget-packed **pavilions**, themed on the elements of earth, air, fire and water. You're encouraged to get your hands on a huge variety of interactive exhibits, games and machines – operating a real JCB, filling diggers and barrows, blasting a rock face or investigating a twister, for example. On the hour, everyone decamps to the main hall for the **Big Melt**, when the original arc furnace is used in a bone-shaking light and sound show that has visitors gripping the railings.

### ARRIVAL AND DEPARTURE

**By train** Sheffield's train station is on the eastern edge of the city centre.
Destinations Leeds (every 12min; 40min–1hr 19min); London (hourly; 2hr 30min); York (every 30min; 53min).
**By bus** Sheffield Interchange bus and coach station lies

### SHEFFIELD AND AROUND

about 200yd north of the train station. Buses run to and from most regional and national centres – including all the main South Yorkshire towns; London (every 30 min; 2hr); Birmingham (every 20min; 1hr 10min); Liverpool (hourly; 2hr) and Manchester (every 30min; 1hr).

### GETTING AROUND AND INFORMATION

**By bus** Local buses depart from High Street or Arundel Gate.
**By tram** The Supertram system (⊛ supertram.com) connects the city centre with the Meadowhall shopping centre (see box opposite), Halfway, Herdings Park, Malin Bridge and Middlewood, with the stations in between giving comprehensive access to most of the city and connections to the Park and Ride scheme.

**Transport info** For fare and timetable information, visit the Mini Interchange travel centre on Arundel Gate, behind the Crucible Theatre (Mon–Fri 7am–6pm, Sat 9am–5pm; ☎ 01709 515151 or 0114 201 2675, ⊛ sypte.co.uk).
**Tourist office** Unit 1, Surrey Street (Mon–Fri 9.30am–1pm & 1.30–5pm, Sat 9.30am–1pm & 1.30–4pm; ☎ 0114 221 1900, ⊛ welcometosheffield.co.uk).

### ACCOMMODATION

**Houseboat Hotels** Victoria Quays ☎ 0114 232 6556 or ☎ 07974 590264, ⊛ houseboathotels.com. Something different – three moored houseboats, available by the night, with en-suite bathrooms and kitchens. You get exclusive use of your own boat, for one to four people. Single occupancy **£79**; families **£99**; boats for four adults **£159**
**Leopold Hotel** 2 Leopold St ☎ 0114 252 4000, ⊛ leopold hotel.co.uk. Once a boys' grammar school, this place is immaculately modernized but retains some original features. Centrally located, the hotel backs onto remodelled Leopold

Square, which has an appealing array of places to eat. **£99**
**Mercure St Paul's Hotel** 119 Norfolk St ☎ 0114 278 2000, ⊛ mercure.com. Sandwiched between the Peace Gardens and Tudor Square, this modern hotel couldn't be more central. Comfortable rather than innovative, with understated (if a little anodyne) decor and fine views over the city the higher you go. **£94**
**University of Sheffield** ☎ 0114 289 3500. Self-catering student rooms in the Endcliffe student village (mid-July to late Sept) can be booked through the university. Within walking distance of the city centre. **£44**

### EATING

★**The Forum** 127–129 Devonshire St ☎ 0114 272 0569, ⊛ forumsheffield.co.uk. A vibrant mixture of bar, café, music venue and boutique mall, with a lively clientele who use it as a breakfast stop, lunch spot, after-work bar, dinner venue, comedy club and night club. Mon–Thurs & Sun 9am–1am, Fri & Sat 9am–3am.
★**Nonna's** 535–541 Ecclesall Rd ☎ 0114 268 6166, ⊛ nonnas.co.uk. Italian bar/restaurant with a great reputation and a family feel. Authentic Italian cuisine (menus have English descriptions). Mains £14–19. Mon–Sun 8.30am–11pm.

**Silversmiths** 111 Arundel St ☎ 0114 270 6160, ⊛ silversmiths-restaurant.com. A "kitchen nightmare" turned around in 2008 by Gordon Ramsay in his TV show, city-centre *Silversmiths* supplies top-notch Yorkshire food from local ingredients – venison sausages and pies, spinach tart with Yorkshire Blue cheese – in a 200-year-old silversmith's workshop. Tues is pie night (£8.95) and there's a three-course set menu on Wed and Thurs (£17.90), and a similar early bird (4.45–6.45pm) and dinner menu (mains £12.50–15.50) at weekends. Reservations recommended. Tues–Thurs 5.30–11.30pm, Fri & Sat 4.45pm–midnight.

**12**

## THE MEADOWHALL CENTRE

Since it opened in 1990 on the site of a derelict steelworks, the **Meadowhall Centre** (☎0845 600 6800, ⓦmeadowhall.co.uk) has dominated Sheffield shopping like a colossus, pulling in thirty million shoppers a year from all over the north of England. Blamed from the start for urban decay as far away as Scunthorpe, it was expected to decimate city-centre shopping in the rest of South Yorkshire. Twenty-five years later, the jury's still out. With hundreds of shops under one roof, it's either Meadowheaven or Meadowhell, depending on your point of view. But even those who hate it find its weatherproof nature and free parking hard to resist.

## DRINKING, NIGHTLIFE AND ENTERTAINMENT

For the best insight into what makes Sheffield tick as a party destination take a night-time walk along **Division St** and **West St** where competing theme and retro bars go in and out of fashion. Locals and students also frequent the bars and pubs of **Ecclesall Rd** (the so-called "golden mile"), out of the centre to the southwest.

**Crucible, Lyceum and Studio** Tudor Square ☎0114 249 6000, ⓦsheffieldtheatres.co.uk. Sheffield's theatres put on a full programme of theatre, dance, comedy and concerts. The *Crucible*, of course, has hosted the World Snooker Championships for thirty years. It also presents the annual Music in the Round festival of chamber music (May), and the Sheffield Children's Festival (late June or July).

**Crystal** 23–32 Carver St ☎0114 272 5926, ⓦcrystalbar .uk.com. A former scissor factory provides stunning premises for this airy bar/nightclub, good for drinks and great for a night out. Thurs–Sat 10pm–3am.

★**Devonshire Cat** 49 Wellington St, Devonshire Green ☎0114 279 6700, ⓦdevonshirecat.co.uk. Renowned ale house with wide variety of domestic and imported beers, plus good pub food (£7.75–14.25) with drinks matched to every selection. Mon–Thurs 11.30am–11pm, Fri & Sat 11.30am–1am, Sun noon–10.30pm; food served Mon–Sat 11.30am–8pm, Sun noon–6pm.

★**Fat Cat** Alma St ☎0114 249 4801, ⓦthefatcat .co.uk. Bought by real ale enthusiasts in 1981 after a brewery sell-off, the *Fat Cat* is now a Sheffield institution offering a wide range of bottled and draft beers, ciders and country wines, and a hearty pub-grub menu (meals around £4.50). With its open fires, polished mahogany bar and etched mirrors, and its total absence of flashing gaming machines and piped music, this is pub-going as it used to be. Daily noon–11.30pm; food served Mon–Fri noon–3pm & 6–8pm, Sat noon–7pm, Sun noon–2pm.

**Leadmill** 6–7 Leadmill Rd ☎0114 221 2828, ⓦleadmill.co.uk. In the Cultural Industries Quarter, this place hosts live bands and DJs most nights of the week, with a comedy club on Wed.

**Plug** 14 Matilda St ☎0114 241 3040, ⓦthe-plug.com. Mid-sized music venue featuring everything from live acoustic folk to diverse club nights, including the award-winning "Jump Around".

**Sheffield City Hall** Barker's Pool ☎0114 278 9789, ⓦsheffieldcityhall.com. Year-round programme of classical music, opera, mainstream concerts, comedy and club nights, in a magnificent, renovated concert hall.

**The Showroom** / Paternoster Row ☎0114 275 7727, ⓦshowroom.org.uk. The biggest independent cinema outside London, and also a popular meeting place, in its relaxed café-bar.

## SHOPPING

Sheffield has all the national chain stores and other shops you'd expect in the city centre, with top-end shops concentrated particularly along **Fargate** and **High St** on one side of the Peace Gardens and budget alternatives along **The Moor** on the other. The trendiest shopping is to be found in the **Devonshire Quarter**, based on Division St, while due south there's a new **indoor market** at 77 The Moor (Mon–Sat 8.30am–5.30pm), replacing the old Castlegate Market. Out-of-town shopping is dominated by the **Meadowhall Centre** (see box above), an easy tram ride three miles east of the centre.

# Leeds and around

Yorkshire's commercial capital, and one of the fastest-growing cities in the country, **LEEDS** has undergone a radical transformation in recent years. There's still a true northern grit to its character, and in many of its dilapidated suburbs, but the grime has been removed from the impressive Victorian buildings and the city is revelling in its new persona as a booming financial, commercial and cultural centre. The renowned **shops**, **restaurants**, **bars** and **clubs** provide one focus of a visit to contemporary Leeds – it's certainly Yorkshire's top destination for a day or two of conspicuous consumption and indulgence. Museums include the impressive **Royal Armouries**, which hold the national arms and armour collection, while the **City Art Gallery** has one of the best collections of British twentieth-century art outside London. Beyond the city, a number of major attractions are accessible by bus or train: north of town lies the stately home **Harewood House**, while south of Leeds, the neighbouring town of **Wakefield** is home to the stunning **Hepworth Gallery** and not far from the gritty **National Coal Mining Museum** and the **Yorkshire Sculpture Park**.

## City Art Gallery

The Headrow • Mon & Tues 10am–5pm, Wed noon–5pm, Thurs–Sat 10am–5pm, Sun 1–5pm • Free • ☎ 0113 247 8256, ⊛ leeds.gov.uk

Sharing a building with the Central Library, the **City Art Gallery** has an important collection of largely nineteenth- and twentieth-century paintings, prints, drawings and sculptures, some on permanent display, others rotated. There's an understandable bias towards pieces by **Henry Moore** and **Barbara Hepworth**, both former students at the Leeds School of Art; Moore's *Reclining Woman* lounges at the top of the steps outside the gallery.

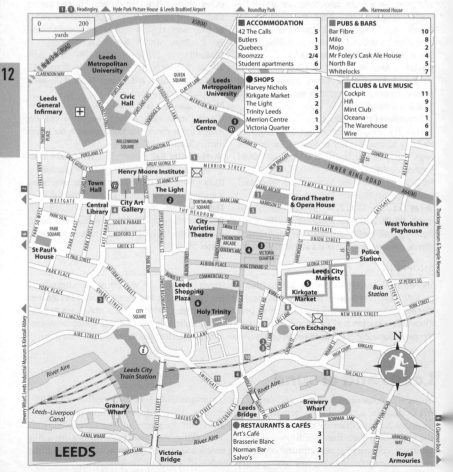

**12**

## Henry Moore Institute

The Headrow • Tues–Sun 11am–5.30pm • Free • ☎ 0113 246 7467, ⓦ henry-moore.org.co.uk

The City Art Gallery connects with the adjacent **Henry Moore Institute**, which, despite its misleading name, is devoted not to Moore himself but to temporary exhibitions of sculpture from all periods and nationalities.

## Royal Armouries

Armouries Drive • Daily 10am–5pm • Free • ☎ 0113 220 1999, ⓦ armouries.org.uk • Bus #28 from city centre

On the south side of the riverbank beckons the spectacular glass turret and gunmetal grey bulk of the **Royal Armouries**, purpose-built to house the **arms** and **armour** collection from the Tower of London. One of the best museums of its type in the world, its five enormous galleries hold beautifully displayed weapons for war, tournaments and hunting, armour and other artefacts dating from Roman times onwards. Particularly spectacular are the reconstruction of a tiger hunt; the Indian elephant armour (the heaviest armour in the world) consisting of 8500 iron plates; fabulously decorated ceremonial suits of full plate armour; a Sikh "quoit turban" which carried a blood-curdling array of throwing quoits; garrotting wires and knives; Samurai, Mongol and Indian armour and weapons; and many ornate guns, from a reconstruction of an enormously long Essex punt gun to an exquisite Tiffany-decorated Smith and Wesson .44 Magnum.

## Thackray Museum

Beckett St • Daily 10am–5pm, last admission 3pm • £7 • ☎ 0113 244 4343, ⓦ thackraymuseum.org • Bus #16 #42 #49 #50 #50A or #61 from the city centre (all around 15min, all stop outside the museum)

Essentially a medical history museum, and a hugely entertaining one, the **Thackray Museum**, next to St James' Hospital, has displays on subjects as diverse as the history of the hearing aid and the workings of the human intestine. It's gruesome, too, with a film of a Victorian limb amputation in a gallery called "Pain, pus and blood".

**12**

## Leeds Industrial Museum

Off Canal Rd, between Armley and Kirkstall Rd, 2 miles west of the centre • Tues–Sat 10am–5pm, Sun 1–5pm • £3.10 • ☎ 0113 263 7861 • Bus #5 or #67

For Leeds' industrial past, visit the vast **Leeds Industrial Museum**. There's been a mill on the site since at least the seventeenth century, and the present building was one of the world's largest woollen mills until its closure in 1969. Although most of its displays naturally centre on the **woollen industry**, and famous offshoots like Hepworths and Burtons, the cinema and printing in the local area are also covered.

## Kirkstall Abbey

Abbey Rd, about 3 miles northwest of the city centre • **Abbey** Tues–Sun: April–Sept 10am–4.30pm; Oct–March 10m–4pm • Free • ⓦ leeds.gov.uk/kirkstallabbey • **Museum** Tues–Fri & Sun 10am–5pm, Sat noon–5pm • £3.60 • ☎ 0113 230 5492 ⓦ www.leeds.gov.uk/ abbeyhouse • Buses #33, #33A or #757 from city centre

The bucolic ruins and cloisters of **Kirkstall Abbey**, which was built between 1152 and 1182 by Cistercian monks from Fountains Abbey, are well worth a visit. The former gatehouse now provides the setting for the family-friendly **Abbey House Museum**, which takes a look at Victorian Leeds.

## Temple Newsam

Off Selby Rd, 4 miles east of Leeds **House** Tues–Sun: April–Sept 10.30am–5pm; Oct–March 10.30am–4pm • £3.70 • **Rare breeds farm** Tues–Sun: April–Sept 10am–5pm; Oct–March 10am–4pm • £3.30 • ☎ 0113 264 7321, ⓦ leeds.gov.uk/templenewsam • On Sun bus

#63a runs to the house from central Leeds and during the rest of the week #19 and #19a run to Colton, from where it is less than a mile's walk; during summer hols, #10 bus runs directly to the house

The Tudor-Jacobean house of **Temple Newsam** shows many of the paintings and much of the decorative art owned by Leeds City Art Gallery. There are paintings from the sixteenth to the nineteenth centuries, furniture (including a number of Chippendale pieces), textiles and tapestries, silver, porcelain and pottery. The estate is over fifteen thousand acres and also contains Europe's largest **rare breeds farm**, where you can see four breeds of pigs, six of sheep, eight of poultry and no fewer than nine of cattle.

## Harewood House

Harewood, 7 miles north of Leeds • Opening hours vary widely according to day and season; check website for full details • Freedom ticket, covering all parts of house and gardens £14 • ☎ 0113 218 1010, 🌐 harewood.org • Frequent buses run to Harewood from Leeds, including the #36 (every 20min, every 30min on Sun)

**Harewood House** – still the home of the Earl and Countess of Harewood – is one of the UK's greatest country mansions. It was created in the mid-eighteenth century by an all-star team: designed by John Carr of York, with interiors by Robert Adam, furniture by Thomas Chippendale and paintings by Turner, Reynolds, Titian and El Greco, all sitting in beautiful **grounds** landscaped by Capability Brown. Tours take in the below-stairs kitchen and servants' quarters as well as innumerable galleries, halls, reception rooms and staircases, dripping with antiques and priceless art treasures, while added attractions include an adventure playground and gardens – including the famous bird garden. Numerous special events, special-interest tours and talks on things like bee-keeping, photography and food keep things lively. Incidentally, the village is pronounced "Harewood" as it is spelt, while the house is pronounced "Harwood".

## Hepworth Gallery

Gallery Walk, Wakefield • Tues–Sun 10am–5pm • Free • ☎ 01924 247360, 🌐 hepworthwakefield.org • From Leeds, take a train to Wakefield Westgate and walk, or a bus to Wakefield city centre, then a local bus to Doncaster Rd (a 5min walk) or Bridge St (next to the gallery); alternatively, Wakefield's freecitybus (🌐 wymetro.com) links all major parts of town, including the Hepworth Gallery

Opened in May 2011, the £35million **Hepworth Gallery** was the largest new gallery to open outside London for decades. A cuboid concrete riverside building designed by Sir David Chipperfield, it has ten display areas housing a wonderful collection of Dame Barbara Hepworth's work – not only finished sculptures, but also working models in plaster and aluminium, lithographs and screen prints. You can even see her original workbench and tools. Other contemporary artists are represented, too, and a flow of new exhibits is assured by close cooperation with the Tate. There's a café and shop, and a children's playground within its pleasant surroundings.

## National Coal Mining Museum

Caphouse Colliery, Overton, about 10 miles south of Leeds, halfway between Wakefield and Huddersfield (on the A642, signposted from M1) • Daily 10am–5pm; last tour 3.15pm • Free • ☎ 01924 848806, 🌐 ncm.org.uk • Train from Leeds to Wakefield Westgate, then from the station the #128 bus goes right past the museum, while #232 passes nearby

While the gentry enjoyed the comforts of life in grand houses like Harewood (see above), just a few miles away generations of Yorkshiremen sweated out a living underground. Mining is now little more than a memory in most parts of Yorkshire, but visitors can get all too vivid an idea of pit life through the ages at the excellent **National Coal Mining Museum**. Based in a former pit, Caphouse Colliery, the highlight is an underground **mine tour** (1hr 30min; warm clothes required; arrive early in school hols; no under-5s) with a former miner as your guide.

# Yorkshire Sculpture Park

West Bretton, outside Wakefield, a mile from the M1 (junction 38) • Daily 10am–5pm (galleries, restaurant and café 10am–4pm) • Free, parking £7.50/day, £5 for 1–2hr • ☎ 01924 832631, ⊛ ysp.co.uk • Train from Leeds to Wakefield Westgate, then bus #96 (Sun #435/436) – a fair bit of walking is necessary

The Yorkshire country estate at West Bretton now serves as the **Yorkshire Sculpture Park**. Trails and paths run across five hundred acres of eighteenth-century parkland, past open-air "gallery spaces" for some of Britain's most famous sculptors. The two big local names represented here are Henry Moore (1898–1986), born in nearby Castleford, and his contemporary Barbara Hepworth (1903–75), from Wakefield. The **visitor centre** is the place to check on current exhibitions and pick up a map – the restaurant has great views over Moore's monumental pieces.

## ARRIVAL AND INFORMATION
## LEEDS AND AROUND

**By train** National and local Metro trains use Leeds Station in the city centre.

Destinations Bradford (every 20min; 20min); Carlisle (every 2hr; 2hr 40min); Harrogate (every 30min; 34min); Hull (hourly; 1hr); Knaresborough (every 30min; 45min); Lancaster (4 daily; 2hr); Liverpool (hourly; 1hr 50min); London (every 30min; 2hr 20min); Manchester (every 15min; 1hr); Scarborough (every 30min–1hr; 1hr 20min); Settle (every 2hr; 1hr); Sheffield (every 10–15min; 40min–1hr 25min); Skipton (every 15–30min; 45min); Wakefield (Westgate & Kirkgate; every 10–15min; 12min); York (every 10–15min; 25min).

**By bus** The bus station is to the east of the centre behind Kirkgate Market, on St Peter's Street, though many buses stop outside the train station as well. Buses run from the bus station to all parts of the city, the suburbs, the rest of West Yorkshire and, via National Express, the rest of the country.

Destinations Bradford (10–30min; 25min); Halifax (every 30min; 1hr 16min); London (hourly; 4hr 25min); Manchester (every 30min–1hr; 1hr 5min–1hr 45min); Wakefield (every 10min; 31min); York (hourly; 1hr).

**Public transport information** The Metro Travel Centres at the bus and train stations have up-to-date service details for local transport; information is also available from Metroline on ☎ 0113 245 7676 or ⊛ wymetro.com.

**Tourist office** The Arcade (Mon 10am–7pm, Tues–Fri 9am–7pm, Sat 9am–5.30pm, Sun 10am–4pm; ☎ 0113 242 5242, ⊛ leeds.gov.uk or ⊛ leedsliveitloveit.com).

## ACCOMMODATION

There's a good mix of **accommodation** in Leeds. Cheaper lodgings lie out to the northwest in the student area of Headingley, though these are a bus or taxi ride away. The tourist office offers an accommodation **booking line** on ☎ 0800 808050.

★**42 The Calls** 42 The Calls ☎0113 244 0099, ⊛42thecalls.co.uk. Converted riverside grain mill, where rooms come with great beds and sharp bathrooms. Being next to the Centenary footbridge, it can sometimes suffer from noisy passers-by. **£85**

★**Butlers** Cardigan Rd, Headingley, 1.5 miles northwest of the centre ☎0113 274 4755, ⊛butlershotel.co.uk. This hotel offers cosy, smart, traditionally furnished rooms on a suburban street; it is next to and associated with *Boundary*. **£69**

★**Quebecs** 9 Quebec St ☎0113 244 8989, ⊛theeton collection.com. The ultimate city-boutique lodgings, boasting glorious Victorian oak panelling and stained glass, offset by chic rooms. Online deals can cut costs considerably. **£170**

**Roomzzz** 12 Swine Gate; also at 2 & 361 Burley Rd, ☎0113 233 0400, ⊛roomzzz.co.uk. Self-catering, one- and two-bedroom apartments in contemporary style, at three locations – Swine Gate is the most central. All come with great kitchens and widescreen TVs. Reduced rates if you book more than a week in advance. **£88**

**Student apartments** Clarence Dock ☎0113 343 6100, ⊛universallyleeds.co.uk. Self-catering rooms near the Royal Armouries, available every summer holiday (mid-July to mid-Sept). First night **£48**, then **£21**

## EATING

★**Art's Café Bar and Restaurant** 42 Call Lane ☎0113 243 8243, ⊛artscafebar.co.uk. A relaxed hangout for drinks, dinner or a lazy Sunday brunch. Mediterranean flavours dominate the well-priced menu, and the wine list is excellent. Mains £10.95–16.50. Daily noon–11pm (Sat till late).

★**Brasserie Blanc** Victoria Mill, Sovereign St ☎0113 220 6060, ⊛brasserieblanc.com. One of the seventeen restaurants established by French celebrity chef Raymond Blanc all over the country, the Leeds branch is a 5min walk from the train station. Housed in an old mill, with plain brick walls, vaulted ceilings and iron pillars, it offers good food in smart but unstuffy surroundings at unthreatening prices. Set two-course menus from £11.50 (lunch) and £14 (dinner). Mon–Fri noon–2.45pm & 5.30–10pm, Sat noon–10.30pm, Sun noon–9pm (bar open all day).

**Norman Bar** 36 Call Lane ☎0113 234 3988,

**12**

Ⓦnormanbar.co.uk. A boho-chic interior with a juice bar, Asian noodle/stir-fry/dim sum menu, and varied club nights. Attracts mainly a young clientele. Light bites £3.95–4.95 (3 for £10). Wed noon–midnight, Thurs & Fri noon–3am, Sat noon–4am.

**Salvo's** 115 Otley Rd, Headingley ☎0113 275 5017,

Ⓦsalvos.co.uk. Mention pizza to Leeds locals and they'll think of *Salvo's*, though there's a classy Italian menu as well – mains £15.95–19.50 – and a choice list of daily specials. It really is worth the trek out from the centre. Mon–Thurs noon–2pm & 6–10pm, Fri & Sat noon–2pm, Sun noon–9pm.

## DRINKING

**Bar Fibre** 168 Lower Briggate ☎0870 120 0888, Ⓦbarfibre.com. One of Leeds' finest gay-friendly bars comes with plenty of attitude. There's food during the day at *Café Mafiosa*, and regular alfresco parties in the courtyard outside (summer) and roaring fires inside (winter). Mon–Wed & Sun noon–1am, Thurs & Fri noon–3am, Sat noon–4am.

**Milo** 10–12 Call Lane ☎0113 245 7101. Unpretentious, intimate and offbeat bar, with DJs most evenings, ringing the changes from old soul and reggae to indie and electronica. Mon–Thurs 5pm–2am, Fri 4pm–3am, Sat noon–3am, Sun noon–2am.

★**Mojo** 18 Merrion St ☎0113 244 6387, Ⓦmojobar .co.uk. A great bar with classic tunes ("music for the people" – an eclectic mix with a swerve towards soul), American food, and a classy drinks menu with lots of cocktails. Mon–Thurs 5pm–3am, Fri–Sun 5pm– 4am.

★**Mr Foley's Cask Ale House** 159 The Headrow ☎0113 242 9674. Super Victorian pub near the Town Hall, with several bars on different levels, draught beers listed on a blackboard with strengths and tasting notes, and bottled beers from around the world. Food is served, too, from around a fiver. Mon–Thurs 11am–11pm, Fri & Sat 11am–midnight; Sun noon–7pm.

★**North Bar** 24 New Briggate ☎0113 242 4540, Ⓦnorthbar.com. The city's beer specialist has a massive selection of guest beers (more Belgian than bitter) plus cold meats and cheeses to nibble on. Mon & Tues 11am–1am, Wed–Sat 11am–2am, Sun noon–midnight.

★**Whitelocks** Turk's Head Yard, off Briggate ☎0113 245 3950, Ⓦwhitelocksleeds.com. Leeds' oldest and most atmospheric pub retains its traditional Victorian decor and a good choice of beers. Mon–Thurs 11am–midnight, Fri & Sat 11am–1am, Sun 11am–11.30pm.

## NIGHTLIFE

When the pubs close you can move on to one of the city's DJ bars or **clubs**, many of which have a nationwide reputation – not least because Leeds lets you dance until 5am or 6am most weekends. For information about **what's on**, your best bets are the fortnightly listings magazine *The Leeds Guide* (Ⓦleedsguide.co.uk) or the daily *Yorkshire Evening Post*.

**Cockpit** Bridge House, Swinegate ☎0113 244 1573, Ⓦthecockpit.co.uk. The city's best live music venue, plus assorted indie/new wave club nights.

**Hifi** 2 Central Rd ☎0113 242 7353, Ⓦthehificlub.co.uk. Small club playing everything from Stax and Motown to hip-hop or drum 'n' bass. Live comedy from top comics.

**Mint Club** 8 Harrison St ☎0113 244 3168, Ⓦthemintclub.com. Up-to-the-minute beats (there's a "no-cheese" policy), and the best chill-out space in the city.

**Oceana** 16–18 Woodhouse Lane ☎0113 243 8229, Ⓦoceanaclubs.com/leeds. Choose between dance, chart, r'n'b and indie in the Venetian Grand Ballroom; 1970s and

1980s disco on Europe's largest illuminated dancefloor; or bars decked out like a Parisian boudoir or ski lodge. Some comedy nights.

**The Warehouse** 19–21 Somers St ☎0113 234 3535, Ⓦtheleedswarehouse.com. Refurbished in 2010, with a completely new sound system. House, electro and techno bring in clubbers from all over the country, especially for Saturday's Technique night.

**Wire** 2–8 Call Lane ☎0113 234 0980, Ⓦwireclub .co.uk. A good indie/alternative dance/rock/electronic club associated with *Hifi* (see above) with weekly club nights and individual events.

## ENTERTAINMENT

**City Varieties** Swan St, Briggate ☎0113 243 0808, Ⓦwww.cityvarieties.co.uk. One of the country's last surviving music halls, it hosts a wide range of acts and was from 1953 to 1983 the venue for the TV series "The Good Old Days".

**Grand Theatre and Opera House** 46 New Briggate ☎0870 121 4901, Ⓦleedsgrandtheatre.com. The regular base of Opera North (Ⓦoperanorth.co.uk) and Northern Ballet (Ⓦnorthernballet.com) also puts on a full

range of theatrical productions.

**Hyde Park Picture House** Brudenell Rd, Headingley ☎0113 275 2045, Ⓦhydeparkpicturehouse.co.uk. The place to come for classic cinema with independent and art-house shows alongside more mainstream films; get there on bus #56.

**West Yorkshire Playhouse** Quarry Hill ☎0113 213 7700, Ⓦwyp.org.uk. The city's most innovative theatre has two stages, plus a bar, restaurant and café.

12

## LEEDS CONCERTS AND FESTIVALS

**Temple Newsam**, four miles east of the centre (see p.593) hosts numerous concerts and events, from plays to rock gigs and opera. Roundhay Park is the other large outdoor venue for concerts, while Bramham Park, ten miles east of the city, hosts the annual **Leeds Carling Festival** (ⓦleedsfestival.com) at the end of August with rock/indie music on five stages. August bank holiday weekend heralds the **West Indian Carnival** in the Chapeltown area of Leeds.

## SHOPPING

Leeds is one of the best cities outside the capital for **shopping**, with numerous independent shops, a throng of classy emporia in the beautifully restored **Victoria Quarter** (ⓦv-q.co.uk) – the "Knightsbridge of the North" – and other arcades that open off **Briggate**. Other options include the shopping complex **The Light** (ⓦthelightleeds.co.uk), the city-centre malls – such as the **Merrion Centre** (ⓦmerrioncentre.co.uk), off Merrion St and the new **Trinity Leeds complex** (ⓦtrinityleeds.com) in Albion Street, not forgetting the eight hundred traders in the Edwardian **Leeds City Markets** in Kirkgate.

**Harvey Nichols** 107–11 Briggate ☏0113 204 8888, ⓦharveynichols.com/leeds. Harvey Nicks, who opened their first branch outside London here in the Victoria Quarter in 1996, are the lodestone for this chi-chi shopping district. Mon–Wed 10am–6pm, Thurs 10am–8pm, Fri & Sat 10am–7pm, Sun 10.30am–5pm.

**Kirkgate Market** ⓦleedsmarket.com. The largest covered market in the north of England, housed in a superb Edwardian building. If you're after tripe, haberdashery or big knickers, this is the place to come. Mon–Sat 8am–5.30pm.

# Bradford and around

12

**BRADFORD** has always been a working town, booming in tandem with the Industrial Revolution, when just a few decades saw it transform from a rural seat of woollen manufacture to a polluted metropolis. In its Victorian heyday it was the world's biggest producer of worsted cloth, its skyline etched black with mill chimneys, and its hills clogged with some of the foulest back-to-back houses of any northern city. A look at the Venetian-Gothic **Wool Exchange** building on Market Street, or a walk through **Little Germany**, northeast of the city centre (named for the German wool merchants who populated the area in the second half of the 1800s) provides ample evidence of the wealth of nineteenth-century Bradford.

Contemporary Bradford, perhaps the most multicultural centre in the UK outside London, is valiantly rinsing away its associations with urban decrepitude, and while it can hardly yet be compared with neighbouring Leeds as a visitor attraction, it has two must-see attractions in the **National Media Museum** and the industrial heritage site of **Saltaire**. The major annual event is the **Bradford Mela** (ⓦbradford-mela.info), a one-day celebration of the arts, culture and food of the Indian subcontinent, held in June or July.

## National Media Museum

Pictureville • Tues–Sun 10am–6pm • Free, screenings £7.50 • ☏0870 701 0200, ⓦnationalmediamuseum.org.uk

The main interest in the centre of Bradford is provided by the superb **National Media Museum**, which wraps itself around one of Britain's largest cinema screens showing daily **IMAX** and 3D film screenings. Exhibitions are devoted to every nuance of film and television, including topics like digital imaging, light and optics, and computer animation, with fascinating detours into the mechanics of advertising and news-gathering.

## Saltaire

3 miles northwest of Bradford towards Keighley • 1853 Gallery Mon–Fri 10am–5.30pm, Sat & Sun 10am–5pm • Free • ☏01274 531163, ⓦsaltsmill.org.uk • Trains run from Bradford Forster Square, or take bus #679 from the Interchange

The city's extraordinary outlying attraction of **Saltaire** was a model industrial village

---

**TOP 5 MUSEUMS OF SCIENCE AND INDUSTRY**

**Kelham Island Museum** Sheffield. See p.589

**Magna** Rotherham. See p.590

**National Coal Mining Museum** Wakefield. See p.594

**National Media Museum** Bradford. See p.597

**National Railway Museum** York. See p.616

---

built by the industrialist Sir Titus Salt. Still inhabited today, the village was constructed between 1851 and 1876, and centred on **Salt's Mill**, which, larger than London's St Paul's Cathedral, was the biggest factory in the world when it opened in 1853. The mill was surrounded by schools, hospitals, parks, almshouses and some 850 homes, yet for all Salt's philanthropic vigour the scheme was highly paternalistic: of the village's 22 streets, for example, all – bar Victoria and Albert streets – were named after members of his family, and although Salt's workers and their families benefited from far better living conditions than their contemporaries elsewhere, they certainly were expected to toe the management line. Salt's Mill remains the fulcrum of the village, the focus of which is the **1853 Gallery**, three floors given over to the world's largest retrospective collection of the works of Bradford-born **David Hockney**.

## ARRIVAL AND DEPARTURE
## BRADFORD AND AROUND

**By train** Bradford has two train stations: Bradford Forster Square, just north of the city centre, offers routes to suburbs, towns and cities to the north and west of the city, while Bradford Interchange, off Bridge St, south of the city centre, serves destinations broadly south and west of the city.

Destinations from Bradford Forster Square Ilkley (every 30min; 31min); Keighley (every 30min; 20min); Leeds (every 30min; 22min); Skipton (every 30min; 39min).

Destinations from Bradford Interchange Halifax (every 15min; 12min); Leeds (every 15min; 23min); Manchester (every 30min; 1hr); Todmorden (every 30min; 35min).

**By bus** Bradford Interchange is the departure point for regional buses to the rest of West Yorkshire; there's also a National Express coach station here for long-distance services.

Destinations Halifax (every 10min; 40min); Huddersfield (every 20min; 40min); Leeds (every 30min; 30–45min); Liverpool (every 30min–2hr; 3–4hr); London (every 25–90min; 5–6hr); Manchester (every 10min–2hr; 1–2hr); Newcastle (every 2hr; 3hr 30m–4hr 45min); Wakefield (every 20min; 1hr 10min).

## GETTING AROUND AND INFORMATION

**By bus** Bradford's handy free citybus service (Mon–Fri 7am–7pm, every 10min) links the Interchange with Forster Square, Kirkgate, Centenary Square, the National Media Museum, the University and the West End

(ⓣ 0113 245 7676, ⓦ wymetro.com).

**Tourist office** Britannia House, Broadway (Mon 10am–5pm, Tues–Sat 9am–5pm; ⓣ 01274 433678, ⓦ visitbradford.com).

## EATING

With nearly a quarter of its population having roots in south Asia, Bradford is renowned for its south Asian food shops and restaurants, and was crowned "Curry Capital of England" in 2011. The city boasts literally hundreds of **Indian restaurants**.

**Akbar's** 1276 Leeds Rd, Thornbury ⓣ 01274 773311, ⓦ akbars.co.uk. The original in a chain that now has branches across the north of England (and one in Birmingham). It's famed for the quality of its south Asian cuisine, offering a wide range of chicken, lamb and prawn curries and is hugely popular, so at weekends you may end up waiting, even when you've booked. Most dishes well under £10. Mon–Fri 5pm–midnight, Sat 4pm–midnight, Sun 2–11.30pm.

★**Mumtaz** 386–410 Great Horton Rd ⓣ 01274 522533, ⓦ mumtaz.co.uk. *Mumtaz* is probably even more highly regarded than *Akbar's* (there's another one at Clarence Dock in Leeds), with plaudits from everyone from Dawn French and Amir Khan, through Shilpa Shetty and Frank Bruno, to Queen Elizabeth II herself (or so its website claims). With its delicious Kashmiri food – a range of *karahi* and biryani dishes, with meat, fish and vegetarian options – and smart decor, it's always busy with locals and visitors from all over the country. Remember, though – no alcohol. Expect to pay around £30/person. Mon–Thurs & Sun 11am–midnight, Fri & Sat 11am–1am.

# Haworth

Of English literary shrines, probably only Stratford sees more visitors than the quarter of a million who swarm annually into the village of **HAWORTH**, eight miles north of Bradford, to tramp the cobbles once trodden by the Brontë sisters. In summer the village's steep Main Street is lost under huge crowds, herded by multilingual signs around the various stations on the **Brontë trail**. The most popular local walk runs to **Brontë Falls** and **Bridge**, reached via West Lane (a continuation of Main St) and a track from the village, signposted "Bronte Falls", and to **Top Withens**, a mile beyond, a ruin fancifully (and erroneously) thought to be the model for the manor, Wuthering Heights (allow 3hr for the round trip). The moorland setting beautifully evokes the flavour of the book, and to enjoy it further you could walk on another two and a half miles to **Ponden Hall**, claimed by some to be Thrushcross Grange in *Wuthering Heights*.

## Brontë Parsonage Museum

Church St • Daily: summer 10am–5.30pm; winter 10am–5pm • £7.50 • ☎ 01535 642323, ⓦ bronte.org.uk

First stop in Haworth should be the **Brontë Parsonage Museum**, a modest Georgian house bought by Patrick Brontë in 1820 and in which he planned to bring up his family. After the tragic early loss of his wife and two eldest daughters, the surviving four children – Anne, Emily, Charlotte and their dissipated brother, Branwell – spent most of their short lives in the place, which is furnished as it was in their day, and filled with the sisters' pictures, books, manuscripts and personal treasures. The **parish church** in front of the parsonage contains the family vault; Charlotte was married here in 1854.

**12**

### ARRIVAL AND INFORMATION · HAWORTH

**By train** The nicest way of getting to Haworth is on the steam trains of the Keighley and Worth Valley Railway (Easter week, school hols, July & Aug daily; rest of the year Sat & Sun; day rover ticket £15; ☎ 01535 645214, ⓦ kwvr .co.uk); regular trains from Leeds or from Bradford's Forster Square station run to Keighley, from where the steam train takes 15min to Haworth.

**By bus** Bus #662 from Bradford Interchange runs to Keighley (every 10min; 50min); change there for the #663, #664 (not Sun) or #665 (every 20–30min; 16–24min).

**Tourist office** 2–4 West Lane (daily: April–Sept 10am–5pm; Oct–March 10am–4pm, except Wed from 10.30am); ☎ 01535 642329, ⓦ haworth-village.org.uk).

### ACCOMMODATION AND EATING

**Apothecary** 86 Main St ☎ 01535 643642, ⓦ the apothecaryguesthouse.co.uk. Traditional guesthouse opposite the church, in a seventeenth-century building with oak beams, millstone grit walls and quaint passages. The rear rooms, breakfast room and attached café have moorland views. **£55**

**Wilsons of Haworth** 15 West Lane ☎ 01535 643209, ⓦ wilsonsofhaworth.co.uk. Top-end B&B with all the bells and whistles you might expect in a quality boutique

hotel; its five luxurious rooms (four doubles and a single), are in a converted row of weavers' cottages within sight of the Bronte museum. **£89**

**YHA Haworth** A mile from the centre at Longlands Hall, Lees Lane, off the Keighley road ☎ 0845 371 9520, ⓦ yha.org.uk. YHA hostel overlooking the village; Bradford buses stop on the main road nearby. Closed Mon–Fri Nov to mid-Feb. Dorms **£15**; doubles **£49**

# The Yorkshire Dales

The **Yorkshire Dales** – "dales" from the Viking word *dalr* (valley) – form a varied upland area of limestone hills and pastoral valleys at the heart of the Pennines. Protected as a National Park (or, in the case of Nidderdale, as an Area of Outstanding Natural Beauty), there are more than twenty main dales covering 680 square miles, crammed with opportunities for outdoor activities. Most approaches are from the south, via the superbly engineered **Settle to Carlisle Railway**, or along the main A65 road from towns such as **Skipton**, **Settle** and **Ingleton**. Southern dales like **Wharfedale** are the most visited, while neighbouring **Malhamdale** is also immensely popular due to the fascinating scenery squeezed into its narrow confines around **Malham** village. **Ribblesdale** is more sombre, its villages popular with hikers intent on tackling the famous **Three Peaks** – the mountains of Pen-y-ghent, Ingleborough and Whernside. To the northwest lies the more remote **Dentdale**, one of the least known but most beautiful of the valleys, and further north still **Wensleydale** and **Swaledale**, the latter of which rivals Dentdale as the most rewarding overall target. Both flow east, with Swaledale's lower stretches encompassing the appealing historic town of **Richmond**.

## GETTING AROUND AND INFORMATION    THE YORKSHIRE DALES

**On foot** The Pennine Way cuts right through the heart of the Dales, and the region is crossed by the Coast-to-Coast Walk, but the principal local route is the 84-mile Dales Way (⊛ dalesway.org.uk). Shorter guided walks (5–13 miles; April–Oct Sun & bank hols £3) are organized by the National Park Authority and Dalesbus Ramblers (⊛ dalesbusramblers.org.uk).

**By bike** The Dales has a network of over 500 miles of bridleways, byways and other routes for mountain bikers (⊛ mtbthedales.org.uk). The main touring cycle route is the

circular 130-mile Yorkshire Dales Cycle Way (⊛ cyclethedales .org.uk), which starts and finishes in Skipton.

**By public transport** Bus timetables (⊛ dalesbus.org) are available at tourist offices across the region, as are *Dales Explorer* timetable booklets, or consult ⊛ traveldales.org.uk.

**National Park Centres** There are useful National Park Centres (⊛ yorkshiredales.org.uk) at Grassington, Aysgarth Falls, Malham, Reeth and Hawes (April–Oct daily10am–5pm; Nov–March Sat & Sun 10am–4pm; closed Jan, except for Hawes which is open all year).

# 12  Skipton

**Skipton** (Anglo-Saxon for "sheep town") sits on the Dales' southern edge, at the intersection of the two routes that cradle the National Park and Area of Outstanding Natural Beauty – the A65 to the western and the A59/61 to the eastern dales. A pleasant market town with a long history, it is defined by its **castle** and **church**, by its long, wide and sloping **High Street**, and by a **water system** that includes the Leeds and Liverpool Canal, its spur the Springs Canal and the Eller Beck.

## ARRIVAL AND INFORMATION    SKIPTON

**By train** Trains run from/to Leeds (every 30min–2hr; 54min) and Bradford (every 30min; 49min), and there's a daily service to London (every 30min; 3hr 10min with one change). The train is by far the best way of getting to Dentdale/Ribblesdale: Dent (every 2hr; 46min); Settle (every 30min–1hr 25min; 30min–1hr).

**By bus** Buses run from Skipton up Wharfedale towards

Buckden (every 2hr; 1hr), to Malham (every 2–3hr; 35min) and Settle (every 2hr; around 40–50min). Links to the rest of the Dales are more difficult, and usually involve using trains and/or changing buses.

**Tourist office** Town Hall, High Street (Mon–Sat 9.30am–4pm, first Sun in the month 10am–4pm; ☎ 01756 792809, ⊛ cravendc.gov.uk).

## ACCOMMODATION AND EATING

**Herriot's Hotel** Broughton Rd ☎ 01756 792781, ⊛ herriotsforleisure.co.uk. A short walk along the canal towpath from the centre of Skipton, in a Victorian listed building, the boutique-style hotel and its restaurant, *Rhubarb*, both offer cheerful decor and lots of original features. Rooms vary in size and price, and there are frequent packages available. **£125**

**The Woolly Sheep Inn** 38 Sheep St ☎ 01756 700966,

⊛ woollysheepinn.co.uk. Pleasant town centre Timothy Taylor tavern which offers a good range of pub food (from £8) along with sandwiches, steaks and pasta dishes. The nine rooms are comfortable and well furnished, though some are small. Convivial, but can be noisy. Mon–Wed 10am–11pm, Thurs 10am–midnight, Fri & Sat 10am–1am, Sun noon–11pm; food served Mon–Fri & Sun 11.30am–9pm, Sat 11.30am–8pm. **£80**

# Ilkley

The small town of **ILKLEY** holds a special place in the iconography of Yorkshire out of all proportion to its size, largely because it's the setting of the county's unofficial anthem *On Ilkley Moor baht 'at*. Vibrant and stylish, Ilkley has plenty to see, including an interesting church, a couple of museums and enough top-end shops, bars and restaurants to keep visiting urbanites happy

## All Saints Church
Church St • Office hours Mon, Tues & Thurs 9.15am–1.15pm, Wed 10–11.30am, Fri 9.15am–12.30pm; ☎ 01943 431126

Ilkley's parish church, **All Saints**, was established in AD 627 by King Edwin of Northumbria and Bishop Paulinus of York, whose carved heads you can see in the entrance porch. Inside, highlights include three impressive eighth-century Saxon crosses, a family pew dating from 1633 and a Norman font made of Ilkley Moor stone with a seventeenth-century font cover complete with pulley and counterweight for raising and lowering it.

## Manor House Museum
Castle Yard, Church St • Tues 1–5pm, Wed–Sat 11am–5pm, Sun 1–4pm • Free • ☎ 01943 600066

Tucked in just behind All Saints Church, the **Manor House Museum** stands on the site of an original Roman fort (you can see a section of the Roman wall at the rear of the building). The museum contains a collection of Roman artefacts from the fort and surrounding area, and exhibits and information about Ilkley's prehistory and its growth as a Victorian spa town.

## Ilkley Moor
A 20min walk from the town centre

Dominating Ilkley's southern skyline is its famous **moor**, somehow smaller yet more forbidding than you might expect. Far from being a remote wilderness, it is very much part of the town's fabric: a place where people can walk, climb or ponder the immensities of time reflected in its ancient rock formations and prehistoric markings. Look out for the Swastika Stone, the Twelve Apostles, the famous Cow and Calf, and a host of cup-and-ring marked rocks. Excellent **information** boards adorn the moor's car parks, and there's more information available at the White Wells Spa Cottage Visitor Centre (Sat & Sun 2–5pm, ☎01943 608035), on Wells Road, up on the moor.

**12**

### ARRIVAL AND INFORMATION                                              ILKLEY

**By train** Ilkley station, in Station Plaza in the town centre, is the terminus of a line which links the town to Leeds and Bradford (every 30min; 31min).

**By bus** The bus station is next to the train station.
Destinations Bolton Abbey (every 2hr; 17min); Leeds (every 30min; 1hr); Malham (6 daily; 1hr 10min); Skipton (6 daily; 30min).

**Tourist office** Station Road (April–Sept Mon–Sat 9.30am–4.30pm; Oct–March Mon–Sat 10am–4pm, Tues from 10.30am; ☎01943 602319, ⊛visitilkley.com).

### EATING AND DRINKING

**Bar t'at Ale and Wine Bar** 7 Cunliffe Rd ☎01943 608888. With an irresistible name, a huge selection of wines and beers and a good atmosphere, this place also offers a decent range of light lunches, sandwiches, and main meals (£9.50–12.50). The toilets need upgrading, though. Daily noon–11pm; food served Mon–Fri noon–2.30pm & 5.30–9pm, Sat noon–9pm, Sun noon–6pm.

★**The Box Tree** 35–37 Church St ☎01943 608484, ⊛theboxtree.co.uk. One of Yorkshire's handful of Michelin-starred restaurants, offering inventive modern French cuisine in mellow surroundings. There are fixed-price menus at £30 (lunch), £40 (dinner), £60 (called A la carte, though it's not) and £75 (Gourmand). Wed 7–9.30pm, Thurs–Sat noon–2pm & 7–9.30pm, Sun noon–3.30pm.

★**The Flying Duck** 16 Church St ☎01943 609587. Occupying the town's oldest pub building, this real ale pub sports old stone walls, beamed ceilings and stone-flagged and wooden-floored rooms. Also has its own brewery in a barn at the rear. Mon–Thurs 11am–11pm, Fri & Sat noon–midnight, Sun noon–11pm.

**Piccolino** 31–33 Brook St ☎01943 605827, ⊛individualrestaurants.com. Large Italian restaurant in the centre of Ilkley, one of a chain across the country. The star attraction is a roof terrace with terrific views across the town and (this is England after all) a retractable roof and space heaters. Good food (mains around £16–23) and staff helpful. Mon–Sat 10am–11pm, Sun 10am–1.30pm.

# Wharfedale

The River Wharfe runs south from just below Wensleydale, eventually joining the Ouse south of York. The best of **Wharfedale** starts just east of Skipton at **Bolton Abbey**, and then continues north in a broad, pastoral sweep scattered with villages as picture-perfect as any in northern England. The popular walking centre of **Grassington** is the main village.

## Bolton Abbey

**BOLTON ABBEY**, five miles east of Skipton, is the name of a whole village rather than an abbey, a confusion compounded by the fact that the place's main monastic ruin is known as **Bolton Priory** (daily 9am–dusk; free; ☎01756 710238, ⓦboltonpriory.org .uk). The priory is the starting point for several popular riverside **walks**, including a section of the **Dales Way** footpath that follows the river's west bank to take in Bolton Woods and the **Strid** (from "stride"), an extraordinary piece of white water two miles north of the abbey, where softer rock has allowed the river to funnel into a cleft just a few feet wide. Beyond the Strid, the path emerges at **Barden Bridge**, four miles from the priory, where **Barden Tower** shelters a tearoom.

### ARRIVAL AND INFORMATION                                    BOLTON ABBEY

**By train** For the loveliest approach to Bolton Abbey, take the Embsay and Bolton Abbey Steam Railway – the station is 1.5 miles by footpath from the priory ruins. The trains (late July and Aug 5 daily; rest of year schedule varies, check website; day rover £9; ☎01756 710614 or ☎795189, ⓦembsayboltonabbeyrailway.org.uk) start from Embsay, 2 miles east of Skipton – the trip from Embsay to Bolton Abbey takes 15min.

**Tourist information** The main source of information is the estate office (Bolton Abbey, ☎01756 718009, ⓦboltonabbey.com) and there's an information point at Cavendish Pavilion, a mile north of Bolton Abbey.

### ACCOMMODATION AND EATING

**Cavendish Pavilion** ☎01756 710245, ⓦcavendish pavilion.co.uk. A riverside restaurant and café, a mile north of Bolton Priory serving roasts, casseroles and the like at good prices. March–Oct daily 10am–5pm; Nov–Feb Mon–Fri 10am–4pm.

## Grassington

**GRASSINGTON** is Wharfedale's main village, nine miles from Bolton Abbey. The cobbled Market Square is home to several inns, a few gift shops and, in a converted lead miner's cottage, a small **Folk Museum** (April–Oct Tues–Sun 2–4.30pm; free; ☎01756 753287, ⓦgrassingtonfolkmuseum.org.uk) filled with domestic equipment and artefacts relating to local crafts and farming.

### ARRIVAL AND INFORMATION                                    GRASSINGTON

**By bus** #72/72R buses to Grassington run roughly hourly (not Sun in winter) from Skipton (33min) and then, six times a day, on up the B6160 to Kettlewell, Starbotton and Buckden in upper Wharfedale.

**National Park Centre** Hebden Road, across from the bus stop (April–Oct daily 10am–5pm; for winter hours, check with centre; ☎01756 751690, ⓦyorkshiredales.org.uk).

### ACCOMMODATION AND EATING

★**Angel Barn Lodgings/Angel Inn** Hetton, 4 miles southwest of Grassington ☎01756 730263, ⓦangelhetton.co.uk. The Dales' gastropub par excellence has five immaculate rooms and suites. Over the road in the inn, Modern British food is served either in the bar/brasserie or more formal restaurant. Brasserie daily noon–1.45pm & 6–9.30pm; restaurant Mon–Sat 6–9.30pm, Sun noon–1.45pm. £150

**Ashfield House** Summers Fold ☎01756 752584, ⓦashfieldhouse.co.uk. Lovely seventeenth-century house, off the square, with a walled garden. The owner is very knowledgeable about the area. Special room rate offers are often available. Dinner is served, mainly to guests, for £36/person. £100

★**Grassington Lodge** 8 Wood Lane ☎01756 752518, ⓦgrassingtonlodge.co.uk. A splash of contemporary style – coordinated fabrics, hardwood floors, Dales photographs – together with a pleasant front terrace enhance this comfortable village guesthouse. £90

12

## Upper Wharfedale

**KETTLEWELL** (Norse for "bubbling spring") is the main centre for **upper Wharfedale**, with plenty of local B&B accommodation plus a youth hostel. It was also one of the major locations for *Calendar Girls*, the based-on-a-true-story film of doughty Yorkshire ladies who bared all for a charity calendar.

### ARRIVAL AND DEPARTURE                                    UPPER WHARFEDALE

**By bus** There's a Sun and bank hol bus service (#800) from Leeds to Hawes, connecting the top end of Wharfedale with Wensleydale, via Ilkley, Grassington and Kettlewell, among other stops. It takes 3hr 10min for the whole trip, and 1hr 5min from Kettlewell to Hawes.

### ACCOMMODATION AND EATING

**Blue Bell Inn** Kettlewell ✆01756 760230, ⊛bluebellkettlewell.co.uk. Pretty seventeenth-century coaching inn that's very much a traditional pub and serves good, no-nonsense pub grub (lasagne, meat and potato pie and the like; main courses £10–15). Mon–Thurs & Sun noon–10.30pm, Fri & Sat noon–11pm; food served noon–5pm & 6–9pm. **£80**

**Racehorses Hotel** Kettlewell ✆01756 760233, ⊛racehorseshotel.co.uk. Comfortable, recently refurbished hotel in what was once the *Blue Bell Inn's* stables. The food is a cut above your standard bar food (home-made paté, for example, or rare-breed belly pork); main courses start at £11. Daily noon–2pm & 6–9pm. **£90**

# Malhamdale

A few miles west of Wharfedale lies **Malhamdale**, one of the National Park's most heavily visited regions, thanks to its three outstanding natural features of **Malham Cove**, **Malham Tarn** and **Gordale Scar**. All three attractions are within easy hiking distance of **Malham village**.

**12**

## Malham

**MALHAM village** is home to barely a couple of hundred people who inhabit the huddled stone houses on either side of a bubbling river. Appearing in spectacular fashion a mile to the north, the white-walled limestone amphitheatre of **Malham Cove** rises 300ft above its surroundings. After a breath-sapping haul to the top, you are rewarded with fine views and the famous limestone pavement, an expanse of clints (slabs) and grykes (clefts) created by water seeping through weaker lines in the limestone rock. A simple walk (or summer shuttle-bus ride) over the moors abruptly brings **Malham Tarn** into sight, its waterfowl protected by a nature reserve on the west bank. Meanwhile, at **Gordale Scar** (also easily approached direct from Malham village), the cliffs are if anything more spectacular than at Malham Cove. The classic circuit takes in cove, tarn and scar in a clockwise **walk from Malham** (8 miles; 3hr 30min).

### ARRIVAL AND INFORMATION                                        MALHAM

**By bus** Malham village is served year-round by bus from Skipton (3 daily; 35min) and the seasonal Malham Tarn shuttle (Easter–Oct Sun & bank hols 4 daily; 25min) which runs between Settle and the National Park Centre.
**National Park Centre** At the southern edge of the village (April–Oct daily 10am–5pm; for winter hours, check with centre; ✆01729 833200, ⊛yorkshiredales .org.uk).
**Website** A good online source of tourist information is ⊛malhamdale.com.

### ACCOMMODATION AND EATING

★**Buck Inn** Cove Road ✆01729 830317, ⊛buckinn malham.co.uk. Pleasant pub popular with walkers. With good, locally sourced food – especially sausages, pies and steaks (main courses £10–22) – comfortable rooms, and a relaxed attitude to muddy boots, this is the ideal base for a walking holiday. Daily noon–3pm & 6–9pm. **£80**

**Miresfield Farm** Across the river from the Buck Inn and Lister Arms ✆01729 830414, ⊛miresfield-farm .com. The first house in the village, by the river, with lovely rural views. The country-pine-bedecked rooms vary in size, and there's a small campsite with toilet and shower. Breakfast available. **£64**

**YHA Malham** Centre of village, next to the Lister Arms pub ☎ 0845 371 9529, ⓦ yha.org.uk. A purpose-built hostel that's a good bet for families and serious walkers. Open all year. Office open 7–10am & 5–10.30pm. Dorms £13; doubles £49

# Ribblesdale

The river Ribble runs south along the western edges of the Yorkshire Dales, starting in the bleak uplands near the Ribblehead Viaduct, flowing between two of Yorkshire's highest mountains, **Ingleborough** and **Pen-y-ghent**, and through the village of **Horton in Ribblesdale** and on to **Settle**, the upper dale's principal town.

## Settle

**Ribblesdale**, west of Malhamdale, is entered from **SETTLE**, starting point of the **Settle to Carlisle Railway** (see box opposite). The small town has a typical seventeenth-century market square (market day Tues), still sporting its split-level arcaded shambles, which once housed butchers' shops, and the **Museum of North Craven Life** (April–Oct Tues 10.30am–4.30pm & Thurs–Sun 12.30–4.30pm; £2.50; ☎ 01524 251388) housed in the eccentric Folly, dating from the 1670s and earning its name from the strange combination of styles, and the curiously upside-down look created by the fact that there are far more windows on the ground floor than on the first and second – it seems surprising that it hasn't fallen down. The museum contains fairly random odds and ends from the history of the town, and that of the construction of the Settle to Carlisle railway.

### ARRIVAL AND INFORMATION                                SETTLE

**By train** The train station, less than a 5min walk from Market Place, down Station Road, is served by the famous Settle to Carlisle railway, one of the most scenic lines in Britain (see box opposite).

**By bus** Regular #58 buses connect Settle with Skipton (2 daily; 46min); #11 buses go north to Horton-in-Ribblesdale (Mon–Sat every 2hr; 21min); while #581

(every 2hr; 31min) runs to the western Dales. The Malham Tarn shuttle (Dalesbus #881; Easter–Oct Sun & bank hols 4 daily) makes a stop at Settle en route to Malham (25min) and Ingleton (25min).

**Tourist information** In the town hall, just off Market Place (Mon–Sat 9.30am–4pm; ☎ 01729 825192). They can provide hiking maps and pamphlets.

### ACCOMMODATION AND EATING

**The Lion** Duke St ☎ 01729 822203, ⓦ thelionsettle .co.uk. Offers comfortable rooms (which cost around £27 more at weekends) and a wide range of locally sourced fish, meats, pies and sausages, with a fine choice of cheeses (mains £7.95–17.95). Mon–Thurs 8am–10pm, Fri & Sat 8am–10.30pm, Sun 8am–9pm. £95

**Ye Olde Naked Man Café** Market Place ☎ 01729

823230. For non-alcoholic drinks and good plain food this café is the best bet. Don't be put off by the twee name – the building was once an undertaker's, and the name is a reference to the old Yorkshire saying, "you bring now't into't world and you take now't out". Mon, Tues & Thurs–Sun 9am–5pm, Wed 9am–4pm.

## Horton in Ribblesdale

The valley's only village of any size is **HORTON IN RIBBLESDALE**, a noted walking centre which is the usual starting point for the famous **Three Peaks Walk** – namely the 25-mile, 12-hour circuit of Pen-y-ghent (2273ft), Whernside (2416ft) – Yorkshire's highest point – and Ingleborough (2373ft).

### ARRIVAL AND INFORMATION                    HORTON IN RIBBLESDALE

**By bus** The #11 service from Settle runs every 2hr (20min).

**Tourist and hiking information** The *Pen-y-ghent Café* (see opposite) doubles as a tourist office and an unofficial headquarters for the Three Peaks walk. They operate a clocking in/clocking out system; walkers who complete the

route within a 12hr period become eligible to join the Three Peaks of Yorkshire Club. They no longer provide automatic back-up should walkers fail to return - this safety service is temporarily suspended. Opening hours are complicated, so phone to check.

## THE SETTLE TO CARLISLE RAILWAY

The 72-mile **Settle to Carlisle** line – hailed by some as "England's most scenic railway" – is a feat of Victorian railway engineering that has few equals in Britain. In particular, between Horton and Ribblehead, the line climbs 200ft in five miles, before crossing the famous 24-arched **Ribblehead viaduct** and disappearing into the 2629yd Blea Tunnel. Meanwhile, the station at **Dent Head** is the highest, and bleakest, mainline station in England. The journey from Settle to Carlisle takes 1hr 40min, so it's easy to do the full **return trip** in one day (£40.60). If you're short of time, ride the most dramatic section between Settle and Garsdale (30min). There are connections to Settle from Skipton (20min) and Leeds (1hr); full **timetable** details are available from National Rail Enquiries (☏0845 748 4950) or on ⓦsettle-carlisle.co.uk.

### EATING

**Pen-y-ghent Café** ☏01729 860333. A local institution for more than forty years, not only supplying much-needed hot drinks, snacks and meals, but also information and advice to walkers. Roughly Feb half-term hols to mid-Oct

Mon & Wed–Fri 9am–5.30pm, Sat 8am–6pm, Sun 8.30am–5.30pm; closed mid-Oct to Boxing Day; Jan & Feb hours vary.

## The western Dales

The **western Dales** is a term of convenience for a couple of tiny dales running north from **Ingleton**, and for **Dentdale**, one of the loveliest valleys in the National Park. Ingleton has the most accommodation, but **Dent** is by far the best target for a quiet night's retreat, with a cobbled centre barely altered in centuries.

### Ingleton and around

The straggling slate-grey village of **INGLETON** sits upon a ridge at the confluence of two streams, the Twiss and the Doe, whose beautifully wooded valleys are easily the area's best features. The 4.5-mile **Falls' Walk** (daily 9am–dusk; entrance fee £6; ☏01524 241930, ⓦingletonwaterfallstrail.co.uk) is a lovely circular walk (2hr 30min) taking in both valleys, and providing viewing points over its waterfalls.

Just 1.5 miles out of Ingleton on the Ribblehead/Hawes road (B6255) is the entrance to the **White Scar Cave** (Feb–Oct daily 10am–5pm; Nov–Jan Sat & Sun same hours, weather permitting; £9.50; ☏01524 241244, ⓦwhitescarcave.co.uk). It's worth every penny for the tour (1hr 20min) of dank underground chambers, contorted cave formations and glistening stalactites.

### ARRIVAL AND INFORMATION                    INGLETON AND AROUND

**By bus** Buses stop at the tourist information centre: the #80 runs from/to Lancaster (every 30min; 1hr 10min) and the #581 and #881 from/to Settle (every 30min; 25min).

**Tourist office** Community Centre car park, Main Street (Easter–Sept daily 10am–4.30pm, Nov–March 11am–3pm; ☏01524 241049, ☏visitingleton.co.uk).

### ACCOMMODATION AND EATING

**The Inglesport Café** Main St ☏01524 241146. On the first floor of a hiking supplies store, this café dishes up hearty soups, and potatoes with everything. Mon–Fri 9am–5pm, Sat & Sun 8.30am–5.30pm.

**Riverside Lodge** 24 Main St ☏01524 241359, ⓦriversideingleton.co.uk. Clean and tidy, with eight bedrooms decorated individually (if a little fussily) and

named after flowers. There's a small sauna and play room, and an optional evening meal at £16.50. **£66**

**YHA Ingleton** Sammy Lane ☏015242 41444, ⓦyha .org.uk. This YHA hostel is in an attractively restored Victorian stone house, set in its own gardens, close to the village centre. Reception 7–10am & 5–11pm. Dorms **£21**; doubles **£49**

### Dentdale

In the seventeenth and eighteenth centuries, **Dentdale** supported a flourishing hand-knitting industry, later ruined by mechanization. These days, the hill-farming community supplements its income through tourism and craft ventures, and in **DENT** village itself the main road soon gives way to grassy cobbles.

### ARRIVAL AND INFORMATION                                    DENTDALE

**By train** While the famous Settle to Carlisle railway (see box, p.605) might seem a good alternative to the bus, be warned that Dent station is over 4 miles from the village itself.

**By bus** Most of Dent's bus connections are with towns outside Yorkshire – Sedbergh (April–Oct 5 daily; 15min),

Kirkby Stephen and Kendal (Sat 1 daily; 50min) – though there is a service to Settle.

**Tourist information** Dentdale Heritage Centre, Dent (daily 11am–4pm; ☎01539 625800, ⓦdentvillage heritagecentre.com). A useful website is ⓦdentdale.com.

### ACCOMMODATION, EATING AND DRINKING

★**George & Dragon** Dent centre ☎01539 625256, ⓦthegeorgeanddragondent.co.uk. Opposite the fountain in the centre of the village, the *George & Dragon* is bigger and more expensive than the nearby *Sun*, with ten comfortable rooms (though some are small), good service

and a convivial bar. There's an extensive menu of traditional pub food with a twist (try, for example, the "steak and t'owd tup pie") – mains cost between £10.95 and £17.25. Daily 11am–11pm; food served June–Oct 6–9.30pm, Nov–May 6–8.30pm. **£90**

## Wensleydale

The best known of the Dales, if only for its cheese, **Wensleydale** is also the largest. With numerous towns and villages, the biggest and busiest being **Hawes**, it has plenty of appeal to non-walkers, too; many of its rural attractions will be familiar to devotees of the **James Herriott** books and TV series.

### Hawes

**HAWES** is Wensleydale's chief town, main hiking centre, and home to its tourism, cheese and rope-making industries. It also claims to be Yorkshire's highest market town; it received its market charter in 1699, and the weekly Tuesday market is still going strong. In the same building as the National Park Centre (see opposite), the recently revamped **Dales Countryside Museum** (April–Oct daily 10am–5pm; closed Jan; for winter hours phone ahead; £4; ☎01969 666210, ⓦdalescountrysidemuseum.org.uk) focuses on local trades and handicrafts. Another attraction is the **Wensleydale Creamery** on Gayle Lane, a little way south of the town centre (Mon–Fri 9.30am–4pm, Sat & Sun 9.30am–4.30pm; winter hours vary, phone to check; £2.50; ☎01969 667664, ⓦwensleydale.co.uk). The first cheese in Wensleydale was made by medieval Cistercian monks from ewes' milk; after the Dissolution local farmers made a version from cows' milk which, by the 1840s, was being marketed as "Wensleydale" cheese. The Creamery doesn't make cheese every day, so call first.

### Askrigg

The mantle of "Herriot country" lies heavy on **ASKRIGG**, six miles east of Hawes, as the TV series *All Creatures Great and Small* was filmed in and around the village. Nip into the *King's Arms* on Main Street, where you can see stills from the TV series.

---

### HERE FOR THE BEER

If you're a beer fan, the handsome Wensleydale market town of **Masham** (pronounced Mass'm) is an essential point of pilgrimage. At **Theakston brewery** (tours daily July & Aug 11am–4pm; Jan–June & Sept–Dec 11am–3pm; £6.95, reservations advised; ☎01765 680000, ⓦtheakstons.co.uk), sited here since 1827, you can learn the arcane intricacies of the brewer's art and become familiar with the legendary Old Peculier ale. The **Black Sheep Brewery**, set up in the early 1990s by one of the Theakston family brewing team, also offers tours (daily 11am–4pm, evening tours Thurs & Fri, but call for availability; £6.95; ☎01765 680100, ⓦblacksheepbrewery.com). Both are just a few minutes' signposted walk out of the centre.

## Aysgarth

The ribbon-village of **AYSGARTH**, straggling along and off the A684, sucks in Wensleydale's largest number of visitors due to its proximity to the **Aysgarth Falls**, half a mile below. A marked nature trail runs through the surrounding woodlands and there's a big car park and excellent **National Park Centre** on the north bank of the River Ure (see below).

### Bolton Castle

Castle Bolton village • Feb–March daily 10am–4pm; April–Oct 10am–5pm (restricted winter opening, call for details) • £8.50, gardens only £3 • ☏ 01969 623981, ⊛ boltoncastle.co.uk

The foursquare battlements of **Bolton Castle** are visible from miles away. Completed in 1399, its Great Chamber, a few adjacent rooms and the castle gardens have been restored, and there's also a café that's a welcome spot if you've hiked here – a superb circular **walk** (6 miles; 4hr) heads northeast from Aysgarth via Castle Bolton village, starting at Aysgarth Falls and climbing up through Thoresby.

### ARRIVAL AND GETTING AROUND                                    WENSLEYDALE

**By bus** The #156 route runs along Wensleydale from Leyburn to Hawes (every 2hr; 50 min), calling at Aysgarth and Bolton Castle. Less frequently, the #59 runs once a day along a similar route (1 daily; 47min). The Little White Bus runs from Hawes to Garsdale (2–4 daily; 23min). A post bus service runs between Hawes and Northallerton (Mon–Fri 3 daily; 1hr 45min). There's also a summer Sun and bank hol service (#800) connecting Hawes to Leeds (3hr).

### INFORMATION

**Tourist information** There are National Park Centres at Hawes Dales Countryside Museum, Station Yard (daily 10am–5pm; closed Jan, for winter hours, check with centre; ☏ 01969 666210; ⊛ yorkshiredales.org.uk) and at Aysgarth, by the river (April–Oct daily 10am–5pm; for winter hours check with centre; ☏ 01969 662910). A useful website is ⊛ wensleydale.org.

### ACCOMMODATION AND EATING

**Herriot's** Main St, Hawes ☏ 01969 667536, ⊛ herriotsinhawes.co.uk. Small, friendly guesthouse in an eighteenth-century building off the market square. There are just six rooms – some of which have fell views. Good hearty breakfasts are cooked to order. **£79**

**Herriot's Kitchen** Main St, Hawes ☏ 01969 667536, ⊛ herriotsinhawes.co.uk. Light lunches, Yorkshire cream teas and a variety of cakes, together with their own preserves made on the premises. Easter–Nov Mon, Tues & Thurs–Sat 10am–4.30pm, Sun 11am–4.30pm; Nov–March Tues, Sat & Sun same hours.

**The Old Dairy Farm** Widdale, 3 miles west of Hawes ☏ 01969 667070, ⊛ olddairyfarm.co.uk. Once the home of the original Wensleydale dairy herd, this farm offers luxurious and contemporary accommodation, with fine dining available (main courses around £15). While nonresidents are welcome to dine, there are no fixed opening hours – it is essential to phone first. **£140**

# Swaledale

Narrow and steep-sided in its upper reaches beyond the tiny village of Keld, **Swaledale** emerges rocky and rugged in its central tract around Thwaite and Muker before more typically pastoral scenery cuts in at **REETH**, the dale's main village and market centre (market day is Fri). Its desirable cottages sit around a triangular green, where you'll find a couple of pubs, a hotel, a **National Park Centre** (see p.608) and the **Swaledale Museum** (May–Oct daily 10am–5pm; £3; ☏ 01748 884118, ⊛ swaledalemuseum.org), containing an interesting hotchpotch of material on the geology, industry, domestic life and people of the valley. Downriver, the dale opens out into broad countryside and the splendid historic town of **Richmond**.

## Richmond

**RICHMOND** is the Dales' single most tempting destination, thanks mainly to its magnificent **castle**, whose extensive walls and colossal keep cling to a precipice above the River Swale. Indeed, the entire town is an absolute gem, centred on a huge cobbled market square backed by Georgian buildings, hidden alleys and gardens. Market day is Saturday, augmented by a farmers' market on the third Saturday of the month.

### Richmond Castle

Riverside Rd • April–Sept daily 10am–6pm; Oct–Nov daily 10am–5pm; Nov–March Sat & Sun 10am–4pm • £4.90; EH • ☎ 01748 822493, Ⓦ english-heritage.org.uk

Most of medieval Richmond sprouted around its **castle**, which, dating from around 1071, is one of the oldest Norman stone fortresses in Britain. The star turn is, without doubt, the massive **keep** – which was built between 1150 and 1180 – with its stone staircases, spacious main rooms and fine battlements. From the top, the **views** down into the town, across the turbulent Swale and out across the gentle countryside, are out of this world. For more splendid views, with the river roaring below, take a stroll along Castle Walk, around the outside of the curtain walls.

### Richmondshire Museum

Ryder's Wynd, off the Victoria Rd roundabout at the top of King St • April–Oct daily 10.30am–4.30pm • £3 • ☎ 01748 825611, Ⓦ richmondshiremuseum.org.uk

For a fascinating chunk of Richmond history, visit the charming **Richmondshire Museum**, off the northern side of the market square. It's full of local treasures, covering subjects as varied as lead mining and toys through the ages, with reconstructed houses and shops recreating village life, and even the set from the TV series *All Creatures Great and Small*.

### Theatre Royal

Victoria Rd • Tours mid-Feb to mid-Dec Mon–Sat 10am–4pm, on the hour; suggested £3.50 donation • ☎ 01748 825252, Ⓦ georgiantheatreroyal.co.uk

Richmond's tiny Georgian **Theatre Royal** (1788) has the diminutive feel of a toy theatre made from a shoe box. One of England's oldest theatres, it features a sunken pit with boxes on three sides and a gallery above; it is open for both performances and tours.

### Easby Abbey

A mile southeast of the town • April–Sept daily 10am–6pm; Oct daily 10am–5pm; Nov–March daily 10am–4pm • Free; EH • Ⓦ english -heritage.org.uk

A signposted walk runs along the north bank of the River Swale out to the golden stone walls of **Easby Abbey**. The evocative ruins are extensive, and in places – notably the thirteenth-century refectory – still remarkably intact.

### ARRIVAL AND INFORMATION                                         SWALEDALE

**By train** There are regular services into Wensleydale and lower Swaledale on the heritage Wensleydale Railway from Leeming to Redmire, and to Darlington, 10 miles to the northeast, on the main east-coast train line.

**By bus** The main transport hub is Richmond, where buses stop in the market square. Bus #159 runs between Masham, Leyburn and Richmond, while bus #30 (infrequent, not Sun) runs up the valley along the B6270 as far as Keld, 8 miles north of Hawes and at the crossroads of the Pennine Way and the Coast-to-Coast path.

Destinations from Richmond Leyburn (hourly; 25 min); Masham (Mon–Sat hourly; 55min); Ripon (Mon–Sat hourly; 1hr 15min).

**Tourist office** 2 Queens Road, Richmond (daily 9.30am–5.30pm; ☎ 01748 850549, Ⓦ richmond.org.uk).

**National Park Centre** Hudson House, Reeth (April–Oct daily 10am–5pm; Nov, Dec, Feb & March Sat & Sun 10am–4pm; ☎ 01748 884059).

### ACCOMMODATION AND EATING

#### RICHMOND

**Frenchgate Hotel** 59–61 Frenchgate ☎ 01748 822087, Ⓦ thefrenchgate.co.uk. Georgian townhouse hotel with eight rooms and walled gardens. Its food (set menu £39) has an excellent reputation – spiced loin of Yorkshire rabbit, for example, or Reg's duck breast. Breakfast Mon–Fri 7.30–9.30am, Sat & Sun 8–10am, lunch daily noon–2pm, dinner daily 6–9.30pm. **£118**

**Frenchgate House** 66 Frenchgate ☎01748 823421, ⓦ66frenchgate.co.uk. Three immaculately presented rooms, plus breakfast with the best – panoramic – view in town. **£85**

★**Millgate House** Millgate ☎01748 823571, ⓦmillgatehouse.com. Shut the big green door of this Georgian house and enter a world of books, antiques, embroidered sheets, handmade toiletries, scrumptious breakfasts and the finest (and least precious) hosts you could wish for. No credit cards. **£110**

**Rustique** Finkle St ☎01748 821565, ⓦrustiqueyork .co.uk. The clue to *Rustique*'s ambience lies in its name – it concentrates on rustic French food and wine in a bistro setting. The atmosphere is busy and cheerful, and the food's lovely, and very reasonably priced (two courses £13.95, three for £15.95). Daily noon–9pm.

★**Whashton Springs** Near Whashton, 3 miles north of Richmond on Ravensworth Rd ☎01748 822884, ⓦwhashtonsprings.co.uk. This working Dales farm offers a peaceful night in the country in rooms (in the main house or round the courtyard) filled with family furniture. **£76**

**REETH**

**King's Arms** High Row ☎01748 884259, ⓦthekingsarms .com. Attractive eighteenth-century inn on the green, offering a range of meals and snacks using locally sourced food, and rooms, all of which are en suite. Daily 11am–11pm; food served daily noon–2.30pm & 6–9pm. **£70**

**STONESDALE MOOR**

★**Tan Hill Inn** ☎01833 628246, ⓦtanhillinn.com. Reputedly the highest inn in Britain (1732ft above sea level), and claims to be the highest wi-fi hotspot. It's certainly one of the most rural – you might well find sheep in the bar. The seven rooms are comfortable, and the menu covers all the old pub favourites (mains £6.50–14.50). April–Aug daily 10am–9.45pm; Sept–March daily noon–3pm & 7–9pm. Dorms **£25**, doubles **£80**

# Ripon and around

The attractive market town of **RIPON**, eleven miles north of Harrogate, is centred upon its small **cathedral** (daily 8.30am–6pm; donation requested; ☎01765 602072, ⓦriponcathedral.org.uk), which can trace its ancestry back to its foundation by St Wilfrid in 672; the original crypt below the central tower can still be reached down a stone passage. The town's other focus is its **Market Place**, linked by narrow Kirkgate to the cathedral (market day is Thurs, with a farmers' market on the third Sun of the month). Meanwhile, three restored buildings – prison, courthouse and workhouse – show a different side of the local heritage, under the banner of the **Yorkshire Law and Order Museums** (all daily: Workhouse 11am–4pm; Prison & Police and Courthouse 1–4pm; combined ticket £9.50; ☎01765 690799, ⓦriponmuseums.co.uk). Just four miles away lies **Fountains Abbey**, the one Yorkshire monastic ruin you must see.

## Fountains Abbey and Studley Royal

4 miles southwest of Ripon off the B6265 · Feb & March daily 10am–5pm; April–Oct daily 10am–6pm; Oct–Jan Sat–Thurs 10am–5pm; free guided tours of abbey April–Oct daily · £10.50; NT & EH · ☎01765 608888, ⓦfountainsabbey.org.uk · #139 bus from Ripon (Mon, Thurs & Sat 4 daily; 15min)

It's tantalizing to imagine how the English landscape might have appeared had Henry VIII not dissolved the monasteries: **Fountains Abbey** gives a good idea of what might have been. The abbey was founded in 1133 by thirteen dissident Benedictine monks and formally adopted by the Cistercian order two years later. Within a hundred years, Fountains had become the wealthiest Cistercian foundation in England, supporting a magnificent **abbey church**. The **Perpendicular Tower**, almost 180ft high, looms over the whole ensemble, while equally grandiose in scale is the undercroft of the **Lay Brothers' Dormitory** off the cloister, a stunningly vaulted space over 300ft long that was used to store the monastery's annual harvest of fleeces. Its sheer size gives some idea of the abbey's entrepreneurial scope; some thirteen tons of wool a year were turned over, most of it sold to Venetian and Florentine merchants who toured the monasteries.

A riverside walk, marked from the visitor centre car park, takes you through Fountains Abbey to a series of ponds and ornamental gardens, harbingers of **Studley Royal** (same times as the abbey), which can also be entered via the village of Studley Roger, where there's a separate car park. This lush medley of lawns, lake, woodland and **Deer Park** was laid out in 1720 to form a setting for the abbey, and there are some scintillating views from the gardens, though it's the cascades and water gardens that command most attention.

**ARRIVAL AND INFORMATION**            **RIPON AND AROUND**

**By bus** Ripon is served by #36 buses from/to Harrogate (every 10–25min; 35min) and Leeds (every 20–35min; 1hr 30min); the bus station is just off Market Place.
**Tourist information** Ripon Town Hall, Market Place

(April–Oct Mon–Sat 10am–5pm, Sun 10am–1pm; Nov–March Thurs & Sat 10am–4pm; closes daily 1–1.30pm year round; ☎01765 604625, ⍟ripon-internet.com).

**ACCOMMODATION AND EATING**

**The Old Deanery** Minster Rd ☎01765 600003, ⍟theolddeanery.co.uk. Luxurious contemporary hotel opposite the cathedral. The innovative menu (main courses

from £15.95) features dishes such as belly of pork or fried stone bass. Mon–Sat noon–2pm & 7–9pm, Sun 12.30–2.30pm. **£125**

# Harrogate

HARROGATE – the very picture of genteel Yorkshire respectability – owes its landscaped appearance and early prosperity to the discovery of Tewit Well in 1571. This was the first of more than eighty ferrous and sulphurous springs that, by the nineteenth century, were to turn the town into one of the country's leading spas. Tours of the town should begin with the **Royal Baths**, facing Crescent Road, first opened in 1897 and now restored to their late Victorian finery. You can experience the beautiful Moorish-style interior during a session at the **Turkish Baths and Health Spa** (separate sessions for men and women; from £15; ☎01423 556746). Just along Crescent Road from the Royal Baths stands the **Royal Pump Room**, built in 1842 over the sulphur well that feeds the baths. The town's earliest surviving spa building, the old Promenade Room of 1806, is just 100yd from the Pump Room on Swan Road – now housing the **Mercer Art Gallery** (Tues–Sat 10am–5pm, Sun 2–5pm; free; ☎01423 556188) and its changing fine art exhibitions.

To the southwest (entrance opposite the Royal Pump Room), the 120-acre **Valley Gardens** are a delight, while many visitors also make for the botanical gardens at **Harlow Carr**, on Crag Lane (daily March–Nov 9.30am–6pm, Nov–Feb 9.30am–4pm; £8.75; ☎01423 565418, ⍟rhs.org.uk), the northern showpiece of the Royal Horticultural Society. These lie 1.5 miles out, on the town's western edge – the nicest approach is to walk (30min) through the Valley Gardens and pine woods, though bus #6 (every 20min) will get you there as well.

**ARRIVAL AND INFORMATION**            **HARROGATE**

**By train** The station is on Station Parade, on the eastern edge of the town centre. There are regular services from/to Leeds (every 30min; 37min).
**By bus** The bus station is next to the train station on Station Parade and is served by #36 buses from/to Leeds (every

15min–1hr; 40min) and Ripon (every 15min–1hr; 32min).
**Tourist office** In the Royal Baths on Crescent Road (April–Oct Mon–Sat 9am–5.30pm, Sun 10am–1pm; Nov–March Mon–Sat 9am–5pm; ☎01423 537300, ⍟visitharrogate .co.uk).

**ACCOMMODATION**

**Acorn Lodge** Studley Rd ☎01423 525630, ⍟acornlodgeharrogate.co.uk. A guesthouse with big-hotel aspirations (luxury fittings, individual decor, jacuzzi, in-room massages) but B&B friendliness (and tariffs). Well placed for the town centre (a 5 min walk). **£89**
**Balmoral Hotel** Franklin Mount ☎01423 508208, ⍟balmoralhotel.co.uk. Boutique hotel (whose strapline promises "a touch of opulence") occupying a rather grand

terrace of three Edwardian houses a few mins' walk from the town centre. Spacious rooms, luxurious fittings and helpful service make this a winner. **£110**
**Studley Hotel** Swan Rd ☎01423 560425, ⍟studleyhotel.co.uk. Mid-sized independent hotel with attached Thai restaurant. The attractive rooms vary in size and cost, and service is good, though the restaurant can get very busy. You can find surprisingly good rates online. **£119**

12

## EATING AND DRINKING

**Betty's** 1 Parliament St ☎01423 502746, ⓦbettys .co.uk. A Yorkshire institution with branches in several North Yorkshire towns (they've refused to open any outside the county), *Betty's* has a uniquely old-fashioned air, with a wrought-iron canopy, large bowed windows, a light airy room, waiting staff in starched linen, and baking that harks back to the past. While they are known for cakes, speciality teas and coffees, they also offer delicious breakfasts and mains – summer vegetable pancakes, for instance, or garlic and thyme chicken. No reservations (except for afternoon tea Fri–Sun), so you may have to wait. Daily 9am–9pm.

**Le D2** Bower Rd ☎01423 502700, ⓦled2.co.uk. Quality French food and excellent service in unpretentious surroundings, and at affordable prices – two courses for £12.95 at lunch and £21 in the evening. Tues–Thurs noon–2pm & 6pm–late, Fri & Sat noon–2pm & 5.30pm–late.

**The Tannin Level** 5 Raglan St ☎01423 560595, ⓦtanninlevel.co.uk. Popular brasserie, smartly understated, with a Michelin-trained cook and super locally sourced food. Earlybird two courses £12.95, à la carte mains around £15–25. Mon–Thurs noon–9pm, Fri & Sat noon–9.30pm, Sun noon–8pm.

**Winter Gardens** Royal Baths, Parliament St ☎01423 877010. For rock-bottom prices, you can't beat *Wetherspoon's*, a pub chain renowned for revitalizing interesting buildings. This is one of their best – all wrought iron, glass and ornate staircases. Daily 7am–11pm.

# York and around

**YORK** is the North's most compelling city, a place whose history, said George VI, "is the history of England". This is perhaps overstating things a little, but it reflects the significance of a metropolis that stood at the heart of the country's religious and political life for centuries, and until the Industrial Revolution was second only to London in population and importance. These days a more provincial air hangs over the city, except in summer when it comes to feel like a heritage site for the benefit of tourists. That said, no trip to this part of the country is complete without a visit to York, which is also well placed for any number of **day-trips**, the most essential being to **Castle Howard**, the gem among English stately homes.

In town, the **Minster** is the obvious place to start, and you won't want to miss a walk around the old city **walls**. The medieval city is at its most evocative around the streets known as Stonegate and the **Shambles**, while the earlier Viking settlement is entertainingly presented at **Jorvik**, perhaps the city's favourite family attraction. Standout historic buildings include the Minster's Treasurer's House, Georgian Fairfax House, the Merchant Adventurers' Hall, and the stark remnants of York's **Castle**. The two major museum collections are the incomparable **Castle Museum** and the **National Railway Museum** (where the appeal goes way beyond railway memorabilia), while the evocative ruins and gardens of **St Mary's Abbey** house the family-friendly **Yorkshire Museum**.

### Brief history

An early **Roman** fortress of 71 AD in time became a city – Eboracum, capital of the empire's northern European territories and the base for Hadrian's northern campaigns. Later, the city became the fulcrum of **Christianity** in northern England: on Easter Day in 627, Bishop Paulinus, on a mission to establish the Roman Church, baptized King Edwin of Northumbria in a small timber chapel. Six years later the church became the first minster and Paulinus the first archbishop of York.

In 867 the city fell to the **Danes**, who renamed it **Jorvik**, and later made it the capital of eastern England (Danelaw). Later Viking raids culminated in the decisive **Battle of Stamford Bridge** (1066) six miles east of the city, where English King Harold defeated Norse King Harald – a pyrrhic victory in the event, for his weakened army was defeated by the Normans just a few days later at the Battle of Hastings, with well-known consequences for all concerned.

The **Normans** devastated much of York's hinterland in their infamous "Harrying of the North". Stone walls were thrown up during the thirteenth century, when the city

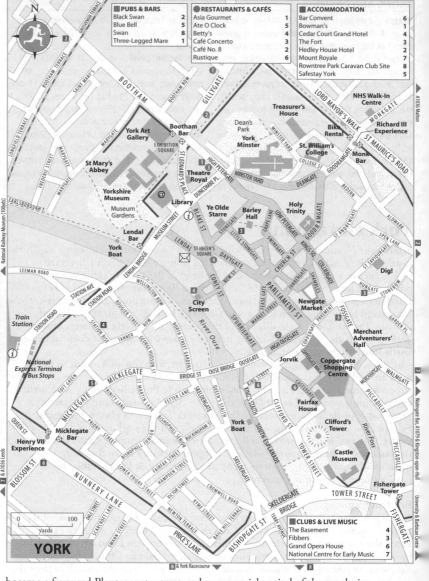

**PUBS & BARS**

| | |
|---|---|
| Black Swan | 2 |
| Blue Bell | 5 |
| Swan | 8 |
| Three-Legged Mare | 1 |

**RESTAURANTS & CAFÉS**

| | |
|---|---|
| Asia Gourmet | 1 |
| Ate O Clock | 5 |
| Betty's | 4 |
| Café Concerto | 3 |
| Café No. 8 | 2 |
| Rustique | 6 |

**ACCOMMODATION**

| | |
|---|---|
| Bar Convent | 6 |
| Bowman's | 1 |
| Cedar Court Grand Hotel | 4 |
| The Fort | 3 |
| Hedley House Hotel | 2 |
| Mount Royale | 7 |
| Rowntree Park Caravan Club Site | 8 |
| Safestay York | 5 |

**CLUBS & LIVE MUSIC**

| | |
|---|---|
| The Basement | 4 |
| Fibbers | 3 |
| Grand Opera House | 6 |
| National Centre for Early Music | 7 |

**YORK**

became a favoured Plantagenet retreat and commercial capital of the north, its importance reflected in the new title of Duke of York, bestowed ever since on the monarch's second son. Although Henry VIII's Dissolution of the Monasteries took its toll on a city crammed with religious houses, York remained wedded to the Catholic cause, and the most famous of the Gunpowder Plot conspirators, **Guy Fawkes**, was born here. During the **Civil War** Charles I established his court in the city, which was strongly pro-Royalist, inviting a Parliamentarian siege. Royalist troops, however, were routed by Cromwell and Sir Thomas Fairfax at the **Battle of Marston Moor** in 1644, another seminal battle in England's history, which took place six miles west of York.

The city's eighteenth-century history was marked by its emergence as a social centre for Yorkshire's landed elite. While the Industrial Revolution largely passed it by, the arrival of the **railways** brought renewed prosperity, thanks to the enterprise of pioneering "Railway King" George Hudson, lord mayor during the 1830s and 1840s. The railway is gradually losing its role as a major employer, as is the traditional but declining confectionery industry, and incomes are now generated by new service and bioscience industries – not forgetting, of course, the four million annual tourists.

# York Minster

Minster Yard • Mon–Sat 9am–5pm, Sun 12.45– 5pm • £10 (including undercroft); combined ticket with tower £15; admission ticket valid for 12 months • Free guided tours of the Minster (1hr) take place Mon–Sat 10am–3pm (subject to availability) and include access to the "Revealing York Minster" and the Orb visitor attractions • ☎ 01904 557200, ⊚ yorkminster.org

**York Minster** ranks as one of the country's most important sights. Seat of the Archbishop of York, it is Britain's largest Gothic building and home to countless treasures, not least of which is an estimated half of all the medieval stained glass in England. The first significant foundations were laid around 1080 by the first Norman archbishop, Thomas of Bayeux, and it was from the germ of this Norman church that the present structure emerged.

### The stained-glass windows

Nothing else in the Minster can match the magnificence of the **stained glass** in the nave and transepts. The **West Window** (1338) contains distinctive heart-shaped upper tracery (the "Heart of Yorkshire"), while in the nave's north aisle, the second bay window (1155) contains slivers of the oldest stained glass in the country. The greatest of the church's 128 windows, however, is the majestic **East Window** (1405), at 78ft by 31ft the world's largest area of medieval stained glass in a single window (currently covered with a tarpaulin bearing an image of the window – the renovation is due to be finished by 2016). You can see an ever-changing selection of the window's most famous stained-glass panels in the odd, inverted-cauldron-shape of "**the Orb**".

### The undercroft, treasury and crypt

The Minster's foundations, or **undercroft**, have been turned into a museum, featuring a new interactive gallery "Revealing York Minster". Among precious relics in the adjoining **treasury** is the eleventh-century *Horn of Ulf*, presented to the Minster by a relative of the tide-turning King Canute. There's also access from the undercroft to the **crypt**, the spot that transmits the most powerful sense of antiquity, as it contains sections of the original eleventh-century church, including pillars with fine Romanesque capitals. Access to the undercroft, treasury and crypt is from the south transept, which is also the entrance to the **central tower**, which you can climb for exhilarating rooftop views over the city.

# Around the walls

The city's superb **walls** date mainly from the fourteenth century, though fragments of Norman work survive, particularly in the gates (known as "bars"), and the northern sections still follow the line of the Roman ramparts. **Monk Bar** is as good a point of access as any, tallest of the city's four main gates and host to the small **Richard III Museum** (daily: April–Oct 10am–5pm; Nov–March 10am–4pm; £3.50; ☎ 01904 615505, ⊚ richardiiimuseum.co.uk). For just a taste of the walls' best section – with great views of the Minster and acres of idyllic-looking gardens – take the ten-minute stroll west from Monk Bar to Exhibition Square and **Bootham Bar**, the only gate on the site of a Roman gateway and marking the traditional northern entrance to the city. A stroll round the walls' entire two-and-a-half-mile length will also take you past the southwestern **Micklegate Bar**, long considered the most important of the gates since it marked the start of the road to London; it's now home to the Henry VII Experience (April–Oct 10am–4pm; Nov–March 10am–3pm; £3.50; ☎01904 615505).

## York Art Gallery

Exhibition Square • Daily 10am–5pm • Free • ☎ 01904 687687, ⓦ yorkartgallery.org.uk

**York Art Gallery** houses an extensive collection of early Italian, British and northern European paintings. The gallery puts on a year-round series of special exhibitions and events, and is noted for its collections of British studio pottery and twentieth-century British painters. It was closed for redevelopment at the time of writing, but should be open by the time you read this; hours and admission charges are likely to remain the same.

## The Yorkshire Museum

Museum Gardens • Daily 10am–5pm • £7.50 • ☎ 01904 687687, ⓦ yorkshiremuseum.org.uk

In the beautiful Museum Gardens between Exhibition Square and the river, next to the romantic ruins of St Mary's Abbey, sits the majestic Grade I listed building of the **Yorkshire Museum.** Five exciting, hands-on galleries comprise the "History of York", a multiscreen, audiovisual display; "Extinct", which covers dinosaurs and more recently extinct creatures; "Meet the People of the Empire" (Roman York); the "Power and the Glory" (Medieval York); and "Enquiry", about how archeology and science can uncover the past.

**12**

## Stonegate

One of York's most picturesque streets, **Stonegate** is as ancient as the city itself. Originally the Via Praetoria of Roman York, it's now paved with thick flags of York stone, which were once carried along here to build the Minster (hence the name). The Tudor buildings that line it retain their considerable charm – **Ye Olde Starre** at no. 40, one of York's original inns, is on every tourist itinerary (you can't miss the sign straddling the street).

### Barley Hall

Off Stonegate • Daily 10am–5pm (4pm In winter) • £5.50; combined ticket with Jorvik £14 • ☎ 01904 543400, ⓦ barleyhall.org.uk

Step through an alley known as Coffee Yard (by the *Olde Starre*) to find **Barley Hall**, a fine restoration of a late-medieval townhouse with a lively museum where you can learn about fifteenth-century life by, among other things, playing period games and trying on costumes. Barley Hall is one one of the Jorvik group of attractions.

## The Shambles

York's most famous street, and one which appears regularly on its promotional brochures, **The Shambles** could be taken as the epitome of the medieval city. Almost impossibly narrow and lined with perilously leaning timber-framed houses, it was the home of York's butchers (the word "shambles" derives from the Old English for slaughterhouse) – old meat hooks still adorn the odd house.

## Jorvik

Coppergate • Daily: April–Oct 10am–5pm; Nov–March 10am–4pm • £9.95, joint ticket with Dig! £14.45, with Barley Hall £14 • ☎ 01904 615505, ⓦ jorvik-viking-centre.co.uk

The city's blockbuster historic exhibit is **Jorvik**, located by the Coppergate shopping centre. Propelling visitors in "time capsules" on a ride through the tenth-century city of York, the museum presents not only the sights but also the sounds and even the smells

of a riverside **Viking city**. Excavations of Coppergate in 1976 uncovered a real Viking settlement, now largely buried beneath the shopping centre outside. But at Jorvik you can see how the unearthed artefacts were used, and watch live-action domestic scenes on actual Viking-age streets, with constipated villagers, axe-fighting and other singular attractions.

## Dig!

St Saviourgate • Daily 10am–5pm • £6; joint ticket with Jorvik £14.45; pre-booking advised • ☎ 01904 615505, ⓦ vikingjorvik.com

Where Jorvik shows what was unearthed at Coppergate, the associated attraction that is **Dig!** illustrates the science involved. Housed five minutes' walk away from the museum, in the medieval church of St Saviour, on St Savioursgate, a simulated dig allows you to take part in a range of excavations in the company of archeologists, using authentic tools and methods. Tours (£1) to visit **Dig Hungate**, York's latest major archeological excavation, start from here.

## Clifford's Tower

Tower St • Daily: April–Sept 10am–6pm; Oct & Nov 10am–5pm; Nov–March 10am–4pm • £4.30; EH • ☎ 01904 646940, ⓦ cliffordstower.com

There's precious little left of **York Castle**, one of two established by William the Conqueror. Only the perilously leaning **Clifford's Tower** remains, a stark stone keep built between 1245 and 1262 to replace the original wooden keep burned down in 1190 AD when it was being used as a refuge by hundreds of Jews trying to escape anti-Semitic riots in the city. Of a rare quatrefoil (clove-leaf) design, perhaps an experiment to improve sight lines between the top of the keep and the base of the walls, it once had two floors with a supporting central column.

## Castle Museum

Eye of York • Daily 10am–5pm • £8.50 • ☎ 01904 687687, ⓦ yorkcastlemuseum.org

Housed in what was once a couple of prisons, displays in the wonderfully inventive **Castle Museum** begin with a series of period rooms from the seventeenth century to the 1980s. There's a large room devoted to Victorian attitudes to birth, marriage and death, followed by a wonderful reconstruction of the sights and sounds of York's Kirkgate during the final years of the nineteenth century, often staffed by people dressed in authentic costume. There are displays, too, of period kitchens (who'd have thought that state-of-the-art equipment from the 1980s could look quite so out of date?), as well as hygiene, costume through the ages, toys and World War II. There's also a superb recreation of the fashion, music and news stories of the 1960s. Finally, the cells in the basement of the prison building contain an affecting series of real-life stories, told by video recordings of actors projected onto cell walls, gleaned from the prison's records.

## The National Railway Museum

Leeman Rd, a 10min walk from the train station • Daily 10am–6pm • Free • ☎ 0844 815 3139, ⓦ nrm.org.uk • A "road train" shuttles visitors here from Duncombe Place next to York Minster (April–Oct daily every 30min; £2)

The **National Railway Museum** is a must if you have even the slightest interest in railways, history, engineering or Victoriana. The Great Hall alone features some fifty restored locomotives dating from 1829 onwards, among them *Mallard*, at 126mph the fastest steam engine ever built. The seemingly interminable restoration of one of the museum's greatest engines – the **Flying Scotsman** – continues. The latest estimate is that it will be finished by the summer of 2015 – but don't hold your breath.

# Castle Howard

15 miles northeast of York off the A64 • Late March to late Oct & late Nov to mid-Dec house daily 11am–4pm, grounds 10am–5pm; grounds also open Jan to late March & Nov to mid-Dec • £14; grounds only £9.50 • ☎ 01653 648333, ⍵ castlehoward.co.uk • The summer Moorsbus (see p.623) comes out here from Helmsley, while some Yorkshire Coastliner buses run from York, Malton or Pickering; you can also take a bus tour from York

Immersed in the deep countryside of the Howardian Hills, **Castle Howard** is the seat of one of England's leading aristocratic families and among the country's grandest stately homes. The grounds especially are worth visiting, and you could easily spend the best part of a day here. The colossal main house was designed by **Sir John Vanbrugh** in 1699 and was almost forty years in the making – remarkable enough, even were it not for the fact that Vanbrugh was, at the start of the commission at least, best known as a playwright and had no formal architectural training. Shrewdly, Vanbrugh recognized his limitations and called upon **Nicholas Hawksmoor**, who had a major part in the house's structural design – the pair later worked successfully together on Blenheim Palace.

Vanbrugh also turned his attention to the estate's thousand-acre **grounds**, where he could indulge his playful inclinations – the formal gardens, clipped parkland, towers, obelisks and blunt sandstone follies stretch in all directions, sloping gently to two artificial lakes. The whole is a charming artifice of grand, manicured views – an example of what three centuries, skilled gardeners and pots of money can produce.

## ARRIVAL AND DEPARTURE YORK

**By train** Trains arrive at York Station, just outside the city walls, a 10min walk from the historic core.
**Destinations** Durham (every 10min; 50min); Harrogate (hourly; 30min); Hull (hourly; 1hr); Leeds (every 10–15min; 25min); London (every 30min; 2hr); Manchester (every 15min; 1hour 25min); Newcastle (every 15min; 1hr); Scarborough (hourly; 50min); Sheffield (every 15–30min; 45min).
**By bus** National Express buses (☎ 0870 580 8080) and most other regional bus services drop off and pick up on Rougier St, 200yd north of the train station, just before Lendal Bridge. Companies include East Yorkshire (for Hull, Beverley and Bridlington; ☎ 01482 592929) and Yorkshire Coastliner (for Leeds, Castle Howard, Pickering, Scarborough and Whitby; ☎ 01653 692556).
**Destinations** Beverley (Mon–Sat hourly, Sun 7 daily; 1hr 10min); Hull (Mon–Sat hourly, Sun 7 daily; 1hr 35min); Leeds (Mon–Fri every 20min; 1hour 20min); Pickering (hourly; 1hr 8min); Scarborough (hourly; 1hr 40min); Whitby (4–6 daily; 2hr 13min).

## GETTING AROUND

**On foot** The historic core is easily explored on foot; from the Minster in the north, for example, to Castle Museum in the south is about a 10min walk. Indeed, one of the best ways to explore the city is to circumnavigate it atop the splendid city walls.
**By taxi** There are taxi ranks at Rougier St, Duncombe Place, Exhibition Square and the train station, or call Station Taxis on ☎ 01904 623332.

## INFORMATION AND TOURS

**Tourist office** 1 Museum St, on the corner with Blake Street (Mon–Sat 9am–5pm, July & Aug to 5.30pm, Sun 10am–4pm ☎ 01904 550099, ⍵ visityork.org). There is also a smaller tourist office at the train station.
**Listings information** The Evening Press (⍵ thisisyork .co.uk), and the monthly What's On York (⍵ whatsonyork .com) provide detailed entertainment, events, festival and exhibition listings for the city.
**Bus tours** City tours by bus – pick up details at the tourist office – cost around £10. York Pullman (☎ 01904 622992, ⍵ yorkpullmanbus.co.uk) offers day-trips to Castle Howard for £17.50, along with several routes to the Dales.
**Walking tours** There are various guided walks available (around £6), including evening ghost walks. There's not much to choose between them, though one is free – the York Association of Voluntary Guides (☎ 01904 550098, ⍵ avgyork.co.uk) offers a guided tour year round (daily 10.15am; 2hr), plus additional tours in summer (April–Oct 2.15pm, and one at 6.45pm June–Aug), from outside the York Art Gallery – just turn up.
**River cruises** The best river operator is YorkBoat (☎ 01904 628324, ⍵ yorkboat.co.uk), who run a variety of cruises from King's Staith and Lendal Bridge (Feb–Nov; cruises from £7.50, families £20).
**York Pass** The York Pass (☎ 01904 550099, ⍵ yorkpass.com) gives free entry to over thirty attractions, not only in the city (eg Barley Hall, Clifford's Tower, Dig! and the Fairfax House) but also elsewhere (Castle Howard, Eden Camp, the North York Moors Railway); it costs £36/£48/£58 for one/two/three days respectively, with reductions if you buy it online.

**12**

## ACCOMMODATION

The main **B&B** concentration is in the side streets off Bootham (immediately west of Exhibition Square), with nothing much more than a 10min walk from the centre.

★**Bar Convent** 17 Blossom St ☎01904 643238, 🖲bar-convent.org.uk. Unique opportunity to stay in a convent. The grand Georgian building houses a museum and café as well as nine single rooms (£33–37 each), twins, doubles and a family room, self-catering kitchen and guest lounge. **£80**

**Bowman's** 33 Grosvenor Terrace ☎01904 622204, 🖲bowmansguesthouse.co.uk. Six spotless rooms in a friendly renovated Victorian terrace B&B off Bootham, within easy reach of the city centre. They provide a permit for free on-street parking. **£80**

★**Cedar Court Grand Hotel** Station Rise ☎0845 409 6430, 🖲cedarcourtgrand.co.uk. Splendid five-star hotel a 2min walk from the train station, housed in what was the 1906 headquarters of the North Eastern Railway. Bags of character, with wonderful views of the walls and the Minster, luxurious rooms, a fine-dining restaurant and relaxing bar. **£175**

**The Fort** Little Stonegate ☎01904 639573, 🖲thefortyork.co.uk. An interesting idea – a "boutique hostel" in the city centre, offering rooms and dorms decorated on themes (log cabin, deep-sea creatures) at a knock-down price. Dorms **£22**; doubles **£78**

**Hedley House Hotel** 3 Bootham Terrace ☎01904 637404, 🖲hedleyhouse.com. Friendly, comfortable small hotel that is at its best in summer, when the outdoor area with sauna/aqua spa comes into its own. Rooms can be a little chilly in winter – especially in the (separate) annexe. Free car parking on first-come, first-served basis. **£115**

**Mount Royale** The Mount ☎01904 628856, 🖲mountroyale.co.uk. Lots of antiques, super garden suites (and cheaper rooms), and a heated outdoor pool in summer. Plus a hot tub, sauna and steam room, and a well-regarded restaurant. **£125**

★**Rowntree Park Caravan Club Site** Terry Ave ☎01904 658997, 🖲caravanclub.co.uk. A wonderful site, the best-located in the city, a 10min walk from the centre, with a back gate that opens onto a street of takeaways, pubs and shops. Open to non-members. Mainly for caravans and motorhomes, but with a small tent enclosure – those with tents must arrive on foot. Advance booking essential, especially at weekends. For motorhome plus 2 adults **£26.20**

**Safestay York** Micklegate House, 88–90 Micklegate ☎01904 627720, 🖲safestayyork.co.uk. In a handsome 1752 building in the centre of the city, with many impressive features. Beds are in dorms (sleeping 4 to 14) and private rooms, all en suite; prices rise at weekends and drop for multi-night stays. Dorms **£16**; doubles **£80**

## EATING

**Asia Gourmet** 61 Gillygate ☎01904 622728. Small, cheerful restaurant in the city centre with prompt service. Mainly Japanese food (sushi a speciality) though other Asian cuisines are available. Main courses £6.50. Tues & Sun 5–10pm, Wed–Sat 5.30–10pm.

**Ate O Clock** 13a High Ousegate ☎01904 644080, 🖲ateoclock.co.uk. The name is dreadful, but the – largely Mediterranean – food is excellent, and there's attentive service and a relaxed atmosphere. A two-course lunch is £9.50, while main dishes are around £14–£20. Music most Fri evenings. Mon 5.30–9pm, Tues–Fri noon–2pm & 6–9.30pm, Sat noon–2.30pm & 5.30–9.30pm.

**Betty's** 6–8 St Helen's Square ☎01904 659142, 🖲bettys.co.uk. Famous across Yorkshire, *Betty's* specializes in cakes and pastries like granny used to make (or not) – try the pikelets or the Yorkshire fat rascals – plus hot dishes and puddings to die for. No reservations. In the basement there's a mirror with the signatures of the hundreds of Allied airmen who used *Betty's* as an unofficial mess during World War II. Daily 9am–9pm.

**Café Concerto** 21 High Petergate ☎01904 610478, 🖲cafeconcerto.biz. Relaxed, Belle Epoque-style bistro facing the Minster, with sheet-music-papered walls and waiting staff in robust aprons. Food is modern European; there are papers to browse. (There's also a two-bedroom apartment available upstairs). Daily 8.30am–10pm.

★**Café No. 8** 8 Gillygate ☎01904 653074, 🖲cafeno8.co.uk. Limited menu using excellent locally sourced produce (Masham sausages, Yorkshire beef and lamb, Ryedale ice cream, beer from Masham) in unpretentious surroundings. Mains cost around £10 during the day, and £14–17 in the evening, or have two courses midweek for £16.50. Its heated garden is a popular spot. Mon–Fri noon–10pm, Sat & Sun 10am–10pm.

**Rustique** 28 Castlegate ☎01904 612744, 🖲rustiqueyork.co.uk. French-style bistro serving excellent-value Gallic food and wine. There are a couple of set menus (two courses £13.95, three £15.95); à la carte features all the classics, including steak frites, moules marinière and confit de canard. Mon–Sat noon–10pm, Sun noon–9pm.

## DRINKING

**Black Swan** Peasholme Green ☎01904 679131, 🖲blackswanyork.com. York's oldest pub is an imposing half-timbered, sixteenth-century tavern, with wonderful details – flagstones, period staircase, inglenook – good beer,

and occasional jazz and folk nights (ⓦ blackswanfolkclub .org.uk). Mon–Sat noon–11pm, Sun noon–10.30pm.
**Blue Bell** Fossgate ☎01904 654904. Built in 1798, the *Blue Bell* is a tiny, friendly local with two rooms, oak-panelling and good real ales. No mobile phones. Recently dropped by the *Good Beer Guide* because of concerns regarding access. Mon–Sat 11am–11pm, Sun noon–10.30pm.

★**The Swan** 16 Bishopgate ☎01904 634968. Lovely local, a Tetley Heritage Inn that offers convivial surroundings, well-kept real ale and a really friendly atmosphere a few minutes from the city centre. Mon–Wed 4–11pm, Thurs 4–11.30pm, Fri 4pm–midnight, Sat noon–midnight, Sun noon–11pm.

## TOP 5 YORKSHIRE PUBS
**Duke of York** Whitby. See p.632
**Fat Cat** Sheffield. See p.591
**Star Inn** Harome. See p.626
**The Swan** York. See opposite
**Whitelocks** Leeds. See p.596

**Three-Legged Mare** 15 High Petergate ☎01904 638246. A converted shop provides an airy outlet for York Brewery's own quality beer. No kids, no juke box, no video games. It's named after a three-legged gallows – it's there on the pub sign, with a replica in the beer garden. Mon–Sat 11am–midnight, Sun noon–11pm.

## NIGHTLIFE AND ENTERTAINMENT

York has its fair share of theatres and cinemas, and **classical music concerts** and recitals are often held in the city's churches and York Minster. Major annual events include the **Viking Festival** (ⓦ vikingjorvik.com) every Feb and the **Early Music Festival** (ⓦ ncem.co.uk), perhaps the best of its kind in the country, held in July. The city is also famous for its **Mystery Plays** (ⓦ yorkmysteryplays.co.uk), traditionally held every four years – the next are planned for 2018.

**The Basement** 13–17 Coney St, below City Screen cinema ☎01904 612940, ⓦ thebasementyork.co.uk. An intimate venue with a variety of nights – from music to comedy to arts events. The first Wed of every month is "Café Scientifique" – a free evening of discussion surrounding current issues in science, while Sun night sees stand-up comedy (7–10pm). Live music events are scattered through the week, along with cabaret, burlesque and club nights. Most nights 8–11pm.
**City Screen** 13–17 Coney St ☎0870 758 3219, ⓦ picturehouses.co.uk. The city's independent cinema is the art-house choice, with three screens, a Riverside café-

bar, and licensed restaurant.
**Fibbers** 8 The Stonebow ☎01904 651250, ⓦ fibbers .co.uk. York's primary live music venue, *Fibbers* regularly puts on local and nationally known bands in a lively atmosphere – consult website for details.
**Grand Opera House** Cumberland St at Clifford St ☎0844 871 3024, ⓦ grandoperahouseyork.org.uk. Musicals, ballet, pop gigs and family entertainment in all its guises.
**The National Centre for Early Music** St Margaret's Church, Walmgate ☎01904 632220, ⓦ ncem.co.uk. Not just early music, but also folk, world and jazz.

**12**

# Hull

HULL – officially Kingston upon Hull – dates back to 1299, when it was laid out as a seaport by Edward I. It quickly became England's leading harbour, and was still a vital garrison when the gates were closed against Charles I in 1642, the first serious act of rebellion of what was to become the English Civil War. Fishing and **seafaring** have always been important here, and today's city maintains a firm grip on its heritage with a number of superb visitor attractions.

## The Maritime Museum

Queen Victoria Square • Mon–Sat 10am–5pm, Sun 1.30–4.30pm • Free • ☎01482 300300, ⓦ hullcc.gov.uk

The city's maritime legacy is covered in the **Maritime Museum**, housed in the Neoclassical headquarters of the former Town Docks Offices. With displays on fishing, whaling and sailing, this provides a valuable record of centuries of skill and expertise, not to mention courage and fortitude, now fading into the past. Highlights include the whaling gallery, with whale skeletons, fearsome exploding harpoons, the sort of flimsy boats in which whalers of old used to chase the leviathans of the deep, a crow's nest made of a barrel, and oddities such as a whalebone seat, a blubber cauldron and a group of Narwhal tusks. An exhilarating and humbling experience.

## The Museums Quarter

Between High St and the River Hull • All attractions Mon–Sat 10am–5pm, Sun 1.30–4.30pm • Free • ☎ 01482 300300, ⊛ hullcc.gov.uk

Over towards the River Hull, you reach the **Museums Quarter** and **High Street**, which has been designated an "Old Town" conservation area thanks to its crop of former merchants' houses and narrow cobbled alleys. At its northern end stands **Wilberforce House**, the former home of William Wilberforce, which contains fascinating exhibits on slavery and its abolition, the cause to which he dedicated much of his life. Next door is **Streetlife**, devoted to the history of transport in the region and centred on a 1930s street scene. The adjoining **Hull and East Riding Museum** is even better, with showpiece attractions including vivid displays of Celtic burials and an impressive full-size model of a woolly mammoth.

## The Deep

Tower St • Daily 10am–6pm, last entry 5pm • £11.50 • ☎ 01482 381000 , ⊛ thedeep.co.uk

Protruding from a promontory overlooking the River Humber, Hull's splendid aquarium, **The Deep**, is just ten minutes' walk from the old town. Its educational displays and videos wrap around an immense 30ft-deep, 2.3-million-gallon viewing tank filled with sharks, rays and octopuses. There's an underwater tunnel along the bottom of the tank, together with a magical glass lift in which you can ascend or descend through the water while coming eye to eye with some of the more intriguing denizens of the deep.

### ARRIVAL AND INFORMATION                                           HULL

**By train** Hull's train station is situated in the Paragon Interchange off Ferensway. There are direct trains between London and Hull, while the city is also linked to the main London–York line via Doncaster as well as to the East Yorkshire coast.

Destinations Bempton (every 30min; 55min); Beverley (Mon–Sat every 25min, Sun 6 daily; 13min); Bridlington (every 30min; 42min); Filey (around 10 daily; 1hr10min); (Leeds (hourly; 1hr); London (6 daily; 2hr 45min);

Scarborough (every 2hr; 1hr 30min); York (hourly; 1hr 10m).
**By bus** The bus station is near the train station in the Paragon Interchange off Ferensway. Buses run to all parts of the region including York (2hr) and the East Coast (1hr40min to Bridlington; 2hr30min to Scarborough).
**Tourist office** Carr Lane at Queen Victoria Square (Mon–Sat 10am–5pm, Sun 11am–3pm; ☎ 01482 223559, ⊛ visithull andeastyorkshire.com). Here you can pick up the entertaining "Fish Trail" leaflet, a self-guided trail that kids will love.

### ACCOMMODATION

**Holiday Inn Hull Marina** Castle St ☎ 0871 9422 9043, ⊛ holiday-inn.com. Rooms at the city's best central hotel overlook the marina, and there's a restaurant and bar, plus an indoor pool, gym, sauna and plenty of parking. **£61.50**
**Kingston Theatre Hotel** 1–2 Kingston Square

☎ 01482 225828, ⊛ kingstontheatrehotel.com. This straightforward, good-value hotel on the city's prettiest square, across from Hull New Theatre, is a 5min walk from the city centre, yet in a quiet neighbourhood. Street parking only (but there's a public car park nearby). **£67.50**

### EATING AND DRINKING

**Cerutti's** 10 Nelson St ☎ 01482 328501, ⊛ ceruttis .co.uk. Facing the old site of the Victoria Pier (now replaced by a wooden deck overlooking the river), this Italian restaurant is especially good for fish dishes. The atmosphere is busy and friendly, and there are frequent special events including live jazz. Main courses are around £13–23, but look out for two- and three-course deals. Mon–Fri noon– 2pm, Mon–Sat 6.45–9.30pm.
**The George** The Land of Green Ginger ☎ 01482 226373. Venerable pub on Hull's most curiously named street – see if you can find England's smallest window. Mon noon–6pm, Tues–Thurs noon–11.00pm, Fri & Sat noon–midnight, Sun noon–10pm.
**Pave Café-Bar** 16–20 Princes Ave ☎ 01482 333181,

⊛ pavebar.co.uk. Nice laidback atmosphere with lots going on – live jazz/blues and comedy nights, and readings by the likes of Alexei Sayle, Will Self and Simon Armitage – and a comprehensive menu of home-cooked food served till 7pm (most mains well under £10). Mon–Thurs & Sun 11am–11.00pm, Fri & Sat 11am–11.30pm.
**Taman Ria Tropicana** 22 Princes Ave ☎ 01482 345640, ⊛ tropicana-hull.co.uk. Specifically Malay (rather than the more generic Malaysian) cuisine. All food is halal, and pork is never used. Check with staff regarding how spicy different dishes are. The "three dishes for £11" option is a good way to try things out. Tues–Sat 5–10.30pm.
**Ye Olde White Harte** 25 Silver St ☎ 01482 326363, ⊛ yeoldewhiteharte.com. Dating back to the sixteenth

century, this place has a pleasant courtyard garden, flagged floors, open brickwork and well-polished furniture,

and serves traditional pub grub (mains £5.50–£7.50). Mon–Sat 11am–midnight, Sun noon–midnight.

## ENTERTAINMENT

**Hull Truck Theatre Company** 50 Ferensway ☎ 01482 323638, ⓦ hulltruck.co.uk. Renowned theatre, where,

among other high-profile works, many of the plays of award-winning John Godber see the light of day.

# Beverley

With its tangle of old streets, cobbled lanes and elegant Georgian and Victorian terraces **BEVERLEY**, nine miles north of Hull, is the very picture of a traditional market town. More than 350 of its buildings are listed, and though you could see its first-rank offerings in a morning, it makes an appealing place to stay.

## Beverley Minster

Minster Yard North • March, April, Sept & Oct Mon–Sat 9am–5pm, Sun noon–4.30pm; May–Aug Mon–Sat 9am–5.30pm, Sun noon–5.30pm; Nov–Feb Mon–Sat 9am–4pm, Sun noon–5.30pm • Free, but donations requested • ☎ 01482 868540, ⓦ beverleyminster.org

The town is dominated by the fine, Gothic twin towers of **Beverley Minster**. The **west front**, which crowned the work in 1420, is widely considered without equal, its survival due in large part to architect Nicholas Hawksmoor, who restored much of the church in the eighteenth century. The carving throughout is magnificent, particularly the 68 misericords of the oak **choir** (1520–24), one of the largest and most accomplished in England. Much of the decorative work here and elsewhere is on a musical theme. Beverley had a renowned guild of itinerant minstrels, which provided funds in the sixteenth century for the carvings on the transept aisle capitals, where you'll be able to pick out players of lutes, bagpipes, horns and tambourines.

**12**

## St Mary's

Corner of North Bar Within and Hengate • April–Sept Mon–Fri 10am–4.30pm; Oct–March Mon–Fri 10am–4pm, Sun before and after services only • Free • ☎ 01482 869137, ⓦ stmarysbeverley.org

Cobbled Highgate runs from the Minster through town, along the pedestrianized shopping streets and past the main Market Square, to Beverley's other great church, **St Mary's**, which nestles alongside the **North Bar**, sole survivor of the town's five medieval gates. Inside, the chancel's painted panelled ceiling (1445) contains portraits of English kings from Sigebert (623–37) to Henry VI (1421–71), and among the carvings, the favourite novelty is the so-called "Pilgrim's Rabbit", said to have been the inspiration for the White Rabbit in Lewis Carroll's *Alice in Wonderland*.

## ARRIVAL AND INFORMATION                                                      BEVERLEY

**By train** Beverley's train station on Station Square is just a couple of mins' walk from the town centre and the Minster. Destinations Bridlington (every 30min; 30min); Hull (every 30min; 15min); Sheffield (hourly; 1hr 41min).

**By bus** The bus station is at the junction of Walkergate and Sow Hill Road, with the main street just a minute's walk away. Destinations Bridlington (hourly; 1hr) Driffield (hourly;

25min); Hull (every 30min–1hr; hourly; 40min); Scarborough (hourly; 1hr 16min)

**Tourist office** 34 Butcher Row in the main shopping area (Apr–Sept Mon–Fri 9.30am–5.30pm, Sat 9.30am–4.30pm, Sun 10am–3.30pm; Oct–March Mon–Fri 10am–5pm, Sat 10am–4.30pm; ☎ 01482 391672, ⓦ visithullandeastyorkshire.com).

## ACCOMMODATION AND EATING

★ **Cerutti 2** Station Square ☎ 01482 866700, ⓦ ceruttis.co.uk. Occupying what was once the station waiting rooms, *Cerutti 2*, run by the same family as *Cerutti's*

in Hull, specializes in fish, though there are meat and vegetarian options too (mains around £12–23). Popular with locals, so it's as well to book, especially at weekends.

Tues–Sat noon–2pm & 6.45–9.30pm.
**King's Head Hotel** 37–38 Saturday Market ☎01482 868103, ⓦkingsheadpubbeverley.co.uk. Tucked into a corner of busy Saturday Market, this period building has contemporary decor inside. It's a Marston's pub, with food from £7, and it can be noisy, especially at weekends, but the rear rooms are quieter, and ear plugs are provided. Mon–Thurs

9am–11pm, Fri & Sat 9am–1am, Sun 11am–11pm; food served Mon–Sat 10am–9pm, Sun 10am–8pm. **£79.95**
★**YHA Beverley Friary** Friar's Lane ☎0845 371 9004, ⓦyha.org.uk. Beautiful medieval monastic house in the shadow of the Minster. What it lacks in luxury it makes up for in atmosphere, location and, of course, economy. Dorms **£18**; triples **£69**

# The East Yorkshire coast

The **East Yorkshire coast** curves south in a gentle arc from the mighty cliffs of Flamborough Head to Spurn Head, a hook-shaped promontory formed by relentless erosion and shifting currents. There are few parts of the British coast as dangerous – indeed, the Humber lifeboat station at **Spurn Point** is the only one in Britain permanently staffed by a professional crew. Between the two points lie a handful of tranquil villages and miles of windswept dunes and mud flats. The two main resorts, **Bridlington** and **Filey**, couldn't be more different, but each has its own appeal.

## Bridlington and around

The southernmost resort on the Yorkshire coast, **BRIDLINGTON** has maintained its harbour for almost a thousand years. The seafront promenade looks down upon the town's best asset – its sweeping sandy **beach**. It's an out-and-out family resort, which means plenty of candyfloss, fish and chips, rides, boat trips and amusement arcades. The historic core of town is a mile inland, where in the largely Georgian Bridlington Old Town the **Bayle Museum** (April–Sept Mon–Fri 10am–4pm; £1; ☎01262 674308) presents local history in a building that once served as the gateway to a fourteenth-century priory. Every November, Bridlington hosts a highly regarded World Music Festival, **Musicport** (ⓦmusicportfestival.com), which pulls in some very big names.

Around fourteen miles of precipitous 400ft-high cliffs gird **Flamborough Head**, just to the northeast of Bridlington. The best of the seascapes are visitable on the peninsula's north side, accessible by road from Flamborough village.

## Bempton

From **BEMPTON**, two miles north of Bridlington, you can follow the cliff-top path all the way round to Flamborough Head or curtail the journey by cutting up paths to Flamborough village. The **RSPB sanctuary** at **Bempton Cliffs**, reached along a quiet lane from Bempton, is the best single place to see the area's thousands of cliff-nesting birds – it's the only mainland gannetry in England. Bempton also has the second-largest **puffin colony** in the country, with several thousand returning to the cliffs each year. Late March and April is the best time to see the puffins, but the bird sanctuary's **Visitor Centre** (daily March–Oct 9.30am–5pm, Nov–Feb 9.30am–4pm; parking £5; ☎01262 851179, ⓦrspb.org.uk) can advise on other breeds' activities.

## Filey

**FILEY**, half a dozen miles north up the coast from Bempton, is at the very edge of the Yorkshire Wolds (and technically in North Yorkshire). It has a good deal more class as a resort than Bridlington, retaining many of its Edwardian features, including some splendid panoramic gardens. It, too, claims miles of wide sandy beach, stretching most of the way south to Flamborough Head and north the mile or so to the jutting rocks of **Filey Brigg**, where a nature trail wends for a couple of miles through the surroundings.

| ARRIVAL AND GETTING AROUND | THE EAST YORKSHIRE COAST |
|---|---|

**By train** Bridlington and Filey are linked by the regular service between Hull and Scarborough, and there are regular trains between York and Scarborough, further up the coast.

**By bus** There are buses from York to Bridlington (every 2hr; 1hr 45min), plus a service from Hull to Scarborough (every

2hr; 2hr 50min) via Bridlington and Filey. There's also an hourly service between Bridlington, Filey and Scarborough, while the seasonal Sunday Spurn Ranger service (Easter–Oct; ☎01482 222222) gives access to the isolated Spurn Head coastline (though it can no longer go all the way to the point owing to erosion).

# The North York Moors

Virtually the whole of the **North York Moors**, from the Hambleton and Cleveland hills in the west to the cliff-edged coastline to the east, is protected by one of the country's finest National Parks. The heather-covered, flat-topped hills are cut by deep, steep-sided valleys, and views here stretch for miles, interrupted only by giant cultivated forests. This is great walking country; footpaths include the superb **Cleveland Way**, one of England's premier long-distance National Trails, which embraces both wild moorland and the cliff scenery of the North Yorkshire coast. Barrows and ancient forts provide memorials of early settlers, mingling on the high moorland with the battered stone crosses of the first Christian inhabitants and the ruins of great monastic houses such as **Rievaulx Abbey**.

| GETTING AROUND | THE NORTH YORK MOORS |
|---|---|

**By train** The steam trains of the North Yorkshire Moors Railway (see box, p.627) run between Pickering and Grosmont and on to Whitby. At Grosmont you can connect with the regular trains on the Esk Valley line, running either 6 miles east to Whitby and the coast, or west through more remote country settlements (and ultimately to Middlesbrough).

**By bus** The main bus approaches to the moors are from Scarborough and York to the main towns of Helmsley and

Pickering – pick up the free *Moors Explorer* timetable booklet from tourist offices and park information centres (or consult ☎01482 592929 or ⓦeyms.co.uk). There are also seasonal Moorsbus services (April–Oct; ☎01845 597000, ⓦmoors.uk.net/moorsbus) connecting Pickering and Helmsley to everywhere of interest in the National Park. There are several departures daily in the school summer hols, fewer at other times (at least every Sun & bank hol Mon).

**12**

| INFORMATION |
|---|

**National Park Visitor Centres** There are two National Park Visitor Centres for the North York Moors, one in Danby (April–Oct daily 10am–5pm, Aug to 5.30pm; for winter hours check with centre; ☎01439 772737), and the other in Sutton Bank (April–July & Sept–Oct daily 10am–5pm, Aug daily 9.30am–5.30pm; for winter hours check with centre; ☎01845 597426). Both offer exhibitions,

pamphlets and maps, a café and a shop. The National Park's website is ⓦnorthyorkmoors.org.uk.

**Cleveland Way Project** Provides maps and information about the route, including an annual, downloadable accommodation guide (☎01439 770657, ⓦnationaltrail.co.uk/ClevelandWay).

## Thirsk

The market town of **THIRSK**, 23 miles north of York, made the most of its strategic crossroads position on the ancient drove road between Scotland and York and on the historic east–west route from dales to coast. Its medieval prosperity is clear from the large, cobbled **Market Place** (markets Mon & Sat), while well-to-do citizens later endowed the town with fine Georgian houses and halls. However, Thirsk's main draw is its attachment to the legacy of local vet Alf Wight, better known as James Herriott. Thirsk was the "Darrowby" of the Herriott books, and the vet's former surgery, at 23 Kirkgate, is now the hugely popular **World of James Herriott** (daily: March–Oct 10am–5pm; Nov–Feb 10am–4pm; £8.50; ☎01845 524234, ⓦworldofjamesherriot.org), crammed with period pieces and Herriott memorabilia.

## ARRIVAL AND INFORMATION

**By train** The train station is a mile west of town on the A61 (Ripon road); minibuses connect the station with the town centre.

Destinations Middlesbrough (hourly; 44min); Manchester (hourly; 1hr 50min); London (every 2hr; 2hr 30min).

**By bus** Buses stop in the Market Place.

Destinations Northallerton (every 2hr; 25–30min); Ripon (every 2hr; 41min); York (every 1–2hr; 1hr).

**By car** Thirsk is just a 30min drive from York, making it an easy day-trip.

**Tourist office** 49 Market Place (Jan–March Mon–Sat 10am–3pm; April–June & Sept–Dec Mon–Sat 10am–4pm; July & Aug Mon–Sat 9.30am–4.30pm; ☏ 01845 522755, ⊚ visit-thirsk.org.uk).

## ACCOMMODATION AND EATING

**Gallery** 18 Kirkgate ☏ 01845 523767, ⊚ gallerybedandbreakfast.co.uk. An award-winning B&B with three comfortable rooms and excellent breakfasts in an eighteenth-century Grade II-listed building. It's on a main street, and can get noisy when the pubs close. **£70**

**Golden Fleece** Market Place ☏ 01845 523108, ⊚ goldenfleecehotel.com. Good rooms and a nice busy atmosphere in this charming old coaching inn nicely

located on Thirsk's large cobbled square. They serve locally sourced food, too. Mon–Sat noon–3pm & 6.30–9.15pm, Sun noon–2pm & 6.30–9pm. **£95**

**The Poplars** Carlton Miniott ☏ 01845 522712, ⊚ thepoplarsthirsk.com. Near the station and the racecourse, this B&B offers clean rooms and "cottages" (actually cabins; three-night minimum stay). All have their own access. **£65**

# Osmotherley and around

Eleven miles north of Thirsk, the little village of **OSMOTHERLEY** huddles around its green. The pretty settlement gets by as a hiking centre, since it's a key stop on the **Cleveland Way** as well as starting point for the brutal 42-mile **Lyke Wake Walk** to Ravenscar, south of Robin Hood's Bay.

## Mount Grace Priory

On the A19 • April–Sept daily 10am–6pm; Oct daily 10am–5pm; Nov–March Sat & Sun 10am–4pm • £5.60; NT & EH ☏ 01609 883494, ⊚ nationaltrust.org.uk/mount-grace-priory, ⊚ english-heritage.org.uk • #80/#89 from Northallerton, then a 30min walk

An easy two-mile walk from Osmotherley via Chapel Wood Farm, the fourteenth-century **Mount Grace Priory** is the most important of England's nine Carthusian ruins. The Carthusians took a vow of silence and lived, ate and prayed alone in their two-storey cells, each separated from its neighbour by a privy, small garden and high walls. The foundations of the cells are still clearly visible, and one has been reconstructed to suggest its original layout.

## Sutton Bank

The main A170 road enters the National Park from Thirsk as it climbs 500ft in half a mile to **Sutton Bank** (960ft), a phenomenal **viewpoint** from where the panorama extends across the Vale of York to the Pennines on the far horizon. While you're here, call in at the **National Park Visitor Centre** (see p.623) to pick up information on the **walks** and off-road **bike rides** you can make from here.

## Kilburn

To the south of the A170, the **White Horse Nature Trail** (2–3 miles; 1hr 30min) skirts the crags of Roulston Scar en route to the **Kilburn White Horse**, northern England's only turf-cut figure, 314ft long and 228ft high. You could make a real walk of it by dropping a couple of miles down to pretty **KILBURN** village (a minor road also runs from the A170, passing the White Horse car park) which has been synonymous with woodcarving since the days of "Mouseman" Robert Thompson (1876–1955), whose woodcarvings are marked by his distinctive mouse motif. The **Mouseman Visitor Centre** (Easter–Oct daily 10am–5pm; Nov & Dec Wed–Sun

11am–4pm; £4.50; ☎01347 869102, ⓦroberthompsons.co.uk) displays examples of Thompson's personal furniture.

## Coxwold

Most visitors to the attractive village of **COXWOLD** come to pay homage to the novelist **Laurence Sterne**, who is buried by the south wall (close to the porch) in the churchyard of **St Michael's**, where he was vicar from 1760 until his death in 1768. **Shandy Hall**, further up the road past the church (house May–Sept Wed & Sun 2.30–4.30pm; gardens May–Sept daily except Sat 11am–4.30pm; also by appointment; house & gardens £4.50, gardens only £2.50; ☎01347 868465, ⓦlaurencesternetrust.org.uk), was Sterne's home, now a museum crammed with literary memorabilia. It was here that he wrote *A Sentimental Journey through France and Italy* and the wonderfully eccentric *The Life and Opinions of Tristram Shandy, Gentleman*.

## Helmsley and around

One of the moors' most appealing towns, **HELMSLEY** makes a perfect base for visiting the western moors and Rievaulx Abbey. Local life revolves around a large cobbled market square (market Fri), dominated by a boastful monument to the second earl of Feversham, whose family was responsible for rebuilding most of the village in the nineteenth century. The old **market cross** now marks the start of the 110-mile **Cleveland Way**. Signposted from the square, it's easy to find **Helmsley Castle** (daily: April–Sept 10am–6pm; Oct–Nov 10am–5pm; Nov–March Sat & Sun 10am–4pm; £5.20; EH; ☎01439 770442, ⓦenglish-heritage.org.uk), its unique twelfth-century D-shaped keep ringed by massive earthworks.

### Rievaulx Abbey

Just over 2 miles northwest of Helmsley off the B1257 • April–Sept daily 10am–6pm; Oct to early Nov daily 10am–5pm; mid-Nov to March Sat & Sun 10am–4pm • £6.20; EH • ☎01439 798228, ⓦenglish-heritage.org.uk

From Helmsley you can easily walk across country to **Rievaulx Abbey** on a signposted path (1hr 30min). Founded in 1132, the abbey became the mother church of the Cistercians in England, quickly developing into a flourishing community with interests in fishing, mining, agriculture and the woollen industry. At its height, 140 monks and up to five hundred lay brothers lived and worked here, though numbers fell dramatically once the Black Death (1348–49) had done its worst. The end came with the Dissolution, when many of the walls were razed and the roof lead stripped – the beautiful ruins, however, still suggest the abbey's former splendour.

### Rievaulx Terrace

On the B1257, a couple of miles northwest of Helmsley • Feb–Nov daily 11am–5pm • £5.95; NT • ☎01439 798340 (summer) or ☎01439 748283 (winter), ⓦnationaltrust.org.uk/rievaulx-terrace

Although they form some sort of ensemble with the abbey, there's no access between the ruins and **Rievaulx Terrace**. This half-mile stretch of grass-covered terraces and woodland was laid out as part of Duncombe Park in the 1750s, and was engineered partly to enhance the views of the abbey. The resulting panorama over the ruins and the valley below is superb, and this makes a great spot for a picnic.

### ARRIVAL AND INFORMATION                              HELMSLEY AND AROUND

**By bus** Buses from Scarborough (every 1hr 15min; 1hr 36min) and Pickering (every 1hr 15min; 35min) stop on or near the Market Place. In addition, seasonal Moorsbus services (April–Oct; ☎01845 597000, ⓦmoors.uk.net /moorsbus), connect Helmsley to most places in the National Park.

**Tourist information** There's no tourist office in Helmsley, but English Heritage are happy to answer queries where they can on ☎01439 770442. For the Cleveland Way, contact ☎01439 770173 or check ⓦryedale.gov.uk.

12

## ACCOMMODATION, EATING AND DRINKING

**Black Swan** Market Place ☎01439 770466, ⓦblackswan-helmsley.co.uk. An interesting Tudor/Georgian ex-coaching inn right on the main square, with a comfortable bar, airy restaurant, award-winning tearoom and charming, attentive staff. The hotel is progressively refurbishing its rooms. Daily 11am–11pm or later at weekends. Restaurant daily 7.30–9.30pm; tearoom daily 10am–5.30pm. **£144**

**Feathers Hotel** Market Place ☎01439 770275, ⓦfeathershotelhelmsley.co.uk. Pub serving restaurant food – all the staples, from £11.95 – and with a surprisingly large choice of rooms. Mon–Sat 11.30am–midnight, Sun 11.30am–11pm; food served Mon–Fri noon–2.30pm & 5.30–9pm, Sat noon–9pm, Sun noon–8.30pm. **£80**

★**Feversham Arms** 1 High St ☎01439 770766, ⓦfevershamarmshotel.com. One of Yorkshire's top hotels, multi-award-winning, luxurious yet unpretentious.

It has a pool, underground car park, spa and a terrific fine-dining restaurant. Look out for special deals. Mon–Sat noon–2.30pm & 6.45–9.30pm; Sun 12.30–2.30pm & 6.45–9.30pm. **£196**

★**Star Inn** Harome, 2 miles southeast of Helmsley ☎01439 770397, ⓦthestaratharome.co.uk. The *Star* is not only a spectacularly beautiful thatched inn, but also one of Yorkshire's longest-standing Michelin-starred restaurants. Food is classic British and surprisingly affordable (main courses around £19–24), and the atmosphere is blessedly unpretentious. Accommodation is available in a separate building, and there's an associated shop/deli across the road. Mon 6–11pm, Tues–Sat 11.30–3pm & 6–11pm, Sun noon–11pm; food served Mon 6.15–9.30pm, Tues–Sat 11.30am–2pm & 6.15–9.30pm, Sun noon–6pm. **£150**

## Hutton le Hole

Eight miles northeast of Helmsley, one of Yorkshire's quaintest villages, **HUTTON LE HOLE**, has become so great a tourist attraction that you'll have to come off-season to get much pleasure from its stream-crossed village green and the sight of sheep wandering freely through the lanes. Apart from the sheer photogenic quality of the place, the big draw is the family-oriented **Ryedale Folk Museum** (mid-Jan to March & Nov to early Dec daily 10am–4.30pm, April to Oct 10am–5.30pm; £7; ☎01751 417337, ⓦryedalefolkmuseum.co.uk), where local life is explored in a series of reconstructed buildings, notably a sixteenth-century house, a glass furnace, a crofter's cottage and a nineteenth-century blacksmith's shop.

### ARRIVAL AND INFORMATION                                                                           HUTTON LE HOLE

**By bus** The #174 travels from/to Pickering once a day (30min).

**National Park Information Centre** At Ryedale Folk

Museum (mid-Jan to March & Nov to early Dec daily 10am–4.30pm, March to Oct 10am–5.30pm; ☎01751 417367). They have a list of local B&Bs.

### ACCOMMODATION AND EATING

**The Barn Hotel** Hutton-le-Hole ☎01751 417311, ⓦthebarnhotel.info. Comfortable en-suite rooms and tearooms serving home-made cakes, scones, sandwiches and hot specials. Food served March–Oct daily 10.30am–4.30pm. **£79**

**The Crown** Hutton-le-Hole ☎01751 417343, ⓦcrownhuttonlehole.com. Spacious real ale pub where

you can sit outside and enjoy the peace of the village. They serve traditional, freshly cooked food, too; you can eat well for under a tenner. Typically open daily 11am–10pm (later when busy); food served Mon–Thurs 11.45am–2.15pm & 5.30–8.15pm, Fri & Sat 11.45am–2.30pm & 5.30–8.30pm, Sun 11.45am–6pm; the pub is closed Mon & Tues during winter.

## Pickering

The biggest centre for miles around, **PICKERING** takes for itself the title "Gateway to the Moors", which is pushing it a bit, though it's certainly a handy halt if you're touring the villages and dales of the **eastern moors**. Its most attractive feature is its motte and bailey **castle** on the hill north of the Market Place (April–Sept daily 10am–6pm; Oct–Nov 10am–5pm; £4.20; EH; ☎01751 474989, ⓦenglish-heritage.org.uk) reputedly used by every English monarch up to 1400 as a base for hunting in nearby Blandsby Park. The other spot worth investigating is the **Beck Isle Museum of Rural Life** on Bridge Street

## THE NORTH YORKSHIRE MOORS RAILWAY

The **North Yorkshire Moors Railway** (T 01751 472508, W nymr.co.uk) provides a double whammy of nostalgia, with the rolling stock, station furniture and smell of steam conjuring up images of bygone travel (especially to those who remember rail in the mid-twentieth century), while the countryside through which the trains pass is reminiscent of an England which in many places has disappeared. Lately, the railway has been attracting a younger generation, too, as a result of its connection with the **Harry Potter films**: Goathland Station was used in the first of the Harry Potter films as **Hogsmeade**, where Harry and co disembarked from the *Hogwarts Express*.

The line, completed by George Stephenson in 1835 just ten years after the opening of the Stockton and Darlington Railway, connects **Pickering** with the Esk Valley (Middlesbrough–Whitby) line at **Grosmont**, eighteen miles to the north. Scheduled **services** operate year-round (limited to weekends and school hols Nov–March), and a **day-return ticket** costs £19. Daily services also run on the Esk Valley line from Grosmont to the nearby seaside resort of Whitby from April to early November, with a return fare from Pickering of £25.

(Feb–Nov daily 10am–5pm; £6; T 01751 473653, W beckislemuseum.org.uk), which has reconstructions of a gents' outfitters and barber's shop, a case full of knickers, and a painting of two giant Welsh guardsmen produced by Rex Whistler for a children's party. **Market** day in town is Monday, and there's a farmers' market on the first Thursday of the month.

### ARRIVAL AND INFORMATION — PICKERING

**By train** The steam trains of the North Yorkshire Moors Railway (see box above) run between Pickering and Grosmont and on to Whitby. The station is a 5min signposted walk from the main street.

**By bus** Buses stop outside the library and tourist office, opposite the Co-op in the centre of town.

**Destinations** Helmsley (hourly; 35min); Scarborough (hourly; 53min); Whitby (4–6 daily; 1hr 4min); York (hourly; 1hr 10min).

**Tourist office** The Ropery, Pickering (March–Oct Mon–Sat 9.30am–5pm, Sun 9.30am–4pm; Nov–Feb Mon–Sat 9.30am–4pm; T 01751 473791, W ryedale.gov.uk).

### ACCOMMODATION AND EATING

The tourist office can help with **B&Bs**, though Whitby, just a 20min drive away on the coast, is the better overnight destination (see p.630).

★ **The White Swan** Market Place T 01751 472288, W white-swan.co.uk. Delightful traditional coaching inn, fully refurbished and updated, with contemporary and traditional bedrooms, and fine Modern British food (mains from £13.95). Daily 7.30am–11pm, food served noon–2pm & 6.45–9pm. £149

# The North Yorkshire coast

The **North Yorkshire coast** is the southernmost stretch of a cliff-edged shore that stretches almost unbroken to the Scottish border. **Scarborough** is the biggest resort, with a full set of attractions and a terrific beach. Cute **Robin Hood's Bay** is the most popular of the coastal villages, with fishing and smuggling traditions, while bluff **Staithes** – a fishing harbour on the far edge of North Yorkshire – has yet to tip over into a full-blown tourist trap. **Whitby**, between the two, is the best stopover, with its fine sands, good facilities, abbey ruins, Georgian buildings and maritime heritage – more than any other local place Whitby celebrates Captain Cook as one of its own. Two of the best sections of the **Cleveland Way** start from Whitby: southeast to Robin Hood's Bay (six miles) and northwest to Staithes (eleven miles), both along thrilling high-cliff paths.

### INFORMATION — THE NORTH YORKSHIRE COAST

**Tourist information** W discoveryorkshirecoast.com is a useful source of online information, and there are tourist offices at Scarborough (see p.629) and Whitby (see p.632).

# Scarborough

The oldest resort in the country, **SCARBOROUGH** first attracted early seventeenth-century visitors to its newly discovered mineral springs. To the Victorians it was "the Queen of the Watering Places", but Scarborough saw its biggest transformation after World War II, when it became a holiday haven for workers from the industrial heartlands. All the traditional ingredients of a beach resort are still here in force, from superb, clean sands and kitsch amusement arcades to the more refined pleasures of its tight-knit old-town streets and a genteel round of quiet parks and gardens. In addition to the sights detailed below, make sure to drop into the **Church of St Mary** (1180), below the castle on Castle Road, whose graveyard contains the tomb of Anne Brontë (see p.705), who died here in 1849.

## Rotunda Museum

Vernon Rd • Tues–Sun 10am–5pm • £3 • ☎ 01723 353665, ⓦ rotundamuseum.co.uk

The second-oldest purpose-built museum in the country (the oldest is in Oxford), the **Rotunda Museum** was constructed to the plans of William Smith, the founder of English geology, and opened in 1829. A fascinating building in its own right, it has recently been updated to include in its venerable shell some high-tech displays on geology and local history. The Dinosaur Coast Gallery is particularly child-friendly.

## Art Gallery

The Crescent • Tues–Sun 10am–5pm • £3 • ☎ 01723 384503 ⓦ scarboroughartgallery.co.uk

Scarborough's **Art Gallery**, housed in an Italianate villa, contains the town's permanent collection – largely the work of local artists, and including paintings, posters and photography – which gives an insight into the way the town has been depicted over the centuries.

## Scarborough Castle

Castle Rd • April–Sept daily 10am–6pm; Oct daily 10am–5pm; Nov to mid-Feb Sat & Sun 10am–4pm • £5; EH • ☎ 01765 608888, ⓦ english-heritage.org.uk

There's no better place to acquaint yourself with the local layout than **Scarborough Castle**, mounted on a jutting headland between two golden-sanded bays. Bronze and Iron Age relics have been found on the wooded castle crag, together with fragments of a fourth-century Roman signalling station, Saxon and Norman chapels and a Viking camp, reputedly built by a Viking with the nickname of Scardi (or "harelip"), from which the town's name derives.

## The bays

The miniature **North Bay Railway** (Easter–Sept daily 10am–4pm; ☎ 01723 368791, ⓦ nbr.org.uk) runs up to the **Sea Life Centre and Marine Sanctuary** on the North Bay at Scalby Mills (daily 10am–5pm; £16.20, £8.10 if ordered online; ☎ 01723 373414, ⓦ visitsealife.com/scarborough), distinguished by its white pyramids. From the harbourside, short **cruises** and **speedboat trips** shoot off throughout the day in the summer. For unique entertainment, head for Peasholm Park, where **naval warfare**, in the shape of miniature man-powered naval vessels, battle it out on the lake (July & Aug Mon, Thurs & Sat; £3.90; details from the tourist office).

The **South Bay** is more refined, backed by the Valley Gardens and the Italianate meanderings of the South Cliff Gardens, and topped by an esplanade from which a **hydraulic lift** (April–Sept daily 10am–5pm) chugs down to the beach.

## ARRIVAL AND DEPARTURE
SCARBOROUGH

**By train** The train station is at the top of town facing Westborough.

Destinations Hull (every 2hr; 1hr 30min); Leeds (hourly; 1hr 16min); York (hourly; 50min).

**By bus** Buses pull up outside the train station or in the surrounding streets. National Express services (direct from London) stop in the car park behind the station.

Destinations Bridlington (hourly; 1hr 18min); Filey

(hourly; 30min); Helmsley (hourly; 1hr 30min); Hull (hourly; 1hr 30min); Leeds (hourly; 2hr 40min); Pickering (hourly; 1hr); Robin Hood's Bay (hourly; 38min); Whitby (hourly; 1hr); York (hourly; 1hr 35min).

## GETTING AROUND AND INFORMATION

**By bus** Open-top seafront buses (Feb–Nov daily from 9.30am, every 12–20min; £2 return) run between North Bay to the Spa Complex in South Bay.

**Tourist offices** Scarborough has two sources of tourist information; one inside the Brunswick Shopping Centre on Westborough (April–June & Sept Mon, Tues & Thurs–Sat 9.30am–5.30pm, Wed 10am–5.30pm, Sun 11am–4.30pm; July & Aug same hours except Sun 10.30am–4.30pm; check for winter hours; ☎01723 383636), and the other on Sandside by the harbour (daily: April–June, Sept & Oct 10am–5.30pm; July & Aug 9.30am–7pm, ☎01723 383636).

## ACCOMMODATION

**Beiderbecke's** 1–3 The Crescent ☎01723 365733, ⓦbeiderbeckes.com. Boutique hotel in a sedate terrace (dating from 1832) on the South Cliff, with free parking. Rooms are comfortable and the bar is old-fashioned (in a good way), with live jazz on Sats. They have a stylish, reasonably priced brasserie, too. **£130**

**Crescent Hotel** The Crescent ☎01723 360929. A spacious, slightly old-fashioned hotel catering for both holiday-makers and business folk, with friendly, helpful staff, comprehensive facilities and a fine restaurant, all housed in mid-nineteenth century splendour. **£107**

**YHA Scarborough** Burniston Rd, 2 miles north of town ☎01723 361176, ⓦyha.org.uk. In an early seventeenth-century water mill a 15min walk from the sea, this is a good hostel for families with kids. Dorms **£13**; private rooms (for four) **£60**

## EATING AND DRINKING

**Café Fish** 19 York Place, at the intersection with Somerset Terrace ☎01723 500301. More of a top-end fish restaurant than a fish-and-chip shop, where a two-course dinner with wine could feature fish curry, steamed mussels or Thai fishcakes, and will cost from about £30. Gets very busy at weekends. Daily 5.30–10pm.

**Café Italia** 36 St Nicholas Cliff ☎01723 501973. Enchanting, tiny, authentic Italian coffee bar. They stick to what they're good at: excellent coffee, ice cream and cakes. Daily 9am–9pm.

**Golden Grid** 4 Sandside ☎01723 360922, ⓦgoldengrid.co.uk. The harbourside's choicest fish-and-chip establishment, "catering for the promenader since 1883". Offers grilled fish, crab and lobster, a fruits-de-mer platter and a wine list alongside the standard crispy-battered fry-up. Decent portions of fish from £7.80. Easter–Oct Mon–Thurs 10am–8.30pm, Fri 10am–9pm, Sat 10am–9.30pm, Sun 11am–6.30pm; Nov–Easter opens 11am, closing varies.

## ENTERTAINMENT

**Scarborough Open Air Theatre** Burniston Rd ☎01723 818111, ⓦscarboroughopenairtheatre.com. Europe's largest open air theatre, built in 1932, hosts a range of top-end concerts and gigs by the likes of Jessie J, Boyzone, Status Quo.

**Stephen Joseph Theatre** Westborough ☎01723 370541, ⓦsjt.uk.com. Housed in a former Art Deco cinema, this premieres every new play of local playwright Alan Ayckbourn and promotes strong seasons of theatre and film. There's a good, moderately priced café/restaurant and a bar open daily except Sun.

# Robin Hood's Bay

The most heavily visited spot on this stretch of coast, **ROBIN HOOD'S BAY** is made up of gorgeous narrow streets and pink-tiled cottages toppling down the cliff-edge site, evoking the romance of a time when this was both a hard-bitten fishing community and smugglers' den par excellence. From the upper village, lined with Victorian villas, now mostly B&Bs, it's a very steep walk down the hill to the harbour. The **Old Coastguard Station** (Jan, March, Nov & Dec Sat & Sun 10am–4pm, Feb daily 10am–4pm, April–Oct daily 10am–5pm, late Dec Mon–Wed, Sat & Sun 10am–4pm; free; NT; ☎01947 885900; ⓦnationaltrust.org.uk/yorkshire-coast) has been turned into a visitor centre with displays relating to the area's geology and sealife. When the tide is out, the massive rock beds below are exposed, split by a geological fault line and studded with fossil remains. There's an easy circular walk (2.5 miles) to **Boggle Hole** and its youth hostel, a mile south, returning inland via the path along the old Scarborough–Whitby railway line.

## ARRIVAL AND GETTING AROUND | ROBIN HOOD'S BAY

**By bus** Robin Hood's Bay is connected to Whitby by Arriva #93 buses (hourly; 20min) and to Scarborough by Arriva #93 buses (hourly; 40min).

**By bike** A couple of miles northwest of Robin Hood's Bay

at Hawsker, on the A171, Trailways (☎01947 820207, ⓦtrailways.info) is a bike rental outfit based in the old Hawsker train station, perfectly placed for day-trips in either direction along the disused railway line.

## INFORMATION

**Tourist information** Though you can pick up a lot of information at the Old Coastguard Station (Jan, March, Nov & Dec Sat & Sun 10am–4pm, Feb daily 10am–4pm, April–Oct daily 10am–5pm, late Dec Mon–Wed, Sat &

Sun 10am–4pm, ☎01947 885900), the nearest official tourist offices are in Whitby (see p.632) and Scarborough (see p.629).

## ACCOMMODATION AND EATING

Many people visit Robin Hood's Bay as a day-trip from Whitby. You can ask about accommodation in Whitby's tourist office (see p.632), or simply stroll the streets of the old part of the village to see if any of the small cottage **B&Bs** has vacancies. There are three good **pubs** in the lower village, two of which offer rooms – food at the *Bay Hotel* is the best.

**Bay Hotel** On the harbour ☎01947 880278, ⓦbayhotel.info. At the traditional start or end of the Coast-to-Coast Walk, this inn offers rooms and bar meals, with main courses at around £9–£11. Mon–Sat 11am–11pm, Sun noon–11pm; food served noon–2pm & 6.30–9pm. **£70**

**Swell Café** Old Chapel, Chapel St ☎01947 880180, ⓦswell.org.uk. A gift shop and café in an old Wesleyan Chapel, built in 1779, where John Wesley himself once

preached. They serve a good range of snacks, sandwiches, cakes, teas and coffees, and alcoholic drinks, and there are great coastal views from its terrace tables. Daily 10am–4.15pm or later if busy.

**YHA Boggle Hole** Boggle Hole, Fylingthorpe ☎0845 371 9504, ⓦyha.org.uk. In a former mill in a wooded ravine about a mile south of Robin Hood's Bay at Mill Beck, this hostel has a great location near the beach. Dorms **£18**; doubles **£59**

# Whitby

If there's one essential stop on the North Yorkshire coast it's **WHITBY**, with its historical associations, atmospheric ruins, fishing harbour, lively music scene and intrinsic charm. The seventh-century cliff-top **abbey** here made Whitby one of the key foundations of the early Christian period, and a centre of great learning. Below, on the harbour banks of the River Esk, for a thousand years the local herring boats landed their catch until the great **whaling** boom of the eighteenth century transformed the fortunes of the town. Melville's *Moby Dick* makes much of Whitby

---

## BRAM STOKER AND DRACULA

The story of **Dracula** is well known, but it's the exact attention to the geographical detail of Whitby – little changed since Bram Stoker first wrote the words – which has proved a huge attraction to visitors. Using first-hand observation of a town he knew well – he stayed at a house on the West Cliff, now marked by a plaque – Stoker built a story which mixed real locations, legend and historical fact: the grounding of Count Dracula's ship on Tate Hill Sands was based on an actual event reported in the local papers.

It's hardly surprising that the town has cashed in on its **Dracula Trail**. The various sites – Tate Hill Sands, the abbey, church and steps, the graveyard, Stoker's house – can all be visited, while down on the harbourside the Dracula Experience attempts to pull in punters to its rather lame horror-show antics. Keen interest has also been sparked among the **Goth** fraternity, who now come to town en masse a couple of times a year (in late spring and around Halloween) for a vampire's ball, concerts and readings.

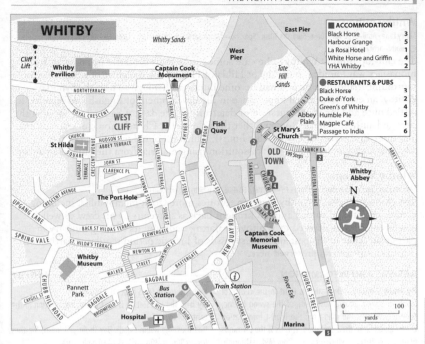

**WHITBY**

Whitby Sands

East Pier

West Pier

Cliff Lift

Whitby Pavilion

Captain Cook Monument

Tate Hill Sands

NORTH TERRACE

THE ESPLANADE

EAST TERRACE

ROYAL CRESCENT

**WEST CLIFF**

1

Fish Quay

Pier Road

AMBER PASS

HENRIETTA ST

Abbey Plain

St Mary's Church

St Hilda

CHURCH SQUARE

HUDSON ST
ABBEY TERRACE

CRESCENT AVENUE

HAVELOCK PL

WELLINGTON TERRACE

2

**OLD TOWN**

199 Steps

CHURCH LA.

2

CHURCH ST

Whitby Abbey

LANGDALE TERRACE

JOHN ST

CLARENCE PL

SANDGATE

AELFLEDA TERRACE

ABBEY LANE

**N**

UPGANG LANE

CRESCENT AVENUE

SKINNER STREET

CLIFF STREET

ST ANNE'S STAITH

SILVER ST

3
3
4

STREET

BRIDGE ST

GRAPE LANE

5

**The Port Hole**

BACK ST HILDAS TERRACE

FLOWERGATE

NEW QUAY RD

**Captain Cook Memorial Museum**

SPRING VALE

ST. HILDA'S TERRACE

NEWTON ST

BRUNSWICK ST

BAXTERGATE

CHURCH STREET

THE ROPERY

**Whitby Museum**

WALKER

STREET

**Pannett Park**

CHUBB HILL ROAD

CAYGILL ST

BAGDALE

BAGDALE T.

BROOMFIELD T.

BAGDALE

Bus Station

SPRING HILL

ALBION TERRACE

WINDSOR TERRACE

6

ⓘ

*Train Station*

River Esk

LANGBOURNE ROAD

CHURCH STREET

0    100
yards

**Hospital** ✚

**Marina**

▼ 5

**12**

whalers such as William Scoresby, and James Cook took his first seafaring steps from the town in 1746, on his way to becoming a national hero. All four of Captain Cook's ships of discovery – the *Endeavour, Resolution, Adventure* and *Discovery* – were built in this town.

Walking around Whitby is one of its great pleasures. Divided by the River Esk, the town splits into two halves joined by a swing bridge: the cobbled **old town** to the east, and the newer (mostly eighteenth- and nineteenth-century) town across the bridge, generally known as **West Cliff**. **Church Street** is the old town's main thoroughfare, barely changed in aspect since the eighteenth century, though now lined with tearooms and gift shops. Parallel **Sandgate** has more of the same, the two streets meeting at the small **marketplace** where souvenirs and trinkets are sold, and which hosts a farmers' market every Thursday.

## Captain Cook Memorial Museum

Grape Lane • Daily: Feb–March 11am–3pm; April–Oct 9.45am–5pm • £4.80 • ☎ 01947 601900, ⓦ cookmuseumwhitby.co.uk

Whitby, understandably, likes to make a fuss of Captain Cook, who served an apprenticeship here from 1746–49 under John Walker, a Quaker ship owner. The **Captain Cook Memorial Museum**, housed in Walker's rickety old house, contains an impressive amount of memorabilia, including ships' models, letters, and paintings by artists seconded to Cook's voyages.

## Church of St Mary

At the north end of Church Street, you climb the famous **199 steps** of the Church Stairs – now paved, but originally a wide wooden staircase built for pall-bearers carrying coffins to the **Church of St Mary** above. This is an architectural amalgam dating back to 1110, boasting a Norman chancel arch, a profusion of eighteenth-century panelling, box pews unequalled in England and a triple-decker pulpit – note the built-in ear trumpets, added for the benefit of a nineteenth-century rector's deaf wife.

## Whitby Abbey

Abbey Lane • April–Sept daily 10am–6pm; Oct 10am–5pm; Nov–March Sat & Sun 10am–4pm • £6.60; EH • ☎ 01947 603568, ⓦ english-heritage.org.uk

The cliff-top ruins of **Whitby Abbey** are some of the most evocative in England. Its monastery was founded in 657 by St Hilda of Hartlepool, daughter of King Oswy of Northumberland, and by 664 had become important enough to host the **Synod of Whitby**, an event of seminal importance in the development of English Christianity. It settled once and for all the question of determining the date of Easter, and adopted the rites and authority of the Roman rather than the Celtic Church. You'll discover all this and more in the **Visitor Centre** (same hours), which is housed in the shell of the adjacent mansion, built after the Dissolution using material from the plundered abbey.

## Whitby Museum

Pannett Park • Tues–Sun 9.30am–4.30pm • £5 • ☎ 01947 602908, ⓦ whitbymuseum.org.uk

The gloriously eclectic **Whitby Museum** features more Cook memorabilia, including various objects and stuffed animals brought back as souvenirs by his crew, as well as casefuls of exhibits devoted to Whitby's seafaring tradition, its whaling industry in particular. Some of the best and largest fossils of Jurassic period reptiles unearthed on the east coast are also preserved here.

### ARRIVAL AND INFORMATION WHITBY

**By train** Whitby's train station is right in the centre of town on Station Square, just south of the swing bridge, conveniently over the road from the Tourist Information Centre and next to the bus station. Whitby is the terminus of the Esk Valley line, which runs here from Middlesbrough, and which connects with the steam trains of the North Yorkshire Moors Railway at Grosmont, which run south to Pickering (see box, p.627). Destinations Danby (4–5 daily; 40min); Great Ayton (4–5 daily; 1hr 5min); Grosmont (4–5 daily; 16min); Middlesbrough (4–5 daily; 1hr 30min).

**By bus** The bus station is next to the train station in the centre of town.

Destinations Robin Hood's Bay (hourly; 19min); Staithes (every 30min; 30min); York (4–6 daily; 2hr).

**Tourist office** On the corner of Langborne Road and New Quay Road, across the road from the train station (daily: April–June & Sept–Oct daily 9.30am–6pm; July & Aug 9.30am–7pm; Nov–March 9.30am–4.30pm; ☎ 01723 383636, ⓦ discoveryorkshirecoast.com or ⓦ visitwhitby.com).

### ACCOMMODATION

**Black Horse** 91 Church St ☎ 01947 602906, ⓦ the-black-horse.com. Four simple en-suite guest rooms above this fine old pub (see below), each named after one of Captain Cook's ships. **£60**

**Harbour Grange** Spital Bridge, Church St ☎ 01947 600817, ⓦ whitbybackpackers.co.uk. Backpackers' hostel right on the river (eastern side) with 24 beds in five small dorms. Self-catering kitchen and lounge; 11.30pm curfew. **£18**

★**La Rosa Hotel** 5 East Terrace ☎ 01947 606981, ⓦ larosa.co.uk. Eccentric B&B with themed rooms done out in extravagantly individual style courtesy of auctions, eBay and car boot sales. Great fun, with terrific views of the harbour and the abbey. Breakfast picnic delivered in a basket to your door. Street parking. **£110**

**White Horse and Griffin** 87 Church St ☎ 01947 604857, ⓦ whitehorseandgriffin.co.uk. In the centre of Whitby's old town, with wonderful views of the harbour. Nicely renovated rooms (and several cottages) with many original features. It's full of character, but can be noisy. **£70**

★**YHA Whitby** Abbey House, East Cliff ☎ 0845 371 9049, ⓦ yha.org.uk. Flagship hostel in a Grade 1 listed building next to the Abbey Visitor Centre. Stunning views, good facilities and a Victorian conservatory, tearoom and restaurant. Rates include breakfast and entry to the abbey. Dorms **£15**; doubles **£59**

### EATING AND DRINKING

**Black Horse** 91 Church St ☎ 01947 602906, ⓦ the-black-horse.com. Lovely old pub (parts date from the seventeenth century) in the heart of the old town, with real ales and food served all day, including tapas, Yorkshire cheeses and local seafood. Easter–Nov Mon–Sat 11am–11pm, Sun noon–11pm; Dec–Easter noon–4pm & 7–11pm.

★**Duke of York** 124 Church St ☎ 01947 600324, ⓦ dukeofyork.co.uk. In a great position at the bottom of the 199 steps, this is a warm and inviting pub, with beams, nautical memorabilia, church pews and views across to the harbour and West Cliff. Come for good real ales, modern

> ## WHITBY FOLK WEEK
>
> Whitby has a strong **local music** scene, with an emphasis on folk and world music. During the annual **Whitby Folk Week** (w whitbyfolk.co.uk), held the week preceding the August bank holiday, the town is filled day and night with singers, bands, traditional dancers, storytellers and music workshops. The best place to find out more **information** is at *The Port Hole*, 16 Skinner Street (t 01947 603475), a Fair Trade craft shop that's also the HQ of local collective Musicport (w musicportfestival.com), who put on gigs from big names in the world/folk scene and hold a renowned annual World Music Festival in Bridlington in November.

pub food and music. Daily Mon–Thurs & Sun 11am–11pm, Fri 11am–11.30pm, Sat 11am–midnight; food served noon–9pm.

**Green's of Whitby** 13 Bridge St t 01947 600284, w greensofwhitby.com. A few yards from the swing bridge, and reckoned by many to be the best restaurant in Whitby, friendly and unpretentious *Green's* has a lively bistro downstairs and a more formal dining room on the first floor, with the same menu and prices available in both (mains around £11–£20). Ingredients are locally sourced, with lots of good fish and meat dishes. Mon–Fri noon–2pm & 6.30–9.30pm, Sat & Sun noon–10pm.

★**Humble Pie** 163 Church St t 07919 074954, w humblepiemash.com. Tiny sixteenth-century building serving a range of pies, cooked fresh to order – steak, stout and leek, Romany, Homity, haggis and neep, and many more – with mash and peas. The decor is 1940s, with World War II background music. All pies £5.99; soft drinks only. Mon–Sat noon–8pm, Sun noon–4pm.

**Magpie Café** 14 Pier Rd t 01947 602058, w magpiecafe.co.uk. Said by Rick Stein to be one of the best fish-and-chip shops in the country, the *Magpie* has served food from its 1750-built premises since the start of World War II. To call it a fish-and-chip shop is a bit disingenuous – although it provides the normal takeaway service, it also serves lesser-known fish like Woof and John Dory in its restaurant (prices from £10.95, depending on fish) and has an extensive wine list. Usually daily 11.30am–9pm, but check before coming.

**Passage to India** 30–31 Windsor Terrace t 01947 606500, w passagetoindia.eu. Stylish tandoori restaurant near the station, with bright red-and-black decor, great food, and friendly, efficient service. Main courses around £8–12; look out for the Tandoori king prawn *karahi*, or the Lam Kam. Mon–Thurs 5.30pm–midnight, Fri 5.30pm–1am, Sat noon–1am, Sun noon–midnight.

**12**

# Staithes

Beyond Whitby Sands, a fine coastal walk starts at Sandsend, leads through pretty Runswick Bay, and reaches, in around four hours, the fishing village of **STAITHES**. An improbably beautiful grouping of huddled stone houses around a small harbour, the village is backed by the severe outcrop of Cowbar Nab, a sheer cliff face that protects the northern flank of the village. James Cook worked here in a draper's shop before moving to Whitby, and he's remembered in the **Captain Cook and Staithes Heritage Centre**, on the High Street (Feb–Nov daily 10am–5pm; Dec & Jan Sat & Sun 10am–5pm; £3; t 01947 841454, w captaincookatstaithes.co.uk), which recreates an eighteenth-century street among other interesting exhibits. Other than this, you'll have to content yourself with pottering about the rocks near the harbour – there's no beach to speak of – or clambering the nearby cliffs for spectacular views. At **Boulby**, a mile and a half's trudge up the coastal path (45min), you're walking on the highest cliff (670ft) on England's east coast.

## ACCOMMODATION
## STAITHES

**Endeavour House** 1 High St t 01947 841029 (rooms), t 07969 054556 (restaurant), w endeavour-restaurant .co.uk. Three lovely doubles in this restaurant-B&B located in a two-centuries-old house by the harbour. Parking available in municipal (£6/day) and private (Glen Vale, £5/day) car parks. There's also a restaurant, run separately from the B&B, with a bistro-type menu (mains from £11.95). Opening times vary – phone for details. **£85**

# The Northeast

TYNE BRIDGE AT NIGHT, NEWCASTLE

**13**

# The Northeast

Remote and breathtakingly beautiful, the county of Northumberland forms the bulk of the northeast of England. An enticing medley of delightful market towns, glorious golden beaches, wooded dells, wild uplands and an unsurpassed collection of historical monuments, it's undoubtedly the main draw in the Northeast, and where you should focus the majority of your time. South of Northumberland lies the county of Durham, famous for its lovely university town and magnificent twelfth-century cathedral, while to the southeast and edged by the North Sea is industrial Tyne and Wear. It's home to the busy and burgeoning metropolis of Newcastle upon Tyne, a dynamic and distinctive city crammed with cultural attractions, great shops and an exceptionally energetic nightlife.

While its most recent past is defined by industry and in particular post-industrial hardship, the Northeast has an eventful early history: Romans, Vikings and Normans have all left dramatic evidence of their colonization, none more cherished than the 84-mile-long **Hadrian's Wall**, built by the Romans in 122 AD to contain the troublesome tribes of the far north. Thousands come each year to walk along parts, or all, of the Wall, or to cycle the nearby National Route 72. Neighbouring Northumberland National Park also has plenty for outdoors enthusiasts, with the huge **Kielder Water** reservoir, and surrounding footpaths and cycleways.

As well as Roman ruins, medieval **castles** scatter the region, the best-preserved being Alnwick, with its wonderful gardens, and stocky Bamburgh, on the coast. The shoreline round here, from Amble past Bamburgh to the Scottish border town of Berwick-upon-Tweed – and officially the end of Northumberland – is simply stunning, boasting miles of pancake-flat, dune-backed beach and a handful of off-shore islands. Reached by a tidal causeway, the lonely little islet of **Lindisfarne** – Holy Island – where early Christian monks created the Lindisfarne Gospels, is the most famous, while not far away to the south, near Seahouses, the **Farne Islands** are the perfect habitat for large colonies of seabirds including puffins, guillemots and kittiwakes.

South of Northumberland, the counties of **Durham** and **Tyne and Wear** better illustrate the Northeast's industrial heritage. It was here in 1825 that the world's first railway opened – the Darlington and Stockton line – with local coal and ore fuelling the shipbuilding and heavy-engineering companies of Tyneside. Abandoned coalfields, train lines, quaysides and factories throughout the area have been transformed into superb, child-friendly tourist attractions.

**GETTING AROUND**                                                      **THE NORTHEAST**

**By public transport** The main East Coast train line runs along the coast from London King's Cross to Edinburgh, calling at Darlington, Durham, Newcastle and Berwick-upon-Tweed, while cross-country trains and buses serve smaller towns and villages inland. In the more remote areas public transport is spotty, so it's best to have your own car or bike.

LINDISFARNE CASTLE, HOLY ISLAND

# Highlights

**❶ Durham Cathedral** Said to be the finest Norman building in Europe, this awe-inspiring cathedral soars above the River Wear. **See p.641**

**❷ Beamish Museum** Exceptional open-air museum that recreates the Northeast's industrial past. **See p.644**

**❸ Killhope Lead Mining Museum** Put on a hard hat and get down the pit to see what life was really like for the Weardale coal miners. **See p.648**

**❹ Newcastle nightlife** From raucous clubs and chic wine bars to cosy boozers and chilled-out indie gigs, there's something for everybody. **See p.658**

**❺ Hadrian's Wall** Walk the length of the greatest Roman monument in England. **See p.662**

**❻ Northumberland castles** Northumberland is littered with beautiful castles, telling of a violent past ridden with ferocious battles and embittered family feuds. **See p.668**

**❼ Holy Island** A brooding lump of rock reached by a tidal causeway, this is a cradle of Christianity, where the splendid, illuminated Lindisfarne Gospels were created. **See p.673**

**HIGHLIGHTS ARE MARKED ON THE MAP ON PP.638–639**

# THE NORTHEAST

## HIGHLIGHTS

1 Durham Cathedral
2 Beamish Museum
3 Killhope Lead Mining Museum
4 Newcastle nightlife
5 Hadrian's Wall
6 Northumberland castles
7 Holy Island

N

0    miles    10

NORTH SEA

Farne Islands

Seahouses
Beadnell
Newton-by-the-Sea
Embleton
6 Dunstanburgh Castle
Craster
Holy Island
Waren Mill
7
Bamburgh
6
Alnmouth
Warkworth
Amble
6
A1068
Belford
6 Chillingham Castle
Eglingham
Alnwick
A1
Newton-on-the-Moor
Ashington
Bedlington
Berwick-upon-Tweed
Scremerston
Beal
B6525
Wooler
A697
B1340
Cragside
Rothbury
A697
Morpeth
Edinburgh
Tweed
A698
A1
A697
Etal
Ford
Crookham
Heatherslaw Light Railway
Etal Castle
Branxton
The Cheviot (2674ft)
NORTHUMBERLAND NATIONAL PARK
Otterburn
Cambo
Wallington
Norham Castle
Coldstream
Cornhill-on-Tweed
Kirk Yetholm
THE CHEVIOT HILLS
Byrness
REDESDALE
Greenhaugh
Tarset
Stannersburn
SCOTLAND
Tweed
A697
A68
KIELDER FOREST PARK
Kielder
Kielder Water
Leaplish
Belvedere
Tower Knowe
Falstone
Edinburgh

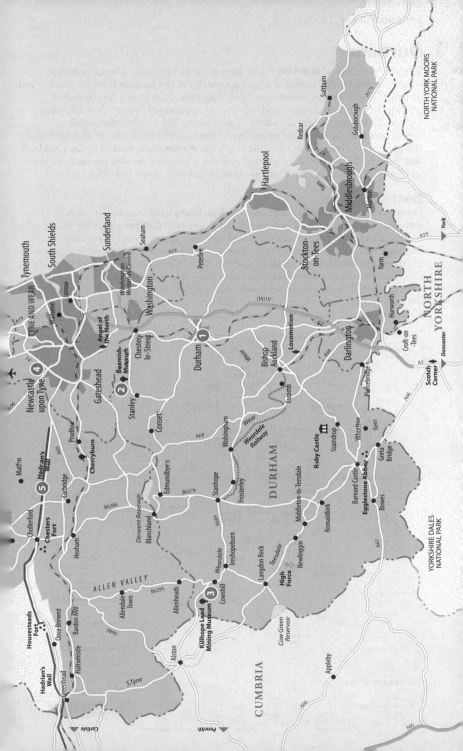

**13**

# Durham

The handsome city of **DURHAM** is best known for its beautiful Norman **cathedral** – there's a tremendous view of it as you approach the city by train from the south – and its flourishing university, founded in 1832. Together, these form a little island of privilege in what's otherwise a moderately sized, working-class city. It's worth visiting for a couple of days – there are plenty of attractions, but it's more the overall atmosphere that captivates, enhanced by the omnipresent golden stone, slender bridges and glint of the river. The heart of the city is the **marketplace**, flanked by the Guildhall and St Nicholas Church. The cathedral and church sit on a wooded peninsula to the west, while southwards stretch narrow streets lined with shops and cafés.

## Brief history

Durham's history revolves around its cathedral. Completed in just forty years, the cathedral was founded in 1093 to house the shrine of **St Cuthbert**, arguably the Northeast's most important and venerated saint (see box opposite). Soon after Cuthbert was laid to rest here, the bishops of Durham were granted extensive powers to control the troublesome northern marches of the Kingdom – a rabble of invading Picts from Scotland and revolting Norman earls – ruling as semi-independent **Prince Bishops**, with their own army, mint and courts of law. At the peak of their power in the fourteenth century, the office went into decline – especially in the wake of the Reformation – yet clung to the vestiges of their authority until 1836, when they ceded

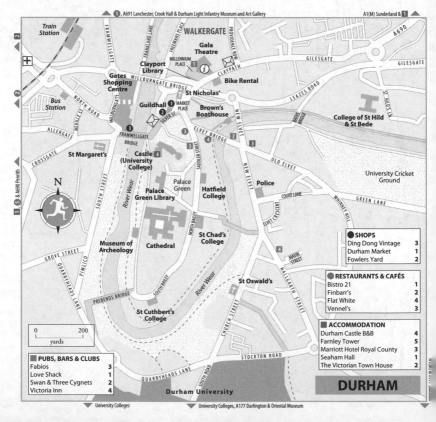

> **ST CUTHBERT**                                                                    13
>
> Born in North Northumbria in 653, **Cuthbert** spent most of his youth in Melrose Abbey in
> Scotland, from where he moved briefly to Lindisfarne Island, which was at that time a
> well-known centre of religious endeavour. Preferring the peace and rugged solitude of the
> Farne Islands, he lived on Inner Farne for thirty years. News of his piety spread, however, and he
> was head-hunted to become Bishop of Lindisfarne, a position he accepted reluctantly.
> Uncomfortable in the limelight, he soon returned to Inner Farne, and when he died his
> remains were moved to Lindisfarne before being carted off to Durham Cathedral.

them to the Crown. They abandoned Durham Castle for their palace in Bishop
Auckland (see p.644) and transferred their old home to the fledgling Durham
University, England's third-oldest seat of learning after Oxford and Cambridge.

## Durham Cathedral

July & Aug Mon–Sat 9.30am–8pm, Sun 12.30–8pm; Sept–June Mon–Sat 9.30am–6pm, Sun 12.30–5.30pm • Donation requested;
Cathedral Highlights Pass (£5) covers entry to the Monks' Dormitory, the Treasures of St Cuthbert and the audiovisual displays • Guided
tours April–Oct 2–3 daily • **Tower** Mon–Sat 10am–4pm, Sun 1–2.30pm; access sometimes restricted, call to check **Monks' Dormitory**
April–Oct Mon–Sat 10am–4pm, Sun 2–4.30pm **Treasures of St Cuthbert** Mon–Sat 10am–4.30pm, Sun 2–4.30pm • £5 • ☎ 0191 386
4266, ⓦ durhamcathedral.co.uk

From the marketplace, it's a five-minute walk up Saddler Street to **Durham Cathedral**,
considered a supreme example of the Norman-Romanesque style. The awe-inspiring
**nave** used pointed arches for the first time in England, raising the vaulted ceiling to new
and dizzying heights. The weight of the stone is borne by massive pillars, their heaviness
relieved by striking Moorish-influenced geometric patterns. A door on the western side
gives access to the **tower**, from where there are beautiful views. Separated from the nave
by a Victorian marble screen is the **choir**, where the dark Restoration stalls are
overshadowed by the 13ft-high **bishop's throne**. Beyond, the **Chapel of the Nine Altars**
dates from the thirteenth century. Here, and around the **Shrine of St Cuthbert**, much of
the stonework is of local Weardale marble, each dark shaft bearing its own pattern of
fossils. Cuthbert himself lies beneath a plain marble slab, his shrine having gained a
reputation over the centuries for its curative powers. The legend was given credence in
1104, when the saint's body was exhumed in Chester-le-Street for reburial here, and was
found to be completely uncorrupted, more than four hundred years after his death on
Lindisfarne. Almost certainly, this was the result of his fellow monks having
(unintentionally) preserved the body by laying it in sand containing salt crystals.

Back near the entrance, at the west end of the church is the **Galilee Chapel**; begun
in the 1170s, its light and exotic decoration is in imitation of the Great Mosque of
Córdoba. The chapel contains the simple tombstone of the **Venerable Bede** (see
p.660), the Northumbrian monk credited with being England's first historian. Bede
died at the monastery of Jarrow in 735, and his remains were first transferred to the
cathedral in 1020.

### The Monks' Dormitory and Treasures of St Cuthbert

A large wooden doorway opposite the cathedral's main entrance leads into the spacious
**cloisters**, flanked by what remains of the monastic buildings. On the right of the
passage lies the **Monks' Dormitory** with its original twelfth-century oak roof – it now
houses the cathedral library. At the end of the passage, in the undercroft, the **Treasures
of St Cuthbert** exhibition displays some striking relics, including the cathedral's original
twelfth-century lion-head Sanctuary Knocker (the one on the main door is a replica),
and a splendid facsimile copy of the Lindisfarne Gospels (the originals are in the British
Library in London). A couple of interesting **audiovisual displays** detail the history of
the cathedral, too.

**13**

# Palace Green Library

Palace Green • Tues–Fri 10am–4.45pm, Sat & Sun noon–4.45pm • £4.50 • ☎ 0191 334 2972, ⦿ dur.ac.uk/palace.green/whatson

**Palace Green Library**, between the cathedral and the castle, shows off a wonderful collection of the university's treasures, including medieval manuscripts and incunabula – early printed books. The library is divided into four separate galleries, including one devoted to the History of the Book. Exhibitions change but could feature anything from Japanese enamel pots to Chinese imperial textiles and ancient Egyptian relics.

# Durham Castle

Easter & July–Sept daily tours 10am, 11am, noon & hourly 2–5pm; rest of the year daily 2pm, 3pm & 4pm • free, tours £5 • ☎ 0191 334 3800, ⦿ durhamworldheritagesite.com

**Durham Castle** lost its medieval appearance long ago, and the university subsequently renovated the old keep as a hall of residence. It's only possible to visit the castle on a 45-minute guided tour, highlights of which include the fifteenth-century kitchen, a climb up the enormous hanging staircase and the Norman chapel, one of the few surviving interiors from the period. It's notable for its lively Romanesque carved capitals, including a green man, and what may be the earliest surviving depiction anywhere of a mermaid. Note that out of term-time you can stay here (see opposite).

# Crook Hall

Frankland Lane, Sidegate • Easter weekend–Sept Sun–Wed 11am–5pm, Sept–Easter weekend Sun, Mon & Tues 11am–3pm • £7 • ☎ 0191 384 8028, ⦿ crookhallgardens.co.uk

**Crook Hall** is a hidden gem in Durham, and well worth making the effort to find. A rare mix of medieval, Jacobean and Georgian architecture, with origins dating from the twelfth century, it's said to be one of the oldest inhabited houses in the area. You can explore its rambling rooms, complete with period furniture and rickety staircases, as well as a series of beautifully tended, themed gardens, including the ethereal Silver and White garden, the Shakespeare Garden, planted with herbs used in Elizabethan times, and the delightful Secret Walled Garden. The flower-swathed **coffeeshop** serves delicious cream teas (£3.90 per person).

# Durham Light Infantry Museum and Art Gallery

Aykley Heads • Wed–Sun 10.30am–4pm • £3.50 • ☎ 0300 026 6590, ⦿ www.dlidurham.org.uk

Just north of the city centre and set in pleasant open parkland, the **Durham Light Infantry Museum and Art Gallery** tells the story of the DLI, one of the most famous county regiments in the British Army, from their beginnings in 1181, via World War I (when it lost twelve thousand soldiers) to its last parade in 1968. Exhibits include splendid uniforms, a huge collection of more than three thousand medals and weapons, and personal items including letters and photographs. Upstairs, the art gallery features temporary exhibitions showcasing work from emerging and established artists.

## ARRIVAL AND INFORMATION
## DURHAM

**By train** Durham's train station is on North Road, a 10min walk from the centre of the city.

**Destinations** Berwick-upon-Tweed (every 30min; 1hr 10min), Darlington (frequent; 20min); London (every 30–60min; 3hr); Newcastle (frequent; 15min); York (frequent; 50min).

**By bus** It's a 5min walk to the city centre from the bus station on North Road.

**Destinations** Bishop Auckland (frequent; 30min); Chester-le-Street (frequent; 20min); Darlington (every 20min; 1hr 10min); Middlesbrough (every 30min; 55min); Newcastle (Mon–Sat every 30min, Sun 4–6 daily; 50min); Stanhope (Mon–Fri 4 daily; 45min).

**Tourist information** 2 Millennium Place, off Claypath (Mon–Sat 9.30am–5.30pm, Sun 11am–4pm; ☎ 0191 384 3720, ⦿ durhamtourism.co.uk).

## GETTING AROUND

**Cathedral Bus** A minibus runs two routes around Durham serving the train station, the bus station, the marketplace and the cathedral. Tickets cost £1 and are valid all day.

## ACCOMMODATION

**Durham Castle B&B** ☎0191 334 4106, ⒲dur.ac.uk. Out of term-time you can have the unique experience of staying in Durham Castle. Accommodation ranges from standard rooms with shared bathrooms to two grand "state rooms", one with a four-poster and seventeenth-century tapestries. Breakfast is served in the thirteenth-century Great Hall. **£75–195**

**Farnley Tower** The Ave ☎0191 375 0011, ⒲farnley -tower.co.uk. A 10min walk up a steep hill west from the centre, this fine stone Victorian house has thirteen comfortable rooms with bright, co-ordinated fabrics. The best rooms have sweeping city views. They also run a smart restaurant, *Gourmet Spot*. **£95**

**Marriott Hotel Royal County** Old Elvet ☎0191 386 6821, ⒲marriotthotels.com. Elegant and luxurious, the *Marriott* has long been regarded as Durham's top hotel. Rooms have huge beds, marble-trimmed bathrooms and comfortable sitting areas. There's a fitness centre and a swimming pool, as well as a selection of restaurants and bars. **£99**

**Seaham Hall** Lord Byron's Walk, Seaham, 10 miles northeast of Durham ☎0191 516 1400, ⒲seaham -hall.co.uk. Perched on a cliff-top overlooking the sea, this hip, exclusive hotel makes a great coastal base for city sightseeing – Durham is only a 20min drive away. It's known for its luxurious spa and pampering treatments and has a wonderful restaurant; spa, dinner, bed and breakfast packages are available. **£195**

**The Victorian Town House** 2 Victoria Terrace ☎0191 370 9963, ⒲durhambedandbreakfast.com. This friendly and tranquil B&B features three en-suite rooms: one twin, one double and one family room. It's located on a quiet and attractive backstreet backed by gardens and is a 5min walk from the station. **£90**

## EATING

**Bistro 21** Aykley Heads ☎0191 384 4354, ⒲bistrotwentyone.co.uk. Housed in a lemon-yellow building a 10min walk from the DLI Museum and Art Gallery, *Bistro 21* serves excellent, seasonal cuisine; mains start at £16.50 and could include fishcakes with a parsley cream and buttered spinach or a juicy sirloin steak with triple-cooked chips. The interior is fresh and pretty, with wooden tables, wicker chairs and whitewashed walls. Mon–Sat noon–2pm & 6–10pm, Sun noon–3.30pm.

**Finbarrs** Waddington St, Flass Vale ☎0191 370 9999, ⒲finbarrsrestaurant.co.uk. This chic restaurant in leafy surroundings serves up anything from full English breakfasts and banana pancakes to dinners of Moroccan lamb with golden raisins; the sweet cherry and pistachio sundaes are delicious. Mains from £15. Mon–Sat 7–9.30am, noon–2.30pm & 6–9.30pm, Sun 7.30–10.30am & noon–9pm.

**Flat White** 21a Elvet Bridge ☎07789 951149, ⒲flatwhitedurham.co.uk. Durham's hippest café, serving barista-standard coffee and hearty sandwiches served on wooden boards (£5). Sit outside in the sun, or inside at tables made from old sewing machines. Mon–Sat 9.30am–5pm, Sun 10am–4pm.

**Vennel's** Saddler's Yard, Saddler St ☎0191 375 0571. Named after the skinny alley or "vennel" where it stands – near the junction with Elvet Bridge – this café serves up generous sandwiches, salads, quiche (£5–6) and tasty cakes in its sixteenth-century courtyard. Daily 10am–5pm.

## DRINKING

Walkergate is the area to head for if you're after loud, lively bars and mainstream nightclubs pumping out cheesy music, but there are also plenty of quieter establishments and more traditional, laidback pubs.

**Fabios** 66 Sadler St ☎0191 383 9290, ⒲fabiosdurham .com. Just above *La Spaghettata* pizzeria, *Fabios* occupies a series of rooms filled with comfy, rug-draped sofas and chalked-up blackboards offering drinks from around £3. The atmosphere is cool and relaxed, with music a melange of rap, r'n'b and dance. Jazz nights every Wednesday. Daily 6pm–2am.

**Swan & Three Cygnets** Elvet Bridge ☎0191 384 0242. Sitting proudly at the end of Elvet Bridge overlooking the River Wear, this loud and cheery pub serves cheap drinks and is filled with a mixed crowd of locals and students. Mon–Sat 11am–11pm, Sun noon–10.30pm.

**Victoria Inn** 86 Hallgarth St ☎0191 386 5269, ⒲victoriainn-durhamcity.co.uk. With its three open fires and rickety wooden stools, this cosy, traditional pub specializes in local ales – try the creamy Tyneside Blonde or the hoppy Centurion Bitter – and stocks more than thirty Irish whiskeys. Mon–Sat noon–3pm & 6–11pm, Sun noon–3pm & 7–11pm.

**13**

## NIGHTLIFE AND ENTERTAINMENT

Durham's **clubs**, frequented by students during the week and locals at the weekends, are scattered through the city centre and in Walkergate. There's generally no dress code, but the locals tend to make an effort. In addition to shows at the Gala Theatre, you can catch regular **classical concerts** at venues around the city, including the cathedral. Ask the tourist office for more details.

**Gala Theatre** Millennium Place 📞0191 332 4041, ⓦgaladurham.co.uk. A modern venue staging music of all kinds, plus theatre, cinema, dance and comedy.
**Love Shack** Walkergate 📞0191 384 5757, ⓦloveshackdurham.com. Large, popular club with two bars, snug booths and a sleek dancefloor. Music is an energetic mix of contemporary club tunes and cheesy classics. Wed & Thurs 10pm–2am, Fri & Sat 8pm–2am.

## SHOPPING

★ **Ding Dong Vintage** 45 The Gates 📞07887 536409, ⓦdingdongvintage.com. A hectic jumble of wonderful vintage clothes, hats, bags, shoes and jewellery. The men's section includes an assortment of watches, medals and regimental uniforms. Mon–Sat 10am–5.30pm.
**Durham Market** Market Place ⓦdurhammarkets .co.uk. Durham's Indoor Market holds a variety of stalls including a haberdashers, sweet shop and fishmongers. Mon–Sat from 9am–5pm.

**Farmers' Market** Market Place ⓦdurhammarkets .co.uk. Fresh local produce sold on the third Thursday of every month. 9am–3.30pm.
**Fowlers Yard** Silver St, behind the marketplace ⓦfowlersyarddurham.co.uk. A series of workshops showcasing local trades and crafts. Drop by to watch the craftspeople at work, commission a piece or buy off-the-cuff. Opening hours vary.

# Around Durham

The county of Durham has shaken off its grimy reputation in recent years and recast itself as a thriving tourist area. The well-to-do market towns of **Bishop Auckland** and **Barnard Castle** make great day-trips from Durham, and there's plenty of excellent walking and cycling in the wilds of the two Pennine valleys, **Teesdale** and **Weardale**. You'll find some top-class museums in the area, too, including **Beamish**, **Locomotion** and the **Bowes Museum**.

## Beamish Museum

10 miles north of Durham, off the A693 • April–Oct daily 10am–5pm; Nov–March Tues–Thurs, Sat & Sun 10am–4pm; in winter, only the town, pit colliery and tramway are open • April–Oct £18; Nov–March Tues–Thurs £9, Sat & Sun £18; 20 percent discount if you get here by bus • 📞0191 370 4000, ⓦbeamish.org.uk • Waggonway #28/28A runs from Newcastle (April–Oct daily, Nov–March Sat & Sun; every 30min; day returns from £2.60); bus #128 runs hourly from Durham (April–Oct Sat only)

The open-air **Beamish Museum** spreads out over three hundred acres, with buildings taken from all over the region painstakingly reassembled in six main sections linked by restored trams and buses. Complete with costumed shopkeepers, workers and householders, four of the sections show life in 1913, before the upheavals of World War I, including a **colliery village** complete with drift mine (regular tours throughout the day) and a large-scale recreation of the High Street in a **market town**. Two areas date to 1825, at the beginning of the northeast's industrial development, including a **manor house**, with horse yard, formal gardens, vegetable plots and orchards. You can ride on the beautifully restored steam-powered carousel, the **Steam Galloper** – dating from the 1890s – and the **Pockerley Waggonway**, which is pulled along by a replica of George Stephenson's *Locomotion* (see opposite), the first passenger-carrying steam train in the world.

## Bishop Auckland

**BISHOP AUCKLAND**, a busy little market town eleven miles southwest of Durham, grew up slowly around its showpiece building, **Auckland Castle**, and became famous

---

**TRAILS AND CYCLEWAYS**

**Coast to Coast (C2C)** ⓦ c2c-guide.co.uk. This demanding cycle route runs 140 miles from Whitehaven to Sunderland.
**Hadrian's Wall Path** ⓦ visithadrianswall.co.uk. An 84-mile waymarked trail allowing you to walk the length of this atmospheric Roman monument.
**National Route 72** ⓦ cycle-routes.org

/hadrianscycleway. Cycle path that runs the length of Hadrian's Wall.
**Pennine Way** ⓦ thepennineway.co.uk. This 270-mile-long footpath starts in the Peak District National Park, runs along the Pennine ridge through the Yorkshire Dales, up into Northumberland, across the Cheviots, and finishes in the Scottish Borders.

---

throughout England as the homeland of the mighty Prince Bishops. Today the town has paled into lesser significance but still offers enough for a pleasant hour or two's wander.

### Auckland Castle

**Castle** Easter–June & Sept Sun & Mon 2–5pm; July & Aug Sun 2–5pm, Mon & Wed 11am–5pm · £8 **Deer park** Daily 7am–dusk · Free · ☎ 01388 602576, ⓦ aucklandcastle.org

Looking more like a Gothic mansion than a traditional castellated castle, **Auckland Castle** has been the official residence of the Bishop of Durham since 1832, although its origins are in fact much older. Founded in 1183, the palace was established as a hunting lodge for the Prince Bishops and is set within acres of lush parkland. Most of the rooms are today rather sparsely furnished, save the splendid seventeenth-century marble-and-limestone chapel and the long dining room, with its thirteen paintings of Jacob and his sons by Francisco de Zurbarán, commissioned in the 1640s for a monastery in South America. After you've seen the castle, stroll around the parkland and into the adjacent **Bishop's Deer Park**, with its Deer House dating from 1760.

### Binchester Roman Fort

Daily: Easter–June & Sept 11am–5pm; July & Aug 10am–5pm · £2.55 · ☎ 0191 370 8712, ⓦ durham.gov.uk

From the town's marketplace, it's a pleasant twenty-minute walk along the banks of the River Wear to the remains of **Binchester Roman Fort**. While most of the stone fort and a civilian settlement that occupied the area remain hidden beneath surrounding fields, the bathhouse with its sophisticated underground heating system (hypocaust) is visible. Excavations are ongoing.

---

**ARRIVAL AND INFORMATION**                                                      **BISHOP AUCKLAND**

**By train** Bishop Auckland is the end of the line for trains from Darlington (26min); the station is on Newgate Street.
**By bus** Buses terminate at Saddler Street.

**Destinations** Durham (frequent; 40min), Newcastle (frequent; 1hr 25min).

---

## Locomotion (National Railway Museum Shildon)

Shildon, 12 miles south of Durham · Daily: April–Sept daily 10am–5pm; Oct–March 10am–4pm · Free · ☎ 01388 777999, ⓦ nrm.org.uk · Trains from Durham and Darlington to Bishop Auckland stop at Shildon station, a 2min walk from the museum. Buses #1 and 1B (to Crook and Tow Law) run from Darlington (Mon–Sat every 30min), stopping at Dale Rd, a 15min walk from the museum

The first passenger train in the world left from the station at Shildon in 1825 – making this the world's oldest railway town. It's a heritage explored in the magnificently realized **Locomotion** (also known as National Railway Museum Shildon), the regional outpost of York's National Railway Museum. It's less a museum and more an experience, spread out around a 1.5mile-long site, with the attractions linked by free bus from the reception building. Depots, sidings, junctions and coal drops lead ultimately to the heart of the museum, **Collection** – a gargantuan steel hangar containing an extraordinary array of seventy locomotives, dating from the very earliest days of steam. With interactive children's exhibits, summer steam rides, rallies and shows, it makes an excellent family day out.

**13**

# Barnard Castle

Affectionately known as "Barney", the honey-coloured market town of **BARNARD CASTLE** lies fifteen miles southwest of Bishop Auckland. The middle of the town is dominated by the splendid octagonal **Market Cross**; built in 1747 and formerly functioning as a market for dairy and butter, it now serves a more mundane purpose as a roundabout.

## The castle

Galgate • Daily: April–Sept 10am–6pm; Oct 10am–5pm; Nov–March Sat & Sun 10am–4pm • £4.60; EH • ☎ 01833 638212, ⓦ english -heritage.org.uk

The skeletal remains of the town's **castle** sit high on a rock overlooking the River Tees. It was founded in 1125 by the powerful Norman baron Bernard de Balliol – thus the town's name – and later ended up in the hands of Richard III. Richard's crest, in the shape of a boar, is still visible carved above a window in the inner ward.

## Bowes Museum

Half a mile east of the town centre • Daily 10am–5pm • £9.50 • ☎ 01833 690606, ⓦ bowesmuseum.org.uk

Castle aside, the prime attraction in town is the grand French-style chateau that constitutes the **Bowes Museum**. Begun in 1869, the chateau was commissioned by John and Josephine Bowes, a local businessman and MP and his French actress wife, who spent much of their time in Paris collecting ostentatious treasures and antiques. Don't miss the beautiful Silver Swan, a life-size musical automaton dating from 1773 – every afternoon at 2pm he puts on an enchanting show, preening his shiny feathers while swimming along a river filled with jumping fish.

## Egglestone Abbey

A mile southeast of Barnard Castle, off the B6277 • April–Oct 10am–6.30pm; rest of the year limited opening hours • Free; EH • ⓦ english -heritage.org.uk

It's a fine mile-long walk from the castle, southeast (downriver) through the fields above the banks of the Tees, to the lovely shattered ruins of **Egglestone Abbey,** a minor foundation dating from 1195. A succession of wars and the Dissolution destroyed most of it, but you can still see the remnants of a thirteenth-century church and the remains of the monks' living quarters, including an ingenious latrine system.

### ARRIVAL AND INFORMATION

**BARNARD CASTLE**

**By bus** Buses stop either side of Galgate.
Destinations Bishop Auckland (Mon–Sat 6 daily; 50min); Darlington (Mon–Sat every 30min; Sun hourly; 45min); Middleton-in-Teesdale (Mon–Sat hourly; 35min); Raby Castle (Mon–Sat hourly; 15min).

**Tourist office** Flatts Road, at the end of Galgate by the castle (April–Oct Mon–Thurs & Sat 9.30am–5pm, Fri 9.30am–4.30pm, Sun 10am–4pm; Nov–March Mon–Sat 10am–3pm; ☎ 01833 696356).

### ACCOMMODATION

**Homelands** 85 Galgate ☎ 01833 638757, ⓦ homelandsguesthouse.co.uk. An assortment of pretty rooms with lots of floral soft furnishings and comfortable beds. The owners are very knowledgeable about the area and can recommend plenty of good walks. Breakfast is great, featuring delicious fruit salads and generous cooked options. **£70**

### EATING AND DRINKING

**Blagraves House** 30–32 The Bank ☎ 01833 637668, ⓦ blagraves.com. Supposed to be the oldest house in Barnard Castle, dating back 500 years, this refined restaurant – oozing atmosphere, with its low oak wooden beams, open log fires and plush furnishings – specializes in traditional British cuisine. Dishes such as pan-fried fillet of beef cost from £23. Tues–Sun 7–10pm.

**The Bridge Inn** Whorlton, 4 miles east ☎ 01833 627341, ⓦ thebridgeinn-whorlton.co.uk. Cosy country pub, with open fires and flagstone floors, in the picturesque village of Whorlton. The food is traditional pub grub – sausages and mash, chicken pie and the like for around £10. Mon–Thurs & Sun noon–11pm, Fri & Sat noon–midnight

# Teesdale

13

**TEESDALE** extends twenty-odd miles northwest from Barnard Castle, its pastoral landscapes on the lower reaches beginning calmly enough but soon replaced by wilder Pennine scenery. Picturesque little villages like **Middleton-in-Teesdale** and Romaldkirk pepper the valley, while natural attractions include the stunning **Cow Green Reservoir** in Upper Teesdale, home to the indigenous Teesdale Violet and the blue Spring Gentian.

## Raby Castle

Staindrop, 8 miles northeast of Barnard Castle • Easter week, May, June & Sept Sun–Wed 1–4.30pm; July & Aug Sun–Fri 1–4.30pm • Gardens same days 11am–5pm • £10, park & gardens only £6 • ☎ 01833 660202, ⓦ rabycastle.com

Eight miles from Barnard Castle, up the A688, beckon the splendid, sprawling battlements of **Raby Castle**, reflecting the power of the Neville family, who ruled the local roost until 1569. The Neville estates were confiscated after the "Rising of the North", the abortive attempt to replace Elizabeth I with Mary Queen of Scots, with Raby subsequently passing to the Vane family in 1626, who still own it today. You can explore the interior, with its lavish bedrooms, dining room, kitchen and drawing rooms filled with furniture and artwork dating from the sixteenth and seventeenth centuries.

## Middleton-in-Teesdale

Surrounded by magnificent, wild countryside laced with a myriad of public footpaths and cycling trails, the attractive town of **MIDDLETON-IN-TEESDALE** is a popular base for walkers and cyclists. A relaxed little place, it was once the archetypal "company town", owned lock, stock and barrel by the London Lead Company, which began mining here in 1753. Just a few miles out of town is a famous set of waterfalls, **Low Force** and **High Force**.

### High Force

Daily 10am–5pm • £1.50, car park £2 • Minibuses from the town centre on Wed only (2 daily; 15min)

Heading on the B6277 northwest out of Middleton-in-Teesdale, you'll first pass the turning off to the rapids of **Low Force**. Another mile up the road is the altogether more spectacular **High Force** waterfall, a 70ft cascade that tumbles over an outcrop of the Whin Sill ridge and into a deep pool. The waterfall is on private Raby land (see above) and is reached by a short woodland walk.

### ARRIVAL AND INFORMATION

### MIDDLETON IN TEESDALE

**By bus** There are hourly bus services to Middleton-in-Teesdale from Barnard Castle (35min).

**Tourist office** Market Place (restricted hours, though usually daily 10am–1pm; ☎ 01833 641001).

### ACCOMMODATION AND EATING

★ **The Old Barn** 12 Market Place ☎ 01833 640258, ⓦ theoldbarn-teesdale.co.uk. In a very central location next to the tourist office, this sympathetically converted barn has three attractive B&B rooms with rustic furniture, elegant iron beds and Egyptian cotton sheets. There's a little patio garden to chill out in after a hard day's walking. **£68**

**Rose & Crown** Romaldkirk, 4 miles southwest ☎ 01833

650213, ⓦ rose-and-crown.co.uk. Beautiful ivy-clad eighteenth-century coaching inn set on the village green and next to a pretty Saxon church. Beneath the tastefully decorated rooms is a refined restaurant (mains from £16), serving accomplished dishes such as pan-fried woodpigeon with juniperberry sauce and grilled pancetta, a more relaxed brasserie (mains from £10), and a cosy bar with a wood fire. **£67.50**

# Weardale

Sitting to the north of Teesdale, the valley of **WEARDALE** was once hunting ground reserved for the Prince Bishops, but was later transformed into a major centre for lead-mining and limestone quarrying; this industrial heritage is celebrated at the excellent **Killhope Lead Mining musueum** and the **Weardale Museum** near Irehopesburn. The main settlement is **Stanhope**, a small market town with a pleasant open-air heated swimming

**13**

pool (ⓦ£3.65; woaspa.co.uk), perfect for cooling off after a long walk in the hills. Just to the east, the village of Wolsingham was a renowned pilgrimage centre in the Middle Ages, while neighbouring Frosterley features the remnants of an eleventh-century chapel.

## Weardale Museum

Ireshopeburn, 9 miles west of Stanhope • Easter, May–July & Sept Wed–Sun 2–5pm; Aug daily 2–5pm • £3 • ☏ 01388 517433, ⓦ www .wearmaledmuseum.co.uk

At Ireshopeburn, west of Stanhope, the **Weardale Museum** tells the story of the dale, in particular its lead mining and the importance of Methodism (the faith of most of the county of Durham's lead miners). There's a reconstructed miner's house as well as the "Wesley Room", dedicated to the founder of Methodism, John Wesley, and filled with his writings, books and belongings.

## Killhope Lead Mining Museum

5 miles west of Ireshopeburn and 12 miles east of Stanhope • April–Oct daily 10.30am–5pm • £8.20 including mine visit • ☏ 01388 537505, ⓦ www.killhope.org.uk • Request bus stop on bus #101 (see below)

If you're keen to learn about Weardale's mining past, a visit to **Killhope Lead Mining Museum**, five miles west of Ireshopeburn, is an absolute must. After many successful years as one of the richest mines in Britain, Killhope shut for good in 1910, and now houses a terrific, child-friendly museum that brings to life the difficulties and dangers of a mining life. The site is littered with preserved machinery and nineteenth-century buildings, including the Mine Shop where workers would spend the night after finishing a late shift. The highlight of the visit comes when you descend Park Level Mine – you'll be given wellies, a hard hat and a torch – in the company of a guide who expounds entertainingly about the realities of life underground, notably the perils of the "Black Spit", a lung disease which killed many men by their mid-forties.

### ARRIVAL AND INFORMATION                                                                         WEARDALE

**By bus** Bus #101 runs roughly hourly between Bishop Auckland and Stanhope, calling at Wolsingham and Frosterley. **Durham Dales Centre** On Stanhope's main road, the Dales Centre houses the tourist office (daily: April–Oct 10am–5pm; Nov–March 10am–4pm; ☏ 01388 527650, ⓦ durhamdalescentre.co.uk) and a café.

### GETTING AROUND

**By bus** Apart from #101, buses are relatively irregular and spotty round these parts. It's best to use the minibuses run by the Weardale Bus Company (☏ 01388 528235, ⓦ weardale-travel.co.uk).

**Weardale Railway** This volunteer-run steam railway chugs along from Bishop Auckland (see p.644) to Stanhope, stopping at Wolsingham and Frosterley on request; for up-to-date timetables and fares see ⓦ weardale-railway.org.uk.

### ACCOMMODATION

**AP Dowfold House** Crook, 6 miles east of Wolsingham ☏ 01388 762473, ⓦ dowfoldhouse.co.uk. Wonderful, relaxed B&B in a Victorian house surrounded by lush gardens and with splendid views out over Weardale. Breakfast, served in the elegant dining room, is the highlight, with lashings of free-range eggs, locally sourced sausages and bacon, home-made bread and jams. <u>£76</u>

### EATING AND DRINKING

★**Black Bull** Frosterley ☏ 01388 527784, ⓦ blackbullfrosterley.com. Hop off the Weardale Railway (see above) and into this traditional pub with beams, ranges, oak tables and flagstone floors. The ales are excellent, as is the food, which is hearty and delicious; mains, like herb-crusted lamb shoulder with apricot and walnut stuffing, start at £10. Thurs–Sat 11am–11pm, Sun 11am–5pm; food served till 2.30pm on Sun.

# Allen Valley

The B6295 climbs north out of Weardale into Northumberland, soon dropping into the **Allen Valley**, where heather-covered moorland shelters small settlements that once made their living from lead mining. The dramatic surroundings are easily viewed from a series of river walks accessible from either of the main settlements: **Allenheads**, at the top of the valley, twelve miles from Stanhope, where handsome stone buildings stand close to the river, or **Allendale Town**, another four miles north. Allendale is a quiet, rural spot – New Year's Eve excepted, when the villagers celebrate pagan-style by throwing barrels of burning tar onto a huge, spluttering bonfire – and is a good place to base yourself for local walking, with a small supermarket and several friendly pubs, all centred on the market square.

### ARRIVAL AND GETTING AROUND                                          ALLEN VALLEY

**By bus** Bus # 688 runs from Hexham to Allendale and Allenheads.

### EATING AND DRINKING

**Allenheads Inn** Allenheads ☎ 01434 685200, ⓦ allenheadsinn.co.uk. A popular stop for cyclists on the C2C route, this pub provides beer and inexpensive bar meals, and has seven rooms which get booked up quickly in summer. Mon–Fri 4–11pm, Fri & Sat noon–midnight. **£78**

**King's Head** Market Place, Allendale ☎ 01434 683 681, ⓦ thekingshead-allendale.co.uk. A handsome eighteenth-century stone-built pub serving Marston's cask ales and Jennings' Cumberland Ale as well as classic pub grub: fish and chips, scampi and burgers. In summer you can eat outside on the village square. Daily noon–11pm.

## Blanchland

A trans-moorland route into Northumberland, the B6278 cuts north from Weardale at Stanhope for ten wild miles to **BLANCHLAND**, a handful of lichen-stained stone cottages huddled round an L-shaped square that was once the outer court of a twelfth-century abbey. The village has been preserved since 1721, when Lord Crewe bequeathed his estate to trustees on condition that they restored the old buildings, as Blanchland had slowly fallen into disrepair after the abbey's dissolution.

### ARRIVAL AND DEPARTURE                                                    BLANCHLAND

**By bus** Bus # 733 runs connects Blanchland with Consett.

### EATING AND DRINKING

★ **Lord Crewe Arms Hotel** 10 miles north of Stanhope off the B6278 ☎ 01434 675251, ⓦ lordcrewearms blanchland.co.uk. Once the abbot's lodge, this hotel's nooks and crannies are an enticing mixture of medieval and eighteenth-century Gothic, including the vaulted basements, two big fireplaces and a priest's hideaway stuck inside the chimney. You can eat in the restaurant (mains from £15), or more cheaply in the public bar in the undercroft. **£140**

# Tees Valley

Admittedly not much of a tourist hotspot in comparison to Northumberland or Durham, the **TEES VALLEY** – once an industrial powerhouse and birthplace of one of the greatest developments in Britain, the public steam railway – nevertheless has some enjoyable attractions. **Darlington**, with its strong railway heritage, is a pleasant place to spend a day, while Middlesbrough's **MIMA** and Hartlepool's **Maritime Experience** (Daily: April–Oct 10am–5pm; Nov–March 11am–4pm; £10; ☎ 01429 860077, ⓦ hartlepools maritimeexperience.com) are extremely worthwhile, the latter particularly if you have children to entertain.

## Darlington

Abbreviated to "Darlo" by the locals, the busy market town of **DARLINGTON** hit the big time in 1825, when George Stephenson's "Number 1 Engine", later called *Locomotion*, hurtled from here to nearby Stockton-on-Tees at the terrifying speed of fifteen miles

**13**

per hour. The town subsequently grew into a rail-engineering centre, and didn't look back till the closure of the works in 1966. The origins of the rest of Darlington lie deep in Saxon times. The monks carrying St Cuthbert's body from Ripon to Durham (see p.640) stopped here, the saint lending his name to the graceful riverside church of **St Cuthbert**. The market square, one of England's largest, spreads beyond the church up to the restored and lively **Victorian covered market** (Mon–Sat 8am–5pm).

## Head of Steam

North Rd Station, a 20min walk up Northgate from the marketplace • April–Sept Tues –Sun 10am–4pm, Oct–March Wed–Sun 11am–3.30pm • £4.95 • ☎ 01325 460532, ⓦ www.darlington.gov.uk

Darlington's railway history is celebrated at the wonderful little **Head of Steam** museum, which is actually the restored 1842 passenger station on the original Stockton and Darlington railway route. The highlight is Stephenson's *Locomotion No. 1*, a tiny wood-panelled steam engine, the first-ever steam train to carry fare-paying passengers. Other locomotives jostle for space alongside, including the shiny, racing-green *Derwent*, the oldest surviving Darlington-built steam train. These, along with a collection of station and lineside signs, uniforms, luggage, a reconstructed ticket office and carriages, successfully bring to life the most important era in Darlington's existence.

### ARRIVAL AND INFORMATION

**DARLINGTON**

**By train** The train station is on Bank Top, a 10min walk from the central marketplace: from the train station walk up Victoria Road to the roundabout and turn right down Feethams.

Destinations Bishop Auckland (frequent; 25min); Durham (frequent; 20min); Newcastle (frequent; 35min).

**By bus** Most buses stop outside the Town Hall on Feethams.

Destinations Barnard Castle (Mon–Sat every 30min, Sun hourly; 45min); Bishop Auckland (Mon–Sat every 30min, Sun hourly; 1hr); Durham (every 20min; 1hr 10 min).

**Tourist office** Leaflets about the town and surroundings are available at the library on Crown Street (Mon & Tues 9am–6pm, Thurs 10am–6pm, Wed & Fri 9am–5pm, Sat 9am–4pm; ☎ 01325 462034).

### ACCOMMODATION

**Clow Beck B&B** Croft-on-Tees, 2 miles south ☎ 01325 721075, ⓦ clowbeckhouse.co.uk. Very welcoming B&B with thirteen individually decorated rooms named after flowers and set round a pretty landscaped garden. The owner is also an accomplished chef, creating delicious breakfasts – the Skipton sausage is very tasty – and evening meals (mains from £17). **£135**

**Rockliffe Hall** Hurworth-on-Tees, 5 miles south ☎ 01325 729999, ⓦ rockliffehall.com. Swanky hotel in a redbrick Victorian Gothic pile between the villages of Croft-on-Tees and Hurworth, which lays claim to having the UK's longest golf course. The rooms are cool and luxurious, and there's a spa and three restaurants. **£175**

### EATING AND DRINKING

★ **Bay Horse** 45 The Green, Hurworth, 5 miles south ☎ 01325 720663, ⓦ thebayhorsehurworth.com. This exquisite pub has a roaring fire, exposed wooden beams, comfy bar stools and chalked-up menus. Tuck into delicious meals such as venison sausage with fondant potatoes and

Yorkshire gravy (£13.95) and make sure you leave room for their puds; the sticky toffee pudding with green apple ice cream (£6.50) is fabulous. Mon–Sat 11am–11pm, Sun noon–10.30pm; no food served Sun evening.

## Middlesbrough Institute of Modern Art

Middlesbrough, 15 miles east of Darlington, on Centre Square, a 10min walk from the train station • Tues, Wed, Fri & Sat 10am–4.30pm, Thurs 10am–7pm, Sun noon–4pm • Free • ☎ 01642 726720, ⓦ visitmima.com

The stunning **Middlesbrough Institute of Modern Art (MIMA)** is one of the few tourist draws in the industrial town of Middlesbrough. Bringing together its municipal art collections for the first time, changing exhibitions concentrate on fine arts and crafts from the early twentieth century to the present day, with a heavy emphasis on ceramics and jewellery. The collection features work by David Hockney, L.S. Lowry and Tracey Emin, among others.

## Saltburn

13

South of the Tees estuary along the coast, it's not a difficult decision to bypass the kiss-me-quick tackiness of Redcar in favour of **SALTBURN**, twelve miles east of Middlesbrough, a graceful Victorian resort in a dramatic setting overlooking extensive sands and mottled red sea-cliffs. Soon after the railway arrived in 1861 to ferry Teessiders out to the seaside on high days and holidays, Saltburn became a rather fashionable spa town boasting a hydraulic **inclined tramway**, which still connects upper town to the pier and promenade, and ornate **Italian Gardens** that are laid out beneath the eastern side of town. The **Smugglers Heritage Centre** (April–Sept Wed–Sun 10am–6pm; £2), set in fishermen's cottages to the east of the pier, is a vivid recreation of Saltburn's darker past.

### ARRIVAL AND INFORMATION                                                      SALTBURN

**By train** There are regular train services from Newcastle (1hr 40min) and Durham (1hr 30min) via Darlington (50min) and Middlesbrough (25min).
**By bus** Frequent buses from Middlesbrough stop outside the train station (40min).

**Tourist office** In the railway station buildings and has a list of accommodation vacancies (Tues–Sat 9am–5pm, closed lunch hour; Oct–May closed Sun & Mon; ☎01287 622422, ⓦ www.redcar-cleveland.gov.uk).

# Newcastle upon Tyne

Vibrant and handsome, **NEWCASTLE UPON TYNE** has emerged from its industrial heyday and its post-industrial difficulties with barely a smut on its face. Its reputation for lively nightlife is just the tip of the iceberg; with its collection of top-class art galleries, museums and flourishing theatre scene – not to mention the shopping – the city is up there with the most exciting in Britain.

The de facto capital of the area between Yorkshire and Scotland, the city was named for its "new castle" founded in 1080 and hit the limelight during the Industrial Revolution – Grainger Town in the city's centre is lined with elegant, listed classical buildings, indicating its past wealth and importance as one of Britain's biggest and most important exporters of coal, iron and machinery. The decline of industry damaged Newcastle badly, signalling decades of poverty and hardship – a period recalled by Antony Gormley's mighty statue the **Angel of the North**, which, since its appearance in 1998, has become both a poignant eulogy for the days of industry and a symbol of resurgence and regeneration.

## Castle Keep

Castle Garth • Mon–Sat 10am–5pm, Sun noon–5pm • £4 • ☎0191 233 1221, ⓦ www.castlekeep-newcastle.org.uk

Anyone arriving by train from the north will get a sneak preview of the **Castle Keep**, as the rail line splits the keep from its gatehouse, the **Black Gate**, on St Nicholas Street. A wooden fort was built here over an Anglo-Saxon cemetery by Robert Curthose, illegitimate eldest son of William the Conqueror, but the present keep dates from the twelfth century. There's a great view from the rooftop over the river and city.

## St Nicolas Cathedral

At the junction of St Nicholas St and Mosley St • Sun–Fri 7.30am–6.30pm, Sat 8am–4pm • Free • ☎0191 232 1939, ⓦ stnicholascathedral.co.uk

The **St Nicolas Cathedral**, dating mainly from the fourteenth and fifteenth centuries, is remarkable chiefly for its tower; erected in 1470, it is topped with a crown-like structure of turrets and arches supporting a lantern. Inside, behind the high altar, is one of the largest funerary brasses in England; it was commissioned by Roger Thornton, the Dick Whittington of Newcastle, who arrived in the city penniless and died its richest merchant in 1429.

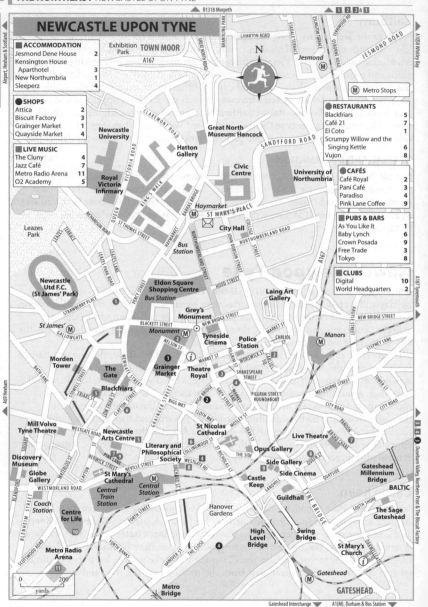

## NEWCASTLE UPON TYNE

**■ ACCOMMODATION**
| | |
|---|---|
| Jesmond Dene House | 2 |
| Kensington House Aparthotel | 3 |
| New Northumbria | 1 |
| Sleeperz | 4 |

**● SHOPS**
| | |
|---|---|
| Attica | 2 |
| Biscuit Factory | 3 |
| Grainger Market | 1 |
| Quayside Market | 4 |

**■ LIVE MUSIC**
| | |
|---|---|
| The Cluny | 4 |
| Jazz Café | 7 |
| Metro Radio Arena | 11 |
| O2 Academy | 5 |

**● RESTAURANTS**
| | |
|---|---|
| Blackfriars | 5 |
| Café 21 | 7 |
| El Coto | 1 |
| Scrumpy Willow and the Singing Kettle | 6 |
| Vujon | 8 |

**● CAFÉS**
| | |
|---|---|
| Café Royal | 2 |
| Pani Café | 3 |
| Paradiso | 4 |
| Pink Lane Coffee | 9 |

**■ PUBS & BARS**
| | |
|---|---|
| As You Like It | 1 |
| Baby Lynch | 6 |
| Crown Posada | 9 |
| Free Trade | 3 |
| Tokyo | 8 |

**■ CLUBS**
| | |
|---|---|
| Digital | 10 |
| World Headquarters | 2 |

Ⓜ Metro Stops

## Quayside

From between the castle and the cathedral a road known simply as The Side – formerly the main road out of the city, and home to the excellent **Side Gallery** – descends to Newcastle's **Quayside**. The river is spanned by seven bridges in close proximity, the most prominent being the looming **Tyne Bridge** of 1928, symbol of the city. Immediately west is the hydraulic **Swing Bridge**, erected in 1876 by Lord Armstrong so that larger vessels could reach his shipyards upriver, while modern road and rail lines

## NEWCASTLE ORIENTATION

Visitors are encouraged to think of the city as **Newcastle Gateshead**, an amalgamation of the two conurbations straddling the Tyne. On Gateshead Quays are the **BALTIC** contemporary arts centre and Norman Foster's **Sage** music centre, and on the opposite side, Newcastle's **Quayside** is where you'll find much of the city's nightlife. The city splits into several distinct areas, though it's only a matter of minutes to walk between them. The **castle** and **cathedral** occupy the heights immediately above the River Tyne, while north of here lies the city centre, **Grainger Town**. Chinatown and the two big draws of the **Discovery Museum** and the **Life Science Centre** are west of the centre, while east is the renowned **Laing Gallery**. In the north of the city, on the university campus, is the **Great North Museum: Hancock** and even further north, through the landscaped Exhibition Park, is the **Town Moor**, 1200 acres of common land where freemen of the city – including Jimmy Carter and Bob Geldof – are entitled to graze their cattle. The old industrial **Ouseburn Valley**, home to an alternative cultural scene, interesting galleries, the excellent **Seven Stories** children's museum and some popular bars, is a short walk east along the river from the city centre.

cross the river on the adjacent **High Level Bridge**, built by Robert Stephenson in 1849 – Queen Victoria was one of the first passengers to cross, promoting the railway revolution. Beyond the Tyne Bridge is an area of riverside apartments, landscaped promenades, public sculpture and pedestrianized squares, along with a series of fashionable bars and restaurants centred on the graceful **Gateshead Millennium Bridge**, the world's first tilting span, designed to pivot to allow ships to pass.

### BALTIC

By the Millennium Bridge • Daily except Tues 10am–6pm, Tues 10.30am–6pm • Free • ☎ 0191 478 1810, ⓦ balticmill.com

Fashioned from an old brick flour mill, **BALTIC** sits on the Gateshead riverbank, by the Millennium Bridge. Designed to be a huge visual "art factory", it's second only in scale to London's Tate Modern. There's no permanent collection here – instead there's an ever-changing calendar of exhibitions and local community projects, as well as artists' studios, education workshops, an art performance space and cinema, plus a rooftop restaurant with uninterrupted views of the Newcastle skyline.

### The Sage Gateshead

St Mary's Square, Gateshead Quays • Daily 9am–11pm • ☎ 0191 443 4661, ⓦ sagegateshead.com

Sitting on the riverbank, the **Sage Gateshead** is an extraordinary billowing steel, aluminium and glass concert hall complex, best seen at night when it glows with many colours. It's home to the Royal Northern Sinfonia orchestra and Folkworks, an organization promoting British and international traditional music, and there's something on most nights – from music concerts to workshops and lectures, as well as the Gateshead International Jazz Festival every April. The public concourse provides marvellous river and city views, and there are bars, a café and a brasserie.

## Ouseburn Valley

The **Ouseburn Valley**, fifteen minutes' walk up the River Tyne from Millennium Bridge, was once at the heart of Newcastle's industrial activities but became a derelict backwater in the mid-twentieth century. A jumble of old Victorian mills and warehouses, the area has seen a remarkable rejuvenation, as artists, musicians, businesses and even residents move in. Lime Street, home to the quirky **Cluny** music bar (see p.659), artists' workshops and the nationally renowned **Seven Stories**, is the hub, but there are plenty of attractions nearby including Europe's biggest commercial art space – the **Biscuit Factory** – an art-house cinema, riding stables and a small working farm.

**13**

## A WEEKEND IN NEWCASTLE

### FRIDAY NIGHT

There's no point in wasting time: put on your glad rags and head into town for a raucous night out, Geordie-style. Warm up with a glass of wine at the cosy **Vineyard** bar or a pint at the **Crown Posada**, and then move on to one of the **Mr Lynch** bars –try *Florita's* or *Baby Lynch* – for a cocktail or three and some dancing. Hardcore party people can finish up their night a **club** – *World Headquarters* and *Digital* are the pick of the bunch.

### SATURDAY

Blow the cobwebs away with a breezy walk along the **Quayside**, admiring the melee of beautifully constructed bridges and striking modern buildings that fringe the riverbank. Spend an hour or two in the contemporary art museum, **The Baltic**, and then pop back over the river to the old town, stopping off at the diminutive **Side Gallery**. After all that art, it's time for lunch at lively Sardinian café, *Pani*. In the afternoon, indulge your inner child at the colourful **Seven Stories** literature museum in the Ouseburn Valley. While you're in the area, don't miss a visit to the **Biscuit Factory**, if only for a cup of coffee and a cake in their cute café. The best place to spend Saturday night is at the artsy **Cluny** bar, particularly if there's live music or a theatre recital going on.

### SUNDAY

Explore Newcastle's architectural heritage – take a trip up to the gloomy **castle** and the adjacent **cathedral**, and then follow the ruins of the old city wall and medieval towers along **Stowell Street**. For lunch you could choose one of the many **Chinese restaurants** near the wall, or tuck into a large Sunday roast at the snug and traditional *Blackfriars*. Walk off your meal and expand your scientific knowledge at the **Centre of Life** museum, and the nearby **Discovery Museum**. If you're all partied and museumed out, put your feet up and munch on popcorn at Newcastle's art-house cinema, **The Tyneside**.

## Seven Stories

30 Lime St • Mon–Sat 10am–5pm, Sun 10am–4pm • £7 • ☎ 0845 271 0777, ⊛ sevenstories.org.uk

Housed in a beautifully converted Victorian riverside mill and spread over seven floors, **Seven Stories** celebrates the art of children's books through displays of original artwork, manuscripts and related documents. The bright, interactive exhibitions change regularly but highlights include original sketches taken from Noel Streatfield's *Ballet Shoes*, material from *Charlie and the Chocolate Factory* by Roald Dahl, Philip Pullman's early drafts, and the unpublished novel by Enid Blyton, *Mr Tumpy's Caravan*. Kids get the opportunity to dress up and create their own art works; there is also a simple café.

## Grainger Town

The heart of the city is known as **Grainger Town**, one of the best-looking city centres in Britain. Thrown up in a few short mid-nineteenth-century years by businessmen-builders and architects such as Richard Grainger, Thomas Oliver and John Dobson, the area is known for its classical facades of stone lining splendid, wide streets, and in particular, **Grey Street**, named for the second Earl Grey (he of the tea), prime minister from 1830 to 1834. In 1832, Grey carried the Reform Act – which granted seats in the House of Commons to large cities that had developed during the Industrial Revolution, like Newcastle – through parliament, an act commemorated by **Grey's Monument** at the top of the street. The restored **Grainger Market** (Mon–Sat 9am–5pm), nearby, was Europe's largest covered market when built in the 1830s, and is today home to the smallest branch of Marks & Spencer, known as the Original Penny Bazaar.

## Centre for Life

Times Square, off Westmorland Rd and Scotswood Rd • Mon–Wed & Fri–Sat 10am–6pm, Thurs 10am–8pm, Sun 11am–6pm; last admission 3.30pm • £12 • ☏ 0191 243 8210, ⓦ life.org.uk

A five-minute walk west of Central Station, the sleek buildings of the **Centre for Life** reach around the sweeping expanse of Times Square. This ambitious "science village" project combines bioscience and genetics research with a science visitor centre that aims to convey the secrets of life using the latest entertainment technology. Children find the whole thing enormously rewarding – from the sparkling Planetarium to the motion simulator – so expect to spend a good three hours here, if not more.

## Discovery Museum

Blandford Square • Mon–Fri 10am–4pm, Sat & Sun 11am–4pm • Free • ☏ 0191 232 6789, ⓦ twmuseums.org.uk

The **Discovery Museum** concentrates on the maritime history of Newcastle and Tyneside, as well as their role in Britain's scientific and technological developments. Highlights include the Tyneside-invented *Turbinia* – which dominates the entrance to the museum – the first ship to be powered by a steam turbine, as well as the Newcastle Story, a walk through the city's past with tales from animatronic characters along the way.

## Literary and Philosophical Society

23 Westgate Rd • Mon, Wed & Thurs 9.30am–7pm, Tues 9.30am–8pm, Fri 9.30am–5pm, Sat 9.30am–1pm • Free • ☏ 0191 232 0192, ⓦ litandphil.org.uk

Known as the **Lit and Phil**, this temple-like public library and learned society occupies one of the city's finest Georgian buildings: the domed roof, stucco ceilings and wrought-iron galleries are well worth a look. Established in 1825, it now runs a programme of recitals, jazz concerts, talks and exhibitions.

## Laing Art Gallery

New Bridge St • Tues–Sat 10am–5pm, Sun 2–5pm • Free • ⓦ twmuseums.org.uk

The **Laing Art Gallery**, in the east of the city, is home to the northeast's premier art collection: the permanent display is a sweep through British art from the seventeenth century to today, featuring sculpture from Henry Moore and a large collection of John Martin's fiery landscapes, along with a smattering of Pre-Raphaelites, so admired by English industrial barons. Another permanent display highlights a superb collection of Newcastle silver dating from the seventeenth century and some colourful 1930s glassware by George Davidson.

## Great North Museum: Hancock

Barras Bridge • **Hancock Museum** Mon–Fri 10am–5pm, Sat 10am–4pm, Sun 11am–4pm • Free; planetarium £2.50 • ☏ 0191 222 6765, ⓦ twmuseums.org.uk **Hatton Gallery** Mon–Sat 10am–5pm • Free • ☏ 0191 222 6059, ⓦ twmuseums.org.uk

A five-minute walk north from Haymarket Metro stop, the **Great North Museum: Hancock** is a clunkily named amalgamation of four museums, the best of which are the Great North Museum, housed in the Hancock building, and the nearby Hatton Gallery. The **Great North Museum** has an engaging mishmash of natural history exhibits – there's a knobbly T-Rex skeleton, some stuffed animals and an aquarium – historical artefacts such as the large-scale replica Hadrian's Wall, and a planetarium. The little **Hatton Gallery**, a two-minute walk away on the university's campus, is famous for housing the only surviving example of German Dadaist Kurt Schwitters' *Merzbau* (a sort of architectural collage); it also hosts a variety of temporary exhibitions.

**13**

**By plane** Newcastle International Airport is 6 miles north of the city (☎ 0871 882 1121, ⓦ newcastleairport.com). It is linked by the Metro to Central Station (every 7–15min 5.45am–midnight; 22min; £3.30) and beyond. You can also take a taxi into the centre (around £17).

**By train** Central Station is a 5min walk from the city centre or Quayside, and has a Metro station.

Destinations Alnmouth (hourly; 30min); Berwick-upon-Tweed (hourly; 45min); Carlisle (hourly; 1hr 30min); Darlington (frequent; 35min); Durham (frequent; 15min); Hexham (every 30min; 40min); London (frequent; 2hr 45min–3hr 15min); York (frequent; 1hr).

**By bus** National Express coaches stop on St James's Boulevard, not far from Central Station, while regional

buses stop at Haymarket bus station (Haymarket Metro). Gateshead Interchange is a big bus station served by local and national buses, linked by Metro to the city centre.

Destinations Alnmouth (every 30min; 1hr 30min); Alnwick (every 30min; 1hr 20min); Bamburgh (Mon–Sat 3 daily; Sun 2 daily; 2hr 30min); Beamish (April–Oct daily, Nov–March Sat & Sun; every 30min; 1hr); Berwick-upon-Tweed (Mon–Sat 8 daily; 2hr 30min); Carlisle (Mon–Sat hourly; 2hr 10min); Chester-le-Street (frequent; 45min); Craster (Mon–Sat 7 daily, Sun 4 daily; 1hr 50min); Durham (Mon–Sat every 30min, Sun 4–6 daily; 50min); Hexham (hourly; 50min); Middlesbrough (Mon–Sat every 30min; 1hr); Rothbury (Mon–Sat hourly, Sun 2 daily; 1hr 30min); Seahouses (Mon–Sat 3 daily, Sun 2 daily; 2hr 10min); Warkworth (daily every 30min; 1hr 20min).

## GETTING AROUND

**By Metro** The convenient, easy-to-use Tyne and Wear Metro (daily 5.30am–midnight, every 5–10min or 10–20min in the evening) connects the city centre with the airport and runs out to the suburbs. You can buy a Metro Day Saver ticket for unlimited rides (from £2.60).

**By bus** All city and local buses stop at Eldon Square shopping centre. Quaylink buses connect major attractions in Newcastle and Gateshead Quays with Newcastle Central Station, Haymarket Bus Station and Gateshead

Interchange. Buses run frequently daily (day ticket £2).

**By bike** Rent bikes at Saddle Skedaddle, Ouseburn Building, Albion Row (daily 9am–6pm; from £25/day; ☎ 0191 265 1110, ⓦ www.skedaddle.co.uk).

**By taxi** There are taxi ranks at Haymarket, Bigg Market (in the city centre between Grey Street and Grainger Street) and outside Central Station. To book, contact Noda Taxis (☎ 0191 222 888 or 232 7777, ⓦ noda-taxis.co.uk) at Central Station.

## INFORMATION AND TOURS

**Public transport information** Nexus Traveline has shops at the Central Station, Haymarket, Monument and Gateshead Metro stations (☎ 0871 200 2233, ⓦ nexus.org.uk).

**Tourist office** The main tourist office is at 8–9 Central Arcade, Market Street (Mon–Fri 9.30am–5.30pm, Sat 9am–5pm, Sun 10am–4pm; ☎ 0191 277 8000, ⓦ newcastlegateshead.com).

**Tours** City tours and various tours to Hadrian's Wall, Northumberland and Durham are run by Castle City Tours (from £40 per group of seven people max;

☎ 07780 958679, ⓦ newcastlecitytours.co.uk) while River Escapes Cruises' sightseeing boats (£6/10/12; ☎ 01670 785666, ⓦ riverescapes.co.uk) depart most weekends throughout the year, and other days in summer, from the Quayside. A hop-on hop-off, open-top sightseeing bus departs from Central Station (April–Oct daily, Nov & Dec Sat & Sun; every 30min–1hr; £8; ☎ 01789 299123, ⓦ city-sightseeing.com). Saddle Skedaddle (see above) also organizes C2C tours and trips to Hadrian's Wall.

---

## NEWCASTLE ART GALLERIES

**Biscuit Factory** 16 Stoddart St, Ouseburn ☎ 0191 261 1103, ⓦ thebiscuitfactory.com. Britain's largest commercial art gallery, displaying and selling anything from pendulum clocks and carved wooden tables to ceramic teapots and quirky necklaces. Free. Mon–Fri 10am–4pm, Sat 10am–6pm, Sun 11am–6pm.

**Globe Gallery** 53–57 Blanford Sq ☎ 0191 597 9377, ⓦ globegallery.org. Contemporary arts space that supports local, up-and-coming artists; there's a variety of exhibitions and one-off events. Free. Wed–Sat 11.30am–5pm.

**Northern Print** Stepney Bank, Ouseburn ☎ 0191 261 7000, ⓦ northernprint.org.uk. Little gallery that sells affordable prints by local artists. You can also learn how to make prints at the studio's workshop. Free. Wed–Sat noon–4pm.

**Side Gallery** 5–9 Side ☎ 0191 232 2208, ⓦ amber -online.com. A long-established, collectively run space with a strong specialism in social documentary photography. Free. Tues–Sat 11am–5pm, Thurs till 7pm, Sun noon–4pm.

## ACCOMMODATION

Budget **hotel chains** offer plenty of good-value rooms in the city centre and down by the Quayside, while the biggest concentration of small hotels and guesthouses lies a mile north of the centre in popular, student-filled Jesmond, along and off Osborne Road: take bus #33 from Central Station or Haymarket.

★**Jesmond Dene House** Jesmond Dene Rd, Jesmond ☎0191 212 3000, ⓦjesmonddenehouse.co.uk. An imposing Arts and Crafts house in a very peaceful wooded valley. The sleek, boldly decorated rooms are decked out in decadent velvet and silk furnishings and have enormous bathrooms with underfloor heating. There's fine dining in the garden-room restaurant and breakfasts are particularly luxurious, with smoked salmon, a range of cooked meats and champagne on offer. Rates vary; book well in advance. **£110**

**Kensington House Aparthotel** 5 Osborne Rd ☎0191 281 8175, ⓦkensingtonaparthotel.com. Twenty-three upmarket apartments of varying sizes, conveniently situated near Jesmond Metro. The decor is modern and sleek, with wood floors, cream carpets and marble kitchen surfaces. Beds are kitted out with luxurious Egyptian cotton sheets and feather down duvets. Six apartments have disabled access. **£115**

**New Northumbria** 61–69 Osborne Rd, Jesmond ☎0191 281 4961, ⓦthenewnorthumbriahotel.co.uk. In a prime position along Osborne Road among the popular, student-filled restaurants and bars, *New Northumbria* has 55 rooms, all with large beds and unfussy decor. There's a bar downstairs and an Italian restaurant attached. **£70**

**Sleeperz** 15 Westgate Rd ☎0191 261 6171, ⓦsleeperz.com/newcastle. A great-value option in the heart of town, part of a little chain that marries functionality with good design. Despite the city-centre location, the 98 compact but comfortable rooms provide a quiet respite from Saturday-night mayhem, and there's a funky breakfast bar/café downstairs. **£52**

## EATING

Newcastle has a great variety of places to eat, from expensive, top-quality restaurants showcasing the talents of young and creative chefs, to fun, relaxed cafés and budget-friendly Chinese restaurants (mostly around Stowell Street in Chinatown). The popular chain restaurants are down by the Quayside.

★**Blackfriars** Friars St ☎0191 615945, ⓦblackfriarsrestaurant.co.uk. Housed in a beautiful stone building dating back to 1239, *Blackfriars* offers superb traditional British dishes using local ingredients. Mains could include pork loin with a bacon and cheese Gateshead floddie (potato cakes, originating from Gateshead, and traditionally eaten for breakfast) or a Doddington cheese and onion Wellington with chive cream sauce, and, for afters, dig into sticky toffee pudding with green grape ice cream and Brown Ale caramel (mains from £12, puddings from £6). Booking recommended. Mon–Sat noon–2.30pm & 5.30–late, Sun noon–4pm.

**Café 21** Trinity Gardens ☎0191 222 0755, ⓦcafetwentyone.co.uk. Stylish Parisian-style bistro with crisp white tablecloths, leather banquettes, a classic French menu and slick service. Expect dishes like confit of duck with Lyonnaise potatoes (£19) or wild mushrooms on toasted brioche and a poached egg (£12), and delicious desserts – the Florentine doughnut with strawberry jam & crème chantilly (£7.20) is particularly good. Mon–Sat noon–2.30pm & 5.30–10.30pm, Sun 12.30–3.30pm & 6.30–10pm.

**Café Royal** 8 Nelson St. Bright and buzzy café with great smoothies, coffees and delectable home-made breads and cakes – try the raspberry scones with clotted cream (£3.50) or hazelnut twists (£2). Mon–Sat 8am–6pm.

**El Coto** 21 Leazes Park Rd ☎0191 261 0555, ⓦelcoto.co.uk. Cute and cosy, this great tapas place has an extensive, good-value menu featuring all the usuals, such as *patatas bravas* and marinated sardines – dishes cost around £5, though paella goes for £10 per person. Daily noon–11pm.

**Pani Café** 61–65 High Bridge St, off Grey St ☎0191 232 4366, ⓦpaniscafe.co.uk. On a side street below the Theatre Royal, this lively Sardinian café has won a loyal clientele for its good-value sandwiches, pasta and salads (mains around £8). Mon–Sat 10am–10pm.

**Paradiso** 1 Market Lane ☎0191 221 1240, ⓦparadiso.co.uk. Mellow café-bar hidden down an alley off Pilgrim Street – the snack food in the daytime becomes more substantial at night, with truffle risotto, salmon steaks and the like. There are set menus throughout the day (two courses from £9.95, three courses from £12.95) as well as à la carte. You can dine outdoors in good weather. Mon–Thurs 11am–2.30pm & 5–10.30pm, Fri & Sat 11am–10.45pm.

**Pink Lane Coffee** 1 Pink Lane ☎07841 383085, ⓦpinklanecoffee.co.uk. The best coffee in town: their beans are slow roasted and the milk is Northumbrian Pedigree. Exposed light bulbs, reclaimed furniture and brickwork tiling makes for a stylish interior. Mon–Fri 7.30am–6pm, Sat 9am–5pm, Sun 10am–4pm.

**Scrumpy Willow and the Singing Kettle** 89 Clayton St ☎0191 221 2323. Wonderful little organic café/restaurant with a relaxed atmosphere and pretty, shabby-chic decor – think candles, mirrors and rickety wood furniture. It's great for vegetarians and vegans: pop in for a tasty brunch of eggs Benedict, porridge or pancakes. The evening menu features locally sourced meat and fish including a delicious Kielder

**13**

lamb with farm vegetables and pearl barley. Mains from £6.95. Mon–Sat 10am–8pm, Sun 11am–4pm.
**Vujon** 29 Queen St ☎ 0191 221 0601, ⓦ vujon.com. The city's classiest Indian restaurant, housed in an elegant building by the Quayside, serving dishes a cut above the ordinary, from venison Jaipur-style with chilli jam (£15.90) to the spicy duck *salan* (£14.90). Mon–Sat 11.30am–2pm & 5.30–11.30pm, Sun 5.30–11.30pm.

## DRINKING

Newcastle's boisterous pubs, bars and clubs are concentrated in several areas: in the **Bigg Market** (between Grey St and Grainger St), around the **Quayside** and in the developing **Ouseburn** area, where bars tend to be quirkier and more sophisticated; in **Jesmond**, with its thriving student-filled strip of café-bars; and in the mainstream leisure-and-cinema complex known as **The Gate** (Newgate St). The **gay** area, known as the "Pink Triangle", focuses on the Centre for Life, spreading out to Waterloo Street and Westmorland and Scotswood roads. Top drinking brew is Newcastle Brown – an ale known locally as "Dog" – produced in this city since 1927.

**As You Like It** Archbold Terrace ☎ 0191 281 2277, ⓦ asyoulikeitjesmond.com. The top bar in the Jesmond area, and part of the *Mr Lynch* chain (see below). Incongruously sitting beneath an ugly tower block, this funky bar/restaurant has a relaxed vibe, exposed brick walls and a mishmash of furniture. The Supper Club (ⓦ thesupperclubjesmond.com), a late-night club night on Fri–Sun (10pm–2am) features jazz, blues and soul. Sun–Thurs noon–midnight, Fri & Sat noon–2am.

**Baby Lynch** 26 Collingwood St ☎ 0191 261 8271, ⓦ babylynch.com. Part of a Newcastle-based chain (includes *As You Like It, Nancy Bordellos, Floritas, Madame Koo* and *Mr Lynch*), but still cool for it, *Baby Lynch* oozes 1970s chic with its retro wooden floorboards, cosy booths and bamboo loungers. The cocktail menu is extensive and very tempting (cocktails from £4.95). It gets busy later on, with the overspill from next-door *Floritas*. Fri–Sun 7pm–3am.

**Crown Posada** 31 Side ☎ 0191 232 1269, ⓦ crownposadanewcastle.co.uk. A proper old man's boozer: local beers and guest ales in this small wood-and-glass-panelled Victorian pub. You might fancy the dark, malty Hadrian's Gladiator (£3.80) or opt for the golden, hoppy Tyneside Blonde (£3.80). Mon–Wed noon–11pm, Thurs 11am–11pm, Fri 11am–midnight, Sat noon–midnight, Sun noon–10.30pm.

★ **Free Trade** St Lawrence Rd ☎ 0191 265 5764. Walk along the Newcastle Quayside past the Millennium Bridge and look for the shabby pub on the hill, where you are invited to "drink beer, smoke tabs" with the city's pub cognoscenti. Cask beer from local microbreweries, a great free juke box and superb river views from the beer garden. Mon–Thurs 11am–11pm, Fri & Sat 11am–midnight, Sun noon–11pm.

**Tokyo** 17 Westgate Rd ☎ 0191 232 1122, ⓦ tokyonewcastle.co.uk. The dark, sleek main bar's handsome enough, but follow the tealights up the stairs to the outdoor "garden" bar lined by plants and trees, giving the area a secret, exclusive feel. A pre-club favourite for Shindig (see below). Sun–Thurs 5pm–midnight & Fri & Sat 4pm–1am.

## NIGHTLIFE

Newcastle's biggest club night is **Shindig**, taking place on Saturdays and switching locations around the city. See ⓦ shindiguk.com for the latest. Gigs, club nights and the gay scene are reviewed exhaustively in *The Crack* (monthly; free; ⓦ thecrackmagazine.com), available in shops, pubs and bars.

### CLUBS

**Digital** Times Sq ☎ 0191 261 9755, ⓦ yourfutureisdigital.com/newcastle. The city's top club, with an amazing sound system pumping out a variety of musical genres. If you like cheesy classics, look out for Born in the Sixties nights, while house, funk and disco fans will get their fix on Saturday's Love nights. Mon & Thurs 10.30pm–2.30am, Fri & Sat 10.30pm–3.30am.

**World Headquarters** Carliol Square, East Pilgrim St ☎ 0191 281 3445, ⓦ welovewhq.com. Smallish and down-to-earth club that's always packed. Music is a medley of house, hip-hop, soul and r'n'b and reggae. Downstairs

---

## EAT! NEWCASTLE

August sees Newcastle's foodie festival EAT! take to the streets, rooftops and nearby countryside. The programme is imaginative and varied, with recent events including a **supper club at Dunston Staiths**, an epic wooden structure once used for loading coal; foraging classes; **fishing workshops at Tynemouth pier**; and an attempt to break the world record for the longest-ever cooking demonstration. There's also street stalls, a **food heroes market** and foodie **walking tours**. To find out what's on, see ⓦ newcastlegateshead.com/eat-festival.

there's a comfy lounge area with squashy sofas and a pool table. Entry fee around £10. Fri & Sat 10.30pm–3am.

## LIVE MUSIC VENUES

★ **The Cluny** 36 Lime St, Ouseburn Valley ☎ 0191 230 4474, ⓦ theheadofsteam.co.uk. Based in an old whisky bottling plant, this is the best small music venue in the city, with something going on most nights, from quirky indie bands to contemporary punk-pop. *Cluny 2*, around the corner at 34 Lime Street (same hours), is its spacious sister venue, with less frequent gigs. Sun–Thurs noon–11pm, Fri & Sat noon–1am.

**Jazz Café** 23–25 Pink Lane ☎ 0191 232 6505, ⓦ jazzcafe-newcastle.co.uk. Slick and intimate jazz club in inauspicious surroundings, hosting top-quality jazz from 9.30pm on Friday and Saturday nights. Tues–Sat 11am–2am.

**Metro Radio Arena** Arena Way ☎ 0844 493 4567, ⓦ metroradioarena.co.uk. The biggest concert and exhibition venue in the Northeast; star appearances have included Lady Gaga, Dolly Parton and Tom Jones. Book popular gigs well in advance.

**O2 Academy** Westgate Rd ☎ 0844 477 2000, ⓦ o2academynewcastle.co.uk. Housed in the former bingo hall, this mainstream venue hosts a variety of big names and local talent.

## ENTERTAINMENT

**Live Theatre** 27 Broad Chare ☎ 0191 232 1232, ⓦ live.org.uk. Enterprising theatre company that aims to find and develop local, and particularly young, talent – the attached *Caffe Vivo* is good for coffee by day and pre-theatre meal deals by night.

**Mill Volvo Tyne Theatre** 111 Westgate Rd ☎ 0844 493999, ⓦ millvolvotynetheatre.co.uk. Beautifully restored Victorian theatre with a wide range of plays, comedy shows and gigs.

**Side Cinema** 5–9 Side ☎ 0191 232 2000, ⓦ amber-online.com. A quaintly dishevelled fifty-seat cinema:

they run an imaginative programme combining arthouse movies with live music.

**Theatre Royal** 100 Grey St ☎ 0844 811 2121, ⓦ theatreroyal.co.uk. Drama, opera, dance, musicals and comedy; also hosts the annual RSC season in Nov.

**Tyneside Cinema** 10 Pilgrim St ☎ 0845 217 9909, ⓦ tynesidecinema.co.uk. The city's premier art-house cinema, with coffee, light meals and movie talk in the Art Deco cinema café. The gorgeous restored decor includes Persian-inspired gilded stucco, stained glass and mosaic floors.

## SHOPPING

**Attica** 2 Old George Yard, off Highbridge ☎ 0191 261 4062, ⓦ atticavintage.co.uk. Excellent vintage shop selling all sorts of clothing for men and women – there's a great selection of glamorous evening wear, jewellery and hats as well as some quirky furniture dating from the 1950s, 1960s and 1970s. Mon–Sat 10.30am–5.30pm.

**Biscuit Factory** 16 Stoddart St, Ouseburn ☎ 0191 261 1103, ⓦ thebiscuitfactory.com. Airy art gallery (see box, p.656) packed with paintings, ceramics, sculptures, jewellery and furniture – all for sale. Prices range from £10 to over £2000. Mon–Fri 10am–5pm, Sat 10am–6pm, Sun 11am–5pm.

**Farmers' Market** Grey's Monument. Central market selling wonderful locally sourced fruit and veg, jams, meats and fish. First Fri of each month 9.30am–2.30pm.

**Grainger Market** Grainger Town. One of the city's oldest and best shopping experiences: a centrally located Georgian market painted in pastel colours and featuring old fashioned fishmongers, butchers and a hardware store, alongside delis, gift shops and a French café. Mon & Wed 9am–5pm, Tues & Thur–Sat 9am–5.30pm.

**Quayside Market** Busy, popular market down on the quayside selling locally produced food, clothes and art and crafts including jewellery. Sun 9.30am–4pm.

## DIRECTORY

**Hospital** Royal Victoria Infirmary, Queen Victoria Road (☎ 0191 233 6161, ⓦ newcastle-hospitals.org.uk) has 24hr A&E services and a Minor Injuries Unit (daily 8am–9pm). The Westgate Walk-in Centre at Newcastle General Hospital, Westgate Road, is open daily (8am–8pm).

**Police** Corner of Market and Pilgrim Streets ☎ 0191 214 6555.

# Around Newcastle

There are a number of attractions near Newcastle, all accessible by Metro. The train runs east towards **Wallsend**, where **Segedunum** fort marks the beginning of Hadrian's Wall, while further east **Bede's World** pays homage to Christianity's most important historian. Further out, near Sunderland, is the splendid **Washington Wildfowl Centre**, while the Angel and the Goddess of the North are two striking pieces of public art.

# 13

## Segedunum

Budle St, Wallsend, 4 miles east of Newcastle • April–May & Sept–Nov daily 10am–4.30pm; June–Aug 10am–5pm; Nov–March Mon–Fri 10am–2.30pm • £5.50 • ☎ 0191 236 9347, ⓦ twmuseums.org.uk/segedunum • Newcastle Metro to Wallsend

**Wallsend** was the last outpost of Hadrian's great border defence and **Segedunum**, the "strong fort" a couple of minutes' signposted walk from the Metro station, has been admirably developed as one of the prime attractions along the Wall. The grounds contain a fully reconstructed bathhouse, complete with heated pools and colourful frescoes, while the "wall's end" itself is visible at the edge of the site, close to the river and Swan Hunter shipyard. From here, the **Hadrian's Wall Path** (see box, p.664) runs for 84 miles to Bowness-on-Solway in Cumbria; you can get your walk "passport" stamped inside the museum.

## Bede's World

On the edge of Jarrow, 5 miles east of Newcastle • Daily Feb–March 10am–4.30pm; April–Sept 10am–5.30pm • £5.50 • ☎ 0191 489 2106, ⓦ bedesworld.co.uk • Newcastle Metro to Jarrow, from where it's a 20min walk through the industrial estate

**Bede's World** sits at the edge of the town of **JARROW** – ingrained on the national consciousness since the 1936 **Jarrow Crusade**, when 201 people marched three hundred miles down to London to protest against the government's refusal to ease unemployment and poverty in the Northeast. The complex explores the life of Venerable Bede (673–735 AD), who lived here as a boy, growing to become one of Europe's greatest scholars and England's first historian – his *History of the English Church and People*, describing the struggles of the island's early Christians, was completed at Jarrow in 731. Exhibits include extracts from Bede's writings and various archeological finds, and outside there's a reconstructed monastic village; children will enjoy the small farmyard complete with pigs, goats and sheep.

## Angel of the North

6 miles south of Newcastle upon Tyne, off the A167 (signposted Gateshead South) • Bus #21 or #22 from Eldon Shopping Centre; there's car parking at the site

Since 1998, Antony Gormley's 66ft-high **Angel of the North** has stood sentinel over the A1 at Gateshead. A startling steel colossus that greets anyone travelling up from the south by rail or road, it's sited on top of a former coal-mining site, acknowledging the area's most emotive industry.

## Goddess of the North

Cramlington, 9 miles north of Newcastle upon Tyne • Daily dawn–dusk, café & visitor centre 9.30am–4.30pm • ⓦ northumberlandia.com • There's a train station at Cramlington located 2.5 miles from the site, or take bus #X13 from Newcastle

The Angel of the North (see above) has a rival in Charles Jencks' **Goddess of the North** (or *Northumberlandia*) nine miles north in Cramlington. Made out of 1.5 million tonnes of earth from Shotton mine and an epic 34m-high and 400m-long, the recumbent naked Goddess was unveiled in 2013.

---

### THE GEORDIE NATION

Tyneside and Newcastle's native inhabitants are known as **Geordies**, the word probably derived from a diminutive of the name "George". There are various explanations of who George was (King George II, railwayman George Stephenson), all plausible, none now verifiable. Geordies speak a highly distinctive dialect and accent, heavily derived from Old English. Phrases you're likely to come across include: haway man! (come on!), scran (food), a'reet (hello) and propa belta (really good) – and you can also expect to be widely addressed to as "pet" or "flower".

---

## 13 Washington Wildfowl and Wetlands Centre

Pattinson, 10 miles east of Newcastle • Daily: April–Oct 9.30am–5.30pm; Nov–March 9.30am–4.30pm • £9.50 • ☎ 0191 416 5454,
Ⓦ wwt.org.uk • Bus #8 from Sunderland stops at the Waterview Park, a short walk from the wildfowl centre; from Newcastle, take the
metro to Washington

Taking up one hundred acres of the north bank of the River Wear in Pattinson (formerly District 15), the popular **Washington Wildfowl and Wetlands Centre** is a lush conservation area of meadows, woods and wetlands that acts as a winter habitat for migratory birds, including geese, ducks, herons and flamingos. In summer, you can watch fluffy ducklings hatch in the Waterfowl Nursery.

## Sunderland

**SUNDERLAND** is fifteen miles east of Newcastle and shares that city's long history, river setting and industrial heritage – but cannot match its architectural splendour. However, it's worth a trip to visit the Sunderland Museum, easily accessible by Metro from Newcastle.

### Sunderland Museum

Burdon Road • Mon–Sat 10am–5pm, Sun 2–5pm • Free • Ⓦ twmuseums.org.uk/sunderland

The **Sunderland Museum** does a very good job of telling the city's history, relating how Sunderland ships were once sent around the world, and also has much to say about the city's other major trades, notably its production of lustreware and glass. The **Winter Gardens**, housed in a steel-and-glass hothouse, invite a treetop walk to view the impressive polished-steel column of a water sculpture.

### Riverside

Across the River Wear, the landscaped **Riverside** is actually the oldest settled part of the city: walk up Fawcett Street and then Bridge Street from the centre and cross Wearmouth Bridge (around 20min). Along the north bank of the river, in front of the university buildings, the early Christian church of **St Peter** (674 AD) is the elder sibling of St Paul's Church at Jarrow and displays fragments of the oldest stained glass in the country.

#### ARRIVAL AND INFORMATION                                                    SUNDERLAND

**By Metro** The main stop for Metros from Newcastle (30–35min) is in the central train station opposite The Bridges shopping centre.
**Tourist information** The tourist office (Mon–Sat 9am–5pm, bank hols 10am–4pm; ☎ 0191 553 2000, Ⓦ sunderland.gov.uk) is behind the central station on the main shopping drag at 50 Fawcett Street.

# Hadrian's Wall

**Hadrian's Wall** (Ⓦ visithadrianswall.co.uk) was constructed in 122 AD at the behest of the Roman Emperor Hadrian. Keen for peace and safety within his empire, fearing attacks from Pictish Scotland, Hadrian commissioned a long wall to act as a border, snaking its way from the Tyne to the Solway Firth. It was built up to a height of 15ft in places and was interspersed by milecastles, which functioned as gates, depots and mini-barracks. The best-preserved portions of the Wall are concentrated between **Chesters Roman Fort**, four miles north of Hexham, and Haltwhistle, sixteen miles to the west, which passes **Housesteads Roman Fort**, **Vindolanda** and the **Roman Army Museum**. Most people come to walk or cycle the length of the Wall, but if you're only planning to walk a short stretch, start off at Housesteads and head west for sweeping views. There are plenty of interesting places to stay and eat around and along the Wall, including the handsome market town of **Hexham** (see p.665).

## Chesters Roman Fort

Four miles north of Hexham • Daily: April–Sept 10am–6pm; Oct–Nov 10am–5pm; Nov–April Sat & Sun 10am–4pm • £5.60; EH • ☎ 01434 681379, ⓦ english-heritage.org.uk

Beautifully sited next to the gurgling River Tyne, **Chesters Roman Fort**, otherwise known as Cilurnum, was built to guard the Roman bridge over the river. Enough remains of the original structure to pick out the design of the fort, but the highlight is down by the river where the vestibule, changing room and steam range of the garrison's **bathhouse** are still visible, along with the furnace and the latrines.

## Housesteads Roman Fort

Around 8 miles west of Chesters • Daily: April–Sept 10am–6pm; Oct–March 10am–4pm • £6.40; EH & NT • ☎ 01434 344525

**Housesteads Roman Fort** is one of the most popular sites on the Wall. The fort is of standard design but for one enforced modification – forts were supposed to straddle the line of the Wall, but here the original stonework follows the edge of the cliff, so Housesteads was built on the steeply sloping ridge to the south. Enter via the tiny **museum**, and walk across to the south gate; next to this lies the ruins of a garrison of up to one thousand infantrymen. It's not necessary to pay for entrance to the fort if you're simply walking along the Wall west from here; the three-mile hike takes in wonderful views as it meanders past **Crag Lough** and over to **Steel Rigg** (which has a car park).

## Vindolanda

Access from behind Once Brewed Visitor Centre • Daily: mid- to end March & Oct 10am–5pm; April–Sept 10am–6pm; reduced hours in winter, call in advance • £6.25, joint admission with Roman Army Museum £10 • ☎ 01434 344277, ⓦ vindolanda.com

The garrison fort of **Vindolanda** is believed to have been built and occupied before the construction of the Wall itself. Guarding the important central section of the east–west supply route across Britain, a series of early forts in this location were built of timber, eventually replaced with a stone construction during Hadrian's reign. Preserved beneath the remains of the stone fortress, these early forts are now being excavated – around three to four hundred volunteers take part every day. The museum contains the largest collection of Roman leather items ever discovered on a single site – sandals, purses, an archer's thumb guard – and a fascinating series of **writing tablets** dating to 90 AD. The earliest written records found in Britain, they feature shopping lists, duty rotas and even a birthday party invitation from one Claudia Severa to Sulpicia Lepidina.

## Roman Army Museum

7 miles west of Vindolanda • Daily: mid- to end March & Oct 10am–5pm; April–Sept 10am–6pm; reduced hours in winter, call in advance • £5.25, joint admission with Vindolanda £10 • ☎ 01434 344277, ⓦ vindolanda.com

The **Roman Army Museum** aims to illustrate how the Roman soldiers stationed here lived. There's everything from armour and weapons – including javelins, shields and swords – to a full-size chariot and a wagon. It's all very entertaining, and successfully brings to life the ruins you may just have seen at Vindolanda.

**13**

## ALONG HADRIAN'S WALL

The best way to visit the Wall is to walk or cycle the length of it. The **Hadrian's Wall Path** (ⓦnationaltrail.co.uk/hadrians-wall-path) runs for 84 miles alongside the Wall itself from Wallsend (see p.660) to Bowness-on-Solway. It takes on average seven days to complete and there's an optional Passport system (May–Oct) involving collecting a series of stamps to prove you've done it. The **National Route 72** (signposted NCN 72; ⓦcycle-routes.org/hadrians cycleway), shares some of the same route as the Footpath, and runs from South Shields to Ravenglass in Cumbria. There's bike hire in Newcastle (see p.656).

### ARRIVAL AND INFORMATION

**By train** The nearest train stations are on the Newcastle–Carlisle line at Corbridge, Hexham, Bardon Mill and Haltwhistle.

**Tourist office** Once Brewed Visitor Centre (April–Oct daily 9.30am–5pm, Sat & Sun 10am–3pm; ☏01434 344396) is

### HADRIAN'S WALL

just off the B6318. It has exhibitions about the Wall and Northumberland National Park, access to Vindolanda (see p.663), a tearoom, toilets and a hostel next door (see below). The #AD122 bus (see below) stops here.

### GETTING AROUND

**By car** The B3618 (aka Military Road) runs alongside the Wall. All museums and forts are accessible by car and there's parking at all major sights, Once Brewed Visitor Centre and Steel Rigg.

**By bus** The little #AD122 (known as the "Hadrian's Wall bus"; Easter–Oct up to 5 times daily in each direction) runs from Newcastle to Corbridge, Hexham, and all the Wall

sites and villages, before heading on to Carlisle and Bowness-on-Solway (the end of the Hadrian's Wall Path). There's also a year-round hourly service on the #685 bus between Newcastle and Carlisle, and other local services from Carlisle and Hexham, which provide access to various points along the Wall.

### ACCOMMODATION

In addition to the B&Bs in the countryside around the Wall, Hexham (see opposite), Haltwhistle and Corbridge have a good selection of accommodation.

★**Carraw B&B** Military Rd, Humshaugh ☏01434 689857, ⓦcarraw.co.uk. It's not often you can say "I've slept on Hadrian's Wall", but here you can – this beautiful B&B, run by a friendly couple, is built right next to Hadrian's masterpiece and boasts stunning views. Lovely homely touches, like home-made shortbread and cake on arrival, hot-water bottles and luxurious toiletries make this place really special. Delicious breakfasts – the nutty granola is a winner. Pitches £12.50. **£98**

**Hadrian's Wall Camping and Caravan Site** Melkridge Tilery, 2 miles north of Melkridge, just south of B6318 ☏01434 320495, ⓦhadrianswallcampsite.co.uk. Friendly, family-run site half a mile from the Wall, with showers, café, washing machine and dryer, and bike storage; breakfast and evening meals available. There's also a heated bunk barn sleeping 10 people (£15 per person). Open all year. Pitches **£12**, camper van **£15**

**Langley Castle** A686, Langley-on-Tyne, 2 miles south of Haydon Bridge ☏01434 688888, ⓦwww.langley castle.com. Suitably regal rooms – four-poster beds, sumptuous furnishings and beautiful bathrooms with

saunas and spa baths – in this turreted medieval castle. The cheaper rooms are in the grounds, looking onto the castle. There's also an atmospheric restaurant, cocktail bar, lounge and gardens. **£195**, castle rooms **£245**

**Twice Brewed Inn** Military Rd ☏01434 344534, ⓦtwicebrewedinn.co.uk. Just 50 yards up from Once Brewed Visitor Centre and hostel, this friendly community pub has simple rooms, a beer garden, local beers on tap and perhaps the Northeast's largest selection of rums (54 of them). En-suites are slightly pricier. **£59**

★**Willowford Farm** Gilsland ☏01697 747962, ⓦwww.willowford.co.uk. Strictly speaking just over the Northumbrian border in Cumbria, but this farmhouse B&B still makes a lovely, tranquil base to explore the Wall. Rooms are in converted farm buildings and decked out with pretty wooden beams and large beds. Packed lunch £6. **£80**

**YHA Once Brewed** Military Rd, Once Brewed ☏0845 371 9753, ⓦyha.org.uk. Basic and welcoming youth hostel next to the visitor centre. They have plenty of walking leaflets, a restaurant and self-catering facilities. Dorms **£19.50**, family rooms **£37.50**

### EATING AND DRINKING

★**Barrasford Arms** Barrasford, 9 miles north of Hexham ☏01434 681237, ⓦbarrasfordarms.co.uk.

Endearingly ramshackle, welcoming and homely, this country pub serves great traditional British food with a French twist; dishes could include Cumbrian outdoor-reared chicken with haricot bean and tomato stew (£12) and for pudding sticky pistachio meringue with orange mascarpone (£5). Booking advisable. Mon 6.30–11pm, Tues–Thur noon–2pm & 6.30–11pm, Fri noon–2pm & 6.30–midnight, Sat noon–midnight, Sun noon–11pm; food served Mon 6.30–9pm, Tues–Sat noon–2pm & 6.30–9pm, Sun noon–3pm.

**Battlesteads Country Inn and Restaurant** Wark-on-Tyne, 12 miles north of Hexham ☎01434 230209, ⓦbattlesteads.com. In a charming little village by a trickling stream, this locally renowned restaurant with a lovely beer garden uses fresh produce sourced from within a 30-mile radius. Leave room for their famed whisky and marmalade bread and butter pudding (£5.75). Best to book. Food served daily noon–3pm & 6.30–9.30pm.

**General Havelock Inn** Haydon Bridge ☎01434 684376. Eighteenth-century inn that specializes in tasty Modern British food, from crab cakes and Cumberland sausages to chocolate brûlée and ice-cream sundaes. Great locally brewed ales on offer, too. Main meals average around £17. Food served daily noon–3pm & 6–11pm.

# Hexham

HEXHAM is the only significant stop between Newcastle and Carlisle, and however keen you are on seeing the Wall, you'd do well to give this handsome market town a night – or even make it your base.

The focal point is the **abbey**, whose foundations were originally part of a fine Benedictine monastery founded by St Wilfrid in 671. Claimed, according to contemporaneous accounts, to be the finest this side of the Alps, the church – or rather its gold and silver – proved irresistible to the Vikings, who savaged the place in 876. It was rebuilt in the eleventh century as part of an Augustinian priory, and the town grew up in its shadow.

## Hexham Abbey
Daily 9.30am–5pm • ⓦ www.hexhamabbey.org.uk

The stately exterior of **Hexham Abbey** dominates the west side of the central marketplace. Entry is through the south transept, where there's a bruised but impressive first-century tombstone honouring Flavinus, a standard-bearer in the Roman cavalry, who's shown riding down his bearded enemy. The memorial lies at the foot of the broad, well-worn steps of the canons' **night stair**, one of the few such staircases – providing access from the monastery to the church – to have survived the Dissolution. The chancel, meanwhile, displays the inconsequential-looking **frith-stool**, an eighth-century stone chair that was once believed to have been used by St Wilfrid, rendering it holy enough to serve as the medieval sanctuary stool.

## The Old Gaol
Hallgate • April–Sept Tues–Sat 11am–4.30pm; Oct–Nov & Feb–March Tues & Sat 11am–4.30pm • £3.95 • ☎01434 652349, ⓦwww .tynedaleheritage.org

Britain's first purpose-built prison, **Hexham Old Gaol** occupies a solid sandstone building to the east of the abbey. It was commissioned by the powerful Archbishop of York in 1330, and constructed using stone plundered from the Roman ruins at Corbridge. Inside there's an entertaining museum extolling the virtues and pitfalls of medieval crime and punishment.

### ARRIVAL AND INFORMATION · HEXHAM

**By train** The train station sits on the northeastern edge of the town centre, a 10min walk from the abbey.
Destinations Carlisle (hourly; 50min); Haltwhistle (hourly; 20min); Newcastle (hourly; 50min).

**By bus** The bus station is off Priestpopple, a few minutes' stroll east of the abbey.

Destinations Bellingham (Mon–Sat hourly; 45min); Newcastle (hourly; 50min).

**Tourist office** In the main Wentworth car park, near the supermarket (April–Oct Mon–Sat 9.30am–5pm, Sun 11am–4pm; Nov–March Mon–Sat 9.30am–4.30pm; ☎01434 652220, ⓦvisithadrianswall.co.uk).

**13**

## ACCOMMODATION

**Hallbank** Hallgate, behind the Old Gaol ☎01434 605567, ⓦhallbankguesthouse.com. A restored house in a quiet town-centre location, with eight very comfortable rooms and an associated coffee shop/restaurant. Evening meals available on request. **£90**

**Matfen Hall** Matfen, 10 miles northeast of Hexham ☎01661 886500, ⓦmatfenhall.com. Large, ritzy country hotel surrounded by acres of green parkland harbouring a golf course and driving range. There's a spa and a good, fine dining restaurant. It's a popular spot for weddings. **£185**

## EATING AND DRINKING

★**Bouchon Bistrot** 4 Gilesgate ☎01434 609943, ⓦbouchonbistrot.co.uk. Very stylish restaurant in a handsome terraced townhouse, serving sophisticated French dishes such as lamb shank "de 5 heures" with sautéed potatoes (£15.50) and crème caramel with *langues du chat* (£4.95). Tues–Sat noon–2pm & 6–9.30pm.

**Dipton Mill Inn** Dipton Mill Rd, 2 miles south of Hexham ☎01434 606577, ⓦdiptonmill.co.uk. A lovely, traditional country pub covered in ivy. While the food is excellent – good pub grub like steak and kidney pie and vegetable casserole – it's most famous for the home-brewed ales, made at Hexhamshire Brewery. Try Old

Humbug, named after the landlord. Mon–Sat noon–2.30pm & 6–11pm, Sun noon–3pm.

★**Rat Inn** Anick, 2 miles northeast of Hexham ☎01434 602814, ⓦtheratinn.com. In a glorious hillside location overlooking Hexham, this quaint pub has a roaring fire in winter and a pretty summer garden. The food is all locally sourced – try the braised local beef in Allendale beer (£10.50). Booking essential for Sunday lunch. On Mondays in summer there are fresh sandwiches available for lunch (from £3.95). April–Sept daily noon–11pm; Oct–March Mon–Fri noon–3pm & 6–11pm.

# Northumberland National Park

Northwest Northumberland, the great triangular chunk of land between Hadrian's Wall and the coastal plain, is dominated by the wide-skied landscapes of **Northumberland National Park** (ⓦnorthumberlandnationalpark.org.uk), whose four hundred windswept square miles rise to the Cheviot Hills on the Scottish border. The bulk of the Park is taken up by **Kielder Water and Forest nature reserve**, a superb destination for watersports and outdoor activities; the small town of **Bellingham** on the eastern edge of the park makes a good base for the reserve, as do **Rothbury** and **Wooler**, both of which also provide easy access to some superb walking in the craggy **Cheviot Hills**.

## Kielder Water and Forest

Surrounded by 250 acres of dense pine forest **Kielder Water** is the largest reservoir in England. The road from Bellingham follows the North Tyne River west and skirts the forested edge of the lake, passing an assortment of visitor centres, waterside parks, picnic areas and anchorages that fringe its southern shore. Mountain biking, hiking, horseriding and fishing are some of the land-based activities on offer, and of course watersports (waterskiing, sailing, kayaking and windsurfing) are hugely popular, too. The mass of woodlands and wetlands means that **wildlife** is abundant – you might spot badgers, deer, otters, ospreys and red squirrels. **Leaplish Waterside Park**, on the western flank of the reservoir, is the best place to head if you're visiting for the first time and need to get your bearings.

### Leaplish Waterside Park

Birds of Prey Centre daily 10.30am–4pm • Flying demonstrations summer 1.30pm & 3pm, Oct–March 2pm • £7 • ☎01434 250400, ⓦkwbopc.com

**Leaplish Waterside Park** is a purpose-built hub of lodges (see opposite) with cafés and a restaurant, a visitor centre (see opposite) and a Birds of Prey Centre where you can see a variety of handsome, sharp-taloned beasts, from owls and falcons to vultures and some inscrutable ospreys.

## ARRIVAL AND INFORMATION

**By bus** The #880 from Hexham serves the visitor centres of Tower Knowe, Leaplish (by request) and Kielder Castle via Bellingham (2 daily Tues & Sat). The #714 from Newcastle upon Tyne runs on Sundays (1 daily) to Tower Knowe, Leaplish (by request) and Kielder Castle.

**Visitor centres** Tower Knowe: from Bellingham, the first

## KIELDER WATER AND FOREST

visitor centre you come to as you head anti-clockwise round the reservoir (daily: April–June & Sept 10am–5pm; July & Aug 10am–6pm; Oct 10am–4pm; ☎0845 155 0236); Leaplish: western flank of the reservoir (Feb–Oct daily 9am–5pm; ☎01434 251000); Kielder Castle: at the northernmost point of the reservoir (daily 10am–5pm; ☎01434 250209).

## GETTING AROUND

**By bike** Purple Mountain (April–Oct 9am–5pm; Nov–March Sat & Sun 9am–5pm; ☎01434 250532, ⓦpurplemountain .co.uk) and the Bike Place (Mon–Sat 10am–6pm; ☎0845 634 1895, ⓦthebikeplace.co.uk) are both near Kielder Castle Visitor Centre, and both offer day rental from £20.

**By car** The nearest petrol station is in Bellingham (14 miles away; closed Sun). For parking, you can buy one ticket at

your first stop (£4) that's valid for all other car parks throughout the day.

**By ferry** The 74-seater Osprey Ferry (☎01434 251000) sails round the reservoir, with stops at Leaplish, Tower Knowe and Belvedere. Tickets (day pass £6.75, short journeys from £4.40) are available at Tower Knowe or Leaplish; prior booking is necessary.

## ACCOMMODATION AND EATING

**Hollybush Inn** Greenhaugh, 12 miles east of Kielder Water ☎01434 240391, ⓦhollybushinn.net. Super little pub in a remote village serving great ales and food, and with four simple and attractive bedrooms upstairs. **£65**

**Kielder Lodges** Leaplish Waterside Park ☎0870 240 3549, or Hoseasons ☎01502 502588, ⓦhoseasons .co.uk. Scandinavian-style self-catering lodges, all with access to the park's pool, sauna, bar and restaurant. Bring plenty of midge repellent. Weekly rates from **£335**

★**Pheasant Inn** Stannersburn ☎01434 240382, ⓦthepheasantinn.com. A traditional country pub on the

road from Bellingham, the *Pheasant Inn* has eight very comfortable bedrooms (including one family room). The highlight is the food, though, served downstairs in the cosy restaurant; expect game pies, Northumbrian cheeses and plenty of fish (mains around £12 in the evening). Booking recommended. Restaurant daily 8–9am & 7–9pm; bar meals noon–2pm & 7–9pm. **£85**

**YHA Kielder** Butteryhaugh, Kielder village ☎0845 371 9126, ⓦyha.org.uk. Well-equipped activity-based hostel, with some two- and three-bedded rooms plus small dorms. Dorms **£16.40**, family rooms **£34.95**

# Rothbury and around

**ROTHBURY**, straddling the River Coquet thirty miles northeast of Hexham, prospered as a late Victorian resort because it gave ready access to the forests, burns and ridges of the **Simonside Hills**. The small town remains a popular spot for walkers, with several of the best local trails beginning from the **Simonside Hills** car park, a couple of miles southwest of Rothbury. Nearby, the estates of **Cragside** and **Wallington** are good options if you want to take a break from hiking.

## Cragside

1 mile east of Rothbury • House: March–Oct Sat & Sun 11am–5pm, Tues & Fri 1–5pm; gardens: March–Oct 10am–7pm • £15.85, gardens only £9.25; NT • ☎01669 620333, ⓦnationaltrust.org.uk/cragside

Victorian Rothbury was dominated by Sir William, later the first Lord Armstrong, the wealthy nineteenth-century arms manufacturer, shipbuilder and engineer who built his country home at **Cragside**, a mile to the east of the village. He hired Richard Norman Shaw, one of the period's top architects, who produced a grandiose Tudor-style mansion entirely out of place in the Northumbrian countryside. Armstrong was an avid innovator, and in 1880 Cragside became the first house in the world to be lit by hydroelectric power. The surrounding **gardens**, complete with the remains of the original pumping system, are beautiful and there's a pleasant tearoom for a light snack.

## Wallington

13 miles south of Rothbury • House: March–Oct Mon & Wed–Fri 1–5pm, Sat & Sun 11am–5pm; gardens: daily 10am–7pm • £9.70, gardens only £6.70; NT • ☎01670 773967, ⓦnationaltrust.org.uk/wallington

**13**

South of Rothbury, down the B6342, stands **Wallington**, an ostentatious mansion rebuilt in the 1740s by Sir Walter Blackett, the coal- and lead-mine owner. The house is known for its Rococo plasterwork and William Bell Scott's Pre-Raphaelite murals of scenes from Northumbrian history. Children will love the collection of dolls' houses, one of which has thirty-six rooms and was originally fitted with running water and a working lift. However, it's the magnificent **gardens and grounds** that are the real delight, with lawns, woods and lakes laced with footpaths. There are events, concerts and activities throughout the year, as well as a café and farm shop on site.

### ARRIVAL AND INFORMATION

**By bus** Buses from Newcastle stop outside the *Queen's Head* pub in the centre (hourly; 1hr 20min).
**National Park Visitor Centre** Near the cross on Church

### ROTHBURY AND AROUND

Street (April–Oct daily 10am–5pm; Nov–March Sat & Sun 10am–3pm; ☎01669 620887, ⓦtheheartof northumberland.co.uk).

### ACCOMMODATION

★**Hillcrest** 200yd from Rothbury centre ☎01669 621944, ⓦhillcrestbandb.co.uk. Superb B&B in a pretty Georgian house, with two beautifully decorated bedrooms – wooden floorboards, antique furniture, exposed walls and the like – with an intriguing past (the owner will explain). Wonderful breakfasts, too. **£75**
**Thistleyhaugh** Longframlington, 5 miles east of Rothbury ☎01665 570629, ⓦthistleyhaugh.co.uk.

Gorgeous, ivy-smothered Georgian farmhouse with five luxurious chintzy bedrooms. They serve delicious three-course dinners (7pm; £20) and hearty breakfasts. **£80**
★**Tosson Tower** Great Tosson, 2 miles southwest of Rothbury ☎01669 620228, ⓦtossontowerfarm.com. Eight lovely rooms on this little working farm in a quiet hamlet with spectacular views out over the Cheviot Hills. Plus some charming self-catering cottages. **£80**

## Wooler and around

Stone-terraced **WOOLER** – rebuilt after a terrible fire in the 1860s – is a one-street market town twenty miles north of Rothbury. It's the best base for climbs up **the Cheviot** (2674ft), seven miles to the southwest and the highest point in the Cheviot Hills. From *Wooler Youth Hostel* at 30 Cheviot St, it's four hours there and back; from Hawsen Burn, the nearest navigable point, it's two hours walking there and back. Wooler is also a staging-post on the Pennine Way and the lovely **St Cuthbert's Way** (from Melrose in Scotland to Lindisfarne).

### Chillingham Castle

6 miles southeast of Wooler • April–Oct Sun–Fri noon–5pm • £9 • ☎01668 215359, ⓦchillingham-castle.com
**Chillingham Castle** started life as an eleventh-century tower. The castle was augmented at regular intervals until the nineteenth century, but from 1933 was largely left to the elements for fifty years, until the present owner set about restoring it in his own individualistic way: bedrooms, living rooms and even a grisly torture chamber (designed to "cause maximum shock") are decorated with historical paraphernalia.

### Chillingham Wild Cattle

Off the A697 between Alnwick and Belford, signposted The Wild White Cattle • April–Oct Mon–Fri tours hourly 10am–noon, 2pm–4pm, Sun 2pm, 3pm & 4pm; winter by appointment • £15 • ⓦchillinghamwildcattle.com

> ### TOP 5 NORTHUMBRIAN CASTLES
> **Alnwick Castle** See p.670
> **Bamburgh Castle** See p.673
> **Chillingham Castle** See above
> **Dunstanburgh Castle** See p.671
> **Warkworth Castle** See opposite

In 1220, Chillingham Castle's adjoining 365 acres of parkland were enclosed to protect the local wild cattle for hunting and food. And so the **Chillingham Wild Cattle** – a fierce, primeval herd with white coats, black muzzles and black tips to their horns – have remained to this day, cut off from mixing with domesticated breeds. It's possible to visit these unique relics, who number around ninety, but only in the company of a warden, as the animals are potentially dangerous and need to be protected from outside infection. The visit takes about two hours and involves a short country walk before viewing the cattle at a safe distance – the closest you're likely to get to big game viewing in England. Bring strong shoes or walking boots if it's wet.

### ARRIVAL AND INFORMATION

**By bus** The bus station is set back off High Street.
**Destinations** Alnwick (Mon–Sat 9 daily; 45min); Berwick-upon-Tweed (Mon–Sat 9 daily; 50min).
**Tourist office** Cheviot Centre, Padgepool Place (leaflets

### WOOLER AND AROUND

and accommodation information available Mon–Fri 9am–5pm; staffed desk Easter–Oct daily 10am–4.30pm; Nov–March Sat & Sun 10am–2pm; ☎01668 282123).

### ACCOMMODATION AND EATING

**Milan** 2 High St, through the arch of the Black Bull hotel ☎01668 283692, ⓦmilan-restaurant.co.uk. Good-value Italian restaurant with exposed brick walls and a jolly ambience, serving large pizzas (from £6.75), pasta dishes (from £7.95) and plenty of meat and fish options. It's a very popular place, so book ahead. Daily 5–10pm.

**Tilldale House** 34 High St ☎01668 281450, ⓦtilldalehouse.co.uk. Snug seventeenth-century stone cottage in the middle of town with three en-suite bedrooms. With enormous, soft beds, deep-pile carpets, an open fire and great breakfasts, it makes a very cosy and enticing base after a long day hiking in the hills. **£58**

# The Northumberland coast

Stretching 64 miles north of Newcastle up to the Scottish border, the low-lying **Northumberland coast** is the region's shining star, stunningly beautiful and packed with impressive sights. Here you'll find the mighty fortresses at **Warkworth**, **Alnwick** and **Bamburgh** and the magnificent Elizabethan ramparts surrounding **Berwick-upon-Tweed**, while in between there are glorious sandy beaches as well as the site of the Lindisfarne monastery on **Holy Island** and the seabird and nature reserve of the **Farne Islands**, reached by boat from Seahouses.

## Warkworth

**WARKWORTH**, a peaceful coastal hamlet set in a loop of the River Coquet a couple of miles from Amble, is best seen from the north, from where the grey stone terraces of the long main street slope up towards the commanding remains of **Warkworth Castle**. From the castle, the main street sweeps down into the village, flattening out at Dial Place and the Church of St Lawrence before curving right to cross the River Coquet; just over the bridge, a signposted quarter-mile lane leads to the **beach**, which stretches for five miles from Amble to Alnmouth.

### Warkworth Castle

April–Oct daily 10am–5pm; rest of the year limited opening hours, call before visiting; Duke's Rooms Wed, Sun & bank hols • £5.20; EH • ☎01665 711423, ⓦenglish-heritage.org.uk

Ruined but well-preserved, **Warkworth Castle** has Norman origins, but was constructed using sandstone during the fourteenth and fifteenth centuries. Home to generations of the Percy family, the powerful earls of Northumberland, it appears as a backdrop in several scenes of Shakespeare's *Henry IV, Part II*. The cross-shaped keep contains a great hall, a chapel, kitchens, storerooms and the Duke's Rooms, which are kitted out in period furniture and furnishings.

### Warkworth Hermitage

Weather permitting April–Sept Wed & Sun 11am–5pm; rest of the year limited opening hours, call before visiting • Combined ticket with castle; EH • ☎01665 711423, ⓦenglish-heritage.org.uk

**13**

A path from the churchyard heads along the right bank of the Coquet to the boat that shuttles visitors across to **Warkworth Hermitage**, a series of simple rooms and a claustrophobic chapel that were hewn out of the cliff above the river some time in the fourteenth century, but abandoned by 1567. The last resident hermit, one George Lancaster, was charged by the sixth earl of Northumberland to pray for his noble family, for which lonesome duty he received around £15 a year and a barrel of fish every Sunday.

### ARRIVAL                                        WARKWORTH

**By bus** The easiest way to get here by public transport is by train to Alnmouth, followed by the bus (hourly; 30min).

## Alnmouth

It's three miles north from Warkworth to the seaside resort of **ALNMOUTH**, whose narrow centre is strikingly situated on a steep spur of land between the sea and the estuary of the Aln. It's a lovely setting and has been a low-key holiday spot since Victorian times, and is particularly popular with golfers: the village's nine-hole course, right on the coast, was built in 1869 (it's claimed to be the second oldest in the country) and dune-strollers really do have to heed the "Danger – Flying Golf Balls" signs which adorn Marine Road.

### ARRIVAL AND DEPARTURE                                    ALNMOUTH

**By train** Trains pass through from Berwick to the north (every 2hr; 20min) and Newcastle to the south (hourly; 30min).

**By bus** There are local bus services from Alnwick and Warkworth, and the regular #X18 Newcastle–Alnwick bus also passes through Alnmouth and calls at its train station, 1.5 miles west of the centre.

### ACCOMMODATION AND EATING

**Red Lion** 22 Northumberland St ☎01668 30584, ⓦredlionalnmouth.com. Six spacious and modern rooms, with pine furniture, cream walls and fresh bathrooms, above a popular, traditional pub. The beer garden is perfect for sunny days, and the menu has everything from big open sandwiches (from £4.95) to sirloin steak (£17.50). **£85**

## Alnwick

The appealing market town of **ALNWICK** (pronounced "Annick"), thirty miles north of Newcastle and four miles inland from Alnmouth, is renowned for its **castle** and gardens – seat of the dukes of Northumberland – which overlook the River Aln. It's worth spending a couple of days here, exploring the medieval maze of streets, the elegant gatehouses on Pottergate and Bondgate and the best **bookshop** in the north.

### Alnwick Castle

April–Oct daily 10am–6pm • £14.50; castle and garden £22 • ☎01665 511100, ⓦ alnwickcastle.com

The Percys – who were raised to the dukedom of Northumberland in 1750 – have owned **Alnwick Castle** since 1309. In the eighteenth century, the first duke had the interior refurbished by Robert Adam in an extravagant Gothic style – which in turn was supplanted by the gaudy Italianate decoration preferred by the fourth duke in the 1850s. There's plenty to see inside, including remains from Pompeii, though the **interior** can be crowded at times – not least with families on the *Harry Potter* trail, since the castle doubled as Hogwarts School in the first two films.

### Alnwick Garden

Daily 10am–6pm; Grand Cascade and Poison Garden closed in winter • £13.75; garden and castle £26.25 • ☎01665 511350, ⓦ alnwickgarden.com

The grounds of the castle are taken up by the huge and beautiful **Alnwick Garden**, designed by an innovative Belgian team and full of quirky features such as a bamboo labyrinth maze, a serpent garden involving topiary snakes, and the popular **Poison Garden**, filled with the world's deadliest plants. The heart of the garden is the computerized Grand Cascade, which shoots water jets in a regular synchronized display, while to the west is Europe's largest treehouse with a restaurant within (see below). The walled Roots and Shoots community veg garden (no ticket required) is a delight.

### Barter Books

Wagonway Rd • April–Sept daily 9am–7pm; Oct–March Mon–Wed & Fri–Sun 9am–5pm, Thurs 9am–7pm • ☎ 01665 604888, ⓦ barterbooks.co.uk

Housed in the Victorian train station on Wagonway Road, and containing visible remnants of the ticket office, passenger waiting rooms and the outbound platform, the enchanting **Barter Books** is one of the largest secondhand bookshops in England. With its sofas, murals, open fire, coffee and biscuits – and, best of all, a model train that runs on top of the stacks – it is definitely worth a visit.

### ARRIVAL AND INFORMATION ALNWICK

**By bus** The station is on Clayport St, a couple of minutes' walk west of the marketplace.
Destinations Bamburgh (Mon–Sat 7 daily, Sun 4 daily; 1hr 15min); Berwick-upon-Tweed (Mon–Sat 6 daily, Sun 3 daily; 1hr); Craster (Mon–Fri 7 daily, Sat 4 daily; 35min); Wooler (Mon–Sat 9 daily; 45min).

**Tourist office** 2 The Shambles, off the marketplace (April–June & Sept–Oct Mon–Sat 9.30am–5pm, Sun 10am–4pm; July & Aug daily 9am–5pm; Nov–March Mon–Fri 9.30am–4.30pm, Sat 10am–4pm; ☎ 01665 511 333, ⓦ visitalnwick.org.uk).

### ACCOMMODATION

**Tate House** 11 Bondgate Without ☎ 01665 660800, ⓦ stayinalnwick.co.uk. In a pretty Victorian house opposite Alnwick Gardens, this B&B has three comfortable bedrooms with spotless bathrooms and nice little touches such as hot-water bottles, iPod docks and DVD players. **£75**

**YHA Alnwick** 4–38 Green Batt ☎ 01665 604661, ⓦ yha .org.uk. A handsome Victorian courthouse nicely converted into a hostel with some private rooms. You're a stroll away form the gardens and castle, and there's a bus stop right outside the front door. Dorms **£18.50**, doubles **£39**

### EATING

**Alnwick Garden Treehouse** Alnwick Gardens ☎ 01665 511852, ⓦ alnwickgarden.com. Glorious restaurant in the enormous treehouse in Alnwick Gardens (you don't have to pay the garden entry fee to visit). There's an open fire in the middle of the room and even tree trunks growing through the floor. Simple meals (sandwiches, quiche and soup) for lunch and in the evening, expensive but tasty mains – honey-glazed duck with braised red cabbage (£18.50) for example, and a refreshing kirsch and blackcurrant sorbet

(£4.95) for pudding. Mon–Wed 11.30am–2.45pm, Thurs–Sun 11.30am–2.45pm & 6.30pm–late.
**Station Buffet Barter Books** Wagonway Road ☎ 01665 604888, ⓦ barterbooks.co.uk. Set in the old station waiting room at Barter Books this unique café serves home-made food including hamburgers, sandwiches, salads and cakes (meals around £7). April–Sept daily 9am–7pm; Oct–March Mon–Wed & Fri–Sun 9am–5pm, Thurs 9am–7pm.

## Craster and around

The tiny fishing village of **CRASTER** – known for its kippers – lies six miles northeast of Alnwick, right on the coast. It's a delightful little place, with its circular, barnacle-encrusted harbour walls fronting a cluster of tough, weather-battered little houses and the cheery *Jolly Fisherman* pub. Other villages worth visiting round here include **Newton-on-Sea** and **Beadnell**, both exuding wind-swept, salty charm. The **coastline** between Dunstanburgh and Beadnell is made up of the long sandy beaches Northumberland is famous for.

### Dunstanburgh Castle

April–Sept daily 10am–5pm; Oct daily 10am–4pm; Nov–March Mon & Thurs–Sun 10am–4pm • £4.30; NT & EH • ☎ 01665 576231, ⓦ nationaltrust.org.uk/dunstanburgh-castle/

Looming in the distance, about a thirty-minute walk northwards up the coast from

**13**

Craster, is stunning **Dunstanburgh Castle**. Built in the fourteenth century, in the wake of civil war, its shattered remains occupy a magnificent promontory, bordered by sheer cliffs and crashing waves.

| ARRIVAL | CRASTER AND AROUND |
|---|---|

**By bus** Bus #18 runs from Alnwick to Craster every 2hr (30min).

## ACCOMMODATION

**Old Rectory** Howick, 2 miles south ☎ 01665 577590, ⓦ oldrectoryhowick.co.uk. Just 400yds from the wind-whipped North Sea, this fantastic B&B sits in its own peaceful grounds and has extremely pretty bedrooms and comfortable sitting areas. Superb breakfasts feature plenty of cooked options, including Craster kippers. **£90**

## EATING AND DRINKING

There's not much in the way of fine dining round these parts; most villages simply have a traditional pub serving decent meals. Craster's beloved **kippers** are smoked at L. Robson & Sons (☎ 01665 576223, ⓦ kipper.co.uk) in the centre of the village; they also sell salty oak-smoked salmon.

**Jolly Fisherman** 9 Haven Hill ☎ 01665 576461. Just above the harbour, this pub has sea views from its back window and a lovely summer beer garden. Not surprisingly for a pub opposite L. Robson & Sons, it serves plenty of fish – crab sandwiches, kipper pâté and a famously good crabmeat, whisky and cream soup. Mon–Fri 11am–3pm & 7–11pm, Sat & Sun 11am–11pm.

**Ship Inn** Low Newton-by-the-Sea, 5 miles north ☎ 01665 576262, ⓦ shipinnnewton.co.uk. Great, rustic pub in a coastal hamlet serving dishes using ingredients from local suppliers – there's plenty of L. Robson smoked fish on the menu. Mains from £7. Ales are supplied by their own brewery next door. Dinner reservations advised. Mon–Sat 11.30am–11pm, Sun 11am–11pm.

# Seahouses and the Farne Islands

Around ten miles north from Craster, beyond the small village of Beadnell, lies the fishing port of **SEAHOUSES**, the only place on the local coast that could remotely be described as a resort. It's the embarkation point for boat trips out to the wind-swept **Farne Islands**, a rocky archipelago lying a few miles offshore.

## The Farne Islands

Owned by the National Trust and maintained as a nature reserve, the **Farne Islands** (ⓦ farne-islands.com) are the summer home of hundreds of thousands of migrating seabirds, notably puffins, guillemots, terns, eider ducks and kittiwakes, and home to the only grey seal colony on the English coastline. A number of boat trips potter around the islands – the largest of which is Inner Farne – offering birdwatching tours, grey seal-watching tours and the Grace Darling tour, which takes visitors to the lighthouse on Longstone Island, where the famed local heroine (see opposite) lived.

| ARRIVAL AND INFORMATION | SEAHOUSES AND THE FARNE ISLANDS |
|---|---|

**By bus** Buses run from Alnwick to Craster every 2hr (1hr).
**By boat** Weather permitting, several operators in Seahouses run daily boat trips (2–3hr; from £13) starting at around 10am. Wander down to the quayside, or contact either the National Trust Shop or the tourist office (see below). During the breeding season (May–July) landings are restricted to morning trips to Staple Island and afternoons to Inner Farne. Landing fees for the islands are payable to the National Trust (£5–6).
**Tourist information** National Trust Shop, 16 Main Street (☎ 01665 721099), by the Seahouses traffic roundabout. The tourist office is located in the main car park.

## ACCOMMODATION

★**St Cuthberts** Seahouses ☎ 01665 720456, ⓦ stcuthbertshouse.com. Award-winning B&B in a beautifully converted 200-year-old chapel. Rooms cleverly incorporate period features like the original arched windows with lovely modern touches such as wet rooms, flatscreen TVs, comfy dressing gowns and slippers. Breakfast is all locally sourced, from the sausages and the eggs to the kippers and the honey. **£105**

# Bamburgh

**13**

One-time capital of Northumbria, the little village of **BAMBURGH** (ⓦbamburgh.org
.uk), just three miles from Seahouses, lies in the lee of its magnificent **castle**. Attractive
stone cottages – holding the village shop, a café, pubs and B&Bs – flank each side of
the triangular green, and at the top of the village on Radcliffe Road is the diminutive
**Grace Darling Museum**. From behind the castle it's a brisk, five-minute walk to two
splendid sandy **beaches**, backed by rolling, tufted dunes.

## Bamburgh Castle

April–Oct daily 11am–5pm • £9.95 • ☎ 01668 214515, ⓦ bamburghcastle.com

Solid and chunky, **Bamburgh Castle** is a spectacular sight, its elongated battlements
crowning a formidable basalt crag high above the beach. Its origins lie in Anglo-Saxon
times, but it suffered a centuries-long decline – rotted by sea spray and buffeted by winter
storms, the castle was bought by Lord Armstrong (of Rothbury's Cragside; see p.667) in
1894, who demolished most of the structure to replace it with a hybrid castle-mansion.
Inside there's plenty to explore, including the sturdy keep that houses an unnerving
armoury packed with vicious-looking pikes, halberds, helmets and muskets; the King's
Hall, with its marvellous teak ceiling that was imported from Siam (Thailand) and carved
in Victorian times; and a medieval kitchen complete with original jugs, pots and pans.

## Grace Darling Museum

Radcliffe Rd • Easter–Oct daily 10am–5pm; Oct–Easter Tues–Sun 10am–4pm • Free • ☎ 01668 214910, ⓦ rnli.org.uk

The **Grace Darling Museum** celebrates the life of famed local heroine Grace Darling. In
September 1838, a gale dashed the steamship *Forfarshire* against the rocks of the Farne
Islands. Nine passengers struggled onto a reef where they were subsequently saved by Grace
and her lighthouseman father, William, who left the safety of the Longstone lighthouse to
row out to them. *The Times* trumpeted Grace's bravery, offers of marriage and requests for
locks of her hair streamed into the Darlings' lighthouse home, and for the rest of her brief
life Grace was plagued by unwanted visitors – she died of tuberculosis aged 26 in 1842,
and was buried in Bamburgh, in the churchyard of the thirteenth-century St Aidan's.

### ARRIVAL AND DEPARTURE
### BAMBURGH

**By bus** A regular bus service links Alnwick and Berwick-upon-
Tweed with Bamburgh, stopping on Front Street by the green.
Destinations Alnwick (Mon–Sat 7 daily, Sun 5 daily; 1hr

15min); Berwick-upon-Tweed (Mon–Sat 3 daily, Sun 2 daily;
40min); Craster (Mon–Sat 7 daily, Sun 5 daily; 30–40min);
Seahouses (Mon–Sat 7 daily, Sun 5 daily; 10min).

### ACCOMMODATION AND EATING

**Copper Kettle** 21 Front St ☎01668 14315,
ⓦcopperkettletearooms.com. Sweet little tearoom,
with a sunny sitting area out the back, serving tasty cakes,
teas and coffees – try the fruit loaf or the tempting carrot
cake with icing. Also light meals such as sandwiches (£5),
jacket potatoes (£6.50) and pies (£6). Daily 10am–6pm.

**Victoria Hotel** Front St ☎01668 214431,
ⓦvictoriahotel.net. This smart boutique hotel has
elegant rooms in a variety of sizes – one with lovely castle
views – a couple of relaxing bars and a more expensive
brasserie (dinner only). Rates include breakfast. **£80**

# Holy Island

It's a dramatic approach to **HOLY ISLAND** (ⓦwww.lindisfarne.org.uk), past the barnacle-
encrusted marker poles that line the three-mile-long causeway. Topped with a stumpy
**castle**, the island is small (just 1.5 miles by one), sandy and bare, and in winter it can
be bleak, but come summer day-trippers clog the car parks as soon as the causeway is
open. Even then, though, Lindisfarne has a distinctive and isolated atmosphere. Give
the place time and, if you can, stay overnight, when you'll be able to see the historic
remains without hundreds of others cluttering the views. The island's surrounding tidal
mud flats, salt marshes and dunes have been designated a **nature reserve**.

**13**

## Brief history

It was on **Lindisfarne** (as the island was once known) that St Aidan of Iona founded a monastery at the invitation of King Oswald of Northumbria in 634. The monks quickly established a reputation for scholarship and artistry, the latter exemplified by the **Lindisfarne Gospels**, the apotheosis of Celtic religious art, now kept in the British Library. The monastery had sixteen bishops in all, the most celebrated being the reluctant **St Cuthbert**, who never settled here – within two years, he was back in his hermit's cell on the Farne Islands, where he died in 687. His colleagues rowed the body back to Lindisfarne, which became a place of pilgrimage until 875, when the monks abandoned the island in fear of marauding Vikings, taking Cuthbert's remains with them.

## Lindisfarne Priory

Priory & museum April–Sept daily 10am–6pm; Oct daily 10am–5pm; Nov–Jan & March Sat & Sun 10am–4pm; Feb daily 10am–4pm • £5.40; EH • ☎ 01289 389200, ⊛ english-heritage.org.uk

Just off the village green, the tranquil, pinkish sandstone ruins of **Lindisfarne Priory** date from the Benedictine foundation. The **museum** next door displays a collection of incised stones that constitute all that remains of the first monastery.

## Lindisfarne Castle

March–Oct Tues–Sun, hours vary according to tide but always include noon–3pm; Jan & Feb Sat & Sun 10am–3pm • £7.40; NT • ☎ 01289 389244, ⊛ nationaltrust.org.uk/lindisfarne-castle

Stuck on a small pyramid of rock half a mile away from the village, **Lindisfarne Castle** was built in the middle of the sixteenth century to protect the island's harbour from the Scots. It was, however, merely a decaying shell when Edward Hudson, the founder of *Country Life* magazine, stumbled across it in 1901. He promptly commissioned Edwin Lutyens (1869–1944) to turn it into an Edwardian country house, and installed a charming walled garden in the castle's former vegetable gardens, to designs by Gertrude Jekyll.

### ARRIVAL AND INFORMATION                                                    HOLY ISLAND

**By bus** The #477 bus from Berwick-upon-Tweed to Holy Island (35min) is something of a law unto itself given the interfering tides, but basically service is daily in August and twice-weekly the rest of the year.
**Crossing the causeway** The island is cut off for about

5hr a day. Consult tide timetables at a tourist office, in the local paper or at ⊛ lindisfarne.org.uk
**Castle shuttle** A minibus trundles the half a mile to the castle from the main car park, The Chare (every 20min 10.20am–4.20pm; £1).

### ACCOMMODATION AND EATING

Due to the size of the island and the small number of B&Bs, it's imperative to **book in advance** if you're staying overnight.

★**Bamburgh View** Fenkle St ☎ 01289 389212, ✉ bamburghview@btinternet.com. Sweet, friendly B&B very near the priory, with three airy, wood-floored rooms, good showers and generous breakfasts. **£85**
**Café Beangoose** Selby House ☎ 01289 389083, ⊛ cafebeangoose.co.uk. Overlooking the green, this excellent restaurant is in a family home, its small rooms complete with knick-knacks and snoozing cats. Meals are hearty and locally sourced: braised beef, sea trout and the like for around £11. Holiday cottages available (£885/ week). May–Oct daily dinner; hours depend on tides.

**St Aidan's Winery** In the modern building behind the green ☎ 01289 389230 ⊛ lindisfarne-mead.co.uk. If you're keen to sample some of the world-famous Lindisfarne mead, this is the place to come. They also sell home-made chutneys, biscuits and jams. Hours depend on tides.
**The Ship** Marygate ☎ 01289 389311. The best pub on the island; friendly and traditional, with open fires and wood-panelled walls. The ales are good, as is the inexpensive pub grub. They have four cosy, en-suite rooms upstairs. **£104**

# Berwick-upon-Tweed

Before the union of the English and Scottish crowns in 1603, **BERWICK-UPON-TWEED**, twelve miles north of Holy Island, was the quintessential frontier town, changing hands no fewer than fourteen times between 1174 and 1482, when the Scots finally ceded the stronghold to the English. Interminable cross-border warfare ruined Berwick's economy, turning the prosperous Scottish port of the thirteenth century into an impoverished English garrison town. By the late sixteenth century, Berwick's fortifications were in a dreadful state and Elizabeth I, fearing the resurgent alliance between France and Scotland, had the place rebuilt in line with the latest principles of military architecture. Berwick was reborn as an important seaport between 1750 and 1820, and is still peppered with elegant **Georgian mansions** dating from that period.

Berwick's **walls** – one and a half miles long and still in pristine condition – are no more than 20ft high but incredibly thick. They are now the town's major attraction; it's possible to walk the mile-long circuit (1hr) round them, allowing for wonderful views out to sea, across the Tweed and over the orange-tiled rooftops of the town. Protected by ditches on three sides and the Tweed on the fourth, the walls are strengthened by immense bastions.

## Barracks

April–Sept Mon–Fri 10am–6pm; Oct–March limited opening hours • £4.20; EH • ☎ 01289 304493, ⓦ english-heritage.org.uk

The town's finely proportioned **Barracks**, designed by Nicholas Hawksmoor (1717) functioned as a garrison until 1964, when the King's Own Scottish Borderers regiment decamped. Inside there's the rather specialist **By the Beat of the Drum** exhibition, tracing the lives of British infantrymen from the Civil War to World War I, as well as the King's Own Scottish Borderers Museum, the Berwick Borough Museum and the **Gymnasium Gallery** of contemporary art.

### ARRIVAL AND INFORMATION                    BERWICK-UPON-TWEED

**By train** From the train station it's a 10min walk down Castlegate and Marygate to the town centre.
Destinations Durham (every 30min; 1hr 10min); Edinburgh (hourly; 45min); Newcastle (hourly; 45min).
**By bus** Most regional buses stop on Golden Square (where Castlegate meets Marygate), though some may also stop in front of the train station.
Destinations Bamburgh (Mon–Sat 6 daily, Sun 2 daily; 40min); Holy Island (Aug 2 daily, rest of the year 2 weekly; 35min); Newcastle (Mon–Sat 7 daily; 2hr 15min); Wooler (Mon–Sat 9 daily; 50min).

**Tourist office** 106 Marygate (April, May & Oct Mon–Sat 10am–5pm; June–Sept Mon–Sat 10am–5pm & Sun 11am–3pm; Nov–March Mon–Sat 10am–4pm; ☎ 01289 330733).
**Tours** The tourist office can book you onto a walking tour of town (Easter–Oct Mon–Fri 2 daily; £4.50; ⓦ explore -northumberland.co.uk) or onto the Hidden Berwick tour (April–Sept Sun–Fri, 1 daily; £6), which includes entry into an eighteenth-century gun bastion not usually open to the public.

### ACCOMMODATION

**No.1 Sallyport** Bridge St ☎ 01289 308827, ⓦ sallyport.co.uk. Berwick's most luxurious B&B, with six sensational rooms in a seventeenth-century house. The two spacious doubles and four lavish suites (£40 more) are elegantly furnished. They also have a little café full of delicious goodies, and serve simple dinners in the evenings. __£110__
**Queen's Head** 6 Sandgate ☎ 01289 307852, ⓦ queensheadberwick.co.uk. One of the best pubs in

town has six snug rooms, including a family room. Great evening meals and breakfasts, too (mains around £15). __£90__
**YHA Berwick** Dewars Lane ☎ 0845 371 9676, ⓦ yha .org.uk. Set in a remarkable eighteenth-century granary building which, thanks to a fire in 1815, has a lean greater than the Leaning Tower of Pisa. Thirteen en-suite rooms, some private and family, plus a bistro and gallery. Dorms __£18__, doubles __£78__

### EATING, DRINKING AND ENTERTAINMENT

**Barrel's Ale** 59 Bridge St ☎ 01289 308013, ⓦ thebarrels.co.uk. Atmospheric pub specializing in (frequently changing) cask ales, lagers and stouts. It's also a great music venue, hosting an eclectic mix of jazz, blues, rock and indie bands. Mon–Thurs noon–11.30pm, Fri–

Sat noon–1am, Sun noon–midnight.
**The Maltings** Eastern Lane ☎ 01289 330999, ⓦ maltingsberwick.co.uk. Berwick's arts centre has a year-round programme of music, theatre, comedy, film and dance and a licensed café.

TOURISTS AT STONEHENGE, C. 1900

# Contexts

# History

England's history is long and densely woven. From obscure beginnings, England came to play a leading role in European affairs and more latterly, with the expansion of the British Empire, the whole globe. What follows is therefore a necessarily brief introduction: we have offered some more detailed accounts in our "Books" section (see p.703).

## The Stone Age

England has been inhabited for the best part of half a million years, though the earliest archeological evidence, dating from around 250,000 BC, is scant, comprising the meagre remains of bones and flint tools from the **Stone Age (Palaeolithic)**. The comings and goings of these migrant peoples were dictated by the fluctuations of successive Ice Ages. The next traces – mainly roughly-worked flint implements – were left much later, around **40,000 BC**, by cave-dwellers at Creswell Crags in Derbyshire, Kent's Cavern near Torquay and Cheddar Cave in Somerset. The last spell of intense cold began about 17,000 years ago, and it was the final thawing of this **last Ice Age** around 5000 BC that caused the British Isles to become separated from the European mainland.

The sea barrier did little to stop further migrations of nomadic hunters, drawn by the rich forests that covered ancient Britain. In about 3500 BC a new wave of colonists arrived from the Continent, probably via Ireland, bringing with them a **Neolithic culture** based on farming and the rearing of livestock. These tribes were the first to make some impact on the environment, clearing forests, enclosing fields, constructing defensive ditches around their villages and digging mines to obtain flint used for tools and weapons. Fragments of Neolithic pottery have been found near Peterborough and in Wiltshire, but the most profuse relics are their graves, usually stone-chambered, turf-covered mounds (called **long barrows**). These are scattered throughout the country, but the most impressive are at Belas Knap in Gloucestershire and at Wayland's Smithy in Oxfordshire.

## The Bronze Age

The transition from the Neolithic to the **Bronze Age** began around 2500 BC with the importation from northern Europe of artefacts attributed to the **Beaker Culture** – named from the distinctive cups found at many burial sites. In England as elsewhere, the spread of the Beaker Culture along European trade routes helped stimulate the development of a comparatively well-organized social structure with an established aristocracy. Many of England's stone circles were completed at this time, including **Avebury** and **Stonehenge** in Wiltshire, while many others belong entirely to the Bronze Age – for example, the Hurlers and the Nine Maidens on Cornwall's Bodmin Moor. Large numbers of earthwork forts were also built in this period, suggesting endemic tribal warfare, a situation further complicated by the appearance of bands of **Celts**, who

| 5000 BC | 3952 BC | 2500 BC | 55 BC |
|---|---|---|---|
| As the ice sheets retreat, the sea floods in, separating Britain from continental Europe. | The date of the Creation – as determined by the careful calculations of the Venerable Bede (673–735). | The start of the Bronze Age – and the construction of dozens of stone and timber circles. | Chickens reach England for the first time – courtesy of Julius Caesar. |

arrived in numbers from central Europe in around 600 BC, though some historians have disputed the whole notion of a Celtic migration, preferring instead the notion of cultural diffusion along well-established trade routes.

## The Iron Age

By 500 BC, the **Britons** – with or without a significant Celtic infusion – had established a sophisticated farming economy and a social hierarchy that was dominated by a druidic priesthood. Familiar with Mediterranean artefacts through their far-flung trade routes, they developed better methods of metal-working, ones that favoured **iron** rather than bronze, from which they forged not just weapons but also coins and ornamental works, thus creating the first recognizable English art. Their principal contribution to the landscape was a network of hill forts and other defensive works stretching over the entire country, the greatest of them at **Maiden Castle** in Dorset, a site first fortified during the Neolithic period. Maiden Castle was also one of the first English fortifications to fall to the Romans in 43 AD.

## Roman invasion

Coming at the end of a long period of commercial probing, the Roman invasion had begun hesitantly, with small cross-Channel incursions led by **Julius Caesar** in 55 and 54 BC. Britain's rumoured mineral wealth was a primary motive, but the spur to the eventual conquest that came nearly a century later was anti-Roman collaboration between the British Celts and their cousins in France. The subtext was that the **Emperor Claudius**, who led the invasion, owed his power to the army and needed a military triumph. The death of the king of southeast England, Cunobelin – Shakespeare's Cymbeline – presented Claudius with a golden opportunity and in August 43 AD a substantial Roman force landed in Kent, from where it fanned out, soon establishing a base along the estuary of the Thames. Joined by a menagerie of elephants and camels for the major battles of the campaign, the Romans soon reached **Camulodunum** (Colchester) – the region's most important city – and within four years were dug in on the frontier of south Wales.

### Resistance and defeat

Resistance to the Romans was patchy. **Caractacus** of the Catuvellauni orchestrated a guerrilla campaign from Wales until he was captured in about 50 AD, but this was nothing when compared with the revolt of the East Anglian Iceni, under their queen **Boudica** (or Boadicea) in 60 AD. The Iceni sacked Camulodunum and Verulamium (St Albans), and even reached the undefended new port of Londinium (London), but the Romans rallied and exacted a terrible revenge. The rebellion turned out to be the last major act of resistance and it would seem that most of the southern tribes acquiesced to their absorption into the empire. In the next decades, the Romans extended their control, subduing Wales and the north of England by 80 AD. They did not, however, manage to conquer Scotland and eventually gave up – as signified by the construction of **Hadrian's Wall** in 130 AD. Running from the Tyne to the Solway, the wall marked the northern limit of the Roman Empire, and stands today as England's most impressive remnant of the Roman occupation.

| 43 AD | 60 AD | 130 AD | 313 |
|---|---|---|---|
| The Roman Emperor Claudius invades Britain – and he means business. | An affronted and enraged Boudica and her Iceni sack Roman Colchester. | Hadrian's Wall completed; Scots kept at bay (at least for a while). | The Emperor Constantine makes Christianity the official religion of the Roman Empire. |

## Roman England

The written history of England begins with the **Romans**, whose rule lasted nigh on four centuries. For the first time, the country began to emerge as a clearly identifiable entity with a defined political structure. Peace also brought prosperity. Commerce flourished and cities prospered, including the northerly Roman town of Eboracum (York) and **Londinium**, which soon assumed a pivotal role in the commercial and administrative life of the colony. Although Latin became the language of the Romano-British ruling elite, local traditions were allowed to coexist alongside imported customs, so that Celtic gods were often worshipped at the same time as Roman ones, and sometimes merged with them. Perhaps the most important legacy of the Roman occupation, however, was the introduction of **Christianity** from the third century on, becoming firmly entrenched after its official recognition by the Emperor Constantine in 313.

## The Anglo-Saxons

By the middle of the fourth century, Roman England was subject to regular **raids** by Germanic Saxons and Picts from Scotland and itinerant Scots from northern Ireland were harrying inland areas in the north and west. Economic life declined, rural areas became depopulated, and as central authority collapsed, so a string of military commanders usurped local authority. By the start of the fifth century England had become irrevocably detached from what remained of the Roman Empire and within fifty years the **Saxons** had begun settling England themselves. This marked the start of a gradual conquest that culminated in the defeat of the native Britons in 577 at the Battle of Dyrham (near Bath) and, despite the despairing efforts of such semi-mythical figures as **King Arthur**, the last independent Britons were driven deep into Cumbria, Wales and the southwest. So complete was the Anglo-Saxon domination, through conquest and intermarriage, that some ninety percent of English place names today have an Anglo-Saxon derivation.

The Anglo-Saxons went on to divide England into the **kingdoms** of Northumbria, Mercia, East Anglia, Kent and Wessex. In the eighth century, the central English region of **Mercia** was the dominant force, its most effective ruler being **King Offa**, who was responsible for the greatest public work of the period, **Offa's Dyke**, an earthwork marking the border with Wales from the River Dee to the River Severn. Yet, after Offa's death, **Wessex** gained the upper hand, and by 825 the Wessex kings had taken fealty from all the other English kingdoms.

### Christianity wins the day

At first, the pagan Anglo-Saxons had little time for **Christianity**, which only survived among the Romano-Britons in the westerly extremities of the country. This was soon to change. In 597, at the behest of Pope Gregory I, **St Augustine** landed on the Kent coast accompanied by forty monks. **Ethelbert**, the overlord of all the English south of the River Humber, received the missionaries and gave Augustine permission to found a monastery at **Canterbury** (on the site of the present cathedral), where the king himself was soon baptized, followed by ten thousand of his subjects at a grand Christmas ceremony. Despite some short-term reversals thereafter, the Christianization of England proceeded quickly, so that by the middle of the seventh century all of the Anglo-Saxon kings had at least nominally adopted the faith. Tensions between the Augustinian

| 597 | 793 | 796 | 1066 |
|-----|-----|-----|------|
| St Augustine lands in Kent with instructions to convert Britain to Christianity. | In a surprise attack, Viking raiders destroy the monastery at Lindisfarne. | Death of King Offa, the most powerful king in England and long-time ruler of Mercia. | King Harold, the last Saxon king of England, catches an arrow in the eye at the Battle of Hastings. |

missionaries and the Romano-British (Celtic) monks inevitably arose, but were resolved by the **Synod of Whitby** in 663, when it was agreed that the English Church should follow the rule of Rome, thereby ensuring a realignment with the European cultural mainstream.

## The Viking onslaught

The supremacy of Wessex in the early ninth century was short-lived. Carried here by their remarkable longboats, the **Vikings** – by this time mostly **Danes** – had started to raid the east coast towards the end of the eighth century. Emboldened by their success, these raids grew in size and then turned into a migration. In 865, a substantial Danish army landed in East Anglia, and within six years they had conquered Northumbria, Mercia and East Anglia. The Danes then set their sights on Wessex, whose new king was the formidable and exceptionally talented **Alfred the Great**. Despite the odds, Alfred successfully resisted the Danes and eventually the two warring parties signed a truce, which fixed an uneasy border between Wessex and Danish territory – the **Danelaw** – to the north. Ensconced in northern England and the East Midlands, the Danes soon succumbed to Christianity and internal warfare, while Alfred modernized his kingdom and strengthened its defences.

Alfred died in 899, but his successor, **Edward the Elder**, capitalized on his efforts, establishing Saxon supremacy over the Danelaw to become the de facto overlord of all England. The relative calm continued under Edward's son, **Athelstan** and his son, **Edgar**, who became the first ruler to be crowned **king of England** in 973. However, this was but a lull in the Viking storm. Returning in force, the Vikings milked Edgar's son **Ethelred the Unready** ("lacking counsel") for all the money they could, but payment of the ransom (the Danegeld) brought only temporary relief and in 1016 Ethelred hot-footed it to Normandy, leaving the Danes in command. The first Danish king of England was **Canute**, a shrewd and gifted ruler, but his two disreputable sons quickly dismantled his carefully constructed Anglo-Scandinavian empire and the Saxons promptly regained the initiative.

## 1066

In 1042, the resurgent Saxons anointed Ethelred's son, **Edward the Confessor**, as king of England. It was a poor choice. Edward was more suited to be a priest than a king and he allowed power to drift into the hands of his most powerful subject, Godwin, Earl of Wessex, and his son Harold. On Edward's death, the Witan – effectively a council of elders – confirmed **Harold** as king, ignoring several rival claims including that of William, Duke of Normandy. William's claim was a curious affair, but he always insisted – however improbable it may seem – that the childless Edward the Confessor had promised him his crown. Unluckily for Harold, his two main rivals struck at the same time. First up was his alienated brother **Tostig** along with his ally King Harald of Norway, a giant of a man reckoned to be seven feet tall. They landed with a Viking army in Yorkshire and Harold marched north to meet them. Harold won a crushing victory at the battle of **Stamford Bridge**, but then he heard that **William of Normandy** had invaded the south. Rashly, he dashed south without gathering reinforcements, a blunder that cost him his life: Harold was famously defeated at the **Battle of Hastings** in 1066 and, on Christmas Day, William the Conqueror was installed as king in Westminster Abbey.

| 1085 | 1102 | 1190 | 1216 |
|---|---|---|---|
| The Normans start work on the Domesday Book, detailing who owns what, does what and lives where. | By the terms of the Synod of Westminster, clergy are forbidden to marry. | King Richard complains that in England it is "cold and always raining," and joins the Third Crusade. | King John loses the Crown Jewels in The Wash (not the wash); much royal grumpiness ensues. |

# The Normans

**William I** imposed a Norman aristocracy on his new subjects, reinforcing his rule with a series of strongholds, the grandest of which was the **Tower of London**. Initially, there was some resistance, but William crushed these sporadic rebellions with great brutality – Yorkshire and the north were ravished and the fenland resistance of Hereward the Wake was brought to a savage end. Perhaps the single most effective controlling measure was the compilation of the **Domesday Book** in 1085–86. Recording land ownership, type of cultivation, the number of inhabitants and their social status, it afforded William an unprecedented body of information about his subjects, providing a framework for the administration of taxation, the judicial structure and ultimately feudal obligations.

William died in 1087, and was succeeded by his son **William Rufus**, an ineffectual ruler but a notable benefactor of religious foundations. Rufus died in mysterious circumstances – killed by an unknown assailant's arrow while hunting in the New Forest – and the throne passed to **Henry I**, William I's youngest son. Henry spent much of his time struggling with his unruly barons, but at least he proved to be more conciliatory in his dealings with the Saxons, even marrying into one of their leading families. On his death in 1135, the accession was contested, initiating a long-winded civil war that was only ended when Henry II secured the throne.

# The early Plantagenets (1154–1216)

Energetic and far-sighted, **Henry II**, the first of the **Plantagenets**, kept his barons in check and instigated profound administrative reforms, most notably the introduction of trial by jury. Nor was England Henry's only concern, his inheritance bequeathing him great chunks of France. This territorial entanglement was to create all sorts of problems for his successors, but Henry himself was brought low by his attempt to subordinate Church to Crown. This went terribly awry in 1170, when he sanctioned the murder in Canterbury Cathedral of his erstwhile drinking companion **Thomas à Becket**, whose canonization just three years later created an enduring Europe-wide cult.

The last years of Henry's reign were riven by quarrels with his sons, the eldest of whom, **Richard I** (or Lionheart), spent most of his ten-year reign crusading in the Holy Land. Neglected, England fell prey to the scheming of Richard's brother **John**, the villain of the Robin Hood tales, who became king in his own right after Richard died of a battle wound in France in 1199. Yet John's inability to hold on to his French possessions and his rumbling dispute with the Vatican over control of the English Church alienated the English barons, who eventually forced him to consent to a charter guaranteeing their rights and privileges, the **Magna Carta**, which was signed in 1215 at Runnymede, on the Thames.

# The later Plantagenets (1216–1399)

The power struggle with the barons continued into the reign of **Henry III**, but Henry's successor, **Edward I**, who inherited the throne in 1272, was much more in control of his kingdom than his predecessor. Edward was a great law-maker, but he also became obsessed by military matters, spending years subduing Wales and imposing English

| 1220 | 1237 | 1256 |
|---|---|---|
| Work begins on York Minster and Salisbury Cathedral – heady days for stone masons. | The Treaty of York, signed by Henry III of England and Scotland's Alexander II, sets the Anglo-Scottish border. | The calendar is getting out of sync, so in England a decree installs a leap year – one leap day every four years. |

jurisdiction over Scotland. Fortunately for the Scots – it was too late for Wales – the next king of England, **Edward II**, proved to be completely hopeless and in 1314 Robert the Bruce inflicted a huge defeat on his guileless army at the battle of **Bannockburn**. This reverse spelt the beginning of the end for Edward, who was ultimately murdered by his wife Isabella and her lover Roger Mortimer in 1327.

**Edward III** began by sorting out the Scottish imbroglio before getting stuck into his main preoccupation – his (essentially specious) claim to the throne of France. Starting in 1337, the resultant **Hundred Years War** kicked off with several famous English victories, principally Crécy in 1346 and Poitiers in 1356, but was interrupted by the outbreak of the **Black Death** in 1349. The plague claimed about one and a half million English souls – some one third of the population – and the scarcity of labour that followed gave the peasantry more economic clout than they had ever had before. Predictably, the landowners attempted to restrict the concomitant rise in wages, thereby provoking the widespread rioting that culminated in the **Peasants' Revolt** of 1381. The rebels marched on London under the delusion that they could appeal to the king – now **Richard II** – for fair treatment, but they soon learnt otherwise. The king did indeed meet a rebel deputation in person, but his aristocratic bodyguards took the opportunity to kill the peasants' leader, **Wat Tyler**, the prelude to the enforced dispersal of the crowds and mass slaughter.

Running parallel with this social unrest were the clerical reforms demanded by the scholar **John Wycliffe** (1320–1384), whose acolytes made the first translation of the Bible into English in 1380. Another sign of the elevation of the common language was the success enjoyed by **Geoffrey Chaucer** (c.1343–1400), a wine merchant's son, whose *Canterbury Tales* was the first major work written in the vernacular and one of the first English books to be printed.

## The houses of Lancaster and York (1399–1485)

In 1399, **Henry IV**, the first of the **Lancastrian** kings, supplanted the weak and indecisive Richard II. Henry died in 1413 to be succeeded by his son, the bellicose **Henry V**, who promptly renewed the Hundred Years War with vigour. Henry famously defeated the French at the battle of **Agincourt**, a comprehensive victory that forced the French king to acknowledge Henry as his heir in the Treaty of Troyes of 1420. However, Henry died just two years later and his son, **Henry VI** – or rather his regents – all too easily succumbed to a French counter-attack inspired by **Joan of Arc** (1412–1431); by 1454, only Calais was left in English hands.

It was soon obvious that **Henry VI** was mentally unstable, and consequently, as the new king drifted in and out of insanity, two aristocratic factions attempted to squeeze control: the Yorkists, whose emblem was the white rose, and the Lancastrians, represented by the red rose – hence the protracted **Wars of the Roses**. The Yorkist **Edward IV** seized the crown in 1471 and held on to it until his death in 1483, when he was succeeded by his 12-year-old son **Edward V**, whose reign was cut short after only two months: he and his younger brother were murdered in the Tower of London, probably at the behest of their uncle, the Duke of Gloucester, who was crowned **Richard III**. Richard did not last long either: in 1485, he was defeated (and killed) at the battle of Bosworth Field by Henry Tudor, Earl of Richmond, who took the throne as Henry VII.

| 1277 | 1290 | 1295 |
|---|---|---|
| Well armed and well organized, Edward I of England embarks upon the conquest of Wales. | Edward I of England expels the Jews from his kingdom, one of several medieval pogroms. | Edward I much vexed when France and Scotland sign a treaty of mutual assistance – the start of the "Auld Alliance". |

# The Tudors (1485–1603)

The opening of the **Tudor** period brought radical transformations. A Lancastrian through his mother's line, **Henry VII** promptly reconciled the Yorkists by marrying Edward IV's daughter Elizabeth, thereby ending the Wars of the Roses at a stroke. It was a shrewd gambit and others followed. Henry married his daughter off to James IV of Scotland and his son to Catherine, the daughter of Ferdinand and Isabella of Spain – and by these means England began to assume the status of a major European power.

Henry's son, **Henry VIII** is best remembered for his multiple marriages, but much more significant was his separation of the English Church from Rome and his establishment of an independent Protestant Church – the **Church of England**. This is not without its ironies. Henry was not a Protestant himself and the schism between Henry and the pope was triggered not by doctrinal issues but by the failure of his wife **Catherine of Aragon** – widow of his elder brother – to provide Henry with male offspring. Failing to obtain a decree of nullity from Pope Clement VII, he dismissed his long-time chancellor Thomas Wolsey and turned instead to **Thomas Cromwell**, who helped make the English Church recognize Henry as its head. One of the consequences was the **Dissolution of the Monasteries**, which conveniently gave both king and nobles the chance to get their hands on valuable monastic property in the late 1530s.

In his later years Henry became a corpulent, syphilitic wreck, six times married but at last furnished with an heir, **Edward VI**, who was only nine years old when he ascended the throne in 1547. His short reign saw Protestantism established on a firm footing, with churches stripped of their images and Catholic services banned, yet on Edward's death most of the country readily accepted his fervently Catholic, half-sister **Mary**, daughter of Catherine of Aragon, as queen. She returned England to the papacy and married the future Philip II of Spain, forging an alliance whose immediate consequence was war with France. The marriage was deeply unpopular and so was Mary's foolish decision to begin persecuting Protestants, executing the leading lights of the English Reformation – Hugh Latimer, Nicholas Ridley and Thomas Cranmer, the archbishop of Canterbury.

## Elizabeth I

Queen Mary, or 'Bloody Mary' as many of her subjects called her, died in 1558 and the crown passed to her half-sister, **Elizabeth I**. The new queen looked very vulnerable. The country was divided by religion – Catholic against Protestant – and threatened from abroad by Philip II of Spain, the most powerful ruler in Europe. Famously, Elizabeth eschewed marriage and, although a Protestant herself, steered a delicate course between the two religious groupings. Her prudence rested well with the English merchant class, who were becoming the greatest power in the land, its members mostly opposed to foreign military entanglements. An exception was, however, made for the piratical activities of the great English seafarers of the day, sea captains like Walter Raleigh, Martin Frobisher, John Hawkins and Francis Drake, who made a fortune raiding Spain's American colonies. Inevitably, Philip II's irritation with the raiding took a warlike turn, but the **Spanish Armada** he sent against England in 1588 was defeated, thereby establishing England as a major European sea power. Elizabeth's reign also saw the efflorescence of a specifically English Renaissance – **William Shakespeare** (1564–1616) is the obvious name – the only major blip being the queen's reluctant execution of her cousin and rival **Mary, Queen of Scots**, in 1587.

| 1314 | 1349 | 1380s | 1485 |
|---|---|---|---|
| At the Battle of Bannockburn, Robert the Bruce's Scots destroy an English army. | The Black Death reaches England and moves on into Scotland the year after. | Geoffrey Chaucer begins work on *The Canterbury Tales* and changes the face of English literature forever. | Battle of Bosworth Field ends the Wars of the Roses. |

## The early Stuarts (1603–1649)

The son of Mary, Queen of Scots, James VI of Scotland, succeeded Elizabeth as **James I** of England in 1603, thereby uniting the English and Scottish crowns. James quickly moved to end hostilities with Spain and adopted a policy of toleration towards the country's Catholics. Inevitably, both initiatives offended many Protestants, whose worst fears were confirmed in 1605 when **Guy Fawkes** and a group of Catholic conspirators were discovered preparing to blow up king and Parliament in the so-called **Gunpowder Plot**. During the ensuing hue and cry, many Catholics met an untimely end and Fawkes himself was tortured and then hanged, drawn and quartered. At the same time, many Protestants felt the English state was irredeemably corrupt and some of the more dedicated **Puritans** fixed their eyes on establishing a "New Jerusalem" in North America following the foundation of the first permanent **colony** in Virginia in 1608. Twelve years later, the **Pilgrim Fathers** landed in New England, establishing a colony that would absorb about a hundred thousand Puritan immigrants by the middle of the century.

Meanwhile, James was busy alienating his landed gentry. He clung to an absolutist vision of the monarchy – the **divine right of kings** – that was totally out of step with the Protestant leanings of the majority of his subjects and he also relied heavily on court favourites. It was a recipe for disaster, but it was to be his successor, **Charles I**, who reaped the whirlwind.

### Charles I and the Civil War

**Charles I** inherited James's penchant for absolutism, ruling without Parliament from 1629 to 1640, but he over-stepped himself when he tried to impose a new Anglican prayer book on the Scots, who rose in revolt, forcing Charles to recall Parliament in an attempt to raise the money he needed for an army. This was Parliament's chance and they were not going to let it slip. The **Long Parliament**, as it became known, impeached several of Charles's allies – most notably Archbishop Laud, who was hung out to dry by the king and ultimately executed – and compiled its grievances in the Grand Remonstrance of 1641.

Facing the concerted hostility of Parliament, the king withdrew to Nottingham where he raised his standard, the opening act of the **Civil War**. The Royalist forces ("Cavaliers") were initially successful, leading to the complete overhaul of key regiments of the Parliamentary army ("Roundheads") by **Oliver Cromwell** and his officer allies. The **New Model Army** Cromwell created was something quite unique: singing psalms as they went into battle and urged on by preachers and "agitators", this was an army of believers whose ideological commitment to the parliamentary cause made it truly formidable. Cromwell's revamped army cut its teeth at the battle of Naseby and thereafter simply brushed the Royalists aside. Meanwhile, an increasingly desperate Charles attempted to sow discord among his enemies by surrendering himself to the Scots, but as so often with Charles's plans, they came unstuck: the Scots handed him over to the English Parliament, by whom – after prolonged negotiations, endless royal shenanigans and more fighting – he was ultimately **executed** in January 1649.

## The Commonwealth

For the next eleven years, England was a **Commonwealth** – at first a true republic, then, after 1653, a **Protectorate** with Cromwell as the Lord Protector and commander in

| 1536 | 1588 | c. 1592 | 1603 |
| --- | --- | --- | --- |
| Anne Boleyn loses her head; another wife of Henry VIII comes to an untimely end. | Spanish Armada meets a watery end; England gleeful; Elizabeth I relieved. | First performance of Shakespeare's *Henry VI, Pt 1*, at the Rose Theatre, London. | King James unites the crowns of Scotland and England. |

chief. Cromwell reformed the government, secured advantageous commercial treaties with foreign nations and used his New Model Army to put the fear of God into his various enemies. The turmoil of the Civil War and the pre-eminence of the army unleashed a furious legal, theological and political debate throughout the country. This milieu spawned a host of leftist sects, the most notable of whom were the **Levellers**, who demanded wholesale constitutional reform, and the more radical **Diggers**, who proposed common ownership of all land. Nonconformist religious groups also flourished, prominent among them the pacifist **Quakers**, led by the much persecuted George Fox (1624–91), and the **Dissenters**, to whom the most famous writers of the day, John Milton (1608–74) and John Bunyan (1628–88), both belonged.

Cromwell died in 1658 to be succeeded by his son **Richard**, who ruled briefly and ineffectually, leaving the army unpaid while one of its more ambitious commanders, General Monk, conspired to restore the monarchy. Charles II, the exiled son of the previous king, entered London in triumph in May 1660.

## The Restoration

A Stuart was back on the English throne, but **Charles II** had few absolutist illusions – the terms of the **Restoration** were closely negotiated and included a general amnesty for all those who had fought against the Stuarts, with the exception of the regicides: those who had signed Charles I's death warrant. Nonetheless, there was a sea-change in public life with the re-establishment of a royal court and the foundation of the **Royal Society**, whose scientific endeavours were furthered by Isaac Newton (1642–1727). The low points of Charles's reign were the **Great Plague** of 1665 and the 1666 **Great Fire of London**, though the London that rose from the ashes was an architectural showcase for Christopher Wren (1632–1723) and his fellow classicists. Politically, there were still underlying tensions between the monarchy and Parliament, but the latter was more concerned with the struggle between the **Whigs** and **Tories**, political factions representing, respectively, the low-church gentry and the high-church aristocracy. There was a degree of religious toleration too, but its brittleness was all too apparent in the anti-Catholic riots of 1678.

## James II and the Glorious Revolution

**James II**, the brother of Charles II, came to the throne in 1685. He was a Catholic, which made the bulk of his subjects uneasy, but there was still an indifferent response when the Protestant **Duke of Monmouth**, the favourite among Charles II's illegitimate sons, raised a rebellion in the West Country. Monmouth was defeated at Sedgemoor, in Somerset, in July 1685 and nine days later he was beheaded at Tower Hill; neither was any mercy shown to his supporters: in the **Bloody Assizes** of Judge Jeffreys, hundreds of rebels and suspected sympathizers were executed or deported. Yet, if James felt secure he was mistaken. A foolish man, James showed all the traditional weaknesses of his family, from his enthusiasm for the divine right of kings to an over-reliance on sycophantic favourites. Even worse, as far as the Protestants were concerned, he built up a massive standing army, officered it with Roman Catholics and proposed a **Declaration of Indulgence**, removing anti-Catholic restrictions. The final straw was the birth of James's son, which threatened to secure a Catholic succession, and, thoroughly

| 1605 | 1642 | 1660 | 1669 |
|---|---|---|---|
| Gunpowder Plot: Guy Fawkes et al plan to blow up the Houses of Parliament, but fail. | The Civil War begins when Charles I raises his standard in Nottingham. | The Restoration: Charles II takes the throne – and digs up the body of Oliver Cromwell to hammer home his point. | Samuel Pepys gives up his diary, after nine years of detailed jottings. |

## KINGS AND QUEENS SINCE 1066

### HOUSE OF NORMANDY
William I (William the Conqueror) 1066–87
William II (William Rufus) 1087–1100
Henry I 1100–35
Stephen 1135–54

### HOUSE OF PLANTAGENET
Henry II 1154–89
Richard I (Richard the Lionheart) 1189–99
John 1199–1216
Henry III 1216–72
Edward I 1272–1307
Edward II 1307–27
Edward III 1327–77
Richard II 1377–99

### HOUSE OF LANCASTER
Henry IV 1399–1413
Henry V 1413–22
Henry VI 1422–61 & 1470

### HOUSE OF YORK
Edward IV 1461–70 &1471–83
Edward V 1483
Richard III 1483–85

### HOUSE OF TUDOR
Henry VII 1485–1509
Henry VIII 1509–47

Edward VI 1547–53
Mary I 1553–58
Elizabeth I 1558–1603

### HOUSE OF STUART
James I 1603–25
Charles I 1625–49
Commonwealth and Protectorate 1649–60
Charles II 1660–85
James II 1685–88
William III and Mary II 1688–94
William III 1694–1702
Anne 1702–14

### HOUSE OF HANOVER
George I 1714–27
George II 1727–60
George III 1760–1820
George IV 1820–30
William IV 1830–37
Victoria 1837–1901

### HOUSE OF SAXE-COBURG-GOTHA
Edward VII 1901–10

### HOUSE OF WINDSOR
George V 1910–36
Edward VIII 1936
George VI 1936–52
Elizabeth II 1952–

alarmed, powerful Protestants now urged **William of Orange**, the Dutch husband of Mary, the Protestant daughter of James II, to save them from "popery" – and that was precisely what he did. William landed in Devon in 1688 and, as James's forces melted away, he speedily took control of London in the **Glorious Revolution** of 1688. This was the final postscript to the Civil War – although it was a couple of years before James and his remaining Jacobites were finally defeated in Ireland at the **Battle of the Boyne**.

## The last Stuarts
**William and Mary** became joint sovereigns after they agreed a **Bill of Rights** defining the limitations of the monarchy's power and the rights of its subjects. This, together with the **Act of Settlement of 1701** made Britain a **constitutional monarchy**, in which the roles of legislature and executive were separate and interdependent. The model was broadly consistent with that outlined by the philosopher and political thinker **John Locke** (1632–1704), whose essentially Whig doctrines of toleration and social contract

| 1678 | 1684 | 1703 | 1707 |
|---|---|---|---|
| John Bunyan, the Protestant preacher and reformer, writes his *Pilgrim's Progress*. | Isaac Newton observes gravity – but is probably not hit on the head by an apple. | "The Great Storm", a week-long hurricane, blasts through southern England. | The Act of Union merges the Scottish Parliament into the English Parliament. |

were gradually embraced as the new orthodoxy. Ruling alone after Mary's death in 1694, William regarded England as a prop in his defence of Holland against France, a stance that defined England's political alignment in Europe for the next sixty years.

After William's death, the crown passed to **Anne**, the second daughter of James II. Anne was a Protestant – an Anglican to be exact – but her popularity had more to do with her self-proclaimed love of England, which came as something of a relief after William's marked preference for the Dutch. During Anne's reign, English armies won a string of remarkable victories on the Continent, beginning with the Duke of Marlborough's triumph at Blenheim in 1704, followed the next year by the capture of Gibraltar, establishing a British presence in the Mediterranean. These military escapades were part of the Europe-wide **War of the Spanish Succession**, a long-winded dynastic squabble which rumbled on until the 1713 Treaty of Utrecht all but settled the European balance of power for the rest of the century. Otherwise Anne's reign was distinguished mainly for the 1707 **Act of Union**, uniting the English and Scottish parliaments.

Despite her seventeen pregnancies, none of Anne's children survived into adulthood. Consequently, when she died in 1714, the succession passed from the Stuarts to the Hanoverians in the person of the Elector of Hanover, a non-English-speaking, Protestant who became George I of England – all in accordance with the terms of the Act of Settlement.

## The Hanoverians

During **George I**'s lacklustre reign, power leached into the hands of a Whig oligarchy led by a chief minister – or prime minister – the longest serving of whom was **Robert Walpole** (1676–1745). Meanwhile, plans were being hatched for a **Jacobite Rebellion** in support of **James Edward Stuart**, the "Old Pretender". Its timing appeared perfect: Scottish opinion was moving against the Union, which had failed to bring Scotland tangible economic benefits, and many English Catholics supported the Jacobite cause too, toasting the "king across the water". In 1715, the Earl of Mar raised the Stuart standard at Braemar Castle, and just eight days later he captured Perth, where he gathered an army of more than ten thousand men. Mar's rebellion took the government by surprise. They had only four thousand soldiers in Scotland, but Mar dithered until he lost the military advantage. There was an indecisive battle at Sheriffmuir, but by the time the Old Pretender landed in Scotland in December 1715, six thousand veteran Dutch troops had reinforced government forces. The rebellion disintegrated rapidly and James slunk back to exile in France with his tail between his legs.

Under **George II**, England became embroiled in yet another dynastic squabble, the War of the Austrian Succession (1740–48), but this played second fiddle to the **Jacobite Rebellion** of 1745, when the Young Pretender, **Charles Stuart** (Bonnie Prince Charlie), and his Highland army reached Derby, just 100 miles from London. There was panic in the capital, but the Prince's army proved too small – he had failed to rally the Lowland Scots, never mind the English – and his supply lines too over-extended to press home his advantage, and the Jacobites retreated north. A Hanoverian army under the Duke of Cumberland caught up with them at **Culloden Moor** near Inverness in April 1746, and hacked them to pieces. The prince lived out the rest of his life in drunken exile, while in Scotland wearing tartan, bearing arms and playing bagpipes

| 1715 | 1745 | 1781 |
|---|---|---|
| First Jacobite Rebellion: James Stuart ("The Old Pretender") raises a Scottish army, but is defeated. | Second Jacobite Rebellion: Charles Stuart (Bonnie Prince Charlie) invades England with a Scots army, but is defeated at Culloden. | Opening of the Iron Bridge – the first iron bridge the world had ever seen – over the River Severn. |

were all banned. Most significantly, the government prohibited the private armies of the highland chiefs, thereby destroying the military capacity of the clans.

## Empire and colonies

At the tail end of George II's reign, the **Seven Years War** (1756–63) harvested England yet more overseas territory in India and Canada at the expense of France; and then, in 1768, with **George III** now on the throne, **Captain James Cook** stumbled upon New Zealand and Australia, thereby extending Britain's empire still further. The fly in the ointment was the deteriorating relationship with the thirteen colonies of North America, which came to a head with the **American Declaration of Independence** and Britain's subsequent defeat in the **Revolutionary War** (1775–83). The debacle helped fuel a renewed struggle between king and Parliament, enlivened by the intervention of John Wilkes, first of a long and increasingly vociferous line of parliamentary radicals. It also made the British reluctant to interfere in the momentous events taking place across the Channel, where France, long its most consistent foe, was convulsed by revolution. Out of the turmoil emerged the most daunting of enemies, **Napoleon Bonaparte** (1769–1821), whose stunning military progress was interrupted by Nelson at **Trafalgar** in 1805 and finally stopped ten years later by the Duke of Wellington (and the Prussians) at **Waterloo.**

## The Industrial Revolution

England's triumph over Napoleon was underpinned by its financial strength, which was itself born of the **Industrial Revolution**, the switch from an agricultural to a manufacturing economy that transformed the face of the country within a century. The earliest mechanized production was in the Lancashire **cotton mills**, where cotton-spinning progressed from a cottage industry to a highly productive factory-based system. Initially, river water powered the mills, but the technology changed after James Watt patented his **steam engine** in 1781. Watt's engines needed **coal**, which made it convenient to locate mills and factories near coal mines, a tendency that was accelerated as **ironworks** took up coal as a smelting fuel, vastly increasing the output from their furnaces. Accordingly, there was a shift of population towards the Midlands and the north of England, where the great coal reserves were located, and as the industrial economy boomed and diversified, so these regions' towns mushroomed at an extraordinary rate. Sheffield was a steel town, Stoke-on-Trent was famed for its pottery, Manchester possessed huge cotton warehouses, and Liverpool had the docks, where raw materials from India and the Americas flowed in and manufactured goods went out. Commerce and industry were also served by improving transport facilities, principally the digging of a network of **canals**, but the great leap forward came with the arrival of the **railway**, heralded by the Stockton–Darlington line in 1825 and followed five years later by the Liverpool–Manchester railway, where George Stephenson's *Rocket* made its first outing.

Boosted by a vast influx of immigrant workers, the country's population rose from about eight and a half million at the beginning of George III's reign to more than fifteen million by its end. As the factories and their attendant towns expanded, so the rural settlements of England declined, inspiring the elegiac pastoral yearnings of Samuel Taylor Coleridge and William Wordsworth, the first great names of the **Romantic movement**. Later Romantic poets such as Percy Bysshe Shelley and Lord Byron took a more socially

| **1783** | **1815** | **1819** | **1824** |
|---|---|---|---|
| End of the American War of Independence – the American colonies break from Britain. | Final defeat of Napoleon at the battle of Waterloo. | Peterloo Massacre: in Manchester, the cavalry wade into a crowd who are demanding parliamentary reform. Many are killed. | Charles Dickens' father is imprisoned as a debtor; his son never forgets. |

engaged position, but much more dangerous to the ruling class were the nation's factory workers, who grew restless when mechanization put thousands of them out of work.

## The Chartists – and social reform

Industrial discontent coalesced in the **Chartists**, a broad-based popular movement that demanded parliamentary reform – the most important of the industrial boom towns were still unrepresented in Parliament – and the repeal of the hated **Corn Laws**, which kept the price of bread artificially high to the advantage of the large landowners. Class antagonisms came to boiling point in 1819, when the local militia bloodily dispersed a demonstration in support of parliamentary reform in Manchester in the so-called **Peterloo Massacre**.

Tensions continued to run high throughout the 1820s, and in retrospect it seems that the country may have been saved from a French-style revolution by a series of judicious parliamentary acts: the **Reform Act** of 1832 established the principle (if not actually the practice) of popular representation; the **Poor Law** of 1834 did something to alleviate the condition of the most destitute; and the repeal of the Corn Laws in 1846 cut the cost of bread. Furthermore, there was such a furore after six Dorset labourers – the **Tolpuddle Martyrs** – were transported to Australia in 1834 for joining an agricultural trade union, that the judiciary decided it was prudent to overturn the judgement six years later. Significant sections of the middle classes supported progressive reform too, as evidenced by the immense popularity of **Charles Dickens** (1812–70), whose novels railed against poverty and injustice. Indeed, the middle classes had already played a key reforming role in the previous century when John Wesley (1703–91) and his **Methodists** led the anti-slavery campaign. As a result of their efforts, **slavery** was banned in Britain in 1772 and throughout the British Empire in 1833 – albeit long after the seaports of Bristol and Liverpool had grown rich on the backs of the trade.

## The Victorians

Blind and insane, **George III** died in 1820. His two sons, **George IV** and **William IV**, were succeeded in their turn by his niece, **Victoria**, whose long reign witnessed the zenith of British power. The economy boomed – typically the nation's cloth manufacturers boasted that they supplied the domestic market before breakfast, the rest of the world thereafter – and the British trading fleet was easily the mightiest in the world. The fleet policed an empire upon which, in that famous phrase of the time, "the sun never set" and Victoria became the symbol of both the nation's success and the imperial ideal. There were extraordinary intellectual achievements too – as typified by the publication of Charles Darwin's *On the Origin of Species* in 1859 – and the country came to see itself as both a civilizing agent and, on occasion, the hand of (a very Protestant) God on earth. Britain's industrial and commercial prowess was best embodied by the engineering feats of **Isambard Kingdom Brunel** (1806–1859) and by the **Great Exhibition** of 1851, a display of manufacturing achievements without compare.

With trade at the forefront of the agenda, much of the political debate crystallized into a conflict between the Free Traders – led by the Whigs, who formed the **Liberal Party** – and the Protectionists under Bentinck and **Disraeli**, guiding light of the **Conservatives**, descended from the Tories. Parliament itself was long dominated by the duel between Disraeli and the Liberal leader **Gladstone**, the pre-eminent statesmen of

| 1834 | 1841 | 1858 |
|---|---|---|
| Tolpuddle Martyrs: agricultural workers from Dorset are transported to Australia for daring to organize. | Thomas Cook organizes his first package tour, taking several hundred temperance campaigners from Leicester to Loughborough. | English engineer Isambard Kingdom Brunel builds the iron-hulled SS *Great Eastern*, the largest ship in the world. |

the day. It was Disraeli who eventually passed the Second Reform Bill in 1867, further extending the electoral franchise, but it was Gladstone's first ministry of 1868–74 that ratified some of the century's most far-reaching legislation, including compulsory education and the full legalization of trade unions.

## Foreign entanglements

In 1854 troops were sent to protect the Ottoman empire against the Russians in the **Crimea**, an inglorious fiasco whose horrors were relayed to the public by the first-ever press coverage of a military campaign and by the revelations of Florence Nightingale, who was appalled by the lack of medical care for the soldiers. The **Indian Mutiny** of 1857 was a further shock to the imperial system, exposing the fragility of Britain's hold over the Indian subcontinent, though the status quo was brutally restored and Victoria took the title Empress of India after 1876. Thereafter, the British army was flattered by a series of minor wars against poorly armed Asian and African opponents, but promptly came unstuck when it faced the Dutch settlers of South Africa in the **Boer War** (1899–1902). The British ultimately fought their way to a sort of victory, but the discreditable conduct of the war prompted a military shake-up at home that was to be of significance in the coming European war.

# World War I and its aftermath (1914–1939)

Victoria died in 1901, to be succeeded by her son, **Edward VII**, whose leisurely lifestyle has often been seen as the epitome of the complacent era to which he gave his name. It wasn't to last. On August 4, 1914, with **George V** now on the throne, the Liberal government declared war on Germany, thereby honouring the Entente Cordiale signed with France in 1904. Hundreds of thousands volunteered for the British army, but their enthusiastic nationalism was not enough to ensure a quick victory and **World War I** dragged on for four miserable years, its key engagements fought in the trenches that zigzagged across northern France and Flanders in Belgium. Britain and her allies eventually prevailed, but the number of dead beggared belief, undermining the authority of the British ruling class, whose generals had shown a lethal combination of incompetence and indifference to the plight of their men. Many looked admiringly at the Soviet Union, where Lenin and his Bolsheviks had rid themselves of the Tsar and seized control in 1917.

After the war ended in 1918, the sheer weight of public opinion pushed Parliament into extending the **vote** to all men 21 and over and to women over 30. This tardy liberalization of women's rights owed much to the efforts of the radical **Suffragettes**, led by Emmeline Pankhurst and her daughters Sylvia and Christabel, but the process was only completed in 1929 when women were at last granted the vote at 21. The royal family itself was shaken in 1936 by the **abdication of Edward VIII**, following his decision to marry a twice-divorced American, Wallis Simpson. In the event, the succession passed smoothly to his brother **George VI**, but the royals had to play catch-up to regain their popularity among the population as a whole.

## Hard times

During this period, the **Labour Party** supplanted the Liberals as the second-largest party, its strength built on an alliance between the working-class trade unions and

| 1892 | 1865 | 1871 | 1909 |
|---|---|---|---|
| Liverpool Football Club founded – years before Chelsea. | William Booth from Nottingham founds the Salvation Army, in the East End of London. | The explorer Stanley "finds" the missionary Dr David Livingstone in Africa. | Lord Baden-Powell forms the "British Boy Scouts". |

middle-class radicals. Labour formed its first government in 1923 under **Ramsay MacDonald** (1866–1937), but the publication of the **Zinoviev Letter**, a forged document that purported to be a letter from the Soviets urging British leftists to promote revolution, undermined MacDonald's position and the Conservatives were returned with a large parliamentary majority in 1924. Two years later, a bitter dispute between the nation's pit men and the mine-owners spread to the railways, the newspapers and the iron and steel industries, thereby escalating into a **General Strike**. The strike lasted nine days and involved half a million workers, provoking the government into draconian action – the army was called in, and the strike was broken. The economic situation deteriorated even further after the crash of the New York Stock Exchange in 1929, which precipitated a worldwide depression. Unemployment topped 2.8 million in 1931, generating mass demonstrations that peaked with the **Jarrow March** from the Northeast of England to London in 1936.

### The Empire reorganises

Abroad, the structure of the **British Empire** was undergoing profound changes. After the cack-handed way the British had dealt with Dublin's 1916 Easter Rising, the status of **Ireland** was bound to change. There was a partial resolution in 1922 with the establishment of the Irish Free State, but the six counties of the mainly Protestant North (two-thirds of the ancient province of **Ulster**) chose to "contract out" and stay part of the United Kingdom – and this was to cause endless problems later. In 1926, the **Imperial Conference** recognized the autonomy of the British dominions, comprising all the major countries that had previously been part of the Empire. This agreement was formalized in the 1931 Statute of Westminster, whereby each dominion was given an equal footing in a Commonwealth of Nations, though each still recognized the British monarch.

# World War II

When Hitler set about militarising Germany in the mid-1930s, the British government adopted a policy of appeasement and made few preparations. Consequently, when Britain declared war on Germany after Hitler's invasion of Poland in September 1939, she was poorly prepared. After embarrassing military failures during the first months of **World War II**, the discredited government was replaced in May 1940 by a national coalition headed by the charismatic **Winston Churchill** (1874–1965), whose bulldog steadfastness and heroic speeches provided the inspiration needed in the backs-against-the-wall mood of the time. Partly through Churchill's manoeuvrings, the United States became a supplier of foodstuffs and munitions to Britain and this, combined with the US's breaking-off of trade links with Japan in June (in protest at their attacks on China), may have helped precipitate the Japanese bombing of Pearl Harbor on December 7, 1941. Once attacked, the US immediately joined the war, declaring against both Japan and Germany, and its intervention, combined with the stirring efforts of the Soviet Red Army, swung the military balance. In terms of casualties, World War II was not as calamitous as World War I, but its impact upon British civilians was much greater. In its first wave of **bombing** of the UK, the Luftwaffe caused massive damage to industrial centres such as London, Coventry, Manchester, Liverpool, Southampton and Plymouth.

| 1912 | 1926 | 1946 | 1950 |
|------|------|------|------|
| Bad news: the *Titanic* sinks and Captain Scott and his men die on the ice in the Antarctic. | Britain's first-ever General Strike: a nine-day walkout in support of the coal miners. The workers lose (again). | Death of John Maynard Keynes, one of the most influential economists of all time. | Soap rationing ends in Britain – a general clean-up follows. |

Later raids, intended to shatter morale rather than factories and docks, battered the cathedral cities of Canterbury, Exeter, Bath, Norwich and York. By 1945, nearly a third of the nation's houses had been destroyed or damaged, over 58,000 civilians had lost their lives, and nearly a quarter of a million soldiers, sailors and airmen had been killed.

## Postwar England (1945–79)

Hungry for change (and demobilization), voters in 1945's immediate postwar election replaced Churchill with the Labour Party under **Clement Attlee** (1883–1967), who set about a radical programme to **nationalize** the coal, gas, electricity, iron and steel industries. In addition, the early passage of the National Insurance Act and the National Health Service Act gave birth to what became known as the **welfare state**. However, despite substantial American aid, rebuilding the economy was a huge task that made **austerity** the keynote, with the rationing of food and fuel remaining in force long after 1945. This cost the Labour Party dear in the general election of 1951, which returned the Conservatives to power under the leadership of an ageing Churchill. The following year, King George VI died and was succeeded by his elder daughter, who, as **Queen Elizabeth II**, remains on the throne today.

Meanwhile, in 1949, Britain, the United States, Canada, France and the Benelux countries signed the **North Atlantic Treaty** as a counterbalance to Soviet power in Eastern Europe. This was clear enough, but there remained confusion over Britain's imperial – or rather post-imperial – role and this was revealed by the **Suez Crisis** of 1956, when Anglo-French and Israeli forces invaded Egypt to secure control of the Suez Canal, only to be hastily recalled following international (American) condemnation. This shoddy fiasco laid bare the limitations on Britain's capacity for independent action and the Conservative prime minister, **Anthony Eden** (1897–1977), whose judgement had been so appalling, was forced to resign. His replacement, the pragmatic, silky-tongued **Harold Macmillan** (1894–1986), accepted the end of empire, but was still eager for Britain to play a leading international role – and the country kept its nuclear arms, despite the best efforts of the Campaign for Nuclear Disarmament (CND).

### Boom and bust

The dominant political figure in the 1960s was **Harold Wilson** (1916–1995), a witty speaker and skilled tactician who was Labour prime minister from 1964 to 1970 – and again from 1974 to 1976. The 1960s saw a boom in consumer spending, pioneering social legislation (primarily on homosexuality and abortion), and a corresponding cultural upswing, with London becoming the hippest city on the planet. But the good times lasted barely a decade: the Conservatives returned to office in 1970 and although the new prime minister, the ungainly **Edward Heath** (1916–2005), led Britain into the brave new world of the **European Economic Community** (**EEC**), the 1970s was an era of recession and industrial strife. Labour returned to power in 1974, but ultimately a succession of public-sector strikes and mistimed decisions handed the 1979 general election to the Conservatives under its new leader **Margaret Thatcher** (1925–2013). The pundits were amazed by her success, but as events proved, she was primed and ready to break the unions and anyone else who crossed her path.

| 1951 | 1955 | 1962 | 1967 |
|---|---|---|---|
| Britain's first supermarket opens in south London. Shopping trolleys become a new traffic hazard. | Fashion designer Mary Quant opens her first shop in London. Skirt hems are about to rise. | The Beatles hit the big time with their first single, *Love Me Do*. | First withdrawal from a cash dispenser (ATM) in Britain – at a branch of Barclays. |

## Thatcher and Major (1979–1997)

Thatcher went on to win three general elections, but pushed the UK into a period of sharp social polarization. While taxation policies and easy credit fuelled a consumer boom for the professional classes, the erosion of manufacturing and the weakening of the welfare state impoverished a great number of the population. Thatcher won an increased majority in the 1983 election, largely thanks to the successful recapture of the **Falkland Islands**, a remote British dependency in the south Atlantic, retrieved from the occupying Argentine army in 1982. Her electoral domination was also assisted by the fragmentation of the Labour opposition, particularly following the establishment of the Social Democratic Party, which had split in panic at what it perceived as the radicalization of the Labour Party, but ended up amalgamating with what remained of the Liberal Party to form the **Liberal Democrats** in 1988.

### Trouble and strife

Social and political tensions surfaced in sporadic urban rioting and the year-long **miners' strike** (1984–85) against colliery closures, a bitter industrial dispute in which the police were given unprecedented powers to restrict the movement of citizens. The violence in Northern Ireland also intensified, and in 1984 IRA bombers came close to killing the entire Cabinet, who were staying in a Brighton hotel during the Conservatives' annual conference. The divisive politics of Thatcherism reached their apogee when the desperately unpopular **Poll Tax** led to her overthrow by Conservative colleagues who feared annihilation if she led them into another general election. The beneficiary was **John Major** (b.1943), a notably uninspiring figure who nonetheless managed to win the Conservatives a fourth term of office in 1992, albeit with a much reduced Parliamentary majority. While his government presided over a steady growth in economic performance, they gained little credit amid allegations of mismanagement, incompetence and feckless leadership, all overlaid by endless tales of Tory "sleaze", with revelations of extramarital affairs and financial crookery gleefully blazed by the British press. There was also the small matter of ties with Europe: a good chunk of the Conservative Party wanted a European free-trade zone, but nothing more, whereas the **Maastricht Treaty** of 1992, which the UK government signed, had the spank of political/federal union with the EEC rebranded as the **European Union (EU)**; right-wing Tories were apoplectic and their frequent and very public demonstrations of disloyalty further hobbled the Major government.

---

### THE ROYALS – AND DIANA

The 1990s were a troubled time for the **Royal Family**, whose credibility fissured with the break-up of the marriage of Prince Charles and Diana. Revelations about the cruel treatment of Diana by both the prince and his entourage damaged the royals' reputation and suddenly the institution itself seemed an anachronism, its members stiff, old-fashioned and dim-witted. By contrast, **Diana**, who was formally divorced from Charles in 1994, appeared warm-hearted and glamorous, so much so that her death in a car accident in Paris in 1997 may actually have saved the Royal Family as an institution. In the short term, Diana's death had a profound impact on the British, who joined in a media-orchestrated exercise in public grieving unprecedented in modern times.

---

| 1970 | 1975 | 1985 | 1994 | 1999 |
|------|------|------|------|------|
| First Glastonbury Festival held – music lovers get used to mud. | First North Sea oil comes ashore. | The bitter, year-long miners' strike is crushed by Margaret Thatcher. | The Channel Tunnel opens to traffic. | The Scottish Parliament and the National Assemblies for Wales and Northern Ireland take on devolved powers. |

## The Blair years (1997–2007)

Wracked by factionalism in the 1980s, the **Labour Party** regrouped under Neil Kinnock and then John Smith, though neither of them reaped the political rewards. These dropped into the lap of a new and dynamic young leader, **Tony Blair** (b.1953), who soon pushed the party further away from traditional left-wing socialism. Blair's cloak of idealistic, media-friendly populism worked to devastating effect, sweeping the Labour Party to power in the **general election of May 1997** on a wave of genuine popular optimism. There were immediate rewards in enhanced relations with the EU and progress in the Irish peace talks, and Blair's electoral touch was soon repeated in Labour-sponsored **devolution referenda**, whose results semi-detached Scotland and Wales from their more populous neighbour in the form of a Scottish Parliament and Welsh Assembly.

Labour won the **general election of June 2001** with another parliamentary landslide. This second victory was, however, accompanied by little of the optimism of before. Few voters fully trusted Blair and his administration had by then established an unenviable reputation for the laundering of events to present the government in the best possible light. Nonetheless, the ailing Conservative Party failed to capitalize on these failings, leaving Blair streets ahead of his political rivals in the opinion polls when the hijacked planes hit New York's World Trade Center on **September 11, 2001**. Blair rushed to support President Bush, joining in the attack on Afghanistan and then, to the horror of millions of Brits, sending British forces into **Iraq** alongside the Americans in 2003. Saddam Hussein was deposed with relative ease, but neither Bush nor Blair had a coherent exit strategy, and back home Blair was widely seen as having spun Britain into the war by exaggerating the danger Saddam presented with his supposed – indeed nonexistent – **WMDs** (Weapons of Mass Destruction).

### Domestic investment

On the domestic front Blair proceeded with a massive and much-needed investment in **public services** during his second term, with education and health being the prime beneficiaries. There was also a concerted attempt to lift (many of) the country's poorer citizens out of poverty. These achievements did not, however, secure the recognition they deserved. This was partly a consequence of the method: though committed to public service investment, Labour failed to trust its employees. The result was a top-down, command-and-control system in which central government imposed all sorts of targets – performance indicators and the like – in a welter of initiatives and regulation that confused almost everyone.

With the Conservatives still at reactionary sixes and sevens, Blair managed to win a **third general election in May 2005**, though not before he had promised to step down before the next general election thereafter – by any standard, a rather odd way to secure victory. After the election, Blair teased and tormented his many political enemies with promises of his imminent departure, but finally, in June 2007, he did indeed move on, to be succeeded by his arch-rival, the Chancellor of the Exchequer, Gordon Brown.

### Gordon Brown and the crash

A deeply obsessive man, **Gordon Brown** (b.1951) proved to be an extraordinarily clumsy Prime Minister with a tin ear for the public mood. He failed to create a

| 2005 | 2007 | 2009 |
|---|---|---|
| The Civil Partnership Act comes into effect, allowing couples of the same sex to have legal recognition of their relationships. | Smoking banned in enclosed public places in England and Wales. | Economic crisis prompts the Bank of England to reduce interest rates to a record low of 0.5%: misery for savers; (some) pleasure for spenders. |

coherent narrative for either himself or his government, even managing to secure little credit for his one major achievement, the staving-off of a banking collapse during the worldwide **financial crisis** that hit the UK hard in the autumn of 2007–08. Brown's bold decision to keep public investment high by borrowing vast sums of money almost certainly prevented a comprehensive economic collapse in 2008 and 2009, though equally his failure to properly regulate the banks beforehand helped create the crisis in the first place.

In the build-up to the **general election of 2010**, both main political parties – Conservative and Labour – as well as the Liberal Democrats, spoke of the need to cut public spending more or less drastically, manoeuvring the electorate away from blaming the bankers for the crash, if not indeed capitalism per se. In the event, none of the three was able to secure a Parliamentary majority in the election, but an impasse was avoided when the Liberal Democrats swapped principles for power to join a **Conservative–Liberal Democrat coalition**, which took office in May 2010 with the Conservative David Cameron as Prime Minister.

## Back to the future – England today

An old Etonian with a PR background, **David Cameron** (b.1966) made a confident and sure-footed start, keeping his ideological cards well hidden (if indeed he has any), while his government limbered up in the background for a savage attack on the public sector dressed up as the need for austerity following the financial crash. All seemed set fair, with the Liberals suitably supine, but key policy initiatives soon began to run aground and the coalition zigzagged between decision and revision, for example in its plans to transform (that is, part privatise) the Health Service.

And so it has continued: the evisceration of public services has carried on apace, but the coalition still lacks a coherent plan and muddle and confusion engulf many of its initiatives. It's true that the UK has finally emerged from the post-2007 recession – and the Conservatives are keen to claim the credit – but pay lags behind inflation; the gap between the rich and the poor continues to widen; house prices, especially in London, have shot through the roof; and Britain's relationship with the EU remains problematic. Fortunately for Cameron, the leader of the Labour Party, the hapless Ed Miliband (b.1969), does not seem to have much of a plan either and the Liberals are facing an electoral pasting for joining the coalition; indeed, only **Nigel Farage** (b.1964), the jokey leader of the EU-hating, right-wing UKIP has managed to sting the Conservatives where it hurts.Underwhelmed by their political class, the English have withdrawn into mass indifference and/or a sullen acceptance of the status quo, though over the border, the wily **Alex Salmond**, leader of the **Scottish Nationalists**, did galvanise support for his vision of an independent Scotland in the referendum of September 18, 2014. The Nationalists came within a hair's breadth of achieving victory, and breaking up the United Kingdom, but the most remarkable feature of the referendum was the high turn-out – an astounding 84 percent. At time of writing, the fall-out from the referendum is impossible to gauge, but the first casualty has been Salmond himself, who resigned as Scotland's First Minister.

| 2011 | 2012 | 2013 | 2014 |
|---|---|---|---|
| Murdoch media empire in crisis over illegal phone-hacking: *News of the World* newspaper closed. | London hosts the Olympic Games. | Same-sex marriage legalised in England and Wales; Scotland follows in 2014. | Severe storms buffet chunks of England; part of the South Devon railway swept out to sea. The Scots reject independence in September's Scottish referendum. |

# Architecture

If England sometimes seems like a historic theme park, jam-packed with monuments and buildings recalling a long and fascinating past, it's because physical evidence of its long history is so ubiquitous. Despite the best efforts of Victorian modernizers, the Luftwaffe and twentieth-century town planners, every corner of the country has some landmark worthy of attention, whether it be a Neolithic burial site or a postmodern addition to a world-famous gallery.

## Pre-1066 origins

Dating from the **fourth millennium BC**, the oldest traces of building in England are the **Neolithic long barrows** (burial sites) and habitations, consisting of concentric rings of ditches and banks. The most famous of all English prehistoric monuments is the stone circle of **Stonehenge** on Salisbury Plain, which was begun in around 3000 BC and extensively modified over the next thousand years. This, as well as nearby **Avebury**, probably had an astronomical and sacred significance. Less grandiose **stone circles and rows** survive from the Lake District to Bodmin Moor, while **hut circles** on the moors of the West Country are associated with the Bronze Age – **Grimspound**, on Dartmoor, is one of the best examples, dating from about 1200 BC. The **Celts**, who arrived in numbers in around 600 BC, left behind a series of hill-top defensive works, ranging from simple circular earthworks to the vast complex of **Maiden Castle** in Dorset. The best preserved Iron Age village of this period is **Chysauster**, Cornwall, consisting of stone houses arranged in pairs. The **Romans** brought order, peace and a slew of **public buildings**, including the surviving amphitheatre in **Chester** and baths in **Bath**. Two of Roman Britain's principal towns, **Colchester** and **St Albans**, retain impressive remains, while the palace at **Fishbourne** in West Sussex, built around 75 AD, is a prime example of a wealthy provincial villa.

### The Anglo-Saxons

The most enduring relics of **Anglo-Saxon** construction were **stone-built churches**, though those that survived were subject to constant modifications, as was the case with two of the earliest English churches, both in **Canterbury** – St Peter and St Paul, and the town's first cathedral, both dating from around 600 AD. The most impressive of all Saxon churches, however, lies in the Midlands, at **Brixworth** in Northamptonshire, erected around 670, and distinguished by the systematic use of arches. The later Anglo-Saxon era was scarred by Viking incursions, though an emergent native style can be discerned in the churches and monasteries erected in the tenth century, many of which show a penchant for quirky decoration, as in the spiral columns in the crypt at St Wystan's Church in Repton, Derbyshire.

## Norman architecture

In the early eleventh century, Anglo-Saxon England's architectural insularity faded away as Continental influences wafted across the Channel. When Edward the Confessor rebuilt **Westminster Abbey** (1050–65), he followed the Norman – or Romanesque – style, while French architectural styles became the dominant influence in both castles and churches following the Norman conquest of 1066. The earliest Norman castles followed a "motte and bailey" design, consisting of a central tower (or keep) placed on a mound (the motte) encircled by one or more courts (the baileys). Most such castles were built of wood until the time of the Plantagenet Henry II, though some were stone-constructed from the beginning, including those at **Rochester** and **Colchester** and the **White Tower** at the **Tower of London**, the most formidable of all the Norman strongholds.

Once the country had been secured, the Normans set about transforming English churches. Many – for example at **Canterbury, York, St Albans, Winchester, Worcester** and **Ely** – were rebuilt along Romanesque lines, with cruciform ground plans and massive cylindrical columns topped by semicircular arches. The finest Norman church was **Durham Cathedral**, begun in 1093 and boasting Europe's first example of large-scale ribbed vaulting. An increasing love of decoration was evident in the spectacular zigzag and diamond patterns on its colossal piers, in the elaborately carved capitals and blind arcading in Canterbury Cathedral, and in the beak-head moulding in Lincoln Cathedral.

## The Transitional style

The twelfth century witnessed a dramatic increase in the wealth and power of England's **monastic houses**. The **Cistercians** were responsible for some of the most splendid foundations, establishing an especially grand group of self-sufficient monasteries in Yorkshire – **Fountains, Rievaulx** and **Jervaulx** – which all featured examples of the pointed arch, an idea imported from northern France. The reforming Cistercians favoured a plain style, but the native penchant for decoration gradually infiltrated their buildings, as at **Kirkstall Abbey** (c.1152), near Leeds. Other orders, such as the **Cluniacs**, showed a preference for greater elaboration from much earlier, as in the extravagantly ornate west front of Norfolk's **Castle Acre** priory (1140–50).

Profuse carved decoration and pointed arches were distinctive elements in the evolution of a **Transitional style**, which, from the middle of the twelfth century, represented a shift away from the purely Romanesque. The use of the pointed arch, alongside improvements in masonry techniques and the introduction of new systems of buttressing and vaulting, meant taller buildings, proportionally larger windows and more slender piers.

## Early English style

**Gothic** architecture began in earnest in the last quarter of the twelfth century, when Gothic motifs were used at **Roche Abbey** and **Byland**, both in Yorkshire, but it was the French-designed **choir** at **Canterbury Cathedral** (1175–84) that really established the new style. This first phase of English Gothic, lasting through most of the thirteenth century, is known as **Early English** (or Pointed or Lancet), and was given its full expression in what is regarded as the first truly Gothic cathedral in England, **Wells**, largely completed by 1190.

Begun shortly afterwards, **Lincoln Cathedral** takes the process of vertical emphasis further, with wall-shafts soaring all the way to the ceiling, while adding an even greater profusion of decoration. The strong influence of Lincoln, however, was resisted by the builders of **Salisbury Cathedral** (1220–65), one of the most homogeneous of the Early English churches.

The **rebuilding of Westminster Abbey** in 1220 epitomises a transitional phase in the evolution of Gothic architecture. This became the most French of English churches, as shown in the flying buttresses added to support its greater height and in the lavish use of **window tracery**, created by subdividing each window with moulded ribs (or mullions).

## The Decorated and Perpendicular styles

The development of complicated **tracery** is one of the chief characteristics of the **Decorated** style, which reached its apotheosis around the end of the thirteenth and the beginning of the fourteenth century, when the cathedral at **Exeter** was almost completely rebuilt with a dense exuberance of rib vaulting and multiple moulding on its arches and piers. **York Minster**, rebuilt from 1225 and the largest of all English Gothic churches, introduced **lierne vaulting**, whereby a subsidiary, essentially ornamental, rib is added to the roof complex. Intricately carved roof bosses and capitals are other common features of Decorated Gothic, as is the use of the **ogee curve** – a curve with a double bend in it.

The prevalent style in the second half of the fourteenth century was the **Perpendicular**, the first post-Norman architecture unique to England and one that emphasized a more rectilinear and less flamboyant design. In **Gloucester Cathedral** (rebuilt 1337–57), for example, this can be seen in the massive east window, in which the tracery is organized in vertical compartments, to maximize the light, while the cloister features the first fully developed **fan vault**.

The Wars of the Roses dinted the construction of new "prestige" buildings in the second half of the fifteenth century, though many parish churches eagerly embraced the new Perpendicular style and work did begin on the remarkable **King's College Chapel**, Cambridge, though this was only completed after the Tudors took the throne, its fan vaulting extended over the whole nave and harmonized with the windows and wall panelling. The Tudors commissioned a number of new buildings too, including Henry VII's splendid **St George's Chapel** at Windsor and **Henry VII's Chapel** in Westminster Abbey, where the dense sculptural detail took vaulting to the limit, with the lavish use of decorative pendants – a rare element in English design.

## The Renaissance

The impact of **Renaissance** architecture during the Tudor period was largely confined to small decorative features, such as the Italianate embellishments at **Hampton Court Palace**. The championing of new and innovative designs often devolved to powerful landowners as typified by the grand mansions of **Burghley House**, Lincolnshire (1552–87), **Longleat**, Wiltshire (1568–80), and **Hardwick Hall** in Derbyshire (1591–96) – celebrated in local rhyme as "Hardwick Hall, more glass than wall".

The full spirit of the Renaissance did not find full expression in England until **Inigo Jones** (1573–1652) began to apply the lessons learned from his visits to Italy, and in particular from his familiarity with Palladio's rules of proportion and symmetry. Appointed Royal Surveyor in 1615, Jones changed the direction of English architecture, with prominent London works including the **Banqueting House**, Whitehall (1619–22); the **Queen's House** at Greenwich (1617–35); and **St Paul's Church**, Covent Garden (1630s), the focal point of the first planned city square in England.

## Wren and the Baroque

The artistic heir of Inigo Jones, **Christopher Wren** (1632–1723) had already established himself as a mathematician and astronomer before turning to architecture shortly after the Restoration of 1660. Wren's work was never so wholeheartedly Italianate as that of Jones, and his first building, Oxford's **Sheldonian Theatre**, demonstrated an eclectic style that combined orthodox classicism with **Baroque** inventiveness and French and Dutch elements.

The bulk of Wren's achievement is to be seen in London, where the **Great Fire of 1666** led to a commission for the building of no less than 53 churches. The most striking of these buildings display a remarkable elegance and harmony, notably **St Bride** in Fleet Street, **St Mary-le-Bow** in Cheapside, **St Stephen Walbrook** alongside Mansion House and, most monumental of all, **St Paul's Cathedral** (1675–1710), with its massive central dome.

Wren also rebuilt, extended or altered several royal palaces, including the south and east wings of **Hampton Court** (1689–1700). Other secular works include **Trinity College Library**, Cambridge (1676–84), the **Tom Tower of Christ Church**, Oxford (1681–82) – a rare work in the Gothic mode – and, grandest of all, **Greenwich Hospital** (1694–98), a magnificent foil to the Queen's House built by Inigo Jones, and to Wren's own Royal Observatory (1675).

# Hawksmoor and Vanbrugh

Work at Greenwich Hospital was continued by Wren's pupil, **Nicholas Hawksmoor** (1661–1736), whose distinctively muscular Baroque is seen to best effect in his London churches, primarily **St George-in-the-East** (1715–23) and **Christ Church**, Spitalfields (1723–29). His exercises in Gothic pastiche include the western towers of **Westminster Abbey** (1734) and **All Souls College**, Oxford (1716–35), while the mausoleum at Castle Howard in Yorkshire (1729) shows close affinities with the Roman Baroque.

The third great English architect of the Baroque era was **John Vanbrugh** (1664–1726), principally known as a dramatist and lacking any architectural training when he was commissioned to design a new country seat at **Castle Howard** (1699–1726). More flamboyant than either Hawksmoor or Wren, Vanbrugh went on to design numerous other grandiose houses, of which the outstanding example is the gargantuan **Blenheim Palace** (1705–20), the high point of English Baroque.

# Gibbs and Palladianism

The peace that followed the Treaty of Utrecht (1713) precipitated a rush to the Continent by English aristocrats and artisans. The most obvious effect was the rebirth in England of the **Palladian** architecture introduced by Inigo Jones a century before – a style that was to dominate the secular architecture of the eighteenth century. The Palladian movement was championed by a Whig elite led by **Lord Burlington** (1694–1753), whose own masterpiece was **Chiswick House** in London (1725), a domed villa closely modelled on Palladio's Villa Rotonda. Burlington collaborated with the decorator, garden designer and architect **William Kent** (1685–1748) on such stately piles as **Holkham Hall** in Norfolk (1734), whose imposing portico and ordered composition typify the break with Baroque dramatics.

In the field of church architecture, the most influential architect of the time was **James Gibbs** (1682–1754), whose masterpiece, **St Martin-in-the-Fields** in London (1722–26), with its steeple sprouting above a pedimented portico, was widely imitated as a model of how to combine the Classical with the Gothic. Elsewhere, Gibbs designed **Senate House** (1722–30) and the **Fellows' Building** at King's College (1723–49), both in Cambridge, and Oxford's **Radcliffe Camera** (1737–49), which drew heavily on his knowledge of Roman styles.

The Palladian idiom was further disseminated by such men as **John Wood** (1704–54), designer of **Liverpool Town Hall** (1749–54) but better known for the work he did in **Bath**, helping to transform the city into a paragon of town planning. His showpieces there are **Queen Square** (1729–36) and the **Circus** (1754), the latter completed by his son, **John Wood the Younger** (1728–81), who went on to design Bath's **Royal Crescent** (1767–74). Georgian Bath was further developed by **Robert Adam** (1728–92), the most versatile and refined architect of his day, who designed the city's **Pulteney Bridge** (1769–74). Adam's forte, however, was in designing elaborate decorative interiors, best displayed in **Syon House** (1762–69) and **Osterley Park** (1761–80), both on the western outskirts of London, and **Kenwood** (1767–79) on the edge of Hampstead Heath. Adam's chief rival was the more fastidious **William Chambers** (1723–96), whose masterpiece, **Somerset House** on London's Strand (1776–98), is an academic counterpoint to Adam's dashing originality.

---

## LANDSCAPE GARDENING

One area in which English designers excelled in the eighteenth century was **landscape gardening**, whose finest exponent was **Capability Brown** (1716–83). All over England, Brown and his acolytes modified the estates of the landed gentry into idealized "Picturesque" landscapes, often enhancing the view with a romantic "ruin" or some exotic structure such as a Chinese pagoda or Indian temple. One of Brown's earliest and most spectacular designs was at **Stowe** in Buckinghamshire, while **Chatsworth** in the Peak District combined his vision with the talents of **Joseph Paxton**, who contributed to the estate in the following century.

# The nineteenth century

The greatest architect of the late eighteenth and early nineteenth centuries was **John Nash** (1752–1835), whose Picturesque country houses were built in collaboration with the landscapist **Humphrey Repton** (1752–1818). Nash is associated above all with the style favoured during the **Regency** of his friend and patron the Prince of Wales (afterwards George IV), a decorous style that made plentiful use of stucco. A prolific worker, Nash was responsible for much of the present-day appearance of such **resorts** as Weymouth, Cheltenham, Clifton (in Bristol), Tunbridge Wells and Brighton, site of his orientalized Gothic palace, the **Brighton Pavilion**. In central **London**, his constructions include the **Haymarket Theatre** (1820), the church of **All Souls**, Langham Place (1822–25), and **Clarence House** (1825), not to mention the layout of **Regent's Park** and **Regent Street** (from 1811), and the remodelling of **Buckingham Palace** (1826–30). The pared-down Classical experiments of Nash's contemporary, **Sir John Soane** (1753–1837), presented a serious-minded contrast to Nash's extrovert creations. Little remains of his greatest masterpiece, the **Bank of England** (1788–1833), but his idiosyncratic style is well illustrated by two other London buildings – his own home, **Sir John Soane's Museum** on Lincoln's Inn Fields (1812–13) and **Dulwich Art Gallery** (1811–14).

Nash and other exponents of the Picturesque also dabbled in a version of the **Gothic** style, and when Parliament voted a million pounds for the construction of new Anglican churches in 1818, two-thirds of these were built in a Gothic or near-Gothic style, inaugurating the so-called **Gothic Revival**. The pre-eminence of neo-Gothic was confirmed when the **Houses of Parliament** were rebuilt in that style after the fire of 1834. The contract was given to Charles Barry (1795–1860), the designer of the classical Reform Club, but his collaborator, **Augustus Welby Pugin** (1812–52), was to become the unswerving apostle of the neo-Gothic. Another eminent architect, **George Gilbert Scott** (1811–78) expressed his neo-Gothic predilections in the extravaganzas of **St Pancras Station** (1868–74) and the **Albert Memorial** (1863–72), both based on Flemish and north Italian Gothic models, while **Truro Cathedral** (1880–1910) was a scholarly exercise in French-influenced Gothic.

Nonetheless, the Victorian age was nothing if not eclectic: many public buildings continued to draw on Renaissance and Classical influences – notably the town halls of Birmingham and Leeds (1832–50 & 1853–58) – and the Catholic **Westminster Cathedral** (1895–1903) was a neo-Byzantine confection. The architectural stew was further enriched by a string of engineer-architects, who employed cast iron and other manufactured materials in such works as Joseph Paxton's glass-and-iron **Crystal Palace** (1851, burned down in 1936). The potential of iron and glass was similarly exploited in **Newcastle Central Station** (1846–55), the first of a generation of monumental railway stations incorporating classical motifs and rib-vaulted iron roofs.

## Ruskin, Morris and Charles Voysey

**John Ruskin** (1819–1900) and his disciple **William Morris** (1834–96), leader of the Arts and Crafts Movement, rejected these industrial technologies in favour of traditional materials – brick, stone and timber – worked in traditional ways. Morris was not an architect himself, but he did plan the interior of his own home, the Red House in Bexley, Kent (1854), from designs by Philip Webb (1831–1915). The Arts and Crafts Movement also influenced **Charles Voysey** (1851–1941), whose clean-cut cottages and houses eschewed all ostentation, depending instead on the meticulous and subtle use of local materials for their effect. The originality of Voysey's work and that of his contemporaries M.H. Baillie Scott

> **TOP FIVE MODERN BUILDINGS**
>
> **Eden Project** Cornwall, 2001 (see p.346)
> **Imperial War Museum North**
> Manchester, 2002 (see p.521)
> **Sage Gateshead** 2004 (see p.653)
> **Selfridges** Birmingham, 2003 (see p.451)
> **Tate Modern, London** 1948–63 & 2000
> (see p.84)

(1865–1945) and Ernest Newton (1856–1922) was later debased by scores of speculative suburban builders, though not before their refreshingly simple style had found recognition first in Germany and then across the rest of Europe.

## The twentieth century

Revivalist tendencies prevailed in England throughout the early decades of the twentieth century, typified by **Edwin Lutyens** (1869–1944), whose work moved from the Arts and Crafts style through to classicized structures, neo-Georgianism and the one-off, faux-medieval **Castle Drogo** on the edge of Dartmoor (1910–30). An awareness of more radical trends did, however, surface in isolated projects in the 1930s, for example **Senate House** in London's Bloomsbury (1932), designed by **Charles Holden** (1875–1960), who was also responsible for some of London's Underground stations, notably **Arnos Grove** (1932). The **Tecton group**, led by the Russian immigrant Lubetkin, also created several examples of the austere International Modern style, most notably London Zoo's **Penguin Pool** (1934). The UK's first public building built in the modernist style was the sleek, streamlined **De La Warr Pavilion** in Bexhill-on-Sea, Sussex, designed by Erich Mendelsohn and Serge Chermayeff in 1935, and described by Mendelsohn as a "horizontal skyscraper".

### 1945 to 1980

The German bombing of World War II created a national **housing crisis** of immense proportions: by 1945, nearly a third of the nation's houses had been destroyed or damaged. City planners up and down the country set about the problem with vim and gusto – but, with one or two notable exceptions, they got the solutions very wrong. Terraced houses were associated with slums, so they were knocked down by the thousand, but all too often they were replaced by **tower blocks** in a pale imitation of the modernist style proclaimed by the likes of Corbusier: modernism had gained a foothold in England after London's 1951 **Festival of Britain**. As if that wasn't enough, speed of reconstruction – rather than quality – was often the key criterion and, convinced that the motor car was the future, roads were ploughed through a host of English cities almost willy-nilly.

   Nevertheless, although the general situation was pretty dire, there were some noteworthy architectural achievements in the 1950s and 1960s, including **Basil Spence**'s (1907–76) startling replacement of the bombed **Coventry Cathedral** (1951–59); Denys Lasdun's (1914–2001) ziggurats at the **University of East Anglia** in Norwich (1963); and the **Royal Festival Hall** (1949–51), a triumphant modernist departure from the traditional model for classical music venues.

### 1980 to 2000

In the late twentieth century, English architecture was stranded between a popular dislike for the modern and a general reluctance among its practitioners to return to the architectural past. **Prince Charles** also entered the debate: his famous comment in 1984 on plans for the new Sainsbury Wing at London's National Gallery ("a monstrous carbuncle on the face of a much-loved and elegant friend") resulted in a replacement of the original design with a much safer Neoclassical pastiche – and initiated a general backtracking on architectural modernism. More positively, a string of leading architects adjusted to the new state of play by adopting a more fluent, sinuous or even whimsical style in their new commissions – and the general public responded well. **Norman Foster** (b.1935) chipped in with the glass-tent terminal at **Stansted Airport** (1991) and **Michael Hopkins** (b.1935) produced both the eye-catching Mound Stand for Lord's Cricket Ground (1985–87) and the wood-panelled auditorium at the **Glyndebourne Opera House** (1994). Even the money-is-power **Lloyd's Building** (1978–86) by **Richard Rogers** (b.1933) was partly redeemed by its hive-like interior.

## The 2000s and beyond

In London, the early years of the twenty-first century produced an array of prestigious, public buildings including Rogers' **Millennium Dome** (1999, now the O2 arena) erected in Greenwich; the spectacular transformation of Giles Gilbert Scott's South Bank power station into **Tate Modern** (2000) by Herzog & de Meuron; the Olympic Games **Aquatic Centre** (Zaha Hadid, 2011); and, by the Norman Foster group, both the **Great Court** (2000) at the British Museum and the **Greater London Assembly** building (2002). Exciting and fresh work also appeared in less likely places, as within the hallowed Victorian frontage of **St Pancras Station**, overhauled and reopened to grand acclaim in 2007, and at Richard Rogers' controversial but ultimately triumphant **Terminal 5** at Heathrow Airport (2008). Even more controversial were the city-slicker skyscrapers that, in a vulgar assertion of the power of money, transformed London's skyline. Behemoths like **The Gherkin** (officially 30 St Mary Axe; 2004), the **Heron Tower** (Kohn Pederson Fox, 2011) and Renzo Piano's **Shard** (2012) were generally well received by both architects and business leaders, but many Londoners found – and find – them daunting and aesthetically distasteful.

### Beyond London

Outside the capital, most of Britain's big cities have invested in eye-catching, prestige developments with prime examples being Gateshead's **BALTIC** arts centre (Ellis Williams Architects, 2002); Manchester's stunning **Imperial War Museum North** (Libeskind, 2002); **Nottingham Contemporary** art gallery (Caruso St John, 2009); Leicester's **Curve** theatre (Rafael Viñoly, 2008); **Sage Gateshead** (Foster and Partners, 2004); and the redevelopment of Liverpool's Paradise Street as **Liverpool One**, opened in 2008–09. Most of these structures are stand alone – or nearly stand alone – but in Birmingham they have shown more ambition, reconfiguring the whole of the city centre by not only refurbishing existing buildings (as in the Ikon Gallery and The Rotunda) but also erecting superb new structures, among which three stand out: the billowing **Selfridges** department store (Future Systems, 2003); the netted **Birmingham Library** (Francine Houben, 2013); and **The Cube** tower block, complete with its startling cladding (MAKE, Ken Shuttleworth, 2010).

# Books and literature

A tour of literary England could take several lifetimes. Many of the world's most famous writers were born, lived and died here, leaving footprints that reach into every corner of the country. Writers' birthplaces, houses, libraries and graves are a staple of local tourist industries, while in places like Stratford-upon-Avon and Grasmere, literature and tourism have formed an unbreakable symbiosis. England even has one quintessential bookish destination, Hay-on-Wye, the town on the Anglo–Welsh border that is entirely devoted to the buying, selling and enjoyment of books – its annual literary festival (every May) is the nation's biggest book-related jamboree.

## Literary England

For readers and book-lovers of all ages, there's something deeply satisfying about immersing yourself in **English literature**'s natural fabric, whether it's tramping the Yorkshire moors with the Brontë sisters or exploring the streets of Dickens' Rochester. And for every over-trumpeted sight in "Shakespeare Country" or "Beatrix Potter's Lakeland" there are dozens of other locales that contemporary English writers have made unquestionably their own, from Martin Amis's London to P.D. James's East Anglia. To plan a route following in the footsteps of your favourite author, turn to Itineraries (see p.24).

### Criminal England

Contemporary **crime writers** have moved well beyond the enclosed country-house mysteries of Agatha Christie. Colin Dexter's morose Inspector Morse flits between Town and Gown in **Oxford** in a cerebral series of whodunnits, while in the elegantly crafted novels of P.D. James it's the remote coast and isolated villages of **East Anglia** that often provide the backdrop. The other English "Queen of Crime", Ruth Rendell, sets her long-running Inspector Wexford series in "Kingsmarkham" – inspired by Midhurst in **West Sussex**, surely the most crime-ridden country town after over twenty Wexford novels. **London**, of course, preoccupies many writers, from Derek Raymond or Jake Arnott recreating Sixties villainy to Rendell again, writing as Barbara Vine, at home with the capital's suburban misfits, drop-outs and damaged. Val McDermid, and her sassy private eye, Kate Brannigan, nail contemporary **Manchester**, and the seedier side of the city also gets a good kicking in the noir novels of Nicholas Blincoe. **Yorkshire** of the 1970s and 1980s is dissected in David Peace's majestic Red Riding quartet about corrupt police; Reginald Hill's popular Dalziel and Pascoe series portrays a more traditional pair of Yorkshire detectives, but in his Joe Sixsmith private-eye novels it's a re-imagined **Luton** that forms the backdrop. Graham Greene gave us seedy **Brighton** first; Peter James' policeman, Roy Grace, digs further into its underbelly, while in **Portsmouth** it's Graham Hurley's Joe Faraday charged with keeping the peace. Britain's rural areas don't escape the escalating body count either. Peter Robinson's Inspector Banks series is set in the **Yorkshire Dales**, and for Stephen Booth and his Derbyshire detective Ben Cooper it's the wilds of the **Peak District**.

### Dickensian England

The name of **Charles Dickens** has passed into the language as shorthand for a city's filthy stew of streets and gallery of grotesques. But although any dark alley or old curiosity shop in London might still be considered "Dickensian", it's a different matter trying to trace the author through his works. He was born in **Portsmouth**, though spent his younger years in **Chatham** and **Rochester**, in Kent (and set most of his last book, *The Mystery of Edwin Drood*, in the latter). Is this Dickensian England? Perhaps, though many of the most famous books – including *Oliver Twist, David Copperfield, Bleak House* and *Little Dorrit* – are set or partly set in a **London** that Dickens unquestionably made his own. His unhappy early experiences of the city – the boot-blacking factory at the age of twelve, his father's spell in a debtors' prison, working as a law clerk – form the basis of many of Dickens' most trenchant pieces of social analysis. Yet only one of his London houses survives (now the Charles Dickens Museum in Bloomsbury), and he only lived in that for two years. To the north then, finally, for Dickensian England, to the fictional "Coketown" of *Hard Times*. Dickens went to Preston and other **Lancashire** mill towns to gather material for his "state-of-the-nation" satire about the social and economic conditions of factory workers, while in **Barnard Castle** (County Durham) he found the heartbreaking neglect of schoolchildren that underpinned the magnificent *Nicholas Nickleby*.

## Haworth and the Brontës

Quite why the sheltered life of the **Brontë** sisters, Charlotte, Emily and Anne, should exert such a powerful fascination is a puzzle, though the contrast of their pinched provincial existence in the Yorkshire village of **Haworth** with the brooding moors and tumultuous passions of their novels may well form part of the answer. Their old home in the village parsonage and the family vault in the parish church only tell half the story. As Charlotte later recalled, "resident in a remote district… we were wholly dependent on ourselves and each other, on books and study, for the enjoyments and occupations of life". Charlotte's *Jane Eyre*, the harrowing story of a much-put-upon governess, sprang from this domestic isolation, yet it was out on the bleak moors above Haworth that inspiration often struck, and where works like Emily's *Wuthering Heights* and Anne's *The Tenant of Wildfell Hall* progressed from mere parlour entertainments to melodramatic studies of emotion and obsession.

## Shakespeare Country

Warwickshire in the West Midlands is – as the road signs attest – "Shakespeare Country", though to all intents and purposes it's a county with just one main destination – **Stratford-upon-Avon**, birthplace in 1564 of England's greatest writer. So few facts about **Shakespeare**'s life are known that Stratford can be a disappointment for the serious literary pilgrim, its buildings and sights hedged with "reputedlys" and "maybes" – after 500 years, still the only incontrovertible evidence is that he was born in Stratford, and lived, married, had children and died there. Real Shakespeare country could just as easily be London, where his plays were written and performed (there was no theatre in Stratford in Shakespeare's day). But, from the house where he was born

---

### POETIC ENGLAND

From *The Canterbury Tales* onwards, **English poets** have taken inspiration from the country's people and landscape. Traditionally, much was made of England's rural lives and trades, by poets as diverse as Northamptonshire "peasant poet" John Clare and A.E. Housman, whose nostalgic *A Shropshire Lad* is one of English poetry's most favoured works. For poets like Cumbria's Norman Nicholson it was working people, their dialect and industry that inspired, while in Yorkshire-born (and later Devon resident) Ted Hughes, savage English nature found a unique voice. Perhaps there's something about the north in particular that engages and enrages poets: Philip Larkin, famously, spent the last thirty years of his life in Hull; the self-proclaimed "bard of Salford", John Cooper Clarke, skewered Manchester in his early machine-gun-style punk poems; and Huddersfield-born Simon Armitage continues to report "from the long, lifeless mud of the River Colne". Meanwhile, dub poet Linton Kwesi Johnson uses Jamaican patois in devastating commentaries on the English social condition ("Inglan is a bitch").

(probably) to the church in which he's buried (definitely), Stratford at least provides a coherent centre for England's Shakespeare industry – and it's certainly the most atmospheric place to see a production by the Royal Shakespeare Company.

## Wordsworth's Lake District

**William Wordsworth** and the **Lake District** are inextricably linked, and in the streets of Cockermouth (where he was born), Hawkshead (where he went to school) and Grasmere (where he lived most of his life), you're never very far from a sight associated with the poet and his circle. Wordsworth's views on nature and the natural world stood at the very heart of all his poetry, and it's still a jolt to encounter the very views that inspired him – from his carefully tended garden at Rydal Mount to the famous daffodils of Gowbarrow Park. It wasn't just Wordsworth either. The "**Lake Poets**" of popular description – Wordsworth, Samuel Taylor Coleridge and Robert Southey – formed a clique of fluctuating friendships with a shared passion for the Lakes at its core.

# A bibliography

The bibliography we've given here is necessarily selective, and entirely subjective. Most of the books reviewed are currently in print, though if your local bookshops can't help, then Amazon almost certainly can (ⓦamazon.co.uk; ⓦamazon.com). The ★symbol indicates titles that are especially recommended.

## TRAVELS AND JOURNALS

**Peter Ackroyd** *London: The Biography; Albion*. The capital is integral to much of Ackroyd's works and in *London* the great city itself is presented as a living organism, with themed chapters covering its fables, follies and foibles. Meanwhile, in the massively erudite *Albion*, Ackroyd traces the very origins of English culture and imagination.

★**Bill Bryson** *Notes From A Small Island*. After twenty years living and working in England, Bryson set off on one last tour of Britain before returning to the States – though in the end he couldn't resist his new country and now lives in Norfolk. His snort-with-laughter observations set the tone for his future travel and popular science best-sellers.

**Paul Kingsnorth** *Real England*. Kingsnorth's personal journey through his own "private England" is partly a lament for what's being lost – village greens, apple varieties, independent shops, waterways, post offices – and partly a heartfelt howl against globalization.

**Stuart Maconie** *Pies and Prejudice; Adventures on the High Teas*. A Lancastrian exile explores the north of England in *Pies*, in which you can find out where the north starts (Crewe station, apparently) and unravel the arcane mysteries of northern dialect, dress and delicacies. *Adventures* continues his engaging investigation of the country, this time of the mythical "Middle England" so beloved of social commentators, and there are more national ruminations in *Hope and Glory*.

**Ian Marchant** *The Longest Crawl*. The pub – so central to English life and landscape – is dissected in this highly

entertaining account of a month-long crawl across the country, involving pork scratchings, funny beer names and lots of falling over.

**Harry Pearson** *Racing Pigs and Giant Marrows; The Far Corner*. The subtitles tell you all you need to know about content – "Travels Around North Country Fairs" and "A Mazy Dribble Through North-East Football" respectively – though they don't tell you that you'll laugh until your sides ache. Pearson was at it again in the more recent *The Trundlers* – the cricketing pitfalls, peculiarities and even premonitions of death that afflict the medium-paced bowler.

**J.B. Priestley** *English Journey*. The Bradford-born playwright and author's record of his travels around England in the 1930s say nothing about contemporary England, but in many ways its quirkiness and eye for English eccentricity formed the blueprint for the later Brysons and Therouxs.

**W.G. Sebald** *Rings of Saturn*. Intriguing, ruminative book that is a heady mix of novel, travel and memoir, focusing ostensibly on the author's walking tour of Suffolk.

**Iain Sinclair** *London Orbital*. After spending a couple of years walking around the "concrete necklace" of the M25, the erudite Sinclair delves into the dark and mysterious heart of suburban London.

**Paul Theroux** *The Kingdom by the Sea*. Travelling around the British coast in its entirety in 1982 to find out what the British are really like leaves Theroux thoroughly bad tempered. No change there then.

## GUIDEBOOKS

★**Simon Jenkins** *England's Thousand Best Churches; England's Thousand Best Houses*. A lucid, witty pick of

England's churches and houses, divided by county and with a star rating – for the book on houses Jenkins includes all

## WINDOWS ONTO ENGLAND'S PAST

In his celebrated diary, **Samuel Pepys** recorded an eyewitness account of daily life in London from 1660 until 1669, covering momentous events like the Great Plague and the Great Fire. The plague of 1665 also takes centre stage in *Journal of a Plague Year* by **Daniel Defoe** (author of *Robinson Crusoe*), a fictional "observation" of London's tribulations actually written sixty years later, while the same author's *Tour Through the Whole Island of Great Britain* (1724) was an early sort of economic guide to the country in the years immediately before the Industrial Revolution. Later, the changing seasons in a Hampshire village were recorded by **Gilbert White**, whose *Natural History of Selborne* (1788) is still seen as a masterpiece of nature writing. By 1830, **William Cobbett** was bemoaning the death of rural England and its customs in *Rural Rides*, while decrying both the growth of cities and the iniquities suffered by the exploited urban poor. These last were given magnificent expression in *The Condition of the Working Class in England*, an unforgettable portrait of life in England's hellish industrial towns, published in 1844 as **Friedrich Engels** worked in his father's Manchester cotton mills. Journalist **Henry Mayhew** would later do something similar for the Victorian capital's downtrodden in his mighty *London Labour and the London Poor* (1851). **George Orwell** was therefore following in a well-worn path when he published his dissections of 1920s' and 1930s' working-class and under-class life, *Down and Out in Paris and London* (1933) and *The Road to Wigan Pier* (1937), giving respectively a tramp's-eye view of the world and the brutal effects of the Great Depression on the industrial communities of Lancashire and Yorkshire. A later period of English transformation was recorded in *Akenfield* (1969), the surprising best-seller by **Ronald Blythe** that presented life in a rural Suffolk village on the cusp of change. Craig Taylor's update, *Return to Akenfield* (2006), and **Richard Askwith**'s *The Lost Village* (2008) show that interest in ordinary English rural life endures today, while in *The Plot* (2009), **Madeleine Bunting** presents an innovative through-the-ages biography of a secluded acre of land owned by her father that gets to the very heart of the English spirit.

sorts of curiosities, from caves in Nottingham to prefabs in Buckinghamshire. Sales were so good that Jenkins has had another stab at the same format in 2013 with *England's 100 Best Views*.

**Sam Jordison and Dan Kieran** *Crap Towns; Crap Towns II; Crap Towns Returns: Back by Unpopular Demand.* The books that made local councils all over England as mad as hell – utterly prejudiced but tongue-in-cheek accounts of the worst places to live in the country. We daren't even repeat the names of the "winners", we'll only get letters of complaint (or cheers of agreement).

**Iain Pattinson** *Lyttleton's Britain*. Great British jazz man and bandleader Humphrey Lyttleton presented the roving radio comedy panel game *I'm Sorry I Haven't A Clue* for 40 years until his death in 2008. His barbed town introductions (". . . from the Malvern Hills. . . it is possible to catch a sight of Birmingham, despite the many, clearly posted warning signs") form a laugh-out-loud gazetteer to many of England's towns and cities.

**A. Wainwright** *A Pictorial Guide to the Lakeland Fells* (7 vols). More than mere guidebooks could ever be, the beautifully produced small-format volumes of handwritten notes and sketches (produced between 1952 and 1966) have led generations up the Lake District's mountains and down through its dales. The originals have now been revised to take account of changing routes and landscapes.

## HISTORY, SOCIETY AND POLITICS

**Julian Baggini** *Welcome to Everytown: A Journey into the English Mind.* The prolific Baggini's "Everytown" is Rotherham – or rather postcode S66, supposedly containing the most typical mix of household types in the country. As a philosopher, his six-month stay there wasn't in search of the English character, but rather their "folk philosophy" (ie, what they think). The result? A surprising, illuminating view of mainstream English life.

**Catherine Bailey** *Black Diamonds – the Rise and Fall of an English Dynasty.* Thoroughly researched book telling the tale of the feuding, coal-owning Fitzwilliam family, powerful aristocrats who were holed up in Wentworth, their lavish Yorkshire mansion, for generation after generation.

**Andy Beckett** *When the Lights Went Out.* Enough time has elapsed to make 1970s Britain seem like a different world (the title is reference to the power cuts during the industrial unrest of 1974), but Beckett's lively history brings the period to life.

**John Campbell** *The Iron Lady: Margaret Thatcher.* Campbell has been mining the Thatcher seam for several years now and this abridged paperback version, published in 2012, hits many political nails right on the head. By the same author, and equally engaging, is his 1987 *Aneurin*

*Bevan and the Mirage of British Socialism* as well as his latest work, a biography of Roy Jenkins.

**Lynsey Hanley** *Estates.* The story of social housing (the council "estates" of the title) hardly sounds like a winning topic, but Hanley's "intimate history" brilliantly reveals how class structure is built into the very English landscape (albeit a land that tourists rarely see).

**Christopher Hill** *The World Turned Upside-Down; God's Englishman: Oliver Cromwell and the English Revolution.* A pioneering Marxist historian, Hill (1912–2003) transformed the way the story of the English Civil War and the Commonwealth was related in a string of superbly researched, well-written texts – among which these are two of the best.

★**Eric Hobsbawm** *Industry and Empire.* Ostensibly an economic history of Britain from 1750 to the late 1960s charting Britain's decline and fall as a world power, Hobsbawm's (1917–2012) great skill was in detailed analysis of the effects on ordinary people. Also *Captain Swing*, focusing on the eponymous labourers' uprisings of nineteenth-century England, and his magnificent trilogy, *The Age of Revolution 1789–1848, The Age of Capital 1848–1875*, and *The Age of Extremes 1914–1991*; there's nothing better.

**David Horspool** *Why Alfred Burned the Cakes.* Little is known of the life of Alfred the Great, king of Wessex, and arguably the first king of what would become "England", but Horspool adds a welcome new dimension to the myths and legends. And in case you were wondering about the cakes, Alfred probably didn't.

**Roy Jenkins** *Churchill: A Biography.* Churchill biographies abound (and the man himself, of course, wrote up his own life), but politician and statesman Jenkins adds an extra level of understanding. Jenkins (1920–2003) specialized in political biogs of men of power, so you can also read his take on the likes of Gladstone, Asquith and Roosevelt.

**Owen Jones** *Chavs: The Demonization of the Working Class.* A trumpet blast from the political left – and a yell of moral/political outrage at the way the media treat the working class. The youthful Jones is articulate, fiery and witty – so expect his character to be assassinated in the media if he becomes (even more) effective.

★**David Kynaston** *Austerity Britain, 1945–51.* Comprehensive vox pop that gives the real flavour of postwar England. Everything is here, from the skill of a Dennis Compton cricket innings through to the difficulties and dangers of hewing coal down the pit, all in a land where there were "no supermarkets, no teabags, no Formica, no trainers ... and just four Indian restaurants". Also recommended is Kynaston's follow-up volumes *Family Britain, 1951–1957* and *Modernity Britain, 1957–1959*.

**Diane Purkiss** *The English Civil War: A People's History.* The English story of revolution, given a human face – the clue is in the subtitle. Purkiss dodges the battles and armies,

focusing instead on the men who fought and the women who had to feed and tend them. If you like it, try Purkiss's follow-up *Literature, Gender and Politics During the English Civil War.*

★**Andrew Rawnsley** *The End of the Party.* Arguably Britain's most acute political journalist, Rawnsley cross-examines and dissects New Labour under Blair and Brown to withering effect.

**Sheila Rowbotham** *Hidden from History.* Last published in 1992, this key feminist text provides an uncompromising account of 300 years of women's oppression in Britain alongside a cogent analysis of the ways in which key female figures have been written out of history.

**Simon Schama** *A History of Britain* (3 vols). British history, from 3000 BC to 2000 AD, delivered by the country's major TV historical popularizer (the books followed the series). Schama's the best at this kind of stuff, writing in a clear and lucid style.

**James Sharpe** *Remember, Remember the Fifth of November; Dick Turpin.* A crisp retelling of the 1605 Gunpowder Plot, which also helps put the English phenomenon of Bonfire Night into context. In *Dick Turpin*, subtitled "The Myth of the English Highwayman", Sharpe stands and delivers a broadside to the commonly accepted notion of Turpin and his ilk – not romantic robbers but brutal villains after all. If you warmed to Sharpe's themes, then move onto his *A Fiery & Furious People: A History of Violence in England.*

**Lytton Strachey** *Queen Victoria.* Strachey (1880–1932) is often credited with establishing a warmer, wittier, more all-encompassing form of biography, with his *Queen Victoria* (1921) following on from his ground-breaking *Eminent Victorians* (1918). Many others have followed in trying to understand Britain's longest reigning monarch, but few match Strachey's economy and wit.

**A.J.P. Taylor** *English History 1914–45.* Thought-provoking, scintillatingly well-written survey from Britain's finest populist historian (1906–90). When it first appeared it was the fifth and final volume of the Oxford History of England. Also *The Origins of the Second World War, The Struggle for Mastery of Europe 1848–1918* and *The First World War: An Illustrated History*, a penetrating analysis of how the war started and why it went on for so long and including a savage portrayal of Britain's high command; first published in 1963, but never surpassed.

★**E.P. Thompson** *The Making of the English Working Class.* A seminal text – essential reading for anyone who wants to understand the fabric of English society – tracing the trials and tribulations of England's emergent working-class between 1780 and 1832.

**Michael Wood** *In Search of England: Journeys into the English Past.* Historian Wood was an early TV historian and consequently his books are highly readable. *In Search of*

## ZEITGEIST NOVELS

Which English novels since the war best capture the spirit of the age in which they were written? Here's our choice.

**1984**, George Orwell (1949). When the clocks strike thirteen in the first sentence, you know something's wrong with wartime England.

**Lucky Jim**, Kingsley Amis (1954). "Angry Young Man" writes funniest book of the century.

**Saturday Night and Sunday Morning**, Alan Sillitoe (1958). Factory life and sexual shenanigans in working-class Nottingham.

**Billy Liar**, Keith Waterhouse (1959). Cloying Yorkshire provincialism meets laugh-out-loud fantasy on the eve of the Swinging Sixties.

**A Clockwork Orange**, Anthony Burgess (1962). Droogs, crime and violence in a dystopian England.

**The History Man**, Malcolm Bradbury (1975). The "campus novel" par excellence.

**London Fields**, Martin Amis (1989). Literary London's favourite bad boy writes ferociously witty, baleful satire or pretentious drivel – you decide.

**The Buddha of Suburbia**, Hanif Kureishi (1990). Youth culture, identity and the immigrant experience.

**Fever Pitch**, Nick Hornby (1992). The modern masculine obsession with football started here?

**Bridget Jones's Diary**, Helen Fielding (1996). Thirty-something female neurosis, rehashed from an original newspaper column (and then again in film).

**White Teeth**, Zadie Smith (2000). Mixed families, mixed races, mixed religions, mixed England.

**Saturday**, Ian McEwan (2005). England's finest contemporary writer addresses the state of the nation and upper-middle-class angst.

**South of the River**, Blake Morrison (2007). The first heavyweight literary despatch from the decade of Blair and New Labour.

**One Day**, David Nicholls (2009). Dexter and Emma. Short-term pleasure and long-term commitment battle it out.

**Life after Life**, Kate Atkinson (2013). Clever, interrogative stuff in a world with no absolutes.

---

*England* delves into the myths and historical record behind the notion of England and Englishness, while other "In search of…" titles shed new light on the Dark Ages, Shakespeare and the Domesday Book.

## ART, ARCHITECTURE AND ARCHEOLOGY

**John Betjeman** *Ghastly Good Taste, Or, A Depressing Story of the Rise and Fall of English Architecture.* Classy – and classic – one-hundred-page account of England's architecture written by one of the country's shrewdest poet-commentators. First published in 1970.

**William Gaunt** *Concise History of English Painting.* Books covering the broad sweep of English painting are thin on the ground, but this succinct and excellently illustrated book provides a useful introduction to its subject, covering the Middle Ages to the twentieth century in just 288 pages; it is, however, a little dated – it was published in 1964.

★**Owen Hatherley** *A Guide to the New Ruins of Great Britain.* No good news here from this angry rant of a book, which rails against – and describes in detail – the 1990s architectural desecration of a string of British cities in the name of speculation masquerading as modernisation.

**Nikolaus Pevsner** *The Buildings of England.* If you want to know who built what, when, why and how, look no further than this popular architectural series, in 46 county-by-county volumes. This magisterial project was initially a one-man show, but after Pevsner died in 1983 later authors revised his text, inserting newer buildings but generally respecting the founder's personal tone.

**Francis Pryor** *Home: A Time Traveller's Tales from Britain's Prehistory.* The often arcane discoveries of working archeologists are given fascinating new exposure in Pryor's lively archeological histories of Britain. Everything from before the Romans to the sixteenth century is examined through the archeologist's eye, unearthing a more sophisticated native culture than was formerly thought along the way. This latest book concentrates on family life, but other Pryor titles include *Britain in the Middle Ages*; *Britain BC* and *Britain AD: A Quest for Arthur, England and the Anglo-Saxons.*

**Brian Sewell** *Naked Emperors: Criticisms of English Contemporary Art.* Trenchant, idiosyncratic, reviews – often attacks – on contemporary art from this leading critic and arch debunker of pretension. Few would want to plough through all 368 pages of the assembled reviews – but dip in and yelp with glee, or howl with irritation.

# Sixty years of English pop

England's sixty-year-plus heritage as a source of inspirational rock'n'roll is indisputable: the country's historic role as the hub of the British Empire, absorbing immigrants from around the world, and its openness to US culture have allowed it to assimilate diverse styles and rhythms – jazz, blues, ska, soul and reggae – and bred a distinctive domestic brand of popular music. Local acts soaked up the delicious musical juices seeping out of the shebeens, developing, for example, a taste for ska matched only in Kingston, Jamaica, and a white audience for US black music that Tamla Motown would envy. England's best music has come from its cities, nourished by fashions from the urban mix and flavoured from the cultural melting pot. Here is a brief survey of some of its major cities, region by region, and the musical legacies they have created.

## London

Inevitably, **London** has the bulk of the history and is home to the widest range of international influences. Traditionally, artists on the way up had to make the trek to the capital to perform, to record and to sign a contract. Management and publishing companies lurked on the cheaper outskirts of the West End theatre and entertainment district, and there was a domestic "Tin Pan Alley", centred on **Denmark Street** in London's West End. In the 1950s, entrepreneurs such as Larry Parnes created menacing-sounding stage personae (**Tommy Steele**, **Marty Wilde** and **Billy Fury**) and stalked the cappuccino bars of Soho to find compliant star material they could reshape as the ideal "all-round entertainer". The whole sordid scene was spoofed in the 1959 film, *Espresso Bongo*, starring **Cliff Richard**.

As the industry blossomed in the early 1960s, the demonic, London-based **Rolling Stones** provided contrast and foil to The Beatles' thumbs-up attitude, bringing shade and cool to the otherwise permanent sunshine of pop music. Acts such as **The Who** and **The Small Faces** were among the most successful of the "**beat groups**" who terrified the locals before heading to the US, following in the wake of the Fab Four, in a "British Invasion". The archetypal Sixties' London band, **The Kinks**, recorded some of the most thoughtful, poignant and enduring pop charmers of the era, in between bouts of breaking equipment and scrapping onstage.

Swinging London was still the place to be when a wave of hippy lifestyles and free love washed over England from sunny California, while the now-demolished UFO on Tottenham Court Road kick-started British psychedelia, booking **Pink Floyd** – originally a blues outfit from Cambridge – and **Soft Machine** in as house bands, hosting the first "light show" and promoting the **14 Hour Technicolor Dream** at Alexandra Palace in 1967 – London's most notorious gig of the decade.

### Glitter to punk and beyond

When the beautiful dreams wore off, English pop returned to primitive stomping with **glam rock** and **glitter**. For a while, East-End-boy-turned-bopping-elf **Marc Bolan** and his band T. Rex ruled the roost, but iconic British rock band, **Queen**, and **David Bowie** proved more enduring. The latter's theatrical flirtations with gayness/bisexuality and Weimar Republic decadence mutated almost beyond recognition in the mid- to late Seventies into **punk rock**, a movement whose roots lay both in US garage bands and early 1960s British pop. Typically those swastika-toting, bondage-clad rockers had no interest in politics at all, however, and just wanted a potent tool for baiting the bourgeoisie. The iconoclastic **Sex Pistols** were joined by such bands as **The Clash**, **The Damned**, **The Jam** and **Siouxsie & The Banshees**, and for a few ecstatic months, punk ruled. The flame burned out quickly, however, and was followed by a confusing mix of **post-punk** scenes pulling in different directions, from rockabilly to a skinhead revival with a taste for high-speed **ska**.

Those left unmoved by the lack of glamour shown by most of these new movements turned back to the superficial fashion wars of nightclubs, and a squadron of **New Romantics** headed by such London-formed acts such as **Duran Duran**, **Spandau Ballet**, **Culture Club** and **Adam & The Ants**. Chart success led to world-cracking tours, with George Michael even taking **Wham!** from London to Beijing in 1985, becoming the first western pop act to gig in Red China.

In the late 1980s, the rise of ecstasy and the affection for the **house** and **techno** scenes of Chicago and Detroit laid the roots for the UK's enduring dance music culture, which for many began at Danny Rampling's euphoric *Shoom* night in Southwark. And in the mainstream, the frills and ruffles of the decade eventually gave way to a search for "roots" and a "back to basics" movement in which the substance of lyrics and melody were considered more important than looks. Indeed, the quest for authenticity in music in the Nineties threw up a slew of big names, including **Blur**, **Suede** and **Elastica** in London, and saw Camden reinvented as the capital of "Britpop".

### 2000 onwards

For a moment, the Camden school endured in the shape of **The Libertines** (and their offshoots **Dirty Pretty Things**), but it was soon overshadowed by the harsh, hectic East London **grime** sound and South London's more minimal **dubstep**, both bastardized fusions of hip-hop, R&B and the weirder end of the dance spectrum. The London scene is, however, broad enough to take in a gamut of other musical styles currently making waves, from folk-influenced acts such as **Mumford and Sons**, **Laura Marling** and **Noah and the Whale**, to the smart, provocative pop of **Florence and the Machine** and the acoustic rap of **Plan B**.

## The northwest

As one of England's major ports, postwar **Liverpool** was home to a substantial immigrant population – Irish and West Indians in particular – with strong commercial links to the New York pop scene via the maritime traffic between the two cities. When they hit big in 1963, **The Beatles** brought moptops, R&B and genuine passion to a pop scene stuffed with insipid novelty tunes and crooning balladeers. From *Please Please Me* to *Hey Jude*, their music furnished a constant reassuring backing track to the rest of the decade. Their success yanked the whole Merseyside music scene into the national spotlight, from **Cilla Black** to **Billy J. Kramer & The Dakotas**, but when The Beatles made the long drive down to London, the media attention moved away. Britain's most influential and long-serving DJ **John Peel** flew the flag for Liverpool in the 1970s, but Liverpudlian pop had to wait until the next decade for its resurgence, in the form of **The Teardrop Explodes** and **Echo And The Bunnymen**. Throughout the Eighties and Nineties, kids would hook up at Probe Records before moving on for a night raving at local superclub, *Cream*. Meanwhile, Beatle-influenced melodic pop rippled on in the love songs to heroin of **The La's** and the robust beauties of **The Boo Radleys** and continued in the 2000s in such flavours as **The Zutons** and **The Coral**, and more recently bands such as **The Wombats** and Lancashire's own **Elbow**.

### Manchester

**Manchester**'s contribution to English pop music is, if anything, even more impressive than Liverpool's. The city boasts or boasted Morrissey's beloved Salford Lads' Club,

Factory Records, Granada TV and the BBC's main northern studios, while *Wigan Casino* – home of Northern Soul – is not far away, though it's the hedonistic nights at *The Haçienda* that excite the most wistful smiles. Furthermore, the list of Manchester bands is endless; from Sixties pop success stories such as **Herman's Hermits** to more recent chart-toppers such as **The Ting Tings**, the city's role as musical capital of the north continuing unchallenged. Manchester and its environs was the second city of English punk, and it nurtured a more sardonic, thoughtful crop of post-punk acts, including **Buzzcocks**, **The Fall** and Macclesfield's **Joy Division** (who morphed into New Order on the death of singer Ian Curtis), that showed more genuine artistry and greater resilience than the perhaps more fashion-led London bands. From the Eighties, two bands, **The Smiths** and **New Order**, despite coming from opposite ends of the pop spectrum, stand out in particular. While Morrissey's ruminations on confused sexuality, shyness and solitude gave a voice to a generation left cold by the mainstream pop world of the mid-80s, it was New Order that had the more far-reaching effect. Having embraced the new hedonism of synth-powered dance music, their music inspired an ecstasy-driven dance-all-night lifestyle that ultimately created local superclub **The Haçienda**. From this developed the "**Madchester**" scene that threw up **The Happy Mondays**, **The Stone Roses**, **The Charlatans** and **James**. After "Madchester", the Manchester scene lost some of its energy – the early Nineties' most successful Mancunian act was manufactured boy band, **Take That**. But the city retained its swagger in the soap-opera squabbles of **Oasis**'s Gallagher brothers, and its taste for downbeat realism with bands such as **The Verve**, and more recently, **Doves**, **Elbow** and Wigan's **Starsailor**.

## The Midlands

While **Brumbeat** donated its fair share of acts to the early to mid-Sixties scenes – with **Spencer Davis Group** and **Traffic** deserving special attention for pushing basic beat

---

### ENGLAND'S POP SHRINES

**Alley of love, Brighton** Hometown of some of England's finest pop stars, Brighton was also the location of the main beachfront action in the movie of The Who's mod opera, *Quadrophenia*.

**Glastonbury** Home to the country's biggest and oldest music festival, which takes place on a farm some miles from town and attracts some 175,000 revellers.

**Town & Country Club, Leeds** The city's best-loved major venue for the final years of the last millennium (now corporatized as the O2 Academy).

**Eric's, Liverpool** Crucible of the alternative and underground scene from the Seventies onward; on the same street as *The Cavern*.

**Abbey Road Studios, London** The Beatles' permanent recording HQ in the capital, and birthplace to countless classic recordings from Pink Floyd to Radiohead.

**Soho, London** Stand in the centre of Soho Square, throw a brick in any direction and you'll hit a revered institution, recording company office, musicians' unlicensed club or aspiring superstar. Seek out 23 Heddon St for that essential Ziggy Stardust tribute pic.

**Isle of Wight** Following the famous 1970 festival, it was 32 years before the island dared/was allowed to host another such event and the second-coming Isle of Wight Festival is now a musical mainstay. More alternative and folksy is the island's Bestival, a second key stop on the festival trail.

**Salford Lads' Club, Manchester** Featured on the cover of The Smiths' album *The Queen Is Dead*, the club once boasted Allan Clarke of The Hollies among its members.

**The Twisted Wheel, Manchester** Northern Soul venue par excellence, the *Twisted Wheel* played it fast, loud, heavy and all night long. The list of visiting bands reads like a Motown/Stax greatest-hits set.

**The Leadmill, Sheffield** Boasting more than 25 years as the city's top venue, the *Leadmill* has been an A-listed must-play gig for acts as diverse as Cabaret Voltaire, Killing Joke and The Fall in the Eighties to today's sleek young turns such as The Long Blondes and Reverend & The Makers.

music forward to the edge of psychedelia – it was not till the era of **Black Sabbath** and **Led Zeppelin**, at the end of the decade, that Brummie pop came alive. Then – as chart pop grew to thrive on hairstyles, glitter and dinosaur stomp – local boy **Roy Wood** escaped The Move and Electric Light Orchestra to emerge as front man to **Wizzard**, while **Slade**'s Noddy Holder sported trousers even more raucous than his gravelly voice. At the tail-end of the Seventies, **The Beat** and Coventry's **The Specials** were at the forefront of a ska revival, and a decade later, all the best "Grebo" (a term coined by **Pop Will Eat Itself**'s Clint Mansell, for a brand of pop aimed at wannabe motorcycle outlaws) bands talked like they had day jobs as Brummie diesel mechanics.

## The West Country

England's southwest has always had a reputation for left-field mavericks, from Dorset's **PJ Harvey** to Cornwall's dance iconoclast **Aphex Twin**. The region's biggest city, and one of England's great ports, **Bristol** has been associated since the 1990s with trip-hop, a catch-all term encompassing artists as diverse as **Portishead**, **Tricky** and **Massive Attack**, who rejected the guitar-led Britpop scene in favour of a darker, spacier and more down-tempo sound.

## The northeast

**Newcastle**'s pop pedigree ranges from **The Animals** in the 1960s through to folk/rock band **Lindisfarne**, punk heroes **Penetration** and **Angelic Upstarts**, Police front man **Sting**, plus **Dubstar** in the Nineties and **Maximo Park** in the 2000s. Heavy-metal, heavy-duty **Satan** also came from Newcastle – while **Durham** sent us the mixed charm and cynicism of **Prefab Sprout** in the Eighties. Softer warblers have included **Cheryl Fernandez-Versini** (née Tweedy, formerly Cole), ah bless, and the mercurial **Bryan Ferry**, a bit less of ah bless.

## Yorkshire

**Hull** weighs in with Mick Ronson and Mick Woodmansey, the linchpins of Bowie's **Spiders From Mars** in the early Seventies; **Everything But The Girl**, who emerged transcendent in the Eighties; and pop punks and local darlings **The Housemartins**, who delighted in articulating the depressing realities normally scorned by chart acts. Rival **Leeds** responded with such politicized bands as **The Mekons**, **Gang of Four** and **Chumbawamba**, while **Soft Cell** and **Sisters of Mercy** provided a counterpart to the pop cheeriness of the post-punk era, paving the way for **The Wedding Present**'s guitar onslaught. More recently, the **Kaiser Chiefs** and the **Pigeon Detectives** have spearheaded a new wave of Leeds-based indie rockers.

### Sheffield

**Dave Berry** and **Joe Cocker** led **Sheffield**'s Steel City invasion in the Sixties, with the punishing stylings of **Def Leppard**, **Cabaret Voltaire** and others maintaining the city's metal-bashing traditions long after the cutlery factories had closed down. The city has also given us a more stylish brand of pop than other regional conurbations in the form of the glossy magazine tunes of **The Human League** and elegant sophistication of **ABC**. **Pulp**'s domination of the thinking-teen's playlist kept the city in the limelight in the 1990s, while **Warp Records** championed an eclectic selection of techno, ambient and rock music. By the late 2000s, though, the baton of elegant sneering, backed up by solid musicianship, had been passed to the **Arctic Monkeys**, and frontman Alex Turner's side band, **The Last Shadow Puppets**.

# Film

England has produced some of the world's greatest films, actors and directors, but for all that it's well-nigh impossible to get critics to agree what exactly constitutes an English film (or indeed, where English film stops and British film starts). Take sci-fi-horror classic *Alien* – a 20th Century Fox movie that launched the career of Sigourney Weaver, but was filmed at London's Shepperton Studios, directed by Tyne and Wear-born Ridley Scott and starred English RADA-trained classical actor John Hurt. Or the multi-garlanded *Slumdog Millionaire*, set in Mumbai with an Indian cast but adapted for the screen and directed by Englishmen Simon Beaufoy and Danny Boyle and entirely financed in the UK. We've concentrated on covering films that are at least set in England (with one or two rare exceptions). The ★symbol indicates films that are especially recommended.

## THE 1930S AND 1940S

★ **Brief Encounter** (David Lean, 1945). Wonderful weepie in which Trevor Howard and Celia Johnson teeter on the edge of adultery after a chance encounter at a railway station. Noël Coward wrote the clipped dialogue; the flushed, dreamy soundtrack features Rachmaninov's *Piano Concerto No.2*.

**Brighton Rock** (John Boulting, 1947). A fine adaptation of Graham Greene's novel, featuring a young, scary Richard Attenborough as the psychopathic Pinkie, who marries a witness to one of his crimes to ensure her silence. Beautiful cinematography and good performances, with a real sense of film noir menace.

**Fires Were Started** (Humphrey Jennings, 1943). This outstanding wartime documentary relates the experiences of a group of firemen through one night of the Blitz. The use of real firemen rather than professional actors, and the avoidance of formulaic heroics, gives the film great power as an account of the courage of ordinary people who fought, often uncelebrated, on the home front.

★ **Great Expectations** (David Lean, 1946). An early film by one of Britain's finest directors – also responsible for *Lawrence of Arabia* and *Bridge on the River Kwai* – this superb rendition of the Dickens novel features magnificent performances by John Mills (as Pip) and Finlay Currie (as Abel Magwitch). The scene in the graveyard will (should) make your hair stand on end.

**Henry V** (Laurence Olivier, 1944). With dreamlike Technicolor backdrops, this rousing piece of wartime propaganda is emphatically cinematic rather than "theatrical", the action spiralling out from the Globe Theatre itself. Olivier is a brilliantly charismatic king, and the atmospheric pre-battle scene where he goes disguised among his men is heartachingly muted.

**I Know Where I'm Going!** (Michael Powell and Emeric Pressburger, 1945). Powell and Pressburger made some of the finest British films of all time (see also *A Matter of Life and Death*, *The Life and Death of Colonel Blimp*, *Black Narcissus*, *The Red Shoes* and *A Canterbury Tale*), all of which expose the peculiarities of the British character and reveal hidden depths and longings. In this delightful romance, Wendy Hiller's modern young woman, who knows what she wants and how to get it, is stymied in her goals by the mysterious romanticism of the Scottish islands and their inhabitants.

**Jane Eyre** (Robert Stevenson, 1943). Joan Fontaine does a fine job of portraying Jane, and Orson Welles is a suavely sardonic Rochester – the scene where he is thrown from his horse in the mist hits the perfect melodramatic pitch. With the unlikely tagline "A Love Story Every Woman Would Die a Thousand Deaths to Live!", it briefly features a young Elizabeth Taylor as a dying Helen Burns.

**Kind Hearts and Coronets** (Robert Hamer, 1949). As with the best of the Ealing movies, this is a savage comedy on the cruel absurdities of the British class system. With increasing ingenuity, Dennis Price's suave and ruthless anti-hero murders his way through the d'Ascoyne clan (all brilliantly played by Alec Guinness) to claim the family title.

★ **Rebecca** (Alfred Hitchcock, 1940). Hitchcock does Du Maurier: Laurence Olivier is wonderfully enigmatic as Maxim de Winter, and Joan Fontaine glows as his meek second wife, living in the shadow of her mysterious predecessor.

**The Thirty-Nine Steps** (Alfred Hitchcock, 1935). Hitchcock's best-loved British movie, full of wit and bold acts of derring-do. Robert Donat stars as innocent Richard Hannay, inadvertently caught up in a mysterious spy ring. In a typically perverse Hitchcock touch, he spends a generous amount of time handcuffed to Madeleine Carroll,

fleeing across the Scottish countryside, before the action returns to London for the film's great music-hall conclusion.
★ **Wuthering Heights** (William Wyler, 1939). The version of Emily Brontë's novel that everyone remembers, with Laurence Olivier as the dysfunctional Heathcliff and Merle Oberon as Cathy. It's tense, passionate and wild, and lays proper emphasis on the Yorkshire landscape, the best of all possible places for doomed lovers.

## 1950 TO 1970

**Billy Liar!** (John Schlesinger, 1963). Tom Courtenay is Billy, stuck in a dire job as an undertaker's clerk in a northern town, spending his time creating extravagant fantasies. His life is lit up by the appearance of Julie Christie, who holds out the glamour and promise of swinging London.

**Carry On Screaming** (Gerald Thomas, 1966). One of the best from the Carry On crew, with many of the usual suspects (Kenneth Williams, Charles Hawtrey, Joan Sims) hamming it up with the usual nudge-nudge merriment in a Hammer Horror spoof.

**Far From the Madding Crowd** (John Schlesinger, 1967). An imaginative adaptation of Hardy's doom-laden tale of the desires and ambitions of wilful/wishful Bathsheba Everdene. Julie Christie is a radiant and spirited Bathsheba, Terence Stamp flashes his blade to dynamic effect, Alan Bates is quietly charismatic as dependable Gabriel Oak, and the West Country setting is sparsely beautiful.

★ **Kes** (Kenneth Loach, 1969). The unforgettable story of a neglected Yorkshire schoolboy who finds solace and liberation in training his kestrel. As a still-pertinent commentary on poverty and an impoverished school system, it's bleak but idealistic. Pale and pinched David Bradley, who plays Billy Casper, is hugely affecting. Loach at the top of his game.

★ **The Ladykillers** (Alexander Mackendrick, 1955). Alec Guinness is fabulously toothy and malevolent as "Professor Marcus", a murderous con man who lodges with a sweet little old lady, Mrs Wilberforce (Katie Johnson), in this skewed Ealing comedy.

**A Man for All Seasons** (Fred Zinnemann, 1966). Sir Thomas More takes on Henry VIII in one of British history's great moral confrontations. Robert Bolt's wry screenplay, muted visuals and a heavenly host of theatrical talent (including Orson Welles as Cardinal Wolsey) add to the spectacle if not the tension, which is where the film dithers.

★ **Night and the City** (Jules Dassin, 1950). Great film noir, with Richard Widmark as an anxious nightclub hustler on the run. It's gripping and convincingly sleazy, and the London streetscapes have an Expressionist edge of horror.

**Saturday Night and Sunday Morning** (Karel Reisz, 1960). Reisz's monochrome captures all the grit and dead-end grind of Albert Finney's life working in a Nottingham bicycle factory – and his anarchic rejection of pretty much everything that surrounds him. The way out: heavy drinking and heavy petting (if not more).

★ **This Sporting Life** (Lindsay Anderson, 1963). One of the key British films of the 1960s, and a classic of the gritty "kitchen sink" genre. It's the story of a Northern miner turned rugby league star with the young Richard Harris giving a great (and singularly muscular) performance as the inarticulate anti-hero, able only to express himself through physical violence.

## THE 1970S AND 1980S

★ **Babylon** (Franco Rosso, 1980). A moving account of black working-class London life. We follow the experiences of young Blue through a series of encounters that reveal the nation's insidious racism. Good performances and a great reggae soundtrack: an all too rare example of Black Britain taking centre stage in a British movie.

**Comrades** (Bill Douglas, 1986). In 1830s England, a group of farm workers decide to stand up to the exploitative tactics of the local landowner, and find themselves prosecuted and transported to Australia. Based on the true story of the Tolpuddle Martyrs, this combines political education with a visually stunning celebration of working lives.

**Distant Voices, Still Lives** (Terence Davies, 1988). Beautifully realized autobiographical tale of growing up in Liverpool in the 1940s and 1950s. The mesmeric pace is punctuated by astonishing moments of drama, and the whole is a very moving account of how a family survives and triumphs, in small ways, against the odds.

★ **Get Carter** (Mike Hodges, 1971). Vivid British gangster movie, featuring a hard-nosed, hard-case Michael Caine as the eponymous hero-villain, returning to his native Newcastle to avenge his brother's death. Great use of its Northeastern locations and a fine turn by playwright John Osborne as the local godfather.

**Hope and Glory** (John Boorman, 1987). A glorious autobiographical feature about the Blitz seen through the eyes of 9-year-old Bill, who revels in the liberating chaos of bomb-site playgrounds, tumbling barrage balloons and debris shrapnel.

**The Last of England** (Derek Jarman, 1987). Jarman's most abstract account of the state of the Eighties Britain. Composed of apparently unrelated shots of decaying London landscapes, rent boys, and references to emblematic national events such as the Falklands War, this may not be to all tastes, but it is a fitting testament to Jarman's unique talent.

**Monty Python and the Holy Grail** (The Monty Python team, 1974). You can't get much more English than the surreal Monty Python crew, and this daft movie, loosely based on the stories of King Arthur and the Holy Grail, remains fresh and funny today with its exuberant combination of histrionics, slick slapstick and clever wordplay.

**My Beautiful Laundrette** (Stephen Frears, 1985). A slice of Thatcher's Britain, with a young, on-the-make Asian, Omar, opening a ritzy laundrette in London. His lover, Johnny (Daniel Day-Lewis), is an ex-National Front glamour boy, angry and inarticulate when forced by the acquisitive Omar into a menial role in the laundrette. The racial, sexual and class dynamics of

their relationship mirror the tensions in the city itself.

**Withnail and I** (Bruce Robinson, 1986). Richard E. Grant is superb as the raddled, drunken Withnail, a "resting" actor with a penchant for drinking lighter fluid. Paul McGann is the "I" of the title – a bemused spectator of Withnail's wild excesses, as they abandon their grotty London flat for a remote country cottage, and the attentions of Withnail's randy Uncle Monty (Richard Griffiths).

## THE 1990S

**Bhaji on the Beach** (Gurinder Chadha, 1993). An Asian women's group takes a day-trip to Blackpool in this issue-laden but enjoyable picture. A lot of fun is had contrasting the seamier side of British life with the mores of the Asian aunties, though the male characters are cartoon villains all.

**East Is East** (Damien O'Donnell, 1999). Seventies Salford is the setting for this lively tragi-comedy, with a Pakistani chip-shop owner struggling to keep control of his seven children as they rail against the strictures of Islam and arranged marriages. Inventively made, and with some delightful performances.

**Elizabeth** (Shekhar Kapur, 1998). Cate Blanchett is stunning in this visually beautiful, Gothic production, where the young, innocent Elizabeth slowly adapts to the role of the "Virgin Queen" to secure her survival. It's better than its sequel *Elizabeth: The Golden Age* (2007), which also stars Blanchett, and focuses on the defeat of the Spanish Armada. But don't take it all as historical gospel.

**The Full Monty** (Peter Cattaneo, 1997). Set in Sheffield, where six unemployed former steel workers throw caution to the wind and become male strippers, their boast being that all will be revealed in the "full monty". Unpromising physical specimens all, they score an unlikely hit with the local lasses. The film was itself an unlikely hit worldwide and the long-awaited striptease is a joy to behold (well almost).

**Howards End** (James Ivory, 1992). A superb Anthony Hopkins leads the way in this touching recreation of E M Forster's celebrated novel. From the prolific Merchant-Ivory team, who produced a string of exquisite period films, renowned for their elegiac settings.

**Lock, Stock and Two Smoking Barrels** (Guy Ritchie, 1998). Ritchie may be much derided for his marriage to Madonna and his mock Cockney (mockney) accent, but this – his breakout film – was a witty and inventive comedy-meets-heist movie that gave gangland heavies a "geezer" re-boot.

**The Madness of King George** (Nicholas Hytner, 1994). Adapted from a witty Alan Bennett play, this royal romp is handsomely staged, with the king's loopy antics (a wonderfully nuanced performance from Nigel Hawthorne)

played out against a cartoon-like court and its acolytes. Rupert Everett is superb as the effete Prince Regent.

★**Nil by Mouth** (Gary Oldman, 1997). With strong performances by Ray Winstone as a brutish south Londoner and Kathy Burke as his battered wife, this brave and bleak picture delves deep into domestic violence and drug/drink addiction. Brace yourself.

**The Remains of the Day** (James Ivory, 1993). Kazuo Ishiguro's masterly novel of social and personal repression translates beautifully to the big screen. Anthony Hopkins is the overly decorous butler who gradually becomes aware of his master's fascist connections, Emma Thompson the housekeeper who struggles to bring his deeply suppressed feelings to the surface. Call a counsellor.

**Richard III** (Richard Loncraine, 1995). A splendid film version of a renowned National Theatre production, which brilliantly transposed the action to a fascist state in the 1930s. The infernal political machinations of a snarling Ian McKellen as Richard are heightened by Nazi associations, and the style of the period imbues the film with the requisite glamour, as does languorously drugged Kristin Scott-Thomas as Lady Anne.

**Secrets and Lies** (Mike Leigh, 1996). Serious-minded, slice-of-life ensemble drama charting a dysfunctional family's hidden secrets, from infidelity to reconciliation–and all seen through the prism of class. Mike Leigh at his most penetrating.

**Sense and Sensibility** (Ang Lee, 1995). Ah, the English and their period dramas. They are all here – Rickman, Winslett, Thompson, Grant, Robert Hardy et al – in this tone-perfect recreation of Jane Austen's sprightly story of love, money and, of course, manners.

★**Trainspotting** (Danny Boyle, 1996). High-octane dip into the heroin-scarred world of a group of young Scotsmen both at home and in London; includes what might be the best cinematic representation of a heroin fix ever.

**Wonderland** (Michael Winterbottom, 1999). One Bonfire Night in London as experienced by three unhappy sisters. Winterbottom's use of real locations, natural light and 16mm film gives it a naturalistic air that's also dreamlike, an effect heightened by Michael Nyman's haunting score.

## 2000 TO 2010

**24 Hour Party People** (Michael Winterbottom, 2002). Steve Coogan plays the entrepreneurial/inspirational Tony Wilson (1950–2007) – the man of many quotes–in this

fast-moving recreation of the early days of Manchester's Factory Records (late 1970s/80s). Stunning soundtrack too.

**Atonement** (Joe Wright, 2007). This adaptation of Ian

McEwan's highly literary novel of misunderstanding and regret benefits from strong performances from Keira Knightley and James McAvoy, as well as fluent plotting.

**Bend It Like Beckham** (Gurinder Chadha, 2003). Immensely successful film focusing on the coming of age of a football-loving Punjabi girl in a suburb of London. Both socially acute and comic.

★**Bronson** (Nicolas Winding Refn, 2009). The subject matter may seem unappetizing – Welsh criminal Bronson (Tom Hardy) is reputed to be the most violent man ever locked up in a British prison – and it's not easy viewing, but Refn's take on this unusual anti-hero is inventive, creative and insightful. Notable also for the appearance of a Rough Guide author as an extra – but blink and you'll miss him.

**Control** (Anton Corbijn, 2007). Ian Curtis, the lead singer of Joy Division, committed suicide in 1980 at the age of 23. This biopic tracks his life in and around Manchester, based on the account provided by his wife, Deborah. Some have raved over Sam Riley's portrayal of Curtis, others have been less convinced, but as an evocation of the early days of Factory Records it's hard to beat.

**Dirty Pretty Things** (Stephen Frears, 2003). A tumbling mix of melodrama, social criticism and black comedy, this forceful, thought-provoking film explores the world of Britain's illegal migrants.

**Gosford Park** (Robert Altman, 2001). Astutely observed upstairs-downstairs murder mystery set in class-ridden 1930s England. The multi-layered plot is typical of the director, the script, from Julian Fellowes, is more nuanced than some of his later TV work, and the who's who of great British actors is led by the superb Maggie Smith.

**Harry Potter and the Philosopher's Stone** (Chris Columbus, 2001). The first film in a series about hero Harry Potter's life at wizard school did wonders for the English tourist industry with its use of places such as Alnwick Castle as

locations. The subsequent films are also darkly enjoyable, with excellent ensemble casts – Spall, Gambon, Rickman et al.

**In the Loop** (Armando Iannucci, 2009). Look what we have to put up with from our politicians, screams Iannucci, in this satire on the opaque and corrupt meanderings of our leaders and their assorted advisors.

**The Queen** (Stephen Frears, 2006). Dame Helen Mirren became an official national treasure after taking on the role of Her Majesty in this PR movie for the palace, which covers the crisis in the monarchy after the death of Princess Diana. Michael Sheen does a great Tony Blair impression, while Sylvia Sims brings a dash of humour to the role of Queen Mum.

**Sexy Beast** (Jonathan Glazer, 2000). Gangster thriller distinguished by the performances of Ray Winstone and more especially Ben Kingsley, who plays one of the hardest, meanest criminals ever. Delightful cameos by an evil Ian McShane and a debauched James Fox, too.

**Shaun of the Dead** (Edgar Wright, 2004). Shuffling and shambolic zombies roam and groan the streets of London in this zom-com, horror-romp that made a name for Simon Pegg. Follow-up films in the same vein–The World's End (2013) – have, however, been notably unfunny, making critics wonder if Pegg has anything left in his crypt/locker.

★**This is England** (Shane Meadows, 2007). British cinema rarely ventures into the East Midlands, but this is where Shane Meadows is at home. Set in the early 1980s, this thoughtful film deals with a young working-class lad who falls in with skinheads – the good-hearted ones to begin with, the racists thereafter.

★**Vera Drake** (Mike Leigh, 2004). Moving story of a 1950s working-class woman, who performs illegal abortions from the goodness of her heart and without thought for either money or the legal consequences, which eventually threaten to destroy her and her close-knit family. A powerful counterblast to the anti-abortion lobby.

## 2010 ONWARDS

**The King's Speech** (Tom Hooper, 2010). Colin Firth is suitably repressed as the vocally challenged King George VI who is given the confidence to become king by Geoffrey Rush's exuberant Australian speech therapist, and there are superb performances from Helena Bonham Carter as his imperious wife (later to become the Queen Mother) and Guy Pearce as the spoiled, tormented Edward VIII.

**Made in Dagenham** (Nigel Cole, 2010). Good-hearted, good-natured film about the struggle for equal pay in the car industry in 1960s England. Sweet packaging for a tough industrial message.

**Mr Nice** (Bernard Rose, 2010). Picaresque tale of one-time drug king and (supposedly) very good egg, Howard Marks (Mr Nice himself) from baffled beginnings to stoned (very stoned) fame and fortune via imprisonment and hostile drug cartels. Rhys Ifans is perfect as the drug-addled hero, Chloe Stevens Sevigny as his wife.

**Philomena** (Stephen Frears, 2013). Coogan and Dench, cynic and innocent, take the high road to find a long-lost child taken from Philomena (Dench), once a single, unmarried mother. Thumbs down to the Ireland of the 1950s in general and the Catholic church in particular. Heartwarming stuff.

★**Sightseers** (Ben Wheatley, 2012). Murder, mayhem, sadism and psychosis on a caravan holiday in the Midlands and the North. Never, but never before, has Crich Tramway Museum seemed so dangerous. This is horror with ironic flair – so avert your eyes strategically or prepare to grimace.

**Wuthering Heights** (Andrea Arnold, 2011). Arnold, whose breakthrough movies were set in urban council estates – Red Road (2006), which used CCTV to tell a story of obsession in Glasgow, and Fish Tank (2009), a searing coming of age tale – demonstrates a lyrical eye for the natural world in her arty, elemental reworking of Emily Brontë's romantic tragedy. The emotions are bruisingly raw.

# Small print and index

## A ROUGH GUIDE TO ROUGH GUIDES

Published in 1982, the first Rough Guide – to Greece – was a student scheme that became a publishing phenomenon. Mark Ellingham, a recent graduate in English from Bristol University, had been travelling in Greece the previous summer and couldn't find the right guidebook. With a small group of friends he wrote his own guide, combining a highly contemporary, journalistic style with a thoroughly practical approach to travellers' needs.

The immediate success of the book spawned a series that rapidly covered dozens of destinations. And, in addition to impecunious backpackers, Rough Guides soon acquired a much broader readership that relished the guides' wit and inquisitiveness as much as their enthusiastic, critical approach and value-for-money ethos.

These days, Rough Guides include recommendations from budget to luxury and cover more than 120 destinations around the globe, as well as producing an ever-growing range of ebooks.

Visit **roughguides.com** to find all our latest books, read articles, get inspired and share travel tips with the Rough Guides community.

## Rough Guide credits

**Editors**: Rachel Mills, Melissa Graham
**Layout**: Anita Singh
**Cartography**: Animesh Pathak, James Macdonald
**Picture editor**: Raffaella Morini
**Proofreader**: Stewart Wild
**Managing editor**: Mani Ramaswamy
**Senior editor**: Natasha Foges
**Assistant editor**: Payal Sharotri

**Production**: Janis Griffith
**Cover design**: Nicole Newman, Michelle Bhatia, Anita Singh
**Editorial assistant**: Rebecca Hallett
**Senior pre-press designer**: Dan May
**Programme manager**: Gareth Lowe
**Publisher**: Joanna Kirby
**Publishing director**: Georgina Dee

## Publishing information

This tenth edition published February 2015 by
**Rough Guides Ltd**,
80 Strand, London WC2R 0RL
11, Community Centre, Panchsheel Park,
New Delhi 110017, India
**Distributed by Penguin Random House**
Penguin Books Ltd,
80 Strand, London WC2R 0RL
Penguin Group (USA)
345 Hudson Street, NY 10014, USA
Penguin Group (Australia)
250 Camberwell Road, Camberwell,
Victoria 3124, Australia
Penguin Group (NZ)
67 Apollo Drive, Mairangi Bay, Auckland 1310,
New Zealand
Penguin Group (South Africa)
Block D, Rosebank Office Park, 181 Jan Smuts Avenue,
Parktown North, Gauteng, South Africa 2193
Rough Guides is represented in Canada by Tourmaline
Editions Inc. 662 King Street West, Suite 304, Toronto,
Ontario M5V 1M7
Printed in Singapore
© Rough Guides 2015

Maps © Rough Guides
Contains Ordnance Survey data © Crown copyright and
database rights 2015

## Help us update

We've gone to a lot of effort to ensure that the tenth edition of **The Rough Guide to England** is accurate and up-to-date. However, things change – places get "discovered", opening hours are notoriously fickle, restaurants and rooms raise prices or lower standards. If you feel we've got it wrong or left something out, we'd like to know, and if you can remember the address, the price, the hours, the phone number, so much the better.

Please send your comments with the subject line "**Rough Guide England Update**" to @mail@uk .roughguides.com. We'll credit all contributions and send a copy of the next edition (or any other Rough Guide if you prefer) for the very best emails.

Find more travel information, connect with fellow travellers and plan your trip on ⓦroughguides.com.

## Acknowledgements

**Samantha Cook** Thanks to Rob Humphreys and Claire Saunders, co-authors on my chapters, who made it all easy and loads of fun; Rachel Mills, for an excellent editorial experience; and Greg Ward for everything, always.

**Keith Drew** Thanks to Tanya Miller, Mani Ramaswamy and Rachel Mills, and especially to Kate, Maisie, Joe and Lilah.

**Matthew Hancock and Amanda Tomlin** Thanks go to Melissa and Rachel for their excellent editing; Sue Emerson at the Isle of Wight tourist board; Wightlink ferries; *Into the Woods* shepherd's hut and treehouse; all at the very friendly staff at *The Pig*; the National Trust; English Heritage; and to Alex and Olivia for their patience and enthusiasm.

**Emma Harrison** Thanks to Visit Isle of Man, the guard at Douglas Station and Rachel Mills, for excellent guidance.

**Phil Lee** would like to thank editor, Rachel Mills, for all the help she has given during the preparation of this new edition of the Rough Guide to England. Special thanks also to Tom Marlow at Marketing Birmingham; Michelle Marriott-Lodge at the *Castle Hotel*, Hereford; Delysia Hart and Daniella White for their Birmingham tips and hints; Dave Robson for his hospitality in Shrewsbury; and Emma Rees and Marnie Darling Rees for always cheering me up.

**Claire Saunders** Thanks and love to Ian, Tom and Mia.

**Ann-Marie Shaw** would like to thank Andy Parkinson and Joe Keggin at Marketing Manchester and Liverpool respectively for pointing me in the most interesting directions; Mary Colston, Martin Jones and Katie Bentley for their warm hospitality; Rachel Mills for her flexible and patient editing; and, above all, Mike, George, Ruby, Lily and Cracks for putting up with all the gallivanting.

**Jos Simon** Thanks to Welcome to Yorkshire, the National Trust, English Heritage and the YHA for information, and to Melissa Graham and Rachel Mills for sympathetic editing.

**Helena Smith** Thanks to David Brookbranks at NewcastleGateshead, Roger Domeneghetti at Visit County Durham and Natalie Wood at Northumberland Tourism.

**Steve Vickers** would like to thank the team at Rough Guides, especially Natasha Foges, Rachel Mills and Mani Ramaswamy. Thanks also to Melissa Graham for her careful editing. Research wouldn't have been possible without help from Leanne and Dan at Bunk Campers. Finally, thanks to Kev, Dan and Cara for the laughs along the way.

## ABOUT THE AUTHORS

**Jules Brown** has written for Rough Guides since 1986 and is the author of the *Rough Guide to the Lake District*.

**Samantha Cook** is a writer and editor born and based in London. She is the co-author of the Rough Guides to London, Vintage London and Kent, Sussex & Surrey, the sole author of the Rough Guides to New Orleans and Chick Flicks , and a contributor to many others.

**Keith Drew** grew up on the edge of the Mendips and spent his Saturday afternoons at the Rec in Bath, which he fondly recalls, and his Saturday evenings on Park Street in Bristol, which he can't really remember at all. A Managing Editor at Rough Guides, he is also co-author of the *Rough Guide to Bath, Bristol and Somerset*.

**Matthew Hancock and Amanda Tomlin** are authors of the *Rough Guide to Britain* and the *Rough Guide to Hampshire, Dorset and the Isle of Wight*. Matthew Hancock is also the author of the Rough Guides to Portugal, Madeira, Lisbon and the Algarve.

**Emma Harrison** is a writer and editor based in Liverpool. She is Editor of The Independent Map Company and a keen traveller, with a particular interest in the Northwest of England.

**Rob Humphreys** has lived in London for over twenty years. He has travelled extensively in Scotland and Central Europe writing books for Rough Guides. He is a qualified City of London Tour Guide and spends his spare time directing shows on the Puppet Theatre Barge.

**Phil Lee** has been writing for Rough Guides for well over twenty years. His other books in the series include Canada, Norway, Belgium & Luxembourg, Bruges, Amsterdam, and Mallorca & Menorca. He lives in Nottingham, where he was born and raised.

**Claire Saunders** grew up in Brighton. After almost ten years of working as an editor and then Managing Editor at Rough Guides in London, she moved back down to Sussex, where she now lives in Lewes and works as a freelance writer and editor.

**Ann-Marie Shaw** has edited countless Rough Guides, contributed to several others – most recently *Make the Most of Your Time on Earth* – and written for publications including The Big Issue in the North. She lives in Cheshire with her partner and three children.

**Jos Simon** was raised on the Llŷn Peninsula and settled in Yorkshire after teaching in various other parts of the country. He fulfilled a long-held ambition to describe his adopted home county by writing the Rough Guide to Yorkshire, and contributing to the Rough Guides to England and Britain.

**Helena Smith** comes from Scotland and lives in Hackney, east London. When she isn't travelling, Helena blogs about food and community at eathackney.com.

**Matthew Teller** (matthewteller.com) is a journalist, broadcaster and travel writer living tantalisingly close to the unfashionable northeastern fringes of the Cotswolds. He has written for Rough Guides for almost twenty years, and tries to keep his blog QuiteAlone.com up to date. He tweets @matthewteller.

**Steve Vickers** is a freelance journalist and guidebook author. He's contributed to more than a dozen Rough Guides titles and has worked for BBC Radio 4, the Independent, the Washington Post and the Observer, among others. You can follow him on Twitter @StevenJVickers

## Readers' updates

Thanks to all the readers who have taken the time to write in with comments and suggestions (and apologies if we've inadvertently omitted or misspelt anyone's name):

Belinda Archer, Fleur Ball, Silvia Barbantani, Roger & Lesley Barnett, Ali Bell, John Benjamin, Edward Braisher, Zoe Bremer, Jacky Bright, Sally Chesters, Patti Collins, Stephen Cook, Cat Coombes, David Cronshaw, Ian Davies, Dalan de Brí, Annabella Forbes, Emma Forbes, Ben Goodhall, Frank Gordon, Robert Harding, Nick Hart, Jennie Harvey, Sally Holden, Caroline and John Horder, Ed Hutchings, Harry Kretchmer; Kirsty Laifa; Stefanie Lüdtke, Colm Magee, Lucy Mellor, Celli Moriarty, Kenneth Nichol, Laura Norton, Martin Peters, Keith Resnick, Rebecca Reynolds, Claire Shirlaw, Adrian Smith, David Stubbs, David Walsh, Chris Williamson, Jennifer Wood, Jenny Wood, Tim Woods and Grace Wylie.

## Photo credits

All photos © Rough Guides except the following:
(Key: t-top; c-centre; b-bottom; l-left; r-right)

p.1 Alan Copson/Getty Images
p.4 Paul Williams – Funkystock/imageBROKER/Corbis
p.5 Hoberman Collection/Corbis
p.9 Atlantide Phototravel/Corbis (tl); RJT Photography/Alamy (tr); Paul Harris/JAI/Corbis (b)
p.11 Andy Hill/Randy Pike (t); Michael Hudson/Alamy (c); Greg Elms/Getty Images (b)
p.13 Paul Weston/Alamy (t); Neil Farrin/JAI/Corbis (b)
p.14 Alan Copson/AWL Images
p.15 Matt Cardy/Getty Images (t); Charles Bowman/Alamy (c); Natalie Sternberg/4Corners (b)
p.16 Design Pics/Corbis (t); Alan Copson/JAI/Corbis (b)
p.17 Jeff Morgan 09/Alamy (t); Matt Cardy/Thermae Bath Spa (cl); Jim Dyson/Getty Images (cr); Martyn Goddard/Corbis (b)
p.18 Christopher Furlong/Getty Images (t); Sandra Raccanello/4Corners (c); Blackpool Pleasure Beach (b)
p.19 Christopher Furlong/Getty Images (tl); Akbar's Restaurants (tr); Justin Foulkes/4Corners (br)
p.20 James Emmerson/Robert Harding Picture Library (t); honister.com (cr); Pawel Libera/Latitude (b)
p.21 Education Images/UIG/Getty Images (t); Robert Workman/Aldeburgh Music (c); Maurizio Rellini/4Corners (b)
p.22 Adam Burton/Robert Harding Picture Library (tr); People's History Museum (c); Roger Coulam/Getty Images (b)
p.23 Massimo Borchi/4Corners (t); Pietro Canali/4Corners (b)
p.24 David Cheshire/Loop Images/Corbis
p.26 Ashley Cooper/Corbis
pp.48–49 Alan Copson/Getty Images
p.51 Steve Vidler/Corbis
p.93 Erin Smallwood/Getty Images (t); Photononstop/Getty Images (b)
p.131 View Pictures/UIG/Getty Images
p.143 Jon Lambert/Whitstable Oyster Festival (t)
p.169 Dave Cole/Alamy Images (bl)
pp.178–179 Guy Edwardes/2020VISION/Nature Picture Library Corbis
p.181 Louise Heusinkveld/Getty Images
p.199 colin@vertiworks.co.uk (t); Matt Jacques/Dreamstime.com (b)
pp.230–231 Andrea Pucci/Getty Images
p.233 Francisco Martinez/Alamy
p.251 Cheltenham Racecourse (t); EURASIA PRESS/Photononstop/Getty Images (b)
pp.276–277 Adrian Dennis/AFP/Getty Images
p.279 Andy Short/Thermae Bath Spa
p.299 Tim Graham/Corbis (t)
p.315 Adam Burton/Robert Harding Picture Library
p.333 The Seafood Restaurant (t)
p.357 Sebastian Wasek/Robert Harding Picture Library
pp.372–373 Tim Stocker Photography/Getty Images
pp.420–421 Dave Porter Peterborough UK/Getty Images
p.423 Peter Cook/Royal Shakespeare Company
p.437 Alan Copson/JAI/Corbis
p.455 Selfridges Birmingham (t); The Print Collector/Getty Images (bl); Ian Dagnall/Robert Harding Picture Library (br)
pp.472–473 Travelpix Ltd/Getty Images
p.475 Tom Martin/JAI/Corbis
p.503 Frank Fell/Robert Harding World Imagery/Corbis (t); Lincolnshire Wildlife Trust/Barrie Wilkinson (bl); Paul Smith (br)
pp.510–511 Ian Bramham Photography/Getty Images
p.513 Ant Clausen Photography/Giants Spectacular
p.535 Ian Canham/Alamy (t); Blackpool Pleasure Beach (b)
pp.552–553 Jeremy Lightfoot / Robert Harding World Imagery/Corbis
p.555 2/Allan Baxter/Ocean/Corbis
p.567 honister.com (br)
pp.582–583 John Dowle/Getty Images
p.585 Andrea Pistolesi/Getty Images
p.615 www.turkishbathsharrogate.co.uk (br)
pp.634–635 Danny Birrell Photography/Getty Images
p.637 Ian Dagnall/Alamy
p.661 Axiom Photographic/*/Design Pics/Corbis (t); Nick Cable/Getty Images (c); Beamish Museum (b)
p.676 Chris Hellier/Corbis

**Front cover & spine** Peak District National Park © Alan Copson/AWL Images
**Back cover** Beach huts in Southwold, Suffolk © Nadia Isakova/AWL Images (t); Canal boat on River Avon, Stratford-upon-Avon © Jane Sweeney/AWL Images (bl); Great Court, British Museum, London © Alan Copson/AWL Images (br)

# Index

Maps are marked in grey

# Y

# Z

# Map symbols

The symbols below are used on maps throughout the book

| | | | | | | | |
|---|---|---|---|---|---|---|---|
| ✈ | Airport | ▒ | Vineyard/winery | 🏖 | Beach | ▬▬▬ | Pedestrian road |
| ★ | Bus stop | ⊠ | Gate | 〰 | Swamp | ⋯⋯⋯ | Steps |
| ⊖ | London Underground station | ∴ | Ruin | ⌒ | Bridge | ▬•▬ | Railway |
| 🚢 | Boat | ✡ | Synagogue | 🌊 | Waterfall | •–•– | Cable car |
| P | Parking | ⊙ | Memorial/statue | ▲ | Mountain peak | ▮ | Building |
| @ | Internet café/access | 🕌 | Mosque | ⌃ | Mountain range | ⇨ | Church (town maps) |
| (i) | Information office | 🏛 | Stately home/historic house | ⌂ | Cave | ◯ | Stadium |
| ✚ | Hospital | 🏠 | Abbey | ♜ | Castle | ▭ | Market |
| ✉ | Post office | ✝ | Church (regional maps) | ♟ | Museum | ▢ | Beach |
| ⊤ | Public gardens | 🏛 | Monument | ▬▬ | Motorway | ▦ | Park |
| ⩙ | Spring/spa | ⌄ | Viewpoint | — | Main road | ⊡ | Cemetery |
| ✗ | Battlefield | 🗼 | Lighthouse | — | Minor road | | |
| ♦ | Point of interest | 🏊 | Swimming pool | - - - - | Path | | |

## Listings key

| | |
|---|---|
| ▪ | Accommodation |
| ● | Café/restaurant |
| ▪ | Bar/club |
| ● | Shop |

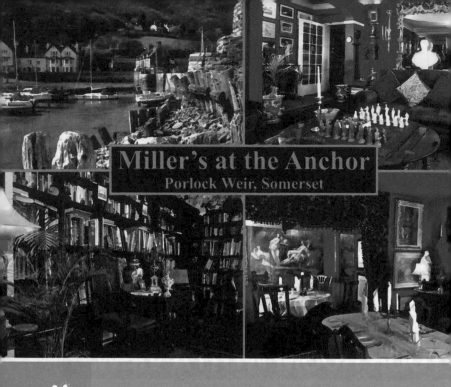

Miller's at the Anchor
Porlock Weir, Somerset